W9-CPO-016

LUTHERAN BIBLE
COMPANION

Volume 1: Introduction and Old Testament

LUTHERAN BIBLE
COMPANION

Volume 1: Introduction and Old Testament

*A Practical Tool for Church Workers
and Laypeople*

Drawn from the consultant materials of 27 scholars for *The Lutheran
Study Bible* project and from numerous faithful resources; supplemented
in view of recent research, including articles by Horace D. Hummel, Paul
L. Maier, Andrew E. Steinmann, and others.

GENERAL EDITOR
EDWARD A. ENGELBRECHT

FOREWORD BY GREGORY P. SELTZ

Whoever would know God and have eternal life should read [the
Bible] with diligence and search for its testimony of Christ, God's Son.
—Martin Luther (*What Luther Says* § 245)

CONCORDIA PUBLISHING HOUSE • SAINT LOUIS

Copyright © 2014 Concordia Publishing House
3558 S. Jefferson Avenue, St. Louis, MO 63118-3968
1-800-325-3040 • www.cph.org

CONTENTS

VOLUME 1

VOLUME 2

Alphabetical Order of Biblical Books, Including Apocrypha

FOREWORD

Jesus says, "You search the Scriptures because you think that in them you have eternal life; and it is they that bear witness about Me" (Jn 5:39). The apostle John says at the end of his Gospel, "These [things] are written so that you may believe that Jesus is the Christ, the Son of God, and that by believing you may have life in His name" (Jn 20:31). And the apostle Paul encourages all people to "Let the word of Christ dwell in you richly" (Col 3:16). The Bible is an incredible book of God's promises and actions to redeem and restore the world to Himself. In the Scriptures there is life and salvation.

That's why in my more than 25 years of ministry, as the Lutheran Hour Speaker, as the Director and Professor of the Cross-Cultural Ministry (Concordia University Irvine), and as a "church planting" pastor in the urban centers of the United States, my main goal was to introduce people to Jesus Christ and to deepen their knowledge of His Word, the Bible. If that is your desire, to know Christ Jesus with an ever deepening knowledge of the Old and New Testaments, then reading the Holy Scriptures with this wonderful resource, the *Lutheran Bible Companion* (*LBC*), will do just that.

WHY THIS BOOK?

Well, first, let's remember that not only is the Bible the most incredible book in all of human history, it is also a unique book. In fact, there is no other sacred book like it. It actually is a collection of books and letters, written over a span of 1,500 years, by over 40 authors from every walk of life—from peasants, to fishermen, to doctors, to priests, to kings. And these writings were written during times of peace, times of war, times of hopelessness, and times of great anticipation. In these writings are unique words, even now for times like this. For the Bible is a book of God's saving actions *in history*. Compared to all religious literature in the world, no other sacred book ties God's promises *for all* to specific people, places, times, and cultures like the Bible. To know the Word of God through the "words of God" is to study them in their context, to seek to know how they were understood, and to know with confidence that the God of the Bible can translate and deliver that message to you and me too.

So how does one go about studying a wonderfully unique book such as the Bible? Good question. Even those who have great desire to know the

Scriptures (among them many of my parishioners, my elders, my students, and even my "seeker" friends and family) have dived into the Word only to get lost, get off track, or to be diverted by some challenge for which they had no answer or no idea of where to look. That's why the *Lutheran Bible Companion* is such a valuable resource. It is a cradle of scholarship—historical, archaeological, theological, and biblical—that allows the reader to start anywhere in the Bible and see the big picture even as one studies a specific book. This Bible Companion is a resource that helps the seeker and the serious Bible student to take the Scripture at its word, to see its major themes, to understand its desired impact, and to let it "dwell in you richly" so that you might see it as it is—God's historically rooted Word of grace, life, and salvation for all those who believe.

BASICS FIRST

I love the fact that the Bible Companion begins with basic articles concerning the Bible as a whole. In this day and age, so many read the Bible from their point of view alone. That may be a good way to start, but the big question that remains is this: how does the Bible wish to be read? The opening articles give practical advice about how to read and study the Bible from the Bible's own perspective. Before critiquing, criticizing, or even applying the Word of God, let the Bible have its say on its own terms. The opening articles then delineate how the Lord works through His Word with such different, yet powerful, themes as Law and Gospel. They orient the reader to the miraculous unity of the Scriptures, giving one confidence that the Scripture will be its own interpreter, and trust that the Holy Spirit will indeed work through the Word. The articles at the end of the Bible Companion concerning "Archaeology, Ancient Literature, the Church" and "the historically unique way that the Bible came to us," provide even more valuable resources that give the committed Bible student a Word-driven orientation to the Scripture's contents that will only enhance its clarity and purpose in one's life.

The Bible Companion also deals with questions that modern readers might ask concerning the nature of the teachings of the Bible. Articles about miracles, science and the Bible, ancient customs and their application to today—all these are taken head-on, showing the serious student that the Bible is indeed a Word for all ages, for all people, for all times, because the God of the Scriptures, as the writer of the Hebrews says, "is the same yesterday and today and forever" (13:8).

Helpful Details

My favorite part of the *Lutheran Bible Companion* is the detailed information that is brought to bear on every book in the Bible itself. Whether it's information about Genesis, creation, and the promised Savior; or Moses, the Torah, and the exodus; or David, the covenant, and the temple; or even the historical and theological facts concerning the Gospels or the Epistles of St. Paul, the *Lutheran Bible Companion* lays valuable, necessary information at the Bible student's fingertips. In preparing my five lectures, "Footsteps of Paul—Footprints of Grace," for the "Footsteps of Paul" sojourn through Asia Minor, Greece, and Italy, this Bible Companion was an invaluable resource for me in my study of the Book of Acts and the Pauline Epistles. The summary sections for chapters, the Law and Gospel themes and doctrinal summaries for each book, the comments from prominent Lutheran theologians, the practical application section and the "Questions People Ask" about the individual book being read—these brought fresh ideas and depth to sections of the Bible that I've read many times before. And the wonderful pictures, illustrations, graphs, and maps provided a glimpse of what was to come on my trip. They will help the Bible "come alive" for you, the reader. And if all that is not enough, there is a "Further Study" section that will offer the average lay reader, Bible study leader, school teacher, professor, and pastor resources that will make the study of the Bible enjoyable and fruitful. In fact, with the Bible at the center and the Bible Companion at the ready, you can read the Bible for "all its worth."

For many today, the Bible remains a closed book. But it doesn't have to be that way. The *Lutheran Bible Companion* is a resource that will help open the Scriptures for any reader of the Word. It can help anyone (as we Lutherans like to say) to truly read, mark, learn, and inwardly digest the Bible, "God's saving word for you." This is a resource that needs to be on every person's shelf, or even better, in their hands.

Great Places in History

One of the great opportunities that I have as the Lutheran Hour Speaker is to lead people in tours of the Holy Land, the lands of St. Paul, and of course, Germany. I've been privileged to preach an Easter sermon right next to the actual empty tomb of Jesus, and a Reformation sermon from the pulpit where Luther himself preached. I've gotten to see these incredible places together with many of the faithful, the great places in history where the faith took root, such as Jerusalem, Antioch, Ephesus, and even Rome. There is nothing like seeing the "dirt level place" where the Gospel promises given to Abraham, Isaac, and Jacob began. But, if you can't see them in person, see them in this wonderful resource, the *Lutheran Bible Companion*. With the Bible and the Companion together, I know that you, like me, will be blessed in your study of God's Word, rooted and anchored in His gracious gifts, to live graced, abundant lives in Him.

> To that end, may God richly bless you.
> Rev. Gregory P. Seltz
> Speaker, The Lutheran Hour

EDITOR'S PREFACE

Lutherans who study the Bible, preach, or teach in English have never had their own comprehensive handbook of the Bible. They have contented themselves with works of varying value by other Christians. From the respectable *Halley's Bible Handbook*, which first appeared as a pamphlet in 1922, to volumes that promote theology of glory, confusion of Law and Gospel, and criticism of the Bible—the Lutheran reader has had to settle for less than helpful resources or search a variety of works to get at the insights needed for basic Bible study. For these reasons, a *Lutheran Bible Companion* was needed.

Earlier generations of Lutherans could look to Luther's introductions to the biblical books if they were printed in their German Bibles. They might reach for Michael Walther's *Harmonia* (1626), Johann Georg Benedikt Winer's *Biblische Realwörterbuch* (1833), the *Concordia Self-Study Commentary* (1971), or other resources. Yet even these fine, earlier resources were not comprehensive. A better resource was needed, especially one that both church workers and laity could use and consult together. From the beginning of *The Lutheran Study Bible* project, we had this work for a Bible companion in mind since we could not possibly supply comprehensive tools within the Study Bible.

DEVELOPING THE BIBLE COMPANION

This companion is the last in a series of works that began in 2003 when we organized the Grow in His Word research project in the Adult Bible Study area at Concordia Publishing House. That research project focused on how people read the Bible and what questions came to mind for them as they read portions of the English Standard Version (ESV). The project led to our publication of *The Lutheran Study Bible* (*TLSB*; 2009) and *The Apocrypha: The Lutheran Edition with Notes* (*ALEN*; 2012).

To aid our writers for these projects, we consulted with 27 Lutheran Bible scholars. The *Lutheran Bible Companion* (*LBC*; 2014) reflects the directions provided by these scholars who guided our setting of dates, descriptions of biblical authors and texts, and referred us to helpful commentaries for developing notes. These scholars include the following:

Rev. Dr. David L. Adams	Rev. Dr. Walter A. Maier III
Rev. Dr. Mark E. Braun	Rev. Dr. Christopher W. Mitchell
Rev. Dr. Lane A. Burgland	Rev. Dr. Timothy E. Saleska
Rev. William W. Carr Jr.	Rev. Dr. Peter J. Scaer
Rev. Dr. Paul E. Deterding	Rev. Dr. Vilson Scholz
Rev. Dr. Roland Cap Ehlke	Rev. Dr. Bruce G. Schuchard
Rev. Dr. Daniel L. Gard	Rev. Charles R. Schulz
Rev. Dr. Charles A. Gieschen	Rev. Dr. Robert A. Sorensen
Rev. Adolph L. Harstad	Rev. Dr. Andrew E. Steinmann
Rev. Dr. Horace D. Hummel	Rev. Mark P. Surburg
Rev. Dr. Arthur A. Just	Rev. Dr. Dean O. Wenthe
Rev. Dr. Jeffrey Kloha	Rev. Dr. John R. Wilch
Rev. Dr. R. Reed Lessing	Rev. Dr. Thomas M. Winger
Rev. David I. M. Lewis	

Since our goal for *LBC* was to create a volume that was not only up-to-date but also comprehensive, we drew extensively upon some older resources loved by our readers. These include Horace D. Hummel's *The Word Becoming Flesh: An Introduction to the Origin, Purpose, and Meaning of the Old Testament* (1985), Raymond F. Surburg's *Introduction to the Intertestamental Period* (1975), Martin H. Franzmann's *The Word of the Lord Grows: A First Historical Introduction to the New Testament* (1981), William F. Arndt's *Bible Difficulties and Seeming Contradictions* (1987), and Erwin L. Lueker's *The Concordia Bible Dictionary* (1963), as well as other CPH publications. The result is a comprehensive, two-volume reference work that has unique historical and theological depth, reflecting the Lutheran tradition of biblical interpretation and application.

Special thanks are due to our designer, Stacy Johnston, who contributed so greatly to the visual content, as well as our production editors, Laura L. Lane and Sarah J. Steiner, proofreader Kari Vo, and production coordinator Pam Burgdorf. Additional thanks to Rev. Roy Askins, who updated the Bible Dictionary and created the index. We praise God for their dedicated service.

We trust that you will enjoy getting to know the Bible better as you call on the Holy Spirit who inspired the Holy Scriptures and as you consult this companion to learn more about the history, culture, setting, and teaching of the Scriptures. May God grant you life by His Word (Psalm 119:25).

Rev. Edward A. Engelbrecht, STM
Concordia Publishing House
Senior Editor, Bible Resources
General Editor, *Lutheran Bible Companion*

The David Waterfalls, located in the Engedi reservation, Negeb, Israel.

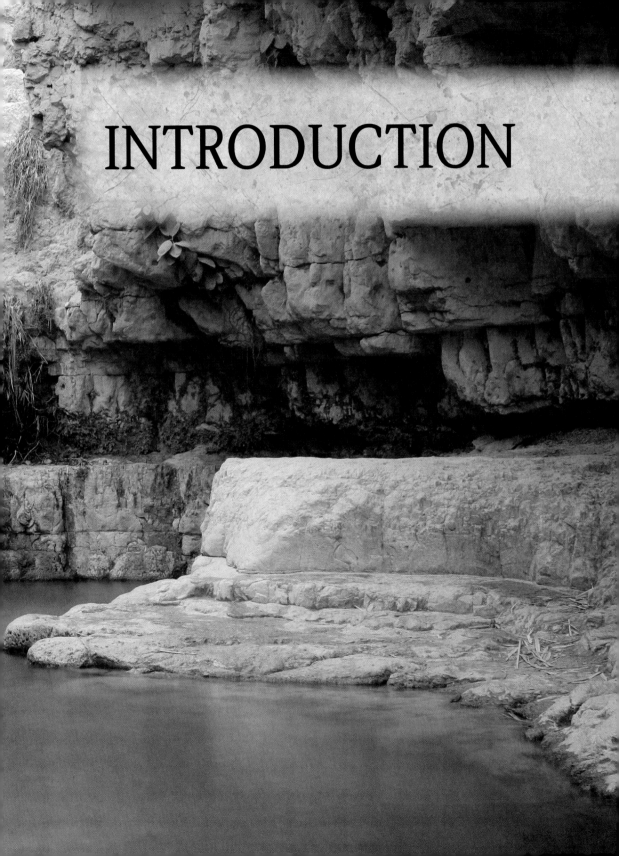

INTRODUCTION

HOW TO USE THIS BIBLE COMPANION

With most books, a reader simply opens to the beginning and starts reading. That is usually not how people first encounter the Bible. For example, one may first learn about passages quoted from the Bible, read Bible stories as children, hear public readings from the Bible at church, or attend a Bible study with a friend. Because of these common ways of coming to the Scriptures, people rarely start on page one of the Bible and read to the end. They typically start with passages from the prophet Moses or from the Lord Jesus and soon develop a host of questions about what they are seeing and how it applies to their lives; in other words, they perceive right away that God speaks to us spiritually through the Bible.

That is why a Bible Companion is such a valuable tool. It is designed to get you to answers for your spiritual questions no matter where you are reading in the Bible. In general, it includes:

- Background information about the Bible and biblical books
- Summary commentaries on each book
- Pictures, illustrations, and maps for understanding the Bible
- Recommended tools for further study
- Bible Dictionary for summaries of information

In keeping with good learning practices, (1) start reading about a particular book of the Bible with the "Overview" column of summary information. Then read about (2) the book's setting, writing, and content. (3) Finally, though most of this companion will be readily understandable, occasionally causing you

FINDING PASSAGES IN THE BIBLE

The Bible includes numerous books that are divided into chapters and verses, such as the following:

Book	chapter	verse
John	3:	16

To find information about a specific book of the Bible in this resource, look up the book's location in the table of contents (p v) or the alphabetical book list (p xiii). You can also find information about a biblical book by discovering its page number in the Bible Dictionary at the end of volume 2.

66 books of the authoritative Scripture (the canon)

14 books of the Apocrypha that Luther translated for his edition of the Bible

✚ 5 additional books of the Apocrypha used by other Christians

85 books all together

to look up a word or two in the Bible Dictionary, there are some more challenging articles. These are set apart and often distinguished by a picture of a ragged set of scholarly books (e.g., p 10). Read these articles only after gaining insight from studying the other material.

Despite the Bible's appearance, it is not just one book. It is actually an ancient collection of books that first took shape in the fourth century AD when book publishing first allowed many, many pages to be sewn together under one cover. Modern editions of the Bible sometimes include only the

THE LAW

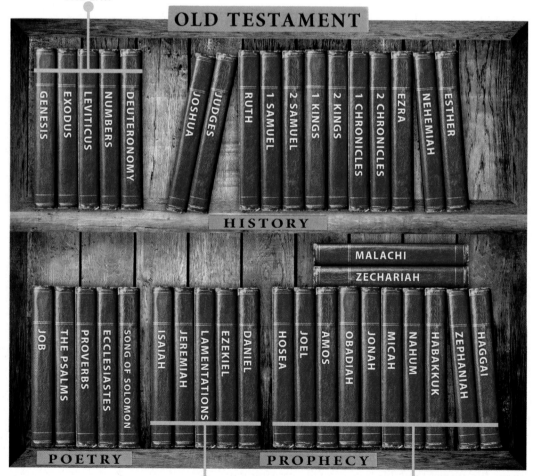

OLD TESTAMENT

GENESIS · EXODUS · LEVITICUS · NUMBERS · DEUTERONOMY · JOSHUA · JUDGES · RUTH · 1 SAMUEL · 2 SAMUEL · 1 KINGS · 2 KINGS · 1 CHRONICLES · 2 CHRONICLES · EZRA · NEHEMIAH · ESTHER

HISTORY

MALACHI
ZECHARIAH

JOB · THE PSALMS · PROVERBS · ECCLESIASTES · SONG OF SOLOMON · ISAIAH · JEREMIAH · LAMENTATIONS · EZEKIEL · DANIEL · HOSEA · JOEL · AMOS · OBADIAH · JONAH · MICAH · NAHUM · HABAKKUK · ZEPHANIAH · HAGGAI

POETRY   PROPHECY

MAJOR PROPHETS   MINOR PROPHETS

66 books of the authoritative Scriptures (known as "the canon"). Other editions may also include an additional set of books known as the Apocrypha. The order of books may be different depending on the publisher. What could be more confusing for someone who has never read the Bible before! For these reasons, the *Lutheran Bible Companion* covers 85 books (see p xxv).

The illustration below shows how all these books are typically grouped together and how one would encounter them in *The Lutheran Study Bible* and *The Apocrypha: The Lutheran Edition with Notes*.

GOSPELS,
LIFE OF CHRIST

HISTORY OF THE
EARLY CHURCH

THE APOSTLE PAUL'S LETTERS
TO SPECIFIC CONGREGATIONS
OR PERSONS

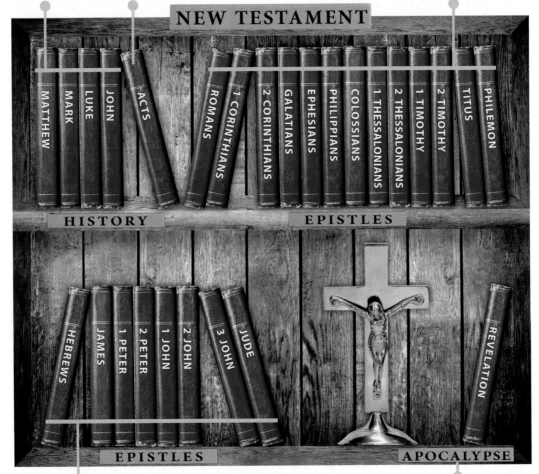

LETTERS TO CHRISTIANS IN GENERAL

VISIONS OF THINGS TO COME

THE COMPOSITIONS

BOOKS IN OTHER
CHRISTIAN TRADITIONS

APOCRYPHA

JUDITH · WISDOM OF SOLOMON · TOBIT · ECCLESIASTICUS · BARUCH · LETTER OF JEREMIAH · 1 MACCABEES · 2 MACCABEES · OLD GREEK ESTHER · SUSANNA · BEL AND THE DRAGON · PRAYER OF AZARIAH · SONG OF THE THREE HOLY CHILDREN · PRAYER OF MANASSEH · 1 ESDRAS · 2 ESDRAS · 3 MACCABEES · 4 MACCABEES · PSALM 151

HISTORIES   THE ADDITIONS   PRAYERS AND
SONGS

Old Testament + New Testament = The Christian Canon

You may notice that the chart of books on the previous pages is also divided into "testaments." We use this term today in legal documents, as in "last will and testament." It means "agreement," "covenant," or "promise." The term *Old Testament* refers to the first 39 books of the Bible in which God revealed Himself and His will to His people before the promised Savior, Jesus Christ, was born. The term *New Testament* refers to the 27 books of the Bible inspired by God after Jesus appeared.

The third set of books, written during the time between the testaments, is called "the Apocrypha." This name probably comes from a Greek word that means "hidden," because in the early years they were kept at churches as helpful books to read, but they were not read publicly before the congregation. Even today at Lutheran churches, public readings of the Bible are drawn from the Old Testament and the New Testament as God's inspired and authoritative Word, whereas the Apocrypha may be read privately or in study groups for devotion or edification.

The teachings and practices of the Lutheran Church are drawn from and guided by the authoritative, canonical books of the Old and New Testaments. If you are reading or studying the Bible for the first time, perhaps the best place to start is the Gospel of John—one of Luther's favorite books—which is introduced on p 319. It tells the story of Jesus the Savior in simple language but with thought-provoking depth. If you have general questions about the Bible, perhaps begin by consulting the Table of Contents and the Bible Dictionary (found at the end of volume 2). You may also wish to explore the articles beginning on p xxix.

HOW TO READ AND STUDY THE HOLY BIBLE

As you open your Bible to read and study, begin with this little prayer, drawn directly from Scripture passages.

Pray

Speak, Lord, for Your servant hears.

Please show me now Your ways,

that I may gain Christ and be found in Him, not having a righteousness of my own that comes from the Law, but that which comes through faith in Christ.

Your Word is a lamp to my feet and a light to my path. Give me life, O Lord, according to Your Word,

and I will declare Your greatness. Amen.

Remember

1Sm 3:9; the Lord speaks to us through His Word.

Ex 33:13; the Lord speaks to us in two basic ways: Law and Gospel.

Php 3:8–9; Scripture teaches us about Christ and His righteousness.

Ps 119:105, 107; Scripture faithfully guides our lives.

Ps 145:6; Scripture leads us to declare the Lord's ways to others.

Read the following essay to deepen your understanding of what the Bible is and how to read and study it.

AN INTRODUCTION TO STUDYING THE HOLY BIBLE

For thousands of years, people have turned to the Bible for wisdom, comfort, and hope; the Bible has changed their lives. Lutherans read the Bible, or hear it read at church, because they believe that through Holy Scripture God answers essential questions about life, death, and eternal life. They believe that God works through the message of the Scripture to call them to repentance and take away their sins. However, those who read and study the Bible may also feel challenged and, at times, confused by what the Bible says.

Learning from a Challenging Passage

The first recorded example of someone publicly reading the text of the Bible (Ex 24) illustrates important truths about the Bible as well as challenges in understanding it and applying it. After the Lord rescued the Israelites from Egypt, He spoke certain laws and promises to the prophet Moses. Moses began to write down God's Word, the first person named as doing so. The first things Moses recorded and read to the people are now part of the Book of Exodus.

> Moses wrote down all the words of the LORD. . . . And he sent young men of the people of Israel, who offered burnt offerings and sacrificed peace offerings of oxen to the LORD. . . . *Then he took the Book of the Covenant and read it in the hearing of the people.* And they said, "All that the LORD has spoken we will do, and we will be obedient." And Moses took the blood [of the sacrifices] and threw it on the people and said, "Behold the blood of the covenant that the LORD has made with you in accordance with all these words." (Ex 24:4–8, emphasis added)

This first known example of Bible reading introduces many of the truths and the challenges (throwing blood?) you will meet when you read the Bible. This essay will prepare you to study such truths and challenging texts. It will also show how all of Holy Scripture (including Ex 24) continually points to the most important truth: the Lord grants you forgiveness, life, and salvation through the blood of His Son, Jesus Christ. For Jesus taught:

> Truly, truly, I say to you, whoever hears My word and believes Him who sent Me has eternal life. . . . I am the way, and the truth, and the life. No one comes to the Father except through Me. . . . The Helper, the Holy Spirit, whom the Father will send in My name, He will teach you all things and bring to your remembrance all that I have said to you. (Jn 5:24; 14:6, 26)

I. THE LORD WORKS THROUGH HIS WORD

A. The Lord Speaks through His Word, Jesus Christ

From eternity, Jesus Christ is "the Word" of God (Jn 1:1; cf Heb 1:1–2). All other words from God truly come through Christ.

B. The Lord Speaks through the Words of the Bible

The meaning and use of the Bible ultimately belong to the One who first guided the writing of the words: the Lord. The first texts of the Bible came from the Lord speaking and from Moses writing down the Lord's Word for our sake, as Ex 24:4 shows.

At the time of the exodus, Moses recorded that the children of Israel did not truly know Him (Ex 3:13–15). They had lost His earlier promises to Abraham (e.g., Gn 12:1–3) and could not know the Lord's mind or His gracious heart toward them (1Co 2:9–12). They could not love Him or trust in Him, even if they were religious. For the people to know the Lord's gracious heart, they had to hear from the Lord. So He introduced Himself, revealing and bestowing His grace through the Word. (The Gospel of God's Word is a *Means of Grace*.)

The apostle John also writes that this communication from the Lord was essential:

> The law was given through Moses; grace and truth came through Jesus Christ. No one has ever seen God [the Father]; the only God [the Son], who is at the Father's side, He has made [the Father] known. (Jn 1:17–18)

In Exodus, the Lord introduced Himself to the people by giving them the Law through Moses. Yet, as John explains, the Lord was not finished revealing who He was. John calls Jesus "the Word" (Jn 1:1, 14) and explains that we most fully know the Father through the revelation of His Son—the Gospel of Jesus Christ.[1]

C. The Lord Works in Two Ways: Law and Gospel

When the Lord speaks His Word, He reveals that He works with people in two basic ways, or teachings (e.g., God's self-revelation in Ex 34:5–7). Lutherans call these two ways *Law* and *Gospel*, though they may be described with other terms, as biblical and Christian history show (see p xxxix). These ways, or teachings, appear throughout Scripture. The Law and the Gospel show God's ways of working with us as a Father. They help us focus on His purpose for Scripture.

We need to focus on Law and Gospel and distinguish them because people come to the Bible with so many different interests and demands. These often interfere with interpreting and applying the Father's Word. For example, the Bible includes history, but it was not written just to be a history book. The Bible includes poetry, but it was not written as a guide to fine literature. It includes a coherent worldview, but it was not written as a book of philosophy. Focusing on Law and Gospel helps us use the Bible for what it truly is: a book about the heavenly Father's gift of salvation through Jesus Christ.

When the heavenly Father spoke to Moses in Ex 24, He spoke laws, or rules, for the people to obey. In view of these laws, He spoke threats and punishments if the people did not obey. Just as an earthly father has rules for his household, the heavenly Father has laws for His creation. Passages that command good

---

1   For example, various Old Testament passages point forward to the truth that God is three in one (triune). However, the persons of the Trinity are more fully revealed only later, in the New Testament, at the announcement of Jesus' birth (Lk 1:35) and Baptism (Mt 3:16–17). With Jesus—the Word—comes the fullest revelation of who the Lord is.

works or threaten punishment for sin are passages of God's *Law*. This is God's first way of working with people.

In Exodus, the Father also promises mercy for the people (e.g., 34:6–7a). The people have peace with God through the blood of the offerings (24:5). He will be their God and care for them. Just as a loving earthly father has mercy on his children, so the heavenly Father is gracious and merciful. All His promises reach fulfillment in Jesus Christ, through whom the Father created the world and bestows blessings, life, and salvation (Jn 1:1–4). Passages that declare God's forgiveness, life, and salvation in Christ are passages of the *Gospel* (e.g., Jn 3:16–17). Such passages appear in both the Old Testament and the New Testament (see below). The Gospel is God's second way of working with people, the way by which He saves them.

As you discover the Law and the Gospel throughout the Scripture, bear in mind how they work together. The Law cannot save sinners. But the Law has essential functions. For example, through the Law, the Lord shows us our sins and drives us to repentance. In this way, the Law serves the central and most important message of the Bible: the Gospel, through which God saves us. The entire pattern of biblical history describes God commanding and condemning through the Law and then forgiving and saving through the Gospel. Though parts of Scripture proclaim nothing but the Law, the Gospel still predominates, because the Law serves the purpose of the Gospel.

D. The Lord Makes Promises and Fulfills His Word

The Bible is divided into two testaments. The Old Testament describes the creation of the universe and the creation of a special nation, Israel. The Lord established Israel as His chosen people by giving them the Law and the Gospel-promises (Ex 19:5–6; 24). Just as God works through means to accomplish His purposes, He chose to work through Israel to fulfill His promises of salvation.

The New Testament describes how the Lord fulfills the Law and Gospel-promises of the Old Testament through the life, death, and resurrection of Jesus Christ. It also reveals how the Lord sends His Word of salvation to all nations. Through the preaching of the Gospel, the Lord created His Church—all who trust in Jesus Christ for the forgiveness of sins. The Church is the "new Israel," promised in the Old Testament and fulfilled in the New Testament.

E. The Lord Does Not Lie

After the Lord spoke to His people and His Spirit moved the prophets and apostles to preach and write, their words were collected into books. (The Bible is not a single book but a collection of books.) Just as God works through means, such as Baptism and the Word, to accomplish our salvation, He worked through the prophets and apostles, who "spoke from God as they were carried along by the Holy Spirit" (2Pt 1:21).

> The Bible is the "Holy Scripture" because God the Holy Spirit gave to His chosen writers the thoughts that they expressed and the words that they wrote (verbal inspiration). Therefore, the Bible is God's own Word and truth, without error (inerrancy). (*Luther's Small Catechism with Explanation*, question 3)

At times, people have assumed that the books of Scripture must contain errors, falsehoods, or useless materials because human beings wrote them down. However, Martin Luther continually pointed out that "God cannot lie" (cf Nu 23:19; Ti 1:2; Pss 12:6; 18:30; Pr 30:5; Jn 3:31–33). Because God's Spirit worked through the writers of Scripture, it is God's infallible Word and is completely reliable.

Over the centuries, people copied the books of Scripture with great care because they recognized them as God's Word. Although we no longer have the original documents written by Moses, Peter, or others, we do have the text faithfully preserved. For example, scholars have carefully studied the thousands of handmade copies of the New Testament. They have recognized that, though minor differences exist between the copies, the books of Scripture were so faithfully recorded that no doctrine has been lost.

The English Standard Version is an excellent and reliable translation of the Hebrew, Aramaic, and Greek texts of the Bible. Just as we call the writings of the prophets and apostles "God's Word," we call reliable translations of the Bible "God's Word."

II. Scripture Interprets Scripture

As our reflection on Ex 24 has shown, helpful principles of interpretation flow from the Law and Gospel teachings of Scripture.

A. The Scripture Focuses on Jesus Christ

As stated above, the Gospel of Jesus Christ is the most important teaching of Holy Scripture. Although many passages do not explicitly refer to Jesus, all the books of Holy Scripture serve the saving purpose of Jesus. For this reason, Jesus said, "You search the Scriptures because you think that in them you have eternal life; and it is they that bear witness about Me" (Jn 5:39). Jesus explained that He and His saving work were the true focus of all God's Word (Lk 24:44–48). So no matter what part of Scripture you read, understand it in view of Jesus Christ and His work (see p xliii).

B. The Scripture Agrees within Itself

Because Jesus is the focus of all of God's Word, the books of Scripture have remarkable agreement. The stories, proverbs, teachings, and other passages present the Law, which drives us to Christ, and the Gospel, which proclaims Christ.

When readers miss the Law and Gospel distinction in Scripture, the Scripture may appear contradictory to them. For example, one might read Ex 24 and conclude that the Israelites were to save themselves by their obedience to the Law and not through faith in the promised Christ. However, the purpose of the Law is to reveal sin so that people will see their need for the Savior (Gal 3:21–22). At first, the Law seems to contradict the Gospel. In fact, the Law serves the Gospel, and Jesus Christ stands forth as the focus.

C. The Scripture Is Understood through Context

The focus of the books of Scripture on Christ and His work and their agreement with one another do not destroy the particular experiences, struggles, and concerns of the biblical writers. Although some passages speak about humanity in general, the prophets and apostles most often wrote for a particular group of people at a particular moment in history. As a result, to fully understand Scripture and to treasure the breadth of the ways it proclaims the Law and the Gospel of Jesus, each passage must be considered in its historical context.

No book or passage should have an alien meaning forced on it. For example, when reading that Moses "took the blood [of the sacrifices] and threw it on the people" (Ex 24:8), a reader should not conclude that God wants us to sacrifice animals today so that we, too, can pour blood on one another. Nor should one shy away from the historical and grammatical meaning of Moses' words because they seem offensive to one's ideas about cleanliness or animal rights. A reader should not spiritualize the words, as though Moses only showed the blood to the people and then poured it on the altar on their behalf (e.g., the Rabbinic Midrash Tanna'im).

Instead, an interpreter should diligently compare the text with other passages of Scripture, beginning with the book of Scripture the text appears in or books by the same writer (in this case, Moses). For example, in Ex 29, blood is applied to the priests as a means of consecration (vv 19–20; cf Lv 8:22–30).

The Epistle to the Hebrews tells us that Moses mingled the blood with water before sprinkling it on the people (9:19). In view of these passages, Ex 24:8 grows clearer. The sacrificial blood was diluted with water, which was sprinkled on the people for their consecration.

Because the people were unclean (sinful, as pointed out by the Law), they needed atonement for their sins and consecration through the sacrifices (blessings of God's mercy, which pointed forward to the sacrificial death of Jesus—the Gospel). In this way, the particular historic message of the passage is respected and more fully understood in view of God's work of salvation.

At times, even with careful study, a passage of Scripture will remain unclear. In such cases, readers should not fall into endless speculation or try to resolve every mystery. Instead, they should let the clearest passages of Scripture guide their understanding of biblical doctrine.

III. THE HOLY SPIRIT BLESSES THE USE OF GOD'S WORD THROUGH FAITH

A. The Holy Spirit Opens Scripture to Us through Faith

Since Holy Scripture is a book of salvation, we can understand it only through faith (1Co 2:12–16). Reason certainly has its place in reading Scripture (e.g., considering the grammar and history). But reason alone is never enough, for reason cannot grasp the spiritual truths of God's Word (cf Jn 3:1–8).

Likewise, our own reason, experiences, interests, and opinions are distorted by the effects of sin, which cloud and confuse us about the meaning and use of God's Word (Jn 3:9–10). This is one reason why people will read the same passage but arrive at vastly different interpretations. The Holy Spirit must open the Scripture for us through faith (Jn 3:31–36).

B. The Holy Spirit Creates the Congregation of the Faithful through the Word

Faith is not something that people naturally possess and offer to God (Jn 1:9–13). For someone to believe in Jesus and understand Scripture, the Holy Spirit must create faith in that person's heart (Jn 3:5–6).

The word *trust*, a synonym for faith, can help us understand how this takes place. You can't have genuine trust in someone you've never met or interacted with. Trust is created through the words and actions of one person toward another. The Holy Spirit creates faith, or trust, in Jesus when God speaks and interacts with that person through His Word, Holy Baptism, and the Lord's Supper (God's Means of Grace), which are administered by the Church. Through these means, a person comes to know God, to trust Him, and to belong to Him in the congregation of the faithful.

C. The Holy Spirit Leads Us to Confession of Faith with the Church

Never imagine that believers exist without the Church. Someone may object to this by asserting that a person could come to faith while reading the Bible at home, without ever going to a church. But how would that person receive a copy of the Bible? Of course, he or she would receive it from someone else. God called someone to prepare that Bible and distribute that Bible, work carried on by the Church! In other words, the Holy Spirit is always working through the Church—through believers like you—to spread the Word to other people. The Lord has entrusted His Word to the Church for this purpose (Ps 145:4–13). Luther wrote:

> The Spirit has His own congregation in the world, which is the mother that conceives and bears every Christian through God's Word [Galatians 4:26]. Through the Word He reveals and preaches, He illumines and enkindles hearts, so that they understand, accept, cling to, and persevere in the Word. (LC II 42)

When the Holy Spirit calls someone to faith, He likewise calls that person to serve in the congregation of the faithful (2Tm 3:16–17). A Christian should not set out to interpret Scripture for himself, in isolation from other believers. God's people meditate on Scripture together (1Tm 4:13) and interpret Scripture in view of Scripture.

Life together in the Church requires unity, because people cannot dwell together long without agreement (1Co 1:9–10). Holy Scripture is the basis of Christian unity (Jn 17:17–21). However, for centuries, most people did not have a personal copy of the Bible. The length of the Scripture makes it difficult for most people to commit it to heart in its entirety. Likewise, false teachers clouded the faithful interpretation of Scripture, as noted above. Each of these factors threatened the unity of the faithful, which the Holy Spirit had created through the Word.

For these reasons, the early Christians prepared short confessions of faith (e.g., "No one can say 'Jesus is Lord' except in the Holy Spirit" [1Co 12:3]; the Apostles' Creed, based on 1Co 15:3–4 and other passages). They also prepared longer confessions based on Scripture in order to distinguish truth from falsehood (e.g., the Nicene Creed and the Athanasian Creed). The Lutheran reformers did the same when they prepared their confessions to address medieval abuse and neglect of Scripture. Lutherans treasure these faithful creeds and confessions because they support and encourage the unity of the Church and stand as examples of faithful reading of Scripture.

The need for these "rules of faith" should call us to humility, to acknowledge that our own reason, experiences, interests, and opinions are distorted by the effects of sin. Just as surely as a child needs the faithful guidance of parents and teachers to learn how to read, new believers also need the community of faith to learn how to read the Holy Scripture. Even Jesus—the Word of God in the flesh—humbly listened to the teachers at the temple in Jerusalem (Lk 2:46). The creeds and confessions are a written record of how God's people faithfully interpret Scripture.

Parents nurture their children in the faith when they read Bible stories to them and bring them to church. Adult converts grow in the faith when they gather with the faithful, where God's Word is publicly read and studied (2Tm 1:13–14).

Conclusion

When Moses first read God's Word to the people of Israel (Ex 24), the Holy Spirit worked through the Law and the Gospel of the Word to create and consecrate a community of faith. The Lord entrusted His life-giving Word to the community and still leads it today through the Word. The Holy Spirit adds to this community all who are baptized into Christ, trusting in the death and resurrection of Jesus Christ for the forgiveness of sins, which is the central message of Scripture.

From the Lord,

through the prophets and apostles,

in the community of faith that confesses God's Word,

we receive the Gospel-promise of our salvation in Christ and

return to the Lord our heartfelt service, prayers, and praise.

General Editor

Law and Gospel: Identifying God's Ways with Mankind

In the sixteenth century, the great reformer Martin Luther wrote the first treatise on distinguishing Law and Gospel. However, Luther's work was hardly new, since Scripture and its interpreters had always made this distinction. The following quotations show the long history of distinguishing God's two ways. These examples will help you recognize terms of Law and Gospel and apply His ways in your life as you read the Scripture.

Examples from Scripture

The Lord Commands and Promises, Curses and Blesses (c 2090 BC):

> Now the LORD said to Abram, "Go from your country and your kindred and your father's house to the land that I will show you. And I will make of you a great nation, and I will bless you and make your name great, so that you will be a blessing. I will bless those who bless you, and him who

dishonors you I will curse, and in you all the families of the earth shall be blessed." (Gn 12:1–3)

The Lord Reveals His Two Ways (c 1446 BC):

"Now therefore, if I have found favor in Your sight, please show me now Your ways, that I may know You in order to find favor in Your sight. Consider too that this nation is Your people." . . . The LORD passed before him and proclaimed, "The LORD, the LORD, a God merciful and gracious, slow to anger, and abounding in steadfast love . . . for thousands, forgiving iniquity and transgression and sin, but who will by no means clear the guilty, visiting the iniquity of the fathers on the children and the children's children, to the third and the fourth generation." (Ex 33:13; 34:6–7)

Jesus Preaches Repentance and Forgiveness (c AD 28):

Jesus came into Galilee, proclaiming the gospel of God, and saying, "The time is fulfilled, and the kingdom of God is at hand; repent and believe in the gospel." (Mk 1:14–15)

He opened their minds to understand the Scriptures, and said to them, "Thus it is written, that the Christ should suffer and on the third day rise from the dead, and that repentance and forgiveness of sins should be proclaimed in His name to all nations, beginning from Jerusalem." (Lk 24:45–47)

The Apostle Paul Distinguished the Work of Law and Gospel (c AD 53):

The Scripture, foreseeing that God would justify the Gentiles by faith, preached the gospel beforehand to Abraham. . . . Is the law then contrary to the promises of God? Certainly not! For if a law had been given that could give life, then righteousness would indeed be by the law. But the Scripture imprisoned everything under sin, so that the promise by faith in Jesus Christ might be given to those who believe. (Gal 3:8, 21–22)

Examples from the Early Church

The Creator's Twofold Power (c 207):

Both [testaments] belong to [God] who says: "I kill, and I make alive; I wound, and I heal" (Deuteronomy 32:39). We have already made good the Creator's claim to this twofold character of judgment and goodness, "killing in the letter" through the law, and "quickening in the Spirit" through the Gospel (2 Corinthians 3:6). (Tertullian, *ANF* 3:452–53)

The Law and the Promise Cannot Be Mixed (c 380):

> The [Gospel's] promise was distinguished from the Law, and since it is different it cannot be mixed [with the Law], for a condition [of the Law] invalidates the promise. (Tyconius, Rule 3)

The Law Kills and the Gospel Gives Life (c 386–98):

> In the Law, he that has sin is punished; here, he that has sins comes and is baptized and is made righteous, and being made righteous, he lives, being delivered from the death of sin. The Law, if it lay hold on a murderer, puts him to death; the Gospel, if it lay hold on a murderer, enlightens, and gives him life. (John Chrysostom, *NPNF1* 12:307)

The Old Testament Proclaimed Righteousness through Christ (c 412):

> His words are, "The righteousness of God is manifested" (Romans 3:21). . . . This is witnessed by the law and the prophets; in other words, the law and the prophets each testify about it. The law, indeed, does this by issuing its commands and threats, and by justifying no one. It shows well enough that it is by God's gift, through the help of the Spirit, that a person is justified. The prophets [show this righteousness] because it was what they predicted that Christ accomplished at His coming. (Augustine, *NPNF1* 5:88–89)

Examples from the Medieval and Reformation Eras

Confess the Lord in Two Ways (Twelfth Century):

> Let [your works] confess Him in two ways, let them be clad, as it were, in a double robe of confession. That is: confession of your own sins, and of the praise of God. . . . Let the humility of confession of your imperfection supply what is lacking in your daily life. For that imperfection is not hidden from God's eyes. If He has commanded that His precepts should be diligently kept (Psalm 119:4) it is in order that, seeing our constant imperfection and our inability to fulfill the duty that we ought to do, we may fly to His mercy, and say, "Your steadfast love is better than life" (Psalm 63:3a). And not being able to appear clad in innocence or righteousness, we may at least be covered in the robe of confession. (St. Bernard of Clairvaux, *The Life and Works of St. Bernard of Clairvaux: The Advent and Christmas Sermons* [London: John Hodges, 1889–96])

The Law Demands, the Gospel Gives (1540):

> The Gospel proclaims repentance and the promise of grace and eternal life. The promise should be diligently distinguished from the Law. And although the Law has certain promises of its own, nevertheless, these differ from the unique promise of the Gospel. Moreover, the promises of the Law require the condition of perfect obedience as is said in the first commandment: "I will do good to those who love me" [cf Dt 5:10]. But the evangelical [Gospel] promise—about remission of sins, justification, and the gift of eternal life—is gratuitous, offered on account of Christ, without a condition of our merits or our worthiness. (Philip Melanchthon, *Commentary on Romans*. Translated by Fred Kramer. [St. Louis: Concordia, 1992], p 22)

Why We Distinguish Law and Gospel (1580):

> The distinction between the Law and the Gospel is a particularly brilliant light. It serves the purpose of rightly dividing God's Word [2 Timothy 2:15] and properly explaining and understanding the Scriptures of the holy prophets and apostles. We must guard this distinction with special care, so that these two doctrines may not be mixed with each other, or a law be made out of the Gospel. When that happens, Christ's merit is hidden and troubled consciences are robbed of comfort, which they otherwise have in the Holy Gospel when it is preached genuinely and purely. For by the Gospel they can support themselves in their most difficult trials against the Law's terrors. (FC SD V 1)

From these examples, one can easily see why the preacher and writer C. F. W. Walther concluded, "If you wish to be an orthodox teacher, you must present all the articles of faith in accordance with Scripture, yet [you] must also rightly distinguish Law and Gospel" (*Law and Gospel: How to Read and Apply the Bible* [St. Louis: Concordia, 2010], p 35).

THE UNITY OF THE SCRIPTURE

The unity of Scripture is not imposed upon Scripture but found there.

—Robert D. Preus, *Doctrine Is Life*

Our English word *Bible* comes from the Greek word for "a book." It came into English by way of medieval Latin, when book technology allowed all the Sacred Scripture to be gathered under one cover—the Bible as we think of it today. But the idea that the Sacred Scripture is unified and, indeed, one book is hardly a medieval or modern notion. The unity of Scripture is already taught in the Scripture itself as the following points will reveal.

The Chief Character of the Scripture

While teaching beside the Bethesda pool in Jerusalem, Jesus told a group of Judeans, "You search the Scriptures because you think that in them you have eternal life; and it is they that bear witness about Me" (Jn 5:39). Like other rabbis,

Jesus spoke of the Old Testament Scripture as a united testimony.[1] But unlike other rabbis, Jesus joined the purpose of the Scripture—salvation for eternal life—to the key character of the Scripture, Himself as the promised Savior (cf Lk 24:44–47). Since all the Scripture bears witness to Jesus, Jesus understood and taught that the Scripture was unified.

The One Author of the Scripture

St. Paul also taught this unity of Scripture. Shortly before his execution under Emperor Nero (AD 68), Paul wrote to his son in the faith, Timothy, a younger Christian leader:

> From childhood you have been acquainted with the sacred writings, which are able to make you wise for salvation through faith in Christ Jesus. All Scripture is breathed out by God and profitable for teaching, for reproof, for correction, and for training in righteousness, that the man of God may be competent, equipped for every good work. (2Tm 3:15–17)

Paul attributes all the Sacred Scripture to the work of God and understands the Scripture as focused on salvation through Jesus. He demonstrates the early Christian belief that the Scripture is unified in its teaching (cf 2Tm 1:13–14 about Christian doctrine generally).

The Fulfillment of Prophecy

The unity of the Scripture is graphically illustrated by the way it is interconnected through promises and fulfillments as well as commentary on earlier texts. (You can find an example of how the Scripture builds on other passages of Scripture in the chart on p xlvii in *The Lutheran Study Bible*.) The sheer number of such examples speaks to the unity of the Scripture. The writers saw themselves as teaching in continuity with what God had previously revealed (cf 2Tm 3:15–17).

The Unity of the Covenants

Scripture itself teaches that the revelation of God was delivered under a "covenant," or "testament," first given to Abraham and confirmed/renewed through

---

1 Collection and canonization of Scripture began already in the Old Testament with the Law of Moses. The Law, Psalms, and Prophets were read, studied, and explained together at the temple and in Jewish synagogues, as early Jewish and Christian testimony shows (e.g., 1Macc 12:9; 2Macc 2:13; 15:9; 4Macc 18:10; Ecclus Prologue; *Against Apion* 1:38–40; Philo, *On the Contemplative Life* 75, 78; Mishnah Yadayim 3:5; *Letter of Aristeas* 155, 317–18; Mt 22:23–46; Lk 24:44; Ac 13:15; 28:23). Jesus and the disciples continued this practice, focusing on the fulfillment of Old Testament prophecies in the person and work of Jesus (Mt 5:17; 11:13–15; Lk 16:16; Jn 1:45; Ac 13:15; Rm 3:21–22). The New Testament teachers and writers assumed the unity of the Old Testament Scripture. The New Testament is more or less a commentary on the Old Testament in view of the life, death, and resurrection of Jesus. For more on the transition from early Judaism to early Christianity, see Oskar Skarsaune, *In the Shadow of the Temple: Jewish Influences on Early Christianity* (Downers Grove, IL: InterVarsity Press, 2002), 279–93.

Moses (Gn 17:9; Ex 2:24; chs 3–6; Lv 26:42; Dt 1:8; 29:12–13; Jsh 24). Although many covenants are described in the Old Testament, Jeremiah saw the covenant given to Abraham and confirmed through Moses as *the* covenant (Jer 31:32), which the people of Israel broke. He then prophesied a second covenant, or "new covenant" (Jer 31:31–33; cf Is 59:20–21; Gal 3:17).

When Jesus instituted the Lord's Supper, He proclaimed the establishment of this new covenant (Mt 26:28; Mk 14:24; Lk 22:20). Paul refers explicitly to an old covenant (2Co 3:14) and a new covenant established in Christ (1Co 11:25; 2Co 3:6). The writer to the Hebrews affirms this understanding of God's revelation by citing Jeremiah (Heb 8:8; 9:15; 12:24; cf Jn 1:17).

The two great covenants of Scripture—the old and the new—relate to each other as prophecy and fulfillment. The first covenant pointed forward to the second, which would fulfill God's plan of redemption. This relationship of old and new, of prophecy and fulfillment, likewise reveals the unity of the Scripture.

A comment should be added about the enduring usefulness of the Old Testament. What is true and good always applies. When Jesus fulfilled the laws and promises of the Old Testament, He did not abolish them (Mt 5:17–18; Rm 3:31). They are not now useless to us, for God still uses them for our instruction (1Co 10:11).

In Christ, our relationship to the Old Testament has changed. Christ fulfilled the laws and the ordinances so that they can no longer condemn those who live by faith in Christ (Rm 7:6; Gal 3:23–26). The ministry of the new covenant outshines the glory of the old (2Co 3:7–18). The civil and ceremonial laws and ordinances of the Old Testament no longer apply to us as laws and ordinances (Eph 2:11–22), but they still stand as testimonies of God's holiness and mercy. They teach us about the goal, or "end," of the ministry of salvation: the deliverance from evil that God brought about in Christ.

Law and Gospel

Interpreting and applying the Scripture as a unified body of teaching is perhaps best understood through the study of Law and Gospel (see p xxxix). God's Law condemns our sin and drives us to despair of our own righteousness. Yet this harsh message of the Law prepares us for God's other great message: the forgiveness of sins in Christ. Although the Law and the Gospel are very different teachings and must be distinguished, they drive toward a unified purpose: our salvation.

As demonstrated in our *TLSB* notes on Ex 34:6–7, Law and Gospel are the enduring themes of all the Scripture. They are the ways of God with mankind. Their constant use unifies the Scripture.

Speak, Lord, for Your Servant Hears

Whenever you study a passage of Scripture, keep these broad truths and themes in mind. They will help you understand the meaning of the passage and how it applies to your life. Treasure the Holy Bible as God's dear gift to you. It is His message of your personal salvation.

The northern region of Israel.

THE PURPOSE AND LANGUAGE OF THE BIBLE

One great danger for people who engage in studies of the Bible is that the Bible may become for them a book of puzzles and problems, which engage them to such an extent that they are reading the Scriptures solely with an eye to difficulties. It is very regrettable if anyone uses the Book of Life in such a fashion. The same thing is true of the person who reads the Bible merely on account of the exalted poetry it contains or its pure, forceful language. It is true also of the person who wishes to use it simply as a source book in historical and archaeological research, and of the students who have been told that the Bible contains some of the best short stories that were ever written and who page through the sacred volume in quest of great literature. These people are right in a way—the Bible does offer what they are looking for; and yet they are wrong, because, in searching for pearls, they fail to lay hold of the one truly precious pearl, the pardon of God provided by the sacrifice of Jesus Christ. These people are as foolish as the prisoner who is sent a letter of pardon by the governor and who admires the envelope, the seal, the beautiful script of the governor's note, but fails to acquaint himself with its contents.

The purpose of the Scriptures is beautifully stated by Paul in 2Tm 3:15–17: "From childhood you have been acquainted with the sacred writings, which are able to make you wise for salvation through faith in Christ Jesus. All Scripture is breathed out by God and profitable for teaching, for reproof, for correction, and for training in righteousness, that the man of God may be competent, equipped for every good work." To bring us to faith in Christ Jesus, to teach us divine, heavenly truths, to correct us when we fall into error or sinful ways of living, to inform us as to the ways in which our God delights, and finally to lead us to heaven, that is the real purpose of the Bible.

The Worldview of the Bible

We are frequently asked, "Is not the worldview which meets us in the Scriptures an antiquated one, long exploded by the research of scientists?" For example, some read the Bible as though it taught that the earth was a flat surface supported by pillars at its four corners, which go down through the waters of the oceans. The sky, they suppose, was regarded as an overarching canopy or firmament that held back the rain and the floods until its windows were opened to pour them down. The tower of Babel needed only to be built a bit higher so that ancient man could reach these canopy-heavens.

We should examine such characterizations of the Bible. They are typical and similar to ones we hear almost every day. Let us look at them. Does the Bible say that the earth is flat? No. The view mentioned is simply an interpretation that the critic puts on the words of Scripture. It is true that in Ps 136:6 the holy writer sends up praise to our great God, "to Him who spread out the earth above the waters, for His steadfast love endures forever." But would it be fair to conclude that the Bible teaches the earth is flat and not a sphere? The context in which the statement is found must be considered. The passage quoted occurs in a poem, and we know that it is one of the properties of poetry to employ bold figures of speech. Why, then, interpret these words literally rather than figuratively? Besides, it would seem to require a good deal of boldness to say that those who speak of the earth being laid out above the waters look upon the earth as a plane rather than as a ball. Does the writer or speaker who designates the section of the United States east of the Rocky Mountains as the Great Plains thereby deny the global form of our earth?

To continue, what shall we say of the Bible's reference to the four corners of the earth? In Is 11:12 we read that the Lord will "gather the dispersed of Judah from the four corners of the earth." But we ask, "Does this prove that the Scriptures teach the earth is a quadrangular body, with four corners jutting out into space?" Obviously, the term "four corners" is equivalent to the four points of the compass. We are here dealing with an easily understood figure of speech. We can point to another statement of the same prophet, in which he, according to the rules of literalists, is denying that the earth has any corners at all, ascribing to it a circular form (Is 40:22): "It is He [the Lord] who sits above the circle of the earth." How foolish to assert on the basis of such figurative expressions that the Bible teaches this or that view on a question of astronomical geography!

Pillars of the Earth

The critic also states that the Bible pictures the four corners of the earth supported by pillars going down through the waters that are around it and under it. First Samuel 2:8, Hannah's hymn of praise, declares of our great God: "The pillars of the earth are the LORD's, and on them He has set the world." While nothing is said here about the pillars going down through the waters that are around and under the earth, pillars of the earth, to be sure, are spoken of, and it is claimed that the world has been placed upon them. But let the critic consider the context. These words are part of a hymn replete with metaphors that in poetic language express the conviction that God has created and now sustains the universe. Rather than conclude from a poetic phrase that the Bible is actually teaching the existence of colossal pillars on which the globe is resting, one should give equal consideration to Jb 26:7, where in words wonderfully sublime the sacred writer says: "He [the Lord] stretches out the north over the void and hangs the earth on nothing." These passages are not contradictory. In bold but beautiful imagery, both exalt the infinite power of our great God, in whom we live and move and have our being.

Furthermore, offense is taken at Gn 1:6–8 and other passages about the "expanse" (KJV, firmament) above the earth. The Hebrew word in question signifies expanse. We today speak of the expanse, or the heavens above us, referring to the sky or the atmosphere. Perhaps our critic's chief difficulty lies in the reference to the waters above the expanse (Gn 1:7), which, it is true, have been a puzzle to many Bible readers. But how simple is the solution when we think of the clouds and other less concentrated vapors floating far above the earth as the waters above the expanse!

There remains the assertion that according to the view of the biblical writers, the expanse is only a little way up and might have been reached from the top of the tower of Babel if the latter had attained the height intended for it. It is true, we read in Gn 11 that the people who lived immediately after the flood, having settled in the land of Shinar, said to one another: "Come, let us build ourselves a city and a tower with its top in the heavens" (v 4). Is there anything so very strange in this statement? We call our high buildings skyscrapers, and the

Germans call theirs "cloudscrapers" (*Wolkenkratzer*). Is there much difference between the boastful language of the early inhabitants of Babel and our own terminology? They employed an expression which they probably knew well enough to be an exaggeration, and it is not so much their language as the spirit in which they spoke that condemned them. To sum up, if no better arguments against the worldview of the Bible can be presented than those just examined, the Bible has little to fear on this score.

The truth of the matter is that the Bible speaks of the great facts of the physical universe only in a general way. It has some very important things to tell us about the world in which we live, things with which science cannot acquaint us, such as the origin of the world, its preservation, its purpose, and its ultimate end. On all these points positive information is granted us in the Scriptures. But when we come to matters such as the nature of light, the number of the planets, the law of gravitation, or the cellular structure of living beings, it has nothing to say.

That God could have given us authoritative revelations on all the moot questions of science is of course very true. But just as evident is the fact that He did not. Does not the wisdom and love of God here manifest itself in a remarkable way? An authoritative book on the wonders and secrets of science would not have been understood two thousand years ago, when few instruments or devices were available for accurate and penetrating observation of natural phenomena. And how many would understand such a book today? Theoretical physics is grasped by few people. Suppose such theories were contained in the Bible. What would be the purpose? The respective section would be much like the famous mathematical passage in Plato's *Republic*, section 546, which, it seems, virtually no one today is able to understand. Since the Bible was written to serve everyone regardless of age or degree of culture, we can well understand why the theories and formulae of science are not recorded on its pages.

The Language of the Bible

We readily admit, of course, that the language of the Bible is popular and not that of our modern textbooks of physics and astronomy. Natural phenomena, when alluded to, are spoken of in terms that were current at the time and in the region where the respective biblical book arose. Just as people today, astronomers included, who hold the Copernican view that the earth revolves around the sun and rotates on its own axis, nevertheless speak of sunrise and sunset, so the biblical books employ the popular language of their day, which is based on appearance rather than on strict scientific fact. We speak of darkness coming on, just as though darkness were something positive and not simply the absence of light; of death seizing a person and of a drought visiting the countryside. In our everyday speech, our eyes catch a glimpse of an object, while in reality the eyes merely receive the picture of an object sent by means of light. Our whole language is permeated with expressions, many of them highly pictorial, built on the appearance of things. Our God through the holy writers addresses us in our own language, so that we may understand Him. Naturally, the peculiarities and idioms of our own speech are not avoided. This fact also accounts for what we call the anthropomorphisms (expressions in which God is spoken of as if He had a human body) and anthropopathisms (expressions which apparently ascribe changeable human emotions to God) of the Bible.

We cannot accept the statements that the Bible teaches an outmoded view of the universe. Such an assumption is simply incompatible with the conviction that the Bible comes from the great God, who is "the Father of lights with whom there is no variation or shadow due to change" (Jas 1:17). Whatever the Bible says, no matter what the subject may be, is true. But at the same time we would warn the reader against making hasty inferences from figurative expressions or popular descriptive phrases current in the language of the day when the Bible was written and universally used to designate certain physical phenomena in an attempt to show what the Bible teaches as to the mechanism of our world. Just as little as Gn 8:21 is to be taken literally, when Moses says: "The LORD smelled the pleasing aroma," so little must the following words, found likewise in the account of the flood (Gn 7:11), "The windows of the heavens were opened," be interpreted to teach that the sky is a solid roof with windows inserted here and there. We cannot approve of the principles of interpretation which, on the basis of the psalmist's allusion to "wings of the wind" (Ps 104:3), would attribute to the Bible the teaching that the wind is a being equipped with wings.

Conclusion

The worldview taught in the Scriptures has to do with other things than those that scientists dwell on. The theme of the Bible is not physical phenomena per se, but the divine power manifesting itself in them. The holy writers do not wish to teach us the number of miles around the earth, but they urge all people to consider the question expressed in these majestic words of Isaiah (40:12): "Who has measured the waters in the hollow of His hand and marked off the heavens with a span, enclosed the dust of the earth in a measure and weighed the mountains in scales and the hills in a balance?" The aims of the Bible are not intellectual, but spiritual. What it says about the universe is meant to teach us lessons which we need for our souls. Where this is borne in mind, there will not be much danger of a person's becoming overly literal in interpreting the Scriptures.

THE NATURE OF BIBLICAL MIRACLES

A frequent criticism of the Bible is that it relates things that are improbable or downright impossible; in other words, that it reports miracles as historical facts. The accounts under consideration are not attacked as difficult to understand, but as untrue. Here we clearly have a large class of passages causing difficulty to some people, and we have to look a little more closely at them. A miracle is an act that transcends human powers of accomplishment and human ability of explanation. It is not an unnatural occurrence, but a supernatural one. At times it may be exactly like a natural event (also called an "act of providence"); but the conditions under which it takes place are such that we classify it as a miracle, for instance, when rain comes in answer to prayer, as in the case of Elijah (1Ki 18:41–46; Jas 5:17–18).

When a miracle takes place, God Himself intervenes and makes His presence felt in a special manner. Egypt was visited by a destructive hailstorm when Pharaoh refused to let the children of Israel depart in obedience to the command of God (Ex 9:22–35). Although hailstorms are perfectly natural occurrences, this particular one constituted a miracle because of its extraordinary vehemence and because it was sent by God as a special sign and as a punishment for the wickedness of the Egyptian king. The Bible is full of reports of miraculous happenings. The chain of such events begins in the first chapter, in the story of the creation of the world (Gn 1), and it continues to the last chapter, where the message of an angel who brought revelations to John is recorded (Rv 22:8). These miracles are of many different kinds, some occurring in nature, others, on and in people; some visible, others invisible; some bringing health, others bringing punishment; some performed without human agents, others, through prophets and apostles. If we were to take everything miraculous out of the Bible, how little there would be left!

Why Are the Accounts of Miracles Rejected by Some People?

It is just this miraculous element in the Scriptures that is the chief stumbling block for many people when they are asked to submit to the guidance of the Bible. Unbelievers and agnostics who publicly and loudly oppose the divine character of the Scriptures object especially to the accounts of miracles. These critics contend that miracles are impossible and that hence all these narratives of supernatural occurrences must be untrue. Miracles are not happening today; they did not happen in ancient times either—so runs the argument. What shall we say?

If a person does not believe in a personal God who has made and who governs the universe, heaven and earth and all they contain, it is natural for him or her to reject the Scripture accounts of miracles. The atheist is consistent when refusing to believe they can occur. But we hope that no reader of this book will say in his heart: "There is no God" (Ps 14:1). It is of no use to argue with such people about the credibility of the Scriptures. Agreement has to be reached on something more basic before there can be profitable discussion, namely, on the question of the existence of God. The biblical narratives throughout presuppose the grand truth that God "exists and that He rewards those who seek Him" (Heb 11:6).

It cannot be denied, however, that there are people who do not wish to be atheists, but who nevertheless doubt the possibility of miracles. God works according to certain laws (the laws of nature), they maintain, and nothing can happen that is contrary to these laws. This is an extraordinary position to assume, we reply. To believe in an almighty and omniscient God, on the one hand, and to deny, on the other, that He can set aside, suspend, or transcend the laws of nature is an obvious inconsistency. Who or what should we regard as God? The law of nature or the One who has made nature with its laws?

Two Important Considerations Concerning Miracles

We have to say that it is unscientific to begin with the assumption that miracles cannot happen. How does one know? Science demands that an investigator have an open mind. The question whether miracles do happen is entitled to the same fair treatment as other questions. Just as one would hardly deny in advance that a new comet has been discovered, so one should not presuppose that miracles are out of the question. The position of Voltaire, who is said to have declared that, even if a miracle were performed in the marketplace before his eyes, he would not accept it, is grossly unscientific. The only question which is justified is whether there is any proof that the miracles related in the Scriptures actually occurred.

In a brilliant little book on radical Gospel criticism (*Die Modernen Darstellungen des Lebens Jesu*) Gerhard Uhlhorn (1826–1901), a celebrated German theologian, looks at whether the position that the biblical miracles did not happen is tenable from the point of view of the scientific historian. For argument's sake, he waives the inspiration of the Scriptures. One miracle the fair-minded critic may admit, Uhlhorn points out, is the greatest of them all: the resurrection of Christ. Even if one regards the New Testament as nothing but a collection of ordi-

THE NATURE OF BIBLICAL MIRACLES

nary human documents, one may grant that this event occurred; the recorded evidence for it is simply overwhelming. The same conclusion is reached, for instance, by the English author who, assuming the pen name Frank Morison, in 1930 published a book entitled *Who Moved the Stone?* What makes the verdict most impressive is that Morison started out to prove the very opposite of what he ultimately found to be true. A similar experience is described more recently by a former legal editor of *The Chicago Tribune*, Lee Strobel, who became a Christian in 1981 after investigating the facts of Christianity. The remarkable cases of Lord Lyttleton and Gilbert West are also very heartening instances of this nature. The former set out to disprove the miraculous element in the conversion of Paul, the latter the resurrection of Christ. When they met to compare notes, they confessed that they had been conquered by the evidence of the Bible. It is not in keeping with the plan of this book to insert here a lengthy discussion on the evidence for the resurrection of our Savior. We must be content with quoting a paragraph from Frederic W. Farrar's *Life of Christ* (chapter 62) in which he summarizes well the facts that even the unbeliever, if fair-minded, may grant:

> That His body had not been removed by His enemies; that its absence caused to His disciples the profoundest amazement, not unmingled in the breasts of some of them with sorrow and alarm; that they subsequently became convinced, by repeated proofs, that He had indeed risen from the dead; that for the truth of this belief they were ready at all times themselves to die; that the belief effected a profound and total change in their character, making the timid courageous and the weak irresistible; that they were incapable of a conscious falsehood and that, even if it had not been so, a conscious falsehood could never have had power to convince the disbelief and regenerate the morality of the world; that on this belief of the resurrection were built the still universal observance of the first day of the week and the entire foundations of the Christian Church these at any rate are facts which even skepticism itself, if it desires to be candid, can hardly fail, however reluctantly and slowly, to admit.

Firmly believing, then, that the merely historical evidence for the resurrection of Jesus is absolutely convincing, we say that here we have a miracle whose acceptance is not conditioned by belief in the infallibility of the Bible and whose actual occurrence cannot be successfully denied. But if this one miracle took place, then the possibility of the occurrence of miracles has to be granted, and the position of those who deny that miracles ever happened becomes untenable. Considerations like this should help persons who balk at Bible stories of miraculous events to overcome their prejudice and to listen to the message of the Scriptures.

Miracles and Our Times

Miracles do not happen today, we are told. Why should we assume that they occurred in the past? Is it really true that there are no longer any miraculous events? There are but few believers in the Savior who cannot point to an occasion where God heard their prayer when the outlook was desperate and He furnished them the help they needed.

An explanation that has frequently been advanced regarding fewer signs and wonders in our own day, and which does not seem farfetched, is that miracles are no longer needed as they were in the days when the Church was founded. At that time, when skepticism and unbelief were encountered by the disciples of Jesus on all sides and the question was heard, "How will these people prove that the new message they proclaim is true?" it was of utmost importance that confirmation should come to their proclamation by special acts of God. In fact, St. Paul referred to miracles as "signs of a true apostle" since God worked such miracles through the apostles most of all (2Co 12:12). Now that the Church is established, it is sufficient that its message be proved true by the influence of the Holy Spirit in the lives of Christians. The fact that there may be fewer spectacular signs and wonders in our days therefore can well be accounted for and need not disturb anyone.

Clearness of the Accounts

As we examine a little more closely some biblical accounts of miracles, we shall soon perceive that these narratives do not need many comments, as though they were unclear. They are wonderful and awe-inspiring, but not unclear, as a rule.

The story of the collapse of Jericho's walls can be understood by every reader of ordinary intelligence; no commentary is required to elucidate its language. How God did it, what unseen forces He summoned to hurl the proud battlements to the ground, whether He perhaps sent an ordinary earthquake, which rocked the region so violently that the walls were rent and thrown down, is something we cannot tell because the inspired narrative is silent on this point. But what we wish to stress here is that it is not the account that is hard to understand, but the manner in which the event took place. If we believe that God is omnipotent and that He can and will intervene to help His children in mysterious ways, then these reports of miracles will present no difficulty.

No Freak Miracles

Another feature worth noting is that many of the miracles follow what we term natural law, though at the same time transcending it. When Jesus feeds the five thousand (Mt 14:13–21), how does He do it? He might have removed their hunger with a word; for with God nothing is impossible. But instead of employing such a method, He provides bread to feed the people, satisfying their hunger and sustaining their lives by the usual means. When the children of Israel were pursued by Pharaoh and, it seemed, would not be able to escape because the sea formed what appeared to be an insuperable barrier to further flight, God prepared a way for them so that they could cross to the other side without difficulty. It is clear that by the exercise of His omnipotence He might have saved them from Pharaoh's grasp in a different way. For instance, He could have transported the whole host through the air to a region of safety. Instead of this, Israel has to march just as it marched before.

The lesson that this suggests is an important one. God does not perform freak miracles. He helps His children through His power, but, as a rule, it is by using the very channels along which His gifts ordinarily come to them. A certain country is visited by a disastrous drought and the resulting famine. Relief comes from God, not in the form of gold falling down from heaven, but in the shape of rain and a few years of plenty. The cancer patient prays to God for help in what appears to be a case of fatal illness. God preserves his life, not by one majestic command, but through surgery and medication. The plagues in Egypt are very instructive if viewed in this light (cf Ex 7–12). In almost every instance they consisted of a visitation that might arise in the ordinary course of events, and yet a miraculous element was attached to each one, manifesting itself in the time when the plague occurred and in its peculiar virulence.

The Healing of a Boy Who Had a Demon

Some readers may be perplexed by what is recorded in Mk 9:29: "[Jesus] said to them, 'This kind [of demons] cannot be driven out by anything but prayer.'" Jesus was speaking to His disciples. On their journey through Galilee they had performed miracles of healing and had expelled demons. In the instance reported in Mk 9:14–29, they had not been able to bring about the expulsion. Jesus chides them for their unbelief, but says in conclusion: "This kind cannot be driven out by anything but prayer." Was there, then, something more than faith required on this occasion? Must the saying of Jesus in which He depicts the power of faith as sufficiently great to move mountains be modified and held not to pertain to the healing of certain cases of demon possession? That is not what Jesus is saying. He is reminding His disciples that an affliction like that of the poor boy they had been dealing with was so dreadful, so terrifying in its nature that strong faith was needed if they wanted to help such an unfortunate sufferer and that their faith had to be strengthened through earnest prayer before entering upon this battle with Satan.

Do People Work Miracles Today?

In this connection let us examine a passage, Mk 16:17–18 (cf also Lk 10:19), in which Jesus definitely promises that miraculous powers will attend those who believe. Must it not, then, be conceded that certain modern groups which appeal to miraculous healings in proof of their possession of the truth are standing on solid scriptural ground? We reply: Let us not cast doubts upon the Word of God by putting a question mark alongside the promises of the Savior. He bestows grand powers on believers, that is certain. But equally clear is the warning that if people claim to possess miraculous gifts, but contradict the revealed Word of God in any point, they are not to be followed. Such powers as they possess or pretend to possess, if used to propagate error, are not from God, but from the Prince of Darkness.

In the Old Testament God warns the children of Israel not to follow a prophet who leads them to believe in other gods, in spite of signs and wonders which he may perform. In Dt 13:1–3 God tells them:

> If a prophet or a dreamer of dreams arises among you and gives you a sign or a wonder, and the sign or wonder that he tells you comes to pass, and if he says, "Let us go after other gods," which you have not known, "and let us serve them," you shall not listen to the words of that prophet or that dreamer of dreams. For the Lord your God is testing you, to know whether you love the Lord your God with all your heart and with all your soul.

And in the New Testament a similar note is sounded when Paul depicts the "lawless one" as appearing "by the activity of Satan with all power and false signs and wonders" (2Th 2:9). Miracles, taken by themselves, are not an absolute proof of the genuineness of the claims a teacher or preacher may put forth. The Church is built on the foundation of the apostles and prophets (Eph 2:20), and if any would lay a different foundation, they are not to be listened to, be their signs ever so spectacular and numerous.

Another important point to remember is that miracles are granted by God and must not be "attempted." To try to perform them without having the assurance that God wants us to engage in them would be tempting the Lord, which in every case is a very reprehensible act (cf Mt 4:7). The apostles, when sent out on their first missionary journey, performed miracles as a matter of course. In Matthew 10:8 and parallel passages, we are told that Jesus bestowed this faculty on them and ordered them to do such works. Yet there were even occasions when miracles did not attend the ministry of Jesus due to people's lack of faith (Mt 13:58).

Finally, miracles were to follow those who believe (Mk 16:17). The context shows that the preaching of the Gospel is most important, not miracles. If people make miracles the chief factor in their ministry, giving them precedence over everything else, we can be sure that their work is not in keeping with the will of God. How little did the apostles, when they preached the word in the various parts of the world, put their miraculous gifts into the foreground! Arriving in a certain town, they did not gather the people to stage some spectacle before them; but they preached the Good News of the kingdom of God established by the work and sacrifice of our Lord Jesus Christ. In the course of their stay in that town, if occasion arose, miracles might be performed, testifying that this new message was indeed the power of God unto salvation to everyone who believes. But there was no thought of making a display of supernatural powers merely to attract the curious or to entertain the multitudes.

THE LAND OF
THE BIBLE

No one who experiences the geography of the Promised Land will disagree with the appropriateness of God's name for this special place. He called it the land of milk and honey. This name not only distinguishes the Promised Land and its natural resources from the desolate deserts around it but also alludes to the geographical diversity found here. In the north, generous precipitation favors the farmer. Rain gives rise to rich agricultural fields that flower and bloom, providing natural resources the bees need to make *honey*. In the south, dryer conditions favor pastoral pursuits. Here the Bedouin children tend the family goat herd that is the source of the *milk* they drink. When God speaks of this entire land, He labels it "a land flowing with milk and honey" (Dt 11:9), acknowledging the dominance of agriculture in the north and pastoral pursuits in the south.

The borders of the Promised Land are discussed in several Bible passages. Nevertheless, precise drawing of borderlines is not always possible. For example, Nu 34 implies that the borders of the Promised Land terminate at the Jordan River, while Jsh 12 and Ezk 47 imply that the Promised Land extended east of the Jordan River to the Syrian Desert, and included the territory from the Arnon River to Mount Hermon. Detailed discussion of these matters occurs in other sources, so our purposes will best be served by describing the boundaries of the Promised Land in a more general way.

Perhaps the easiest way to describe the borders of the Promised Land is via the limits imposed by natural boundaries at every cardinal compass point. The northern boundary of Israel is formed by the Lebanon and Anti-Lebanon mountains. The southern boundary is the Wilderness of Zin and the Wadi el-Arish (River of Egypt). The western boundary of the Promised Land is the Mediterranean Sea. The eastern boundary is the Syrian Desert.

When we define them as such, we are extending the borders of the Promised Land to the ultimate limit permitted by the biblical authors. Nevertheless, this still leaves us with a land that is significantly smaller than most envision. From north to south, the Promised Land measures approximately 200 miles. From east to west, the distance between the sea and desert varies between 80 and 105 miles (averaging 90 miles in width). These dimensions of the Promised Land describe an area of approximately 12,000 square miles. Invariably, new visitors to Israel are struck by how much smaller the land is than they had anticipated.

The far northern region of Israel.

THE DIVERSITY OF THE LAND

Although this land is very small, it is a land with significant geographical diversity. Within the 200 miles of the northern and southern boundaries, one may experience every climate and ecological zone between sub-alpine and sub-tropical. We can walk in the snow among the pine forests of Mount Hermon, among the palm trees in Jericho, and past acacia trees in the desert of the Judean Wilderness. On the same day in August, the average high temperature at Jericho may be 102 degrees, while just 15 miles away in Jerusalem the temperature may be 75 degrees. One hundred miles to the north, snow may be gleaming on the fields of Mount Hermon. Mountain tundra, deserts, seashores, and marshy jungles are all part of the complex landscape that made up ancient Israel. Because being in one place in Israel is not like being in another, no single picture of the land will honor this great diversity in geography. To fully grasp the geography of Israel, we must compose a picture album that is filled with a great variety of images. As the readers turn the pages of their Bibles, they must also be ready to turn the pages in their picture albums. Even the story of Jesus, which occurs in a relatively small region, is set against a myriad of geographical settings. To fully appreciate the unique nature of each story, we must place it within its own unique geographical context.

We will begin to unpack this geographical diversity by dividing the Promised Land into four geographical zones: the coastal plain, the central mountain zone, the Jordan rift valley, and the eastern plateau. In the following paragraphs, a brief summary of each zone will prepare you to understand more detailed descriptions.

Green and red lettuce growing in the Sharon region.

Just as Abram and Sarai immigrated to Canaan 4,000 years ago at the Lord's command, "Lift up your eyes and look from the place where you are, northward and southward and eastward and westward. . . . Arise, walk through the length and breadth of the land" (Gn 13:14, 17).

Like the representatives of Israel sent to spy out the land, "Go up into the Negeb and go up into the hill country, and see what the land is . . . whether the land is rich or poor, and whether there are trees in it or not. Be of good courage and bring some of the fruit of the land" (Nu 13:17–18, 20).

The Coastal Plain

On the western side of the Promised Land we find a large plain with gently rolling hills. The coastal plain stretches 190 miles from Rosh HaNiqra in the north to the Wadi el-Arish in the south. The width of the plain varies from 50 yards to 15 miles, and grows wider and slightly higher in elevation as one travels south. The majority of this zone is an undulating plain with very low, rolling hills, most reaching no higher than 150 feet above sea level. As this region has a blanket of soil that has washed down from the central mountains, it is the most fertile of the zones and receives between 16 and 25 inches of annual precipitation. Standing in the heart of this plain, the traveler is overwhelmed not only by its fertility but also by its openness. The lower elevation of this gently rolling terrain favors international merchants and, in turn, the armies of empires who want to grow rich by taxing the merchants moving goods up and down the coast.

Herd of goats grazing in the mountains of Samaria, Israel.

Central Mountain Zone

Traveling east from the coastal plain, we meet the rising terrain of the central mountain zone. This zone extends through the heart of the country from Upper Galilee in the north to the foothills of the Negeb in the south. The mountains of this region rise abruptly and dramatically, forming a sharp contrast with the coast to its west and the Jordan Valley to its east. Elevations in these mountains average between 1,500 and 3,000 feet above sea level, with many segments reaching over 3,300 feet. The mountains themselves are neither snowcapped nor forested, giving them a harsh and rocky appearance.

The degree of fertility and accessibility varies from north to south in the region. In general, the central mountain zone is the least fertile and least accessible of the four zones. It does not favor either the farmer or the international traders. The narrow valleys provide less surface area for planting and produce a much smaller harvest. The rugged mountains that rise above those valleys force north-south travelers onto exposed, undulating ridgelines. East-west travel through the zone becomes all but impossible at most places due to the topographic relief imposed by the mountains. In many places, an east-west trip inland would encounter up to five ridgelines, each separated by deeply cut valleys requiring thousands of feet in elevation change. Given the poor prospects for agriculture and trade, one may wonder who would want to live in this sort of place. The answer is simple: the individual wishing to live in the most secure portion of the country. International invaders rarely entered this zone due to its reduced economic value and rugged terrain.

The Sea of Galilee rests in the northern portion of the Jordan rift valley.

Jordan Rift Valley

Traveling eastward from the Mediterranean Sea, the third zone the traveler meets is the Jordan rift valley. And what a valley it is! This zone is part of the Afro-Arabian rift valley, one of the longest and deepest intrusions in the earth's surface. It extends over 4,000 miles from Turkey to the great lakes of Africa. Within Israel, one can trace the primary fault line by following the streambed of the Jordan River. The valley begins at the base of Mount Hermon and follows the river during its 160-mile run, through the Sea of Galilee and to the southern end of the Dead Sea. This rift that primarily runs from north to south has also spawned a number of significant east-west valleys that radiate into the mountains. Such valleys provide the easiest passage for travelers moving east and west through the central mountain zone.

Perhaps the most striking feature of this zone is its elevation. The great majority of the Jordan rift valley is below sea level. The surface of the Sea of Galilee lies at 700 feet below sea level. The surface of the Dead Sea is the lowest place on earth's surface at 1,300 feet below sea level. As one might expect, the effects of this deep, geologic scar in the crust of the earth makes its presence felt in more than one way. Within archaeological sites along the rift, there is clear evidence of devastating earthquakes that have reshaped the land and destroyed magnificent structures. Today, the Jordan rift valley still comes alive with brief tremors. While such tremors give occasional testimony to the geological dynamics of this valley, hot springs that dot the region offer a continuous reminder of the dynamic forces at work just beneath the surface. These springs, frequently visited by the ancient inhabitants for their soothing and healing qualities, are still used by modern visitors who feel the need for such a hot bath.

An olive grove near the shore of Galilee.

Fertility and accessibility vary greatly along the run of the Jordan rift valley. The northern portions of the valley are more fertile than those lying farther south, but even the more fertile portions of this zone are less desirable than the fields of the coastal plain. The Jordan rift valley is more accessible than the mountains lying either to its east or west, but travel and trade are made more difficult by the climate. The oppressive heat of the summer months, coupled with malaria-infested swamps, discourage significant travel through most of this region.

Eastern Plateau

The eastern plateau, the final zone to be discussed, lies at the greatest distance from the Mediterranean Sea. The eastern plateau rises sharply and dramatically from the Jordan rift valley, forming a mountain-like facade. It then levels off and tilts east, descending to the fringes of the Syrian Desert. This zone boasts mountain peaks that reach 5,000 feet above sea level. The dominant characteristic of the zone, however, is its plateau-like appearance.

From the air, it presents itself as a high tableland that runs 250 miles from the base of Mount Hermon to the Gulf of Aqaba, varying in width from 30–80 miles. This tableland is incised by several deep canyons that carry runoff water from the mountains to the Jordan rift valley.

Rocky hills and fields near Syria.

In the northern stretches, the fertility of this plateau rivals that of the coastal plain. But as one moves south, fertility begins to diminish. Eventually, the rainfall becomes so scarce that shepherding, rather than agriculture, dominates the economy. The plateau did favor north-south trade, but the route was less desirable than the one on the coastal plain due to the significant canyons one needed to cross east of the Jordan River.

THE PLANTS AND ANIMALS OF THE LAND

The tremendous diversity in geography presented in the four zones of Israel supports very diverse plant and animal communities within ancient Israel. By contrast to many of us living a more urban lifestyle, animals and plants would have been a regular part of people's lives during biblical times. At the time of Jesus, 80 to 90 percent of the population was engaged in agricultural pursuits. When we consider the fact that the animal and plant communities of Israel are likely to be very different than those regularly experienced by the readers of this book, we conclude that most of us have a lot to learn about this dimension of God's Promised Land. A detailed look at the flora and fauna of Israel lies outside the scope of this article, but we will take a few moments to introduce this fascinating dimension of God's Promised Land.

Plant life in Israel must find a way to cope with the unique rainfall cycle. Virtually all of the rain falls within 50 consecutive days in the winter, therefore plants have adopted various ways in which they adapt themselves to this cycle and the years of drought that they regularly encounter. Some plants increase their water intake through enlarged root systems, while others edit their physical growth to collect the summer dew more efficiently.

Trees in the Galilee hills.

Still other plants limit the amount of water they lose through transpiration. As plants vary in the degree and nature of adaptation, it is not unusual to find different forms of vegetation on opposing sides of the same hill—plants on one side are enjoying a moist environment, while those on the other side have a drier environment. Given these challenging growing conditions, one might expect there to be fewer plants. But, in fact, Solomon is said to have described the plant life of his kingdom in some detail (1Ki 4:33). That is no small feat given that over 2,800 species of flowering plants alone grow in Israel.

As people such as Joshua or David walked the countryside, the principal forest cover they experienced was the maquis. The maquis is a cluster of plants comprised of various tree species (typically oak and terebinth) that grow no higher than about 15 feet. The trees grow very closely to one another creating a dense thicket at the base that is difficult to penetrate. Today the impact of significant deforestation has robbed the land of its former appearance. This deforestation began in the biblical period as a product of agricultural clearing, denuding by flocks, and the use of wood during various wars.

Domesticated plants also surrounded the people we know from our Bibles. Those plants played a key role in their lives by providing food, shelter, and income for the residents of the land. The Bible makes frequent reference to seven agricultural products expected from the land when the land was producing well. They are wheat, barley, grapes, olives, figs, pomegranates, and honey (Dt 8:8). We know that the diet of the Israelites also included various legumes and vegetables as well as cucumbers, watermelons, onions, leeks, and garlic.

Wildlife is another dimension of God's creation that is rich and varied in the Promised Land. Over five hundred different species of birds have been observed in Israel, from the sparrow to the stork to the ostrich. Of those, 120 are migrants that are regularly observed during their migration season. The ancient residents of Israel also had a chance to see reptiles and mammals that you may have only encountered in a zoo. This includes the hippo, crocodile, tortoise, gazelle, ibex, lion, bear, wolf, and cheetah. Some of these animals became a food source for the people in this land, while others posed a threat to business and travel.

THE CHOSEN LAND

This land that is so unique in topography, flora, and fauna is God's chosen land. Before we leave this general introduction to Israel, let us pause for a moment to consider why the Lord would have chosen this land rather than another to be the Promised Land. Biblical authors repeatedly clarify that God created every acre of land on the earth's surface. The land of Israel was not the only land available to Him. So why would He choose this land rather than another? The inspired writers only hint at the answer. But by combining theology and geography we propose the following explanation: God chose Israel to be the land of hope because it was suited for proclaiming a message and because it inspired faith.

A Land Suited to Proclaim a Message

In order to better understand why this land is so powerful in proclaiming a message to the world, we first need to place it within the larger geographical context of the Fertile Crescent. The Fertile Crescent is a semicircle of land that extends from the Mediterranean Sea to the Persian Gulf. The north side of this arch is bound by that portion of the Alpine-Himalayan mountain

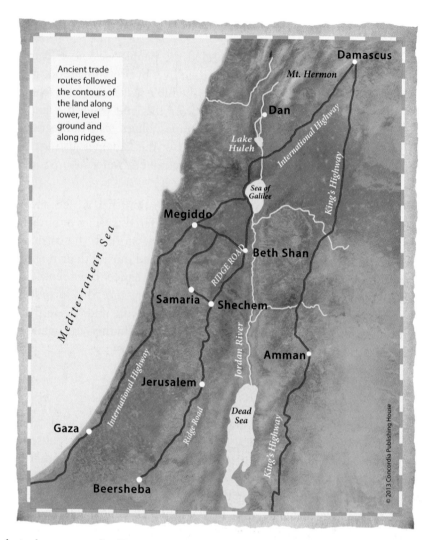

Ancient trade routes followed the contours of the land along lower, level ground and along ridges.

chain known as the Taurus, Kurdistan, and Zargos Mountains. The south side of this arch terminates in the Arabian and Syrian Desert. Between the mountains and the desert is a relatively arable land. The more northern portions of this arch receive sufficient rain to grow grain. In the southern portions of this arch, water may be diverted by irrigation canals from the Tigris and Euphrates Rivers to water the agricultural fields. In this arch between the rugged mountains and desiccating desert, the Fertile Crescent provided the natural resources needed to carry on life. The key here is water. If we take a map and mark the land watered by the Nile, the Tigris, and the Euphrates Rivers, as well as those areas receiving more than 12 inches of annual precipitation, we will have marked the Fertile Crescent.

This arch is the home of the ancient Assyrian and Babylonian empires mentioned in the Old Testament. Among these more sophisticated people, we find the roots of modern culture that we take for granted. In this crescent, art, music, literature, and mathematics find their earliest recorded beginning.

The Fertile Crescent was not only the seat of ancient culture but it was also the key to international transportation and trade. A highway that we will call the International Highway follows this arch. It courses through this arch for 1,770 miles from southern Egypt to the head of the Persian Gulf via a route between mountains and desert. Merchants traveled this highway buying and selling to everyone along the way. In the Promised Land, this usable arch narrows to approximately 30 miles west of the Sea of Galilee. That makes Israel a land bridge from which the economy of the world could be controlled. It was this factor more than any other that consistently brought the larger empires of the Fertile Crescent to Israel. It became a tax station from which those empires could tax the goods carried by the merchants on the International Highway.

But that highway carried another commodity that the empires could not tax: the news of the day. If you had a message to deliver in the ancient world, you could either send messengers scurrying along the International Highway, or you could position yourself at a key point along that highway and speak a message that would be carried by others to the farthest reaches of the inhabited world. God did both. The apostles would travel this road, but even before they reached places well beyond the boundaries of Israel, the message of the Gospel had arrived ahead of them carried by other travelers on this ancient road. As the land of Israel is the crossroads linking Asia, Africa, and Europe, it becomes a podium. Clearly one of the reasons that the Lord chose this land to be a stage for much biblical history was that the world would regularly come past this podium and carry what it heard to the farthest reaches of the world.

A Land that Inspires Faith

The second reason that God may have selected Israel as His chosen land is that it inspires faith in its residents. Faith is a quality highly praised by God in His message to us. As the psalmist says, "The LORD takes pleasure in those who fear Him, in those who hope in His steadfast love" (Ps 147:11). God wants His people to turn to Him in faith. This quality is particularly desirable in the messengers who would speak from the podium in the Promised Land. They were to speak their message with faith and conviction. Israel is a land that inspires such faith. The messengers who live in this land do not live in comfort and security, but are harassed both by distant empires and local tribes. They live threatened by the Egyptian and Mesopotamian empires that bring their armies to ravage the land and control the international economy. On only a few occasions in history have those who lived in this land actually controlled their own political destiny. Typically such autonomy only existed when the empires were weakened or distracted by other national and international events. The inhabitants of this land not only feared the empires but also the raiders that would sweep in from the desert at harvest time.

But perhaps the most significant factor that inspired faith in this land was the lack of Israel's natural resources compared to its neighbors. It possesses no gold and very few minerals. But most significantly it is a land without an adequate supply of fresh water. The ancient inhabitants of Israel absolutely depended on rainfall to water their fields, fill their cisterns, and animate the springs. God promised to send that rain (Dt 11:13–15) and invited the people to put their faith in Him.

Why did the Lord select this land to be the Promised Land? The biblical writers do not lead us directly to the answer. But by combining what they do say with a sensitivity to the geography of Israel, we may propose that the Lord selected this land because it was an apt podium for the delivery of His message as well as a destitute land that invited the messengers in that podium to renew their faith in the Lord's promises.

Adapted from John A. Beck, *The Land of Milk and Honey: An Introduction to the Geography of Israel* (St. Louis: Concordia, 2006), 11, 19–27.

THE TIME OF THE BIBLE: A CHRONOLOGY

Calculations based on the biblical record make it possible to date many events and the lives of people who participated in those events. Biblical history did not merely occur "once upon a time" as storytellers say. Biblical and Christian religion is historical, since God's supernatural revelation entered ordinary space and time. (See "History and God's People," p 193.)

Stone Age culture shows some evidence of record keeping. (See the interesting overview of research in Richard Rudgley, *The Lost Civilizations of the Stone Age* [New York: The Free Press, 1999].) However, historians and archaeologists typically date the development of writing as we know and use it today to the end of the fourth millennium BC and associate early writing with Mesopotamia and Egypt. The genealogies of Genesis 5; 10–11 are incomplete, so historians cannot effectively calculate dates from them (see p 7). The first dateable person in the Bible is Abram (Abraham), who was born in Mesopotamia near the end of the third millennium BC and later traveled to Egypt (Gn 12).

Calculating Dates

The following chronology allows the reader to compare the biblical record of events with parallel records of events in world history, with special attention to the civilizations that most often interacted with the people of Israel. Users should be aware that scholars of history may differ considerably when dating specific kings and events (e.g., dates proposed for the early dynasties of Egypt often differ by as much as 50 years). Although historians may fix some dates on the basis of astronomical events described in ancient texts, they estimate most dates by comparing lists of kings and events.

Historians also sometimes have difficulty determining the dates for biblical persons and events after Abram. (E.g., dates for the exodus and conquest are hotly debated in academic circles.) Dating usually grows easier and clearer as one moves forward in history (e.g., for Israel, dates from the kingdom period and forward are more easily calculated). We are grateful to Andrew Steinmann, whose research on the dates of biblical persons and events was especially helpful for the development of the tables below. Bracketed notes represent a proposed construction based on biblical and historical contexts.

EVENTS FROM CREATION TO THE FLOOD

BIBLICAL RECORD	RECORDS OF OTHER CIVILIZATIONS
Creation in six days (Gn 1–2)	Creation accounts in Mesopotamia and other cultures have similarities with biblical themes but differ markedly in theology.
Fall into sin (Gn 3)	
Children of Adam and Eve (Gn 4–5; 10). Moses may refer to an earlier resource for his information: *The Book of the Generations of Adam* (see *TLSB* note, Gn 5:1; see also pp 5–9).	
Noah called to build the ark (Gn 6)	Flood accounts in various world cultures describe a great worldwide flood during which a hero rescues animals and mankind (e.g., *Sumerian Kings List, Atrahasis Epic, Eridu Flood Story*, and *Epic of Gilgamesh*). Such flood accounts are not limited to Mesopotamia.
The flood (Gn 7–8)	
God's promise to Noah (Gn 9)	
The tower of Babel (Gn 11)	The *Sumerian Epic of Enmerkar* refers to a common language spoken by all people.

Although writing began at an earlier date (e.g., Sumerian records of commerce may date to c 3300 BC), recorded history began when the Egyptians used hieroglyphs to describe the unification of Upper and Lower Egypt under Menes in c 3100 BC. After this point, it becomes possible to calculate dates for persons and events, though many difficulties still result because of the variety of calendars, writing systems, and styles used by ancient people.

Anatolia, Greece, and Rome	Egypt and Africa	Dates	Syria, Canaan, and Israel	Mesopotamia and Persia
DATEABLE, RECORDED HISTORY				
	Menes unites Upper and Lower Egypt; 1st Egyptian Dynasty	c 3100 BC	Gebal/Byblos serves as an important trade center with Egypt; Jericho is a long-established city	
	2nd Dynasty begins	2890	Temple gifts at Gebal/Byblos bear the name of Egyptian ruler Khasekhemui	

Anatolia, Greece, and Rome	Egypt and Africa	Dates	Syria, Canaan, and Israel	Mesopotamia and Persia
		c 2700		Sumerian royal inscriptions begin; early dynasty of Sumerians emerging; name of ruler Enmebaragesi found in archaeological remains from this time
	Djoser reigns; 3rd Dynasty; Imhotep builds step pyramid	2686		
		c 2500		Writings in Mari
	5th Dynasty	c 2494		
		c 2400		Writings in Assyria
	6th Dynasty	c 2345		
		c 2334	Sargon conquers Syrian states; they yield various goods to him	Sargon I of Akkad; followed by Akkadian Dynasty
		c 2290–2250	Ebla flourishes as trade center between Mediterranean region and Mesopotamia	

Detail of the Standard of Ur; Sumerian.

Anatolia, Greece, and Rome	Egypt and Africa	Dates	Syria, Canaan, and Israel	Mesopotamia and Persia
THE PATRIARCHS OF ISRAEL				
		2166 BC		Abram born (Gn 11:27–32)
	Intermediate period; invaders divide and disrupt Egypt	c 2160–2040		
		c 2150		Gutians invade and disrupt Ur
		c 2156		Sarai born (Gn 17:17)
		c 2112–c 2095		Ur-Nammu, founder of the 3rd Sumerian Dynasty of Ur and the Sumerian legal code, builds step pyramid
		c 2100	Amorite invasion destroys Gebal/Byblos	
		2091		Abram moves from Haran to Canaan (Gn 12:4)
		2067	Abram given the name Abraham, circumcised with Ishmael (Gn 17:1–6, 24–25)	
	Egyptian Middle Kingdom	c 2040–1786		
		c 2030	Sarah dies (Gn 23:1–2)	
		2026	Isaac marries Rebekah (Gn 25:20)	
		2006	Jacob and Esau born (Gn 25:24–26)	
		2004		Dynasty of Ur-Nammu ends

Model of a grain storage house with scribe and men carrying sacks of grain; Egyptian (2040–1650 BC).

Anatolia, Greece, and Rome	Egypt and Africa	Dates	Syria, Canaan, and Israel	Mesopotamia and Persia
Minoan culture builds palaces on Crete		c 2000	Pottery imported from Cyprus reaches Canaan	
	Mentuhotep unites Egypt; 12th Dynasty begins with powerful pharaohs	1991	Abraham dies (Gn 25:7)	
		1966	Esau marries Judith (Gn 26:34)	
		1943	Ishmael dies (Gn 25:17)	
Hittites emerging in Anatolia; Greek pottery uses hieroglyphic script		c 1900		
	[Joseph sold into slavery in Egypt (Gn 37:2, 12–28)]	inter 1901– 1897		
		1894		Sumuabum establishes Amorite Dynasty at Babylon
		1886	Isaac dies (Gn 35:28–29)	
	[Joseph enters service in Pharaoh's court (Gn 41:46)]	inter 1888– 1884		
	Jacob goes to Egypt (Apr; Gn 47:9, 28; Ex 12:40–41)	1876		

Hittite king, Tudhaliya, held in the hand of god Sharuma.

Anatolia, Greece, and Rome	Egypt and Africa	Dates	Syria, Canaan, and Israel	Mesopotamia and Persia
	Jacob dies (Gn 47:28)	1859		
		c 1830		Iakhdunlim strengthens Mari
	[Joseph dies (Gn 50:22, 26)]	inter 1808–1804		Assyrians build temple to Sumerian god Enlil
ISRAEL IN EGYPT				
Linear A script at Crete		c 1800–1450 BC		Hurrians spreading influence
		1792–1750		Hammurabi of Babylon
	2nd Intermediate Period	1786–1567		
		c 1775	Aleppo, an important trade center under the ruler Iarimlim	Mari flourishes as a trade center, as recorded in the archives of Alalakh
		1756		Hammurabi destroys Mari
	Hyksos invade and dominate Egypt	c 1750		
Labarnas founds Hittite Empire		c 1680		
		c 1670		Asshur (Akkadian/Assyrian) Dynasty emerges
Hattusilis I expands Hittite Empire	17th Dynasty established at Thebes	c 1650	N. Syria falls to the Hittites	Kassite Dynasty emerges in Babylon
Mursilis I leads Hittites to victory over Aleppo and Babylon		c 1590	Aleppo defeated	Hittites defeat Amorite Dynasty of Babylon
	Hyksos expelled	c 1580–1570		

Anatolia, Greece, and Rome	Egypt and Africa	Dates	Syria, Canaan, and Israel	Mesopotamia and Persia
	Ahmose begins New Kingdom; 18th Dynasty	c 1570	Fleeing Hyksos occupy Sharuhen, Egyptians destroy the city	
Telipinus issues edict regulating Hittite succession and courts		1530		
	Moses born (Ex 7:7; Dt 34:7); Thutmose I claims Syria	1526		
Mycenaeans trade with Canaanites		c 1500	Mycenaean designs influence Canaanites	Mitanni Empire emerges in N. Mesopotamia under Saustatar
	Amenhotep II quells rebellion in Orontes Valley	1488	Cities of the Orontes Valley revolt against Egyptian rule	

Fresco from the Minoan palace at Knossos.

THE EXODUS AND THE CONQUEST

Anatolia, Greece, and Rome	Egypt and Africa	Dates	Syria, Canaan, and Israel	Mesopotamia and Persia
	Thutmose III destroys coalition at Megiddo	c 1468 BC	Canaanite Prince of Kadesh coalition defeated	
	Thutmose III co-regent with Amenhotep II, who campaigns in Asia	c 1450		
Destruction of Greek palaces (e.g., Knossos)	1st Passover; exodus (Apr; Ex 12:6; 1Ki 6:1; Nu 33:3)	1446	Passover in Sinai (Apr; Nu 9:1); Israel arrives at Wilderness of Sin (May; Ex 16:1) and Wilderness of Sinai (May/June; Ex 19:1)	

Canaanite bronze bulls; Late Bronze or Early Iron Age.

Anatolia, Greece, and Rome	Egypt and Africa	Dates	Syria, Canaan, and Israel	Mesopotamia and Persia
		1445	Tabernacle set up (Mar/Apr; Ex 40:2,17); census taken (Apr/May; Nu 1:1–2, 18); Israel leaves Wilderness of Sinai (May; Nu 10:11)	
		1444	Israel leaves Kadesh (Dt 2:14)	
	Thutmose IV makes peace with Mitanni Empire; Amarna Letters	c 1425		Mitanni and Egyptians cease long struggle over Syria
		1407	Israel arrives at Wilderness of Zin (Apr/May; Nu 20:1); Aaron dies (July/Aug; Nu 33:38)	
			Moses addresses Israel (Dec/Jan; Dt 1:3)	
		1406	Israel crosses the Jordan (Apr; Jsh 4:19); 1st Passover in the land (Jsh 5:10)	
Hittite New Kingdom emerges		1400	Joshua gives Hebron to Caleb (Jsh 14:10)	
		1399–1375	Death of Joshua and the elders (Jgs 2:6–10)	

THE JUDGES OF ISRAEL

Anatolia, Greece, and Rome	Egypt and Africa	Dates	Syria, Canaan, and Israel	Mesopotamia and Persia
	Akhenaton (Amenhotep IV) introduces monotheistic religious reforms	c 1379 BC	Judges lead Israel c 300 years	
Hittite expansion under Suppiluliumus I		c 1375	Hittites retake Syria	

Anatolia, Greece, and Rome	Egypt and Africa	Dates	Syria, Canaan, and Israel	Mesopotamia and Persia
Hittites defeat Mitanni		c 1360	Cities of Syria ally with Mitanni and suffer defeat from the Hittites	Hittites and Ashuruballit I defeat Mitanni ruler Tushratta; Mitanni becomes part of Hittite Empire
	Ramses I begins 19th Dynasty	1332	Eglon oppresses Israel	
		c 1307–1275		Adad-nirari I of Assyria defeats Kassites and Mitanni
Battle of Kadesh between Hittites and Egyptians	Ramses II defeated at Kadesh	1286		
Troy violently destroyed		c 1275		Shalmaneser I defeats Mitanni; builds 2nd capital at Calah
		1236	Jabin oppresses Israel	
		1234		Tukultininurta I defeats Kassite Dynasty of Babylon; however, Kassites regain control
	Sea Peoples invade Egypt	1230		
Hattusus burned; Hittite Empire collapses	Senakht begins 20th Dynasty	c 1200		
Sea Peoples (Philistines?) invade coast of Canaan	Egyptian influence diminished	1190	Philistine cities emerging in Gaza	
		1124–1103		Nebuchadrezzar I (Assyrian) makes Babylon his capital
		c 1114–c 1076		Tiglath-pileser I of Assyria expands empire and wins victories against Babylon

Anatolia, Greece, and Rome	Egypt and Africa	Dates	Syria, Canaan, and Israel	Mesopotamia and Persia
	21st Dynasty (Tanite); Egyptian weakness	1085		
		1099–1060	Eli, priest and judge (1Sm 4:15, 18); on Samuel, see pp 277–78; *Ant* 6:294	
		1060	Ark in Philistine territory (1Sm 6:1)	

THE KINGDOM OF ISRAEL

Anatolia, Greece, and Rome	Egypt and Africa	Dates	Syria, Canaan, and Israel	Mesopotamia and Persia
Collapse of Mycenaean culture; Linear B script no longer used		c 1050 BC		
		1048–1009	Saul reigns over Israel (1Sm 13:1; Ac 13:21)	
		1039	David born (2Sm 5:1–5)	
		1010–1009	David lives in Philistine territory (1Sm 27:7)	
		1009–970	David reigns seven years in Hebron, then over all Israel in Jerusalem (2Sm 5:5; 1Ki 2:11)	
	Pharaoh's daughter marries Solomon	970–931	Reign of Solomon (1Ki 12:42)	
		967–960	Temple built and dedicated (1Ki 6:1; 2Ch 3:1–2; 2Ch 7:7–10)	

The Gezer Calendar, in Hebrew.

Anatolia, Greece, and Rome	Egypt and Africa	Dates	Syria, Canaan, and Israel	Mesopotamia and Persia
THE DIVIDED KINGDOMS: ISRAEL AND JUDAH				
	Shoshenq I founds 22nd Dynasty	945 BC		
		931	Israel divided under Rehoboam	
		927	Shishak (Shoshenq I) invades Israel (1Ki 14:25; 2Ch 12:2)	Ashur-dan II revives Assyria
Phoenician temple built on Crete; Etruscans emerging in Italy		c 900		
		898	Asa's reform/ covenant (May/June; 2Ch 15:10–12)	
		883–859		Ashurnasirpal II of Assyria expands his empire, slaughtering prisoners and deporting conquered people
		871	Jehoshaphat sends teachers throughout Israel (2Ch 17:7)	
		858–824	N. Syria falls to Shalmaneser; Damascus besieged	Shalmaneser III of Assyria
		855–853	No war between Israel and the Arameans (1Ki 22:1)	
		853	Battle of Qarqar between Aramean kings and Assyrians	
		841–835	Athaliah rules Judah; Joash hidden in temple	

Anatolia, Greece, and Rome	Egypt and Africa	Dates	Syria, Canaan, and Israel	Mesopotamia and Persia
		c 828–824		Rebellion complicates Assyrian succession; Shamshi-Adad emerges as ruler with help of Babylonians
	23rd Dynasty begins	817		
	Tyrians found Carthage	c 813	Jerusalem temple repaired (2Ki 12:6–7)	
		804	Damascus conquered	Adad-nirari III of Assyria takes over Syria
Etruscan city-states emerge in central Italy		c 800		
		c 783–773		Shalmaneser IV of Assyria
1st Olympiad		775	Jotham born (2Ki 15:32–33; 2Ch 27:1)	
		773	Shalmaneser IV leads unsuccessful campaign against Damascus	
		744–727		Tiglath-pileser III of Assyria
		740	Hezekiah born (2Ki 18:1–2; 2Ch 29:1); Isaiah's vision (Is 6)	
Greeks colonize locations around the Mediterranean		c 734–580		
		724–722	Samaria besieged (2Ki 18:9–10)	

ISRAEL IN EXILE

		722 BC	Fall of Samaria to Assyrians	
		721–705		Sargon II of Assyria

Anatolia, Greece, and Rome	Egypt and Africa	Dates	Syria, Canaan, and Israel	Mesopotamia and Persia
	25th Dynasty of Shabaka (Cushite)	716		
		715	Hezekiah repairs temple (2Ch 29:3; Is 14:28–32)	
		704–681		
		c 701	Sennacherib besieges Jerusalem (2Ki 18:13; Is 36:1); Hezekiah's sickness; Hezekiah pays tribute to Sennacherib	
Carchemish preserves Hittite script and culture to this point		700		
	Assyrians occupy Egypt	671		Esarhaddon takes Egypt; height of Assyrian Empire
		668–c 627		Ashurbanipal, last great ruler of Assyria
	26th Dynasty begins; Psamtik expels Assyrians	664–663		
2nd Messenian War		650		
		633	Jehoiakim born (2Ki 23:36; 2Ch 36:5); Josiah seeks the Lord	
Cylon attempts coup in Athens		c 630		

Assyrian soldiers from the walls of Sennacherib's palace.

Balustrade of Phoenician-Israelite style, from Jehoiakim's palace.

Anatolia, Greece, and Rome	Egypt and Africa	Dates	Syria, Canaan, and Israel	Mesopotamia and Persia
		629	Josiah purges high places (2Ch 34:3)	
		628	Jeremiah called to be a prophet (Jer 1:1–2)	
		625–605		Nabopolassar of Neo-Babylonia
		623	Book of the Law found in the temple; Josiah's Passover (Apr 15; 2Ch 35:1, 19)	
Etruscan Dynasty of Tarquius begins		616	Jehoiachin born (2Ki 24:8; 2Ch 36:9)	
		c 612–609		Chaldeans and Medes destroy Assyrian rule
	Pharaoh Neco defeated at Carchemish	605	Nebuchadnezzar besieges Jerusalem (2Ki 24:1); Judeans first removed from Judah (Jer 24, 36, 45–46; Dn 1)	
		604–562		Nebuchadnezzar of Neo-Babylonia
		604	Fast proclaimed; Baruch reads scroll (inter Nov 24–Dec 23; Jer 36:9–10, 22)	
	Egyptians repel Babylonians	601	Jehoiakim rebels against Nebuchadnezzar	Babylonians turned back near Gaza
Phocaea Greeks colonize Spain		600		
		599	Nebuchadnezzar takes captives (Jer 52:28)	
		597	Nebuchadnezzar besieges Jerusalem (2Ki 24:10; 2Ch 36:10)	

Anatolia, Greece, and Rome	Egypt and Africa	Dates	Syria, Canaan, and Israel	Mesopotamia and Persia
Solon's reforms in Athens		594	Hananiah confronts Jeremiah (Jer 28:1); Hananiah dies (Jer 28:17)	
		593		Ezekiel's 1st vision (July 31; Ezk 1:1–2)
		589	Siege of Jerusalem (Jer 32:1–2; 39:1; 52:4; Ezk 24–25)	
		587	Final siege of Jerusalem begins (2Ki 25:1; Ezk 24:1–2)	Oracles against Egypt (Ezk 29:1–2) and Pharaoh (Ezk 30:20–22; 31:1–2)

JUDAH IN EXILE

Anatolia, Greece, and Rome	Egypt and Africa	Dates	Syria, Canaan, and Israel	Mesopotamia and Persia
		587 BC	Wall of Jerusalem breached (July 29; 2Ki 25:3–4; Jer 39:2; 52:6–7); Nebuzaradan burns the temple (Aug 28; Jer 52:12–13); Gedaliah killed (2Ki 25:25; Jer 41:1–2)	
		573		Ezekiel's vision of a new Jerusalem (Ezk 40–48)
		inter 573–569		Nebuchadnezzar's 2nd dream and humiliation (Dn 4)
Croesus of Lydia		561		Evil-merodach of Neo-Babylonia; Jehoiachin freed from prison (2Ki 25:27; Jer 52:31)

Detail of the Babylonia Ishtar Gate.

Anatolia, Greece, and Rome	Egypt and Africa	Dates	Syria, Canaan, and Israel	Mesopotamia and Persia
Homer's poems set down in writing		c 560		Nergal Shar Usur of Neo-Babylonia
		559–529		Rise of Persian Empire under Cyrus II
		553		Ancient of Days vision (Dn 7)
Cyrus defeats Lydians; Persian pressure drives Phocaeans west to Italy and Spain		551		Goat and ram vision (Dn 8); Cyrus II of Persia defeats Croesus of Lydia; Ionian Greeks become Persian subjects
JUDEANS RETURN FROM EXILE				
		538 BC		Cyrus rules Babylon; Cyrus's decree (Ezr 1:1; 5:13; 6:3)
		537	Altar in Jerusalem rebuilt (Ezr 3)	
		536	2nd temple begun (inter Apr 29–May 28; Ezr 3:8)	Daniel in mourning; prince of Persia opposes angel (Apr 3–23; Dn 10:2, 13)
Greeks attempt westward expansion	Carthage and Etruscans halt Greek expansion	c 535		
		530	Work on temple halted (Ezr 4:24)	
	Achaemenid 27th Dynasty under Cambyses	525		Cambyses II of Persia (528–523 BC)
		522–486		Darius I of Persia
		520	Messages of Haggai and Zechariah (Hg 1–2; Zec 1)	

Anatolia, Greece, and Rome	Egypt and Africa	Dates	Syria, Canaan, and Israel	Mesopotamia and Persia
		516	2nd temple finished (Feb 21; Ezr 6:15)	Darius campaigns against Scythians
Roman republic founded		509		
Cleisthenes reforms Athenian constitution toward democracy	Carthage concludes peace treaty with Rome	c 508		
Ionian revolt against Persia		499		Persians mobilize against Ionian tyrants
Battle of Marathon; Greeks defeat Persians		490		Darius defeated at Marathon
		486	Letter written to Xerxes (Ezr 4:6)	
Greeks defeat Persians at Thermopylae, Artemisium, Salamis		480		Greeks defeat huge Persian force
		478		Xerxes of Persia marries Esther (Est 2:16–17)
		474		Haman issues edict about Jews (Apr 17; Est 3:12); Mordecai issues counter-edict (July 23; Est 8:9)
		464–424		Artaxerxes I of Persia
1st Peloponnesian War		460–446		
Athenians support Inaros's revolt	Lybian Prince Inaros revolts against Persians	459		

A Persian two-headed griffin in the ancient city of Persepolis, Iran.

Anatolia, Greece, and Rome	Egypt and Africa	Dates	Syria, Canaan, and Israel	Mesopotamia and Persia
		458	Ezra arrives in Jerusalem (Oct 31; Ezr 7:8–9)	Ezra leaves Babylon (Apr 8; Ezr 7:9); Ezra leaves Ahava River (Apr 19; Ezr 8:31)
	Herodotus in Egypt	c 450		
Athens makes peace with Persia		449		
Canuleian Law (Roman)		445	Walls of Jerusalem completed (Oct 3; Ne 6:15); Nehemiah holds convocation (Oct 8; Ne 7:73; 8:2)	Nehemiah requests leave to go to Jerusalem (inter Apr 13–May 11; Ne 2:1–5)
		433/432		Nehemiah returns to Susa (Ne 13:6)
Great Peloponnesian War		431–404		

THE TIME BETWEEN THE TESTAMENTS

Anatolia, Greece, and Rome	Egypt and Africa	Dates	Syria, Canaan, and Israel	Mesopotamia and Persia
		423–405 BC		Darius II of Persia
	Priests of Khnum and Persians destroy Jewish temple in Egypt	410		
	Amyrtaeus rebels, establishes Saite 28th Dynasty	c 405		
Peloponnesian War ends		404		
		404–359/358		Artaxerxes II of Persia
Gauls capture Rome		390		
	30th Dynasty	380		

Anatolia, Greece, and Rome	Egypt and Africa	Dates	Syria, Canaan, and Israel	Mesopotamia and Persia
Philip II of Macedon		359–336		
		358–338		Artaxerxes III of Persia
	Carthage concludes treaty with Rome	348		
1st Samnite War begins; Roman power expands	31st Dynasty under Artaxerxes III	343		Persians attack at Pelusium
Rome wins Latin War		341		
Dissolution of Latin League		338		Artaxerxes III murdered; Arses (Xerxes II) rules Persia
Alexander rules Macedonia		336		
	Darius III takes Egypt	335		Darius III rules Persia until 331
Alexander defeats Persians at Issus		333		
	Alexander proclaimed pharaoh	332	Alexander takes Judea away from Persians	
Alexander the Great dies at Babylon		323		
	Ptolemy I founds Ptolemaic Dynasty (Greek)	305		Seleucus I Nicator founds Seleucid Dynasty (Greek)
1st Punic War; Roman power expands	Carthaginians lose territory to Rome	264–241		
2nd Punic War		218–202		

Alexander the Great.

Anatolia, Greece, and Rome	Egypt and Africa	Dates	Syria, Canaan, and Israel	Mesopotamia and Persia
	Ptolemy IV defeats Antiochus III	217	Battle of Raphia secures Ptolemaic rule of Judea	Antiochus III defeated at Raphia
	Scopus defeated; Ptolemies lose Judea, make peace with Seleucids	198	Battle of Panias; Jews in Egypt and Judea are separated from one another politically	Antiochus III takes over Judea
Romans defeat Antiochus III at Smyrna		190		Antiochus III loses much of Asia Minor to Rome, faces financial trouble
		174	Jason bribes Antiochus III to secure the high priesthood at the Jerusalem temple	
		171	Menelaus, a non-Levite, purchases the priesthood at Jerusalem; Jason removed	
		c 168	Mattathias dies	
Romans conquer Macedonia	Antiochus IV Epiphanes engaged in war with Egypt	167	Antiochus IV orders pigs to be sacrificed to Olympian Zeus at the Jerusalem temple, leading to the Maccabean revolt; sacrilege continues for 2½ years	Antiochus IV Epiphanes forces Syrian laws on Judeans
		166	Battle of Beth-horon	
		165	Judas Maccabeus leads rebellion against Seleucids	
		164	Maccabees retake and purify Jerusalem; Hanukkah established	
		153	Jonathan officiates as high priest at Feast of Booths	Syrian conflict between Demetrius I and Alexander Balas; Seleucid Kingdom declines; knowledge of cuneiform script is lost

Anatolia, Greece, and Rome	Egypt and Africa	Dates	Syria, Canaan, and Israel	Mesopotamia and Persia
		147	Battle of Jamnia	
3rd Punic War; Romans destroy Corinth	Romans destroy Carthage	146		
	Infighting divides Ptolemies	145		
		141	Simon takes Akra, enters Jerusalem	Parthians begin to take over Mesopotamia
		135	Ptolemy murders Simon, last son of Mattathias; John Hyrcanus accepts Syrian rule	Antiochus VII Sidetes besieges Jerusalem
		104–103	Aristobulus rules	
		103–76	Alexander Jannaeus rules	
		76–67	Alexandra rules	
Romans fight slave war with Spartacus		73–71		
		67–63	Aristobulus II rules	
Romans establish Idumean Dynasty under Antipater		63	Idumean Dynasty under Antipater	
Caesar's Gallic Wars		59–51		
Crassus defeated at Carrhae		53		Battle of Carrhae; Parthians defeat Romans
	Cleopatra VII and Ptolemy XIII enthroned	52		

Anatolia, Greece, and Rome	Egypt and Africa	Dates	Syria, Canaan, and Israel	Mesopotamia and Persia
Julius Caesar crosses the Rubicon and becomes Roman dictator		49–44		
	Cleopatra's son Caesarion born	47	Herod made tetrarch of Galilee	
Caesar assassinated		44		
		43	Malchus poisons Antipater	
Octavian (Augustus) and Antony defeat Cassius and Brutus at Philippi		42	Herod the Great and Phasael made tetrarchs of Judea	
Octavian appoints Herod ruler of Judea		40	Herod flees from Parthians to Rome, returns as ruler	Parthians invade Judea but later withdraw
Battle of Actium; Egyptians withdraw	Egyptians claim victory at Actium	31		
Rome rules Egypt until AD 642	Antony and Cleopatra commit suicide	30		
Augustus, 1st Roman emperor		27 BC–AD 14		
		14–4 BC	Family feuds trouble Herod	

Anatolia, Greece, and Rome	Egypt and Africa	Dates	Syria, Canaan, and Israel	Mesopotamia and Persia
		THE NEW TESTAMENT		
		4 BC	Angel appears to Zechariah (c Nov 15; Lk 1:8–22)	
		3 BC	The annunciation (inter Apr 17–May 16; Lk 1:26–38); John the Baptist born (Aug; Lk 1:57–66)	
	Holy family in Egypt	2 BC	Jesus born (mid Jan to early Feb; Mt 1:25; Lk 2:1–7); Magi visit; flight to Egypt (mid to late in the year; Mt 2)	
		1 BC	Death of Herod the Great (after Jan 10; Mt 2:19); return to Nazareth (Mt 2:19–23)	
		AD 6	Judas the Galilean leads revolt against Rome; Judea, Samaria, and Idumaea combined to form the Roman province of Judea	
		c 10	Rabbi Hillel dies	
		11	Jesus in temple before the elders (c Apr 8–22; Lk 2:42)	
Tiberius, Roman emperor		14–37		
Revolt in Gaul; grain shortages cause unrest in Rome		21		
		29	Baptism of Jesus (Fall; Lk 3:1–2)	
		30	Jesus at Passover (c Apr 8; Jn 2:20)	

Coin issued by Herod the Great.

Anatolia, Greece, and Rome	Egypt and Africa	Dates	Syria, Canaan, and Israel	Mesopotamia and Persia
		32	Jesus at Passover (c Apr 15; Jn 6:4); Jesus arrives at Feast of Booths (c Oct 14; Jn 7:14); Feast of Booths (Oct 17 or 18; Jn 7:37)	
Roman Senators unable to pay debts; subsidized by Emperor Tiberius		33	Triumphal entry (Sun, Mar 29); Last Supper (Thurs eve, Apr 2); crucifixion (Fri, Apr 3); resurrection (Sun, Apr 5); ascension (May 14; Lk 24:51; Ac 1:9); Pentecost (May 24)	Jews of Parthia, Media, Elam, and Mesopotamia travel to Jerusalem for Pentecost
	Ethiopian eunuch baptized, returns home (Ac 8:26–39)	35		
		35–42		Revolt of Seleucia on the Tigris against Parthian rule
		36	Paul's conversion (Ac 9:1–31)	
Caligula (Gaius), Roman emperor		37–41	Josephus, Jewish historian, born	
Caligula.	Philo of Alexandria leads Jewish delegation to Rome	c 39	Caligula attempts to place statue of himself in Jerusalem temple	
		41	Martyrdom of James (late Mar; Ac 12:2); Peter in prison (Apr; Ac 12:3–4); Passover (May 4; Ac 12:4); Peter leaves Jerusalem (May; Gal 2:11)	
		41–44	Herod Agrippa I rules Judea	

Anatolia, Greece, and Rome	Egypt and Africa	Dates	Syria, Canaan, and Israel	Mesopotamia and Persia
Claudius, Roman emperor		41–54		
Peter on mission in Asia Minor (Spr/Sum; 1Pt 1:1–2); [in Corinth (Fall); at Rome (mid Nov)]		42	Peter in Antioch (May 41–Apr 42; Gal 2:11)	
		44	Herod Agrippa at festival in Caesarea (Mar 5; Ac 12:19); death of Herod Agrippa (Mar 10; Ac 12:21–23)	
		47–48	Paul's 1st missionary journey (Ac 13:1–14:28)	
Paul goes to Macedonia; Barnabas and John Mark go to Cyprus (mid May; Ac 15:36–16:10)		49	Conference in Jerusalem (Ac 15:1–35); Peter goes to Antioch (Feb; Gal 2:11); Paul confronts Peter (Apr; Gal 2:11)	
		49–56	[Peter in Antioch (seven years)]	
Paul's 2nd missionary journey (Ac 15:39–18:22)	Philo of Alexandria leads second Jewish delegation to Rome	49–51		
Paul's 3rd missionary journey (Ac 18:23–21:17)		52–55		
Nero, Roman emperor		54–68		
		55–57	Paul imprisoned in Caesarea (Ac 23:23–26:32)	

Fresco found in a Roman home.

Anatolia, Greece, and Rome	Egypt and Africa	Dates	Syria, Canaan, and Israel	Mesopotamia and Persia
Paul's journey to Rome (Ac 27:1–28:16)		57–58		
Paul in custody in Rome (Ac 28:17–31)		58–60		
		62	Martyrdom of James, the Lord's brother	
Paul assigns Titus at Crete (Ti 1:5)		64–65		
Paul in Ephesus, where he leaves Timothy (Spr–Sum; 1Tm 1:3)		65		
	Tiberias Julius Alexander, of Jewish descent, appointed Roman prefect of Egypt	66		
		66–70	Jewish revolt against Romans	
Peter and Paul martyred		68		
Emperor Vespasian		69–79		
		70	Titus destroys Jerusalem temple; Rabbon Yohanan ben Zakkai at Yavneh Academy	Jerusalem Jews settle in Babylonia, which becomes the new center of Judaism
		c 73	Fall of Masada	
Emperor Titus		79–81		
Emperor Domitian		81–96		
		c 90–115	Rabbon Gamaliel II at Yavneh Academy	

Anatolia, Greece, and Rome	Egypt and Africa	Dates	Syria, Canaan, and Israel	Mesopotamia and Persia
Jews revolt in Cyprus	Jews revolt in Egypt and Cyrene	115–17		Trajan captures Mesopotamia; Jews revolt
	Founding of Antinoöpolis by Emperor Hadrian	130		
		132–35	Bar Kokhba revolt; death of Rabbi Akiva, Yavneh Academy leader who hailed Bar Kokhba as the messiah	

View of the Masada stronghold in the Judean wilderness. In the right foreground is the earthen ramp constructed by Roman soldiers to breach the fortress. In the background is the Dead Sea and the mountains where the ancient Moabites lived.

c

GENERAL TOOLS FOR STUDYING THE BIBLE

There are an overwhelming number of resources available for study of the Bible. The following collection describes some of the best resources, especially for Lutherans, which may supplement use of this companion. The categories of resources are listed alphabetically. Although many of the resources are recently published, classic and unsurpassed resources are also included. When a resource is suitable for lay/Bible class use, the descriptions below make that clear. Readers may wish to seek out electronic or computer-based versions of the works, or Bible study software that allows detailed searches of the biblical text (cf "concordances" below).

For commentaries on particular books of Scripture, refer to the section titled "For Further Study" that appears at the end of each description of a biblical book (e.g., p 56). The Bible and the Apocrypha referenced throughout this companion are:

The Lutheran Study Bible. Edward A. Engelbrecht, gen. ed. St. Louis: Concordia, 2009. ✥ Based on the ESV and designed for lay/Bible class use, *The Lutheran Study Bible* (*TLSB*) includes more than 26,000 study notes, 220 thematic articles, 36 maps, and numerous other features. *Lutheran Bible Companion* (*LBC*) is a companion volume for *TLSB* as well as other editions of the Bible used by Lutherans.

The Apocrypha: The Lutheran Edition with Notes. Edward A. Engelbrecht, gen. ed. St. Louis: Concordia, 2012. ✥ A study Bible-treatment of the Apocryphal books that appeared in the Luther Bible, also including books used by other Christian traditions. Introduces the intertestamental era, includes maps, articles, descriptions of Jewish and Christian literature, as well as an extensive topical index. Based on the ESV; designed for lay/Bible class use.

Ancient Texts of the Bible

Aland, Kurt, and Barbara Aland. *The Text of the New Testament: An Introduction to the Critical Editions and to the Theory and Practice of Modern Textual Criticism.* 2nd ed. Translated by Erroll F. Rhodes. Grand Rapids: Eerdmans, 1989. ◊ A translation of a widely used introductory textbook. Reviews editions from Nestle to the present, the transmission and a description of the manuscripts, an introduction to modern editions, resources, and an introduction to the practice of New Testament criticism, based on 12 basic rules. Includes charts of textual contents of manuscripts and papyri as well as pictures of selected manuscripts.

Challoner, Richard, ed. *The Holy Bible: Douay-Rheims Version.* Charlotte, NC: Saint Benedict Press, 2009. ◊ Translation of the Latin Vulgate into English for Roman Catholic readers. Since the Vulgate was the Bible of the Western Church throughout the medieval era, the Douay-Rheims version is valuable for historical studies of Scripture and theology.

Pietersma, Albert, and Benjamin G. Wright, eds. *A New English Translation of the Septuagint.* Oxford: Oxford University Press, 2007. ◊ The ancient Greek translation of the Old Testament was cited by New Testament writers, widely used in the Early Church, and is still the preferred version among Eastern Orthodox Christian theologians. This edition includes introductions to the texts and their translation, a most valuable historical resource.

Tov, Emanuel. *Textual Criticism of the Hebrew Bible.* 3rd rev. exp. ed. Minneapolis: Fortress, 2011. ◊ The state-of-the-art examination of scholarly views by a recognized expert in the field. Academic and detailed study.

Würthwein, Ernst. *The Text of the Old Testament: An Introduction to the Biblia Hebraica.* 2nd English ed. Translated by Erroll F. Rhodes. Grand Rapids: Eerdmans, 1995. ◊ A translation of a widely used introductory textbook, which describes the different types of Hebrew and Old Testament manuscripts and how scholars engage with them. Academic but less technical than Tov's study.

Archaeology and the Bible

Mazar, Amihai. *Archaeology of the Land of the Bible, 10,000–586 B.C.E.* Vol. 1 of the Anchor Bible Reference Library. New Haven: Yale University Press, 1992. ◊ A survey by a widely respected expert who works from the perspective of Near Eastern archaeology and relates it to biblical studies.

Meyers, Eric M., ed. *The Oxford Encyclopedia of Archaeology in the Near East.* 5 vols. New York: Oxford University Press, 1997. ◊ Includes the work of experts, presented in over 1,100 articles, with illustrations and maps. Provides the broad cultural context of Israel's history.

Shanks, Hershel, gen. ed. *Biblical Archaeology Review.* Biblical Archaeology Society, 1975–Present. ◊ Popularly written to bridge between professional archaeologists and non-experts who are interested in biblical studies. Articles written by both Jews and Christians representing a broad variety of perspectives; therefore, use with discernment.

Stern, Ephraim. *Archaeology of the Land of the Bible: The Assyrian, Babylonian, and Persian Periods (732–332 B.C.E.).* Vol. 2 of the Anchor Bible Reference Library. New Haven: Yale University Press, 2001. ◊ A companion volume to the work of Mazar, covering the remainder of the Old Testament era.

———, ed. *The New Encyclopedia of Archaeological Excavations in the Holy Land.* 4 vols. Jerusalem: Israel Exploration Society and Carta; New York: Simon & Schuster, 1993. ◊ Describes more than 400 sites in Israel, Jordan, and the Sinai wilderness. Prepared by archaeologists and other experts in the field of study.

Atlases and Geographies of the Bible

Aharoni, Yohanan, Michael Avi-Yonah, Anson F. Rainey, Ze'ev Safrai, and R. Steven Notley. *The Carta Bible Atlas.* 5th rev. and exp. ed. Jerusalem: Carta, 2011. ◊ Formerly known as *The Macmillan Bible Atlas.* A series of two-color maps; covers biblical history and includes the defeat of Bar Kokhba in AD 135. Follows late dating from patriarchs through the time of Samuel. Helpful period maps plus historical description of the period.

Beck, John A. *The Land of Milk and Honey: An Intro-duction to the Geography of Israel*. St. Louis: Concordia, 2006. ♪ An ideal introduction for lay/Bible class use, with interpretive, theological, and even devotional observations. A pleasure to read.

Currid, John D., and David P. Barrett. *Crossway ESV Bible Atlas*. Wheaton, IL: Crossway, 2010. ♪ Large and well-illustrated atlas for canonical Scripture, including 175 maps, illustrations; it does not cover the Apocrypha or intertestamental era.

Curtis, Adrian, ed. *Oxford Bible Atlas*. 4th ed. New York: Oxford University Press, 2007. ♪ Best of the Bible atlases. Features well-done, easy-to-read maps together with a summary of history and extensive gazetteer.

Canon of the Bible

Bruce, F. F. *The Canon of Scripture*. Downers Grove, IL: InterVarsity Press, 1996. ♪ A historical and theological survey by a Protestant scholar. Accessible for lay/Bible class readers.

Childs, Brevard S. *Introduction to the Old Testament as Scripture*. Minneapolis: Fortress, 2011 reprint. ♪ Childs presents introductory essays on the problem of the canon, canon and criticism, and text and canon. He then shows how Jews of the intertestamental period selected the writings that are found in the Old Testament and rejected other writings current in their time. He stresses that the 39 books of the Old Testament are not only a source of the Judeo-Christian tradition but also a product of that tradition.

McDonald, Lee Martin, and James A. Sanders, eds. *The Canon Debate*. Peabody, MA: Hendrickson, 2002. ♪ A collection of historical and theological essays from Protestant, Roman Catholic, and Jewish scholars.

Metzger, Bruce M. *The Canon of the New Testament: Its Origin, Development, and Significance*. Oxford: Clarendon Press, 1997. ♪ A historical and theological survey from a New Testament scholar.

Steinmann, Andrew E. *The Oracles of God: The Old Testament Canon*. St. Louis: Concordia, 1999. ♪ A historical and theological survey from an Old Testament scholar and chronologist.

Chronology of the Bible

Chilton, Bruce. *Redeeming Time: The Wisdom of Ancient Jewish and Christian Festal Calendars*. Peabody, MA: Hendrickson, 2002. ♪ Examines the calendars used in Judaism and Christianity, explaining their rhythmic character and their practices in the first century with the aim of making their views of time comprehensible to readers today.

Finegan, Jack. *Handbook of Biblical Chronology: Principles of Time Reckoning in the Ancient World and Problems of Chronology in the Bible*. Rev. ed. Peabody, MA: Hendrickson, 1998. ♪ Especially helpful for exploring the different methods of time reckoning in Egypt, Mesopotamia, Israel, and how they relate to one another. Also surveys various Jewish and Christian chronological systems.

Steinmann, Andrew E. *From Abraham to Paul: A Biblical Chronology*. St. Louis: Concordia, 2011. ♪ Identifies dateable persons and events in the Bible, coordinating between information in the Bible and extrabiblical sources. Comprehensive, including the intertestamental era.

Concordances of the Bible

Mounce, William D. *The Crossway Comprehensive Concordance of the Holy Bible (ESV)*. Wheaton, IL: Crossway Books, 2002 ♪ A companion to the ESV translation, treating nearly 14,000 biblical terms. Computer based searching of the ESV is also available on the publisher's website. Handy for lay/Bible class use.

Nave, Orville J., ed. *Nave's Topical Bible*. Nashville: Nelson, 1979. ♪ This reference work, first published in 1897, allows readers to explore the Bible through brief encyclopedic entries and collections of texts arranged topically so that one may rapidly discover biblical teaching on a particular topic. Based on the KJV.

Strong, James, ed. *The Exhaustive Concordance of the Bible*. Peabody, MA: Hendrickson, 2007. ♪ The most widely used English concordance, based on the KJV, with English terms distinguished by the Hebrew, Aramaic, and Greek terms they represent. Adaptable for lay/Bible class use.

Young, Robert, ed. *Young's Analytical Concordance to the Bible*. Rev. ed. Nashville: Nelson, 1980. ⟐ Based on the W. B. Stevenson revision in 1922. Contains more analytical features than Strong's. Especially valuable for those with basic knowledge of Hebrew, Aramaic, or Greek.

Cultural Setting of the Bible

De Vaux, Roland. *Ancient Israel: Its Life and Institutions*. 2 vols. Translated by John McHugh. New York: McGraw-Hill, 1965. ⟐ Cultural overview. Excellent for Old Testament background that is also absolutely crucial for the New Testament.

Hallo, William W., and K. Lawson Younger Jr. *The Context of Scripture*. 3 vols. Leiden: Brill, 2003. ⟐ Includes canonical compositions, monumental inscriptions, and archival documents from ancient Near Eastern cultures that existed alongside biblical Israel. More thorough and up-to-date for literature than Pritchard.

King, Philip J., and Lawrence E. Stager. *Life in Biblical Israel*. Louisville; Westminster, 2001. ⟐ A cultural overview prepared by noted archaeologists, focused on the Iron Age. Includes color pictures and illustrations.

Klinck, Arthur W., and Erich H. Kiehl. *Everyday Life in Bible Times*. 3rd ed. St. Louis: Concordia, 1995. ⟐ An ideal resource for lay/Bible class use. Includes graphic illustrations.

Meeks, Wayne A. *The First Urban Christians: The Social World of the Apostle Paul*. 2nd ed. New Haven: Yale University Press, 2003. ⟐ A now classic application of sociological methods to biblical studies.

Pritchard, James B., ed. *The Ancient Near East: An Anthology of Texts and Pictures*. 2 vols. Princeton, NJ: Princeton University Press, 1958, 1976. ⟐ Both volumes shed much light on history, life, and events in the ancient Near East in the Old Testament era. More concise than Hallo-Younger and includes a wealth of visuals.

Skarsaune, Oskar. *In the Shadow of the Temple: Jewish Influences on Early Christianity*. Downers Grove, IL: InterVarsity Press, 2002. ⟐ A readable description of how Christian thought and practice emerged from first century Judaism.

Thompson, J. A. *Handbook of Life in Bible Times*. Downers Grove, IL: InterVarsity Press, 1987. ⟐ A beautifully illustrated presentation of life in the biblical era, with maps and charts. Divided into seven parts: I. introductory survey; II. people at home; III. food and drink; IV. industry and commerce; V. culture and health; VI. warfare; VII. religion. Cross-references in margins and selected bibliographies at the end of each chapter. A valuable aid but some inaccuracies occur here and there.

Encyclopedias of the Bible

Freedman, David Noel, ed. *The Anchor Bible Dictionary*, 6 vols. New York: Doubleday, 1992. ⟐ Encyclopedic in size and character. Reflects current views for archaeology, geography, biblical criticism, etc. A valuable resource due to its careful editing, scholarship, and comprehensiveness. However, it does not consistently include Christian and evangelical theological perspectives.

Tenney, Merrill C., and Moisés Silva, eds. *The Zondervan Encyclopedia of the Bible: Revised Full-Color Edition*. 5 vols. Grand Rapids: Zondervan, 2009. ⟐ Features concise articles with good content by evangelical scholars. Beautifully illustrated.

History in the Bible

Bright, John. *A History of Israel*. 4th ed. Louisville: Westminster, 2000. ⟐ Provides a very knowledgeable history of the Old Testament era. Bright seeks to portray God's often unfaithful people in their total context. In this he is perhaps unsurpassed. He holds a critical perspective, but this title is one of the best Old Testament histories when used with careful discernment.

Franzmann, Martin H. *The Word of the Lord Grows: A First Historical Introduction to the New Testament*. St. Louis: Concordia, 1981. ⟐ A careful study of the New Testament on the basis of its own witness and that of the Early Church with a helpful stress on the theological content of each of the books.

Hummel, Horace D. *The Word Becoming Flesh: An Introduction to the Origin, Purpose, and Meaning of the Old Testament.* St. Louis: Concordia, 1985. ⍟ Written from a careful biblical viewpoint. The author examines the introductory questions of the Old Testament and analyzes its interpretation and criticism. He highlights the theology of the Old Testament and its implications for the proper understanding of Scripture. This is Christological, Lutheran exegesis at its finest.

Jeremias, Joachim. *Jerusalem in the Time of Jesus.* Philadelphia: Fortress, 1969. ⍟ This book, by one of the greater Lutheran exegetes of the twentieth century, gives access to the world of Jesus and the character of life in Jerusalem. Indispensable for reading the New Testament.

Kitchen, K. A. *On the Reliability of the Old Testament.* Grand Rapids: Eerdmans, 2006. ⍟ A noted Egyptologist examines the historical character of biblical events, arguing for the Bible's accuracy by citing extrabiblical evidence from ancient Near Eastern literature and archaeology. He argues for a thirteenth century date for the exodus rather than the traditional fifteenth century date.

Lessing, R. Reed, and Andrew Steinmann. *Prepare the Way of the Lord: An Introduction to the Old Testament.* St. Louis: Concordia, 2013. ⍟ A seminary level text by Lutheran scholars covering recent and enduring issues in Old Testament interpretation.

Middendorf, Michael P., and Mark Schuler. *Called by the Gospel: An Introduction to the New Testament.* Eugene, OR: Wipf & Stock, 2007. ⍟ A survey from Lutheran theologians of New Testament books and theology, written for university students.

Steinmann, Andrew, ed. *Called to Be God's People: An Introduction to the Old Testament.* Eugene, OR: Wipf & Stock, 2006. ⍟ A survey from Lutheran theologians of Old Testament books and theology, written for university students.

History of the Bible

Ackroyd, P. R., et al., eds. *The Cambridge History of the Bible.* 3 vols. Cambridge: Cambridge University Press, 1963–70. ⍟ A careful investigation into the history of the Bible in Western Christianity, covering the ancient, medieval, and Reformation eras to present.

Norton, David. *A History of the Bible as Literature.* 2 vols. Cambridge: Cambridge University Press, 1993. ⍟ A more recent historical investigation, which provides special insights on the King James Version and the changing views of translation and literary value.

Trebolle Barrera, Julio. *The Jewish Bible and the Christian Bible: An Introduction to the History of the Bible.* Translated by Wilfred G. E. Watson. Grand Rapids: Eerdmans, 1998. ⍟ From an expert on the Dead Sea Scrolls, who describes the formation of the canon in Judaism and Christianity, translations of biblical texts, and schools of interpretation.

Interpretation and Application of the Bible

Archer, Gleason L. *New International Encyclopedia of Bible Difficulties.* Grand Rapids: Zondervan, 2001. ⍟ A more thorough apologetic work from an evangelical scholar.

Arndt, William. *Bible Difficulties and Seeming Contradictions.* Edited by Robert G. Hoerber and Walter R. Roehrs, St. Louis: Concordia, 1987. ⍟ The brilliant work of William Arndt updated. Prepared by Lutheran theologians.

Bonhoeffer, Dietrich. *Meditating on the Word.* 2nd ed. Lanham, MD: Rowman & Littlefield Publishers, Inc., 2000. ⍟ A collection on meditation drawn and translated from Bonhoeffer's writings, which emphasizes love for God's Word and its value for life.

Burgland, Lane. *How to Read the Bible with Understanding.* 2nd ed. St. Louis: Concordia, 2015. Forthcoming. ⍟ Excellent for lay/Bible class use, explaining the basic practices of biblical interpretation, the literary qualities of biblical books, and how the Bible developed.

Hauser, Alan J., and Duane F. Watson, eds. *A History of Biblical Interpretation.* 2 vols. Grand Rapids: Eerdmans, 2003. ⍟ A collection of scholarly essays on biblical interpretation, presented in chronological order, beginning with the intertestamental era.

Preus, Jacob A. O. *Just Words: Understanding the Fullness of the Gospel*. St. Louis: Concordia, 1997. ♫ Explores the many ways in which the Scripture presents the Gospel as creation, commerce, legal language, personal statements, sacrifices, and deliverance.

Thiselton, Anthony C. *New Horizons in Hermeneutics*. Grand Rapids: Zondervan, 1992. ♫ A high-level treatment of hermeneutics, semiotics, literary theory, speech-act theory, reader-response theory, and other modern theories of interpretation. A standard advanced reference work.

Voelz, James W. *What Does This Mean? Principles of Biblical Interpretation in the Post-Modern World*. Rev. 2nd ed. St. Louis: Concordia, 2013. ♫ A seminary level hermeneutics textbook written for the Lutheran tradition, discussing textual criticism, semantics, and application in view of postmodernism.

Walther, C. F. W. *Law and Gospel: How to Read and Apply the Bible*. St. Louis: Concordia, 2010. ♫ A new translation of the classic lectures delivered in 1884–85, which present the many aspects of the most important distinction in evangelical, Lutheran, biblical interpretation. Readable for lay/ Bible class learners; essential for preachers and teachers.

Theology of the Bible

Childs, Brevard S. *Old Testament Theology in a Canonical Context*. Minneapolis: Fortress, 1990. ♫ The canonical approach views history from the perspective of Israel's faith as reflected in the Old Testament and seeks to follow the biblical text in its theological use of history. Scripture serves as a continuing medium through which the saving events of Israel's history are appropriated by each new generation of faith.

Floysvik, Ingvar. *When God Becomes My Enemy: The Theology of the Complaint Psalms*. St. Louis: Concordia, 1997. ♫ A study of the most challenging psalms, in which the ancient Israelites perceived that God caused their suffering and prayed for Him to change His course of action.

Gibbs, Jeffrey A. *Jerusalem and Parousia: Jesus' Eschatological Discourse in Matthew's Gospel*. St. Louis: Concordia, 2000. ♫ Gibbs' treatment of the Eschatological Discourse (Mt 24–25) is invaluable, approaching the text from the perspective of narrative criticism, resulting in an insightful running commentary on much of Matthew. Gibbs' emphasis on the eschatological orientation of Matthew is essential for a proper understanding of the Gospel.

Gieschen, Charles, ed. *The Law in Holy Scripture: Essays from the Concordia Theological Seminary Symposium on Exegetical Theology*. St. Louis: Concordia, 2001. ♫ A collection of scholarly essays addressing questions surrounding Law and Gospel in Holy Scripture, especially in view of the "New Look at Paul."

Hurtado, Larry W. *Lord Jesus Christ: Devotion to Jesus in Earliest Christianity*. Grand Rapids: Eerdmans, 2003. ♫ Surveys the New Testament and early Christian literature to document the devotion to and worship of Jesus as one with God. Overturns earlier critical theories about the evolution of Christian theology.

Translations of the Bible into English

Bruce, F. F. *History of the Bible in English*. 3rd ed. Cambridge, UK: Lutterworth Press, 2003 reprint. ♫ Sketches the history from the beginning of the English translations to the present. He stresses the principles that lie behind each translation.

Poythress, Vern S., and Wayne A. Grudem. *The Gender-Neutral Bible Controversy: Muting the Masculinity of God's Words*. Nashville: Broadman & Holman Publishers, 2000. ♫ Argues against the "political correctness" movement that has corrupted some recent Bible translations.

Ryken, Leland. *The Word of God in English: Criteria for Excellence in Bible Translation*. Wheaton, IL: Crossway, 2002. ♫ Describes the debates about Bible translation, argues against "dynamic equivalence" in favor of literal and essentially literal approaches.

REFERENCE
GUIDE

ABBREVIATIONS

= ....means the wording is the same or virtually so
AD ....*anno Domini* (in the year of [our] Lord)
Aram .... Aramaic
BC .... before Christ
c ....circa
cf .... confer
ch .... chapter
chs .... chapters
esp .... especially
Grm ....German
Gk ....Greek
Hbr..............Hebrew
lit .... literally
NT .... New Testament
OT .... Old Testament
p ....page
pp ....pages
v .... verse
vv ....verses

Canonical Scripture

Gn .... Genesis
Ex .... Exodus
Lv .... Leviticus
Nu ....Numbers
Dt ....Deuteronomy
Jsh .... Joshua
Jgs .... Judges
Ru .... Ruth
1Sm .... 1 Samuel
2Sm ....2 Samuel
1Ki .... 1 Kings
2Ki .... 2 Kings
1Ch ....1 Chronicles
2Ch ....2 Chronicles
Ezr .... Ezra
Ne ....Nehemiah
Est .... Esther
Jb .... Job
Ps ....Psalms

Pr .... Proverbs
Ec .... Ecclesiastes
Sg ....Song of Solomon
Is ....Isaiah
Jer...................... Jeremiah
Lm ....Lamentations
Ezk ....Ezekiel
Dn .... Daniel
Hos .... Hosea
Jl ....Joel
Am ....Amos
Ob .... Obadiah
Jnh ....Jonah
Mi .... Micah
Na .... Nahum
Hab ....Habakkuk
Zep .... Zephaniah
Hg ....Haggai
Zec ....Zechariah
Mal ....Malachi
Mt .... Matthew
Mk .... Mark
Lk .... Luke
Jn ....John
Ac .... Acts
Rm ....Romans
1Co ....1 Corinthians
2Co ....2 Corinthians
Gal ....Galatians
Eph .... Ephesians
Php .... Philippians
Col .... Colossians
1Th ....1 Thessalonians
2Th ....2 Thessalonians
1Tm ....1 Timothy
2Tm ....2 Timothy
Ti .... Titus
Phm .... Philemon
Heb .... Hebrews
Jas ....James
1Pt ....1 Peter
2Pt ....2 Peter

1Jn . . . . 1 John
2Jn . . . . 2 John
3Jn . . . . 3 John
Jude . . . . Jude
Rv . . . . .Revelation

The Apocrypha

Jth. . . . . Judith
Wis. . . . . .The Wisdom of Solomon
Tob . . . . Tobit
Ecclus. . . . . Ecclesiasticus (Sirach)
Bar . . . . Baruch
Lt Jer . . . . The Letter of Jeremiah
1Macc . . . . .1 Maccabees
2Macc . . . . .2 Maccabees
Old Grk Est. . . . . .Old Greek Esther
Sus . . . . .Susanna
Bel . . . . .Bel and the Dragon
Pr Az . . . . .The Prayer of Azariah
Sg Three. . . . . .The Song of the Three
Holy Children
Pr Man. . . . . .Prayer of Manasseh

Other Books

1Esd . . . . 1 Esdras
2Esd . . . . 2 Esdras
3Macc . . . . 3 Maccabees (Ptolemaika)
4Macc . . . . .4 Maccabees
Ps 151. .Psalm 151
1En . . . . *1 Enoch*
2En . . . . *2 Enoch*
Jub . . . . *Jubilees*

Commonly Cited Works and Authors

AB series. | The Anchor Bible Commentary

ACCS | Ancient Christian Commentary on Scripture. Thomas C. Oden, gen. ed. 29 vols. Downers Grove, IL: InterVarsity Press, 2000–2009.

AE | Luther, Martin. *Luther's Works.* American Edition. Vols. 1–30: Edited by Jaroslav Pelikan. St. Louis: Concordia, 1955–76. Vols. 31–55: Edited by Helmut Lehmann. Philadelphia/Minneapolis: Muhlenberg/Fortress, 1957–86. Vols. 56–75: Edited by

Christopher Boyd Brown. St. Louis: Concordia, 2009–.

ANF | Roberts, Alexander, and James Donaldson, eds. *The Ante-Nicene Fathers: The Writings of the Fathers Down to AD 325.* 10 vols. Buffalo: The Christian Literature Publishing Company, 1885–96. Reprint, Grand Rapids, MI: Eerdmans, 2001.

Ant | Josephus, Flavius. *Antiquities of the Jews.* In *The Works of Josephus.* Translated by William Whiston. Peabody, MA: Hendrickson Publishers, 1987.

Ap | Apology of the Augsburg Confession. From *Concordia.*

ALEN | Engelbrecht, Edward A., gen. ed. *The Apocrypha: The Lutheran Edition with Notes.* St. Louis: Concordia, 2012.

CBCA | Cambridge Bible Commentaries on the Apocrypha.

CC | Concordia Commentary series. St. Louis: Concordia, 1996–.

CC 2Pt/Jude | Giese, Curtis P. *2 Peter and Jude.* CC. St. Louis: Concordia, 2012.

CC Col | Deterding, Paul E. *Colossians.* CC. St. Louis: Concordia, 2003.

CC Dn | Steinmann, Andrew E. *Daniel.* CC. St. Louis: Concordia, 2009.

CC Jnh | Lessing, R. Reed. *Jonah.* CC. St. Louis: Concordia, 2007.

CC Lk1 | Just, Arthur A. *Luke 1:1–9:50.* CC. St. Louis: Concordia, 1996.

CC Mt1 | Gibbs, Jeffrey A. *Matthew 1:1–11.* CC. St. Louis: Concordia, 2006.

CC Rv | Brighton, Louis A. *Revelation.* CC. St. Louis: Concordia, 2004.

Concordia | McCain, Paul Timothy, ed. *Concordia: The Lutheran Confessions.* 2nd ed. St. Louis: Concordia, 2006.

Ep | Epitome of the Formula of Concord. From *Concordia.*

FC | Formula of Concord. From *Concordia.*

GWFT | God's Word for Today. Bible study series. St. Louis: Concordia, 1994–.

ICC — International Critical Commentary.

K&D — Keil, C. F., and F. Delitzsch. *Biblical Commentary on the Old Testament.* Translated by J. Martin et al. 25 vols. Edinburgh, 1857–78.

KJV — King James Version of Scripture.

LBC — Engelbrecht, Edward A., gen. ed. *Lutheran Bible Companion.* St. Louis: Concordia, 2014.

LC — Large Catechism of Martin Luther. From *Concordia.*

LCHS — Lange, John Peter. Lange's Commentary on the Holy Scriptures. Edited by John Peter Lange and Philip Schaff. 25 vols. New York: Charles Scribner's Sons, 1893.

LL — LifeLight. Bible study series. St. Louis: Concordia, 1999–.

LSB — Commission on Worship of The Lutheran Church—Missouri Synod. *Lutheran Service Book.* St. Louis: Concordia, 2006.

LSB Altar Book — Commission on Worship of The Lutheran Church—Missouri Synod. *Lutheran Service Book: Altar Book.* St. Louis: Concordia, 2006.

LXX — Septuagint. Koine Greek Old Testament.

MT — Masoretic text.

NAC — New American Commentary. 38 vols. Nashville: Broadman & Holman, 1991–2010.

NCBC — New Century Bible Commentary.

NICNT — New International Commentary on the New Testament.

NICOT — New International Commentary on the Old Testament.

NIGTC — New International Greek Testament Commentary.

NPNF1 — Schaff, Philip, ed. *A Select Library of Nicene and Post-Nicene Fathers of the Christian Church*, Series 1. 14 vols. New York: The Christian Literature Series, 1886–89. Reprint, Grand Rapids, MI: Eerdmans, 1956.

NPNF2 — Schaff, Philip, and Henry Wace, ed. *A Select Library of Nicene and Post-Nicene Fathers of the Christian Church*, Series 2. 14 vols. New York: The Christian Literature Series, 1890–99. Reprint, Grand Rapids, MI: Eerdmans, 1952, 1961.

OTL — Old Testament Library.

PBC — People's Bible Commentary. 41 vols. St. Louis: Concordia, 1994, 2005.

RHBC — Reformation Heritage Bible Commentary. St. Louis: Concordia, 2013–.

SC — Luther, Martin. *Luther's Small Catechism with Explanation.* St. Louis: Concordia, 1986.

SD — Solid Declaration of the Formula of Concord. From *Concordia.*

Steinmann — Steinmann, Andrew E. *From Abraham to Paul: A Biblical Chronology.* St. Louis: Concordia, 2011.

StL — *Dr. Martin Luthers Sämmtliche Schriften.* Herausgegeben von Dr. Joh. Georg Walch. Neue revidirte Stereotypausgabe. St. Louis: Concordia, 1880–1910.

ThC E1 — Gerhard, Johann. *Theological Commonplaces. Exegesis 1, On the Nature of Theology and On Scripture.* Edited with annotations by Benjamin T. G. Mayes. Translated by Richard J. Dinda. St. Louis: Concordia, 2009.

TLSB — Engelbrecht, Edward A., gen. ed. *The Lutheran Study Bible.* St. Louis: Concordia, 2009.

TNTC — Tyndale New Testament Commentaries.

TOTC — Tyndale Old Testament Commentaries.

WA DB — *D. Martin Luthers Werke: Deutsche Bibel* [Luther's Works, Weimar Edition: German Bible]. 12 vols. in 15. Weimar: H. Böhlau, 1906–.

WA TR — *D. Martin Luthers Werke: Tischreden.* 6 vols. Weimar: H. Böhlau, 1912–21.

WBC — Word Biblical Commentary.

MAPS AND DIAGRAMS

TRANSLITERATION GUIDELINES

References to the Hebrew, Aramaic, and Greek texts of the Bible appear at various places in *LBC*, especially in the Bible Dictionary. Transliterated terms were included to support in-depth study of the text. Readers who do not desire to study a foreign term or phrase may skip over it just as one may skip over etymological information in an English dictionary.

A transliterated word in *LBC* is usually a lexical form, but may also be (1) a form in a specific text, or (2) a form found in English usage (e.g., Baal).

Hebrew and Aramaic Transliteration

Hebrew Consonants	English Consonants
א : alef	ʾ
ב : bet	b
ג : gimel	g
ד : dalet	d
ה : he	h
ו : waw	w
ז : zayin	z
ח : chet	ch
ט : tet	t
י : yod	y
ך or כ : kaph	k
ל : lamed	l
ם or מ : mem	m
ן or נ : nun	n
ס : samek	s
ע : ayin	ʿ
ף or פ : pe	p; f; or ph
ץ or צ : tsade	ts
ק : qof	q
ר : resh	r
ש : sin/shin	s; sh
ת : taw	t; th

Hebrew Vowels	English Vowels
patach	a
furtive patach	a
qamets	a
final qamets he	ah
seghol	e
tsere	e
tsere yod	e
short hireq	i
long hireq	i
hireq yod	i
qamets chatuph	o
holem	o
full holem	o
short qibbuts	u
long qibbuts	u
shureq	u
chatef qamets	o
chatef patach	a

Greek Transliteration

Greek Letters	English Letters
α : alpha	a
β : beta	b
γ : gamma	g
γ : gamma nasal (before γ, κ, ξ, χ)	n
δ : delta	d
ε : epsilon	e
ζ : zeta	z
η : eta	e
θ : theta	th
ι : iota	i
κ : kappa	k
λ : lambda	l
μ : mu	m
ν : nu	n
ξ : xi	x

Greek Letters	English Letters
o : omicron	o
π : pi	p
ρ : rho	r
ρ : initial rho (or in medial double rho)	rh
σ and **ς** : sigma	s
τ : tau	t
υ : upsilon (not in diphthong)	y
υ : upsilon (in diphthong)	u
φ : phi	ph
χ : chi	ch
ψ : psi	ps
ω : omega	o
' : rough breathing mark	h

Adapted from *The SBL Handbook of Style* (Peabody, MA: Hendrickson Publishers), 1999, 28–29.

An angel grips the sword by which Abraham would sacrifice his son Isaac. Behind Abraham appears a ram whom God sent as a substitute for the sacrifice. This dramatic Old Testament event foreshadowed the sacrifice of Jesus as the Lamb of God who takes away the sin of the world, illustrating the unity of the two testaments.

THE OLD TESTAMENT

THE VALUE OF THE OLD TESTAMENT

The Old Testament has basic relevance in the life of every Christian because through it comes not only the revelation of the origin of the world in which we live but also the origin of sin, how it brought down God's curse, and how God gave His loving promise to free mankind from the dreadful results of the curse of sin. No one can properly appreciate the Old Testament who does not discover the golden thread of prophecy that assures mankind of the coming of the Messiah, identified in the New Testament as Jesus Christ, the Savior of the World. Luther wrote,

> Christ says in John 5[:39], "Search the Scriptures, for it is they that bear witness to me." . . . The ground and proof of the New Testament is surely not to be despised, and therefore the Old Testament is to be highly regarded. And what is the New Testament but a public preaching and proclamation of Christ, set forth through the sayings of the Old Testament and fulfilled through Christ? (AE 35:235–36)

In reading the Old Testament, it is necessary to be aware that it reflects cultures, customs, and conditions quite different from those that current readers have experienced. It must be recognized that the writers employ various literary forms in order to communicate the truth of God's revelation. This volume will help you with these goals.

Interpretation and Application

When Jesus Christ, having risen from the dead on Easter morning, walked with two men on the first Easter afternoon on their way to Emmaus and found them confused about His death and reports of His resurrection, Luke tells us that He opened unto them the Scriptures: "Beginning with Moses and all the Prophets, He interpreted to them in all the Scriptures the things concerning Himself" (Lk 24:27). Later when Paul had been brought as a prisoner to Rome, he called the leaders of the Jews in Rome together and "From morning till evening he expounded to them, testifying to the kingdom of God and trying to convince them about Jesus both from the Law of Moses and from the Prophets" (Ac 28:23).

These are the examples we will follow in the presentation of the books of the Old Testament. We believe this is key to a proper understanding and application of God's Old Testament revelation, namely, the faith that these writings were inspired by God "to make [us] wise for salvation through faith in Christ Jesus" (2Tm 3:15). Reading from this perspective, every book of the Old Testament carries a meaningful and faith-strengthening message for the reader and reduces the inclination to get lost in mere questions and problems of language and culture and authorship and chronology.

Mosaic of the Transfiguration in the Vatican Museums.

THE BOOKS OF MOSES

The Torah or Pentateuch

Scribes of the Old Testament, New Testament persons, and believers through the centuries held that Moses wrote the first five books of the Bible, known as the Books of Moses. Several passages in the books point to this history (Ex 17:14; 24:4, 7; Nu 33:2; Dt 31:9–11), as well as other passages of the Old Testament (e.g., Jsh 8:31–33; 2Ki 14:6; Ezr 3:2) and the New Testament (Mk 12:26; Lk 24:27; Ac 7:37–38; 28:23; Rm 10:5).

However, in the eighteenth century, critical scholars raised questions about the authorship. For example, they noticed differences in the vocabulary of various portions of the Books of Moses. They also noticed that some passages presented information that would not have been available at the time of Moses or that seemed out of place, such as the following:

Gn 14:14—"Dan" was not used for a region until the time of the Judges

Gn 36:31—Refers to kings ruling over Israel, which did not occur until the reign of Saul

Ex 11:3; Nu 12:3—Compliments for Moses, which seem unlikely to come from Moses himself

Nu 35:14; Dt 4:46—Use the expression "beyond the Jordan," which could imply Israel had already settled west of the Jordan

Dt 34:5–12—The account of Moses' death

These observations led scholars to propose theories about the authorship, which ultimately meant a

Nile River.

thoroughly reconstructed view of the history of Israel, ideas of revelation, and evolutionary development of Israelite religion. For example, Richard Simon (1638–1712) wondered whether Moses simply edited these books, wrote parts of them, or perhaps did not write them at all. French scholar Jean Astruc (1685–1766) noticed that in some parts of Genesis a certain Hebrew word for "God" is used (Elohim), but in other parts a word for "Lord" is used (Yahweh; see *TLSB*, p 1227). Astruc proposed that this happened because Moses used different sources, which had different names for God. Biblical critic J. G. Eichhorn (1752–1827) and other German scholars (e.g., K. H. Graf and J. Wellhausen) developed Astruc's ideas more radically. Their search to discover whether the Books of Moses included other sources resulted in their documentary hypo-thesis, or JEDP theory, which assumed that Moses was not the author. They concluded that a much later editor drew the books together from four sources: the Jahwist, Elohist, Deuteronomist, and Priestly writers (hence J, E, D, P

Steps leading to the Canaanite era city of Dan (Laish), eighteenth century BC.

as an abbreviation for the theory). Their views became standard in liberal schools of theology and are still taught today.

However, in the twentieth century, scholars such as J. F. H. Gunkel (1862–1932) began to question aspects of the JEDP theory. Others rejected it altogether. Now, in the twenty-first century, most scholars have abandoned the practice of the JEDP theory in favor of methods that interpret large sections or entire books as whole literary compositions. Conservative biblical scholars have always attributed these five books to Moses. Archaeology and study of the texts have affirmed the antiquity of the books. For an overview of a common, critical approach to these issues, see "The JEDP Theory" on pp 10–11.

Evidence of Sources in the Bible

The Bible itself clearly teaches that Moses used other sources—written and oral—for composing the first five books of Scripture. Moses' most important source was God Himself; God dictated portions of the books to him (cf Ex 24:3). But Moses also mentioned or quoted the following potential sources:

The Book of the Generations of Adam (Gn 5:1)

The Saying about Nimrod (Gn 10:9)

The Saying about the Mount of the LORD (Gn 22:14)

The Tradition of the Sinew (Gn 32:32)

The Statute of Joseph (Gn 47:26)

The Song of Moses (Ex 15:1–18)

The Song of Miriam (Ex 15:20–21)

The Memorial for Joshua (Ex 17:14)

The Book of the Covenant (Ex 24:7)

The Tablets of the Testimony (Ex 24:12; 25:16)

The Registration of Elders (Nu 11:26)

The Book of the Wars of the LORD (Nu 21:14–15)

The Song of the Well (Nu 21:17–18)

The Song of Heshbon (Nu 21:27–30)

The Book of the Law (Dt 29:21; 30:10; 31:26)

When giving place-names, Moses also may have drawn on written or oral sources (cf Gn 11:9; 16:14; 26:33; 33:17; 35:20; Dt 3:14). A few passages possibly indicate later editing to provide clarity (see *TLSB* notes, Gn 14:14; 36:31).

Responding to Critical Views

The literary and the historical reconstructions of critical scholarship conflicted drastically with the Bible's own presentation of Israel's history and religion. Accepting the critical views in the JEDP theory means adopting a fundamentally different version of the Christian faith, beginning with radically different understandings of the nature of revelation and of biblical inspiration and authority. In view of this, conservative scholars have offered different explanations for the observations noted above.

First, the pivotal argument for Mosaic authorship is at once biblical and Christological. Not only do both Testaments repeatedly refer to these books as Mosaic, but Christ Himself does as well. A few of these examples might by themselves legitimately be considered mere traditional usages, with "Moses" becoming a traditional name for the books. However, the cumulative evidence makes plain that real Mosaic authorship was meant by the biblical writers who cited the books.

Second, we have already noted above a few undeniable but marginal signs that the Books of Moses were updated for the sake of later readers. Scribes likely provided brief notes that helped the reader understand the setting in their own day during the kingdom period (Gn 14:14; 36:31) or from their perspective of time and place (Ex 11:3; Nu 12:3; 35:14; Dt 4:46).

Third, one may also note that in the Books of Moses, as in other biblical books, there are signs of modernization of the language as it developed. English readers can best understand what this means by placing the 400-year-old King James Bible alongside a more modern translation, such as the Revised Standard Version and the English Standard Version, both of which stem from the King James. The differences in the English of these versions are dramatic, but the updating of the language has little affected the meaning of the texts. Readers of Hebrew observe something similar in the Hebrew of the Books of Moses. Much of the Hebrew text is written in ordinary, classical Hebrew, which likely means it was updated at the time of David and Solomon—the Golden Age of Hebrew literature some centuries after Moses.

However, poems in the Books of Moses often read differently from the stories. The poems appear to be written in a more archaic form of Hebrew. Another modern example can help us understand why. Worshipers today tend to prefer older versions of hymns and prayers, which best preserve the poetry and agree with what the worshipers memorized over years of using the hymns or prayers (the Lord's Prayer is an excellent example of this conservative tendency). The ancient Israelites likewise preferred to have their poems unchanged or little changed. The poems in the Books of Moses now stand as reminders of what older Hebrew looked like and sounded like because these poems were not updated as the stories and other texts were.

Fourth, it is especially apparent in the Prophetic Books, as we shall see later, that there was some rearrangement or transmission of the prophetic oracles for specific literary purposes, whether by the prophets themselves or by disciples (see pp 700–713). Something similar may have happened in portions of the Books of Moses. Certain stylistic differences, in accord with the customary usages of the scribes, might easily have arisen in that connection. Mosaic authorship need not be taken in so narrow a sense as to attribute every contour of the language to Moses himself. (For example, someone else most likely wrote the story of Moses' death.) Theologically, this need not conflict with the biblical teaching about the Bible's inspiration anymore than our faith in its inspiration today prevents editors and translators from preparing new editions of Holy Scripture.

Title of the Books

The Hebrew name for the Books of Moses is "Torah." (The Greek title is "Pentateuch"). The conventional translation of "Torah" with "Law" is most lamentable. If it were possible to turn back the clock and expunge misleading renditions from our Bibles, this would surely be the place to start. It indisputably is one of the major culprits in reinforcing the stubborn prejudice that somehow the Old Testament is more legalistic.

If it were possible, it might be better not to translate the word, but simply to transliterate the Hebrew word "Torah," as is the common Jewish practice. The word means something much more than Law; it means "instruction." It relates both the impossible demand of God upon fallen man as well as the good news of God's own meeting of His demand in the covenant—and in the promises attached to it. "Word of God" is often a superb equivalent of Torah as parallel examples in Hebrew poetry show (e.g., Is 2:3 and Mi 4:2; and examples in Ps 119 and in Dt).

THE JEDP THEORY

Critical scholars, such as Julius Wellhausen (1844–1918), settled on a theory of how the Books of Moses were written by assigning different parts of the books to different proposed authors or editors. This theory remains commonly used among liberal critical scholars of the Bible. The following is a summary of their ideas.

J-Author

Also known as the "Yahwist." Wrote in the tenth or ninth century BC in the kingdom of Judah during the early stirrings of the Israelite prophetic movement. His writings have an ethical tone and teach that Yahweh is the only God, while remaining tolerant of Canaanite religious practices. The J-author wrote about Israel's history in a creative and uninhibited manner. For liberal theologians, this proposed writer is the model of good religion.

E-Author

Also known as the "Elohist." Wrote or edited in the ninth or eighth century BC in the Northern Kingdom of Israel (Ephraim). Introduced greater accent on law and covenant when describing Israel's history. Sharply rejects the Canaanite religion and emphasizes God's exclusive covenant with Israel. Writes more detailed traditions about the work and character of Moses, the archetypical lawgiver. (Cf Ex 20–24.)

D-Author

Also known as the "Deuteronomist." Wrote or edited in the seventh century BC at Jerusalem. Required worship only at one central sanctuary and limited the priesthood to the Levites. Compromised views between priestly and prophetic, ceremonial and ethical religion. (Cf the Book of Deuteronomy.)

P-Author

Also known as the "Priestly" author. Wrote or edited in the sixth or fifth century BC at the time of the exile or afterward when the remnant of Israel was a theocratic community rather than a kingdom. Focused on temple worship and God's glory at Sinai. Wrote in a dry, formal, precise style preferring lists, genealogies, rubrics, and exact measurements. (Cf Ex 25–Nu 10.) For liberal theologians, this proposed writer is the model of bad, legalistic religion.

The theory presents numerous problems for itself, as the practitioners themselves have noted. For example, the proposed J-author and the E-author are difficult to distinguish so that some scholars speak of JE or the "narrative source," which really leaves only two "sources" for the first four books of the Bible (JE and P). Due to the speculative character of the theory, more and more scholars are studying the Books of Moses as they were received in Israel and preserved in the manuscripts rather than trying to reconstruct the books and their history.

GENESIS

In Abraham all families of the earth will be blessed

The name for Genesis comes from the book's Greek title. The word means "birth" or "genealogy," topics that are important to the stories of Genesis and to its structure. It may be helpful to look at Genesis as an overview of world history written especially for the people of Israel, to define God's place for them in history. In fact, a greater period of history is compressed in this first book of the Old Testament than in all the remaining 38 books combined. The following paragraphs offer comment on Genesis as history and highlight significant features of its character and structure.

Origins or Beginnings

The first 11 chapters report real, empirical history, just as much as the rest of the Bible. Yet we are generally not yet able to investigate its history as readily as later epochs. History always retains its mysterious character because we study past events from afar, and we are not able to repeat them as we can scientific experiments. Speaking theologically, *divine* work in history as well as in the natural world is ultimately recognized as a matter of revelation and faith. Although Genesis is factual, it provides something more as well. It points us to the meaning of the past in a way that helps us make sense of the present, just as the Gospels tell the stories of Jesus' life while explaining His greater role in history and in eternity.

The accounts of Genesis are not adaptations of older Near Eastern legends and myths as some have proposed.

OVERVIEW

Author
Moses the prophet

Date
Written c 1446–1406 BC

Places
See maps, pp 25, 29.

People
Adam; Eve; Cain; Abel; Seth; Noah; Shem; Canaan; Abraham; Sarah; Lot; Melchizedek; Hagar; Ishmael; Abimelech; Isaac; Rebekah; Laban; Jacob (Israel); Esau; Rachel; Leah; sons of Israel; Dinah; Tamar; Potiphar; Manasseh; Ephraim

Purpose
To trace the passing of the promise of God's Savior from generation to generation, to all Israel and to all nations

Law Themes
The curse and death that come with sin and disobedience; humankind's slavery to evil; families divided by sin

Gospel Themes
The promise of a Savior; God gives blessings, life, and freedom; God's goodness and covenant promise for the faithful

Memory Verses
The image of God (1:26–27); the trees of Eden (2:16–17); the promised Deliverer (3:15); man's heart is evil (6:5; 8:21); all families blessed through Abraham (12:3; 18:18; 26:4); righteous through faith (15:6); scepter of Judah (49:10–12)

TIMELINE

	Creation
c 2091 BC	Call of Abraham
2026 BC	Isaac marries Rebekah
1876 BC	Jacob goes to Egypt
1446 BC	Exodus from Egypt

Ripening pomegranates at a garden in Israel remind us of the bounties of Eden.

The many undeniable parallels with Near Eastern literature point in the opposite direction: the extrabiblical tales are garbled reflections of the biblical accounts. The biblical God is not a mythological construct—He is a real, personal being. Genesis states a uniquely biblical assumption: the Creator alone is eternal. On that premise the Bible explicitly bases not only creation itself but also God's judgment and our salvation.

Modern theories of origins, even "theistic evolution," fail to break with paganism at the point of *ultimate* beginnings, no matter how far back the date for evolution is pushed. In a way, evolution founders more on the biblical teaching about the fall than on creation itself. The Bible teaches that God made all things good and that evil was a corruption of that created perfection. To hold that God made things corrupt or incomplete to begin with undermines the biblical view of God and the need for redemption.

Grammatically, it is impossible to try to calculate a date for creation based on the meaning of "day" (Hbr *yom*). The word is undeniably used in Hebrew (as in English) in a variety of ways. Yet in the context of Gn 1, its ordinary 24-hour sense is certainly the most natural sense.

We are bound by the clear biblical impression of a relatively *young* earth, but we are in no position to attempt to fix a precise date; in a fully biblical context it is not an important matter but one we must note. It is not a question of whether the Bible is true, or of letting extrabiblical evidence overrule the Bible's testimony, but of what truth the Bible is teaching on this point. The uncertainties about dates based on Genesis arise primarily because of the biblical numbers, especially in the genealogies and chronologies. Not only does the Bible *sometimes* use numbers symbolically, but the word *son* especially is often used in derivative senses of "descendant," or of cultural and political connections. This makes it difficult to simply add up the ages in Genesis and calculate a date for creation.

The twofold account of creation (Gn 1–2) provides a "wide-angle" introduction to all of creation and zooms in for a "close-up" of the Bible's primary interest: mankind. The small amount of repetition in the text need not bother us; abundant ancient Near Eastern examples illustrate that repetitious writing was common, especially in epic material (there are countless applications in the Bible).

In 2:4a we meet the word *toledoth* (sometimes translated "generations") for the first of 10 times in Genesis. Critics read 2:4a as the conclusion of a priestly creation account—the problem being, however, that everywhere else *toledoth* introduces a section instead of concluding it. The expression plays a structural role in Genesis (see p 18). It consistently both concludes and introduces. It appears to signal major points where the line of God's chosen people is narrowed down en route to the Chosen One. In Gn 2, then, *toledoth* would signal the first narrowing of the line, from all of nature to mankind. So understood, it also helps fuse chs 1 and 2 into a structural unity.

The story of salvation does not begin with Gn 12, as critics commonly hold, but at Gn 3:15, the "first mention of the Gospel" (*protevangelium*). The prophecy of salvation here must be integrated with other themes in the Book of Genesis: promise, blessing, election—and probably, as noted, "toledoth" as well.

Chapter 10 is the famous "Table of Nations." Quite a few of the place-names are locatable and the Ebla tablets appear to describe one of the persons. The "Eber" of 10:21 (again in 11:14) appears to be the same as one of the major kings of Ebla (c 2300 BC). When the genealogy is continued in 11:10, it is only the line of Eber and Peleg that is picked up to lead us into the world of the patriarchs.

The Patriarchs

Problems of historical confirmation continue with the story of the patriarchs. From the cultural history of the times (especially the findings at Mari and Nuzi) we can document names and customs which appear to parallel or illuminate those recorded of the patriarchs. The fact that some of these customs are different from the later standard Israelite laws or customs helps confirm their historicity, because if the texts were written centuries later, they would scarcely have preserved the customs of the forefathers—or even known of the existence of such usages. More conservative, archaeologically oriented scholars such as William Albright, G. Ernest Wright, and Nelson Glueck dated the patriarchs either in the Middle Bronze I or II eras (c 2100–1700 BC) and associated their migrations with the massive Amorite movements of the times. Their conservative scholarly consensus still influences current discussions of biblical archaeology.

A bearded dignitary of Ebla, wearing a fleece coat and holding an axe. (Carbonized wood, c 2300 BC.)

Genesis 14 remains a historical and literary puzzle. Earlier attempts to associate Amraphel with Hammurabi cannot be sustained. One notes especially the designation of God as El Elyon ("God Most High"; v 18), a title that can be formally paralleled at Ugarit ("Aliyan," applied to Baal). It seems to have been especially common in patriarchal times (alongside "Shaddai," often translated the same way, but so far unparalleled in other Near Eastern literature).

Jabbok River, which flows westward into the Jordan River.

Especially significant is the change of Jacob's name to "Israel" at the Jabbok ford (32:22–32). This narrative is probably to be read both on the personal and on the tribal level, because "Israel" ever after remains the covenant people's major self-designation ("sons of Israel"). To provide a modern comparison, it is the "baptismal name," the "*Christian* name" of the people, and is best explained along those lines. Yet the people remain "Jacob," which in prophetic address often alternates with the new name. They are at the same time saints and sinners (*simul justus et peccator*).

The Joseph section contains many examples of Egyptian customs. It begins in ch 37, only to be interrupted promptly by the Judah and Tamar episode in ch 38. Obviously, part of the reason for this interruption is interest in the tribe of Judah, the forebearer of David—and the Messiah. We may also have an example here of a literary device that was common in antiquity but alien to us: Joseph temporarily disappears from the reader's sight at the same time that in the narrative itself he disappears from his father and brothers!

Jacob's blessing in ch 49 is important linguistically because of its many archaic poetic features, and even more so theologically because of the Davidic/messianic reference in connection with the blessing given Judah.

The closing words of Genesis, "in Egypt," set the stage for the Book of Exodus. Historically, however, there ensues a long interval, a veritable dark age in our knowledge of the Israelites.

Historical and Cultural Setting

According to traditional biblical chronology, the era of the patriarchs began during Egypt's Eighth Dynasty. The Egyptians had already chronicled nearly 1,000 years of successive pharaohs, providing helpful scaffolding for comparison with events described in Genesis. In fact, great pharaohs had completed the pyramids before Abram and Sarai visited Egypt during a famine in Canaan (Gn 12). The lack of rainfall at this time contributed to economic decline in the region, weaker pharaohs, and eventual civil war in Egypt during the First Intermediate Period. Mentuhotep II (2010–1960 BC) reunified Egypt, introducing the Middle Kingdom Period. A court official, Amenemhat I (1938–1908 BC) founded the Twelfth Dynasty with powerful pharaohs. When Joseph was sold into Egypt, the Egyptians were prospering again, completing great works of literature such as *The Prophecies of Neferti* and *The Tale of Sinuhe*. Effective leadership stabilized the land, making it an attractive place for the sons of Jacob to settle (1876 BC). During the Second Intermediate Period (1786–1567 BC), Egypt was at war with a new foreign power: the Hyksos of Asia. The Hyksos invaded (c 1750) and ruled in the Nile delta for centuries until the rulers of Upper Egypt expelled them (c 1580–70). Pharaoh Ahmose established the New Kingdom and the Eighteenth Dynasty not long before the birth of Moses (1526), with which the Book of Exodus begins.

Amorite soldier leading a prisoner.

However, Egypt was just one of the great powers at the time of the patriarchs. Abram was born further to the east in Mesopotamia, at the city of Ur near the Persian Gulf, which also had a flourishing civilization. When Abram was young, the Gutians invaded Ur (c 2150 BC). The Amorite invasion of Mesopotamia (c 2100) may have caused the move of Abram's family to the west. He moved from Haran to Canaan in 2091 BC. Canaan became the setting for most of Genesis (chs 12–50) with visits to Egypt interspersed until Joseph moved the family to Egypt for a stay of 430 years.

According to Genesis, Abram and Sarai witnessed the progress of Near Eastern civilization all along the Fertile Crescent—the agricultural and inhabitable lands that stretched from the Nile, up the Mediterranean coast, along the Litani and Orontes river valleys, toward the Upper Euphrates and Tigris rivers that flow into the Persian Gulf. It might seem amazing that this

Continued on p 21.

OUTLINE

Genesis is the prologue for the central story of the exodus in the Books of Moses. The book is unified and also divided by the tenfold repetition of Hbr *toledoth*, "generations." This term, uniquely used by Moses, introduces each new section of the book by recounting the history of generations or families. Only the genealogy of Israel is carried forward through Genesis to Ex 1:1–5.

The broad outline of the book is very simple. Chapters 1–11 report the primeval history of the entire human race, and chs 12–50 report the beginning of the history of election in the patriarchs. The latter may be subdivided into chs 12–26, Abraham and Isaac; chs 27–36, Jacob and Esau; and chs 37–50, Joseph. Chapters 1–11 set the stage for the patriarchal covenant and promise, as chs 12–50 lead up to an initial fulfillment in the exodus and the covenant at Sinai. Hence the title of the Book is appropriate in many respects: "Genesis" or "beginning" in various aspects.

I. The Book of the Ancients (1:1–11:26)

  A. Beginnings (chs 1–4)

    1. Setting: creation of the heavens and the earth (1:1–2:3)

    2. The fall and God's judgment (2:4–3:24)

    3. Aftermath of the fall (ch 4)

  B. Descendants of Adam (ch 5)

  C. The Flood (chs 6–9)

    1. Setting of the flood (6:1–8)

    2. The flood (6:9–8:22)

    3. Aftermath of the flood (ch 9)

  D. Table of Nations (ch 10)

  E. Tower of Babel (11:1–9)

  F. Descendants of Shem (11:10–26)

II. The Book of the Patriarchs (11:27–37:1)

  A. Descendants of Terah (11:27–32)

B. Story of Abraham (12:1–25:18)

  1. God calls Abram (ch 12)

  2. Abram receives a blessing (chs 13–14)

  3. God makes a covenant with Abra(ha)m (chs 15–17)

  4. Abraham intercedes for Sodom before its destruction (chs 18–19)

  5. An heir for Abraham (chs 20–24)

  6. Conclusion of the story of Abraham (25:1–18)

C. Story of Jacob (25:19–37:1)

  1. Jacob and Esau (25:19–34)

  2. Isaac as Abraham's heir (ch 26)

  3. Jacob receives the blessing (27:1–40)

  4. Jacob flees Esau's vengeance (27:41–33:20)

    a. Esau's anger (27:41–28:9)

    b. Jacob at Bethel (28:10–22)

    c. Jacob in Paddan-aram (29:1–30:43)

    d. Jacob returns to Canaan (31:1–33:20)

  5. Conflict with the Shechemites (ch 34)

  6. Jacob fulfills his vow (35:1–15)

  7. Transitionary material (35:16–37:1)

    a. Deaths of Rachel and Isaac (35:16–29)

    b. Generations of Esau (ch 36–37:1)

III. The Book of Joseph (37:2–50:26)

  A. Joseph and His Brothers (37:2–36)

    1. Introductory note (37:2a)

    2. Joseph sold into slavery (37:2b–36)

  B. Excursus—Judah and Tamar (ch 38)

    1. Judah's family (38:1–5)

    2. Tamar's situation (38:6–11)

    3. Tamar and Judah (38:12–30)

  C. Joseph Prospers Despite Injustice (ch 39)

    1. Joseph at Potiphar's house (39:1)

    2. Joseph prospers (39:2–6a)

3. Potiphar's wife (39:6b–18)

4. Joseph imprisoned (39:19–23)

D. Joseph Interprets Dreams in Prison (ch 40)

  1. Joseph, the cupbearer, and the baker (40:1–8)

  2. The cupbearer's dream (40:9–15)

  3. The baker's dream (40:16–19)

  4. The cupbearer and the baker are judged (40:20–23)

E. Joseph Interprets Pharaoh's Dream (41:1–45)

  1. Pharaoh's dream (41:1–8)

  2. The cupbearer remembers Joseph (41:9–13)

  3. Pharaoh reveals his dream (41:14–24)

  4. Joseph interprets Pharaoh's dream (41:25–36)

  5. Joseph is rewarded (41:37–45)

F. Joseph Serves Pharaoh (41:46–57)

  1. Seven years of plenty (41:46–49)

  2. Joseph's sons (41:50–52)

  3. Seven years of famine (41:53–57)

G. Sons of Jacob Come to Egypt (ch 42)

  1. Jacob sends his sons to buy grain (42:1–5)

  2. Joseph accuses his brothers of spying (42:6–17)

  3. Joseph offers a deal and plays a trick (42:18–25)

  4. The brothers discover the trick (42:26–28)

  5. The brothers return home (42:29–38)

H. The Brothers Go to Egypt a Second Time (chs 43–45)

  1. Jacob sends his sons for grain again (43:1–15)

  2. Joseph's steward receives the brothers (43:16–25)

  3. Joseph receives the brothers (43:26–34)

  4. Joseph plays a second trick (44:1–13)

  5. Interview: Joseph reveals himself (44:14–45:15)

  6. Pharaoh hears of Joseph's brothers (45:16–20)

  7. The brothers return to Jacob (45:21–28)

I. Jacob Goes to Egypt (46:1–47:12)

  1. Jacob sets out for Egypt (46:1–7)

  2. Genealogy of Jacob's descendants (46:8–27)

  3. Joseph meets Jacob (46:28–34)

4. Pharaoh welcomes Joseph's family (47:1–10)

5. Joseph's family settles in Egypt (47:11–12)

J. The Hebrews in Egypt (47:13–31)

    1. Joseph acquires lands for Pharaoh (47:13–26)

    2. Summary note on the Hebrews in Egypt (47:27–28)

    3. Joseph swears to return Jacob's body to Canaan (47:29–31)

K. Jacob Blesses Ephraim and Manasseh (ch 48)

    1. Jacob adopts Ephraim and Manasseh (48:1–7)

    2. Jacob blesses Ephraim and Manasseh (48:8–22)

L. Jacob Blesses His Sons (49:1–28)

    1. Introduction (49:1–2)

    2. Blessings on the sons of Jacob (49:3–27)

    3. Conclusion (49:28)

M. Deaths of Jacob and Joseph (49:29–50:26)

    1. Death of Jacob (49:29–33)

    2. Embalming of Jacob (50:1–3)

    3. Burial of Jacob (50:4–14)

    4. Joseph's brothers fear vengeance (50:15–21)

    5. Death of Joseph (50:22–26)

couple would travel so far until one considers that they lived as herders, accustomed to moving with their animals in search of pasture. Genesis ends with the herders settling in Goshen, "the best of the land" of Egypt (47:6).

COMPOSITION

Author(s)

See pp 4–11.

Date of Composition

See pp 4–11.

Purpose/Recipients

The Book of Genesis describes God's work as Creator of all things and creator of Israel through His chosen servant, Abraham. Using the thematic term *generations* (Hbr *toledoth*), Genesis traces the passing of God's promised salvation from generation to generation, culminating in the promises to the sons of Israel and especially to Judah, from whom the kings of Israel would descend—including Jesus of Nazareth, whom the New Testament describes as the Messiah and promised offspring of Abraham. In this way, Genesis defines the people of Israel and their unique, God-given role in becoming a blessing to all the families of the earth (12:3).

Literary Features

Genre

Torah, the traditional Hebrew name for the Books of Moses, applies well to Genesis (see pp 4–11). The work contains genealogies (cf chs 5; 11) and poems (e.g., ch 49) but is predominantly historical narrative, which some scholars characterize as family or tribal history in the case of the patriarchs (chs 12–50). Genesis may contain one of the most ancient texts known to man, "the book of the generations of Adam" (ch 5), a chronicle of mankind listing persons from before the great flood.

Characters

Genesis begins with **God** (1:1) and ends with the "sons of Israel" (50:25). In other words, the book begins with the Creator as the main character and transitions to focus on His creation and the particular family He creates (18:9–14) and chooses (12:1–3). Along the way, the reader meets many of the most beloved and despised characters in the Bible, such as the following:

Adam and **Eve** are presented as the first human beings. They were real, historical persons who likely dwelt in the region we call Mesopotamia today. God placed them in a special environment, the Garden of Eden, from which they were to fill the earth with their offspring and subdue the whole of God's created world.

The **serpent** appears in ch 3 as a major character and antagonist to human beings before slithering out of the story. Moses described the serpent as no ordinary snake but a rational character that could speak and reason with Eve. These circumstances caused critical scholars to propose that the account is rooted in mythology. However, this was not the conclusion of early Jewish and Christian writers, who saw in the serpent the embodiment of someone far more sinister: Satan or the devil, as explicitly identified in the last book of the Bible (Rv 12:9; 20:2).

Noah is presented as a faithful but flawed servant of God through whom the Lord saved the human race. His story is found in numerous extrabiblical accounts, most famously in the *Enuma Elish* saga of Mesopotamian literature, which dates to the second millennium BC. This interesting parallel points to the antiquity of the information recorded in the first chapters of Genesis.

Abraham and **Sarah** were originally named Abram and Sarai (chs 12–16). God specifically chose Abram and brought him to faith through His promise of offspring through whom all nations would be blessed. This unique promise distinguished Abraham and Sarah's descendants as the chosen people of God through whom the Savior would come (cf 3:15; 12:1–3). Abraham also received the covenant of circumcision (ch 17; the occasion of their name changes) that helped distinguish his descendants and their religious faith and commitment from their neighbors.

The *Enuma Elish* is a Babylonian story of creation, written in cuneiform. Pictured here is one of seven tablets, which date from the eighth or seventh centuries BC.

Jacob and **Esau**, Abraham and Sarah's grandsons, are the next major figures in Genesis. The brothers are opposed to each other from the womb and described as if opposites in character (25:19–28). Genesis explains how the second son, Jacob, became the inheritor of God's promise to Abraham and how Esau departed from the faith and culture of the family. It likewise explains how Jacob received the covenant name, Israel (32:22–32; 35:1–15), and had 12 sons that became the 12 tribes of Israel.

Joseph is the main character of the longest narrative in Genesis, the eleventh son of Jacob, who like his father was threatened and persecuted by his brothers. They sold him as a slave and he ended up in prison in Egypt. The story then explains how God providentially delivered Joseph and elevated him to the highest rank in the land. When Joseph was suddenly reintroduced to his brothers, he used his position first to chasten them and drive them to repentance. Then he rescued them from a famine, resettling them in Egypt. The story explains how the descendants of Joseph received a double inheritance in Israel through his two sons Ephraim and Manasseh. At the time Moses wrote, the combined strengths of Joseph's descendants was second only to the tribe of Judah (cf Nu 1:27, 33, 35), which foreshadowed their influential role in Israel's future.

Judah was the fourth son of Jacob, who received a minor narrative in Genesis (ch 38), a significant role in the story of Joseph (44:14–34), and the most substantial prophetic blessing from his father (49:8–12), who foresaw that Judah would become Israel's ruling tribe.

Narrative Development or Plot

As a large, complex book, Genesis does not present a single plotline or story, though the author provides an overarching structure through the 10 divisions of the book and the transferring of God's promise from Adam and Eve through a sacred line of persons from Seth to Noah, to Abraham, Isaac, and Jacob, whom God renames "Israel." (See "Purpose," p 22; see also the outline above.) To read summaries of the major stories in Genesis, see "Characters" above.

Resources

See p 7.

Text and Translations

The traditional Hebrew text of Genesis, like that of the other Books of Moses, is well preserved. The Samaritans preserved their own version of the book, which includes some unique readings. The LXX text of Genesis is a very literal rendering of the Hebrew, with occasional passages clearly providing a Greek idiom. Nineteen fragments of Genesis manuscripts were found at Qumran, most of which support the traditional Hebrew text. Other finds included commentaries on the Book of Genesis, the Genesis Apocryphon, and *Jubilees*, which retells stories from Genesis.

DOCTRINAL CONTENT

Summary Commentary

Chs 1–4 God's first act, the creation, is an act of grace. God acts freely to reflect His character, making the world "very good" (1:31). He takes great care to place man and woman in the garden to care for the things that He created. Ch 2 is a more detailed account of creation, focusing on the creation of humankind. The serpent tempts Adam and Eve to sin. With the words that God speaks to the serpent, to Eve, and to Adam after their disobedience, He sets the course for the rest of biblical history. Here there is judgment for sin, but also the first hint that the effects of the fall will one day be undone when the serpent is crushed (3:15). Chapter 4 begins with a mur-

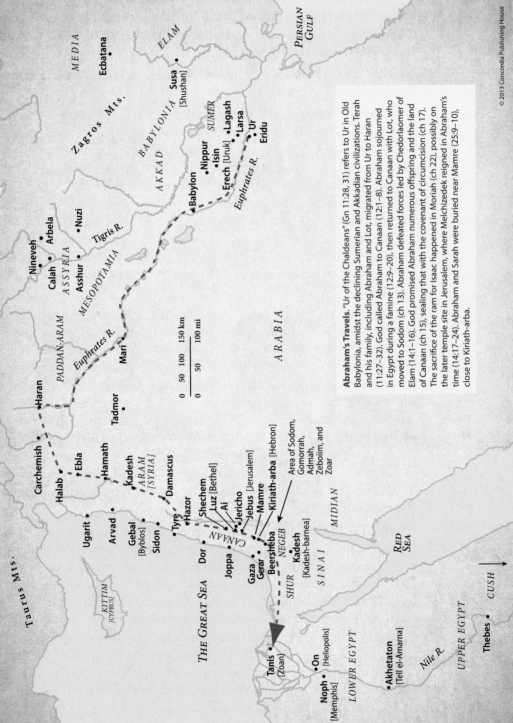

Abraham's Travels. "Ur of the Chaldeans" (Gn 11:28, 31) refers to Ur in Old Babylonia, amidst the declining Sumerian and Akkadian civilizations. Terah and his family, including Abraham and Lot, migrated from Ur to Haran (11:27–32). God called Abraham to Canaan (12:1–8). Abraham sojourned in Egypt during a famine (12:9–20), then returned to Canaan with Lot, who moved to Sodom (ch 13). Abraham defeated forces led by Chedorlaomer of Elam (14:1–16). God promised Abraham numerous offspring and the land of Canaan (ch 15), sealing that with the covenant of circumcision (ch 17). The sacrifice of the ram for Isaac happened in Moriah (ch 22), possibly on the later temple site in Jerusalem, where Melchizedek reigned in Abraham's time (14:17–24). Abraham and Sarah were buried near Mamre (25:9–10), close to Kiriath-arba.

© 2013 Concordia Publishing House

der and traces how the shadow of violence lengthens until Lamech perverts God's intention for marriage. But we also learn of the birth of Seth, through whom God's promise will continue.

Ch 5 The genealogical summary advances the story to the next major development—the flood.

Chs 6–9 Seth's descendants increasingly participate in the evil that overwhelms God's creation, preferring their own inclinations toward beauty and power over God's clear will for their lives. God threatens judgment but also salvation for His chosen family. Faithful Noah and his family experience the greatest horror this earth has known, but the ark carries them up and away from the destruction and total devastation by the great flood. Noah demonstrates extraordinary patience and willingness to listen and obey God while confined in the ark for more than a year. God reassures Noah and his family that He will never again send a universal flood. The problem of sin reappears with Noah's sinful drunkenness, which results in tragic consequences for his family.

Chs 10–11 The Table of Nations describes the origins and interrelationships of many nations of the world. The list is important because it is the only document of its kind in existence and demonstrates the common descent of all human beings from Noah. Most important to the list are the Canaanites and Shemites, around whom the stories of the Old Testament will revolve. To curtail the pride and evil design of early humankind, God intervenes to make it difficult for family groups and tribes to communicate with one another, thereby causing them to disperse to different regions of the Near East and beyond. Sin weighs heavily on the human race as spans of life are drastically shortened. After the human race has again turned away from God, the history of salvation and the messianic promise is narrowed to one man, Abram, the son of Terah of the line of Shem.

Chs 12–19 God calls Abram to faith, giving him a promise that God Himself would fulfill for all people. Although God promises Abram that he will possess the land that God will give him, Abram still finds no secure place in which to dwell. Then a land dispute arises between Abram's and Lot's herdsmen. Abram—for the sake of peace within the clan—decides they need to part and relinquishes to Lot the right of first choice. Next, the land of Canaan is torn by marauding invaders, who sweep up Lot in their conquest. But God in His grace provides deliverance. The Lord fulfills His promise to bless Abram, doing so through the ministry of Melchizedek, the priest of God Most High, who presents Abram with a feast.

God credits righteousness to Abram simply on the basis of His covenant promise and faith. To the promise, He adds the visible sign of animal sacrifice, by which God shows Abram that He is committed. Sarai seeks alternative means for fulfilling God's promise of a son by giving her servant, Hagar, to Abram. When God provides a son to Hagar, discord and strife arise because of jealousy and pride. Abram receives both a new name (Abraham) and the sign of the covenant promise God had given His people.

Divine messengers, on their way to Sodom and Gomorrah to deliver judgment, visit Abraham and Sarah to announce that Sarah will bear the child of promise. Abraham begs the Lord to spare the wicked cities for the sake of the righteous. Lot and his small family are spared the destruction of Sodom, but Lot and his daughters, driven by weakness and fear, resort to evil means to preserve their family line. And still God is patient, even granting protection to their offspring.

Desolate south end of the Dead Sea near the region of ancient Sodom.

20:1–25:18 When in Egypt, Abraham is deceptive in pretending that Sarah is only his sister, but God intervenes to protect him from the harm of his own doing. Twenty-five years after the promise was first given (12:2), a child is born to Abraham and Sarah. His name is Isaac, "he laughs," calling to mind the past laughter of his parents and describing their joy upon his birth. When Sarah becomes alarmed at Ishmael's behavior toward Isaac, Abraham determines to dismiss Ishmael and Hagar from his household. The climax of Abraham's life of faith comes when he who loves his son Isaac so much is willing to offer him as a sacrifice to his Lord. Abraham finds great relief when God provides a ram in the thicket instead. Sarah's death is the occasion for a significant development: Abraham purchases a plot of ground in the Promised Land, a testimony to his confidence in God's promises and to his concern for his wife's remains. Abraham sends his servant to find a wife for his son Isaac. Rebekah and her parents consent to the proposal. Though they have not met, Isaac and Rebekah consent to a marriage that will be filled with God's blessing and love. Abraham makes clear that Isaac alone is his heir. Abraham dies a blessed death and is given a proper burial by his sons Isaac and Ishmael.

25:19–27:46 The Lord chooses to give His special blessing to Jacob, who does not deserve this gift either by birth order or by virtue. This comes about as Esau disdains his birthright, and Jacob schemes against his brother.

Neither is worthy of the Lord's favor and the honor to carry on the promise. Nevertheless, when a severe famine forces Isaac to relocate his family, the Lord appears to him with words of comfort. In this adversity, the Lord promises to Isaac the same favor He did to Abraham: His caring presence, land, offspring, and blessedness to all people. Although Isaac doubts the Lord's protection and lies to Abimelech, the Lord provides Isaac with agricultural prosperity and the respect of local rulers. Deceptive Jacob, scheming Rebekah, unwitting Isaac, and impulsive Esau all fall short of the Lord's perfect standard, which allows Jacob to steal Esau's birthright.

Chs 28–33 Isaac gives Jacob a command and a blessing: Jacob must leave home, go to his relatives, and not marry a Canaanite wife. Before he departs, Isaac gives Jacob the blessing of Abraham, a blessing that includes the land of Canaan, many descendants, and ultimately the dignity of being an ancestor of the Messiah. Esau chooses a wife from Abraham's family (Ishmael) in order to please Isaac, which may indicate repentance for previously dishonoring his parents. God appears to Jacob in a vision with ascending and descending angels. He tells how all nations will be blessed through the line of Jacob. In thankfulness, Jacob vows to build an altar for the worship of the true God and to tithe. Jacob's sin falls back upon him. Just as he deceived his brother Esau, the firstborn, so also Laban deceives Jacob regarding a firstborn daughter. Laban's daughters Leah and Rachel contend with each other regarding childbearing and Jacob's affection. The Lord finally grants Rachel a child and thus removes her reproach (30:23). Laban deceives Jacob by taking away the livestock he promised. Nonetheless, the Lord blesses Jacob by miraculously prospering his livestock and granting him shrewdness with honesty. Laban's deception leads to dispute. Jacob flees back to Canaan where he faces the conse-

Hands carved into a basalt stele indicate that pillars, such as the one set up by Jacob (Gn 28:22), could represent people worshiping. This Canaanite collection of pillars comes from Hazor.

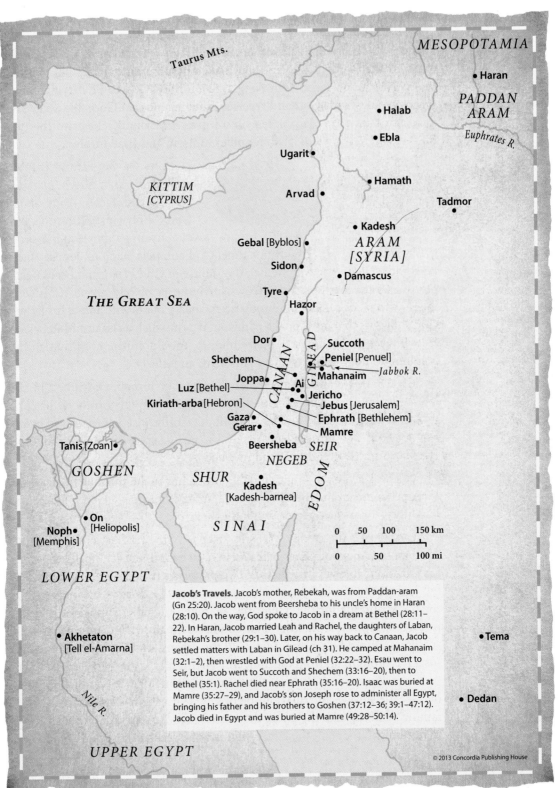

Taurus Mts.

MESOPOTAMIA

● Haran

PADDAN ARAM

● Halab

● Ebla

Euphrates R.

Ugarit ●

● Hamath

● Tadmor

Arvad ●

KITTIM [CYPRUS]

● Kadesh

ARAM [SYRIA]

Gebal [Byblos] ●

Sidon ●

● Damascus

Tyre ●

THE GREAT SEA

Hazor ●

Dor ●

CANAAN

GILEAD

Succoth
Peniel [Penuel]
Mahanaim

Shechem ●

Joppa ●

Ai ●

Jabbok R.

Luz [Bethel]

Jericho ●

Kiriath-arba [Hebron]

Jebus [Jerusalem]

Gaza ●

Ephrath [Bethlehem]

Gerar ●

Mamre

Beersheba

SEIR

Tanis [Zoan] ●

NEGEB

GOSHEN

SHUR

Kadesh [Kadesh-barnea]

EDOM

On [Heliopolis] ●

Noph ● [Memphis]

SINAI

| 0 | 50 | 100 | 150 km |
| 0 | 50 | 100 mi |

LOWER EGYPT

● Akhetaton [Tell el-Amarna]

● Tema

Jacob's Travels. Jacob's mother, Rebekah, was from Paddan-aram (Gn 25:20). Jacob went from Beersheba to his uncle's home in Haran (28:10). On the way, God spoke to Jacob in a dream at Bethel (28:11–22). In Haran, Jacob married Leah and Rachel, the daughters of Laban, Rebekah's brother (29:1–30). Later, on his way back to Canaan, Jacob settled matters with Laban in Gilead (ch 31). He camped at Mahanaim (32:1–2), then wrestled with God at Peniel (32:22–32). Esau went to Seir, but Jacob went to Succoth and Shechem (33:16–20), then to Bethel (35:1). Rachel died near Ephrath (35:16–20). Isaac was buried at Mamre (35:27–29), and Jacob's son Joseph rose to administer all Egypt, bringing his father and his brothers to Goshen (37:12–36; 39:1–47:12). Jacob died in Egypt and was buried at Mamre (49:28–50:14).

● Dedan

Nile R.

UPPER EGYPT

© 2013 Concordia Publishing House

quences of deceiving his brother, Esau. Faced with possible death, Jacob turns to the Lord in prayer, then makes preparations to aid his family's safety. Alone and faced with danger, Jacob finds God to be his adversary. Jacob wrestles with God and receives a new name and God's blessing. The next day, God turns Jacob's fear into joy as Esau approaches and the two brothers are reconciled. Jacob humbles himself, and Esau forgives.

A flint knife was the tool of circumcision. This Egyptian example dates from c 3100 BC.

Chs 34–36 Family trouble reappears when Shechem rapes Dinah, and Jacob's sons abuse God's holy institution of circumcision so they can massacre the men of Shechem. About this time, God compels Jacob to get rid of the false gods. He journeys to Bethel, the "house of God." He again hears God's promises and worships. Yet sorrows surround Jacob. He learns of his son's incest with Jacob's concubine and also the death of his wife and of his father. God shows us that for the sake of devout parents such as Isaac and Rebekah, He will give good things to their children, the Edomites, even though the children do not imitate their parents' faith and life.

Ch 37 This chapter introduces the story of Joseph, continued in chs 39–48. Joseph is favored by his father but hated by his brothers. Joseph's prophetic dreams only raise tensions in the family. Joseph is betrayed by his brothers and sold into slavery. Yet God spares Joseph's life in order to fulfill His plan and the dreams He had revealed.

Ch 38 The sins of Onan, Judah, and Tamar make this one of the most sordid chapters of the Bible. Yet despite human sinfulness, God is at work in Judah's family, as Jacob later prophesies (49:10).

Chs 39–42 The story returns to Joseph. With steadfast faith, he resists the temptation of Potiphar's wife. Yet in return for his godly life, Joseph loses his job and is thrown into prison. Two prisoners from Pharaoh's household tell Joseph their dreams. Joseph explains that the dreams mean death for the baker and life for the cupbearer. Yet when the chief cupbearer is freed, he forgets about Joseph. Then Pharaoh has a dream. His fortune-tellers and sorcerers cannot help him understand the dreams that God sent. Therefore, Joseph is brought up from the dungeon. Giving all the glory to God, he interprets the dreams and warns of the coming famine. Pharaoh exalts Joseph to oversee the storage and distribution of Egypt's great harvests. As the years of famine begin to take their toll, there is enough surplus to share with those in need throughout all the land. The sons of Israel enter Egypt for food and unknowingly fulfill Joseph's earlier dream they had resented (37:5–8). Joseph begins a test to determine his brothers' treatment of his father and Benjamin, and to encourage repentance and a renewed relationship with God.

Chs 43–45 Joseph—motivated by love for Benjamin and his other brothers—tests his brothers to learn whether they will be jealous or abandon their youngest brother, as they had Joseph. He prepares a final test to determine whether his brothers will allow Benjamin to be enslaved and bring further grief to their father. Their refusal to leave Benjamin behind, and Judah's sacrificial offer of himself to spare both brother and father, show that their hearts have genuinely changed. Joseph reveals himself, reassuring his brothers. With Pharaoh's support, he sends for his father and family. Jacob is finally convinced that his son is alive.

"Famine Stele," though written in Ptolemaic times, tells of a seven-year famine during the reign of the Pharaoh Djozer (3rd Dynasty, third millennium BC).

46:1–49:27 Jacob leaves Canaan for Egypt only when he knows it is the Lord's will. The Lord is not limited by geography. He *will fulfill* His promise to make Abraham's seed a great nation in Egypt. Israel's children are called by name (ch 46) as they journey to Egypt. Powerful, wealthy Pharaoh humbly receives the blessing of Jacob, a lowly Hebrew, whose son addresses the famine by centralizing all Egypt's resources in a sharecropping system. Jacob (Israel) adopts and blesses Joseph's sons. Though born in Egypt to an Egyptian mother, they have full status as "children of Israel," people through whom God will bless the world. The blessing (testament) of Jacob is a prophecy about each son and his tribe. All 12 sons are blessed as participants in the promise that began with Abraham, emphasizing return to the land. Jacob concentrates on Reuben, Simeon, Judah, and Joseph—the first two negatively, the latter two positively. Jacob's testament promises great blessings, including the height of God's goodness: messianic kingship for Judah's line. Jacob's predictions are not uniformly happy. The reality of sin includes judgment (Simeon and Levi), oppression (Issachar), warfare (Gad, Benjamin), and other distress. Though Joseph will prosper in many ways, the greatest gift to Jacob's descendants is Judah's scepter (49:10).

49:28–50:26 Jacob insists on burial in Canaan, Israel's permanent home. He receives the most ornate funeral in the Bible, which also shows Joseph's importance. Jacob's sons fear that only their father's presence has prevented Joseph's revenge for their earlier hatred and violence. But Joseph consoles them and speaks kindly to them. The death of Joseph after 93 years in Egypt closes the first Book of Moses, but Joseph's request for final burial in Canaan reminds us that the story has only begun.

Specific Law Themes

Following the account of a perfect creation and God's gift of life, Genesis describes the corruption of creation and the intrusion of death as a consequence of sin. The curse of sin and death immediately manifests itself in the sin of Cain, who takes the life of his brother, Abel, dividing the family (4:8). From there, sin spreads perpetually to all the families of the earth. Every person is enslaved by sin since "every intention of the thoughts of his heart" is only evil continually (6:5) and even Noah, the last righteous man on earth (6:8–9), falls into flagrant sin after God rescues him from the flood. Families are repeatedly shown to be cursed and divided by sin.

Specific Gospel Themes

Recognizing the dominating themes of curse, sin, and death allows one to see most clearly the other great family of themes in Genesis. God gives life and blessing in creation, and immediately after the fall He promises restoration through the gift of a champion who will overcome the tempter (3:15). As the book narrows to focus on the descendants of Seth, Noah, and Abraham, one reads the promise of blessing for all families on earth (12:1–3), which is repeated to later generations.

Specific Doctrines

Genesis recounts events prior to the formation of Israel as God's chosen people. The succeeding books in the Old Testament record what God did for and through Israel. Therefore, Genesis is often said to present a prehistory to the main content of the Old Testament. But it is more than that.

Genesis and the Rest of the Bible

Genesis should also be viewed in the larger perspective of the entire "mystery of revelation" leading through Israel to God's final act of salvation in Jesus Christ. When Paul, for example (in Gal 3:16–25), reviews the entire Old Testament period "until the offspring [Christ] should come" (v 19), the covenant with Abraham is not preliminary but basic to God's entire plan of salvation. All that followed, including the covenant at Sinai, implemented the promise to Abraham. At Mount Sinai the Law "was added because of transgressions" (v 19), as a "guardian" (v 24) to remind humanity constantly of its sinfulness and need for redemption.

The entire history of Israel, therefore, may actually be considered a grand interlude between the promise to Abraham and its fulfillment in Jesus Christ. The Sinai covenant of Law did not annul the promise but represents the way God chose "that the promise by faith in Jesus Christ might be given to those who believe" (Gal 3:22). Israel was elected to inherit and bear the promise of grace; the covenant of Mount Sinai was to remind Israel constantly of its need for grace and at the same time to assure it that God's plan of salvation was being carried out. God gave the covenant of Sinai to Israel for a limited time and purpose. Since these aspects are now fulfilled, "we are no longer under a guardian" (v 25). In contrast with the Sinai covenant, the promise to Abraham was not merely first but also preeminent and permanent. It underlies all God's deeds for and through Israel. In this framework, all the accounts of Genesis have meaning and relevance.

The events in Genesis introduce the Book of Exodus, but they also provide the proper perspective for the entire Old Testament as well as the New. Genesis emphasizes that salvation is by the promise of grace and not through the Law—and that the succeeding history of Israel recounts God in action to fulfill that promise. As such, Genesis controls the interpretation of the entire Old Testament by writing across each page: Abraham "believed God, and it was counted to him as righteousness" (Gal 3:6; cf Gn 15:6).

The call of Abraham, therefore, divides Genesis into two majestic pillars that bear up the temple of Scripture—not only the vestibule but also its entire sublime edifice. If we pull them down, we have removed not a supposedly inconsequential foreword to the Bible but foundational truths that support the whole structure of biblical teaching. These two pillars of truth are:

1. The God who chose Abraham and his offspring is the eternal and almighty Creator, and His foremost yet rebellious creatures need redeeming mercy (Gn 1–11).
2. The God of the universe, a gracious Creator, will restore fallen humanity through Abraham's offspring (Gn 12–50).

Firsts in Genesis

Genesis has also been rightly called "the book of beginnings," for it recounts how the world and humanity began, how marriage originated, how people became sinful, and how God directed the affairs of nations during the first millennia of history. But beneath this compressed recital of events from Adam to Abraham's grandsons lies the principle that controlled the selection and presentation of the materials themselves: God's desire to portray Himself as fulfilling His promise to bring salvation. God, who promised to redeem humanity, created the universe and therefore has the power to direct all things to achieve His purpose. The sin of the first parents—and of their offspring, begotten in their marred image of God—establishes the need for the saving acts of God's grace. In a selective and schematic account of the nations, general world history quickly narrows to Abraham, the father of believers.

Key Texts in Genesis

Theologians through the centuries have turned to the first part of Genesis in support of numerous doctrines. The narratives of the lives of Jacob and Joseph have been cited less often because they are largely historical and continue themes already present in the earlier chapters (cf, e.g., the way the New Testament authors quote the earlier chapters of Genesis rather than the later chapters).

Creation is an obvious doctrine of Genesis to which theologians turn repeatedly. Although the Psalms and other books of Scripture describe God's work as Creator, Genesis provides the definitive account of God's created order, with focus on the creation of mankind in God's image (1:26–27). God's mandate that mankind be fruitful and multiply (1:28), as well as His creation of marriage (2:18–25), define what it is to be human and how we shall live. His creation of the Sabbath rest (2:3) also caught the attention of theologians describing worship and created order. (Cf Luther's exposition of 4:26 as another text on worship; AE 1:262–63.) After the flood, God's description of capital punishment established the need for orderly and just government, due to the image of God in mankind (9:6).

God's command not to eat of the tree of the knowledge of good and evil, with the threat of death, revealed the Law to Adam (2:17; cf 4:7; 6:3, 5; 8:21). Applied in ch 3, the Law taught about the nature and origin of temptation and of sin. In the same chapter, theologians recognized the first proclamation of the Gospel when God promised a deliverer born of the woman (3:15; the *protevangelium*). From the beginning, Genesis established the Law and Gospel distinction and dynamic for teaching the faith and extended that teaching in the promises and responsibilities of the covenants. Through the chosen people, the offspring of Abraham, the Lord would bless all nations

(12:3; 17:7; ch 22, esp v 18). The New Testament confirmed that in Jesus Christ God fulfilled these promises of the everlasting covenant so that all who trust in Christ are declared righteous through faith (15:6).

Application

What Adam did and came to be is not merely a memory but a sad reality in all people from Adam and Eve through Abraham, Isaac, and Jacob down to today: "Sin came into the world through one man, and death through sin" (Rm 5:12). There is no exception to the rule: where there is life, there is death. But another Adam was to come and bring the good news: where there is death, there is life. "The son of Adam, the son of God" (Lk 3:38), "the last Adam" (1Co 15:45), was and remained "the image of the invisible God" (Col 1:15). Therefore, "those who receive abundance of grace and the free gift of righteousness reign in life through the one man Jesus Christ" (Rm 5:17); for "by a man [*the* Man: Christ] has come also the resurrection of the dead" (1Co 15:21).

Chs 1–4 Even after the fall and the coming of sin, much of the goodness that God built into creation remains. It is not the existence of evil and suffering that requires an explanation; it is the existence of goodness and beauty and love that is most remarkable. A world without God cannot explain such things. With the words that God speaks to the serpent, to Eve, and to Adam after their disobedience, He sets the course for the rest of biblical history. There is no way back to Eden. The only way for Adam and Eve and their descendants is forward to the cross. The long story culminates in Jesus Christ, the Seed of the woman, but it does not end there. Today, we are part of the unfolding story.

A ram rears up on its hind legs to reach the branches of the "tree of life," an ancient Near Eastern artistic theme that dates from the foundation of civilization at Ur.

Ch 5 Genealogies teach an important theological lesson: God perseveres in the fulfillment of His promises. God does not become bored with His plan or discouraged by Satan's efforts to derail it. Like God's people before us, we often wander from God's path. Yet, God works patiently to set the course right again and to draw us back to Himself.

Chs 6–9 Recognizing that the human heart is a continual source of evil, God's patience is about to give way to judgment. But God also plans to have mercy. Even as Noah finds favor in the eyes of the Lord, so also the faithful of all times have God's favor on account of the promised Savior. Although dwarfed by Noah's experience, all Christians experience turbulence in their lives that can lead them to the brink of despair. But through Noah, God has demonstrated that He will lift up and save His faithful people whom He has cleansed in Holy Baptism. People of faith do not always demonstrate such patience and often act on their own, even under less trying circumstances than those of Noah. But God is patient when His people are not; in Christ, He provides forgiveness and deliverance when His people do not have the patience of Noah. God is faithful to His covenants, even when people are not. The message of every rainbow tells us He is faithful to His promise to provide a Savior. Noah's sinful drunkenness reminds us that the biblical heroes were sinful men and women who lived by faith in the forgiveness of sins.

Chs 10–11 The Table of Nations shows that from the Shemites would come the good news that God was remembering His promise of the Seed that would crush the head of the evil one (3:15). Like the story of the fall, the story of Babel shows that rebellion against God ultimately leads to divisions among people. People are driven away from paradise and from one another. Yet the Lord was preparing to gather and bless all nations in the birth of the living Word from the line of Shem.

Chs 12–19 God's Spirit works faith, when and where He pleases, through the Word. He is faithful to do as He has said. He made Abram into a great nation, blessing all the world through the Son. What an example Abram sets for true, godly living! As God rescued Lot through Abram and his 318 well-trained men, so He watches over and cares for us. He sent a Redeemer to rescue us. God credits righteousness to Abram simply on the basis of His covenant promise and faith. Like Sarah, we may doubt and even laugh at God's purposes for us. Despite such moments of weakness, the Lord reassures His saints not only of His omnipotence but also of His forgiveness, as Sarah realized when she gave birth to Isaac in her old age. Intercede in prayer for those who have not yet repented of their wickedness. Take comfort in the truth that God spares the wicked for the sake of one righteous man—Jesus Christ.

20:1–25:18 Left to our own devices, our scheming makes a mess of our lives and brings affliction to those around us. How impatient and untrusting we can become when things do not go as we think they should, even over short periods of time, even when God has clearly promised that all things will work together for good. Despite clear promises from God, we also become overly concerned about matters in our lives that irritate us or cause us to doubt His promises. But as with Abraham and Sarah, God takes our human weakness into consideration. The climax of Abraham's life of faith comes when he who loves his son so much is willing to offer him as a sacrifice to his Lord. Often we fail tests of faith that do not begin to compare to Abraham's. Thankfully, there was an even greater sacrifice when God the Father in heaven offered the sacrifice of His beloved Son to secure forgiveness for our failures. Like Abraham, we should instruct our children about the Lord and should bury the bodies of the faithful departed with honor. Such burial is a confession of the resurrection, that Christ will return and raise us from the dead to be gathered to Him.

25:19–28 God's ways are not our ways. When we come before God on the basis of rights, claims, and human justice, we fall. Our hope cannot rest on human nature or accomplishments. We share in this fallen humanity and often act like these biblical figures. Despite this sorry state, Christ became our substitute. He loved us and gave Himself up for us, a fragrant offering and sacrifice to God. He was cursed so we may be blessed (Gal 3:13).

Chs 26–33 Parents today should carefully raise their children to seek a godly Christian spouse, and children should honor and obey their parents according to God's Word. This is God's command. In opposition to the Fourth Commandment, we have often disrespected our parents and others in authority. God's Law condemns our disobedience and calls us to sincere repentance. We have much to be thankful for. Christ is our gateway to heaven. Thanks be to God, the Church's Bridegroom deals faithfully. He covers our debt with the sacrifice of His life and love so that we may be His. Deception leads to dispute between relatives, which threatens to break out into open warfare. Such an outcome is avoided because God steps in. Family feuds, often fueled by deceit, continue to plague relationships today. We need God to step into our lives, into our families. In Him and in His Word there is no deceit. Trust Him to forgive the contrite sinner and to quiet the angry heart. Go to Christ for pardon and for peace.

Face of a Canaanite painted on pottery (Beth-shan, c 1300 BC).

Chs 34–36 One sin leads to another. Zeal for a right cause is good, but moderation and due process are also required.

God-fearing people such as Jacob sometimes have children who fall into great sin and shame. And even those who receive God's promises, such as Rachel and Isaac, are still subject to death. Mourning is a part of life in a sin-broken world. When sorrows surround you, call on the Lord in prayer. Remember and celebrate His promises, which are guaranteed to you in Jesus' death and resurrection. Because Jesus conquered death and sin, we have comfort in the midst of all troubles.

Bits of silver were weighed and used like money. These ingots date from the sixth century BC.

Ch 37 We can expect that those who love virtue will be hated and envied by the wicked. Yet we should also pursue humility and avoid arrogance. When sin is not dealt with, it breeds even more wickedness. Joseph's brothers let their hatred lead to betrayal and lies. Many years later, God's Son was betrayed by His friend, not for 20 shekels but for 30 pieces of silver. Yet this also took place so that God could fulfill His plan for our salvation.

Ch 38 Sexual sins lead to trouble and heartache in this life. Yet God does not cast away those who were conceived and born out of wedlock, but He preserves those who fear Him, just as He preserved Perez. Through Judah's son Perez, the line that would eventually give birth to the Savior was preserved (cf Mt 1:3). So let us flee from sexual immorality, being mindful that God punishes unchastity. And let us confess our sins as Judah did, knowing that God, for the sake of Jesus Christ, will forgive all who repent.

Chs 39–42 Pursue chastity and flee fornication, as Joseph did. Mark and avoid the bad example of Potiphar's wife, who slandered Joseph. People so easily forget those who helped them, and they neglect to honor God, who delivered them. Although others may forget us, even if our father and mother forsake us, the Lord will take care of His people and remember them in His mercy (Ps 27:10). Like Joseph, we should praise God for any good thing we have. In hard times, those who have should share with those who have not. Here is comfort: after long periods of suffering, at just the right time, the Lord will give help to His people, just as He did for Joseph. Through His Son, Jesus, God rules over us and gives us what we need: pardon, provision, and peace.

Chs 43–45 Joseph's conduct is like God's. He displays both generosity and severity, seeking repentance. The brothers' fear comes from the alienating power of sin. The Lord reminds us to humbly acknowledge and take responsibility for our sin. When Judah mediates with his father and with Joseph, and shows himself willing to be enslaved in place of his brother, this prefigures the saving work of his descendant, Jesus, who gave Himself as mediator, ransom, and sacrifice for the world. Let us not quarrel in our Christian journey, but hold fast to the mercy and doctrine that God has revealed. In Christ, our sin is forgiven, and God gives us the joy of reconciliation and new life.

46:1–49:27 Like Jacob, seek the Lord's guidance and blessing for your plans. He has revealed His will for our deeds and our salvation in His Word. Where He has not spoken, He gives us freedom to make reasonable choices. Spiritual blessings take precedence over temporal ones. People who put earthly security and temporal blessings first often take desperate measures to keep things that death will someday take from them. Just as blessing came to mighty Pharaoh through a lowly shepherd, so also the kingdom of God and His righteousness come to believers in humble forms—an infant in a manger; a man dying on a cross; words, water, bread, wine—yet in them are hidden God's majesty. The Seed of Abraham culminates in an eternal kingdom for Judah's descendants, fulfilled in the Messiah, Jesus.

49:28–50:26 The grief at Jacob's death reflects the reality of sin, death's cause (cf 2:17), and yet also the dignity of the human body. Our funeral customs are a way of confessing that God has promised to raise the dead. Christ Jesus has conquered death for our sake (1Co 15:55–57). Sin penetrates flesh and spirit and can lead people to despair. To console despairing sinners, God causes the Gospel of reconciliation in Christ to be preached. Joseph's life illustrates one of God's promises for obedience to the Law—prosperous, long life (Ex 20:12). Despite his long, prosperous life, Joseph looks forward, not back: "God *will* surely visit you" (Gn 50:25). The coming gift is the Lord Himself, His visitation, fulfilled in part in the exodus from Egypt. But even the exodus pales before God's final visitation in the Messiah (Lk 1:68) and its culmination when the bones of Joseph and all the redeemed are raised to immortality.

CANONICITY

As part of the Torah, the most important portion of the Hebrew Scriptures for the Jews, the Book of Genesis was treasured. Christians received the book without question.

Lutheran Theologians on Genesis

Luther

"In his first book [Genesis] Moses teaches how all creatures were created, and (as the chief cause for his writing) whence sin and death came, namely by Adam's fall, through the devil's wickedness. But immediately thereafter, before the coming of the law of Moses, he teaches whence help is to come for the driving out of sin and death, namely, not by the law or men's own works (since there was no law as yet), but by 'the seed of the woman,' Christ, promised to Adam and Abraham, in order that throughout the Scriptures from the beginning faith may be praised above all works and laws and merits. Genesis, therefore, is made up almost entirely of illustrations of faith and unbelief, and of the fruits that faith and unbelief bear. It is an exceedingly evangelical book." (AE 35:237)

"We assert that Moses spoke in the literal sense, not allegorically or figuratively [about the creation], i.e., that the world, with all its creatures, was created within six days, as the words read. If we do not comprehend the reason for this, let us remain pupils and leave the job of teacher to the Holy Spirit." (AE 1:5)

"The line of descent was traced from Adam, through many patriarchs, down to Noah, and from there down to Abraham. During this time the church suffered great damage, for ungodliness had increased to such an extent that even the descendants of the saints were carried away into error. Therefore it was necessary for Moses to point out how in this great peril God accomplished the rebirth of the church, lest it collapse entirely and true religion be utterly blotted out.

"This account deserves our attention as an extraordinary example of mercy. It should encourage and persuade us that God will preserve the church also in our own time, when everything is threatening religion with destruction. Despite the great importance of their content the preceding accounts are very brief [chs 1–11]. In these which follow, however, the Holy

Spirit will speak at greater length and will discuss everything in greater detail. Accordingly, up to this point the church looks like a brook that is flowing along peacefully; but now it receives accessions and rushes along with the roar of a real river until, through the marvelous blessing of God, the holy nation expands into a vast ocean and fills the world with its name." (AE 2:245)

For more of Luther's insights on this book, see *Lectures on Genesis* (AE 1–8).

Gerhard

"*The first Book of Moses* is called *bere'shith* ['In the beginning'] by the Hebrews from its initial word; the rabbis call it *sepher yetsirah*, 'the Book of Creation'; the Greeks, *Genesis* ['Genesis'], and this name the Latin Church has kept. The reason for the name is twofold: first, because it describes the 'generations of heaven and earth' (as Moses says, Gen. 2:[4]) and, second, because it sets forth the genealogy of the patriarchs (c. 5 and elsewhere).

"Some think that this same book is called the book *hayashar*—'of the upright man' or 'of the right and just (*eutheon*) men' (Josh. 10:13; 2 Sam. 1:18)—because it describes the history of the patriarchs Abraham, Isaac, and Jacob, whom the Cabalists call with the special title 'upright men.' . . .

"Furthermore, Genesis has fifty chapters and gives a history of 2,368 years, namely, from the creation of the world to the death of Joseph. It can be divided into six sections according to the number of the patriarchs: Adam, Noah, Abraham, Isaac, Jacob, and Joseph. It can also be divided into the history of the time before the flood and after the flood. Jerome tells us in *Genes.* that there was a prohibition among the Jews that no one should read Genesis 1 or tell it to others before he was thirty years old. Our blessed Luther thinks that there was no need for such a prohibition because all of Scripture was a sealed book for them because of the veil placed before their eyes.

"The chief reasons why Moses, the lawgiver of the Israelites, wanted to begin his writing with the history of creation and of the patriarchs are these: (1) So that, from the description of those things that he could not have known except by divine revelation, he might acquire authority for his teaching. Augustine, *De civ. Dei*, bk. 18, c. 40: 'Do we believe one who tells the past rather than one who has also foretold things that would happen, which we now see happening?' (2) So that there might be a definite foundation of faith in the Church against the opinions of the heathen about the eternity or origin of the world. (3) In order to teach the people of Israel the majesty of the Creator and move them to obedience. (4) To set before the Israelites their own forefathers as examples of the rewards for godliness and the punishments meted out for wickedness. Eusebius, *Praepar. evang.*, bk. 7, c. 3: 'Before he set down the laws, he impressed the lives of their ancestors on the minds of men. Thus after exhorting them with the rewards of the good and the punishments of the wicked to embrace virtue and flee wickedness, he finally put the laws into their midst.' (5) To teach that one must seek or invoke no other God but Him who is the Creator of the world and who with a sure word has revealed Himself to men right from the beginning of the world." (ThC E1 § 119)

Traditional depictions of Moses often include *cornuta* (Latin "horns") due to a mistranslation in the Vulgate. Jerome, the translator, mistook "shone" (Hbr *quaran*) for "horned" (Hbr *qeren*). Later readers concluded that God put horns on the head of Moses rather than the radiance that the Bible actually describes (Ex 34:29–35). The anti-Semitic idea that Jewish people have horns, which they hide under their hats, arose from this tragic mistranslation. Fresco-Mosaic.

QUESTIONS PEOPLE ASK ABOUT GENESIS

The Creation of the World (Gn 1)

The first chapter of the Bible has been the battleground of Christians who have striven to uphold the authority of the Scriptures and of skeptics who have endeavored to destroy that authority by means of ammunition taken from the arsenal of science. We cannot approach Gn 1 without a feeling of deep awe when our God affords us, as it were, a glimpse into His workshop. As He relates what He did in the beginning, let us adore Him. To all of the attacks made upon Moses' account of creation the Christian can draw attention to the obvious fact that not one of the critics was present when the universe was created to observe that stupendous event, but that all the critics have to say on this subject rests on inferences, a circumstance that ought to make them very modest in offering their opinions, to say the least. Furthermore the Christian can tell the critics that they cannot be aware of all the gigantic forces, the catastrophes and upheavals, which the Creator may have employed to give our earth its present form. Let the geographical strata be studied by all means, but let us here as elsewhere beware of confusing investigation and interpretation.

Skull from Neolithic Jericho, one of the oldest continuously inhabited cities on earth. Plaster overlayed bone with shells to form the eyes.

We admit, of course, that what Moses relates is utterly inconsistent with the evolution theory, which is widely taught these days. But we maintain that the theory of evolution, which teaches a gradual development of living beings from lower to higher forms of life, by its very nature cannot be proved, for there is no way of studying this supposed development in the laboratory. It has been well said that Charles Darwin's *The Origin of Species* has much to say about species and presents evidence that some people believe indicates the origin of new species, but has little to say about evolution itself. For nowhere does he or anyone else demonstrate a way in which the degree of change required by evolution could occur. New breeds of animals and plants may arise, but these are not new "kinds" in the sense of Genesis.

Did Adam Die Immediately after the Fall?
(Gn 2:17; 5:5)

Initially, a comparison of Gn 2:17 and 5:5 is puzzling. Adam was told that on the day on which he would eat of the forbidden tree he would die, yet he continued to live for many centuries after his first transgression. How shall we explain this difficulty? Two points will show that no discrepancy exists. For one thing, Adam did die when he ate of the forbidden fruit. What he experienced was not physical death, it is true, but spiritual death. He became dead in trespasses and sins; that terrible state that consists of inward separation from God, the Source of all life, set in (cf Eph 2:1, 5). Thus the threat of God was literally fulfilled—Adam died when he became disobedient. Besides, this spiritual death brought on the doom of physical death. When Adam issued from the hands of the Creator, he was immortal; but after he had committed his first sin, his condition was different. He had now become subject to corruption and started on the journey to the grave. God did not tell Adam that in the day he ate of the forbidden fruit he would be put to death or would be executed, but that he would die—which implies that he would have a mortal body that would slowly waste away. We are fully justified in saying that Adam began to die in paradise immediately after he had permitted himself to be led into sin. God created our first parents vigorous and healthy. They represented the human race still in its youth. As a result, the process of destruction affected them more slowly than it affects us today.

Stone vase from Nippur (c 3000–2340 BC) featuring a serpent.

The Serpent (Gn 3)

In the third chapter of the Bible we meet the sad story of how Adam and Eve, having been beguiled by the tempter, fell into sin, losing the innocence that was theirs when they were issued from the hands of the Creator. There are a number of questions prompted by this narrative, such as "How could evil enter the world, which was good, indeed perfect, when the work of creation was completed?" Here we face a mystery for which we can offer no other explanation than the one given in divine revelation, namely, that the tempter brought sin into the world. If the inquiry is pushed beyond this point and the question is asked, "How could Satan, who evidently was created as a good creature, become perverted and an enemy of God?" we are not able to give an answer. It is a question on which God has not thought it necessary to inform us in His Holy Word.

Of all the various details of the story, however, there is none that to such an extent elicits inquiry and discussion as the statements pertaining to the serpent. Does Moses here wish to say that the serpent is a rational animal, gifted with human (or more than human) intelligence, having the faculty of speech, and that it, besides, is a wicked, ungodly creature opposing the plans of the Lord and causing enmity between Him and people, His foremost creatures on earth? Some scholars have considered it necessary to have recourse to rather fanciful interpretations in order to defend the Scriptures against the charge of investing the serpent with reason and intelligence. There have been those who have made an allegory out of the whole story and have declared the serpent to stand for evil desires arising in people and causing their downfall. The view has been expressed that the serpent represents intelligence devoid of conscience, as we see such intelligence operating in criminals who use all their intellectual powers for furthering their evil purposes and apparently have entirely suppressed the voice of conscience. There is no reason, however, why we should regard this account as an allegory. The story itself does not say that it is not to be taken literally, and there are no other passages in the Scriptures that direct us to give it a figurative interpretation. It must be remembered that a deviation from the literal sense is not justified unless the Scriptures themselves suggest such a course. Bowing to the plain statements of God's Holy Word, we must assume that a real serpent was present when the fall of humanity occurred and that out of its mouth came the words recorded whereby Adam and Eve were induced to become disobedient to God.

Several facts must not be lost sight of as we ponder this story. The whole account indicates sufficiently that something extraordinary and supernatural occurred when the serpent spoke. In the second chapter of Genesis we are told that Adam gave names to all the beasts of the field and the fowl of the air, but that "there was not found a helper fit for him" (v 20). Here we have the declaration that among the beasts there was no fit companion for him. All of them were of an inferior order, not possessing the eminent mental and moral gifts with which Adam was endowed. The serpent was no exception. It lacked the faculty of speech and reason and moral insight as much as did all the other beasts. Such is the conclusion we arrive at when reading Gn 2. Coming to the narrative in the next chapter and reading of the serpent's speaking and leading Adam and Eve astray, the readers will feel at once that here a mysterious evil power is beginning to give evidence of its existence of which the Scriptures have not spoken before, and they will see that the serpent was merely the instrument of this evil force. We must recall here, too, that according to Gn 1:31 "God saw everything that He had made, and behold, it was very good." The serpent is included in this comprehensive statement. When it is pictured as the tempter, the reader must conclude on the basis of the preceding narrative that the holy writer does not mean to describe the serpent itself as deceiving humanity, but is speaking of a mysterious somebody or something making use of the serpent. But why does this evil person or power employ the serpent for its purposes? We have the reply in Gn 3:1: "Now the serpent was more crafty than any other beast of the field that the LORD God had made." When Adam and Eve observed the various animals about them, they soon noticed that the serpent was characterized by a remarkable shrewdness or slyness, which could not but deeply impress the person who watched it. Perhaps this attribute made it less amazing that the serpent spoke than if coherent words had come from the mouth of some other animal. It has been conjectured quite plausibly that because of this attribute this beast was used by the tempter in his attack on Adam and Eve. In other passages of the Bible, too, the serpent is pictured as possessing shrewdness. We are all acquainted with the admonition of the Savior addressed to His disciples to be "wise as serpents" (Mt 10:16). Here, then, it appears, we have a sufficient explanation of the course the tempting power pursued when it chose the serpent as its instrument.

In the above paragraph we have spoken of the tempter or the tempting power in vague terms. Now we must inquire whether the revelation of God does not throw some light on the being that made use of the serpent in the Garden of Eden. And here we can say that, while there are not many passages of the Scriptures that allude to this subject, definite information on the enemy responsible for the fall of humanity is contained in divine revelation. From the Old Testament we learn that besides the holy angels of God there is an evil angel called Satan (Jb 1:6–12). The name Satan means "adversary." The Book of Job does not say when he became an enemy of humanity seeking to lead people into sin; it merely states the fact that he delights in doing injury and in seeing people turn against the Creator.

The remarkable story in 1Ki 22:20–23 likewise presupposes that in the invisible world there is a being or beings whose aim is to deceive and to work destruction. It is in the New Testament, however, that fuller light is shed on this mysterious subject. In 2Pt 2:4 we read: "God did not spare angels when they sinned, but cast them into hell and committed them to chains of gloomy darkness to be kept until the judgment"; and a parallel passage in Jude (v 6) says: "And the angels who did not stay within their own position of authority, but left their proper dwelling, He has kept in eternal chains under gloomy darkness until the judgment of the great day."

From other books of Scripture we learn that there were angels who did not remain in the state of righteousness in which they had been created, but who sinned, leaving their own habitation, the mansions of heaven, and who were cast down by God to hell, being barred forever from the beautiful home that they left. It is here that we have the origin of evil in the universe. One of these fallen angels is Satan, and it was he who employed the serpent in his successful endeavor to lead humanity into sin (Jb 1:6–12; 1Ki 22:20–23; 2Pt 2:4; Jude 6; Rv 12).

The Flood (Gn 6–8)

The biblical account of the great flood that destroyed humanity (with the exception of Noah and his family) is said to be out of harmony with scientific views. The representation of the flood as a universal one is attacked, and certain details are objected to, such as the gathering of pairs of animals from all over the earth in Noah's ark to keep the various species from becoming extinct. Christians readily admit that the account of the flood contains many features that we have to class as miraculous, that is, as things that we cannot understand. But the inability of Christians to explain an event that is contained in the revelation of God is not for them sufficient ground to reject the narrative as untrustworthy. They know that God performs miracles, and it is just as easy for Him to work a million of them as one.

Critics may not deny that a great flood occurred on earth. On the one hand, traditions among many nations distinctly assert that such a flood took place. The Roman poet Ovid in his *Metamorphoses* gives an interesting and picturesque description of a terrible flood that brought destruction upon the whole human race except two people. The source from which Ovid obtained the material for his account of the great flood was Greek literature, where, a number of centuries before his day, without known influence coming from the Bible, the flood was remembered as a great event in the early history of humanity. Since stories of this nature exist with many peoples, it is valid to conclude that a flood occurred, the memory of which was preserved in traditions handed down from one generation to the next.

On the other hand, the surface of the earth witnesses to the occurrence of a great flood in the distant past. On high mountains in various parts of the world traces of such a visitation are plainly discernible. With evidence of this kind, it is not reasonable to deny the occurrence of a great flood that proved destructive to humanity.

The *Epic of Gilgamesh* features the heroic King of Uruk (c 2600 BC) who survived a great flood sent by the gods. Here he wrestles a lion.

Magnitude of the Flood (Gn 7)

Some assert that Moses erred when he described the great flood as universal. In Gn 7 the sacred narrative says: "And the waters prevailed so mightily on the earth that all the high mountains under the whole heaven were covered. . . . And all flesh died that moved on the earth, birds, livestock, beasts, all swarming creatures that swarm on the earth, and all mankind" (vv 19, 21). It is asserted that such a great flood would violate laws of hydrostatics by the accumulation of such a great mass of water. But could not the God who created the waters also manipulate them in such a way that the results spoken of in Gn 7 would follow?

To the statement that the geological strata as they are found today contradict the occurrence of a worldwide flood in historic times, we reply that no one knows what conditions were like at that time and what forces were at work in the different parts of the world, constituting probably a great diversity of factors, which, while operating simultaneously, at times did not leave the same traces.

The sacred account does not speak only of tremendous rains but, in referring to the fountains of the great deep that opened at this time, seems to be pointing to earthquakes occurring when the great visitation descended upon the earth. Some commentators think that the masses of water necessary to cover the whole earth would have been too vast to let us entertain the thought that such an occurrence actually happened. But consider that three-fourths of the earth's surface is water and that the almighty arm of our God could easily hurl these tremendous masses of water upon the mainland.

The Age of Abraham When He Left Home
(Gn 11:26, 32; 12:4; Ac 7:4)

In these four passages an apparent contradiction looms up. If Terah was 70 years old when Abram was born and lived to be 205 years old, then Abram was 135 years old at the time of his father's death. And if he left Haran only after his father's demise, he must have been a man of at least 135 years when the migration into the land of promise was undertaken. That contradicts the statement that Abram was 75 years old when he departed from Haran (Gn 12:4). But all this rests on an assumption that is not demanded by the text, namely, on the theory that Abram was the oldest of the sons of Terah and was born when his father was 70 years old. It is true that Gn 11:26 says: "When Terah had lived 70 years, he fathered Abram, Nahor, and Haran." There Abram is mentioned first, which may be due to his having been the firstborn. But there may just as well have been some other reason, for instance, that Abram was the most prominent of the sons of Terah and for that reason is given the first place in the list. If we assume, as we may well do, that Abram was the youngest of the three brothers named, and that he was born when his father was 130 years old, his age at the time of his father's death would have been 75, and Gn 12:4 and Ac 7:4 would be in perfect harmony.

Intermarriage of Brothers and Sisters
(Gn 20:11–12; Lv 20:17)

It has often been said that the marriage of Abraham to Sarah, his half sister, was something that God strictly prohibits in the Bible and that therefore He ought not to have showered His blessings on this couple. The praise that Scripture bestows on Abraham is held to be unwarranted in view of what is termed his incestuous marriage. The difficulty vanishes if we consider that in the early ages of the history of the world God had not forbidden marriages between brothers and sisters. In fact such marriages had to take place at the start if the plan of God to let the whole human race descend from one man and one woman should be carried out. (Cf the words of Paul in Ac 17:24–26.) Cain, and quite probably Seth, married their sisters. That they had sisters is evident from Gn 5:4. Did they commit a sin by doing so? No. Such a union was not yet forbidden. It was thus at the time of Abraham. God had not yet declared a marriage of this kind contrary to His will (cf Lv 18:6–18). Therefore the apparent contradiction here is removed if we bear in mind that the passages from Genesis and Leviticus refer to different periods in the world's history.

Does God Tempt Us? (Gn 22:1 [KJV]; Jas 1:13)

How shall we explain that the Bible denies that God ever tempts people and yet in some translations says that He does? The solution lies in the meaning of the word *tempt*. This term is used in a good sense and in a bad sense. When employed in a good sense, it means to try or to test a person in such a way that the disposition of the heart and the innermost convictions will become apparent in order that all concerned may receive indisputable proof as to the person's character. Used in a bad sense, it means to entice people to do evil in order to destroy them. All afflictions sent to us by God may be called trials, or temptations, intended for our good, and as such they should be welcomed by us. James himself, who affirms that God tempts no one (Jas 1:13), had admonished his readers a few verses before, "Count it all joy, my brothers, when you meet trials of various kinds, for you know that the testing of your faith produces steadfastness" (1:2–3). It was a testing of this kind that God brought upon Abraham. It was a severe trial, in which the faith of Abraham was proved to be genuine and sturdy and undoubtedly was greatly strengthened. At the end of it the glorious promises that God had given him were reaffirmed. But the term is likewise used to designate experiences of the opposite kind—veiled attacks intended to lead people into eternal damnation. When James says of God: "He Himself tempts no one," he is speaking of allurements that are designed by the powers of evil and have as their object our ultimate and eternal misery. Such temptations, of course, do not come from God.

An additional comment on the Sixth Petition of the Lord's Prayer, "Lead us not into temptation," may be enlightening in this connection. This petition has often been understood as saying that God brings temptations upon His children. As a matter of fact, it says nothing of the kind. It simply expresses the prayer that God would lead us so that our enemies will not be able to execute their wicked designs against us, namely, to lure us into sin. The meaning of the prayer is: "Guide us so that Satan will not have an opportunity to put stumbling blocks in our way." These words, then, do not contradict the statements of James that God tempts no one.

Number of Abraham's Sons (Gn 25:6; Heb 11:17)

Abraham had only one son, and Abraham had several sons—both statements are true. He himself would have made either one of them as the occasion required. Isaac was the only son whom Sarah had borne him, the only one who was to be in the direct line of ancestry to the Messiah. Isaac was the only heir of the vast possessions of Abraham. Therefore, while it is true that Abraham had sons by concubines, the statement that Isaac was his only son is justified and not in conflict with the passages that speak of Ishmael and the sons of Keturah.

Can God Be Seen? (Gn 32:30; Jn 1:18)

Besides the above passages, a number of others must be considered; for instance, in Ex 33:20 God says to Moses: "You cannot see My face, for man shall not see Me and live." On the other hand, we read in Ex 24:9–10: "Then Moses and Aaron, Nadab, and Abihu, and seventy of the elders of Israel went up, and they saw the God of Israel. There was under His feet as it were a pavement of sapphire stone, like the very heaven for clearness."

It might appear as if these passages are in total disagreement with one another. Yet harmonization is not difficult at all. Jesus tells us that God is a spirit (Jn 4:24), from which it follows that He cannot be seen. That His essence is invisible is an unalterable fact. But this invisible and glorious God may grant to human beings special manifestations of Himself, reflections of His glory, some unmistakable signs of His presence. He may, for the benefit of people, provide a visible form in addressing them (e.g., the burning bush, Ex 3). Upon beholding these manifestations, people will say that they have seen God, and they are justified in speaking this way even though they have not seen that most blessed, omniscient, and all-wise Spirit, but merely certain manifestations of Him or the form that He temporarily provided. To use a humble illustration, when we see sparks fly from a wire that is electrically charged, or when we see lightning zigzag across the sky, we say that we have seen electricity; however, we know very well that we have not seen electricity but merely light that indicates its existence.

Cattle graze on the banks of the Nile River as in Pharaoh's dream (Gn 41).

Number of People in Jacob's Family (Gn 46:27; Ac 7:14)

A well-known difficulty confronts us here. Moses states that the family of Jacob numbered 70 persons when it came to Egypt, while Stephen speaks of 75. We may quote here from an article in the *Concordia Theological Monthly*: "The discrepancy vanishes when we compare the Septuagint text of the latter passage. Stephen was a Greek-speaking Jew, and presumably he had learned the Holy Scriptures in the Greek version, the Septuagint. In the Septuagint the number of souls belonging to the family of Jacob is computed as 75. Which text is right, that of the Hebrew Bible or that of the Septuagint? They are both right. The figure 70 in the Hebrew text, which is followed in our English Bible, is arrived at by including Joseph, his two sons, and Jacob himself. The figure 75 in the Septuagint version is due to the inclusion of some additional descendants of Joseph. In Genesis 46:20 the Hebrew text reads: 'And to Joseph in the land of Egypt were born Manasseh and Ephraim, whom Asenath, the daughter of Poti-Pherah priest of On, bore unto him.' The Septuagint has these same words and then makes the following addition: 'Manasseh had sons, whom his Syrian concubine bore him, namely, Machir. Machir begat Galaad. The sons of Ephraim, the brother of Manasseh, were Sutalaam and Taam. The son of Sutalaam was Edom.' Thus three grandsons and two great-grandsons of Joseph are mentioned in the Septuagint account, who are not named in the Hebrew text, and in the summary of the Septuagint they are counted with the others. It may seem strange that these descendants of Joseph, some of whom had not yet been born at the time of Jacob's removal to Egypt, are enumerated in this list. Perhaps the explanation is that Joseph lived to see these descendants and that they became prominent afterwards as the heads of families (cf. Gen. 50:23). But whatever the reasons may have been for drawing up the list in the form in which it has been handed down, it clearly is not justifiable to speak of a discrepancy between Genesis and Acts at this point" (From "Some Difficulties in the Speech of Stephen," by W. Arndt. Vol. 4 [February 1924]: p. 35).

Burial Place of Jacob and His Sons
(Gn 50:13; Jsh 24:32; Ac 7:15–16)

A twofold difficulty meets us here. The Genesis account says that Jacob was buried in the cave that Abraham had bought from Ephron, the Hittite, while Stephen apparently says that Jacob was buried at Shechem. Furthermore, the Book of Joshua states that Joseph was buried in the parcel of ground that Jacob had bought at Shechem, while Stephen says that the fathers, that is, the sons of Jacob, to whose number Joseph belonged, were laid in the tomb that Abraham bought for a sum of money from the sons of Hamor, the father of Shechem.

Let it be noted with respect to the first point that Acts 7:16 does not necessarily say that Jacob was among those buried at Shechem. The subject of the verb "were carried back" need not be "Jacob and our fathers," but merely "our fathers." We might render vv 15 and 16 thus: "And Jacob went down into Egypt, and he died, he and our fathers, and they [namely, the fathers] were carried back to Shechem." That would imply that the sons of Jacob were buried at Shechem. There is no other passage in the Bible that narrates such a burial, but neither is there any passage that denies it. A rabbinical tradition relates that the brothers of Joseph were given burial at Shechem, where his own remains found their last resting place, and there is no reason why this tradition should be rejected as unhistorical.

Thus, as far as the burial place of Jacob is concerned, the apparent discrepancy between Gn 50:13 and Ac 7:15–16 vanishes as soon as we note that the latter passage need not be interpreted as referring to the burial of Jacob, but it may well be taken as speaking merely of the place where his sons were laid to rest.

Stairs and city gate of Shechem, near which Joseph was buried (Jsh 24:32).

Probably a little more difficulty is caused by the fact that the Book of Joshua states that the place where Joseph was buried at Shechem had been bought by Jacob, while Stephen says that this parcel of ground had been bought by Abraham. Various solutions of the difficulty have been proposed. A fully satisfactory explanation seems to be furnished by the assumption that Abraham, when he came to Canaan, bought a piece of land from Hamor, the father of Shechem, in order to have a place in which to erect an altar. In the course of time he moved to other places, and the land he had purchased was again occupied by the former owners and their descendants. One hundred eighty-five years later Jacob came into that vicinity and bought the same piece of land that his grandfather had purchased. Under this assumption, which is not an unnatural one, the difficulty created by the two passages is removed. The Old Testament, it is true, does not mention a purchase of land on the part of Abraham at Shechem, but either through tradition or through direct revelation from God Stephen may have known that such a transaction took place.

We may note one more possible solution of the difficulty. Several prominent exegetes hold that Stephen is alluding in one statement both to the purchase of a burial place by Abraham from Ephron the Hittite and to the purchase of a parcel of land by Jacob from Hamor, the father of Shechem. Genesis records both these transactions, mentioning, with reference to each, the seller and the buyer (25:9–10; 33:18–19), while Stephen, it is held, speaks of both as if they constituted one purchase. Matthias Flacius, a Lutheran theologian of marvelous acumen and learning, is one of the interpreters who holds this view. He states: "Stephen has not the time, as he is hurrying through so many stories, to narrate the separate ones in detail. Therefore he combines in one two distinct sepulchers, places, and purchases in such a way that he mentions the real buyer of the one story, omitting the seller, and again mentions the real seller of the other story, omitting the buyer, uniting by a diagonal line, as it were, two of the four factors in his abridged account."

Another illustrious Lutheran theologian, Johann Bengel, quotes these words of Flacius with approval and points out that Stephen also at several other places in his speech condenses his account of events or statements in similar fashion; for instance, in Ac 7:7, where words spoken to Abraham and to Moses are combined and made to appear as one statement. To many a Bible reader the solution of Flacius and Bengel will commend itself as a good alternative to the one presented previously.

FURTHER STUDY

Lay/Bible Class Resources

Davis, John J. *Paradise to Prison: Studies in Genesis*. Salem, WI: Sheffield Publishing Co., 1998 reprint. ♪ A good, popularly written one-volume commentary for general issues, but weaker on theology.

Jeske, John C. *Genesis*. PBC. St. Louis: Concordia, 2003. ♪ Lutheran author. Excellent for Bible classes. Based on the NIV translation.

Kidner, Derek. *Genesis*. TOTC. Downers Grove, IL: InterVarsity Press, 1967. ♪ Compact commentary interacting with a variety of English translations. British evangelical author.

Life by His Word. St. Louis: Concordia, 2009. ♪ More than 1,500 reproducible one-page Bible studies covering each chapter of the canonical Scriptures. Page references to *The Lutheran Study Bible*. CD-Rom and downloadable.

Rosin, Laine. *Genesis: Rooted in Relationship*. GWFT. St. Louis: Concordia, 1994. ♪ Lutheran author. Thirteen-session Bible study, including leader's notes and discussion questions.

Wenthe, Dean, Timothy Huber, Jesse Yow, and Roland Ehlke. *Genesis, Parts 1 and 2*. Leaders Guide and Enrichment Magazine/Study Guide. LL. St. Louis: Concordia, 2000–2001. ♪ Two in-depth, nine-session Bible studies covering the Book of Genesis with individual, small group, and lecture portions.

Church Worker Resources

Aalders, G. C. *Genesis*. 2 vols. Grand Rapids: Zondervan, 1981. ♪ Translated from Dutch commentary published in 1949. Good textual analysis. Addresses critical objections. Reformed theological perspective.

Hamilton, Victor P. *The Book of Genesis*. 2 vols. NICOT. Grand Rapids: Eerdmans, 1990. ♪ Evangelical scholar emphasizing God's promise of reconciliation.

Leupold, Herbert C. *An Exposition of Genesis*. 2 vols. Grand Rapids: Baker, 1942. ♪ Lutheran. A careful exposition by a conservative scholar.

Luther, Martin. *Lectures on Genesis*. Vols. 1–8 of AE. St. Louis: Concordia, 1958–70. ♪ The great reformer's lectures from 1535–45, which reflect his mature approach to biblical interpretation. Lengthy comments that are rewarding with patient, discerning reading. Luther consulted the Hebrew text and reflected on the application of the prophecies and their New Testament fulfillment.

Matthews, Kenneth. *Genesis*. 2 vols. NAC. Nashville: Broadman and Holman, 1996, 2005. ♪ Insightful evangelical commentary based on the NIV.

Academic Resources

Cassuto, Umberto. *A Commentary on the Book of Genesis.* 2 vols. Jerusalem: Magnes Press, 1961–64. ♠ Jewish author who stresses Mosaic authorship. Filled with helpful comments by a gifted philologist.

Gunkel, Hermann, and Mark E. Biddle. *Genesis.* Mercer Library of Biblical Studies. Macon, GA: Mercer University Press, 1997. ♠ The starting point for all discussions of form criticism in Genesis. Dated, but still useful for understanding the presuppositions of form critics and their heirs. Available in a good English edition translated from the 1910 German edition.

K&D. *Biblical Commentary on the Old Testament: The Pentateuch.* Vol. 1. Grand Rapids: Eerdmans, 1959 reprint. ♠ Lutheran scholar. A careful handling of theological issues in Genesis. Makes purposeful use of both Hebrew and Aramaic. This century-and-a-half old work should not be overlooked. Despite its age, it remains a most useful commentary on the Hebrew text.

Lange, John Peter. *Genesis.* LCHS. New York: Charles Scribner's Sons, 1893. ♠ A helpful, older example of German biblical scholarship, based on the Hebrew text, which provides references to significant commentaries from the Reformation era forward.

Sailhamer, John. *The Pentateuch as Narrative: A Biblical-Theological Commentary.* Library of Biblical Interpretation. Grand Rapids: Zondervan, 1992. ♠ Helpful emphasis on the Pentateuch as literature. Insightful on how the parts of the book fit together, what the author expresses, and the manner of expression.

Skinner, J. *A Critical and Exegetical Commentary on the Book of Genesis.* 2nd ed. Edinburgh: T&T Clark, 1930. ♠ A classic in the tradition of the JEDP theory. Often the best place to start to understand the main line of critical thinking, though obviously now dated even from their perspective.

Speiser, Ephraim A. *Genesis.* Vol. 1 of AB. New York: Doubleday, 1964. ♠ Although critical, Speiser provides useful information on the Near Eastern setting. Theologically weak.

von Rad, Gerhard. *Genesis.* OTL. Rev. ed. Philadelphia: Westminster, 1973. ♠ A very popular title in critical circles. Often supplements the form critical work of Hermann Gunkel. Must be used with careful discernment.

Wenham, Gordon J. *Genesis.* 2 vols. WBC. Dallas: Word, 1987, 1994. ♠ A valuable general resource that one should consult. Wenham is more or less conservative as an interpreter, though sometimes aligning with critical scholarship.

Westermann, Claus. *Genesis: A Commentary.* 3 vols. Trans. by John J. Scullins. Minneapolis: Augsburg, 1984–86. ♠ A highly technical work that summarizes the state of research with much comparative material, excursus, and linguistic notes. Minimal theology. Standard critical approach that is both influential and important, especially for the interpretation of Genesis in the twentieth century. An almost inexhaustible mine of references to other articles and materials, especially on technical (historical, linguistic, and literary) issues.

EXODUS

*I will take you to be
My people, and
I will be your God*

To the descendants of Abraham, Isaac, and Jacob, God seemed to have forgotten His promises; the time seemed endless. "The time that the people of Israel lived in Egypt was 430 years" (Ex 12:40). During these centuries God apparently had not moved to fulfill His promise to give possession of Canaan to Abraham's descendants. The patriarchs had lived temporarily in the Promised Land, but now the sons of Jacob were again in a foreign land.

Exodus gives no reason for this gap in salvation history, for God alone knows the "times or seasons that the Father has fixed by His own authority" (Ac 1:7). But these silent years speak loudly of the need to depend on the promises of God, for with Him even a thousand years are but a day (Ps 90:4), and without Him nothing will or can happen.

Near the beginning of Exodus, God said to Moses, "I have remembered My covenant" (Ex 6:5). This statement bridges the intervening time. What God would do was as much a gift of undeserved goodness as the promises given to Abraham. His descendants also would be right with God as they received the assurance of His forgiving mercy. They, like Abraham, responded to His promise with obedience of faith.

The Book of Exodus gets its name from one of the major events it records—a matter of only a chapter (14), but of such towering significance theologically

OVERVIEW

Author
Moses the prophet

Date
c 1446 BC

Places
Egypt; Midian; Mount Horeb (Mount Sinai); land of Goshen; Red Sea; wilderness of Shur; Marah; Elim; wilderness of Sin; Rephidim; Massah; Meribah; wilderness of Sinai

People
Joseph; Pharaoh; Egyptian taskmasters; Shiphrah; Puah; Moses; Amram; Jochebed; Miriam; Pharaoh's daughter; Jethro (Reuel); Zipporah; Gershom; Eliezer; elders of Israel; Aaron; foremen of the people of Israel; magicians of Egypt; Nadab; Abihu; Eleazar; Ithamar; Amalekites; Joshua; Hur; Oholiab; Bezalel

Purpose
The Lord reintroduces Himself to Israel, rescues them from Egypt, and gives them a covenant of laws and sacrifices

Law Themes
Plagues against unrepentant Egypt; God gives the Ten Commandments and requires an oath to fulfill the Law

Gospel Themes
God remembers and fulfills His promises to the patriarchs; atonement through sacrifice

Memory Verses
The Ten Commandments (Ex 20:1–17); the Lord's two ways (Ex 34:6–7)

TIMELINE

Between 1808 and 1804 BC		
		Joseph dies
1529 BC	Aaron born	
1526 BC	Moses born	
1446 BC	Exodus from Egypt	
1399–1379 BC	Death of Joshua and the elders	

An artist's aerial view of the Nile River Delta.

that the extension of the name to the entire book is entirely justified. Exodus plays a role in the Old Testament comparable to the Gospels in the New. The exodus event is the heart of the Old Testament "gospel," and the word *redeem* comes to be forever bound to it.

Historical and Cultural Setting

Exodus first records the phenomenal growth of the Israelites from the mere 70 people who had first migrated to Goshen, and then the conflict this occasioned, especially with the rise of a hostile dynasty (presumably to be associated with the expulsion of the Hyksos by native Egyptian forces, c 1580–1570 BC). According to a traditional chronology of the Bible, Moses would have been born near the end of the Hyksos period. (See "Historical and Cultural Setting" for Genesis, p 17.) During the reign of Ahmose, the pharaoh who expelled the Hyksos, there are records of two rebellions, one by a Nubian leader in southern Egypt and a second led by Tetian, who attempted a coup centered at Nefrusi, a city in the former Hyksos territory. Both rebellions were harshly suppressed. Egyptians at this time tended to fear foreigners, but within a few generations the pharaohs were marrying foreign wives for political reasons and bringing non-Egyptian children into Egypt for training in Egyptian ways. From the expulsion of the Hyksos to 1390 BC, most of the rulers of Egypt have names ending in "-mose," surprisingly similar to the name of the biblical prophet. When Moses fled into the Sinai region and settled among the Midianites, he fled to a region that was of marginal interest to the Egyptians, who had to stay focused on the major powers to their south and northeast.

Pharaoh Thutmose III.

The traditional date for the exodus, 1446 BC, occurs during a high point in Egyptian military power due to the successful Asian offensive of Pharaoh Thutmose III (c 1479–25), who made seventeen military campaigns into the Syria-Canaan region, including his critical victory at Megiddo (c 1468 BC). However, he was also frequently in Egypt, which would allow for his confrontation with Moses. Critics point out that Egyptian records never expressly mention Israel until the much later Merneptah Stele of c 1212–1203 BC, the earliest mention of Israel as a distinct people in an extrabiblical text. One should note that Egyptian records, though more extensive than most ancient cultures, are far from complete. Since the Bible records that Israel later approached Canaan from the east and settled in the central highlands, it describes Israel fleeing a powerful pharaoh by entering areas that were of lesser interest to the Egyptians, who typically marched their troops up the coast to meet trade partners and armies further north in Lebanon and Syria.

Increased linguistic knowledge has generally forced much earlier dating for the Song of Moses (ch 15), a few critics even conceding that it may actually stem from an eyewitness. Most critical reservations have lingered over 15:13–17, which appears to presuppose the later events of the conquest and even possession of Zion. But parallels with the Ugaritic literature discovered at Ras Shamra make actual Mosaic authorship perfectly plausible for also this part of the poem.

The children of Israel arrived at Sinai three months after the exodus, and dwelt there until the departure recorded in Nu 10:33. The first phase of the revelation at Sinai climaxes in the impressive covenant ratification ceremony in Ex 24. Most of the laws in the Covenant Code have numerous undeniable parallels in the ancient Near Eastern literature. For example, specific ceremonial statutes went along with ancient Israel's status as a state, as was the case with most political units before modern times; worship of Yahweh was the established religion. Exodus ends with the consecration of the tabernacle by the descent of the same "glory" (Hbr *kabod*, God's "incarnational" presence), which had led them from Egypt, now to take up permanent residence above the Mercy Seat in the Most Holy Place.

COMPOSITION

Author(s)

See pp 4–11.

Date of Composition

See pp 4–11.

Purpose/Recipients

The Book of Exodus presents God's deliverance of His people from the tyranny of the Egyptian Pharaoh, and the formal establishment of the covenant with the descendants of Abraham, Isaac, and Jacob. The theme of Exodus is

THE DATE OF THE EXODUS

The date of the exodus, or whether there was even such an event, has been a major focus of scholarly discussion. The following paragraphs briefly describe the chief views.

Merneptah Stele.

Exodus as Legend. This view is common among critical and liberal scholars who do not consider the biblical account as historically accurate (e.g., 1Ki 6:1, which states that Israel came out of Egypt 480 years before Solomon began to build the temple at Jerusalem). They acknowledge that Israel must have emerged as a nation at some point in history. An obvious date after which Israel could not have arisen is c 1212–1203 BC, the time at which the Merneptah Stele was engraved, which mentions Israel as a people settled in Canaan. Critical scholars may regard the story of the exodus as the product of memories about people leaving Egypt to settle elsewhere. For example, Manetho's accounts about the movement of Semitic peoples out of Egypt are regarded as background for the development of an exodus legend. See p 68.

Late Date of the Exodus. This is a compromise view proposed by some evangelical scholars. It regards the exodus as a real event but does not regard the biblical record of Israel's chronology as fully accurate. A key passage for this view is Ex 1:11, which refers to the Egyptian cities of Pithom and Raamses. The latter city is concluded to be Pi-Ramesses, dating from the thirteenth or twelfth centuries. As a consequence, a thirteenth-century exodus seems most likely to these scholars. For a critique of this view, see Steinmann, pp 54–64.

Traditional Date of the Exodus. This long-standing view, and the one preferred in the *LBC*, is based on the straightforward calculation of years from the building of the temple at Jerusalem to the departure from Egypt, as described in 1Ki 6:1, which gives one a date of c 1446 BC. For a thorough explanation of the traditional view, see Steinmann, pp 45–53.

"I will take you to be My people, and I will be your God" (Ex 6:7), which taught Israel about its unique place among the nations. The first part of the book (chs 1–19) tells of the mighty deeds of God to create this nation by delivering it out of Egypt's house of bondage. In the second part (chs 20–40), God makes clear at Mount Sinai how the people are to acknowledge Him as their covenant God.

Literary Features

Genre

Exodus is largely historical narrative but enfolds several other genres within it: Chapter 15 is poetry. Chapters 20–23 are the book of the covenant, which is similar to suzerain-vassel covenants between other Near Eastern nations of the second millennium BC, especially the Hittite covenants. Within the book of the covenant, as well as chs 12 and 24, are legal and ceremonial texts. Chapters 25–31 are building instructions, with the construction report appearing in chs 35–40. Exodus is an obvious compilation of these elements but with the unified purpose of reporting Israel's transition from subservience to Pharaoh to the service of Yahweh.

After the second battle of Kadesh (1259 BC), Ramses II recorded in hieroglyphics the peace treaty between Egyptians and Hittites. Biblical convenants resemble Hittite treaties.

Characters

Moses is the major character, whose life can be divided into three 40-year periods: Moses' birth and life in Egypt (Ex 1), Moses' exile in Midian near Mount Sinai (Ex 2–4), and Moses' leadership of God's people from Egypt to Mount Nebo (Ex 5–Dt 34). God providentially rescued Moses when he was a baby, but Moses grew up living among the pagan Egyptians. In events that anticipate the main narrative, Moses seems to have retained or learned that he was a Hebrew, for when he saw a fellow Hebrew beaten by an Egyptian, he intervened to rescue his countryman. He killed the Egyptian and was forced to flee to Midian and Sinai, a path on which he would later lead Israel. At Sinai, God called Moses to return to Egypt and deliver Israel from its bondage. He did so famously through the miraculous series of plagues

Continued on p 67.

OUTLINE

The contents of Exodus divide almost equally into historical and legal material (the latter predominating in the rest of the Books of Moses). Chapters 1–18 bring us through the exodus to Mount Sinai, and chs 19–40 begin the legislation revealed at Sinai. In chs 25–31 we have God's instructions concerning the tabernacle ("prescriptive"), and in chs 35–40 the report of how they were carried out to the letter ("descriptive"). The latter is slightly abbreviated, but otherwise the texts are virtually identical, except for the tense of the verbs. This type of almost verbatim rehearsal is common in ancient texts.

I. Israel Enslaved in Egypt (chs 1–11)

  A. Israel in Egypt (ch 1)

    1. Israel's growth (1:1–7)

    2. Slave labor (1:8–14)

    3. Attempted extermination (1:15–22)

  B. Moses the Deliverer (ch 2)

    1. Birth and rescue of Moses (2:1–10)

    2. Moses' flight to Midian and marriage to Zipporah (2:11–22)

    3. God plans to rescue His people (2:23–25)

  C. God's Plan of Deliverance (chs 3–4)

    1. God reveals Himself to Moses (3:1–12)

    2. God reveals His divine name (3:13–17)

    3. God gives Moses instructions (3:18–22)

    4. The staff, the signs, and Aaron (4:1–17)

    5. Moses' return to Egypt (4:18–23)

    6. Zipporah circumcises their son (4:24–26)

    7. Aaron sent to be Moses' mouth (4:27–31)

  D. Preparation and Confrontation with Pharaoh: the 10 Plagues (chs 5–11)

    1. Making bricks without straw (ch 5)

    2. God promises deliverance (6:1–13)

and passage through the Red Sea, which God provided. Moses had a unique relationship with God. He could approach God's nearer presence and experience His glory as no one else could. Moses became the epitome of the Old Testament prophet, harshly rebuking the sins of Israel but also interceding for them.

Aaron, Moses' brother, was selected by God to act as Moses' spokesman (4:14, 27) and worked alongside his brother throughout the exodus. An exception, which illustrates the malleable character of Aaron, happened when Moses was on Mount Sinai. The people of Israel, intent on having an idol for their worship, pressed Aaron to create the idol for them. When Moses confronted Aaron, the latter offered a weak explanation for his actions (32:24). Despite Aaron's flaws, the Lord selected him as Israel's high priest.

Levites are the descendants of Levi, one of Jacob's sons (Gn 35:23). They formed the tribe from which Moses and Aaron came. God consecrated the Levites due to their zeal at the critical moment when Israel was divided over whether to heed Moses or to follow their inclination toward idolatry. They were singled out for special service at the tabernacle. Just as the narratives of Genesis defined the tribes of Judah, Ephraim, and Manasseh, so the Book of Exodus defined the Levites. The next book of Moses, Leviticus, would define the priestly family of Aaron and their service.

Pharaoh is the Egyptian title for the supreme ruler of Egypt. Exodus refers to two Egyptian rulers: (A) the "new king" (1:8) who did not know Joseph, enslaved and persecuted the Israelites, and sought to punish Moses; and (B) the pharaoh of the exodus who steadfastly resisted Moses' requests to let Israel go and who pursued Israel to the destruction of his own troops. In both cases, the pharaoh is depicted as a harsh ruler.

The historical identification of which pharaohs are intended has led to considerable study. But the biblical authors did not provide specific names or revealing character descriptions. Egyptian records of the period do not clearly describe Israel or the exodus. As a result of these factors, it is difficult to confirm the identities of the pharaohs. In fact, Egyptian chronology is itself a matter of dispute, which prevents a simple side-by-side comparison with a biblical chronology. Nevertheless, historians have discussed some pharaohs as possible candidates. Ahmose I and Thutmose III are among those mentioned for traditional biblical chronology. In fact, the early Jewish historian Josephus (c AD 37–100) cited an account of the Egyptian priest Manetho (c 280 BC), who referred to a "Tuthmosis" driving shepherds out of Egypt to settle in Jerusalem (*Against Apion* 2:15). This might appear to be a direct reference to the events of Exodus. However, Manetho's account may confuse the expulsion of the Hyksos with the flight of the Israelites, since both of these events would be associated with Egypt's Eighteenth Dynasty according to traditional chronology. Scholars who argue for a later date of the exodus propose Seti I and Ramses II as possible pharaohs, but this approach usually assumes inaccuracies in the biblical records.

Narrative Development or Plot

Although a large portion of the Book of Exodus is instructions about laws, building, and worship, these sections are part of the broader story of Israel's redemption from Egypt. The book begins where Genesis leaves off, with a list of the sons of Israel and reference to Joseph's life and death in Egypt. God's gracious redemption is emphasized in saving Moses' life through Pharaoh's daughter (chs 1–2) and providing for his servant in the wilderness so that Moses' life anticipates the redemption and providence that forms the central story of the book: the rescue of Israel from the Egyptians. Everything that happens in Exodus happens in view of this event, which became central to Israel's story throughout its history.

Before redeeming Israel, the Lord punished the Egyptians for their cruelty through a series of plagues that

The dry, modern Red Sea wilderness likely received more rainfall in the second millenium BC, according to archaeological surveys.

devastated the land until, climactically, the firstborn children of Egypt died, while the Lord drew away Israel as His firstborn son. The dramatic flight from Egypt ended when Pharaoh's army drowned in the Red Sea. For the next few months, the Israelites traveled to Mount Sinai where the Lord gave them His covenant, the beginnings of the Law, and instructions for building the tabernacle. The story of the golden calf, as an interlude, emphasizes that there is only one God and that Israel needs the discipline and instruction of the Law. The book ends with Israel gladly fulfilling God's command to build the tabernacle and God filling the tabernacle with His same glory that led the people out of Egypt.

Resources

As noted above, Exodus is compiled using a variety of texts, notably the Song of Moses (15:1–18), the song of Miriam (15:20–21), the memorial for Joshua (17:14), the book of the covenant (24:7), and the tablets of the testimony (24:12; 25:16). See p 7.

Text and Translations

The traditional Hebrew text of Exodus, like that of the other Books of Moses, is well preserved. The Samaritans preserved their own version of the book, which includes some unique readings. The LXX text of Exodus is a very literal rendering of the Hebrew, with occasional unique readings. Seventeen fragments of Exodus manuscripts were found at Qumran, which support the traditional Hebrew text. *Jubilees* retells the stories of Exodus up to the giving of the Law at Mount Sinai.

DOCTRINAL CONTENT

Summary Commentary

Ch 1 Israel emerges as a people. God's blessing and the fulfillment of His promise gives growth to the nation and preserves His people in a foreign land. As a last resort to halt the growth of Israel, Pharaoh commands the Egyptians to collaborate in the mass killing of Hebrew boys (v 22).

Ch 2 Moses, born of believing Hebrew parents (Heb 11:23), is raised in Pharaoh's household and "instructed in all the wisdom of the Egyptians" (Ac 7:22), enjoying the best of two worlds. Although God is not mentioned, He is accomplishing His purposes to redeem Israel. God later humbles Moses before calling him to lead Israel out of Egypt, letting him feel the sufferings of his people and making Moses realize how totally inadequate he is to save them, since this former prince must live as a fugitive in the household of a Midianite priest. God hears Israel's cry for deliverance. He does not forget Israel but remembers His covenant with their fathers.

Chs 3–4 What begins as just another day tending sheep changes dramatically when God confronts Moses at the burning bush on the holy mountain. I AM makes His presence known in fire and word and discloses His special name. He sends Moses on what seems to him an impossible mission. Moses resists the Lord's call to lead Israel out of Egypt because of his focus on his own shortcomings and the doubts of his people. Moses may not be the best speaker, but that does not matter because he will be speaking God's Word (4:12). Moses returns to Egypt as an act of faith. Confronting Pharaoh with God's demands and confronting the people whom he fears (4:1) proves a daunting assignment. Yet Moses obeys, and the people believe.

Chs 5–11 Pharaoh makes the burdens of Israel heavier, leading Moses and the people to frustration. As a Levite, Moses has good family connections, but this does not translate into an eager willingness to serve the Lord. According to God's plan of salvation, Moses and Aaron are His "god" and "prophet" who speak His Word before Pharaoh in order to rescue the Israelites from 430 years of bondage.

The Lord strikes at the very heart of Pharaoh's idolatry by striking the Nile and the resources provided by the river, which are associated with Egyptian gods. He begins to deliver His people from Egypt through water, by which He will later destroy Pharaoh's army and set Israel apart. The pattern of the plagues sets a recurring theme of sin, oppression (the plagues), repentance, and deliverance. Magicians, sorcerers, and charlatans cannot stop the power of God. The plagues follow repeatedly as God's judgment increases in magnitude. The Lord distinguishes between Egypt and Israel by protecting His people in Goshen from the plagues. Pharaoh wants the Israelites to sacrifice and worship according to his expectations, but Moses could never allow this. Despite the number of times Pharaoh goes through the cycle of sin, oppression, regret, and deliverance, God will not be mocked. Pharaoh seeks compromise and even forgiveness, but his pride still refuses to bend to the will of God. In ch 11 God's final judgment is about to come upon Pharaoh and Egypt. The hardened king will see that God's patience has come to an end and His wrath is imminent.

12:1–15:21 The Lord explains the Passover. Then the final plague takes place at midnight; as all Egypt lies in deep sleep, every firstborn son dies. Pharaoh comprehends that this plague is certainly God's punishment. The exodus has begun; salvation has arrived by God's grace. After 430 years in Egypt, many of them spent in slavery, Israel begins its exodus into religious freedom, which centers on freedom to worship and sacrifice to the one true God. In 12:43–51, the Lord gives supplementary regulations concerning the Passover due to the fact that Egyptians and likely other persons (v 38) have joined themselves to the Israelites. The Lord also sets Israel apart by instituting observances that help them remember their freedom won in the exodus. At the Red Sea God miraculously brings Israel through the waters, but this is more than simply passing a geographic barrier. When Israel crosses through the sea, they leave behind slavery and a future of death in Egypt for freedom and a future of life with God. Israel is powerless to make this drastic change on its own, but God intervenes to provide the way. Moses praises the Lord for victory and anticipates future victories (15:1–21).

A modern Seder meal of bitter herbs (horseradish and romaine lettuce), a paste of fruit and nuts, a hard boiled egg and a bone of lamb or goat.

15:22–18:27 The Lord patiently supplies Israel with drinking water and meets Israel's need for food with bread from heaven. However, when the Israelites ignore God's simple rules for its collection and consumption, they provoke an exasperated rebuke from God (16:28–29). Israel does not understand at the time, but God is blessing them through this experience, training them in the rhythms of work and Sabbath rest. When Israel again runs out of water, they grumble instead of turning to God, their Rock, for help. God in His graciousness does not deal with them according to their folly but furnishes the water they desperately need. Israel then learns firsthand as they fight enemies such as Amalek that success depends on the Lord. Without the Lord's direction and strength, they will lose. Moses serves as chief mediator between God and the Israelites, and God uses Moses and his subordinates to teach the people about Himself through His Law.

Chs 19–24 At Mount Sinai, God establishes His covenant with Israel. God reminds His people that He graciously rescued them in the exodus, impresses them with His majesty and presence, and establishes a covenant with them to guide their service as a "kingdom of priests." Ch 20 marks the beginning of the book of the covenant (20:22–23:19), in which the Ten Commandments are explained and applied. Through Moses, God gives a variety of "guiding decisions," precedent-setting legislation that would guide Israel's courts throughout the coming generations. The Lord regulates human relations with sensitivity toward the poor and powerless, yet also with high regard for impartial justice. He connects the Sabbath with regula-

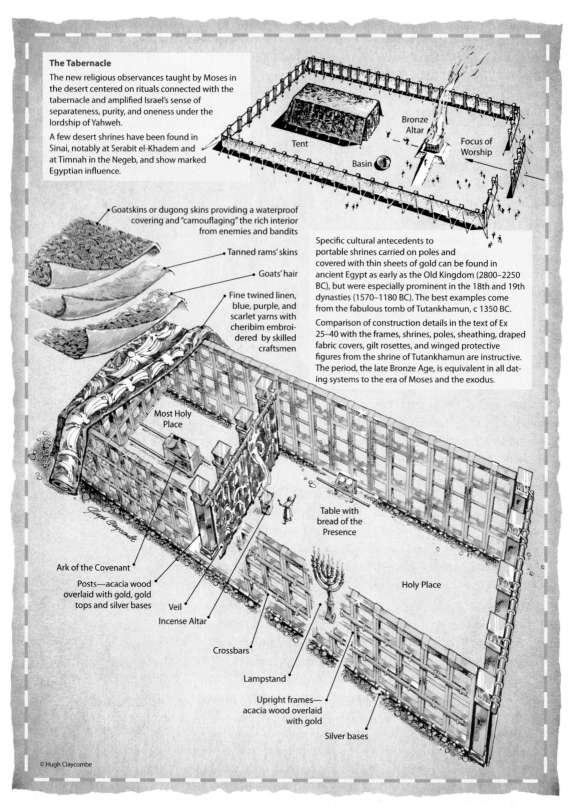

The Tabernacle

The new religious observances taught by Moses in the desert centered on rituals connected with the tabernacle and amplified Israel's sense of separateness, purity, and oneness under the lordship of Yahweh.

A few desert shrines have been found in Sinai, notably at Serabit el-Khadem and at Timnah in the Negeb, and show marked Egyptian influence.

Tent

Bronze Altar

Focus of Worship

Basin

Goatskins or dugong skins providing a waterproof covering and "camouflaging" the rich interior from enemies and bandits

Tanned rams' skins

Goats' hair

Fine twined linen, blue, purple, and scarlet yarns with cheribim embroidered by skilled craftsmen

Specific cultural antecedents to portable shrines carried on poles and covered with thin sheets of gold can be found in ancient Egypt as early as the Old Kingdom (2800–2250 BC), but were especially prominent in the 18th and 19th dynasties (1570–1180 BC). The best examples come from the fabulous tomb of Tutankhamun, c 1350 BC.

Comparison of construction details in the text of Ex 25–40 with the frames, shrines, poles, sheathing, draped fabric covers, gilt rosettes, and winged protective figures from the shrine of Tutankhamun are instructive. The period, the late Bronze Age, is equivalent in all dating systems to the era of Moses and the exodus.

Most Holy Place

Table with bread of the Presence

Ark of the Covenant

Posts—acacia wood overlaid with gold, gold tops and silver bases

Holy Place

Veil

Incense Altar

Crossbars

Lampstand

Upright frames— acacia wood overlaid with gold

Silver bases

© Hugh Claycombe

tions on rest (cf Ex 20:8–11) and worship (cf Dt 5:12–15). Rest refreshes the body; worship refreshes the soul. God promises to drive out Israel's enemies ahead of them if they remain faithful to Him and to the covenant given them through Moses. Moses then ascends Mount Sinai to receive the terms of the covenant God makes with His people, concluding the book of the covenant.

Chs 25–31 The Lord tells Moses to build a sanctuary in which He will dwell. Though God is present everywhere, He locates His saving presence in the tabernacle, where He has promised to be found. The Lord speaks to Moses from the Mercy Seat, the place of the Commandments and the atonement—His Law and His Gospel-mercy. The tabernacle and its furniture are laid out according to the specifications God gave on the mountain (25:40; Ac 7:44). Israel's worship is not spontaneous or haphazard but is carefully organized to honor the Creator, who set creation in order by carefully arranging space, boundaries, and the passage of time. (Cf Gn 1:1–2:3.) Specific limits mark the holiness of the Lord, limiting the approach of humans to Him. The beautiful priestly attire reflects the beauty of God as well as the office in which the priests minister (Ex 28). God consecrates the Aaronic priesthood to consecrate His people, who are to be a kingdom of priests (19:6). Plans for construction are revealed. Craftsmen, imbued with the Spirit of God, are named.

Chs 32–34 While Moses is on the mountain, Israel soon doubts God's promises and turns to idolatry. The Lord sends Moses to confront them. Their idol is unable to help them, and they experience punishment. Fully aware of their sin, the Israelites strip off their ornaments to show their repentance and sorrow. Moses goes back up the mountain and receives an extraordinary gift: God speaks to him face-to-face, as to a friend (though without seeing God directly). Moses asks to learn God's ways and see God's glory. He is permitted to see a glimpse of God's presence. After coming back down the mountain, Moses veils himself because the Israelites, in their sinfulness, are terrified to see a manifestation of God's glory.

Chs 35–40 God calls the people again to share in His Sabbath rest. Offerings, materials, and laborers pour into the work site to begin the task. What God spoke, Moses reveals to Bezalel and Oholiab, who in turn train the craftsmen. Beginning with the ark and Mercy Seat, as the single most holy piece of furniture, the elements of the tabernacle are constructed. Bezalel erects the court boundary. Entering from the east, one comes first to the place of sacrifice: the bronze altar signifying the importance that atonement has for Israel. The Lord lives among His people in the tabernacle and leads them to life and salvation.

Specific Law Themes

One of the major Law themes is the sequence of plagues whereby God punishes the Egyptians for the years of oppression against Israel. The Lord told Moses that He raised up this stubborn pharaoh specifically for this purpose. In this way, Exodus teaches that God plans for the punishment of the wicked and may even drive them to it. The Ten Commandments and the many legal statutes governing Israel's relationship to the Lord, including oaths to fulfill the Law, are likewise a major element of the book. God's holiness restricts access to Him and requires practices of cleansing and atonement.

Specific Gospel Themes

God graciously hears and remembers His promises to His people, even when years of distance from Him have taken place. Redemption and rescue are the greatest themes of Exodus. The Lord provides for the people's redemption through the blood of the Passover Lamb, and its benefits are realized in the separation and consecration of Israel from their pagan neighbors, culminating in the passage through the Red Sea, which saves Israel but destroys the Egyptians. The sacrifices of the tabernacle touch on these themes through the blood of atonement and consecration, which is even sprinkled directly on the people (24:8).

Specific Doctrines

The importance of Passover and the Feast of Unleavened Bread for the Lord, for Israel, and also for Christians can scarcely be overstated. The feast for Christians climaxes at Holy Week and Easter when Jesus, the Lamb of God, was sacrificed.

The laws of the covenant (like most of the subsequent legislation) must be seen in proper theological perspective. We could partly describe them as illustrations or examples of faithful response to redemption, which would also account for some of the minor variations in different codes. Special comment seems mandatory only in the case of the so-called *lex talionis*, the "eye for an eye" law governing retaliation in 21:24. The law directs *restraint*, not cold-blooded retribution. We here see ancient Israel in its role as a state rather than as a church, and the law's intent is to safeguard people from excessive punishment with as much "love" as is possible in that realm. When in the world of power, retributive justice must operate; the law insists that the punishment must correspond to the severity of the infraction.

The Ark of the Covenant

The ark of the covenant was the centerpiece of the Israelite tabernacle. The ark was a box covered with gold, 44 in. long by 26.4 in. wide and high, with carrying poles for the wilderness journey to the Promised Land. Centered within the tabernacle (portable temple), the ark was later placed within Solomon's permanent temple.

Once a year, the high priest entered the Most Holy Place to appear before the Lord (Lv 16:34). This part of the Day of Atonement ceremony included sprinkling of the blood from animals upon the cover of the ark of the covenant (Lv 16:14). Israelite people prayed over animals to be sacrificed, placing on them their own sin and guilt (Lv 16:21). Blood was a substance that embodied both physical and spirtual life, and was sprinkled on the sacred space between the cherubim.

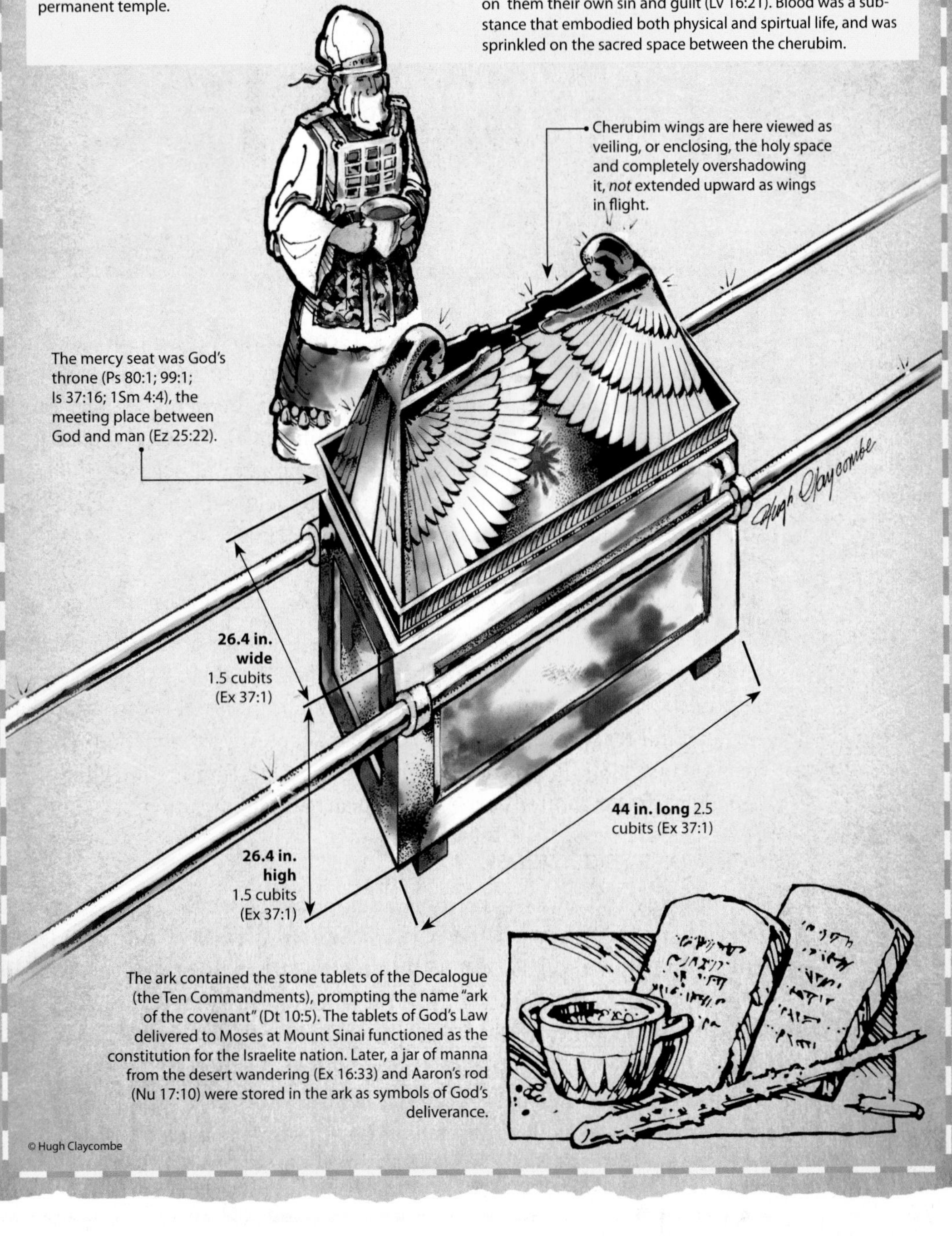

Cherubim wings are here viewed as veiling, or enclosing, the holy space and completely overshadowing it, *not* extended upward as wings in flight.

The mercy seat was God's throne (Ps 80:1; 99:1; Is 37:16; 1Sm 4:4), the meeting place between God and man (Ez 25:22).

26.4 in. wide
1.5 cubits
(Ex 37:1)

26.4 in. high
1.5 cubits
(Ex 37:1)

44 in. long 2.5 cubits (Ex 37:1)

The ark contained the stone tablets of the Decalogue (the Ten Commandments), prompting the name "ark of the covenant" (Dt 10:5). The tablets of God's Law delivered to Moses at Mount Sinai functioned as the constitution for the Israelite nation. Later, a jar of manna from the desert wandering (Ex 16:33) and Aaron's rod (Nu 17:10) were stored in the ark as symbols of God's deliverance.

© Hugh Claycombe

The gilded chest from Tutankhamun's tomb (c 1322 BC) was constructed and carried on poles like Israel's ark of the covenant (Ex 25:10–22).

The word *pattern* (Hbr *tabnith*) is theologically very important for chs 25–40. It appears at the beginning of the section (25:9). The tabernacle and its ritual are a reflection, a miniature, a copy of the heavenly temple. There is God's eternal throne (ultimately the entire universe), but God must become "incarnate" in a special dwelling place among mankind because of its alienation in sin. The same language and idea is applied to the tabernacle's successor, the temple (and by extension to the entire Holy City, Zion), as well as to Christ, both His incarnation and the fulfillment in Him of God's eternal purpose for the temple of the entire creation (cf e.g., Hebrews and Revelation).

The conclusion of Exodus highlights the theology of the tabernacle and temple to be found throughout the Bible. The "Word becoming flesh" message of the Old Testament is especially evident in God's incarnational and sacramental real presence in the sanctuary, centering above the Mercy Seat in the Most Holy Place. In Exodus and the Old Testament, "glory" (Hbr *kabod* or Gk *doxa*) often carries such incarnational meaning.

Key Texts in Exodus

The first key text may strike the reader as odd, though it is important to remember that Exodus is the book of Scripture where God provides the fuller stipulations of His Law, a fact that has naturally drawn the attention of interpreters to that topic. In ch 1, the story of the Hebrew midwives demonstrates that God rewards those who fear Him and honor His commands (1:21). In other words, the book begins with an example of how Israel must live if the people are to distinguish themselves as God's people, different from nations such as the Egyptians, who oppress the helpless.

When God reveals His covenant name to Moses, "I AM WHO I AM" (3:14), He introduces the mystery of His greatness. He invites Moses to speak the name, to share it with Israel and to call upon Him in faith. The name "I AM" and also the nature of God are in a sense hidden and mysterious to us.

Theologians have frequently turned to a series of passages in Exodus when discussing the will of God and the will of mankind. God reveals to Moses beforehand that Pharaoh will not listen to him and that ultimately the Lord will harden Pharaoh's heart (3:19; 4:21; 7:3). Indeed, God raised up Pharaoh for the purpose of displaying His power and making His name known among the nations. This does not mean that God predestined Pharaoh for destruction. It is noteworthy that during the first five plagues Pharaoh hardened his own heart with stubbornness, but Moses records dramatically that the Lord hardened Pharaoh's heart after the sixth plague (9:12). The story leaves room for the human will as well as God's will in mercy and justice. God's later declaration, "I will be gracious to whom I will be gracious, and will show mercy on whom I will show mercy" (33:19) continues this theme and invites one to ponder the mysteries of election and grace.

Exodus returns to one of the opening themes of Genesis and introduces a moral and ceremonial law in connection with it: observance of the Sabbath, which becomes a repeated emphasis beginning at ch 16. The fact that Sabbath observance entered into the Ten Commandments amplified importance of the observance in distinction from other Old Testament ceremonial laws.

The Ten Commandments (20:1–17) are the core text of the book of the covenant and remain foundational to religious practice and to modern legal systems. To fend off suspicion that the Old Testament is legalistic, it is grammatically noteworthy that the Ten Commandments use indicative rather than imperative verbs. These state what the believer who has experienced God's grace will voluntarily do, not commands of what he must do to deserve or earn God's love. They represent the boundaries of God's kingship, beyond which the believer will not stray, but within which he is essentially free to respond joyfully and voluntarily, as illustrated by the rest of the laws of the Old Testament.

Because of Jesus' teaching about swearing oaths, Ex 22:11 has been a text in constant discussion. Another law about speech is likewise important. Exodus 22:28 forbids cursing God as well as one's ruler, showing the importance the Lord places on government and those who administer it, while raising questions about what a believer should do when rulers are wicked, such as the Egyptians who had enslaved Israel.

A man with a coil of rope approaches a bull. The Egyptians and other Mediterranean people admired the strength of bulls and venerated them.

A favorite passage of preachers must be Ex 32:6 when Israel "rose up to play" before the golden calf and thus offended their Savior. When their bellies were full, their minds and hearts turned away from God, illustrating the dangers of prosperity, luxury, and gluttony.

Arguably, the most important text in Exodus is God's self confession, in which He declares that He is both merciful and just (34:6–7). The passage describes God's two ways of working with Israel, which become constant themes in Old Testament history and in Christian theology, embodied in the proper distinction between Law and Gospel. Apart from the repetition of some hymnic phrases, the words of Ex 34:6–7 are the most often cited by other Old Testament writers (Cf Dt 5:9; 7:9; Ne 9:31; Jer 32:18; Dn 9:4; Jl 2:13; Mi 7:18–20) indicating their core role in Old Testament doctrine and the unity of scriptural teaching.

Application

The Book of Exodus established the Old Testament priesthood and the pattern of worship for God's people. The public administration of the general worship rites of a holy people in a holy tabernacle was restricted to a holy (i.e., specially designated) group: the tribe of Levi. And within this tribe, only Aaron and his descendants were sanctified or consecrated for the specific function of the priesthood proper (28:1). But not even all priests were permitted to perform all the rites. Aaron was to be "holy to the Lord" in a special way—as the priest or high priest. Only he and the firstborn among his descendants, for example, would be eligible to enter the Most Holy Place while one of them served as high priest.[1] And to emphasize their holy functions, all officiants in the sanctuary were to wear "holy garments" (28:2–4; 39:1–30) and were to be consecrated in an ordination ceremony (29:1–37; 40:12–15).

Amid all these specifics about holy worship (between the directions, chs 24–31, and their performance, chs 34–40) is inserted (chs 32–34) perhaps the most unholy and humiliating account of Israel's early life: its breaking of the covenant by the worship of the golden calf at the same time that the cov-

---

1   Later the nonpriestly Levites, i.e., those not of Aaron's family, were designated to be "ministers" of the priests (cf Nu 3–4).

enant was established. That God forgave them testifies clearly that the God of the covenant truly is a God of mercy and forgiveness, a point for us to remember as we labor together in God's kingdom and notice one another's strengths and weaknesses. All that God did for and through Israel of old was prophetic history (1Co 10:1–6). It pointed forward to the consummation of His eternal plan of salvation through His Son, Jesus Christ. The exodus from Egypt and the making of the covenant at Mount Sinai are events of history, both Israel's history as well as the history of the people of the new covenant—"a chosen race, a royal priesthood, a holy nation, a people for His [God's] own possession" (1Pt 2:9). The latter became God's people just as did the first—not by merit but by the saving and forgiving mercy of God.

The purpose of both covenants is the same: that God's people of all ages may "proclaim the excellencies of Him who called you out of darkness into His marvelous light" and "be holy in all your conduct" (1Pt 2:9; 1:15).

The continuous nature of the covenant is witnessed on a holy mountain where "Moses and Elijah . . . appeared in glory and spoke of His departure [Gk: His exodus], which He was about to accomplish [Gk: fulfill] at Jerusalem" (Lk 9:30–31). In His death Jesus entered once and for all into the Most Holy Place, sprinkling not the blood of goats and calves but His own blood, "thus securing an eternal redemption" (Heb 9:12). It is the blood of the new covenant because it is God's yes and amen of the fulfillment of His old covenant promises. The old covenant was God's signature of promise; the new covenant validates the promise.

Ch 1 Israel emerges as a people and thrives. Pharaoh imagines that he can thwart God's will. Consider how God provides for, supports, protects, and preserves His Church day by day. God blesses us as He blessed Israel, yet He has also revealed to us His greatest blessings in His only-begotten Son. As a last resort to halt the growth of Israel, Pharaoh commands all his people to collaborate in the mass killing of Hebrew boys (v 22). When evil in this world seems to triumph and we struggle on account of our weakness, we can call to mind the women who feared God and were blessed by Him.

Ch 2 As the story of Moses shows, even when God does not seem to be at work in our lives, we can be certain that His good and gracious will is being done among us. God humbles us as He humbled Moses. He does this so that at the proper time He may raise us up in Christ (1Pt 5:6).

Chs 3–4 "Without God's Word we can have no God" (AE 13:386). What was true for Moses is true for us as well. God is present for us and speaks to us in His Word. We have no hope for salvation except through God's Word and promise. Like Moses, we Christians have been called to speak God's

Word in faith. Luther calls faith the "skill above all skills. It is the work of the Holy Spirit alone" (AE 14:59). There is no other way to explain the faith of Moses and of the people, and there is no other way to explain our faith. By our own reason and strength, we cannot believe in Jesus Christ. But because "the Holy Spirit has called me by the Gospel," I bow my head and worship (SC, Third Article).

Chs 5–11 Why does God wait and put people through such suffering? "Faith does not despair of the God who sends trouble. Faith does not consider Him angry or an enemy. . . . Faith rises above all this and sees God's fatherly heart behind His unfriendly exterior" (AE 14:59). He gives His name to Israel and calls them to trust Him. According to God's divine plan of salvation, Moses and Aaron are His "god" and "prophet" who speak His Word before Pharaoh in order to rescue the Israelites from 430 years of bondage. God's plan moves forward. The intensity of temporal punishment increases; God remains slow to anger and desires to deliver sinners by His grace. People who trust Christ the Lord are drawn closer to Him in times of tribulation, seeking His forgiveness, comfort, strength, and healing for the sake of His cross and resurrection. Pharaoh mocks God with false repentance, but the Lord is unmoved. Sinners cannot bargain with God by conceding some of their sins or by amending behaviors. God sees through it all. Call on God's mercy. Jesus is always ready to forgive.

The granite peaks of Mount Sinai.

12:1–15:21 Passover marks a new era for the people of Israel and foreshadows the new, spiritual Israel in Christ, the perfect Lamb who takes away the sin of the world (1Co 5:7; Heb 7:27). The troubles of Israel's departure from Egypt are merely the introduction to a new life of liberty, which comes with burdens and responsibilities. God Almighty preserves His people from the destroyer and brings Israel out of the land of bondage by grace alone. Teach about this salvation to your children. Also explain our exodus from sin and death granted through our Lord Jesus. Jesus offered Himself as the perfect, "once for all" sacrifice (Heb 10:10). He purifies us from our sin and consecrates us so that God can call us His own.

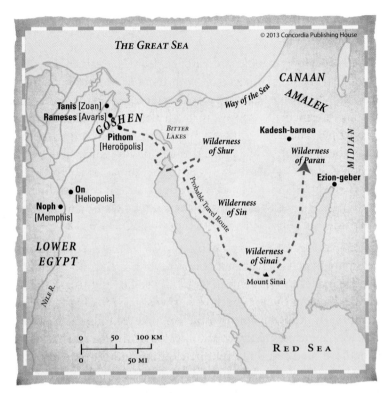

The Exodus. God led His people through the wilderness, not by the Way of the Sea (Ex 13:17–18). Many sites on their route cannot be located with certainty. The Israelites journeyed from Rameses in Goshen to Succoth (12:37), which may be Pithom. They marched to Etham, on the edge of the wilderness (13:20). God ordered them to Pi-hahiroth to bait a trap for Pharaoh (14:1–4). Then God led His people through the Red Sea, trapping the Egyptians under the waters (14:5–31); see *Ant* 2:315, 324–25. The Israelites traveled into the Wilderness of Shur to Marah (15:22–25) and Elim (15:27). They came via Dophkah and Alush to Rephidim (Nu 33:13–14; Ex 17:1), where they defeated the Amalekites (Ex 17:8–16). Through the Wilderness of Sinai, they came to Mount Sinai (Ex 19–40). Israel went to Kibroth-hattaavah, Hazeroth (Nu 11:34–35), and then into the Wilderness of Paran (12:16). God commanded Israel to remain in the wilderness for 40 years (Nu 14:20–35).

He knows our situation, meets us where we are, and walks with us by day and night to bring us into His kingdom.

15:22–18:27 We need water to refresh our bodies; without it, we die. And if we go without spiritual refreshment, we will die eternally. However, God meets this spiritual need for us just as certainly as He quenched Israel's thirst at Marah. We likewise need the rhythms of work and rest. These rhythms still apply for us today because we require both physical rest and rest from our sins through the righteous labors of Jesus. He was stricken

Himself for what they deserve. Christ Jesus is the Rock of Israel and our Rock of salvation.

Chs 19–24 God's people are rescued from slavery in Egypt by His grace. God establishes His covenant with them at Mount Sinai. Yet sinfulness prevents the people from approaching God personally. God graciously appoints an intermediary, Moses, through whom He makes His covenant with His people. The Lord comforts His people by reminding them first of His mercy toward them. God protects the poor and vulnerable by building compassion and respect for justice into Israel's social laws. His two ways of Law and Gospel manifest themselves constantly for our good. By the blood of the covenant, the Lord anticipates the forgiveness of sins in Jesus, who would become "sin" for us in order to redeem us (2Co 5:21).

Chs 25–31 Organized worship, patterned on God's Word and the life of our Savior, honors God's works of creation, redemption, and sanctification, by which He makes us His beloved people. Specific limits mark the holiness of the Lord, limiting the approach of humans to Him. Due to our sins, we cannot approach the Holy One of Israel and live. Through Christ's work on the cross, we have access to the court, the Most Holy Place in heaven (cf Heb 4:14). The Lord required that even the clothing and movement of the high priest would bring glory and offer praise. Reassess your offering of praise and service to the Lord. Give all glory to Jesus, who diligently bore your guilt and consecrates you by grace. God consecrates the Aaronic priesthood to consecrate His people, who would be a kingdom of priests (Ex 19:6). Our High Priest, Jesus, set aside this old order of sacrifices to offer Himself once for all (Heb 10:8–10). Value the service of each person, but give all glory to the Lord, who forgives your sins and makes you one in Christ.

Chs 32–34 Israel soon doubts God's promises and turns to idolatry. We, too, may grow impatient or doubt God's promises. In fear or doubt, we may turn to idols of our own: anything that we "fear, love, and trust" more than the true God. He invites our repentance and our prayers and has promised to hear us and answer. He works with us in His grace. How blessed are we to be called the friends of God. John tells us that no one has ever seen God's full presence and glory, for it would be too much for a sinner to bear. Yet, we see God when Christ Jesus covered Himself in our flesh and lived among us (Jn 1:18). Sinful hearts may also stumble over God's verdict that the effects of sin will harm anyone other than the sinner. Could it be fair that the fathers' sin affect the third and fourth generation (Ex 34:7)? But the results of sin in one person's life often do impact others. We learn patterns of sin from our parents and often suffer the effects of others' sin. But the Lord's steadfast love, mercy, and grace are greater than any sin, because He has atoned for our sin. His mercy abounds for thousands of generations (34:7), far more than the effects of sin. Because of Christ, we see the Lord and live in His glorious grace.

Chs 35–40 Our true rest is in the one true God, who grants life, peace, and all blessings. For God's people, work begins as an act of faith motivated by God's Word. He works through a plan, through means, and through people. When the fullness of time came (Gal 4:4), Jesus enacted the plan laid before eternity (Eph 1:4) and built a heavenly city with foundations (Heb 11:10; Rv 21:9–27). In the Gospels, Jesus compares the tabernacle and Herod's temple with the temple of His body (Mt 27:40; Jn 2:19–22), by which we have full remission of sin. By the temple of Jesus' body, we approach the Father. The glory of the Lord continues in Word and Sacrament, through which Christ lives in and with us.

CANONICITY

As part of the Torah, the most important portion of the Hebrew Scriptures for the Jews, the Book of Exodus was treasured. Christians received the book without question.

Fresco-Mosaic of the high priest Aaron.

LUTHERAN THEOLOGIANS ON EXODUS

Luther

"[In Exodus] when the world was now full and sunk in blindness so that men scarcely knew any longer what sin was or where death came from, God brings Moses forward with the law and selects a special people, in order to enlighten the world again through them, and by the law to reveal sin anew. He therefore organizes this people with all kinds of laws and separates it from all other peoples. He has them build a tent, and begins a form of worship. He appoints princes and officials, and provides his people splendidly with both laws and men, to rule them both in the body before the world and in the spirit before God. . . .

"For the law has three kinds of pupils. The first are those who hear the law and despise it, and who lead an impious life without fear. To these the law does not come. They are represented by the calf worshipers in the wilderness, on whose account Moses broke the tables of the law [Exod. 32:19]. To them he did not bring the law.

"The second kind are those who attempt to fulfill the law by their own power, without grace. . . . For the law shows that our ability counts for nothing without Christ's grace.

"The third kind of pupils are those who see Moses clearly, without a veil. These are they who understand the intention of the law and how it demands impossible things. . . . For if Christ's glory did not come alongside this splendor of Moses, no one could bear the brightness of the law, the terror of sin and death. These [third kind of] pupils fall away from all works and presumption and learn from the law nothing else except to recognize sin and to yearn for Christ. This is the true office of Moses and the very nature of the law." (AE 35:237, 245–46)

For more of Luther's insights on the Ten Commandments, see *Ten Sermons on the Catechism* (AE 51:137–61) and *Eight Sermons at Wittenberg* (AE 51:79–83).

Gerhard

"*The second Book of Moses* is called *shemoth* from its second word. The Greeks call it *Exodos* ["Exodus"], and the Latins have kept this nomenclature because it describes the departure of the children of Israel from Egypt. It has forty chapters and contains the history of the 142 years from the death of Joseph to the building of the tabernacle. It can be divided into the antecedents, the actual departure, and the consequences; also into the birth and rearing of the Israelite church. Some divide the entire account into the departure of the Israelites and their stay at Mount Sinai. We can set up six parts that make up the total account: (1) The life of Moses and his ambassadorship to Pharaoh. (2) The plagues of Egypt that confirmed Moses' authority. (3) The exodus of the Israelites from Egypt, their crossing of the Red Sea, and their travels in the wilderness. (4) The establishment of the church and commonwealth after the Decalogue and other forensic laws were published. (5) The sin of the people and their reconciliation with God. (6) The erection of the tabernacle and the preparation of the things pertaining to divine worship." (ThC E1 § 120)

Baby Moses presented to Pharaoh's daughter (Ex 2).

QUESTIONS PEOPLE ASK ABOUT EXODUS
The Magicians of Egypt (Ex 7–9)

The Egyptian magicians tried to imitate the miracles that Moses and Aaron performed in the name of Yahweh to prove the authenticity of their message. Perhaps more strange than any other part of this narrative is the story of the magicians throwing down their rods and changing them into serpents (7:10–12). How must these performances be viewed? When the Lord called Moses to go to Pharaoh and to Israel with a special message, He gave him several signs, and one of these consisted of Moses throwing his rod on the ground and changing it into a serpent, which, however, was again turned into a rod when Moses took it by the tail (4:2–5). It is evident that we are here dealing with a divine miracle. But what shall we say about the wise men and the sorcerers, the magicians of the Egyptians who "did the same by their secret arts. For each man cast down his staff, and they became serpents" (7:11–12)? Must we conclude that it was through divine power that they gave this exhibition? It is plain that what happened was something supernatural; none possess this ability in their own right.

It has been suggested that perhaps the rods of the magicians were serpents that had been put into a state of rigidity by their masters and which began to move when they were thrown down on the ground. This might be accomplished by squeezing the nape of the animals' necks, rendering them immobile. However, some will note that the text says rods were thrown down and became serpents. If this is taken literally, one should not conclude that what the magicians did was accomplished through divine power. The Lord would not assist His enemies in

Papyrus Westcar records magic events in the court of Pharaoh Cheops
(seventeenth century BC) including the parting of lake water.

The exodus was the chief Old Testament example of God's redemption and power to save Israel. It is the Old Testament "gospel." This early depiction is from the Dura Europos synagogue, c AD 245.

their efforts to counteract the influence of His own servants, Moses and Aaron. There remains the possibility that it was through Satan that the magicians accomplished their feats. That it is Satan who operates in cases where opposition to God and His will is accompanied by miraculous performances is evident from 2Th 2:9, where the Scriptures say of the "lawless one" that his coming "is by the activity of Satan with all power and false signs and wonders." This means that Satan is supplying the power for the miraculous signs of the lawless one. Here we have a key for the supernatural exhibitions that are done by unbelievers. Satan is assisting these enemies of God, and with his aid they do things that surpass human understanding. It is very true that the veil of deep mystery rests on this whole subject because God has not given us much instruction on it.

Christians know that Satan is strong, but they know, too, that God alone is omnipotent. How Satan brought about those marvelous happenings in Egypt we cannot say. He has faculties and means at his command that are beyond our understanding; but supernatural deeds need not be looked upon as almighty deeds. When we say that the angels are stronger than we, we do not ascribe almighty powers to them. If we adhere to the letter of the Scriptures in explaining the part the magicians played as being in reality the work of Satan, admitting, however, our ignorance of the methods or means he employed, we shall be following a safe course. If this story makes the power of the devil appear very formidable, the child of God will find comfort in that part of the narrative which says that Aaron's rod swallowed up the rods of the magicians (Ex 7:12), God manifesting His superiority to Satan. And the following narrative not only tells of the inability of the magicians to bring forth gnats, which compelled them to confess, "This is the finger of God" (8:19), but when the plague of boils struck the Egyptians, the magicians likewise were among the victims and could not stand before Moses (9:11). We are thus shown that, while Satan can do marvelous things, he cannot do all things and cannot successfully contend against God.

The Plagues of Egypt and the Passage through the Red Sea (Ex 7–15)

The Book of Exodus reports a remarkable series of impressive miracles that God performed when the time had come to take His people out of bondage. Some interpreters have concluded that the plagues with which God afflicted the Egyptians were more legendary than miraculous. It is true that similar plagues in all probability occurred now and then in that country.

On this account some assert that we are not dealing here with punishments that Yahweh sent upon the recalcitrant Egyptians, but with events as natural as eclipses. They conclude it was merely superstition that gave a higher significance to the plagues, overlooking several obvious considerations: (1) These visitations were of unusual severity. (2) They came in close succession. (3) They fell upon the land according to the Word of the Lord spoken by Moses and Aaron. There were other features connected with these plagues that made them stand out as divine visitation. For instance, the final plague did not attack children in general, but merely the firstborn. It was noticed that in every house it was the firstborn who was smitten, and in this manner everyone was made to see that a special divine punishment had come upon the nation. In general, God in these visitations followed His usual method of not working grotesque wonders, performing unnatural things. Instead He employed forces that are at hand and that operate in their accustomed fashion to accomplish His design.

When the Israelites had left Egypt with Pharaoh pursuing them, God, in rescuing His people, performed another miracle, one that is remembered more than any other in Hebrew literature. He divided the sea and led the Israelites safely to the other side, while Pharaoh and his hosts were destroyed. Here, too, God employed a natural means to achieve His purpose. We read in Ex 14:21–22: "Then

Moses stretched out his hand over the sea, and the LORD drove the sea back by a strong east wind all night and made the sea dry land, and the waters were divided. And the people of Israel went into the midst of the sea on dry ground, the waters being a wall to them on their right hand and on their left." Notice that an east wind blows and makes the bottom of the sea dry enough for passage.

In discussions of the miracle the assertion has frequently been made that an extraordinary ebb set in which made it possible for the Israelites to reach the opposite shore in their flight, while their pursuers, who were too late for passage, were overwhelmed by the returning tide. But it is clear that such a view violates the plain words of Holy Scripture, which says, "the waters being a wall to them [the Israelites] on their right hand and on their left." If merely an unusual ebb had been responsible for the passageway, there would not have been water on both sides. While holding to the principle just enunciated as to the method of God's working His miracles, we must not alter the scriptural account, but leave its sense unimpaired. What particular forces God employed in restraining the waters we do not know, but His Word, telling us that He did separate the waters, is sufficient evidence for believing children of God that the sea was divided in some miraculous way.

Length of Israel's Sojourn in Egypt
(Ex 12:40; Gn 15:13; Gal 3:17)

The subject of the above texts is the length of the sojourn of Israel in Egypt, immediately after which sojourn the Law was given on Mount Sinai. No one should find it difficult to reconcile the first two statements, 400 being a round number, while 430 gives the actual number of years Israel stayed in Egypt. But the words of Paul (Gal 3:17) seem to be in conflict with Genesis and Exodus, since they say that from the time the promise was given to the promulgation of the Law was 430 years. Paul seems to lessen the number of years the children of Israel lived in Egypt considerably. From the time Abram was called and given the promise to the departure of Jacob for Egypt is a period of 215 years. This way of reckoning would leave only 430 minus 215 years for Israel's sojourn in the land of bondage. But here again we are proceeding on an assumption that is not necessary. Why must we assume that Paul is thinking of the first time or of one of the occasions when God gave a promise to Abraham? The apostle simply says that the covenant cannot be annulled by the law, which was given 430 years later. No valid objection can be raised to letting the period of 430 years begin when Jacob took up his abode in Egypt. We recall that when this patriarch was on his way to Egypt, the Lord spoke to him in a vision at night and gave him reassuring promises (Gn 46:2–4). The Scriptures do not record that the Lord repeated His promises to Jacob while the latter lived in Egypt; thus we may say that the direct promissory declarations of God to the patriarchs ceased at the time when Jacob went to live with Joseph and that we have good reason to assume that Paul in making his calculation is figuring from this point of time. Under this premise, Paul, as well as Ex 12:40, records Israel's sojourn in Egypt as 430 years. All pertinent Scripture passages are then in complete agreement.

The interpretation just given is that which is favored by some commentators. It is only fair that we mention another interpretation, which has many adherents. According to some, Paul is merely quoting from the Septuagint, which was the version of the Old Testament known to his readers, and he is disregarding all critical questions pertaining to the subject under discussion. The Septuagint reads in Ex 12:40: "The sojourn of the sons of Israel which they sojourned in the land of Egypt and in the land of Canaan was 430 years." The object of Paul was by no means to discuss the length of the sojourn of the Israelites in Egypt, but simply to point out that the Law had been given a long time after the declaration of the promise. We can well understand why he does not in this case, as he does on other occasions, reject the Septuagint version and adopt that of the original Hebrew. There is no warrant for assuming that the Old and the New Testament are contradicting each other.

Did the Egyptians Lose All Their Horses?
(Ex 9:3, 6; 14:9)

How could Pharaoh pursue the Israelites with a large army, including horsemen and chariots, if all his horses had died (9:3, 6)? We may note three points.

The word *all* in such cases is a relative concept, a figure of speech called hyperbole or exaggeration. When a heavy frost in spring shatters the hopes for an abundant fruit crop in a certain locality, we may say that the whole crop has been destroyed, though a few isolated apples and peaches will appear on the trees. Our remark simply states that, generally speaking, there will be no fruit crop, or that the surviving fruit is not worth mentioning. It probably was the same situation when a dread pestilence overtook the cattle and horses in Egypt. The loss was so general that the animals which remained were very few in number and hardly worth considering. We say a hailstorm has destroyed the whole wheat crop. Do we mean to state that every single stalk of wheat has been broken? No! We would consider such an interpretation of our remark unfair. Let us grant the holy writers the same privilege in the use of terms and literary figures that we ourselves employ.

Moses indicates in his narrative that the plague affected not all the cattle of the Egyptians, but only those that were in the field (9:3). The account then permits us to assume that the horses of Pharaoh that he kept in his forts ready for immediate service escaped the pestilence.

The animals belonging to the Israelites were not stricken, as we see from 9:4, 7. It may be that immediately after the cessation of the plague Pharaoh filled the gaps in his supply of war horses by taking as many horses from the Israelites as he could, under some pretext or other.

The Destructiveness of the Seventh Plague
(Ex 9:19, 27)

It has been said that these two passages contain conflicting statements because v 19 warns the Egyptians that every man and beast found in the field when the hail storm comes would die, and yet v 27 says that Pharaoh sent men to Moses and Aaron while the storm was raging. In reality there is no difficulty here. We may assume that there were intermissions in the storm, periods of less violence, when the leaders of Israel could well be called. It must also be remembered that v 19 speaks of men and beasts "in the field." Did Pharaoh have to send servants out into the field in order to call Moses and Aaron? That is not likely. In all probability these men were not far away from the royal palace.

Egyptian farmers working fields. Wall painting from the Tomb of Unsu (1540 BC).

The Making of Images (Ex 20:4; 25:18, 20)

A critic may contend that here the Book of Exodus contradicts itself, forbidding in one passage what it encourages in the other. But let the prohibition in 20:4 be read in connection with v 5, and it will be seen at once that it has reference to images made to be worshiped, either as representations of the deity before which one

Relief carving of a bull from the Luxor temple.

intends to bow or images of creatures that a person wishes to adore. The whole passage (20:3–6) is a stern commandment forbidding idolatry. The question of whether it is ethical or moral to make images if one does not put them to idolatrous uses does not enter into the discussion at all. The whole difficulty therefore disappears if we bear in mind that 20:4 speaks of idolatry practiced by means of images and not of the making of images in general.

Did the Lord Sanction Adultery? (Ex 20:14; Nu 31:18)

This pair of passages presents so little difficulty from the point of view of harmonization that it would not have been listed if it were not for the frivolous use that some unbelieving writers make of Nu 31:18. They maintain that the order contained in this passage was given so that the immoral desires of the Israelites might be served. If that were the case, then God would indeed be contradicting Himself, since in Ex 20:14 and in numerous other passages He forbids sexual immorality. But is the import of Nu 31:18 correctly understood by these critics? The command of God has its correct explanation in the fact that the women mentioned in Nu 31:18 had not been active in misleading the Israelites to participation in the immoral worship of Peor. Therefore, they were permitted to live, though they had to become the slaves of the Israelites. There was no sexual motive to which they owed their preservation.

Worship of God in the Wilderness (Ex 24:4; Am 5:25)

If Amos were denying that the children of Israel in the wilderness made any offerings to the true God, he would be contradicting Ex 24:4 and a number of other texts. So much is clear. But is that the intention of his words? What he denies in his question is that the children of Israel brought offerings to Yahweh for the space of 40 years. They did not have settled agricultural practices from which sacrifices might regularly be brought but received their chief sustenance from the daily manna the Lord supplied.

Also, Amos's question may recall Israel's problems with idolatry. While the Israelites had dedicated themselves to the service of Yahweh, they at times fell into idolatrous ways—for instance, when they induced Aaron to make the golden calf and proclaimed: "These are your gods, O Israel, who brought you up out of the land of Egypt!" (Ex 32:4). During their 40 years of wandering, the Israelites were by no means always faithful to the true God, but there were occasions when they flagrantly set aside the First Commandment. Amos 5:25 agrees with similar passages (Is 43:23; cf Lv 17:7; Dt 4:19) in describing this.

Therefore, it is right to say that Israel in the wilderness worshiped the true God and also that Israel did not bring sacrifices and offerings to God in the wilderness for 40 years.

God's Attitude toward Fraud (Ex 3:21–22; Lv 19:13)

The text from Leviticus has the endorsement of conscience: defrauding one's neighbor is a sin. But how shall we reconcile with it the command God gives the Israelites to borrow articles of silver and of gold from their Egyptian neighbors with the intention of taking these things along when their hurried exodus would take place? Let it be remembered that the Israelites were fully entitled to these valuables as payment for the long and arduous service that had been exacted from them. The Egyptians could not maintain that the loss that they suffered was an undeserved one. The Israelite women were to ask the Egyptians outright for these objects, and God would move the hearts of the Egyptians in such a way that they would not refuse to give the articles to the Israelites.

It may be thought that the last words of v 22, "So you shall plunder the Egyptians," indicate that a kind of fraud was intended and was to be practiced. The term *plunder* actually implies a result of military victory rather than common robbery. In fact, the Hebrew word can mean "deliver," as though Israel was rescuing these articles from the Egyptian oppressors! The prophecy of God simply says that the Egyptians would willingly part with their belongings at the request of the Israelites but would afterwards regret that they had readily yielded up their property to their former servants, feeling that they had suffered a great loss.

Is God a Lover of Peace? (Ex 15:3; Rm 15:33)

Do these two texts contradict each other? It is true that the one pictures God as a mighty warrior, while the other calls Him the God of peace. But not even according to our human standards are these two attributes irreconcilable. Some of our great war heroes were essentially of a peaceful disposition. The two passages simply supplement each other. The Bible describes God as both just and loving, almighty and merciful, a terror to all who do evil and at the same time the support of all who are His children, as one who avenges unrighteousness and yet is peaceful and a promoter of peace. To all who accept God as He has revealed Himself to us in the Bible, the above texts are not conflicting.

Egypt's Abu Sinbel temple wall showing slaves that were used for building the temple. God commanded Israel not to treat slaves and foreigners the way the Egyptians had treated them (Ex 20:10).

Why Was the Law of the Sabbath Given?
(Ex 20:11; Dt 5:15)

Many Bible readers have noticed that the commandment enjoining the keeping of the Sabbath day is motivated differently in Ex 20:11 and Dt 5:15. The former passage bases the Sabbath law on the resting of the Lord on the seventh day after the creation of the world and hallowing this day; the second, on the rest that the Lord provided for Israel after the years of wearisome toil in Egypt. It is true that the Sabbath law is not promulgated for the same reason in both passages. But does this constitute a discrepancy? The simple explanation is that God gave this commandment for several reasons, and on the one occasion the one is named, on the other occasion the other. Similarly we may say to someone, "Believe in Jesus because He is the true God"; at another time we may say, "Believe in Jesus because He is the only Redeemer." We are not thereby contradicting ourselves, for we are not denying the second time what we said the first time, but are simply giving an additional reason.

Attitude Toward One's Parents (Ex 20:12; Lk 14:26)

How can we harmonize the great commandment teaching respect and honor toward our parents with the saying of Jesus that everyone who wishes to be His disciple has to hate father and mother? There is a verbal difficulty here, but no real one. We must remember, to begin with, that Jesus Himself emphasized the commandment, "Honor your father and your mother," in the strongest possible manner. With stinging words He rebuked the Pharisees and scribes for setting aside this commandment when it conflicted with their own self-made regulations (Mk 7:9–13)! Hence from the purely historical point of view it would be impossible to assume that Jesus in Lk 14:26 means to abrogate the great commandment that speaks of the proper attitude toward one's parents. Again, the same Jesus who taught that we should love even our enemies would certainly not command His followers to nurse hatred of their parents in their hearts. When He says that His disciples must hate father and mother, He is employing the word *hate* in a peculiar sense.

A little searching in the Bible will show that the term "to hate" was used in the sense of "to love or value less." The most striking proof for this meaning is found in the story of Jacob, of whom the sacred narrative says: "He loved Rachel more than Leah, and he served Laban another seven years" (Gn 29:30). And then Moses continues (v 31): "When the LORD saw that Leah was hated . . ." Thus Moses, in describing the attitude of Jacob toward Leah, uses two terms that evidently equate loving less and hating. The second is simply more vivid and expressive than the first. Here we have proof that the Bible employs the word *hate* now and then in a figurative sense, denoting not the opposite of love but a lesser degree of love. What Jesus demands is that the highest love of His disciples be given to Him. "Whoever loves father or mother more than Me is not worthy of Me" (Mt 10:37)— that is the thought expressed here. Our devotion to Jesus should be so strong, so pure, of so elevated a nature, that in comparison with it our attachment to human beings, even to those to whom we owe our lives, must dwindle.

Validity of the Sabbath Law (Ex 31:16–17; Col 2:16)

The difficulty here lies in the fact that the one text seems to ascribe perpetual validity to the Sabbath law, while the other very emphatically declares that this law has been abrogated in the New Testament era. But all those who find a contradiction here have failed to notice that the text from Exodus very plainly says that the Sabbath law has been given to the children of Israel; that the Sabbath was to be a sign between Yahweh and the children of Israel forever. As long as Israel was God's chosen people, set apart from all other nations, this law was in force. In the New Testament the situation has changed. There is no longer any nation that God regards as His own in a special sense. The covenant that He made with Israel on Mount Sinai has been fulfilled. The covenant that the Lord made through the redemption of Christ embraces all nations (cf Jn 4:21–24; Ac 10:15). The meaning of Ex 31:16–17 may be given thus: As long as there are children of

Israel (in the particular sense of covenant people), the Sabbath must be observed. "Forever" in this case means perpetually, as long as the conditions apply. When the law said that under certain conditions a person would be a servant forever (Ex 21:6), that meant, of course, as long as that person lived or until the Year of Jubilee. The law did not imply servitude after death. Hence, when God says to Israel: "[The Sabbath] is a sign forever between Me and the people of Israel," that meant as long as the nation was in existence as God's peculiar people. The same explanation applies to the laws respecting circumcision, sacrifices, and other external ordinances (cf Gn 17:7; Ex 12:14; Lv 3:17; 6:13, 18).

Can Weariness Be Ascribed to God?
(Ex 31:17; Is 40:28)

The text from Isaiah agrees with all the conceptions that we have noted from the Scriptures concerning God—that He is almighty, infinite, unchangeable, a spirit, and not subject to fatigue and exhaustion. The statements made several times in the Scriptures that God rested (e.g., Gn 2:2–3), and especially the text from Exodus quoted above, saying that God was refreshed, seem to conflict with this picture. First we should mention that the phrase "God rested" had for the Hebrews the significance, "God ceased to work." The Hebrew verb translated "rested" is *shabat,* from which the word *Sabbath* is derived. One may find "to cease" as the first meaning listed for this verb in a Hebrew lexicon. Genesis 8:22 illustrates the point: "While the earth remains, seedtime and harvest, cold and heat, summer and winter, day and night, shall not cease." "Shall not cease" is a translation of the verb *shabat.* Here, the meaning "to rest," in our sense of the term, would be out of place. Hence there can be no doubt that *shabat* really has the significance "to stop." If it is given this meaning in Ex 31:17, the difficulty caused by the verb "rested" has been disposed of.

But now the question arises, "What of the statement that God was refreshed"? Like all other peoples, so the Hebrews, too, had their figures of speech which were not intended to be understood literally. If we translate "God was refreshed" literally from the Hebrew of Ex 31:17, the rendering would be, "God breathed freely," namely, like one who had just labored strenuously. Evidently this is merely a picturesque expression in keeping with eastern forms of speech. This literary device that describes God in human ways is called anthropomorphism ("having human form"). In this case the meaning is simply that God finished the task He planned to perform.

FURTHER STUDY

Lay/Bible Class Resources

Cole, R. Alan. *Exodus.* TOTC. Downers Grove, IL: InterVarsity Press, 1972. ♬ Compact commentary interacting with a variety of English translations. A popular but generally helpful evangelical treatment of the text.

Grundmann, Fred. *Exodus: By His Mighty Hand.* GWFT. St. Louis: Concordia, 1995. ♬ Lutheran author. Thirteen-session Bible study, including leader's notes and discussion questions.

Kern, Alma, John R. Wilch, Paul Raabe, Leland Stevens, Jan Brunette, and Edward A. Engelbrecht. *Exodus: Parts 1 and 2.* Leaders Guide and Enrichment Magazine/Study Guide. LL. St. Louis: Concordia, 2003. ♬ Two in-depth, nine-session Bible studies with individual, small group, and lecture portions.

Life by His Word. St. Louis: Concordia, 2009. ♬ More than 1,500 reproducible one-page Bible studies covering each chapter of the canonical Scriptures. Page references to *The Lutheran Study Bible.* CD-Rom and downloadable.

Ramm, Bernard L. *His Way Out: A Fresh Look at Exodus.* Ventura, CA: Regal Books, 1974. ♬ Solid and delightfully written.

Wendland, Ernst H. *Exodus.* PBC. St. Louis: Concordia, 2005. ♬ Lutheran author. Excellent for Bible classes. Based on the NIV translation.

Church Worker Resources

Davis, John D. *Moses and the Gods of Egypt: Studies in Exodus.* 2nd ed. Grand Rapids: Baker, 1986. ♬ A study of Exodus with special reference to the first 12 chapters in the light of recent archaeological and historical studies. Popularly written and thoroughly conservative. Especially helpful in relating the ten plagues to Egyptian gods.

Sarna, Nahum. *Exploring Exodus: The Origins of Biblical Israel.* New York: Schocken, 1996. ♬ A comparison of the biblical exodus account with Egyptian, Assyrian, Canaanite, and Babylonian history and culture, which emphasizes the value of the biblical narrative.

Academic Resources

Cassuto, Umberto. *Commentary on the Book of Exodus.* Publisher's Row/Varda Press, 2005. ♬ Rabbinic scholar. Work translated from the Hebrew edition published in the 1960s. Focused on the Masoretic text, its value as literature, and philology. Rejects JEDP.

Childs, Brevard S. *The Book of Exodus.* OTL. Philadelphia: Westminster, 1974. ♬ A useful, moderately critical resource. Carefully traces the history of interpretation and reacts against the more critical handling of the text. A "biblical theology" product.

Durham, John I. *Exodus.* WBC. Dallas: Word, 1987. ♬ More recent, full-length, academic commentary. Mildly critical, but often helpful, if used with caution.

Fretheim, Terence E. *Exodus: Interpretation Bible Commentary.* Louisville: Westminster John Knox Press, 1991. ♬ Exegetical and theological commentary from a moderate critic seeking contemporary application of the text.

K&D. *Biblical Commentary on the Old Testament: the Pentateuch.* Vol. 2. Grand Rapids: Eerdmans, 1959 reprint. ♬ A careful handling of theological issues in Exodus by a Lutheran scholar. Makes purposeful use of both Hebrew and Aramaic. This century-and-a-half old work should not be overlooked. Despite its age, it remains a most useful commentary on the Hebrew text.

Lange, John Peter. *Exodus.* LCHS. New York: Charles Scribner's Sons, 1876. ♬ A helpful, older example of German biblical scholarship, based on the Hebrew text, which provides references to significant commentaries from the Reformation era forward.

LEVITICUS

You shall be holy, for I the Lord your God am holy

Among the ruddy granite peaks at the south end of the Sinai wilderness, the Lord gave the Law to His people through the prophet Moses. About 40 years earlier, Moses climbed a particular peak to view the burning bush where the Lord introduced Himself (c 1446; Ex 3). Moses would refer to this peak as "the mount of the LORD" (Nu 10:33). It never became a part of Israel's territory, though it may have been a place of pilgrimage for believers as early as the ninth century BC (1Ki 19). According to early Christian tradition, Jebel Musa is the particular peak hallowed by God's nearer presence when He consecrated Israel and set apart the tribe of Levi for priestly service at the newly erected tabernacle.

The name Exodus ("the way out") shows that the Book of Exodus tells about God's people on their way out of Egypt. In a similar way, the name Leviticus (drawn from "Levites") tells us that in the Book of Leviticus we learn about the duties of the people in their worship life, led by the Levites. This focus on worship follows naturally after the account of the construction of the tabernacle, the place for worship and sacrifice, in the last chapters of Exodus.

Although the Book of Leviticus seems to stand independently, it is actually part of a broader record of the moral, ceremonial, and civil laws God gave to Israel through Moses during the year Israel spent at Mount Sinai. The 56 chapters from Ex 20–Nu 8 contain very little history (as one finds in the other 97 chapters of Genesis,

View from the summit of Jebel Musa, believed to be Mount Sinai. The events of Leviticus likely took place on a nearby plain.

OVERVIEW

Author
Moses the prophet

Date
c 1445 BC

Places
Wilderness of Sinai; tabernacle in the Israelite camp

People
Moses; Aaron and his sons: Nadab, Abihu, Eleazar, Ithamar; elders and congregation of Israel

Purpose
To teach Israel how God shares His holiness with them and how they should live in His holiness

Law Themes
Uncleanness; sin requires blood sacrifices; diseases resulting from sin; walking in God's statutes and commands

Gospel Themes
Cleansing; atonement; redemption; "I am the LORD your God"; consecration; rest

Memory Verses
Teach the people (10:10–11); holy to the Lord (11:45; 20:26); atonement (16:30–34); sacrifice only to the Lord (17:1–5)

TIMELINE

1529 BC	Aaron born
1526 BC	Moses born
1446 BC	Exodus from Egypt
c 1445 BC	Events of Leviticus
1406 BC	Israel crosses the Jordan

Exodus, and Numbers). They are mostly laws and present a unique body of material within the broader composition of the books. Divisions between Exodus, Leviticus, and Numbers may have resulted from practical necessity, such as the length of text that could commonly fit on a scroll. Leviticus may, therefore, be a scroll-length division capped off with, "These are the commandments that the LORD commanded Moses for the people of Israel on Mount Sinai" (Lv 27:34). These factors illustrate how the Books of Moses were likely composed together and in view of one another with the worship focus of Leviticus standing at their heart. Such an observation may also encourage modern readers to understand the value that the content of Leviticus held in the eyes of ancient Israel.

Entrance to a copper mine at Timna, Israel, north of the Gulf of Aqaba.

Historical and Cultural Setting

As noted in the introduction to Exodus, in the fifteenth century BC Sinai was of remote interest to the Egyptians, who traveled the "way of the sea" to reach more strategic locations in western Asia such as Lebanon and Syria. The Egyptians had established successful copper and turquoise mines in the Sinai region, as evident from the ancient slag piles and mines explored by archaeologists. But Israel would have enjoyed relative peace in the rocky valleys to which God led them since the Egyptians commonly reached their mines by ship rather than by land.

The other regional power was the Midianites, whose civilization was centered east of the Gulf of Aqaba. Whatever the political or cultural development of the Midianites may have been during this period, the Midianites we meet in Moses' account were friendly to Israel and assisted them in the wilderness (Ex 2–4, 8; Nu 25, 31). Israel spent about a year encamped at Sinai in c 1445 BC before setting out for the Promised Land, following the Levites who bore the ark of the covenant.

COMPOSITION

Author(s)

See pp 4–11.

Date of Composition

Leviticus describes events in c 1445 BC while Israel was at Mount Sinai. See pp 4–11.

Purpose/Recipients

Temple for the Egyptian goddess Hathor at Timna copper mines.

As the shortest book of the Pentateuch, Leviticus may seem like the longest because of its profusion of details about worship. The book is important because, as part of the covenant, it provides fuller instruction for Israel's relationship to God. Rather than introduce new or different instructions, Leviticus elaborates, applies, and implements principles already set forth in Exodus, explaining what it means to be God's holy people.

Literary Features

Genre

As noted above, Leviticus is primarily a legal code that includes a few stories that illustrate the gravity of the Law.

Characters

As a legal code, the Book of Leviticus includes few characters, some of whom were introduced in Exodus. Moses, a member of the tribe of Levi, acts as God's Lawgiver. His brother Aaron is consecrated as high priest, while Aaron's sons are consecrated as priests. The elders of Israel are mentioned as a distinct body of leaders who represent their distinct tribes and the whole congregation of Israel in some rituals (4:15; 9:1). Under the Law, Israel may be treated collectively, i.e., God may judge them all together but He may also call on the congregation as a unit to mete out punishment on an individual (e.g., ch 24).

Chapter 10 focuses specifically on the sons of Aaron, Nadab and Abihu, who violated God's Law and suffered immediate death. They were replaced by Aaron's other sons, Eleazar and Ithamar, who served nobly. Eleazar would further distinguish himself as a leader, as described in the Book of Numbers (see p 129).

One other group deserves mention: the Canaanites. The Lord refers to them as negative examples whom Israel must not imitate (18:3).

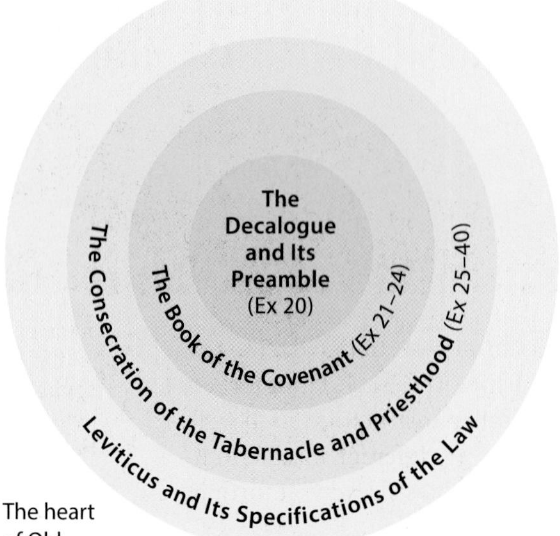

Narrative Development or Plot

Although Leviticus stands as an independent Book of Scripture, it continues from the story of Exodus. God chose to present the Law as successive and ever-widening concentric circles begun in Exodus, as illustrated here.

Although the multitude of individual directives in Leviticus may seem bewildering, keep in mind the whole picture—an entire complex of legislation designed to instruct the Israelites on how they are to respond to God's covenant of undeserved goodness and grace. Its recurring theme (as throughout the Pentateuch) is "You shall be holy, for I the LORD your God am holy" (Lv 19:2; cf 11:45; Ex 19:6).[1] To be a holy nation, Israel, inwardly and outwardly, is to be separated from all that defiles. They are dedicated to God by a life of purity.

These requirements provide a general structure to Leviticus. Holiness requires, first of all, cleansing from sin by a sacrificial atonement. Such a holy people then express desire for reconciliation with God and enjoy the resultant communion with God by presenting various offerings. A holy people also will give evidence of dedication to God by observing God's ordinances for a life that is consecrated to Him according to His will.

Leviticus also contains three historical events that highlight obedience (and disobedience) to the covenant: (1) Moses, following the prescriptions in Ex 29, consecrates those who are to serve in the tabernacle (Lv 8–9). (2) Nadab and Abihu, two sons of Aaron, fail to follow the directions of sacri-

The heart of Old Testament law was the Ten Commandments (Decalogue) to which the Lord added other moral, ceremonial, and civil laws.

The Decalogue and Its Preamble (Ex 20)

The Book of the Covenant (Ex 21–24)

The Consecration of the Tabernacle and Priesthood (Ex 25–40)

Leviticus and Its Specifications of the Law

---

1 The word *holy* and its derivatives occur some 130 times in Leviticus.

fice and are consumed by fire (10:1–7). (3) A man is punished (stoned) for violating the law against blasphemy (24:10–23).

Resources

Unlike the other Books of Moses, Leviticus does not refer explicitly to other ancient documents. Nonetheless, scholars typically refer to chs 11–15 as the "manual of purity" because of its unified content. (Chs 1–7 may be referred to as the "manual of offerings"; see outline.) A portion of Leviticus may also sometimes be referred to as a legal "code," though the book itself does not describe any element circulating as an independent document.

Text and Translations

The traditional Hebrew text of Leviticus, like that of the other Books of Moses, is well preserved. The Samaritans preserved their own version of the book, which includes some unique readings. The LXX text of Leviticus is a very literal rendering of the Hebrew, with occasional passages providing a more clearly Greek idiom. Seventeen fragments of Leviticus manuscripts were found at Qumran, which support the traditional Hebrew text.

DOCTRINAL CONTENT

Summary Commentary

Chs 1–3 In His grace, God provides a means through which He can "dwell" among sinners: the sacrifice of animals on behalf of the people. Through the sacrifices and grain offerings, God also provides His Old Testament priests with food. The remaining grain becomes most holy once the priest burns the memorial portion. Through the peace offering on high holy days and special occasions, God provides meat for a sacrificial banquet, which a family could share with invited guests (7:11–36; 19:5–6; 23:37). Peace offerings acknowledge God's grace toward His people.

4:1–6:7 God, who abhors all sin, distinguishes sins of error from those of intent. Because of sin, God could no longer dwell with the Israelites as He desired. To this end, God gave the sin offering for the deliverance of those who inadvertently sinned against Him (cf 4:20, 26, 31, 35). The Lord also describes the sacrifice and compensations of the guilt offering for mending relationships with God and with neighbor.

6:8–7:38 God would have fellowship with His people only after atoning for their sin through sacrifice. The people had to be ritually clean to partici-

Continued on p 106.

OUTLINE

The theocratic nation has been organized, the covenant ratified (justification), and the tabernacle erected, but before Israel continues its journey to the Promised Land, it also needs regulations regarding worship in the tabernacle and the ensuing holiness of life. Leviticus supplies that need.

The book's outline is impressively simple, all of it concerned with the sanctification requisite to serve the holy God. Chapters 1–16 mostly record laws concerning the removal of the defilement (unholiness or uncleanness) separating man and God, and chs 17–26 again summarize and illustrate the behavior appropriate to the purified people of God (the so-called Holiness Code). Chapter 27 might be viewed as an independent appendix.

I. Israelite Involvement in the Divine Service (chs 1–15)

  A. Manual of Offerings (chs 1–7)

    1. Voluntary, God-pleasing offerings (chs 1–3)

      a. Divine legislation for private offerings (1:1–2)

      b. Regulations for burnt offerings (1:3–17)

      c. Regulations for grain offerings (ch 2)

      d. Regulations for peace offerings (ch 3)

    2. Mandatory offerings for atonement (4:1–6:7)

      a. Regulations for sin offerings (4:1–5:13)

      b. Regulations for guilt offerings (5:14–6:7)

    3. Consumption of holy food (6:8–7:38)

      a. Daily public offering (6:8–18)

      b. Daily grain offering of high priest (6:19–23)

      c. Occasional offerings of Israelites (6:24–7:21)

      d. Prohibited food: fat and blood (7:22–27)

      e. Priest's portion of peace offerings (7:28–36)

      f. Conclusion of the manual of offerings (7:37–38)

pate in the meal God prepared for them (7:19–21). This section concludes God's manual of offerings, a precise manual meant to be strictly followed by priests and individuals. Here is God's framework to prepare an unholy people to dwell with a holy God.

Chs 8–10 Moses consecrates Aaron as high priest and Aaron's sons as priests. Aaron then begins his priestly duties with God's approval. The story of Nadab and Abihu's thoughtlessness shows us that God is present in grace and in wrath. The God who justifies sinners also condemns those who will not sanctify the Lord.

Ch 11–15 These laws are sometimes called the manual of purity. Each dietary regulation was lovingly put in place so that God might protect His people from death, such as what was experienced by Nadab and Abihu, who died because of their impurity. Childbirth also made a woman ceremonially unclean. The rules in ch 12 exempt the new mother from the rigors of the Law and her typical role in family/community life. They also promise cleansing and restoration. Infectious skin diseases, whether of the body or of clothing, make individuals unclean. Priestly legislation keeps God's people clean, so that God might dwell among them and bless them (cf Ex 25:8). Leviticus shows that disease is a consequence of the fall into sin, which isolates God's people outside the boundaries He established, but God provides the means to readmit those whose skin disease is healed. Infected individuals and homes must be removed from God's presence. In His mercy, God provides His priests with purification rites to cleanse individuals and homes. Ritual impurity separates God from His people. God's declaration that semen and menstrual blood cause uncleanness prevents His people from engaging in ritual prostitution. Chapter 15 shows God providing a means to remove impurity and to make His people clean again.

Ch 16 Once a year, on the 10th day of the seventh month, God implemented a mandatory Day of Atonement. Ritual sacrifices cleansed the sanctuary, tent of meeting, altar, priests, and the entire congregation from their sins. The chief cleansing agent was blood, which pointed forward to Jesus' sacrifice.

Chs 17–22 These laws apply to the sanctuary. God proclaims His dwelling place as the exclusive place for sacrifices. He does not want His people running after false gods. He also forbids the wanton killing of birds and other animals. Chapter 18 shows that sexual purity is so important to God that He issues decrees detailing how to protect it. Only intercourse between a husband and wife is approved by God. By His grace, He also chooses to dwell among His people and shower them with blessings. By His hand, they were delivered from the corruption of Egypt; by His hand, they would drive out the Canaanites and settle in their land; and by His hand, the land would bring forth its abundance. In response for all He has done, God commands the loyalty of His people.

God sets His priests apart. They determine what is holy and what is common (10:10). Such an important responsibility requires rules to protect their consecration before God so that they would not die as did Nadab and Abihu. All the people are responsible for helping priests maintain their sacred status before God. Leviticus shows that our God is a holy God who shares His holiness with His people. By keeping God's ordinances, the Israelites reflect God's love back to Him and to one another. Failure to keep God's commands destroys any assurance of God's acceptance of their sacrifice and of them.

Ch 23 Chapter 23 represents a liturgical calendar for the Israelites. All such festivals and Sabbaths prefigure Christ (Col 2:16–17). Remembrance of God's deliverance of the Israelites from Egypt was the most important component in their liturgical calendar. He made redemption the chief theme of their service. Ritual celebrations also remind the Israelites of God's blessing of the harvest. The Day of Atonement was the great day of rest in the Sabbath month (Lv 23:32), with no work performed the entire day. Like Passover, the Day of Atonement commemorated God's mercy and was an annual call to repentance and faith. The Feast of Booths concluded the festive half of the liturgy that began at Passover and commemorated Israel's safe travel on the way to the Promised Land.

24:1–16 Aaron or his sons receive a series of special ordinances: first, attend the lamps twice daily to maintain light in the Holy Place. The second ordinance involves the bread of the Presence. Each Sabbath, the high priest sets 12 new loaves before the Lord (v 8). The third ordinance (vv 1–4) deals with God's holy name. God equates this blasphemy with the sin of idolatry because it undermined true worship. Blasphemers were cursed by God (cf Mt 25:41).

24:17–25:55 God establishes a system for administering justice based on equity and compensation for loss, which deals with personal injury, use of property, and debt. Just as humankind needs a Sabbath rest, so the land needs rest. Because the land belongs to God, it was returned to Him every seventh year. The Year of Jubilee also provides God's people with restored freedoms since freedom, family, property rights, and devotion make a nation strong. Land is God's gift to His people through their tribes and clans. At all times, land sold by a poor family member could be redeemed. God expects

His people to honor Him for His great provisions by treating others with respect (Ex 20:12–17). Those who entered bond-service because of debts were to be treated with respect, for they did not belong to their master but to God.

Ch 26 This chapter presents the twin themes of blessings and curses found throughout the Lord's teaching. Failure to obey God's statutes, rules, and laws results in punishment. God's discipline intensifies as the disobedience intensifies against Him. One by one, God removes His blessings in order to lead His people back to Him in repentance, that He may again shower them with His grace (2Pt 3:9).

Ch 27 Leviticus concludes by showing how all God's people are involved in the stewardship of God's house. Based on how God has blessed them, each Israelite provides materials and finances for the maintenance of God's sanctuary for the ongoing operation of the Divine Service.

Samaritan Passover sacrifice on Mount Gerizim.

Specific Law Themes

Leviticus addresses problems of both physical and spiritual uncleanness, emphasizing the holiness or uniqueness of God and His people. Because mankind is sinful, blood sacrifices are necessary to hallow them. Sacrifices bring together (1) the problem of sin causing death with (2) substitutionary death bringing about life. Diseases are also regarded as resulting from sin so that healing and cleansing are not merely medicinal or hygienic activities but spiritual acts. Leviticus returns to earlier biblical themes of *walking* before God by keeping His statutes and commands.

Specific Gospel Themes

The Law themes in Leviticus typically have Gospel counterparts. Uncleanness is overcome by cleansing, offense is removed through atonement, and loss is restored through redemption.

The Lord reminds Israel 49 times, "I am the LORD your God," emphasizing the exclusive relationship God provides them through the covenant. They belong to the Lord and He belongs to them. He consecrates them as a kingdom of priests and gives them rest (Sabbath).

Specific Doctrines

Few texts tend to be as opaque and forbidding to the modern reader as these laws of Leviticus. The texts themselves contain little explicit theology. Both aversion to ritual and spiritualistic prejudices may hinder readers from comprehending the holistic assumptions of biblical theology: sin has corrupted the whole person, body as well as spirit, and the remedy must correspond.

Purity and Marriage

Leviticus 18 continues to serve as a crucial source of teaching on purity in matters of sexuality and marriage, as the Church Fathers emphasized it over the centuries. The prohibitions are not simply negative but actually begin with a promise that those who observe them "shall live by them" (18:5). In an era of dreaded communicable diseases that are indeed life threatening, one may readily see the practical value of this teaching. God painstakingly restricts human sexual practices to a husband and a wife alone.

Love Your Neighbor

A second passage that has always caught the attention of theologians, including Jesus and the Jewish teachers during His ministry, is "You shall love your neighbor as yourself: I am the LORD" (19:18). The broader teaching warns against hatred and urges clear communication and relationships rather than vengeance that seeks personal gain at another person's expense. The New Testament emphasizes that love is the fulfilling of the Law, which puts the seemingly humdrum statutes of Leviticus in a different light.

Sacrifice, Atonement, and Satisfaction

In one sense, the New Testament's prominent typological use of the subjects in Leviticus should end any thought that the teachings are obscure from us today. "Vicarious satisfaction," "Lamb of God," etc., are scarcely comprehensible apart from an understanding of these passages of the Law. The typological connection would be impossible if Old Testament worship were informed by merely ritual theology rather than by grace.

We must first understand Old Testament sacrifice on its own terms. At the same time, if biblical theology is a unity, we must also approach it in essentially the same way as the New Testament teaches us to regard *our* "sacrifices" of money, time, etc. Sacrifice likewise had a "eucharistic" aspect; it was a prayer-act of thanksgiving accompanying and confirming, as it were, the verbal prayers thanking God for His covenant gifts. Further, the sacrifices were God-ordained means of grace for atoning for sin and satisfying His righteous wrath. This list of things to consider illustrates just how Leviticus is in its content and teaching.

Sacrifices as Sacraments

From an earthly perspective, Israel's sacrifices have much in common with sacrifices all over the world, but Israel's sacrifices are *sacraments*. From God's side they belong to the realm of justification: God used them to hallow His people and declare them just or righteous. One major evidence of this is the fact that no sacrifices were valid for willful, deliberate sins (committed "with a high hand"); these, if repented of, were apparently covered only by the comprehensive offering on the Day of Atonement.

Three sacrificial motifs may be helpfully distinguished: (1) gift (of thanksgiving); (2) communion; and (3) atonement and/or satisfaction. Conspicuous by its absence is a sacrifice that usually prevailed in surrounding paganism: feeding of the gods. Sometimes the Bible even explicitly polemicizes against such notions (Ps 50; Mi 6). Each of the three biblical motifs is especially prominent in certain sacrifices: gift in the whole burnt and grain offerings; communion in the peace offerings, and forgiveness in the sin and guilt offerings. All three motifs, however, also interpenetrate one another—all of the concepts seem to be present in all sacrifices.

Two teachings also dominate the last half of Leviticus: atonement (*kaphar*) and satisfaction (*qodesh*). In both we meet the same holism of the physical and the spiritual, the ritual and the ethical, which we encountered in connection with "uncleanness," and which the modern mind finds so difficult. Possibly the term *sacramental* is the best term for describing the unity of internal and external aspects found in gift, communion, and atonement/satisfaction.

Atonement (expiation) is not simply the same as "forgiveness," but implies a decontamination, a cleansing of a physical as well as a spiritual order. Sin here is not only in the mind or will, but a negative force (a miasma) that invades all parts of the material world as well. Something as physical as blood is necessary to effect atonement, as though the physical heat of the sacrificial blood was removing the icy deadliness of divine wrath, so that God and man might endure one another's presence in peace.

Sacrifices, Grace, and Holiness

We must give full weight to the biblical emphasis that the true God Himself graciously provides the means by which His righteous wrath may be allayed. In a way, this was the point of the entire covenant, old as well as new. When seen this way, *atonement* and *satisfaction* become virtual synonyms, but both are likely to be misunderstood without the corrective emphasis supplied by the other.

The situation is similar with *holiness*. Our common definition of the term, "without sin," is acceptable only if accompanied by a comprehensive, despiritualizing definition of "sin." Objects and bodies are "holy" or "unholy" in the Bible as well as minds and wills. God is "wholly other," separated from the "common" or "secular." Holiness certainly is not merely *one* of His attributes. Sometimes the Bible reserves the idea of holiness entirely for God and describes its gracious communication to mankind under the rubric of His "glory." An old saying summarizes it aptly: "God's glory is His holiness revealed, His holiness is His glory concealed."

Reading through the ritual complexities of Leviticus is not an act of penance, but it may lead to repentance. It should drum into modern ears the inviolability of God's laws within every detail, within every area of one's relationship to Him and to other people. Leviticus teaches what Jesus taught: "You therefore must be perfect, as your heavenly Father is perfect" (Mt 5:48). People today, too, are unholy unless they love their neighbor as themselves (Lv 19:18; cf Mt 22:39 and parallel passages). In a day that has lost the sense of the holy, the Book of Leviticus should be read. St. Paul wrote:

> Are we to continue in sin that grace may abound? By no means! How can we who died to sin [sacrificed] still live in it? Do you not know that all of us who have been baptized into Christ Jesus were baptized into His death? We were buried therefore with Him by baptism into death, in order that, just as Christ was raised from the dead by the glory of the Father, we too might walk in newness of life. (Rm 6:1–4)

This famous New Testament passage is replete with themes from Leviticus, reminding us of how central the book's teaching is to Christian doctrine.

Application

Chs 1–3 Just as the Israelites faithfully confessed their sins and prayed to the Lord during their sacrifices, present your confession of sins and prayers of repentance and faith before Him in the name of "the Lamb of God, who takes away the sin of the world!" (Jn 1:29). At the Lamb's invitation, we come to the Lord's Table, where we receive His true body and blood, a holy meal God Himself prepares for the forgiveness of sins. Jesus' death was God's great peace offering for the world, since the Father brought about our peace and reconciliation through Jesus.

Holy Communion is the Passover celebration that Jesus revised for His disciples.

4:1–6:7 Just as God's Old Testament people publicly confessed their sins during divine worship, God's people today confess their sins of thought, word, and deed. In the Law, the Lord calls us to something far greater than self-interest. He wants us to mend relationships with others. Praise God, His attitude toward us is merciful and self-giving; He desires our atonement.

6:8–7:38 God's people today eat a meal in His presence each time they partake of Holy Communion as God's priests (cf 1Pt 2:9). Christ's body was offered as a sin offering and a reparation offering to God. By His incarnation and atoning sacrifice, Jesus Christ is today our Immanuel, "God with us" to save us.

Chs 8–10 Jesus is our great High Priest (Heb 2:17; 3:1; 7:26). We come before Him as sinners in need of consecration. As with the Old Testament priests, it is God's cleansing that makes us holy. In Baptism, God washes us clean (1Co 6:11). He anoints us with the Holy Spirit (2Co 1:21–22). Christ Himself consecrates us as priests (Eph 5:26–27). God's people, the beneficiaries of His grace, should serve the Lord in reverence and awe (Heb 12:28–29).

Chs 11–15 Through the Law, God distinguished Israel and provided for their purification. These laws illustrate those themes of purification in our lives. We witness the minute details of God's Law. We also see God's grace and His hand of protection providing guidelines for what is clean and unclean for His Old Testament people.

Ch 16 The New Testament teaches that by His death, Jesus offered the perfect sacrifice and entered the heavenly sanctuary with His blood (Heb 9:11–14), opening the way for believers to enter into God's presence (Heb 6:20). In His blood alone is your atonement.

Chs 17–22 God's Law continues to reveal us as sinners deserving death (Rm 3:9–20), but Jesus reveals that He came not to condemn but to save sinners (Jn 3:17–18). Through Baptism, He grants new life in His Word (Rm

6:1–11; 1Co 6:9–11). Recognize that God made His people holy by grace, and in the Law He guides them away from the self-destructive customs of the nations. In the Gospel of Jesus Christ, believers have freedom from their sins, freedom to please God as His beloved, chosen people.

Ch 23 All Old Testament festivals and Sabbaths prefigure Christ (Col 2:16–17). The life of Jesus Christ shapes the Christian liturgical calendar, granting rest not only for our weary bodies but also for our weary souls. He is our Passover, the Bread of Life, our Pentecost, Atonement, and shelter. Walk with Him by faith. His peace will comfort you in all circumstances.

24:1–16 Aaron or his sons attend the lamps twice daily to maintain light in the Holy Place. As you serve the Lord daily, rejoice and attend the light of His Word, which enlightens the sanctuary of the heart. Jesus is the light of the world (Jn 8:12; 9:5). He gives His flesh as bread for all believers (Jn 6:51) and grants life (Jn 6:53–55). Hallow God's name (Mt 6:9), call on His name (1Co 1:2), and do everything in His name (Col 3:17).

24:17–25:55 All we have belongs to the Lord, our Maker and Redeemer. Honor Him with your property and life, even as He blesses and prospers you in His loving care. Those in Christ are likewise beneficiaries of God's grace (Ac 10:39–43). Because we are released from our debts, we are called to have mercy on others, to release them from their debt (Mt 6:12). We now await the restoration promised in the heavenly Jubilee (Ac 3:21).

Ch 26 Failure to walk with God brings painful consequences (Lv 26:14–39). Therefore, cling to God's Word, especially His promise that His people belong to Him (v 13). God's discipline intensifies as the disobedience intensifies against Him. One by one, God removes His blessings in order to lead His people back to Him in repentance, that He may again shower them with His grace (2Pt 3:9). The epitome of God's grace is seen at the cross, where His Son died to remove the curse brought by sin (cf 1Jn 1:9).

Ch 27 The collection of our offerings during the liturgy supports the services of God's house today (cf Ac 4:34–5:11). Our offerings are part of the holy work of God's people for the benefit of the world (Rm 15:27; 2Co 9:12). Through our offerings, we bear witness to what God has done through Calvary's cross.

CANONICITY

As part of the Torah, the most important portion of the Hebrew Scriptures for the Jews, the Book of Leviticus was treasured. Christians received the book without question.

LUTHERAN THEOLOGIANS ON LEVITICUS

Luther

"The special topic of the third book [Leviticus] is the appointment of the priesthood, with the statutes and laws according to which the priests are to act and to teach the people. There we see that a priestly office is instituted only because of sin, to disclose sin to the people and to make atonement before God, so that its entire function is to deal with sin and sinners. For this reason too no temporal wealth is given to the priests; neither are they commanded or permitted to rule men's bodies. Rather the only work assigned to them is to care for the people who are in sin." (AE 35:237–38)

Gerhard

"*The third Book of Moses* is called *Wayiqra'* by the Hebrews from the first word of the book. The Greeks and Latins call it 'Leviticus' because, most of all, it treats the Levitical priesthood and the Levitical or ceremonial laws. It has twenty-seven chapters and contains the history of one month, namely, of the first month of the second year after the departure from Egypt. Jerome, Epistle *ad Paulin.*, writes: 'In it almost every syllable breathes the heavenly mysteries because its figures lead us to Christ, the one great High Priest of the New Testament.' With regard to its objects it can be divided into three parts, the first of which treats *sacred things*; the second, *sacred persons*; the third, *sacred acts*." (ThC E1 § 121)

Questions People Ask About Leviticus

Leviticus: Outmoded or Relevant?

Leviticus introduced God's demand for holiness, which did not end with the old covenant. Consider just a few passages from the new covenant:

> Present your members as slaves to righteousness leading to sanctification. (Rm 6:19)

> Present your bodies a living sacrifice, holy and acceptable to God. (Rm 12:1)

> Let us cleanse ourselves from every defilement of body and spirit, bringing holiness to completion in the fear of God. (2Co 7:1)

> We should be holy and blameless before Him. (Eph 1:4)

> [He] called us to a holy calling, not because of our works but because of His own purpose and grace. (2Tm 1:9)

> As He who called you is holy, you also be holy in all your conduct. (1Pt 1:15)

Like Israel, the people of the new covenant must be holy in order to be in communion with God, and they must give evidence of that communion in holy worship and holy lives. Though many of the laws in Leviticus no longer apply (Gal 3:19–25), the book (indeed, all the Law) still provides profitable instruction in holy living (Rm 7:6; 12:1–2; 2Tm 3:16–17).

But since unholiness awaits God's people at every corner of life, they (like Israel) must be *accounted* holy:

> For in Him all the fullness of God was pleased to dwell, and through Him to reconcile to Himself all things, whether on earth or in heaven, making peace by the blood of His cross. And you, who once were alienated and hostile in mind, doing evil deeds, He has now reconciled in His body of flesh by His death, in order to present you holy and blameless and above reproach before Him. (Col 1:19–22)

This reconciliation is once and for all; every sin becomes contemporary with it and is atoned. The Lamb of God, slaughtered 20 centuries ago, gave benefit for

115

sins committed today as well as for Israel's sins long ago, for "it is impossible for the blood of bulls and goats to take away sins" (Heb 10:4).

The sacrifices of the Old Testament have been abrogated because they pointed forward to the blood of Christ, who has come. Yet even the New Testament believer (who is, at the same time, a sinner with "natural" thinking) needs to read of them and hear again and again the underlying theology:

Sin is not a trivial matter. Every breaking of God's will, including unwitting sin, has deadly consequences.

People can do nothing to make themselves acceptable to God. Their forfeited lives can be redeemed only by an atonement, a substitution, that God has "given on the altar."

People daily need to seek the forgiving mercy of God.

Total redemption calls forth a total response and commitment to God. Holy living is living wholly to God. "You therefore must be perfect, as your heavenly Father is perfect" (Mt 5:48).

The Israelites of old may not have understood or anticipated all this—or needed to. They had faith in the promised deliverance of God, a deliverance fulfilled in the coming of the Deliverer, the Lamb of God, who was offered as the final, perfect sacrifice. They received forgiveness and salvation through their trust in the promised deliverance. Whenever Israel brought sacrifices to confess sins and beg forgiveness, God accepted the sacrifices and used them as a channel of His forgiving mercy. Of this Luther says very fittingly and decisively:

We treat of the forgiveness of sins in two ways. First, how it is achieved and won. Second, how it is distributed and given to us. Christ has achieved it on the cross, it is true. But he has not distributed or given it on the cross. . . . He has distributed and given it through the Word, as also in the gospel, where it is preached. He has won it once for all on the cross. But the distribution takes place continuously, before and after, from the beginning of the world. For inasmuch as he had determined once to achieve it, it made no difference to him whether he distributed it before or after [the cross], through his Word, as can easily be proved from Scripture. . . . When we consider the application of the forgiveness, we are not dealing with a particular time, but find that it has taken place from the beginning of the world. So St. John in the Book of Revelation [13:8] says that the Lamb of God was slain before the foundation of the world. (AE 40:213–15)

By God's design, the sacrifices pointed beyond themselves to the Sacrifice by which the old sacrifices were valid as means of God's grace.

Were Sacrifices Pleasing to God?

Leviticus 1:9 commands: "Its entrails and its legs he shall wash with water. And the priest shall burn all of it on the altar, as a burnt offering, a food offering with a sweet aroma to the LORD."

Isaiah 1:11 asks: " 'What to Me is the multitude of your sacrifices?' says the LORD. 'I have had enough of burnt offerings of rams and the fat of well-fed beasts. I do not delight in the blood of bulls, or of lambs, or of goats.' "

In a number of passages in the writings of Moses, as in Lv 1:9, the children of Israel were ordered to offer up sacrifices to God, and they were told that these sacrifices were a sweet aroma, that is, that they were pleasing and acceptable to the Lord. That seems to be contradicted by the Isaiah passage, which has several parallels in the Psalms and the writings of the prophets, where apparently it is declared that God does not delight in the sacrifice of animals. We have here an interesting case, which shows that in considering apparent discrepancies the context in which the respective passages are found must be studied carefully. Examine carefully the first chapter of Isaiah, beginning at v 10. You will soon see that the Lord is not protesting against the offering up of sacrifices as such but against the manner and the spirit in which these sacrifices were brought by the contemporaries of Isaiah who did not repent and trust in the Lord's mercy. God tells the inhabitants of Jerusalem that He is weary not only of their burnt offerings but also of their appointed feasts and even of their prayers. Evidently their whole worship was an abomination to Him. Why? Because, as v 15 says, their hands were full of blood. They were a wicked generation. To escape the punishment they had merited and at the same time to be given an opportunity to continue their sinning, they offered up many sacrifices. Their opinion was that the mere performance of outward ceremonies would please God and thus furnish them the opportunity they coveted to continue in the path of evil. Wherever burnt offerings were brought in such a spirit, they proceeded from a deceitful heart and aroused God's anger instead of pleasing Him.

When God prescribes the numerous sacrifices mentioned in the laws of Moses and promises His blessings upon those who bring them, He always presupposes that the hearts of the worshipers are believing, humble, and obedient. At the time of the prophets the worship of Yahweh had degenerated largely into an external ceremonialism, which was offensive to God. The above remarks also apply, for instance, to Jer 6:20, where Yahweh declares sacrifices unacceptable. But, as 6:19 shows, He takes this attitude on account of the wickedness of those who offered them. A comparison with prayer will be helpful here. God has commanded prayer in a number of texts. But if the prayer is mere lip service, hypocritical worship, God abhors it. God does not in Is 1:11 contradict Lv 1:9. He merely expresses the pertinent additional truth that sacrificial worship, if not proceeding from a believing heart, is offensive in His sight.

A rock badger.

The Rock Badger and the Hare

In the listing of clean and unclean animals in Lv 11:5–6, two animals—the rock badger (a small mammal) and the hare—are here classified as ruminants (animals that chew their cud); however, according to zoology they do not belong to this classification. Critics have not been slow in saying that here Moses becomes guilty of an undeniable error. The law in question stated that animals that both chewed the cud and parted the hoof might be eaten, but those that did merely one or neither of these two things should be considered unclean.

The famous German biblical scholar Karl F. Keil says in his commentary on Leviticus:

> The hare and hyrax [badger] . . . were also unclean because, although they ruminate, they do not have cloven hoofs. It is true that modern naturalists affirm that the two latter do not ruminate at all, as they do not have the four stomachs that are common to ruminant animals; but they move the jaw sometimes in a manner which looks like ruminating, so that even Linnaeus affirmed that the hare chewed the cud, and Moses followed the popular opinion.

G. E. Post writes in *Hasting's Dictionary of the Bible, vol. 2* (under *hare*): "The hare is a rodent and not a ruminant. The statement (Lev. 11:6; Deut. 14:7) that it cheweth the cud is to be taken phenomenally, not scientifically." As Henry Baker Tristram well says:

> Moses speaks of animals according to appearances, and not with the precision of a comparative anatomist, and his object was to show why the hare should be interdicted, though to all appearance it chewed the cud, namely, because it did not divide the hoof.

Additionally, hares are known to chew their droppings that may be further digested (they have two kinds of droppings). Re-chewing their droppings produces a digestive process similar to rumination. As the experts above explain, we must remember that Moses is giving the children of Israel some practical rules that are to guide them in their choice of food. For that reason their own terms and their own descriptions are employed in designating clean and unclean animals. When all is considered, the difficulty that people have found in these verses must vanish.

Eating of Sacrificial Meals

Leviticus 7:15 asserts: "The flesh of the sacrifice of his peace offerings for thanksgiving shall be eaten on the day of his offering. He shall not leave any of it until the morning." (Cf Lv 22:30.)

Leviticus 19:6 declares: "It shall be eaten the same day you offer it or on the day after, and anything left over until the third day shall be burned up with fire."

Here we have an interesting case showing how important it is that the context be studied carefully when discrepancies seem to arise in the Scriptures. If we read merely these two verses, we seem to be dealing with a pair of passages that contradict each other. The one says that of the sacrificial offering nothing shall be left until the following day, while the other states that on the next day parts of the sacrifice may be eaten. However, the verse following Lv 7:15 clarifies the whole situation. Leviticus 7:16 says: "But if the sacrifice of his offering is a vow offering or a freewill offering, it shall be eaten the day that he offers his sacrifice, and on the next day what remains of it shall be eaten." We see that a certain class of the offerings discussed in 7:15–16 was of such a nature that a part of it could remain until the next day and then be eaten.

Leviticus 19:6 states the general rule, embracing both kinds of offerings—those that had to be eaten the day when they were brought and those that could be eaten on the following day—while 7:15 speaks only of those sacrifices of which no remainder was to be left until the next day. But the following verse states that there was an exception to the rule just mentioned.

Levirate Marriage

God commanded that a man shall not marry his brother's wife (Lv 20:21) yet He also gave the law of the so-called levirate marriage, which enjoined that if a man had died childless, his brother should marry his widow and that the firstborn of the second union should be considered the offspring of the deceased brother (Dt 25:5–10; cf Mt 22:24). First, one should recognize that the one brother's death releases his wife from the bonds of marriage so that she is free to remarry (cf Rm 7:2–3). It is also necessary to remember that we have in Dt 25:5–10 a regulation intended merely for the children of Israel, to be in effect for the time of the Old Testament. It was a law of importance among this people, where tribal connections and keeping the paternal inheritance intact were matters of great importance; but nowhere in the Scriptures is it taught as belonging to the moral law, which is binding upon all people to the end of the world. This marriage was not something the surviving brother had to undergo whether he wished to or not. Deuteronomy 25:7–10 shows that while it was expected of him to enter upon it, he could say: "I do not wish to take her," and there was nothing that could compel him to act contrary to this decision.

The question still remains whether the Mosaic Law is not contradicting itself here, enjoining in the one instance what it forbids in the other. Obviously this is not the case. Deuteronomy 25:5 does not set aside the general law, expressed in Lv 20:21; it merely enacts an exception.

Human Sacrifices

Leviticus 27:28–29 states: "But no devoted thing that a man devotes to the LORD, or anything that he has, whether man or beast, or of his inherited field, shall be sold or redeemed; every devoted thing is most holy to the LORD. No one devoted, who is to be devoted for destruction from mankind, shall be ransomed; he shall surely be put to death."

Deuteronomy 12:30–31 says: "Take care that you not be ensnared to follow them, after they have been destroyed before you, and that you do not inquire about their gods, saying, 'How did these nations serve their gods?—that I also may do the same.' You shall not worship the LORD your God in that way, for every abominable thing that the LORD hates they have done for their gods, for they even burn their sons and their daughters in the fire to their gods."

The Bible, both directly and by implication, condemns the slaughter of human beings in an endeavor to gain favors from a deity. Various passages can be cited in proof of this position besides the text from Deuteronomy quoted above (e.g., Lv 18:21; 20:2). Some scholars, while admitting that these texts forbid human sacrifices, maintain that in other passages of the Bible such sacrifices are sanctioned and that the Bible contradicts itself. They point especially to the Leviticus text listed above as furnishing evidence for their contention.

Leviticus 27:28–29 is grossly misinterpreted if a sanction of human sacrifices is found there. It should be observed that this passage does not speak of sacrifices at all. The chapter gives instruction as to the keeping of vows by which something is set apart for the Lord. In that connection vv 28 and 29 discuss the meaning of a special act, the significance of which was to devote something to destruction or make it a *cherem,* to use the Hebrew term. If someone had vowed to give something to the Lord, he could, so the chapter informs us, redeem the object that he had promised to present to God. But it was different if the thing had been pronounced a *cherem.* If a living being was thus designated, its life was forfeited. The presupposition evidently is that God Himself or the properly constituted authorities had to pronounce a person guilty of death if the law of *cherem* was to apply. Just as little as a person had the right to kill a human being at will, not even a slave belonging to him (cf Ex 21:20), so little could he pronounce anyone a *cherem* at will, even if the person in question was his slave. The intention of the passage is to bring out the solemn meaning of the term *cherem* and to remind the Israelites that they must not put that which had lawfully been devoted to destruction into the same category with things vowed, the redemption of which was possible.

Assyrian illustration of human sacrifice.

In Jsh 6:17 God declared that everything that was in Jericho, the human beings included, was to be *cherem.* We see this particular law in operation in Jsh 6:21: "Then they devoted all in the city to destruction [literally, "made a *cherem*"], both men and women, young and old, oxen, sheep, and donkeys, with the edge of the sword." In this case God Himself had declared the whole city set apart for destruction. According to Nu 21:2 the Israelites declared the cities of an enemy a *cherem,* that is, to be the object of complete destruction. A comparison of all the passages where the term is used will show that in every case it is presupposed or stated expressly that the wrath of God was kindled against those who were so designated. We therefore have no instance here of human sacrifices sanctioned or demanded by the law of God, but merely a solemn and stern way of sentencing an evildoer or a number of evildoers to death.

Some people point to the command given by God to Abraham to offer up his son Isaac (Gn 22:2). They claim that here at any rate a human sacrifice was sanctioned, even ordered by God. It is true that God told Abraham: "Take your son, your only son Isaac, whom you love, and go to the land of Moriah, and offer him there as a burnt offering." But we notice that it was not at all the intention of God to let Abraham kill his son. We must not overlook that Gn 22:1 says, "God *tested* Abraham." What He planned to bring about was a state of willingness on the part of Abraham to part with what he loved most on earth if the Lord required it. God intervenes and shows that He does not desire human sacrifices. He provides a ram, indicating that the offering up of animals is acceptable to Him (for the time of the Old Testament) to serve as types of the Lamb of God, who takes away the sins of the world. Thus Gn 22 does not sanction human sacrifices, but rather implies that they are contrary to the divine will.

Probably the most celebrated passage on which the critics rely in their charge that the Bible in certain places endorses the offering up of human beings is the one that relates to the vow of Jephthah (Jgs 11:30–40). This hero had promised that whatever would come forth from the doors of his house to meet him when he returned from fighting the people of Ammon should belong to Yahweh, and he would offer it up for a burnt offering. Unfortunately, it was his only daughter who came out to meet him. He was exceedingly grieved, but, so the narrative informs us, kept his vow. In considering this story, we must bear in mind that Jephthah, in making his vow, acted entirely on his own initiative, being carried forward by a lofty enthusiasm and burning zeal for the liberation of Israel. Evidently his opinion was that since he expected an unusual favor from God, he ought to have recourse to an unusual method of showing his gratitude in case his prayer should be granted. The narrative does not say that Jephthah was under orders from God in this matter. Neither is the action of Jephthah endorsed or praised. The holy writer relates the events with perfect objectivity, passing no judgment on the vow of Jephthah, since the outcome of the affair condemns his rashness sufficiently. If Jephthah sacrificed his daughter, ending her life prematurely, he did it without divine warrant. In that case he merely added a second sin to the first. That he made a vow of the kind recorded was wrong; if he kept it, he committed an additional wrong. If the question is asked how a man of Jephthah's station could do something that in the Law of Moses had been declared wicked and abominable, the answer is that he lived in a period of Israel's history when the mandates of God were largely forgotten and the influence of the heathen nations surrounding Israel was very strong. The Book of Judges bears ample testimony to the religious deterioration that manifested itself in Israel at this time. Hence the action of Jephthah need not cause surprise at all.

It must be remembered also that the narrative does not expressly say that Jephthah offered up his daughter as a burnt offering. Many commentators believe it is possible to interpret the story as implying that Jephthah compelled his daughter to remain unmarried. They think that Jephthah offered up his daughter in a spiritual way, consecrating her for service at the tabernacle for the rest of her life and devoting her to celibacy. If this interpretation is adopted, all difficulty disappears. But whether one accedes to the view of the commentators last mentioned or not, the above discussion has shown that no contradiction exists between the texts forbidding human sacrifices and the story of Jephthah, inasmuch as the vow of Jephthah and its execution are simply narrated, like various other reprehensible acts of prominent people, without being given divine approval.

In support of the interpretation of Jephthah's vow presented above, it needs to be stressed that in response to it his daughter "wept for her virginity" but not the more hideous prospect of an impending death. While the possibility of a lifelong childlessness would indeed have been a fate provoking deep grief, it strains credulity to believe that there was cause for intense and protracted wailing if she was to remain a virgin for only "two months" (v 37) more and then was to suffer death. The statement that "she had never known a man" (v 39) perhaps indicates that she remained alive and continued celibate during the remainder of her days.

In opposing this view some scholars have taken issue with the translation of Jephthah's promise: "*whatever* comes out . . . I will offer *it* up for a burnt offering," insisting that he said: "*whoever* comes forth . . . I will offer *him* up." However they must admit that both versions are grammatically possible since the Hebrew, like other Semitic languages, has no neuter gender and distinguishes only a masculine and a feminine gender.

It is apparent moreover that the pronouns "whatever" and "whoever" have no literal equivalents in the Hebrew text. They serve in English to introduce a relative clause in rendering the meaning of the Hebrew masculine participle, translated more literally: "the one coming forth." By using such a general term Jephthah increased the dramatic suspense since neither he nor others could foresee the identity of the one coming forth to meet him. At the same time he allowed himself a choice of action in carrying out the terms of the vow. If a human being was to be the one to greet him, he would dedicate him or her "to be the LORD's" for a lifetime of service and (in the sense of an alternative) in case it was an animal, he would "offer it up for a burnt offering." It could also be maintained that, strictly speaking, the antecedent of the masculine pronoun "him" demanded a male person and excluded the possibility of a female victim.

It is significant to find that Jephthah is mentioned as one of the heroes of faith in Hebrews (11:32). It may appear highly unlikely that he would have been accorded this distinction if he had actually committed human sacrifice.

This thirteenth-century manuscript illumination depicts Jephthah sacrificing his daughter by putting her to death (bottom left panel). In fact, he may have offered her to lifelong service at the tabernacle or at another shrine (cf Ex 38:8; Jgs 11:37; 1Sm 1:22–28; 2:22).

FURTHER STUDY

Lay/Bible Class Resources

Dunker, Gary. *Leviticus: Life in the Blood.* GWFT. St. Louis: Concordia, 2005. ♪ Lutheran devotional writer. Eleven-session Bible study, including leader's notes and discussion questions.

Harrison, Roland K. *Leviticus: An Introduction and Commentary.* TOTC. Downers Grove, IL: InterVarsity Press, 1980. ♪ Compact commentary interacting with a variety of English translations and some Hebrew terms in transliteration. Generally evangelical; not theologically profound.

Lenz, Mark J. *Leviticus.* PBC. St. Louis: Concordia, 2003. ♪ Lutheran author. Excellent for Bible classes. Based on the NIV translation.

Life by His Word. St. Louis: Concordia, 2009. ♪ More than 1,500 reproducible one-page Bible studies covering each chapter of the canonical Scriptures. Page references to *The Lutheran Study Bible.* CD-Rom and downloadable.

Stirdivant, Mark, and R. Reed Lessing. *LifeLight: Wilderness Wanderings.* Leaders Guide and Enrichment Magazine/Study Guide. LL. St. Louis: Concordia, 2012. ♪ An in-depth, nine-session Bible study covering key texts of Leviticus, Numbers, and Deuteronomy, with individual, small group, and lecture portions.

Church Worker Resources

Bonar, Andrew A. *A Commentary on the Book of Leviticus.* 4th ed. London: Banner of Truth, 1966. ♪ A classic resource that tends toward application for preaching.

Noordtzij, A. *Leviticus: The Bible Student's Commentary.* Grand Rapids: Zondervan, 1982. ♪ Helpful exegetical insights; somewhat popular.

Wenham, Gordon. J. *The Book of Leviticus.* NICOT. Grand Rapids: Eerdmans, 1979. ♪ A most helpful resource.

Academic Resources

DeVaux, Roland. *Ancient Israel: Religious Institutions.* 2nd ed. Garden City, NY: Doubleday, 1968. ♪ Mildly critical. One of the best available resources on Israel's worship.

Gardiner, Frederic. *Leviticus.* LCHS. New York: Charles Scribner's Sons, 1876. ♪ A helpful, older example of German biblical scholarship, based on the Hebrew text, which provides references to significant commentaries from the Reformation era forward.

Gerstenberger, Erhard. *Leviticus.* OTL. Louisville: Westminster John Knox, 1996. ♪ Translation of a German critical commentary that proposes a late date for the composition for the book.

Gray, George B. *Sacrifice in the Old Testament: Its Theory and Practice.* New York: KTAV, 1971. ♪ Although critical, this is an important study on the role of sacrifice in the worship of Israel.

Hartley, John E. *Leviticus.* WBC. Dallas: Word, 1992. ♪ Evangelical scholar emphasizing the book's theology. Attributes much of the book to Moses.

K&D. *Biblical Commentary on the Old Testament: The Pentateuch.* Vol. 2. Grand Rapids: Eerdmans, 1971 reprint. ♪ A careful handling of theological issues in Leviticus by a Lutheran scholar. Makes purposeful use of both Hebrew and Aramaic. This century-and-a-half old work should not be overlooked. Despite its age, it remains a most useful commentary on the Hebrew text.

Kleinig, John W. *Leviticus.* CC. St. Louis: Concordia, 2004. ♪ Lutheran authors. Insightful scriptural connections between the Old Testament and its system of sacrifice and regulations and its New Testament fulfillment through the atoning death and resurrection of Jesus Christ.

Milgrom, Jacob. *Leviticus: A Book of Ritual and Ethics.* A Continental Commentary. Minneapolis: Fortress, 2004. ♪ A more compact commentary from the author of the Anchor Bible commentary.

———. *Leviticus.* Vols. 3, 3A, and 3B of AB. New York: Doubleday, 1991, 2000. ♪ Thorough commentary on historical and textual issues from a Jewish critical scholar. Less helpful on theology.

NUMBERS

The Lord bless you and keep you

A reader easily recognizes in Numbers its progressive outline of events. By the end of the book, Israel is on the plains of Moab, across the Jordan River from Jericho, poised for the final step of crossing the river to conquer Canaan. Exodus 19:2 gave the previous progress report: They had "encamped in the wilderness . . . before the mountain." Numbers provides the intervening events.

The Book of Numbers received its title in the Septuagint and Western translations from the two censuses recorded in chs 1 and 26. Yet in this case the Hebrew name (derived, as usual, from one of the opening words), "in the wilderness," is more descriptive. In some respects the book is a collection and quite innocent of an outline, though, upon deeper inspection, it is clear that it continues a pattern of composition established at least as early as Ex 12. Its structure is basically historical, interspersed with additional legislation.

Historical and Cultural Setting

As noted in the introductions to Exodus and Leviticus, Israel withdrew from Egypt during a high point in Egyptian power. But God led them into a wilderness region that shielded them from Egyptian ambitions. Assisted by a Midianite priest, whose daughter Moses had married, Israel ate the food God supplied (manna) and began to forage in the wilderness. They encountered a number of semi-nomadic groups and minor kingdoms, such as the Amalekites of southern

The southern wilderness of Israel (Negeb) blossoms when watered by spring rains.

OVERVIEW

Author
Moses the prophet

Date
1445–1406 BC

Places
Wilderness of Sinai; Wilderness of Zin; see map, p 140

People
Moses; Aaron; Levites; elders and chiefs of Israel; Miriam; 12 spies; Korah; Dathan; Abiram; Sihon; Og; Balak; Balaam

Purpose
To describe how the Lord preserves Israel despite the obstacles from Sinai to Canaan

Law Themes
Duties; uncleanness; punishment for complaining; rebellion; cursing

Gospel Themes
Redemption; "I am the LORD your God"; consecration; purification; atonement; blessing

Memory Verses
Aaronic benediction (6:24–27); God's Word is true (23:19); star of Jacob (24:17)

TIMELINE

1526 BC	Moses born
1446 BC	Exodus from Egypt
1445 BC	Census taken
1407 BC	Israel arrives at Plains of Moab
1406 BC	Israel crosses the Jordan

Regional powers mined turquoise and other precious stones in the wilderness. This Egyptian pectoral decoration is inlaid with turquoise and carnelian.

Canaan, the kingdom of Arad west of the Dead Sea, and the Amorites and Moabites east of the Dead Sea. Israel's growing strength apparently intimidated the leadership of the Midianites, a group with whom they previously had peaceful relations. The end of Numbers describes the Midianites aligning with the Moabites against Israel. Under Moses, Israel conquered and began to settle the regions east of the Jordan River where they prepared to invade the Promised Land.

Archaeological evidence suggests that the wilderness through which Israel wandered was not as arid and desolate as it is today. Likewise, the people they encountered were not always Bedouin-like tribesmen but settled civilizations with distinguishing artifacts. Most of the groups mentioned above were already noted in Genesis.

COMPOSITION

Author(s)

See pp 4–11.

Date of Composition

See pp 4–11.

Purpose/Recipients

Numbers, like Leviticus, adds another concentric circle of covenant legislation to the core provisions of Exodus (cf diagram, p 102). The pattern of blended legislation and history remains the same, but history takes a much more prominent place in Numbers than in Leviticus, and the laws are more incidental and largely occasioned by circumstances. See p 101.

In contrast to Leviticus (at Sinai and covering just a few months), the events in Numbers take place at more than 40 places and during 38 years. In a general way, Leviticus tells us what God *said* to the covenant nation, while Numbers (more like Exodus) tells us what God *did* to bring Israel to the Land of Promise. As a result, its legislative sections are interwoven into the historical narrative. In fact, Numbers contains some of the most dramatic events of the Old Testament.

Literary Features

Genre

As noted above, the Book of Numbers is history, presented in chronological and geographical order, recounting the travels and experiences of Israel from Sinai to the borders of Canaan. Interspersed with the history are various laws. Numbers includes other documents or quotations of documents; especially noteworthy are the censuses and the poems of ch 21. For more on this feature, see "Resources," p 130.

Characters

As a history, Numbers presents a wealth of characters, beginning with the familiar and long-suffering sons of Levi: Moses and Aaron. (See pp 63, 67.) Their tribe receives special duties in connection with the tabernacle so that the Levites become a special semi-priestly group within Israel, designated to assist the sons of Aaron, who are priests. Moses and Aaron's sister, first described in Exodus, appears again when Miriam and Aaron oppose Moses' marriage to a Cushite woman, illustrating dynamics of family life among these leaders of Israel as well as Moses' special standing before God. The story of Miriam, and that of the daughters of Zelophehad (ch 36), show that Israelite women were not silent and passive when it came to family matters.

Bronze figure riding a donkey, reminiscent of the Balaam story in Nu 22–24.

The censuses and some stories introduce tribal chiefs and elders, who acted as representatives of their people. Joshua of Ephraim and Caleb of Judah show themselves bold and faithful among 12 spies Moses sent into Canaan. These same heroic figures reappear in later books, taking on further responsibility. In contrast with the heroism of Joshua and Caleb appear the Levite Korah and the Reubenites Dathan, Abiram, and On, who lead a rebellion against Moses and Aaron. Aaron's son, Eleazar, succeeds him as high priest, through whom a priestly dynasty would continue for centuries.

Several Gentiles appear as significant characters who oppose Israel but suffer condemnation and defeat: the kings Sihon of the Amorites, Og of Bashan, Balak of Moab, and the prophet Balaam.

Narrative Development or Plot

Numbers begins at Sinai with a census and with preparations (marching orders) for the journey to the Promised Land (1:2–10:10). Israel left Mount Sinai (10:11–13) and marched northward to Canaan but was prevented from immediately attaining the goal. As punishment for rebelling against God, Israel was sentenced to 40 years (2 completed plus 38 more years) of wandering in the wilderness.

Although the Israelites continued to rebel against their God-appointed leaders, after 38 years they arrived again at the point of their previous northernmost advance, Kadesh (20:1). From Kadesh (20:22), in the fortieth year of the exodus, they skirted the lands of Edom (21:4), moved northwest into the plains of Moab (Amorite territory along the Jordan River north of Moab), and conquered it (21:21–25). Numbers concludes with Israel on the plains of Moab.

Resources

As noted above, Numbers draws its name from the censuses of chs 1 and 26, which likely existed as independent compositions adapted for the book's history. Along with the censuses appear references to some specific compositions: a registry of elders (11:26), the "Book of the Wars of the LORD" (21:14–15), the Song of the Well (21:17–18), and the Song of Heshbon (21:27–30). The last three compositions are poetic and show archaic elements like those found in the poems of Exodus (see p 7). Mention of these resources reveals the composite nature of Numbers, by which Moses or his editor supplemented the history.

Text and Translations

The traditional Hebrew text of Numbers, like that of the other Books of Moses, is well preserved, though not as well as other Books of Moses (e.g., problems appear in ch 21). The Samaritans preserved their own version of the book, which includes some unique readings. The LXX text of Numbers is a very literal rendering of the Hebrew, which is often wooden and reveals the weaknesses of the translator(s). Seven fragments of Numbers manuscripts were found at Qumran, which support the traditional Hebrew text.

The Legislative Sections of Numbers

Laws and directives of all kinds are scattered throughout Numbers.

Old Laws

Many legislative sections contain directives already given in Exodus and Leviticus (cf Nu 28:6: "ordained at Mount Sinai") but are here elaborated and their meaning deepened. Among these are:

The removal of unclean persons from the camp (5:1–4) and restitution for wrongs done (5:5–10). The laws of sacrifice, emphasizing the meal offerings (ch 15). The rights and duties of the Levites (ch 18). The laws regarding offerings on established feast days and regarding vows (ch 28–30). The cities of refuge (35:9–34).

New Laws

Other sections deal with entirely new provisions, such as:

The law of jealousy (5:11–28), which submits a wife to a test resembling an ordeal when a husband suspects her of unfaithfulness.

Regulations governing the vows of a Nazirite (6:1–21), meaning "one separated" (not "Nazarene"). Although all Israel is holy, these volunteer Nazirite vows demonstrate extraordinary consecration to God.

The cleansing of the Levites (8:5–26), who, like the priests, were admitted to their appointed service in the tabernacle only after the proper rite of installation.

Tassels (with one blue thread) on the garment corners (15:37–41) were to help a person "remember all the commandments of the LORD."

Tassel on a Jewish garment.

Purification through the ashes of a sacrificial red heifer (ch 19), mixed in water with the ashes of cedar, hyssop, and scarlet yarn, would cleanse a person defiled by contact with a corpse (5:2; 9:6).

Laws of inheritance (27:1–11; cf 36:1–12) provide that a man without sons could pass his inheritance also through his daughters, provided that they married men of their own tribe.

The offerings for the seven days of unleavened bread (28:17–25).

Laws Temporary and Permanent

Some of the laws and provisions were designed only for the period of wilderness wandering—for example, the grouping of the tribes about the tabernacle, the marching formations, the signals for beginning and ending a journey, and exclusion from the camp for various reasons.

Other laws were to apply immediately and to remain in force ever afterward—for example, blowing the trumpets for directing the movement of camps on their journey (10:2), in war, and in celebration of appointed feasts and the regulations regarding the consecration and function of priests and Levites.

Many prescriptions deal only with the conquest and possession of Canaan—for example, driving out all the inhabitants of Canaan (33:50–56); marking the boundaries of the land (ch 34); assigning 48 cities to the Levites (ch 35), six as cities of refuge in the case of manslaughter.

Finally, some rites were to begin when they came into the land (15:2)—for example, meal offerings (impossible in the desert) were to accompany the animal sacrifices (chs 15; 28; 29).

Laws in a Framework of Events

Like Exodus and Leviticus, Numbers does not codify laws according to subject matter. But some legislative material and some new directives are added as certain situations develop.

The rights and duties of the Levites are enumerated in connection with their location within the camp, the formation of which required the taking of the census (chs 1–4). Further clarification of Levitical authority resulted from the uprising of the Levite Korah (16:1–7). The allotment of 48 cities to the Levites (ch 35) follows the provisions for dividing "the land to you for inheritance"

(34:16–29). The Levites' purification for service appears in the context of the completion of the tabernacle (ch 8; cf 7:1).

The law regarding female inheritance (27:1–11; 36) grew out of the second census, during which a man named Zelophehad was found to have only daughters (26:33).

After the defeat of the Midianites, rules for the conduct of war became necessary (31:14–31).

Such obvious connections do not always exist. For example, though laws regarding the removal of unclean persons from the camp (5:1–4) follow the setting up of the camp (chs 1–4), the immediately following statutes (i.e., regarding restitution for wrong, the law of jealousy, and the prescription for a Nazirite; 5:5–6:21) have no direct connection with the camp itself.

Particularly after their arrival on the plains of Moab (22:1), legislation tends to anticipate the future (e.g., chs 28–29, concerning offerings in the land, mentioned after Moses' successor is named in 27:12–23).

The explicit reference to future sacrifices "when you enter the land of Canaan" (34:1) appears to support the conclusion of some scholars that sacrifices were suspended for the 38 years after Israel's exclusion from Canaan (14:39–45). Other factors also favor this view. For example, Scripture makes no reference to the performance of sacrifices or to the setting up of the tabernacle during these 38 years. Even such a basic ceremony as circumcision was neglected (Jsh 5:5–8). Centuries later, the prophet Amos would ask (expecting a negative reply), "Did you bring to Me sacrifices and offerings during the forty years in the wilderness, O house of Israel?" (Am 5:25; later quoted by Stephen, Ac 7:42).

OUTLINE

The presentation of Israel's history in Numbers has the feel of a journey. The inclusion of legal material often corresponds to the historical situation.

I. From Mount Sinai to Kadesh (chs 1–12)

  A. First Census (chs 1–4)

    1. Israel's warriors (1:1–46)

    2. Levites exempted (1:47–54)

    3. Arrangement of the camp (ch 2)

    4. Sons of Aaron (3:1–4)

    5. Duties of the Levites (3:5–39)

    6. Redemption of the firstborn (3:40–51)

    7. Duties of the Kohathites (ch 4)

  B. Final Preparations for the Journey (5:1–10:10)

    1. Unclean people (5:1–4)

    2. Confession and restitution (5:5–10)

    3. Test for adultery (5:11–31)

    4. Nazirite vow (6:1–21)

    5. Aaron's blessing (6:22–27)

    6. Offerings at the tabernacle's consecration (ch 7)

    7. Seven lamps (8:1–4)

    8. Cleansing of the Levites (8:5–22)

    9. Retirement of the Levites (8:23–26)

    10. Passover celebrated (9:1–14)

    11. Cloud covering the tabernacle (9:15–23)

    12. Silver trumpets (10:1–10)

  C. Journey to Kadesh (10:11–12:16)

    1. Israel leaves Sinai (10:11–36)

    2. People complain (11:1–15)

    3. Elders appointed to aid Moses (11:16–30)

    4. Quail and a plague (11:31–35)

    5. Miriam and Aaron oppose Moses (ch 12)

II. From Kadesh to Transjordan (chs 13–21)

   A. Refusal to Invade Canaan (chs 13–14)

      1. Twelve spies and their mixed report (ch 13)

      2. People rebel, are punished and defeated (ch 14)

   B. Religious Questions (chs 15–19)

      1. Laws about sacrifices and unintentional sins (15:1–31)

      2. Sabbath breaker executed (15:32–36)

      3. Tassels on garments (15:37–41)

      4. Korah's rebellion (ch 16)

      5. Aaron's staff buds (ch 17)

      6. Duties of priests and Levites (ch 18)

      7. Laws for purification (ch 19)

   C. Journey to Moab and Conquest of Transjordan (chs 20–21)

      1. Death of Miriam (20:1)

      2. Waters of Meribah (20:2–9)

      3. Moses strikes the rock (20:10–13)

      4. Edom refuses passage (20:14–21)

      5. Death of Aaron (20:22–29)

      6. Arad destroyed (21:1–3)

      7. Bronze serpent (21:4–9)

      8. Arriving in Moab (21:10–20)

      9. Conquest of Transjordan (21:21–35)

III. Israel on the Plains of Moab (chs 22–36)

   A. Balaam Blesses Israel, but Israel Disobeys (chs 22–25)

      1. Balak summons Balaam (22:1–21)

      2. Balaam's donkey and the angel (22:22–41)

      3. Balaam's first oracle (23:1–12)

      4. Balaam's second oracle (23:13–30)

      5. Balaam's third oracle (24:1–14)

      6. Balaam's final oracle (24:15–25)

      7. Baal worship at Peor (25:1–9)

      8. Zeal of Phinehas (25:10–18)

   B. Second Census and New Laws (chs 26–30)

      1. Census of the new generation (ch 26)

Doctrinal Content

Summary Commentary

Chs 1–4 Through a census, the Lord shows Moses that Israel has grown mightily. He also sets the Levites apart for special service; their duty is spiritual, not military. God charges the Levites with moving, maintaining, and protecting the tabernacle, God's dwelling place. As an added means of protection, He instructs the Israelites to camp around the tabernacle; the Levites serve as the final defense against defilement (1:52–53). When encamped, the Israelites face the tent of meeting, showing the centrality of God's place for their lives. Aaron's sons are set apart to serve as God's high priests. They would be the anointed leaders of the tabernacle and later the temple, down to the first century, when Herod's temple would be destroyed in AD 70. The Lord chooses the Levites to assist the sons of Aaron, His anointed priests. Each Levitical clan performs assigned duties for the care and security of the sanctuary (tent of meeting) and its precious contents (3:25, 31, 36–37). According to the Law, the firstborn sons belong to the Lord (Ex 34:20). In their place, God appoints the Levites and allows for the redemption of all firstborn Israelite sons, foreshadowing redemption through Christ (Heb 9:12).

Chs 5–6 The ground is holy wherever the tent of meeting lodges. Defilement means death, for uncleanness is rooted in sin. God's Law will be Israel's wisdom and understanding in the sight of the people (Dt 4:6). For example, God provides recourse should a man suspect his wife of adultery, a most serious matter (Ex 20:14). Also, Nazirite vows are made voluntarily before God. The length of vows can vary, but once a vow is made, God requires fulfillment (Nu 6:21). In the Aaronic benediction, the divine name Yahweh is used three times in reference to the triune nature of God.

Chs 7–8 Each leader of the 12 tribes of Israel presents his offering to God at the tabernacle dedication. Leaders give thanks to God for bringing them out of Egypt to establish His covenant with them. No windows shed light into the Lord's sanctuary, so the lampstands are truly a light shining in the darkness (8:1–4). Israel's sin is transferred to the Levites, who transfer this sin to sacrificial animals. Only by the blood of sacrificial animals are the Levites cleansed of their sin and allowed to serve the priests of the Most High God. "It is the blood that makes atonement by the life" (Lv 17:11). A Levite could begin service at age 25. Once a Levite reached 50, he could assist younger Levites, but he could no longer do the work required at the tabernacle.

9:1–10:10 God commands Moses to celebrate Passover anew as a memorial of His great deliverance. All people were to participate, even if they could not observe the event on the same dates. At God's directive, the Israelites move away from Mount Sinai. The pillar of cloud/fire symbolizes His gracious hand over His covenant community. Blasts on the silver trumpets signal the time to move, but they also serve the purpose of calling leaders of the entire community to assemble at the tent of meeting. God Himself leads His people toward the land promised long ago (Gn 12:7).

10:11–12:16 The Israelites march to the Promised Land; the ark of the covenant leads the way (10:33). However, the grumbling begins only three days into the journey. Earlier, we learned of Moses' helplessness as Israel's

The common quail migrates through Israel in the spring and the fall.

leader—one man amid a throng of rebellious people. Mercifully, God grants 70 elders to help Moses. When God sends quail to the people, they greedily hoard it, gathering at least 6 bushels per person. They eat some and dry the rest to eat later. Then Moses faces a new rebellion when Miriam and Aaron claim equal status with their younger brother. They learn the danger of challenging God's authority.

Chs 13–14 God permits the spies to enter the Promised Land at the Israelites' request (Dt 1:22). Twelve spies, one from each tribe, are sent; among them is Moses' successor, Joshua. The land is just as God had described it to Moses, flowing with milk and honey (Ex 3:8; Nu 13:27). Yet 10 of the 12 spies fear the inhabitants of the land (13:31), thereby doubting God. The doubt of 10 spies poisons the entire camp with rebellion. Moses argues that if God were to destroy the Israelites for their rebellion, God's holy name would be defamed. So Moses appeals to God for mercy. Those persons 20 years and older will not see the land God promised. Yet God will not bring destruction on all Israel for their disobedience. Caleb, Joshua, and the next generation will inhabit the new land. The Israelites now completely change plans and go to war, but again ignore God's Word. Sham obedience meets with God's resistance.

Ch 15 God reassures the people that after the older generation has passed away, He will fulfill His promise to the younger generation. God then restates the rules for dealing with unintentional sin through sin offerings (Lv 4). Yet, a man gathering wood shows contempt for God's Word. God considers this blasphemous because the man's act follows God's restatement about deliberate sin (Nu 15:22–31). In the tassels added to their garments, God provides a visible reminder for the Israelites of His Word and His presence among them.

Chs 16–19 The rebellion of Korah and his followers threatens the lives of the Lord's servants and the unity of the congregation. Yet when the Lord's punishment falls on the rebels, the Lord's servant Aaron rushes into the midst of the plague to save the people. God supports Aaron's priesthood by a miracle that distinguishes Aaron from the leaders of the 12 tribes. In the budding of Aaron's staff, He provides a visual reminder of God's seal of approval on the Levitical priesthood. Although the latest rebellion against the Lord comes from the Levites through Korah, God does not dismiss the Levites but reaffirms them in their calling. He provides for their forgiveness and their inheritance. He also provides a means to cleanse those who had touched a corpse or accidentally came in contact with a bone of a dead person or a grave.

Chs 20–21 In the 40th year, a new generation of Israelites arrives where the nation stood 38 years before. Those over the age of 20 have died. Yet Moses faces more grumbling over water from the new generation. As before, Moses and Aaron humble themselves before the Lord at the entrance to the tent of meeting, and God opens His hand of mercy. However, Moses' words "shall we" indicate that he and Aaron were claiming credit for the miracle of water, not attributing it to God. Moses appeals to the Edomites for passage on the basis of history, and he promises to pay for water. Yet, Edom denies them passage. Moses and Aaron install Eleazar as high priest. Aaron dies for his

A honeybee approaches almond blossoms in Israel, the "land of milk and honey."

disbelief at Meribah, which means "quarreling" (20:12). In death, he joins the rebellious generation who were lost in the wilderness. The Canaanite king of Arad learns of the movement of the Israelite nation and responds by attacking some of the outlying citizens, carrying some into captivity. As Moses guides God's people in the direction of the Red Sea, away from their primary objective of the Promised Land, rebellion begins anew and God punishes people with fiery serpents. God carries His people to the east side of the Jordan River. Finally, 40 years of wilderness wandering are about to end. For a second time, the Israelites seek permission to travel the King's Highway. This time, they are denied its use by Sihon, king of the Amorites. The Israelites lay claim to Sihon's land, which later became a home for the tribes of Reuben and Gad (32:1–5). Og, a second Amorite king, marches against the Israelites. The Lord delivers another victory. The Israelites now lay claim to all the land east of the Jordan. This territory is later given to the half-tribe of Manasseh.

Chs 22–25 Fearful Balak summons the soothsayer Balaam to curse the Israelites. God works with the situation by emphasizing the importance of His Word, which must be fulfilled. As Balaam mocked the Lord by ignoring His Word, the Lord now comically mocks Balaam: so great is God's Word, it can make a donkey speak! God presents the first of Balaam's four oracles. Balaam cannot curse the people whom God has not cursed (23:8). For a second time, seven altars are constructed—this time atop Pisgah (23:14).

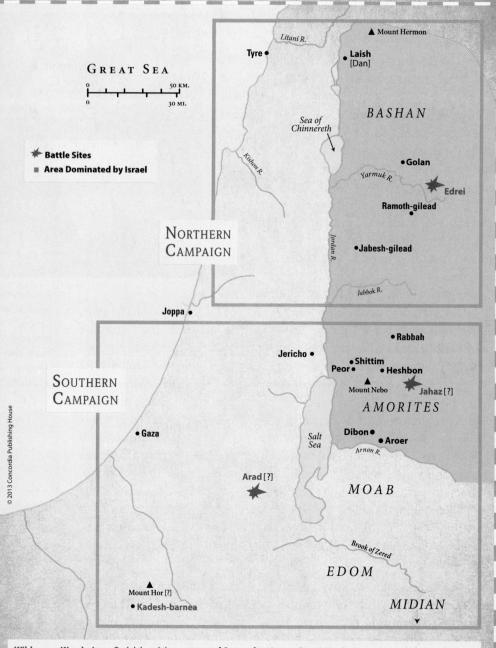

GREAT SEA

0 ——————————— 50 KM.
0 ——————————— 30 MI.

🟅 **Battle Sites**
⬛ **Area Dominated by Israel**

Litani R.

Tyre •

• Laish
  [Dan]

▲ Mount Hermon

Sea of Chinnereth

BASHAN

Kishon R.

•Golan

Yarmuk R.

🟅 Edrei

Ramoth-gilead •

**NORTHERN
CAMPAIGN**

Jordan R.

•Jabesh-gilead

Jabbok R.

Joppa •

**SOUTHERN
CAMPAIGN**

• Rabbah

Jericho •

•Shittim

Peor • • •Heshbon

• Gaza

*Salt
Sea*

▲
Mount Nebo

🟅 Jahaz [?]

AMORITES

Dibon •
• Aroer

Arnon R.

Arad [?]
🟅

MOAB

Brook of Zered

EDOM

▲
Mount Hor [?]
• Kadesh-barnea

MIDIAN
↓

© 2013 Concordia Publishing House

Wilderness Wanderings. God delayed the conquest of Canaan for 40 years (Nu 13–14; Dt 1:19–46). Israel often stayed near Kadesh-barnea (Nu 33:36). Aaron died on Mount Hor (Nu 20:22–29; 33:37–39). Israel destroyed Arad and surrounding cities (Nu 21:1–3). Edom refused passage to the east (Nu 20:14–21), so the Israelites went perhaps as far south as Ezion-geber to skirt Edom (Nu 21:4; Dt 2:8). They camped in the Valley of Zered and along the Arnon River (Nu 21:12–13). At Jahaz, they defeated the Amorites who had occupied part of Moab (Nu 21:21–30; Dt 2:24–37). They defeated Bashan at Edrei (Nu 21:31–35; Dt 3:1–7). Next they camped east of Jericho at Shittim (Nu 25). After they defeated the Midianites (Nu 31), Israel controlled the Transjordan from the Valley of the Arnon to Mount Hermon (Dt 3:8–10). Moses died on Mount Nebo (Dt 34).

The results are the same. God does not change His mind as humans do (23:19). What God has blessed must remain blessed; therefore, Balaam must bless Israel as well. He can say only what God has commanded him to say. God's Word is changeless, and He dwells with His people to bless them. For a third time, God will not allow Balaam to curse the Israelites. Instead, Balaam blesses them and recites God's litany of love. The fourth and final oracle occurs immediately after Balaam's encounter with Balak and has to do with future events: a messianic prophecy of a star coming out of Jacob. Yet Balaam worms his way into the spiritual lives of Israel and causes them to forsake God for the worship of Baal. In response, Phinehas strikes on the Lord's behalf, stopping the idolatrous actions of Zimri and Cozbi.

Chs 26–29 Opposite the Jordan River and Jericho, the Lord commands another census. The records show God's faithfulness in preserving His people. A particular example follows: contrary to many grievances presented in Numbers, the daughters of Zelophehad approach Moses with humble demeanor to seek his counsel. The Lord hears their request and answers with grace and mercy. Death is near for Moses, who desires that God would provide a new leader. Otherwise, the people would wander like "sheep that have no shepherd" (27:17). In His mercy, God raises up Joshua, one of the two spies who returned from the Promised Land with a favorable report (cf 28:18; 14:6–9). With the older generation buried in the wilderness, God begins grooming the younger generation as faithful stewards of His Law.

Ch 30 Vows made to God—made in His name—are to be carried out faithfully. When these vows are not fulfilled, they reflect poorly on God's good name and shame His people. Dependents need the approval of their father or husband to make a binding vow.

Chs 31–32 Moses is given a final assignment. He is to oversee the destruction of a group of Midianites who had tempted Israel to idolatry and brought a plague among them. God acts forcefully to protect His people from falling away. Phinehas, the son of Eleazar the high priest, coordinates the attack. The victory secures the east bank of the Jordan, from which the Israelites will conquer Canaan. The Reubenites and Gadites desire the good land east of the Jordan to raise livestock. They vow to fight beside their brothers in the conquest of Canaan (fulfilled in Jsh 22:1–6).

Chs 33–35 Moses recounts Israel's travels. God guides Israel every step of the way to the Promised Land. He now does not want the religions of the heathen Canaanites to influence the Israelites or to lead them astray as did the Midianites. He has already given the Israelites the Promised Land. Yet, the Lord still calls them to faithful action, to live and serve according to the promise. The Lord works through the drawing of lots and assigns the territory He wishes various tribes to inhabit (cf Jsh 14–20). Eleazar and Joshua oversee the process as God's representatives. God had selected the Levites to help the priests. Their cities of refuge would protect individuals accused of accidental killing. Such individuals find safety from "the avenger of blood" in the appointed cities. To protect the innocent, God establishes a system of justice with two witnesses (35:30).

Ch 36 For each tribe to retain its territory, God commands that Zelophehad's daughters choose husbands within their own tribe. Numbers ends with a brief summary statement that all regulations therein came by God's hand.

Specific Law Themes

Like the Books of Exodus and Leviticus, Numbers emphasizes the duties of Israel before God, especially the need to distinguish between the clean and the unclean. While traveling in the wilderness, the Israelites repeatedly complain and rebel against God. He punishes them to drive them toward repentance. Those suspected of sin are under the threat of a curse, that is, under threat of punishment.

Specific Gospel Themes

The themes of God's mercy likewise are consistent with those found earlier in Exodus and Leviticus. The Lord is the redeemer of Israel who proclaims to them, "I am the LORD your God." He provides for the consecration, purification, atonement, and blessing of the people whom He continues to sustain and guide toward the Promised Land.

Specific Doctrines

Though the value of the Book of Numbers remains much the same as for Leviticus, the new covenant reader finds embedded in this book a special blessing that his or her own appointed "Aaron" (that is, the pastor) pronounces in worship: the Aaronic blessing (6:24–26):

> The LORD bless you and keep you;
> the LORD make His face to shine upon you
>   and be gracious to you;
> the LORD lift up His countenance upon you
>   and give you peace.

Here, if nowhere else in the Book of Numbers, the old and new covenants meet. Old Testament Israel and its spiritual descendants have the same history of salvation and the same giver of blessing, grace, and peace. All are numbered in God's heavenly "Book of Numbers" because the Mediator between God and humanity "was numbered with the transgressors" (Is 53:12; Mk 15:28)—transgressors of both covenants. No one is a mere number, a statistical digit to be added into a total. Each is a "you" (singular), who is blessed and kept in peace.

In Nu 14:18 Moses quotes back to the Lord His earlier self-confession (cf Ex 34:6–7), which is the most referenced statement of the Old Testament. Since sinners perpetually give birth to more sinners, all stand in need of a gracious God who abounds in steadfast love toward sinners. A further weighty passage emphasizes God's integrity, who "is not man, that He should lie" (Nu 23:19), a passage much loved by Luther, who drew comfort from the fact that God would not fail to keep His promises and that His Word—the Scriptures—were reliable.

An important text for establishing liturgical practice for ordination and appointment to service in God's name is 27:18. It describes Moses laying his hands on Joshua as a sign that God was setting Joshua apart.

Application

Chs 1–4 The strength of God's people does not depend on size and military strength but on His Word and grace. As God charges the Levites with moving, maintaining, and protecting the tabernacle, God's dwelling place, all the people huddle about His sacred dwelling and enjoy the blessings of His presence. Christ dwells in our midst and incorporates us into His holy tabernacle, the Church. Pray for the leaders of your congregation and community, that they may walk in the ways of the Lord. He will hear your prayer for Jesus' sake and lead you into a blessed future. Just as the Lord consecrated the Levites to care for the tabernacle and to support the services of the sanctuary, He likewise calls and consecrates His people today to support the ministry of the Word. God entrusts us with His Gospel message of reconciliation through His Son, Jesus Christ. That message must be kept undefiled (Gal 1:8) by proper training for ordained ministers of the Gospel (2Tm 2:2) and for all believers. Those whom the Lord calls, He also equips by grace.

Chs 5–6 Our corporate prayer of Confession reminds us that "we are by nature sinful and unclean" and that our salvation comes through God's mercy alone (*LSB*, p 167). Freely honor the Lord's mercy by making restitution and by showing mercy toward others. Note from this text that God designed human sexuality for the blessed estate of marriage. Yet He also offers forgiveness through Christ for those who err and repent. God, who does not take lightly any vow made to Him, faithfully keeps His vows, including that of Gn 3:15, which promised your salvation in Christ. What a blessing it is to know that God the Father blesses all aspects of our lives, that God the Son has redeemed us poor, miserable sinners, and that God the Holy Spirit calls us by the Gospel.

Chs 7–8 The offerings of Israel commemorate God's favor, which we still enjoy due to the sacrifice of Christ's blood at Calvary (cf 1Co 5:7). We light candles to symbolize the Lord's presence among us through His Word and Sacraments. God's light is Jesus Christ (Jn 1:4), who conquers death and grants eternal life (Rm 6:23b). Israel's sin is transferred to the Levites, who transfer this sin to sacrificial animals. Only by the blood of sacrificial animals are the Levites cleansed of their sin and allowed to serve the priests of the Most High God. "It is the blood that makes atonement by the life" (Lv 17:11). At Calvary, Jesus redeemed all humans from sin (Heb 9:15) as foreshadowed in the Old Testament sacrifices. We receive these blessings now through the New Testament ministry. As God provided for the Levites' retirement in good health, the Church should show appropriate care for the health of faithful church workers, for the Lord bears the burdens of us all and carries us through life unto life everlasting.

9:1–10:10 Just as the Lord continually sought the good and unity of Israel, He seeks our good and unity in the services of His precious Word, which describes our creation, redemption, and sanctification as His people through faith in Christ, our Passover Lamb. He sustains us on the journey of faith through His Means of Grace. Scripture teaches that a trumpet blast will also signal our call to heaven on the Last Day (1Th 4:16).

10:11–12:16 The Israelites march to the Promised Land; the ark of the covenant leads the way (10:33). The Lord deals gently with His people by providing constant guidance and sound leadership. Today, pray for your leaders, that the Lord would bless and keep them and guide them in thoughtful service to His people, whom Christ redeemed with His precious blood. When tempted to grumble, think of Christ at Gethsemane and how He turned His pains into prayers. Like Moses, you may at times feel frustration and become angry with the Lord. Thanks be to God, He is "slow to anger and abounding in steadfast love and faithfulness" (Ps 86:15). In all circumstances, the Lord leads us to confess, "Blessed be the name of the LORD" (Jb 1:21), for He truly does bless us and supply our needs (cf Mt 6:11). God's punishment is swift, yet merciful. Our Lord is a Lord of both Law and Gospel, by which He always calls people to repentance and pronounces grace.

Chs 13–14 Just as the Lord gave His people a challenging mission, anticipating great faithfulness, He likewise challenges us. When you face challenges, do not collapse in doubt. Instead, call on your gracious Lord, who redeemed you and will lead you. His Word remains good. Call on Him in repentance, for He grants faith by grace through His precious Word. What a blessing to know that our humble prayers are heard by the very Creator of heaven and earth. Because of Christ's obedience, we dare to call Him "Abba, Father." Consider how God does not deliver what the Israelites truly deserve for their insolence. Instead, He shows mercy by raising up a new generation to inherit His promise. Hear God's gracious call to repentance each day. Rejoice in the Word and in God's forgiveness through Christ, the Savior.

Acacia trees in Sinai.

Ch 15 After the cloud of punishment comes the rainbow of God's grace. In Confession and Absolution, He provides us forgiveness for our unintentional sin, as well as willful sin and despising of God's Word, which have damnable consequences if we persist in them. Yet Jesus, Lord of the Sabbath, has fulfilled all the requirements of the Law for our sake (Mt 5:17). In the cross of God's Son, we witness the ultimate reminder of God's Law and Gospel, His wrath and grace.

Chs 16–19 Aaron's intercession reminds us of Christ's intercession for us; He came among us to save us. Properly ordained and installed leadership is a blessing from God, not a curse. Respect those in authority over you by praying for them in patience and by trusting without envy. Exercise diligent care for the church workers called to your congregation or school. Rejoice that the Lord distributes His life-giving and purifying Word to you through them.

Chs 20–21 Rebellion has a cost, but God is ever ready to start afresh and fulfill His promises. When struggles and complaints hamper you, turn to the Lord in humble prayer. As you serve each day, reflect by asking yourself, "How has God made me a blessing to others in my duties?" Though you will stumble in faith, as Moses did, know that your merciful Father will not cast you aside. Seek peace and fairness within your family. Above all things, pray for the forgiveness of sins as you forgive those who trespass against you (Mt 6:12). How blessed is the mercy of Jesus, our Brother (Heb 2:10–18). The Lord calls His people to peace, which He pronounces through His ministers in the word of blessing (Nu 6:24–26). As Moses guides God's people in the direction of the Red Sea, away from their primary objective of the Promised Land, rebellion begins anew. Those in Israel who repented received God's salvation by looking to the sign of His mercy in faith (21:9). What an excellent precursor of God's redemption through the cross. Those who look upon the cross in faith are saved. He will keep His Word to you too. God protects His people and overthrows the false religions of the nations.

Chs 22–25 God cannot be manipulated, and His Word must not be twisted for sinful purposes. Treasure the Word. Share it confidently, because the Word is God's power for working repentance and forgiving sins. As Christians, we, too, are often oblivious to the many spiritual and earthly forces that seek our destruction. Thankfully, God is not oblivious to them and stretches out His mighty hand to protect us. The future belongs to God. Rebellion, sin, or sinister means will not deter His plan of salvation through Christ. Balaam worms his way into the spiritual lives of Israel and causes them to forsake God for the worship of Baal. The situation is reminiscent of the worship of the golden calf (Ex 32). As at that time, God's anger against sin causes the death of thousands; yet it saves tens of thousands more. God is a God of both Law and Gospel. He metes out punishment to drive people to repentance but also has compassion on His wayward sons and daughters. He always gives Himself fully for His people as demonstrated by Christ's sacrifice on the cross for us.

Chs 26–29 Pray that God's Word and heritage will be maintained in your family. His abiding love can see you through every plague and trouble. The prayer of the upright pleases God (Pr 15:8). He has our good at heart in all His teaching. He is always ready to provide for His beloved flock through our Good Shepherd, Jesus.

Ch 30 Our word must be our bond, including our word of repentance when we do not live up to our words. God's Word does not fail us. As you pray about the path of life ahead, consider how your choices will affect others. Discuss matters with them, as appropriate. Pray for the Lord's guidance, and seek understanding in His Word.

Chs 31–32 The tactics described in these chapters were meant for this specific situation and cannot be used by people today as a guide to "holy war." Vengeance belongs to God (Dt 32:35) and is enacted through His chosen authorities, not by individuals. Pray for the safety and peace of soldiers, police, and all in such callings. When you make promises, keep your word, for the Lord will hold you responsible. Rejoice that He keeps His Word responsibly, promising and delivering His blessings and care.

Chs 33–35 The Lord walks with you and remains ever faithful, calling you to repentance, faith, and a blessed future. God's people today should avoid all syncretism with other religions, lest the teaching of God's Word be corrupted. As you interact with others who do not know or believe in Christ, pray for their deliverance, life, and salvation. As you face new challenges, consider that the Lord has already prepared your way. His gift and inheritance cannot be taken from you. The Lord leaves nothing to chance or accident but thoroughly prepares for His people's bodily needs, peace, and blessing. Entrust your life and ways to Him, for He cares for you!

Ch 36 For each tribe to retain its territory, God commands that Zelophehad's daughters choose husbands within their own tribe. Numbers ends with a brief summary statement that all regulations therein came by God's hand. He willingly bends an ear to hear even the most routine request and acts on each person's behalf with righteousness and mercy. In Christ, God cares for each individual.

CANONICITY

As part of the Torah, the most important portion of the Hebrew Scriptures for the Jews, the Book of Numbers was treasured. Christians received the book without question.

LUTHERAN THEOLOGIANS ON NUMBERS

Luther

"In the fourth book [Numbers], after the laws have been given, the princes and priests instituted, the tent and form of worship set up, and everything that pertains to the people of God made ready, then the whole thing begins to function; a test is made as to how well the arrangement operates and how satisfactory it is. This is why this very book says so much about the disobedience of the people and the plagues that came upon them. And some of the laws are explained and the number of the laws increased. Indeed this is the way it always goes; laws are quickly given, but when they are to go into effect and become operative, they meet with nothing but hindrance; nothing goes as the law demands. This book is a notable example of how vacuous it is to make people righteous with laws; rather, as St. Paul says, laws cause only sin and wrath." (AE 35:238)

"Therefore we see that these many laws of Moses were given not only to prevent anyone from choosing ways of his own for doing good and living aright, as was said above, but rather that sins might simply become numerous and be heaped up beyond measure. The purpose was to burden the conscience so that the hardened blindness would have to recognize itself, and feel its own inability and nothingness in the achieving of good. Such blindness must be thus compelled and forced by the law to seek something beyond the law and its own ability, namely, the grace of God promised in the Christ who was to come. Every law of God is good and right [Rom. 7:7–16], even if it only bids men to carry dung or to gather straw. Accordingly, whoever does not keep this good law—or keeps it unwillingly—cannot be righteous or good in his heart. But human nature cannot keep it otherwise than unwillingly. It must therefore, through this good law of God, recognize and feel its wickedness, and sigh and long for the aid of divine grace in Christ." (AE 35:244)

Gerhard

"*The fourth Book of Moses* is called *Wayedaber* by the Hebrews from its first word. The Greeks call it *Arithmoi* and the Latins "Numbers" because in it the tribes that left Egypt are counted, and it lists the number of the forty-two dwelling places in the wilderness. At the beginning there is a listing of the men among the people who were fit for military service and, later, of the Levites destined for the public administration of divine worship. It has thirty-six chapters and contains the history of thirty-eight years, nine months, and twenty days: from the first day of the second month of the second year after the exodus to the first day of the eleventh month of the fortieth year after the exodus. It describes the wandering of the Israelites through the wilderness and both the preparation preceding it and their situation following it, at which occasion the lawgiver intersperses examples of obedience honored with rewards and disobedience visited with punishments." (ThC E1 § 122)

Nomads' desert camp in the Negeb, southern Israel.

QUESTIONS PEOPLE ASK ABOUT NUMBERS

The Large Number of Israelites at the Exodus

A difficulty encountered in the Old Testament involves numbers that appear to be excessively high. Only a few instances need be cited to illustrate this phenomenon.

In Nu 3 the total number of newborn males in the one tribe of Levi is given as 22,000 (v 39) whereas the sum of the firstborn sons of all twelve tribes amounts to only 22,273 (v 43). At the dedication of the temple Solomon offered 22,000 oxen and 120,000 sheep (1Ki 8:63; 2Ch 7:5). According to 1Ch 29:4 David gave to the house of the Lord 3,000 talents of gold and the princes supplied another 5,000 talents of gold (29:7; a talent weighed over 60 pounds).

In dealing with such figures we must keep in mind two basic principles. In the first place, the numbers of the original text should not be regarded as fanciful inventions and therefore impossible and false. They were meant to represent a counting of persons and items that conformed to the facts in the case. In the second place, every effort should be made to determine what the original text actually said and how it came to read as it does.

It is a known fact that mistakes in numbers are the main source of misprints even in modern publications despite proofreaders and editorial scrutiny. The transmission of numerical data in the Old Testament manuscripts was no exception. But the problem was aggravated by factors unique to the recording of figures in the Hebrew language. The writers and copyists did not have Arabic numerals. The word for a number had to be spelled out in consonants without affixed vowels. When abbreviations, consisting of the first letter of the word, came into use, they became an additional source of confusion (a modern parallel: the letter "t" can stand for 2, 3, 10, 20, 1,000, etc.). The individual letters of the alphabet were also pressed into service to designate figures—for example, "a" for 1. The first letter of the Hebrew alphabet could also be the abbreviated spelling for the word *thousand*. Groupings of vertical and horizontal strokes appear in ancient Aramaic documents to specify the number of thousands and hundreds in a given figure. These and similar factors encountered by copyists of the ancient manuscripts may account for many numerical difficulties in the present text.

A much debated large number is the figure of Israel's population, recorded in Nu 1 and 26. Here a census of the people, twice compiled by Moses at the time of the exodus, itemizes figures "by fathers' houses" of those who were "from twenty years old and upward, all in Israel who are able to go to war" (1:2–3). When the contingents of men capable of bearing arms, supplied by each tribe and computed individually, are added, their total is given as 603,550 in 1:46 and 601,730 in 26:51. Agreeing in round figures, these totals are made up of individual entries for each tribe that, however, vary greatly in the two lists. Simeon, for example, is credited with 59,300 warriors in 1:23, but with only 22,200 in 26:14.

It is a matter of simple arithmetic to conclude that if each of the 600,000 soldiers came from a family of only two or three members, the entire population of Israel at the time consisted of c 2,500,000 people.

Taken at face value, this figure provokes some disconcerting questions. For example, how could these millions manage to pass through the opened sea with the Egyptian chariotry in hard pursuit?" If two million people settled in Canaan, the density of population would have been several times as great as that of the most densely populated countries of Europe. Furthermore, Moses told the escaped slaves several times that the seven nations which they were to displace were "greater and mightier" than they (Dt 4:38; 7:1; 9:1; 11:23). Those mentioned specifically were the Hittites, the Girgashites, the Amorites, the Canaanites, the Perizzites, the Hivites, and the Jebusites.

Various commentators have attempted to reduce this large figure and to make it more compatible with their understanding of circumstances prevailing at the time of the exodus. None of these, however, is acceptable if it is designed to question or eliminate the miraculous intervention of God to protect and sustain His chosen people during their sojourn in the desert.

British scholar J. W. Wenham offered one of the solutions (see "Large Numbers in the Old Testament." *Tyndale Bulletin* [1967]: 19–53). He points out that it is apparent that most of the high figures involve the Hebrew word for *thousand*, *'eleph*. However, this word also means "family" or "clan" (Nu 1:16; 10:4: "heads of the tribes of Israel"; cf Jsh 22:21, 30). When the same consonants are supplied with different vowels, the word designates "chiefs" (Gn 36:15–18; Ex 15:15). It is suggested, therefore, that in many instances this Hebrew word *'eleph* did not represent a number, as the later copyists assumed, but referred to an individual: a military leader of thousands, a commander of a large group, an officer, a fully equipped soldier. During the generations when Israel was under foreign domination this military meaning of the word was lost so that the copyists of the text understood it only as a number (a modern parallel would be "foremen" spelled "four men" and so interpreted).

Taking the word *'eleph* in the sense of a commander and the word for hundred to mean a contingent of soldiers, Wenham suggests that the text of the census figures originally meant to say: 580 leaders of 235 contingents, each of which consisted of some 25 to 100 men. The total fighting force is then estimated at 18,000 men and the entire population at about 72,000. The second census in Nu 26 is computed to reach comparable results, as well as that taken by David and recorded in 2Sm 24:9 and 1Ch 21:5. It should be noted that such a large group of people still was in need of bread from heaven and water from a rock to keep them alive during 40 years of desert wandering. Such proposals are admittedly tentative, incomplete, and receptive to further study.

At What Age Did the Levites Begin Their Service?

Numbers 4:3, 47 affirms: "From thirty years old up to fifty years old, all who can come on duty, to do the work in the tent of meeting. . . . From thirty years old up to fifty years old, everyone who could come to do the service of ministry and the service of bearing burdens in the tent of meeting. . . ."

Numbers 8:24 declares: "This applies to the Levites: from twenty-five years old and upward they shall come to do duty in the service of the tent of meeting."

First Chronicles 23:3, 24, 27 asserts: "The Levites, thirty years old and upward, were numbered, and the total was 38,000 men. . . . These were the sons of Levi by their fathers' houses, the heads of fathers' houses as they were listed according to the number of the names of the individuals from twenty years old and upward who were to do the work for the service of the house of the LORD. . . . For by the last words of David the sons of Levi were numbered from twenty years old and upward."

One may rightly wonder why different ages are mentioned. Careful observation provides solutions. According to 8:24 the Levites were eligible for *service in the tent of meeting* at the age of 25. The difference in the wording of the two passages appears to envisage a different kind of service at the lower age from the full exercise of official duties at the age of 30. Regarding 1Ch 23:24, one may observe that the Levites began to minister at the age of 30. "By the last words of David" they were to be *registered* for service at the age of 20.

One should note also that after the return from Babylon, when the temple was being restored, Levites were appointed "from twenty years old and upward, to supervise the work of the house of the LORD" (Ezr 3:8). Two factors apparently played a part. First, only 74 Levites returned from Babylon (Ezr 2:40; Ne 7:43). Since the Levites were in short supply, it was perhaps necessary to appoint younger men to this service. Second, these Levites were concerned only with the building project as advisers or foremen. They were not engaged in the sacrifice and worship at the temple, since the sanctuary had not yet been rebuilt. Thus the fact that they were under 25 would not be a disturbing issue, particularly in a time of short supply of Levites.

The Number of Fatalities

Numbers 25:1, 9 records: "While Israel lived in Shittim, the people began to whore with the daughters of Moab. . . . Nevertheless, those who died by the plague were twenty-four thousand."

First Corinthians 10:8 states: "We must not indulge in sexual immorality as some of them did, and twenty-three thousand fell in a single day."

Two attempts have been made to harmonize the 23,000 in 1 Corinthians with the 24,000 in Numbers. In our opinion both are weak solutions. One is based on the supposition that Paul's phrase "in a single day" may imply that another thousand perished in the next few days. Such a premise seems to be forcing the texts. Another wishes to refer the apostle's statement to the incident of the golden calf (Ex 32:6–8, 35) when God also sent a plague. No statistic on the fatalities from that plague is given (32:35), though 3,000 fell by the sword (32:28). This attempt is also weak since Paul refers to the golden calf in the previous verse (1Co 10:7) as an example of idolatry, while he connects the death of the 23,000 with sexual immorality. Likewise each of the following verses is said to refer to a specific and different event: tempting Christ (10:9) parallels Nu 21:4–8, and grumbling (10:10) recalls Nu 14:2–3, 26–38. So this attempt also is weak and forced.

No doubt a better solution is the realization that we have here large round numbers rather than an exact figure. Round numbers, of course, may vary. In the case of the fatalities in ancient Israel, an exact number of 23,456 or 23,521 might be reported in round numbers either as 23,000 or as 24,000. Similar is the practice today of stating the population of cities, states, and countries in round numbers.

It might also be noted that the addition of the phrase "in a single day" (not recorded in the Old Testament) may imply that Paul uses information from some rabbinic tradition, as he does in 2Tm 3:8, where the names of Jannes and Jambres are given without being included in Ex 7:11, 22.

Mount Nebo, from which Moses viewed the Promised Land.

FURTHER STUDY

Lay/Bible Class Resources

Kuske, Paul W. *Numbers*. PBC. St. Louis: Concordia, 2005. ♪ Lutheran author. Excellent for Bible classes. Based on the NIV translation.

Life by His Word. St. Louis: Concordia, 2009. ♪ More than 1,500 reproducible one-page Bible studies covering each chapter of the canonical Scriptures. Page references to *The Lutheran Study Bible*. CD-Rom and downloadable.

Rake, Tim. *Numbers: Faith in the Wilderness*. GWFT. St. Louis: Concordia, 2007. ♪ Lutheran author. Thirteen-session Bible study, including leader's notes and discussion questions.

Stirdivant, Mark, and R. Reed Lessing. *LifeLight: Wilderness Wanderings*. Leaders Guide and Enrichment Magazine/Study Guide. LL. St. Louis: Concordia, 2012. ♪ An in-depth, nine-session Bible study covering key texts of Leviticus, Numbers, and Deuteronomy with individual, small group, and lecture portions.

Wenham, Gordon J. *Numbers: An Introduction and Commentary*. TOTC. Downers Grove, IL: InterVarsity Press, 1981. ♪ Brief, somewhat popular; a good supplement. Too liberal on authorship, etc., but often very helpful.

Church Worker Resources

Ashley, Timothy R. *The Book of Numbers*. NICOT. Grand Rapids: Eerdmans, 1993. ♪ Evangelical commentary with emphasis on linguistics. Less theological.

Noordtzij, A. *Numbers: The Bible Student's Commentary*. Grand Rapids: Zondervan, 1983. ♪ A sequel to the volume on Leviticus. Too liberal on authorship, etc., but often very helpful.

Academic Resources

The Book of Numbers is the most neglected portion of the Pentateuch in modern scholarship. The selection of current commentaries is limited.

Ashley, Timothy R. *The Book of Numbers*. NICOT. Grand Rapids: Eerdmans, 1993. ♪ Evangelical commentary founded on philology and theology, based on the final form of the text. Some discussions of critical views.

K&D. *Biblical Commentary on the Old Testament: The Pentateuch*. Vol. 3. Grand Rapids: Eerdmans, 1971 reprint. ♪ Much detailed information on translation of Hebrew and location of places. A careful handling of theological issues in Numbers by a Lutheran scholar. This century-and-a-half old work should not be overlooked. Despite its age, it remains a most useful commentary on the Hebrew text.

Lange, John Peter. *Numbers*. LCHS. New York: Charles Scribner's Sons, 1890. ♪ A helpful older example of German biblical scholarship, based on the Hebrew text, which provides references to significant commentaries from the Reformation era forward.

Milgram, Jacob. *Numbers*. JPSTC. Philadelphia: The Jewish Publication Society, 2003. ♪ A Jewish commentary that views the book as history, providing traditional Torah commentary and scholarly insights

Romer, Thomas. *The Books of Leviticus and Numbers*. Levven: Peeters, 2008. ♪ A collection of academic papers illustrating the current state of critical opinions and arguing for the importance of these books in the Torah.

DEUTERONOMY

You shall love the Lord your God

Deuteronomy continues where Numbers leaves off. The setting and time remain the same: the plains of Moab east of the Jordan in the fortieth and final year of the exodus.[1] The two books also share an immediate and explicit concern for the people and the covenant "when you enter the land of Canaan" (Nu 34:2). But in Deuteronomy a greater urgency dominates its message. The long-awaited event is about to happen, and the people must prepare for it. They must remember their past and commit themselves to the future under God's gracious covenant.

"Deuteronomy" is a misnomer, based on the Septuagint's mistranslation of 17:18. The Hebrew there commands the king to prepare "a copy of this law," but the Greek translators mistakenly rendered it "this second law" (*deuteronomion touto*). That would imply that the book consists mostly of *repetition* of laws already encountered in previous books. This misunderstanding still appears to be widespread—or at least it is a charitable explanation for the common neglect of what is theologically one of the most important books in the Old Testament. There is some repetition of previous laws here, no doubt, but Deuteronomy's major thrust is the theology of the Torah ("instruction"), that is, the good news of the Gospel, which empowers and motivates all valid obedience before God. The frequency of its citation in the New Testament is no accident!

Deuteronomy represents Moses' last cycle of covenant instruction. Clearly centered in the Decalogue, this final concentric circle of legislation supplements and occasionally modifies previous laws (cf diagram, p 102). The following example illustrates the relationship of Deuteronomy to previous legislation as well as its deliberate adaption of known laws to changing conditions.

---

1 Verse 1 seems to indicate that Moses delivered the substance of these addresses when Israel first arrived at Kadesh two years after leaving Egypt. When they returned to Kadesh 38 years later, the new situation demanded that the same directions be given again.

View from the Jordan Valley, looking toward Israel's central highland.

OVERVIEW

Author
Moses the prophet

Date
1407/1406 BC

Place
Plains of Moab

People
Moses; Joshua; priests and Levites; judges, elders, and chiefs of Israel; Sihon and Og

Purpose
To present the renewal of the Sinai covenant for God's people before they entered the Promised Land

Law Themes
Devoted to destruction; hard-hearted; laws of the covenant; snare of idolatry; cursing

Gospel Themes
Redemption; "I am the LORD your God"; inheritance; righteousness by God's Word; promises of the covenant; God's love and calling; atonement; faithfulness; blessing

Memory Verses
Fair judgment (1:17); God's unchanging Word (4:2); the Lord is one (6:4–7); false prophets and the new prophet (18:15–22); God wounds and heals (32:39)

TIMELINE

1526 BC	Moses born
1446 BC	Exodus from Egypt
1407/1406 BC	Moses addresses Israel in Moab; Israel crosses the Jordan
1400 BC	Joshua gives Hebron to Caleb

In 16:1–12 the directions for the celebration of the Passover assume an acquaintance with earlier instructions for it (e.g., Ex 12:1–20) and repeat only some of the provisions. But Deuteronomy adapts one point: as long as Israel was encamped at the tabernacle in the wilderness, this festival was to be observed within each household. But after the conquest, Israel was to leave its households (Dt 16:5) and still gather "at the place that the LORD your God will choose to make His name dwell in it" (v 6). In Canaan, attendance at the central sanctuary would require the worshipers to assemble there no matter how far from their homes. As the second example, note that during the journey all animals that were to be eaten had to be slaughtered at the door of the tabernacle (Lv 17) except when anyone catches "any beast or bird that may be eaten" (v 13). Such a requirement would be unrealistic and punitive in Canaan. Therefore,

> When the LORD your God enlarges your territory, . . . and you say, "I will eat meat," . . . you may eat meat whenever you desire. If the place that the LORD your God will choose to put His name there is too far from you, then you may kill any of your herd or your flock, . . . and you may eat within your towns. (Dt 12:20–21)

Deuteronomy includes some sections of legislation applicable only to settled life in Canaan—e.g., concerning false and true prophets (13:1–11; 18:20–22), concerning the kingship (17:14–20), and concerning the conduct of war (ch 20). Deuteronomy represents Israel's transition from a nomadic life in the wilderness to a settled life in the Promised Land. It presents itself as a farewell sermon from Moses, who announced that the Lord would supply other prophets for leading the people in the future.

Historical and Cultural Setting

According to the traditional chronology of the Bible, Pharaoh Amenhotep II (1426–1400 BC) would have ruled Egypt while Moses preached this last message to Israel on the plains of Moab. Amenhotep's armies successfully traveled up the Mediterranean coast to the Orontes River where they defeated the Mitanni. In later campaigns they would overcome rebellions in Syria and secure trade relations with the Babylonians, the Hittites, and the Mitanni. The Egyptians maintained vassal relationships with the rulers of Canaan at this time. However, the mountainous territories of the Canaanites stood between Israel and the Egyptians, limiting direct interaction.

COMPOSITION

Author(s)

There is no reason why the entire Book of Deuteronomy had to be delivered as one continuous sermon from Moses' lips. Like the later prophetic oracles, Moses or an editor may well have edited and shaped the book in language as well as in arrangement.

Amenhotep II dominated the coastal region of Canaan but not the highlands.

Very few would care to argue that the final chapter (Moses' death and burial) stems from Moses (not theologically impossible, but historically unlikely). That, plus other concluding material, makes plain that the bulk of Deuteronomy was welded into the entire Pentateuch at some later date, presumably after—but not too long after—Moses' death. Little more can be said with any certainty, but such assumptions are entirely compatible both with the biblical data and with the doctrine of verbal inspiration. For more on authorship, see pp 4–11 and "Resources," p 166.

Moses' Place in History

Moses' death marks the end of an epoch. "There has not arisen a prophet since in Israel like Moses, whom the LORD knew face to face" (34:10). By God's choice and grace, Moses was "the man of God" and "the servant of the LORD" (33:1; 34:5).

Moses mediated a covenant that endured for centuries, and then its outward forms ended. When *the* Prophet, the Word made flesh, arrived, what was preparatory in the old covenant for God's ultimate covenant was absorbed in fulfillment. As God's spokesman, Moses transmitted to and defined for Israel a way of life with God based on faith in the promise of His unearned, merciful forgiveness. "By it [faith] the people of old received their commendation" (Heb 11:2), and it is still possible to be saved only by faith, by "looking to Jesus, the founder and perfecter of our faith" (12:2). Faith in God's forgiveness (the faith of both covenants) is valid for only one reason: the Lamb of God who took away the sins of the world.

The demand of the Law (God's call for full outward and inward devotion to Him) also remains in force. It was fulfilled by Him who was put under the curse of the law (Gal 3:10–13), but He did not destroy the Law (Mt 5:17–20). For He also requires, "If you love Me . . . keep My commandments" (Jn 14:15). No less demanding than the Mosaic Law, His commandments are identical with the Old Testament summary of its law:

> You shall love the Lord your God with all your heart and with all your soul and with all your mind. This is the great and first commandment. And a second is like it: You shall love your neighbor as yourself. On these two commandments depend all the Law and the Prophets. (Mt 22:37–40; cf Dt 6:5; Lv 19:18)

Therefore, Jesus could make the sweeping and unqualified statement, "Moses . . . wrote of Me" (Jn 5:46). Not a verse or chapter only, but all the words of this prophet point to Him and come to rest in Him.

On the road to Emmaus, when Jesus explained to the two disciples "in all the Scriptures the things concerning Himself" (Lk 24:27), He began with Moses.

Date of Composition

According to traditional chronology and interpretation, Moses wrote the book in c 1407/1406 BC after addressing the people on the plains of Moab. The critical penchant is to attempt to construct an evolutionary pattern, with Deuteronomy representing the language in the age of King Josiah (640–609 BC) in contrast to the classical "Golden Age" prose of writers during the reign of King Solomon (970–931 BC). But do we really have sufficient evidence or controls for such a construct, other than arguments in a circle? The critics sometimes compare the texts with the extrabiblical Lachish letters (early sixth century), though these letters are too brief to prove anything in this respect. From about the same date are the prose sections of the Book of Jeremiah, which are often considered major evidence. Less certainly, there are the homiletical sections of the Historical Books of uncertain date (often considered a "Deuteronomic history," of a piece with Deuteronomy originally, and hence yielding another argument in a circle). But, if Moses, the great pioneer, had set the pace, is it so unlikely that prophets and other writers would sometimes continue to use the same idiom for centuries, especially when dealing with similar topics? One would have little difficulty providing parallels in various homiletical traditions of the West (e.g., the influence of the KJV and the Luther Bible on English and German writers).

Purpose/Recipients

Use of history to elucidate and emphasize the key elements of the covenant becomes more meaningful when one considers the circumstances and the concerns of Moses. Previously, the people had in their midst the mediator of the covenant, but they had not often listened to him. Moses therefore makes one final grand plea for faithfulness to the covenant obligations. Knowing that he is about to die, Moses is concerned that Israel follow his successor as God's appointed one.

An entirely new generation faced Moses. Not one (save Joshua and Caleb) of the original "signers" of the covenant at Sinai was present. This was a new people. They could shrug off all responsibility and say, "Our fathers may have said, 'All that the Lord says, we will do,' but *we* have made no such promise." Does this new generation standing before Moses truly believe that the covenant made at Sinai was made with and for them and was not just a thing of the past? If so, do they understand with their heart, soul, and mind the implications of obedient commitment?

Furthermore, Israel had arrived just recently on the plains of Moab; yet two-and-a-half tribes already were situated in their permanent lands. Would they renege on helping the other tribes? When the people have taken possession of the land and have begun to enjoy its fruits, will they still feel a need for the Lord? Or will they be tempted to say, "The covenant was made in the wilderness for the wilderness; it does not apply to life in Canaan"? Would Israel actually kill or drive out the idolatrous people of Canaan and destroy their places of worship? These concerns shape the discourses in Deuteronomy and reveal the urgency in what Moses has to say "today" (4:40, et al.) if the covenant is to remain in force after the conquest of Canaan.

The Kadesh Treaty established peace between the Hittites and Egyptians. The form of such treaties has parallels with the biblical covenants.

Literary Features

Genre

Deuteronomy is written in the form of a suzerain-vassal treaty like those in use among the Hittites and like the book of the covenant (Ex 19:24; studies of the Hittite suzerainty treaties have demolished the critical theory that "covenant" *must* represent a later development in Israel when priestly writers introduced legalistic ideas about serving God). Moses presents the covenant in the form of an address or farewell sermon to the people, beginning with a historical prologue (Dt 1:6–3:29), followed by moral (chs 4–11), civil (chs 19–25), and ceremonial stipulations (chs 12–18, 26). Chapters 27–28 describe a liturgy for confirming the covenant, followed by admonitions toward renewal (chs 29–30). The last chapter describes the succession of Joshua as leader and the death of Moses.

In most of Deuteronomy, events of the past (often in story form) are interwoven into the fabric of Moses' long discourses about the covenant and its laws. Deuteronomy differs from Numbers in the way it relates history to legislation. In Numbers, instruction was given as historical situations arose. In Deuteronomy, history becomes a part of the instruction itself as Moses underscores God's presence and activity in all the events that brought Israel to that time and place (events for the most part already recorded in Exodus through Numbers).[2] The language is distinctive enough in many respects, e.g., many subordinate clauses are used (syntaxis) in contrast to the "and—and" coordination of most Hebrew narrative (classical parataxis). Likewise the style is often expansive, if not at first glance rambling and repetitious. Such is characteristic of sermons in all ages. Many similar hortatory passages appear elsewhere in the Pentateuch.

---

2   In some instances Deuteronomy adds a new feature or detail not previously included. E.g., in Nu 13:1–2 the spies were sent by Moses at God's command. Dt 1:22–23 adds that Israel originally had requested this precautionary measure. Additional examples can readily be found.

OUTLINE

I. Preamble (1:1–8)

II. Historical Prologue (1:9–4:43)

  A. The Appointment of Leaders (1:9–18)

  B. Spies Sent Out (1:19–25)

  C. Rebellion against the Lord (1:26–46)

  D. Wanderings in the Desert (2:1–23)

  E. Defeat of Sihon, King of Heshbon (2:24–37)

  F. Defeat of Og, King of Bashan (3:1–11)

  G. Division of the Land (3:12–20)

  H. Moses Forbidden to Cross the Jordan (3:21–29)

  I. Obedience Commanded (4:1–14)

  J. Idolatry Forbidden (4:15–31)

  K. The Lord Is God (4:32–40)

  L. Cities of Refuge (4:41–43)

III. Stipulations of the Covenant (4:44–26:19)

  A. Moral Law (4:44–11:32)

    1. Introduction to the Law (4:44–49)

    2. The Ten Commandments (ch 5)

    3. Love the Lord your God (ch 6)

    4. Driving out the nations (ch 7)

    5. Do not forget the Lord (ch 8)

    6. Not because of Israel's righteousness (9:1–6)

    7. The golden calf (9:7–29)

    8. Tablets like the first ones (10:1–11)

    9. Fear the Lord (10:12–22)

    10. Love and obey the Lord (ch 11)

  B. Ceremonial Law (12:1–16:17)

    1. The one place of worship (ch 12)

    2. Worshiping other gods (ch 13)

    3. Clean and unclean food (14:1–21)

    4. Tithes (14:22–29)

    5. The year for canceling debts (15:1–11)

    6. Freeing servants (15:12–18)

    7. The firstborn animals (15:19–23)

    8. Passover (16:1–8)

    9. Feast of Weeks (16:9–12)

    10. Feast of Booths (16:13–17)

Characters

Moses is the chief figure in Deuteronomy, which also refers to Joshua, the priests and Levites, and other leaders in Israel. For more on these figures, see pp 63, 67, and 129.

Narrative Development or Plot

Moses' great concern on the plains of Moab was that the covenant not become a thing of the past. The introduction to his discourses reflects his desire to make a lasting impression on his hearers: "Moses undertook to explain this law" (1:5). The Hebrew word for "explain" actually means "to engrave" and is used only here as "explain." Moses wanted to *inscribe*—indelibly write—this law on the hearts of his people; for the time was coming soon when he would no longer be alive to repeat it himself. Moses therefore provided for the law to be engraved[3] on stone (27:1–8) soon after his death when "you cross over the Jordan."

אָנֹכִי ה' ‎ לֹא תִּרְצָח
לֹא יִהְיֶה ‎ לֹא תִּנְאָף
לֹא תִשָּׂא ‎ לֹא תִּגְנֹב
זָכוֹר אֶת ‎ לֹא תַעֲנֶה
כַּבֵּד אֶת ‎ לֹא תַחְמֹד

Listings of the Ten Commandments have differed for different groups. This Jewish example begins with Ex 20:2 (Dt 5:6), "I am the LORD."

Deuteronomy shows how Moses put all his powers of persuasion and oratory into applying the law to his listeners. He appealed; he illustrated; he pleaded; he threatened; he summarized; he itemized; he repeated. His words are charged with a sense of crisis and finality. They reflect the warm compassion in the heart of a man whose life since the burning bush had been devoted to his people. He shows urgent concern for the future based on years of experience with a fickle people.

Second, he worked to persuade the present generation of Israelites, old and young, to become part of God's plan, to "enter into the sworn covenant of the LORD your God, which the LORD your God is making with you today" (29:12). In 28 chapters he explains the past, present, and future significance of the covenant. Only then (in ch 29) does he expect Israel to act on the basis of his instruction and to enter into the covenant as did their fathers.

---

3 The same Hebrew word for "explain" is used here as in 1:5. The word occurs once elsewhere of writing on stone: in Hab 2:2 where two verses later the famous words to be inscribed include "the righteous shall live by his faith."

Moses taught well. Certain lessons are repeated again and again, as if to engrave them. Yet they all have one major objective: to enable the Israelites to see themselves in the perspective of the unchanging covenant of the unchanging God. The outcome was to be a whole-souled participation.

Resources

Moses referred three times to "this Book of the Law" (29:21; 30:10; 31:26; cf 28:58, 61; 29:20, 27; 31:24) suggesting that much of the Book of Deuteronomy was composed when he delivered his message to explain and renew the covenant. The title was later applied to the whole of the five Books of Moses, perhaps as early as the time of Joshua (Jsh 8:31, 34; 23:6), who may have made editorial additions to the books or adjoined his own work to them (24:26).

Text and Translations

The traditional Hebrew text of Deuteronomy, like that of the other Books of Moses, is well preserved. The Samaritans preserved their own version of the book, which includes some unique readings. The LXX text of Deuteronomy is a literal rendering of the Hebrew, with occasional passages clearly providing a Greek idiom. Thirty fragments of Deuteronomy manuscripts were found at Qumran, most of which support the traditional Hebrew text. After Psalms, it was the most common book of the Bible among the scrolls.

DOCTRINAL CONTENT

Summary Commentary

Late Bronze Age sword from a tomb near the Canaanite city of Acco.

1:1–8 Through many trials, God raises a new generation in Israel and brings them to the plains of Moab just east of the Jordan River. The Promised Land is in sight.

1:9–3:22 In His great love, God establishes a judicial system administered by God-fearing men selected from among the Israelites. Moses retells the story of the Israelites' rebellion. Although God promised to drive out the Canaanites, the Israelites listened to the 10 spies instead and recoiled in fear. As a result, an entire generation of Israelites died in the desert. Their disobedience causes God to withdraw His presence and delay giving them the Promised Land. After 40 years, God teaches His faithfulness to a new generation and prepares them as a father prepares his dear children. God's promise of land for the Edomites, Moabites, and Ammonites means that the Israelites must pass farther north. God leads the charge to drive the Amorites from the land. The Israelites' victories belong only to God. Stubborn King Sihon places his army in God's path, and it is swallowed up as easily as Pharaoh's army in the Red Sea. Moses presents Israel's victory over Og, the apportionment of land east of the Jordan River, and the installation of Joshua.

3:23–4:43 Sin and its consequences walk hand in hand. Moses' consequence was that he did not enter the Promised Land at that time. God desires to dwell among His people, but a holy God cannot live among an unholy people. So God lovingly establishes His ordinances, including the Ten Commandments. Through Moses, God warns the Israelites of the perils of following pagan gods. Consequences would include forfeiting the land, though God retained ownership of it (Lv 25:23). Moses also reminds the people that with fire and wonders God has established Himself as the God of Israel. No other god has led a people away from their captors, conquered their enemies, and established them in a new land. The Lord provides refuge for His people east of the Jordan.

4:44–6:25 The conquest of Canaan is underway. Territories once belonging to Sihon and Og are under full control of the Reubenites, Gadites, and the half-tribe of Manasseh. Moses presents God's Word to the Israelites, including many laws and promises. Moses also recounts how all of the Israelites assembled at Mount Sinai to hear God present guidelines for a holy relationship with Him and with one another. God desires to shower His people with blessings, but their hearing and following of His Word is required for Him to dwell among them.

Chs 7–11 God's hand is raised against the inhabitants of Canaan, whose sin has ripened before God, causing His action. God, not the Israelites on their own, will drive the Canaanites from the Promised Land. He plans to fulfill His promise to Israel's greatest ancestors: Abraham, Isaac, and Jacob. God weaves a pattern of worship into the lives of the Israelites. By trusting God's promises and keeping His commands, they honor His name and show God's grace to the nations surrounding them (4:6). Their disobedience dishonors God's name. He will soon lead the Israelites into Canaan, a land that 40 years earlier they had called unconquerable. But God Himself will lead the charge with "consuming fire" (9:3). By retelling the story of the golden calf (Ex 32), Moses teaches a new generation about the consequences of disobeying God's commands. The entire nation was about to forfeit their status as God's chosen people. But God mercifully turned away from their sin. Only Moses' prayer of intercession spared them. God inscribed two new tablets with His precious commands and promised to lead the Israelites into Canaan. He desires that those who love Him realize that He has the awesome power to forgive sins. In respect of this power, and in honor due His holy name, the Israelites are to reflect God's love back to Him in their words and actions. In so doing, they witness God's love to the nations around them and to the foreigners among them. Soon the Israelites will cross the Jordan River to begin conquering the land God had promised to Abram so many years before.

12:1–16:17 The Lord calls His people to cleanse the land of all places of false worship. He would provide for them a place to receive His presence in grace and blessing. The Lord warns His people to fear Him, especially when they are tempted to worship the gods and follow the abominable customs of the people whose land they are to possess. As members of His household, they must avoid mimicking the self-destructive behaviors of their pagan neighbors. The Israelites were to adopt new and distinct table manners, eating only clean food. God would provide for His people through the land that He was giving them. He commands them to use their portion for worship and to provide for the needy. Since the Lord would generously provide for His people, He commands them to be generous with one another. At the Passover festival, the people would remember the way God delivered them from slavery in Egypt. The Feast of Booths includes foreigners, who are also called to celebrate God's gracious provision of the harvest.

16:18–18:22 God commands impartiality in judges because He is Himself impartial in judgment (Rm 2:11). He forbids all forms of false worship even as He provides for instruction in the truth. Difficult legal cases require special consideration, and the people are to respect the decisions. God will allow His people to have a king, but only on certain conditions. Note well the focus on God's Word in this description of a good and godly king. Though the Levitical priesthood will not have an inheritance of land that will provide their sustenance, the Lord Himself will be their inheritance. They are to share in the offerings that are brought to the Lord. As Israel enters the Promised Land, they will be exposed to the influences of the false, occultist worship practices of the nations surrounding them, which they are to avoid.

Criteria for identifying false prophets and false prophecy are given. God will provide a source of revelation to communicate with His people: He will send a line of prophets that will culminate in the great Prophet promised here, the Lord Jesus Christ.

Ch 19 God gives statutes covering both unintentional and intentional killings. God gives each family of His people an allotment of land, and the property boundaries of neighbors are to be respected (cf 5:19, 21). Laws are given concerning witnesses who bring accusations against others, and safeguards concerning them are given to ensure justice.

Ch 20 God gives statutes governing warfare. God's moral will is not to be suspended but is to guide and direct our actions, even in matters of war. In the face of danger, God encourages His people with the promise of His presence and the assurance that He fights for them to give them the victory.

Ch 21 The Lord provides laws regarding violence and family, beginning with a sacrifice for an unsolved murder. He emphasizes the value of human life by describing the atonement that must be made for it. Israel is given laws governing the marrying of female captives. God expects Israel to act differently than the world around them. God has established marriage for the good of men and women. The inheritance rights of the firstborn are safeguarded. God assures fair treatment and proper inheritance, which helps stabilize family life. Persistent and utter rebellion against parental authority is covered by a law that demands capital punishment if there is no repentance. God demands that the integrity of the family be maintained by honoring fathers and mothers as His representatives to their children. To despise one's mother and father is to despise God Himself and threaten the well-being of the larger community. Executed criminals are not to be left hanging but must be buried the same day. They are cursed by God and will defile God's gift, the land of promise, which God had hallowed.

Chs 22–25 God gives a variety of laws governing brotherly love, maintaining distinctions in the created order, and keeping Israel unto Himself, such as laws concerning marriage, promiscuity, adultery, rape, and incestuous adultery. These laws protect individuals, the integrity of the family unit, and the social stability and purity of the nation. Other laws in this section protect the weak from the strong.

Ch 26 God's grace to Israel is celebrated as they are reminded of deliverance from slavery in Egypt, the gift of land, and being a holy people chosen as the Lord's treasured possession. Also described is Israel's response in the offering of firstfruits, the payment of the tithe for the sake of the needy, and a promise to keep the Lord's command.

Chs 27–30 The Lord's command regarding Mount Ebal emphasizes the importance of God's written Word and God's desire that His people respond joyfully with sacrifices of praise. The old covenant promised blessings to those who kept God's Law and curses to anyone who did not (cf Gal 3:10). In fact, Moses forcefully details the dreadful consequences of disobeying the voice of the Lord God. These punishments would not be the result of the natural cycles of history. Moses repeatedly identifies the Lord as the One who sends the curses. In this farewell speech, Moses emphasizes several important truths: the Lord's gracious care for every Israelite, the responsibility of each person to abide by God's covenant, and the certainty that anyone who turns away from the Lord will be punished. Individual responsibility is highlighted. The Lord's declaration to His people to choose life is inseparable from His covenant of grace that He established with them.

Chs 31–34 Moses' introduction of Joshua as his successor begins with acknowledging God's judgment on his own disobedience, which disqualified him from entering the Promised Land. Israel could have no relationship with the Lord God apart from His Word. Israel's very existence depended upon the Lord. In response to His grace, Israel was to engage in regularly reading the Law and instructing future generations about the one true God, who led them through the wilderness to the Promised Land. Employing the Law, Moses prophesies that Israel will be unfaithful. Yet, he also encourages Joshua to be strong and repeats God's promise that He will bring them into the Promised Land (31:23). Moses' song likewise prophesies Israel's apostasy and professes the one true God. For His name's sake and in His compassion, He would vindicate His people and vanquish the enemy. The Lord reminds Moses that he has disqualified himself from entering the Promised Land due to breaking faith with Him. Yet, in His mercy, God permits Moses to see the Promised Land from a distance. The conclusion of Deuteronomy signals a transition in leadership from Moses to Joshua, a transition from the oral communication of the Word to the written communication of the Word, a transition from the wilderness wanderings to the eventual occupation of the Promised Land. Moses' final messages to the people include both warnings (in the words of a song) and promises (in the words of a blessing).

Specific Law Themes

Moses admonished the people of Israel to devote the wicked Canaanites to destruction. He likewise warned Israel against hard-heartedness, lest they end up like the Canaanites. Deuteronomy provides numerous laws of the covenant in preparation for the settlement in the Promised Land. When the people move into the land, they must avoid the snare of idolatry, which has led the Canaanites astray. Moses has the Israelites take oaths of loyalty subject to the curse of the Law if they should disobey it, that is, they will surely suffer the penalties God threatens.

Specific Gospel Themes

Deuteronomy caps the theme of redemption that began with the story of the exodus. God has brought them to the new land He promised as an inheritance. As in Leviticus and Numbers, Moses repeats God's covenant declaration: "I am the LORD your God." God's Word, the Torah-instruction Moses proclaims and writes, will be the righteousness of the people. The covenant includes not just stipulations but numerous promises of the covenant, with attendant blessings. God emphasizes His love for and faithfulness to Israel, since He called their fathers to become His chosen people.

Grapevines are trailed along the ground to preserve their moisture. Although the climate is drier today, the Promised Land may still yield a bountiful harvest.

Specific Doctrines

Although each of Moses' discourses has its own emphasis, seven points weave back and forth between them, providing a continuous, unified whole.

1. The Covenant Land As "Promised Land"

The opening words of the first sermon stress Israel's conquest of Canaan as part of a long-range plan of God.

See, I have set the land before you. Go in and take possession of the land that the LORD swore to your fathers, to Abraham, to Isaac, and to Jacob, to give to them and to their offspring after them. (1:8)[4]

The conquest of Canaan would not be a national achievement or the result of natural cause and effect. Without the promise to the fathers there would be no conquest. The Promised Land was to be theirs only as heirs of the promise.

2. Continuing Validity of the Covenant

Moses recalled many events of the past to show how God had been fulfilling this promise ever since the exodus began. But most often he called attention to the history of the past few months: the defeat of the Amorite kings, Og and Sihon, the most recent link in the chain of events that firmly bound this people to the covenant made with the patriarchs. Moses' purpose seems obvious—everyone in his audience had experienced the event. Though many had been born after other victories, no one could say of this one, "I don't know whether your story is true." This victory over the Amorites proved to all, young and old, that they had overcome not by their own strength but by God's. Possession of the land would be possible only because "I give it to you."

Moses also had to impress on his listeners in sharp and precise language the contemporary nature and continuing validity of the covenant. Therefore, he said to people who were but children or not even born yet at the time of Sinai,

The LORD our God made a covenant with us in Horeb. Not with our fathers did the LORD make this covenant, but with us, who are all of us here alive today. The LORD spoke with *you* face to face at the mountain, out of the midst of the fire. (5:2–4, emphasis added)

With an eye toward asking this new people to commit itself to the covenant, Moses emphasized that thereby they would enter into a relationship with God identical to what He had established with their fathers at Horeb (Mount Sinai). The presuppositions, terms, and obligations of the covenant had not changed after 40 years—and they were to remain unchanged. To be the covenant people, Israel is required always

to fear the LORD your God, to walk in all His ways, to love Him, to serve the LORD your God with all your heart and with all your soul, and to keep the commandments and statutes of the LORD. (10:12–13)

---

4   Moses recalls this oath to the fathers about 25 times in Deuteronomy.

The basis and foundation of instruction in God's will were laid down once and for all in the Ten Commandments engraved on two tables of stone (4:13). Now Moses engraves them on his hearers' hearts by repeating them verbatim (5:6–21) before using them as the text of an extended sermon (5:22–11:32). Israel's covenant status depends on continued obedience to these basic and all-embracing requirements of undivided loyalty to God.

3. Covenant Forms and Ceremonies

Furthermore, God had required at Sinai that the people observe outward forms and ceremonies. Moses proceeded to remind the living generation also of these covenant obligations to be

> a people holy to the LORD your God, and the LORD has chosen you to be a people for His treasured possession, out of all the peoples who are on the face of the earth. (14:2; cf 7:6)

The moral, ceremonial, social, and political expressions of their separation from all other nations and total consecration to God were designed not merely for the desert, but

> you shall be careful to do [them] in the land that the LORD, the God of your fathers, has given you to possess, all the days that you live on the earth. (12:1)

Moses repeats many of these provisions in his second discourse (chs 12–26), fully expounding some and making minor adjustments in a few to meet the needs of life in the Promised Land.

4. The Covenant of God's Grace

Just as the Ten Commandments remained the same, so did the terms of the covenant shaping God's relationship to His people. The covenant would never be based on merit. It would remain His instrument of grace to a people that had not and never would deserve what He had bound and pledged Himself to give in the promises to the patriarchs and to the fathers at Sinai.

The covenant had to be of grace. From the beginning Israel stubbornly had broken the covenant often, shamefully, and defiantly. Moses reminds them:

> Remember and do not forget how you provoked the LORD your God to wrath in the wilderness. From the day you came out of the land of Egypt until you came to this place, you have been rebellious against the LORD. (9:7)

173

5. Obedience and Repentance

In view of Israel's past performance, Moses rightly worried whether the people would or could continue as the covenant nation. If the people persist in breaking the covenant by their disobedience, God has no obligation to keep them as His covenant people. He even will deprive them again of the land they have not quite inherited.

On the other hand, the God who began the covenant with the patriarchs and the fathers at Sinai also promises to continue to show mercy to those who love Him and keep His commandments. As in the past, He will receive back into His grace those who penitently plead for His forgiving mercy. God's power has not grown weaker. He can and will bless beyond expectation, for

> Behold, to the LORD your God belong heaven and the heaven of heavens, the earth with all that is in it. Yet the LORD set His heart in love on your fathers and chose their offspring after them, you above all peoples, as you are this day. (10:14–15)

6. Future Temptation to Break the Covenant: Ease in Canaan

Moses anticipated unprecedented occasions of temptations to break the covenant once Israel had crossed the Jordan and taken possession of the land. If a previous generation had been willing to surrender God for the easy life of Egypt (compared to the wilderness), will not this generation also quickly forget God once it enjoys what the Promised Land has to offer? Thus, Moses warns,

> Take care lest you forget the LORD your God . . . when you have eaten and are full and have built good houses and live in them, and when your herds and flocks multiply and your silver and gold is multiplied and all that you have is multiplied . . . [and] you say in your heart, "My power and the might of my hand have gotten me this wealth." (8:11–13, 17)

7. Future Temptation to Break the Covenant: Idolatry

Similarly, Moses was apprehensive of Israel's future exposure to idolatry. If they had "played the harlot" at their first contact with idolatrous practice in Moab (Nu 25), what would they do when they encountered it at every turn in Canaan? God therefore directed the Israelites to exterminate the idolatrous people of Canaan and to destroy their places of worship, their altars, and all their paraphernalia for idolatry.

In this context the direction from God to set up an altar on Mount Ebal after the entry into Canaan takes on importance. This is one of 18 times in Deuteronomy in which God specifies that "you shall seek the place that the LORD your God will choose, out of all your tribes to put His name and make His habitation there" (12:5).

In Canaanite idolatry, the gods could be manipulated to do the bidding of the people. Not so with the one God, Yahweh. He is not at the disposal of His worshipers wherever or whenever they desire to put Him into their service by magic and incantation. Nor is He a force of nature to be controlled. Since He is God the Almighty, *He* will choose the places of worship according to His good pleasure and according to the requirements of developing circumstances.

The excavator of a stone structure on Mount Ebal interpreted it as a worship site, possibly even as the altar built by Joshua (Dt 27). Others regard the structure as the base of a tower, though some concede that the many animal bones there suggest the site was used for sacrifice.

Moses wanted Israel to enter the Promised Land forewarned and forearmed. To do so, they had to keep the First Commandment above all: "You shall have no other gods before Me" (5:7). Moses explained this commandment and summed up its positive teaching in the great *Shema* (so-called for its opening Hebrew word), "Hear, O Israel: The LORD our God, the LORD is one!" (6:4), which became a creedal statement about God's essence for Jews and Christians. The Lord calls His people to wholehearted love, loyalty, and life commitment—a deepening of the First Commandment to have no other gods. In fact, He must impart such gifts and trust through His teachings (cf 30:6, 19; 32:39).

In 12:8, 28, 32; 27:6 God makes clear that His Word is to be our guide in matters of both faith and works. The believer is not allowed to set up His own Law. The Word is a norm and guide for life, which God has prepared in advance for us to use (Eph 2:10). He promises ongoing access to His life-giving Word through the gifts of prophets who will speak it to Israel. Chapter 18 provides a key text anticipating a prophet like Moses, which was fulfilled in the appearing of Jesus (Ac 3:22–23; 7:37). Despite the prominence of the Shema, Luther regarded the prophecy of Jesus as the chief passage of the book.

Application

1:1–8 God's covenant promise is sure. He keeps His word to His people, including His word to you. Rejoice in the Lord's faithfulness as you share His testimonies with others.

1:9–3:22 We have a faithful Judge in heaven who wishes not to condemn us but to deliver us from sin. We are wrong to trust the word of others over the Word of God. Our victories, too, belong to God. Our salvation is only by God's hand, not our own. By His Son's precious blood, we are justified; by His Spirit, we are sanctified.

3:23–4:43 Forgiven sinners rejoice that the consequences of sin no longer bring eternal separation from God. Through the Word, the Lord leads us to faith and to keep His commands faithfully; He shows forth His blessings in our lives. Such a God is worthy of our worship and praise. In Christ, He declares us His very own people and prepares an everlasting home for us.

4:44–6:26 The Lord promises many and great blessings to those who receive His testimonies. Sinful men and women need an intermediary between themselves and God. Though Moses served in that capacity at Sinai, Jesus Christ fills that role in a much greater way for you and for me (1Tm 2:5–6; cf Rm 8:1–2). God's Holy Spirit now dwells within all believers. Indeed, we become God's dwelling place (1Co 3:16).

Ch 7–11 Today, through Jesus Christ, believers are led into the promised land of eternal life. Each time we look upon the empty cross, we are reminded of God's promise of redemption fulfilled in Christ. Yet how easily Christians today look upon themselves as self-made, dishonoring God in the process. Our salvation came at a terrible price: it cost God the life of His Son, a gift we are to remember in Holy Communion until Christ comes again in His glory (1Co 11:26). God calls His people to come before Him and seek His forgiveness in order that He might "cleanse us from all unrighteousness" (1Jn 1:9). Pray for yourself and others who face temptation. Take comfort in the promise that Jesus intercedes for you and will be with you amid all struggles. By God's grace, we repent of our stubbornness. Through Baptism, we are made new creatures (Rm 6:4), counting ourselves dead to sin and alive to God (6:11).

12:1–16:17 God forbids us from worshiping Him in ways that seem good to us but that are contrary to His Word. As members of God's household (Eph 2:19), we, too, must leave behind all those behaviors and habits that damage ourselves and the Christian community (5:1–7). God calls us to share with our neighbor in need from the abundance of our possessions (cf Eph 4:28; Lk 10:25–37). Because God provides for us, we do not need to be anxious about our sustenance in this life (Mt 6:31). As we celebrate the Lord's Supper "in remembrance" of Jesus, we receive the freedom from sin that He alone gives. Together we experience the true unity that comes from access to God's grace in Christ Jesus.

16:18–18:22 In this we stand warned: there will be tribulation and distress for all who do evil, including those within the household of God. We did not choose God, but He chose us (Jn 15:16). We can be rightly confident that He will keep us in true faith and lead us through death to eternal life. When the Law of God convicts us, we must not seek to escape judgment by trying to gain other people's approval for our sinful actions. Our gracious God comes to us in His Word, warning us of snares and pitfalls, reminding us of our relationship to Him as His beloved children, and encouraging and comforting us with the assurance of His love and forgiveness. God graciously desires to speak to us to give to us what we cannot live without, the Word that has the power to bring us to repentance (Rm 3:20, Law), make us alive to eternal life (Rm 1:16, Gospel), and keep us in the truth (Jn 8:31–32). As God provided for the needs of the Levitical priests through the gifts of His people, God's people are moved by His grace in Christ Jesus to support those who labor among them, especially in preaching the life-giving Gospel of Jesus.

A "Seat of Moses" from which a rabbi would teach (Chorazim synagogue, Galilee; fourth century AD).

Ch 19 God has given life—all life, from conception on—and reserves the right to take it. He deals bountifully with us to care for our physical needs in this life, but even more, He has given us an inheritance in heaven, secured for us and marked out by Christ Jesus! His perfect justice is seen at the cross, where payment was made in full for sin. There, Jesus became a curse for us; the One who knew no sin was made sin for us (2Co 5:21).

Ch 20 We have been given the promise of our Savior's constant presence with us, even on the battlefields we tread. In your struggles, call on Him, for He has promised grace, wisdom, and every blessing in your hour of need.

Ch 21 In satisfying His divine justice, God sent His own Son into this world to make the expiatory sacrifice, the atonement, for our lives on the cross of Calvary, there shedding His lifeblood for the guilt of our sins. The model for marriage is that of the Bridegroom, Christ, who gave Himself up unto death and applied the benefits of His death and resurrection to her in Holy Baptism. Since He gives all things to us by grace, there is no basis for rivalry based on our merits. In Christ Jesus, we are assured of an inheritance imperishable, undefiled, and unfading, kept in heaven for us! God gave Israel and us the gift of a Savior, His Son, who was hung on a tree to redeem us. He hallows us from the curse of the Law by becoming a curse for us.

Chs 22–25 Our Savior, Jesus, opened for us the door to heaven so that we are set free from concern for self and are enabled to turn our attention to serving others (cf Jn 13:34). Our God has also blessed us with the institution of marriage to provide family, companionship, and a God-pleasing outlet for sexual desire. All who approach Him with broken hearts are received by Him, for "now in Christ Jesus you who once were far off have been brought near by the blood of Christ" (Eph 2:13). Since God is always with us, we dare not live as though He is not present or in ways that would dishonor Him. In all circumstances, the Lord does not simply tolerate sin but calls people to repent and to have their hearts changed by His Word of grace. Thanks be to God for His compassion toward us! His Son loved us more than Himself, and He died for our sins.

Ch 26 Like Israel, our joyful response is to serve the Lord with good works. Baptism celebrates God's grace to us: deliverance from the slavery of sin, the promise of an inheritance in God's heavenly land, and being declared a saint even now.

Chs 27–30 The Lord encourages us to treasure His Word rather than the words of man. To say "Amen" to God's law is not enough. God demands perfect obedience (Jas 2:10). Threat and promise, Law and Gospel, are the ways of God with humankind. Here, the blessings come from the renewal of the covenant, and the curses that follow anticipate the need for the new covenant in the blood of Christ, which was shed for our blessing and pardon. Moses taught them, and teaches us, that a relationship with God means a circumcision of the heart, i.e., faith rooted in the heart and soul. Such faith lives in obedience to the one true God, who gathers and blesses His people.

Chs 31–34 Jesus, whose name is a form of the Old Testament name Joshua, is our deliverer and leader in life. The Promised Land of heaven stands open before us. The promises in Moses' blessing point to the One "counted worthy of more glory than Moses" (Heb 3:3), namely Christ, because while Moses was a faithful servant of God who spoke God's Word, Christ is Son of God (3:6), whom God appointed heir of all things (1:2). "For the law was given through Moses; grace and truth came through Jesus Christ" (Jn 1:17).

Underneath Are the Everlasting Arms

The last recorded words of Moses are his blessing on the individual tribes of Israel (Dt 33). Like many of the "judgments and statutes" that Moses presented, his parting words about tribal prosperity may leave modern readers untouched (except for some appreciation of its poetic imagery and language).

But as the Aaronic Blessing (Nu 6:24–26) draws today's readers into the circle of the old covenant, so do some of the closing words of Moses' blessing. God pronounces it on us, too, for we share in the blessing on Israel of old. Together with Israel, believers of all ages bow their heads before the same God and receive the same assurance: "The eternal God is your dwelling place, and underneath are the everlasting arms" (Dt 33:27).

Moses' arms had grown weary in the battle with the Amalekites and soon now would be rigidly helpless in death. Yet he knew that the arms of God are always present with everlasting strength. They remain outstretched even when God says today as He did to Moses, "Return, O children of man" (Ps 90:3).

God led Israel out of Egypt and into Canaan with "an outstretched arm" (Dt 26:8) also for people today. For out of those tribes of the desert came He who put God's arms under all His people. Because He takes away the sins of the world, every believer can confidently repeat Jesus' dying words to God, "Father, into Your hands I commit My spirit" (Lk 23:46).

CANONICITY

As part of the Torah, the most important portion of the Hebrew Scriptures for the Jews, the Book of Deuteronomy was treasured. Christians received the book without question.

LUTHERAN THEOLOGIANS ON DEUTERONOMY

Luther

"In the fifth book [Deuteronomy], after the people have been punished because of their disobedience, and God has enticed them a little with grace, in order that by his kindness in giving them the two kingdoms they might be moved to keep his law gladly and willingly, then Moses repeats the whole law. He repeats the story of all that has happened to the people (except for that which concerns the priesthood) and explains anew everything that belongs either to the bodily or to the spiritual governing of a people. Thus Moses, as a perfect lawgiver, fulfilled all the duties of his office. He not only gave the law, but was there when men were to fulfill it. When things went wrong, he explained the law and re-established it. Yet this explanation in the fifth book really contains nothing else than faith toward God and love toward one's neighbor, for all God's laws come to that. Therefore, down to the twentieth chapter, Moses, in his explanation of the law, guards against everything that might destroy faith in God; and from there to the end of the book he guards against everything that hinders love." (AE 35:238–39)

"Moses beautifully repeats and edits into brief compass the whole history, the good deeds and the wonders of God, at the same time mentioning also the deeds of godless men. He intends to declare the glory and magnificence of God and thus to coax the people to trust the divine goodness and to fear His wrath, so that, taught by experience, they might become ready to receive His Law from the heart. For the best preparation of all for hearing the Law and for moving the hearer is that which takes place through the evangelical praise of the mercy and the wrath of God." (AE 9:16)

"For first of all Moses teaches godliness. He preaches faith amply and richly. He attaches the most beautiful ceremonies, by which the common people must be grasped and held, to keep them from making up their own, which God hates. Then he busies himself with the ordering of civil government and the nurture of mutual love, and he directs and arranges everything with the most suitable and just laws. Nothing here is foolish or useless, but everything is necessary and useful, as he will easily understand who knows what it is to manage government among people that are a little too free and wise in their own estimation, as this Jewish nation was. In such circumstances it is often necessary to ordain and do and permit things that would otherwise be laughed at and hissed down with very good reason. I do not think that God wanted to shape people by means of such ceremonies for any reason other than that He saw that the masses were most moved and captivated by those surface displays. To keep them from being empty masks and mere spectacles, He added His Word, the stuff and substance behind the masks, as it were, that by it they might become serious and meaningful, and the people themselves might know that what they did pleased God, and that if they themselves devised others without the Word, mere games and trumpery would result." (AE 9:6–7)

For more of Luther's insights on this book, see *Lectures on Deuteronomy* (AE 9).

Gerhard

"*The fifth Book of Moses* is called *'eleh hadebarim* by the Hebrews from its first words. The Greeks call it *Deuteronomion*, as if to say 'the repeated Law,' because, as Irenaeus says (bk. 4, c. 1, p. 223): 'In it there is a recapitulation of the entire Law. Consequently, it contains an epitome of the former books.' The fact that the rabbinic scholars call it *mishnah*, 'the repeated reading,' agrees with this name, for it is nothing else but, as they write, 'the recollection of prior matters that are written in the other books.' It has thirty-four chapters and contains the history of the final two months of the fortieth year after the exodus. It can be divided into *doctrinal matters* involving moral, ceremonial, and forensic laws; *historical matters*; and *prophetic matters*. Philo, *De mundo*, thinks that Moses himself gave these five books their Greek names. It is, however, more likely that the Septuagint translators thought up these Greek titles.

"These are the five Books of Moses, or the books written by Moses, and they are included under the number five. Thus the Hebrews call them *chumash*; the Greeks, *Pentateuchos*. The Talmudists and Cabalists, from the fact that 'light' is mentioned five times in the beginning of Genesis 1, think that those five books were signified because they were like lights and thus may be safely trusted. (See Weidner, preface to *Loc. fid. Christ.*, p. 8.) Nevertheless we must note that Joshua added the final chapter of Deuteronomy after the death of Moses, as we gather from Josh. 24:26.

"Some claim that Ezra did this. Josephus asserts that, when Moses was about to die, he wrote his death in the sacred volumes because he was afraid that the Jews would declare that God had taken him up because of his excellent virtues. The Hebrews divide the entire Pentateuch into fifty-two divisions or titles: Genesis into eleven; Exodus into eleven; and Leviticus, Numbers, and Deuteronomy into ten each. They also mark these divisions with their first words, calling the first *br'shith* [Gen. 1:1]; the second, *nch* [Gen. 6:8]; the third, *lk lk* [Gen. 12:1]; and so on to the last. All the *pesukim*—that is, verses—into which the Jews divide the entire Pentateuch number 5,830.

"Both the Israelite and Christian churches have always considered these five Books of Moses as canonical. Nevertheless they did not for that reason exclude the rest of the books from the canon, something that the Sadducees (so named from Zadok) once did, who accepted nothing as Scripture except the Books of Moses. As a result of this, Christ proves against them the resurrection of the dead, which they were denying, from Moses (Matt. 22:32). The Samaritans, or Samarites, conspired with the Sadducees in this error, from which the Sadducees also went to the temple of the Samaritans built on Mount Gerizim.

"On the other hand, Ptolemy (after whom the Ptolemites were named) divided the Law of Moses into three parts and, in fact, made the author of one the creator of the world; of the second, Moses; and of the third, the elders of the synagogue. By 'creator of the world' he did not understand the true God but some middle divinity between God and the devil. Therefore he was rejecting the entire Law (Epiphanius, *Haeres.* 33). The Antitactae said that it was a law of the second God; therefore they thought it was piety to resist the Law by living wickedly. Simon Magus taught that it was a law of a sinister power." (ThC E1 §§ 123–24)

QUESTIONS PEOPLE ASK ABOUT DEUTERONOMY

God's Omniscience

Deuteronomy 8:2 demands: "And you shall remember the whole way that the LORD your God has led you these forty years in the wilderness, that He might humble you, testing you to know what was in your heart, whether you would keep His commandments or not."

Acts 1:24 reports: "And they prayed and said, 'You, Lord, who know the hearts of all, show which one of these two You have chosen.'"

When the Bible says that God knows the hearts of all people, and again, that God tests human beings to know what is in their hearts, does it not contradict itself? This matter has puzzled Bible readers time and again. The answer, however, is not as difficult as it might seem. First, there is no passage in the Scriptures that says that God does not know all things. Those statements that speak of God's testing the hearts of people do not say that He does not know the thoughts of their hearts. This is not a case of one passage affirming what the other denies. Second, when the Bible says that God puts humans to the test to know their hearts, the implication evidently is that God subjects them to certain visitations, which will reveal that what God knew beforehand concerning their hearts is absolutely true. It means that evidence is furnished that corroborates God's judgment. For instance, a professor of chemistry, lecturing to her class, says: "Now I will apply an acid to this substance to see what the result will be." She speaks in this way though she knows the result perfectly well beforehand. When God sends trials to know what is in a person's heart, He is doing something that He would not have to do for Himself but that is very wholesome for the individual concerned. When Abraham showed himself obedient, being willing to sacrifice his only son at the Lord's command, evidence was furnished that he trusted God and would obey Him. Thereby his own faith was strengthened, and all who doubted his loyalty to God could be referred to this unsurpassed act of obedience. The texts quoted do not therefore contradict each other. Deuteronomy 8:2 and similar passages merely teach that God now and then sends trials upon people that show what is in their hearts and thus corroborate the judgment of God's omniscience.

Treatment of Enemies

Deuteronomy 20:16–18 enjoins: "But in the cities of these peoples that the LORD your God is giving you for an inheritance, you shall save alive nothing that breathes, but you shall devote them to complete destruction, the Hittites and the Amorites, the Canaanites and the Perizzites, the Hivites and the Jebusites, as the LORD your God has commanded, that they may not teach you to do according to all their abominable practices that they have done for their gods, and so you sin against the LORD your God."

Luke 6:35–36 urges: "But love your enemies, and do good, and lend, expecting nothing in return, and your reward will be great, and you will be sons of the Most High, for He is kind to the ungrateful and the evil. Be merciful, even as your Father is merciful."

First John 4:16 affirms: "We have come to know and to believe the love that God has for us. God is love, and whoever abides in love abides in God, and God in him."

Do the declarations of the New Testament that God is love and that His children must be merciful as He is merciful fit with the command of God to annihilate the Canaanites and to put even the children of these enemies to the sword? It might seem that here there is a wide chasm that can never be bridged. However, consider the following.

The nations that inhabited Canaan just prior to its occupation by Israel, under the leadership of Joshua, were extremely wicked. Several times God, in proclaiming His statutes and forbidding abominations and vices, says that on account of their gross sins He is casting out the native people of Canaan before Israel (cf Lv 18:24–30). If ever nations challenged the wrath of the Almighty to destroy them by their addiction to horrible forms of wrongdoing, these nations did. The crimes were such that human reason cried out against them.

We must not forget that the God who is love is likewise a just God. He is willing to forgive and to help, but if His love is unceasingly rejected and spurned, then the sinner who does not want mercy will get justice. Just as surely as there is a heaven, there is a hell. We may find it difficult according to our way of thinking to harmonize the doctrine of eternal damnation with that of God's grace. But the former is taught in the Scripture just as clearly as the latter. The punishment of God upon wicked nations is totally in keeping with what the Bible tells us of the justice of God. The only problem remaining is that all the inhabitants without exception, even the children, were to be killed, and that no opportunity was given these people to repent. The next points address these objections.

Assyrian prisoners of war are led to a life of slavery in Egypt (Temple of Ramses II, Abydos).

Was there anything so extraordinary in the command that all inhabitants without exception were to be punished by death? In the flood, all men, women, and children who inhabited the earth (except Noah and his family) were destroyed. When Sodom and Gomorrah were burned, the destruction of the inhabitants was total, Lot and his daughters being the only ones who escaped. It is perfectly true that these facts do not constitute an argument that will clear up the difficulty confronting us here. But it is helpful to remember that the conquest is not as unique as we might first imagine.

We must not overlook the fact that if the true religion was to be preserved in Israel, the heathen nations of Canaan had to be not merely subjected, but exterminated or driven out. Remaining in the land, even as slaves, they constituted a constant menace to the purity of the worship of the Israelites, as is abundantly proven by the pernicious influence that was exerted by such people who were permitted to remain or who came in contact with Israel along its borders.

Also, would slavery or mass imprisonment (which did not exist at this time) be preferable? Few would agree that they would. To be sure, war raises the greatest ethical issues, involving battle, refugees, prisoners, and occupation of conquered communities. Every modern military and police force wrestles with these issues. However, readers should also note that "pure" pacifism raises similar ethical issues, such as toleration for tyranny, murder, abuse, slavery, and moral compromise. Biblical history shows God advocating proactive resistance of evil, including the use of force at times.

The initial strikes of the conquest took place over about seven years, during which time Joshua pursued God's plan of destroying the Canaanites. The effect of such conquest ultimately led to what God described in Ex 23:27–31, that when faced with so great a threat, the Canaanites would withdraw. Although this observation does not end all objections, it does show how the strategy of conquest was finally intended to preserve Israel and to displace the Canaanites.

Did Moses Grow Infirm in Old Age?

Deuteronomy 31:2 reads: "And he said to them: 'I am 120 years old today. I am no longer able to go out and come in. The LORD has said to me, "You shall not go over this Jordan."'"

Deuteronomy 34:7 records: "Moses was 120 years old when he died. His eye was undimmed, and his vigor unabated."

The difficulty created by these two passages lies in the fact that the first one seems to describe Moses as having become infirm through old age, while the second expressly says that his eyes had not been dimmed and his natural vigor had not abated. It should be observed that any person who reaches 120 years old must be described as vigorous! Deuteronomy 31:2 does not assert that Moses had become the victim of weakness, which is usually incidental to old age. The great man of God merely says, "I am no longer able to go out and come in." Undoubtedly Moses had come to the Jordan, and he knew that he was not to cross this river with the hosts of Israel. Thus his words may merely mean, "I shall have to leave you." The term "to go out and to come in" is used of the function of leaders (cf Nu 27:17). Therefore, the expression may indicate that Moses could no longer be the leader of Israel. If we interpret his words in this fashion, the two passages listed are not contradictory.

FURTHER STUDY

Lay/Bible Class Resources

Braun, Mark E. *Deuteronomy*. PBC. St. Louis: Concordia, 2005. ☙ Lutheran author. Excellent for Bible classes. Based on the NIV translation.

Dunker, Gary. *Deuteronomy: God's Word for a New Generation*. GWFT. St. Louis: Concordia, 2008. ☙ Lutheran devotional writer. Thirteen-session Bible study, including leader's notes and discussion questions.

Life by His Word. St. Louis: Concordia, 2009. ☙ More than 1,500 reproducible one-page Bible studies covering each chapter of the canonical Scriptures. Page references to *The Lutheran Study Bible*. CD-Rom and downloadable.

Stirdivant, Mark, and R. Reed Lessing. *LifeLight: Wilderness Wanderings*. Leaders Guide and Enrichment Magazine/Study Guide. LL. St. Louis: Concordia, 2012. ☙ An in-depth, nine-session Bible study covering key texts of Leviticus, Numbers, and Deuteronomy with individual, small group, and lecture portions.

Thompson, John A. *Deuteronomy: An Introduction and Commentary*. TOTC. Grand Rapids: Zondervan, 1974. ☙ Generally helpful evangelical resource. Compact verse-by-verse commentary interacting with a variety of English translations.

Church Worker Resources

Craigie, Peter C. *The Book of Deuteronomy*. NICOT. Grand Rapids: Eerdmans, 1976. ☙ A careful, lucid exposition of the biblical text. Verse-by-verse format. Emphasizes the theme of covenant.

Luther, Martin. *Lectures on Deuteronomy*. Vol. 9 of AE. St. Louis: Concordia, 1958–70. ☙ The great reformer's lectures from 1525, which reflect his mature approach to biblical interpretation. Luther consulted the Hebrew text and reflected on the application of the prophecies and their New Testament fulfillment.

Ridderbos, J. *Bible Student's Commentary: Deuteronomy*. Grand Rapids: Zondervan, 1984. ☙ Useful for verse-by-verse commentary.

Academic Resources

K&D. *Biblical Commentary on the Old Testament: The Pentateuch*. Vol. 3. Grand Rapids: Eerdmans, 1971 reprint. ☙ This century-and-a-half old work from Lutheran scholars should not be overlooked. Despite its age, it remains a most useful commentary on the Hebrew text.

Nelson, Richard D. *Deuteronomy: A Commentary*. OTL. Louisville: Westminster John Knox, 2002. ☙ A more recent, respectable critical commentary that also provides literary and rhetorical analysis.

Schröder, Fr. Wilhelm Julius. *A Commentary on the Holy Scriptures: Deuteronomy*. LCHS. New York: Charles Scribner's Sons, 1890. ☙ A helpful older example of German biblical scholarship, based on the Hebrew text, which provides references to significant commentaries from the Reformation era forward.

von Rad, Gerhard. *Deuteronomy*. OTL. Philadelphia: Westminster, 1966. ☙ A critical commentary from a respected representative of that approach, who focuses on theoretical history and textual notes rather than theology.

THE BOOKS OF HISTORY

Be strong and very courageous, being careful to do according to all the law that Moses My servant commanded you. Do not turn from it to the right hand or to the left, that you may have good success wherever you go. This Book of the Law shall not depart from your mouth, but you shall meditate on it day and night, so that you may be careful to do according to all that is written in it. For then you will make your way prosperous, and then you will have good success. (Jsh 1:7–8)

With these words, the Lord sets before Joshua His plan for Israel's future and the two ways that the writers of the Books of History would judge Israel's leaders and events. These historians would distinguish (1) Israel's failure to keep God's Word revealed to Moses and (2) Israel's faithfulness to God's Word. The Books of History record the consequences of condemnation under God's Law and the blessings that flow from God's gracious promises. In these two ways, God's Word through Moses anticipated Israel's life and future, the failure or prosperity that would come with sin or with faith.

The forested central highlands of Canaan became the focus of the conquest for Israel and would become the backbone of their new and powerful kingdom at the juncture of three continents: Africa, Asia, and Europe. The pine groves and meadows pictured here are near Jerusalem.

Sources Cited in the Books of History

The writers of the Books of History reference numerous other collections and documents in their works. The following list is not exhaustive, but it illustrates the number and variety of the documents. There is probably duplication within the list because the writers likely referred to the same documents by different titles.

The Book of the Law of Moses (Jsh 1:8)

The Book of Jashar (Jsh 10:13)

The Description of the Land (Jsh 18:9)

The Book of the Law of God (Jsh 24:26)

The Commandments of the Lord (Jgs 3:4)

The Officials and Elders of Succoth (Jgs 8:14)

The Rights and Duties of the Kingship (1Sm 10:25)

The Law of Moses (1Ki 2:3)

The Book of the Acts of Solomon (1Ki 11:41)

The Book of the Chronicles of the Kings of Israel (1Ki 14:19)

The Book of the Chronicles of the Kings of Judah (1Ki 14:29)

The Book of the Law/the Covenant (2Ki 22:8–23:27)

The Law of the Lord (1Ch 16:40)

The Chronicles of King David (1Ch 27:24)

The Chronicles of Samuel the Seer (1Ch 29:29)

The Chronicles of Nathan the Prophet (1Ch 29:29)

The Chronicles of Gad the Seer (1Ch 29:29)

The History of Nathan the Prophet (2Ch 9:29)

The Prophecy of Ahijah the Shilonite (2Ch 9:29)

The Visions of Iddo the Seer (2Ch 9:29)

The Chronicles of Shemaiah the Prophet (2Ch 12:15)

The Chronicles of Iddo the Seer (2Ch 12:15)

The Story of the Prophet Iddo (2Ch 13:22)

The Prophecy of Azariah the Son of Obed (2Ch 15:8)

The Book of the Kings of Judah and Israel (2Ch 16:11)

The Book of the Law of the Lord (2Ch 17:9)

The Chronicles of Jehu the Son of Hannani (2Ch 20:34)

The Book of the Kings of Israel (2Ch 20:34)

The Story of the Book of the Kings (2Ch 24:27)

The Book of Moses (2Ch 25:4)

The Vision of Isaiah the Prophet (2Ch 32:32)

The Chronicles of the Seers (2Ch 33:19)

The Laments (2Ch 35:25)

The Book of the Kings of Israel and Judah (2Ch 36:8)

The Letter to Artaxerxes (Ezr 4)

The Book of the Records (Persian; Ezr 4:15)

The Book of the Genealogy (Ne 7:5)

The Book of the Chronicles (Ne 12:23)

The Book of the Chronicles (Persian; Est 2:23)

The Book of Memorable Deeds (Persian; Est 6:1)

The Book of the Chronicles of the Kings of Media and Persia (Persian; Est 10:2)

Although many of these sources are lost, some titles listed above may be names for books of Scripture. Most significantly, there are numerous references throughout the Books of History to the "Law," which refers to one or more of the Books of Moses (the Pentateuch). This shows the continuing importance and influence that the Books of Moses played in guiding the style and themes of later writers.

The Books of History also include numerous references to letters during the kingdom period, such as the Letter to Artaxerxes listed above. Scribes may have collected these for the different kings and used them as a basis for writing comprehensive historical accounts (e.g., 2Sm 11:14; see *TLSB*, p 1900). There are also ref-

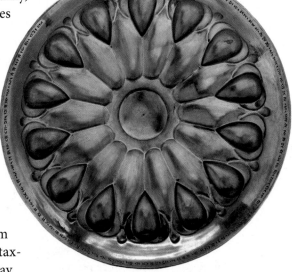

Silver bowl of Artaxerxes I (464-424 BC) shows the skill of Persian craftsmen. The inscription states, "Artaxerxes, the great king, king of kings. King of countries, son of Xerxes the king, of Xerxes (who was) son of Darius the king, the Achaemenian, in whose house this silver drinking-cup (was) made."

erences to oral prophecies, such as the Prophecy of Azariah the Son of Obed listed above, and chronicles, or historical accounts.

Unlike the other Books of History, Judges lacks the numerous references to other documents. However, Judges shows special interest in oral accounts of naming (1:17, 26; 6:24, 32; 10:4; 15:17, 19; 18:12), which was also of interest to Moses (see p 7).

Relation to One Another in the Scriptures

Joshua, Judges, 1 and 2 Samuel, and 1 and 2 Kings were known by the rabbis as "the Former Prophets." Their writings followed the ministry and the manner of Moses, so their works naturally followed his in the Hebrew Scriptures. The rabbis placed Ruth, Esther, Ezra, Nehemiah, and Chronicles in the general category of "Writings." Editors for the Septuagint brought all these books together as a running history of Israel from the death of Moses to the reestablishment of the temple after the Babylonian exile.

Critical scholars have assumed that the theological and historical perspectives of the Former Prophets were shaped by a common editor, the Deuteronomist, who interpreted Israelite history in view of the covenant blessings and curses described in Dt 27–28. Clearly, Moses' farewell sermon in Deuteronomy influenced the content and writing of these books; an editor must have brought these books together in the canon of Scripture.

However, one should note that the books of the Former Prophets were written by authors from different eras who shared a common theology of history, which they drew from Moses. For example, Joshua was written by Joshua. Judges was clearly authored before the kingdom period, and 1 and 2 Samuel date from the united monarchy. These accounts and their interests are followed by 1 and 2 Kings, which record the history of the divided monarchies down to the time of the Babylonian exile. (See chronology, pp lxxxiii–lxxxviii.)

Aside from Ruth, which was likely written to honor the rule of David, the other Writings were penned after the exile and served the purpose of strengthening and reestablishing the remnant of God's people after that national crisis. Ezra, Nehemiah, and 1 and 2 Chronicles are like the Former Prophets in style, emphasizing the curses and blessings of the Law of Moses. Ruth and Esther are wonderfully plotted stories about faithful women.

History and God's People

As the size and scope of the Books of History show, history is an important field of study for God's people. St. Paul wrote about the history of Israel: "Now these things took place as examples for us, that we might not desire evil as they did" (1Co 10:6). The stories of the Israelites stand in Scripture like sermon illustrations for the teachings of Moses.

In his *Preface to Galeatius Capella's History*, Luther wrote about the value and use of history with specific reference to Judges, Kings, Chronicles, Ezra, and Nehemiah.

> Upon thorough reflection one finds that almost all laws, art, good counsel, warning, threatening, terrifying, comforting, strengthening, instruction, prudence, wisdom, discretion, and all virtues well up out of the narratives and histories as from a living fountain. It all adds up to this: histories are nothing else than a demonstration, recollection, and sign of divine action and judgment, how He upholds, rules, obstructs, prospers, punishes, and honors the world, and especially men, each according to his just desert, evil or good. And although there are many who do not acknowledge God or esteem him, they must nevertheless come up against the examples and histories and be afraid lest they fare like those individuals whom the histories portray. They are more deeply moved by this than if one were simply to restrain and control them with mere words of the law or instruction. Thus we read not only in the Holy Scriptures, but also in the books of pagans how they cited as witnesses and held up the examples, words, and deeds of forebears when they wanted to carry a point with the people or when they intended to teach, admonish, warn, or deter. The historians, therefore, are the most useful people and the best teachers, so that one can never honor, praise, and thank them enough. . . . One can see especially in the books of Judges, Kings, and Chronicles that among the Jewish people such masters were appointed and retained. That was also the case among the kings of Persia who had such libraries in Media, as one can gather from the book of Ezra and Nehemiah [Ezra 6:2]. (AE 34:275–76)

How fitting that the Lord of history, the promised Son of David (2Sm 7:8–16), should Himself become man and part of history in order to be our Savior. In Him, we see the Law of Moses fulfilled and the promised Kingdom come.

Prophets and Historians

It is not entirely clear how or why Joshua, Judges, Samuel, and Kings came to be called "the Prophets." The title may have arisen merely from early Jewish traditions of prophetic authorship of these works. This is not impossible, but, at best, does not appear to suffice as an answer.

It is certainly more helpful, and perhaps also more accurate, if we understand the title as characterizing the contents of the books as well. Then these works are understood as exhibiting prophetic *theology*, as the "sermon illustrations" preceding the "sermons" of the prophets themselves.

It may even be argued that "Former Prophets" is a much better and more accurate designation than our "Historical Books." For better or for worse, "history" for modern readers implies certain standards of objectivity, comprehensiveness, chronology, and usually also secular perspective, to which these biblical books do not correspond. When the biblical books diverge from our notion of history, the stage is set for doubts and questions of various sorts. This is not only true of the historical-critical method, which programmatically measures ancient texts unfairly, but comparable difficulties may easily arise also for the more ordinary reader.

Ancient and Modern History

Accordingly, it must be accented that these histories are unabashedly written to make a point. The writers select and present events as it serves their purposes. The fact that we can scarcely hear such language except in a negative sense only illustrates the problem. Possibly the recent realization that complete objectivity is an impossibility in such matters has softened the difficulty for modern audiences, but probably not a lot.

The Hebrew Bible does not include a specific word for history but uses general terms for writing, such as "words," "scroll," or "genealogy." Our ideas of history come from the Greeks. When we stress that the "history" presented here is not the same as the modern type, this should not imply that what is presented is somehow less than true. Rather, the books speak factually as well as theologically, even though many questions we might raise remain unanswered. What the Holy Spirit offers us is not *less* than history, but infinitely more. The *ultimate* concern is with *inner* history of the books.

Theology of History

The basic pattern illustrated throughout the Former Prophets is that of reward for obedience or faithfulness, and retribution or punishment for unfaithfulness. That scheme is commonly criticized as, at best, hopelessly simplistic and probably mechanistic and legalistic as well. Some critics condescendingly concede only a certain long-range, pragmatic truth to the principle, and many are motivated by a universalistic aversion to the entire idea of divine retribution.

The correct understanding commends itself readily, even humanly speaking, if we remain aware of the theological scope of the material. Instead of judging externally (politically, sociologically, psychologically), the viewpoint is concerned with what is *ultimately* true. As the Latter Prophets preached tirelessly, the Word of God is always operative in either blessing or cursing, Law or Gospel. What we have is a theology of history.

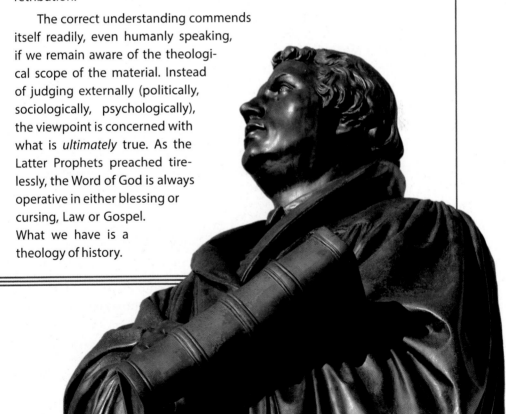

Hexateuch, Heptateuch, Octateuch, and Deuteronomic History

In the late medieval era, scholars began to use the Latin term *pentateuchus* (from Gk for "five books") to describe the five Books of Moses. In later centuries, scholars used related terms to describe a variety of theories about how the first books of the Bible were composed, edited, or collected. These terms may appear in commentaries and other literature on the Bible. The following entries will help you understand these terms and the basic theories that stand behind them.

Tetrateuch. "Four books." Based on the theory that the first four books of the Bible were edited or compiled from the same set of sources: J, E, and P. In this view, the Book of Deuteronomy is thought to represent its own source or tradition: D. For more on the JEDP theory, see pp 10–11.

Pentateuch. "Five books." A common title for the five Books of Moses.

Hexateuch. "Six books." Noting that the Book of Joshua built upon the Books of Moses and its opening words assumed the existence of a "Book of the Law" (1:8), scholars proposed that the first six books of the Bible were edited or compiled from the same JEDP sources.

Heptateuch. "Seven books." A theory similar to hexateuch, but including the Book of Judges, which assumes the story of Joshua in its opening words (1:1).

Octateuch. "Eight books." A theory similar to heptateuch, but including the Book of Ruth, which assumes the account of the Judges (1:1).

Deuteronomic History. Proposed by Martin Noth (1902–68). Assuming the tetrateuch theory, Noth proposed that Deuteronomy was the first volume in a series of works that shared the same theology of covenant curses for disobedience and blessings for faithfulness (cf, e.g., Dt 27–28). This proposed history collection encompassed the biblical books of Deuteronomy through 2 Kings.

JOSHUA

Be strong and very courageous, being careful to do according to the Law

The grassy plains of Moab give way to drier hills on the east and the salty shores of the Dead Sea on the southwest. The plains form a northward path of green, alongside the tree-lined shores of the Jordan. In this setting, at Abel-Shittim, the Lord urged Joshua to meditate upon the Law of Moses and to lead the people of Israel across the Jordan River. Because of Moses' earlier mistakes in the wilderness, his bones would remain behind on Mount Nebo. In contrast, the people carried with them the bones of Joseph, to be buried at Shechem in the heart of the homeland God promised.

The Book of Joshua is not an idealized reconstruction of the past. It includes the miraculous, but it also lays bare the failures of individuals, of tribes, and of Israel as a whole. At the same time, many facts about Canaanite history are left unmentioned, facts available only through archaeology and the ancient records found in Israel and in the surrounding areas.

When reading Joshua, it is crucial to remember that the Old Testament does not purport to be world history (not even the history of Israel in the strict sense of the word) but a theological history. It is therefore highly selective in its choice of the material used to tell how salvation came to earth. Gauged by this standard, a conquering campaign by a world empire may be a mere trifle in comparison with the piling up of a few stones to form an altar at Shechem. Therefore, scholars cannot always fit this covenant history into the framework of parallel cir-

The Oasis of Jericho, one of the oldest continuously inhabited sites in the world, as seen against the surrounding desert.

OVERVIEW

Authors
Joshua; an unknown writer

Date
c 1406–1375 BC

Places
Transjordan; Jericho; Gilgal; Ai; Gibeon; central highlands of Canaan; Shiloh; Shechem; see maps, pp 211, 212

People
Joshua; Caleb; Rahab; Achan; Adonizedek; Eleazar; Phinehas

Purpose
To record how the Lord fulfilled His promise to give Canaan as an inheritance to Israel

Law Themes
Devotion to destruction; Achan's greed; inheritance; cities of refuge; the Law of Moses; memorials

Gospel Themes
Joshua's name; covenant renewal; the Lord's promises fulfilled; cities of refuge; memorials

Memory Verses
Meditate on the Word (1:7–8); my house will serve the Lord (24:14–15)

TIMELINE

1526 BC	Moses born
1446 BC	Exodus from Egypt
1406–1400 BC	Conquest under Joshua
1399–1375 BC	Deaths of Joshua and the elders
1099–1060 BC	Eli's priesthood and judgeship

199

THE CONQUEST AND ARCHAEOLOGY

For a long time, the American "Albright school" especially has persuaded many to believe at least the substantial historicity of the biblical accounts.

Critics, partly in the absence of archaeological evidence, presumed that the Book of Joshua artificially described a slow protracted infiltration of people with much independent guerilla activity. Only much later did these infiltrators see themselves as a distinct and unified people of Israel. More recent sociological reconstructions propose that a great variety of dispossessed and disaffected elements, both native Canaanites and newcomers, joined forces against the aristocratic oppression of the Canaanite city-states (the Israelites serving as a catalyst for a peasant revolt). Such a thesis is not totally incompatible with the biblical data, but one should not accept the theory as fully compatible with the Scriptures either.

As these theories show, the conquest raises numerous historical and interpretive issues. The topic provides an example of the frequent ambiguity of the archaeological evidence. For example, when archaeologists discover a layer of destruction at a site, they often struggle to determine who caused the destruction. It must also be conceded that, at least at the present, the accumulated archaeological evidence is not only often ambiguous, but does not conform to typical interpretations of the scriptural accounts, precisely in the cases of Jericho, Ai, and Gibeon where the most biblical detail has been preserved.

The very location of Ai (the name means "ruin") is debated; the traditional site had lain in ruins for centuries already at the time of Joshua. Evidence of Late Bronze occupation is also meager at Gibeon. There are various ways to explain these current archaeological difficulties, but we should not pretend as though the difficulties are not there.

Ironically, much better evidence of Late Bronze destructions, presumably by the Israelites, is evidenced in the excavations of sites that the Bible mentions more in passing: Hazor, Lachish, Debir, Eglon, etc. It is worth noting that there is no archaeological evidence of a destruction of Shechem at this time, just as Jsh 8:30 indicates. As noted above, the absence of the Philistines in the wars of Joshua also appears to fit the archaeological evidence: Joshua might have swept all the way to the Mediterranean coast (and assign Simeon and Dan territory there), but the Philistines would have swept down from the North and displaced Israel, perhaps only a very short time later.

cumstances in secular history. Some questions must remain unanswered.

God's marching orders to Joshua had not included the occupation of the land. The people were to "go over this Jordan . . . into the land that I [God] am giving to them" (1:11), but nothing is said of Joshua's leadership in attaining this ultimate goal. Joshua's work is restricted to a "softening up" operation against the enemy. This limitation is made explicit in the account of the allotment of the land (chs 13–21, particularly 13:1). There God reminds Joshua of his advanced age and of the big task he leaves unfinished: "There remains yet very much land to possess." Then follows a list of the areas that remain, that were unpossessed at this juncture, and the promise of God: "I Myself will

drive them out from before the people of Israel. Only allot the land to Israel for an inheritance" (13:1–6). Acting on pure faith, therefore, Joshua was to divide the land and give it as an inheritance before it was conquered or possessed. (Although the land was allotted, the next step, the full occupation of the land, was thwarted by Israel's lassitude and weak faith—as reported later.)

Some biblical locations, such as Hazor pictured here, are easily identified by archaeologists.

Historical and Cultural Setting

To understand this history, four basic factors in the account must be placed into clear perspective. First, chapters 13–21 provide a summary record. Other battles with the Canaanites took place in addition to those briefly described here (cf the list of 31 defeated kings in 12:7–24). "Joshua made war a long time with all those kings" (11:18).

Second, when more is added beyond a mere mention of names, the detail demonstrates that without the miraculous intervention of God, Israel could not have won a victory (much less have ever set foot into Canaan). What was impossible became easy when the Lord gave victory; what seemed easy (like attacking Ai) became impossible without Him.

Third, Joshua's achievements must not be exaggerated beyond what the account expressly states. He directed the joint effort of all the tribes, but that joint effort had a limited goal. It is that limited goal to which we turn our attention in the next four paragraphs.

The round structure at the center is the remains of a neolithic tower at Jericho. The site was badly weathered in antiquity so that the ruins of Joshua's conquest (Late Bronze Age) were likely not preserved.

That it was a joint effort can be seen in the attention called to the two and a half tribes east of the Jordan who participated in the campaigns west of the Jordan and their dismissal by Joshua at the end of these battles. This joint effort contrasts strongly with the later attempts by individual tribes to take possession of their assigned territories.

But Joshua's assignment was not to lead Israel until it occupied all of Canaan, not even until it had occupied the territories where God's people had achieved military victory. The record clearly distinguished between victory in battle and the permanent settlement of Israel.

Joshua sought to (and did) eliminate the most imminent threat to Israel's foothold in Canaan, and he did this as the leader of a military supplied by a united people. When he finished this task, the back of Canaanite power was broken, and so "the land had rest from war" (11:23).

During this period of rest, Joshua carried out God's second objective: allotting the land. Note that Joshua supervised only the allotment; he did not direct a unified endeavor to possess the land on behalf of the individual tribes.

The fourth basic factor to keep in perspective is the distinction between taking the land in battle and occupying or possessing it. If the difference is obscured, the Book of Joshua may seem to conflict with the account in the Book of Judges. With careful reading, one can detect this nuance in ch 12. This summary of events begins by listing the kings of the land whom the children of Israel defeated, and whose land they possessed "beyond the Jordan" (v 1). The second part of the chapter lists "the kings of the land whom Joshua and the people of Israel defeated on the west side of the Jordan, . . . and Joshua gave their land to the tribes of Israel as a possession according to their allotments" (v 7). The verb "possessed" (or "take possession") is conspicuously absent in connection with Joshua's activity with the people as a whole. True, Joshua gave certain areas of Canaan "as a possession," but in this modifying clause, the meaning is that he gave the territory "to be a possession."

The silence regarding Egypt poses a different problem. Joshua makes not one mention of the Eighteenth Dynasty of Pharaohs and their armies despite Egypt's earlier subjugation of Canaan, the incorporation of Canaan into the empire, and the repeated forays by Egypt into Canaan, even after Egypt had lost the earlier and more effective control of this territory. In fact, Egypt isn't mentioned in the Scriptures at all between the exodus and the time of Solomon.

However, one may note that campaigns by Egypt at this time followed the highway up the coast and through the inland plains, whereas Israel's initial foothold remained restricted to the highland ridge. Therefore, the Egyptians also may have been one of the reasons the tribes did not dispossess the cities in the plains. God, of course, could have destroyed them during Joshua's time just as He had at Moses' time if Israel had trusted Him to do so. Cf Nu 13–14.

An Egyptian scarab bearing the name of Thutmose III and found at Gezer.

An apparently premature reference to the Philistines also presents a historical problem. Extrabiblical sources state that the main body of these sea peoples settled on the southern coast of Canaan after 1200 BC. Although the Book of Joshua mentions no clash with these newcomers, it does refer to "the regions of the Philistines" as one of several areas that remain to be possessed after Joshua's death (13:1–2). But it may have been more than a century after Joshua's death before the Philistines were in a position to defend their regions against Israel's attempt to dispossess them. (For similar references to the Philistines, see Ex 13:17 and 23:31.)

COMPOSITION

Authors

Jewish tradition consistently understands the "Joshua" heading to refer to authorship of the book as well as its contents. The situation could be quite comparable to authorship of the Books of Moses, even with respect to the burial notices at the end. (Unlike the Books of Moses, however, we have no later scriptural notices attributing the book to Joshua, nor are there compelling internal indications in that direction.)

CRITICAL VIEWS OF JOSHUA

Advocates of the JEDP theory were confident that Joshua, as the final member of the "Hexateuch," had the same literary history as the preceding five books (see pp 196–97). The resulting picture was one of a composite JE for the first 12 chapters, a D revision, and finally a P revision, which contributed most of the rest of the book (the teaching and the statistical material, respectively). Joshua 24, however, was usually considered E because of its locale at Shechem. E was sometimes held responsible for the fiction of a unified campaign in contrast to J's better historical memory.

This approach has largely fallen out of favor today, especially with the preference for Martin Noth's "Deuteronomic history" hypothesis. It is debatable, however, whether Noth's hypothesis has really changed things much. Noth simply thought of a great variety of independent materials (some of it possibly even contemporary with the events) organized within a Deuteronomic framework.

Form criticism, however, has again tried to move behind the written sources, with results that are not generally very congenial. "Cult-legends" are thought to account for the heavy liturgical cast of much of the material, regardless of how much actual history may be involved. Especially Gilgal and Shechem figure prominently in these speculations. "Hero-legends," especially of Joshua, and various explanations of ruins and rites, are also thought to have contributed. The fact that detailed narratives of conquest are preserved only in the Gilgal-Jericho-Ai-Gibeon series suggests to many critics that only tales from the "Rachel tribes" (or maybe only the tribe of Benjamin) were preserved in later times, and that Joshua had originally spearheaded the conquests of only these groups. Allegedly, then, the quasi-historical Benjaminite tradition became normative for all of Canaan, and a local hero, Joshua, became the conquistador of the entire land. (The real course of the invasion of Canaan is often thought to have been three-pronged—Judah from the south, Benjamin from the east, and "Joseph" from the north—but that plainly flies in the face of the biblical data.)

Date of Composition

Joshua would have written most of the book between c 1406–1375 BC, with account of his death likely added by another writer. Internal evidence for authorship of the book at the time of Joshua includes the various references to Sidon instead of Tyre as the major Phoenician city, the absence of the Philistines as a threat, and the "we" notices in 5:1, 6, 13 (KJV), etc., indicating direct input from Joshua at least at those points.

There are, however, indications of composition after the time of Joshua, unless these are to be regarded again as minor editorial additions. These include not only the burials at the close of the book and the repeated "until this day" statements, but also the reference to the later Danite migration to the north in 19:47, and the citation of the "Book of Jashar" in 10:12 (which also includes David's lament over Jonathan and could scarcely have been intact until after the latter event). Probably latest of all is the apparent distinction between the two kingdoms of Israel and Judah in 11:21. None of this evidence would, however, necessarily imply a later date than the united monarchy, or possibly the early divided monarchy.

Purpose/Recipients

The covenant with the patriarchs and with Israel at Sinai is the central, controlling factor of everything recorded in Joshua, which emphasizes that the covenant includes "terms"—requirements on the part of God as well as of Israel. Through Israel, God would fulfill His part of the covenant, His promise to carry out His plan of salvation for all the nations of the earth. Israel must be faithful as the covenant nation; its history depends on it. The Book of Joshua makes crystal clear that Israel succeeds or fails in the measure that it remains God's instrument. In every age God blesses those whom He chooses, and He curses those who defy Him. This simple formula solves the great question of history that otherwise remains despite every explanation of human cause and effect.

As the Book of Joshua bears witness, human beings are unable to produce this salvation-bringing history. Only Yahweh can effect the miraculous defeat of the Canaanites as He directs the course of history for His purpose.

The correlation between history and the covenant did not begin either with Moses or at the time of Joshua. God had decreed salvation from the beginning, from the promise to Adam and Eve (Gn 3:15)—and even before the foundation of the world (Eph 1:4). The Book of Joshua merely presents another act in the drama of salvation. Since the redemption of the world by the blood of the new covenant was God's ultimate purpose, every chapter of the old covenant is God's footprint in His undeviating and merciful march to Calvary.

The Book of Joshua marks a significant milestone in Israel's history: "Not one word of all the good promises that the LORD had made to the house of Israel had failed; all came to pass" (Jsh 21:45; cf Ex 24 for a similar previous milestone). The author emphasizes that God solidly built His way of salvation on the roadbed of historical achievement. Events happen only in accordance with the fixed and unalterable principles of the Maker and His promises.

Therefore, the conquest does not develop artificially or magically. Blessings do not fall mechanically and ready-made into Israel's lap. Israel must labor to make them come true, and proper was the admonition to "be strong and courageous" (1:6, 9).

Literary Features

Genre

As noted in the introduction to the Former Prophets, the Book of Joshua is a history written with prophetic or theological perspective. The presentation of history describes (1) the blessings and successes Israel received as they faithfully followed God's ways and (2) the curses or condemnations they experienced when they departed from God's ways. The book also includes military campaign accounts, a land survey, Joshua's farewell address, and a service of covenant renewal.

Characters

The central character is **Joshua** as the leader of Israel. His career parallels that of Moses in several ways. Perhaps the most striking similarity occurred when the "commander of the LORD's army" encountered Joshua and commanded him: "Take off your sandals from your feet, for the place where you are standing is holy ground" (5:13–15; cf Ex 3:5).

Other similarities include: God's promise to be with Joshua as He was with Moses (1:5), the people's promise of loyalty (1:16–18—though Moses often had to deal with their rebelliousness and unfaithfulness), the miraculous crossing of the Jordan River on dry land (3:14–17), reinstituting the Passover and the rite of circumcision (5:2–10), the writing of the Law on tables of stone (8:32), and reestablishing the covenant (24:1–25).

But Joshua's leadership of Israel also differed from that of Moses in two ways. First, no lapse from faith is recorded of Joshua as it is of Moses (but less of Joshua's personal history than is given for Moses). Second, though Moses had to cope with a rebellious people at every turn, no general revolt against Joshua is mentioned. In fact, the book's closing notes that "Israel served the LORD all the days of Joshua, and all the days of the elders who outlived Joshua, and had known all the work that the LORD did for Israel" (24:31). Yet the author of this book, by including particularly those events similar to the life of Moses, stressed the continuity of Israel's history under the undeviating purpose of God.

Despite human frailties and instability, God's dealings with His people as a whole often revolve around individuals who have become great because of their service to the God who chose them. Thus, this book bears the name of Moses' "understudy," and its contents constitute another chapter that ends as the next one begins—"after the death of Joshua" (Jgs 1:1).

Scripture does not provide enough detail to determine the length of this Joshua epoch. Two items are mentioned: (1) Joshua was 110 years old when he died (24:29), and (2) his parting addresses to the people shortly before his death took place "a long time afterward, when the LORD had given rest to Israel from all their surrounding enemies" (23:1). But Joshua's age when the book opens is not told. Thus one can only conjecture that the span may have been about 50 years, based on the assumption that Joshua was at least 20, of "arms bearing age," when he spied out the land (Ex 33:11). That plus the 38 additional years in the wilderness would make him close to 60 years old when Moses died, and an additional 50 years would bring him to 110 at his death.

Narrative Development or Plot

The Book of Joshua opens during the first month of the Israelite year, Abib 1406 BC, as the Lord encourages Joshua in his new calling. Joshua sends spies into the land to investigate their first obstacle: Jericho. The Israelites travel to the east bank of the Jordan and await Joshua's direction. They cross the river and set up two memorials of the miracles and blessings God provides. On the eleventh day of Abib, they circumcise those who were not circumcised in the wilderness and then celebrate their first Passover in the land. As the people begin to eat the first fruit of the land and observe the seven-day Feast of Unleavened Bread, the manna that sustained them in the wilderness stops falling from heaven. These events demonstrate God's faithfulness to His promises.

OUTLINE

I. The Lord Prepares Israel to Inherit the Land (1:1–5:12)

   A. Transition and Setting (1:1)

   B. The Lord Encourages Joshua to Take Possession of the Land (1:2–9)

   C. Joshua Commands Officers to Muster the People (1:10–11)

   D. Joshua Reminds the Transjordan Tribes of Duty toward All Israel (1:12–15)

   E. The Transjordan Tribes Respond (1:16–18)

   F. The Spies and Rahab (ch 2)

   G. Crossing before Conquest (chs 3–4)

   H. Interlude between Crossing and Conquering (5:1–12)

II. The Lord Causes Israel to Capture the Land Inheritance (5:13–12:24)

   A. Encounter with the Divine Commander (5:13–15)

   B. Central Campaign (chs 6–8)

   C. Southern Campaign (chs 9–10)

   D. Northern Campaign: Defeat of Jabin and the Kings of the North (11:1–15)

   E. Review of Israel's Victories (11:16–12:24)

III. The Lord Allots the Land Inheritance to Israel (chs 13–21)

   A. The Lord Commands Joshua to Allot the Land (13:1–7)

   B. The Allotment Carried Out (13:8–21:42)

   C. Summary Statements: God Has Now Given the Land Promised Long Ago (21:43–45)

IV. The Lord's War Victory Enables Israel to Live in the Land Inheritance as Heirs of All His Covenant Promises (chs 22–24)

   A. Joshua Blesses and Dismisses the Transjordan Tribes from Shiloh (22:1–9)

   B. Israel Remains One Covenant Nation (22:10–34)

   C. Joshua's First Farewell Sermon (ch 23)

   D. Covenant Renewal at Shechem (24:1–28)

   E. Three Saints Await Resurrection in the Promised Land: Memorials to the Lord's Fulfilled Promises (24:29–33)

The story continues with a series of military campaigns during which the Lord teaches the people that He alone is the source of their strength and victory. The account begins with a visit from "the commander of the army of the Lord" (5:14), who greets Joshua the way the Lord greeted Moses at Sinai. The first battles take Jericho and cities of the central highlands. Israel turns southward, then northward to meet threats from various coalitions of Canaanites. By the end of ch 12, the military efforts cease and Joshua allots land to individuals and tribes, a dominating feature of the book that emphasizes the fulfillment of promises to the patriarchs and the importance of the land in biblical theology.

In the last portion of the book, Joshua blesses and dismisses the Transjordan tribes who helped conquer the land. He leads the people in a service of covenant renewal, calling upon them to remain steadfast in serving the Lord. The book closes with a brief record of the memorials provided for Joshua, Joseph, and Eleazar the high priest.

Resources

As noted above, the Book of Joshua not only stems from the promises about the land in the Book of Moses (e.g., Gn 12:1; 15:12–21; 17:8; 26:2–4; etc.) but also the curses and warnings regarding the Canaanites (9:24–27). On the life of Moses as a model for relating the life of Joshua, see pp 206–7. The Book of Joshua explicitly mentions other documents, such as the Book of the Law of Moses (1:8), the Book of Jashar (10:12–13), the Description of the Land (18:9), and the Book of the Law of God (24:26).

Text and Translations

The Hebrew text of Joshua includes relatively few variants and is in good order. The LXX expands the text in some place, but is, overall, 4 or 5 percent shorter than the Hebrew text. Codex Vaticanus is substantially different from the Hebrew.

DOCTRINAL CONTENT

Summary Commentary

Ch 1 The Lord encourages Joshua with assurances of success and promises of His presence through His empowering Word as Joshua begins the critical work of conquering and allotting the Promised Land to Israel. He assumes command and encourages the people, especially the three eastern tribes, who in turn encourage Joshua that they will support the conquest.

Ch 2 Joshua sends two spies to Jericho, where they find a people filled with fear, but they also find a person who shares their faith: Rahab the prostitute, who believes the reports about the Lord.

The Jordan River at flood stage (cf Jsh 3:15).

3:1–5:12 With the ark of the covenant of the Lord leading Israel, the waters of the Jordan pile up in a heap, allowing Israel to cross safely on dry land. They safely and miraculously enter the Promised Land, and Joshua is exalted (3:7). The stone memorials will serve to teach the power of God in judgment and salvation. In the Promised Land, the nation resumes the practice of circumcision, the sign and seal of God's covenant with His people, by which He rolls away the reproach of Egypt at Gilgal. Israel celebrates its spiritual holidays, as the Lord provides for its worldly needs.

5:13–8:35 Before the campaign to conquer the central highlands, Joshua has a surprise encounter with the commander of the army of the Lord, who will provide him success in battle. As a woman of faith in the Lord, Rahab is kept safe in the middle of the destruction of unrepentant Jericho; she becomes part of Israel. However, the sin of one man, Achan, results in defeat and death for the Israelites at Ai. Guilty Achan is caught by the Lord, confesses before Joshua, and is stoned at the Valley of Achor. After the sin of Achan has been punished and Joshua does all that the Lord commanded, Israel successfully destroys the city of Ai. This event rededicates the people to the covenant and announces to those in the Promised Land that God had come to claim the land. The Law is written in stone to remind the people that it has not gone away.

Chs 9–10 The southern campaign begins with a Canaanite ruse. Because Joshua and the Israelites neglect to seek the Lord's counsel, they fall for the deceit of the Gibeonites and make a treaty that they must honor. When the kings in Canaan set out to destroy Gibeon for its covenant with Israel, Joshua honors that covenant and God delivers Gibeon (10:11). Joshua captures and destroys the five Canaanite kings who tried to hide in a cave

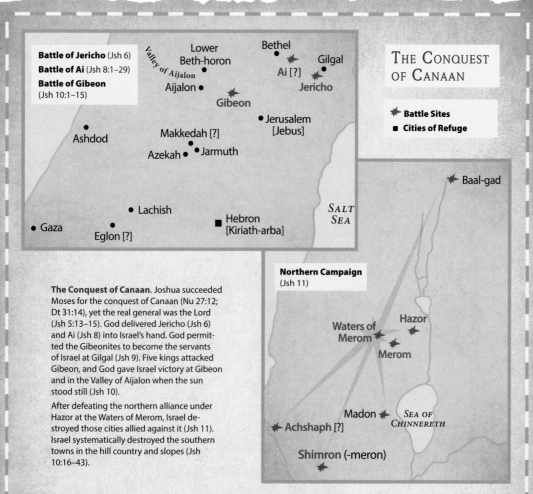

THE CONQUEST OF CANAAN

Battle of Jericho (Jsh 6)
Battle of Ai (Jsh 8:1–29)
Battle of Gibeon
(Jsh 10:1–15)

⚹ **Battle Sites**
■ **Cities of Refuge**

Lower
Beth-horon
Bethel
Gilgal
Ai [?]
Valley of Aijalon
Aijalon •
Jericho
Gibeon
• Jerusalem
[Jebus]
Ashdod •
Makkedah [?]
Azekah • • Jarmuth

• Lachish
*SALT
SEA*
• Gaza
Eglon [?] •
■ Hebron
[Kiriath-arba]

The Conquest of Canaan. Joshua succeeded Moses for the conquest of Canaan (Nu 27:12; Dt 31:14), yet the real general was the Lord (Jsh 5:13–15). God delivered Jericho (Jsh 6) and Ai (Jsh 8) into Israel's hand. God permitted the Gibeonites to become the servants of Israel at Gilgal (Jsh 9). Five kings attacked Gibeon, and God gave Israel victory at Gibeon and in the Valley of Aijalon when the sun stood still (Jsh 10).

After defeating the northern alliance under Hazor at the Waters of Merom, Israel destroyed those cities allied against it (Jsh 11). Israel systematically destroyed the southern towns in the hill country and slopes (Jsh 10:16–43).

Northern Campaign
(Jsh 11)

⚹ Baal-gad

Hazor
Waters of
Merom
Merom
Madon ⚹ *SEA OF
CHINNERETH*
⚹ Achshaph [?]

⚹ Shimron (-meron)

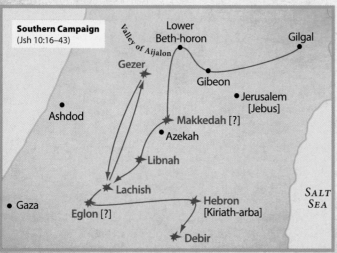

Southern Campaign
(Jsh 10:16–43)

Lower
Beth-horon
Gilgal
Valley of Aijalon
Gezer
Gibeon
• Jerusalem
[Jebus]
Ashdod •
Makkedah [?]
• Azekah
• Libnah
Lachish
*SALT
SEA*
• Gaza
Eglon [?]
Hebron
[Kiriath-arba]
⚹ Debir

Other cities conquered included Arad, Adullam, Aphek, Carmel, Dor, Geder, Goiim, Hepher, Hormah, Jokneam, Kedesh, Lasharon, Makkedah, Megiddo, Tappuah, Taanach, and Tirzah.

Cities that the Israelites failed to take were Jerusalem, which David would later conquer, and the five Philistine cities: Ashdod, Ashkelon, Ekron, Gath, and Gaza.

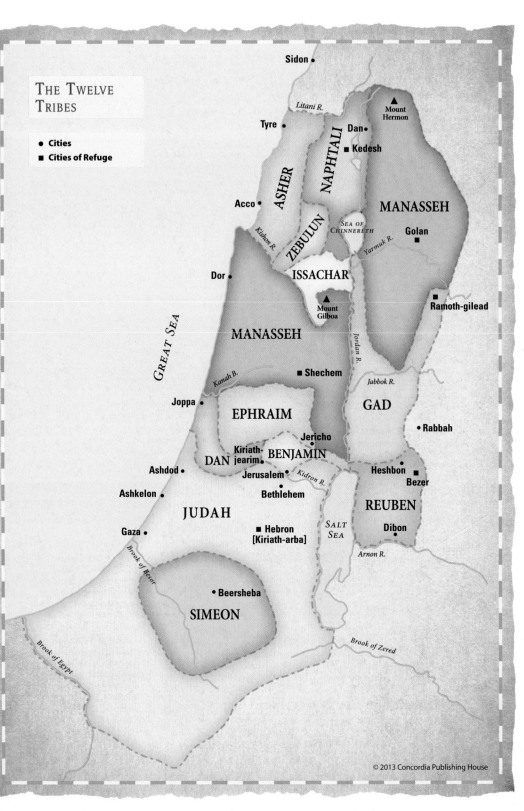

that later became their tomb. The Lord leads His people through a series of successive victories over cities in southern Canaan.

Chs 11–12 The initial conquest of the land under the leadership of Joshua is completed. By the hand of God, Joshua gives the Israelites the land as their inheritance. This list of defeated enemies serves as a reminder that no power, no matter how great or glorious, can withstand the power of the Lord. How remarkable that Joshua, once a slave in Egypt, becomes a conqueror of so many kings! It is because the Lord is with him.

Chs 13–14 Even with much already accomplished to bring the people of God into their promised possession, much remains to be done for the promises to be completely fulfilled. The promise of the land to Abraham's descendants finds earliest fulfillment in the tribes east of the Jordan. Then, final preparations and explanatory remarks are given before the land is apportioned to the remaining tribes. The first allotment begins with Caleb.

Chs 15–19 Judah receives precedence in the allotment of land. Joshua describes the failures of Ephraim to drive out the Canaanites. The tribes of Joseph move to lay claim to the promises of God by inheriting their land. But they forget His promises about acquiring His blessings. Settling the land of Canaan was not an overnight event. God's servant Joshua needed to remind, encourage, and direct the people in this matter, lest they become negligent in following God's promises to their completion. Benjamin, one of the smallest tribes, receives its allotment between Judah and Ephraim, the two most powerful tribes. Simeon's clans receive land and cities within the boundaries of Judah. Consequences of the rash actions of Simeon and Levi were visited upon their descendants. The disbursement of inheritance continues with Zebulun. Issachar receives as inheritance the area west of the Jordan and south of the Sea of Chinnereth. Asher's allotment runs along the Great Sea north of Mount Carmel, upward to the territory of the pagan city of Sidon. Naphtali's portion and inheritance is in the north. Dan fails to gain its inheritance. As a strong leader, Joshua receives his portion last! The allotment of land begins with Caleb, one of the faithful spies; it ends with Joshua, the other faithful spy.

Chs 20–21 At the Lord's direction, Joshua appoints six cities of refuge, demonstrating the Lord's desire for both justice and mercy. The Lord also provides for the tribe of Levi, and with that, the author proclaims with praise that the Lord has kept all of His promises.

Chs 22–24 In the first of his three farewell sermons, Joshua dismisses the eastern tribes after they faithfully finished the work they promised to do. A misunderstanding about a symbolic altar occurs but is peacefully resolved.

In the second of Joshua's three farewell sermons, he addresses the leaders of Israel with warnings against serving other gods and reminds them of the Lord's faithfulness and victories for Israel. At Shechem, Joshua summarizes for Israel the history of salvation by grace, from the call of Abraham to the victories under Joshua. As the Mosaic covenant is formally renewed, Joshua and the people boldly profess their faithfulness to the God who redeemed them and gave them victory. Three graves in the Promised Land (of Joshua, Joseph, and Eleazar) attest to the faithfulness of the Lord in fulfilling His promises.

Specific Law Themes

The Book of Joshua is a continual demonstration of God's wrath against the Canaanites, and sometimes the Israelites. The Canaanites are devoted to destruction for persisting in wickedness for generations. The Israelites, in contrast, are chastened according to the covenant. Memorials to their failings are raised. Knowing that Israel will continue in the struggle against sin even after they settle in the land, the Lord provides cities of refuge to which perpetrators of manslaughter may flee and receive mercy. The Lord holds Joshua to the standard of the Law.

Specific Gospel Themes

Even the name of Joshua points to the Lord's promised blessings; it means "The Lord saves" and is the Old Testament form of the name Jesus. The book emphasizes that the Lord fulfills His promises, which is confirmed by the direction provided to Joshua throughout the book and especially in the conquest and allotment of the Promised Land. The cities of mercy illustrate God's provision for mercy in cases of accidental death, a measure that softened the cultural vigilante practice of blood-vengeance. Several memorials remind generations to come of the Lord's mighty deeds to provide for His people.

Specific Doctrines

Regardless of questions about the relationship between the Books of Deuteronomy and Joshua, the one follows the other naturally as simple historical sequel, continuing the narrative from the death of Moses to the death of Joshua. The contents of Joshua must be seen as a fulfillment of the promises so often repeated in the Books of Moses.

Jesus and Joshua

The figure of Joshua is a type of Christ and the Promised Land; crossing the Jordan is a type of His benefits. Another expression of the same theme is "rest," used repeatedly in both Testaments (e.g., Dt 3:20; Jsh 1:15; Ps 95:11; Mt 11:28; Heb 3:11; 4:11). Since Baptism makes us members of His body, we already now share in His kingdom of grace, and await the consummation in the kingdom of glory.

Joshua's name pointed to Jesus, because "Joshua" and "Jesus" are one and the same names (Hebrew and Aramaic respectively), both meaning "salvation, victory," etc. The prophetic qualities of Joshua and of the Promised Land converge in Jesus. Unfortunately, in modern times the "land" motif has almost been spiritualized into nonexistence, so much so that many Christians experience special difficulty in appropriating this major Old Testament theme.

Reshef, west Semitic deity of plague and war, was worshiped from Syria to Egypt.

Even after Christ's advent and the writings of the New Testament, we live like the people of Israel, awaiting the fulfillment of God's promises: we live in the time of the "not yet." We wait and hope for the *fulfillment* in Christ's reappearing—though now we often prefer the term *consummation*, so as not to demote Christ to merely one person in a series. After Christ, there can no longer be "fulfillment" in the strict sense, but only an end or climax of His fulfillment in the eternal kingdom.

"Holy" War?

A war of conquest, even a "holy" war explicitly commanded by Yahweh, creates problems for many readers. The *cherem* or sacral ban called for the total extermination of the enemy. Some critics seek to evade the issue by viewing it as largely just later Deuteronomic rhetoric, intended only to stir the audience to uncompromising opposition to Canaanite religion, but that is scarcely a solution.

External evidence indicates that such usages were common in antiquity, when there was no such thing as nonsacral warfare and there was no such thing as prison rehabilitation programs. What did you do with a defeated enemy in a subsistence economy? The options were kill them or enslave them, both of which are unappealing for people today.

In a way, the whole point of the Book of Joshua is that the conquest of the land was in accordance with the divine purpose, and to reject this is virtually to reject the entire book in its theological dimension.

Liberal failure to distinguish church and state, both in biblical and modern applications, compounds the problems. If we remember that Old Testament Israel was a political as well as a spiritual unit, we will neither think that it can be used as a direct model for the political action of the "*church militant*" nor will we spiritualistically imagine that it would have been possible for Israel to conquer Canaan only in some realm of the Spirit. Nor will we forget that ultimately the warfare is total, involving bodies as well as souls, the physical real estate of this planet as well as "the spiritual forces of evil in the heavenly places" (Eph 6:12). And only stupidity could imagine that there could ever, in any real world—spiritual or material—be a victory or salvation without corresponding defeat and damnation.

Canaanites commonly built their walls with rough stones like those in the foreground. However, a gateway required cut stones as seen in the background at Shechem.

Renewal of the Covenant

After God had graciously formed Jacob's descendants into His covenant people and named them as His own, He provided them a choice for the future: "If you will . . . then I will . . . " Joshua presented this if/then choice to the people at Shechem in the renewal of the covenant. They could continue on the path God established for them, or they could follow the road to destruction by rejecting the covenant.

Israel's success and failure are in direct proportion to courage of faith and obedience. God put His power over all the earth at Israel's disposal, but only as Israel tapped the resources of the Creator by trusting His promises and enacting the responsibilities of the Law could Israel overcome all odds. This axiom enables the reader to understand the Bible's terse statements of what Israel achieved and what it failed to accomplish in taking possession of Canaan. "By faith the people crossed the Red Sea as on dry land. . . . By faith the walls of Jericho fell down" (Heb 11:29–30). Walls crumbled and armies were routed when Israel armed itself with faith in God. Conversely, in the absence of the obedience of faith when and because Israel sinned and "transgressed My covenant" (Jsh 7:11), Israel suffered defeat. In the defeat at Ai, Israel's natural resources and strength could have been sufficient to overwhelm the enemy (v 3). God therefore made it clear that without faith resulting in obedience there would be no victory. Even after the death of Joshua, the strength or weakness of Israel always remained in strict proportion to the faithfulness of the tribes to the covenant. None of the tribes could occupy its allotted territory without divine aid.

God's miraculous help was needed because some of the odds or circumstances that the tribes faced were overwhelming by human standards. Judah, for example, was no match for the people of the plains and their chariots of iron (Jgs 1:19). But the true problem was lack of confidence in God's help or the courage of faith to attempt the impossible. Iron chariots were nothing against the power of God in Joshua's obedience to the covenant (Jsh 11:6, 9; cf Dt 20:1). Nor were they a problem later when "the Lord routed Sisera and all his chariots and all his army before Barak with the edge of the sword" (Jgs 4:15). If by faith the walls of Jericho fell, there was no fortress in Canaan that could have withstood the trumpet blasts of Israel's faith.

All the while, God was channeling this miraculous help through circumstances that outwardly appeared to follow a natural pattern of cause and effect. A wind or landslide dammed up the Jordan (3:13–16; cf Ex 14:21), and hailstones helped defeat the army of the coalition of five kings headed by Jerusalem (Jsh 10:11). A naturalistic philosophy of history would say that these phenomena happened at an auspicious time, that Israel "got the breaks." But the faithful are able to see God's hand at work and sing,

> He [God] turned the sea into dry land;
> > they passed through the river on foot.
> There did we rejoice in Him,
> > who rules by His might forever. (Ps 66:6–7)

The Law of Moses

The stories of the Old Testament have always served as sources for illustrating the meaning of the Ten Commandments and other portions of the Law of Moses, in keeping with the apostle Paul's comment, "These things took place as examples for us, that we might not desire evil as they did" (1Co 10:6). The Book of Joshua notes that, in violation of the First Commandment, Israelites continued to cling to idols from Egypt even after years of wandering in the wilderness and settling in the Promised Land (24:14). The leaders of Israel feared a return to false worship (ch 22). Oaths taken in God's name (Second and Eighth Commandments) must not be broken (9:18); the example of Rahab and other biblical figures raised questions about whether it was wrong to lie (cf Zec 8:16–17). The Lord's admonition for Joshua to meditate on the Law (Jsh 1:7–8) shows its usefulness in preparing us for good works.

Application

Ch 1 Joshua begins the critical work of conquering and allotting the Promised Land to Israel. If left alone in our sin and weakness, we would not be able to serve God and to become successful in His eyes. Yet, God enables us through the promises of His Scriptures. He makes us strong and courageous for service. God is at work by the power of His Word to create unity and cooperation between leaders and followers.

Ch 2 Joshua sends two spies to Jericho, where they meet Rahab the prostitute. The God of free and faithful grace grants forgiveness, safety, and peace to repentant sinners, who are justified by grace through faith in Christ and who perform works that prove their God-given faith (Rm 3:22, 24; Jas 2:25–26).

3:1–5:12 Today, you can find direction and purpose in the Lord Jesus as "the way" (Jn 14:6). He who did wonders at the Jordan will lead you through this life and land you safely in the heavenly Canaan. Although our sin brings us reproach before God, the Lord removes our guilt through His appointed means today (Baptism). Awareness of God's saving grace and generous gifts leads us to set right priorities and to "seek first the kingdom of God and His righteousness" (Mt 6:33).

5:13–8:35 When we think we have the strength to fight our spiritual enemies, we are on our way to defeat. God is a God of justice, who cannot let sin go unpunished. Yet God is also a God of love, whose justice was satisfied when His Son took the punishment for the sin of the world. The Lord delivers us, through faith in Jesus, from the destruction awaiting this present evil age. After the sin of Achan has been punished and Joshua does all that the Lord commanded, Israel successfully destroys the city of Ai. The story of Achan is an example of God's judgment and sentence against all sin and sinners. Thanks be to God. The Word was given by God in Christ, the Rock of Ages, so forgiveness and life might be written on our hearts.

Chs 9–10 How often do we judge things based on appearance and act without consulting the Lord and His Word? When confronted by strife, do we try to handle it ourselves, or do we call on the Lord to save and help us? When the Lord promises victory, He brings it to pass. No matter how great or how many challenges face you, cling to the Lord's promises and pray based on them. Consider the deliverance that came by God's hand as you reflect on the challenges you face.

Chs 11–12 Joshua, by the hand of God, gives the Israelites the land as their inheritance. The Lord has said, "Do not be afraid" (11:6). Fear should not affect our faithfulness to the will and direction of the Lord. How remarkable that the Lord is also with you and will strengthen you to overcome all that would enslave you.

Chs 13–14 Though God has established a place for His people to dwell eternally, many things conspire to rob us of that promised inheritance and peace. The first allotment begins with Caleb. The story of Caleb reminds us of God's judgment on faithless Israel (the conquest was delayed) and God's faithfulness to the faithful (His promises are completed to Caleb). Throughout, Caleb shows that the Lord is the strength of the faithful.

Chs 15–19 The assigning of land to Judah points to our end-times promised land through Christ, who came from the tribe of Judah. In contrast, the failures of Ephraim to drive out the Canaanites warn us against neglecting our spiritual battles as Christians. The Lord equips us for these struggles, giving us His Spirit and the Word. Benjamin's land would become the heartland of the kingdom of Israel. No matter how small we may seem to others in the Church or the world, we can take confidence, because the Lord makes plans for us and promises our salvation. When the Lord challenges us, He also equips us by His good Word and Spirit. When we fail and fall into sin, we will be tempted to give up completely on what we know is good and right. Yet, when we are at our lowest, the Lord remembers us in His mercy.

Chs 20–21 Our God of grace "is our refuge and strength, a very present help in trouble" (Ps 46:1). As the Lord provided for the Levites, He promises that when we seek first His kingdom and His righteousness through Christ, He will grant us what we need for this life (Mt 6:33).

Chs 22–24 Commitment, responsibility, and faithfulness to our word are not always present among us. Believers still carry their old sinful natures; therefore, misunderstandings or false accusations sometimes flare up among them. But the power of God's Word and Spirit working in our hearts can bring about genuine reconciliation and peace. We deserve none of the good that God gives us. Yet, pray for courage. His saving grace and His Spirit can enable us to boldly confess His name.

CANONICITY

As evident from the history-based psalms and other passages of the Old Testament, the story of Joshua and the conquest was central to ancient Israelite belief. The Book of Joshua was welcomed by Jews and early Christians without dispute (cf, e.g., the comments of Jesus son of Sirach in Ecclus 46:1–10).

Lutheran Theologians on Joshua

Luther

"Joshua, however, denotes Christ, because of his name and because of what he does. Although he was a servant of Moses, yet after his master's death he leads the people in and parcels out the inheritance of the Lord. Thus Christ, who was first made under the Law (Gal. 4:4), served it for us; then, when it was ended, He established another ministry, that of the Gospel, by which we are led through Him into the spiritual kingdom of a conscience joyful and serene in God, where we reign forever." (AE 9:43)

"Joshua also fulfilled it [Dt 27–28] after the city of Ai was taken (Josh. 8:30 ff.); there both the blessings and the curses were read before the whole people, and burnt offerings and thankofferings were made, as Moses says here. Of course, this was done that through the external show the crude people (as I have said) might be stirred to remember the Law, for people are moved by outward ceremonies more than by bare words alone. . . .

"[Moses] recounts no blessings here, but only cursings, although he assigns seven tribes to blessings and it is written in Joshua that blessings were also recounted (Joshua 8:33 ff.). I think that the reason for this was that Moses shows himself to be the minister of sin and death through the Law, which holds all under a curse (Gal. 3:10). Finally this people of the Law perished through the curse. But Joshua adds blessings, that he might point to Christ, who blesses all who are under the curse of the Law and yearn for Him. On account of Christ, Judah is classified among those who ought to stand forth to receive a blessing, because He [Christ] was to come from Judah." (AE 9:258–59)

"This [Jsh 24:19–20] was the farewell speech of Joshua. He admonishes the people with extraordinary feeling, as if he would say, 'I fear that you will provoke God's wrath again. If so, God will punish you, for he can't tolerate this. If you provoke him and fall away from him, God will be angry,' etc. Another solution is that the earlier words [24:14–15] were said of the ungodly and the later words [vv 19–20] of the godly, just as we have many psalms in which, here and there, people are praised and are lifted up to heaven and immediately after are put down into hell; by synecdoche, in the former case the godly in the whole people are spoken of, and in the latter case the ungodly. We do the same thing in our churches when we preach; we praise those among the people who are good and then, on the other hand, we reprove the bad and the ungodly. So the church is called holy, although only the smallest part of it is actually holy." (AE 54:301)

Gerhard

"The Greeks call *the Book of Joshua*: *Iesous Naue*, because it contains the history of the things that Joshua, the servant of Moses, had done, things that Joshua himself consigned to writing by God's will. Augustine (*Q. 12 in lib. Judic.*) has doubts as to who wrote the Book of Joshua. Some attribute it to Ezra and others to a prophet. The title, however, indicates that Joshua wrote it, a fact that Munsterus confirms in c. 1 of Joshua. You see, it is called 'the Book of Joshua' not merely with respect to its object but also with respect to its instrumental efficient cause, as we conclude from Josh. 24:26.

"There is a report that Ezra added to the end of the book the things that were written after the death of Joshua. Theodoret thinks that the entire book was taken long after Joshua's death from an ancient commentary whose title was 'the Book of the Just,' taken from the words of Josh. 10:13: 'Is this not written in the Book of the Just?'

"It has twenty-four chapters and contains the history of the eighteen years from Moses' death to Joshua's death. It describes the history: (1) of the entry of the Israelites into the land of Canaan under the leadership of Joshua; (2) of the vanquishing of the Canaanites; and (3) of the distribution of the land among the tribes of Israel. It also can be divided into a history of Joshua's affairs (1) in war and (2) in peace. It contains 645 verses." (ThC E1 §125)

QUESTIONS PEOPLE ASK ABOUT JOSHUA

The Morality of War and the Covenant

As one of the covenant stipulations, God required that Israel annihilate the Canaanites and all the inhabitants of the land, and all booty of war was to be destroyed or dedicated to the Lord.

> When the LORD your God gives them over to you, and you defeat them, then you must devote them to complete destruction. You shall make no covenant with them and show no mercy to them.... In the cities of these peoples that the LORD your God is giving you for an inheritance, you shall save alive nothing that breathes. (Dt 7:2; 20:16)

Israel obeyed (usually). "Then they devoted all in the city to destruction ... with the edge of the sword" (Jsh 6:21).

Some who read Joshua have claimed that this passage (6:21) reflects a low standard of morality on the part of Israel, that Israel's morals and conception of God had not moved beyond a low level of development—and that this God of bloody savagery has nothing in common with the loving Father of the forgiving Jesus, who directed God's people to "love your enemies and pray for those who persecute you" (Mt 5:44).

A Canaanite bronze scimitar sword, which was badly bent.

But this charge forgets that the God of love also is the God who sends wrath on all workers of iniquity. Without His wrath, His love is reduced to impotence and sentimentality. Without His wrath, there would have been no cleansing flood at the time of Noah, no purging of the land of Sodom and Gomorrah, and ultimately no need for His Son to take on Himself the Father's wrath for the sins of the whole world.

Behind this charge against the picture of God in Joshua lies the more difficult yet real question of evil in the world. How can God idly stand by while nations war against nations, while the destructive forces of nature devastate more cities than Israel ever did, while individuals deliberately and premeditatively select innocent victims for torture, abuse, and murder? Although whole tomes have been written on this subject, it is treated but briefly here.

The reader of Joshua (as well as most of the Old Testament) must keep in mind that God there provides a condensed history of His involvement with humanity to bring about the salvation of the world through the Seed to be born out of His covenant people, Israel. That goal of God cannot let sinful nations or peoples stand in the way—and that included the pagan peoples of Canaan who could lead Israel into idolatry (as actually happened because Israel did not obey God's command utterly to destroy them). On the other hand, God at times chose to use sinful nations to accomplish His purposes. For example, God later chose Assyria and Babylon to be His agents of punishment against the Northern and Southern Kingdoms and then chose a Persian, Cyrus, to be His agent against Babylon and to be the one who let God's people return from Babylon to the Promised Land (2Ch 36:14–23).

The problem of evil in the world lies not with a God in whom "steadfast love and faithfulness meet; righteousness and peace kiss each other" (Ps 85:10) but with a humanity that is sinful from its mother's womb (51:5), even from Eve and Adam. The solution is not in redefining God but in receiving the salvation He provides through His Son, our Savior.

What Joshua, son of Nun, achieved has meaning only as a preparation for and a promise of Jesus, son of Mary and Son of God. The land conquered by Joshua was a perishable inheritance, but Jesus, the mediator of the new covenant, provided "an inheritance that is imperishable, undefiled, and unfading, kept in heaven for you" (1Pt 1:4). "The gospel . . . is the guarantee of our inheritance until we acquire possession of it" (Eph 1:13–14). But as in Israel's day, "everyone who is sexually immoral or impure . . . has no inheritance in the kingdom of Christ and God" (5:5).

Therefore, together with Joshua, God's people of every age must and can renew their covenant with God (Jsh 24:15).

The Sins of Evildoers Visited upon Others

Joshua 7:1 narrates: "But the people of Israel broke faith in regard to the devoted things, for Achan the son of Carmi, son of Zabdi, son of Zerah, of the tribe of Judah, took some of the devoted things. And the anger of the LORD burned against the people of Israel."

In contrast, Ezk 18:20 declares: "The soul who sins shall die. The son shall not suffer for the iniquity of the father, nor the father suffer for the iniquity of the son. The righteousness of the righteous shall be upon himself, and the wickedness of the wicked shall be upon himself."

These two passages are representative of two groups of texts that may prove perplexing to Bible readers and may seem to contradict each other. The sin of Achan brings the wrath of God upon the children of Israel. Similarly in Ex 20:5 God threatens to visit the sins of the fathers upon the children to the third and fourth generation of those who hate Him. On the other hand, Ezk 18:20 expresses a sentiment that immediately meets with our approval, namely, that the guilty shall die, no one else. Let the reader bear in mind the following points, and the difficulties will be resolved.

No person is absolutely pure and innocent. If the evildoing of one person brings disaster upon himself and another person, the latter cannot maintain that he is being dealt with unjustly. He also is a sinner who has deserved the punishment of God. Though he may not have committed the same sin that the first person committed, he has his own forms of wrongdoing.

All that we do reacts either favorably or unfavorably upon our fellow human beings. Good deeds prove a blessing not simply to ourselves but to others as well; our evil deeds have the same range of influence. An alcoholic may bring ruin not only to his own person but also inflicts misery on his family and friends. In a moral world, a great responsibility for the welfare of others is laid upon us. The sentinel forsaking his post causes the rout of the whole army. So Achan by his theft brought the anger of God upon all Israel.

This is one of the ways in which God punishes sin. Parents who recklessly squander their belongings must as a consequence not merely endure poverty themselves, but must (and this frequently is a far greater punishment) witness the suffering of their children. This fact is one of the considerations that must deter us from transgressing. Achan ought to have resisted the temptation to take from the things that were accursed, not simply for his own sake but for the people's sake as well.

Still the words of Ezk 18:20 are literally true. God does not impute the guilt of the wicked to the innocent. The child shall not bear the guilt of the parent, nor shall the parent bear the guilt of the child. God knows how to distinguish between the wicked and the God-fearing even when they live under the same roof. "The soul who sins shall die." Death here is a term for eternal damnation—the second, the real death. To be sure, pious children often are thrown into misery because their parents have led a life of unbridled foolishness. But let it be remembered, on the one hand, that this fact does not mean that God has condemned these children and turned away from them in anger; and on the other hand, that these temporal sufferings may be a blessing in disguise, sent upon God's children as a chastisement, in accordance with the maxim, "For the Lord disciplines the one He loves" (Heb 12:6).

Thus we see that Jsh 7:1 and Ex 20:5 set forth the terribleness and the far-reaching, sad consequences of wrongdoing; Ezk 18:20, however, speaks of the guilt attached to wickedness and of eternal damnation coming upon impenitent sinners. The point of view is a different one in each case. If this distinction is borne in mind, the passages will be found to be in complete agreement.

Joshua Bidding the Sun to "Stand Still"

In Jsh 10:12–14 we have one of the most remarkable narratives in all the Scriptures. In the midst of a great battle against five kings of the Amorites, Joshua commanded the sun and moon to "stand still." It must not be overlooked that "Joshua spoke to the LORD" (v 12). The general of Israel turned to God in prayer. His command addressed to the sun was not the mandate of a haughty potentate, who, like Xerxes, thought that even the forces of nature ought to be subject to him, but the utterance of faith, which trusts that with God nothing is impossible. Full of confidence in God's help and feeling certain that what he was about

Valley of Aijalon as seen from Gibeon.

to do had divine sanction, he spoke to the sun and moon, the words amounting to a prayer for God's intervention on Israel's behalf.

There are a number of interpretations proposed for this passage: some interpreters find here no miraculous intervention in the regular course of nature. Poetic in form and language, they think the account is merely a figurative way of saying that the day was long enough to permit Israel to destroy the fleeing enemy. It is similar to Deborah's exclamation: "The stars . . . fought against Sisera" (Jgs 5:20).

Other commentators insist that this day was miraculously prolonged beyond the normal 24 hours. The believer has no reason to doubt that He who created "the heavens and the earth . . . and all the host of them" could control the work of His "fingers" (Gn 2:1; Ps 8:3; Is 34:4). He had the power to stop the vast machinery of the universe with its myriads of interlocking gears.

A third interpretation finds the miraculous element in the fact that God at the right moment commandeered the forces of nature as He did in Egypt and at Jericho. Here at Gibeon, He sent a barrage of hailstones. The accompanying storm prolonged the darkness of the night. Under its cover the Israelites had surprised the enemy and then were able to complete the pursuit of the fleeing allies. Accordingly the result of God's intervention was sustained darkness rather than additional hours of sunlight. The meaning of the Hebrew verbs describing the phenomenon is cited in support of this view. "Stand still" has the basic meaning to "be silent" and then by analogy to "cease" or "desist" from a given activity. "Stopped," literally "stand," at times has the same connotation of stopping to function. "Go down," literally "enter," is used of the disappearance of the sun in the west. Used in connection with the preceding verbs it means that the sun did not come into view for about a whole day.

Another possible view is that the words "did not hurry" (v 13) may imply a slowing of movement so that the rotation required 48 hours rather than the usual 24. It has been pointed out that the worship of the sun and the moon by the Canaanites might have induced God to bring about the utter defeat of these peoples by the agency of their supposed divinities in order to manifest to the world the futility of their belief as well as of every other form of idolatry. Whether this proposal is right or not, we can rest assured that some great and benign purposes of our great God were served when He heard the prayer of Joshua.

FURTHER STUDY

Lay/Bible Class Resources

Dunker, Gary. *Joshua: The Lord's Promise Fulfilled.* GWFT. St. Louis: Concordia, 2006. ♪ Lutheran author and devotional writer. Eleven-session Bible study, including leader's notes and discussion questions.

Harstad, Adolph. *Joshua.* PBC. St. Louis: Concordia, 2003. ♪ Lutheran author. Excellent for Bible classes. Based on the NIV translation.

Harstad, Adolph. *Joshua.* Leaders Guide and Enrichment Magazine/Study Guide. LL. St. Louis: Concordia, 2006. ♪ An in-depth, nine-session Bible study covering the Book of Joshua with individual, small group, and lecture portions.

Hess, Richard S. *Joshua: An Introduction and Commentary.* TOTC. Downers Grove, IL: InterVarsity Press, 1996. ♪ A most useful compact commentary, written by an evangelical scholar. Hess gives special attention to the tribal allotments.

Life by His Word. St. Louis: Concordia, 2009. ♪ More than 1,500 reproducible one-page Bible studies covering each chapter of the canonical Scriptures. Page references to *The Lutheran Study Bible.* CD-Rom and downloadable.

Church Worker Resources

Harstad, Adolph. *Joshua.* CC. St. Louis: Concordia, 2004. ♪ Lutheran author. The best available commentary for interpretation of Joshua's theology and its application. Archaeology considered from a conservative perspective.

Howard, David M. *Joshua.* NAC. Nashville: Holman Reference, 1998. ♪ A useful commentary on Joshua, based on the NIV translation.

Woudstra, Marten H. *The Book of Joshua.* NICOT. Grand Rapids: Eerdmans, 1981. ♪ A helpful exposition by a conservative theologian in the Reformed tradition; restrained emphasis on typology.

Academic Resources

Boling, Robert G., and G. E. Wright. *Joshua.* Vol. 6 of AB. New York: Doubleday, 1982. ♪ Linguistically helpful, archeological emphasis; critical in viewpoint.

Davis, John J. *Conquest and Crisis: Studies in Joshua, Judges, and Ruth.* Grand Rapids: Baker, 1969. ♪ A useful resource by a conservative scholar.

Fay, F. R. *A Commentary on the Holy Scriptures: Joshua.* LCHS. New York: Charles Scribner's Sons, 1889. ♪ A helpful, older example of German biblical scholarship, based on the Hebrew text, which provides references to significant commentaries from the Reformation era forward.

Hawk, L. Daniel. *Joshua.* Berit Olam. Collegeville, MN: The Liturgical Press, 2000. ♪ Commentary focused especially on the structure of the Hebrew text, which Hawk treats as a literary whole.

K&D. *Biblical Commentaries on the Old Testament: Joshua, Judges and Ruth.* Grand Rapids: Eerdmans, 1971 reprint. ♪ This century-and-a-half old work from Lutheran scholars should not be overlooked. Despite its age, it remains a most useful commentary on the Hebrew text.

JUDGES

Everyone did what was right in his own eyes

From the low plains of the Jordan to the heights of Hebron, the Israelite tribe of Judah began its campaign to possess the land Joshua allotted to them. The battle would literally be uphill (Jgs 1:2). Under Joshua's leadership, the future looked bright and optimistic. Israel was well on the way to claiming possession of its inheritance. Faithful to God and obedient to Joshua, His covenant representative, the unified tribes broke the power of vastly superior forces in Canaan. What was begun (and achieved) by united action and the power of a common faith could be expected to be completed when each tribe, in the same faith, made its way into its allotted territory.

The Lord was still with them. Yet the obstacles facing each tribe were as formidable and insurmountable as the opposition in the days of Joshua. Walls as high as those of Jericho would have to give way, and chariots of iron like those of Jabin (Jsh 11:1–9) needed to be destroyed by an army lacking even shield or spear (Jgs 5:8). Encouraged and fortified by the Lord's help in the past, Israel could expect to march on to complete victory.

But those bright prospects vanished, and dark disappointment settled over Israel in the Book of Judges. No tribe succeeded in driving out the inhabitants and fully occupying its assigned land. Instead, territory was lost. One tribe (Dan) was entirely dispossessed (ch 18) and had to find another area to

From the heights of Mount Tabor, Israelite leaders could observe the approach of the Canaanite chariots and stay out of their reach until the Kishon River hindered Canaanite maneuvers, making them vulnerable to attack.

OVERVIEW

Author(s)
Unknown

Date
Written c 1000 BC

Places
Cities throughout Israel and Canaan, especially in the central highlands, which Israel conquered first and held

People
Joshua, Deborah, Gideon, Samson, and other judges; the tribes of Israel; Canaanites; Philistines; Moabites; Midianites; Ammonites

Purpose
To present Israel's declining spiritual state and the Lord's mercy, by which He forgave them and held them together

Law Themes
Israel's failure to conquer the Promised Land; transgression of the covenant; cowardice; idolatry; unfaithful Levites; doing what's right in one's own eyes

Gospel Themes
The Lord provides saviors and judges; the Lord answers Israel's cry for help; the angel of the Lord; the Spirit of the Lord

Memory Verses
The Lord's enemies and friends (5:31); 11 tribes repent (20:26); wayward Israel (21:25)

TIMELINE

1399–1375 BC	Death of Joshua and the elders
1217–1178 BC	Deborah
1157 BC	Eli born
1099–1060 BC	Eli's priesthood and judgeship
1088 BC	Oppression by the Midianites and Philistines begins

Canaanite fertility goddess, Astarate (cf Asherah, Ishtar). Through intermarriage, the Israelites adopted such goddesses, as described in Jgs 3.

inhabit. Joshua's last words had warned of this ominous future: "If you forsake the LORD and serve foreign gods, then He will turn and do you harm and consume you, after having done you good" (Jsh 24:20).

The opening chapters of Judges (1:1–3:6) set the stage for this dismal picture in Israel's history. To connect it with the previous period, the state of affairs at Joshua's death are once more mentioned (2:1–10), and the section elaborates on the covenant cause-and-effect theme. God had given success to the first phase of capturing Canaan; now Israel was assigned the task of dispossessing the inhabitants and fully occupying the land.

But the people did not obey the Lord. "They went after other gods; . . . And they provoked the LORD to anger" (2:12). Thus they created for themselves a situation that led to their undoing. The Lord warned them, "Their gods shall be a snare to you" (2:3). Israel's lack of faith was the reason that it did not accomplish what God promised to do for and through the nation.

Such inactivity aroused the displeasure of the Lord (vv 1–5), and Judges shows to what wickedness this dallying with God's promise led. When Israel does not act aggressively, sins of omission (due to a lack of faith) lead inevitably to sins of commission, and Israel slides downhill into every vice against God and neighbor, into gross idolatry and wickedness of every kind. "Where there is no prophetic vision [and the Law is ignored,] the people cast off restraint" (Pr 29:18).

So it was that "everyone did what was right in his own eyes" (Jgs 21:25), but what they did was "evil in the sight of the LORD" (2:11). Anarchy prevailed. Religious, social, political, and moral principles disappeared. Even civil war broke out (ch 20). These were dark ages for Israel.

Historical and Cultural Setting

The Book of Judges mentions a time of persecution preceding the work of each major judge (six total) as well as a time of rest after deliverance. But with the exception of Shamgar, it lists only the duration of the judgeship of each minor judge. As a result, the recording of the years is incomplete and unclear.

Although the years given in the Book total 410 years,[1] 1Ki 6:1 gives a total of 480 years[2] from the time "after the people of Israel had come out of the land of Egypt" (1446 BC) and the fourth year of Solomon (968 BC). After subtracting time for Saul, David, and Solomon, about 300 years remain for the judges. One must consider how the 410 total years fit with the c 300 years calculated from the exodus to the service of Eli. (Jephthah, the second-to-last judge, reminds the Ammonites [in Jgs 11:26] that some 300 years had passed since they suffered defeat under Moses.)

A number of factors allow for this reduction. One need not assume from Scripture that the events of Judges took place one after the other rather than simultaneously. For example, the phrase "The LORD . . . sold them into the hand of the Philistines and into the hand of the Ammonites" (10:7) may introduce both Jephthah's deliverance from the Ammonites (10:6–12:7) and Samson's forays against the Philistines (chs 13–16). With one exception, all the periods of rest and one of oppression are reckoned in terms of 40 years (i.e., a generation) or a multiple of it. Some of these are likely round figures denoting a generation.

Judges recounts the stormy history of God's people after the conquest. Pockets of unconquered Canaanite city-states, the emergence of the Philistines as a major threat, and the recurrent apostasy and disunity of the tribes themselves contributed to making the period anything but tranquil.

From archaeological data we know that the period that followed the invasion of the "Sea Peoples" (the Philistines are the best known representatives), which had annihilated all the great political powers of the area, was a time of greatest possible ferment throughout the ancient Near East. Into the vacuum swept many of the nomadic desert tribes of which the Israelites themselves had partly been harbingers. But the Book of Judges shows that Israel suffered from similar nomadic invasion once they had settled down. Typically, however, the biblical writer is interested in that broader picture, only as it impinges on Israel's history, and specifically as God employs one or the other of those historical agents as instruments of His wrath upon a disloyal people. This leads to focus problems in the historical interpretation of the book.

---

1   The total includes 111 years of opposition and the major judges, 70 years of the minor judges, 226 years of rest, and 3 years of Abimelech.

2   Paul mentions in round figures that God gave them judges for "about 450 years" (Ac 13:20). No doubt he is referring to the years of the judges in their totality, from Joshua to Samuel.

CRITICAL VIEWS OF JUDGES

Critical scholars have considered the tribal structure in this period an "amphictyony," an association of states dedicated to a common religion and its defense. Greek examples inspired these ideas about the period of the judges. This hypothesis envisioned a central shrine, with each tribe retaining full internal and political independence. This view was often combined with a "covenant renewal festival" hypothesis, which purported to describe periodic meetings of the tribes or their representatives at the shared religious center. Amphictyonic officials were supposedly limited to religious functions, such as "covenant mediator" or major preacher at the festivals.

These ideas increasingly came under sharp attack, and it remains to be seen if they will survive. No other hypothesis has won acceptance among the scholars, and many today would not care to venture beyond the sorry picture Judges itself paints: a clear memory of Moses and Sinaitic covenant, but honored more in the breach than in the observance, and precious little unity—political, religious, or otherwise.

Much modern critical scholarship envisions the liturgies of this period as the first major creative incubator of many of Israel's later traditions, religious as well as literary. However, a more fundamental clash between the biblical record and critical hypothesis is scarcely conceivable! The Bible describes this period as one of moral and religious decay rather than one during which the beliefs of Israel developed or matured.

COMPOSITION

Author(s)

The Talmud attributes authorship to Samuel—an opinion which is by no means impossible, and which does not lack for defenders today (at least among conservatives). But finally one must admit that the author is unknown.

Date of Composition

Various indications suggest that the final form of the book might have been put together after the time of Samuel, such as the refrain that there was "no king in Israel." This would not necessarily point to a date later than the united kingdom. However, in 18:30 we read that Jonathan's descendants were priests in Dan "until the day of the captivity of the land," which almost certainly brings us down to the time of the fall of the Northern Kingdom in the eighth century. It must always be conceded that these rather marginal comments might have been editorial updates made long after the composition of the main work itself.

Purpose/Recipients

As the introduction above indicates, the Book of Judges describes examples of unfaithfulness to the covenant and their consequences, reminding readers of the need to walk in the way of the Lord continually. The book may also support the need for a king who could offer a common defense for the nation and unify the tribes.

Literary Features

Genre

Like the Books of Moses and Joshua, the Book of Judges is a theological history. It illustrates the curses for sin and the blessings for faithfulness through examples from Israel's history. Critics often viewed the introduction to Judges (1:1–2:5) as a conclusion for the first six books of Scripture (the Hexateuch theory; see pp 196–97). In this view, the heart of the book was added later, characterized by a variety of stories organized around a Deuteronomic framework. However, such a Deuteronomic comment is missing not only in the final chapters of the book, but also in the case of Abimelech and the minor judges. This undermines confidence in the critical theory.

Characters

The biblical "judge" (Hbr *shophet*) does not have the same courtroom associations as the modern term. The biblical usage is ancient; the biblical writer used the term in a broader, almost double, sense.

On the one hand, we have evidence from Ugarit, Mari, Ebla, and even Carthage (a Phoenician colony) for the term's use as a virtual synonym for "king"—or at least "ruler." In sociological terms judges were charismatic leaders, men of the hour who proved themselves and won acceptance by their success. Once the deliverance had been won, many of them apparently continued to wield some authority. The extrabiblical usage shows that "judge" implies not so much unique acts of deliverance as a sustained series of acts of government, maintaining justice by means of righteous judgments. The Hebrew term for such ordered rule, *mishpat* (often translated "justice" or "judgment") is derived from the same root as the term for judge (*shophet*).

At the same time, the biblical writer is plainly interested in a broader sense of the term. As rulers, both kings and judges make many judgments, implying either acquittal or condemnation. When God is the subject in relation to His faithful, covenant people, the ordinary assumption is that His judgment will be one of acquittal or salvation, in faithfulness to His promises. God is the real judge of His people; that is a point of the book as a whole. The biblical writer helps bring out this nuance of "judge" by often paralleling it (cf 2:16) with the term *saviors* or *deliverers* (*moshi'im*, derived from the same Semitic root as the names Joshua and Jesus). Possibly it is significant that the noun "judge" is never used directly of an individual in the book.

The problem is complicated slightly by the appearance of both "major" and "minor" judges in the book. The six minor judges are Shamgar, Tola, Jair, Ibzan, Elon, and Abdon, about which very little information has been preserved. It may simply have not served the writer's overriding theological concerns to include more information about these leaders. Possibly they were more the ordinary Semitic type of judge (in the sense of "ruler") with few charismatic attainments, and were included only for the sake of completeness.

It should be noted in passing that especially in Numbers we meet a tribal functionary called a *nasi'* ("prince"). His precise role is also unclear, but apparently some regular administrative machinery is reflected in the title. In contrast, the *shophet* or "judge" may have arisen in times of great emergency and continued in authority on a different level.

Narrative Development or Plot

Having told in ch 1 how it came about that Israel's conquest was incomplete, the writer proceeds in ch 2 to describe the consequences: Israel by its own lack of faith was about to be "Canaanized" and lose its mission as God's instrument of salvation to the nations. Therefore, since Israel's occupation of Canaan would no longer serve His purposes, "[God] will no longer drive out before them any of the nations that Joshua left when he died" (2:21). But He did not abandon His people forever. God let their enemies afflict them, and when Israel repented, He sent a deliverer, a judge (2:11–19). From these broad points, the account moves into a series of historical examples.

The accounts probably overlap somewhat, but the accounts of the major and minor judges (3:7–16:31) are presented largely in chronological order. The incidents in the dual epilogue (chs 17–21) are more difficult to date but probably took place early in the period. The era extended from the death of Joshua (c 1399 BC) to the beginning of the reign of Saul, the first king of Israel's united monarchy (c 1048 BC). While the entire period thus comprised slightly more than three centuries, Othniel did not come to leadership until an entire generation had died after the death of Joshua (cf 2:10). In addition, Samuel must also be included within this chronology prior to 1048 BC. Several judges may have ruled simultaneously in separate locations.

Resources

The Book of Judges begins with the assumption that readers will know the story of Joshua (1:1; 2:1–10). It mentions "the commandments of the LORD," which may refer to the Books of Moses or at least an oral account of laws Israel was to observe (3:4). The story of Gideon describes a written resource, listing officials and elders (8:14).

Text and Translations

The traditional Hebrew text poses no serious problems, but we have two different recensions reflected in the Septuagint. Qumran evidence makes it likely that both Greek versions were based on variations already in the Hebrew textual tradition.

What is usually considered the earlier of the Greek uncials (Alexandrinus, representing the "Lucianic" recension) also offered the translation which is found in the majority of LXX manuscripts. But it is precisely these which diverge most from the Masoretic Hebrew text. The other edition, best represented by Vaticanus (uncial B), is much closer to the Masoretic

OUTLINE

text, but, at least from the Greek textual standpoint, would not ordinarily be accorded the same weight.

The degree of the differences involved should not be exaggerated. As usual with textual variations, matters of great substance are rarely implicated, and doctrinal matters even less so. At the same time, the variations dare not be glossed over.

Doctrinal Content

Summary Commentary

1:1–3:6 After the optimistic, faith-filled account in Joshua, Jgs 1 introduces the disappointing next phase of Israelite history. The various tribes of Israel allow the Canaanites to remain in the land, which creates a powerful temptation for Israelites to adopt their culture and worship their gods. Israel's failure to drive out its Canaanite opponents is not caused by military weakness but rather by spiritual weakness.

The Israelites know who the Lord is, but they no longer experience His blessed presence among them. They made God their enemy because of their unfaithfulness. Israel would no longer enjoy the blessings promised in Lv 26:1–13 and Dt 28:1–14 under the Lord's covenant; instead, the Israelites would find themselves engaged in a struggle against their pagan neighbors. Yet even in these dark times, God does not withdraw His mercy from His people but raises up a series of champions to be their "saviors."

3:7–31 Othniel, the ideal judge, is God's first champion to rescue Israel from a powerful foreign oppressor. God gave Othniel His Spirit and victory. In contrast, the treachery-filled victory of Ehud over Eglon and the Moabites is told in greater detail than the account of Othniel's victory over Cushan-rishathaim (3:9–11). The summary about Shamgar differs from the surrounding accounts (3:31). There is no announcement that Israel did evil in the eyes of the Lord and no mention that they cried out to Him; no mention that the Lord raised up His person to save them, or that Shamgar was clothed with the Spirit, or that God acted in this judge's behalf.

Chs 4–5 After Israelite armies led by Barak defeat Jabin and the Canaanites, an Israelite woman kills Sisera the Canaanite general by pounding a tent peg through his skull. The Song of Deborah and Barak is a poetic and vivid retelling of the Lord's victory over the Canaanites, especially praising Jael's triumph over Sisera.

Chs 6–8 Gideon's initial call to be a judge reveals his demoralized spirit and weak character, yet with the assurance of the Lord's presence, he makes a first assault on the Baal worship in his own community. Gideon's act of tearing down the Baal altar arouses antagonism. He receives an outpouring of the Holy Spirit to empower him for battle and win the support of neighboring Israelite tribes. Despite a clear revelation of the Lord's will, Gideon twice puts the Lord to a test, hoping to gain certainty for his faltering faith.

After Gideon's army is reduced to a frighteningly low number, he gains confidence when he overhears a dream in the Midianite camp. In pursuit of the Midianites, Gideon acts magnanimously toward the Ephraimites jealous of his victory, but bitterly toward other countrymen. After the victory, Gideon's apparently pious refusal of kingship masks a heart already sold to monarchy. His request for gold from his supporters allows him to make an idol that leads Israel into idolatry. Despite military success, prestige, and wealth, Gideon's judgeship brings Israel little lasting good. One of his many sons will now seek to gain the crown Gideon ceremoniously rejected.

Ch 9 Abimelech, Gideon's illegitimate son, brutally murders his 70 brothers and has himself appointed king in Shechem. One brother, however, manages to escape and in a parable warns that Abimelech is unworthy of the office. The first attempt at kingship in Israel fails miserably, not because monarchy is an unacceptable form of government but because Abimelech is an unworthy candidate.

10:1–5 Following the discredited kingship of Abimelech, the Lord provides rescue and safety through two "minor" judges: Tola and Jair. Even good judges like Jair are affected by the sins of the culture—polygamy and a thirst for wealth.

10:6–12:7 Israel's spiritual well-being deteriorates after the deaths of Tola and Jair. During oppression from the Ammonites, Israel is left to beg for a leader to repulse this latest threat. Despite Jephthah's outcast status, he is selected to lead the Israelite armies against the Ammonites. He argues that Israel has proper claim to the lands east of the Jordan after living there three centuries. Jephthah's carefully crafted speech and military victory over the Ammonites are overshadowed by his rash vow to sacrifice the first thing that comes out to him from his doorway—which turns out to be his only child. The tribe of Ephraim, in its pride and jealousy, is angry at not participating in the glory of Jephthah's victory and threatens to kill the Gileadites. Instead, identifying their enemies by their regional dialect, the Gileadites defeat Ephraim, killing 42,000 of their fellow Israelites.

12:8–15 Three "minor" judges are mentioned: Ibzan, Elon, and Abdon. But nothing is said of their deeds, other than that two of them have large families. Unlike other judges, these deal with no invaders, no civil war, and no dramatic sins. Nevertheless, the people still need to be judged through God's servants who apply His Law.

Chs 13–16 The Lord's messenger appears to a barren woman, promising that she will bear a son who must live as a Nazirite and who will save

In this early Christian wall painting, Samson threatens the Philistines with the jawbone of an ass (Jgs 15:15–17). Such jawbones were used to make cutting tools, such as sickles, for Israelite farmers.

Israel from the Philistines: Samson. The story jumps to his adult years, when Samson sees a Philistine woman and urges his parents to approve an inappropriate marriage with her. Samson is strong physically, but weak morally. Although his long hair marks him externally as a Nazirite, he violates God's Law repeatedly and disrespects his parents.

Samson goes to claim his bride, only to find that her father has married her to someone else. Enraged, Samson begins a personal conflict with the Philistines. Samson's weakness for women proves to be his doom when Delilah coaxes from him the secret of his strength. Bereft of all of his powers, Samson is at the mercy of the Philistines. As Samson is weak and humiliated, the Philistines ascribe their victory to their god Dagon. In that hour, Samson turns to God in faith. He pushes down the columns that support the roof of the pagan temple, destroying thousands of the enemy.

Chs 17–18 A dishonest Ephraimite named Micah uses cursed treasure to create idols, which he worships as the true God of Israel. He even hires a wandering Levite to serve as the priest of his idolatrous shrine. The Danites believe it is too difficult to take the inheritance assigned to them, so they look for easier prey. Acting with cruelty and idolatry, they head north and found the city of Dan.

Chs 19–21 A Levite travels to find his concubine. Though the woman has sinned, the family makes a great effort to be reconciled. However, the Levite soon abandons her to wicked Benjaminites. The violent death of the

Levite's concubine illustrates the low point of wickedness during this period in Israel's history. The Levite tells the Israelites about the abomination committed by the Benjaminites, so the shocked tribes, unified for the first time since Joshua's day, resolve to punish their kindred tribe. A civil war begins.

After the carnage against the Benjaminites, the Israelites begin to mourn the near eradication of one of their kindred tribes. They have compassion for the 600 survivors and hope to restore the tribe. So the elders devise a plan to come up with wives for the Benjaminites.

Specific Law Themes

The Book of Judges records Israel's ultimate failure to conquer the Promised Land despite God's promises and support. After the death of Joshua, the next generation transgresses the covenant. They descend into cowardice before Israel's enemies and adopt pagan habits and idols. The most egregious examples are witnessed in the stories of unfaithful Levites. The book concludes by stating that everyone was doing what was right in his own eyes (21:25).

Specific Gospel Themes

Throughout the period and despite Israel's moral decline, the Lord provided saviors and judges to lead the people. The Lord continued to heed the cries of His people, sending His angel and granting His Spirit to chosen leaders.

Specific Doctrines

By breaking the simple command to "make no covenant with the inhabitants of this land" (Jgs 2:2; cf Ex 23:32), Israel began its downfall. Israel was to be His arm of justice against Canaanite peoples whose measure of wickedness was full and overflowing.

Fraternization and intermarriage with idolaters led to idolatry. The chain reaction of unbelief continued as Israel "abandoned the LORD, the God of their fathers . . . [and] went after other gods, from among the gods of the peoples who were around them . . . and served the Baals and the Ashtaroth" (Jgs 2:12–13) and "the gods of Syria, the gods of Sidon, the gods of Moab, the gods of the Ammonites, and the gods of the Philistines" (10:6). Baalism proved attractive to Israel particularly at this point in its history. When Israel's nomadic way of life gave way to a sedentary agricultural economy, the fertility worship of Baal seemed to offer an abundance of crops, increase in flocks, and the birth of the next generation. Some Israelites even doubted whether the Deliverer from Egypt had divine jurisdiction in Canaan, or whether the land belonged to the local Baal, whose prerogative it was (as the Canaanites assured the Israelite newcomers) to grant the necessary grain and cattle.

Indications are that Israel first rationalized a "small" accommodation to the First Commandment: they would continue to worship Yahweh but would do so through the forms of Baalism. Accommodation to Baalism, a "peaceful coexistence" with it, seemed to grassroots Israel a practical way to assure a livelihood. But such syncretism denies in theory and practice the one and only God, who had already prescribed the forms of worship and who had already limited worship of Him to the place(s) He would designate. In addition, the sensual and sensuous ingredients of Baal worship were seductive and enticing compared to the austere and imageless rites required for Yahweh.

What began as a small accommodation ran amok. When the people rejected God, they also rejected loving their neighbors—and ultimately abused them. That progression may seem a long way down, but Judges teaches that it can be a tiny step. (Cf the men of the city of Ophrah who were willing to kill Gideon because he had destroyed his father's altar to Baal; 6:25–30.)

Once Baalism had taken root, it was difficult to eradicate. Centuries later, the prophets still were condemning Israel for this idolatry (e.g., 1Ki 16:31; Jer 2:8). If only Israel had remembered the words of Moses: "Hear, O Israel: The LORD our God, the LORD is one" (Dt 6:4).

The Book of Judges is in many respects an illustration of God's patience, especially with wayward and sinful people. God gave Israel a long time (about 300 years, the period of the judges) to live as a covenant nation without a national representative to preserve its unity. But lack of faith repeatedly dissolved the nation's bond and resulted in confusion and defeat. Each time that happened, God called Israel back to orderly covenant living. He chose leaders from various tribes to correct the disorders that had arisen and to give the tribes an opportunity to make a fresh start. But neither severity nor kindness on the part of God succeeded. After such attempts, "the people of Israel [again] did what was evil in the sight of the LORD" (Jgs 2:11 et al.). Sadly, Judges is the episodic recital of Israel's failures to live as a divinely governed people.

Canaanite gold and silver figure of Baal.

We marvel at God's patience. We tire of reading the recurring pattern of (1) gross infidelity, (2) repentance under chastisement, (3) relief from disaster under a deliverer (a "judge"), and (4) the inevitable relapse into the same evil. But every true formula and repetition of history must contain the monotonous, unimaginative, and unvarying perversity of the human heart—and the unending justice and mercy of God.

God's Purpose for Israel

God had one purpose in creating Israel and giving Canaan as an inheritance. In His covenant with the patriarchs and with Israel at Mount Sinai, He had made it clear that Israel was to be a means to an end: to bring the blessings of salvation to all nations.

God had His own inscrutable reason for electing Israel as the chosen nation, but He reveals some of the reasons why He directed the course of Israel's history at the time of the conquest as He did. He would, first of all, give Israel physical possession of the land in a way most advantageous to the conquerors: "The LORD your God will clear away these nations . . . little by little, . . . lest the wild beasts grow too numerous for you" (Dt 7:22; cf Ex 23:29–30).

This pattern of gradual conquest also committed Israel to learn to be true spiritual heirs of the land. During such a protracted period, they could conquer only by faith and in obedience to the covenant. Only as "a kingdom of priests" (Ex 19:6) were they to displace the kings of Canaan.

The people had ample opportunity to learn this lesson. But after Joshua's death, Israel lacked the faith to be God's covenant nation and thus did not dispossess the Canaanites. (Two of the few successful tribal leaders were Caleb, Joshua's fellow spy into Canaan under Moses, and Othniel, Caleb's nephew [Jgs 1:11–20].)

God did not deviate from His announced program for Israel. As long as the Canaanites remained, they served to test Israel "to know whether Israel would obey the commandments of the LORD, which He had commanded their fathers by the hand of Moses" (Jgs 3:4). This situation remained for a long time, as can be seen from the Book of Judges. Even a new generation, which "had not experienced all the wars in Canaan" (v 1), was not permitted to possess the land without learning to wage war as God's people (i.e., to conquer by faith in Him and for His ends).

The Law of Moses

Like other Historical Books, Judges serves as a ready source of examples regarding the Ten Commandments. The angels mourned over our idolatry and disobedience (2:1–4). Gideon's house was punished for breaking the First Commandment (8:27) by reintroducing idolatry, even though Gideon acted with good intentions. The oath to Jephthah shows that pledges of loyalty are acceptable in some cases (11:10). Violations of the Sixth Commandment led to personal and community disasters (chs 19–22).

Christology and Church

The angel of the Lord (ch 13) was commonly regarded as a manifestation of Christ before His incarnation, whose name was especially holy and unspeakable (13:18). Samson's allegory of the plowing heifer (14:18) was applied to the Church, which plows with God's Word and makes it known.

Application

1:1–3:6 After the optimistic, faith-filled account in Joshua, Jgs 1 introduces the disappointing next phase of Israelite history. Because of spiritual weakness, believers today also experience suffering, disappointments, and even death. Yet the Lord faithfully calls us to repentance amid our sufferings. He suffered for our sins and renews us by the Gospel.

Where the Law shows us our sin, the Gospel shows us the Father's loving heart in Jesus. He cures our spiritual blindness and leads us to seek Him and worship Him with new hearts. Without sincere faith, it is impossible to please God and rightly receive His blessings. How wonderful that God promises to stand by us, despite our wavering faith. "If we are faithless, He remains faithful—for He cannot deny Himself" (2Tm 2:13).

3:7–31 The treachery-filled victory of Ehud shows how God uses the people available to Him to achieve His larger purposes. Despite our misdeeds and selfish motives, God blesses us. His grace is sufficient for us too. In all things, He works for the good of those who love Him (Rm 8:28).

Chs 4–5 Barak does not demonstrate strong faith, but many Christians can sympathize with his misgivings. We, too, can be weak and slow to act. Yet the Lord is with us, alongside us. Jesus went ahead of us to the cross and through death to everlasting life. He will lead us to the victory ground of heaven.

Chs 6–8 Gideon seems an unlikely figure to become a future champion of Israel. Yet the Lord of surprising, unearned grace seeks sinners and equips them to accomplish great things. As Gideon was clothed by the Lord, so the Holy Spirit clothes us with the righteousness of Christ Jesus. Jesus said that an evil and adulterous generation looks for a sign (Mt 12:39). But when the Lord wishes to give us a sign, we are arrogant to reject it (cf Is 7:10–14). We are tempted to criticize Gideon's lack of decisiveness, but we, too, need repeated assurance that God will keep His promises. Fight the good fight of faith; our warfare is not against flesh and blood but against the

The spring of Ein Harod, by which Gideon tested his men (Jgs 7:1–8).

enemies of the Savior (Eph 6:12). He has won the victory, which is ours through faith.

Ch 9 The Lord calls us to act with integrity when we choose our leaders or when we speak up against them. Through God's Word we learn genuine integrity, which the Holy Spirit produces in sinners through the Word of Christ, our Savior. How frequently rulers exploit people rather than seeing leadership as an opportunity for service!

10:1–5 Even good judges like Jair are affected by the sins of the culture—polygamy and a thirst for wealth. How blind we may be to the besetting sins of our culture! God's grace stepped into our world in the person of Jesus, who rode a donkey in humility so that He might teach and serve the people.

10:6–12:7 Spiritual gullibility leads people to believe anything that suits their desires. God is remarkable in His persistent mercy and in His willingness to begin anew with us. Christians may appear an unimportant minority on earth, with no particular claim to power, and losing influence as society becomes more and more secular. Yet God still guides the affairs of the world in the interest of His people.

12:8–15 Ibzan, Elon, and Abdon—living out both their spiritual offices (in their judgeships) and temporal offices (in their families)—stand as examples of the doctrine of vocation. Nothing is recorded of their good works. Yet, God was still pleased with them on account of their faith.

Chs 13–16 God's Word comes to us with special purpose. The Lord strengthens us for our special mission of serving Him in a hostile world.

Despite Samson's sinfulness, "the Spirit of the LORD" comes upon him for the sake of God's purposes. The Holy Spirit works through Samson to accomplish "great salvation" for His people. Samson rightly confesses that this is God's gift, for He is the true Judge and Savior. When we are weak and broken spiritually (or perhaps also physically), we finally despair of ourselves. In that hour, Christ is the true strong man for us spiritually. Samson carried the gates of a city, but Jesus carried the cross and all our sin.

The torch-bearing foxes of Jgs 15 appear on a floor mosaic of a c fourth century synagogue in lower Galilee. The colored tiles on the right likely depict Samson's robe, belt, and cloak.

Chs 17–18 God's commands are often difficult to obey, but acting on our own impulses only multiplies sin. Even at our worst, the Lord has chosen and ordained for us a Savior, our true High Priest, Jesus Christ, who is the only way to salvation. The Lord had generously provided the Danites with priests and a sanctuary at Shiloh, where He promised to meet with them and grant them His mercy. Even so, the Lord meets with us and blesses us through the means He has ordained: the Word and the Sacraments.

Chs 19–21 Sins, like the concubine's and the Levite's, still wound and divide families today. These manipulations of morality are a final example of the moral degradation that comes from everyone doing what is right in his own eyes. God pours out His wrath on sinners, but He saves a remnant by His grace. Lord, have pity! Deliver the Church, Your Bride, from evil.

CANONICITY

As is evident from the history-based psalms, the stories of the period of the judges were important to Israel's history, though they illustrated the weaknesses of the people. The Book of Judges was welcomed by Jews and early Christians without dispute (cf e.g., the comments of Jesus son of Sirach from Ecclus 46:11–12).

Fresco-Mosaic of Samson killing a lion.

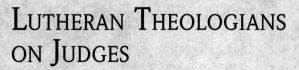

Lutheran Theologians on Judges

Luther

"The historians, therefore, are the most useful people and the best teachers, so that one can never honor, praise, and thank them enough." (AE 34:276)

"It is necessary to know the scope of this word [judges] in Hebrew; for it denotes also an official position itself or the administration of law, as in Ps. 1:5: 'The godless shall not stand in the judgment,' which others would render, 'in rule'; likewise Ps. 72:1: 'God, give judgment to the king.' Hence it is used in the name of the Book of Judges, which in Latin would be called the book of princes, rulers, governors, or magistrates." (AE 9:49)

"He calls leaders 'saviors,' as we find in the Book of Judges (Judg. 3:9), where He sent them many saviors, that is, leaders to lead them and take charge of them, to be in the lead if they ever had to fight with enemies." (AE 18:204)

"In the book of Judges one can see the good that God did through Ehud [Judg. 3:15–30], Gideon [Judg. 6:11–8:28], Deborah [Judg. 4:4–5:31], Samson [Judg. 13:2–16:31], and other individuals, though the people were not worthy of it." (AE 46:192–93)

Gerhard

"*The Book of Judges* is called by the Hebrews *Shoftim* and by the Greeks *Kritai*. Nothing certain is evident regarding the intermediate author of this book. In the prologue to this passage, Cardinal Hugh [of St. Cher] writes that 'someone has written into the records the activities of the judges of his time. Samuel or Ezra or Jeremiah or Hezekiah gathered this material into a single volume.' This conjecture about Hezekiah is confirmed by the fact that his secretaries are said to have gathered some of Solomon's proverbs into one book (Prov. 25:1).

"It is called the 'Book of Judges' because it contains the history under the rule of the judges. It describes: the condition of the state of Israel from the death of Joshua to the priesthood of Eli; how, during that time, the Israelites with oft-repeated apostasy frequently departed from God and, because of this, were afflicted by God with due punishments; and how, after their conversion to God at the hand of the judges that were divinely raised up from the various tribes, they again were freed from the power of their foes. Augustine, *De civit. Dei*, bk. 18, c. 13: 'At the times of the judges there alternated among the people of God both humilities of the hardships because of their sins and the prosperities of consolation because of God's mercy.'

"It has twenty-one chapters and contains a history of 299 years: forty years from Joshua's death to the death of Othniel (Judg. 3:11); eighty years from Othniel's death to the deaths of Ehud and Shamgar (Judg. 3:30); ten years from Ehud's and Shamgar's deaths to the death of Deborah (Judg. 5:31); forty years from Deborah's death to the death of Gideon (Judg. 8:21); three years from Gideon's death to the death of Abimelech (Judg. 9:22); twenty-three years from Abimelech's death to the death of Tola (Judg. 10:2); twenty-two years from Tola's death to the death of Jair (Judg. 10:3); six years from Jair's death to the death of Jephthah (Judg. 12:7); seven years from Jephthah's death to the death of Ibzan (Judg. 12:9); ten years from Ibzan's death to the death of Elon (Judg. 12:11); eight years from Elon's death to the death of Abdon (Judg. 12:14); twenty years from Abdon's death to the death of Samson (Judg. 16:31); one year from Samson's death to the priesthood of Eli. If you add up all these, they total 299 years. This book can be divided into twelve parts according to the number of the judges whose origin, life, and accomplishments it describes. This usage Jerome expresses in these words (Epistle 103 *ad Paulinum*): 'In the Book of Judges there are as many figures as there are princes of the people.' It contains six hundred verses." (ThC E1 § 126)

Questions People Ask about Judges

The Omnipotence of God

Judges 1:19 records: "And the LORD was with Judah, and he took possession of the hill country, but he could not drive out the inhabitants of the plain because they had chariots of iron."

Matthew 19:26 reads: "But Jesus looked at them and said, 'With man this is impossible, but with God all things are possible.'"

That God is almighty is asserted in a number of passages of the Bible. At first sight the text from the Book of Judges seems to contradict these assertions. However, a closer study of this passage will reveal that there is no conflict here at all. When the holy writer says, "And he took possession of the hill country," it is not the Lord who is spoken of, but Judah, and hence it is not the Lord who could not drive out the inhabitants of the valley, but Judah. If the Lord had so wished, He could, of course, have made Judah strong enough to annihilate the inhabitants of the lowland also. But this action was not in keeping with His divine plan. The difficulty presented by the two texts quoted above vanishes the moment we examine Jgs 1:19 as it is clearly and accurately translated in the New King James Version, where it states "they could not drive out. . . ." The King James Version incorrectly implies that the Lord could not drive out the people in the lowland since it reads, "and He . . . could not" instead of "but they could not."

Here is a convenient place to examine another passage that apparently contradicts the statement that God is almighty. Hebrews 6:18 states: "It is impossible for God to lie." This passage says in so many words that a certain thing is impossible for our God. However, this statement does not in the least deny that He possesses omnipotence. What does omnipotence mean? Simply that our God can do whatever He wishes to do. It is very true: God cannot lie, God cannot sin, God cannot cease to be, but neither does He wish to do these things. We see, then, that the correct conception of omnipotence will solve the apparent difficulty presented by Heb 6:18.

Joshua—Judges—Jesus

Although Joshua is not specifically called a judge, the judges are called "Joshuas" (i.e., saviors). They did their part to keep open the channels of the covenant "that we should be saved from our enemies and from the hand of all who hate us" (Lk 1:71). But they merely paved the way for the coming of *the* Joshua, the Savior, Joshua/Jesus of Nazareth.

More wonderful in birth than Samson, perfect in obedience beyond all these saviors of Israel, Jesus did more than lead the fray against the enemies of humanity; He directed the full brunt of their attack on Himself to His own death. It was no futile act of desperation like that of Samson; the Lord rose from the grave in triumph over the vanquished foe. The result: not rest merely for a generation or two, but endless rest.

A Bronze Age bichrome jug decorated with ibex and palms, found at Tel Yin'am, Galilee.

FURTHER STUDY

Lay/Bible Class Resources

Cundall, Arthur E., and Leon Morris. *Judges and Ruth.* TOTC. Downers Grove, IL: InterVarsity Press, 1968. ♫ Cundall uses a somewhat critical approach in his comments on Judges. Morris draws on archaeological information in his exposition of Ruth.

Dunker, Gary. *Judges: God's Grace through Savior-Judges.* GWFT. St. Louis: Concordia, 2007. ♫ Lutheran author and devotional writer. Eleven-session Bible study, including leader's notes and discussion questions.

Lawrenz, John C. *Judges/Ruth.* PBC. St. Louis: Concordia, 2005. ♫ Lutheran author. Excellent for Bible classes. Based on the NIV translation.

Life by His Word. St. Louis: Concordia, 2009. ♫ More than 1,500 reproducible one-page Bible studies covering each chapter of the canonical Scriptures. Page references to *The Lutheran Study Bible.* CD-Rom and downloadable.

McGuire, Brent, Timothy Rake, and Gary Dunker. *Judges.* Leaders Guide and Enrichment Magazine/Study Guide. LL. St. Louis: Concordia, 2007. ♫ An in-depth, nine-session Bible Study covering the Book of Judges with individual, small group, and lecture portions.

Church Worker Resources

Block, Daniel I. *Judges, Ruth.* NAC. Nashville: Broadman & Holman, 1999. ♫ Focuses on the books as literature and how they communicate theologically.

Davis, Dale Ralph. *Such a Great Salvation: Expositions of the Book of Judges.* Grand Rapids: Baker, 1990. ♫ A devotional or homiletical commentary from an evangelical scholar.

Wood, Leon J. *The Distressing Days of the Judges.* Grand Rapids: Zondervan, 1975. ♫ A fact-filled resource from a Reformed scholar.

Younger, K. Lawson, Jr. *Judges, Ruth: The NIV Application Commentary.* Grand Rapids: Zondervan, 2002. ♫ Written by an evangelical scholar, with emphasis on applying the text for today's reader.

Academic Resources

Boling, Robert B. *Judges.* Vol. 6A of AB. New York: Doubleday, 1975. ♫ Philologically excellent, with a critical emphasis in its construction of history. Very little on the theology of the Book.

Cassel, Paulus. *Judges.* LCHS. New York: Charles Scribner's Sons, 1889. ♫ A helpful, older example of German biblical scholarship, based on the Hebrew text, which provides references to significant commentaries from the Reformation era forward.

Gunn, David M. *Judges.* Blackwell Bible Commentaries. Oxford: Backwell, 2005. ♫ A survey of how the Jews and Christians have interpreted the book over the centuries.

K&D. *Biblical Commentaries on the Old Testament: Joshua, Judges and Ruth.* Grand Rapids: Eerdmans, 1971 reprint. ♫ This century-and-a-half old work from Lutheran scholars should not be overlooked. Despite its age, it remains a most useful commentary on the Hebrew text.

Schneider, Tammi J. *Judges.* Berit Olam. Collegeville, MN: Liturgical Press, 2000. ♫ A Jewish scholar who applies the methods of literary criticism and treats the books as a unified composition.

Soggin, J. Alberto. *Judges: A Commentary.* OTL. Louisville: Westminster John Knox, 1981. ♫ Written from a critical perspective with focus on historical interests.

RUTH

Your people shall be my people, and your God my God

Climbing downward from the heights of Bethlehem toward the Jordan Valley, one may see the vivid green promise of the plains of Moab stretching to the east. This was the path of a Judean family seeking relief from famine, likely caused by drought on the highlands of Judah. But it was also a retreat from the Promised Land that Israel was to conquer under Joshua and the Judges. The story of this family begins with tears and desperation before giving way to hope.

The Book of Ruth supplements Judges in several ways. It records a bit of delightful history of that period and supplies further evidence of God's faithfulness to His promises. The scope of the story is not national or tribal as is Judges. It is limited to individuals, and the plot is laid within the confines of family life. What happens to this little family in its domestic struggles concerns God as much as the big issues of national survival.

When the heroine of the story "happened to come" to a certain field (2:3), God was giving her a chance to reap the reward of faith and faithfulness. She had not in vain taken refuge under the wings of Israel's God (v 12). At the right juncture of small circumstances, God prepared a man to spread his wing of protection over her (3:9).

OVERVIEW

Author(s)
Unknown

Date
Written c 1000 BC

Places
Bethlehem in Judah; Moab

People
Ruth; Naomi; Elimelech; Mahlon; Chilion; Orpah; Boaz; unnamed relative; Obed; Jesse; David

Purpose
To show that the Lord demonstrates His faithfulness by providing for Ruth's family a redeemer, who secures their heritage among God's people

Law Themes
The frailty of life; God allows suffering; selfish disregard for family

Gospel Themes
The Lord's kindness; God welcomes the nations by grace; redemption; inheritance; the genealogy of Jesus, the Redeemer

Memory Verses
Ruth's faithfulness (1:16–17); Boaz's blessing (2:11–12); the women's blessing (4:14–15)

TIMELINE

1217–1178 BC	Deborah
1157 BC	Eli born
1099–1060 BC	Eli's priesthood and judgeship
1088 BC	Oppression by the Midianites and Philistines begins
1060 BC	Death of Eli

Bedouin women gather remnants of wheat in the Judean Hills. They have erected a booth for shelter from the sun.

The story of Ruth also portrays the exception to the general picture of anarchy and lawlessness during the time of the judges. Then, as always, a faithful remnant lived in Israel—wholesome, decent, magnanimous people. Home ties were close; marriage was sacred; purity and restraint of passions had not vanished. If family life was sound, albeit by exception, Israel could hope for national healing and health.

The Book of Ruth, which could be called "A Rose Growing out of the Muck of Iniquity," provides dramatic relief from the strain of general horror and savagery during the period of the judges.

Historical and Cultural Setting

One can argue on philological grounds for the plausibility or possibility of the story taking place in the era of the judges, as the opening verse states. Critics usually conclude that the private-life aspects of the story are fictional (though why this family should not retain a memory of its background remains unclear). Yet they may also concede that the story presents a genuine memory of temporary migration from Judah to Moab in time of famine. The tradition of David's partial Moabite ancestry will often also be conceded. Nonetheless, this poses various historical solutions and problems. For example, it would explain why David sent his parents to Moab for safekeeping while he was a fugitive from Saul (1Sm 22:3–4), but it makes even more puzzling David's unusually harsh treatment (perhaps half of them massacred) of the conquered Moabites later on as he is building his empire (2Sm 8; presumably some treachery must have been perpetrated, of which we are not informed).

The Book of Ruth does not provide specific help for knowing when the events took place during the time of the judges. The genealogy (4:18–22) records at least three generations from David to Boaz. But the early genealogy is obviously abbreviated, highlighting only the most important forebearers. For more on the genealogy, see "Date of Composition."

COMPOSITION

Authors

The Talmudic ascription to Samuel (as happens likewise with the Books of Judges and Samuel) can safely be dismissed as "unscientific," but no more plausible suggestion seems ever to have been made.

Date of Composition

According to Ru 1:1, these events happened "in the days when the judges ruled," but only two generations before the time of David; for Obed (Ruth's son) was "the father of Jesse, the father of David" (4:17). Very likely, this family story took place during the time of Eli, with which the books of Samuel open.

The genealogy from Perez to David (vv 18–22) no doubt is only partial. Salmon, the sixth link, who married Rahab after the fall of Jericho (cf Mt 1:5) perhaps some 250–300 years earlier, was probably a genealogical father of Boaz.

The date of the writing is difficult to pin down. The usual critical conclusion is fifth century, alleging that Ruth was written in opposition to the policies of Ezra and Nehemiah, against marriage to foreign wives. Besides that presumed historico-political occasion, other arguments are also adduced, but just as debatably. The book's presence in the writing portion of the Hebrew canon certainly does not imply lateness of composition; especially the five Megilloth were all brought together in this position out of liturgical motives, regardless of date.

Earlier critics appealed to alleged Aramaisms and other supposed linguistic indications of lateness. Since the discovery of "Aramaisms" in pre-Israelite Canaanite texts, however, most of that "evidence" has evaporated. Dialectical variation, perhaps reflecting provincial speech around Bethlehem, seems better to explain the speech idiosyncrasies of the book than any hypothesis of late composition. Whatever the explanation of these relatively few peculiarities, it must be stressed that they are exceptional. In general, the language and style of the Book of Ruth is pure, classical Hebrew, on a par with Samuel and palpably different from what we encounter in later books, e.g., Esther, Chronicles, or Nehemiah.

If one says "classical Hebrew," he implies a date perhaps as early as the united monarchy itself, and scarcely later than the middle of the divided monarchy (thus perhaps 900–700 BC). Since David is mentioned by name in the genealogy (assuming its origination with the rest of the book), the book can scarcely date earlier than his reign. Perhaps it is even to be dated sometime within his reign, as many conservatives hold, because no subsequent kings are mentioned, not even the renowned Solomon. That conclusion is not absolutely necessary, however, since "David" would suffice to establish the lineage of the entire dynasty, and messianic interests might even have made it desirable to stop with his name. Really, it is not possible to be any more precise.

Purpose/Recipients

The author intended to relate an episode of history before the kingdom period, and there is not much to suggest that his purposes extended far beyond that. The concluding genealogy must indicate that there was some interest to relate the genealogy of David. (The very fact that David's ancestress is described as a Moabitess is a major argument for the book's historicity, as is often pointed out since that fact would be so easily used against the family.) To attribute any profound further "purposes" to the author requires reading between the lines of his straightforward narrative.

It is plausible to assume that a subsidiary purpose may have been to counteract one-sidedly dark portraits of the quality of life in the period of the judges (as in Jgs 19–21) and then also to suggest examples of right living under the covenant, of piety and fidelity, of home life and family solidarity for all times. It was all the more significant to see those ideal qualities exemplified in a family that welcomed a foreigner, and indirectly, at least, the point is surely made that the covenant was not limited by national, political, or racial boundaries. These various purposes probably overlap and are all to be related to the book's theological stance.

Literary Features

Genre

The Book of Ruth is a family history with national interest, due to the genealogy of David in ch 4. Form critics inevitably suggest that the book is popular legend or a novella, a somewhat broader and perhaps slightly more positive term (as concerns historicity) than the English term *novel*, but mostly just suggesting some well-wrought, relatively brief artistic product.

Characters

A novelistic or legendary understanding of the Book of Ruth is often accompanied by an attempt to interpret the names in the book as symbolic. Like most names, especially in Hebrew, those in the Book of Ruth do undeniably have a meaning (though often debatable when it comes to specifics), but that is a far cry from establishing that they were contrived for the storyteller's purposes. Their historicity is at least strongly suggested by the fact that their types, if not the actual names, are all well attested in ancient documents.

Linguistically, the meaning of "Ruth" is the most difficult of all to establish. The translation of "(female) companion" is satisfying to proponents of a novelistic theory, but scientifically unlikely. Not much more firmly based are derivations from two other roots, yielding meanings such as "attractive" (from *ra'ah*, "to see") or "refreshing" (*rwh*). The symbolists like to associate "Orpah" with the Hebrew for "neck" and interpret it as "stiff-necked, stubborn, disloyal," or the like, allegedly symbolizing her willingness to leave Naomi and return home, but every indication is that that association is equally fanciful. Similarly, the association of "Boaz" with "strength" is only one of various possibilities. "Mahlon" and "Chilion" have been interpreted as "sickness" and "failing," respectively, but also without any good foundation; the latter name is attested at Ugarit, and both are good Late Bronze types, but we have no real clue to their meaning. The most common biblical *type* of name, of course, is "Elimelech," probably meaning, "The King [Yahweh] is my God." But the only name for which we have any warrant in the book itself for making anything of is "Naomi," meaning "delightful/pleasant," on which the bearer herself puns in 1:20, suggesting that she be called Mara ("bitter") instead.

A woman's face (Phoenician ivory carving).

Narrative Development or Plot

This lovely story portrays the blessings that God in His providence bestows on individuals who live out the covenant, reestablished under Joshua at Shechem, as they promised: "The LORD our God we will serve, and His voice we will obey" (Jsh 24:24). Commentators vie with one another in praising form and content of this masterful short story, known by the heroine's name. In reality, her mother-in-law, Naomi, plays the most significant role of the drama.

Because of a famine, Naomi's husband had taken her and their two sons from Bethlehem to "sojourn in the country of Moab" (Ru 1:1). After the death of her husband and two sons, Naomi planned to return to Judah, for the famine was over (v 6). Ruth, the Moabite widow of one of Naomi's sons, insisted on casting her lot with Naomi and Naomi's God. So the stage was set for the main plot of the story, leading to a happy ending: the marriage of Ruth to Boaz. Naomi directed Ruth's "chance" acquaintance with prosperous Boaz. In guileless simplicity, Ruth followed Naomi's instructions, and Naomi's trust in Boaz's integrity, kindness, and sense of duty to the extended family was not misplaced.

The Book of Ruth is not merely or primarily a love story but a history of God's people, albeit on a small scale. Naomi, Ruth, and Boaz knew and responded in faith to the promises and provisions of Israel's God. The son born to Boaz and Ruth, Obed, became the heir of her previous husband and his clan. To indicate Ruth's and Boaz's compliance with this stipulation, the child was given to Naomi and reckoned as her son (4:13–17).

At the same time, this family anecdote flows like a small rivulet into the main stream of larger covenant history. Ruth became the great-grandmother of David, from whom issued great David's greater Son, born at Bethlehem to fulfill all covenant promises (4:21–22; cf 1Ch 2:12–15; Mt 1:5–6).

Although the story is simple, the modern reader needs an acquaintance with four laws and customs of that day in order to understand the development of the plot.

1. Naomi and Ruth use their covenant right of the poor to glean in someone else's field at harvesttime (cf Lv 19:9; 23:22; Dt 24:19). This was necessary after they returned from Moab either because the ancestral field had not been sown or because its crop belonged to someone else. Note the words of Boaz (Ru 4:3): "Naomi . . . is selling the parcel of land which belonged to our brother Elimelech."

2. The main action of the book hinges on the duties of the kinsman. Covenant legislation provided for "redemption" of land sold by an impoverished relative (Lv 25:23–28). "A close relative[1] of his clan" (v 49) had this obligation.

3. Mosaic Law also decreed the so-called levirate marriage (Dt 25:5–10). The brother-in-law (Latin: *levir*) was required to marry the widow of a childless marriage. Custom seems to have extended this statute to apply to more distant relatives as well. Neither Boaz nor the relative closer than he (Ru 3:12) was the brother-in-law of Ruth, yet the latter agreed to act as the "deliverer" of the property. But when Boaz informed the other relative of the duty also to play the part of a *levir*, he backed off, leaving Boaz free to buy "all that was Elimelech's"—and thereby also to claim the right to marry Ruth (4:9–10).

---

1 The frequent Hebrew word in Ruth translated "relative" is related to the verb "to redeem" and the noun "redemption." A "redeeming relative" fulfilled his duty as a relative by delivering or saving the needy one from his or her predicament.

OUTLINE

Ruth: A Drama of Faithfulness

The history of Ruth clearly divides according to its chapters into four acts. Each act may conveniently be divided into two unequal scenes.

Act I   The Dilemma

> Scene A—Prologue: Tragedy (Famine in Israel; deaths of father and sons in Moab; 1:1–5)

> Scene B—Setting: Return (Naomi returns with Ruth but no heir; 1:6–22)

Act II   The Hope

> Scene A—Acceptance (Boaz welcomes Ruth to his field and to Israel; 2:1–17)

> Scene B—Nourishment (Widows are temporarily cared for; 2:18–23)

Act III   The Risk

> Scene A—Strategy (Naomi proposes daring plan for permanent solution; 3:1–6)

> Scene B—Challenge (Ruth challenges Boaz to redemption and marriage; 3:7–18)

Act IV   The Solution

> Scene A—Climax: Sacrifice (Boaz acts to solve dilemma; 4:1–12)

> Scene B—Epilogue: Heir (Fidelity is blessed eventually with descendant King David; 4:13–22)

4. To confirm the release of property rights, the closer kinsman drew off his shoe before witnesses at the gate of the city. This strange custom was based on part of the regulation of Dt 25:8–10 concerning the public repudiation of one who refused to perform the duty of the *levir*. In that case, the widow drew off the relative's shoe and spat in his face, perhaps to shame him (or another relative) into compliance.

Possible Sites Where Elimelech Settled

Journeys of Naomi and Ruth. An Israelite would not usually leave his inheritance, because it was really on loan from the Lord (Lv 25:23). Such a move would normally result in punishment or condemnation. The Book of Ruth, however, does not condemn Elimelech and his family, who probably exhausted all other resources before leaving for Moab.

Moab had become Israel's enemy (Nu 22–24). Yet, at this time, no specific ban on marrying Moabite women existed, as it did later in the Old Testament (Ezr 9:1–15; Ne 13:23–28).

At times, the Lord encouraged the patriarchs to seek refuge in a foreign land (Abraham and Jacob in Egypt; Isaac and David among the Philistines). As he did for these others, God delivered Naomi and Ruth, the foremother of David and Jesus.

Resources

The genealogy of ch 4 was drawn from tribal history.

Text and Translations

The Hebrew text is well-preserved, and the ancient translations derive from the traditional Hebrew text. Because the text is so easy to understand, the Book of Ruth is commonly read by students who have completed their introductory studies in Hebrew grammar.

A careful reader will note even in English translation—and it is much more obvious in the original Hebrew—that the Book of Ruth comes from a different "school" of history than the surrounding books, particularly Judges (or most of it). However, the last chapters of Judges (19–21) may possess certain linguistic features in common with Ruth, while their portraits of life in that period are almost opposite to each other.

DOCTRINAL CONTENT

Summary Commentary

Ch 1 Elimelech and his sons struggle during a famine and move to Moab to preserve their family. Ruth refuses to stay in Moab when Naomi determines to go back to Bethlehem, even though her sister-in-law stays in Moab. Naomi confesses the bitterness she feels on returning to Bethlehem without her husband and sons. Yet Ruth is with her still, and will live in Israel and adopt their God.

Ch 2 The Lord brings Ruth and Boaz together in mutual honor. We see a wonderful reversal in the fortunes of Ruth and Naomi.

Ch 3 Naomi acts in faith and hope as she sends Ruth to Boaz as a potential redeemer. These women do not simply take matters into their own hands. Their actions are based on the principles of God's Word regarding care for families in ancient Israel.

Ch 4 Boaz acts boldly on behalf of Naomi and Ruth to secure their future and family inheritance. The Lord blesses Boaz and Ruth with marriage and with a child; Naomi's friends celebrate His merciful redemption. The Book of Ruth ends with a summary of the genealogy of King David. The drama of God's mercy has come full circle. Those seemingly abandoned by God now see His mighty arm of blessing reaching out to them.

Specific Law Themes

The story of Ruth illustrates the frailty of life as the family withers during a merciless famine. The fact that God allows such suffering is a sobering aspect of an otherwise hope-filled history. The failure of the redeemer in ch 4 reminds us of family responsibilities and how many fail to live up to them.

Specific Gospel Themes

The Book of Ruth is ultimately a story of God's kindness; He graciously welcomes the nations among His chosen people. It likewise focuses on God's provision for redemption and inheritance by which families are strengthened and maintained. Finally, the book provides an important connection to Israel's greatest Old Testament king and to great David's greater Son, Jesus.

Specific Doctrines

One of the first matters to require attention is the real import of Ruth's oft-quoted speech in 1:16–17, expressing her resolve to accompany Naomi. One should take care neither to read into Ruth's words more than is actually said nor fail to hear them in total context. As usual in the Old Testament, the cultural and the religious, the political and the theological, are intertwined. Ruth expresses herself in terms of personal and familial loyalty. Ruth's "conversion" is nowhere described, yet the context gives ample clues that she speaks out of covenantal convictions, and these must be highlighted: the use of "Yahweh" in Ruth's oath (the only time in the book on Ruth's lips), the use of "loaded" theological terms in the context, such as God's "visiting" His people (1:6), or His "kindness" (*chesed*, 1:8). Similar vocabulary is artfully used throughout the book, but it is rarely apparent in English translation.

Second, there is the questionable matter of Ruth's clandestine visit to Boaz at the threshing floor (ch 3). At Naomi's instigation, it is plain that the purpose of the visit is to prod Boaz into exercising his role as "redeemer" (*go'el*), as Ruth explicitly calls him when he awakens (3:9). Both biblical parallels (Ezk 16:8; Dt 22:30; 27:20) and modern Arabic custom make plain that Ruth's request to Boaz to spread his "wings" (i.e., the corner of a garment) over her meant a request for marriage; that was the specific way Boaz should function as "redeemer" (cf below), somewhat in fulfillment of his own prayer in 2:12. In other phrases sexual double entendre seems obvious in the Hebrew: words such as *lie, know*, and especially in this context, *feet*—which can be a euphemism for the genitals in Hebrew idiom, but which, like the other words, can also be taken at face value, and obviously must be here. The language may imply that the couple began their relationship inappropriately, but such wordplay does not force the conclusion. It is surely no accident that Boaz praises Ruth (3:10) for the honor she shows, as he agrees to pursue the matter promptly. Behind all of this, however, and central to the book's plot and significance, is the idea of "redemption."

Levirate Redemption

Levirate laws were widely known in Israel's environment but also differed widely in detail, and we must reckon with the possibility of provincial variation in the Book of Ruth. Furthermore, even if one ascribes all the legal "codes" to Moses, it is plain that the various collections, taken individually, are each incomplete and often only illustrative. Hence, it may well be that the combination of levirate and redemption responsibilities evidenced in Ruth may have been more common than our few sources would indicate. Likewise, the assumption by a more distant relative of the levirate responsibility when a woman had no brothers-in-law, as Ruth did not, may or may not have been regular practice. And since "redemption" was concerned with persons as well as property, bringing it into connection with *marriage* of persons may not have been that unusual a step either. The differences in the shoe symbolisms of Dt 25:9 and Ru 4:7–8 probably refer to entirely different situations and are not to be compared at all.

Whatever the sociological particularities, Boaz plainly exercises his obligations as both levir and redeemer. The marriage blessing of Ru 4:11–12 is prominently represented in later Jewish and Christian nuptial ceremonies. Both it and the book's concluding genealogy (4:18–22) anchor in Boaz's ancestor, Perez (Judah's child by Tamar; Gn 38), by marriage into which line Ruth becomes an ancestress of David and an inner participant in the messianic promises to which it was heir. Its fulfillment is heralded by incorporation into the genealogy of Mt 1 at the head of the New Testament, ending with "Joseph the husband of Mary, of whom Jesus was born, who is called Christ" (v 16).

It is because the genealogy sets the narrative in its broader redemptive context that the book's featuring "redemption" is so significant (the verb *ga'al* is used 20 times in the four chapters). The Book of Ruth is the Bible's major example of "redemption" in the social context. That background needs to be stressed for full understanding of the theological expression. The first point of extension of the metaphor is the perception of God as Israel's relative via the covenant, and thence as helper of the helpless, the defender of the defenseless. (Cf also Job's "Redeemer" in Job 19:25.) The "redeemer's" concern is not only for persons in an interior, psychological sense, but also for their property, land, or inheritance. The Old Testament's theological application centers on the exodus (Ex 15:13), but it is developed especially in Is 40–55 to describe the "exodus" from Babylon. Because of Boaz's "redemption" of Ruth, and their union, the ultimate exodus becomes possible in the Redeemer, Christ. More detailed word study would also have to point out that in New Testament usage *redeem* has been enriched by merger with the Old Testament companion concept of "ransom."

The widow's plea ostracon asks a king for rights to her husband's property.

It is also fruitful to read Ruth as "messianic history," that is, noting from the book that the levirate and *go'el* institutions, concerned as they were with preserving family name, seed, and inheritance, found their ultimate fulfillment in Christ and His kingdom.

Application

The Book of Ruth was read in the synagogue for the Festival of Weeks (the time of barley harvest), or Pentecost, which has its place above all in the New Testament festival of Pentecost. Filled with the Holy Spirit, the apostle

Peter proclaimed salvation to Israel and to "all who are far off, everyone whom the Lord our God calls to Himself" (Ac 2:39). As a Moabitess, Ruth's good fortune was a foreshadowing of that redemption for all. Boaz redeemed only a parcel of ground, but the "Redeeming Relative" of the fulfillment has restored to humanity an inheritance in heaven by the redemption that He paid with His blood.

Ch 1 Like Elimelech, you may struggle against unexpected changes in the economy or in your family. God gives you freedom in making family and business decisions, but He also gives you the blessings and guidance of His Holy Word. Like Ruth, boldly confess faith in the Lord and commitment to your family. Intermittent times of suffering are used by God to humble us. In due time, God raises us up to see His mercy and care more clearly.

Ch 2 The Lord brings Ruth and Boaz together in mutual honor. We see a wonderful reversal in the fortunes of Ruth and Naomi. In times of darkness and suffering today, we may doubt God's Father-heart toward us. Yet God promises that He works all things for our good (Rm 8:28–39).

Ch 3 Naomi and Ruth do not simply take matters into their own hands. Their actions are based on the promises about redemption in God's Word, which sets a marvelous example for us. We can always approach our Redeemer, Jesus.

Ch 4 God calls us to act with wisdom on behalf of the helpless, to perpetuate their life and share with them the inheritance of eternal life in His name. As the Lord blesses you, let others know of His kindness so that they may celebrate with you. He restores your life and guarantees your future through the blessings of His beloved Son.

CANONICITY

The position of the Book of Ruth in the Hebrew canon as the second of the Writings (Megilloth) is obviously determined by the chronological sequence of the liturgical festivals for which these works were used (beginning with Canticles for Passover). The connection with the Feast of Weeks (*Shabu'oth*; Pentecost) is apparently based on the notice of Ru 1:22 that Naomi and Ruth returned to Bethlehem "at the beginning of barley harvest." The Septuagint's relocation of the book, influenced by more Western and probably also more secular notions of history, was determined by the opening words (1:1) dating the narrative "in the days when the judges ruled." Jews and Christians received the book without question.

LUTHERAN THEOLOGIANS ON RUTH

Luther

"Ruth, who followed her mother-in-law Naomi, says (Ruth 1:16): 'Your people shall be my people, and your God my God.' Although she did not belong to the holy people—for she was a Moabitess—she was nevertheless saved because she clung in faith to the God of Israel." (AE 3:133)

"God has always been accustomed to collect a church for Himself even from among the heathen. Thus Ruth was a Moabitess, and Rahab was a Canaanite woman. They are numbered in the genealogy of Christ (Matt. 1:5). Nor were these the only women who attached themselves to the godly, but many other Canaanites did so along with them. Not that Ruth or Rahab partook of the forgiveness of sins because they were on the wrong path. No, they were converted; they received the Word from the Israelites. This means, of course, that a heathen or unbeliever became a believer. For after believing the Word which he heard, he was a member of the church and no longer a heathen." (AE 8:135–36)

"This passage is an exposition of the law in Deuteronomy 25 [:5], namely, that if the brother of the deceased man is unwilling, then the next to him in blood kinship should marry her. Besides, Ruth didn't demand that Boaz marry her." (AE 54:301)

Gerhard

"*Ruth.* The author of this book is unknown. It consists of four chapters in which it describes the history of the Moabite woman Ruth, how she was placed into God's people through her marriage to Boaz, David's forefather, and in this way was in the genealogy of the Savior. For this reason this history has been especially marked and holds a special place. The Jesuit Sandaeus writes that the Protestants 'erased the Book of Ruth from the sacred canon' (in *Thema seculare de deserenda Synagog. Protestant.*, thesis 27). Either he is greatly deceived or lies boldly, for none of us denies that the Book of Ruth is canonical. The opinions of interpreters vary with regard to the time at which the history described in this book occurred. The Chaldean paraphraser says, 'Ruth was the daughter of King Eglon of Moab,' who is mentioned in Judg. 3:12. However, no authority of Scripture proves this nor is it likely that a king's daughter wanted to marry a foreigner's son, abandon her fatherland and ancestral area, and go off to another land to look for food. Rabbi D. Kimchi, on Ruth 1, and other rabbinic scholars claim that 'Boaz, who married Ruth, is the judge whom Judg. 12:8 calls 'ibtsan (Ibzan),' who immediately followed Jephthah. From a comparison of Matt. 1:5 and the end of this book, Tremellius tries to show that this history occurred at the time of Deborah. Augustine, on the other hand, refers the time of this account to the beginning of the kings (*De doctrin. Christ.*, bk. 2, c. 8). Josephus (*Antiq.*, bk. 5) and Cardinal Hugh [of St. Cher] apply it to the time of the priest Eli, which almost coincides with Augustine. The account of Ruth, however, seems older, for it is written as having occurred in the days of one of those judges who is described in the Book of Judges. In a doubtful matter it is better to suspend judgment than to define something rashly. The account of this book can be divided into the antecedents, act, and consequences of the marriage contracted between Boaz and the widow Ruth. It contains eighty-five verses." (ThC E1 § 127)

QUESTIONS PEOPLE ASK ABOUT RUTH

One of the main features of the story seems to create a conflict. Boaz's marriage to a Moabite woman seems not to conform to the covenant specification in Dt 7:3, which prohibited marriage with non-Israelite women. On the other hand, intermarriage with Moabites was not expressly forbidden in this passage. Although Dt 23:3 states that "no Ammonite or Moabite may enter the assembly of the LORD. Even to the tenth generation," this prohibition may refer not to intermarriage but to the exclusion of male Moabites from worship rites.

God's laws were designed to keep Israel from losing identity as the chosen people of God. There is room in His goodness to acknowledge Ruth's surrender of homeland, nationality, and paganism in her desire to serve the true God of Israel.

Later, after the return of the exiles from Babylonia and at the time of Ezra and Nehemiah, intermarriage of Israelites with "the people of the land" (including Moabites) was a serious problem (Ezr 9:1–4; cf 10:2–3). Some scholars have concluded that Ruth was written as a historical novel after the return from Babylonia in order to counteract Ezra's prohibitions against mixed marriages. But if the book were a novel, it would have carried no weight at Ezra's time because it would improperly attribute "impure blood" to Israel's great King David! In fact, the story attributes "impure blood" to Israel's *greatest* king (Mt 1:5). Jesus is the Savior of all humanity, old covenant and noncovenant people equally.

Le geſſe.

FURTHER STUDY ━━━━━━━━━━━━━━━━━━

Lay/Bible Class Resources

Cundall, Arthur E., and Leon Morris. *Judges and Ruth.* TOTC. Downers Grove, IL: InterVarsity Press, 1968. ♪ Cundall uses a somewhat critical approach in his comments on Judges. Morris reflects archaeological information in his exposition of Ruth.

Dunker, Gary. *Ruth: Your God Will Be My God.* GWFT. St. Louis: Concordia, 2008. ♪ Lutheran author and devotional writer. Eleven-session Bible study, including leader's notes and discussion questions.

Lawrenz, John C. *Judges/Ruth.* PBC. St. Louis: Concordia, 2005. ♪ Lutheran author. Excellent for Bible classes. Based on the NIV translation.

Life by His Word. St. Louis: Concordia, 2009. ♪ More than 1,500 reproducible one-page Bible studies covering each chapter of the canonical Scriptures. Page references to *The Lutheran Study Bible.* CD-Rom and downloadable.

McGuire, Brent, Timothy Rake, and Gary Dunker. *Ruth/Esther.* Leaders Guide and Enrichment Magazine/Study Guide. LL. St. Louis: Concordia, 2008. ♪ An in-depth, nine-session Bible Study covering the Books of Ruth and Esther with individual, small group, and lecture portions.

Church Worker Resources

Hubbard, Robert L., Jr. *The Book of Ruth.* NICOT. Grand Rapids: Eerdmans, 1988. ♪ A literary commentary by an evangelical scholar. Less technical and more theological.

Academic Resources

Bush, Frederic. *Ruth/Esther.* WBC. Dallas: Word, 1996. ♪ A thorough commentary focused especially on the literary qualities of the book and theological implications. Prepared by an evangelical scholar with critical assumptions.

Campbell, Edward F., Jr. *Ruth.* Vol. 7 of AB. New York: Doubleday, 1975. ♪ Strong on philology; generally helpful.

Cassel, Paulus. *Ruth.* LCHS. New York: Charles Scribner's Sons, 1889. ♪ A helpful, older example of German biblical scholarship, based on the Hebrew text, which provides references to significant commentaries from the Reformation era forward.

K&D. *Biblical Commentaries on the Old Testament: Joshua, Judges and Ruth.* Grand Rapids: Eerdmans, 1971 reprint. ♪ This century-and-a-half old work from Lutheran scholars should not be overlooked. Despite its age, it remains a most useful commentary on the Hebrew text.

Nielsen, Kirsten. *Ruth: A Commentary.* Louisville, KY: Westminster John Knox Press, 1997. ♪ A helpful application of recent literary critical methods.

Wilch, John R. *Ruth.* CC. St. Louis: Concordia, 2006. ♪ Lutheran author treating every term and phrase of the Hebrew text to draw out the Book's theology. The best available commentary.

Tree of Jesse from the *Psaultier d'Ingeburg de Danemark.*

1 AND 2 SAMUEL

I will raise up a faithful priest before My anointed one

High ridges and domed hills line the routes through Ephraim, at the heart of Israel. Along these routes ran Ephraim's troops. They followed their tribesman, Joshua, as well as judges such as Ehud, Deborah, Gideon, and Tola. But they fled from Jephthah, when arrogance led to civil war (Jgs 3, 4, 7, 10, 12). Ephraim was a leading tribe of Israel; their territory was a crossroad—the home of the tabernacle at Shiloh, but also a home to unconquered Canaanites and a point of entry for foreign armies. As the first Book of Samuel begins, the latest invaders on the coastal plain, the Philistines, sharpen their iron weapons.

God had chosen Israel "to be a people for His treasured possession, out of all the peoples who are on the face of the earth," to be "a people holy to the Lord your God" and "a kingdom of priests" (Dt 14:2; 26:19; Ex 19:6). Its holiness, which made it different from the other nations, was to be above all its *spiritual* relationship with God through faith.

But also its political administration was to be different. Kings governed the nations around Israel; Israel alone had been the exception. In Egypt and in the Tigris and Euphrates Valley, absolute monarchies held sway, some as incarnate sons of the gods. Even

In David son of Jesse's poetry, a horn referred to one's power and triumph (Ps 18:2). This horn-shaped ivory vase encircled with gold bans (fourteenth century BC) was found at Megiddo.

OVERVIEW

Author(s)
Unknown

Date
Written c 970 BC

Places
Regions of Benjamin/Ephraim, Philistia, and Judah (see maps, pp 212, 290, 292)

People
The prophet Samuel; King Saul and Jonathan; David, the son of Jesse; Hannah; the priests: Eli, Hophni, and Phinehas; Goliath and the Philistines

Purpose
To reveal the Lord's faithfulness toward Israel in establishing His rule through Samuel, Saul, and David, despite the people's unfaithfulness

Law Themes
Barrenness; covetousness; neglect of fatherly duties; unfaithfulness; rejection of God's rule; failure to keep God's Word; rash vows; jealousy; divination

Gospel Themes
The Lord provides leaders; the Lord promises an everlasting kingdom and priesthood; victory in the Lord's name; godly friendship; blessings through the tabernacle; David's mercy

Memory Verses
Hannah's prayer (2:1–10); a new priesthood (2:30–31, 35); the Lord calls Samuel (3:10–11); obedience better than sacrifice (15:22–23); the battle is the Lord's (17:45–47)

• •

TIMELINE

1157 BC	Eli born
1099–1060 BC	Eli's priesthood and judgeship
1088 BC	Oppression by the Midianites and Philistines begins
1048–1009 BC	Reign of Saul
1009–970 BC	Reign of David

the small city-states in Canaan were headed by autocratic kings. Significantly, it was not so in Israel. Their king was "the Lord of hosts."[1]

Historical and Cultural Setting

Israel's form of government is called a *theocracy*. In the covenant, God had provided for Israel's government. His statutes were to promote and establish internal order. The Lord of hosts would direct the people in battle through leaders especially appointed for the needs of the moment. And God had commissioned Israel as a tribal confederacy to complete the conquest of Canaan after the death of Joshua.

Yet Israel became a monarchy after centuries of existence without a king because of its lack of faith in its true King, the Lord of hosts. After Joshua, the individual tribes failed to take God at His word; they did not trust His promise of help in taking full possession of the land. God tried for a long time—the whole period of the judges—to call Israel back to live by faith in His promises. Instead, Israel repeatedly sank close to being just another secular people like those around them. Israel sold its birthright for the pottage of Canaan's materialism and sensual worship. Despite the judges' frequent deliverance of Israel from punishment at the hands of its enemies, a thorough change of heart did not result. Israel always reverted to its common pattern, and always the Lord "gave them over to plunderers" (Jgs 2:14). Chaos would reign again, and the Philistines threatened to engulf the nation.

Israel tried to escape this situation of its own making not by the repentance and faith of a people of God but by being still more like the Canaanites: "Appoint for us a king to judge us *like all the nations*" (1Sm 8:5, emphasis added). "The thing displeased Samuel" (v 6). He recognized their request for what it was: a rejection of God's help in favor of human security, the desire to live by sight rather than by faith.

God answered their request with an emphatic no. God would not let His people become "Canaanized" and secularized. He would not give them a king as a substitute for Himself and so let them reject Him (10:17–19). At the same time He instructed Samuel "to obey their voice" (8:9). Long-suffering in the face of Israel's unwillingness to rise to the challenge of its destiny, He would come to the aid of its weak faith by giving it a visible and tangible representative of His rule, of His kingship, in the person of a human king.

Scripture gives abundant evidence that God did not relinquish His rule to an earthly king and let Israel be "like all the nations." First, Israel would

---

1   The expression "the Lord *zebaoth*," ("Lᴏʀᴅ of hosts" or "armies") occurs for the first time in Scripture on the lips of Samuel's mother, Hannah (1Sm 1:11).

not crown men on the basis of their proven abilities. God Himself chose Saul and David, obscure and untried men, and directed Samuel to find them and to anoint them for office. Second, God would permit no glorification or cult of the king. The king's person had no status except as the mediating executive of the covenant. He would rule in God's name, by God's Spirit, and for God's purposes. Third, one law applied to both king and subjects: covenant fidelity. In battle, for example, "the LORD saves not with sword and spear" (17:47), and neither would the king. Victory would be assured only "if both you [the people] and the king . . . will follow the LORD your God; . . . but if you will not obey the voice of the LORD, but rebel against the commandment of the LORD, then the hand of the LORD will be against you and your king" (12:14–15).

The monarchy, different from a tribal confederacy of course, would result in outward changes of administration. Samuel called attention to these (8:10–18): concentration of power in the hands of a king, conscription of armed forces from all the tribes, requisition of national resources, and taxation for the support of the court and its administrative offices. And there was no guarantee that succeeding kings would not abuse their power and make oppressive and arbitrary demands on their subjects (as later history proved they did).

Samuel tried to forestall such autocratic evils. Because the king was bound to rule within the framework of the established covenant, Samuel specified "the rights and duties of the kingship, and he wrote them in a book[2] and laid it up before the LORD" (10:25).

The way to Israel's golden age was a fierce and bloody struggle. Humanly speaking, David's empire could become a reality only because the great powers of the Fertile Crescent were not then (about 1000 BC) in a position to extend their domination into Canaan. Egypt had lost control of the area completely; Babylonia's first empire (Hammurabi's) had crumbled; Hittite power had been swept away by peoples from the islands and coasts of the Aegean Sea; Assyria had crushed the Hurrians (founders of the kingdom of Mitanni) but needed a few more centuries to consolidate its gains before becoming the mistress of the ancient world. David, of course, did not create this favorable international situation, but he exploited the providential timing of world events to the full.

Depiction of a Semitic king. Idrimi of Alalakh rebelled against his Mitanni overlords and fled to Canaan. He later petitioned the Mitanni and was restored to his throne (sixteenth century BC).

---

2   This document likely incorporated and elaborated the terms set down in Dt 17:14–20.

COMPOSITION

Author(s)

The following paragraphs speak less about the author of Samuel and more about the various ancient traditions for naming the book, how or whether to divide it, and how to relate it to what we know as the Books of Kings.

Jewish tradition attributed the first part of the book to Samuel and the rest to Gad and Nathan. There is apparent evidence of later composition, possibly pointing again to the period after the fall of Samaria, though quite certainly to the early divided monarchy for at least the major sources. The author had recourse to various records. In noncovenant nations such annals were written not by free men but by groveling sycophants under the direct control of the king. But Israel's prophets, who by divine authority directed even kings to act in faithful adherence to the covenant, recorded what God did through the nation and through individuals to implement His covenant promises. Thus the author of Samuel likely had before him the book "of Samuel the seer, . . . the Chronicles of Nathan the prophet, . . . [and] the Chronicles of Gad the seer" (1Ch 29:29) and used these sources to achieve his above-stated purpose—a history not of David but of the kingdom of God.

Book Divisions

In the Hebrew canon, at least as far back as we can trace it, the books of Samuel and Kings are distinguished from each other by the names we know, but neither one is internally subdivided into "First" and "Second." (By holding all of Samuel as one book and all of Kings as one book, the Jews could count *four* Former Prophets, balancing with the four Major Prophets.)

The internal subdivisions for each book apparently started with the Septuagint. However, the Septuagint does not distinguish "Samuel" and "Kings" from each other by title. Rather, it presents both together as one unified history of the united and divided kingdoms, with the title, "Books of the Kingdoms" (*basileiōn*), but still with essentially our four divisions. The same fourfold arrangement entered the Vulgate, where Jerome, however, substituted "Kings" for "Kingdoms" (perhaps partly reflecting his Hebrew influences). Hence, at least until very recently, Roman Catholic literature has referred to "I–IV Kings."

About the time of the Reformation, the Septuagint's internal subdivisions were introduced into editions of the Hebrew text, each pair of books, however, retaining its original title in the Hebrew Masoretic tradition. In this way, a compromise of Greek and Hebrew titles entered into Protestant Bibles.

In many ways the consistent Greek use of "Kingdoms" instead of an initial "Samuel" is more appropriate to the contents, since Samuel plays a diminishing role after 1Sm 15.

Date of Composition

Major portions of the book were likely written during the reigns of Saul and David as tradition attests. See "Authors."

Purpose/Recipients

The writer is intent on tracing history and evaluating individuals and events according to their contribution to or hindrance of God's ultimate goal for history. A strict chronological arrangement of events is of only secondary consideration. This disregard of chronology surfaces particularly in the stories of David. His victories over the surrounding nations and those of his administrative personnel, for example, are given brief summaries in 2Sm 8. Then one of those victories (over the Ammonites and Syrians, 8:3–12) is given in more detail in ch 10 and in 12:26–31. The closing chapters (2Sm 21–24) also supplement the previous biographical accounts of David. For example, ch 21 evidently occurred before 2Sm 16:8 (in which David is cursed for the action in 21:1–14).

Literary Features

Genre

The account of the rise of Israel from near extinction to empire glory is unique in ancient national histories. Israel's great change in status from vassalage to empire took place within the span of about a century—Eli: 40 years (1Sm 4:18); Samuel: no length of time indicated; Saul: 40 years (Ac 13:21); David: 40 years (2Sm 5:4). God did not design Scripture to be a national history in the usual sense. The center of interest is not Israel as a state or nation but as God's chosen people and instrument. The sacred record does not report events according to their importance for or glory of the state or king. In fact, decisive battles grudgingly are given a few lines of space while whole pages are devoted to moral and religious issues in the lives of individuals. The selection and elaboration of materials are governed by their value to God's cause-and-effect covenant history. Defeat came to those who frustrated God's purposes, but success crowned the efforts of those who advanced His kingdom. "David became greater and greater, for the LORD, the God of hosts, was with him" (2Sm 5:10).

Because the Books of Samuel devote much space to representative individuals under the covenant, the stories throb with human interest and emotion. The loftiest motives of friendship, loyalty, and piety vie against treachery, betrayal, and desecration of everything sacred. Across this stage of history march villains who are and remain wicked, heroes who fall and cannot rise again, and fallen saints who do not repent.

The end of 1 Samuel has characteristics of a travel narrative, including the following locations where David went and persons he visited:

1. David to be with Samuel at Ramah and Naioth (19:18–24);
2. a secret meeting with Jonathan (ch 20);
3. Ahimelech, the priest, at Nob (21:1–9);
4. Achish, the Philistine king, at Gath (21:10–15);
5. the cave of Adullam (22:1–5);
6. the forest of Hereth (22:5);
7. Keilah (23:1–13);
8. the cities of Ziph and Engedi in the wilderness of Judah (23:14–24, 29);
9. the city of Carmel, where David married Abigail (ch 25); and
10. the cities of Gath and Ziklag in Philistia (ch 27; 29:6; 30:26; 2Sm 1:1).

Characters

Eli

Eli, the second-to-last of the judges, was an old man when he entered the record. There is no indication of what he had accomplished during the 40 years of his judgeship. But the fact that he could function as the high priest at the central sanctuary at Shiloh presupposes some stability within Israel. Though God-fearing and pious, he lacked the aggressiveness and firmness required of an administrator. His judgeship (and life) ended at the news of the death of his undisciplined sons, of the defeat of Israel in battle, and of the loss of the ark to the Philistines. Never had such a disgrace been heaped on Israel! His newborn grandson's name, Ichabod (literally, "where is glory"), characterized the degrading situation: "The glory has departed from Israel" (1Sm 4:19–22).

Samuel

Samuel has always been a difficult figure to classify, but that probably answers to his position on the threshold of one of the major transitions in Israel's political and theological history, namely from theocracy to monarchy. In many ways he is the last and greatest of the "judges," and even his venal sons, Joel and Abijah (1Sm 8:2), are so described.

Presumably Samuel was also a priest, because he was Eli's successor, and his conflict with Saul (1Sm 13:13) implies that he alone had the right to sacrifice. Conversely, Saul's behavior may foreshadow much later interference in worship affairs by the monarchy.

In many respects, Samuel must also be understood as the first of the great prophets (cf Ac 13:20), and from here on we meet many of them also in the historical books. First Samuel 9:9 indicates that he was a "seer," yet his "prophecy" towers head and shoulders above other prophets and leaders in that day. As the great prophets of later times spearheaded a "back to Moses" reformation after the devastations of Baalism, so Samuel can be understood as leading Israel's first great religious revival after her "first love" had failed in the period of the judges (cf esp 1Sm 7). His famous "Behold, to obey is better than sacrifice" oracle against Saul (15:22–23) is in many respects the essence of the prophetic message.

Thus, Samuel is a veritable "second Moses," representing virtually all offices in Israel as no one had since Moses. It is no accident that Jer 15:1 views Moses and Samuel together as great mediators and intercessors for Israel. In this, as in other respects, Samuel anticipates both Elijah and Christ. Typologically, not as much is usually made of Samuel as many other figures, but there appears to be no good reason for that neglect.

In many respects, Moses had functioned as a "king," as Samuel likewise functioned as a "judge." (Note the reaction of the Bethlehemites at his coming in 1Sm 16:4.) Samuel strenuously resists the people's request for a king, but then accedes to it (1Sm 8–9). He anoints Saul but is also Saul's undoing. Samuel's attitude is typical of Dt 17:14–15—kingship is recognized as one of God's great gifts to His people, alongside of a realistic awareness of the extent to which it could also be a magnet for syncretism and a focus of apostasy.

Much is often made of the fact (and apparently rightly so) that Samuel does not anoint Saul (or David) as "king" (*melek* in the proper sense), but only as *nagid*, usually translated "prince" (1Sm 9:16; 10:1, 13:14, though *melek* is used in other passages in the context, apparently in a more popular sense). Apparently, Samuel hoped to satisfy the people's demand for centralized authority without opening the floodgates to the pagan, Canaanite ideology that almost necessarily came with *melek*. Samuel did not really succeed, and Saul's failure, too, can probably be laid in part to his inability to synthesize the ways of the Lord with lordly rule. First with David (and Nathan) is kingship grafted successfully into native Israelite stock, and *nagid* and *melek* come to be virtual synonyms, as we often meet them in later literature.

Finally, it should be stressed, as Samuel clearly illustrates, that "prophecy," humanly speaking, arises in Israel largely as a counterpoise to kingship. One of prophecy's major and standing tasks is to call the throne to account, especially to remind it that the absolutist, mythological, and "divine right" models of paganism are inappropriate for the covenant society of Israel. And when kings fade after the exile, prophets soon disappear from the scene too.

Samuel died before David became king over Israel (1Sm 25:1), but his anointing of this shepherd of Bethlehem was an act of faith that was not put to shame.

Samuel's stature in God's drama of salvation is reflected in the Magnificat of Mary (Lk 1:46–55). At the prospect of the birth of the Savior, Mary is constrained to praise the mercy of God in words similar to those in which Hannah, Samuel's mother, had rejoiced in God's deliverance of His people (1Sm 2:1–10).

Saul

Eli and Samuel, like Moses, were descendants of Levi. The first king of Israel was a Benjaminite. Tall, handsome, popular, devout, courageous, resolute, and open to the Spirit of God, Saul seems to have had all the necessary qualifications of royalty.

He was appointed to the kingship by three separate and distinct ceremonies at three different places but with one common factor: Samuel as "master of ceremonies."

At the first ceremony, in "the land of Zuph" and at "the outskirts of the city" of Ramah, Samuel anointed Saul in private to be "prince" over His people (1Sm 9:27–10:1). Perhaps in order not to overwhelm the peasant Saul, Samuel refrained from calling him the future king but used a more general term. Yet Saul was assured of divine sanction and aid for a totally unexpected position of leadership in Israel. And Saul was given three signs to help him believe that the Lord had chosen him for this undreamed-of role and distinction (10:1–7).

The second ceremony, at Mizpah, sought to persuade the people that God was granting their request for a king and that God had chosen Saul, the son of Kish. This was done through the casting of lots, administered by Samuel (vv 17–27). Most of the people were convinced of Saul's right to the kingship by this method, though some still repudiated him.

Saul's general acceptance as king took place at still a third convocation, this time at Gilgal. The people called it a "renewing" of the kingdom and sanctified it with peace offerings (11:14–15).[3]

Saul had excellent personal assets and for a time rendered valuable service to his people. Nevertheless, he died a failure, rejected by God. His mistakes may appear trivial and pardonable on the surface, but neither God nor Samuel, His spokesman, acted unjustly in declaring this first king a failure.

First, Saul did not wait for Samuel to sacrifice before a battle but took on himself the right to officiate (13:5–15). Second, he chose to disobey God's command to destroy everything and everybody after a victory over the Amalekites; he spared the king and the best of the booty (ch 15).

These sins appear as slight offenses in comparison to the heinous crimes of later kings, including David's murder and adultery. But no man of clay dare presume to dictate to God how He is to administer either His long-suffering mercy or His punitive justice in the life of an individual or of a whole nation. Any attempt to do so fashions God in the image of one's own idolatrous thinking. This precise sin of dethroning God was the base of Saul's sin. Who was king in Israel, Saul or the Lord of hosts? In his royal person Saul challenged the validity and binding character of God's established order for His people. Israel was a "church"; Saul wanted to make it a "state." Israel was governed by a "constitution"; Saul wanted to be dictator (cf 14:24–30). God did not tolerate such an arrogant challenge to His rulership at this critical juncture, the beginning of the monarchy. Truly, God judges the heart.

From the gate of Beth-shan (Tel Beit She'an), one can see distant Mount Gilboa where King Saul and his sons were slain by the Philistines who then displayed their bodies on the walls of Beth-shan.

---

3   Because these three acts of "coronation" are interspersed with accounts of other events, the author may have arranged his material in a nonchronological sequence.

After the Lord had "rejected him from reigning over Israel . . . the Spirit of the LORD departed from Saul, and a harmful spirit from the LORD tormented him" (16:1, 14).

Saul's monarchy did not seriously alter Israel's national structure as a confederacy of tribes. Saul seemingly derived financial support by some taxation (17:25) and took steps toward forming a standing army (14:52). But there is no evidence that he established a bureaucratic chain of command. He built no castle but kept his "royal residence" in his native Gibea. Only a few intimates (including his cousin Abner) constituted his modest court. With these minor adaptions to a monarchy Saul appears to have overcome some initial opposition to his person and to have kept the loyalty of the entire nation (10:27).

Militarily, Saul's reign accomplished little. At his death (hastened by his own hand, 31:4) Israel was again at the mercy of the Philistines, who dominated all of Canaan west of the Jordan River. Ishbosheth, Saul's son, sought safety east of the Jordan and there set up a pretense of rulership.

David

The first Book of Samuel had recorded David's anointing by Samuel (1 Sm 16:1–13), his entry into Saul's service (16:14–18:30), and his flight from Saul (chs 19–31). The second book, "after the death of Saul," tells of David's rise to power. Because of his significance for Israel's history, his life's account receives more space in the Old Testament than that of any other character.

David was the youngest of eight sons of Jesse. As so often happens, God chose the person who was least likely to succeed to be the instrument of His might and power. Perhaps 10 years or so elapsed after Samuel had anointed David before he became king of all Israel at the age of 30 (2Sm 5:4). These intervening years, filled with high drama and severe testings of faith, included some realistic training for David.

The author selects a number of incidents from this period to set forth (1) God's providential guidance of His protégé and (2) David's willingness to let God choose the road to the throne. (Again, these accounts may not be in chronological order, nor can the exact circumstances surrounding each situation be established.) The bulk of 1Sm 19–31 reports Saul's persecution of David and the latter's resultant flights for safety.

After Saul's death, the tribe of Judah acclaimed David as king (2Sm 2:1–4). When Saul's son Ishbosheth was assassinated by two fellow Benjaminites, and Saul's cousin and army commander Abner (1Sm 14:50) was murdered, "all the tribes of Israel came to David at Hebron . . . [where] they anointed

David king over Israel" (2Sm 5:1, 3). From this time on, his path to power within and without rose steadily.

Governmental functions developed more fully under David than under Saul's initial monarchy, and control was centralized in the person of the king. The list of David's officials for the various functions of state (civil and military) in 2Sm 8:15–18 and 20:23–26 indicates a well-developed government operation. For example, David had appointed Joab as commander-in-chief of the army. The chain of command seems to have involved two upper echelons known as the "Three" and the "Thirty." Three distinct army groups apparently formed the nucleus of David's armed forces: a detachment of 600 veterans of David's battles prior to Saul's death, a troop named after the city of Gath and under the command of Ittai, and a bodyguard referred to as "Cherethites [Cretans] and Philistines." Judicial powers were vested in the king (15:2) and were delegated by him to others. Finances necessary for the maintenance of this host of "servants of the king" and for his standing army were raised by taxation. There was even an official "in charge of the forced labor" (20:24—but NKJV: "in charge of revenue").

David appears to have had no difficulty in administering his far-flung empire, but he failed to master himself and to maintain order in his own family. His sin against the sanctity of life and the family (i.e., adultery with Bathsheba and the planned death of her husband, Uriah—ch 11) touched off a chain reaction of incest, rape, murder, intrigue, and revolution in his own household. His son Absalom's coup and death completely unnerved the king. In his grief (19:4–8) he forgot his duties to the nation, and he made several decisions that showed he had lost the ability to feel instinctively what action was proper and fitting in a given situation. (Cf the appointment of Amasa to replace Joab and David's treatment of Mephibosheth, Saul's son—19:11–30.)

Regardless of the circumstances, royal sin is no less censurable and self-destructive than the wickedness of ordinary people under God's Law. And the prophet Nathan had the courage to speak the words of indictment to David: "You are the man!"

Though both Saul and David sinned against God and His covenant, the difference between Saul's deep-seated presumption and David's moral lapses must be kept in mind. David repented "out of the depths" (Ps 130), and

Aramaic inscription found in Dan (ninth century BC) mentions the battles of Ben Hadad, King of Aram, against the House of David.

pardon was pronounced with divine finality. Heinous and black though his crimes had been, David's submission to God's sanctions left him a usable though chastened instrument of God's rule over His people. In contrast to Saul, David showed himself responsive to God's ordinances and did not willfully set aside the Law to further the power of the crown.

The events and the words of David preserved for us in chs 21–24 come from various periods of David's reign (see outline; see also pp 300–301).

Narrative Development or Plot

The Book of Judges documented Israel's repeated failures to function as God's instrument to bring about His covenanted promise of salvation to all people. The bright exception of Ruth only confirmed the general rule of this dark period. And the first part of 1 Samuel seems to be merely another chapter in the record of this dreary state of affairs.

An Israelite cistern at Shiloh, where Eli and his sons led worship at the tabernacle. Precious water was reserved at every opportunity.

In the opening chapters of Samuel, Israel's dissolution had worsened. The Philistines continued as God's scourge on the unfaithful people. Samson's earlier skirmishes had held the Philistines in check only temporarily, and after his ignominious death, they invaded Israel in force. In fact, Israel's humiliation at their hands reached hitherto unplumbed depths. The Philistines destroyed the center of Israel's worship at Shiloh and bore away as a trophy of war Israel's holiest possession: the ark of the covenant (1Sm 4:5). The well-ordered and precisely defined worship of the Lord (established at Mount Sinai) could no longer be maintained.

God's extreme punishment was provoked by a progressive breakdown of religious and moral rectitude that reached even into the highest places: the family of the high priest, Eli. His sons, one of whom was destined to hold this most sacred position, "did not know the LORD, . . . treated the offering of the LORD with contempt, . . . [and] lay with the women who served at the entrance to the tent of meeting" (2:12–22).

As before, God raised up a judge to deliver Israel from the Philistines. So important was his activity that the records of this and the succeeding periods are identified by his name: Samuel. He "judged Israel all the days of his life" (7:15).

But these dreary opening chapters also betoken a better day. Samuel's weapon of deliverance was not strength of arms but the power of prayer; he "cried out to the Lord for Israel, and the Lord answered him" (7:9). Like Moses and like the prophets who would arise later, Samuel was an intercessor (cf Jer 15:1). As a mediator of the Word of the Lord, he called Israel back to covenant faithfulness. At his urging, "the people of Israel put away the Baals and the Ashtaroth, and they served the Lord only" (1Sm 7:4).

But the change was not complete, so Samuel tried by an unprecedented move to continue it until it became permanent. When he "became old, he made his sons judges over Israel. . . . Yet his sons did not walk in his ways but turned aside after gain. They took bribes and perverted justice" (8:1–3).

Nevertheless, this judge and prophet helped restore Israel in its role as God's chosen people. At God's behest Samuel supplied Israel with permanent leadership in the person of a king, first Saul and then David. Under the former, order was restored only partially and temporarily. At his death, the Philistines controlled more Israelite territory than before and seemed to have all the Promised Land in their grip.

But Samuel also had anointed David to be the next king in Israel. This "man after His [God's] own heart" (13:14) again made Israel the instrument of God's holy purposes. The reversal of conditions during David's reign was nothing short of miraculous. Chaos gave way to order, disintegration and dissolution to stability, degradation and disgrace to Israel's golden age of glory. This physical and spiritual reestablishment of the covenant people is the story of the Books of Samuel, though the latter portion of the history shows how David's infidelity nearly ruined everything until God led him to repentance.

Resources

As noted above, tradition attributes the book to the writings of Samuel, Gad, and Nathan. At least a portion of this idea may be upheld by noting that Samuel wrote about the rights and duties of kings (1Sm 10:25) and that documents by these prophets were expressly mentioned in Chronicles (1Ch 29:29; 2Ch 9:29). The unity and homogeneity of the "court history" section (2Sm 9–20) is often contrasted with greater unevenness in much of the rest

Continued on p 288.

OUTLINE

A nation's fate often is determined by its leadership. So also this period in the history of Israel is told in terms of its representatives: Eli, Samuel, Saul, and David. Their roles furnish the following outline of the two books of Samuel:

I. Birth of Samuel and Religious Environment in Israel (1Sm 1–3)

  A. Faithful Family: Elkanah and Hannah (1Sm 1:1–2:11)

    1. God makes the barren fruitful: Hannah bears a son (1Sm 1:1–20)

    2. Hannah returns to the Lord what He had first given her (1Sm 1:21–28)

    3. Hannah's "Magnificat" (1Sm 2:1–11)

  B. Unfaithful Family: Eli's Sons (1Sm 2:12–36)

    1. Eli's sons in the Lord's house versus Samuel in the Lord's house (1Sm 2:12–26)

    2. Bitter fruit of unfaithfulness (1Sm 2:27–36)

  C. Call and Initial Ministry of Samuel (1Sm 3)

    1. Call of Samuel (1Sm 3:1–18)

    2. The Word of the Lord remains with Samuel (1Sm 3:19–21)

II. Movement of the Ark, Emblem of the Lord's Presence (1Sm 4:1–7:2)

  A. The Lord Refuses to Manifest His Presence through the Ark (1Sm 4:1–11)

  B. The Lord's Withdrawal of His Presence (Glory) (1Sm 4:12–22)

  C. The Lord Manifests His Presence through the Ark (1Sm 5)

  D. The Lord's Presence at the Ark Returns (1Sm 6:1–7:2)

III. What's at Stake in the Governance (Rule) of Israel (1Sm 7:3–8:22)

A. Israel Repents and God Delivers Them through Samuel (1Sm 7:3–17)

B. A King like the Nations, instead of God through His Judges (1Sm 8)

IV. Transition from Judgeship to Monarchy (1Sm 9–12)

A. Selection and Anointing of Saul (1Sm 9:1–10:8)

B. Public Selection of Saul (1Sm 10:9–27)

C. Saul's Victory at Jabesh Confirms His Selection as King (1Sm 11)

D. Samuel's Warnings: the Blessings and Curses of the Monarchy (1Sm 12)

V. Rise and Crisis of Saul (1Sm 13–15)

A. Saul's Impulsive Sacrifice (1Sm 13:1–14)

B. Campaign from Gibeah and Philistine Detachment at Michmash (1Sm 13:15–14:46)

C. Saul's Limited Success (1Sm 14:47–52)

D. Saul's Third Impulsive Action and Rejection as King (1Sm 15)

VI. Saul Must Decrease, and David Must Increase (1Sm 16–31)

A. Samuel Anoints David; the Spirit Comes to David (1Sm 16:1–13)

B. The Spirit Departs from Saul and Rests on David (1Sm 16:14–23)

C. David Defeats Goliath (1Sm 17)

D. David's Success Angers Saul (1Sm 18)

E. Saul's Family Helps David Avoid Saul's Attacks (1Sm 19–20)

1. Michal thwarts a plot (1Sm 19)

2. Jonathan helps David to escape Israel (1Sm 20)

F. David's Flight from Saul (1Sm 21–31)

1. David at Nob (1Sm 21:1–9)

2. Achish of Gath (1Sm 21:10–15)

3. David escapes to a cave and a forest (1Sm 22:1–5)

4. Saul kills the priestly family at Nob (1Sm 22:6–23)

5. David rescues Keilah (1Sm 23:1–6)

6. Saul tries to capture David (1Sm 23:7–29)

of the book. Other original sources that are often suggested are an ark narrative; a biography of Samuel, especially his infancy; royal archives; etc.

Text and Translations

Unlike Judges and Kings, the major textual difficulties in Samuel come primarily not from the Greek but from the Hebrew—for reasons that entirely elude us. The Greek sometimes follows a different recension, too, but the Hebrew of Samuel has the dubious honor of exhibiting the most poorly preserved text of all the Historical Books, with only Ezekiel and Hosea possibly worse in the whole Old Testament. The amount of textual corruption can be—and sometimes has been—exaggerated, but there is no responsible denying that much of it exists (see an egregious example at 1Sm 13:1). Sometimes parallels in Chronicles, the Septuagint, and now the Qumran scrolls are helpful in attempting a reconstruction of the original.

DOCTRINAL CONTENT

Summary Commentary

1Sm 1–3 The Lord shows His mercy to Hannah and demonstrates that His power is stronger than human weakness by giving Hannah a son. Samuel, dedicated to God even before conception, is a living sign of God's grace. Hannah brings the young Samuel to the presence of the Lord at Shiloh, and she offers a sacrifice of thanksgiving and consecration. In fulfillment of her vow, Hannah gives Samuel to the Lord for the length of his life. Hannah then exults that God has fulfilled His Word.

While Eli's sons abuse their priestly authority and treat with contempt both the worshipers and the sacrifices offered to God, Samuel grows in his service in the Lord's presence. Hannah and Elkanah also experience God's blessing through the ministry of Eli and receive the gift of more children. Eli's sons refuse to listen to their father's rebuke and warning. Eli receives God's condemnation of his priestly service, a judgment that has negative consequences for Eli's whole house. God vows that He will raise up a faithful priest to serve Him according to His will. While the Lord's word of judgment against Eli's house is confirmed through His revelation to Samuel, that same revelation confirms Samuel's own calling as a prophet.

4:1–7:2 After suffering a relatively minor defeat, the Israelites decide to bring the ark from Shiloh to the battlefront, only to suffer a catastrophic military defeat and lose the ark to the Philistines. God's word of judgment is fulfilled in Israel's defeat, the death of Eli's sons, and the capture of the ark. Yet, Eli and his daughter-in-law, after hearing the news, also die. The idol-worshiping Philistines experience the ark not as a means of blessing but as a means of judgment. Not only is their chief god, Dagon, humiliated before the ark, but all the Philistine cities that house the ark experience the "hand" of the Lord in the form of plague. Although the Philistines returned the ark with a guilt offering, and although the ark's return was confirmed by a miraculous sign, the Israelites still had to learn proper reverence toward God's holy things.

7:3–8:22 With Samuel's encouragement, the people of Israel turn to the Lord and cry out for mercy. This marks the beginning of a new era, in which the people of Israel subdue the Philistines, have their land restored, experience peace, and live under the leadership of Samuel the judge. However, with an unseemly desire to be like other nations, Israel's elders ask Samuel for a king, their action being a rebuke to Samuel and a rejection of the Lord as their King. Nevertheless, the Lord tells Samuel to agree to the request for a king, but also to warn the people about what a king will do.

Chs 9–12 The secret selection and anointing of Saul is made public in a national assembly, though Saul is still hesitant about taking on the role. Although Samuel anoints Saul as the king-designate and the Holy Spirit changes Saul, people remain uncertain about his leadership. Yet, in the Spirit of God, Saul acts boldly and strategically. The nation unites in worship and praise to the Lord for the victory by Saul's leadership and by God's hand. By words and a miraculous sign, Samuel powerfully proclaims a message of judgment and promise.

Chs 13–15 Encounters with the Philistines dominate Saul's reign. He serves primarily as a military leader. Because of Saul's act of disobedience and lack of faith, he will lose his kingdom and God's help against the Philistines. Against great odds, the Lord gives Israel a victory over the Philistines through Jonathan, whose name means "the Lord gave." Saul's foolish oath threatens Jonathan's life, but the people rightly intervene. One of the most tragic passages in Old Testament history is recorded here—a stark reminder of the seriousness of not listening to and

A northern prisoner with Philistine hairstyle/ headdress depicted on a faience tile from the mortuary temple of Ramses III. The invasion of the Philstines disrupted Egyptian rule in the Canaanite lowlands.

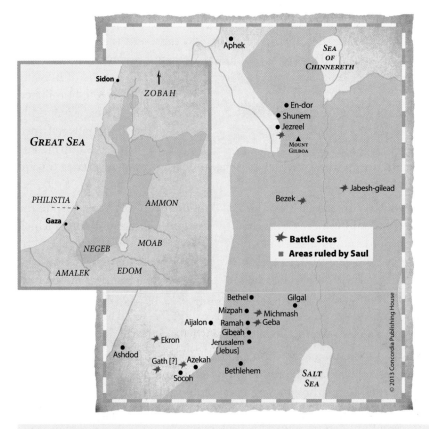

Kingdom and Battles of Saul. Saul defeated Nahash, leader of the Ammonites, at Jabesh-gilead (1Sm 11:1–12). Jonathan routed the Philistines at Geba, but they reassembled with a great force at Michmash (1Sm 13:1–7). God gave Jonathan the victory at Michmash, and Saul pursued them beyond Aijalon (1Sm 14:1–46). David slew Goliath near Azekah and Socoh, whereafter the Israelites pursued the Philistines to Gath and Ekron (1Sm 17). Israel's enemies included Philistia, Zobah, Ammon, Moab, Edom, and Amalek (1Sm 14:47; 15:1–9). Saul fought against all of them. He and his sons, except Ish-bosheth, died on Mount Gilboa in battle against the Philistines (1Sm 31).

following God's Word. Saul fails to carry out the Lord's command to destroy the Amalekites completely, so the Lord will no longer bless his leadership.

Chs 16–20 Samuel's focus is directed away from Saul's ruined potential to what God will do through Jesse's youngest son, David, a man after God's own heart (13:14). David plays music to soothe Saul when an injurious ("evil") spirit brings Saul emotional and mental instability. The gripping story of Goliath and the faith of young David provides a superb example of how God grants victory in the face of impossible odds. Jonathan's unselfish affection for David is seen when Jonathan renounces his own right to the throne—something highly unusual. Saul's jealousy does him no good; meanwhile, David is faithful to the Lord, who gives him success. At the beginning (v 5), middle (v 15), and end of ch 18 (v 30), we are told that David is successful in all he does, because the Lord is with him. Saul's hatred for David results in his attempts to murder him, but the Lord intervenes through Saul's own children. David and Jonathan's friendship displays lasting loyalty and personal self-sacrifice (cf Pr 17:17).

Chs 21–22 David receives the holy bread of the Presence to sustain him during his flight from Saul. Yet he pretends to be insane to escape the predicament at Gath. During David's continued flight, his followers support him and God protects him, directing David through a prophet. David had panicked due to fear (ch 21), but the Lord calmed and directed him. In the remainder of ch 22, the story temporarily leaves David. We see the priesthood nobly suffering at the hands of the godless.

Chs 23–25 The Lord protects His servant and frustrates the plans of the wicked, revealing His will not only in the word of the prophet but also by hindsight in the unfolding of events. Against the overwhelming opposition of Saul and his Ziphite informers, God spares David as Jonathan said He would. David's compassion for vulnerable Saul is motivated by respect for God and His anointed. It is met warmly by Saul, resulting in a temporary truce. Abigail intervenes between David and Nabal, rescuing both from their anger.

Aramean slinger (tenth century BC).

Chs 26–29 Saul again pursues David, who demonstrates that he is a faithful, forgiving servant. Tired of the constant danger and hardship of evading Saul, David shrewdly finds refuge among the Philistines. As with David's previous clever action among the Philistines, the writer makes no indication that the Lord encouraged or approved of David's behavior. Despairing from fear and desperate for reassurance, Saul turns to the occult for answers, having forsaken his relationship with God. As the Philistine army moves northward to battle Israel, David's loyalty will be tested. This difficult situation within the army is resolved when David is removed from the battlefield. Once again, God looked after David's welfare.

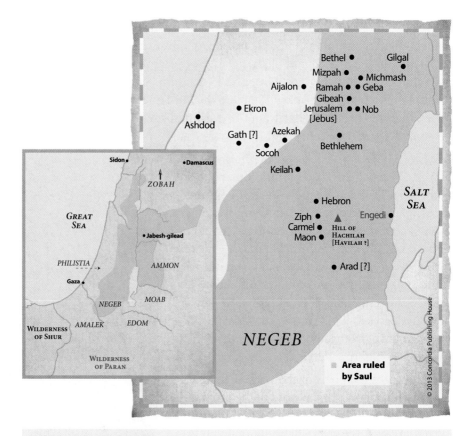

Saul Pursues David. Saul disobeyed God (1Sm 13:5–15; 15). God therefore chose David to be the next king (16:1–13). Saul became jealous of David (18:6–16) and finally pursued David by various ways to Engedi (chs 19–23). David spared Saul's life (ch 24), resulting in a truce and an interlude when all Israel mourned the death of Samuel (25:1). David then went to the Wilderness of Paran and received Abigail as wife in the region of Carmel (25:2–42). Saul pursued David again at the hill of Hachilah, but David again spared Saul's life (ch 26). To escape Saul, David fled to Gath, among the Philistines, where he was given Ziklag as his stronghold (ch 27).

Chs 30–31 The Amalekites raid David's home and take the people captive. David faces his first great crisis as a leader since serving in Saul's army years earlier. The Lord aids David and the people of Ziklag through an unlikely source: an abandoned Egyptian slave, who tells them how to find the Amalekites. The victory God gives David over the Amalekites provides opportunity for him to grow even stronger as a leader. Meanwhile, Saul forfeits his divine blessings by compromising God's Word, and he dies a brutal death at the hands of the very enemy he was chosen to defeat: the Philistines.

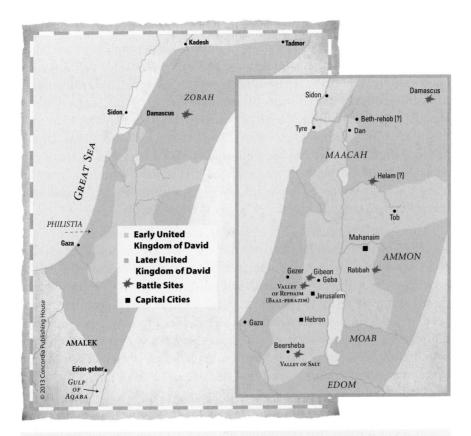

Kingdom of David. David ruled Judah for seven years at Hebron (2Sm 5:5; 1Ch 29:27). Saul's son Ish-bosheth ruled Israel from Mahanaim for two years (2Sm 2:10). David's men scored a victory over Ish-bosheth's force at Gibeon (2Sm 2:10–3:1). David conquered Jerusalem and ruled all Israel from there for 33 years (2Sm 5:1–10; 1Ch 11:1–9). He defeated the Philistines at Baal-perazim and routed them from Geba to Gezer (2Sm 5:17–25; 1Ch 14:8–16). David had victories against the Philistines at Metheg-ammah (location uncertain); against Edom in the Valley of Salt; and against Moab, Zobah, Damascus, and Amalek (2Sm 8; 1Ch 18). He also defeated the Syrians and the Ammonites at Helam (2Sm 10; 1Ch 19) and the Ammonites at Rabbah (2Sm 12:26–31; 1Ch 20:1–3).

2Sm 1–4 An Amalekite confesses to David that he had assisted with Saul's suicide and now expects a reward. Instead, he receives capital punishment for killing the Lord's anointed king. David then mournfully sings not only of his love for his friend Jonathan but also of his respect and admiration for King Saul, a man who had forced him to live as a fugitive for more than 12 years. David inquires of the Lord, moves to the area of Hebron, and is anointed by the men of Judah as their king. When told that the men of Jabesh-gilead have buried Saul, David blesses them and promises to treat them well.

However, Abner makes Saul's son Ish-bosheth king over the northern tribes of Israel, while David reigns over Judah. Competition at Gibeon leads to a fierce battle. The Benjaminites are defeated, but David's nephew Asahel is slain by Abner. The relationship between Ish-bosheth and his general, Abner, deteriorates until, finally, Abner aligns himself with David. Without David's knowledge and in a time of peace, Joab murders Abner to avenge the death of his brother Asahel. King David curses Joab and all his father's house. Although Abner has been his enemy, David leads the mourning at Abner's funeral. Meanwhile, two soldiers of Ish-bosheth murder him and bring his head to David, hoping to receive a reward. Instead, David sentences them to death, but honors his enemy Ish-bosheth.

Chs 5–10 After defeating the Jebusites, David makes Jerusalem his capital over all Israel. The Philistines, disturbed that David is now king over all Israel, attack him twice and are defeated. David inquires of and relies on the Lord for victory. Having defeated the Philistines, David prepares to bring the ark of the covenant to Jerusalem. Uzzah touches the ark, contrary to the Word of God, and is struck dead. Handling the ark properly, David humbles himself as he lays aside his royal robes, puts on a priestly garment, and worships before the Lord as the leader of a kingdom of priests. When Michal sees David humbly dressed as a priest, she begins to mock him.

The Lord tells David and Nathan not what they will do but what He will do and make for David—an everlasting house and kingdom. In humility, David acknowledges that everything the Lord has done and will do for him and for Israel is due solely to the Lord's mercy. The Lord next gives David great victories over the kingdoms around Canaan and Syria and also much wealth as the spoils of war. David rules justly and relies on his ministers of state. When David learns that Jonathan's son is alive, he immediately gives the son Saul's lands and brings him to dine at his table for the rest of his life. However, a new Ammonite king rejects David's offer of peace, listening instead to those who speak evil of him. In the end, Joab and David defeat and humble the Syrian kings by the Lord's hand.

Chs 11–14 David's life goes from triumph to tragedy as the sin of his eye becomes a sin of lust and of deed. He lies with another man's wife and then has the man killed to keep the sin secret. By preaching the Law, Nathan leads David to condemn his own sin. Once David repents, Nathan announces the Gospel: the Lord has put away his sin. Nevertheless, his child of adultery will not survive. Although David prays for his child's recovery, the child dies. David then goes to worship in the Lord's house. David comforts Bathsheba, and she bears him a son. God gives the child a name indicating His love and peace: Solomon. Returning to the theme of conquest, Joab does not take credit for the victory over Rabbah but invites his master David to join him in conquering the city.

A second moral failure threatens to divide the kingdom. Amnon's lust for his sister Tamar leads him to commit a vile crime against her. David, from misguided love for his son or sinful weakness, fails to administer justice. The way is thus paved for further violence in the house of David. Absalom takes the law into his own hands and avenges Amnon's rape of his sister Tamar. Absalom then flees from his father and goes into exile. Thus, the king has lost two sons: the murdered Amnon and the runaway Absalom. One sin leads to another, leaving a trail of consequences along the way. With subtlety, Joab moves the king to show mercy toward Absalom instead of administering justice. David is thereby reconciled with his son only outwardly. Once Absalom has officially been reconciled to the king, he begins to campaign for the throne.

Chs 15–18 David is forced to flee Jerusalem and cross the brook Kidron. While his own son and countrymen conspire against him, he receives fierce loyalty from foreigners. Though David must depart from Jerusalem, he puts his fate into the Lord's hands. Also, his allies will be his eyes and ears in Jerusalem, bringing word to him at the Jordan River. As David flees, Shimei curses him. David recognizes Shimei's cursing as the Lord's justice. He spares Shimei from death, accepts the divine judgment, and entrusts himself to God's mercy in faith. Meanwhile, David's sin is repaid in kind. The evil adultery he committed with Bathsheba is punished by his son Absalom's adultery with his harem. Though apparently at the mercy of his enemies and the elements, David is under the mercy of God. Absalom is defeated by the Lord and hung on a tree. Joab has Absalom killed and brings the war to an end so the rest of Israel is spared. Ahimaaz is anxious to bring news of the victory to David, but he fails to tell about Absalom's death. Expecting an angry reaction from the king, Joab sends a Cushite to bear the message.

Chs 19–20 David's grief over Absalom threatens to undo all that has been accomplished on his behalf. His mourning borders on self-pity and despair, which is neither expedient nor faithful. Having won the war, David has the task of regaining the people's support. The northern tribes of Israel reconsider their decision to follow Absalom. As David retraces his steps to Jerusalem, he meets several of the same people he encountered previously. With mercy, wisdom, and generosity, David crosses over the Jordan, out of the wilderness on his way back to the royal city. For David to return to his throne in Jerusalem, a rebellion among the northern tribes of Israel must be stopped. Though David has been humbled and brought to repentance for his sins, the shadow of rebellion and violence continues to haunt his reign.

Chs 21–24 The remaining chapters describe events from "the days of David." Saul's sons, whether innocent or guilty with their father, now pay the penalty for Saul's crime. In a separate incident, Philistine giants and armies attack, yet David and the armies of Israel are victorious. Due to his old age, David will no longer go out to battle with his troops. In his song of deliverance, David acknowledges that God Almighty trained him for war, provided him with weapons of war, fought for him, and gained for him the victory. Inspired by the Holy Spirit, David speaks forth his last will and testament, prophesying of God's eternal covenant, which would be fulfilled in the kingdom of Christ. Though David certainly makes honorable mention of those who fought bravely alongside him, the faithfulness and loyalty of a warrior seems to be the deciding factor in whether he is included in David's list of mighty men. Joab, a general perceived as disloyal, is excluded from the list. David's obsession with numbers and statistical strength does not belong in matters of faith. God did not command him to record a census, so He punishes Israel because of it.

Specific Law Themes

The Books of Samuel often describe the destructive power of sin and its consequences, especially as they affect families. This is powerfully illustrated in the mockery of Hannah's rival, the covetousness of Eli's sons, and the failure of their father to rebuke them. In a similar way, family difficulties dominate the end of Samuel as David and Bathsheba commit adultery and David's children rebel. Alongside these family troubles is Israel's rejection of the Lord and His servant Samuel in favor of Canaanite-style monarchy. Saul's rashness and jealousy stand at the heart of the work.

Specific Gospel Themes

God's provision for leadership is key to each part of the story, which culminates in promises of an eternal kingdom and faithful priesthood. The Lord raises up lowly David, grants him victory in His name, and transfers the kingdom to David. Along the way, the Lord supplies to His anointed one loyal friends and subjects, such as Jonathan. David restores the tabernacle to its rightful place in the life of Israel, where the true king—the Lord—is enthroned.

Specific Doctrines

God used the monarchy (particularly the reign of David) to reestablish Israel as His nation in order to carry forward His ultimate purpose: to bring His mercy to all nations. This rehabilitation was effected in all areas of Israel's life and illustrates for us the value of sound government.

The Arad fortress near Israel's southern border included its own temple, used for centuries. Pictured here is the Holy of Holies, including two Massebah stones, which might represent worshipers or dieties, and also two altars.

Full possession of the land would be theirs as God carried out His promise. What Joshua had only started and what the individual tribes lacked the faith to do was achieved under David. All opposition of the Canaanites was overcome, and the land "from the river of Egypt to the great river, the river Euphrates" (Gn 15:18) finally became Israel's possession. David's kingdom extended even beyond the borders of Canaan proper and took on the proportions of an empire.

Moral order was restored. No longer could anyone do "what was right in his own eyes" (Jgs 21:25) as in the days of the judges. The Law of Moses was again enforced. Justice prevailed, for the king himself supervised and supplemented the judicial procedures and acted as the court of final appeal. So absolute was the application of justice that not even the king could flout with impunity the rights of his subjects. (E.g., David's murder and adultery were condemned and punished.)

Restoration of Worship

Israel's worship eventually was restored. During the time of the judges, Israel's disobedience had created conditions that made it impossible to observe the unified and ordered system of worship defined in Mosaic Law. In addition, at Samuel's time the Philistines had conquered and destroyed Shiloh (where the sanctuary had been) and had captured the ark of the covenant (1Sm 4:1–11). During foreign occupation and the absence of the ark, festivals such as the Day of Atonement evidently could not be observed. But God still desired and accepted Israel's worship to the extent that it was sincere and that the people were able to observe Mosaic regulations. Therefore, altars were erected at various places during this confused period, and sacrifices acceptable to God were made (Ex 20:24).[4]

Under David's rule conditions gradually returned to the prescribed practice. David brought the ark to Jerusalem and reestablished the priesthood. But he was not destined to build a temple or to reinaugurate the full order of service; God reserved this for David's son Solomon.

The Role of the Prophets

Spiritual life was fortified and directed to a greater degree by the prophets. This office was not new to Israel; both Moses and Joshua had been spokesmen of God to Israel (though the latter is not expressly called a prophet). During the time of the judges "the LORD sent a prophet [unnamed] to the people of Israel" (Jgs 6:8). Furthermore, a human mediator likely is meant in Jgs 10:11: "The LORD said to the people of Israel. . . . " Samuel was also "established as a prophet of the LORD" (1Sm 3:20; cf 15:10).

David, quoted in the New Testament as a prophet himself (Mt 22:42–44), had at his side as counselors the prophets Nathan and Gad. The prophets played an important part during the entire period of the monarchy—and even after that. Some of them left their messages in the books bearing their names; some did not (cf Micaiah, 2Ch 18:6–27). But all the prophets, differing in temperament and endowments, are cast in the same mold of uncompromising integrity in speaking the oracles of God. Unique in the ancient world, they all insisted that Israel's kings submit to covenant obedience, for God's one standard applied to all people. The doctrines and teachings of the prophets did not vary: "Behold, to obey is better than sacrifice, and to listen than the fat of rams" (1Sm 15:22).

The Messianic Kingdom

Because of all these physical and spiritual blessings during Israel's golden age, David's reign became a symbol and prophetic type of the fulfillment of the old covenant in the new: God's promise of a spiritual rule in human hearts. That covenant promise had not changed when the patriarchal system of Abraham changed into a federation of tribes at Sinai, nor did God set a different goal when He permitted the federation to have a monarch to implement the covenant. But now the anointed king (David and his son and offspring) would represent God's rule on earth until from their seed would

---

4   No arbitrary disregard was permissible. Saul's assumption of priestly functions was severely punished (1Sm 13:11–14), as was the profaning of the ark (6:19). Cf 15:22: "Behold, to obey is better than sacrifice, and to listen than the fat of rams."

come the fulfillment of all that they typified so imperfectly: "the Son of God . . . the King of Israel" (Jn 1:49).

The Hebrew word for "anointed one" is *meshiach*, Messiah (Gk, *Christos*). The term "messianic prophesy" therefore may be limited to the covenant promises that refer to the Messiah's royalty and His descent from David.[5] But in a wider sense all Old Testament types and promises may be called messianic. Christ established His royal kingdom by absorbing and fulfilling in His person the function of all the Old Testament prototypes of God's rule—the king as well as the prophet, the anointed high priest, the Servant of the Lord, the Son of Man, the Redeemer, and the Man of Sorrows by whose "stripes we are healed" (Is 53:5).

Like all prophetic types, David's kingdom was an imperfect vehicle. He stooped to unkingly and unmessianic behavior. His "house," intended to occupy "the throne of his kingdom forever" (2Sm 7:13), was swept away by foreign kings. This failure does not impugn God's promise concerning the enduring character of David's dynasty, for the promise was conditioned on the covenant. Despite Israel's frequent failure to live by the covenant, God kept His promises. "My steadfast love I will keep for him [David] forever, and My covenant will stand firm with him" (Ps 89:28; cf Is 55:3; Ac 13:33). And when the time was fulfilled, Mary, the peasant girl of Nazareth, heard the angelic messenger prophesy of her royal son (Lk 1:32–33).

The Law, Prayer, and Repentance

As with other Historical Books, Samuel illustrated the Commandments and other teachings of Moses. Eli loved and tolerated the wickedness of his sons when he should have rebuked them (1Sm 2:29). The examples of Saul (negatively) and David (positively) show us that the Lord must be first in our lives. Saul feared failure and the people more than God (13:8–15; 15:24); Nabal loved his goods above all (ch 25). The many examples of oaths were referenced for demonstrating that some oaths were appropriate and less risky (20:3), while one should use special care in swearing by God's name (1Sm 14:24; 25:22; 2Sm 21:7, 17), as the Second Commandment teaches. Saul's visit to En-dor (1Sm 28) illustrates the sin of invoking someone other than the true God in seeking spiritual aid. The Fourth Commandment applies to the home (1Sm 2:34; 4:11) as well as the government (1Sm 24:7, 11–12; 2Sm 14:20). The Fifth Commandment forbids aiding someone in homicide (1Sm 18:17). The stories of David and Bathsheba, Amnon and Tamar are perhaps the best illustrations of sin against the Sixth Commandment (2Sm

---

5   E.g., Is 9:6–7; 11:1, 11; Jer 23:5–6; Ezk 34:20–24; Am 9:11–12; Zec 9:9–10.

11; 12:9–15; ch 13). Many stories raise questions about the application of the Eighth Commandment (1Sm 16:5; 19:13; 20:28; 21:13; 22:9; 26:1; 2Sm 17:1, 9; 20:9), the boundaries between deceiving and withholding information.

Prayers for physical benefits are encouraged by the examples of Hannah, who sought a child (1Sm 1), and David, who awaited the restoration of his kingdom (2Sm 15) and rejoiced when the Lord delivered him (2Sm 22).

Ministry can be corrupted by an unfaithful life, such as that which led the Lord to remove the priesthood from Eli and his household (1Sm 2:30; 3:12). The Holy Spirit and faith depart from those who persist in manifest sins (1Sm 16:14; 2Sm 11) because the unrepentant resist the Word. In contrast, Nathan's rebuke and David's repentance illustrate the work of God's Word in converting the heart (2Sm 12:13; cf 1Sm 2:6). God can even use the rebukes of sinners for moving someone to repentance (2Sm 16:5–14).

Application

Although many people appear on the pages of the Books of Samuel, David is the chief character. The successors to his throne are evaluated on whether they did "what was right in the eyes of the Lord, according to all that David his father had done" (2Ki 18:3; cf 1Ki 15:3, 11; 2Ki 14:3). His loyalty to God and his importance as God's instrument in promoting His plan of salvation is thereby fully recognized and normative despite a full knowledge of David's defects and shortcomings. The recognition of David magnifies the grace of God rather than idolizes the man.

Samuel anoints David; from the synagogue at Dura Europos.

David was a remarkable leader. God had endowed him with physical charm, a poetic soul, a captivating and inspiring personality, and a sure instinct for choosing the right word and the appropriate action in a given situation—a combination of leadership qualities rarely found in one person.

David gave abundant evidence that a God-fearing leader need not be a blundering fool. He shrewdly exploited each new development for the advancement of his cause. With skill and tact he knew how to ingratiate himself with friend and foe and how to heal the divisions in Israel. His choice of neutral Jerusalem as his capital was a diplomatic triumph. His grief at the death of Saul and Jonathan was sincere and not a mere "playing to the galleries"; he expressed it, and it won him friends. His treatment of Saul's offspring was dictated by kindness as well as by prudence. As pointed out, after the harrowing experience of Absalom's revolt, David was not his old self. But this human and unflattering account only makes his true greatness shine in even greater glory.

David also serves as a negative example of sin and a positive example of repentance. He lives in the record not as a ghost conjured up by a historian but as a man of flesh and blood—tempted always and at times overcome by lust and pride, yet accepted by God's forgiving mercy and usable for a role of glory unattained after him. The messianic promise to David and his house (2Sm 7) marks an important juncture in divine revelation. The human ancestry of the Savior, the Mediator of the new covenant, is identified. The large circle of humanity has been narrowed to Shem (Gn 9:26), of his sons to Abraham (12:3), of his offspring to the tribe of Judah (49:10), and of this tribe to the house of David. Centuries later, Mary, espoused to Joseph the "son of David" (Mt 1:20), received the final definitive announcement: "You will . . . bear a Son . . . and of His kingdom there will be no end" (Lk 1:31, 33).

1Sm 1–3 Hannah's trusting openness to God's Word, and the blessing she received, encourages us to trust that God will deal with us according to His compassionate love. Everything that we have is a gift from the Lord. This means that we have no right to keep anything back from service to God, no matter how dear it is to us. Hannah's prayer also gives us encouragement to look to God for every good thing that we need in life, confident that He will fulfill our deepest desires in eternity through His Anointed One, Jesus Christ.

The story of Eli's sons encourages us that no matter how disordered things may get in our world and even in the Church, God will stand by His gracious Word of blessing. God's rebuke and warning show His desire for our repentance. He will hold us responsible for those in our care. He also assures us He will always provide a means of saving us from our sins through the ministry of the anointed Son of God, Jesus Christ.

4:1–7:2 This account of the Philistines capturing the ark of the covenant stands as a rebuke to us if we believe that God's gracious presence can be manipulated for our purposes to give us license to do our own sinful will. God's word of judgment is fearful and means death to all who have sinned. Our hope lies in His mercy alone. Through repentance and His promised mercy, God gives us the gift of faith so that His presence may bring our healing and salvation (cf Lk 8:43–48).

7:3–8:22 Like the people of Israel, when we live apart from God, we experience frustration and defeat. As God leads us to cry to Him for mercy, He restores us and makes us whole in Christ Jesus. Leadership should be tempered by faith, which calls on the Lord, His guidance, and His blessing. He often gives us what we want, but even more graciously, He gives us what we need—forgiveness, life, and salvation.

Chs 9–12 The Lord's use of life's circumstances is beyond our expectations. Call on the Lord, who always leads in the right way, even when it seems otherwise. The Lord is our "very present help in trouble" (Ps 46:1). In challenging times, God's Spirit empowers you to face the challenge. Knowing that Jesus is indeed our Savior and Lord, we can act confidently as agents of God's kingdom.

Chs 13–15 True refuge resides only in the true God—the God of Abraham, Isaac, and Jacob, the God of Samuel. He acts in "the fullness of time" as when "God sent forth His Son" (Gal 4:4) to forgive all our sins—including our faithless impatience. Though we may fail from the world's perspective, God gives us ultimate spiritual victory and all things in Christ.

Chs 16–20 Because God looks on our hearts (1Sm 16:7), we stand condemned before Him (Jer 17:9–10a). Yet, He leads us to plead: "Create in me a clean heart, O God" (Ps 51:10). Pray to God: "Take not Your Holy Spirit from me" (Ps 51:11). In Christ, the friend of sinners, we have a faithful and forgiving friend who will never leave or forsake us. What others intend for evil against David God turns into good. "Blessed is the one whose transgression is forgiven, whose sin is covered" (Ps 32:1). Give thanks to the Lord for the friends He has blessed you with and the wonderful way He has protected you. Pray to grow in the grace of giving thanks. By grace, God treats all of us infinitely better than we deserve.

Chs 21–31 When troubles and sins surround you, turn to the Lord and His servants for aid. Treasure God's Word as your stronghold. Be prepared to suffer as God's royal priesthood, remembering that God's purpose will not be thwarted. He is watching over you, though His presence may often be hidden by adverse circumstances. Be ready to show compassion even to your enemies, as God in Christ has demonstrated His undeserved love to you. God calls us to listen to the voice of reason and peace. His wisdom and peace, expressed in the godly counsel of His servants, will guide your heart in the way of life. Entrust your future to His care rather than to your cleverness or the world's favor. Acknowledge and rejoice that God's grace and promise are as close at hand as His Word, which will guide you in the paths of life. When the Lord grants success and prosperity to you, consider how this increases your opportunities and your responsibilities. Learn by the examples of Saul and David. By promises and blessings, the King of heaven provides life for you in His Son, Jesus.

2Sm 1–4 God is the author of human life, and He wants innocent human life protected. Yet, He has given the sword to the government for the punishment of evildoers. Like David, we should not delight in our enemies' downfall but commend their families to God in prayer. Sometimes, God's promises call for patience. Inquire of the Lord in His Holy Word and seek reconciliation with enemies. Self-interest and self-glory are sins that plague us all. Jesus, on the other hand, selflessly left His throne on high, died to pay for our sins on the cross, rose, and took the Church as His Bride. The Lord of justice and peace, who sent His Son to bear all injustice for your sake, is your hope in all circumstances.

Chs 5–10 When success comes our way, let us not boast and demand recognition. For our plans to have God's blessing, we must call on Him and submit to the judgment of His Word. Though God disciplines the irreverent, He remains faithful to bless the humble. Do not fear to make merry before the Lord and endure suffering. Our Lord Jesus was not ashamed to humble Himself on the cross to save us from our arrogance.

In all we do for the Lord, we must first consult His Word to find out what is pleasing to Him. When great blessing comes your way, glorify the Lord for His gifts. Our victory comes only when the Lord gives it. Just as David invites Mephibosheth to eat at his table, the Lord Jesus invites us to eat at His table, where He serves us His body and blood. He would have us continually act in good faith toward all. Thanks be to God, who fights for us and covers our shame in the mercy of Jesus.

Chs 11–14 Whenever you try to hide a sin by committing another sin, you are just digging yourself deeper into a hole. Instead, confess! Repentance is the only right preparation for the Gospel. When suffering the earthly consequences of our sin, we also should acknowledge that we deserve them, and we should continue to worship the Lord. In Baptism, the Lord gives us a new, eternal life and gives us the name "Beloved of the Lord." Christ, the Son of David, is the great King of glory, yet He humbled Himself and gives us the benefits and glory of His victory over the devil.

The covetous desires of our hearts, when nurtured instead of resisted, can burst forth into deadly wickedness. We need the Law's restrictions and guidance. Vengeance is not to be taken into our own hands; punishment and discipline are rightly administered through the offices God has established (parents, government). Although fathers love even evil children, the children should not misuse this love, as Absalom did. For Christ's sake, God desires not to punish but to spare His sinful and rebellious children. Christ has righteously coveted our life and voluntarily laid down His life on our behalf. We are justified by His grace alone, through faith in His forgiveness.

Chs 15–18 In suffering, we, like David, should humble ourselves under God's hand and commit ourselves and our paths into His keeping. Life here in this world is often a wilderness journey of weeping and the expectation of death. We are too easily led to make quick judgments, especially when they agree with our expectations. The Lord, however, looks at the heart and is not fooled. Christ Jesus has borne the curse and judgment of God in our stead. For His sake, we are spared the punishment we deserve. We should pray that the Lord would humble us each day, through discipline unto repentance, so that we may not be humbled before Him in the final judgment! In contrast to Absalom, Jesus, the sinless Son of David, was reckoned a rebellious sinner (2Co 5:21) and died on a tree to bear God's curse against the world's sins (Gal 3:13). How blessed are the feet of those who proclaim the Gospel, who tell us that our King Jesus reigns with mercy! Our Father in heaven has opened His merciful heart to us in the outstretched arms of Jesus, the Son of David.

The head of a scepter, from Moza, Israel, shaped like a pomegranate and carved in Egyptian blue (calcium copper silicate).

Chs 19–20 Sometimes our sin is manifested in pride and self-righteousness, other times in despondency and defeatism. We are tempted to manipulate the people and situations around us to our own advantage, and even to seek revenge. Thanks be to God that His heart burns instead with love and mercy for us. For He despises nothing He has made but forgives the sins of all who are penitent for Jesus' sake.

Chs 21–24 Believers will always face warfare with the devil, the world, and the evil desires of the flesh. Whatever good is in us is God's gift alone. In this Word, God sets forth His covenant of grace, an eternal covenant in which Christ rules us, justifies us, and brings us to eternal life. The saints live "by faith," believing God's Son would ransom them from bondage to hell and death. Christ's cross was a sacrifice to appease God's wrath, which now has resulted in the place of God's mercy on earth: the means of grace in the Holy Christian Church.

CANONICITY

The kingdom of David formed the next great story in the history of God's people and became the focus of His promises for the future. The reigns of David and Solomon were high points and served as enduring examples and measures for Israel generally and for the kings of Israel in particular. The Books of Samuel were welcomed by Jews and early Christians without dispute (cf e.g., Ecclus 46:13–47:11).

Background of Jerusalem. Barely 12 acres in size, Jebus, a Canaanite city, could well defend itself against attack, with walls atop steep canyons and shafts reaching an underground water source. Second Samuel 5:7 calls it "the stronghold of Zim." Yet David captured the stronghold and made it his capital.

Mount Moriah

Jerusalem is shown from above and at an angle; and therefore wall shapes appear different from those on flat maps. Wall locations have been determined from limited archaeological evidence; houses are artist's concept.

Hinnom Valley

Kidron Valley

© Hugh Claycombe 1982

Substantial historical evidence, both biblical and extrabiblical, places the temple of Herod (and before it the temples of Zerubbabel and of Solomon) on the holy spot where King David built an altar to the Lord. David had purchased the land from Araunah the Jebusite, who was using the exposed bedrock as a threshing floor (2Sm 24:18–25). Tradition claims a much older sanctity for the site, associating it with the altar of Abraham on Mount Moriah (Gn 22:1–19). Genesis equates Moriah with "the mount of the Lord," and other Old Testament shrines originated in altars erected by Abraham.

Lutheran Theologians on 1 and 2 Samuel

Luther

"St. Anna, the mother of Samuel, sings in 1 Samuel 2:9: 'Not by might shall a man prevail.' St. Paul says in 2 Corinthians 3:5: 'Not that we are sufficient of ourselves to claim anything as coming from us; our sufficiency is from God.' This is a most important article of faith, including many things; it completely puts down all pride, arrogance, blasphemy, fame, and false trust, and exalts God alone. It points out the reason why God alone is to be exalted—because He does all things. That is easily said but hard to believe and to translate into life. For those who carry it out in their lives are most peaceable, composed, and simple-hearted folk, who lay no claim to anything, well knowing it is not theirs but God's." (AE 21:328)

"Although God manipulates and establishes all kingdoms, granting them to whom He will, nevertheless to this people He adds a special word of favor, to let them know that they have the kingdom of God. Therefore in the Book of Samuel they are reproved for having sinned gravely; for in seeking a king they trusted in him as in a man and a human government and did not seek a king in God and through His Word, as He says there (1 Sam 8:7): 'They have rejected Me from being king over them.'

"Moses instructs [a prospective king] to rule with trust in God alone and with the knowledge that he has been appointed and preserved by His Word. Therefore he commands him not to multiply horses (v. 16), that is, not to trust in military might; not to lead the people back into Egypt, that is, not to trust in human favor and strength; not to multiply gold and silver, that is, not to trust in wealth (v. 17); not to multiply wives, that is, not to let his faith be snuffed out by thorns, as Christ calls the pleasures and cares of life, Luke 8:14. On the other hand, he does not forbid him to be strong with horses and military might, as we read that David and Solomon were (1 Kings 4:26); nor does he forbid compacts and alliances with men, like those which Solomon had with the King of Tyre and Egypt (1 Kings 5:12), and David with the Moabites, the Ammonites, and King Toi (2 Sam. 8:9)." (AE 9:169)

"God had ordered Saul to exterminate the Amalekites, insisting that not so much as the hoof of an ox survive. But Saul disobeyed. He did indeed slay all the people, but he spared the fine cattle. He was seized by avarice, so that he did not destroy all the fine beasts. And when the prophet Samuel took him to task for this, asking him to account for the animals that had not been slain, he replied: 'The people spared them, to sacrifice them to the Lord our God.' Samuel now became so incensed that he pronounced a terrible judgment on Saul, saying: 'What does God care about your sacrifice? He demands obedience. God did not command you to sacrifice the animals.' And when Saul continued to justify and defend what he had done, the charge of disobedience was flung into his teeth. He was informed that God regarded disobedience as a sin comparable to idolatry and sorcery (1 Sam. 15:1–31). For if God orders me to do one thing and I do another, and, over and above this, try to justify myself, I am really committing sorcery. As a matter of fact, we are all still wont to do this. If Saul had only said: 'I forgot the command. I did wrong!' his sin would have been remitted." (AE 22:397)

Gerhard

"*The two Books of Samuel.* The author of the *Glossa ordinaria* claims that Samuel wrote the first book up to the part where his death is mentioned (c. 25) and that David added the rest, as well as the second book. There are some who confirm this opinion from 1 Chron. 29:29. Therefore they are called 'the Books of Samuel,' first, by reason of their instrumental efficient cause because Samuel wrote a good part of them; second, by reason of their subject matter and object because the history of Samuel is described in the first part of the first book. In the latter part of the first book, as well as in the second book, the activities are told of the first Israelite kings, Saul and David. As a result of this, among the Greeks and Latins they are also called 1 and 2 Kings. Some think that the prophets Nathan and Gad wrote the latter part of the first book and the second book.

"First Samuel consists of thirty-one chapters and contains the history of eighty years: forty under Eli (1 Sam. 4:18) and forty under Samuel and

Saul (Acts 13:21). With regard to the objects that it describes, it can be divided into three parts: the history (1) of Samuel, the last judge; (2) of Saul, the first king; and (3) of David, chosen in place of Saul. Second Samuel consists of twenty-four chapters and contains the history of the forty years under King David (2 Sam. 5:4–5). It can be divided according to the status of the Davidic kingdom, of which it explains: (1) the beginning, (2) the growth, (3) the end. First Samuel has 797 verses; 2 Samuel, 679." (ThC E1 § 128)

Fresco-Mosaic of King David playing a harp. About 70 psalms are attributed to David.

QUESTIONS PEOPLE ASK ABOUT SAMUEL

Does the Lord Sanction Lying?

1 Samuel 16:1–2 states: "The LORD said to Samuel, 'How long will you grieve over Saul, since I have rejected him from being king over Israel? Fill your horn with oil, and go. I will send you to Jesse the Bethlehemite, for I have provided for myself a king among his sons.' And Samuel said, 'How can I go? If Saul hears it, he will kill me.' And the LORD said, 'Take a heifer with you and say, "I have come to sacrifice to the LORD." ' "

Proverbs 12:22 affirms: "Lying lips are an abomination to the LORD, but those who act faithfully are His delight."

The charge is made that God, who in the text from the Book of Proverbs strictly prohibits lying or deception, in the passage from 1 Samuel commands His prophet to engage in an act of duplicity; that the same God who forbids deceiving people in one passage in another endorses it. A careful consideration will show that the charge is not completely correct. In 1Sm 16:1–2 God orders Samuel to anoint one of the sons of Jesse as king of Israel, and when Samuel points out that this is a very dangerous thing, God orders him to offer up a sacrifice at the house of Jesse and on that occasion to attend to the anointing of the king. There is no reason to charge God with ordering Samuel to do something dishonest in this case. It is true, when Samuel was asked why he was going to the house of Jesse, his reply was, "to sacrifice to the LORD." But was that telling a lie? No, he went also with that very purpose, and nothing compelled him to tell inquirers of all his designs in going to the house of Jesse. There is certainly nothing dishonest with saying that we are going to a friend's house, when we also intend to do business along the way. In that case we are stating the truth, and no one will charge that we are being deceptive in our statement. Secrecy and concealment are not the same as duplicity and falsehood. God is not sanctioning deception; He is merely outlining a course of action for Samuel that will insure his safety.

In this connection 1Ki 22:21–22 may be discussed: "Then a spirit came forward and stood before the LORD, saying, 'I will entice him.' And the LORD said to him, 'By what means?' And he said, 'I will go out, and will be a lying spirit in the mouth of all his prophets.' And He said, 'You are to entice him, and you shall succeed; go out and do so.' " At first reading it might seem as though the Lord is pictured here as the author of the deception to be practiced upon Ahab, the wicked king of Israel. However, a careful reading of the passage will show that the situation was somewhat different. A lying spirit declares himself willing to deceive Ahab. The Lord thereupon says: "Go out and do so." In other words, God permits this evil spirit, who has the intention of leading Ahab astray, to do his work. Without the permission of God he could not have become a lying spirit in the mouths of the prophets of Ahab; but when the Lord withdrew His restraining hand, then the way was open to him. God permitted the evil spirit to practice his deception because He wished to punish Ahab for his idolatry and his other evil ways. We simply have here an instance where one evil deed is punished by another. Hence the text from 1 Kings merely shows that in certain instances God permits deception to be practiced upon the doers of iniquity who have spurned His Word and are impenitent. It does not mean God's people are free to lie.

Did Saul Inquire of God Through Urim?

1 Samuel 22:23 reads: (David said to Abiathar): "Stay with me; do not be afraid, for he who seeks my life seeks your life. With me you shall be in safekeeping."

1 Samuel 28:6 records: "And when Saul inquired of the LORD, the LORD did not answer him, either by dreams, or by Urim, or by prophets."

The Urim and Thummim, it seems evident, were terms to designate the revelation of the will of God by means of lots kept by the high priest. The precise nature of the manner in which the lots functioned for this purpose is no longer ascertainable. The difficulty created by the above passages consists in that Abiathar the high priest was with David, having taken the ephod or sacred robe with him (1Sm 23:9; 30:7), which normally held the lots. Apparently Saul had access to other lots nevertheless and could make inquiry by means of them. But reading 1Sm 28:6 carefully, we notice that the passage does not say that Saul inquired of God through Urim. The writer merely says that God did not answer Saul in any way whatever. The king may have asked for some revelation, leaving the manner to God, but no answer was forthcoming.

In this connection another passage may be discussed, namely, 1Ch 10:14, which says that Saul did not inquire of the Lord, while 1Sm 28:6 seems to state that he did. The situation reflected in these passages was the following: Saul did not turn to the Lord with a prayerful, repentant heart. When he was in the midst of troubles, he did utter cries directed to Yahweh, without, however, repenting of his sins, and hence his pleadings were not prayers at all, and for this reason they were not heard by God.

The Medium of En-dor

Who has not read with feelings of sorrow and pity, and at the same time of awe, the story found in 1Sm 28:5–20, which relates that Saul went to En-dor, where a medium received a prediction from the spirit world of his impending death? A number of matters engage our attention as we enter into a consideration of this account. The Lord no longer was answering the inquiries of Saul because these were not brought

A seven-cupped bowl from the Canaanite temple excavated at Nahariyeh on the North Israel coast.

before Him in a filial attitude, but with a mind bent on doing evil. The sacred text says: "The LORD did not answer him, either by dreams, or by Urim, or by prophets" (1Sm 28:6).

From the stories of Joseph (Gn 37) and Pharaoh (Gn 41), we learn that God at times gave revelations by means of dreams. Another method that He employed was that of Urim. In connection with the breastplate of the high priest we find Urim and Thummim, which in literal translation mean "lights" and "perfections." These names likely stand for some special objects that were in the breastplate and were taken out and used after the manner of lots when the will of God was sought. (However, some think that when the high priest put on the breastplate and prayed to God, a divine revelation was granted him.) The Israelites of the time of Moses and David and probably of many succeeding generations knew how Urim and Thummim were employed. We no longer possess this information. Finally, God often made known His will through prophets whom He sent to Israel and its rulers with a message. In view of the disloyalty of Saul, God at this time did not grant him any directions or guidance in the ways mentioned.

Thereupon Saul, becoming reckless and desperate, fearing the strong army of the Philistines, asked his servants to lead him to a medium who might put him in touch with a spirit able to tell him what to do. In taking this course, Saul completely reversed himself. In former years he had put to death or banished all witches and wizards in Israel, obeying in this respect the will of God, who had strictly forbidden all sorcery and witchcraft. Now he himself sought to obtain the services of one of these practitioners of evil. God had given Israel His Word and the priesthood, and frequently He sent prophets, so that his people had all knowledge needed for their welfare. To pry into the future through witchcraft or divination was branded as a wicked procedure. In His wise providence the heavenly Father has flung a thick veil over the future, and to try to lift it by unauthorized means is impudent and presumptuous.

When Saul had stated his wish and assured the woman of safety, as she would be complying with his request, she asked, "Whom shall I bring up for you?" (1Sm 28:11). Could she really summon a departed spirit from the regions beyond the grave to appear on earth and subject him to questioning? That she pretended to have this ability is evident, and Saul, we see, had no doubt that her powers in this respect were genuine. He told the woman to bring up Samuel. The next thing reported is that, when the woman saw Samuel, she uttered a loud cry and said to the king: "Why have you deceived me? You are Saul" (v 12). The appearance of the visitor from the spirit world was like that which had characterized Samuel during his life, and Saul, hearing the description given by the woman, had no doubt that the old prophet had come. It seems that the king did not see the unearthly visitor. Whether the words of the spirit proceeded out of the mouth of the woman, which is probable, or whether the apparition spoke of its own, cannot be determined with certainty. What Saul heard from the spirit was crushing news, announcing the defeat of Israel and the death of Saul and his sons.

Two Views

Among believing scholars we find two views concerning this remarkable event, which agree in the chief point, namely, in the conviction that it was impossible for the medium and for Satan to summon Samuel or any other one of God's servants who had departed this life out of the beyond. That Satan cannot bring back upon earth the departed saints is implied in Lk 16:22, 26, where the soul of Lazarus is said to be taken into Abraham's bosom, separated by an unbridgeable chasm from the realm of Satan. We may here think also of the words of Jesus spoken to the penitent criminal on the cross: "Truly, I say to you, today you will be with Me in Paradise" (Lk 23:43). When Stephen was put to death, he prayed: "Lord Jesus, receive my spirit" (Ac 7:59). Paul declares that to depart in his case means to be with Christ, which would be far better than the condition he was in here on earth (Php 1:23). When we survey these Scripture texts, the conviction inevitably forces itself upon us that God does not permit Satan or his tools to summon the spirits of the believers to obtain information from them. In this respect both views agree.

There is a difference of opinion, however, on the question whether it was the spirit of Samuel that was seen by the woman or whether what was beheld was Satan himself, who assumed the outward appearance of the great prophet.

The Bible students of the Reformation era and the following century were quite unanimous in the view that Satan played the role of Samuel, deceiving Saul, who was under the impression that he was in contact with the prophet. They admitted, of course, that the story says Samuel spoke to Saul and that the words of the spirit fit the life and the character of Samuel, but they held it quite natural to assume that the spirit is merely given the name by which it was referred to in the remarks of the woman and that the holy writer does not think it necessary to go beyond this terminology. The Scriptures in no other narrative relate the appearance of a spirit of the departed to give information on the future and, furthermore, the Sacred Record emphatically states God was no longer granting communications to Saul; for that reason it does not seem likely that He would permit Samuel to appear on an occasion where in direct violation of divine will incantations were uttered and a spirit was invoked. These are important considerations favoring this view.

On the other hand, there are believing Bible interpreters, most of them of more recent date, who think that it was Samuel himself that came from the spirit world to announce to Saul his doom. While insisting just as strongly as the previous interpreters that witches and Satan are powerless to summon the saints that sleep into the world of the living, they hold that the letter of the narrative plainly points to the appearance of Samuel himself, who, so they explain, was sent by God to make the dire prediction of Saul's defeat and death. They refer to the shriek of the woman, mentioned in v 12, and interpret it as being due to her surprise when Samuel, whom she had not at all expected, appeared; her plan being simply to pretend to get in touch with the departed, while in

A typical royal jar which held royal goods "for the King" (Hbr *lammelek*) found at Lachish but possibly associated with Hebron where David first ruled.

reality she would be obtaining her answer to Saul's inquiries through the agency of Satan. To show that saints can appear here on earth if God so wills it, the case of Moses and Elijah is pointed to, who appeared to Jesus at the transfiguration

313

and were likewise seen by Peter, James, and John. There is no reason to consider such a view unscriptural if one believes that no amount of satanic influence can carry the departed saints back into the sphere of mortals and if one regards the appearance of Samuel as an exceptional instance, brought about entirely by God's intervention to make an ultimate pronouncement of His wrath against the wicked king and to do it through the same prophet who had previously announced God's anger to the disobedient ruler. The words of the spirit: "Tomorrow you and your sons shall be with me" (1Sm 28:19) in this case refer to the beyond, the world of the dead, which Saul was soon to enter—a view that does not deny that in yonder world God's children dwell in bliss, while the wicked are punished.

Did Michal Remain Without Children?

2 Samuel 6:23 reports: "And Michal the daughter of Saul had no child to the day of her death."

2 Samuel 21:8 (KJV) narrates: "The king took . . . the five sons of Michal the daughter of Saul, whom she brought up to Adriel the son of Barzillai the Meholathite."

Michal had no child unto the day of her death, says the one passage, and the other passage states in most Hebrew manuscripts (as reflected in the KJV) that she had five children. The holy writer in his statement in 2Sm 6:23 may intend to say that Michal had no child in her marriage with David. If we assume this to be his meaning, then all difficulty vanishes. A different explanation is that we assume Michal in 2Sm 21:8 to be a copyist's mistake for Merab. (Two Hebrew manuscripts and the LXX do have "Merab" instead of Michal.) If we compare the latter passage with 1Sm 18:19, we see that Merab was the daughter of Saul who was given in marriage to Adriel, the man mentioned in 2Sm 21:8. Thus it seems clear that this passage does not speak of Michal, the wife of David.

Defeat of the Syrians

2 Samuel 10:18 states: "The Syrians fled before Israel, and David killed of the Syrians the men of 700 chariots, and 40,000 horsemen, and wounded Shobach the commander of their army, so that he died there."

1 Chronicles 19:18 says: "The Syrians fled before Israel, and David killed of the Syrians the men of 7,000 chariots and 40,000 foot soldiers, and put to death also Shophach the commander of their army."

The Hebrew text for the passage from 2 Samuel, literally translated, reads: "David killed seven hundred chariots of the Syrians"; for the passage from 1 Chronicles: "David killed seven thousand chariots of the Syrians." Of course, the meaning is that David killed the men that occupied the chariots. The difference in the number of chariots is best explained as due to the error of a scribe, who (especially since letters were used as numerals) could easily write 7,000 instead of 700 or vice versa. With respect to the other divergence between the two passages, 2 Samuel says that David killed 40,000 horsemen, 2 Chronicles that he killed 40,000 foot soldiers in this battle. The Chronicler sought to provide greater detail about the troops; perhaps these warriors could fight both as cavalry and as infantry as the occasion requried. (It is worth noting that some LXX and an old Latin text also have "foot soldiers.") Throughout history, militaries have included mounted infantry that would travel to a battle on horseback or chariots but fought on foot in tightly organized formation.

Did Absalom Have Sons?

2 Samuel 14:27 declares: "There were born to Absalom three sons, and one daughter."

2 Samuel 18:18 affirms: "Now Absalom in his lifetime had taken and set up for himself the pillar that is in the King's Valley, for he said, 'I have no son to keep my name in remembrance.'"

Here we have a conspicuous illustration for the importance of the rule: give heed to the respective dates, and the Scriptures will be found in agreement. Absalom had three sons, and Absalom had no sons, the two texts say. If both were written with respect to the same time in the life of Absalom, we should be confronted with a contradiction. But there is no evidence whatever compelling us to look upon these two statements as having reference to the same period in Absalom's history. Both statements are true. One depicts the situation early in the life of Absalom, the other the situation when he died. Three sons had been born to him, but when he erected a monument to his own memory, they had died. The infant mortality rate in Old Testament times was probably quite high.

Similarly, careful attention to the dates of the respective events will clear up the difficulty caused by the statement in Nu 20:18–21, saying that the Edomites would not permit Israel to journey through their land, and the statement in Dt 2:4, 8, which says that such permission was given. Compare likewise two apparently conflicting references to the extent of Hezekiah's wealth, 2Ki 18:14–16 and Is 39:2, 6.

Who Moved David to Number Israel?

2 Samuel 24:1 asserts: "Again the anger of the LORD was kindled against Israel, and He incited David against them, saying, 'Go, number Israel and Judah.'"

1 Chronicles 21:1 says: "Then Satan stood against Israel and incited David to number Israel."

At first reading these two texts seem to contradict each other, the first text attributing to God what the second one assigns to Satan. No one, however, acquainted with biblical modes of speech will find it difficult to harmonize these two statements. God permitted Satan to influence David in such a way that he proudly ordered a census. This can be expressed thus: "God moved David to number Israel," or it may be given in these words: "Satan provoked David to number Israel." Each statement is true, but does not tell everything pertaining to the origin of the census. Both together give us a comprehensive view of the situation. In 2Sm 24:1 the profound truth is hinted at that God punishes evildoing by permitting sin to beget sin. David and Israel had aroused the anger of Yahweh, who withdrew His hand and let the devil have access to the heart of David.

Similarly it is stated that God hardened the heart of Pharaoh (Ex 10:27). It was Pharaoh himself who hardened his heart, as the sacred narrative says several times. But finally God no longer restrained Pharaoh, and that is described thus: "The LORD hardened Pharaoh's heart." When God allowed Pharaoh to go his own way, he could give free rein to his cruel passions; it was a punishment for the wicked attitude of the Egyptian king, who had so often refused to obey the divine command.

Number of Warriors in Israel at the Time of David

Second Samuel 24:9 states: "And Joab gave the sum of the numbering of the people to the king: in Israel there were 800,000 valiant men who drew the sword, and the men of Judah were 500,000."

First Chronicles 21:5 reports: "And Joab gave the sum of the numbering of the people to David. In all Israel there were 1,100,000 men who drew the sword, and in Judah 470,000 who drew the sword."

There are two points to be considered here. The one account says that when Joab numbered the children of Israel, he found the number of the warriors in Judah to be 500,000. The other account gives the figure as 470,000. The figures are not far apart. Evidently the account in 1 Chronicles is more exact than the other. The writer of 2 Samuel contents himself with stating the number of warriors in round figures. Here, then, there is no discrepancy.

With regard to the number of warriors found in the other tribes of Israel, the case is not so simple. Second Samuel says that they numbered 800,000; 1 Chronicles, that there were 1,100,000 of them. Several commentators propose the following solution, which appears perfectly satisfactory. They suggest that in the account of 2 Samuel the standing army of Israel is not reckoned. The size of this standing army was considerable, as we see from 1Ch 27:1, namely, 288,000 (24,000 x 12), not counting the numerous officers. If this number is added to the 800,000 mentioned in 2 Samuel, we arrive at approximately the same figure as in 1 Chronicles.

Price Paid for the Threshing Floor of Ornan

2 Samuel 24:24 affirms: "But the king said to Araunah, 'No, but I will buy it from you for a price. I will not offer burnt offerings to the LORD my God that cost me nothing.' So David bought the threshing floor and the oxen for fifty shekels of silver."

1 Chronicles 21:25 asserts: "So David paid Ornan 600 shekels of gold by weight for the site."

A superficial reading may find a disagreement between these two passages; but as soon as one inspects them a little more closely, the impossibility of making them oppose each other becomes clear. First, it should be pointed out that Araunah and Ornan are different spellings of the same name. Next, the text from 2 Samuel says that David bought a threshing floor and some oxen. The text from 1 Chronicles declares that he bought the place. It is clear that two different transactions are spoken of. We may assume that David first bought the threshing floor and the oxen for 50 shekels of silver. Later on he may have decided to buy the whole field belonging to Ornan, paying 600 shekels of gold. This was to be the temple site, and naturally more ground than merely a threshing floor was needed. See map, p 305.

FURTHER STUDY

Lay/Bible Class Resources

Baldwin, Joyce. G. *1 and 2 Samuel*. TOTC. Downers Grove, IL: InterVarsity Press, 1988. ♪ Compact commentary consulting the Hebrew and various translations. Written by a British evangelical scholar.

Brondos, Joel, Donna Streufert, and Mark Eddy. *Life of David*. Leaders Guide and Enrichment Magazine/Study Guide. LL. St. Louis: Concordia, 2010. ♪ An in-depth, nine-session Bible Study covering sections of Samuel and Kings with individual, small group, and lecture portions.

Dunker, Gary. *1 and 2 Samuel: God's Grace through Kings*. GWFT. St. Louis: Concordia, 2008. ♪ Lutheran devotional writer. Thirteen-session Bible study, including leader's notes and discussion questions.

Life by His Word. St. Louis: Concordia, 2009. ♪ More than 1,500 reproducible one-page Bible studies covering each chapter of the canonical Scriptures. Page references to *The Lutheran Study Bible*. CD-Rom and downloadable.

Mittelstaedt, John R. *1 & 2 Samuel*. PBC. St. Louis: Concordia, 2005. ♪ Lutheran author. Excellent for Bible classes. Based on the NIV translation.

Payne, David F. *I and II Samuel*. Daily Study Bible. Philadelphia: Westminster, 1982. ♪ A compact commentary on the history and theology of Samuel.

Teske, Steven, and R. Reed Lessing. *1 and 2 Samuel*. Leaders Guide and Enrichment Magazine/Study Guide. LL. St. Louis: Concordia, 2012. ♪ An in-depth, nine-session Bible Study covering the Books of Samuel with individual, small group, and lecture portions.

Church Worker Resources

Arnold, Bill T. *1 & 2 Samuel*. NIV Application Commentary. Grand Rapids: Zondervan, 2003. ♪ Evangelical, theologically informed commentary.

Bergen, Robert D. *1 & 2 Samuel*. NAC. Nashville: Broadman & Holman, 1996. ♪ Evangelical author who is critical of Christological interpretation.

Academic Resources

Anderson, Arnold A. *2 Samuel*. WBC. Dallas: Word, 1989. ♪ Historical-critical, offering considerable comment on possible alternatives to the form or formation of the text before arriving at worthwhile interpretation of the text as received in the Hebrew Bible.

Auld, A. Graeme. *First and Second Samuel: A Commentary*. OTL. Louisville: Westminster John Knox, 2011. ♪ The more recent volume of the OTL series (cf Hertzberg below). Focused on translation of primary texts (MT and Old Greek).

Brueggemann, Walter. *First and Second Samuel*. Interpretation: A Bible Commentary for Teaching and Preaching. Louisville: Westminster John Knox, 1990. ♪ A talented writer and scholar, working from a historical-critical perspective.

Campbell, Anthony F. *1 Samuel*; *2 Samuel*. Forms of the Old Testament Literature. Grand Rapids: Eerdmans, 2003; 2005. ♪ A current form critical study of the text and its hypothetical sources.

Cartledge, Tony W. *1 and 2 Samuel*. Smyth & Helwys Bible Commentary. Macon, GA: Smyth & Helwys, 2001. ♪ Draws out the history and theology of the text; keeps in mind the central place of Jesus in the revelation of God.

Erdmann, Chr. Fr. David. *First and Second Books of Samuel*. LCHS. New York: Charles Scribner's Sons, 1891. ♪ A helpful, older example of German biblical scholarship, based on the Hebrew text, which provides references to significant commentaries from the Reformation era forward.

Hertzberg, Hans Wilhelm. *I and II Samuel*. OTL. Philadelphia: Westminster, 1964. ♪ Written from a critical perspective but including interpretation of the book's theological message as well.

K&D. *Biblical Commentaries on the Old Testament: The Books of Samuel*. Grand Rapids: Eerdmans, 1971 reprint. ♪ This century-and-a-half old work from Lutheran scholars should not be overlooked. Despite its age, it remains a most useful commentary on the Hebrew text.

Klein, Ralph W. *1 Samuel*. WBC. Dallas: Word, 1983. ♪ Especially focused on the textual issues of Samuel. Takes a canonical approach to interpretation.

McCarter, P. Kyle. *I Samuel*. Vol. 8 of AB; New York: Doubleday, 1979; *II Samuel*. Vol. 9 of AB. New York: Doubleday, 1984. ♪ Written from a critical perspective. In expository comments, he addresses the text-critical matters of the Qumran literature.

1 AND 2 KINGS

Turn from your evil ways and keep My Commandments

East of Jerusalem flow two springs: the Gihon, which was the principal source of water for Jerusalem, and the En-rogel, a secondary source further to the south. Streams from both would flow into the Kidron Valley, creating a verdant green contrast to the rocky slopes and city walls where David ruled.

To these springs, which were only about 2,150 feet apart, gathered two groups in c 970 BC. The first group supported the kingship of David's son Adonijah at En-rogel, on the boundary between Benjamin and Judah, the tribes from which Israel's royal families sprang. The second group, nearer to Jerusalem, supported the kingship of David's son Solomon at the Gihon. Each group noisily hailed their choice, but it was to Solomon that the people of Jerusalem rallied that day, ensuring that he would inherit the throne.

As this story shows, the Book of Kings opens with a people divided. Although Solomon efficiently and gloriously united Israel during his reign, more political and cultural divisions emerged shortly after his death and plagued Israel throughout its history. Although the people united to build the temple of the Lord and vowed to abide by His word, they divided to follow different gods and kings. They wandered like the fresh waters of Jerusalem down the Kidron Valley toward the tepid Dead Sea. The Book of Kings tells this complex story over 400 years until the fall of Jerusalem and the apparent end of David's dynasty.

Historical and Cultural Setting

With God's blessing, David and Solomon rose to power while local issues divided the major regional powers in Egypt and Mesopotamia. During the thirteenth century, waves of Sea Peoples invaded the coasts of Canaan and Egypt, settling as rivals to the Pharaohs and to the Israelite tribes. After the death of Rameses XI in 1069 BC, Egypt was ruled by different leaders, one

Olive trees and terraces of the Kidron Valley stand before a wall and cemetery of the Old City in Jerusalem. At the south end of this valley (left), Solomon was anointed king. Beyond the top wall (looking west), he built the temple and its courts.

at Amun in the south and another at Tanis in the north. With two leaders and a divided force, the Egyptians could not assert their strength along the coast of Canaan as they had done for centuries. However, when Egypt was reunited under Shoshenq I (Shishak; 945–925 BC), the Egyptians successfully raided Jerusalem, weakening the kings of Judah. The Egyptians continued to be a force in the region, but they never matched the force of their rivals from the north and west.

To the north of Israel, the Hittite New Kingdom collapsed in c 1180 BC. The Assyrians likewise lost influence after the death of Tiglath-pileser I (1076 BC). This allowed the Arameans, people living in the region of Damascus, to gain strength. Both David and Solomon strengthened Israel and contended with the Arameans or Syrians, preventing them from invading Israel. However, when Israel was divided after the death of Solomon, the northern kings struggled and lost decisive battles against the Arameans, as the Book of Kings records. When Tiglath-pileser III (744–727 BC) restored Assyrian strength, his armies overran Damascus in 732 BC and the Northern Kingdom of Israel in 722 BC. A century later, the Babylonians rose to power and overthrew the Assyrians. They conquered the Southern Kingdom of Judah in 587 BC, likely a generation before the editor of the Book of Kings completed his history.

The Book of Kings and Archaeological Discoveries

Various forms of external evidence illuminate the Bible's testimony about the history of this period. For example, research indicates that Solomon's administration, described in 1Ki 4, was heavily dependent on Egyptian models—there were few native models to follow. In 4:6 we hear for the first time of the system of *corvée* or "forced labor" (cf 5:13), which would ultimately be the empire's undoing. Solomon's "twelve officers" (4:7) apparently oversaw districts that no longer corresponded exactly to the ancient tribal boundaries. Reasons of efficiency may have been involved, but one also suspects a deliberate attempt to break up old loyalties.

International elements contributed to the construction of the temple. This is apparent from the biblical reports themselves of massive Phoenician influence, not least in the employment of the half-Tyrian Hiram as its chief architect (7:13–14). Both in general architectural plan as well as in numerous details, there are many ancient Eastern parallels to Solomon's temple. The parallelism may be exaggerated as well as unduly minimized.

Twelve steles surround a place of worship in Gezer. The city was given to King Solomon by an Egyptian pharaoh (1Ki 9:16).

First Kings 11 signals the beginning of the end of the David-Solomonic empire as a result of Solomon's increasing apostasy. Rezon cultivates old grudges in Damascus (vv 23–25), indicating the resurgence of the Aramean states, which would bedevil the Northern Kingdom throughout its history. David's other two adversaries, Hadad the Edomite and Jeroboam, are given asylum and obviously encouraged by Egypt (vv 14–22 and 26–40). The pharaoh involved is probably the same Shishak who invaded both north and south after the schism. Pharaoh's attack signals both the revival of the great powers to the north and south of Israel after long dormancy, and specifically the beginning of Egypt's meddling pretensions that continued in one form or the other down to the time of Christ.

It is no accident that Jeroboam had been in charge of forced labor (11:28) before his disaffection and flight to Egypt. Nor, probably, is it accidental that the prophet Ahijah, who encouraged him by a dramatic "symbolism" and prophecy (that is, both action and verbal prophecy), hailed from Shiloh (vv 29–39). Ahijah probably represented the old, conservative northern religious order; that order found it even harder than did the loyal circles in the south to stomach Solomon's innovations.

When Rehoboam journeys to Shechem to be crowned king of Israel as well as of Judah (1Ki 12), we are not surprised that the northern grievances turn on the hated *corvée* or "forced labor." Rehoboam not only rudely rebuffs them but pours salt in the wounds by dispatching Adoram to enforce it. Adoram pays for it with his life (v 18), and only Shemaiah the prophet dissuades Rehoboam from further armed misadventure (vv 21–24). The disruption is permanent (c 922 or 931).

It was not until the reign of Omri about a half-century later that the northern capital became fixed in Samaria (1Ki 16:24), which thereafter was often used as the title for the entire country (as also Ephraim, its largest tribe, often was). Jeroboam first situated the capital in the ancient religious center of Shechem, and possibly even for a time across the Jordan in Penuel (12:25), but about 900 BC it was apparently moved to Tirzah (15:21, 33).

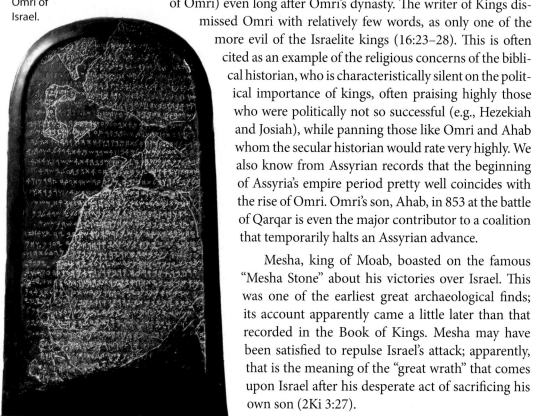

Victory stele of Mesha, king of Moab, thanking the god Chemosh for his victory over king Omri of Israel.

Omri was one of Israel's ablest kings, who not only built Samaria as its capital, but also brought it to the height of its power and influence. We know this primarily from Assyrian sources that refer to Israel as *Bit Humri* (House of Omri) even long after Omri's dynasty. The writer of Kings dismissed Omri with relatively few words, as only one of the more evil of the Israelite kings (16:23–28). This is often cited as an example of the religious concerns of the biblical historian, who is characteristically silent on the political importance of kings, often praising highly those who were politically not so successful (e.g., Hezekiah and Josiah), while panning those like Omri and Ahab whom the secular historian would rate very highly. We also know from Assyrian records that the beginning of Assyria's empire period pretty well coincides with the rise of Omri. Omri's son, Ahab, in 853 at the battle of Qarqar is even the major contributor to a coalition that temporarily halts an Assyrian advance.

Mesha, king of Moab, boasted on the famous "Mesha Stone" about his victories over Israel. This was one of the earliest great archaeological finds; its account apparently came a little later than that recorded in the Book of Kings. Mesha may have been satisfied to repulse Israel's attack; apparently, that is the meaning of the "great wrath" that comes upon Israel after his desperate act of sacrificing his own son (2Ki 3:27).

Detail from the Black Obelisk showing Jehu, king of Israel, prostrating himself before Shalmaneser III, Assyrian king.

Second Kings 10 closes with a notice of Hazael of Damascus encroaching on Israelite territory. On the famous Black Obelisk of archaeological discovery, we see Jehu prostrate before Shalmaneser III of Assyria, whom Ahab had once stopped in his tracks at Qarqar (a step taken by Jehu in part probably to halt Hazael's depredations).

From Assyrian records, we also know that Hezekiah headed a local anti-Assyrian coalition, which Sennacherib could not let go unchallenged for long.

COMPOSITION

Author(s)

The situation of Kings is very similar to that of the other Former Prophets. The Talmud attributes the book to Jeremiah. This is possible, except for its closing verses. Its likelihood is enhanced by the strong similarities between the styles of Deuteronomy and the prose of the Book of Jeremiah. If the tradition about Jeremiah seems like an overly neat simplification, it remains undeniable that the author(s) must have belonged to circles of very much the same mind as Jeremiah. See also "Resources," p 339.

Date of Composition

The notice of Jehoiachin's release gives us a c 561 BC starting point for dating the work, while the total absence of any allusion to the fall of Babylon in 539 or the other momentous events under Cyrus seems to tell us the writing was concluded before these events. If so, the completion of not only Kings, but possibly of all the books associated with the Deuteronomic history may be dated to within those two decades. The majority critical view probably favors the location of this work in defeated Judah, among the survivors of the debacle rather than in Babylon among the exiles, but there are no real grounds for deciding between the two views.

Additionally, there are some other passages in Kings that can be read as stemming from a date earlier than the fall of Jerusalem (1Ki 8:8; 11:36; 2Ki 8:19) or even earlier than the death of Josiah (2Ki 22:20). As a result, most critics assume a double "Deuteronomic redaction," with a first edition of the book appearing in connection with the Josianic reformation (late seventh century) and our present edition appearing in the mid-sixth century BC.

One of the most vexing problems in biblical study is the chronology of the framework of Kings. The situation is like that in Judges, but probably even more difficult to resolve definitively. This is because the framework in Kings uses a double system of dates (nothing like our modern systems was apparently in use anywhere). It gives both absolute dates of the total regnal years of each monarch, and comparative dates (synchronisms) in terms of the regnal year of the king of one kingdom at the time of the accession of a new king in the other. The comparative dates are only used until the collapse of the Northern Kingdom in 722 BC. The chronology problem consists in the discrepancies between the totals of the two systems.

There is no commonly agreed upon solution to the problem. Julius Wellhausen and earlier scholars tended simply to reject the comparative dates as later and purely artificial. Knowledge now of even earlier Assyrian and Babylonian chronologies has made that stance difficult to maintain.

Especially in America, two major solutions are usually employed: (1) the more "conservative" one of Edwin R. Thiele, which assumes an accurate Hebrew text, and a complicated, but consistent, system of co-regencies and shifts in calendric systems and methods of computation in the two kingdoms; (2) that of William F. Albright, who assumes few changes in systems until postdating began under Manasseh, but who is forced to assume many textual errors when things do not otherwise work out.

When it comes to *absolute* chronology, our major anchor is the Assyrian king lists, with occasional reference to eclipses or the like, which can be astronomically determined. When there are synchronisms of Mesopotamian and biblical events, we can often determine the biblical date very accurately. Hence, for many events in the period of the monarchy, scholarly computations often differ by only a year or less. For more on these issues, see Andrew E. Steinmann's *From Abraham to Paul: A Biblical Chronology* (St. Louis: Concordia, 2011), 37–65.

Continued on p 330.

THE BOOKS OF SAMUEL AND KINGS COMPARED

In the Septuagint, an ancient Greek translation of the Old Testament, these books are titled "3 and 4 Kings," whereas the two books of Samuel are labeled "1 and 2 Kings." This grouping does not intend to say that all these books had the same author. But it does call attention to the fact that these four volumes record the history of the monarchy in Israel from its origin in 2 Samuel to its ignominious end in 2 Kings. The continuity of this long story is provided by the opening chapters of 1 Kings, which depict the final years of the reign of David, the hero of 2 Samuel.

But the Books of Kings differ from the Books of Samuel in several respects. In Samuel the events take place in a time span measured by decades; in Kings they cover nearly four centuries. In Samuel there are three main characters (the person bearing the name of the books and two kings); in Kings the action is restricted to the reign of one person (Solomon) until after his death, when some 40 royal individuals are listed or described. About half of them reigned in Israel, the confederation of 10 tribes that seceded from the dynasty of David and lasted about two centuries. During this period, 12 loyal successors of Solomon ruled in Jerusalem. For a little over a century after the fall of Israel, nine more kings acceded to the throne of David. This mélange of leading characters became so complex that for a time kings with the same name (Jehoram) held sway in each kingdom.

Organization

The Books of Kings differ from Samuel also in the way this large number of leading characters is organized into a structured framework. Among the information listed in each case is (1) the time of accession to the throne of the new king in terms of the regnal year of the contemporary monarch in the other kingdom, (2) the age of the king, (3) the length of his reign, and (4) an appraisal of the king's character.

Another feature not found in Samuel but prominent in Kings is the frequent reference to documents containing "the rest of the acts" of a given king. The author had to have access to additional records in reviewing events that occurred over several hundred years. Other authors (e.g., of Judges and Samuel) must have used sources also, but Kings makes more than a passing reference to such compendiums of history. The Books of Kings cite them explicitly some 30 times in stereotypical formulas. The reader is directed to supplementary records in each of the divided kingdoms—in the northern part, "the book of the kings of Israel"; in the southern, "the book of the kings of Judah." The content of these noncanonical works is unknown because they are no longer extant. (Nor are those mentioned in Chronicles; cf 2Ch 9:29; 12:15; etc.)

Rise and Fall

More glaring and crucial than the divergent literary organization of Samuel and Kings is the status of the covenant nation as depicted at the end of each book. In Samuel, an upward movement reaches its culmination in the reign of David, who not only attained full sovereignty and independence for his people but also international fame and imperial recognition. In Kings, a decline soon resulted in deepest degradation and abject humiliation. Because the chosen nation broke the covenant, the holy city and the temple were reduced to ashes, torched by the Babylonian conqueror. The inhabitants of the city and the land were not only reduced to vassalage, but a large number of them were dragged off to the faraway country of the foreign overlord.

The people's hopes for survival were as dead as the dry bones in Ezekiel's vision (Ezk 37). Never again would an earthly descendant of David lay claim to the throne of the covenant nation and rule over it in royal independence. Later confirming this sad state of affairs, the mob reviling Jesus at His trial shouted, "We have no king but Caesar!" (Jn 19:15), the Herods being but Rome's puppets. In order to mock the servile status of the Jewish people, Pilate put this inscription on the cross of the condemned criminal: "Jesus of Nazareth, the King of the Jews" (v 19).

Despite their dreary ending, the Books of Kings remain open to the future. The liberation of the Davidic king Jehoiachin, recorded in the last four verses of 2 Kings (ch 25), may be regarded as a token of the deliverance God had in store for all nations. For, all appearance to the contrary, the Lord of history would not fail to keep His covenant and "the sure blessings of David" (Ac 13:34; cf Is 55:3) to raise up "a horn of salvation for us in the house of His servant David" (Lk 1:69). In God's own way and in the fullness of time, a King would ascend "the throne of His father David . . . of His kingdom there will be no end" (Lk 1:32–33). Although His kingdom was not of this world, "all nations will come and worship" Him, "for He is Lord of lords and King of kings" (Rv 15:4; 17:14; cf 19:16).

A Common Motif

Although differing in several respects, the Books of Samuel and Kings have a basic motif in common, which accounts for their inclusion in that part of the Hebrew canon called the Former Prophets. Though written as royal annals in form and content, the Books of Kings sustain the prophetic proclamation, affirming that everything happens "according to the definite plan and fore-knowledge of God" (Ac 2:23). In keeping with this axiom, the record in Kings presents but another chapter in the history of the chosen nation and documents God's faithfulness in keeping His eternal covenant—its blessings as well as its judgments.

Consequently, the author was particular in choosing data to incorporate in his account. From 400 years of Israel's history, he carefully selected the incidents and situations that bear witness to God's direction of the course of history in order to "remember His holy covenant" (Lk 1:72).

The author's eclectic procedure is evident also in his discriminating use of the sources at his disposal, "the acts of the kings of Israel and Judah." Thus he accords to King Jeroboam of Israel only seven verses, though this monarch reigned for 41 years (2Ki 14:23–29). For the same reason, the author compresses into 18 verses the report of King Manasseh of Judah, whose wicked rule lasted 55 years (21:1–18). Furthermore, it is indicative of the kind of history the author set out to furnish that about one-third of its pages are devoted to telling the stories of two ancient messengers of God's covenant: Elijah and Elisha, the contemporary kings being little more than a foil for their prophetic activity (1Ki 17–21; 2Ki 1–9).

Purpose/Recipients

The book's major concern is about the sole legitimacy of the worship in Jerusalem, but even more basically the sole deity of Yahweh (vs. any and all idolatry). No doubt, this was the chief doctrine of the writer's subject. For example, the kings of Judah who champion true Yahwism at Jerusalem, but tolerate worship at high places (outlying shrines, some of which were probably at times relatively Yahwistic themselves), are only slightly censured. Those who openly encourage or patronize paganism receive no commendations whatsoever. Of all the kings of Judah, only Hezekiah and Josiah receive unconditional praise, and five others receive conditional approbation.

By this same criterion, *all* the kings of Israel are said to have done evil (except for Shallum, who reigned only a month), even when, as in the case of Jehu, power came on the coattails of renewed worship of Yahweh. The recurrent refrain is that "they did not depart from the sins of Jeroboam the son of Nebat, with which he made Israel to sin" (cf 2Ki 13:11; 14:24).

Literary Features

Genre

The "framework" of Kings, as that of Judges, combines chronology with religious judgments. However, whereas the material within the framework of Judges consisted of more disconnected episodes, the histories of the two kingdoms in most of Kings constitute parallel and continuous records. The two histories are integrated by the scheme of narrating the reign of one king to its conclusion, and then describing the reigns of all the kings who came to the throne in the other kingdom during that same period. To one who is basically familiar already with the history (as the original audience surely was), the scheme is simple and effective.

An invariable pattern, with only very minor modifications, is consistently used to describe the kings of Judah: (1) "In the __th year of N[ame], the king of Israel, began N, the son of N, the king of Judah to reign" (that is, a synchronism of the king's accession with the regnal year of the contemporary king of Israel); (2) "He was __ years old when he began to reign"; (3) "and he reigned __ years in Jerusalem"; (4) "and his mother's name was N"; (5) the history of his reign, varying considerably in length and character; (6) the Deuteronomic verdict on the religious quality of his reign (cf below); (7) (the beginning of the conclusion) "and the rest of his acts, and all that he did, are they not written in the book of the chronicles of the kings of Judah?"; (8) "So he slept with his fathers, and they buried him with his fathers in the city of David"; and (9) "N, his son, reigned in his stead."

The framework to the histories of the kings of Israel is slightly shorter: we are told neither the names of their mothers nor their age at accession, and in the conclusion the phrase "was buried with his fathers" is never used. The shorter description undoubtedly implies disapproval of the northern kings. In both forms of the framework, however, very explicit religious judgments are made on the reigns of each king, and these differ drastically in the two kingdoms.

Characters

Although the Books of Kings begin with the great King David, he is present in the story chiefly to introduce his son and successor: **King Solomon**.

Solomon's reign (970–931 BC) represented both a high point in the history of Israel and also a turning point. Solomon's great reign and expansive wealth crescendoed in the building of the Jerusalem temple, which occupies most of the chapters dedicated to him. Unlike his father David, Solomon is a man of peace and diplomacy whose greatness is measured in wisdom rather than heartfelt devotion and in economics rather than military conquest. However, like David, Solomon allows base passions and pride to corrupt his reign and introduce the immediate decline that hounds his successors—idolatry, as carefully explained in 2Ki 17. Despite David's flaws, he remained Israel's greatest ruler and the standard by which Solomon

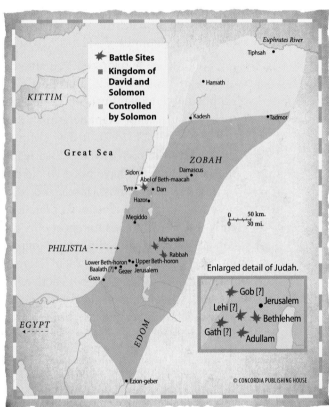

Kingdom of David and Solomon. David experienced civil war in his later years. His army defeated his rebel son Absalom at Mahanaim (2Sm 17:24–18:18) and the rebel Sheba at Abel of Beth-maacah (2Sm 20).

David and his men undertook campaigns against the Philistines at Gob and Gath (2Sm 21:15–22; 1Ch 20:4–8) and at Lehi, Adullam, and Bethlehem (2Sm 23:11–17; 1Ch 11:12–19).

Solomon secured what David had won, taking Hamath and building Hazor, Megiddo, Gezer, Upper and Lower Beth-horon, Baalath, and Tadmor (1Ki 9:15–19; 2Ch 8:3–6). He built a fleet at Ezion-geber (1Ki 9:26; 2Ch 20:36) and sealed pacts with Tyre (1Ki 5:1–12; 10:22; 2Ch 2:3–16; 9:21). Solomon's kingdom stretched from Tiphsah on the Euphrates in the north to Gaza in the south (1Ki 4:24).

Solomon's later apostasy caused God to raise adversaries in Hadad of Edom; Rezon of Damascus and Zobah; Pharaoh Shishak of Egypt; and finally Jeroboam, who would rule Israel over against Rehoboam, Solomon's son, who would rule Judah (1Ki 11).

and all the other kings would be measured (1Ki 11; for more on Solomon, see the introductions to his books: Proverbs, Ecclesiastes, and Song of Solomon).

During the wayward reign of Solomon and others, the Lord did not fail to instruct the covenant people in the way of righteousness and to warn them of the consequences of disobedience to His holy will. For He "warned Israel and Judah by every prophet and every seer, saying, 'Turn from your evil ways and keep My commandments and My statutes' " (2Ki 17:13).

Some of these **prophets** remained unidentified and are called only "a man of God" or "a prophet" (cf 1Ki 13:1, 20). Others are supplied with names but without additional information regarding their persons, as for example, Ahijah the Shilonite and Jehu the son of Hanani (11:29; 16:7). It may seem strange that no mention is made of well-known divine emissaries who also were active during the same time and have filled whole books with the Word of God spoken by them, such as Amos, Hosea, and Micah. Since the inspired author's purpose was to furnish a history of Israel and Judah ruled by kings, he apparently restricted himself to report only the careers of the prophets who made contact with the contemporary occupants of the throne and played a part in directing events during their reigns. Accordingly, the sacred chronicler mentions the prophet Nathan, active in David's struggle to make Solomon his successor. Reference is also made to Isaiah because he delivered God's word to King Hezekiah. But the activities of two other prophets are reported at far greater length, making them two of the most important characters in the book.

Elijah (1Ki 17–21; 2Ki 2:1–12) made the wicked King Ahab the principal target of his ministry. Appearing before the king as if from nowhere (1Ki 17:1), Elijah announced the coming of a severe drought. When it arrived, the Lord supplied His prophet with drink from the brook Cherith and with food brought to him by ravens. Because the brook also dried up, the Lord ordered Elijah to seek refuge beyond the reach of Ahab in Zarephath, a city in the territory of Phoenician Sidon. Here Elijah provided a miraculous supply of flour and oil for the widow who had fed him. And when her son became sick and died, Elijah was granted the power to revive the young boy.

After three years Elijah obeyed the command of the Lord to appear again before Ahab and to announce the end of the drought (1Ki 18:1). On this occasion he demonstrated to the king and an assembly of people that the Lord controlled the forces of nature and was the true God of Israel. For

Northward view from the Carmel Ridge. The Mediterranean Sea is visible on the far left.

in answer to Elijah's prayer, fire rained from heaven and devoured his altar and the sacrifice on it, all thoroughly drenched with water. The prophets of Baal, challenged to prove that their god could do likewise, had already failed miserably, taunted and ridiculed by Elijah. Proved to be impostors, they were seized by the people and executed by the prophet of the Lord.

Elijah now faced the wrath of Ahab's wicked wife, Jezebel. Unnerved by her threat to kill him (1Ki 19:2), as she had already done to other faithful prophets, he fled the land of Israel and sought safety in Beersheba on the southern border of Judah. From there he proceeded farther south to Mount Horeb (Mount Sinai; v 8), sustained on his journey of 40 days and nights by food that an angel had provided for him at the outset. Here where Moses had met with the Lord, the runaway prophet heard from the Lord "the sound of a low whisper" (v 12) to impress on him that he was to resume his ministry motivated by a quiet appeal to his inner self rather than by the dramatic display of God's power over nature that had taken place earlier.

Reinstated as the Lord's emissary, Elijah again confronted Ahab in Samaria (21:17–29) to denounce him for illegally confiscating the vineyard of Naboth, the hereditary owner, after Jezebel had arranged his execution on trumped-up charges of blasphemy. The prophet announced that "the dogs shall eat Jezebel within the walls of Jezreel" (v 23). The king repented of his misdeed and was granted a reprieve from the punishment awaiting him (v 29).

Elijah also transmitted the Word of the Lord to Ahab's successor, Ahaziah (2Ki 1:2–17). The latter sent messengers to Baal-zebub, the god of Ekron, to inquire whether their master would recover from an injury sustained when he fell from an upper room. Prompted by God, Elijah met them on their way and sent word back to the king informing him that he would die. Ahaziah twice sent a captain with 50 men to capture Elijah, but each time they were consumed by fire from heaven. At Ahaziah's third try, the angel of the Lord told Elijah to go to Ahaziah and personally repeat that the king would " 'not come down from the bed to which you have gone up, but you shall surely die.' So [Ahaziah] died according to the word of the LORD" (vv 16–17).

The end of Elijah's career came at Jericho across the Jordan (2:1–12). There suddenly "chariots of fire and horses of fire separated the two of them. And Elijah went up by a whirlwind into heaven" (v 11).[1] Before his spectacular departure and at God's direction he had chosen Elisha—his associate and understudy—as his successor, .

Elisha is also a main character (1Ki 19:16, 19–21; 2Ki 2–9; 13:14–20). Still a young man when he was endowed with a double portion of Elijah's spirit at the latter's translation from this earth (2Ki 2), Elisha served as the Lord's prophet to five successors of Ahab, a period of some 50 years. Like his "father" and mentor, Elijah's successor gave evidence of his divine mission by prophesying through the Spirit of God (3:11–20). By the power of the same Spirit he also performed supernatural feats and wonders.[2] Most of them were done to vindicate himself as the Lord's anointed. In some instances, they resembled acts recorded about Elijah.

Elisha also directed the course of national and international events. At the beginning of his ministry, he carried out the divine directive, previously assigned to Elijah (1Ki 19:15), to confirm that Hazael would be king of Syria (2Ki 8:7–15) and Jehu as king of Israel (9:1–13). At another time he cured Naaman, a commander of the king of Syria, of his leprosy by ordering him to wash seven times in the Jordan (5:1–14).

Even after Elisha's death, his corpse gave evidence of the power that the Lord had granted him during his lifetime. For when his lifeless body came into contact with the mortal remains of a soldier thrown into the same grave, the latter was restored to life (13:20–21).

Narrative Development or Plot

The first two chapters of 1 Kings narrate David's sad final days and Solomon's succession. As noted above, the proposal that they form the conclusion to an original, discrete "History of the Succession" or the like, beginning at 2Sm 7,

Continued on p 338.

---

1   For Elijah's appearance together with Moses at the transfiguration of Jesus, see Mt 17:3.

2   E.g., 1Ki 2:14, 19–22; 4:1–7, 18–37, 38–41, 42–44; 6:1–7, 8–17, 18–20.

OUTLINE

A simplified outline of the books would divide them into three basic parts: (I) the history of Solomon, 1Ki 1–11; (II) the kings of Israel and Judah, 1Ki 12–2Ki 17; and (III) the last kings of Judah, 2Ki 18–25. The following outline provides more detail.

I. David's Reign Ends (1Ki 1:1–2:12)

    A. Solomon Established as King (1Ki 1)

    B. David's Final Advice to Solomon; His Death (1Ki 2:1–12)

II. Solomon's Reign (1Ki 2:13–11:43)

    A. Solomon's Early Reign and Wisdom (1Ki 2:13–4:34)

    B. Building the Temple and Palace (1Ki 5–7)

    C. Dedication of the Temple (1Ki 8:1–9:9)

    D. Further History of Solomon's Reign (1Ki 9:10–10:29)

    E. Solomon's Foreign Wives Turn His Heart from God (1Ki 11)

III. Division of the Kingdom of Israel (1Ki 12:1–24)

    A. Rehoboam Made King, Meets with Jeroboam and the Northern Tribes (1Ki 12:1–15)

    B. Northern Tribes Break from the House of David, Make Jeroboam Their King (1Ki 12:16–24)

IV. Jeroboam I Reigns in Israel (1Ki 12:25–14:20)

    A. Jeroboam's Building Activity and Religious Innovations (1Ki 12:25–33)

    B. Jeroboam, a Prophet, and Another Prophet (1Ki 13:1–32)

    C. Jeroboam's Evil Ways (1Ki 13:33–14:20)

V. Rehoboam, Abijah, and Asa Reign in Judah (1Ki 14:21–15:24)

VI. Nadab, Baasha, Elah, Zimri, and Omri Reign in Israel (1Ki 15:25–16:28)

is plausible. They read like a tale of typical intrigue. If Solomon believed that he was both God's and his father's choice as successor, he certainly acted decisively to help make it come true!

Although attempts are made to stimulate and vivify the senile David through the ministrations of youthful Abishag, the court is awash with intrigue. Adonijah, supported especially by Joab and Abiathar, attempts a *coup d'etat* and has himself sworn in at the spring of En-rogel, a short distance down the Kidron Valley. But his efforts are foiled by the counterplot of Nathan, Bathsheba, Zadok, and Benaiah, who support Solomon and install him at the spring Gihon, at the foot of ancient Jerusalem.

Solomon finds a "show of right" to eliminate all competition as soon as possible. He is only too happy to find reasons to carry out David's deathbed request to even old scores with Joab and Shimei. Adonijah makes a fatal request to marry Abishag, which was at least interpreted as a continuing claim on David's throne. Abiathar, the priest, alone of the principals opposing Solomon, escapes death, but is banished to Anathoth (also Jeremiah's home), thus fulfilling the ancient curse on the house of Eli (1Ki 2:27). Zadok replaces him. "The kingdom was established in the hand of Solomon" (2:46).

After rejoicing in the successes of Solomon and his God-given wisdom, the author notes Solomon's weaknesses and rebellions during his reign. He anticipates the coming trouble that breaks out when Solomon's son, Rehoboam, offends the northern tribal leaders, and his father's enemy, Jeroboam (11:26–40), leads a successful revolt that divides Israel. From that point onward, the book describes and judges the kings of Judah and Israel, culminating in the great theological statement of 2Ki 17, which explains God's reasons for sending Israel into exile. Before long, the sins of Judah lead to the Babylonian conquest and exile of Judah. Second Kings closes with a note of hope that the freeing of King Jehoiachin of Judah anticipates the restoration of the Davidic dynasty.

Resources

The author of Kings himself mentions many of his sources, and there is reason to think that others may have been used. In the first part, "the Book of the Acts of Solomon" is referred to in 1Ki 11:41, and thereafter we have repeated mention of "the Book of the Chronicles of the Kings of Israel" (17 times) and "the Book of the Chronicles of the Kings of Judah" (15 times). The Hebrew phrase translated "Chronicles" is the same as the title of the canonical book, but it is usually assumed that more official archives and annals are implied here than the material found in the heavily theological biblical book by that name. By those references, the author reminds his readers that he is not interested in any exhaustive history or biography, but only in what serves his theological purposes. If the reader is interested in more details, he is, in effect, advised to "go look it up in the library." (Would to God they were available to us as they were to the original readers.)

Besides the sources explicitly cited in the Hebrew text of Kings, the Septuagint attributes Solomon's great prayer at the consecration of the temple (1Ki 8:22–53) to a "Book of the Song." Some suggest that this is really the same "Book of Jashar" that is cited elsewhere (Jsh 10:13; 2Sm 1:18), since the spelling is very similar (a Hbr *yodh* could easily have fallen out; *yashar* becoming *shir*, "song").

Whatever the number or nature of the sources, the so-called Deuteronomic hand is very much in evidence throughout Kings, and in a manner similar to Judges (see pp 10–11). It shows itself in the overall framework, as well as in theological interpretation and commentary. The latter appears

Ancient rulers and scribes were interested in detailed records. In this example, Egyptian scribes are counting the hands of persons killed in battle by Rameses II.

both in short comments, such as those calling attention to the power and fulfillment of the prophetic Word, as well as longer sections (e.g., the concluding meditations on the fall of Israel in 2Ki 17 and of Judah in ch 25).

Text and Translations

As we noted at the beginning of Samuel, the Hebrew Bible had one book of "Kings" until the Reformation, while the Septuagint included Samuel in four books of "Kingdoms." Artificial and unoriginal though its separation from Samuel appears to be, the name Kings or Kingdoms is quite appropriate, for the books narrate the history of the kingdoms from David's last days until after the Babylonian exile. The internal subdivision of Kings (at the death of Ahab) appears to be as arbitrary as that at the end of 2 Samuel. We surmise that it was made mostly on the basis of equality of contents (22 chapters in 1Ki, 25 in 2Ki), probably determined by the space available on scrolls at some point in the history of transmission.

There are more than normal textual problems with Kings. The problems are more like the issues in Judges rather than Samuel. They do not so much arise out of corruptions in the transmission of the Hebrew text as from Septuagint variations from it. To complicate the matter further, the Septuagint manuscript traditions also differ from one another, and these differences may be based on Hebrew prototypes that are not currently available to us. (There are also variations at times in parallel passages in Chronicles.)

Sometimes the LXX text is shorter; other times it contains material not in the Masoretic Hebrew text. Two of the additions are noteworthy. After 1Ki 2:35 and 2:46 in the Septuagint we encounter the "Miscellanies," which do not correspond at all with the Masoretic text at this point. As the name indicates, it is a heterogeneous collection of data especially about Solomon's reign, and its insertion here strongly suggests that at some stage of Greek transmission, the book of "Kingdoms" was divided at this point. A longer addition appears after 1Ki 12:24, containing various traditions about the life and career of Jeroboam I. Some scholars argue that it represents a second and different edition of the story of Israel's division into Northern and Southern Kingdoms, but that is unlikely. Some of these additions appear elsewhere in the Masoretic text, dispersed throughout 1Ki 2–11.

Finally, some scholars argue that in Kings, as elsewhere, the "Vaticanus" and "Lucianic" traditions of the Septuagint are not independent translations of different Hebrew texts but represent rather successive revisions of the Septuagint to bring it into conformity with the Hebrew tradition represented by the Masoretic text.

DOCTRINAL CONTENT

Summary Commentary

1Ki 1:1–2:12 Opening the Book of Kings is the account of the last days of King David. Even before his death, a rivalry between two of his sons develops, as Adonijah prepares to take over the reign. The prophet Nathan shows proper reserve in approaching David, stating facts, and asking the king what his intentions are. When David learns of Adonijah's intentions, David declares that Solomon is to succeed him as king according to God's purposes. David rightly commends God's Word to Solomon as the basis of good judgment and leadership.

2:13–4:34 Though a man of peace, Solomon oversees the deaths of his political enemies. (Scripture does not absolutely approve of Solomon's motives in these cases but does affirm his right and responsibility to govern.) In return for Solomon's selfless request for wisdom, God blesses him

Pillars from King Solomon's great store house in Hazor.

not only with wisdom but also with riches and honor. His legendary wisdom is evident in (1) his dealing with the two prostitutes who claim to have given birth to the same living child, and (2) those he chooses as officials. The reign of Solomon was a fleeting golden time in Israel's history. The wealth he enjoyed was a gift from the gracious God.

Chs 5–7 Solomon, whose name means "peace," prepares international treaties with Hiram of Tyre in order to build the temple. It takes seven years to build the temple. Solomon's house takes almost twice as long to build (13 years), an ominous foreshadowing of Solomon's shifting priorities.

8:1–9:9 When the Levites bring the ark of the covenant to Jerusalem, the cloud filling the Lord's house is nothing less than God's awesome presence—His glory. In a lengthy prayer,

Solomon recalls how the Lord has graciously kept His promises to His people. Although God dwells in heaven, He has chosen to come and bless His people with His presence. The solemn dedication of the temple ends with the awesome sacrifice of thousands of animals and with a feast celebrated by the entire nation of Israel. God then appears to Solomon a second time to emphasize the promises and the demands of the covenant with David's house.

9:10–10:29 Hiram feels cheated in his agreement with Solomon, and the king's glorious building projects include forced labor. (The record of Solomon's acts are a mixture of faithful service to God and self-service.) The queen of Sheba's legendary visit to Jerusalem shows the widespread fame of Solomon's wisdom. Not only does God bless Solomon with great wisdom, but He also blesses him with a great reputation. His fabulous wealth matches his great wisdom; he "excelled all the kings of the earth in riches and in wisdom" (10:23).

Ch 11 The great tragedy of Solomon's reign is that, having married many foreign women and taken hundreds of concubines, he turns from the Lord to worship his wives' idols. The closing years of his reign are troubled as the Lord foretells the division of the kingdom and raises up adversaries to Solomon (e.g., Jeroboam).

12:1–24 Solomon's son Rehoboam foolishly alienates many of the people by laying on them a heavier burden of hard labor than his father had. Rehoboam's arrogance is a warning. His foolish and sinful attitude divides the kingdom, allowing Jeroboam to become king of the northern tribes.

The high place Jeroboam I established at Dan for worship of a golden calf. The metallic structure marks the likely position of the altar for burnt sacrifice. A set of steps (bottom left corner) allowed Jeroboam and his priests to carry the sacrifices up to the altar.

12:25–14:20 Jeroboam sets up rival worship. By making golden calves and temples for the practice of idolatrous religion, he leads the people into sin. A man of God from Judah confronts Jeroboam. Then an old prophet leads the man of God into sin! The prophet Ahijah foretells that Jeroboam's dynasty will come to an end. His reign marks the beginning of a line of northern kings who will continue to lead the people of Israel astray.

14:21–15:32 Idolatry marks Rehoboam's reign over Judah, even though he does not promote it as Jeroboam does in Israel. Rehoboam's son Abijam reigns for only three years, but it is long enough for him to follow in his father's sinful footsteps. King Asa breaks the pattern of wickedness and does what is "right in the eyes of the LORD" (15:11), though the idolatrous high places remain. Switching from Judah to Nadab's reign in the Northern Kingdom, we learn that Nadab, like all the other Israelite kings, does what is "evil in the sight of the LORD" (v 26).

15:33–16:28 Because of the evil of Israel's King Baasha, the Lord predicts that his house, like that of Jeroboam, will be cut off (16:3). After only two years as king, Baasha's son Elah is assassinated (while "drinking himself drunk," v 9). One of his military leaders, Zimri, seizes the throne, but he lasts only seven days as king before the troops conspire against him and make Omri the king. During Omri's reign in Israel civil war breaks out, with half the people following him and half following Tibni. Omri's forces are victorious, and Tibni dies.

16:29–17:24 The next chapters describe the confrontation between King Ahab and the prophet Elijah. Ahab, who marries Jezebel the Sidonian, becomes the most notorious of the long line of wicked kings (16:30). Having predicted a drought to Ahab, the great prophet Elijah goes to the brook Cherith, where the Lord has ravens miraculously provide for him. Through Elijah, the Lord also miraculously provides food for a widow in Zarephath. When the widow's son dies, Elijah raises him back to life by God's power.

Chs 18–19 The famous confrontation between Elijah and the prophets of Baal ends with God demonstrating that He is the only true God and with the execution of the false prophets. After the 3½-year drought, God sends rain when "[Elijah] prayed again" (Jas 5:18). Queen Jezebel seeks to kill Elijah. He flees into the wilderness to Mount Horeb, where centuries earlier, Moses had received the Ten Commandments. When Elijah is discouraged because he feels he is the only prophet left, the Lord comes to him in a "low whisper," encouraging him. Elijah returns to Israel and casts his cloak on Elisha, who will succeed him in God's work.

Ch 20 After describing Elijah's prophetic ministry, the sacred text returns to the history of King Ahab and his wars with Ben-hadad, king of Syria. Speaking through a prophet, the Lord tells Ahab that he will defeat the Syrian forces of Ben-hadad. The Lord allows the smaller Israelite force to crush many Syrians because the Syrian king, Ben-hadad, mocked God's omnipresent rule. Then the Lord's prophet uses a parable to show Ahab his guilt in releasing Ben-hadad, king of Syria.

21:1–22:40 When Naboth refuses to sell his vineyard to Ahab, Queen Jezebel schemes to charge Naboth with cursing God. Having been falsely accused, Naboth is stoned to death, and Ahab takes possession of the vineyard in violation of God's commandment (Ex 20:17). Elijah goes to meet Ahab while he is in Naboth's vineyard. There Elijah boldly prophesies the death of Ahab and his wife, Jezebel. Ahab shows repentance and humbles himself before God. Yet Ahab's false prophets encourage him to fight against the Syrian city of Ramoth-gilead. The Lord's prophet, Micaiah, does not give Ahab a favorable prediction about the war. For this, the king orders that Micaiah be imprisoned. Giving his royal robes to Jehoshaphat, Ahab disguises himself and goes into battle, where he is struck and killed by a "random" arrow.

22:41–2Ki 1:18 The inspired record briefly returns to the Southern Kingdom of Judah and the life and death of King Jehoshaphat, who, like his father Asa, does what is "right in the sight of the LORD" (22:43). It also records the two-year reign of Ahab's son Ahaziah. He and his troops show disdain for the Lord and His servant Elijah, and are condemned with fire and death.

Ch 2 When the Lord takes Elijah to heaven, He also bestows Elijah's office and authority on Elisha, his chief disciple. Through a series of miracles, the Lord removes all doubts about Elisha as Elijah's successor.

3:1–8:6 Through Elisha, the Lord delivers King Jehoram and Jehoshaphat. He delivers a widow from poverty and her sons from slavery. He also returns a kindness shown by a couple at Shunem, and miraculously provides for the sons of the prophets. The Syrian commander Naaman is convinced that the Lord can heal him of leprosy, according to the Lord's Word. Elisha's servant Gehazi pursues Naaman's riches, hoping for great wealth; then he lies to Elisha about what he has done. With a miracle of compassion through Elisha, the Lord delivers a son of the prophets from debt. The Lord settles a war between Syria and Israel through Elisha's leadership. When the Syrians impose a horrific and frustrating siege upon Samaria, Elisha boldly prophesies that the Lord will feed the people. Ironically, He works through helpless, outcast beggars to bring word to Samaria of His victory over Syria and to reveal the bounty of provisions left for the city.

8:7–29 Elisha prophesies the death of Ben-hadad, the rise of Hazael, and the destruction of Israel through Hazael. The gruesome passage records the particular means and persons God used for judging rebellious Israel and brutal Ben-hadad. Judah binds itself to sinful Israel through a marriage alliance when Ahaziah, king of Judah, marries into the family of Joram, king of

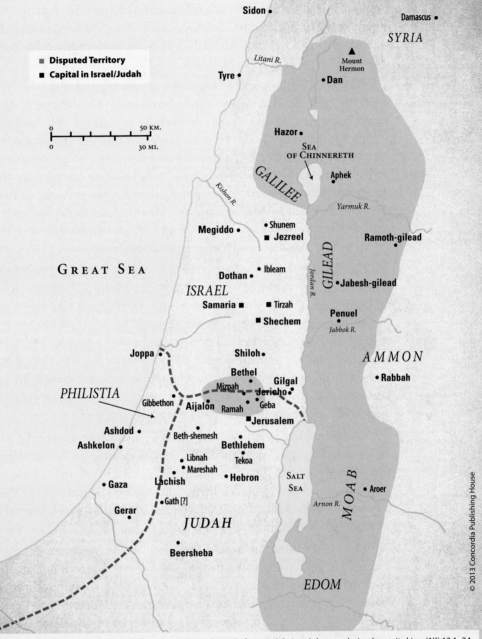

Disputed Territory
Capital in Israel/Judah

Sidon

Damascus

SYRIA

Litani R.

Mount Hermon

Tyre

Dan

0 ————— 50 KM.
0 ————— 30 MI.

Hazor

SEA OF CHINNERETH

Aphek

GALILEE

Kishon R.

Yarmuk R.

GILEAD

Megiddo

Shunem

Jezreel

Ramoth-gilead

GREAT SEA

Dothan

Ibleam

Jordan R.

Jabesh-gilead

ISRAEL

Samaria

Tirzah

Penuel

Shechem

Jabbok R.

Joppa

Shiloh

AMMON

Bethel

Rabbah

Mizpah

Gilgal

PHILISTIA

Jericho

Gibbethon

Aijalon

Ramah

Geba

Ashdod

Beth-shemesh

Jerusalem

Ashkelon

Bethlehem

Libnah

Tekoa

Mareshah

Hebron

SALT SEA

Aroer

Gaza

Lachish

MOAB

Gerar

Gath [?]

Arnon R.

JUDAH

Beersheba

EDOM

© 2013 Concordia Publishing House

Israel and Judah. Solomon's son Rehoboam caused Israel to split from Judah; Israel then made Jeroboam its king (1Ki 12:1–24; 2Ch 10:1–11:4). Jeroboam established Israel's capital first at Shechem (1Ki 12:25), but later apparently moved it to Tirzah (1Ki 14:17). Jerusalem remained the capital of Judah (1Ki 12:18). Periodic coups in Israel destroyed the dynasties of Jeroboam (1Ki 15:27–30), Baasha (1Ki 16:8–13), Zimri (1Ki 16:15–22), Omri (2Ki 9:14–10:14), and Jehu (2Ki 15:8–12). Omri moved Israel's capital to Samaria (1Ki 16:23–24); Jezreel apparently served as a secondary capital (1Ki 21:1). Moab, and then Edom and Libnah, rebelled against Judah (2Ki 3; 8:20–22). Control of territory east of the Jordan passed back and forth between Israel and Syria (2Ki 10:32–33; 13:14–25; 14:23–29). A chaotic succession of kings heralded the fall of Israel to Assyria in 722 BC (2Ki 15:8–17:23).

Israel. They fight alongside each other, and Ahaziah visits Joram when he is wounded. Marriage, mutual defense, and visiting the sick are usually noble acts, blessed by God. But Ahaziah uses them to strengthen his bond with evildoers.

Chs 9–10 Elisha sends a "son of the prophets" to anoint Jehu ruler over Israel, to fulfill God's promise of judgment against the dynasty of Ahab. The Lord's judgment against Ahab's household is fulfilled with vicious irony when Jehu shoots Joram and has his body cast into the vineyard of Naboth. Jehu executes and disdains the body of Jezebel, the wicked queen mother of Israel, bringing the earlier prophecy to absolute completion. Through deception, Jehu wipes out more potential rivals, the servants of Baal, who were closely allied with Ahab's dynasty. He continues to demonstrate his wit and taste for irony (cf 9:11, 34; 10:9, 19). Despite Jehu's excesses, the Lord grants him a long reign and a four-generation dynasty.

Chs 11–12 The bloody dynastic practices of pagan nations and of the Northern Kingdom of Israel erupt in Judah through Athaliah. Amid this vicious purge, the Lord preserves the house of David and the renewal of faithful worship by protecting Joash through his aunt Jehosheba. The Lord emboldens the priest Jehoiada, the Carites, and the guards to place David's heir, Joash, on his rightful throne. Jehoiada leads Joash to have a long and blessed reign. The temple receives much-needed attention from Jehoash, Jehoiada, and other faithful servants. Yet Joash, who began so well, comes to a sorrowful end because he departs from the Lord's way.

Ch 13 In dire threat from the Syrians, Jehoahaz is one of the few Israelite kings to seek the Lord's favor. But Jehoahaz walks in his forebears' ways and renews war with Judah, using the respite from Syria to multiply his sins. The end of Elisha's life signals lingering hope for the Israelites as the Lord's covenant people. But it also signals the loss of their last great prophet, whose service kept them connected to the Lord.

14:1–15:16 Amaziah serves the Lord, yet he overestimates his power and tries to gain influence in the kingdom of Israel, which defeats him. The Lord grants Israel an opportunity to reestablish its kingdom through Jeroboam II, as prophesied by Jonah. He shows remarkable patience for His rebellious people on the basis of His promises and compassion, proclaimed in Dt 32:1–43. Azariah prospers with God's blessing but also faces His judgment, as does Zechariah, ending Jehu's dynasty. Shallum, the conspirator, has a remarkably short reign. Divided loyalties in Israel lead to even greater brutality.

15:17–31 Assyria, the kingdom by which the Lord will eventually punish Israel with exile, now appears and takes tribute. Under such pressure, the Israelites once again conspire against their king, Pekahiah, and establish yet another vulnerable rule. Assyria begins to dismantle Israel during the reign of Pekah and carries away the first captives.

Megiddo of this era included a granary capable of holding 450 cubic meters of provisions, likely for the chariot horses stabled in the city.

15:32–16:20 King Jotham of Judah faces pressure from the kings of Syria and Israel, who tempt him to focus on human alliances and strength rather than on the Lord. After generations of relatively faithful rulers, Judah is led badly astray by Ahaz, who is cowed by the pressures from Israel, Syria, and Assyria. In savage irony, the wicked King Ahaz, who sacrifices his son to a false god, would receive the sign of Immanuel that announced the coming of the Son of God, our Savior (Is 7:10–25; 9:6–7; 11:1–9).

Ch 17 Hoshea, the last king of Israel, placates the Assyrians, conspires against them, and even resists them for three years. All of these strategies fail to save the kingdom. Settled in distant lands, the northern tribes are more or less lost to history (cf, however, the apocryphal book of Tobit). The Lord allows Israel to fall and go into exile as a warning to all generations of believers. Through a priest and teaching about the covenant, the Lord reaches out to the people settled in Israel since He had commanded Israel to deal graciously with sojourners and to teach them the faith and practices of the true God (cf Ex 12:19).

Chs 18–20 The Lord raises up Hezekiah to guide Judah through its most challenging moment, facing the great Assyrian Empire. When an Assyrian official shows disdain for Hezekiah, the people demonstrate their steady trust in their faithful king. Through Isaiah, the Lord comforts Hezekiah and promises to defeat the mocking Assyrians with a mere word. Placing Sennacherib's words before the Lord, Hezekiah asks the Lord to distinguish Himself from the idols of the nations.

Portion of the Canaanite era tunnel under Jerusalem, to which Hezekiah's workmen connected, directing the waters of the Gihon Spring into the city and out of reach of the Assyrians.

After the defeat of the Assyrians, Hezekiah grows ill. The Lord heeds Hezekiah's prayer and heals him. But Hezekiah responds by seeking alliance with the Babylonians, leading to prophecy about the downfall of Judah. Hezekiah callously welcomes this news since it will not happen during his life but during the lives of his descendants.

Ch 21 Ironically, faithful Hezekiah leaves his throne to the worst king in Judah's history, Manasseh, who had 55 years to thoroughly corrupt the people. During Manasseh's reign, the Lord determines to do away with the kingdom of Judah. He does not yet reveal how this will happen. King Amon rejects God's ways also and walks in the ways of evil King Manasseh, his father.

22:1–23:30 Through the faithful guidance of Hilkiah, the Lord instructs Josiah and raises up another faithful king for Judah. King Josiah, Shaphan, and Hilkiah organize the repairs of the temple, contracting faithful workers. Through the prophetess Huldah, the Lord confirms the message that King Josiah learned from the Book of the Law: the Lord would condemn Judah. However, the Lord also promises mercy to Josiah, in view of his repentance. With bitter detail, the writer describes Josiah's campaign to remove all elements of false worship from regions under his rule.

The great and memorable Passover celebrated under Josiah does not fundamentally change matters of faith in Judah. The Lord will sift the people through the Babylonian exile only 26 years later. King Josiah dies due to conflicts over the rising regional power of Babylon. Yet, the Lord fulfills His Word to Josiah by gathering him to the tombs of the kings of Judah.

23:31–24:20 In three short months, Jehoahaz is able to restore false worship in Judah and so overturn his father's reform. The Lord arranges regional politics against Jehoiakim and Judah, determined to avenge the evils committed by Judah's kings. In the surrender of Jehoiachin, the Lord allows the dismantling of the temple David had planned and Solomon had built. He remains repulsed by Judah's evils, rejecting even the vassal rule of Zedekiah.

Ch 25 After Judah's third rebellion, the Babylonians enforce sterner policies, killing off all manner of community leadership and ending Judah's status as a kingdom and a holy land. Despite all that has happened, the Lord provides for the preservation of the "house of David" (cf 2Sm 7:12–17) when former King Jehoiachin is released from prison and his family line is preserved (2Ki 25:27–30).

Specific Law Themes

A major element of the Books of Kings is their constant reference to the precedent for righteousness set by King David. Rulers are compared with him and assessed as good or evil based on their faithfulness to the covenant and especially its teachings about idolatry. Second Kings 17 summarizes this theology and explains that the disobedience of the kings and their people was the cause of their downfall. In contrast, it describes at times how the Lord rewarded and cared for those who pursued righteousness.

Specific Gospel Themes

The Books of Kings illustrate how the Lord established David's household through Solomon's line, from which would come the Messiah's everlasting kingdom. It promised that the Lord's mercies were delivered through the temple services. The final chapter, which describes the freedom of King Jehoiachin, anticipates the restoration of God's people under a future Davidic king. This was later fulfilled in the birth of Jesus, who was titled the Son of David.

Specific Doctrines

The writer for the Books of Kings demonstrated a special, religious viewpoint that is often labeled Deuteronomic. He made no effort to examine matters "objectively" from every possible angle as is sometimes the goal in modern historiography. (As the reader considers this viewpoint, it is proper to remember that all history is selective.) His goal was to understand the history of Israel in view of God's covenant described in the Law of Moses.

There is also an emphasis on wisdom in the Books of Kings. Solomon's interest in wisdom (1Ki 4:29) connects with an international phenomenon, thriving at this time especially in Egypt. The term *wisdom* does not quite mean what the Western ear hears in it. It was often a court phenomenon, concerned with training in statecraft, diplomacy, and the like. On that count, the introduction of formal wisdom to Israel under Solomon certainly rings true.

The Temple

The temple had both vertical (natural) and horizontal (historical) meaning, whereas pagan counterparts were only vertical. The temple was indeed a miniature, a reflection, a microcosm of the heavenly temple (ultimately the universe). What was done at the temple was, as it were, also done in heaven. The uniquely biblical accent is on the horizontal connection with the history of salvation: God temporarily and "incarnationally" takes up residence with His chosen people. He will guide them, together with all of nature and history, toward the temple not made with hands, the new Jerusalem that the New Testament calls the "new heavens and a new earth in which righteousness dwells" (2Pt 3:13; this is the goal of all of history). Both these vertical and horizontal typologies come together also in Christ. Much of the theological significance of the temple is given classical expression in Solomon's great prayer at its dedication (1Ki 8:22–53), which is better called a consecration. It is couched in classical covenant (Deuteronomic) language and thought. A key element in Kings is its rejection of idolatry, yet theologians have noted Solomon's use of images in the temple (1Ki 7:36). Images are presented as useful and acceptable when not applied to idolatrous purposes.

In Old Testament theology, as in the piety and religion of Israel viewed more historically, the importance of the temple can scarcely be exaggerated. It overlaps to a large extent with theologies (and typologies) of the holy city (Jerusalem-Zion) and of the holy land. In fact, a picture of concentric circles is helpful: from His real presence in the Most Holy Place, God's holiness "radiates" outward into all the world; from there, as from His heavenly throne, He judges and rules all that is, with His conquest of the entire world looking toward the final fulfillment of His eternal reign.

It is especially important to emphasize the intimate interconnection of the temple-Zion complex with Davidic-Messianic themes and types. For all practical purposes, David and the Messiah cannot be discussed apart from the temple and Zion, any more than Christ can be considered apart from His body, the Church.

In contrast with David, an important negative example arises in the person of Jeroboam. He instituted an idolatrous form of worship in order to maintain political control over his people. The sins of Jeroboam are mentioned repeatedly (e.g., 1Ki 14:16; 15:30; 16:31; 2Ki 10:29–31; 13:2, 11;

14:24; 15:9, 18, 24, 28) and became proverbial for the writer. Later theologians characterized these sins as self-willed rites and works that arise when people depart from the Scripture as the standard of doctrine and practice.

The Prophets and the Kings

Beginning with 1Ki 17, the biblical writer turns his attention to Elijah, the advance guard of the great prophetic movement that a century later would also produce many biblical books. Not only is this major prophetic figure a northerner, but he also hails from Tishbe in Gilead across the Jordan, more isolated from the syncretism and internationalism of the centers of power. Elijah's major target is Ahab (874–853 BC), and even more so, his Sidonian wife, Jezebel, who as a fanatical devotee of Melqart, the Tyrian Baal, symbolized all that Elijah opposed. Later theologians wrote of Baal worship as a synonym for false worship that led people astray.

Nowhere is the infinite gulf between the two worlds of Israel and Canaan, Yahweh and Baal, better illustrated than in the famous story of Naboth's vineyard (1Ki 21:1–16), which stands as an object lesson for the dangers of coveting, which can only lead to further sins. Two fundamentally different conceptions of kingship are illustrated: the absolutist, "god-man" concept of paganism self-evident to Jezebel, versus the elected, but responsible, incorporation of the promises of God championed by Elijah (and obviously known to Ahab). Also different concepts of "land" are exhibited: Yahweh was the real owner of all land, and it was only lent to His elect people. Real estate was part of the covenant relationship, of the inheritance, the blessings of the promise.

The great historical and theological significance of Elijah must be underscored. To no little extent he can be characterized as embodying the very spirit of prophecy. Much as Samuel had done some two centuries earlier, he sparks a major revival of genuine Yahwism at a time when the fires were burning very low—and one that would continue and grow into the great prophetic movement beginning with Amos a century later.

Especially noteworthy is the way Elijah is implicitly presented as a second Moses, personifying the "back to Moses" character of the entire prophetic revival. (The most striking expression of the parallelism, of course, is Yahweh's theophany to Elijah on Mount Sinai in 1Ki 19, probably at the very spot where He had allowed Moses to see only His back; cf Ex 3.) Thus Elijah personifies messianic expectation (Mal 4:5, and the Gospels). Together with Moses, he witnesses to the fulfillment of both their ministries in Christ on the Mount of Transfiguration (Mt 17:1–13).

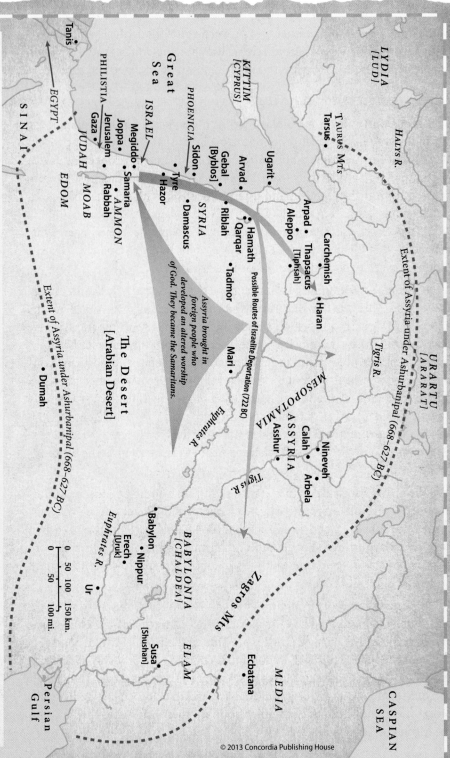

Assyrian Exile of Israel. Assyria was the largest empire since the Old Babylonian dominance of Sumer and Akkad before Abraham. It deported people from Galilee and east of
the Jordan as early as 733 BC and crushed Syria in 732 BC. God permitted Assyria to destroy
idolatrous Israel in 722 BC; Israelites were deported and assimilated into upper Mesopotamia (2Ki 15:8–17:23). Assyria resettled other peoples into Israel (2Ki 17:24–41). Assyria

menaced the entire Near East, at times exacting tribute from the Phoenician cities, Judah,
Edom, Moab, and Ammon, and crushing Israel and Philistia. Assyria checked the power of
Egypt and even incorporated Egypt into its empire for a time. Borders fluctuated with the
power of the kings. Ashurbanipal held a great area, yet Assyria fell to Babylon about 25
years after his death.

LYDIA
[LUD]

HALYS R.

TAURUS MTS

Tarsus •

KITTIM
[CYPRUS]

Carchemish •

Arpad • Thapsacus
Aleppo •   [Tiphsah]

• Haran

URARTU
[ARARAT]

Extent of Assyria under Ashurbanipal (668–627 BC)

Tigris R.

CASPIAN
SEA

Tanis •

EGYPT

Great
Sea

Ugarit •

PHOENICIA
Sidon •
Gebal
[Byblos] •

Arvad •

Hamath
• Qarqar

Riblah •

• Tadmor

Possible Routes of Israelite Deportation (722 BC)

Mari •

Euphrates R.

MESOPOTAMIA

ASSYRIA
Asshur •

Calah •
Nineveh •

• Arbela

Tigris R.

MEDIA

Assyria brought in
foreign people who
developed an altered worship
of God. They became the Samaritans.

SINAI

ISRAEL

Megiddo •
Joppa • Samaria •
Jerusalem •
Gaza •
PHILISTIA

• Tyre
• Hazor

SYRIA
• Damascus

JUDAH

MOAB

AMMON
Rabbah •

EDOM

The Desert
[Arabian Desert]

Extent of Assyria under Ashurbanipal (668–627 BC)

• Dumah

Euphrates R.

Babylon •
Erech
[Uruk] •

Nippur •

BABYLONIA
[CHALDEA]

Zagros Mts

Ur •

Susa
[Shushan] •

ELAM

Echatana •

Persian
Gulf

0   50   100   150 km.
0   50   100 mi.

© 2013 Concordia Publishing House

The stories of Elijah's successor, Elisha, are especially focused on miracles. Among them is Elisha's God-given ability to see the spiritual realities that exist in everyday life. Through Elisha's vision, we learn about the multitude of angels—horses and chariots of fire—that surround and aid God's servants in the struggle against seemingly impossible odds (2Ki 6:15–17).

Second Kings 17 brings us to the end of the Northern Kingdom, after one too many flirtations with Egypt's vain promises. Just as would be true later of Judah, Israel's final years were wracked by conflict between pro-Egyptian and anti-Egyptian factions. The chapter describes the application to Israel of the ruthless Assyrian imperial policy of shuffling populations to break further resistance, and the subsequent rise of the Samaritans. Primarily, though, the writer seizes the occasion for a religious meditation on the theological principles illustrated in the catastrophe. All along, the writer keeps reminding his readers that God had spared Judah because of his promise to David.

Second Kings 25:27–30 closes on the upbeat notice that after Nebuchadnezzar's death, his successor, Evil-merodach ("A devotee of Marduk") elevated King Jehoiachin from ordinary detention to a sort of preferential house arrest (c 561). In the light of the book's constant accent on God's mercy to Judah on account of His promises to David, God's necessary judg-

Assyrian palace walls record the defeat of Lachish and the harsh exile of the Judean people.

ment on His people can only be read as saying that the messianic promise continues.

Application

1Ki 1:1–2:12 The conclusion of David's great reign and epic life reminds us of the mortality of all people, for all are sinners and must die. Yet through the Messiah—great David's greater Son—we have hope and confidence beyond this life to the glories of heaven. Sin and greed lead to dissension—that has not changed. How ugly to witness family rivalry over an inheritance (cf Lk 12:13–15), which is precisely the matter here, especially addressed by the Ninth Commandment. When stakes are high, we may feel the urgency to rob others of their decisions. However, God would have us honor the calling of others by assisting them with facts and good counsel as Nathan does here for David. The Word of His prophets is ever ready to counsel and encourage us in the way of peace, indeed, in the way of life everlasting. David's dying example of concern for his son Solomon, and the kingdom over which he would reign, encourages us in Christlike love and service to our families and others. In His death, Christ supplied fully what we need for our life and peaceable service in His kingdom.

2:13–4:34 God wants us to respect the earthly government under which we live, recognizing that we serve a higher King and are citizens of an everlasting kingdom. Because of our human limitations, we are unable to perfectly fulfill the challenges we face. True wisdom consists of far more than acquiring facts and information. Rather, it is godly wisdom to declare our sinfulness and need for a Savior, and to see in Jesus the One who meets all our needs. The Lord supplies us with able companions for serving our nation and His kingdom. We are priceless to Him, and our names are recorded in the Book of Life through Jesus' work on our behalf.

Chs 5–7 The Lord calls us to live in peace and to trade with others, even those who do not share our faith. Such peaceful relations are a blessing. The Lord also calls us to show concern for the house of worship in which we gather. It is, after all, a reflection of our devotion to the Lord, His Word, and His work. Too often, we neglect the things of God in favor of personal interests. Though the Lord would not have us ignore our home and comforts, He bids us to use all we have for the glory of His name, dedicating ourselves and all to the Architect of heaven. Solomon's magnificent temple with its furnishings, especially those relating to the sacrificial system, pointed to the coming Savior, whose sacrifice, forgiveness, life, and eternal salvation have become ours. Thanks be to God!

8:1–9:9 God's presence reminds us of our unworthiness before Him. God recognizes our weakness; in Solomon's words, "there is no one who does not sin" (8:46). God also mercifully hears our prayers for help, comes to us, and delivers us by His great power and love. We therefore dedicate ourselves so that our hearts may "be wholly true to the LORD our God" (8:61) and that we may share the Good News of Jesus "that all the peoples of the earth may know" the Lord (8:60). For He has forgiven and renewed us by grace.

9:10–10:29 We often complain about not having enough of this world's goods, yet God daily and richly forgives us and continues to shower material blessings upon us. How great is His undeserved goodness! Our lives, too, are a record of sin along with our attempts to serve the Lord. That is why we daily need renewal at the cross of Jesus, in whom we are a new creation, dedicated to godly service. Such is His great love toward us in Christ—becoming poor, that we might be rich.

Ch 11 The tragic fall of Solomon is a warning to believers throughout all ages. If someone so wise and good as Solomon can turn from the Lord, how easily the same thing can happen to us! With a deep sense of humility, we say, "There but for the grace of God go I." Thanks be to God that He blesses us with faithful spouses and dear families hallowed by His grace.

12:1–24 When we shut our minds and hearts to the advice of others—and especially to God's inspired Word—we invite disaster. The Lord of history uses examples such as Rehoboam to work repentance in us. Our greatest asset in life's struggle is God's Word for wisdom, forgiveness, and renewal in Christ.

12:25–14:20 We need to be aware of the subtle giving of our hearts to the idols of false religions, materialism, pleasure, and self-centeredness. The Lord turns us away from these traps and leads us to the worship of the true God, our Savior. The Lord who calls us to faith must likewise keep us in the faith, which He does through daily repentance in conjunction with His Word and Sacrament (Means of Grace). This sacred history relates God's patience with His people, whom He planned to save by the righteous reign of His Son, Jesus Christ.

14:21–15:32 The example that parents set greatly influences their children. Our example for the next generation influences whether they will walk "in all the sins" of their forefathers or whether their hearts will be "wholly true to the LORD" (15:3). Yet the Bible does not teach fatalism. Despite the sins of one generation, the Lord can raise up the next in the right way. Take heart! The Lord intercedes in history. He intercedes in our lives by His gracious Word.

15:33–16:28 How easily sinful human beings slip into gross wickedness and debauchery! Instead of indulging our sinful nature, the Lord cultivates in us "the fruit of the Spirit" (Gal 5:22–23). Such fruit grows within a heart made right through faith in Jesus. But God's grace to families and households persists, even for us. The great King of heaven confirms us as members of His household.

16:29–17:24 Once people reject God's Word, anything goes, as the lives of Ahab and Jezebel attest. Yet by His grace, God can call people from the deepest shadow of darkness to repentance and salvation. In a wicked, harsh, and hostile world, God watches over those who are His. No matter how much everything may seem to be against us, the Lord is with us, a haven of everlasting love. Already in Old Testament stories such as this, we see God's power over death, the height of which is Christ's glorious resurrection from the dead. For us and for our salvation, He has conquered sin, Satan, and death, opening the gates to everlasting life in heaven.

Ivory furniture decoration depicting a sphinx or a cherub. Found in King Ahab's ivory palace.

Chs 18–19 God's protection for Elijah and Obadiah is a comfort to Christians, lest we think that God will allow the wicked to destroy us. No matter how entrenched and powerful the forces of evil are in the world, God is still guiding history for the good of His people, for their everlasting salvation. How powerful is the prayer of a righteous person! We can be sure that the Lord will always be with us, patiently blessing us with His love, mercy, and grace. God's voice speaks to us in the quietness of the inspired pages of Scripture, by which He encourages us with the forgiveness, life, and salvation in Jesus, the Word made flesh. As God raises up Elisha to follow in Elijah's footsteps, so He is now raising up faithful servants of the Gospel to minister to this generation and the next.

Ch 20 The Lord teaches us how He punishes the godless and protects those who call on His name. While the Bible records battles and wars, behind it all, God is still in control for the sake of His people. His merciful goodness is infinite for the sake of His children, whom He protects. Beware of mocking the Almighty, either by insult or by lack of faith in His good and gracious rule. How marvelously our Lord's word continues to instruct us in repentance and in faith, through the Gospel of His kingdom. His gracious rule delivers us from evil.

21:1–22:40 We are constantly tempted to get what we want at the expense of others. Instead of taking from others, Jesus gave Himself for us. In sacrificing His life for the sins of the world, He gave us the priceless treasure of life and salvation. Thanks be to God, His Word does not end with the Law but includes the precious Gospel as a key to forgiveness and heaven. Many false prophets today would mislead us and rob us of the treasures of God's Word. The Holy Spirit gives us insight through the Word to see through all falsehood.

1Ki 22:41–2Ki 1:18 Amid the many examples of godlessness and tragedy, God's Word contains bright examples of those who followed Him. Though 1 Kings ends on a tragic note, we have seen that alongside God's Law and judgment runs His message of the Gospel and forgiveness. The Lord would have us treat His servants with proper respect, pray for them, and hear His Word from them. In this sinful world, God's Word is rare and precious, preserving our lives and delivering us from all condemnation.

Ch 2 The burning desire to serve God and His people through faithful leadership is proper (cf 1 Tm 3:1). If you set your heart on such noble service, walk and talk with the Lord's servants to learn from them His Word and wisdom, by which the Lord will prepare you for your calling. The heavenly Father will send His Spirit to embolden and uplift you, through Jesus, His Son. Though miracles may not follow you (as with Elisha), you have God's miraculous Word in the pages of Holy Scripture by which the Lord will bless you with the comfort of salvation and equip you for every good work.

3:1–8:6 Do not equate poor planning with faith. For all your endeavors, seek God's blessing through prayer and make your plans through the wisdom of His Word. The Lord cares about your finances, your freedom, and every aspect of your life. Plan well for the future, seek His guidance, and turn to Him with your requests. The Lord often provides temporal rewards to His people, acknowledging their faith and kindness. When you seek the Lord in prayer, pour out your heart to Him. Bow before Him and make your petitions known. The Lord has made His heart known for you in the life, death, and resurrection of His only-begotten Son, our Savior. He cleanses us by water and the Word, for His Word gives life and salvation. When you suffer, you will be tempted to blame the Lord or the Church for evil that you witness. May God strengthen you to resist temptation and to call on the

Lord, seek consolation, and find direction in God's prophetic Word, which does not fail. The Suffering Servant, Jesus, knows the depth of your trials. He will bear your sins and griefs as your beloved Savior.

8:7–29 Elisha's tears illustrate the pain of God's heart over the sins and condemnation of His rebellious people. How difficult to apply God's Law when our hearts and God's heart long to show compassion! This text shows the seriousness of sin and its ravages against sinners. When temptation confronts you, do not test the Lord's patience by making peace with wickedness or ungodly relationships but pray that He would guide you through the Word into wholesome relationships. His Word is a lamp for your feet and enlightenment for life everlasting in Christ.

Chs 9–10 Fulfill your calling diligently in the Lord's name, no matter how others may dismiss it or jeer at you. God will fulfill His purpose for you and bless you with the strength for dedicated service. He puts to death and gives life; to us who believe, He gives life everlasting in Christ. Not a letter of His Word shall fail! Pray for your leaders, that they may be not only successful but also just and righteous. Your just and righteous leader, the King of heaven, will hear your pleas and answer according to His good purposes and according to the mercies of Jesus.

Chs 11–12 As an aunt or uncle, commend your nieces and nephews to the Lord's care by looking out for their welfare, praying for them, and turning them over to the security of the Lord's house. The Lord, who Himself studied, learned, and grew as a child, will strengthen and support you in this loving work, even as He forgives your weaknesses and covers your sins. By the Word of His house, the Lord will instruct you in faith, life, and the way of salvation.

Ch 13 God's mercy is abused most when used as an opportunity to do evil. God's favor is ever available, especially for those who sincerely repent of their sins (which Jehoahaz failed to do). The repentant will not have a savior like the Assyrians but will have the true Savior, Christ Jesus, who bears away our sins and establishes an eternal homeland for us.

As the Lord has mercy on you, exercise mercy and kindness toward others. His mercy is the dearest treasure of His great and gracious reign, by which He grants forgiveness for your sins.

14:1–15:16 Faith is not a guarantee of success. Pride leads to downfall. Enact your plans with reflection on God's Word, with prayer, and with wisdom from God. If members of your family have wandered from the faith they professed before the Church, do not stop praying for them or proclaim-

Solomon's Temple

960–587 BC

The temple of Solomon, located adjacent to the king's palace, functioned as God's royal palace and Israel's national center of worship. By its symbolism, the sanctuary taught the rule of the Lord over the whole creation and His special headship over Israel.

The floor plan is a type that has a long history in Semitic religion, particularly among the West Semites. An early example of the tripartite division into *'ulam*, *hekal*, and *debir* (portico, main hall, and inner sanctuary) has been found at Syrian Elba (c 2300 BC) and, much later but more contemporaneous with Solomon, at Tell Ta'yinat in the Orontes basin (c 900 BC). Like Solomon's, the latter temple has three divisions, contains two columns supporting the entrance, and is located adjacent to the royal palace.

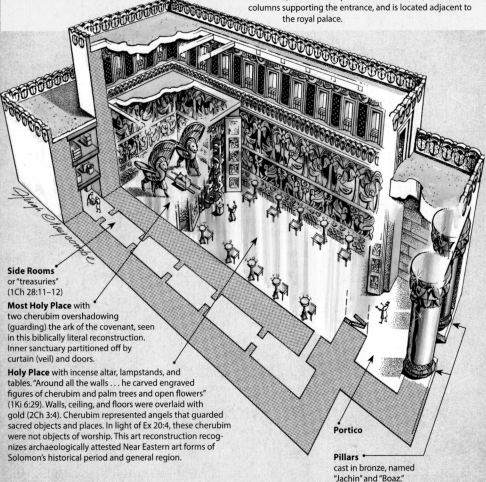

Side Rooms or "treasuries" (1Ch 28:11–12)

Most Holy Place with two cherubim overshadowing (guarding) the ark of the covenant, seen in this biblically literal reconstruction. Inner sanctuary partitioned off by curtain (veil) and doors.

Holy Place with incense altar, lampstands, and tables. "Around all the walls . . . he carved engraved figures of cherubim and palm trees and open flowers" (1Ki 6:29). Walls, ceiling, and floors were overlaid with gold (2Ch 3:4). Cherubim represented angels that guarded sacred objects and places. In light of Ex 20:4, these cherubim were not objects of worship. This art reconstruction recognizes archaeologically attested Near Eastern art forms of Solomon's historical period and general region.

Portico

Pillars cast in bronze, named "Jachin" and "Boaz."

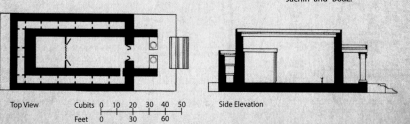

Top View

Side Elevation

| Cubits | 0 | 10 | 20 | 30 | 40 | 50 |
| Feet | 0 | | 30 | | 60 | |

Art Forms of Solomon's Period

Complete biblical descriptions of Solomon's temple are presented in 1Ki 6; 7:13–51; 8:1–20; 1Ch 28–29; 2Ch 3–5.

Did Solomon's temple look like this?
This art only depicts how Solomon's artists might have expressed themselves within their vision and times. The temple was destroyed in 587 BC by the Babylonians, and not one decorative stone has been found. Yet the word pictures of Scripture cannot be rejected. Though inadequate to the task, this selection of artifacts from Solomon's time period provided the artist with, at best, acceptable illustration copy. For example, a small carved ivory from Arslan Tash, Syria became the model for the large cherubim that guarded the ark; costume decor was followed in detail, but the wings were changed, rolling forward and outward to match the sculptured cherubim of the Most Holy Place (2Ch 3:10).

Artifacts (from the floor up) **A.** Ribbonlike design found at the 'Ain Dara temple may have symbolized the endless roll of seasons and years. **B.** Seedpod design from a column base at Tell Ta'yinat. **C.** Lampstand modeled on artifacts from Megiddo and Hazor. **D.** Winged guardian and sacred tree, Nimrud ivories. **E.** Lotus blossoms, Egyptian theme. **F.** Winged guardian, Arslan Tash. **G.** Stylized palm tree featuring heart of new growth, new life, Samaria. **H.** Frieze of palm trees, Arslan Tash. **I.** Window sash and railing styles, Nimrud ivories.

Gold overlaid the floor (1Ki 6:30) and the beams, thresholds, walls, and doors (2Ch 3:7). This sounds extravagant, yet not within its time. Inscriptions of Assyrian kings exclaim, "I covered the walls of [my] temple so it shone like the sun"; another king claims to have applied gold "like plaster, slapping it on." In recent times, sheets of gold were discovered all over large objects in the tomb of King Tutankhamun. Solomon had trade monopolies and also may have benefited from a "gold rush." Lavish gold for the house of God! It was the ancient norm.

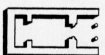

Tell Ta'Yinat Temple. Syria

Solomon's Temple. Jerusalem (Side rooms omitted) 960–587 BC

'Ain Dara Temple. Syria (Side rooms omitted)

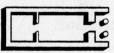

Were Solomon and his temple a myth?
Archaeologists have now found temple foundations that bear strong architectural parallels to Solomon's as described in the Bible, notably at Tell Ta'yinat, discovered in 1936, and at 'Ain Dara, excavated between 1980 and 1985, both in northern Syria. They share what is known as the "long room plan." Since Solomon relied on the architects of King Hiram of Tyre, his temple is indeed an expression of the Syrian long room style and anchors itself in that region and period of history.

ing the Word to them. Rejoice in your freedom to gather with the saints for prayer and to receive the Word and the Sacraments, the greatest treasures. Take your frustrations to the Lord in prayer. His counsel will deliver you from the heat of anger and calm your troubled spirit.

15:17–31 God's people should not put off repentance. Instead, learn to lead your children and grandchildren in a life of repentance, based on God's Law and promised mercy in Christ. When times are difficult, you may feel tempted to turn on those close to you, but that will only bring further despair. Instead, turn to the Lord in prayer, requesting peace and unity through the Gospel, which unites God's people through Baptism in His name and communion in His Supper. Through the Word of Christ, God sets us free.

15:32–16:20 God, of course, is not opposed to alliances, friendships, or trust between His subjects. Indeed, He calls us to faithfulness in such relationships. Yet, He places the greatest importance on trust in His salvation. He is our greatest ally against misplaced faith and false saviors. At all times—even the worst of times—the Lord has us and our salvation on His heart.

Ch 17 All human efforts to hold on to God's blessings and promises—embodied here in the Promised Land—are doomed to fail. Israel received God's call and blessings by grace through faith, which is the only way we receive God's blessings still today. Through the Assyrian exile, the Lord erased the heritage of rebellious Israel. Also, the enduring heritage of the Old Testament passed from Judah, through Jesus, the Son of David, to all people who would receive the promises and blessings of God by grace. The New Testament warns us to guard our doctrine and life lest we fall away from the Lord. God calls us to teach His Word faithfully to each generation, emphasizing His Law (by which the Lord leads us to daily repentance) and His promises of the covenant in Christ (by which He grants us everlasting salvation). He would have us deal kindly and patiently with sojourners and guests among us, proclaiming to them God's Law and Gospel, by which the Lord consecrates for Himself a people.

Chs 18–20 Like Hezekiah, you are to trust and serve the one true God without compromise, presenting a positive testimony of His grace. Be assured: the Lord always leads His people and can raise up faithful leaders for them. Pray for your leaders, entrusting them to Jesus Christ, the Good Shepherd. Have confidence in God's Word, though scoffers and critics may despise it. The Lord performs what He promises and works salvation for all who trust in Him. Call on the Lord, as He invites you to do, and trust,

Hezekiah built this massive wall in Jerusalem to protect against invading Assyrians.

like faithful Hezekiah, that the Lord indeed hears and answers for His mercy's sake, which He has revealed to us in Christ.

Ch 21 Make parenthood and family among your highest priorities, by which you may serve not only this generation, but generations to come. Rather than test God's patience, make daily repentance part of your life. For such repentance to be faithful and not just routine, cling to the teachings of God's Word, which shows you your sins and the ways of God's heritage. Pray for your leaders and look for legitimate ways to condemn their errors (e.g., fair elections; peaceful protest) in order to establish justice in your land. Your just and gracious Ruler in heaven oversees all things. He will bless and keep you according to the grace of His beloved Son.

22:1–23:30 God's people cannot overestimate the value of faithful teachers and counselors for their youth. Do not withhold the teachings of God's Word from the young but teach them right and wrong, truth distinguished from falsehood, during their earliest years. The Lord will not fail to bless those who deal honestly. He deals honestly with us in calling us to repentance and in setting all things right by the faithful service of His beloved Son. Sincere repentance is never in vain, even if someone continues to experience hardship after turning to the Lord. Rather, it is the loving work of God's Holy Spirit through His Word, and His works avail for our salvation. Set your heart to serve the Lord and pray for His help to make changes peaceably. In all circumstances, the God of peace will sustain you for good works. Best of all, He has accomplished your salvation through His beloved Son. When faithful people meet a tragic end, such as soldiers or officers who fall in the line of duty, do not assume that they or their families are being punished by the Lord or that He has forsaken them. Instead, honor the noble who fall too soon in your eyes, offering thanks to God for their noble service. Jesus, too, met an early end (to our notions), but His death was purposefully timed by God for our salvation.

23:31–24:20 How easy to destroy and corrupt! How hard to set things right again! Sins, even when forgiven, continue to bear consequences in our lives. As you consider your life in view of God's Word, consider also the lives and futures of those against whom you sin and ask the Lord for mercy, not only for yourself, but also for those affected by your sins. The Lord does not cast off His people forever but calls them to repent. Ever present in His Word and Sacraments, He administers to us the full blessings of forgiveness.

Ch 25 The holy kingdom of God abides forever because its King, our God and Savior, cannot be overthrown. With God's counsel, adjust to the disappointments you face and make different plans for the future. Most of all, repent of your failures and confess your shortcomings. Your Lord yet has great blessings in mind for you, which He grants in Christ.

CANONICITY

The second century BC Jewish teacher, Jesus son of Sirach, drew upon the Books of Kings for his assessment of famous kings and prophets in Israel (Ecclus 47–49). Scribes at Qumran also valued the texts of Kings. As noted earlier, Rabbinic Judaism attributed the Books of Kings to the prophet Jeremiah (see p 325). New Testament writers frequently referred to the books, illustrating their authority: Mt 12:42 (1Ki 10); Lk 4:25–27 (1Ki 17; 2Ki 7:3; 5:1–14); Ac 7:47 (1Ki 6); Rm 11:2–4 (1Ki 19); Jas 5:17–18 (1Ki 17:1; 18:41–45). Christians received the books into their canon without question.

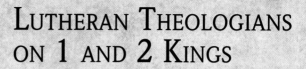

LUTHERAN THEOLOGIANS ON 1 AND 2 KINGS

Luther

"Elijah had killed the 800 prophets with great courage (1 Kings 19:1–3), and no one's power was so great that he feared it; but when Jezebel threatened him, he is struck with such fear that he flees. Before this he was not afraid of the king; now he runs away from a woman.

"Accordingly, all this seems to be foolish; but it shows great understanding and is very helpful, because it is recorded for the comfort of the churches, in order that we may know how merciful God is. We may indeed be evil and weak, provided that we are not found among those who persecute, hate, and blaspheme God. God wants to have patience with our weakness.

"I am neither able nor willing to excuse the fathers, as others do. Indeed, I am glad to hear about the failings and the weaknesses of the saints. But I do not praise these failings and weaknesses as good deeds or virtues. . . . Nor are these things recorded for the sake of the hard, the proud, and the obstinate. No, they are recorded in order that the nature of the kingdom of Christ may be pointed out. In His small flock He has poor and weak consciences that are easily hurt and are not easily comforted. He is a King of the strong and the weak alike; He hates the proud and declares war on the strong." (AE 5:25–26)

Gerhard

"*The two Books of Kings* are called by the Hebrews *melakim* ['Kings']; the Greeks and Latins [call them] 3 and 4 Kings because they reckon 1 and 2 Samuel as Books of Kings also. Various prophets wrote the history of the kings, but we cannot know and define for certain who gathered that [history] into a single volume and compendium. Many attribute it to Ezra.

"Procopius of Gaza, Rabbi Kimchi, and Isidore say that Jeremiah gathered this work into a single volume because the last chapter of the Books of Kings agrees in style, words, and story with the last chapter of the Book of Jeremiah. It appears, however, that this volume was gathered by abridging parts of the books of the days of the kings of Judah and Israel and the writings of the prophets Nathan, Ahijah of Shiloh, Iddo the Seer, and Shemaiah, Hozai,[3] Jehu, and Isaiah, which were quoted quite frequently in 3 and 4 Kings.

"Augustine explains that both are to be numbered with the prophetic books (*De civ. Dei*, bk. 17, c. 1)." (ThC E1 § 129)

Elijah fresco.

---

3   The Vulgate at 2 Chron. 33:19 takes the Hebrew word *chozay*, often translated as "Seers," as a proper noun.

QUESTIONS PEOPLE ASK ABOUT KINGS

The Slaughter of Baal's Prophets

After Elijah's victory over the prophets of Baal at Mount Carmel, he told the people: "Seize the prophets of Baal; let not one of them escape" (1Ki 18:40). The sacred narrative continues: "And they seized them. And Elijah brought them down to the brook Kishon and slaughtered them there." This slaughter of the false prophets has been called murder. Some people have asked whether the practice of persecuting heretics and putting them to death is not here given biblical warrant.

While pondering these questions, we must remember that the ceremonial and civil laws of Moses had not yet been withdrawn. Whereas in New Testament times they were repealed by God Himself, at the time of Elijah and King Ahab they were binding on all Israelites. This law contained some stern provisions for dealing with idolaters. Deuteronomy 13:13–16 and 17:2–5 prescribed the punishment for those who worshiped false gods. The law likewise contained severe legislation against false prophets who would seduce Israel to practice idolatry, the penalty being death (Dt 13:1–5). When the prophets of Baal were executed, they suffered the punishment which the God-given law of Israel had fixed. There was at this time no religious liberty in Israel; the form of government was theocratic, God Himself being the Ruler, the king His governor, and the law of Moses the constitution.

It ought to be clear that this incident does not give anyone the right in our day to persecute people who are of a different faith. When the New Testament dispensation came, the old ceremonial and civil law that God had given through Moses was set aside, as Paul so gloriously declares in his Epistle to the Galatians (see esp Gal 3:24–25 and 5:1). By no means would it be in keeping with the will of God if we today were to proceed against false teachers and prophets with fire and sword. This is apparent from the stern rebuke that Jesus meted out to James and John when they wanted to call down fire from heaven on the Samaritan village that had refused to receive Jesus and His disciples (Lk 9:51–56). The theocracy ceased long ago; there is no lon-

Baal the storm god, covered in gold and silver. The shield and spear are missing.

ger any nation that can be called God's people in the same sense as Israel was in Old Testament times. Now God's children, constituting the spiritual Israel, are found in all parts of the world. It would be wrong to invoke the old Mosaic legislation to guide us in our attitude toward false prophets. That God abhors idolatry and every corruption of His teaching is something that these passages tell us even today, but their direction to put to death those who worship false gods and teach such worship was intended only for the days of the Old Covenant.

Finally, to the question whether Elijah did not transcend the limits of his authority and resort to mob law when he told the people to seize the prophets of Baal, we reply that he was the special ambassador of God and that, since the civil authorities did not enforce the constitution and stop the heinous transgression of the divine law of which these prophets were guilty, as God's messenger he had to intervene and himself carry out the divine will.

The Lying Spirit Sent by God

A passage that arouses discussion in Bible classes is 1Ki 22:19–40, where the sacred historian relates how a lying spirit had entered the prophets of King Ahab, persuading him to proceed against the Syrians, a campaign in which he lost his life. How must we look upon the statement of v 23: "Now therefore behold, the LORD has put a lying spirit in the mouth of all these your prophets"? How can we make this statement, which comes from a prophet of God, agree with the biblical teaching that God is truthful and holy in every respect? A little study will show that there is nothing in this story incompatible with the attributes of our great God.

Micaiah communicates the following facts to Ahab and Jehoshaphat: (1) The counsel of the prophets urging Ahab to proceed to battle was not from God, but from the devil, the enemy of humanity. (2) Ahab's destruction, however, was determined by the Lord, and the campaign against the Syrians was to have a disastrous outcome for the king of Israel. (3) God was using the devil in this instance to accomplish His design, the punishment and downfall of Ahab, who was one of the most wicked kings that disgraced the throne of the ten tribes. We have here a familiar method of God, employing the agencies of evil to punish what is evil. To put it differently, God permitted the devil in this instance to work the harm that he is always intent on accomplishing, but from which he usually is kept by the mighty hand of the Ruler of the universe. There are but few, if any, Bible stories that more vividly portray Satan's constant eagerness to inflict injury and the manner in which God employs the forces of darkness to punish the evildoers.

Destructive Miracles

What should one think about miracles that were done for the very purpose of destroying people's lives, bringing grief and woe to many households? Such an act was performed when Elijah twice let fire fall from heaven and each time a captain and fifty men were consumed (2Ki 1:9–12). We may here think, too, of the death of Pharaoh and his host in the sea when they were pursuing the Israelites (Ex 14:26–31). A few words will be sufficient. When the soldiers described in 2 Kings were killed, God meted out punishment to the wicked rulers whom they served. Whether all, or at least most of them, were themselves ungodly, we do not know, neither need we assume that they were. Many a good Christian soldier has perished on the field of battle; his body suffered, but his soul was saved.

Furthermore, in the case of the two captains, just as in that of Pharaoh, God showed that He will not be mocked. If people think they can oppose the Almighty and openly defy Him, His wrath may quickly manifest itself in their destruction. And finally, the rebuke of Jesus administered to James and John—when they, after the manner of Elijah, wished to call down fire upon the Samaritan village that had refused to give lodging to the little band (Lk 9:52–56)—must not be looked upon as implying a criticism of the action of Elijah. The two cases were entirely different. To mention but one point, for Elijah the fire furnished protection from persecution; James and John, however, wished to avenge an insult offered to their Master and themselves. The rebuke of Jesus indicated that they did not have the right motives in their zeal. We have an illustration here of the famous saying: if two do the same thing, it is not the same (*Si duo idem faciunt, non est idem*). What Elijah did was right. The same act, when attempted by the disciples of Jesus, was wrong, the situation being altogether different.

Contents of the Ark of the Covenant

First Kings 8:9 asserts: "There was nothing in the ark except the two tablets of stone that Moses put there at Horeb, where the LORD made a covenant with the people of Israel, when they came out of the land of Egypt."

Hebrews 9:4 affirms: "the ark of the covenant covered on all sides with gold, in which was a golden urn holding the manna, and Aaron's staff that budded, and the tablets of the covenant."

The contents of the ark of the covenant have aroused a good deal of discussion. The matter of dispute is this: in the one passage the ark is said to have contained the pot of manna and Aaron's rod; in the other it is asserted that they were not in the ark. Apparently a contradiction! And yet, how easily this knot is untied!

We must ask whether the same time is referred to in each case, and the solution is at once evident. The writer of Hebrews makes a general statement referring to events during the lifetimes of Moses and Aaron, from which it is clear that originally, and perhaps for a long period of time, the articles mentioned were kept in the ark. The passage of Kings relates to one particular point of time, namely, the occasion when the ark was placed into the Most Holy Place of Solomon's temple hundreds of years later. By this time the pot of manna and Aaron's rod had been removed—a circumstance not surprising when one considers the many vicissitudes the ark passed through after it had been constructed in the wilderness.

Artist's depiction of the ark of the covenant.

Solomon's Polygamy

We are told in 1Ki 11:3 that King Solomon had a large harem of wives and concubines. Is not marriage to be a union between two persons only? In discussing the case of this wise king, we must remember how emphatically the Bible points to the universality of sin, making only one exception, namely, that of our Savior Jesus Christ. Solomon, with all his piety and wisdom, was a fallible human being, whom we cannot follow in everything he did. It is very true that marriage was instituted to be a union between one man and one woman, a truth confirmed in the New Testament when Jesus says: "the two shall become one flesh" (Mt 19:5), and when Paul, in enumerating qualities that a bishop or pastor must possess, includes the monogamous relationship: "the husband of one wife" (1Tm 3:2).

Many of the saints of the Old Testament disregarded this truth because they were ignorant of it. Surrounded by peoples who practiced polygamy, they gradually lost sight of the teaching of God on this point. The Lord permitted them to continue in this error (cf Ac 17:30), though by the account of the institution of marriage which He gave through Moses (Gn 2:18–24) and through a passage like Dt 17:17 He plainly indicated that polygamy does not have His sanction. God could have interposed some more special legislation, but He refrained.

If any say that the course of the Lord in this case is offensive to them, they have great need of examining their own hearts and conduct and of considering how many things in their own lives God mercifully overlooks—errors, weaknesses, imperfections. It is extremely difficult to overcome the downward pull of one's environment or to rise above the level of the world about us. "Do not be conformed to this world," states a divine law binding for people in all periods of history (Rm 12:2). But how hard a task it is! While condemning polygamy and frankly acknowledging that the saints who practiced it committed a sin, though they did it unwittingly, let us praise the long-suffering of God, who forgives even those errors of which we are not aware and cleanses us from secret faults (Ps 19:12).

Did Asa Remove the High Places?

First Kings 15:14 reads: "But the high places were not taken away. Nevertheless, the heart of Asa was wholly true to the LORD all his days."

Second Chronicles 14:3–4 records: "He took away the foreign altars and the high places and broke down the pillars and cut down the Asherim and commanded Judah to seek the LORD, the God of their fathers, and to keep the law and the commandment."

First of all, it must be understood that a "high place" may refer to a hill where sacrifice was offered, such as Gibeon (1Ki 3:4), or to an elevated structure upon which a sacrifice was offered (cf 2Ch 14:5). The latter are easily removed but one cannot so easily remove a hill or prevent someone from returning to it as a place of sacrifice.

Asa removed many high places and pagan images, according to 2 Chronicles. But total eradication of pagan sacrifice was not achieved, as we see from 1Ki 15:14. Both statements, then, are true. Asa removed the tools of pagan sacrifice, and yet when his reign was ended, an observer could say that, generally speaking, the places of sacrifice were still in favor with the people.

War Between Asa and Baasha

First Kings 15:16 narrates: "And there was war between Asa and Baasha king of Israel all their days."

Second Chronicles 14:5–6 declares: "He [Asa] also took out of all the cities of Judah the high places and the incense altars. And the kingdom had rest under him. He built fortified cities in Judah, for the land had rest. He had no war in those years, for the LORD gave him peace."

The first passage says that there was war between Asa and Baasha, king of Israel, all their days. The second declares that under Asa the land had rest and that he had no war in those years because the Lord had given him rest. The apparent discrepancy between these two passages will disappear if we bear in mind that 1Ki 15:16 need not be understood as saying that Asa and Baasha were campaigning against each other as long as they occupied thrones contemporaneously. The meaning may simply be that there was a feeling of hostility, of bitter enmity, existing between them all the time, an enmity that ultimately resulted in actual warfare. Second Chronicles 16:1 relates that Baasha made an expedition against Judah in the thirty-sixth year of the reign of Asa, a date that will be explained in the following section. Asa had been king about 16 years and Baasha about 12 years when this campaign was inaugurated. It is the only instance of an actual clash of arms between the two kings that is related in the Scriptures. Besides, it will help us to understand the situation if we note that 2Ch 14:6 says that "he had no war in those years," that is, just at the time when he was building walled cities he was not compelled to fight enemies coming against him from the outside. Baasha, it is true, was his rival and enemy also during the years of comparative rest and quiet, but he did not engage in actual warfare against him. The above considerations will completely reconcile the two Bible passages quoted.

When Did Elah Begin to Reign?

First Kings 16:6, 8 states: "And Baasha slept with his fathers and was buried at Tirzah, and Elah his son reigned in his place. . . . In the twenty-sixth year of Asa king of Judah, Elah the son of Baasha began to reign over Israel in Tirzah, and he reigned two years."

Second Chronicles 16:1 says: "In the thirty-sixth year of the reign of Asa, Baasha king of Israel went up against Judah and built Ramah, that he might permit no one to go out or come in to Asa king of Judah."

The text from the Book of Kings says that Baasha died in the twenty-sixth year of Asa. According to the text from Chronicles, Baasha was still alive in the thirty-sixth year of the reign of Asa. The suggestion of Karl F. Keil seems to propose a satisfactory solution. He says in his commentary: "Most commentators and chronologists, and the best of them, regard the thirty-fifth year (and thirty-sixth year) as referring not to the commencement of Asa's reign, but to the separation of the kingdoms. In this case it would coincide with the fifteenth year of Asa's reign, and the war would thus have broken out in the sixteenth, when Baasha was still alive."

Continued on p 374.

KINGS AND PROPHETS OF JUDAH AND ISRAEL

The kingdoms of Judah and Israel began as one kingdom under the rule of Saul (1048–1009 BC). They were divided briefly when David reigned in Hebron (1009–1002 BC) and Saul's son Ish-bosheth (1009–1008 BC) reigned in Mahanaim. Some years after Ish-bosheth was murdered by rivals, David became ruler of all Israel from Jerusalem; he subdued Israel's traditional enemies (1002–970 BC). David's son Solomon succeeded him and further expanded the kingdom (970–931 BC). But Solomon's son Rehoboam did not manage the kingdom well, and it split into Judah and Israel (also called Ephraim in the Old Testament). The chart below presents an overview of the kings of Judah and Israel along with the prophets who served in these kingdoms. (Overlapping dates within a kingdom indicate co-regencies; see shaded areas. Prophets whose names appear in italic have written books of Scripture. Pious kings who introduced reforms are marked with an asterisk.)

Prophets of Judah	Kings of Judah	Reigns in Judah (BC)		Reigns in Israel (BC)	Kings of Israel	Prophets of Israel
Shemaiah	Rehoboam	931–914	10th century BC	931–910	Jeroboam	Ahijah
	Abijam	914–911				
Azariah Hanani Jehu	Asa*	911–870		910–909	Nadab	
				909–887	Baasha	
				886–885	Elah	
				885	Zimri	
				885–880	Tibni	
				885–874	Omri	
Jahaziel Eliezer	Jehoshaphat*	873–848	9th century BC	874–853	Ahab	Elijah Micaiah
				853–852	Ahaziah	Elisha
Obadiah	Jehoram	853–841		852–841	J(eh)oram	
	Ahaziah	841				
Priest Jehoiada	Athaliah	841–835		841–814	Jehu	
Zechariah Joel	Joash*	835–796		814–796	Jehoahaz	

Prophets of Judah	Kings of Judah	Reigns in Judah (BC)		Reigns in Israel (BC)	Kings of Israel	Prophets of Israel
	Amaziah	796–767	8th century BC	798–782	Jehoash	*Jonah*
	Azariah (Uzziah)	792–740		793–753	Jeroboam II	*Amos*
Isaiah						
Micah	Jotham	750–735		753	Zechariah	
				752	Shallum	
				752–742	Menahem	
				742–732	Pekah	
	Ahaz	735–715		742–740	Pekahiah	Oded
				732–722	Hoshea	*Hosea*
Nahum	Hezekiah*	715–686		722	Fall of Samaria	
	Manasseh	696–642	7th century BC	The Assyrians deported people from Galilee and Transjordan as early as 733 BC. They crushed Syria in 732 BC. God permitted Assyria finally to destroy idolatrous Israel in 722 BC. Much of the Israelite population was deported and assimilated into upper Mesopotamia (2Ki 15:8–17:23). Assyria resettled other peoples in Israel (2Ki 17:24–41).		
Habakkuk	Amon	642–640				
Zephaniah Huldah *Jeremiah*	Josiah*	640–609				
	Jehoahaz	609				
Daniel	Jehoiakim	609–598				
Ezekiel	Jehoiachin	598–597	6th century BC	Nebuchadnezzar became king of Babylon in 605 BC. He deported Jehoiachin of Judah and others in 597 BC (2Ki 24:8–17; 2Ch 36:9–10). More deportations occurred in 587 BC after Jerusalem was destroyed (2Ki 25:1–25; 2Ch 36:11–21). Other Judeans escaped to Egypt after further unrest (2Ki 25:22–26), which resulted in a further deportation c 582 BC. The Judeans lived in refugee colonies in the vicinity of Babylon and were not assimilated. In 539 BC, Cyrus of Persia triumphed over the Babylonians. In 538 BC, he approved the return of the Judeans to their homeland.		
	Zedekiah	597–587				
	Fall of Jerusalem	587				
	Restoration	537 BC				

Though the division of the united kingdom was a momentous occasion in the history of Israel, the date when it occurred is not the usual basis in computing the chronological data of the kings who reigned during the divided kingdom. Another solution of the difficulty therefore has been suggested. It proposes to assume that a copyist misread the number 36 for 16 in 2Ch 16:1 and the number 35 for 15 in 2Ch 15:19. Reducing these dates by 20 years would restore harmony to the sequence of the recorded events. See also the section "When did Hoshea Ascend the Throne?" (p 376).

Cessation of Syrian Hostilities against Israel

Second Kings 6:23 reports: "So he prepared for them a great feast, and when they had eaten and drunk, he sent them away, and they went to their master. And the Syrians did not come again on raids into the land of Israel."

Second Kings 6:24 states: "Afterward Ben-hadad king of Syria mustered his entire army and went up and besieged Samaria."

Common sense as well as fairness compel us to assume that any discrepancy here can be only an apparent one. Verse 23, saying that the Syrian raiders "did not come again" into the land of Israel, might be paraphrased, "The Syrians ceased to come into the land of Israel." The supernatural aid afforded the Israelites so frightened the Syrians that they stopped their incursions into the territory of their neighbors to the south. But this cessation of attacks was only temporary. After some time the courage of the Syrians and their lust for booty revived. Benhadad, their king, headed a strong expedition, carrying terror and destruction into the territory of the 10 tribes. The expression, "Syrians did not come again on raids into the land of Israel," simply has a relative sense—"no more" in this connection being equivalent to "no more for the time being." In our everyday speech we frequently use this expression in the same sense. We decline invitations to partake of some more food at the table of a friend by saying, "No more, thank you," which does not mean we will never eat again.

Age of Ahazaiah at His Coronation

Second Kings 8:26 records: "Two and twenty years old was Ahaziah when he began to reign; and he reigned one year in Jerusalem. And his mother's name was Athaliah, the daughter of Omri king of Israel." (KJV)

Second Chronicles 22:2 reads: "Forty and two years old was Ahaziah when he began to reign, and he reigned one year in Jerusalem. His mother's name also was Athaliah the daughter of Omri." (KJV)

Disagreement between these two texts in some translations seems to be undeniable. In all probability 2Ch 22:2 contains a copyist's error. The Hebrew characters for 42 are not strikingly different from those for 22, and it is not a far-fetched assumption that a scribe, in copying the Chronicles, through an oversight wrote 42 instead of 22. Similarly a copyist's error would explain the discrepancy between two ages given for Johoiachin's accession to the throne at 18 (2Ki 24:8) and at 8 (2Ch 36:9–10).

Note that in each case the decade number varies (42 and 22; 18 and 8). If the number notations in the time of Ezra and Nehemiah consisted of horizontal or vertical strokes, or if the manuscript to be copied was blurred or smudged, the copyist could miss one or more of the decade notations.

Length of Jotham's Reign

Second Kings 15:30 affirms: "Then Hoshea the son of Elah made a conspiracy against Pekah the son of Remaliah and struck him down and put him to death and reigned in his place, in the twentieth year of Jotham the son of Uzziah."

Second Kings 15:33 asserts: "He [Jotham] was twenty-five years old when he began to reign, and he reigned sixteen years in Jerusalem."

The difficulty in these verses, following one another with but two intervening verses, is apparent. How could Hoshea, king of Israel, ascend the throne in the twentieth year of Jotham, king of Judah, when the latter reigned only 16 years?

The problem is solved by positing a co-regency for Jotham with his father Azariah, also called Uzziah. Adding the 10 years, during which the son shared the throne with his father, to Jotham's sole reign of 16 years, the event recorded in v 30 could have occurred during his total regency of 26 years. That such a co-regency actually occurred in this instance is confirmed by v 5, which states: "And the LORD touched the king, so that he was a leper to the day of his death, and he lived in a separate house. And Jotham the king's son was over the household, governing the people of the land."

Some propose joint rules of other royal fathers and sons, though no mention is made of their co-regency. This approach commends itself for the simple reason that it enables one to mesh the various chronological data in First and Second Kings.

When Did Hoshea Ascend the Throne?

Second Kings 15:30 reports: "Then Hoshea the son of Elah made a conspiracy against Pekah the son of Remaliah and struck him down and put him to death and reigned in his place, in the twentieth year of Jotham the son of Uzziah."

Second Kings 17:1 reads: "In the twelfth year of Ahaz king of Judah, Hoshea the son of Elah began to reign in Samaria over Israel, and he reigned nine years."

The two numbers given for the beginning of the Israelite Hoshea's reign are synchronized with dates during the rule of two kings of Judah. These questions arise: Did Hoshea begin to reign in the twentieth year of Jotham and/or in the twelfth year of his son and successor Ahaz? Can these dates be harmonized? The difficulty can be solved in part if both kings of Judah are credited with a co-regency.

Accordingly if Jotham shared the throne with his predecessor for 10 years and then ruled for 18 more years as sole regent, a total of 28 years, then Hoshea of Judah could indeed have begun his reign "in the twentieth year of Jotham the son of Uzziah."

The "twelfth year of Ahaz," the other king of Judah, on the other hand, is at odds with this date. It does, however, agree with it if it is assumed that a scribe misread the number 2 for 12. For more on this issue, see Steinmann's *From Abraham to Paul: A Biblical Chronology* (St. Louis: Concordia, 2011).

Egyptian sundial.

The Shadow on the Sundial of Ahaz

When Hezekiah was ill, God heard his prayer for deliverance from what seemed to be certain death and graciously gave him a sign to strengthen his faith in the divine promise that his health would be restored. The episode is related twice in the Scriptures (2Ki 20:8–11 and Is 38:7–8). The sign that God granted the king was a very marvelous one indeed. The shadow indicating the procession of the hours on the sundial that Ahaz had made, instead of moving ahead in its course, was to retreat 10 steps (degrees), thus defying, as it were, natural law and giving evidence of the intervention of the mighty Creator. The sign occurred just as predicted. It has been conjectured that the sundial was near the sickroom of King Hezekiah and was situated so that it could be viewed from there and that hence the king with his own eyes observed the miracle that the Lord worked on his behalf.

What was the nature of the sign that God performed on this occasion? The account in 2 Kings, which is the more detailed one, tells us that the Lord brought the shadow (on the sundial) 10 degrees backward. The precise construction of the sundial is not known to us. It may have consisted of a large pillar or obelisk, throwing its shadow on a huge dial, divided into degrees, or steps (the Hebrew word for degrees, translated literally, signifies steps). As the king and his servants watched the sundial on this particular day, they saw the shadow that marked the time going in the wrong direction. The writer does not say that this was due to the movement of a heavenly body (sun or earth). He furnishes no explanation. His account makes it possible to assume that the miracle was confined to what happened on the sundial, God's almighty power making the shadow move in a direction opposite to the usual one.

In the account of Isaiah, however, the statement is found: "So the sun turned back on the dial the ten steps by which it had declined" (38:8). The sun according to appearances went back 10 degrees. Whether this was done at the usual rate or in shorter time is not stated. Many scholars hold that Isaiah is not referring to a miracle happening in the firmament, but to a miraculous event that occurred on the sundial. The prominence that is given to the dial and the shadow and the degrees in the account strongly supports this view. Since there is no mention of a lengthening of the day, this seems preferable to the view that understands Isaiah to say that the sun reversed its course and shone longer than usually.

What is important is that we do not deviate from the intended sense of the narrative as far as this can be determined. That God could have made the sun according to appearances move eastward instead of westward is as certain to the believing Christian as anything can be. If this were the sense of the inspired account, we should not hesitate a minute to accept it as true. But in all candor we have to say that the meaning of the holy writers seems to be that the gracious sign that God granted Hezekiah consisted in a miraculous happening on the sundial of Ahaz. After all, to make the shadow travel contrary to the laws of light was as much an exhibition of omnipotence as would have been a mandate bringing about the retrogression of the sun in its course in the firmament.

FURTHER STUDY

Lay/Bible Class Resources

Auld, A. Graeme. *I & II Kings*. The Daily Study Bible Series. Louisville: Westminster John Knox, 1986. ♪ Simple treatment with some good insights; based on the RSV translation.

Dunker, Gary. *1 and 2 Kings: God the Promise Keeper*. GWFT. St. Louis: Concordia, 2010. ♪ Lutheran devotional author. Eleven-session Bible study, including leader's notes and discussion questions.

Life by His Word. St. Louis: Concordia, 2009. ♪ More than 1,500 reproducible one-page Bible studies covering each chapter of the canonical Scriptures. Page references to *The Lutheran Study Bible*. CD-Rom and downloadable.

Loy, David, and Erik Rottmann. *1 and 2 Kings*. Leaders Guide and Enrichment Magazine/Study Guide. LL. St. Louis: Concordia, 2013. ♪ In-depth, nine-session Bible study with individual, small group, and lecture portions.

Wiseman, Donald J. *1 & 2 Kings*. TOTC. Downers Grove, IL: InterVarsity Press, 1993. ♪ Semi-conservative, solid scholarship, not overly technical or deep but focused on historical background. Compact commentary that consults other translations.

Wolfgramm, Arno J. *Kings*. PBC. St. Louis: Concordia, 1994. ♪ Lutheran author. Excellent for Bible classes. Based on the NIV translation.

Church Worker Resources

House, Paul R. *1, 2 Kings*. NAC. Nashville: Holman Reference, 1995. ♪ Basically conservative, comfortably in between a popular and more scholarly treatment; good insights.

Inrig, Gary. *I & II Kings*. Holman Old Testament Commentary. Nashville: Broadman & Holman, 2003. ♪ Fairly conservative. More focused on giving ideas to preachers and teachers.

Leithart, Peter. *1 & 2 Kings*. Brazos Theological Commentary on the Bible. Grand Rapids: Brazos Press, 2006. ♪ A uniquely theological approach to the book that does not strive for verse by verse commentary. Written from an ecumenical, creedal perspective.

Patterson, Richard D. and Austel, Hermann J. *1, 2 Kings*. The Expositor's Bible Commentary. Grand Rapids: Zondervan, 1988. ♪ Not overly deep or technical; basically conservative, with helpful insights. Based on the NIV.

Provan, Iain W. *1 and 2 Kings*. New International Biblical Commentary. Peabody, MA: Hendrickson, 1995. ♪ Semi-conservative, ranging between very simple and very deep, technical.

Walsh, Jerome and Robert L. Cohen. *1 and 2 Kings*. 2 Vols. Berit Olam. Collegeville, MN: Liturgical Press, 1996, 2000. ♪ These volumes focus on the canonical form of the text as received rather than speculation on sources. Very helpful reading of the text in its historical as well as narrative contexts.

Academic Resources

Bähr, Karl Chr., W. F. *First and Second Books of Kings*. LCHS. New York: Charles Scribner's Sons, 1890. ♫ A helpful older example of German biblical scholarship, based on the Hebrew text, which provides references to significant commentaries from the Reformation era forward.

Brueggemann, Walter. *1 & 2 Kings*. Smyth & Helwys Bible Commentary. Macon, GA: Smyth & Helwys, 2000. ♫ A higher-critical commentary that provides unusual insights and an interesting way of explaining and applying the biblical text. Many brief excursuses.

Cogan, Mordechai. *1 Kings*. Vol. 10 of AB. New York: Doubleday, 2001. ♫ Standard higher critical work. A more in-depth treatment.

DeVries, Simon J. *1 Kings*. WBC. Dallas: Word, 1985. ♫ More technical and in-depth treatment (especially with regard to translation and text-critical matters). Semi-conservative.

Fretheim, Terence E. *First and Second Kings*. Westminster Bible Companion. Louisville: Westminster John Knox, 1999. ♫ Higher critical, but not aggressively so, with a summarizing, briefer treatment of passages. Some interesting excursuses.

Fritz, Volkmar. *1 & 2 Kings*. A Continental Commentary. Translated by Anselm Hagedorn. Minneapolis: Fortress, 2003. ♫ Higher critical, not overly technical or deep. Some good insights.

Gray, John. *I & II Kings*. OTL. Philadelphia: Westminster, 1963. ♫ Well-informed on Canaanite influences of the period. Critical. Strong on archaeology and comparative religions.

Hobbs, T. R. *2 Kings*. WBC. Dallas: Word, 1985. ♫ A strong literary and theological commentary.

K&D. *Biblical Commentaries on the Old Testament: The Books of the Kings*. Grand Rapids: Eerdmans, 1971 reprint. ♫ This century-and-a-half old work from Lutheran scholars should not be overlooked. Despite its age, it remains a most useful commentary on the Hebrew text.

Montgomery, James A. *A Critical and Exegetical Commentary on the Books of Kings*. ICC. Edinburgh: T&T Clark, 1951. ♫ The historical data is handled well. A strong example of text-critical scholarship.

Seow, Choon-Leong. *The First and Second Books of Kings*. The New Interpreter's Bible, Vol. 3. Nashville: Abingdon, 1999. ♫ Higher critical, more of a summarizing treatment, with some good insights.

Thiele, Edwin R. *The Mysterious Numbers of the Hebrew Kings*. 3rd ed. Grand Rapids: Zondervan, 1984. ♫ A special study on the chronological issues raised by the references to the reigns of the kings.

1 AND 2 CHRONICLES

Yours is the kingdom, O Lord

The books preceding Chronicles present a continuous historical progression from creation and the age of the patriarchs to the formation of the chosen people (Gn–Dt), from Israel's occupation of the Promised Land to the turbulent period of the judges (Jsh–Ru), and from David's and Solomon's days of glory to the fall of Jerusalem and the Babylonian captivity (Sm–Ki).

Surprisingly, the two Books of Chronicles traverse the same millennia as Genesis to Kings. The story begins again with Adam and ends at a point only a quarter-century after the last event in 2 Kings: the liberation of Jehoiachin, king of Judah, from a Babylonian prison in 562 BC (2Ki 25:29). Second Chronicles 36:22–23 adds that when the Persian king Cyrus became the new world ruler in 538 BC, he issued a decree of general amnesty, permitting the exiles to return to their homeland. Although a list of people who dwelt "again in their possessions in their cities" appears in 1Ch 9, and a list of the royal descendants of David in 1Ch 3, no postexilic events are mentioned in Chronicles.

Our English title, "Chronicles," is a fairly accurate rendition of the Hebrew title, which literally says "[The book of] the words/events of the days/times past" (Hbr *[Sepher] dibhre hayammim*). The antiquity of the Masoretic title cannot be ascertained, but

Armies from Africa and broader Asia would clash on Israel's fruitful plains. Israel's failure to follow the Lord made their homeland a minor kingdom, subject to the nations.

OVERVIEW

Author
Unknown, likely a Levite

Date
Written c 430 BC

Places
Jerusalem; Gibeon; Mount Gilboa; Hebron; Ammon; Syria; Zion

People
Saul; David; Solomon; Joab; Nathan; Uzzah; Asaph; Zadok; Levites; the exiles

Purpose
To chronicle for the exiles the rule of David's house and the appointed services of the Levites as a record of how God's people "keep faith"

Law Themes
Breaking faith; exile; failure to follow God's Word; seek the Lord

Gospel Themes
God's blessings and rule through David; the Lord's rule through David's house; God with His servant; atonement at the tabernacle

Memory Verses
A royal throne forever (1Ch 22:9–10); Levites as prophets (1Ch 25:1); my God is with you (1Ch 28:20); David's doxology and prayer (1Ch 29:11, 16–17); the eyes of the Lord (2Ch 16:9); Jehoshaphat's battle plan (2Ch 20:20–22)

TIMELINE

516 BC	Second temple completed
445 BC	Walls of Jerusalem restored
c 430 BC	Chronicles written
334–323 BC	Conquests of Alexander the Great
167 BC	Maccabean revolt

381

it could be as old as a similar title found among the sources it cites. For example, 1Ch 27:24 mentions the "chronicles" of King David (cf 1Ch 29:29; 2Ch 12:15; 20:34; 33:18–19; many more examples in 1–2Ki). The title may have been used for the book from the time it was written.

Cyrus, King of Persia.

Historical and Cultural Setting

As noted above, Chronicles provides a grand historical overview from the dawn of creation to the promised re-creation of Israel from the dust of the Assyrian and Babylonian conquests. For an overview of these conquering empires, see pp 321–22. The immediate context for the compilation and composition of Chronicles is the Persian Empire, which began in c 550 BC when Cyrus the Great overpowered the Medians and incorporated them into his kingdom. The combined power of Medo-Persia allowed him to conquer Babylon in 539 BC, after which he gained the favor of previously conquered people by allowing their exiled people to return to their homelands and rebuild them. Among those approved for return were the people of Judah, who would rebuild the Jerusalem temple for Yahweh with the support of Cyrus (2Ch 36:23; Ezr 1:2–4). The importance of this event for the chronicler is amplified by the fact that he makes it the very last thing mentioned in his work.

COMPOSITION

Author(s)

Tradition has long associated the Book of Chronicles with Ezra the scribe. However, studies on the language and theology of Ezra compared with Chronicles remain inconclusive, if not contradictory (see p 426). Many who would deny any connection make the mistake of including Nehemiah in their statistics, whereas there should be little doubt that his distinctive memoirs have independent, autobiographical origin. The purpose of Chronicles seems thoroughly agreeable with Ezra's religious program: to establish the self-understanding of the postexilic community as essentially a religious entity, revolving around the two divine institutions of the temple and the Davidic dynasty (see below). Perhaps above all, Ezra the Levite seems a natural choice for explaining the prominent Levitical interests of the book. Yet, there are also enough differences with the Book of Ezra that one does well to leave the matter open to other possibilities.

Date of Composition

Scripture nowhere identifies the author of Chronicles, but Jewish tradition suggests that Ezra wrote it. Many modern scholars hold that it forms a trilogy with the books of Ezra and Nehemiah, all three being composed by an anonymous writer called "the Chronicler." In any case, the contents of Chronicles do not require a date of composition later than the last quarter of the fifth century BC.

The book concludes with Cyrus's edict of restoration in 538 BC; it could not be written earlier than that. Many critical scholars located the work of the Chronicler in the Greek period, that is, sometime after Alexander's victories in 333 BC. The main arguments were linguistic and genealogical, but both are very fragile.

Two genealogies are often adduced as evidence of so late a date. One is that of the high priest Jaddua in Ne 12:11. (See our discussion on p 429, but in any case the relevance of that appeal is dependent upon the assumption that the Chronicler is also responsible for Ezra-Nehemiah.) The other is the list of the descendants of Zerubbabel apparently to the sixth generation in 1Ch 3:19–24. If we average 20 years per generation, and subtract 120 years (20 X 6) from 520 (Zerubbabel) that gives us a date of 400 for the composition of Chronicles. This would work, unless one wants to insist that Ezra was the author.[1] The fact that the Septuagint (followed by Vulgate and Peshitta) extends the genealogy to *eleven* generations indicates how easily such lists could be updated. That makes the debate a text-critical one and also demonstrates how spongy the entire argument is for a late date.

Continued on p 386.

---

1   Edward Young, however, mounts a plausible argument that the passage in question covers only *two* generations, down to Pelatiah and Jeshaiah in v 21a, while 21b does not directly continue the line but inserts the names of four other Davidic families *contemporary* with those two, possibly their brothers. Others interpret the evidence to imply *four* generations. Either of these alternatives would yield a date compatible with Ezrahite authorship (c 480 or 440).

CHRONICLES AND THE CRITICS

The historical reliability of Chronicles has often been questioned. We find such questioning even in the Talmud, although the book's canonicity is never known to have been an issue. Earlier higher criticism tended almost automatically to challenge the reliability of nearly every statement that was not taken directly from Samuel or Kings and to view the entire work as simply late Levitical propaganda, allegedly describing what should have happened rather than what did. At most, it was conceded to be a useful collection of practices and their rationalizations at the time of composition, perhaps especially valuable as a witness to the forces that shaped Judaism, but devoid of merit as a historical source for the earlier periods it purported to depict.

One often cited example of this supposed bias is Chronicles' classification of Samuel as a Levite (1Ch 6:1–28) in alleged contradiction of his description as an Ephraimite in 1Sm 1:1–20. Most likely, however, he was a Levite living in Ephraimite territory (cf a similar case in Jgs 17:7). Alternatively, Samuel could have been "adopted" as a Levite since he was entrusted to a Levite family early in life (although it is debated whether this was possible). In any event, were it invention, we might expect more than a passing reference to it.

In recent times, critical skepticism has abated slightly. It is conceded that the Chronicler must have had access to many ancient sources to which he was far closer than any modern historian. Where archaeology has been able to make a judgment about the historical content of Chronicles, it has tended to be favorable. For example, the aqueduct and water system that Hezekiah built for Jerusalem (2Ch 32:30), and the border fortresses built at various times (2Ch 11:5–10; 16:1–6), are all now known to exist.

The Siloam inscription records the drama of digging King Hezekiah's tunnel, which brought water into Jerusalem as preparation for a siege.

Much of the skepticism about Chronicles has to do with its allegedly inflated numbers. Critics, however, appear to have inflated the problem themselves. Of the approximately 20 instances of differing figures in Chronicles and Samuel-Kings, in only about a third of the cases is the higher figure found in Chronicles. Probably simple textual corruption (especially easy in the case of numbers) accounts for the vast majority of the discrepancies (see p 398). At times, however, we may also have to reckon with the possibility of the same symbolic or hyperbolic use of numbers that we occasionally encounter elsewhere in the Scriptures.

The fortifications of Lachish, overrun by Sennacherib in c 701 BC.

The other traditional type of argument in favor of a late date was based on the supposed presence of Greek loanwords—but, again, this depended on conclusions about Ezra-Nehemiah more than Chronicles itself. However, William Albright demonstrated that the words in question were Persian, not Greek. Since then, critical opinion has gravitated increasingly toward a 400 BC date. Some have now defended a late *sixth* century date (divorcing Chronicles from Ezra-Nehemiah). The argument is that only in that period can we document all three of Chronicles' major interests (prophecy, kingship, and temple worship). At best, this is an argument from silence.

Also affecting the question is Chronicles' possible anti-Samaritan attitude. Evidence increasingly indicates that the schism did not become final until John Hyrcanus's destruction of the Samaritan temple in the second century BC, but in other respects that was only the capstone of a friction that went back to the exile itself, and hence we have no handhold here either. Critics often argue further for lateness on the grounds of the Chronicler's alleged historical unreliability, but we shall not even honor the suggestion.

Purpose/Recipients

Chronicles' review of past events is neither simply a condensation of history from Genesis to Kings nor even a balanced summary of Israel's past. Although some accounts here have a counterpart in Samuel and Kings, Chronicles is not designed to repeat the contents of those books.

Chronicles was written with special interest. Note the large number of pages allotted to some phases of history in comparison with others. Of its 65 chapters, almost one-third (19) are taken up with the account of one person, David (1Ch 11–29). By contrast, the eons preceding his reign are compressed into introductory genealogical lists comprising only nine chapters (1Ch 1–9). A similar large space is devoted to the activities of another individual, David's son Solomon (2Ch 1–9). The 400 years of the divided kingdom are covered in just 27 chapters (2Ch 10–36).

As further indication of its special interest, Chronicles not only assigns a disproportionate amount of space to David and Solomon (almost half), but it also restricts its reports on these two kings almost entirely to a single aspect of their reigns. The focus is not their political achievements (which receive only passing attention) or their personal lives (which go practically unnoticed). Rather, interest centers in what these men did to further the spiritual edification of their people at the pinnacle of Israel's outward glory. Chronicles contains extensive and detailed reports on how these men planned, built, and dedicated the temple; how they promoted true worship forms; how they fostered music as a prominent feature of the services; and how they were careful to have only authorized personnel officiate in the temple.

There is a reason that these special interests loom so large in this survey spanning millennia: Chronicles, written after the exile, had something to say from the past to people who recently and barely had survived extinction in the land of their Babylonian captors. Although the people again walked the soil of their fathers, they could not blink away the humiliating fact that they were "slaves" of the Persian king (Ne 9:36–37). Prospects of becoming "a light for the nations" (Is 49:6; cf Lk 2:32) appeared to lie buried in the ruins of the temple and in the rubble of the Holy City.

Israel's history showed that its downfall began when it no longer worshiped God according to His ordinances. Its neglect of prescribed forms of worship was the outward symptom of an internal malady. The neglect proved that the people did not love the Lord with all their heart and with all their soul and with all their might (Dt 6:5). Ritual disobedience proved to be a spring from which flowed all the other foul waters of covenant disloyalty, including the sins against the neighbor.

To this dispirited band of immigrants, Chronicles recalled history from the perspective of God's "everlasting covenant" with David—His "steadfast, sure love for David" (Is 55:3). To those who lamented, "our hope is lost" (Ezk 37:11), the reminder of God's "steadfast, sure love for David" proclaimed, "There is hope for your future" (Jer 31:17). So, for example, each name in the lists of ancient forebears (1Ch 1–9) was not just the bare statistical entry of an archivist. The genealogies going back to Adam were a sustained litany, intoned so persistently as to bring every doubting heart in tune with its message: "All appearances to the contrary, you are the people whom the Creator of all people has chosen in order to bless all the families of the earth" (cf Gn 12:1–3).

For the same reason, Chronicles lets Israel's past glory shine into its dark days of the postexilic period. To a people who now owed a precarious existence to the grace of a foreign ruler, the past sang out: "What these leaders of Israel achieved shows that the Lord of history truly is able to let His kingdom come according to His determinate counsel and will. Nations rise and fall at His command."

But Chronicles reviews history in its unique way for another reason. Although "in great trouble and shame" (Ne 1:3) and in need of encouragement, the nation needed instruction in righteousness. The chosen people were to learn from the past also that they had no future if they obstinately "sinned against [God's] rules, which if a person does them, he shall live by them" (9:29). The cardinal sin was idolatry. It canceled all covenant promises and invoked dire curses. On the other hand, undivided devotion of the heart was to be expressed through rites prescribed by God, by officiants appointed by Him, and in the place designated by Him. Therefore, the temple, once planned by David and built by Solomon but now in ruins, spoke of what had been and again must be central in the relationship of Israel to God. The temple and its proper worship were the heartbeat of the nation; here grace and mercy sustained its life.

Literary Features

Genre

St. Jerome first suggested the translation "Chronicles" (though he did not use it in the Vulgate) by which the West generally knows the book. Perhaps in Hebrew culture the phrase had connotations more nearly like our "history," but certainly "chronicles" is entirely misleading, especially if contrasted with "history," such as one finds in Kings. "Chronicles" implies a mere annal or objective record of events without any principle of selection or further purpose in writing. It applies to the biblical book, if at all, only in the case of the exclusively genealogical first nine chapters. "History," by contrast, connotes a purposeful selection and presentation of materials, and by that criterion there is perhaps no book in the Bible where the term is more fitting. Chronicles must be recognized as the third major historiographic effort of the Old Testament, alongside the history in Samuel-Kings and the pre-Davidic history of especially the Pentateuch. (Chronicles parallels both works, at least formally, in its initial genealogies.)

Characters

As noted above, the chief characters in Chronicles are David and Solomon, whose reigns are described in a most positive light when compared to the accounts in the Book of Kings. The Chronicler focused on their successes, especially those related to the establishment of the temple and its services.

The Chronicler presents evil kings, such as Jehoram, Ahaz, and Manasseh, but also other good kings. The following are examples of those who pleased God, at least during a significant portion of their reigns.

Jehoshaphat was a good king at first and fostered learning of the Scriptures in Judah. But when Syria threatened Canaan, Jehoshaphat allied himself with northern King Ahab (instead of with the Lord of hosts) to do battle (2Ch 18). The war ended when Ahab died (as had been prophesied). But because of his alliance with Ahab, Jehoshaphat incurred the anger of the Lord, who sent some of the surrounding nations to attack Judah. Yet because all Judah and the king himself then called on the Lord, He delivered Judah.

Joash, another good king, restored the temple after collecting a tax on all Judah. But later, when the high priest died, the people turned to their idols, and the Syrians came and looted them. Joash was killed by his own servants.

After one of the kings closed down the temple, **King Hezekiah** reopened it (2Ch 29:3), sanctified it, and restored the sacrifices, the Levitical orders, and the temple treasury. He also ordered the long-neglected Passover to be observed. When King Sennacharib of Assyria came to attack Jerusalem, the angel of the Lord killed the best of the enemy army, forcing Sennacharib to return home (32:1–21).

Eight-year-old **Josiah** (2Ch 34:1) zealously restored the worship of Judah and destroyed idols. In the course of work on the temple, the Book of the Law was found (v 14) and read. Josiah and all Judah repented of their sins, kept the Passover, and offered sacrifices. Josiah was killed in battle with the Egyptians, to the grief of all Judah.

Narrative Development or Plot

Israel's ancestral history begins with Adam in order to place God's people into its proper setting among the peoples of the earth (1Ch 1). This nation was but one of many nations of the earth, yet was chosen by God to be a special nation. The Chronicler lists the 12 tribes according to a double order: the order of birth of the sons of Jacob (briefly noted in 2:1–2) and the order in which the tribes settled the land. Chapter nine ends with a repetition of part of the genealogy of Saul (vv 35–44) as a transition to the next section, which begins with the death of Saul and the rise of David.

As a true man of God, David carried out the command that had been given to Joshua but had never been completely fulfilled: to take the whole land from the nations who inhabited it. It was to reach from the river of Egypt (a desert river south of Judah) to the Euphrates. Under David, the land of Israel reached these dimensions. He achieved this in obedience to God's command—but only with fierce warfare. Because David had "shed much blood," God did not allow him to build the temple (22:7–10). Before David died, he gave Solomon final instructions to build the temple and turned over to him both the plans and all the funds that he had collected for the task (28:11–19).

Ruins of the city Halabia, near the spot where the rule of David and Solomon reached the great Euphrates River.

After Solomon was established on the throne, the Lord appeared to him in a vision and let him ask for the desires of his heart. When Solomon asked only for wisdom and knowledge to rule the people well, the Lord granted him also riches and honor that would be the envy of the world (2Ch 1). And indeed, gold and silver were said to become as common as stones in Jerusalem (1:15; 9:27). The temple was built with all the elegance and beauty available. When the building was finished, Solomon assembled all the leaders of Israel (ch 5) to bring the old tabernacle with all its furnishings up to the temple—especially the ark of the covenant to be placed in the Most Holy Place. There was music and praise, and the glory of the Lord filled the temple. Under the peacetime reign of Solomon, great wealth and pomp flowed into Jerusalem, so much that even the visiting queen of Sheba had to see it to believe it (ch 9) and was astonished.

After the death of Solomon, his son Rehoboam became king. Jeroboam, with the older royal advisors, asked him to lighten the yoke (of taxes) that Solomon had imposed on Israel to build the temples and palaces in Jerusalem. Rehoboam did not take the advice of the elders but followed his young advisors, who urged that he increase the burdens. All of Israel except for Judah and Benjamin forsook Rehoboam and thereafter remained in rebellion until obliterated by Assyria (ch 10). Rehoboam did not try to force the northern tribes back into subjection but instead built up the fortunes and fortresses of Judah (11:2–17).

The remainder of the account describes the character and activities of the various kings of Judah, tracing the history down to Jehoiachin. Some good kings, such as Asa, Jehoshaphat, Joash, Uzziah, Hezekiah, and Josiah,

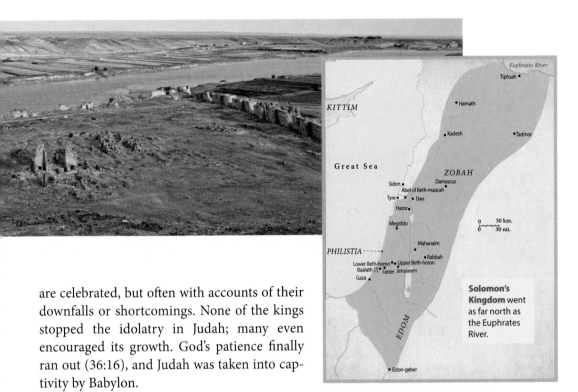

KITTIM

Euphrates River

Tiphsah •

• Hamath

• Kadesh

•Tadmor

Great Sea

ZOBAH

Sidon • Damascus
Abel of Beth-maacah
Tyre • • Dan
Hazor •
Megiddo •

0   50 km.
0   30 mi.

Mahanaim

PHILISTIA - - - - →

• Rabbah
Lower Beth-horon • Upper Beth-horon
Baalath [?] • • Gezer Jerusalem
Gaza •

EDOM

• Ezion-geber

Solomon's Kingdom went as far north as the Euphrates River.

are celebrated, but often with accounts of their downfalls or shortcomings. None of the kings stopped the idolatry in Judah; many even encouraged its growth. God's patience finally ran out (36:16), and Judah was taken into captivity by Babylon.

Despite Israel's unfaithfulness to the covenant, God, ever merciful and gracious, continued to make the descendants of Abraham His instrument to bless and redeem all nations. He kept His promise, spoken "by the mouth of Jeremiah" (v 22), saying, "When seventy years are completed for Babylon, I will visit you, and I will fulfill to you My promise and bring you back to this place" (Jer 29:10). And so it was that "the LORD stirred up the spirit of Cyrus king of Persia" (2Ch 36:22), heir of the Babylonian Empire, to release the enslaved people of God and to aid them in resettling the Land of Promise.

This second exodus from captivity is described in the books of Ezra and Nehemiah.

Resources

The Chronicler mentions many of his sources, and there are evidently others not mentioned. Some 20 of these appear to be mentioned by name, though it seems that sometimes the same source is cited under a slightly different title. The following is a list of major titles: "The Law of the LORD" (1Ch 16:40); "the chronicles of King David" (27:24); "the Chronicles of Nathan

Continued on p 396.

OUTLINE

The Books of Chronicles show us how Israel, Judah, and the house of David stand at the center of God's plan of salvation, fulfilled in the reign of the Messiah. First Chronicles 9 is important to understanding the book's character and composition. Israel's ancestry, traced back to Adam (1Ch 1–8), on the one hand, and the return from the Babylonian captivity, on the other, constitute the framework within which the historical survey of Chronicles runs its course. Repatriated "people of Judah, Benjamin, Ephraim, and Manasseh" had the assurance that they were still a part of all Israel whose genealogies are on record (1Ch 9:3). Jerusalem, David's capital and site of Solomon's temple, was again at the center of things (1Ch 9:1–9). Furthermore, authorized officiants, priests, and their Levitical assistants resumed the worship rites, as "David and Samuel the seer established them" (1Ch 9:22). The last verses introduce David's reign through the repetition of ancestors and descendants of Saul, his only predecessor (1Ch 9:35–44; cf 8:29–40). Although human sin brings consequences, the divine purposes of Israel's God cannot be thwarted—a fact to which 1Ch 9:2–34 points.

I. Nations and Israel in God's Plan of Salvation (1Ch 1:1–9:34)

   A. From Adam to Abraham (1Ch 1:1–27)

   B. From Abraham to Jacob (1Ch 1:28–54)

   C. A Genealogy of David (1Ch 2)

   D. Descendants of David (1Ch 3)

   E. Descendants of Judah (1Ch 4:1–23)

   F. Descendants of Simeon (1Ch 4:24–43)

   G. Descendants of Reuben (1Ch 5:1–10)

   H. Descendants of Gad (1Ch 5:11–22)

   I. The Half-Tribe of Manasseh (1Ch 5:23–26)

   J. Descendants of Levi (1Ch 6)

B. Ahaz's Reign (2Ch 28:1–7)

C. Ahaz and Judah Defeated (2Ch 28:8–15)

D. Ahaz's Alliance with Assyria and His Idolatry (2Ch 28:16–27)

E. Hezekiah's Reign Begins (2Ch 29:1–2)

F. Hezekiah's Reforms (2Ch 29:3–31:21)

G. Hezekiah Depends on the Lord to Defeat Assyria (2Ch 32)

H. Manasseh's Reign and Repentance (2Ch 33:1–20)

I. Amon's Reign and Death (2Ch 33:21–25)

J. Josiah's Reign and Reform (2Ch 34–35)

K. Judah's Decline under Jehoahaz, Jehoiakim, Jehoiachin, and Zedekiah (2Ch 36:1–16)

L. Jerusalem Captured, Burned, and Its People Exiled to Babylon (2Ch 36:17–21)

M. Proclamation of Cyrus (2Ch 36:22–23)

the prophet" (29:29); "the Chronicles of Gad the seer" (29:29); "the prophecy of Ahijah the Shilonite" (2Ch 9:29); "the visions of Iddo the seer" (9:29); "the chronicles of Shemaiah the prophet" (12:15); "[the chronicles of] Iddo the seer" (12:15); "the story of the prophet Iddo" (13:22); "the prophecy of Azariah the son of Obed" (15:8); "the Book of the Kings of Judah and Israel" (16:11); "the Book of the Law of the LORD" (17:9); "the chronicles of Jehu the son of Hanani" (20:34); "the Book of the Kings of Israel" (20:34); "the Story of the Books of the Kings" (24:27); "the Book of Moses" (25:4); "the vision of Isaiah the prophet" (32:32); "the Chronicles of the Seers" (33:19); "the Laments" (35:25); and "the Book of the Kings of Israel and Judah" (36:8). These works had apparently all survived the exile—but did not ultimately survive in the manuscript tradition.

In addition to all these extracanonical sources, however, it seems clear that the Chronicler's major source was a canonical one: Samuel-Kings or its equivalent text that appears in that collection. How direct the relationship was cannot be said with certainty, but there are frequent verbatim parallels. If Kings was not finished until the early exile and Chronicles was written shortly after the exile, the chronological gap between the two would not be great at all.

CYCLES IN CHRONICLES

A cyclical theme emerges in the Chronicles history:

Cycle 1
A. Creation of the World and Israel (1Ch 1–8)
B. Retribution by Exile for Unfaithfulness (1Ch 9:1)
C. Restoration of Israel in Jerusalem (1Ch 9:2–34)

Cycle 2
A. Rise of Saul (1Ch 9:35–44)
B. Retribution for Unfaithfulness (1Ch 10:1–14a)
C. Restoration in David (1Ch 10:14b)

Cycle 3
A. The Ideal Kingdom (1Ch 11–2Ch 9)
B1. Retribution by Division of the Kingdom for Unfaithfulness (2Ch 10:1–36:13)
B2. Retribution by Exile for Unfaithfulness (2Ch 36:14–21)
C. Restoration by Cyrus (2Ch 36:22–23)

Text and Translations

The Hebrew text of Chronicles is fairly well preserved with two areas of weakness. Lists of names are subject to copyist errors. The numbers recorded in the book likewise may have caused problems, as explained below.

Many students of the Bible have found it hard to believe that Chronicles presents accurate history because of the numbers recorded there. Although in most instances they are in full agreement with those found in Samuel-Kings, there are two areas in which the numbers cause difficulty: (1) some of them diverge from the numbers in Samuel-Kings,[2] and (2) some seem too large to be possible. A few examples of each are cited here to illustrate the matter.

---

2 Not all ancient versions of a given Bible passage contain the same number, and not all English Bible translations use the same ancient manuscripts. Therefore, although discrepancies may appear in one translation, they might not appear in another.

DIFFERENCES WITH SAMUEL-KINGS

1. 2Ch 2:2 — 3,600 overseers	1Ki 5:16 — 3,300
2. 2Ch3:15 — 35 cubits	1Ki 7:15—18
3. 2Ch 4:5 — 3,000 "baths"	1Ki 7:26 — 2,000
4. 2Ch 8:18 — 450 gold talents	1Ki 9:28 — 420

Larger Numbers[3]

1. 2Ch 3:4 — 120 cubits	1Ki 6:2 — 30
2. 1Ch 18:4 — 7,000 horsemen	2Sm 8:4 — 1,700
3. 1Ch 19:18 — 7,000 chariots	2Sm 10:18 — 700

Some of these apparent discrepancies may have resulted from mistakes made by ancient copyists of texts. This possibility of error is enhanced in view of the fact that ancient writers did not have modern Arabic numerals at their disposal. It appears that at some time letters of the alphabet were used to signify numbers—letters that could easily have been misread. There is also good reason to believe that a numerical notation in vogue consisted of horizontal and vertical strokes, another source of potential error. (See pp 150–51.)

Although these factors may remove some of the problems of computation encountered in Chronicles, biblical research at present lacks an adequate explanation for every instance. But there is reason to hope that continued textual and archaeological studies will make it possible to understand what the numerical notations in Chronicles actually mean. At the same time, there is no reason to believe that the Chronicler deliberately falsified the account to embellish and glorify the history of Israel.

Copies of the LXX text for Chronicles were corrupted, sometimes significantly. In the Syriac tradition, Chronicles was not at first regarded as canonical. It was preserved in Syriac as a paraphrase rather than as a careful translation.

---

3   In some cases a smaller number is given in Chronicles than in Samuel-Kings. For example, 2Ch 9:25—4,000 stalls; 1Ki 4:26—40,000.

DOCTRINAL CONTENT

Summary Commentary

Ch 1 Through the families of the earth, the Lord unfolds His plan of salvation, focusing on Abraham, the father of all who believe (Rm 4:16). The Lord made Abraham the father of many nations.

Chs 2–3 Although Judah was not the firstborn or the most noble of Jacob's sons, his descendants took the first place among the tribes of Israel and fathered the greatest kings and builders. David's dynasty ruled all Israel for 80 years and the Southern Kingdom of Judah for over 400 years; his descendants continued to lead after the return from the Babylonian exile.

Chs 4–7 The genealogy broadens to include all Israel. Other members of David's family, who increased the family's territory and served with David, are listed. Simeon's descendants and some of their noteworthy successes are listed. They lived peaceably and supportively among Judah's descendants. The Chronicler recounts Reuben's weakness and relationship to Judah, which illustrates why Judah came to lead Israel. Only a little information is recorded about the "sons of Gad" in Scripture, who lived and fought beside the sons of Reuben. The early successes of East Manasseh did not spare them from defeat after they abandoned God's covenant. God punished them specifically through sending the Assyrians. An overview of the priestly tribe of Levi is included, down to the time of David. Although little information about Issachar is presented, the Chronicler records the tribe's great numbers. Benjamin, Jacob's youngest son and the father of one of the smallest tribes, is given the honor of a genealogy, unlike Dan, who receives almost no notice. Summaries of Naphtali and West Manasseh specially note the place of mothers. The touching story of Ephraim's recovery from disaster illustrates brotherly care and personal endurance, as Ephraim became a most powerful tribe in Israel's history. The account of Asher concludes the genealogy of the 12 tribes. Leaders of this far-flung tribe receive special emphasis, though their warriors' strength did not sustain them.

Chs 8–9 A Benjaminite genealogy designed specifically for Saul's family shows that though Saul's tribe was smaller than others, it received special attention because God called them to service as leaders of Israel. The separated people of Israel return to a new unity at Jerusalem.

Chs 10–12 The Chronicler announces the death of Saul but celebrates David's enthronement, overlooking David's struggles. Critics may fault the Chronicler's omission of the graphic details about David's ascent. David wins support from throughout Israel, and his coronation is a great celebration.

Chs 13–17 David strengthens the unity of Israel by consulting the leaders and receiving affirmation, though he fails to bring the ark of the covenant all the way to Jerusalem. God establishes David's house and his household in Jerusalem. David, as the new king, acts as a priest by blessing and ministering to the congregation of Israel. Three psalms are arranged specifically to emphasize Israel's thanks for the Lord's merciful deeds. David establishes two sites for worship and provides for proper services at each. The Lord confirms His everlasting covenant with David, which is fulfilled in the appearing of Jesus, called "Son of David."

Chs 18–20 David demonstrates his abilities as a military and efficient leader. The respect David showed the Ammonite ruler is repaid with humiliation. However, David conquers the Ammonites and defeats even the most formidable warriors, the Philistine giants. Fear of such giants had kept Israel from entering the Promised Land, but the Lord strengthened His people for victory.

Chs 21–22 Though the Lord does not let David build the temple, He allows him to make preparations so that Solomon can accomplish the goal. David tells Solomon to build the temple, affirming that the Lord will be with him in this task.

Chs 23–26 David organizes the Levites for service at Jerusalem according to God's Law because they have earlier been spread throughout the tribes. He also organizes the musicians of the temple as prophets and provides for the protection of the sanctuary and for those who go in and out of its gates. David entrusts many aspects of his rule to the Levites, who could teach and apply the Word in their services.

Chs 27–29 David establishes a comprehensive military program by which the king could call up troops for service. He welcomes the service of tribal leaders and appoints the treasurers, farmers, herders, counselors, and military commanders of his reign. He wisely adapts the older tribal system for the purposes of forming a united nation under the king's central authority. David announces that the Lord chose Solomon as the future king. David receives the plans for the temple from God and carefully passes them on to Solomon, his heir. As king, David leads Israel in giving by setting an example of generosity for the Lord's work. He acts like a priest by leading the assembly of Israel's leaders in prayer. At his death, his son peaceably takes over the leadership of the kingdom.

Solomon worshiped the Lord at the high place at Gibeon, a city in the region of Benjamin that was also set apart for Levites.

2Ch 1 The Lord greatly blesses Solomon, who worships at the Tent of Meeting set up at Gibeon. Chronicles emphasizes how Solomon used the Lord's wisdom in the kingly activities of administration and trade, which strengthened his kingdom.

Chs 2–7 Solomon, whose name means "peace," prepares international treaties with Hiram of Tyre in order to build the temple. Through sacrifices offered by Abraham, David, and now Solomon, the Lord affirms the site for Solomon's temple on Moriah. After the temple is built, the Lord shows His approval by igniting the sacrifices and filling the temple with His glory. He also affirms His promises to David's house.

Chs 8–9 Solomon settles matters with Hiram of Tyre, uses forced labor, and expands his influence. He begins and finishes his reign under the watchful eyes of the Lord's prophets (cf 1Ki 1:32–45), who reviewed his accomplishments and likely also reviewed his failures.

Chs 10–12 Solomon overwhelms the queen of Sheba and forms a trade alliance with her. His wealth expands but his heart turns away from the Lord so that the Lord raises up adversaries to Solomon's rule. When his son, Rehoboam, ascends the throne, he foolishly increases tensions and causes the northern tribes to withdraw and form the kingdom of Israel. Priests, Levites, and citizens of Israel seek the Lord at His temple in Jerusalem, despite the personal and professional hardships it brings. Rehoboam cleverly exploits family relationships to strengthen his hold on Judah. Yet his purposes conflict with the Lord's purposes for families. The Lord proves Himself righteous toward Rehoboam and Judah by punishing their abandonment of His Law and by hearing their confession of sin.

Chs 13–20 The Lord fights against Jeroboam for the sake of Abijah and Judah. Asa reigns in Judah and pleases the Lord. When Azariah speaks God's

Word to Asa, the king courageously brings reform to Judah and to members of the tribes of Israel. Later, Asa stumbles in his faith. But rather than repent, he foolishly lashes out at the Lord's prophet. The Lord strengthens faithful Jehoshaphat so that the fear of the Lord falls upon the nations. In Israel, He raises up the prophet Micaiah to confront wicked King Ahab. In Judah, the Lord calls Jehoshaphat to serve Him with His whole heart—halfhearted commitment simply will not do. By promise, prayer, and praise, the Lord accomplishes Judah's deliverance. The Lord makes Judah rejoice over their enemies, the Moabites, Ammonites, and Meunites.

Chs 21–24 Through a letter from Elijah the prophet, the Lord warns Jehoram that he must face God's punishment. The Lord wills and brings about the downfall of Ahaziah and the house of Ahab. However, Athaliah reigns in her son's stead and destroys the royal family, though the Lord preserves the house of David through Joash. On behalf of the boy king Joash, the priest Jehoiada makes a covenant with the people of Judah based on the Law of Moses. Through sound leadership, the Lord renews the mercies of temple service and the good administration of the kingdom. The Lord guides Joash through the priest Jehoiada and his son Zechariah, but Joash finally rejects the Lord's ways.

Chs 25–26 Amaziah extends the benefits of his father's policies and avenges his father's death. Though the Lord grants Amaziah victories, he rebels against the Lord due to pridefulness. His son, Azariah, succeeds him and continues in the manner of his father so that the Lord makes Azariah a leper. He is succeeded by Uzziah, who did what was right before God but became a victim of pride when he sought to serve in a priestly role at the temple.

Chs 27–31 Jotham orders his ways before the Lord and grows mighty as a result. He learns from both the good example and the bad example of his father, Uzziah. His son, Ahaz, leads Judah astray when he adopts pagan sacrifices. When Syria and Israel overrun Judah and lead away numerous prisoners, the Lord shames the Israelites for mistreating their southern prisoners. Hezekiah leads the priests and Levites in cleansing the temple and restoring the sacrifices. Hezekiah fully restores the temple services according to God's Word and the examples of David and Solomon. Hezekiah also renews the Passover celebration to call the people back to the Lord. The Lord blesses Judah under Hezekiah's rule, and Hezekiah reestablishes the support of the priests and Levites.

Chs 32–36 When the Assyrians besiege Jerusalem, they mock Hezekiah and the Lord. The Lord answers Hezekiah's prayer by annihilating the Assyrian army and forcing their retreat. Hezekiah, blessed with great wealth and power, struggles with pride. This threatens to destroy him, his kingdom, and his descendants. His son, Manasseh, succeeds him and multiplies wickedness in Judah. Through distress and the admonitions of

An Egyptian ivory carving depicts the outcome of the battle of Megiddo. Captive Israelites are led away into slavery.

the prophets, the Lord leads Manasseh to repentance. Amon next becomes king but only reigns two years. His son, Josiah, seeks the Lord and destroys the idolatrous shrines in Judah and all Israel. The Book of the Law is rediscovered and the Lord's ways are restored through Josiah's reform. Josiah leads the people in an exceptional celebration of the Lord's Passover. However, Josiah dies in battle when he confronts Pharaoh Neco at Megiddo.

The Chronicler quickly describes the last kings of Judah (Jehoahaz, Jehoiakim, Jehoiachin, and Zedekiah), who were dominated by Babylon. He likewise records how stubbornness dominates the people of Judah (36:15–16). The Babylonians defeat Judah and destroy Jerusalem, including the temple. They take the Judeans into exile. Yet 70 years later, the Lord stirs the Persian king Cyrus to declare that the Judeans could return home from exile. Ironically, the people who would not hear God's Word from the prophets now hear His decree from the mouth of a foreign ruler who may have been a pagan.

Specific Law Themes

The Chronicler describes Israel and Judah "breaking faith" with the Lord by failing to follow God's Word and seek Him. As a result, He sends them into exile. For extensive comment on these and other themes, see "Specific Doctrines" below.

Specific Gospel Themes

The Chronicler celebrates God's blessings and rule through David as well as through members of David's house. God promises to be with His servants, with the tabernacle and temple representing that abiding presence. They are also the places of atonement, where God is reconciled to His erring people. For extensive comment on these and other themes, see "Specific Doctrines" below.

Specific Doctrines

The Books of Chronicles were written as unabashedly supernaturalistic history. In other words, the writer set out to record God's perspective on events. Although the rest of the "histories" in the Bible also write from a supernatural perspective, Chronicles does so to a greater degree.

In Chronicles, virtually everything is the result of direct divine intervention. In utter contrast to the modern preference for providence, God's relation to history in Chronicles is so extremely close that liberals sometimes style it "manipulative." Because God is on their side, the outcome of Israel's battles is predestined in advance; the significant activity of men seems almost to be limited to prayers and hymns. A good example is Jehoshaphat's battle against Moab and Ammon (2Ch 20). After a prayer and encouragement from the inspired Jahaziel, Jehoshaphat fields an "army" in the form of a temple choir chanting psalms in the wilderness: "And when they began to sing and praise, the LORD set an ambush against the men" and "they all helped to destroy one another" (vv 22–23).

Undoubtedly, there was much more to write about the event. But even an unbelieving writer could accomplish that. Hence, to the Chronicler there was no point in belaboring the matter. What was supremely important was what only the eye of faith could see, the eternal dimensions that transcended time and space.

One consistent application of this accent in Chronicles' theology of history appears in the rigorous presentation of divine reward or retribution. The viewpoint again is common throughout Scripture (cf Ps 1). Yet in Chronicles, retribution comes with a promptness and almost mathematical proportion that would contradict experience if it were really to be taken as simply an experiential account. But as stressed in connection with Wisdom Literature, in total canonical context we must understand an ultimate fulfillment or justification to follow events. One good example of this accent in Chronicles is its added explanation for Josiah's tragic defeat and death at Megiddo; it was because "he did not listen to the words of Neco from the mouth of God, but came to fight in the plain of Megiddo" (2Ch 35:22).

Another feature of Chronicles was especially important to theologians of the Reformation, that is, the emphasis on reforms in the book (e.g., the reformation of worship led by David, 1Ch 22–25; the reforms of later Judean kings, such as Hezekiah, 2Ch 29–31). They saw themselves acting in a similar way by restoring pure forms of worship. They directed their rulers toward the positive examples set by Hezekiah and others.

Community of Faith

Another prominent accent in Chronicles' theology is the concern for the legitimacy of the community (ecclesiology). Theologically it attaches to the pivotal doctrines of election and covenant. The Jerusalem community, the author stresses, was certainly the legitimate heir of the ancient promises, the remnant, the holy seed—*a* fulfillment, even if not *the* fulfillment. In a day of small things (Zec 4:10), the Chronicler boldly proclaims that the entire history of mankind from Adam onward had taken place for the sake of this small community within the vast Persian Empire. Only in the light of the history of election could the significance of the community be properly understood and expounded. Its religion was the only true one on earth, and its temple was mankind's true religious center, the sole earthly abode of the sole deity.

Like the prophets, the Chronicler envisions a reunited Davidic kingdom with its capital at Jerusalem. Some 47 times he speaks of "all Israel" (cf Deuteronomy), and 24 times of "all the people." He misses no opportunity to speak of "evangelistic" missions to the seceded tribes, and delights in reporting occasions when Northerners did come to Jerusalem (e.g., 1Ch 13:2; 2Ch 30:10–11; 34:9).

Elsewhere it appears that even Gentiles are welcome in the temple precincts as long as they come in reverent acknowledgment of Yahweh (e.g., the duplication of that portion of Solomon's dedicatory prayer, 2Ch 6:32–33; 1Ki 8:41–43). All of this, of course, is thoroughly in accord with the mission of the Old Testament as a whole.

Inevitably, the concern for legitimacy centered on the community's leaders, specifically the hierarchy or the Levitical priesthood, not only the Zadokite high priest, but also the lesser clergy, the Levites (cf below). If God's grace and holiness is to be mediated to His people, it must be through duly authorized and "ordained" personnel. Hence the genealogical interest, demonstrating the unbroken succession of the priestly orders back not only to Moses and Aaron but also to Levi, the son of Israel. This picture, too, is no different than the Pentateuch's; here, too, the Chronicler is no innovator but is simply concerned that they be faithful to the ancient revelation, as befitted their exalted calling and status.

Work of the Spirit

In some respects Chronicles is the most "Spirit-filled" book in the Scriptures, precisely because all opposition between spirit and form, physical and spiritual, is ignored. In Chronicles, the Spirit speaks through virtually any agency, even through a pagan king such as Pharaoh Neco, as we noted above. Prophecy may take place at worship or elsewhere. Particularly in Chronicles the chant and psalmody of the Levitical choirs is sometimes characterized as "prophecy," no doubt partly because of external similarities at times (and possibly also common roots) but ultimately in recognition that "all these are empowered by one and the same Spirit" (1Co 12:11). True worship, even the most formal, is spiritual, and has an obviously celebrative and joyful atmosphere (cf below). There is no better refutation in all of Scripture than Chronicles to the earlier critical dogma and prejudice (which still lingers) that the "prophetic religion of the heart" had no room for the "sterile rituals" of the priesthood.

The same Spirit thus inspires not only priest, but king and prophet as well. David, in prophetic manner, himself receives the divine word (1Ch 28:19 even reports his receiving temple plans "in *writing* from the hand of the LORD," parallel to Moses' inspired blueprint for the tabernacle; Ex 25:9). Likewise, David's successors, at least the faithful ones, are favored with direct revelation, which they pass on to others, thus assuming the prophetic role. This general picture, of course, is not unique to Chronicles either, but nowhere so highlighted as by the Chronicler.

Naturally, it is the prophets themselves who are the most common mouthpiece of the Spirit. Especially accented is the role of the prophet as advisor to the (Davidic) king. In fact, one may wonder if Chronicles has not departed entirely from any formal or sociological sense of the word *prophet*, using it totally in its basal biblical sense of any bearer of divine revelation. Many of these prophets are also Levites, but apart from Chronicles' general interest in that group, no particular significance seems to attach to the fact.

The Chronicler does much of his own teaching through extensive quotation of prophetic sermons, oracles, and prayers throughout the book. The characteristic prophetic accent on the need for prayer and repentance thus receives due stress, as well as the consequent summons to faith and action. In his study of sermons in Chronicles, Gerhard von Rad notes at least three elements that usually appear: (1) quotation of an ancient source, often prophetic, i.e., a text; (2) application of the theological principle of that quotation to some aspect of Israel's past, i.e., one of God's mighty acts ("Gospel"); and (3) application of the text to the present, usually a call to faith and action. If taken at face value, we have here a very important entrée to a much neglected subject: the preaching of the Old Testament.

First Chronicles 21 reestablishes an important subtheme in biblical theology: the role of Satan. He is characterized as the primary author of sin because he leads people into temptation and to disobey the Spirit of God. Whereas the book normally focuses on David's successes, it acknowledges here one of his weaknesses.

Israel's Service

The Chronicler's effort to stimulate the rebuilding of Israel as a theocracy works with two interrelated divine institutions: temple (with priesthood) and Davidic monarchy (in the Holy City, Zion). David is the key figure throughout, but let us first explore Chronicles' overriding accent on liturgy or worship. At its heart is the accent that Israel was a worshiping community, a liturgical assembly. All of life is to be worship, service (cf *leitourgia*; one word serves for both the broader and narrower senses of the term in Greek as well as in English). This idea, of course, underlays the priestly materials of the Pentateuch as well, and the prophets had underscored it mightily, but the political concerns of the monarchy often distracted from this center and fostered false notions of the nature of the "kingdom." The Chronicler is motivated to assist the postexilic community in its adjustment from a politically independent society to a religious community without political possibilities. Now that Israel's political glory was a thing of the past, it must be underscored anew that the true vocation of the chosen people was to offer God undefiled worship in the Jerusalem temple. Not national and worldly glory but religious zeal would have to be the source of Israelite greatness and strength from here on. Israel's hope dare not be placed in military strength or political acumen but solely in fidelity to the covenant.

The sad miscarriages of the Maccabean era vividly illustrate how difficult it was for the old Israel to learn this lesson. The Christian inevitably sees God preparing Israel for the coming of the Gospel, but, if honest, he will also be reminded how difficult it has been also for the "new Israel" on earth to stay focused on mission rather than politics.

Worship Themes

In Chronicles' description of worship, three themes stand out: (1) temple and ark; (2) Levites; and (3) choral chant or temple music.

Although the Chronicler's heart appears to be more with the Levites, there is never any suggestion of breaching the traditional distinction between them and the priests, or of evading the priestly supervision of Levitical work (the vast variety of which, in addition to singing and preaching, is amply documented in the book). In fact, sometimes the Chronicler seems more concerned to safeguard the priestly position, e.g., Uzziah's punishment for daring to offer incense (2Ch 26:16–21); or the description of David's sons simply as "chief officials" (1Ch 18:17) instead of as "priests" as in 2Sm 8:18. Similarly, the traditional sacrifices according to the Mosaic rubrics receive ample mention.

Inevitably, the temple receives considerable accent, and not just because it was about the only rallying point the postexilic community had. Much of the relevant material in Kings is reproduced (e.g., much of 2Ch 2–9 comes from 1 Kings) but much is also added; e.g., David's preparations for building

the temple and charge to Solomon (1Ch 22). However, the Chronicler is at pains to stress that the angel of the LORD had specified Ornan's threshing floor as the site of the temple (1Ch 21:18), and that David received heavenly plans for the temple just as Moses once had for the tabernacle (1Ch 28:19). As in 1Ki 8, great accent is put on Yahweh's abiding presence in the temple, not only the center of their present life but also pointing toward the visible return of the LORD to His "temple," the new creation, on the coming day of salvation. God's presence is expressed more often in terms of His "name" associated especially with Deuteronomy, than in terms of His "glory." In a way, this eternal "incarnational" presence of God among His people often receives more stress than the theme of God's mighty acts in the past, such as the exodus, etc., which are little mentioned.

A Canaanite bronze tripod hung with pomegranates reminiscent of the decoration of Solomon's temple.

The ark of the covenant, that is, the center of the temple as the center of God's presence, and hence also a major symbol of the unity of all the tribes of Israel, inevitably is also highlighted. The entire section (1Ch 13–17) describing David's bringing of the ark from the house of Abinadab to Jerusalem is considerably expanded over the parallel pericope in 2Sm 6–7. It details the Levites' role in the preparations for the move as well as in the actual procession. It cannot be proved that a similar procession involving the ark was a recurrent liturgical occasion as many scholars have hypothesized. However, the great detail with which the Chronicler records the event suggests that his interest was not only historical (cf Ps 24, 132, etc., which could describe a ritual of procession that Israel repeated).

The role of the Levites as liturgical singers and musicians is also introduced in connection with the procession of the ark to Jerusalem (1Ch 15:16–24; cf 1Ch 6:31–48). This service becomes a permanent part of the temple liturgy, and in 1Ch 25 the families and courses of the choristers are detailed. They are given an honor beyond that of the ordinary Levite (cf Luther and his high regard for music in the service of God; we discount much critical skepticism which holds the liturgical and genealogical details of 1Ch 23–27 to be a later addition or expansion of 1Ch 6). The liturgical functions of the Levites are characteristically listed in this order (2Ch 8:14): "for their offices of praise and ministry before the priests as the duty of each day required."

The example of Jehoshaphat teaches readers to call boldly on the Lord in exceptional circumstances rather than rely solely on their own will and ability. The story shows that when we err or are ill prepared, God may answer our pleas for mercy. Since worship and prayer stood at the center of life for God's people, the story should not apply only to exceptional situations. We commonly find ourselves asking what we are to do and may call on the Lord at any time (2Ch 20:12).

The Chronicler discloses an exact and detailed knowledge of the musical parts of the typical temple service, especially of its vocal aspects, but not neglecting the instrumental. If it were not for Chronicles, we would know next to nothing about this aspect of Israel's worship (except possibly for the much later Mishnaic descriptions). Attention should be called especially to an often overlooked pericope (1Ch 29), where the eucharistic theme is explicitly associated with sacrifice. The occasion is Solomon's second anointing (v 22b), and after the presentation of the tribes' freewill offerings, David expresses himself in language echoed repeatedly in the Offertories and Eucharistic prayers of Christendom: "For all things come from You, and of Your own have we given You" (v 14b).

Our only other biblical source for this aspect of Israelite worship is, of course, the Psalter. Even more than Leviticus, Chronicles should be absolutely indispensable collateral reading with the Psalms, at least if one aspires to hear them in anything like their original setting. The Chronicler himself quotes the text of many of the psalms sung by the Levites on various occasions, most of which are essentially parallel to some in the Psalter (though usually in varying combinations, suggesting considerable freedom in their actual use). It is these praises especially that give the whole worship theology of Chronicles its distinctive note of supreme joy and thanksgiving.

One notes parallels also with the superscriptions of the Psalms: the word commonly translated "chief musician," and the singers' guilds, Heman, Ethan, and especially Asaph (who is singularly accented, and to which guild hence some suppose that the Chronicler himself belonged). Unfortunately, not even Chronicles gives us enough information to decipher much from the superscriptions, but the Chronicler is a major independent testimony to their antiquity and accuracy.

David and the Messiah

The Chronicler's other focus is "Davidism." The perpetuity of David's house and the functioning of the temple are uttered in one breath, as it were. The entire work could be subtitled, "The History of the Davidic Dynasty, the Recipient of a Divine Promise." Two things stand out in the Chronicler's treatment of the subject: (1) his accent on David instead of Moses; and (2) the fact that he writes at a time when the throne is vacant, with little prospect of any heir of David ever being able to occupy it again.

One must resist the critical temptation to see the Chronicler as downplaying Moses or the Torah as "priestly." As a matter of fact, both Moses and the Books of Moses (Torah) are mentioned much more frequently in Chronicles than in Samuel-Kings. The Torah obviously remains the official standard by which the people order their lives (e.g., Jehoshaphat's instruction in 2Ch 17:9; Josiah's reformation in 2Ch 34; and Ezra's and Nehemiah's labors, if that is to be included). In 2Ch 31 Hezekiah enjoins the people to be faithful in giving "the portion due to the priests and the Levites, that they might give themselves to the Law of the LORD" (v 4).

David does not so much replace Moses as stand on his shoulders. As in all of biblical theology, the covenant with David does not abrogate but extends and applies the ancient promises. In a sense, the whole covenantal relation of God to man is solidified in the man David and what God accomplished through him. It is no contradiction of the above to stress that sometimes David almost appears as a "second Moses," receiving from God's hands the pattern of the temple as Moses had of the tabernacle, and that David is even empowered to make adjustments in ritual and architectural detail, as new circumstances required. In another sense, however, there is a "back to Moses" aspect in the Chronicler's presentation of David, because he now presides over more of a community of faith or a "church" than a state with its political and military preoccupations.

The Chronicler's orientation is surely to the present and the future more than to the past. He evokes memories of presently unrealizable glories partly in order to stress that the ancient dynastic promises are not forgotten in these sad days, nor is God powerless to fulfill them. If Israel will only remain resolutely faithful, she will yet experience even greater glories. The covenant promises to David may be in momentary abeyance, but in God's good time, a "greater than David" will surely rise from among them. One may quibble about the appropriateness of the term *messianic* to describe Chronicle's depictions, but that is surely the import, even though the technical language is not used and the hope is not couched in the futuristic language of the prophets. David is, in a sense, superior to Moses precisely because in him originated the kingdom that still has a lawful claim to rule and that is destined to *messianic* transfiguration.

The genealogies of 1Ch 1–9 not only point a finger at the physical descendants of David among them as a sign and guarantee that David's counterpart will one day take up residence in their midst in the flesh, but they also provide a messianic, future-focused signature to the entire book in the light of God's universal purposes since Adam. We assuredly do not go astray if we press the point that Chronicles' interest in the kingdom of the first David is also an interest in the new David and the new kingdom that will arise in God's good time. The earthly temple, with its foundations in eternity, where God Himself is already "incarnate," constantly points toward that city without a temple where the dwelling of God is forever with men. And the supernal music that reverberates throughout the book is a foretaste of the new song.

On second thought, perhaps Chronicles was chosen to conclude the canon of the old covenant both because of its profound realization that "all theology is doxology" and also because of its magnificent forward thrust toward the new and eternal covenant in great David's greater Son.

Application

1Ch 1 Just as sin divided and corrupted Adam's family, it attacks and tears apart families today. Yet, these genealogies show how the Lord continues to work through families as the faith is preserved and spread from one generation to the next. The Godhead itself shows this, with the Father sending forth His Son for the sake of our salvation (Jn 3:16). Sadly, Abraham's physical (not spiritual) descendants are still in conflict nearly 4,000 years later as the nations of the Near East continually battle one another and draw others into the conflict. Such conflicts can end only through the forgiveness of sins, offered through Abraham's offspring, our Lord Jesus Christ.

Chs 2–3 Although you, like Judah, have stumbled in life, set your heart on serving the Lord and supporting your family. The Lord will hear your prayers of repentance and of blessing for your family. From a small beginning with a Judean shepherd boy, the Lord wrought great things. Today, through prayer and godly leadership, humbly commend your family to God's service. Jesus, David's greatest descendant, will lead you into a blessed future.

Chs 4–7 In any group or family, some will lead, but most will follow. No matter what your calling, bring honor to your family, congregation, employer, and nation by prayer and devoted service. Leadership and inheritance are not blessings one can simply take for granted, because they come with responsibility. God has given you responsibility in His kingdom, no matter what your standing in life. He has also equipped and blessed you with gifts, including the blessings of life and salvation through Christ, our Head. Hebrews 5:10 declares Christ to be the High Priest after the order of Melchizedek, superior to all those of Levi because He Himself is the sacrifice for our sins. He lives forever (Heb 7:23–25) and serves in the greater, heavenly temple (Heb 8–10). Though we suffer much in this life, our Brother Jesus Christ is full of comfort and supports us through our brothers and sisters in the faith.

Chs 8–9 For God's people, honor and nobility are not products of our strength, but of God's calling and the character He develops in us. The Lord renews our service and their hope based on restored faith in His mercy. Though we break faith with the Lord daily, He restores us daily through repentance and faith in Christ, whose mercy is new every morning.

Chs 10–12 The record of God's blessings to David was what the Chronicler's readers needed to remember most. When failures and trials would overwhelm us, the Lord focuses us on His mercy, which can carry us through. The feast that will be celebrated at the end of time will bring together all God's scattered children, not only those of Israel but believers among the separated children of Adam as well (cf 1Ch 1:1, which describes Israel's place in the world). That eternal feast even now sustains the Church on earth. In every celebration of the Lord's Supper, the gathered people of God look beyond the circumstances of life to an eternal day of joy for all nations (cf Mt 26:29; Mk 14:25; Lk 22:15–18; 1Co 11:23–26; Rv 19:6–9).

Chs 13–17 Consensus is often difficult to attain, especially in a large group. Yet the Lord blesses the people's sincere desire for restoring godly practices. Our station in life, whether humble or exalted in the eyes of the world, is established for the sake of God's good purposes. In mercy, He has established our heavenly home through Christ. Indeed, Christ has consecrated you as a priest in His kingdom to bless, thank, and praise God before the nations. He sustains you in this precious service with His very body and blood for the forgiveness of all your sins. Recite the psalm (16:8–36) to express your thanks to God, including specific examples of His mercy in your life. For His steadfast love, which He professes to you through His beloved Son, truly endures forever.

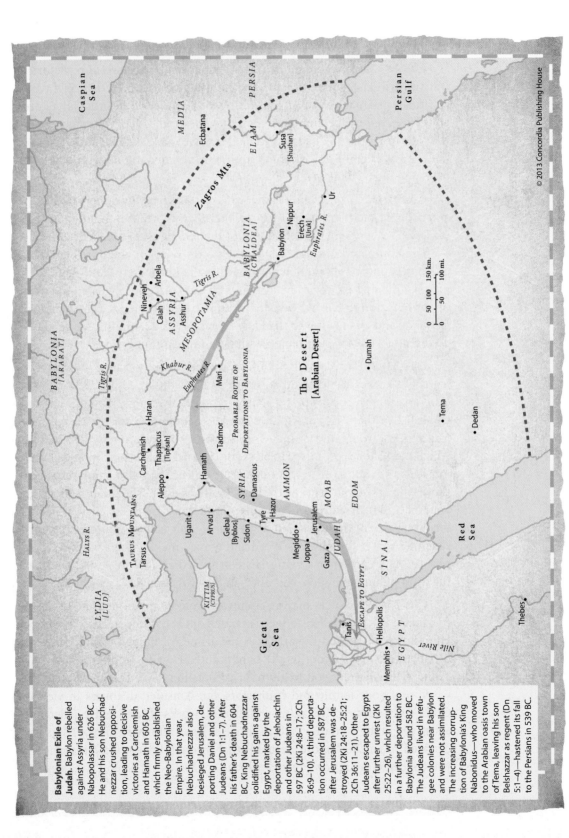

Babylonian Exile of Judah. Babylon rebelled against Assyria under Nabopolassar in 626 BC. He and his son Nebuchadnezzar crushed opposition, leading to decisive victories at Carchemish and Hamath in 605 BC, which firmly established the Neo-Babylonian Empire. In that year, Nebuchadnezzar also besieged Jerusalem, deporting Daniel and other Judeans (Dn 1:1–7). After his father's death in 604 BC, King Nebuchadnezzar solidified his gains against Egypt, marked by the deportation of Jehoiachin and other Judeans in 597 BC (2Ki 24:8–17; 2Ch 36:9–10). A third deportation occurred in 587 BC, after Jerusalem was destroyed (2Ki 24:18–25:21; 2Ch 36:11–21). Other Judeans escaped to Egypt after further unrest (2Ki 25:22–26), which resulted in a further deportation to Babylonia around 582 BC. The Judeans lived in refugee colonies near Babylon and were not assimilated. The increasing corruption of Babylonia's King Nabonidus—who moved to the Arabian oasis town of Tema, leaving his son Belshazzar as regent (Dn 5:1–4)—hastened its fall to the Persians in 539 BC.

© 2013 Concordia Publishing House

Chs 18–20 As a servant of Christ's kingdom, you may enjoy victories. But you will also suffer ridicule and humiliation (Mt 5:10–12). Fight this spiritual warfare with prayer, as is fitting for a soldier of the cross. The Lord, your King, bore your humiliation on the cross and covers your shame with the robe of His righteousness. No matter what colossal challenges face you, the Lord will grant you strength and faithful companions with whom to overcome such challenges.

Chs 21–22 The heavenly Father calls on weak, earthly fathers to care for and support their children. This is especially important in matters of faith (cf Dt 6:7–9), of which the building of the temple is an excellent example. We also commend our children to the Lord's care, praying for them daily and wisely entrusting them with service to the Lord, their family, and their nation. Our success and our future is with the Lord. He entrusted the work of our salvation to His beloved Son, who in turn commended the temple of His body and His spirit into the Father's hands (Lk 23:46), that we might be cleansed by His blood and reign with Him in the resurrection.

Chs 23–26 Throughout Scripture, we see the importance of organized worship services, which God still expects of us today. Although congregations are imperfect because they are composed of sinners, the Lord has still entrusted to them His precious Word and Sacraments for the sake of our forgiveness through the Gospel. Treasure your congregation as the site from which the Lord has promised to bless you. Regard faithful pastors and church musicians with the full respect due their calling, and also show respect to those who assist and serve with them. God has established their service for your faithful instruction and blessing. God's Word applies to every aspect of life, every day of the week. No matter what your calling in life is, the Lord sanctifies that calling by His Word and prayer, making your work a sacred service. As a carpenter serving His earthly father, Joseph, Jesus sanctified the work of human hands. His labor on the cross sanctifies us wholly.

Chs 27–29 Soldiers play an important role in any organized society, a role blessed by God when service is carried out according to His Word. God Himself has organized the angels as the armies of heaven to fight on your behalf and to deliver you. As the Lord granted David wisdom to pursue his calling, He will grant you wisdom for your calling. Like David, listen to the wisdom of your family and counselors, but consider all things in view of God's Word. Honor His calling with fruitful works of service. He called and chose you in the merciful, loving service of Jesus, who paid for your sins and declared you a child of the eternal Father through Baptism in His name. As you conclude the Lord's Prayer each day (cf 29:10–11), keep David's example in mind and humble yourself before the King of heaven. He reigns on your behalf to bless and strengthen you by the grace of His Son, Jesus.

2Ch 1 The Lord meets with us and blesses us at the services of His Word and Sacraments. Do not neglect His appointed Means of Grace. Through these humble means, the Lord grants us the blessings of Jesus' sacrifice. Like Solomon, use your gifts to bless those who work with you and for you. Remember how the Lord works on your behalf in all things, and how He administers the greatest blessings of all: the treasures of His mercy in Christ.

Chs 2–7 The Lord calls us to peace and to serve. The raising and blessing of Solomon's temple demonstrates the Lord's patient planning for our lives and for our salvation in Christ, who gave His life for our sins in view of this hill of sacrifice. Remember that in all things the Lord guides us through His Word, which ignites our hearts and fills our minds with His affirmation. His goodness and steadfast love are surely ours in Christ.

Chs 8–9 Our lives are a record of sin along with our attempts to serve the Lord. Treasure the faithful spiritual leaders the Lord provides for your wisdom and counsel. Both their rebuke and their blessing stem from the Lord's good purposes for you: to call you to repentance and to make you wise unto salvation in Christ.

Chs 10–12 People are not political tools but gifts from our gracious heavenly Father, whereby we may nurture one another in His love. When faithfulness to the Lord comes with challenges, still choose to follow the way of faithfulness, seeking the fellowship of the faithful in the Church. Thanks be to God, He works within our church and our families to strengthen faith and extend His peace through mutual care in His Word. The Lord is always ready to hear our confession and to forgive us. In applying His Law, He always has in mind our good, our repentance, and our salvation.

Chs 13–20 When trouble assails and surrounds you, call out confidently to the Lord. He fights mightily on your behalf and in ways beyond your comprehension, as demonstrated in His victory over Satan at the cross. The Lord likewise calls you to courageous action on behalf of others who need to hear His Word. Take courage! The Lord's Word accomplishes His purposes for the sake of His people, especially His purpose of salvation. Although you, too, will stumble, daily rely on the Lord by calling on Him in prayer and by requesting His forgiveness. Because of His righteousness, He will declare you blameless for the sake of His Son. As He strengthens you, use that strength to honor His name. Daily offer praise to God for His merciful kindness toward you and your loved ones. Daily rejoice in His greatest victory: the cross and resurrection of Jesus.

Chs 21–24 A harsh letter is difficult to write and harder still to receive. Yet as sinners, we all need the rebuke of God's Law against our sins. Above all, we need the call to repentance, forgiveness, and new life that the Lord is always ready to offer. Pray for your household, that God's Word and peace may prevail among you and rule your hearts. Our heavenly Father greatly desires to show mercy to all people. Just as Joash needed the faithful guidance of Jehoiada, children today need faithful guides in life (pastors, teachers, coaches, etc.). Seek such faithful guides and pray for them. Our faithful Lord will raise up godly men and women who know and duly apply His Holy Word for our instruction in righteousness.

Chs 25–26 Enact your plans with the wisdom of God's Word and with humility. We likewise feel the constant pressure to compromise the truth and follow the Lord halfheartedly. Prosperity or sin can divide you from the Lord and His people. Repent daily and focus on the Word. By His faithful and gracious Word, the Lord, who has power to help, will unstop our ears and turn our hearts to hear Him.

Chs 27–31 Learn to respect and emulate all that is good in your parents, for they are God's gift to you. Also seek to grow in the ways of your heavenly Father, who gives life everlasting in the might of His Son. Mistreating one's relatives, as the Israelites did, is doubly shameful. God calls us to treat our extended family with respect and care to lead them to repentance and life. Thankfully, the Lord treats us mercifully by forgiving our sins and reconciling us to the family of God. Renewal is always more than outward cleansing. Through the Word, the Lord cleanses and changes hearts. In Jesus' sacrifice, He atones for all our sins. Today, we regularly celebrate the new Passover—the Holy Supper of Christ, who offered Himself in compassion for our salvation.

Chs 32–36 When headlines disturb you, take comfort in the truth that all the intrigues of the nations are subject to the Lord's plans for His creation and church. When life is good, beware of pride. Even if you are able to fend off all other threats, pride will still assault and defeat you if the Lord does not come to your aid. Like Hezekiah, humble yourself before the Lord and ask for His forgiveness. Recognize your successes as signs of His kindness, which He extends through the blessings of creation and the mercy of Jesus Christ. He is always ready to hear us, just as He heard and had compassion on the wicked king Manasseh. The Holy Spirit will lead you not only to confess your sin but also to put away and avoid temptation. The Lord alone is your God; He is the only Savior, as Judah discovered.

CANONICITY

Chronicles concludes the Writings portion of the Hebrew Bible, and therewith the Old Testament itself in the traditional Masoretic ordering. The arrangement is at least as old as the New Testament: when Jesus calls down upon the hypocrites of His day "all the righteous blood shed on earth, from the blood of righteous Abel to the blood of Zechariah" (Mt 23:35; cf Lk 11:51), He referred to the events described at the end of Chronicles (2Ch 24:20–22). It is a way of saying "from Genesis to Chronicles" (2Ch 24:20–22). That is, He referred to the entire Scriptures of the time. Manuscript evidence at Qumran shows that Jews there had collected and copied the book. Both its canonical position and its unfortunate name in translations may have contributed to its relative neglect and oblivion, apparently all through history, at least in comparison with the other historical books in the Bible, especially Kings.

The fact that its conclusion (2Ch 36:22–23), citing Cyrus's edict of restoration, is identical with the beginning of Ezra (1:1–3a) has often led to the suspicion not only that the two were originally a single work but also that originally Ezra-Nehemiah followed Chronicles in chronological sequence. However, ending with Cyrus's decree would have been preferred, despite its overlap with Ezra, in order to close both book and canon on a promissory note (cf similarly the conclusion of Kings).

The Septuagint introduced changes in both name and canonical position. Instead of "Chronicles," it gave the name "things omitted/passed over" that is, in Samuel and Kings ("Paralipomenon"; a designation, via the Vulgate, still current in Catholicism). If anything, that designation is even less appropriate than "Chronicles," and the misunderstanding it causes did nothing to enhance the importance of the work. (The Septuagintal division of the book into I and II has become universal, however, even being introduced into Hebrew editions shortly before the Reformation.) The more topical relocation of the work after Kings probably led to the impression that it was merely a retelling of the same events—and hence presumably of secondary importance!

LUTHERAN THEOLOGIANS ON CHRONICLES

Luther

Luther specifically commented on the value of Chronicles for teaching the faith.

"When I speak of the title [of Isaiah; 1:1], I do not mean only that you should read or understand the words 'Uzziah, Jotham, Ahaz, Hezekiah, kings of Judah,' etc., but that you should take in hand the last book of Kings and the last book of Chronicles and grasp them well, especially the events, the speeches, and the incidents that occurred under the kings named in the title [of Isaiah], clear to the end of those books. For if one would understand the prophecies, it is necessary that one know how things were in the land, how matters lay, what was in the mind of the people—what plans they had with respect to their neighbors, friends, and enemies—and especially what attitude they took in their country toward God and toward the prophet, whether they held to his word and worship or to idolatry." (AE 35:274)

Gerhard

"*The two Books of Chronicles.* Among the Hebrews there is only one book, which is called *dibdey hayatim,* 'The Words of the Days,' because in them are described individually the deeds and activities of the kings of the people of Israel. Munsterus renders this as 'The Books of Annals.' That is not bad, for they are indeed annals, as Gellius witnesses (*N. A.*, bk. 5, c. 18): '. . . when the history of so many years is set down, observing the order of each year so as to all but demonstrate what took place in each year.' The Greeks and Latins divide this book into two books, and the Greeks call this the book of *Paraleipomena,* as if to say, 'of things passed over.' You see, it explains in summary what was omitted from or not fully described in the Pentateuch, the Books of Joshua, Judges, Samuel, and Kings. The Latins, on the other hand, call it the Book of Chronicles, as if to say, 'The Chronology.' Luther kept this name in his German translation of the Bible.

"Concerning the author of these books, nothing certain is known. Rabbi Salomon and Rabbi D. Kimchi, whose *Perushim* on these books are extant, declare in the beginning thereof that 'they were written by Ezra the lawyer.' This they confirm with the argument that the same words that are at the conclusion of Chronicles occur at the beginning of the Book of Ezra. The same Rabbi Salomon writes in his commentary, c. 7: 'Ezra had found three books of genealogies from which he assembled this.' Jerome (Epistle *ad Paulin.*) calls him 'the epitome of the Old Testament' and says, 'He was so great a man, a man of such quality, that were anyone to wish to take for himself a knowledge of Scripture without him, he would be mocking himself.' He also writes, *Prolog. galeatus*: 'He is the chronicler of all divine history.' The Hebrews place it after the Books of Ezra because they think that Ezra wrote it at the time when the Jewish people had returned to Jerusalem after the Babylonian captivity, something they conclude from the end of his second book. Some think that this is the book mentioned in 1 Kings 15:23; on the other hand, some claim more accurately that it is not that book itself but only an epitome of it." (ThC E1 § 130)

QUESTIONS PEOPLE ASK ABOUT CHRONICLES

Numerical Records

For a description of the challegnes involved with figures in Chronicles and how they relate to figures in the Books of Kings, see pp 397–98.

The Omnipresence of God

Second Chronicles 7:12 (cf v 16) records: "Then the LORD appeared to Solomon in the night and said to him: 'I have heard your prayer and have chosen this place for Myself as a house of sacrifice.'"

Acts 7:48 declares: "Yet the Most High does not dwell in houses made by hands, as the prophet says."

A hurried reading of these two passages might incline one to say that there is a discrepancy; but the disagreement is merely on the surface, namely, in the words employed and not in the meaning expressed. Both passages are true. We are justified in saying that God dwelt in the temple in Jerusalem, as well as in saying that He did not dwell in that temple. He dwelt there in the sense of making it the place of His special revelation and the manifestation of His glory. He did not dwell there if by that is meant inclusion in a certain building. That the words quoted above from 2 Chronicles were not to be understood to mean that God was shut up in the temple in Jerusalem can be seen from the prayer of Solomon at the dedication of the house of God recorded in the sixth chapter of 2 Chronicles, the chapter immediately preceding the one that is said to teach God's confinement in a certain building. Solomon says: "But will God indeed dwell with man on the earth? Behold, heaven and the highest heaven cannot contain You, how much less this house that I have built!" (2Ch 6:18). Thus there is no disagreement here. The one passage merely points to the special favors that God conferred on Israel, the other to the great truth that God is not confined to any locality in the universe.

FURTHER STUDY

Lay/Bible Class Resources

Crown, Stewart. *Chronicles*. Leaders Guide and Enrichment Magazine/Study Guide. LL. St. Louis: Concordia, 2014. ♪ In-depth, nine-session Bible study with individual, small group, and lecture portions. (Forthcoming.)

Dunker, Gary. *1 and 2 Chronicles: I Will Hear from Heaven*. GWFT. St. Louis: Concordia, 2008. ♪ Lutheran devotional author. Eleven-session Bible study, including leader's notes and discussion questions.

Life by His Word. St. Louis: Concordia, 2009. ♪ More than 1,500 reproducible one-page Bible studies covering each chapter of the canonical Scriptures. Page references to *The Lutheran Study Bible*. CD-Rom and downloadable.

Selman, Martin J. *1 and 2 Chronicles: An Introduction and Commentary*. TOTC. Downers Grove, IL: InterVarsity Press, 1994. ♪ Compact commentary focused more on theology than other elements, written by a British evangelical scholar.

Wendland, Paul O. *1 and 2 Chronicles*. 2 Vols. PBC. St. Louis: Concordia, 2005. ♪ Lutheran author. Excellent for Bible classes. Based on the NIV translation.

Church Worker Resources

Braun, Roddy. *1 Chronicles*. WBC. Dallas: Word, 1986. ♪ Broadly helpful treatment of the book from a critical perspective, with significant treatment of background and introductory matters.

Dillard, Raymond B. *2 Chronicles*. WBC. Dallas: Word, 1987. ♪ Dependent on the Braun volume for its introduction. Compatible as a sequel to that volume.

Academic Resources

Japhet, Sara. *1 and 2 Chronicles*. OTL. Louisville: Westminster John Knox, 1993. ♪ Most thorough commentary; from a Jewish scholar. Literary and historical analysis arguing for a single author of a unified composition.

K&D. *Biblical Commentaries on the Old Testament: The Book of the Chronicles*. Grand Rapids: Eerdmans, 1971 reprint. ♪ This century-and-a-half old work from Lutheran scholars should not be overlooked. Despite its age, it remains a most useful commentary on the Hebrew text.

Myers, Jacob M. *I and II Chronicles*. Vols. 12, 12a, and 13 of AB. New York: Doubleday, 1965. ♪ Holds to a single author. Also contends that Israel's worship and covenant guidelines were revealed by God. Stresses recent archaeological finds.

Zöckler, Otto. *A Commentary on the Holy Scriptures: The Book of the Chronicles*. LCHS. New York: Charles Scribner's Sons, 1877. ♪ A helpful older example of German biblical scholarship, based on the Hebrew text, which provides references to significant commentaries from the Reformation era forward.

EZRA AND NEHEMIAH

Return to the Lord, and
He will gather you

The Books of Ezra and Nehemiah together record how the Babylonian captivity, the tomb of Israel's national identity, became the womb of its rebirth. The following paragraphs retrace how this would happen. (On the unity of these books, see "Composition," pp 426–28.)

The people from whom the Christ was to come "according to the flesh" (Rm 9:5) were God's special creation. From Abraham, who "was as good as dead (since he was about a hundred years old) . . . when he considered the barrenness of Sarah's womb" (4:19) would come the Son of promise, "born according to the Spirit" (Gal 4:29). But soon the offspring of the patriarchs, shut up in the dungeon of Egyptian slavery, seemed destined for oblivion. Then God spoke His mighty "let My people go" (Ex 5:1), and a young nation, "a kingdom of priests and a holy nation" (19:6), sprang into being.

But the nation turned out to be a disobedient son, unfaithful to its high calling. When the end came, its capital and temple lay in ruins, its land scorched and occupied by the enemy. With its population decimated and carried into exile, Israel seemed destined to share the fate of all vanquished peoples of antiquity. In the normal course of events, it would have been doomed to extinction in Babylonia, the victim of attrition and absorption by the conqueror.

But God once more spoke a life-giving word, and there was a resurrection of Israel's "dry bones" (Ezk 37:1–14). There was a second exodus, as foretold by the prophets. And in the Promised Land once more, the seed of Abraham continued to be the people by whom the Lord of the nations was to bless "all the families of the earth" (Gn 12:3).

There are two phases in the story of Israel's rehabilitation after Babylon. Though reported in separate books, each stage consists of a construction program in wood and stone followed by a reestablishment of moral and

The magnificent Ishtar Gate from Babylon illustrates the wealth and power of its rulers, who overwhelmed and absorbed the kingdom of Judah.

spiritual foundations. Ezra records the building of the temple (Ezr 1–6); Nehemiah the erection of Jerusalem's walls (Ne 1–7). Ezra the priest alone initiates the first spiritual reform (Ezr 7–10); in the second he has the support and collaboration of Nehemiah (Ne 8:1–13:3), a layman who also takes action independently (13:4–31).

Historical and Cultural Setting

The drama of Israel's restoration opens 60 years before Ezra appears on the scene. In 538 BC, when Jerusalem had been in ruins for half a century, a large contingent of exiles returned to the homeland. Prominent figures in that early period included the two governors, Sheshbazzar and Zerubbabel, and the high priest, Jeshua (Ezr 1:8; 2:2). In their second year the people were ready to begin rebuilding the temple (3:8), but it took over 20 difficult years before the returnees were able to complete it in 516 BC.

The next recorded events are Ezra's return to Jerusalem almost 60 years later (458 BC) and his vigorous campaign against mixed marriages, "for Ezra had set his heart to study the Law of the LORD, and to do it and to teach His statutes and rules in Israel" (7:10).

After another interval of 12 years, Nehemiah received permission from the Persian king to investigate reports that the repatriated exiles were "in great trouble and shame" (Ne 1:3). On his arrival in Jerusalem (445 BC), he at once set to work to make the city safe against attacks from the outside. Overcoming serious difficulties, he built the walls of the city, organized watchmen to guard them, and persuaded the people to repopulate the city enclosed by the walls. In the spiritual re-armament of the people that followed, he yielded initiative to Ezra.

Apparently recalled by the king, Nehemiah left Jerusalem in 433/2 BC. When later he returned, he found it necessary again to correct abuses that had crept in during his absence.

Ezra and Nehemiah, their contributions to Israel's reconstruction made, both vanished from sight as abruptly as they appeared on stage.

Ezra and Nehemiah in the Persian Empire

Israel's rehabilitation in the Promised Land as reported in these books did not materialize overnight. The dates in the summary above make clear that more than 100 years elapsed between the arrival in Jerusalem of the first exiles (538 BC) and the reforms carried out by Nehemiah on his second visit to the city. This century coincided almost exactly with the first half of the duration of the gigantic Persian Empire that stretched from the Indus River through Asia Minor to the Mediterranean Sea and down through Israel to the waters of the Nile. Its turn to be buried under the sands of time would come a hundred years later when Alexander the Great (d 323 BC) became the next world conqueror.

One of the earliest known maps of the world, with Babylon at its center. Assyria, Elam, and other places are also named (700–500 BC).

NEHEMIAH OVERVIEW

Author
Nehemiah, governor of Judah

Date
c 445–432 BC

Places
Susa; Jerusalem's gates, walls, and villages; Beyond the River

People
Nehemiah; Eliashib; Ezra; Artaxerxes; Sanballat; Tobiah; Geshem

Purpose
To demonstrate that all things are possible by God's gracious and providential care

Law Themes
Exile due to sin; illegal marriages; persecution; broken faith by failing to keep God's Word

Gospel Themes
God fulfills His promises of grace; God's providence; restored atonement at the temple; God's hand guides history and the lives of His people, the remnant

Memory Verses
Nehemiah's prayer (1:4–11); building the wall (4:18–23); attending to the Word (8:7b–8)

TIMELINE

587 BC	Jerusalem temple destroyed
538 BC	Cyrus decrees that exiles may return to Judah
516 BC	Second temple completed
445 BC	Nehemiah leads work on walls of Jerusalem
434 BC	Nehemiah returns to Susa

PERSIAN RULERS

In both Ezra and Nehemiah events are dated according to the regnal years of the following Persian rulers:

Cyrus 559–530	Zerubbabel and Jeshua return to Jerusalem
Cambyses 528–523 (not mentioned)	Rebuilding halted
Darius 522–486	Second temple completed 516
Xerxes (Ahasuerus) c 486–465	Events in Esther
Artaxerxes 464–424	Return of Ezra (458) and Nehemiah (445)

Five more kings held the throne in the next century, including another Xerxes, two Dariuses, and two Artaxerxes. Daniel (a contemporary in part with Cyrus) and Esther (a contemporary of Xerxes) both lived at the time of Ezra and Nehemiah but are not mentioned because they were not involved in the reconstruction program in the homeland.

COMPOSITION

Authors

These two books virtually have to be introduced as one, not only on literary grounds but also because of the historical overlap in the careers of the two men. There are also close literary connections with Chronicles, not only because of possibly common authorship (see below) but also for the obvious reason that the conclusion of 2Ch 36 (vv 22–23) is identical with the beginning of Ezra (1:1–3a). The common subject is the decree of Cyrus, and the fact that in Chronicles it is broken off in the middle of a sentence probably indicates that at some point in transmission the two were united. (That, however, by no means demonstrates common authorship.)

Since Ezra-Nehemiah is the chronological sequel to Chronicles, it probably originally followed it, an order to which the Septuagint returned and with which we are now familiar. Presumably, the original order was reversed and Chronicles was placed after Ezra-Nehemiah when the Writings portion of the Hebrew canon was being assembled (see p 1011). The idea apparently was to conclude the canon with a book that chronicled the entire sacred history (as St. Jerome described Chronicles), and perhaps Cyrus's decree was let stand, even though repetitious, in order to close the canonical collection on an optimistic note.

It is often assumed that Ezra and Nehemiah were *originally* one composition, but this is doubtful. The most that can be said with certainty is that they were united very soon. Jesus son of Sirach (c early second century BC) probably knew only a single work, as seems to follow from his mention of Nehemiah, but not Ezra, in his praise of famous men. Josephus and the earliest Christian writers (including the great LXX uncials) present the same picture. In the Masoretic tradition the unity is firmly established, as evidenced not only in the lack of any space between the two but also in the concluding comments and statistics that are only given at the end of Nehemiah for both books (the division was only secondarily introduced shortly before the Reformation).

Evidence that the two books were originally discrete compositions is probably provided both by the appearance of a superscription in Ne 1:1 and, in Masoretic texts, by a marginal notice, "Nehemiah," perhaps witnessing to a memory of their original independence (which led Luther to abandon Vulgate usage [cf below] and label the second book "Nehemiah," as most since him have done). Also indicative of originally independent circulation is the duplication of the list of returning exiles in Ezr 2 and Ne 7:6–68. If so, the two were early combined because of their obvious continuity. Another motive may have been to obtain a total number of canonical books equal to the number of letters in the Hebrew alphabet (22).

The books quote Ezra's and Nehemiah's own words at length, but a fair amount of third-person narrative raises the question whether one of them also completed the entire work. It is just as predictable that tradition assumed one of them was the editor, as that criticism has tended to doubt it. Dogmatism in either direction is unhelpful, but tradition certainly cannot be said to have been disproved, and it still remains as likely an explanation as any (that is, at least someone of Ezra's own generation and closely associated with him). The earliest and perhaps still most likely tradition had the book written by Ezra (together with most of Chronicles) but completed by Nehemiah. Alternatives that Ezra himself incorporated the Nehemiah materials in his final edition, or that Nehemiah appended his entire book to the completed Ezra do not make for a fundamentally different picture.

Second Maccabees preserves a tradition of Nehemiah's extensive library, which, if true, may have a bearing on the question.

Scripture does not make direct statements on the final authorship of these books. According to a widely held theory, they form a literary unit with Chronicles, produced by an unknown person and therefore conveniently called "the Chronicler."[1] There are enough similarities in the three books to suggest that they are the composition of the same writer-editor. Also, a date for one author a century later is advanced because of the inclusion of the genealogy of the high priestly line in Ne 12:1–11.

But other factors favor individual authorship. Rabbinic tradition, counting Ezra-Nehemiah as one book, holds that "Ezra wrote his book" but adds significantly that Nehemiah "finished it." If true, the first-person accounts in both books are not memoirs incorporated by a compiler but separate autobiographical notes by Ezra and Nehemiah themselves. Both writers present statistical materials based on documents current at their own time. And only Ezra contains sections written in Aramaic (Ezr 4:7–6:18; 7:12–28), at that time the language of international diplomacy.

Date of Composition

The Elephantine materials (papyri found at or near Elephantine, Egypt) have removed all reason to doubt a fifth-century date of at least the Aramaic sections of Ezra, and the large number of Persian words throughout adds to the case.

The question is complicated by that of the relation of Ezra-Nehemiah to Chronicles (see p 383). Traditionally the Chronicler was identified with Ezra. Even some modern critical scholars have defended the equation. More often, however, it is agreed that Chronicles and Ezra-Nehemiah have common authorship, but not necessarily by Ezra. (The Nehemiah memoirs are always a special case and are often held to have been appended secondarily at a later time.) That leaves the question of the date of both books wide open. Serious objections have been mounted against that assumption of common authorship (alleged stylistic, linguistic, and conceptual differences), and the pendulum has swung in the direction of either leaving Chronicles out of the picture altogether, or of positing a multilayered process in the development of the material. It appears to be another case where philological arguments (at least until we have vastly more hard data) can only end in a draw, and where by default alone, tradition looks as good as ever.

---

1 Some propose Ezra as the author of the trilogy.

Most of the arguments once adduced for a late third-century date (or later) for Ezra-Nehemiah (and also Chronicles, if they are the same work) have been quietly abandoned, but a couple of them still merit attention. One concerns the mention of a "Jaddua" in Ne 12:11 and 22. If this were the same Jaddua whom Josephus reports as high priest when Alexander the Great entered Jerusalem in 332, we certainly would have evidence of a later hand. At most, however, it might indicate no more than some later, secondary updating of the lists. More likely, Josephus has telescoped several generations, and the Jaddua of Alexander's time was not the son of Johanan mentioned by Nehemiah but his grandson. From the Elephantine letters we know Johanan (grandson of the Eliashib mentioned in Ne 3:1 and 13:4–9, 28) to have been high priest in the last decade of the century. Thus his son, Jaddua, could easily have been of age and in office by 400, and there is no insuperable problem in assuming that Nehemiah lived that long. (The discussion is rendered extremely difficult by the fact that, like "Jaddua," so many of the names of this period are family names or at least repeat themselves in succeeding generations.)

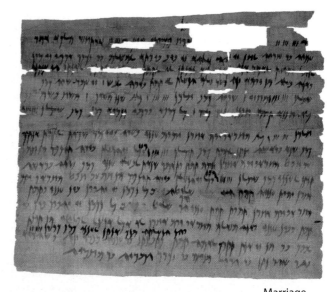

Marriage document, in Aramaic, dated 3rd July, 449 BC, found on Elephantine Island, Egypt. It mentions the family of Ananiah, a Jewish temple official.

Archaeology has disposed of two other erstwhile arguments for lateness. Mention of (Greek) drachmas or darics in Ne 7:71 is no longer taken as evidence of post-Alexandrian composition, because of the now demonstrated use of the standard at Elephantine as well as in the Persian period at Beth-zur (a short distance south of Jerusalem). Similarly, the title "king of Persia" (Ezr 1:1) or reference to "Darius the Persian" (Ne 12:22) is no longer a stumbling block because of ample parallels from antiquity.

Purpose/Recipients

It appears that, except for Ezra's and Nehemiah's strict measures, there would have been nothing left of Old Testament religion. Even if the community had survived the Persians, they would scarcely have been prepared for the onslaughts of Hellenism soon to come in Alexander's wake, not to speak of persecutions of the Maccabean era. Ezra and Nehemiah plainly were convinced that the prophets were right: pagan influences had to be ruthlessly expunged; compromise would be fatal. It was a time of necessary retrenchment, of withdrawal to the center for survival. Not only within subsequent Judaism but also often in Church history (our own age certainly being no exception), there are times when sheer survival is a maximal achievement.

Literary Features

Genre

The Books of Ezra-Nehemiah are a history that is, at least in part, compiled from a variety of primary sources such as letters, lists, and memoirs. The importance of Ezra-Nehemiah as a historical source can scarcely be exaggerated. For all practical purposes, our knowledge of the fifth-century Judean community is almost completely dependent on their testimony. And were it not for their record, our acquaintance with fifth-century Judaism would scarcely be any greater than with the fourth and third centuries—which often barely exceeds zero. We know that the community was in existence, but precious little more.

Characters

The paramount significance of the two figures, **Ezra** and **Nehemiah**, cannot be overstated. Humanly speaking, it seems certain, that, except for their labors, the little community of repatriates would surely have gone under, or at least merged their religious beliefs with those of their neighbors. Hopes of another Davidic ruler physically occupying the throne had apparently died with Zerubbabel, or were at least postponed. Prophets still appeared (cf Ne 6:10–14), but it was no longer their hour—as, for the most part it had not been since the demise of dynastic hopes (cf Zec 13:2–6). The transition to a "theocratic" or priestly (hierocratic) form of government appropriate to the times until the "fullness of time" did not come easily.

Apparently the credit for the success of the community goes equally to both Ezra and Nehemiah. Their cooperation remains a classical example of the necessary interpenetration of the material and the spiritual in God's earthly kingdom—and not only in the Old Testament when "church" and "state" are in principle still united. Without Nehemiah's heroic and draconian measures, Ezra's labors of covenant renewal could scarcely ever have come to fruition, except perhaps for a tiny clique. And without Ezra's religious measures, Nehemiah's administrative reforms would have remained purely external and legal—and probably also very temporary, as indicated by the relapse during his brief return to Persia (Ne 13:6–8).

Outline for Ezra

I. First Return of Exiles and Rebuilding of the Temple (chs 1–6)

  A. Proclamation of Cyrus (1:1–4)

  B. Response to the Proclamation (1:5–11)

  C. List of Returnees (ch 2)

     1. Introduction to the list (2:1–2a)

     2. People of Israel by families (2:2b–20)

     3. People of Israel by location (2:21–35)

     4. Priests of Israel (2:36–39)

     5. Levites, singers, and gatekeepers (2:40–42)

     6. Temple servants (2:43–54)

     7. Sons of Solomon's servants (2:55–58)

     8. Those who could not prove their descent (2:59–63)

     9. Numbers for the whole assembly (2:64–67)

     10. Freewill offerings for the house of God (2:68–69)

     11. Note on location of returnees (2:70)

  D. Rebuilding the Altar (3:1–7)

  E. Rebuilding the Temple (3:8–13)

  F. Adversaries Oppose Rebuilding (4:1–6)

  G. Adversaries' Letter to King Artaxerxes (4:7–16)

  H. King Artaxerxes Orders Rebuilding to Cease (4:17–24)

  I. Rebuilding Begins Again (5:1–5)

  J. Tattenai's Letter to King Darius (5:6–17)

  K. Decree of King Darius (6:1–12)

     1. Decree of Cyrus found (6:1–5)

     2. Response of King Darius to Tattenai (6:6–12)

  L. Temple Finished (6:13–15)

  M. Temple Dedicated (6:16–18)

  N. First Passover in New Temple (6:19–22)

Nehemiah thus fully deserves his reputation as one of the great laymen of the Bible, accomplishing what often only laymen can. His repeated petitions that God "remember" his accomplishments suggest that perhaps he also illustrates the inexperience of many laymen at articulating their faith in a way entirely satisfactory to the clergy. (However, that problem recedes if we recall that the "form" employed was a standard votive one in the Near East, and it can be understood in a theologically acceptable manner.) But, if so, he is also a reminder, especially standing alongside Ezra, that faith and even orthodoxy are not simply to be equated with theological fluency, ideal though that is.

Despite Nehemiah's importance, however, Ezra usually dominates the limelight, and, from a theological or ecclesiastical viewpoint, for good reason. Ezra's role in the "history of religion" is almost incalculable, even from the most detached standpoint. As is sometimes said of Moses, if he did not exist, we should have to invent him! If Moses was Israel's founder (humanly speaking), Ezra was, indeed, as he is often styled, the "father of Judaism."

Ezra's paramount significance in the history of religion can be summarized in two areas: (1) as a scribe, and (2) with respect to the canon. Originally, the term *scribe* applied to any "secretary" or amanuensis (e.g., Baruch to Jeremiah), but particularly of a government post at the head of an administrative division (cf 2Ki 12:11; 25:19). In Ezra's case, it doubtless translated into something like "Secretary of State for Jewish affairs," and Ezra's mission to Jerusalem must have been essentially an implementation of his office's major responsibility. Given the circumstances, however, that is, the intrinsic importance of teaching and expounding the Mosaic revelation, Ezra virtually becomes an incarnation of the term's shift to the meaning of "exegete," "Bible interpreter," etc. (Jer 8:8 may well indicate, however, that the usage was not totally new in Ezra's time.) Wisdom traditions apparently became ever more explicitly wedded to the special revelation of the Torah at about the same time (note the equation of wisdom and law in Ezr 7:25), further enhancing the relevance of the "scribe" to the details of daily living. Only as the interpretations began to move beyond mere exposition of the Word itself did "scribe" begin to assume (at least from the Christian standpoint) some of the negative coloration that it has in the New Testament, trends that would be continued and amplified in subsequent rabbinism.

Narrative Development or Plot for Ezra

As a history, the Book of Ezra focuses on how God restored Judea, the temple, and holiness to Israel. Ezra opens with proclamation of the emperor Cyrus, which almost sounds like the emperor was responding directly to a request from God and in fulfillment of prophecy. Not all of the Judeans were ready to go back to Jerusalem. Ezra details a list and reports that less than 50,000 returned. However, those who returned did so in faithfulness to the Lord and intent upon rebuilding the temple. When the inhabitants of the territory surrounding Jerusalem noticed the reconstruction work, they slandered the Judeans in a message to the king of Persia, warning that the Judeans, with the temple and city rebuilt, would rebel. An order was given to stop the construction, and all building operation on the temple site ceased for the next 15 years.

Ezra introduces two prophets, Haggai and Zechariah, whom God called in 520 BC to urge the people to finish rebuilding the temple. Opposition developed again but was not supported by Darius, so that the temple was finally completed four years later. The end of the book tells of Ezra's personal immigration to Jerusalem at the encouragement of Artaxerxes Longimanus and the work of reformation, particularly in regard to mixed marriages between Judeans and members of Gentile tribes and nations. The book ends with a statement about all those who had married foreign women and had to put them away with their children.

Narrative Development or Plot for Nehemiah

Like the Book of Ezra, the Book of Nehemiah is a history of restoration but with some different focuses. The book begins with Nehemiah learning about the sad state of the exiles in Jerusalem and his prayer that God would have mercy on them. He explains how King Artaxerxes recognizes his distress and grants his request to travel to Jerusalem so that the city walls may be restored. Nehemiah is to serve as governor.

After arriving at Jerusalem, Nehemiah goes out at night to survey the state of the city walls. He then encourages the builders to begin again and supports them in that effort, while also rebuking the Jewish nobles and officials for taking advantage of the poor. The wall is eventually finished and the book provides an account of the exiles who returned to Jerusalem.

The next part of the story describes how Ezra led the people in a service of covenant renewal and in the celebration of the Feast of Booths. By casting lots, it is decided which Judeans will live within Jerusalem. The priests and Levites are entrusted with the services of God's house and participate in the dedication of the new city walls. The book ends with Nehemiah enacting a series of reforms, addressing problems with mixed marriages, cleansing the temple chambers, restoring the inheritance of the Levites, and ending abuses of the Sabbath.

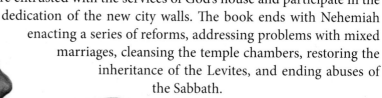

Resources

Considerable scholarly energy has been invested in the attempt to precisely delineate sources used in creating Ezra-Nehemiah. No complete unanimity has emerged, but some of them seem quite obvious and are worthy of note. The two major ones are the two great autobiographical passages, the "memoirs" of both Ezra and Nehemiah. The precise extent of both is often debated, but their existence is usually assumed (though a few regard them as compositions of the Chronicler or someone else). Ezra's memoirs apparently comprise at least the bulk of chs 7–9 where we have

Outline for Nehemiah

I. Nehemiah's First Visit (chs 1–12)

  A. Nehemiah Hears of the Situation in Jerusalem and Prays (ch 1)

  B. Nehemiah Takes Action (ch 2)

    1. He travels to Jerusalem (2:1–10)

    2. He secretly inspects walls and gates (2:11–16)

    3. He organizes repairs in face of opposition (2:17–20)

  C. Builders of Walls Listed by Section (ch 3)

  D. Opposition to Rebuilding (ch 4)

    1. Sanballat and Tobiah (4:1–5)

    2. Plot to attack the workers (4:6–14)

    3. Rebuilding the walls (4:15–23)

  E. Problems Arise (ch 5)

    1. Complaints from the oppressed (5:1–5)

    2. New direction under the Law (5:6–13)

    3. Leading by example (5:14–19)

  F. Completing the Walls (ch 6)

    1. Opposition (6:1–9)

    2. False prophets (6:10–14)

    3. Work on the walls (6:15–19)

  G. Lists of Exiles (7:1–73a)

    1. Protecting Jerusalem (7:1–4)

    2. Discovering and recording the list (7:5–72)

    3. Settling the exiles (7:73a)

  H. Covenant Renewal and Revival (7:73b–10:39)

    1. Ezra reads God's Word (7:73b–8:12)

    2. God's people celebrate Feast of Booths (8:13–18)

    3. God's people fast (9:1–5a)

    4. God's history of grace toward Israel (9:5b–31)

    5. God's people confess their sins (9:32–37)

the first person ("I") used. More precise boundaries can scarcely be fixed because the style is not distinct enough from the surrounding third-person ("he") narratives about Ezra, which, however, may well also stem from Ezra.

Nehemiah's memoirs are more distinctive, possibly because they were not subjected to as much editorial activity (Ezra's respect for his colleague's diary?). They are quite unanimously found in Ne 1–7, and probably constitute at least the bulk of chs 9–13 as well. Their repeated refrain, "Remember me, O my God" or the like (5:19; 13:14, 22, 31) has led to the plausible suggestion that they were modeled somewhat after the memorial inscriptions common in the ancient Near East—not merely memorials for men, but a sort of votive thankoffering to a deity (cf below).

Besides these two memoirs, the third major bloc of material in Ezra-Nehemiah is the Sheshbazzar-Zerubbabel section of Ezr 1–6. All three blocks appear to depend heavily on three types of sources: lists, letters, and official documents of various sorts. The most striking list is that of the expatriates who returned with Zerubbabel, which is duplicated almost verbatim in Ezr 2 and Ne 7. Ezra 8:1–14 details family heads who returned with Ezra, and Ne 12:1–26 lists priests and Levites from Zerubbabel's to Nehemiah's time. Ezra 10:18–24 records those who face excommunication because of marriage to foreign women. Nehemiah 9:38–10:27 is a roster of the signatories to Nehemiah's covenant, as 3:1–32 is of those who had participated in the rebuilding of the walls.

The letters quoted are largely exchanges between the opponents of the new Jewish community and the Persian court—all in Aramaic, like the connecting passages, hence perhaps first brought together in some intermediate Aramaic source. These include the exchange with Artaxerxes in Ezr 4:7–23, and with Darius in 5:6–6:12.

Vase of a Phoenician woman. Her headdress served as a container (fourth century BC).

Included in the latter is Darius's citation of Cyrus's "Edict of Restoration" of 538. It constitutes the major example of the third type of source, namely, official documents. As noted above, besides its citation here in Aramaic, we also meet it in a different Hebrew version at the beginning of the book (Ezr 1:2–4). For a long time the authenticity of the latter was widely questioned on the grounds of the differences in both tone and subject matter. However, even many critics are now convinced that most of the variations are due to the different settings and audiences. The matter-of-fact Aramaic document appears to be a typical memorandum (Persian *dikrona*; Hbr *zikkaron*) of the king's oral decision filed in the royal archives, while the Hebrew version takes the form of an oral proclamation of the king's edict by a herald, town crier, or the like in the audience's own language. The genuineness of also the latter is supported by its formal parallelism with Artaxerxes' letter to Ezra in 7:12–26 (in Aramaic).

All three of the main blocks in Ezra-Nehemiah not only utilize the same three types of material but may also display a similarity of literary structure, by which the components are linked together, especially in certain summary notations (e.g., temple dedication in Ezr 6:13–14 and wall dedication Ne 12:26) and repetitive resumptions (e.g., Ezr 6:22b and Ne 11:1 on working and living in Jerusalem). That type of overall structural unity need not imply free composition, of course, but it probably betrays the hand of the author of the book as it stands, whether Ezra himself or another.

Text and Translations

The Masoretic Hebrew text of Ezra-Nehemiah is well preserved, with variations in spelling. The Qumran fragments of Ezra are compatible with the Masoretic text, again with the presence of spelling variations and some differences in grammar. The LXX text of Ezra-Nehemiah introduces a different matter completely—rewriting. For more on this issue, see *ALEN*, p 269. The Latin and Syriac versions fairly reflect the Hebrew books.

Note should be taken of the presence in Ezra of two sizable portions written in Aramaic: 4:7–6:18 and 7:12–28. (The only real parallel elsewhere in the Bible is Dn 2–7.) It was once widely argued that the type of Aramaic employed required a fairly late date of composition, but archaeological discoveries, especially the Elephantine Papyri from fifth-century Egypt, have long since demolished that skepticism. It plainly was the usual "imperial Aramaic" of the time, the *lingua franca* of the Persian Empire. Thus, it is understandable that Aramaic commences at 4:7 with a letter sent to Artaxerxes, but it is not clear why the Aramaic then continues for a time.

Even the Hebrew of Ezra betrays increasing Aramaic influence, but nowhere so prominently as in Nehemiah's memoirs, where the language is still technically Hebrew, but the underlying syntax and speech patterns appear to be quite thoroughly Aramaic. (Of course, Aramaic increasingly displaced Hebrew in everyday speech, Hebrew being retained in Israel largely as a liturgical language, but recent discoveries underscore that we must not overstate its demise. Especially in the stricter and more nationalistic sects from Maccabean times on and in the time of Christ, Hebrew plainly continued to flourish until at least AD 200.)

Part of the Babylonian Chronicle. The series summarizes principal events from 747 BC to 280 BC. Each entry is separated by a horizontal line and begins with a reference to the year of a king's reign.

Doctrinal Content

Summary Commentary for Ezra

Chs 1–3 The Lord stirs Cyrus the Persian to send home a remnant of the Judean exiles, as prophesied by Isaiah and Jeremiah. Although 42,360 people respond to Cyrus's invitation to return to Judah, relatively few Levites—key temple workers—appear on the list. Within about a year of Cyrus's decree, the Judeans are settling in their homeland and beginning to work on the altar to restore the sacrifices, showing their sincere desire for true worship and for honoring their emperor's decree. The service dedicating the foundation for the new temple stirs deep emotions for the Judeans because of the memory of their shortcomings and because they are eyewitnesses to God's renewed mercy for them.

Ch 4 To maintain pure worship, the Judeans reject the offer from the people of the land, who insist on taking part in building the temple and in joining the worship services. Ezra illustrates the strong and unreasonable opposition that the Judean settlers faced from regional Persian officials. Artaxerxes' response and the violent intervention of local officials stop the civil building projects in Jerusalem, most notably the work on the temple.

Chs 5–6 God's prophets boldly call His people back to the work of the Jerusalem temple. The Persian governor Tattenai discovers the truth about the rebuilding of the Jerusalem temple to the "great God" of heaven. The emperor Darius approves the building of the temple, sponsors its sacrifices, and curses those who would interfere. The God of heaven has so radically changed the circumstances that the government that opposed the project becomes its sponsor. As a result, God's people rejoice in the atonement for all Israel celebrated at the dedication of the Jerusalem temple. They also rejoice in the cleansing and blessings associated with the celebration of the first Passover at the new temple, including the conversion of some people of the land.

Chs 7–8 Through the decree of the pagan ruler Artaxerxes, the Lord provides for the instruction of His people in His Word, as led by Ezra. More leaders and members of their families return from the exile in Babylonia. Near the head of the list are members of the royal household, which had nearly been destroyed. The Lord also helps Ezra discover the Levites and temple servants whose roles at the temple were going unfulfilled. By His hand, Ezra's caravan successfully delivers their offerings to Jerusalem.

Chs 9–10 Ezra expresses remorse and shame when he learns of the unfaithful Judeans' illegal marriages. To resolve the problem, some Judeans make a harsh proposal for immediate divorces, but the counsel of the community wisely requests investigation so they can learn the extent of the problem and propose the best solution. As a result of the earlier investigation, 111 illegal marriages are identified and ended.

Summary Commentary for Nehemiah

Chs 1–2 Nehemiah recalls the report about Jerusalem that prompted his decision to travel there and assist God's people. On behalf of those struggling in Jerusalem, Nehemiah fasts and prays with great empathy as guided by God's Word. Nehemiah asks for an opportunity to help rebuild his homeland, and the king answers favorably, because God is guiding the matter. The Word moves Nehemiah's heart to begin plans for rebuilding Jerusalem's walls.

Chs 3–4 The Judeans eagerly begin work on the walls and gates of Jerusalem under Nehemiah's able leadership. When obstacles arise, Nehemiah encourages ever more vigilant service by reminding the workers that "our God will fight for us."

Chs 5–7 Governor Nehemiah addresses the problems caused by excessive interest rates and taxes and sets an example of generosity for the leaders. However, false prophets attempt to deceive Nehemiah and bring about his death. God's people must always test claims of prophetic authority against the sure Word of prophecy: Holy Scripture (Dt 18:20–22; 1Jn 4:1–3). Nehemiah appoints faithful colleagues to ensure good progress on the next phase of the work and catalogs the status of the community.

Chs 8–10 Nehemiah's efforts result in an opportunity for Ezra and others to teach God's Word to the Judeans. The Word moves their hearts, who sanctify the day of celebration by Word and faith. By studying Scripture, the Judeans learn that they had overlooked celebrating a key feast: the Feast of Booths. The people confess the Lord's enduring mercy promised in the covenant. They were saved by God's grace, not by their obedience. They offer thanks to the Lord for the blessings of the covenant and the atonement provided through the sacrifices.

Chs 11–13 For the sake of security and good order, a number of people willingly agree to occupy Jerusalem, which was only beginning to be restored. With careful organization, the priests and Levites lead the people in worship and in dedicating the city walls. Nehemiah confronts ongoing issues of the Law and holiness, even losing his composure when people violate the covenant (13:25). The book ends with practical measures he enacts.

Specific Law Themes in Ezra

Ezra is grieved because the people broke faith with the Lord by violating His covenant with them. As a result, the Lord has surrendered them to exile among the Gentile nations. Instead of seeking the Lord, the people continually fail to follow God's Word.

Specific Gospel Themes in Ezra

Although the people of Judah rebelled, the Lord did not forget His covenant with their forefather, David. The Lord had blessed them through David's household and, even though the people have gone into exile, He preserved the household of David in order to renew His blessings to the people. The Lord heeds the concerns of His servant, Ezra, and will be with him throughout the struggles he faces. Through Ezra's efforts to reestablish the temple and its sacrifices, the Lord reestablishes atonement for the people of Judah.

Specific Law Themes in Nehemiah

The book opens with Nehemiah's distress over the exiles who returned to Jerusalem but had not been able to restore the community. As he prays about the situation, he painfully recalls the reasons for the community's failures and exile, which originally led to Jerusalem's destruction. After Nehemiah faces opposition from outside the community, he discovers an example of corruption within the community, which will again lead to their destruction: illegal marriage. The people continue to break faith with their Lord.

Specific Gospel Themes in Nehemiah

Nehemiah recalls God's grace and providence in calling Israel His people and preserving them despite their failures. Like Ezra, he focuses on the blessings connected with God's Word and the temple sacrifices and feasts. He sees God's hand guiding the people through history to be the remnant for renewal of the covenant.

Specific Doctrines in Ezra-Nehemiah

The two great prayers of Ezra deserve special note (Ezr 9; also Ne 9, which the LXX attributes to Ezra). Both serve as major refutations of any misunderstanding of Ezra's work as sterile "legalism," "biblicism," etc. Critics often regard them as two recensions of the same prayer, which is unlikely, though like many prayers (especially uttered by the same person), they undeniably have elements in common. The settings are different, though they are in a way merely the positive and negative sides of the same coin: the context of

Ezr 9 is the confrontation with the problem of mixed marriages, while Ne 9 forms a major part of the great ceremony of covenant renewal, the climax of Ezra's labors. From a theological viewpoint, it is one of the Bible's classical statements of salvation history (*Heilsgeschichte*), of the "theology of recital," which anticipates the Gospel of the "mighty acts of God." To its list of acts, the Church will add those of the New Testament fulfillment, climaxing in Christ.

Likewise, from a liturgical viewpoint, we have in Ezra's prayer of Ne 9 one of the noblest liturgical formulae in the Old Testament. It is only technically out of chronological sequence to label it a "Eucharistic prayer," and as a matter of fact it has served as a model for many such prayers in the history of the Christian worship (not to speak of its influence on synagogue worship). It centers in "remembrance" (*anamnesis*), of past acts of Law and Gospel as the basis for present repentance and covenant renewal, as well as of future hope. Revival of the prayer's role today might aid also the present generation in "remembrance" of their Old Testament patrimony.

The Book of Nehemiah teaches that the day of rest was not simply for bodily rest but was especially for devotion to God's Word (Ne 8). It also teaches the value of public confession (Ne 9), which is not focused on enumeration of individual sins but on the acknowledgement that all are sinners in need of God's forgiveness, especially as they draw together for the public ministry of the Word and for the administration of the Sacraments.

Ezra's traditional association with the closing of the Old Testament canon has even more direct significance for Christianity. There is no way to test directly the accuracy of the tradition (and, in any event, only the human, historical aspects of canonization can be "tested" anyway), but there is no reason why the conservative should not grant it essential credence.

Application of Ezra

Chs 1–3 The Lord of heaven and earth continues to govern the nations for the good of His people. Though the news we hear each day is often bad, we can rejoice that the Lord of heaven is at work amid tumultuous events. He also gives each of us a role of service in our local congregation. When you are discouraged or overwhelmed by the needs of your congregation, entrust your cares to the Lord of heaven, who oversees all things for your benefit. The Lord sincerely receives your worship and requests; He has promised to answer according to His goodwill and the mercy He demonstrated in His Son, your Redeemer. By the Word, the Lord lays a foundation for new life and peace in your life.

Ch 4 When God's people today consider the boundaries of pure and faithful worship, and also God's calling to reach out to others, they may feel challenged as they work to fulfill both callings. Clear boundaries in doctrine and practice are necessary because a corrupt gospel is no Gospel at all (cf Gal 1:8). God's people may also face bureaucratic opposition when seeking building permits, etc., for churches and schools. Pray for your governing officials who do not seem to recognize the valuable contribution God's people make in civil life. Underlying the physical struggles of our world are always spiritual struggles. Take courage from the Lord's mastery of His creation and the manner in which He works for the good of His people, especially shown in the civil punishment and glorious resurrection of His Son for our redemption.

Chs 5–6 When your cause is right in the Lord's eyes, do not hesitate to act and to call others to peaceable action. Act confidently, because the Lord will watch over you, bless you, and keep you. Encourage good people to seek public office. The God of heaven rules among us through faithful leaders in both church and state. The great God of our salvation cares for every aspect of our lives. Who knows what changes God may bring? Above all, offer thanks to Him for your salvation by Jesus' sacrifice. Praise God for the blessings of forgiveness you hear and receive in your congregation. There is no greater cause of joy than the pardon of our heavenly King. How great is our calling to proclaim God's mercy and cleansing!

Chs 7–8 Just as the Lord provided for the instruction of His people through Ezra, the Lord converts hearts and extends His gracious rule through the Word for you. He likewise preserved the house of David, thereby preserving for you the promise of a Savior, the Son of David, Jesus. Each believer has a valuable role of service to fulfill in his or her church, whether leading or attending to other duties. Along with your office, the Lord will grant you His Spirit and gifts, which will build you up. Like Ezra, commit yourself body and soul to the Lord's service. For the Lord supports the service of His people; He serves them graciously in Christ.

Chs 9–10 Few topics have grown more sensitive than the issues surrounding marriage. This is ultimately because families fail to believe in or teach what God's Word teaches about the holy blessings of marriage. Like Ezra, express your shame, remorse, and prayers to God when sinful notions of marriage tear at your family. Study and share the teachings of God's Word about marriage. Christ the Bridegroom is also our Redeemer, who removes all our shame and comforts our remorseful hearts.

Application of Nehemiah

Chs 1–2 As you hear of other people's needs, take them to heart as a matter of prayer and concern. God's Word grants confidence in prayer. Call on the Lord to confess your sins and to plead for others; use God's promises as your guide. God's hand is constantly at work in history, though we rarely can foresee and determine what He will do. His hand is on His children to guide them with the love He has for them in Christ. All His promises to you are "Yes" and "Amen" in Christ the Savior.

Chs 3–4 Like Nehemiah and the Judeans, God's people still today have civic duties to fulfill, sharing in the burdens of their family and neighbors. As the Lord gives you strength, support the good works of others, which creates life and improves its quality. Do not let the taunts of unbelievers or naysayers keep you from fulfilling your calling. The great and powerful Lord—He who stooped to bear our burdens and save us in Christ—is with you in your work. Enact every sound plan with confidence in His blessing. Just as He overcame Satan at the cross, He will overcome the obstacles you, too, may face.

Chs 5–7 In politics, words are cheap but goodwill is rare and good deeds are rarer still. When people are unfairly burdened, we can follow Nehemiah's example by relieving them, whether by providing for fairer laws or by helping them directly. As the Lord grants you opportunity, lead others by good example. Abide in God's Word, which is able to make you wise for life and for eternal life through Christ. How great a blessing is a shared burden in service to the One who bore all our burdens at the cross and will share heaven with us too.

Chs 8–10 God's Word is our source of peace and blessing. Support the proclamation of the Word not only by your offerings and service but, most important, by hearing and studying it. Celebrate the holiness of your Lord, who sanctifies you by the Word. Sing the Word in joyful hymns, for in their words, He will grant you strength. Each day, the Lord's people need to partake of God's Word—a feast for the soul. Consume and study the Scriptures daily, for by them the Lord nurtures faith and grants life. As the Lord blesses us, we also respond with offerings of thanks for His gracious gifts in Christ.

Chs 11–13 Volunteer service has great value and may involve great sacrifice. Prayerfully consider how you may voluntarily serve your Lord, your church, and your community. As you serve the Lord, you will also have frus-

Zerubbabel's Temple

516–20 BC

Shown here is a much more modest reconstruction of Solomon's magnificent temple, destroyed by the Babylonians in 587 BC. It is assumed that this "second temple" followed the original floor plan, but funds were limited, craftsmanship was compromised, and its glory was in a spiritual sense only (Hg 1:6–7).

Reconstructed cherubim here guard the ark as before, along with barrier tapestry (curtain or veil), lampstands, tables, and portico pillars. But the walls are plain, with no hint of lavish artistry or gold.

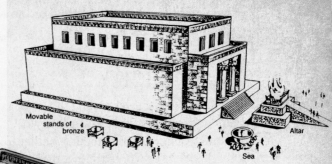

Movable stands of bronze

Altar

Sea

Temple source materials are subject to academic interpretation, and subsequent art reconstructions vary.

On the ark of the covenant, cf Ex 25.

Construction of the second temple was started in 530 BC on the Solomonic foundations leveled a half-century earlier by the Babylonians. People who remembered the earlier temple wept at the comparison (Ezr 3:12). Not until 516 BC, the sixth year of the Persian emperor Darius I (522–486 BC), was the temple finally completed at the urging of Haggai and Zechariah (Ezr 6:13–15).

Archaeological evidence confirms that the Persian period in Judea was a comparatively impoverished one in terms of material culture. Later Aramaic documents from Elephantine in Upper Egypt illustrate the official process of gaining permission to construct a Judean place of worship and the opposition engendered by the presence of various foes during this period.

Of the temple and its construction, little is known. Among the few contemporary buildings, the Persian palace at Lachish and the Tobiad monument at Iraq el-Amir may be compared in terms of technique.

Unlike the more famous structures razed in 587 BC and AD 70, the temple begun by Zerubbabel suffered no major hostile destruction, but was gradually repaired and reconstructed over a long period. Eventually, it was replaced entirely by Herold's magnificent edifice.

trating experiences. Pray for the Lord to grant you strength, to control your anger, and to maintain proper focus on the Word. When frustration gets the better of you, count on the Lord to forgive you and strengthen you for continued service.

CANONICITY

The Book of Ezra was among those copied at Qumran, indicating its interest among Jews. In the second century BC, Jesus son of Sirach celebrated the lasting memory of Nehemiah, whether from his book or from another source (Ecclus 49:13). As noted above, the Books of Ezra and Nehemiah were treated as one in the rabbinic tradition and the Hebrew Bible. The LXX includes the compositions titled after "Esdras," parts of which some scholars regard as a unique composition that could predate the Masoretic Hebrew text, though this appears unlikely. (For more on this, see pp 454–55.) When Jerome translated Ezra and Nehemiah for the Vulgate, he treated them as separate works, which is how they were commonly received among Christians.

St. Jerome.

LUTHERAN THEOLOGIANS ON EZRA-NEHEMIAH

Luther

"The Word of God has this character that it is made known and comes when man is most desperate over everything, when he thinks that nothing is less likely to happen than what the Word of God says most certainly will happen. You see, it does not come to the lazy or the pleasure-seekers. To them it is a source of laughter. Rather it comes to the weak and the oppressed, to those in need. These also finally receive it in such a way that all human boasting vanishes and nothing is credited to our own strength and energies, but all to God alone. . . . You see, here the rebuilding of the temple is ordered against very powerful, very bitter foes. The command is given, I say, to a weak people, few in number, a people against whom stand powerful princes and powerful nations, which lived round about and daily threatened imminent destruction, as one may see in Ezra. For the violence of the neighboring peoples was such that the Jews were forced to build with one hand and to fight with the other to ward off the hostile nations. Yet, against all these fierce and powerful foes this one weak prophet here dares to rise up and prophesy about rebuilding the temple. So he orders this handful of people, who had just recently been snatched from a most burdensome captivity, to stand up against a mad and inflated king who didn't want them to rebuild the temple. . . . Yet it is the Word of God which commands such things, and to it we must listen even though the whole world resists it as the Jews also did listen. You see, when we thus attribute to God the glory of truth, then it happens that everything which first was opposed to us now is compelled to promote and help us in our plans. This is what happened here, where all the very heavy burdens and bitter hindrances were changed into peaceful allies. After all, as the account shows, the king ordered the princes to help the people, whereas before that they had been ordered to resist and oppose them. So, what appeared impossible earlier became very easy because of God's plan. Obviously, this is the way divine mercy, working wonderfully, turns all things into good for those

447

who believe; judgment is turned into salvation for them, sin into righteousness, etc., enemies into friends and subjects. For God, . . . ('The Almighty'), holds all things in His hand. The whole world, kings and princes, too, must obey Him." (AE 18:369–70)

"The word of God—that Jerusalem should be restored and built—went forth in the second year of Darius, about the time that Nehemiah came from Cambyses and began to rebuild Jerusalem, etc. For this was a great event, begun by many—and even promoted by angels, as Zechariah 1[:7–17] declares—yet not by everybody at once on the same day or at the same hour [Ezra 1–6]." (AE 35:304)

"The church is the work of God's hands, and His children are His cultivation. 'Therefore [God says] command Me. You cannot bring the matter to a successful issue. I will do it. Believe Me.' Ezra and Nehemiah carefully read these words of comfort and consoled the people and the king by means of the Word. Let God handle the matter, He will do it properly." (AE 17:129–30)

"I fear the time will come when schoolmasters, pastors, and preachers alike will have to quit, let the word go, and turn to a trade or some other means of stilling the pangs of hunger; just as the Levites had to abandon the worship of God to till the fields, as Nehemiah writes [Neh. 13:10]. Isn't it a crying shame? Up to now, a town with four or five hundred population could turn over to the mendicant monks alone the equivalent of five, six, or seven hundred gulden, besides what bishops, officials, and other bloodsuckers, together with beggars and relic hawkers, have already wrung from them. . . . But when they are asked to contribute one or two hundred gulden toward good schools and pulpits, they cry, 'You would reduce us to rags and make beggars of us! We would have nothing left'; then covetousness and concern for livelihood take over, and the people think they will die of hunger." (AE 45:318–19)

Gerhard

"*The two Books of Ezra* are considered as a single volume among the Hebrews according to Jerome (Epistle *ad Paulinum*) and Lactantius (*Instit.*, bk. 4, c. 11, where he quotes as from the Book of Ezra what is found in 2 Ezra or Nehemiah, c. 9). The same Lactantius (loc. cit.) calls Ezra a prophet, but Augustine doubts 'whether he ought to be called a prophet' (*De civit. Dei*, bk. 18, c. 36). The Greeks and Latins divide it into two books and assign the first to Ezra, the second to Nehemiah.

"Ezra was a scribe, highly skilled in the Law (Ezra 7:1, 6, 11). Jerome says this was Josedech, whose son was the high priest Joshua. (Cf. Ludovicus Vives, commentary on *De civ. Dei*, bk. 18, c. 36.)

"The first Book of Chronicles calls him Josedech. The Hebrews think he was Malachi, the last of the prophets.

"Munsterus wants him to be Nehemiah, whom Ezra 2:63 calls *Hattirschata*,[2] meaning 'cupbearer.' Rabbi Aben Ezra says this is a name of dignity in the Chaldean tongue. Tremellius interprets this as 'agent' or 'ambassador of the king.' Nehemiah was the son of Hecaliah, cupbearer of King Artaxerxes Memnon (Neh. 2:1), who ruled at Susa, the major city of Persia, which was built by Darius Hystaspes (as Pliny, *N. H.*, bk. 6 c. 27, and Athenaeus, *Deipnosoph.*, bk. 12, write) and where Megasthenes and other historians say a famous library was located.

"The first Book of Ezra consists of ten chapters and contains an account of the 146 years from the edict of Cyrus to the nineteenth year of Artaxerxes Memnon. It describes the account of the return of the Jews from their captivity by the leadership of Zerubbabel and of the rebuilding of the temple, along with the beginning of divine worship amid many difficulties. It has two parts: (1) About the return of the Jews from the Babylonian captivity into their homeland. (2) About the beginning of their divine worship and the state of Israel. Zerubbabel restored the temple; Ezra, the worship; and Nehemiah, the city.

"The second Book of Ezra, otherwise called Nehemiah, has thirteen chapters and covers the history of the fifty-five years from the twentieth year of Artaxerxes to the reign of the last Darius.

"This second book is attributed to Ezra (though it was written by Nehemiah) for two reasons: (1) Because it contains what Ezra and Nehemiah did at the same time. (2) Because, among the Hebrews, both books were connected into a single volume, which was divided into two among the Latins.

"In it is described the building of the walls and gates of the city, as well as of those things that Nehemiah established beneficially to correct the state of Israel. It can be divided conveniently into those two parts." (ThC E1 § 131)

---

2   Luther's German Bible and the Vulgate at Ezr 2:63 treat the Hbr word *hatirshatha'* as a proper noun.

QUESTIONS PEOPLE ASK
ABOUT EZRA AND NEHEMIAH

What was the actual *historical* sequence of Ezra and Nehemiah? We can broach here only a few salient aspects of the issue; for further details the reader is referred to the commentaries, larger introductions, or to the fine summary in John Bright's *A History of Israel*.

There is no longer any serious debate about Nehemiah's dates, and his career forms a fixed point in the discussions. The Elephantine texts, written in the last decade of the fifth century, prove that the "Artaxerxes" whom Nehemiah served was Artaxerxes I (464–424). Thus Nehemiah must have first arrived in Judah in 445 (the king's twentieth year) and returned to Persia in 433/2 after a term of about 11 years as governor (Ne 13:6). But after apparently only one year in Ecbatana, he returns for a second term of office of uncertain duration.

The questions all arise about Ezra's relation to Nehemiah. There are three main alternatives. (1) The traditional view assumes that the Artaxerxes associated with Ezra is also Artaxerxes I, as is the case of Nehemiah. Then, the date of Ezra's arrival in that monarch's "seventh year" (Ezr 7:7) can easily be fixed as 458,

An Elephantine letter concerning Passover celebrations, by official order of Armasmes, the governor of Egypt, in accordance with an edict issued by Darius (fifth century BC).

thirteen years *before* Nehemiah. (2) The most common alternative identifies the Artaxerxes of the Ezra narrative with Artaxerxes II (404–358), not bringing Ezra on the scene until 397, well *after* Nehemiah's activity. This construction caught on rapidly among critical scholars after Albin van Hoonacker, a Belgian Catholic, first proposed it in 1880, and it still has many defenders. (3) A third suggestion relates with tradition to Artaxerxes I, but also proceeds on the assumption of a scribal error in the date given in Ezr 7:7, namely, that it originally read "*thirty*-seventh" instead of "seventh," yielding a date of 428 for Ezra's advent, sometime in the middle of Nehemiah's second term in office. (Early on, Julius Wellhausen had suggested "*twenty*-seventh," but it appears to have no defenders today.)

The third alternative is gravely weakened by the total lack of any objective support for the hypothesis in any extant textual witness.

The second proposal—to postpone Ezra's arrival until the reign of Artaxerxes II—is obviously radical, no matter from what viewpoint one sees it. Textually, it involves considerable surgery in order to eliminate the names of both Ezra and Nehemiah wherever, according to the theory, they should not appear. Theologically, of course, it assumes that the biblical writer was thoroughly confused. Historically, probably the most telling argument against it derives from Elephantine again. The Passover Papyrus indicates that already in 419 the cultic affairs of Jews in the Diaspora were being regulated by the Persian king via Jerusalem, and Ezr 7:25 indicates that Ezra's appointment for just such duties was the first of its kind.

That brings us back to the traditional view that Ezra arrived in 458, thirteen years before Nehemiah. None of the many objections tendered against this position are conclusive, and other possibilities can usually be suggested. That Ezra shows no concern about security may indicate only that the neighbors saw purely religious reform as little threat; "security" from them became necessary only after construction of the city walls began (cf Ezr 4:7–23). The charge that, according to the traditional view, Ezra must have failed is unfounded, because the problems involved (mixed marriages, economic abuses) are recurrent ones under any circumstances. Why Ezra waited 13 years before promulgating the Torah cannot be answered with certainty, but it is possible that Nehemiah's extra push first made so grand a ceremony seem feasible. Another sticky point is the mention of a "wall" in Ezr 9:9, well before Nehemiah is on the scene; however the usual Hebrew word for "wall" is not used, and ESV may well be correct in taking it to be figurative for "protection." Also, who can say why Ezra and Nehemiah make virtually no mention of each other? The problem certainly is not unique in biblical literature (cf, e.g., on the prophets). And so it goes with numerous other commonly lodged "objections."

Above all, it appears that external—specifically, archaeological—evidence is increasingly not only taking us out of the realm of supposition and hypothesis but also weighing in on the side of tradition. Elephantine, as we noted, had been helpful all along, and now our understanding of the era is further enhanced by the Wadi Daliyeh Samaritan Papyri and some sixth-century bullae (seals) that mention some of Zerubbabel's immediate family who were connected with Jewish governors who succeeded him. In sum, although the 428 alternative date for Ezra's possible arrival cannot be dogmatically discounted, and though the traditional 458 date suffers from various disabilities (presumably because of the paucity of our information about the period), the latter is still a position that one need have no misgivings about retaining.

Among the many other historical problems of this period, mention must be made of one more, namely the relation between Sheshbazzar (Ezr 1:8; 5:14–16) and Zerubbabel. On the latter we are reasonably well informed (except for the mysterious end of his career), but the problem arises because similar activities are attributed to both. Both are of royal descent, both lead exiles back, both lay foundations of the second temple, both are governors of the province of Judah, etc. It has even been proposed that they are two names of the same person, and, of course, critics are not lacking who simply suppose that the Chronicler (or whoever the author was) got things all mixed up. Suffice it to say here that the most likely explanation appears to be that Sheshbazzar is the same as the "Shenazzar" of 1Ch 3:18, that is, the son of Jehoiachin and uncle of Zerubbabel, that both he and Zerubbabel led groups of returning exiles, and that Sheshbazzar's career as governor of Judah as well as his efforts at rebuilding the temple were short-lived, soon being replaced by Zerubbabel, who far overshadows him.

The Case of Foreign Wives

In the tenth chapter of the Book of Ezra we read about the putting away of strange wives whom some of the returned Israelites had married. It may strike the reader as cruel that the husbands in this case were admonished to put away their wives if they were not of Israel. Was it right for Ezra to introduce such a stern measure, which must have meant a good deal of heartache? Must we today urge people who have married unbelievers to separate from them? The marriages in question were a plain transgression of a commandment that God had given to Israel and that He had not revoked (Dt 7:1–3). Thus marriages with these women were illegal, and it was perfectly right to dissolve them. We assume that the unfortunate women and their children were not mercilessly set adrift, exposed to the danger of perishing from hunger, but that provision was made for their maintenance after they had been separated from God's people. The reason for this strict command of God is added: "For they would turn away your sons from following Me, to serve other gods. Then the anger of the LORD would be kindled against you, and He would destroy you quickly" (7:4). Intermarriage easily leads to indifference, a fact that we observe only too frequently in our own day.

If the accusation should be brought against Ezra that he mixed church and government, insisting that the Scriptures be followed in a matter that at least in part belonged to the sphere of the civil government, we must remember that Israel was a theocracy, where the Books of Moses were the law books according to which all social and political questions were to be decided. With respect to New Testament times, the law given in Dt 7:1–4 has lost its validity. Even if we had no specific statement in the writings of the evangelists and apostles showing that this particular law no longer is binding, we should know that it is not in force for us, for the New Testament informs us, for instance, in Galatians that all these old ordinances have been removed with the coming of Christ (cf Gal 5:1–6). But in addition we have a specific pronouncement of Paul on this subject (1Co 7:12–16), where the believing husband or wife is told not to separate from the unbelieving spouse. Hence the passage in Ezra, while reminding us of the danger lurking in mixed marriages, must not be looked upon in our days as making unbelief on the part of husband or wife justifiable cause for divorce.

Lists of Returned Exiles

In Ezr 2:1–65 and Ne 7:6–67 the names of those are given who returned out of the Babylonian captivity. A comparison of the two lists shows several variations, though the sum total mentioned is the same in each case, namely, 42,360. The following considerations should clear up difficulties. It is quite likely that where so many names and figures had to be copied, errors of transcribers crept in and that these are responsible for some of the variations. In such instances it is not the sacred text that is at fault, but later copyists. Furthermore some of the divergences are caused by a difference in the spelling of certain proper names; these do not really constitute discrepancies. For instance, the name spelled Bani in Ezr 2:10 is evidently the same as Binnui in Ne 7:15.

A striking fact is that if we add the figures given in Ezra, the total is 29,818; in Nehemiah it is 31,089; while each writer states that the total number of the returned exiles is 42,360. Evidently we either have to assume that the copyist through an oversight omitted a number of names with the respective figures, or that the holy writers, in giving the sum total, included families that they had not enumerated. It is not impossible that, in computing the total, they added figures that they had not mentioned in the list and that hence the lists themselves are not, and were not intended to be, exhaustive.

Contributions of the Returned Exiles

Ezra 2:69 narrates: "According to their ability they gave to the treasury of the work 61,000 darics of gold, 5,000 minas of silver, and 100 priests' garments."

Nehemiah 7:70–72 declares: "Now some of the heads of fathers' houses gave to the work. The governor gave to the treasury 1,000 darics of gold, 50 basins, 30 priests' garments and 500 minas of silver. And some of the heads of fathers' houses gave into the treasury of the work 20,000 darics of gold and 2,200 minas of silver. And what the rest of the people gave was 20,000 darics of gold, 2,000 minas of silver, and 67 priests' garments."

Fourth-century coin with Persian king and charioteer.

The passage from Ezra states that the people who had returned gave 61,000 darics of gold, 5,000 minas of silver, and 100 garments. That from Nehemiah states, if we add the figures of the text, that 41,000 darics of gold, 4,700 minas of silver, and 97 garments were given. With regard to the 61,000 darics of gold mentioned in Ezra, commentators are inclined to think that we have here a copyist's mistake, that the figure really ought to be 41,000, as stated in Nehemiah. One would have to admit that such a mistake could easily occur. Concerning the minas of silver and the garments for priests, we see that Ezra contents himself with giving round numbers while Nehemiah submits the exact figures.

There is, of course, another way of approaching these passages. Ezra and Nehemiah may not be speaking of the same people and the same gifts in their enumerations. Both of them say that "some of the heads of families" (Ezr 2:68) made offerings. Ezra may include figures that Nehemiah omits, and vice versa. Under this assumption neither account is intended to be complete. At any rate, the passages given cannot be said to contain insuperable difficulties.

Relation of Ezra to Esdras

In the Septuagint, the united Ezra-Nehemiah appears as "Esdras B" ("Esdras" being simply a Greek version of "Ezra"). The canonical "Esdras B" is thus distinguished from "Esdras A," a work considered apocryphal by Protestantism, but at least "deuterocanonical" by Catholicism (see below). Herewith begins an almost nightmarish variation in terminology. Although Jerome had earlier recognized Ezra-Nehemiah as a unity, in the Vulgate he divided them, labeling Ezra "Esdras I" and Nehemiah "Esdras II," a usage which still prevails in much of Catholicism. The (divided) canonical works having been placed first, the deuterocanonical (apocryphal) "Esdras A" of the LXX now became "Esdras III" in the Vulgate. "Esdras A" always remained just that (the apocryphal work) in the LXX, but at some point Jerome's division of Ezra and Nehemiah was introduced there, too, and now "Esdras B" often came to refer to only Ezra (not both books, as originally), while "Esdras C" was introduced to designate Nehemiah.

As though all this were not enough, we have to reckon in addition with a late first-century AD pseudepigraphical apocalypse named after Ezra (Esdras). It was extremely popular in the Early Church but ultimately excluded from the canon. However, Jerome retained it as an appendix to the Vulgate, placing it after the New Testament together with The Prayer of Manasseh (see 2Ch 33). In the LXX it is referred to simply as the "Esdras Apocalypse" or "Esdras the Prophet," but in the Vulgate it became "Esdras IV."

Enter finally the English (Protestant) versions. Since the titles "Ezra" and "Nehemiah" were now firmly established for Protestants, the apocryphal book became "First Esdras," essentially like the LXX's "Esdras A" rather than Jerome's "Esdras III." Then the apocalyptic work became "II Esdras"—although often also referred to as "IV Ezra" or the "Ezra Apocalypse" (with Vulgate and Septuagint respectively)!

Perhaps the following table will help:

English (Protestant)	Vulgate (RC)	Septuagint
I Esdras (apocryphal)	III Esdras	Esdras A
Ezra	I Esdras	Esdras B (sometimes = Ezra-Nehemiah)
Nehemiah	II Esdras	(Esdras C)
II Esdras (sometimes "IV Ezra" or "Ezra Apocalypse")	IV Esdras	Esdras the Prophet (or "Apocalypse")

The apocryphal Esdras requires further comment. To a certain extent, one can say that, externally considered, it is simply an alternate edition or textual tradition of the canonical Ezra-Nehemiah, not differing much more than the LXX as a whole sometimes differs from the Hebrew Masoretic text (perhaps especially Judges and Kings). It almost appears as if the Western tradition, when confronted with two Greek versions of Ezra-Nehemiah, compromised by accepting both! Although the canonical Hebrew text is generally superior, there are points where the alternate version is very helpful for text-critical purposes.

However, there are also significant differences in content. The apocryphal work appears to be much more exclusively interested in the history of the temple and Israelite worship, as perhaps evidenced also by its omission of Nehemiah's "memoirs" (Ne 1–7), thus possibly also evincing greater affinity with Chronicles. Possibly this is also why 1 Esdras begins with the middle of Josiah's reign (his Passover—a version of 2Ch 35–36) and ends in the middle of a sentence (Ne 8:13a) so that it could serve as a continuation of Chronicles.

Consonant with 1 Esdras's interest in Zerubbabel's rebuilding of the temple, it includes one long and significant pericope not found elsewhere: the "Debate of the Three Bodyguards" (1Esd 3). It purports to explain how it was that Darius was reminded of his earlier promise to support the rebuilding of the temple, namely because Zerubbabel had won a debate concerning the strongest thing in the world. The champions of "wine" and "king" had lost to Zerubbabel's "Women are strongest, but truth is victor over all things"!

The sprawl of modern Jerusalem contrasts dramatically with the ruins described by Ezra and Nehemiah.

FURTHER STUDY

Lay/Bible Class Resources

Brug, John F. *Ezra/Nehemiah/Esther*. PBC. St. Louis: Concordia, 1985. ♪ This short commentary by a Lutheran theologian hits the main points in incisive fashion. The reader does not waste time with the unimportant. It is based on the NIV and most useful for Bible classes.

Kidner, Derek. *Ezra and Nehemiah*. TOTC. Downers Grove, IL: InterVarsity Press, 1979. ♪ A helpful resource by a British evangelical writer; somewhat popular in style and format. Focuses on theology and history.

Life by His Word. St. Louis: Concordia, 2009. ♪ More than 1,500 reproducible one-page Bible studies covering each chapter of the canonical Scriptures. Page references to *The Lutheran Study Bible*. CD-Rom and downloadable.

Church Worker Resources

Breneman, Mervin. *Ezra, Nehemiah, Esther*. NAC. Nashville: Broadman & Holman, 1993. ♪ Written by an evangelical scholar. Less scholarly than Fensham and more popular in writing style. Well worth reading.

Yamauchi, Edwin. "Ezra, Nehemiah" in vol. 4 of *The Expositor's Bible Commentary*. Edited by Frank E. Gaebelein. Grand Rapids: Zondervan, 1988. ♪ Brief but conservative and often helpful.

Academic Resources

Clines, David J. R. *Ezra, Nehemiah, Esther*. NCBC. Grand Rapids: Eerdmans, 1984. ♪ A thorough and well written commentary from a critical viewpoint.

Crosby, Howard. *Nehemiah*. LCHS. New York: Charles Scribner's Sons, 1877. ♪ A helpful older example of German biblical scholarship, based on the Hebrew text, which provides references to significant commentaries from the Reformation era forward.

Fensham, F. Charles. *The Books of Ezra and Nehemiah*. NICOT. Grand Rapids: Eerdmans, 1982. ♪ A recommended academic commentary that is strong on historical issues.

K&D. *Biblical Commentaries on the Old Testament: Books of Ezra, Nehemiah, and Esther*. Grand Rapids: Eerdmans, 1971 reprint. ♪ This century-and-a-half old work from Lutheran scholars should not be overlooked. Despite its age, it remains a most useful commentary on the Hebrew text.

Myers, Jacob M. *Ezra, Nehemiah*. Vol. 14 of AB. New York: Doubleday, 1965. ♪ Very helpful on the archaeological-historical data but focused on critical reconstructions.

Schultz, Fr. W. *Ezra*. LCHS. New York: Charles Scribner's Sons, 1877. ♪ A helpful older example of German biblical scholarship, based on the Hebrew text, which provides references to significant commentaries from the Reformation era forward.

Steinmann, Andrew E. *Ezra and Nehemiah*. CC. St. Louis: Concordia, 2010. ♪ The best and most recent commentary from a Lutheran scholar, providing thorough analysis of the Hebrew text, chronology, and theological reflection.

Williamson, H. G. M. *Ezra, Nehemiah*. WBC. Dallas: Word, 1985. ♪ Scholarly work but can be critical, especially in the "form/structure/setting" section. Generally very useful otherwise.

ESTHER

Deliverance will arise

Esther and Ezra-Nehemiah complement one another most strikingly by their respective portrayals of divine providence. In the latter books, all that happens is ascribed directly to God's action. He "stirred up the spirit of Cyrus" (Ezr 1:1); His "good hand" was on Nehemiah (Ne 2:8). Ezra's review of history mentions no part played by the great men in Israel's past; they were but channels through whom God governed the universe (Ne 9:6–37).

Esther seems to go to the other extreme with only one vague reference to divine providence. God goes unmentioned throughout the book except for this veiled allusion (4:14: "Deliverance will rise for the Jews from another place"). In this scheme of things, people do not express their dependence on Him. Esther provides no prayer for help when disaster threatens; there is no song of thanksgiving when deliverance comes; there is only action—as if everything depended on human courage and resourcefulness. Concern about this feature of the book was so strong at a later time that apocryphal additions to Esther were composed in which lengthy prayers are placed on the lips of Mordecai and Esther, and the deliverance of the Jews is repeatedly attributed to God.

But even without these apocryphal additions, God's guiding hand is clearly present in the book. Despite their noblest efforts, hero and heroine would have gone down to defeat had it not been that favor-

OVERVIEW

Author
Unknown

Date
Written c 400 BC

Places
Susa; Persian Empire from India to Ethiopia

People
Esther; Mordecai; Hegai; Ahasuerus (Xerxes); Vashti; Memucan; Haman

Purpose
To record the Lord's providential deliverance of the Judeans from destruction by their enemies in the Persian Empire

Law Themes
Weakness before one's enemies due to disobedience; the Lord thwarts grudges and hatred

Gospel Themes
Preservation of God's people from whom Jesus would be born; the Lord works constantly for the deliverance of His people

Memory Verses
Mordecai's counsel about courage (4:13–17)

TIMELINE

587 BC	Jerusalem temple destroyed
516 BC	Second temple completed
478 BC	Ahasuerus (Xerxes) marries Esther
474 BC	Mordecai issues edict about Judeans
445 BC	Walls of Jerusalem restored

Ahasuerus (Xerxes I) with two attendants at Persepolis, Iran.

able circumstances made success possible. At crucial points, coincidences beyond their control converged to produce situations that spelled the difference between life and death. Similarly, for example, in Genesis Joseph had seen the same power create the "chance happenings" that determined his life. In both Genesis and Esther, it was not a blind, capricious force but a force that "in all things" deliberately let God "work together for good, for those" for whom it shaped events (Rm 8:28). This force could not be stymied by forces of evil, even if they represented the resources of a world empire. It established a universal tribunal of justice where right and wrong have their day in court. This often unnamed power is "the finger of God" (Ex 8:19; Lk 11:20).

Historical and Cultural Setting

The Book of Esther does not pick up the thread of history where the two preceding books left it, but supplements the record of the same century of postexilic Israel spanned by Ezra and Nehemiah. It tells of events that happened after the rebuilding of the temple (516 BC; Ezr 1–6) but before Ezra's arrival in Jerusalem (457 BC; Ezr 7–10). Esther does not furnish a continuous chronicle of this half-century. The account is limited to a dramatic episode during the early part of the reign of Ahasuerus, or Xerxes (486–466 BC), referred to only in passing in Ezr 4:6.

Esther complements Ezra-Nehemiah also as far as the place of action is concerned. The scene shifts from the newly established community in Jerusalem to provinces within the Persian Empire where many Jews chose to remain rather than return to the homeland. The court of Xerxes is the focus of attention. For more on the broader context, see p 424.

Decorative frieze from the Apandana in Susa.

COMPOSITION

Author

Esther is undeniably another of those (relatively rare) instances where conservatives must agree with liberals on the anonymity of the writing. Many ancient and even some more recent commentators have attributed the book to Mordecai on the basis of Est 9:20 and perhaps also 9:23. While not impossible, the verses do not say that, and the most one could safely infer from them would be that Mordecai's writings and royal records were among the unknown author's sources (cf 10:2).

The writer remains unknown. Only general information about him can be gleaned from the book. He composed it sometime after the death of Xerxes (465 BC) because he refers to the king's biography, "written in the Book of the Chronicles of the kings of Media and Persia" (10:2). He also had access to the records kept by Mordecai (9:20, 23). At the same time he draws on his personal acquaintance with Persian life to put events into their proper setting. His incidental descriptions of the palace in Susa (KJV: Shushan), the royal court (e.g., 1:6–7), and its protocol and customs have been found to be so accurate as to suggest that he was a contemporary of the events he records. A person intimately acquainted with the details is not apt to commit blunders in major historical references (as charged by many critical scholars). From the opening "now in the days of" (1:1) to the closing reference to documentation (10:2) he purports to write what actually happened, not a fanciful historical novel.

Date of Composition

Agreement is not so easy to reach on date of composition. A Maccabean date was once widely defended among critics, especially by those who doubted both the narrative itself and any relation with Purim, but this view is no longer so popular. The idea then tended to be that Haman was Antiochus Epiphanes in disguise, and that the story was fabricated in order to bolster Jewish courage in the dark days of Syrian persecution (quite parallel to the critical view of Daniel, see pp 844–49). It is true that Jesus son of Sirach (c 200) does not mention the book (but neither does he mention Ezra or Daniel), that the festival is not referred to earlier than 2Macc 15:36 (where it is called "Mordecai's day"), and also that Josephus provides the first-known quotation of the book. However, these are all arguments from silence, and may, at most, witness only to the length of time (not necessarily any resistance) that it took for a book and festival originating in the eastern Diaspora to reach the centers of Judaism in Israel and gain common acceptance.

Even critical opinion increasingly inclines toward the view that at least early editions of Esther must root in the Persian period, before Alexander's invasion. Not only is there the absence of Greek influence, but the large amount of Hebrew prose from Qumran (Esther not among it) is plainly of a different character. The Hebrew of Esther probably finds its closest biblical parallel in Chronicles (see pp 382–83), usually dated around 400, except that the vocabulary of Esther reflects distinct Persian influence. There is also the matter of the author's uncanny acquaintance with Persian customs. It is also valid to adduce the accord between the author's description of Xerxes' palace at Susa and the reports of the archaeologist who excavated it (Marcel-Auguste Dieulafoy). Since the palace was destroyed by fire in the reign of Artaxerxes I, some 30 years later, details of its structure would scarcely be remembered much longer. If we add the conservative assumption of historicity to all that, we get a very strong case for Persian origin, possibly even by a contemporary living in Susa or its environs, and perhaps not too long after Xerxes' death in 465. Dates later than the turn of the century would be increasingly hard to defend, though it is impossible to be more precise.

Purpose/Recipients

By any reckoning, one of the purposes of the Book of Esther is to explain the origin and background of the Festival of Purim. It is often opined that the main concern was to sanction a festival that was not commanded in the Torah, but the apparent ease with which Hanukkah and the Ninth of Ab were accepted belies that explanation.

It is quite possible that the Jewish commemoration of Purim more or less coincided with some Persian festival, some of whose popular observances came to be mingled with it. Many parallels to such mingling can be adduced in both Judaism and Christianity (e.g., Santa Claus or Easter eggs). In later times, certainly, the rather "Halloween" type of popular Jewish observance of Purim was encouraged by the fact that it tended to coincide, at least in Europe, with pre-Lenten "carnival" and Mardi Gras merriment. (Cf rabbinical statements that "On Purim anything is allowed," or that drinking could continue until it was no longer possible to distinguish "Cursed be Haman" and "Cursed be Mordecai"!)

Literary Features

Genre

Is the Book of Esther "historical"? There certainly is nothing in the book (not even "miracles" in the strict sense) to suggest that it is not, and to the conservative mind that pretty well settles the matter. Inevitably, that emphatically is not the case for the liberal, and one meets an entire spectrum of critical views about its historicity. Many critical scholars regard the book as a "historical novel," perhaps like the apocryphal tales of Tobit and Judith. The doubts concern not only the narrative itself but also the originality of the connection with the Festival of Purim. The marks of normal Hebrew history-writing, both the "now in the days of" at the beginning and the bibliographical ref-

An illuminated Esther Scroll (c 1620), read at the Feast of Purim.

erence at the close (Est 10:2) to "the Chronicles of the kings of Media and Persia" are often dismissed as mere artifices by the writer, especially since the "Chronicles" mentioned have never been found. To those so inclined, many other skepticisms come very easily, because of our paucity of information about the fifth century BC, specifically of the Persian Empire in that period and the role of the far Eastern Jewish Diaspora in it. However, the author displays a phenomenal knowledge of Persian customs, and numerous Persian loanwords occur in the book. The critics will usually concede that his "local color" is authentic.

Characters

Esther 1–3 introduces the chief actors of a drama full of suspense and sudden reversals. The first to appear on the stage is the **Persian king**. The fate of the Jews, threatened with extinction, is subject to the whims of this all-powerful ruler (ch 1). **Esther**, who became his queen, is the heroine; her cousin and guardian, **Mordecai**, is the hero (ch 2). The villain is Xerxes' grand vizier, **Haman**. The rest of the book plays out the drama to a happy conclusion.

Not surprisingly, "Mordecai" was a quite common name in the neo-Babylonian period. Its presence is scarcely surprising in the successor Persian kingdom, especially among Jews who had migrated there from Babylon, as is explicitly stated in this instance (Est 2:5–6). In fact, in 2:2 another "Mordecai" is mentioned, one of the leaders of the returning exiles, together with Zerubbabel (which is itself almost certainly a Babylonian name meaning "seed of Babylon"). The adoption of such foreign names by the exile scarcely even signifies assimilation, and certainly no necessary syncretism or apostasy from the ancestral faith.

Continued on p 467.

MAJOR HISTORICAL MATTERS IN THE BOOK OF ESTHER

Our discussion proceeds with the usual assumption that King "Ahasuerus" is Xerxes I (486–465 BC). (The original Persian and Hebrew forms of the names are much closer than appears in our translations.) Confusion of names was ancient, however, because the Septuagint consistently has Artaxerxes. Also a minority of modern scholars has attempted to identify Ahasuerus with Artaxerxes II (404–358; see also on Ezr 4:6 and Dn 9:1), but historical problems are only compounded by situating the events a century later.

Detail from the tomb of Xerxes.

If the identification with Xerxes is correct, a very plausible synchronism between the book and well-known world history presents itself, and the puzzling gap in the book between Ahasuerus's third year (Est 1:3) and his seventh (2:16) is readily explained. The great banquet thrown by the king in his third year (483) would correspond to preparations made for the attempted naval invasion of Greece, which came to grief in the famous debacle at Salamis in 480. Herodotus reports that thereafter Xerxes sought escape in his harem, which is readily compatible with Esther's selection in the seventh year (479).

Some critics have charged the author of Esther with poor historical memory because, at superficial reading, he appears in 2:6 to imply that Mordecai had been among the first of Nebuchadnezzar's deportees over a century earlier in 597. The difficulty readily dissolves, however, if we take Kish (Mordecai's great-grandfather) instead of Mordecai as the antecedent of the relative pronoun at the beginning of the verse.

One still unsolvable problem concerns the name of Xerxes' queen. Instead of the biblical "Vashti," Herodotus calls her "Amestris," the daughter of a Persian general, who had long been married to the king (two of their sons joined the campaign against Greece), and he makes no mention of any "Esther." However, Herodotus is also subject to critique; at least one aspect of his characterization of "Amestris" may correspond to "Vashti," namely, her reputation as a cruel and calculating woman, a cause of concern to the king himself. In addition, there is the possibility of dual names, and, above all, if we but recall that it was a polygamous society, the difficulty will scarcely be insurmountable.

Herodotus also reports that a Persian king was supposed to choose his wife from one of seven noble families (cf Est 1:14), and, if so, Esther, a Jewess, would have been ineligible. Of course, Mordecai and Esther do not broadcast her background, but laws of that sort are easily evaded, especially by a despot who regards himself above the law. Esther was also breaking Jewish law by marrying an uncircumcised unbeliever, and this, too, the author reports without overt comment. All of this is undoubtedly related to the book's theological perspective; cf below.

Herodotus's report that the Persian Empire was divided into 20 "satrapies" is often also urged against the book's opening statement (1:1) that Ahasuerus ruled over 127 "provinces." However, there is no reason to assume that the two terms describe the same thing ("province" is probably a subdivision), and other evidence indicates that the number of administrative units in the Persian Empire was not constant. Earlier Assyrian records mention an "Agag" as the name of one of the districts in the later Persian Empire, thereby lending historicity to "Haman the Agagite" (neither a descendant of the Amalekite king, Agag, as Jewish tradition sometimes supposed, nor his symbolic counterpart, as critics who view the book as fiction have sometimes argued).

One earlier critical objection is now clearly seen to be hypercritical, namely that "Pur" (and thence the name of the festival, "Purim") did not really mean "lots," as it is explained in Est 3:7 and 9:24. Archaeology has presented us with Assyrian texts from the early second millennium and later, that use both the noun *puru* and a cognate verb in the requisite sense. Haman's use of dice to determine a date for the extermination of the Jews was vividly illustrated by the uncovering of large numbers of them in the excavations at Susa.

Critical skepticism also once questioned whether a Jew could have risen as high in the Persian administration as Mordecai did, even succeeding Haman in his position as grand vizier, second only to the king, after he had exposed Haman's plot against the Jews (chs 7–8). However, in perhaps our greatest archaeological coup of all in connection with the book, we now have a cuneiform tablet from near Babylon that mentions one "Marduka" as a high official at the court of Susa already during the early years of Xerxes (and possibly even under his predecessor, Darius I). Even many critics concede the identification with Mordecai, and, if so, we have major external testimony toward the historicity of the entire book, and not only of this detail.

In the subsequent reigns of Artaxerxes I and Darius II we have archaeological evidence of many Jews holding important posts (among them Nehemiah, cupbearer to Artaxerxes I), some of them even governors of administrative districts. It has plausibly been suggested that this increasing Jewish prominence in the empire may have stemmed from Mordecai's example and influence, beginning perhaps with the "fear of Mordecai" (9:3) which caused all the officials of the empire to cooperate with him in reversing the intended massacre.

No doubt all the elements of popular storytelling are here, but if that proves anything, it is only that "truth is stranger than fiction." In a certain minimal sense, such narrative ability need in no way conflict with historicity and need not be debated. Certainly, on the purely literary level there is little debate about the author's skillful artistry, making the book an artistic masterpiece, quite apart from more ultimate judgments about it.

Form critics have attempted to isolate original components of the story, and often suggest that it was woven out of three originally independent tales, perhaps from a Jewish midrashic source: Vashti's insubordination, conflict between two courtiers, and Esther's rise and role in saving her people. Scholarly interest in Wisdom Literature had led to the suggestion that in final recension the book was supposed to illustrate that movement's tenets (much as many critics suggest for the Joseph stories in Genesis, or the "legends" in the first part of Daniel). There may be a grain of truth here, however, related to the book's theological idiom (cf below).

At any rate, the latter suggestion is superior to the hypothesis of mythological origins (later "historified" at Jewish hands), which until recently was often quite popular in some critical circles. Originally, the myth should have described the rivalry of the chief gods of Babylon and Elam (an early counterpart of Persia), eventuating in Babylon's political ascendancy over its eastern neighbor. Much was made of the names of the principal characters: Mordecai should be a derivative of Marduk, head of the Babylonian pantheon; Esther is supposedly derived from Ishtar, the popular Mesopotamian goddess of love (and even Esther's Hebrew name, Hadassah, is explained on the basis of the Akkadian word for "bride," a frequent Ishtar epithet); Haman should represent Humman, the chief Elamite deity, Vashti the Elamite goddess Mashti, and so on.

From the foregoing examples it can be seen that though the book arouses skepticism and speculation among critical scholars, many points of that criticism have been addressed by increasing knowledge of the historical context or from reasonable arguments, which finally complement the historical character of the book.

Derivation of the name Esther from Ishtar is not impossible, but much more likely it represents the same Indo-European word as the English "star." Esther's original Hebrew name Hadassah (Est 2:7) is almost certainly a feminine form of the common Hebrew word for "myrtle." "Esther" was perhaps substituted to conceal her Jewish identity (cf 2:10), or it may have been a royal name given her at her coronation.

Narrative Development or Plot

The Book of Esther is an especially well-plotted rescue story, filled with ironic turns that hinge upon the threat of annihilation. The book involves three feasts and their consequences: the feast of Ahasuerus (chs 1–4), the feast of Esther (chs 5–8), and the feast of Purim (chs 9–10). At the center stands beautiful and vulnerable Esther who must abandon a passive role to defy the enemy of her people, the wicked Haman. The character who openly moves Esther to use her relationship to the emperor as the means to overcome adversity is Mordecai, but most interpreters detect allusions to unseen providence—God at work behind the events to bring about deliverance for His people (4:14).

Myrtle plant in bloom. Esther's Hebrew name means "myrtle."

The story anticipates deliverance for the Jews when the emperor honors Mordecai instead of Haman (6:1–13). The plot climaxes when Esther must accuse Haman of wicked intent and convince the emperor to act against him at the same moment when she reveals herself to be a Jew, the subject of Haman's edict of condemnation (7:3–6).

Resources

The writer of Esther referred explicitly to "the book of memorable deeds" (6:1) and "the Book of the Chronicles of the kings of Media and Persia" (10:2). He may also have had access to documents of Mordecai (9:20, 23).

Text and Translations

There are relatively few text-critical problems about the Hebrew text of Esther (cf below). One oddity worth mentioning, however, is the writing of the names of the 10 sons of Haman in the Masoretic text of Esther 9:7–9 in

OUTLINE

A number of commentators note the structure of the Book of Esther (chiasm; see Bible Dictionary in *LBC*, vol. 2). Banquets and other episodes in the first half (chs 1–5) coincide with parallel incidents in the second half (chs 7–10), pivoting on ch 6. While the parallels do not account for all of the material in the Book of Esther, they do establish the framework of an outline. The book is clearly divided in two—the first half depicts the threat to the Judeans, and the second relates the deliverance of the Judeans.

I. Threat to Judeans (chs 1–5)

    A. King's Banquets (1:1–9)

    B. Queen Vashti's Refusal (1:10–22)

    C. Esther Chosen Queen (2:1–18)

    D. Mordecai Discovers a Plot (2:19–23)

    E. Haman Plots against Judeans (ch 3)

    F. Esther Agrees to Help Judeans (ch 4)

    G. Esther Prepares a Banquet (5:1–8)

    H. Haman Plans to Hang Mordecai (5:9–14)

II. Deliverance of Judeans (chs 6–10)

    A. King Honors Mordecai (6:1–13)

    B. Esther Reveals Haman's Plot (6:14–7:6)

    C. Haman Is Hanged (7:7–10)

    D. Esther Saves Judeans (ch 8)

    E. Judeans Destroy Enemies (9:1–19)

    F. Feast of Purim Inaugurated (9:20–32)

    G. Greatness of Mordecai (ch 10)

a perpendicular column, because of ancient folklore (haggadah) that they were hanged over one another.

The additions to the Hebrew text in the Septuagint are surely also indirect evidence of the book's popularity. The Greek text adds some 107 verses not found in the Hebrew, and all indications are that they never were Hebrew but were composed in Greek and probably added to the Septuagint after its initial translation. Just when is uncertain, but Josephus was plainly acquainted with at least some of them. (In Protestant circles they are regarded as apocryphal, and hence [following Jerome's precedent] collected separately under that heading, but they often make little sense apart from their original context.) Some of the additions are simply rhetorical or even fanciful embellishments of the more terse original (e.g., a dream by Mordecai and its interpretation—an explanation of the feast), but many of them plainly have the purpose to amend the "secular" character of the original (e.g., prayers by both Esther and Mordecai), and the name of God, so conspicuous by its absence in the Hebrew text, is now conspicuously intoned. When we say "Septuagint," we mean as usual the "B" or Vaticanus text, but it is to be noted that Alexandrinus is probably a separate translation of the Hebrew (probably based on a separate Hebrew text to begin with), surely further testimony to the book's popularity. See pp 104–15.

Doctrinal Content

Summary Commentary

1:1–2:18 Ahasuerus celebrates his accession to the throne with extravagant drinking parties for government officials and common citizens. He and his wife, Vashti, are not models of moral virtue for believers. Yet God uses the king's dismissal of his wife to allow Esther to become queen. After careful preparation, beautiful Esther meets Ahasuerus, gains his favor, and becomes queen of Persia.

2:19–4:17 The story then moves to focus on Esther's cousin and guardian, Mordecai. Mordecai's discovery of a plot against Ahasuerus means that the king owes him a favor. Haman's extreme prejudice against the Judeans threatens them with annihilation. Mordecai is shocked by Haman's edict and goes into public mourning. Esther gradually comes to realize the seriousness of the situation and pledges her life in an attempt to save her people.

Chs 5–8 Esther does not make her intentions known immediately to the king and to Haman, but waits for exactly the right time. Then Ahasuerus, who is unable to sleep, hears of Mordecai's good deed and decides to honor him. Haman happens to arrive at the court just in time to become the king's agent appointed to honor the hated Mordecai. Haman has hidden from Ahasuerus the full consequences of his murderous plan to wipe out the people of Judah. The king may be deceived, but God is not. Haman's end fulfills the words of Pr 26:27: "Whoever digs a pit will fall into it, and a stone will come back on him who starts it rolling." Ironically, King Ahasuerus then gives Mordecai permission to issue a decree that countermands Haman's decree. The Judeans are given the right to defend themselves if attacked and so take vengeance on their enemies.

Persian staff (seventh–sixth century BC).

Chs 9–10 When the 13th of Adar arrives, the Judeans ably defend themselves. They destroy those who hate them but take no plunder from their enemies. The Festival of Purim is established by Mordecai and Esther to celebrate the destruction of Haman and other Persian enemies. A postscript praises Ahasuerus and Mordecai for providing the people with good government and for seeking their welfare.

Specific Law Themes

The Book of Esther characterizes the weak and precarious state of the Judeans during the exile, who were especially vulnerable to attack and became targets of criticism due to their unique teachings and practices. Esther is rebuked for hiding her distinctiveness (a member of Israel, the covenant people) and her decision to hide from rather than confront the evil that threatens her people. The book also shows how God deals with those who hold grudges and harbor hatred, such as Haman and his family.

Specific Gospel Themes

The story illustrates God's providence, who delivers His people from whom the Savior, Jesus, would eventually be born.

Specific Doctrines

All of the above questions and problems with respect to the Book of Esther pale in comparison with the issue of its theological significance and canonicity. Difficulties of this sort have attended the book almost from the outset, and certainly have not been lessened by modern historical-critical perspectives.

To those tempted to misunderstand the workings of God's providence, the Book of Esther affirms that God expects people to work out their own salvation, even though He bestows it. He lets people reap the fruits of their labor, even though He makes them grow. He lets people rejoice in their accomplishments, even though their actions are not always blameless.

Providence is the term commonly used to describe the author's theological perspective, and we may accept it, provided we do not simply subsume the book under the rubric of "general revelation." Of course, from the divine perspective, the kingdoms on the right (church) and the left (state) are ultimately one, but Esther must ultimately be read as part of the history of *election*, as part of God's special governance for His *chosen* people. Many of these issues come to a head or can be illustrated in one well-known and pivotal verse, namely Est 4:14, Mordecai's admonition to Esther: "Who knows whether you have not come to the kingdom for such a time as this?"

It is very doubtful that Mordecai is simply telling Esther that, if she fails to do her part, deliverance will come to the Jews "from another quarter" (RSV), that is, through some other individual or via some other political agency (though even that would surely suggest "providence"). The Hebrew word here is translated "place" (*maqom*), and it is far more likely that the traditional exegesis is correct which understands the word as the same reverent expression for the divine name that we know well from only slightly later Jewish literature (cf similarly "heaven" in Matthew's "kingdom of heaven").

Ancient die from Tel Dan. (Enlarged.)

This interpretation is reinforced by Esther's request in v 16 that all Jews in Susa "hold a fast on my behalf." We need to recall that fasting was normally accompanied by prayer (of course, to the one true *personal* God). (We also understand then why the LXX adds at this point prayers by both Mordecai and Esther.) In that light, neither will Esther's "If I perish, I perish" be misread as merely human pluck, let alone fatalism. In fact, the entire book and the festival based on it must be read as "chance" or "luck" for which "providence" is often only a euphemism: Haman casts "lots" (Purim) to set a date for the extermination of the Jews, but a personal God, not the roll of the dice or other happenstance, determines "destinies."

Christian misgivings about the Book of Esther have often also fastened on the alleged "nationalism" of the book, or its apparently primarily ethnic approach to the concept of the "people of God." Mindfulness of the "canonical context," as sketched above, will remove some of the problem, but at this point a common Christian difficulty with the Old Testament is met head on: the people of God under the old covenant *were* constituted as state (that is, political and/or cultural or ethnic entity) as well as church.

On the more positive side, however, the book's account of God's providential intervention is also typical of "the eternal miracle of Jewish survival." And the miracle has continued for millennia. Thus, the Book of Esther takes its place in the canon alongside especially Rm 9–11 as a testimony to God's continuing purposes for His ancient olive tree as well as believers from all nations, who together as God's people form the Church. We will reverently own the mystery (Rm 11:25).

Application

1:1–2:18 God's people must resist societal influences that encourage extravagant materialism. God graciously cares for us, providing us with the necessities of daily living (1Tm 6:8). For example, God will often use evil deeds to work His will, as the story of Esther shows. At the beginning of the story, her future looks bright. But perilous times were coming for her and for her people. In all that happens, God is silently at work directing affairs. At the critical moment, Esther would be in a position to play a decisive role in delivering Israel. "God moves in a mysterious way His wonders to perform" (*LSB* 765:1). We walk by faith and not by sight.

2:19–4:17 At a crucial time in the future, when the fate of many Judeans will hang in the balance, Mordecai's good deed will have saving consequences. Events that seem unconnected come together in God's plan to save His people. In contrast, bigotry and intolerance like Haman's continue in our modern world. The danger is that we criticize these attitudes in others but fail to see the log in our own eye (Lk 6:41). Our prejudices can put barriers in the way of people hearing the Good News of salvation. As with Esther, God may provide us with positions, wealth, and talents that enable us to serve the cause of God's people and the Gospel. Thanks be to God, in the fullness of time He sent our Deliverer to redeem us from every failure. Unlike Esther, our Deliverer had to die for His people and the whole world. He freed us to serve under His rule as His witnesses.

Chs 5–8 Ultimately, it is God who inspires Esther's delay in announcing her intentions in order to give Haman more rope with which to hang himself. We are often impatient, eager to hurry things along. When God seems to act too slowly on our behalf, may we still trust His wisdom and continue to pray with confidence, "Your good and gracious will be done." For

God humbles those who glorify themselves. In striking contrast to Haman is Christ Jesus, who "did not count equality with God a thing to be grasped," but humbled Himself for our salvation (Php 2:6–8). A loving Father, not random chance, governs world affairs and rules all things for the good of His people. The hands that were nailed to the cross are the hands of God, who cares for you and me. When we find ourselves entangled in sin and its consequences, our only escape is to turn in repentance to Christ and receive from Him forgiveness and renewal. Self-defense is not forbidden in Scripture, but Jesus has overturned the law of revenge for believers (cf Mt 5:38–39). Leave vengeance to the Lord and the governing officials, who are called to administer justice (Rm 12:19; 13:3–4).

Chs 9–10 God preserves His Old Testament people because from them would come the Savior of the world. God controls history to preserve His elect and fulfill His promises. That is still true today. God works behind the scenes to bring about victory when we are helpless, but God rescues us by sending His Son, who took our sin, our punishment, and our death upon Himself, paying the price for our redemption. We have gotten relief from our enemies. Our sorrow has been turned to joy and our mourning into feasting because the Holy Spirit has worked faith in our hearts. We celebrate our victory at the festivals of Christmas, Easter, and Pentecost.

Persian earring of gold with inlays of turquoise, carnelian, and lapis lazuli (c 525–330 BC).

CANONICITY

In the Hebrew canon, Esther concludes the subcollection of the five festival Megilloth (Hbr "scrolls"), following a chronological order that begins with Passover (with Canticles as its lection). In none of the five instances is the connection more intrinsic than in the case of Esther, actually narrating, as it does, the origin of the feast of Purim, usually occurring toward the end of February or the beginning of March on the Western calendar.

Jewish Views

Esther is the only Old Testament book not represented at Qumran, and though this is conceivably an accident of discovery, it seems possible that the sectarian community rejected the book, especially since there are other indications of the group's Eastern affinities, which should have made them even more favorably disposed toward it. Scholars tend to assume that causes were as follows: its minimal religiosity, the absence of mention of the name of God, Esther's disobedience to the Torah by marrying an unbeliever, etc.

Josephus obviously regarded Esther as canonical, yet the Talmud preserves evidence of later rabbis who denied that the book "defiled the hands" (was holy or canonical). Among the Jewish masses, the book has always been extremely popular, not only because of the lighthearted celebration accompanying Purim but also because of its strongly nationalistic character. To this day, it is customary for worshipers to participate vocally in the contemporization of the story as it is read in Purim synagogue services, expressing rage at mention of Haman's name, repeating after the reader accounts of Jewish victories, etc. The common critical wisdom is that the rabbis may have been reluctant to canonize a book that showed contempt for Gentiles and might thus provoke further anti-Semitism (if they did not object to its very contents), but that they were finally forced into embracing it by popular pressure. Humanly speaking, this is not impossible, but it is purely hypothetical. It is undeniable, however, that increasing persecution of the Jews at the hands of Christendom made it all the easier for Jews to identify with it and view it as ever more precious. Hence, it is at least understandable that Maimonides in the Middle Ages would say that in the days of the Messiah only Esther and the Torah would survive, and there were even rabbis to be found who ranked it above the Law and the Prophets.

Christian Views

In early Christendom, Esther was apparently not nearly so popular as in the Jewish community, but assertions of its rejection there often appear to be exaggerated. Nothing can be concluded from the New Testament's failure to allude to it. The Church Fathers refer to it rarely, but this may be partly due to the fact that Purim found no counterpart in Christian calendars, that is, the book did not readily lend itself to typological exposition. Many Christian canonical lists in the East omit Esther, while in the West it was nearly always included (because it knew of the religious additions in the Septuagint, while the East did not?), but all overt objections appear to have been silenced by the council of Carthage in 397. When Esther is referred to, it is often in close association with Judith (with its very similar theme, deliverance of Jews through a beautiful and brave woman), which was also widely regarded as canonical.

No doubt, however, the same increasingly bad blood between Jews and Christians that enhanced its popularity among the former served as a damper upon its popularity among the latter. From this context, it is hard to disassociate unfortunate comments attributed to Luther: "I am so hostile to the book [2 Maccabees] and to Esther that I wish they did not exist at all; for they judaize too much, and have much heathen perverseness" (WA TR 3:3391b). It is to be noted, however, that the words come from Cordatus's collection of Luther's *Table Talk*. Cordatus's notes indicate that the statement comes from early in 1534 while Luther was "correcting" 2 Maccabees. This may refer to his editorial work on the first edition of the complete German Bible published later that year. Luther likely spoke from frustration with the work he faced since the work on Maccabees was difficult. (See M. Reu, *Luther's German Bible* [Columbus, OH: The Lutheran Book Concern, 1934], 222–23.) In any case, it is surely significant that Luther never attempted to expunge Esther from the canon.

Answering Objections

If, then, we defend the book's inspiration and canonicity, how do we answer the objections raised against it? (It is another classical case where presuppositions will tell much of the story.) There are basically two criticisms of the book: (1) Apart from fasting (Est 4:1–3), it appears to be devoid of distinctively religious practices or concepts. The conception of Judaism is more ethnic and nationalistic than theological. It could even be considered anthropocentric, because the name of God is not mentioned even once, as well as prayer, worship, Jerusalem, temple, etc. (2) The book not only describes the Jews' wholesale slaughter of their enemies in retaliation for the designs on their own lives but appears to exult in and encourage such behavior. On both counts (particularism and vengeance), it is easy to draw superficial contrasts with the spirit of Christianity, but more profound reflection can, at very least, suggest viable alternatives.

The only defensible explanation for the author's lack of explicit religious content is simply that this was the idiom in which the author (under inspiration) elected to write. Except for the statistical anomaly of the total absence of the word *God*, its idiom is not as different from other portions of Scripture as may appear at first blush. Esther is very similar to units such as the Joseph narratives, Ruth, David's court history, etc., where God acts in no overt way, but only hidden "in, with, and under" the fumbles and foibles of mankind, the sum of their actions, whether laudable or reprehensible.

Of course, we understand that this represents no conflicting theology nor mere literary variation, but corresponds factually to God's manner of operation at the time. What looks like pure coincidence in the book is really personal divine guidance and deliverance. The "natural" circumstances it deals with are really supernatural. The very absence of explicit mention of God in the book can be construed as a testimony to His sovereign rule at all times, even when men do not intone His name. "He who keeps Israel will neither slumber nor sleep" (Ps 121:4).

The viewpoint is essentially the same as that of the prophets' predictions of divine use of historical agents such as Assyria and Babylonia to chasten His faithless people. The prophetic parallel can fruitfully be pressed further: the "great reversal" of the fortunes of God's people in Persia that the Book of Esther records can (and must in canonical context) be seen as one historical manifestation of the ultimate goal of all of history that the prophets constantly proclaim. God made both human wisdom and folly work together for His transcendent good, climaxing in Christ.

As usual, "historical" interests took precedence in the Greek world, and the Septuagint removed the book to its familiar position after Ezra and Nehemiah, that is, the last of the Historical Books. Although the type of historiography employed in Esther differs markedly from that of some of the earlier "histories," the new association was not bad, because, at least according to the most likely datings, the events of Esther fall between those recorded in the sixth and seventh chapters of Ezra (the latter recounting Ezra's expedition to Jerusalem in 458, 16 years after the initial Purim, apparently in 474).

Lutheran Theologians on Esther

Luther

"The greater part [of a nation] always belongs to the devil and is idolatrous. Thus there is no doubt that . . . Mordecai and Esther, gained many people. But they were not able to correct the kingdoms in their entirety." (AE 8:93)

"Simple garb and adornment is more fitting for a woman than a wagonload of pearls. I do not want to interpret this [1Tm 2:9] too scrupulously—that rich clothing is forbidden to women. Here we must make exceptions for weddings. . . . a woman adorns herself in honor of her groom but goes about in common fashion otherwise, etc., Scripture commends the adornment for a spouse, etc. . . . After all, a queen must bedeck herself, as did Esther. If she clothes herself with care and good taste, she is not decorating herself but acting in accord with the custom of and allegiance to the people with whom she lives. If it were the custom, then it would be a matter of choice for her so to adorn herself or not. In allegiance to her groom, in honor of her wedding and husband, she should dress otherwise than one dresses in church, where one ought to wear proper clothing." (AE 28:273–74)

"The church, which is thoroughly sanctified in the cross of Christ, has holiness, because she abstains from all that is of the world and the flesh, and she has majesty in all riches, goods, houses, costs, etc. But this majesty [of the church], which is spiritual, is altogether opposite to what men have known. For it does not do great things according to the world; indeed, in this way the lowest contempt and squalor are in her. But she builds magnificent spiritual houses (cf. Prov. 9:1ff.) crammed full with costly banquets, very famous for throngs of peoples and nobles, so that the feast of Ahasuerus [Est 1:5–7] is as nothing here, but in the eyes of the spiritual and the angels." (AE 11:264–65)

Gerhard

"*Esther* is called by the Hebrews *megiylath 'ester*, 'The Volume of Esther.' Melito (Epistle *ad Onesimum*, in Eusebius, bk. 4, c. 25), Athanasius (*Synop.*), and Nazianzen (*Carm. de script.*) exclude this book from the canon. However, the Hebrews and the other teachers of the early Christian Church unanimously acknowledge that it is canonical. Therefore those we mentioned first seem to be speaking about what was added to it, or the appendix.

"Sixtus Senensis (*Biblioth.*, bk. 1, p. 5) thinks that no mention was made of Esther because at those times the authority of this book was not yet firm among all the churches.

"Opinions vary regarding the author of this book. Isidore claims that Ezra wrote it, but Eusebius (*Chron.*) asserts that its author was later than Ezra. The Jew Philo (*Chronol.*) assigns it to Joachim, priest of the Hebrews, son of the high priest Joshua. The Latin fathers claim that Mordecai wrote it, and Esther 9:20 and 23 favor them.

"It has ten chapters and contains an account of ten or, as others wish, twenty years. It describes things that happened to the Jews who did not return to their country but stayed in the kingdom of Persia at the time of King Ahasuerus, who in the secular histories is called Xerxes, son of Darius Hystaspes. Especially, however, it treats the story of Esther, who was honored by a royal marriage and through whom the danger that threatened the necks of the Jews was averted by the miraculous providence and guidance of God. Because the book sets forth a comedy,[1] as it were, we can divide this account conveniently into protasis, epitasis, and catastrophe."[2] (ThC E1 § 132)

---

1   That is, a story presenting a conflict that ends happily. Not necessarily humorous.
2   That is, introduction, increase of tension, and resolution.

FURTHER STUDY

Lay/Bible Class Resources

Baldwin, Joyce. *Esther*. TOTC. Downers Grove, IL: InterVarsity Press, 1984. ♫ Very helpful resource. Baldwin offers a conservative and insightful presentation. Compact commentary based on the NIV, with other translations consulted. Written by a British evangelical scholar.

Brug, John F. *Ezra/Nehemiah/Esther*. PBC. St. Louis: Concordia, 1985. ♫ Although the book is not of a technical nature, Lutheran readers may well find this volume the most helpful. Lutheran author. Excellent for Bible classes. Based on the NIV translation.

Life by His Word. St. Louis: Concordia, 2009. ♫ More than 1,500 reproducible one-page Bible studies covering each chapter of the canonical Scriptures. Page references to *The Lutheran Study Bible*. CD-Rom and downloadable.

McGuire, Brent, Timothy Rake, and Gary Dunker. *Ruth/Esther*. Leaders Guide and Enrichment Magazine/Study Guide. LL. St. Louis: Concordia, 2008. ♫ An in-depth, nine-session Bible Study covering the Books of Ruth and Esther with individual, small group, and lecture portions.

Penhallegon, Philip Werth, *Esther: For Such a Time as This*. GWFT. St. Louis: Concordia, 2008. ♫ Lutheran author and Hebrew teacher. Eleven-session Bible study, including leader's notes and discussion questions.

Church Worker Resources

Allen, Leslie C, and Timothy S. Laniak. *Ezra, Nehemiah, Esther*. Peabody, MA: Hendrickson, 2003. ♫ Part of the New International Biblical Commentary; takes a conservative and biblical approach to the Book of Esther.

Jobes, Karen H. *The NIV Application Commentary: Esther*. Grand Rapids: Zondervan, 1999. ♫ Conservative. As the name of the series implies, strong on contemporary applications.

Academic Resources

Fox, Michael V. *Character and Ideology in the Book of Esther*. 2nd ed. Grand Rapids: Eerdmans, 2001. ♫ Includes commentary and excurses by a Jewish expert on Hebrew literature, writing from a critical perspective. Focuses on literary, historical, and theological elements.

K&D. *Biblical Commentaries on the Old Testament: Books of Ezra, Nehemiah, and Esther*. Grand Rapids: Eerdmans, 1971 reprint. ♫ This century-and-a-half old work from Lutheran scholars should not be overlooked. Despite its age, it remains a most useful commentary on the Hebrew text.

Levenson, Jon D. *Esther*. OTL. Louisville: Westminster John Knox, 1997. ♫ Offers some interesting ideas on the structure and story of Esther, while it flatly rejects Esther's historicity.

Moore, Carey A. *Esther*. Vol. 7B of AB. New York: Doubleday, 1971. ♫ Philologically the most thorough; theologically anemic. Concludes that Esther is a historical novel.

Schultz, Fr. W. *Esther*. LCHS. New York: Charles Scribner's Sons, 1877. ♫ A helpful older example of German biblical scholarship, based on the Hebrew text, which provides references to significant commentaries from the Reformation era forward.

THE BOOKS OF WISDOM AND POETRY

Understanding Biblical Wisdom

> From where, then, does wisdom come? . . . God understands the way to it, and He knows its place. . . . And He said to man, "Behold, the fear of the Lord, that is wisdom, and to turn away from evil is understanding." (Jb 28:20, 23, 28)

With these poetic lines, Job reaches an important conclusion in his debate with three friends. They have come to mourn with him because of his deep suffering and to explain to him why things are the way they are. Job disagrees with them and, in the passage above, concludes that only God understands how things really work in life, death, and suffering. Their debate has to do with wisdom, which, as Job explains, is difficult to find and understand. The issues are described in poetry, which also can be difficult to understand.

Jezreel Valley viewed from Mount Gilboa. King Saul, who reigned foolishly, died with his sons on these heights. The kingdom passed to David, Solomon, and their house, so long as they reigned in wisdom.

This introduction will explore unique features of the Books of Wisdom and Poetry, which stand together in the Old Testament because of their forms, themes, and authorship. It will help you understand these unique and challenging passages of God's Word and their important message. You will find more on these topics in the introductions and articles to particular books.

The Ways of the Creator

The biblical term *wisdom* (Hbr *chokmah*) occurs most often in Job, Proverbs, and Ecclesiastes (c three-fifths of all usages). Whereas numerous psalms recount the history of early Israel and draw wise observations from that history, the main Books of Wisdom and Poetry never talk about the earliest history of Israel (e.g., Abraham, Jacob, and Moses are never mentioned in Job, Proverbs, or Ecclesiastes). These Books of Wisdom and Poetry mention some of Israel's important rulers (e.g., Proverbs mentions David, Solomon, and Hezekiah), but their main focus has to do with God's orderly creation and living in harmony with that order.

Hebrew wisdom was not theoretical or speculative but practical and based on God's ways observed in creation. However, biblical wisdom is not simply a natural knowledge of God and His ways. Nor is it derived from human reason. As Jb 28 shows, wisdom is something God understands (v 23). He has declared it and spoken it (vv 27–28). Wisdom could not be "the fear of the Lord" (v 28) unless the Lord made Himself known. Biblical wisdom is a special revelation from God as surely as the Ten Commandments or the sermons of the prophets. Ultimately, it is knowledge leading to repentance and faith in the Lord.

Wisdom is the art of life, living the way God intended. As a result, biblical wisdom focuses on ethics and spiritual conduct—the way of righteousness. This wise way of life comes from a personal God who is righteous and holy; wisdom is one of His attributes. (When you read the mundane details about life in Proverbs, see in them the intimacy of the Creator's care for His creation.) Wisdom is distinct from philosophy (as recorded by the Greeks), though these disciplines share a common interest in created order, an interest that ultimately developed into what we call science.

Common Themes in Biblical Wisdom

The Books of Wisdom and Poetry display common themes in the following introductory and concluding passages:

> There was a man . . . whose name was Job . . . who feared God and turned away from evil. (Jb 1:1)

> The LORD knows the way of the righteous, but the way of the wicked will perish. (Ps 1:6)

> The fear of the LORD is the beginning of knowledge; fools despise wisdom and instruction. (Pr 1:7)

> Fear God and keep His commandments, for this is the whole duty of man. For God will bring every deed into judgment, with every secret thing, whether good or evil. (Ec 12:13–14)

The themes of (1) fear toward God, (2) the difference between the righteous and the wicked, and (3) the Lord's role as judge appear repeatedly. Wisdom teaches that people may walk along one of two ways or paths: one leading to destruction, the other leading to life.

An exception among the Books of Wisdom and Poetry is the Song of Solomon, which celebrates the wonder of love that "is strong as death. . . . Its flashes are flashes of fire, the very flame of the LORD" (8:6). Here is the only reference to the Lord in the Song, connecting the bond of marital love with His power. The Song of Solomon probably stands with the other Wisdom Books because of its poetic form and its authorship by Solomon the Wise.

Wise Men and Counselors

The Books of Wisdom and Poetry likely had their start as wise sayings offered by judges and teachers in Israel. Their poetic form has its root in the oral culture of the ancient Near East (see "Biblical Poetry," pp 487–90). Numerous biblical passages refer to wise men and counselors who guided decision making for kings and communities (cf Ex 18:13–27; Ru 4:1–2; 1Ki 12:6–8; Jer 18:18; Ezk 7:26). Their wise sayings were collected for instructing the young (1Ki 4:29–34; Pr 25:1). For example, Pr 1–9 presents a series of educational speeches from a father to a son, or from a teacher to his student. Leaders in Israel expected their people to learn wisdom—in fact, the Lord commanded it. Children were expected to learn the texts of the Commandments (Dt 6:4–9), and citizens were expected to learn certain songs (Dt 31:19; 2Sm 1:17–18; Ps 60). Education in wisdom had personal, family, clan, and national importance.

The Wisdom of Amenemope, an Egyptian text from which Solomon may have borrowed.

Many teachings in Israelite wisdom overlap with wise sayings from other cultures. For example, Pr 22:17–24:22 is similar to the Egyptian "Wisdom of Amenemope," which dates from before the time of Solomon. In part, such overlaps occurred because the problems of living are much the same everywhere, regardless of religion, culture, and history. Naturally, similar observations would arise. Yet Scripture also tells us that Solomon "collected" wise sayings. He probably did not limit his collecting to the sayings of Israelites (see chart at right). Since wisdom was based on God's created order, all true wisdom naturally belonged to God and His people.

Conclusions about Wisdom

The early Christian apologist Justin Martyr (c 100–c 165) reflected on the universal presence of God's wisdom as follows:

> Whatever things were rightly said among all men, are the property of us Christians. For next to God, we worship and love the Word who is from the unbegotten and ineffable God, since also He became man for our sakes, that, becoming a partaker of our

CATEGORIES OF WISDOM

Most basic is the proverb (Hbr *mashal*), in simplest form an observation without any imperative or admonition, and often characterized by poetic features (paronomasia, assonance, alliteration, rhyme, puns, or synonymy). Other types are more common outside the Book of Proverbs: riddles (*chidah*; cf Jgs 14:14); fables and allegories (Jgs 9:8–15; 2Sm 12:1–4; 2Ki 14:9; Pr 5:15–23; Ec 12:1–7; often in Ezk; cf on Solomon in 1Ki 4:32–34); hymns and prayers (especially in the Psalter, but cf Jb 5:8–16; and 28; Pr 8); the dialogue (Grm *Streitgespräch*; esp Job); the "confession" or autobiographical narrative (esp Ecclesiastes).

Wisdom in the Bible and the Ancient Near East

Historic Eras	Egyptian/ Western Hellenism	Israel/Judaism/ Christianity	Mesopotamian/ Eastern Hellenism
Creation to the Time of Abraham	Instruction of the Vizier Ptah-Hotep	Genesis opens with the wise distinction between good and evil, life and death.	Sumerian Wisdom Literature
Patriarchal Period		Job	"I Will Praise the Lord" Wisdom
Israelite Kingdom Era	Wisdom of Amenemope	Psalms (esp 1; 19; 37; 104; 107; 147; and 148); Proverbs; Ecclesiastes; Song of Solomon	Ahiqar (Assyrian)
Between the Testaments	Hermetic Literature	Wisdom of Solomon; Ecclesiasticus (Sirach); Wisdom fragments from Qumran Cave 4 (4Q184; 185; 510; 511); Two Ways theme in the Community Rule (1QS)	
NT Era		Sayings of Jesus in the canonical Gospels; James; Two Ways theme in the Didache	
Early Christian/ Rabbinic Era	Western Gnosticism	Rabbinic Pirke Aboth poetry; Sayings of the Desert Fathers	Syriac Menander; Eastern Gnosticism

Genesis begins with God creating life and contrasting the way of life and the way of death. From this theme, first presented by God to Adam under the trees in Eden, comes all biblical wisdom. It is also a major theme in ancient Near East Wisdom Literature. The righteous, who are wise, walk in the way of life as God created it. The wicked, who are foolish, walk in the way of death, which is contrary to God's created order.

sufferings, He might also bring us healing. For all the [ancient] writers were able to see realities darkly through the sowing of the implanted word that was in them. (*ANF* 1:193)

Justin's attitudes reflect a long-standing approach to wisdom in ancient Israel, in Judaism, and among the first Christians. Since truth comes from God, whatever is true belongs to God's people. Yet biblical wisdom is different from that of other cultures and religions because it emphasizes one God as the source of all knowledge and understanding; it focuses on right and wrong and is fulfilled in Christ, our righteousness.

Over time, biblical wisdom focused more and more on the Scriptures—God's Word—where God's ways are faithfully recorded (Ps 1; 119). Just as God's creation is orderly and harmonious, so God's Word is harmonious and orders our steps in the way of life. Biblical wisdom illustrates the faithful living found in the legal sections of the Books of Moses. Ultimately, wisdom embodied two things: Scripture as Wisdom (pursued by Judaism and Christianity) and Christ as Wisdom (pursued by Christianity as described in Colossians and John). The Lutheran hymn writer Erdmann Neumeister (1671–1756) expressed all this most beautifully:

I know my faith is founded

On Jesus Christ, my God and Lord;

And this my faith confessing,

Unmoved I stand on His sure Word.

Our reason cannot fathom

The truth of God profound;

Who trusts in human wisdom

Relies on shifting ground.

God's Word is all-sufficient,

It makes divinely sure,

And trusting in its wisdom,

My faith shall rest secure. (*LSB* 587:1)

Biblical Poetry

One-quarter to one-third of the Old Testament is poetry. In most ancient literature of the Near East, poetry is the preferred form of expression. The biblical Wisdom Books of Job, Proverbs, and Ecclesiastes are almost entirely poetic. Therefore, it was natural for scribes to group together the Wisdom Books with other Poetic Books, such as Psalms and the Song of Solomon. However, poetry is also found throughout the Historical Books and is especially common in the Prophetic Books.

The common poetic style for wisdom is based on the *mashal* (translated "proverb"), which builds on strong contrasts such as good and evil, righteousness and wickedness, life and death. The wise insights are collected into short, pithy sayings. These sayings are often presented in longer speeches (e.g., Jb 3:1–42:6; Pr 1–9).

As stated above, Hebrew poetry is rooted in speech and was probably composed orally. Poetry has its roots in ancient, oral composition, when people told stories or expressed ideas in memorable forms that they would also commit to writing. Today, writing is exactly how we remember things. (Who hasn't said, "Wait, let me get a pen," while on the phone?)

Some prose passages of Scripture may be based on earlier poems. For example, the song of Deborah in Jgs 5 probably predates the prose account in Jgs 4. Moses and the author of Joshua may be quoting earlier poetic works when writing their histories (e.g., note the poetry at Gn 1:27; 2:4, 23; 3:14–19; 4:23–24; 9:6, 25–27; and Jsh 10:12–13).

The Form of Hebrew Poetry

The ESV translators make it easy for you to recognize poetic passages by presenting them in poetic format from short lines (cola) to poetic paragraphs (strophes and refrains) to stanzas (longer passages separated by extra space). In Hebrew, poetry and prose are distinguished by the presence or lack of prose markers—three Hebrew terms commonly found in prose but not often found in poetry. Two of these prose markers are frequently translated as "which" (relative pronoun) and "the" (definite article). The third prose marker is not translated. It stands before a noun to show what the direct object in the sentence is. Because these prose markers appear six to eight times more often in prose, poetic passages feel lean or terse as one reads them in Hebrew.

Attempts to discover and describe a grand system of Hebrew poetry have been challenging. Hebrew poems can have formal meter and structure, but they do not consistently appear in rhyme, cadence, or rhythms of long and short syllables (commonly found in Greek and English poems). Nor do Hebrew poems have a strict number of syllables (like Japanese haiku). In fact, even though a Hebrew poem may evidence clear form in its lines and structure, it is not likely that it shares that same form and structure with other Hebrew poems. Perhaps this is a result of free, oral composition. Masters probably passed on their way of composing a poem to their students, which would explain why many poems show similarity, yet do not conform to specific patterns. Forms are there, guiding the composers but not restricting them. Acrostic poems, which have their outline from the 22 letters of the Hebrew alphabet, have the most obvious structure. Yet even these poems differ significantly from one another, since they may arrange each colon by the alphabet (e.g., Ps 111–12) or by as many as eight lines for each letter (e.g., Ps 119).

Categories of Hebrew Poems

Specific types of Hebrew poetry are difficult to identify. We have some Hebrew names for poetic compositions (e.g., *shir*, *mizmor*, *maskil*, and *qinah*). But the writers did not explain for us the specific features of these poems. We are left to wonder whether these terms describe a specific type of poetry or a poem's content.

Theologian Hermann Gunkel (1862–1932) distinguished a variety of categories for Hebrew psalms: (1) hymns, (2) thanksgiving psalms, (3) royal psalms, (4) laments, (5) penitential psalms, and (6) imprecatory psalms. (Some of Gunkel's categories were based on ancient uses for psalms; e.g., the "seven penitential psalms" were used liturgically by the early Christians.) Such categories can be helpful but should not be applied too strictly, since they are modern categories that may not truly reflect how God's people viewed their poems. Goals or functions can also be used to distinguish Hebrew poems. Some have suggested the following: didactic poetry, liturgical poetry, love poetry, and prophetic poetry.

Parallelism

The most important feature of Hebrew poetry is the use of parallel words, thoughts, sounds, and forms of grammar. Poetic lines (usually two, called *bicola*) may have one or more of these parallels. The parallels may contrast

Papyrus plants flourish along the Nile River and other waterways in the region. They were the source of the earliest paper manuscripts upon which Near Eastern people composed their wisdom and poetry.

with each other, compare to each other, or build upon each other in a variety of ways. Here are some common examples of parallels:

Parallel Grammar

He judges the world with righteousness;
He judges the peoples with uprightness. (Ps 9:8)

These lines have the same grammatical structure: noun, verb, noun, prepositional phrase.

Parallel Sounds

Can papyrus grow [*hayig'eh*] where there is no [*belo'*] marsh?
Can reeds flourish [*yisgeh*] where there is no [*beli*] water? (Jb 8:11)

The sounds of the first line are echoed in the second.

Parallel Thought (comparison)

Like a lame man's legs, which hang useless,
Is a proverb in the mouth of fools. (Pr 26:7)

Parallel Thought (contrast)

Weeping may tarry for the night,
But joy comes with the morning. (Ps 30:5b)

Parallel Thoughts in Steps

The LORD is a stronghold for the oppressed,
A stronghold in times of trouble. (Ps 9:9)

The second line builds on the thought about "stronghold" introduced in the first line.

Word pairs provide the basic building blocks for many parallels. They are words people commonly associate with one another. Examples of English word pairs would be *cat* and *mouse, man* and *woman, night* and *day.* The Hebrews and other ancient composers (such as the Canaanites at Ras Shamra) used word pairs to create and organize their poetic lines. They also paired words with similar meanings or contrasting meanings. Examples of word pairs in the Hebrew poetry above are *world* and *peoples, weeping* and *joy, night* and *morning, oppressed* and *trouble.*

Conclusions about Poetry

Recognizing parallels is an important tool for interpreting Hebrew poems. Since one line relates to the next, the lines often clarify or explain one another. As you read and seek to apply God's Word written in poems, be sure to look for these parallels. They will reveal not just the poem's beauty but, most important, its meaning.

Hebrew word pairs also often work hand in hand with the basic teachings of God's Word: Law and Gospel. Many contrasting word pairs are used again and again in Hebrew poetry and help the reader to distinguish Law and Gospel. Here are some classic Law and Gospel word pairs: *curse* and *bless, hate* and *love, sin* and *mercy, wicked* and *righteous.*

THE WRITINGS

(Hbr *Kethubim*) and Wisdom

In the Hebrew Bible, Books of Wisdom and Poetry appear in the third part of the Hebrew canon. The Hebrew tradition merely gave these texts the nondescript name of "Writings" (*Kethubim*). Of course, the adjective *holy* or *sacred* is implied, and hence the Greek title, "Hagiographa." The following list includes the Writings as ordered in the Hebrew Bible. Those in bold are categorized as Books of Wisdom in later tradition.

Psalms	Lamentations
Job	Esther
Proverbs	Daniel
Ruth	Ezra
Song of Solomon	Nehemiah
Ecclesiastes	Chronicles

To a certain extent, "Writings" means no more than "Etc." or various pieces that fit neither into the Torah nor the Prophets. Beyond that we know too little about the historical circumstances of the formation of the Hebrew canon to say much more. Date of composition obviously plays some role in which books were placed among the Writings; the substance of some of the pieces is obviously earlier (e.g., Ruth).

Clear liturgical influences are apparent in the case of the five Megilloth ("scrolls") in the middle of the hagiographic canon. These five were (and are) the liturgically proper pericopes for five major Jewish festivals (the books listed in the chronological order of the festivals with which they are associated):

Song of Solomon for Passover,

Ruth for Weeks or Pentecost,

Lamentations for *Tish'a b'Ab* (commemorating the fall of Jerusalem),

Ecclesiastes for Booths (Tabernacles), and

Esther for Purim.

One cannot say with certainty how ancient are either the liturgical associations or the canonical positioning, but there is no reason why both should not reach far back into the Old Testament period itself.

With the Septuagint's preference for topical classifications, the Greek translations (followed by nearly all modern versions) redistributed the Writings among the historical, poetical, and prophetic books. However, one can scarcely say that this represented any improvement. There is much poetry elsewhere in the Hebrew Bible, especially in the prophets, and the title "history" raises at least as many questions as it answers for the modern, Western mind.

The Psalter may well have been given final form as a Wisdom Book (cf esp Ps 1). The Hebrew sequence of Psalms, Proverbs, Job may simply wish to highlight the Psalter, while Ecclesiastes was placed in the liturgical sequence of the Megilloth. The Septuagint appears to have rearranged the order to bring together the three works associated with Solomon (Proverbs, Ecclesiastes, and Song of Solomon), but with Psalms intervening between Job and those three.

View toward Mount Hermon in the northern region of Israel. Hebrew wisdom and poetry often comment on the wonders of God's creation.

JOB

Shall we receive good from God, and shall we not receive evil?

The Book of Job mentions no events that can be synchronized with any other known history. There are, however, many indications that the story of Job is ancient. One of the main ones is the name itself, Job, or in Hebrew, *Iyob*. Although we know it also from later Arabic sources, it appears as early as c 2000 BC in an Egyptian Execration Text as *'ybm* (mimated form), and thereafter frequently in the second millennium (in texts such as Amarna, Alalakh, Mari). The other names in the book are also appropriate to the second millennium BC. This is the general period of the biblical patriarchs.

The references in Ezk 14:14 and 20 to "Noah, Daniel, and Job" as paragons of righteousness also point in the same direction. About the antiquity of Noah, there is no question, and the name Dan'el is found in fourteenth-century Ugaritic legends (though there are good arguments for taking the figure here as the contemporary of Ezekiel too).

Parallel Literature

Certain other possible parallels to the biblical Job appear in ancient Near Eastern literature, though these parallels are also difficult to date (and may well rest on even earlier materials). The so-called "Babylonian Job" apparently dates from the latter half of the second millennium and contains harrowing descriptions of an affliction comparable to Job's. But the differences are equally profound, and the Babylonian story begins where the biblical Job leaves off, with thanksgiving for recovery from illness (hence its real title, "I Will Praise the Lord of Wisdom" [*Ludlul Bel Nemequi*], that is, Marduk).

Much older, and in some ways formally much more parallel, is an ancient Sumerian tract, describing how a sufferer cajoles his personal god (cf Job's "umpire," "witness," etc., below) to pity and release him; in a mechanical and almost deterministic sense this Sumerian work recognizes that all suffering is a result of sin, but without the profound moral earnestness and even ques-

Red rock columns of the Timna mining region, south of the Dead Sea. Job 28 describes ancient mining practices that may have been used in this region.

tioning of divine justice which we find in Job. There is also a so-called "Babylonian Theodicy," an alphabetical poem (acrostic) from about 1000 BC (sometimes compared with Ecclesiastes). In dialogue or debate form, it laments that the gods made men sinful but the poem makes no attempt to solve the problem. Probably even more coincidental are the Egyptian "parallels": "The Protests of the Eloquent Peasant," from the early second millennium, "The Dispute over Suicide," from the late third millennium, and others.

Although many of the themes in Job appear in ancient Near Eastern wisdom literature, the book emerges as really without extrabiblical parallel. The main point at the moment, however, is the high antiquity of nearly all of the "parallels" cited, enhancing the likelihood that the biblical text can be similarly dated. If the literary roots of the work are that ancient, the likelihood that the events behind it are as old or older is also increased.

Qesitah hematite weight.

Possibly the strongest evidence for an ancient date is found within the book. The social organization points in that direction, as does the sacrificial offering by the family head rather than by an official priesthood (cf the example of Abraham in Genesis). Likewise, the rarity of the name Yahweh in the book and the preference for the generic terms *Elohim* or the singular *Eloah* suggests antiquity; even more so for the title "Shaddai" (usually translated "Almighty"), which occurs in Job almost twice as often as in all the rest of the Old Testament together. The usage of names of God thus coincides remarkably with what we find in Genesis. Another bit of evidence is the mention of a unit of currency (Hbr *qesitah*), otherwise attested only in Gn 33:19 and Jsh 24:32.

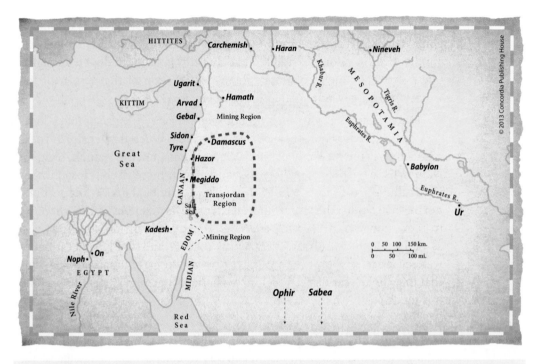

The exact location of Job's home is uncertain. Associations can be drawn with regions east of the Jordan based on other references to "Uz" in Scripture. Uz was the name of the son of Aram and grandson of Shem (Gn 10:22–23; 1Ch 1:17), of Abraham's nephew (Gn 22:21), and of an Edomite, one of the sons of Dishan the Horite (Gn 36:28; 1Ch 1:42). Jer 25:20 notes that "all the kings of the land of Uz" were forced to drink of the cup of God's wrath. Lm 4:21 mentions Uz with Edom. These references look toward the south. Jb 1:3, "people of the east," encompasses people living beyond the Jordan River (from Midian in the south [Jgs 6:3] to Abram-naharaim in the north [also called Mesopotamia; Gn 24:10]. Therefore, Uz is vast. Josephus and early tradition supported a northern location as best suited for the manner of Job's life and the general background of the Book of Job. The Transjordan region was less arid in ancient times.

Historical and Cultural Setting

Some of the evidence mentioned above for antiquity might just as well point toward a non-Israelite (or marginally Israelite) location for the book's original setting and/or composition. Precisely where, however, depends on the location of "the land of Uz" (1:1). Most modern scholars have placed it southeast of Israel, probably somewhere between Edom and northern Arabia. A few have gone so far as to argue that the book represents an example of Edomite wisdom, but there is no way even to test such a hypothesis, which exceeds the evidence at best. Geographical proximity to Edom might be supported by the apparent placement of Uz in that area in Jer 25:20 and Lm 4:21, as well as by the inclusion of Job in 1:3 as among "the people of the east." His vulnerability to raids by Sabeans and Chaldeans (1:15 and 17) associate him with eastern people as well. The Psalm of Habakkuk appears to associate the divine name *Eloah* with Teman, another region in this same general area (whence came Job's "friend," Eliphaz; cf also Elihu's origins in "Buz," apparently in this area). In a postscript the LXX plainly situates Uz "in the regions of Idumea and Arabia," but this is connected with its highly questionable (though not impossible) identification of the person of Job with Jobab, king of Edom, mentioned in Gn 36:33.

Other features in the book do not seem to agree with a southern location of Uz. A few scholars have tried to locate it much farther north (near Antioch or Palmyra, even northern Mesopotamia; but the Hauran, south of Damascus, or perhaps northern Gilead is much more likely). Josephus, as well as both Christian and Muslim traditions, can be found in support of a northern location. The indications of extensive farmland in ch 1 might point to more populous areas such as these. The animals of Job 40–41, as well as other references to reeds or papyrus (cf 8:11 and 40:21) suggest better watered areas, possibly even swamps or river mouths. (Climate studies show that the whole Near Eastern region was better watered in ancient times than it is today.)

Language

Job's geographical location also leads one to consider the language of the book, which unfortunately leads to further debate. Job contains the largest number of words that appear only once in the Bible (*hapax legomena*; about 100 of them). A cursory check of nearly any Hebrew lexicon will demonstrate that Job often uses otherwise familiar words in unusual senses. William F. Albright once even estimated that as much as 45 percent of the book's vocabulary is of less than certain meaning! The challenges occur in the forms of the words, their uses together in sentences, and in their basic meaning. A certain affinity with Ps 139 (also probably a wisdom product) has long been noted, but we know little of its provenance.

Neither is there any agreement about what accounts for the unique wording in the book. An Edomite dialect has often been suggested, but,

Chaldeans of southern Mesopotamia hide in the river reeds to escape the Assyrians.

again, we know too little of that language to check out the hypothesis. The Ugaritic texts at Ras Shamra have enabled satisfactory explanation of many linguistic features (see especially Pope's commentary, p 539), as well as enhancing the likelihood of ancient composition. Nevertheless, as a whole, the style of the work is not very close to that of the Ugaritic epics. As a result, the commentators talk more of northwest Semitic or of Phoenician of the Amarna period. The problem is that the more we seek an explanation in that direction, the less contact we can maintain with the "sons of the east" (unless the events happened in one place and the composition in another). A sort of compromise, the Hauran or northern Transjordan comes into consideration as an area whose dialect might well show influence from many directions. The latter explanation has in its favor its ability to account for the Aramaic coloration of the Hebrew of Job, especially (perhaps) in the Elihu speeches (a major example is the preference of *-in* over *-im* as the masculine plural ending).

Because none of these hypotheses account for everything unusual about the language of the book, some have argued that Job is translated into Hebrew from another language, while still reflecting many features of the mother tongue. Aramaic and Arabic have been major candidates. These explanations, however, have not convinced very many scholars either, so we end up with the same question with which we began. In the end, one may conclude that Uz lay east of Canaan, whether to the north or to the south.

COMPOSITION

Author

The book itself gives no clear indication of who wrote it, when, or where. Its wisdom classification suggests some wisdom teacher as author, but that is not very definite. The wide range of allusions suggests that the writer was widely traveled and well educated, but that also makes it difficult to pin him down to any particular locale. It may be helpful to assert that Job is the author of the book, that is, that there may be a strong autobiographical element to it.

There are Talmudic and Syriac traditions of Mosaic authorship (and hence in the Syriac Peshitta Job follows directly after the Books of Moses), but they do not seem worthy of credence, except possibly as an indication of the antiquity of the composition. We are in no position to improve upon the counsel of St. Gregory, who while the barbarians were pounding on the gates of Rome, insisted that the important thing about the book's authorship was to affirm that the Holy Spirit wrote it.

Date of Composition

Partly because Job is a book of wisdom, it does not make clear reference to broader historical events nor particular theological formulations in a way that would make it easy to date. Some four different periods still have their defenders: (1) that of the Patriarchs; (2) of Solomon; (3) of the late monarchy; and (4) during or after the exile.

Nineteenth-century critics tended to favor a seventh-century origin, and many thought especially of the long reign of Manasseh, when evil and suffering flourished. At least one critic tried to date the work as late as the second century on the grounds that Jb 15:20–30 referred to Alexander Jannaeus. A fifth- or sixth-century date has become usual for critics, though the grounds for the opinion vary.

The Egyptian Barque boat symbolized their ideas about the journey into the afterlife. The Book of Job describes the biblical teaching on this ancient topic by referring to the resurrection of the body.

Arguments for so late a date appear to depend on evolutionistic arguments in a circle. These appeal to Job's allegedly "advanced" theology, especially as it wrestles with the problem of suffering, as though monotheism were not present in Israel earlier, or as though Israel or humanity had never confronted that issue earlier. As long as almost the entire wisdom movement in Israel was thought to be a postexilic phenomenon, it almost followed necessarily that Job had to be composed somewhere in that context.[1]

Closely related is the critics' argument that Job bears witness to a time before the idea of everlasting life and personal immortality was accepted in Israel (cf Jb 19). That entire issue cannot be discussed here, but there is ample evidence also of that belief in Israel as well as in its environs in the earliest times, though it undeniably became more prominent in later periods. If we may turn the tables and argue from parallels, Egyptian wisdom had great interest in preparing for eternity. That at least establishes the possibility that ancient wisdom hoped for immortality.

The appearance of "*the* Satan" (Hbr) in the prologue has encouraged some critics to suggest Persian influence on the book, and date it as late as the fifth or even fourth century. Allegedly, the use of the definite article with "Satan" should align Job with a similar usage in Zec 3, but a little before the usage in 1Ch 21. The prologue's general picture of the heavenly courtroom appears in the early biblical texts (cf Gn 6; Dt 32 and 33; 1Ki 22; and repeatedly in the prophets). In fact the comparable pagan idea of the "assembly of the gods" appears already in second millennium texts in both Canaan and Mesopotamia. This establishes the likelihood that the biblical picture in the prologue of Job was as ancient as many other features of the book.

In sum, conservatives have greater confidence in the historicity of the book's narrative and favor less time between the events and when they were written down. The possibility of a late editing of an essentially earlier work might also be considered, but is just speculation.

So how much earlier should we go in search of a most likely date? In both Jewish and Christian circles it once was common to think of an actual patriarchal date of composition (e.g., Eusebius).

Already Gregory of Nazianzus in the fourth century AD suggested the age of Solomon as the most likely period of composition; he was seconded by Luther, and many modern conservative scholars would concur. The preference for this period pivots on the traditional association of Solomon with wisdom in general. The cosmopolitan atmosphere of the Book of Job might fit that period.

---

1 Critics still widely assume that Job (like Ecclesiastes, allegedly to an even greater degree) is largely protest against mechanical and legalistic "Deuteronomic" doctrines of reward and punishment—but, if Deuteronomy is Mosaic and if the "legalism" is a figment of critical imagination, that argument loses all cogency, at least as a basis for dating. Similarly, although the exile did highlight individual predicaments and accountability, there is ample evidence, both within and without the Bible, that it was anything but a new topic in the seventh century or later.

Nevertheless, it must be conceded that the final word has by no means been spoken on this question, and there is no prospect of a definitive answer until or unless we benefit from a windfall of information far beyond what we presently possess. Fortunately, the question of date is not a theological issue.

Purpose/Recipients

God never reveals to Job the ultimate reason for his trauma, namely the challenge from "the Satan." When the Lord finally does respond to Job's repeated requests—even demands—for a hearing, what He says is about as big a surprise as anything in the book. These divine speeches should not be searched for the answer to the problem of suffering, as is often done (though, of course, in a broader sense they are a major part of the answer). The book is not a treatise leading by rational argument to a conclusion (a *theodicy* in any Western, philosophical sense of the term). God's answer to Job addresses the entire audience of readers or hearers. The overarching point of the book is that the Lord is the Redeemer, despite what we may suffer in this life.

Literary Features

Genre

Franz Delitzsch was apparently the first in modern times to address the question of genre, and his suggestion, following Theodore of Mopsuestia in the fourth century, was that the book was a "drama" (which would not need to imply any historical inaccuracy). Some have followed Delitzsch, but that particular answer meets with little favor today. Drama (at least in any precise sense) appears never to have penetrated the ancient Near East. Attempts at comparisons with other types of classical literatures, tragedies, epics, even Plato's dialogues, have proved no more convincing, though points of contact can be established with nearly all of them. Hence, taken as a whole, it appears best to admit that Job is one of the unique masterpieces of world literature.

Individual components of the book combine to form a virtual anthology of all Old Testament types, with ample parallels also outside of Israel. For example, wisdom themes are obvious in Job's refusal to speak rashly, the emphasis on the efficacy of Job's prayer (42:7–9), and, of course, retribution. Many parts of the poetic section of the book can be explained as a sort of dramatization of individual lament. This helps explain the many affinities with the Psalter that are so evident at points.

Much of the book has a legal or forensic tone, as Job, in effect, accuses God of breach of contract. Courtroom comparisons may explain much, and if we accent the ultimate unity of law and wisdom, one may even think of the covenant lawsuit, so often employed by the prophets. Job's great "negative confession" in ch 31 (a plea of innocence) has prominent parallels in both Egyptian and Babylonian literature. Those cultures also provide examples of disputation, which many see as a point of comparison with the book; their disputations were usually structured along the lines of: (a) mythological introduction, (b) debate between two friends, and (c) divine resolution of the issue.

Although Job and the three friends alternate in speaking, they really do not answer one another and often do not even appear to be speaking to one another. In fact, "answer" regularly in Job follows Hebraic idiom by implying not so much response to conversation as the beginning of a speech, regardless of the context. We probably understand the speakers best if we assume that they were primarily seeking to convince *us*, not one another. They addressed the unseen audience of listeners or readers (and perhaps in a more ultimate sense, God Himself). In modern terms, one might think of an oratory contest rather than a debate. The prize goes to the one who makes the best speech, not to the one who has best rebutted an opponent. Each speech, then, must be considered a self-contained unit, with only minimal direct relation to those preceding and following. The tone becomes more acrimonious as the "dialogue" ensues, but even that judgment may follow from the false assumption of a debate. Neither is it really possible to sustain any clear-cut distinction between the individual themes of the three friends.

Characters

In the Book of Job, **Satan** is mentioned as appearing among the sons of God before the Lord. Satan is not formally introduced and described; it is taken for granted that the children of God reading the book have knowledge of his identity. The account, however, contains some valuable hints as to Satan's characteristics. We are told that he goes "to and fro on the earth" and walks "up and down on it" (Jb 1:7). He appears as a restless being, constantly on the lookout for opportunities to carry out his designs. We furthermore deduce from the story that he is a spirit; for the "sons of God" mentioned in Jb 1:6 must be the holy angels who came before the Lord to receive their orders and to give reports. We may think of the description given of them in Heb 1:14: "Are they not all ministering spirits sent out to serve for the sake of those who are to inherit salvation?" The whole scene depicted in Jb 1:6–12 is something that takes place in the spiritual world, and hence the conclusion is inevitable that Satan, too, is a spirit.

Satan is intent on doing harm as he moves about in the world. With reference to Job he says, in a complaining way, that God has made a hedge around him, making it impossible to inflict injury on this pious man (1:10). The statement is very consoling to us Christians, showing that Satan's power is limited. In doing the mischief he delights in, Satan can go no further than God permits. Although Satan wishes to use misfortunes and afflictions as a means to induce people to curse God (1:11), the story shows that he cannot freely determine the magnitude and weight of these trials. God remains the Sovereign, who "is faithful, and He will not let you be tempted beyond your ability" (1Co 10:13).

Job Mocked by His Wife, by Georges de la Tour.

In 2:9, **Job's wife** (traditionally known as Dinah) makes her only appearance. She is scarcely the ideal helpmeet but she does again become the mother of his children in the restoration at the end of the book. The book itself makes no more of her behavior, but her tempting words to Job did not escape ancient commentators, sometimes spilling over into angry statements about women (cf Eve's primordial role as temptress). Thus, to the question why Satan spared Job's wife, Chrysostom answered that it was because she was "the devil's best scourge" (cf Augustine's *diaboli adjutrix* and Calvin's *organum Satani*). More modern commentators have attempted to excuse her shrewishness as a reflex of love for her husband, which seems equally hard to accept.

The book presents **three friends of Job**—Eliphaz the Temanite, Bildad the Shuhite, and Zophar the Naamathite—and a younger man, Elihu the son of Barachel the Buzite, who breaks into the dialogue to rebuke the others. These characters sit down with Job to discuss problems and propose wise solutions. They are Job's counselors, examples of ancient wise men.

The "wise" may have been one of the four major classes of Israelite intellectual society, alongside of prophet, priest, and king. Sometimes the social role and teaching function of the wise seems to have been quite informal, but at other times it appears likely that we can speak of more formal "schools," or of carefully structured institutions. Elsewhere in the ancient Near East, we know of such structures in connection with both temples and courts, but in Israel we lack details until a very late period.

It is helpful, however, to distinguish three separate settings of Israelite wisdom activity: popular, political, and theological. Probably all three were at work in most periods, but, to a certain extent, they also correspond to three different chronological stages through which the wisdom movement passed. The earliest, and in all ages, the most elementary form of wisdom is that of *family or clan wisdom*, the commonsense expressions of how to get along that form the bedrock of any culture. We see this form in virtually all the biblical literature, and many of the literary collections undoubtedly root there. Beginning with the monarchy, and probably heavily dependent on Egyptian models, we may speak of *court wisdom*, concerned partly with the king as a guarantor of justice and "righteousness" (cf below), but especially concerned to communicate the art and skills of statecraft, political administration, and so on. One may think of biblical reports of Solomon as the fountainhead and patron of biblical wisdom. Third, we plainly can also speak of a *"school" or scribal wisdom*, apparently especially after the exile, and often developing in a more explicitly theological and/or philosophical direction.

This Neo-Assyrian seal impression shows Tiamat, the god of chaos, depicted as a snake or dragon. A bearded god, perhaps Ninurta, god of cosmic order, attacks the beast.

All of this indicates that, whatever the sociological structures, "wisdom" often came close to being synonymous with "culture"—and, in antiquity, that would be always a sacral culture as well. Job's three friends and Elihu represent these wise men whose speeches greatly impress, though turning out to be wrong in the end.

Most of the Lord's second speech is constituted by two long "monster speeches" about **Behemoth** (40:15–24) and **Leviathan** (ch 41). These two formidable creatures, both the work of God's hands (like Job; cf 40:15), are described at great length in the form of rhetorical questions (the latter especially in the case of Leviathan). Can Job enter into conflict with and subdue them? And if not, how does he ever expect to be able to stand before God?

Who are these beasts? The literature on the question is immense. Behemoth is simply the plural of the Hebrew word for "beast" or "cattle," apparently used in 40:15 and perhaps elsewhere (cf Ps 73:22; Is 30:6) as an "intensive plural" for a specific beast of great size and strength (*the* beast *par excellence*). In this plural form, the word is never used with the definite article, suggesting that it is also a proper name (as at least it is usually rendered here). If so, which beast is it? Early commentators usually thought of the elephant. Modern interpreters have inclined toward hippopotamus, though mention of the "lotus" in Jb 40:21–22 has seemed to point toward Egypt, causing some to prefer a crocodile. If so, however, "Jordan" in v 23 is troublesome, and if not emended away, appears to point definitively toward a habitat in Canaan. Does the identity of the animal really matter? In one sense, not very much, especially if the intent is only to describe some huge earthly beast, that is, with no typical or supernatural import. That major issue cannot be settled with reference to Behemoth alone, apart from consideration of the following beast, Leviathan (ch 41).

The name of the second beast much more readily suggests supernatural or typical import. (Liberal commentaries will commonly use the adjective "mythological"; there is no doubt about the name's mythological connections outside the Bible, but the adjective is scarcely defensible in a canonical context.) In Canaanite mythology, Leviathan (Lotan) is well-known as the name of a seven-headed sea-serpent, more or less personifying the ocean itself, which was defeated by Baal at the "creation," a defeat that must annually be repeated ritually if creation is not to revert to chaos. As a literary device, it is used in Is 27:1 and Ps 104:26 (cf Am 9:3) as a picturesque depiction of the monstrous forces of evil that Yahweh has defeated and neutralized. Apparently Rahab ("arrogance") was a name for the same monster, and it is used in the Bible in the same way, with special reference to Egypt (Is 30:7; 51:9; Ps 87:4; 89:10; this name must not be confused with that of the Jericho prostitute in Jsh 2, which is spelled differently in Hebrew).

It is to be noted that both Leviathan and Rahab are mentioned earlier in the book, Leviathan in Jb 3:8, and Rahab in 9:13 and 26:12 (in 7:12 an unnamed sea creature is also alluded to).

The big question (parallel to that of Behemoth above) is whether Leviathan refers to some natural animal. That there is *some* natural reference seems undeniable, but commentators are no more unanimous in identifying it than they are Behemoth. Most think of a crocodile, though there are other identifications (especially whale, if Behemoth is interpreted as a crocodile). There is ample evidence for the presence of crocodiles in Canaanite waters in biblical times, so no Egyptian setting need be sought here either. Crocodiles are mentioned nowhere else in the Bible, so we have no way of knowing whether leviathan was the everyday designation of that beast, or whether the usage indicates a proper noun.

That point returns us to the major exegetical issue surrounding both Behemoth and Leviathan: are they natural or supernatural creatures? If they are merely natural, God's argument in the second part of the second speech is essentially the same as it was in the first speech.

Natural beasts (whatever their precise identification) are partly in view and are part of Yahweh's argument. At the same time, the natural beasts stand for something supernatural. The evidences of this are many. The very language describing the beasts often is otherworldly (e.g., esp 41:18–21). Natural animals were sometimes captured and killed, while the poems describe these monsters as too powerful and ferocious for man to master. Especially if the names are to be capitalized (as proper names), it seems likely that we are dealing with personifications of more than natural animals. Particularly in the case of the second beast, Leviathan, it seems difficult to avoid hearing some of the same ex-mythological or spiritual significance the name has elsewhere in the Bible (cf above). "Leviathan" commonly symbolizes and summarizes the object of God's end times victory. Its poetic signification here is perhaps connected with the primordial creation of Satan and the evil angels.

In other words, the very monstrosity of the earthly animals (again no matter what their precise identification) should remind the audience of the monstrosity of evil. To the original audience perhaps the very names would suggest the association. Both beasts would then represent diabolical power—and, ultimately, the Diabolos or Satan himself (cf the use of the dragon symbol and the "Beast" for Satan in Revelation). In this way, the story of Job comes full circle from the Lord's dialogues with "the Satan" to his defeat in the end.

Narrative Development or Plot

The accusations of Job's friends seem minor when compared with the accusation of Satan, who asks the central question in the Book of Job and sets the theme: "Does Job fear God for no reason?" (Hbr *hinnam*; 1:9). In other words, why should Job or any other person fear, love, and trust in God? Satan wants to show that a person only serves God because He rewards obedience or punishes disobedience. Job's three friends take up this understanding—our relationship to the Almighty is simply a matter of punishment for disobedience or reward for obedience—and they argue with Job about this issue for most of the book (cf chs 3–31).

However, Job understands that something greater is at work between God and humanity. Job confesses faith in a Redeemer, that the Lord is his

OUTLINE

This biblical book has an exceptionally clear and well-marked outline. The prologue and epilogue are prose. All of the speeches are poetry and are clearly demarcated by statements identifying the speaker. So the simplest outline is this:

    1. Prologue in Narrative Prose (chs 1–2)

    2. Dialogue of Speeches in Poetry (3:1–42:6)

    3. Epilogue in Narrative Prose (42:7–17)

Here is a more detailed outline:

    I. Prologue in Narrative Prose (chs 1–2)

    II. Dialogue of Speeches in Poetry (3:1–42:6)

        A. Dialogue between Job and His Three Friends (chs 3–26). These dialogues have three cycles of speeches. After Job's opening lament (ch 3), in each cycle the order of speakers is this: Eliphaz, Job, Bildad, Job, Zophar, Job. In the third cycle, however, Bildad runs short on words and Zophar is at a loss for words. Hence, in the third cycle, Zophar has no speech and Job has no response to Zophar.

        1. Job's opening lament (ch 3)

        2. First cycle (chs 4–14)

          a. Eliphaz (chs 4–5)

          b. Job (chs 6–7)

          c. Bildad (ch 8)

          d. Job (chs 9–10)

          e. Zophar (ch 11)

          f. Job (chs 12–14)

3. Second cycle (chs 15–21)
   a. Eliphaz (ch 15)
   b. Job (chs 16–17)
   c. Bildad (ch 18)
   d. Job (ch 19)
   e. Zophar (ch 20)
   f. Job (ch 21)
4. Third cycle (chs 22–26)
   a. Eliphaz (ch 22)
   b. Job (chs 23–24)
   c. Bildad (ch 25)
   d. Job (ch 26)
B. Job's Monologue (chs 27–31)
C. Elihu's Speeches (chs 32–37)
D. Yahweh's Two Speeches and Job's Two Responses (38:1–42:6)
   1. Yahweh's first speech (38:1–40:2)
   2. Job's first response (40:3–5)
   3. Yahweh's second speech (40:6–41:34)
   4. Job's second response (42:1–6)

III. Epilogue in Narrative Prose: God's Verdict and Job's Restoration (42:7–17)

Savior (9:33–35; 13:15–16; 14:13–14; 16:19–21; 19:24–27); he has learned true wisdom from the Lord, which comes from "fear" (i.e., trust; see "fear" in the Bible Dictionary, *LBC*, vol. 2) and repentance. Despite Job's insights and legendary patience, he sins by attempting to justify himself in his final appeal (ch 31).

At this point, the young man Elihu interrupts the debate (chs 32–37) to condemn Job's self-justification and the self-righteous condemnations of Job offered by Job's friends. Elihu comes closest to understanding the situation. He defends God's justice and builds on Job's insights about repentance and redemption. He perceives that the Lord "delivers the afflicted by their affliction and opens their ear by adversity" (36:15). He hits upon an important biblical truth: God redeems amid and even through suffering.

After the Lord confronts Job (chs 38–41), Job puts into practice what he had earlier confessed. He repents "in dust and ashes" and receives the Lord's redemption (ch 42). In this way, Satan's initial question is answered—Job does not fear the Lord for the sake of wealth or prosperity. He fears the Lord because He calls people to repentance and redeems them.

Resources

As noted above, a variety of similar compositions exist in Egyptian and Mesopotamian literature. Nevertheless, Job is a unique composition in its plot, characters, and doctrine.

Text and Translations

Because the Book of Job is unique, it is scarcely surprising that it has more than its share of textual problems. The variations in all the versions as well as the perplexities of the Hebrew (often evinced by the Masoretes) testify to the antiquity of the problem. Rarely is the modern scholar in a position to do more than add one more opinion to the series.

However, Job is also one of those books where the LXX often differs quite radically from the Masoretic Hebrew text, mostly in the direction of greater brevity, though sometimes apparently displaying considerable freedom. The LXX is some 400 lines or one-sixth shorter than the traditional Hebrew text, resulting in a text-critical problem similar to, though not quite so severe as, that in Jeremiah (see p 759). In the light of present evidence, there is simply no way of knowing for sure whether the autograph text was abbreviated in the Masoretic tradition or abbreviated in the Septuagint tradition. The usual presumption is that the Masoretic text is superior, and it is interesting to note that assumption already apparent in Origen's *Hexapla* (third century AD), where portions of the Hebrew text missing in the Septuagint were supplied from Theodotion's translation.

Striking new evidence on the question came from Qumran, where two fragments of a Targum on the Book of Job were found. They date to the time of Christ (and are thus the earliest Targum known). In general the Targum appears to support the Hebrew text. Yet, there are other times when it favors the LXX, and sometimes it goes its own way. Thus, it renders a very mixed verdict and, at this stage of our knowledge at least, really does not help at all in reaching a solution.

DOCTRINAL CONTENT

Summary Commentary

Chs 1–3 Job has a wonderful—even "perfect"—family and life. Yet Job's devotion to God is not based on self-righteousness. He recognizes the sinful, corrupt nature at work within his family and seeks God's forgiveness (1:5). God agrees to test Job through suffering. Rather than curse God, Job blesses and worships Him. He displays no regret, as though he suspects his loss is the result of sin by someone in his family. He sees God's hand at work in his suffering. Though Job loses virtually all his possessions, he does not lose trust in the Lord. He feels there is nothing he can do. Job's friends also display genuine, appropriate sorrow and care. Even the most optimistic people will reach despair when overwhelmed by pain and suffering.

Chs 4–14 The first cycle of speeches by Job and his friends begins with Job expressing sorrow. Eliphaz tries to comfort Job but only adds to Job's misery. He only offers platitudes. Job harshly accuses Eliphaz and his other friends of failing to provide even the smallest amount of comfort or help. He turns to God with this desperate cry: "Leave me alone" (7:16). Bildad argues backward: sin produces suffering; therefore, all who suffer must have sinned against God. Job responds that he has no hope of fixing the problem with God. God is too powerful and there is no one to mediate between him and God—not even Job's friends. Of the three friends, Zophar is the most vehement in his denunciation of Job. He does not base his speech on visions (Eliphaz) or tradition (Bildad). He simply concludes Job is a terrible sinner, for how else can Job's extreme sufferings be explained? Whereas Zophar has wrongly focused on people's supposed ability to shape their own destiny, Job correctly recognizes God's control. Job rightly sees that the world is in a state of frustration; sin is still so powerfully at work in our world, and even in our lives as believers. Job expresses the hope of forgiveness and life, but struggles with an overwhelming awareness of God's heavy hand upon weak and sinful human beings like himself.

Chs 15–21 In the second cycle, Job's misery only increased through the aggravating words of his friends. Everyone has abandoned him. Even God has treated Job as His enemy. But Job confesses that God will nevertheless be his witness and intermediary at the coming judgment. After Job's great confession of faith in his heavenly witness-mediator, he begins to consider his outward circumstances once again. He describes how the situation was becoming bleaker. Bildad implies that unless Job repents, he will suffer the ravages of death. When Job's physical condition grows closer to death and he considers a permanent memorial to record his innocence, his spirit soars to his only hope: the Redeemer, God Himself. The divine Redeemer will stand on the earth on the Last Day. Job will receive his vindication in his resurrected body, from which he will see the Redeemer with his own eyes. Zophar assumes that the truly righteous are somehow exempt from external miseries and must enjoy prosperity now ("theology of glory"). Job's friends ignore the observable fact that many among the wicked prosper and live seemingly easy lives. By truthfully describing life on earth, Job is reminded to look beyond this life for his hope and righteousness.

Chs 22–26 In the third cycle, Eliphaz's speech calls Job to repentance, and as such, this chapter is profitable for meditating on one's own sin and the need for God's deliverance. Job complains that God seemed distant and impossible to find (23:3). Yet he remains convinced—by faith and not by sight (2Co 5:7)—that God does not change His will (23:13–14). The brevity of this last speech by Job's friends shows they have finally run out of arguments. Bildad's speech is a good sermon for Job and for everyone. Job states that the almighty God has created the heavens and the earth (26:7) and still controls all things (26:8–10). But this work is merely the "outskirts of His ways" (26:14)—as if the entire creation was the hem at the edge of His cloak!

This replica of an Egyptian mural depicts the colorful garments and hairstyle of Semitic tribesmen in the nineteenth century BC.

Chs 27–31 Job refuses to abandon his confidence. He knows and confesses "what is with the Almighty" (27:11), namely, that he will finally be vindicated (27:6), while his enemies will be swept away (27:13–23). He explains that people cannot find wisdom by their own reason or strength. God alone can give it through His declaration—His Word. Job bases his speech on the idea that moral behavior merits God's favor and that immoral behavior earns God's displeasure. If anyone could be justified before God based on good works, it would have been Job. But God's justice is too uncompromising, and His ways on earth are hidden.

Chs 32–37 Elihu now speaks up. He argues that there is no clear correlation between our experience of suffering (or good) and the will of God. He maintains that when Job, a mere human, dictates to God how or when

He must act, Job must be charged with rebellion. Elihu believes that Job has added unbelief to his sin by complaining so bitterly. (In doing so, Elihu fails to consider some understandable human emotion on Job's part.) Elihu counsels Job that the Lord uses affliction not just for our punishment but also for our deliverance. Elihu tells Job to abandon obstinacy and, with proper fear and trust, to submit to God as his Lord, thereby preparing Job for God's visit in the whirlwind (38:1).

Chs 38–42 In the whirlwind, God responds with a mild, yet firm counteraccusation. The Lord reminds Job that He not only created the world but also continues to care for it. Job falls silent. Job finally recognizes his real insignificance in comparison with Behemoth's and Leviathan's might and defiance. In the end, the Lord restores Job. We see him praying for his friends, who, though they seemed friendly, were acting as his spiritual enemies. Job does not accuse his friends and ask for judgment, but follows the Lord's gracious lead and acts as their mediator before the Lord.

Specific Law Themes

The Book of Job presents the disappointing truth that people suffer unduly in a world broken and corrupted by sin. Although no sinner can merit God's mercy or the security of life now or eternally, it seems unfair that outwardly wicked people may escape suffering while nice people do not escape. Job emphasizes that no one—not even he, as one known to be "blameless and upright" (1:1)—can justify himself before God. The book likewise acknowledges that Satan can tempt people, deceive them, and even inflict suffering upon them, while God seems silent or distant.

Specific Gospel Themes

Job shows that the Lord—in apparent silence and distance—may accomplish His good purposes through suffering. Even while His people mourn their losses and suffer in ways that appear unfair to human judgment, the Lord remains the Redeemer of His people, governing creation and life according to His good and gracious will. Job even foresees the blessings of the resurrection of the body, which physically illustrates the sad realities of destruction and the joys of restoration that appear in Job's story and our own.

Specific Doctrines

The book's introduction characterizes Job as "blameless and upright" (1:1; 1:8). The words do not signify absolute moral perfection but are simply the type of observation characteristic of wisdom. The immediate context, however, also suggests a broader context—before God (*coram Deo*). In this sense, "blameless and upright" means "forgiven, justified," though we can hardly expect wisdom to use this more technical theological language.

Satan, in the form of a serpent, tempted Adam and Eve.

The Adversary

"The Satan" (Hbr) is a title, not a personal name, which means "adversary" or perhaps "prosecuting attorney." The picture is not that of an upholder of justice, but of an officious and ambitious barrister who is always searching for excuses to display his legal talents.

The real debate or contest in the book is between God and Satan. The issue is the profoundly biblical one of whether or not God is served for His own sake, out of sheer gratitude and loyalty, or whether, as in Satan's opinion, everyone has his price. God tempts no one, but plainly in the prologue God permits a testing of Job, and in a sense even initiates it (1:8), and this is surely part of the message of the book. It sets the stage for the entire book, though it is not given to us to know the precise supernatural dimensions of his suffering. Job's sublime benediction at the conclusion of the first test (1:21) in many ways anticipates the book's conclusion; it is not to be read as mere resignation or fatalism.

Theologians have referenced the Book of Job to demonstrate that God is not the cause of sin. Satan is the one who tempts to destruction and would deceive us (1:9–12), yet even he is powerless unless God permits his work (1:21). The Lord created mankind good and cares for him, though he is dust (10:8–12) and is contaminated by sin (14:1–4) to the extent that he cannot do good works before God.

The Dialogues

As Job's friends "lecture" on the issues of evil and suffering, they expound virtually every solution to Job's problems:

(a) "confession is good for the soul," even if one is aware of no particular sins, for no one is perfect;

(b) suffering has disciplinary and probationary value;

(c) suffering is frequently temporary and sometimes only apparent;

(d) suffering is inevitable ("Into each life some rain must fall");

(e) suffering is necessarily mysterious and inscrutable.

Every reader will recognize in these speeches not only universal, human wisdom on the subject, but many accents that the Bible affirms elsewhere in more specifically theological dimension.

It is important to stress that the friends can virtually never be faulted for what they say. In fact, the book no doubt wishes to reaffirm the truth of what they say—as far as it goes. Taken out of context, their arguments are often more cogent than Job's, and if it were simply a matter of a human panel of judges, they would probably win over Job. God ultimately faults them because, unmindful of what the reader knows on the basis of the prologue, they have virtually made God a prisoner of His own law. They have forgotten that the ultimate verdict between mankind and God is a relational one, finally transcending laws and codes altogether.

Similar considerations are necessary to understand Job's part of the "dialogue." Like anyone in the throes of deep distress, Job is not concerned to challenge any dogma or theory of suffering, but to make sense out of his own experience in the light of what he knew on the basis of revelation. (As in most wisdom literature, the detailed contents of that revelation receive little expression, but one is bound to misunderstand the book without the presupposition.) Since Job knows that retribution alone cannot explain his plight, he demands a "friendly God" (cf Luther). Job cannot proclaim his own innocence or justify himself because God has become his enemy. He needs God's pronouncement from on high to clear him of wrongdoing. Since God does not respond right away to Job's confession, Job accuses God of being an arbitrary, malicious despot. Since he currently experiences God as an enemy, even a brutish and monstrous one, Job's outcries, sometimes approaching the blasphemous, are understandable, even if not exemplary. (No doubt, to a certain extent they represent an Eastern tradition, ancient as well as modern, of venting emotions that tend to be frowned on in Western cultures.) From a literary standpoint alone, some incomparably beautiful meditations appear on the desirability of the peace and repose of death (3:16–19; ch 7; and perhaps esp ch 14). One should note that Job never decries either the material losses of ch 1 or the sickness of ch 2, but concerns himself throughout exclusively with the real issue, his relationship with God.

Job's Redeemer

As Job fights his way "out of the depths" and strives to regain his spiritual equilibrium, it is widely recognized that his famous "I know that my Redeemer lives" statement of 19:25 is one of the high points in the book.

Ruins at Hazor date from the time of Solomon. At top right appears a chambered city gate where community legal proceeding would take place. Extending from it appears a hollow casemate wall that could be filled with rubble to defend against a seige.

What is not so well-known and widely overlooked is the fact that that passage is only a climactic expression of a motif that surfaces at least three other times. We first meet the theme of the "arbiter" (Hbr *mokhiach*) in 9:33. Job has been depicting God as virtually a bully, before whom he never stands a chance. Even if he should take God to court, it would mean only another display of "might makes right" procedure.[2] Hence, all Job can hope for is an "umpire," a neutral "mediator" (so the LXX translates the word) who will "lay his hand upon us both," and reestablish fair play. Job may have in mind some idea like the personal angel of later thought; in ancient polytheistic contexts each person has a "personal god" who acts as his advocate in the council of the gods, especially when the great gods are too busy to attend to the affairs of individuals.

Chapter 14 is important in the sequence of Job's thought. For the first time the idea of a solution beyond the grave appears to enter Job's thinking, an idea that will not be developed further until the famous passage of ch 19. Most of ch 14 is a general meditation on the brevity of human life; since it is so, why doesn't God simply leave us alone and allow us to enjoy the few

---

2   Note the ex-mythological imagery used to describe God's superior power: trampling the back of the defeated seagod Yam (Jb 9:8; cf 7:12) and overwhelming "the helpers of Rahab" (9:13; cf 26:12; Ps 89:10; and Is 51:9).

days we have (v 6)? But beginning with v 13, Job speaks personally. What if he could be "hidden" (not dead, but given asylum) from God's fury until His apparent tantrum was over? Then, when God called, he would "answer," that is, perhaps be resurrected and returned to earth for a fair trial. But it is too much to hope for at the moment (v 18); people pass on and decay like everything else. In v 12, when Job had rejected the idea the first time, he had used three Hebrew terms that were at least pregnant with the idea of resurrection, and at least in later times they often came to signify just that.

In Jb 16:18–22 the idea of life after death is muted, but Job returns to the ideas foreshadowed in ch 9. Although God and his "miserable comforters" (16:2) have ganged up against Job, he will not give up. Even if God is about to do him in, Job prays that his blood will remain unburied in order to continue to cry to heaven for justice and vindication (cf Gn 4:10; Is 26:21; Ezk 24:7–8). But to do any good, someone must be in heaven to hear his cry and plead his case. And now for the first time Job no longer speaks hypothetically, but, at least momentarily, is sure that "even now, behold, my witness is in heaven" (Jb 16:19).

Who is this "witness" (Hbr *'edh*) or "he who testifies for me" (Hbr *shahed*)? Probably the majority of commentators understand it to be God Himself, that is, that Job here appeals, as it were, "to God against God," to the God of justice and forgiveness, as he knows the true God must really be, against the apparent ogre of a God he is presently experiencing. This understanding is by no means impossible, but both the immediate context and the parallel passages seem to make a third party more likely. Since God in this context is still the accuser and executioner, the "witness" here, like the "arbiter" of 9:33, is more likely an intercessor or intermediary, who will plead with God like "a son of man does with his neighbor" (16:21).

In 17:1–3 Job appears to have lost his certainty and slipped back into the slough of despondency; the passage is not totally clear, but Job seems to say that since he has no witness to his surety in the heavenly court he prays that God Himself may relent and "lay down a pledge" for him. The Christian knows that only the risen Christ fulfills this hope, but how clearly Job himself saw is hard to say. In any event, he plainly has taken a step further in the direction of the certain conviction and profound declaration of 19:25–27.

After another bitter complaint about his treatment at the hands of God and man alike, Job's spirit begins to rise again in 19:25. This time Job evinces no doubts whatsoever, and articulates his hope in terms of a Redeemer (Hbr *go'el*), who surely is roughly comparable to the "arbiter" (Hbr *mokhiach*) and "witness" (Hbr *'edh*) of the preceding passages. The traditional rendition of *go'el* as "Redeemer" is not so much wrong as premature. The basic reference of *go'el* is to a kinsman who is obliged to buy back his less fortunate relatives from slavery, or at least their property from foreclosure (classically illustrated by Boaz in the Book of Ruth). On the first level, Job here appears to do no more than adapt the idea to his situation before God in the celestial courtroom, and something like "vindicator," "champion," "defense attorney" (perhaps explicitly over against Satan as "prosecuting attorney") is acceptable translation. As in ch 16, it is theoretically possible that Job is merely thinking of God Himself, but it seems much more likely that a third party is in mind. (In the light of fulfillment, the difference narrows in the God-man, Christ.)

In the rest of the Old Testament, there is no doubt that the *go'el* image is often applied in a broader sense to God's redemption of His people, particularly in the exodus. If the Book of Job were not wisdom literature with its characteristic reluctance to tie in explicitly with mainstream biblical themes and usages, an interpreter would be much less reluctant to hear *go'el* in that broader sense also in this context. Nevertheless, the conservative will not hesitate to hear the word also here in its broader canonical context (*tota Scriptura*), where there is no doubt about its ultimate applicability only to Christ, our "advocate" (e.g., 1Jn 2:1), "who was delivered up for our trespasses" (Rm 4:25).

We should note that Job's idea of an arbiter-witness-mediator appears at least once more in the book, this time on the lips of the enigmatic Elihu in 33:23. In 33:19–33 it appears that Elihu is picking up and attempting to modify Job's own earlier references to some heavenly champion. In reply to Job's complaints about the silence of God, Elihu argues that God has various ways of communicating with man—but primarily in order to discipline him, and thus evoke repentance. Among those ways is the possibility of "an angel, a mediator," who cannot be expected simply to exonerate Job, but who may convince God that the guilty one has suffered enough, and thus encourages the man's repentance. Elihu states all this only conditionally, and even then his point is several notches below Job's own declarations. Nevertheless, he does pinpoint once again a critical problem in the book, the communication gap between God and man, and the need for an intercessor who will be enough like God to speak to Him, but also enough like man to speak for him. It is not yet the "fullness of time" (Gal 4:4), and the Book of Job carries the theme no further, but in retrospect we recognize here a preparation for the Gospel (*praeparatio evangelica*).

Life after Death

Job confidently asserts that he shall see God "and not another" (i.e., perhaps now reconciled, and no longer as an enemy). The only real issue is whether Job's language implies a resurrection of the body or a more "spiritual" beholding of God (possibly in the intermediate state; the decision turns especially on the meaning of a Hebrew preposition). It is impossible to settle the matter definitively, but mention in the context of "skin," "eyes," and "heart" (literally "kidneys") would seem to favor the interpretation that Job thinks of his future, vindicated existence in bodily terms. In any event, the passage remains one of the peaks of the book, and the Christian will not hesitate to confess the fulfillment in the resurrection. Theologians have always come to ch 19 when teaching the resurrection of the body. Such an affirmation does not contradict Job's earlier oration on the inevitability and finality of death (in one sense, an incontrovertible fact of human experience), but it does insist that that is not all there is and that the ultimate resolution of life's problems lies in eternity.

Job's teaching about the resurrection of the body is affirmed in the resurrection of Christ. (Master Vyssi Brod; fourteenth century AD).

Some also object that, if the traditional understanding is correct, it is strange that the resurrection of the body is never alluded to again in the book. The objection, however, appears to misunderstand the book's primary purpose, as though it gives theoretical answers rather than focus everything toward a proper relation to God. It may well also be true, as many commentators think they discern, that the remainder of Job's discourses have a much calmer and more dispassionate tone, and that Job is able to turn the friend's arguments against themselves. If so, the genuineness of ch 28, even on Job's lips, would be easier to understand (cf both above and below), and it may be no accident that the "dialogue" winds down and sputters out hereafter (Zophar does not even give his expected third speech in the third cycle).

Job's Relationship with God

It bears emphasis that God in His speeches never demands anything like a conversion or even that Job "repent." (The Hebrew word used by Job in 42:6 is not the ordinary one for repentance but rather signifies a more general change of mind, relenting, regretting. In context, this should mean, among other things, that Job vindicates God's confidence in him over against the Satan's sneers: he does worship God from the perspective of disinterested piety, neither expecting reward nor complaining when external rewards do not ensue.) Throughout the book, Job is never required to renounce his stubborn claim that his suffering was undeserved. His often bitter complaints are not only tolerated by God, but we are surely given to understand that such a stance can be the proper one for the person who takes God and His Word seriously (in contrast to any supine resignation or fatalism). Job's main problem all along had been God's silence, and now the mere fact that God is speaking again is (in the context) sufficient to provoke Job's repentance.

Neither should the fact that God rewards Job with material blessings in the "materialistic" conclusion of Job pose a problem for anyone acquainted with the unity of the material and the spiritual in biblical thought. As noted already, wisdom was prone to use nature or creation to discuss spiritual realities. In this context, the unity extends all the way to the "immortality of the soul" and the "resurrection of the body." It is probably no accident that "restored the fortunes" in 42:10 translates the Hebrew phrase commonly applied also to God's final victory.

Job's material possessions are doubled not to highlight materialism or Job's virtues but to underscore the magnitude of grace. As tradition has always taken it, the text probably intimates even more of resurrection thought in that the number of Job's children is *not* doubled, presumably because they were never really lost to him.[3] A Septuagint addition to the book explicitly extends the thought to Job himself: "It is written that he will rise again with those whom the Lord raises up." Certainly together with 19:25–27 this is part of the book's horizon.

Other wisdom pieces (e.g., Pss 49; 73; 139; Dn 12) reinforce explicit resurrection intent in the epilogue of Job; apparently wisdom reflection on the problem of innocent suffering was one of God's major means in nourishing and preparing for His final resolution of the problem of evil in the resurrection of His Son.

---

3   One must note the strange Hebrew numeral in v 13 which might mean "twice seven," that is, 14 sons—though the number of daughters certainly remains the same.

Application

Chs 1–2 In the Book of Job, the Lord puts Satan to the test in order to prove something marvelous for you: Satan cannot snatch you out of the Lord's hand (Jn 10:28–29). Even when all seems right in our families, the Lord calls us to daily repentance, because true peace and devotion flow from His mercy. When friends and family mourn and suffer, abide with them. Share their grief, and look for opportunities to comfort them. Pray to the "God of all comfort" on their behalf, for "through Christ we share abundantly in comfort too" (2Co 1:3, 5).

Ch 3 Scripture does not teach that death is a friend to those who suffer—death is always an enemy (1Co 15:26), but one overcome by the Lord. Commend those who despair to Jesus, who likewise cried, "My God, My God, why have You forsaken Me?" (Mt 27:46) and rose from the dead to say, "Peace be with you" (Jn 20:21).

Chs 4–14 When you reach out to a friend or family member, do not give answers that simply bandage deep hurts. Listen carefully to the sufferer and learn to share the pain. God uses adversity to discipline His people. In the midst of trial, we might doubt God's love for us. But the cross shows us the measure of God's love. By the power of the Holy Spirit, we can see suffering as a tool to refine faith and strengthen our relationship with God in Jesus Christ.

Our righteousness does not determine our well-being, or lack thereof. Rather, it is all in God's hands. When we become discouraged, it is vital that we remember God's wisdom and power. Although Job does not acknowledge God's use of these attributes for our good, in Christ "we know that for those who love God all things work together for good" (Rm 8:28).

Chs 15–21 We must not assume that someone's mental, emotional, and/or spiritual agony is the result of unrepentant rebellion; it could very well be that God is refining that person's faith. Just as the afflictions of Christ overflow into our lives, so also our comfort in Christ overflows; we are being made like our Savior (1Co 1:5; Php 3:10). When we are perplexed in our affliction, may we—through the eyes of faith—see Christ, whose affliction saved us from sin and death!

Regardless of the circumstances and the depth of darkness you may face, call on Jesus Christ, the only mediator between God and all people (1Tm 2:5). Christ is now interceding for you at the right hand of God (Rm 8:34). The Redeemer sees you in your helpless state. As a true Redeemer who buys back His kinsman from bondage, Christ has won you for Himself at the cost of His own flesh and blood. Therefore, we look beyond the injustice we observe and continually confess that our outward predicament does not define God's attitude toward us. While the houses of the wicked remain after earthly storms, the spiritual houses of those in Christ endure forever against sin, the world, and the devil because they are built on the rock that is Christ (Mt 7:24–27).

Chs 22–26 Putting ourselves in Job's place for a moment, who can argue with Eliphaz when he accuses us of failing to love both neighbor (22:5–9) and God (22:12–14) alike? Surely Eliphaz is also correct when he declares that God will listen to our repentant prayers (22:27)! Yet the sufferings Job bears are not because of his sin, as Eliphaz assumes. The Lord humbles him in order to exalt him. This is truly the way of the cross. Though you suffer poverty and injustice, know that the Lord wills your good and desires your salvation. He calls us to humility and contrition. We can offer no defense for ourselves and for our sins; we must throw ourselves entirely on God's mercy. As great as the creation appears in our eyes, our Creator towers above it. Yet, for our salvation, the limitless Creator allowed Himself to be confined to the limits of our humanity when Jesus Christ was conceived by the Holy Spirit and born of the Virgin Mary.

Chs 27–31 Job's faith in God grows stronger in the face of his difficulties, just as iron is strengthened on the anvil and in the forge. No matter what befalls him, Job entrusts all things to his Creator. Job will learn that God has His purpose in suffering. There is no way for humans to see behind the mask of God, to know God's will apart from Scripture. He reveals His gracious will through the Word, not by reason or experience.

Chs 32–37 When we feel trials, we can be comforted knowing that God is not punishing us because of our sin, but is strengthening our faith through testing. "God puts His saints to work in various ways and often holds back the rewards of works-righteousness. He does this so that they may learn not to trust in their own righteousness and may learn to seek God's will rather than the rewards. This can be seen with Job, Christ, and other saints" (Ap V 77). Questioning God's actions in our lives or world may lead to serious sin. But God is patient with us, even as He was with Job.

Allow affliction to open your ears (36:15b) to learn the Lord's purposes, and to open your mouth in praises (36:24). Praise Christ most highly, who delivers you from evil by His agony and bloody sweat. Though we may become distracted by many things in this life, both bane and blessing, God prepares us for His visitation, when all that will matter will be our confidence in His grace through Jesus Christ, our Lord.

Chs 38–42 We might question God and wonder whether He is actually in charge of the daily events of our lives. Coming face-to-face with our Creator brings us to our knees. Yet the fearsome face of the Creator also smiles on Job and shows him mercy. Finally, we admit that we seldom can comprehend God's ways, because sin clouds our understanding. What Job could not do to save himself, God did by sending "His only Son, that whoever believes in Him should not perish but have eternal life" (Jn 3:16).

CANONICITY

Already in the sixth century BC the prophet Ezekiel referred to Job (Ezk 14:12–20), demonstrating the book's influence in Israel.[4] Scribes at Qumran also valued the book. New Testament writers referred to Job (Jas 5:11) and cited his book (Rm 11:35; 1Co 3:19), illustrating its authority. Christians received the book into their canon without question.

Ecce Homo portrait of Christ. Like the Gospels, Job teaches that God works through suffering. Christ delivers us by His "agony and bloody sweat" (The Litany, *LSB*, p. 288).

---

4 The Hebrew text of Ecclus 49:9 mentions "the prophet Job" but the Greek text translates as "enemies with storm."

LUTHERAN THEOLOGIANS ON JOB

Luther

Luther states that the Book of Job "is written for our comfort." It teaches that all people sin and that God's justice is not like human justice:

"The book of Job deals with the question, whether misfortune comes from God even to the righteous. Job stands firm and contends that God torments even the righteous without cause other than that this be to God's praise, as Christ also testifies in John 9[:3] of the man who was born blind.

"Job's friends take the other side. They make a big and lengthy palaver [empty talk] trying to maintain God's justice, saying that he does not punish a righteous man, and if he does punish, then the man who is punished must have sinned. They have a worldly and human idea of God and his righteousness, as though he were just like men and his justice like the justice of the world.

"To be sure, when Job is in danger of death, out of human weakness he talks too much against God, and in his suffering sins. Nevertheless Job insists that he has not deserved this suffering more than others have, which is, of course, true. Finally, however, God decides that Job, by speaking against God in his suffering, has spoken wrongly, but that in contending against his friends about his innocence before the suffering came Job has spoken the truth. So the book carries this story ultimately to this conclusion: God alone is righteous, and yet one man is more righteous than another, even in the sight of God.

"But this is written for our comfort, that God allows even his great saints to falter, especially in adversity. For before Job comes into fear of death, he praises God at the theft of his goods and the death of his children. But when death is in prospect and God withdraws himself, Job's words show what kind of thoughts a man—however holy he may be—holds toward

God: he thinks that God is not God, but only a judge and wrathful tyrant, who storms ahead and cares nothing about the goodness of a person's life. This is the finest part of this book. It is understood only by those who also experience and feel what it is to suffer the wrath and judgment of God, and to have his grace hidden.

"The language of this book is more vigorous and splendid than that of any other book in all the Scriptures. . . . So, for example, when he says something like this, 'The thirsty will pant after his wealth' [Job 5:5], that means 'robbers shall take it from him'; or when he says, 'The children of pride have never trodden it' [Job 28:8], that means 'the young lions that stalk proudly'; and many similar cases. Again, by 'light' he means good fortune, by 'darkness' misfortune [Job 18:8], and so forth." (AE 35:251–52)

Gerhard

"*Job.* The interpreters, both Jews and Christians, vary greatly about this book. Rabbi Moses Ben Maimon (*More Nebuchim*, part 3, sect. 22) denies that Job was ever possible [*in rerum natura*]; therefore he thinks that [Job] is only an example. The Hebrews (Talmud, ordin. 4, tr. 3) do not have the Book of Job in the divine volumes nor do they think that he lived among humans. Ezekiel's testimony, however, refutes this opinion (Ezek. 14:14), and this is in conformity with what we have in James 5:11. In *De verbo Dei*, bk. 1, c. 5, Bellarmine tries to draw Luther into agreement with this error because Luther declares (in *Conviv. sermon.*, title *De patriarchis et prophetis*) that he does 'not believe that all things happened as they are told in the Book of Job'[5] and also because he says (title *De libr. V. et N.T.*): 'The Book of Job is like the argument of a fable for setting forth an example of long-suffering.'[6]

"We respond, however, in this way. (1) The *Table Talk* was not seen, read, nor approved by Luther but had been changed often, mutilated, and added to by private whim of anyone, something that rightly takes genuine trustworthiness from it. (2) Luther himself warns that the things he said in convivial conversation among his friends must not be considered as articles of faith, as Selnecker relates in the preface to the *Table Talk*. (3) In the Ger-

---

5 Cf. StL 22:1415 (*Table Talk*).
6 Cf. StL 22:1422 (*Table Talk*).

man version of the Bible, [Luther] kept the Book of Job among the canonical books and distinguished it from the apocryphal books. (4) Luther's words are quoted out of context, for he adds in the same place: 'I think the Book of Job is true history.' Also: 'Meanwhile, it touches upon the truth of the situation and on the act itself.' (5) Luther only doubts whether Job sets forth everything in external speech or, on the other hand, thought some of it. For in temptations and troubles people generally say few things aloud nor do they generally arrange them in this order. He thinks, therefore, that some learned man at the time of Solomon, or even Solomon himself, put all this into this order. (6) We should accept Luther's words in regard to both order and method of treatment, for this kind of *hysteron proteron* [*prothusteron*] is not at all uncommon in Scripture. (7) Luther does not use the word 'fable' for a fictitious narrative, for in the same place he calls it a true history. Rather, he uses it for the subject of comedy in the same sense that the history of Josephus, reduced into the form of comedy, is generally called 'fable' and the 'arguments of fable.' (8) Let Bellarmine recognize his own words, *De verbo Dei*, bk. 1, c. 9, § *At Hieronymus*: 'The ancients sometimes use the word "fables" not for fictitious matters but for true narrations, as it is said in the last chapter of Luke [v. 15]: "It happened while they were telling stories [*fabularentur*] . . . ." Minucius Felix, at the beginning of the dialogue that he titles *Octavius* calls a true story of someone's sailing voyage a "fable." '

"But let us return to the Book of Job. Rabbi Isaac thinks that this Job was Jobab, king of the Edomites, who is mentioned in Gen. 36:34. Although Rabbi Aben Ezra in his commentary on this passage laughs at this opinion, and though Jerome does not approve it (*QQ. Hebraic. super Genes.*), nevertheless Dr. Zehnerus confirms it with arguments we must not hold in contempt: [(1) *From the circumstances of places.* . . . (2) *From the description of the public offices.* . . . (3) *From the similarity of names.* . . . (4) *From a reckoning of the time.* . . . (5) *From the judgment of various authors.*]" (ThC E1 §§ 134–44)

"The Christian Church has always held the Book of Job in high regard. Jerome speaks about it as follows (*Ad Paulinum*, vol. 3, f. 7): 'It determines all the laws of dialectic with its proposition, assumption, confirmation, conclusion. Every word in it is filled with feelings.' Suidas (loc. cit.) says that it sings far more sweetly than the Homeric and Platonic nightingales and embraces 'an inquiry into the nature of the entire region, the natural orders of animals and birds, and some brilliant tales.' The summary of the whole book is whether God afflicts even the devout. This Job affirms, but his kinsmen deny it.

"It has forty-two chapters, and we can divide it as we do drama into introduction [*protasis*], tension [*epitasis*], and happy reversal [*catastrophe*], yet in such a way that nothing is taken away from historical truth. Some divide it into dialogue and epilogue. In the dialogue, the persons who speak are God, Satan, Job, Job's wife, and four of his kinsmen: Eliphaz, Bildad, Zophar, and Elihu. It is counted quite deservedly among the poetic books of the Old Testament, for Jerome (preface to Job) witnesses that 'this book from the beginning of the third chapter to the sixth line of the last chapter consists of hexametric verses of spondees and dactyls,' though the nature of this meter is unknown to us today." (ThC E1 § 140)

Storm in the Judean wilderness. "The LORD answered Job out of the whirlwind" (Jb 38:1).

THE PLACE OF WISDOM IN THE BIBLE

Great biblical themes of the election of Israel, Sinaitic covenant, exodus and conquest, promises about the people and the land, sacrifice and temple, are almost totally absent from Job and most other Books of Wisdom (except the Psalms), as is most of the semi-technical vocabulary employed elsewhere in the Bible to present them. The theme of "kingship" is not developed in the light of Nathan's oracle to David but is more a matter of etiquette or protocol before royalty anywhere, anytime. In biblical wisdom, "sin" is not a matter of fundamental fallenness and rebelliousness, but of atomistic infractions of a code of conduct. The particular name of Israel's God, "Yahweh," appears often enough but in so casual a way that one can easily substitute "God" or "deity" of almost any sort.

Perhaps the first thing to stress is the difference between an *explicit* theological statement and one that is assumed or implicit. Much of wisdom literature is of the latter type. Yet it must be understood and interpreted in the light of not only the more explicit wisdom statements, but of all of Scripture, of the canonical context. The real subject of wisdom is not just any man but an Israelite. Wisdom's "universalism" involves, indeed, God's claim on all the universe, but one realized and realizable only in His gracious covenant. Its setting is the daily life of people who confessed Yahweh as Creator, Judge, and Redeemer. Its accent on retribution and reward was an assertion of faith, based on revelation, not some naive deduction from experience. Sacred and secular are not distinguished because everything is sacral! The very assumption of an underlying moral order rejects any real secularism.

Outside of the covenant of faith, God's universal claim is only expressed as condemnation (the Law's second use), confronting and condemning all until they convert. The proverbs will only indicate certain moral principles that also the believer will be concerned to teach in the "kingdom on the left hand." Yet, wisdom is understood and applied in its full and true intent only within the covenant, where the full content of God's revelation is proclaimed and received in faith. Both wisdom and righteousness assume a universal moral order. That order (of salvation or new creation) is available only through God's gracious gift of His righteousness (justification by faith).

The main dogmatic category for properly approaching wisdom is the third use of the Law. It represents an alternate mode of expression and type of approach to the illustration of faithful living found in the legal sections of the Books of Moses and is thoroughly harmonious and compatible with them. It concentrates on those aspects of living that the believer shares with all people and where the motivations or any uniqueness will often be unapparent to people. Believers are certainly not less concerned about the ordinary, everyday concerns of living than unbelievers.

Proverbs and maxims dealing with such concerns have a great deal of commonality among all ages and all peoples—precisely because the problems of basic living are much the same, regardless of religion, culture, historical epoch, and so on. Hence, one need not be surprised that biblical wisdom shows phenomenal parallels with its cultural neighbors. As always, it is not a matter of one culture borrowing from another (the question itself is misconceived) but of a cultural continuum. And the differences are infinitely greater than the surface similarities, because the same principles have been transplanted into an entirely different context. The real and ultimate "uniqueness" of biblical (and Christian) life is not in external behavior patterns (respectable citizens of goodwill usually agree on these to a large extent) but in the theological context, motivations, or goals. Faith insists that the real and ultimate "wisdom" is released and established only in the proper relation to God in Christ.

Special Revelation on General Revelation

It may be helpful to compare such wisdom to general revelation or to the order of creation. Biblical wisdom documents are verbally inspired, that is, they represent special revelation, as much as the rest of Scripture. But the topic or aspect of life to which they point is general revelation, natural revelation, or natural law. Written in all hearts, it condemns until the special revelation of the Gospel makes all things new. After conversion, the Christian continues to grow and learn in many respects and from any source, but confessing that the real Source of knowledge is the same as that vouchsafed in Scripture. God's servant actively seeks his place in the world of his Creator with an attitude of "faith seeking understanding" *(fides quaerens intellectum)*. As one made in God's image, this search is part of his quest for God's will in his life. Believing that all truth is ultimately one because its ultimate author is One, the believer utilizes all relevant sources, whatever their earthly mediation. All knowledge is not revealed in Scripture, but all knowledge becomes "wisdom" before God only when ultimately subordinated to, tested, and evaluated in the light of Scripture. In a sense, then, wisdom provides a sampling or exemplars of how the believer confronts the valid aspects of this world's wisdom and employs it to the greater glory of God. He now has at his disposal all the blessings of creation and is intended to exercise the best possible stewardship of them (cf 1Co 3:21b–23).

Two Ways

Only if one keeps this theology in mind will one of the major problems in biblical wisdom be comprehended in a satisfactory way. That is the problem of the apparently naive, if not deterministic, black-and-white contrast between the "two ways," that of the righteous and of the wicked (classically taught in Ps 1; a variety of synonyms are also employed). However, it seems unthinkable that anyone, let alone a wise man, could really believe that life was that simple. The ancients surely knew and experienced as well as we that virtue is not always rewarded, nor vice invariably requited, that the good guys are by no means automatically the richest, happiest, or most successful. Such a literalistic reading would collapse.

The two ways depicted here are found in the hills west of the Jordan River. Biblical wisdom describes God's people daily choosing the way of life rather than death.

One could make amends simply by inserting an "ultimately" or "usually" before the stark black-and-white assertions. This may be supplied from the total canonical context.

Wisdom highlights primarily man's life before God, always under God's searchlight (cf Ps 139). *Every* day is judgment day. Man is always at the cross-roads. His situation is always poised between life and death, order and chaos (the explicit polarities of wisdom throughout). Every choice and activity of his, even the most trivial, is fraught with ultimate consequences. Each thrusts ultimately in one direction or the other.

Only Judgment Day will finally reveal the eternal disjunction of the "two ways." We cannot enter here into the question of how much of this eternal view (eternal life versus eternal punishment) is already present in the Old Testament. Liberals usually reject it out of hand. Although conservatives may stress it too quickly, wisdom's accent on ultimacies argues that such a theology was, at very least, *implicit* throughout mainline Old Testament thought, and often surfaced also in a more explicit way. It is no accident that many of those most explicit assertions appear in wisdom contexts (e.g., Pss 49; 73), and many other wisdom texts are open to it (e.g., Pss 1; 139). In one sense, the full nature of that outcome could not be revealed until the ultimate act itself, the resurrection of our Lord.

Wisdom and Theological Expression

One can observe degrees of theological expression in biblical wisdom. However, it is important to stress that these distinctions are not for constructing a chronological evolution of theology.

On one level, biblical wisdom expresses itself through simple sayings, where theological context is taken for granted. Many wise men apparently did not concern themselves with making their teaching theological. There was no point in all circles of writers rehearsing the same thing in the same way. One may distinguish a second expression of biblical wisdom when "the fear of Elohim/Yahweh" becomes an organizing principle.

Two further and all-important theological expressions of wisdom must be described. One ultimately became more important for Christianity; the other for Judaism. The third accents wisdom as ultimately a Person, a heavenly figure of wisdom dwelling in the midst of and informing all earthly manifestations. The fourth expression is *explicit* identification of wisdom with "Word" as Torah, or of Proverbs as though it were a book of the Pentateuch—identification of general with special revelation, if you will.

It is ironic that the latter two expressions appear most explicitly in literature written *after* the close of the Old Testament canon, in certain apocryphal books. Those developments retain great importance, both for helping us understand the less explicit, earlier canonical literature, and as a bridge to and background for the New Testament (and the Talmud).

Possibly the earliest text that illustrates movement between these levels is the final verse of Jb 28 where the real source and content of wisdom, otherwise ultimately inaccessible to man, is identified as the "fear of the Lord." Already implicit here is a motif to which especially Ecclesiastes gives classical expression: the *limits* of man's "wisdom" and of man's ability to master and govern his own life. Wisdom marks off areas of life that belong to Yahweh alone. Very explicit, and very important, however, is the canonical Pr 8, where wisdom exists before the creation of the universe, and furthermore is God's daily delight and master workman in the labor of creation. It is more than merely a "personification" of wisdom.

The apocryphal Ecclus 24 (esp v 23) stresses the identity of wisdom and Torah. Although the source of wisdom is "the mouth of the Most High" (v 3), *she* is somewhat available to all people. She took root like a tree especially in Zion, where she invites all to eat and drink from her—which, however, will only incite greater thirst or hunger.

Wisdom 7 again develops the personal theme. Here in semi-Hellenistic form, her immanence in all souls and easy access to all people is stressed. As "a pure emanation of the glory of the Almighty" (v 25), she orders all things well, especially in teaching the four cardinal virtues: self-control, prudence, justice, and courage.

Christ among the Doctors by William Holman Hunt.

Wisdom in Christianity and Judaism

As we said, the theme in this development of wisdom formulation that became most important for Christianity (and hence also for Christian understanding and exposition) was the accent on the *personal* element in wisdom. God is indeed immanent in all creation, but (and ultimately more significantly) is also transcendent to it, and hence a genuine "Creator" (and ultimately, "Redeemer," both terms implying a personal being). Nature cannot be the result of impersonal, evolutionistic process, but stems from and is upheld by the personal Word of a personal God. To the believer, nature becomes a transparency of, a window through which one may see, God's eternal design. Natural law cannot finally be eternal, immutable principles but must be expressions of His *personal* will. "Retribution," "reward," etc., cannot be forced into legalistic straitjackets but are overruled by His personal offer of redemption.

It is no accident that much of the Christology of the New Testament is couched in wisdom terms. Christ is wisdom incarnate, in whom the new creation is realized (and the mysticism of the Eastern church has generally found the theme easier to retain and appropriate than the West; cf the repeated refrain, "Wisdom!" in the traditional Byzantine liturgy). Two New Testament passages are especially significant in this connection: Colossians with its cosmic Christology, and John (esp ch 1), where the Logos is both heir to the explicit merger of general and special revelation we have just discussed, and can make contact with the vast amount of comparable Greek thought about the immanent Logos, world-reason, or divine "logic" in all creation. The same wisdom themes continue in New Testament pneumatology: the Spirit of Christ transmits and contemporizes the personal energy of Wisdom Incarnate, of the "Word *made* flesh."

As noted earlier, wisdom was also explicitly identified with the Word, with Torah, with the mainstream of special revelation or salvation history (*Heilsgeschichte*). Much of the development of classical Judaism out of Old Testament Yahwism follows this path. As wisdom merges with Torah, the wisdom-teacher increasingly becomes a "scribe," the expounder of Scripture, and his authority will be enhanced as the synagogue gradually overtakes and replaces the temple. At the very same time, many wisdom techniques and idioms continue to be employed by the rabbis and are gathered in the Talmud (classically in the *Pirqe Aboth*, an early collection of rabbinical proverbs). Under these auspices, wisdom presses not toward the "orthodoxy" of Christianity, but toward the "orthopraxis" or accent on the manner of life (*halakah*) characteristic of Judaism to the present day.

One must be careful about dividing the two emphases. Judaism did not completely deny the personal aspect of wisdom, but obviously did not accept its Christological application. Just as obviously, however, Christianity did not reject the identification of wisdom with the Word: not only were the two parts of Scripture at one in Christ, but both creation and redemption achieved their fullness in the incarnation and resurrection. The unity continues to find expression in the three simultaneous meanings of "Word" in Christian theology: the person of the incarnate Christ, the Gospel about Him, and the Scriptures that define those terms.

QUESTIONS PEOPLE ASK ABOUT JOB

The Abode of the Evil Angels

Job 1:7 narrates: "The LORD said to Satan, 'From where have you come?' Satan answered the LORD and said, 'From going to and fro on the earth, and from walking up and down on it.'"

Jude 6 says: "And the angels who did not stay within their own position of authority, but left their proper dwelling, he has kept in eternal chains under gloomy darkness until the judgment of the great day."

These two texts speak of a matter concerning which God has not thought it necessary or wise to grant us an extensive revelation. Jude writes that the angels who left their beautiful heavenly home are kept in "eternal chains," an expression that evidently describes the prison of hell. In the Book of Job, however, we read that Satan, the head of the evil angels, walks to and fro on the earth, which seems to show that he is not bound. Hence there appears to be a contradiction.

The Bible appears to say that while the evil angels are all imprisoned, a certain freedom of movement and action has been left to them, which permits their activities here on earth. For example, a person may be imprisoned in a penitentiary for life and yet be given the privilege of walking about in the prison yard or even outside of it under certain conditions and restrictions. All that Jude says can well be harmonized with such a view. That God has kept them "under gloomy darkness" would mean that He has assigned hell to them as their abode, from which they can venture forth only as often and as far as He permits.

The statement that Satan came before the Lord among the sons of God (Jb 1:6) raises other questions. Does that not imply that Satan entered heaven? How does this agree with his having been cast out forever from the realms of the blessed?

In looking at these questions, let us remember the remark made above that we are here dealing with events in the spiritual realm, concerning which we have but an inadequate conception. It lies altogether beyond the sphere of the experience of mortals. The language used is that which we use in speaking of human rulers and their courts, and we must conclude that this was the way the author wanted to teach us what happened.

One thing is certain, a communication of thoughts took place between the Lord and Satan. As to the manner in which it was done, we had better not speculate. It must be observed, too, that the narrative does not say that Satan came before God in heaven. The place where he was when he replied to the questions of God is not mentioned. It is true that Satan's abode after his fall is the abyss, the region of eternal darkness, and the almighty power of God will see to it that he will not escape. But the imprisonment is not so complete as to prevent him from roaming about on earth "like a roaring lion, seeking someone to devour" (1Pt 5:8).

We cannot conclude this brief section without saying that what is of chief importance is not the ability to answer the questions concerning Satan that our intellect and especially our curiosity ask, but an earnest endeavor to heed the warnings of the Holy Scriptures against the temptations that Satan will throw across our path until the end of time.

The Sufferings of God's Children

Job 2:3, 7 states: "And the LORD said to Satan, 'Have you considered My servant Job, that there is none like him on the earth, a blameless and upright man, who fears God and turns away from evil? He still holds fast his integrity, although you incited Me against him to destroy him without reason.' . . . So Satan went out from the presence of the LORD and struck Job with loathsome sores from the sole of his foot to the crown of his head."

Proverbs 12:21 affirms: "No ill befalls the righteous, but the wicked are filled with trouble."

No evil will happen to the righteous person, says the Bible. And yet, according to the same Bible, Job, who was a just man, had to suffer evil if ever a man did. How does the declaration in Proverbs fit with the history of Job? The solution lies in the meaning of the term *wicked* (also translated as evil), which in the sense employed in Pr 12:21 describes real hurt or damage to someone. Did Job experience wickedness of this sort? He did not. We must remember that his sufferings were merely temporary, that they led him into a deeper knowledge of God and His ways, that they served as a fire of purification which made him a better person, that they were the precursor of greater wealth and bliss than he had enjoyed before. Paul declares in Rm 8:28 that "for those who love God all things" (and there, according to the context, he would include sufferings) "work together for good"; and thus nothing that must be termed evil or wicked can befall a Christian. For a while it seemed as though Job's lot was a terrible one. In reality it turned out to be blessed.

The End of the Book of Job

There are two speeches by Yahweh at the end of Job (38:1–40:2 and 40:6–41:34). Job submits to the Lord after each speech. But why does this happen twice? What is the function or purpose? It seems impossible to distinguish the two.

Sometimes it is suggested that because Job had challenged both God's power and justice, the first and second speeches should meet those two objections, respectively. However, the different contents of the two speeches do not seem to correspond to that distinction, unless one puts greater weight on 40:8–14 (cf below). At first reading, it would seem that Job had questioned God's justice rather than His power, while God's reply underscores His power and hardly speaks at all to the question of His justice or moral government of human affairs.

The first speech consists almost totally of a series of ironic questions—like "Do you know?" "Were you there?" "Can you too?"—all intended to put the smallness of mankind in bold relief before the Creator. In 38:1–38 we have a review of inanimate nature, followed in 38:39–39:30 by a summary of the wonders of animate nature. Yahweh's first speech ends with a repetition (40:1–2) of the challenge with which it began (38:1–3), and Job's submission is just as brief (40:3–5). Critics have great difficulty with this brief exchange, partly because of its brevity, and a frequent solution is to regard the entire second divine speech as a later addition. If we reject that solution, it still is not easy to decide precisely what the dynamics of the book are at this point. Is Job's submission here insufficient, possibly even insincere or covertly still defiant, so that another sermon is required to finish the task? Job's second submission (42:1–6) is a bit longer, but scarcely different in quality. Perhaps it is best to assume that we have here only a pause, governed by literary or artistic considerations.

After a repetition of the challenge (40:6–9), Yahweh's second speech again divides into two parts, though the first portion is very short. In the first (40:10–14), Job is ironically invited to "play God" by defeating all the forces of evil in the world. Only in these verses, at least at first reading, does God appear to be dealing with the moral issues Job has raised, and the answer is very similar to what both Job and the friends have already asserted in their own ways: justice must be left to God. The positioning of these verses between the nature poems before and after may signal their centrality and importance in the total answer. As always in Scripture, God's ability to redeem is based on His ability to create— and re-create. Redemption finally changes the world as well as people. It is one of wisdom's bedrock emphases that the same order of righteousness is intended to pervade all realms of existence.

FURTHER STUDY

Lay/Bible Class Resources

Andersen, Francis I. *Job: An Introduction and Commentary.* TOTC. Downers Grove, IL: InterVarsity Press, 2008. ♪ A helpful, concise, scholarly, and conservative commentary, though often not as Christological as it should be.

Archer, Gleason L., Jr. *The Book of Job: God's Answer to the Problem of Undeserved Suffering.* Grand Rapids: Baker, 1982. ♪ A useful resource written in popular style by a well respected evangelical theologian and translator.

Honsey, Rudolph. *Job.* PBC. St. Louis: Concordia, 2004. ♪ Lutheran author. Excellent for Bible classes. Based on the NIV translation.

Kidner, Derek. *The Wisdom of Proverbs, Job and Ecclesiastes: An Introduction to Wisdom Literature.* Downers Grove, IL: InterVarsity Press, 2008. ♪ The subtitle explains the focus of Kidner's book, which emphasizes the literary structure and theology of biblical wisdom.

Life by His Word. St. Louis: Concordia, 2009. ♪ More than 1,500 reproducible one-page Bible studies covering each chapter of the canonical Scriptures. Page references to *The Lutheran Study Bible.* CD-Rom and downloadable.

Mason, Mike. *The Gospel According to Job: An Honest Look at Pain and Doubt from the Life of One Who Lost Everything.* Wheaton: Crossway, 1994. ♪ This excellent devotional commentary on selected verses was written by a Christian who suffered torments like those of Job.

Teske, Steven, and LeRoy Leach. *Job.* Leaders Guide and Enrichment Magazine/Study Guide. LL. St. Louis: Concordia, 2011. ♪ An in-depth, nine-session Bible study with individual, small group, and lecture portions. Lutheran authors.

Church Worker Resources

Hulme, William E. *Christian Caregiving: Insights from the Book of Job.* St. Louis: Concordia, 1992. ♪ This small book contains excellent pastoral insights gleaned from the way Job and his friends interact.

———. *Dialogue in Despair: Pastoral Commentary on the Book of Job.* Nashville: Abingdon, 1968. ♪ Helpful for purpose expressed in title.

Academic Resources

Alden, Robert L. *Job*. NAC. Nashville: Broadman, 1993. ♫ It is very good in many respects: conservative isagogically; generally Christological, but not as strongly Christological as Hartley; good on the Redeemer passages. The book is weak on the Yahweh speeches, claiming that the message of whole book is that God is sovereign, in control of all. The author finds no Gospel comfort in Jb 38–42.

Dhorme, Édouard. *A Commentary on the Book of Job*. London: Nelson, 1976. ♫ English translation of the French classic; extensive discussions of text-critical matters.

Driver, Samuel Rolles, and George Buchanan Gray. *A Critical and Exegetical Commentary on the Book of Job*. ICC. 2 vols. Edinburgh: T&T Clark, 1921. ♫ Detailed philology, sometimes dated, but often still the best on the grammatical meaning of the text.

Gordis, Robert. *The Book of God and Man: A Study of Job*. Chicago: University of Chicago Press, 1965. ♫ A Jewish classic.

———. *The Book of Job: Commentary, New Translation and Special Studies*. New York: Jewish Theological Seminary of America, 1978. ♫ Includes text of Job in Hebrew, a translation, word studies, and commentary.

Gray, John. *The Book of Job*. Sheffield: Sheffield Phoenix, 2010. ♫ An important contribution to philological study of Job, drawing on Ugaritic and Arabic texts.

Habel, Norman C. *The Book of Job*. The Cambridge Bible Commentary on the New English Bible. Cambridge: Cambridge University Press, 1975. ♫ Mildly critical, yet considers Job a unity. This commentary generally is excellent in literary matters. Particularly good is its attention to recurring themes and words as the author shows how Job and the friends interact with each other and return to themes they voiced earlier. Unfortunately, Habel fails miserably to interpret the Redeemer passages Christologically, and instead refers them to an angelic mediator, who is neither true God nor true man. In some key places Habel describes a classic Lutheran theological interpretation in terms of Law and Gospel, but then rejects it.

Hartley, John E. *The Book of Job*. NICOT. Grand Rapids: Eerdmans, 1988. ♫ This commentary is probably the most consistently Christological of all the published commentaries. It is not as detailed as Habel, but theologically much better. He relates the Redeemer passages to the crucified and risen Christ (although he fails to treat ch 28 Christologically).

K&D. *Biblical Commentaries on the Old Testament: The Book of Job*. Grand Rapids: Eerdmans reprint (n.d.). ♫ This century-and-a-half old work should not be overlooked. Despite its age, it remains a most useful commentary on the Hebrew text. The philology is dated and not always reliable. Surprisingly, Delitzsch is skeptical of interpreting ch 19 as a resurrection hope.

Pope, Marvin H. *Job*. Vol. 15 of AB. Rev. ed. New York: Doubleday, 1973. ♫ Philologically very helpful, also with reference to Ugaritic comparative materials. This commentary is pretty good on comparative philology and near-Eastern background. Theologically it is weak and not Christological.

Zöckler, Otto, Tayler Lewis, and Llewelyn John Evans. *The Book of Job*. LCHS. New York: Charles Scribner's Sons, 1872. ♫ A helpful older example of German biblical scholarship, based on the Hebrew text, which provides references to significant commentaries from the Reformation era forward.

PSALMS

Lift up your heads

It is almost redundant to underscore the importance of the Psalter, whether in contemporary life or in the history of the Church or the synagogue (or the temple preceding both), whether in public worship or in private devotion. Different communities have employed the Psalms differently. Medieval monks chanted them daily. The Reformed churches exalted psalm paraphrases over "human" hymnody. Lutheran use centered on liturgical elements (Introits, Graduals). The general Protestant accent on individual piety tended to encourage more private use of the Psalter. But as the original use in church and public worship often lessened, the private use lost its urgency too—a process of secularization that Western Christians have not yet learned how to reverse.

We may lament the fact that often the Psalter is virtually the only familiar portion of the Old Testament for many people (and sometimes only Ps 23 or a few similar snippets). The frequent practice of printing the Psalms as an appendix to editions of the New Testament encourages the assumption that little else in the Old is really very relevant. Indeed, Psalms may validly be viewed as an Old Testament in miniature, or as a distillation of its entire message. Yet, if they are consistently used in isolation, they are forced to aid and abet the crime of our age: the divorce of faith and spirituality from history and the totality of Scripture.

Because the Psalter is sublime, technical analysis of the Psalter seems like the dissection of a flower, the intrusion of "science" and reason into the realm of the spirit. Precisely for that reason one must take up arms against the "great shame and vice" of interpreting the Psalter as one's personal prayer book without regard to its history and churchly use, valuing psalms merely as poetry, or investigating them psychologically.

Historical and Cultural Setting

Based on the superscriptions and historical references within the psalms, they were written from as early as the time of Moses (fifteenth century BC) down to the Persian period (fifth century BC) when the Psalter likely

Tambourine, lyre, and harp played by a procession of Aramean (Syrian) musicians whose culture flourished just north of Israel. The same instruments are mentioned in the Psalms.

assumed its final and present form. Our Psalter is a collection of earlier collections, represented in part by the division of the Psalter into five "books," in artificial imitation of the five Books of Moses (see the Outline for the divisions). Possibly there was also a liturgical association of 30 psalms with each of the books in the Pentateuch, reaching a canonical total of 150. Liturgical motives for the collections are evident because each of the five books ends with a doxology (41:13; 72:18–19; 89:52; 106:48; 150).

Book I (Pss 1–41) appears to be a preliminary collection. With the exception of Pss 1–2, 10, and 33, all the superscriptions have the phrase "of David." For that reason, it is sometimes referred to as the "Davidic Psalter." It is often presumed to be the earliest collection (though early individual psalms plainly appear elsewhere). Other than the references to David, the contents are quite miscellaneous, and there is no clear principle of collection and arrangement. The absence of a "Davidic" superscription to Ps 2 is surprising, especially considering its contents. However, there is evidence in the Talmud and some New Testament manuscripts (the Western text of Ac 13:33) that Ps 2 was originally the first psalm in the collection. If so, its superscription may have dropped off when Ps 1 was added (perhaps specifically as an introduction to the entire Psalter).

Book I has another significant characteristic, especially in comparison with Book II (Pss 42–72; and most of Book III [Pss 73–89] as well, which may indicate that Books II and III were together a second collection). Different poetic preferences for the divine name appear in the collections. Book I generally prefers the divine name "Yahweh," whereas in Pss 42–83 the preference is for "Elohim." In fact, the proportions are almost exactly the same in both cases, the preferred name exceeding the other by a ratio of 85 percent to 15 percent. On its face, this could scarcely be accidental; its deliberateness is surely clinched by studying the psalms that appear twice with only trivial variations except for the different names for God: Ps 14 = Ps 53 and Ps 40:13–17 = Ps 70. As a result, Book I is often referred to also as the Yahwistic Psalter and Books II—III as the Elohistic Psalter.[1]

There is ample evidence that at least three different earlier collections lie behind our present "Elohistic Psalter" (Books II—III). Psalms 50 and 73–83 are "Asaph psalms," probably a reference to an ancient and senior guild of temple singers and cymbalists. (Cf the information on Asaph in Chronicles: 1Ch 15:17; 16:4–5; 2Ch 29:30 specifically describes him as a "seer" and author of psalms alongside David.) Similarly, we have "Korah psalms" in 42–49, and again in 84–85 and 87–88 as increments at the end of Book III (cf 1Ch 6:22). Third, we again have "Davidic" psalms in 51–65 and 68–70; there is no telling how or why these psalms of David were separated from those in Book I. Psalm 72 is a lone "Psalm of Solomon" (cf 127), but it concludes by noting the end of "the prayers of David." One must also note that Pss 84–89 again prefer the divine name Yahweh, suggesting that these psalms may have been added after the major Yahwistic and Elohistic collections had been combined. All of this shows how complex the process of forming the Psalter was, a process that we are able to recover only very tenuously.

Books IV and V (Pss 90–150) tell us little about how they were collected. Scholars generally agree that most of these psalms were written later than those in the first three books. It appears that the order of the five books corresponds roughly to the chronological order of their collection. Some very early psalms are, however, embedded in these two books, e.g., Ps 90, attributed to Moses (possibly, then, the earliest in the entire Psalter), and 122; 124; 131; 133; 138–145, which again are Davidic.

Liturgical associations are also much more obvious in the final two books. Since the worship practices associated with Books IV and V are known from later Judaism, the critical instinct is to date both these psalms and their liturgical associations to a later period—at least that of the second temple (finished in 516 BC). However, there appears to be no good reason why these traditions could not also have been current in the first temple.

Psalms 120–134 have the superscription, "A Song of Ascents." These are considered "pilgrim songs," the "ascents" referring to stages in the pilgrimage up to Mount Zion at especially the three great pilgrimage festivals. Only

---

1 Critics feel naturally compelled to relate this phenomenon to the JEDP theory, and sometimes theorize that the two collections took shape in the Southern Kingdom and the Northern Kingdom where the names Yahweh and Elohim were preferred respectively. Unfortunately, there is not a shred of objective evidence to support this.

The rugged setting for St. George's Monastery, just off the old road to Jerusalem, gives one a sense of the challenges ancient pilgrims faced on the climb of nearly 4,000 ft in elevation to reach the Temple Mount.

Ps 122, however, gives clear internal indication of this original association. The Mishnah states that the Levites of the second temple sang them one per step on the climb up to the court of men in the temple.

The "Hallelujah Psalms" are 104–106; 111–113; 115–117; 135; and 146–150. They are called this because of the prominence of that refrain, "Praise the Lord." They are sometimes thought to have been a separate collection. Jewish liturgical tradition also describes a number of psalms in Book V as "Hallel psalms" ("song of praise") but it is not clear how old this tradition was. The ordinary Hallel (Pss 113–118) is often also known as the "Egyptian Hallel" because of its close association with Passover, though it is also used at the other two major festivals and at Hanukkah. At Passover, Pss 113–114 are traditionally sung before the meal (a poetic meditation on the exodus), and Pss 115–118 are sung after it, which may be the "hymn" sung by our Lord after the Last Supper and before Gethsemane (Mt 26:30; Mk 14:26). At least in later times Pss 119–136 (the latter with the refrain, "for His steadfast love endures forever") were often known as the "Great Hallel" (in distinction from the ordinary one).

In Books IV and V we also note doublets or repetitions of psalms, or parts of them, which appeared in the earlier books: 108:1–5 = 57:7–11 and 108:6–13 = 60:5–12. In this connection, we should also note the many partial parallels and different combinations of parts of psalms that occur throughout Chronicles. For example, at 1Ch 16:8–36 we have a song of

Continued on p 551.

THE PSALMS IN ISRAEL'S WORSHIP

Mention must be made of five influential reconstructions of how Israel used psalms in worship. We mention first the most radical one, which, fortunately, was always recognized as such, and today commands little more than historical interest. This was the position of the Swedish "Uppsala school."

The Uppsala School

This school of thought proposed that there was a New Year's festival in Israel that differed only a little from those at Babylon, including a mimed death and resurrection of the king representing the deity, and a sacral mating (Gk *hieros gamos*) between king and prostitute to insure fertility throughout all realms. The most one might concede is that such things may have happened in the darkest days of Israel's apostasy, which the Book of Kings does not blush to recount. In no way could these practices ever have been normative for worship of Yahweh and for biblical faith!

Vast energies have been devoted to debate about whether ancient Israel even celebrated New Year's each autumn. It remains remarkable that the biblical texts never describe a festival like the modern Jewish *Rosh Hashanah*. Both Ugaritic and biblical (Dt 31:10) evidence suggests, at most, a seven-year rather than an annual cycle of autumnal observances. These observations call into question much of the detail of the Uppsala reconstructions.

The Myth and Ritual School

Perhaps most akin to the Swedish Uppsala theory was the British myth and ritual school. Although it grew increasingly conservative in the course of time, it, too, scarcely exists any longer as a recognizably independent school of thought. It will suffice to point out that "myth and ritual" was used here in a neutral sense to describe "the liturgy and story of the liturgy"—a "story" that might be either true or false, either historical or mythological.

Mowinckel's Enthronement Festival

Somewhat more conservative (and increasingly so in later years) than either the Swedes or the British, was the Norwegian Sigmund Mowinckel. His theories have been the most influential of all. With proper adaptation, his *The Psalms in Israel's Worship* still makes worthwhile reading. Although he also located the major festival on a supposed Israelite New Year's, he preferred to describe it as an "enthronement festival," using the enthronement psalms as his key texts

Replica of King Tutankhamun's throne.

(some 43 of which he classified). The liturgical cry, "Yahweh has become king" was the key to his reconstruction. Other elements followed in its wake: re-creation, reestablishment of the monarchy, ritualized battle against chaos, and so on.

Note that Mowinckel included specifically biblical and historical events or themes in his view, such as the exodus, election, and covenant, though they played a relatively minor role. Even in his later, more conservative years, Mowinckel never quite succeeded in anchoring his theory sufficiently in actual biblical history. But the practiced student may make satisfactory adjustments: Israel's kingship was not "divine" in the pagan sense. God was not really enthroned by any liturgical action. His eternal reign, tied to Messianic promise and fulfillment, ever and again came into Israel's midst through Word and Sacrament (cf the Lord's Prayer, "Thy kingdom come").

Kraus's Royal Zion Festival

Two other reconstructions came from Germany.[2] Hans-Joachim Kraus's "royal Zion festival" was a far more biblical and historical-based theory, but it never won many adherents, and little of it has ever been translated into English. As the name indicates, Kraus postulated two principal motifs: (1) God's choice of David and his dynasty and (2) His choice of Jerusalem or Zion as His seat. Kraus proposed that there was a ritual procession to Zion with the ark (Ps 132 as its hymn) and a reenactment of the founding of the Davidic dynasty. The celebration of Yahweh's "enthronement" was a mere commemoration of historical manifestations of Yahweh's power, especially in the deliverance from Babylon. Kraus highlighted some of the Bible's own primary themes: the election of David and Zion (alongside exodus, conquest, and exile). Thankfully, there was a clear break here with the mythological approaches.

---

2   German scholarship remained very cool toward the entire worship approach. Martin Noth, who emphasized oral traditions in forming texts, vigorously opposed centering psalms on worship.

Weiser's Covenant Festival

The fifth major hypothesis was the "covenant festival" of Artur Weiser. Many of the same types of judgments would apply here as in the case of Kraus. In America, Weiser has been far more influential. Part of the reason, no doubt, lay in the Reformed background of much established American biblical scholarship to which the theme of "covenant" was attractive. Furthermore, Weiser's pursuit of the covenant theme in the Psalter often coincided with interest in the Biblical Theology movement, and with the "covenant renewal festival," allegedly centering at Shechem and underlying many biblical narratives. To Reformed Protestants, Weiser's "covenant festival," with its accents on a call to commitment, was an attractive alternative to the more "Catholic" or "sacramental" versions of Mowinckel and others.

Weiser made "theophany" his point of departure by noting the prominence of Yahweh's self-revelation in some liturgical texts (Pss 18; 50; 81; etc.). Through a worship dramatization, Yahweh "shone forth" in the midst of the annual assembly as He had originally at Sinai when the covenant was first sealed with Israel. Other central features in Weiser's scheme fan out from this central act of revelation: rehearsing Yahweh's deeds in history (cf Ps 78), proclaiming God's will (possibly by a covenant mediator representing Moses; cf Ps 81), and recommitting through a ceremony of covenant renewal.

Weiser added a number of other minor themes, which, it should be noted, are very close to Mowinckel's major ones—on the whole, a good summary of the greater biblical basis for Weiser's proposals. Among these were: the celebration of Yahweh's kingship and creative power (Pss 47; 104); His universal judgment over all peoples (Pss 68; 82; 99); enthronement of the Judean king (Pss 2; 45), and others.

All in all, the conservative will probably rate Weiser's commentary as one of the best out of critical circles. The reason will not be out of any favoritism for a covenant festival (which one might take or leave), but because he relates the psalms to central biblical themes.

Avoiding the Influence of Pagan Theology

As the examples above show, reading the Psalms naturally invites one to wonder how they were used and prayed in ancient Israel. Since the psalms rarely explained how they were used, modern scholars have tended to seek examples of how the religions that surrounded Israel used psalm-like writings. This approach proved to be both helpful in some respects as well as confusing and even harmful in others.

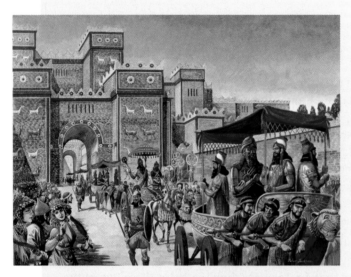

Artist rendition of New Year's Festival in Babylon.

The history of biblical doctrine and practice depends on the assumption of one personal God, His election, and His covenant. As a result, the magical view *(opus operatum)* of pagan worship—like mythology in general—is the absolute opposite of biblical and Christian faith. Pagan and biblical ideas about the nature of worship must be distinguished, something that many critical researchers have failed to do when interpreting the Psalms.

In pagan worship one can really speak of some essentially "timeless" order *(illud tempus)*. In fact, the action of the worship had magical force, priming the cosmic process, actually enthroning the gods anew, causing creation to happen yet another time. Pagan worship simultaneously reaffirmed the divine kingship of the earthly viceroy of the gods, and therewith upheld and maintained the political order and ensured military success throughout at least the coming year. The Babylonian cult of Marduk, peaking at the *akitu* or New Year's celebration, was undeniably of this sort, and it is the major model critics have used to reconstruct preexilic Israelite worship. Allegedly, Yahweh, too, was made king each year and the enthronement psalms were the liturgy of the festival. Simultaneously, the "sonship" of the Davidic ruler was also reestablished, the monster of chaos (Tiamat, Leviathan, Rahab) in both creation and history was subdued for another year, the coming of ample rains and other signs of life and fertility were assured, and so on.

Sacramental Theology and Liturgy

Psalm texts may well have been liturgical components of a ceremony. Yet no magical power inhered in either the Psalms or the dramatic ceremonies they accompanied. We argue that historic Lutheranism offers the biblically distinct view of worship that best comprehends the Psalms and their use. We label it *sacramental theology.* In this view, there is real objective power in connection with the true worship based on Word and Sacrament.[3] This is true whether the worshiper knows it and confesses it or not, but there can be no positive benefit for him apart from his conscious faith and appropriation.

A sound, biblical theology makes Leviticus and Chronicles indispensable complements of the Psalter. Psalms are the Word, the extensions of the sermon, and sometimes even "Words of Institution"—changing the external elements of worship into Means of Grace. The "elements" in the psalms would originally be the accompanying sacrifices at the tabernacle and temple, which were essentially sacraments that comforted Israel with God's forgiveness and peace.

Praying the Psalms Today

The "today" of Ps 95:7b–11 teaches representation or contemporization that is implicit throughout the Psalter. The worshiper is taught to pray as though he were a contemporary praying the psalm with ancient Israel. This simultaneously stresses that the actual ancient history is real, made present and actualized "for me." This updating of the psalm events occurs not only intellectually, spiritually, and verbally, but also physically and sacramentally, with reference to all aspects of being a child of God. The psalms are not *only* the matter of the lone individual's personal relation to God. They solidly anchor conversion and the entire Christian experience in the Means of Grace, in the church, and ultimately then in real incarnational history as well. As Ps 95 illustrates, the ancient texts repeatedly performed this contemporizing function in ancient Israel and continue in Christ to perform it for us. Compare, for example, how we shout "Christ is risen" at our Easter celebrations, remembering its historicity, affirming Christ's presence in our hearts, but also celebrating the work of the Spirit in Word and Sacrament in bringing Christ out of the remoteness of ancient history.

Finally, biblical history always includes and points forward to the goal and climax of all history. In terms of the royal psalms, that means the final consummation of the kingdom of God in the Messiah. Yet, there is always the "now" alongside the "not yet." Word and Sacrament always now offer the totality of what is promised in them. Parallel to the past, present, and future of our human horizon, one must not forget the vertical, the supernatural, the incarnational. Only in the final outcome, in the new creation, will vertical (heavenly) and horizontal (earthly) totally coincide as they did in Paradise at the beginning.

---

3   Word and Sacrament are powerful for either salvation or damnation; cf examples of unworthy reception of the sacrifices and of the Lord's Supper (1Co 11:27; *manducatio indignorum*).

NAMES IN THE PSALMS

Nearly two-thirds of the Psalms have names of Old Testament figures associated with them. However, scholars cannot always tell whether they were written by these persons, for these persons, or about these persons. The chart below shows the names associated with various psalms.

Name	Psalm Association	Contribution
Moses: d c 1406 BC. Prophet who led Israel out of Egypt and received God's Law.	90	Moses led or provided for leadership in worship at the beginning of Israel's independence (Ex 15).
David: 1040–970 BC. Second king of Israel; warrior, prophet, and poet.	3–9; 10?; 11–32; 34–41; 51–65; 68–70; 86; 101; 103; 108–10; 122; 124; 131; 133; 138–45	David appointed 4,000 singers and musicians for the tabernacle. About half of all the psalms are attributed to David.
Jeduthun (Ethan): Time of David; family of Merari?	39	Levites/prophets appointed by David for praise at the tabernacle (1Ch 25:1–3, 6). They used harps, lyres, and cymbals as accompaniment. Different family groups cast lots to determine when they would serve.
Heman: Time of David; family of Kohath.	88	
Asaph: Time of David and Solomon; family of Gershon.	50; 73–83	
Sons of Korah: Time of David and Solomon.	42; 44–49; 84–85; 87–88	Doorkeepers and musicians of the tabernacle and temple.
Solomon: d 931 BC. Israel's third king; wrote Proverbs, Song of Solomon, and Ecclesiastes.	72; 127	Builder of the first temple; 3,000 proverbs and 1,005 songs, but very few psalms, are attributed to Solomon.
Ethan: Time of Solomon.	89	An Ezrahite, renowned for wisdom (1Ki 4:31).
Anonymous: Some of these psalms connect with the psalm that precedes them. Most anonymous psalms are in Book Five of the Psalter.	1–2; 10?; 33; 43; 66–67; 71; 91–100; 102; 104–7; 111–21; 123; 125–26; 128–30; 132; 134–37; 146–50	Pss 113–18 form the "Egyptian Hallel" of later Jewish liturgy, used at festivals. Pss 120–36 form the "Great Hallel."

praise at David's bringing of the ark to Jerusalem, composed of 105:1–15; 96:1–13; and 106:47–48. Likewise in 2Ch 6–7 Solomon includes Ps 132 in his prayer, and the people respond with the refrain from Ps 136. Like the different combinations in the Septuagint, this probably witnesses to the great fluidity, already in very early times, of many psalmic components, at least in actual liturgical usage. It also reinforces the importance of Chronicles for understanding how the psalms were actually used in Israelite worship.

In the Hebrew canon, the Psalter commands pride of place at the head of the Writings (Hbr *kethubim*). As a result, in later Hebrew literature and in the New Testament (Lk 24:44) "Psalms" is sometimes shorthand for all the "Writings."

COMPOSITION

Authors

As noted above, many psalms include superscriptions that apparently indicate authorship. Those mentioning David are both the most frequent and the most significant. Fourteen times additional notations specify the occasion on which David penned the psalm. Almost needless to say, critical scholarship regards these, especially the latter, as historically worthless, and representing only later interpretation (*haggadah* or *midrash*). We have already mentioned the textual variation that justifies some reserve about whether all of these superscriptions are really part of the inspired text, but nowhere are objective grounds to be found for dismissing them out of hand. It seems very difficult to envision circumstances under which anyone could (or would wish to) add such fictional embellishments to psalmody that would already have been universally recognized as canonical. (For more on this issue, see "Date of Composition," pp 553–54.) The superscriptions raise the entire question of the date of the psalms, and specifically the likelihood of whether David composed any of them. The two questions are not entirely identical, of course, but do run parallel to a great extent.

Let us first consider the "of David" (*le-dawid*) superscription. Its traditional translations (already in LXX, which has 15 more of them than the Hebrew) reflect the nearly unanimous opinion that David wrote the psalms. The *le* was traditionally classified as a "*lamedh* of authorship"; in Hab 3:1 it almost certainly has that meaning, and we are now happy to have such a use attested outside the Bible, in Ugaritic texts. But the extrabiblical evidence is also ambiguous: there are times, for example in the Ugaritic epics, where *le-[name]* must refer to the subject, not the author of the composition (e.g.,

Canaanite gods such as *le-Baal, le-Keret,* etc.). Furthermore, even minimal knowledge of Hebrew will tell one that *le* is capable of a tremendous variety of meanings. The Ugaritic usage may also suggest ascription, yielding a translation something like "dedicated to [name]."

The Standard of Ur depicts ancient musicians in Hurrian culture.

A Hurrian hymn text found at Ugarit includes the earliest known example of musical notation.

Another popular alternative understands the entire phrase as meaning something like "Davidic," that is, following his example or tradition, and in this way many scholars think of a "Davidic Psalter" as one of the preliminary collections (alongside ones by the Choirmaster, Asaph, and Korah) underlying the canonical collection. Finally, we may note that it once was popular to argue on the basis of Hurrian usage in the Mari tablets that *dawidum* was originally a common noun meaning no more than "ruler" or "prince," for example, and that in the superscription it originally meant no more than "belonging to the royal ritual," "under crown sponsorship," or the like (cf uses of the Roman name/title "Caesar"). Thus Mowinckel could argue that the superscription meant only "for the use of the david [the monarch]" who happened to occupy the throne at the time. But, at best, a generous amount of conjecture is involved here, as seems to be increasingly recognized.

How can we decide? As usual, mere study of the words (philology) will not give us a definitive answer. Perhaps the safest rule of thumb would be to invoke the ancient maxim, "when in doubt, go with tradition" (*In dubito, pro traditio*). As far as the conservative is concerned, we have sufficient references in the Bible to David's musical interests and mentions of his authorship of specific psalms from both the New Testament and elsewhere in the Old Testament. What is ruled out of court is the common critical supposition that the entire tradition of Davidic authorship is a late, fanciful deduction from traditions such as 1Sm 16:14–23; 2Sm 1:17–27 and 3:31–34; Am 6:5; e.g., describing David as a skillful singer, not to speak of "midrashes" such as 1Ch 22–29 that describe David's reorganization of temple worship, especially its choral aspects. (Very similar considerations would apply to the other proper names in the superscriptions: Korah, Asaph, Solomon, Moses, for instance—and perhaps also additional ones in the LXX; cf 2Ch 29:30 which seems to support that there were "Davidic" and "Asaphic" collections of psalmody in the time of Hezekiah.)

Besides the critics' evolutionary theories about Israel's religion, the other critical arguments against David writing some of the psalms associated with him are quite easily checkmated. Some critics have attacked the frequent references to the "temple" as already built (e.g., Ps 5:7; 27:4; 68:29; 79:1), but a brief concordance study will soon establish that not only "temple," but synonyms such as "house of the Lord" or "tent" were often used very flexibly and interchangeably (cf also 1Sm 1:9, where the tabernacle at Shiloh is referred to as a Hbr *hekal* or "temple"). Second, it is also frequently objected that Davidic psalms sometimes (e.g., 20; 21; 72; 110) refer to the king in the second person, but ample extrabiblical as well as biblical parallels (especially Moses in the Pentateuch) to this usage emasculate the objection, all the more so if, as seems likely, David spoke not only about himself, but also about his (messianic) office.

Date of Composition

Archaeological finds have cleared the way for regarding some psalms and superscriptions as predating David. Linguistic arguments for post-Davidic origin from alleged Aramaisms in certain psalms simply no longer hold water in the light of Ugaritic evidence. Evidence not only enhances the likelihood of earlier dates, but virtually makes impossible the late dates proposed by classical criticism. "Hymnbook of the *second* temple" had once been the great critical slogan. Critical attitudes were already rampant before the Qumran discoveries. However, the vast distance between the canonical psalms and the "psalms of praise" (Hbr *Hodayot*), composed at Qumran in the century or two before Christ, dropped the previous dogma with a single shot.

Egyptian stele with a hymn to Amun.

Ugarit was the major, but not the sole, source of evidence regarding earlier dates. "Psalms" of one sort or the other we now have from almost all over the ancient Fertile Crescent. Egypt produced some as early as the pyramid age (Old Kingdom), and the rough parallels between Ps 104 and Akhenaton's hymn to the sun disk are especially often noted. Moses' schooling in this culture makes plausible the biblical ascription to him of not only Ps 90, but also the extra-Psalter pieces of Ex 15 and Dt 32–33 (in each case we probably have to concede some linguistic updating). Mesopotamia offers psalms already in Sumerian times, and the repertory grows extensive as we move forward through the centuries. The many laments as well as praises to Marduk, chief god of Babylon, are especially noteworthy. As usual in such matters, the parallelism should not be overstated, but the point here is about the cultural context in which psalmic composition was commonplace millennia before David.

Canaan has so far yielded very few "psalms" as such, but it is both geographically and chronologically so much closer to the practices in Israel that its evidence is much more weighty. From Amarna we have only a few possible psalm-fragments, and the Ugaritic literature is largely epic rather than psalmic in nature, but the parallels in vocabulary, phraseology, and prosody are little short of phenomenal. Some psalms so teem with archaic forms that there would be little difficulty in defending a *pre*-Davidic date for them, and it even seems likely that David availed himself of structures and even phrases already at hand. The fact that the Old Testament psalms are theologically unique does not exclude their authors from borrowing composition styles from the surrounding culture.

Among the psalms that are especially archaic in form are 18 (cf 2Sm 22) and 68, but many others are subject to illumination on the basis of Ugaritic studies. The retention of archaic forms by the ancient scribes, even when they were no longer understood, is impressive testimony to the almost frantic care with which the ancient texts were preserved and handed down. In other cases, the texts appear to have been modernized linguistically in the course of transmission before being fixed. (Consider, for comparison, how a prayer or hymn based on the King James Version may be updated for modern use.) Even when linguistic parallels are few, Ugarit often illuminates the meaning of words or concepts (as an example, the "gods" or angels of the heavenly council in Ps 82, who have been unfaithful in their charges over earthly kingdoms; cf Jn 10:31–36).

Purpose/Recipients

The Psalms express hope in the Lord's salvation through prayers and praises. The purpose of each psalm varies depending on its form and content. See "Genre," pp 557–69.

Literary Features

The more topical, Western reordering of biblical books made the Psalter the first of the "poetic" books. The Masoretes or their predecessors recognized the Psalms (together with Job and Proverbs—but only these three) as poetry. Hence, they furnished the Psalms with a somewhat different set of notes (punctuation-cantillation system) than used elsewhere in the Hebrew Bible.

Since that system could not be reproduced in translation, the Septuagint's reclassification of the Psalms was, no doubt, a happy means of advising the reader to recognize the different, poetic nature of the literature. However, until relatively modern times it seems to have escaped attention that far more of the Old Testament is poetry than either of these ancient traditions recognized (especially nearly all of the prophets, and thus—as bears constant emphasis—a high percentage of the entire Old Testament is poetry). The typographical distinction between poetry and prose must be reckoned as one of the major pluses in most modern translations.

Not all aspects of Hebrew poetry are understood or agreed upon. Nonetheless, a discussion of poetry is especially appropriate in the case of the Psalter, because of the intrinsic "splendor of holiness" (cf Pss 29:2; 96:9), that is, the virtual inseparability of aesthetics from worship.

Fortunately, the one feature of Hebrew poetry that is agreed upon (it is also common in other ancient Near Eastern literature) is also the only one that is really accessible to the reader who is limited to translations, namely parallelism. It is a feature that is quite obvious, once pointed out. But since it is not characteristic of Western poetry, it *must* be pointed out! Rhyme is, as such, almost totally absent, but the lavish use of repetition of vowels and consonants (assonance and alliteration, respectively) sometimes has a similar effect. For more on parallelism, see pp 488–90.

In addition to parallelism, most (not all) scholars agree that Hebrew poetry was metrical or rhythmical, but there is no consensus about the details. Early scholars often compared Hebrew meter with the fairly rigid rules of classical Greek and Latin poetry ("quantitative"), but that is today almost unanimously disregarded. A divide between the two (or three) members of a poetic verse is usually evident, but it is not clear how the beats on either side should be counted (if at all). A common solution is to count only the accented or stressed syllables, yielding a sort of "free chant" or "sprung rhythm." The most common scheme (as also at Ugarit) appears to be a two-membered line with three beats or stresses apiece (a 3:3 bicolon or distich), although threefold (tristichs; tricola) and even fourfold (quatrains) examples appear, and sometimes with two or (less frequently) four beats per member.

In addition to parallelism and meter, it seems undeniable that Hebrew poetry also had some sense of stanza or strophic structure. Such patterns appear to have operated quite flexibly; their presence is often easily transferable to translations. The enigmatic "Selah" (discussed below) may have been preceded by refrains (cf Ps 46), and thus may be further evidence of "strophes." At times alphabetic (acrostic) structures (e.g., Ps 119) also give us a sort of stanza arrangement.

Psalms Outside the Psalter

The canonical Scriptures preserve many psalms that, humanly speaking, might just as easily have been included in the Psalter (though in some cases it is debatable whether they are really "psalms" or not). Often called psalms are Hannah's prayer (1Sm 2:1–10), Hezekiah's thanksgiving (Is 38:10–20), Jonah's prayer in the fish (2:3–10), and the "Psalm of Habakkuk" (ch 3). Psalm 18 is reproduced almost precisely in 2Sm 22. In Chronicles we find many psalms (or parts of them, sometimes in different combinations) quoted in connection with historical events. But there is little reason why a number of other texts should not be classified as psalms too: cf "The Song of Moses" in Ex 15 and Dt 32, etc.

Special attention must be called to two genuine psalms at the beginning of the New Testament: Mary's Magnificat (Lk 1:46–55) and Zechariah's Benedictus (Lk 1:68–79). The former, of course, is in many ways only a rendition of Hannah's prayer, and neither piece contains anything out of character with the Old Testament. The fact that both songs are, nevertheless, widely used in Christian worship forms a sort of paradigm not only of the ease with which the psalms are, in fact, likewise employed but also of the hermeneutical principles that must ultimately be spelled out if Christian use of the psalms is to be distinguished from that of the synagogue or of "religion in general."

Fourth century AD synagogue mosaic of David playing a lyre.

Some of the difficulty in determining whether religious poetry is psalmic or not is betrayed in the varying titles of the canonical collection. The Hebrew for "praises" (*tehillim*; the artificial masculine plural apparently indicates a special, canonical collection of praises) applies technically to the many laments and other non-laudatory psalms only in a very broad sense. The conclusion of Book II (Ps 72:20) indicates that the title "prayers" may have been used at some earlier stage, but that, too, is not immediately applicable to all the psalms. Hence, possibly the Greek tradition, from which our own usage is derived, made the wisest choice by calling them *psalmoi* (Lk 20:42; Ac 1:20) technically derived from only one of the various superscriptions (Hbr *mizmor*). Since it means literally "song/hymn," especially one sung to the accompaniment of stringed instrument (*psalterion*), it has very broad applicability. Psalter (*Psalterion*), which appears at the head of some Greek manuscripts, refers to the stringed instrument accompanying *psalmoi* or songs, but in practice it came to mean any "collection of songs" and so virtually merged with the other term.

Genre

As noted earlier, we do not have a thorough or even firm understanding of Hebrew names for different types of psalms. As a result, scholars have developed modern titles to describe what they distinguish as different forms of psalms (form criticism). Two important contributors to this effort were Hermann Gunkel (1862–1932), the father of form criticism, and Claus Westermann (1909–2000), who offered revised categories. Gunkel's approach has found nearly universal acceptance in virtually all camps so that we can do no better than consider and evaluate his major categories (*Gattungen*) individually. Only Westermann's reclassification has had much impact, partly because of his concentration on strictly form-critical questions, partly because he rejected the use of psalms in worship as a point of departure.[4]

Besides a host of "minor" (less frequent) genres, Gunkel originally proposed four major ones: hymns, individual laments, individual thanksgivings, and communal laments. Eventually, as a result of pressure from co-workers, he added a fifth genre, the "royal" psalms. That issue highlights a problem that haunts Gunkel's whole scheme, namely, the interplay of the form in which something was written with the material that the form contains. "Content," of course, is a thoroughly valid consideration for classifying literature as well, and ultimately a reader cannot seal it off from considerations of form. Gunkel's first four categories described certain formal or structural characteristics. These were fairly clear. But in the royal psalms, and some of the minor types, different forms hardly existed. The conservative generally has little difficulty appreciating and appropriating the purely formal analysis, but, all too often, all kinds of reservations must be registered when critics make judgments about the content of psalms.

---

4   In essence, Westermann reduces all categories to two: psalms of lamentation (*Bittpsalmen*) and psalms of praise (*Lobpsalmen*). The latter is really a merger of Gunkel's "hymns" and "thanksgivings," but Westermann himself promptly subdivides them into (a) "declarative" (recalling one definite act of salvation) and (b) "descriptive" (celebrating Yahweh's majesty and power in general) types.

Hymns. One of the most helpful classifications made by Gunkel was "hymn." Gunkel postulated joyous occasions (*Sitz im Leben*) when the people assembled at the sanctuary to praise God. As long as the individual is not excluded from the picture, it is impossible to take exception to such a construction, belonging to the very bedrock of the concept of "worship," as it does. Neither is one very surprised when it is mentioned that externally there is relatively little that is unique about this genre: parallels can be found all over the ancient Near East, especially Babylonia, praising the god(s) for goodness and presumed favors (though neither is it surprising that very often the flavor is one of flattery in order to make the deity yield to personal desires). Individual laments are a fairly distinguishable type, but "communal laments" (which Gunkel classified as a minor form) merge almost imperceptibly with the hymns, one of the weaknesses of the system.

A hymn tends to have a clear fourfold pattern:

(1) An introductory call to praise, usually a plural imperative (often "Hallelujah" = "Praise ye the LORD," or "Praise/bless, my soul," which may well recur as a refrain; occasionally we read "Let me/us sing" etc. [cohortative]);

(2) The reason for the praise, commonly a "for" clause (*ki*-clause or sometimes simply *ki tob* = for He is good, or expressed in Hebrew by means of the "hymnic participle," usually rendered into English by a relative clause, e.g., 103:3 ff);

(3) The corpus, body, or main part of the praise;

(4) Sometimes a renewed call to praise, often in the same words as at the beginning, is included.

Most hymns tend to have a very universal flavor, and hence are easily subject to universal*istic* abuse. They often envision all peoples, even all of nature, joining in the praise and celebrating the climax of God's judgment and salvation. The proper understanding is not to conclude that all people are "anonymous Christians," but to recall God's missionary will. His salvation is *available* to all who believe, offered fully in the present and straining toward the final judgment.

Christian worship has little difficulty in appropriating this part of the Psalter, but certain assumptions are made, and if it is to be genuinely Christian worship, these cannot be allowed to become entirely self-evident and unconscious. When the Christian uses them, he assumes not only the unity of Scripture in promise and fulfillment, but the unity of the Godhead as the common subject of both testaments. The "LORD" or Yahweh of the Old

Testament is also the "God and Father of our Lord and Savior Jesus Christ," whom the Holy Spirit makes our God in Word and Sacrament. The nature and attributes of this God and His works of creation, redemption, and sanctification are essentially the same, but these have also been more fully revealed in the new covenant. The acts of God for which the psalms praise Him are also part of the history of our salvation, but they are accessible to us only through Christ, and to them we add the climactic acts of God on Good Friday and Easter.

Traditionally, one *always* concludes public recitation of a psalm with the Gloria Patri (after which the antiphon, summarizing the psalm's message, is repeated). The Gloria Patri is a symbolic way of stressing that the Psalms (like the rest of the Old Testament) are not Christianized by reading into them some alien meaning, by doing violence to their literary and historical integrity, but by "extending" their literal sense, "reading out" of them together with the New Testament their fulfilled and prophetic meaning in Christ and the Holy Spirit. And also worthy of all acceptance is the liturgical custom of bowing one's head in acknowledgment of and devotion to the saving mystery confessed as the Gloria Patri is recited or chanted.

"Gloria patri" appears at the end of Psalm 109 (108 in Vulgate) of the Lutrell Psalter, fourteenth century.

"Hymn" is so comprehensive a word, however, that one is not surprised that Gunkel found it necessary to subdivide this form. Most of his subdivisions are determined according to subject matter or content, not form.

Besides general hymns, one major subdivision is "Hymns of Zion," praising the holy city of God's election, the place where His name or glory is "incarnate." Examples include Pss 48; 76; and 87. As throughout the Old Testament, Zion is the complement of king/Messiah, and points forward to the Christian Church. The ease with which the Church (at least until the modern era) understood herself as heir to these promises is aptly illustrated by Luther's use of Ps 46 in writing "A Mighty Fortress."

One customarily also speaks of "history" and "nature" hymns. Aspects of these elements are present in nearly all psalms, of course, but are especially prominent in certain ones, justifying a separate classification. The titles

559

Wartburg Castle, where Martin Luther wrote "A Mighty Fortress," based on Psalm 46.

are nearly self-explanatory: "nature" hymns (e.g., Pss 19a, 29, 104, 147–150) praise God especially in His capacity as Creator and Preserver of "nature." Such psalms defend against modern evolutionism as they defended against ancient Baalism. "History" hymns (e.g., Pss 78; 105; 106; 114) recount God's salvific work.

Finally, we may note the subdivision commonly referred to in modern scholarship as the "enthronement" hymns (e.g., Pss 47; 93; 96–99). Usually, the enthronement is that of Yahweh, not the earthly monarch. Their obverse, then, is the "royal psalms" with the elect king as their subject; there is no ultimate reason why these should not be called hymns as well, but, as noted, Gunkel considered them a distinct form. As the name indicates, the "enthronement" psalms celebrate Yahweh's kingship over all the earth, and what follows from it, His "judgment" over all the earth. They are characterized by the refrain, "Yahweh rules." The universal and eternal dimension seems very prominent. Yet because of Mowinckel's theories about the use of psalms for festivals, few parts of the Psalter have attracted as much attention as these psalms. Suffice it to say at this point that the basic issue is whether these psalms describe an eternal state of affairs or whether they celebrate a real enthronement in some sense. As we shall argue below, that is probably a false alternative, but it does raise questions about the aptness of the label "enthronement."

Laments and Thanksgivings. Gunkel counted individual and communal laments as two discrete types. Except in external form and/or setting (*Sitz im Leben*), the two are not always distinguishable. Structurally, the thanksgivings are very similar to the laments, and often we find the two types united in a single psalm (e.g., Ps 22). Gunkel himself compared the two types to the halves of a shell. "Communal thanksgivings" are very rare (Gunkel counted only two: Pss 84 and 122), and, as noted, they merge with hymns.

There are more individual thanksgivings. These include Pss 30; 32; 34; 116; and outside the Psalter, the psalm of Hezekiah (Is 38:10–20) and the psalm of Jonah (2:3–10). But in the individual as well as in the communal categories, the number of laments far outweighs the number of thanksgivings! Should we attach any significance to that fact? There may well be truth to the explanation sometimes offered that the proportion corresponds to our disposition much more readily to petition God than to thank God. If so, the Psalter does not intend to sanctify that failing but represents part of God's condescension and accommodation to our weaknesses. At the same time the imbalance may also reflect a more lively sense of sin among the Old Testament pious than is common among us, and may thus be part of the divine attempt to accommodate our need to lament and repent. Similarly, one might offer as an historical explanation the very difficult lot of the people of God in the Old Testament, which we should then also understand theologically as exemplary of the divine administration of the Law, without which a truly evangelical thanksgiving will never flourish either.

The individual laments are numerically the most common of all (perhaps some 40 in all), and thus form the backbone of the Psalter. A few of them are among the best known in the Psalter, namely the seven "penitential" psalms (6; 32; 38; 51; 102; 130; 143; the Eastern church also counts seven of them, but with a somewhat different listing). That, however, well illustrates how the entire form might just as well be labeled "penitential," which would at least better expose their theological significance than "lament." On the other hand, the careful reader cannot help but note how relatively little *explicit* "penitence" one encounters in the Psalter; no doubt, we are to understand the very descriptions of distress (punishment for sin) as admissions of guilt.

The fact that Ps 32 is today usually classified as a "thanksgiving" rather than as a "lament" also well illustrates the extent to which those two types are the opposite of one another, and sometimes almost interchangeable. In fact, one noteworthy motif sometimes encountered in the laments is the "doxology of judgment" (perhaps best and classically illustrated in Ps 51:4), the profound recognition that the faithful often thank God in most heartfelt and spontaneous fashion in the very midst of lamentation as they experience His Law or judgment.

Formally, laments and thanksgivings are characterized by some half-dozen elements. However, the inspired poets were no slaves to any inherited structure; there is no fixed order to the elements. They commonly begin with a vocative or invocation, "O, LORD," or the like (cf hymns that are regularly introduced by an imperative). The actual plea or petition for help, usually in imperative form ("help, save, have mercy, wake up!") may follow immediately, be delayed, or be repeated at various points. Sometimes the vocative is accompanied by honorific titles of various sorts, often reminding Yahweh of His promises or performances of deliverance in the past, and sometimes chiding Him for His delay or apparent lethargy in responding similarly in the present. The modern reader often comments on what appears to Him as near-irreverence, if not flippancy, at these points. Undoubtedly we witness here not only a certain covenant "intimacy" with the Father, but also a "boldness and confidence" (Luther) that holds God to His promises and will not let go without a blessing (cf Gn 32).

Sooner or later, in greater or lesser detail, one meets the description of the distress or the calamity, which forms the body of these psalms. At first blush, one is easily surprised to note that the misfortune is often depicted at greater length and in more harrowing detail in the thanksgivings than in the laments. It would seem that part of the explanation is psychological: it is common experience that it is easier to relate woes after they are past and relieved than while one is in their throes. Possibly there is also a literary desire to construct an ample foil for the thanksgiving and praise that is the real subject of these psalms.

In the case of the communal laments, there is usually little difficulty in identifying the setting (cf Pss 36; 44; 74; 77; 79; 80; 83). It is invasion, exile, famine, and so on that imperils the entire people and brings them or their representatives to the sanctuary in fasting, supplication, etc. The Book of Joel probably illustrates such a situation, and the historical books preserve other instances.

One of the major issues for interpreting psalms is to determine precisely what problem the author faced, and there is extensive literature on the subject. On the surface the reader meets descriptions of what appears to be sickness, imminent death, false accusation, imprisonment, fiendish enemies, or the like. A highly figurative, but also obviously stylized language, often punctuates these descriptions: attack by troops, menace of wild beasts, "many waters" engulfing the worshiper, parched lips, and body wracked with pain. Are the events literal or picturesque?

If the idea of "justice" at the temple is pursued in its biblical fullness, it will also be brought into connection with the concept of "justification." The "enemies" and "false accusers" will not only be particular historical figures, but transhistorical and metaphysical. The "many waters" motif probably has ultimate roots in mythological depictions of chaos described in the psalms as invading and nearly overwhelming the order God has graciously implanted in the believer's soul.

And then we probably have the major clue to understand the variety of descriptions with their many metaphors. One might say they represent a classical case of the necessity to interpret *both* literally and non-literalistically. Certainly sickness and death remain the common lot of all people. The vast variety of circumstances is deliberate in order to speak to "all sorts and conditions of men." The wide applicability of these psalms is part of their power even when approached as great literature, and all the more so when viewed as inspired Scripture.

The pious throughout the ages have usually sensed this instinctively. The psalms apply to all sorts of unfortunate circumstances that are not explicitly mentioned. But they also point toward something far deeper than any individual's diagnosable ills, whatever their nature and variety. Above all one must not forget that the subject is not primarily the ills of *any* one person anywhere, but, first and foremost, those of the covenant man. They intend to point mankind beyond all superficial diagnoses of his ills, real though they be, to the ultimate problem of alienation from God, of original sin, and so on. God Himself through the Law must supply the right question before the right answer of the Gospel has an audience.

Many of these psalms are explicitly cited in the New Testament as fulfilled in Christ (e.g., Pss 22, 69, 109), but that citation appears to be, in part, illustrative of what applies on the whole to the entire genre. The Christian Church confesses that Christ is the only one who can or who has plumbed the depths of the primal suffering of which these psalms ultimately speak, but whose experience of it was also undeserved and hence was vicarious and redemptive for those who join themselves to Him. Only Jesus can pray these psalms in all their fullness, and only in covenant with Him can the faithful, Old Testament as well as New, pray them validly. Even more profoundly, we insist that through Baptism it is Christ, the last Adam, the "new Israel," who prays these psalms in us and for us before the throne of the Father. And because of His victory, we know that we do not pray them in vain.

The "Self-Righteous" and Imprecatory Psalms. Those who read Psalms as only great religious literature and forget its true theology invite two severe theological problems. These problems surface especially in negative confessions where the righteous sufferer speaks. If liberal interpretations were correct, one could, indeed, regard these confessions as little more than ancient sentiments, only partway along the evolutionary road toward mankind's highest ideals in his never-complete quest for and perception of God.

Both problems appear side by side in Ps 139:19–24. This psalm is usually classified as a "wisdom psalm," and it probably is no accident that we confront the problems because wisdom concentrated on questions of ultimate destinies, retributions, and so on. The first problem is that of alleged "*self*-righteousness," which often easily appears on the surface, not only in Ps 139:23–24, but also in the protests of Job, in the simple distinctions of Ps 1, etc. How easy it is for the ordinary reader to hear such expressions as self-congratulation for mere external respectability, or for the critical theologian to contrast such sentiments with St. Paul's profound theology of sin, among others.

The broader teaching of Scripture will determine the appropriate answer: if the one Author of Scripture does not contradict Himself, those liberal understandings cannot possibly be correct. In the light of the covenant and imputed-righteousness-framework of all of Scripture, orthodoxy naturally hears such words as the forgiven and justified sinner's boasting and glorying solely in Christ. It may well also be true that the speaker is not guilty as accused, but the real point transcends even this historical point. It may be—undoubtedly was—true that many in the Old Testament *mis*understood and *mis*applied such words, as many still do in the new covenant (and correction of such biblical misunderstandings should be high on the pastor's and teacher's agenda).

The second and more grievous problem is that of the cursing (imprecatory or minatory) psalms. How can one "hate them with complete hatred" (Ps 139:22), not to speak of the almost incredible, blood-curdling curses that sometimes escape the psalmist's lips (perhaps especially Pss 35; 58; 69; 83; 109; 137)? How is such apparently sheer spite and unrelieved hatred compatible with Jesus' prayer on the cross, or the message of "Love your enemies" in general? For many liberals the problem appears not only in the overtly imprecatory psalms, but it jars and obtrudes whenever "enemies" are mentioned negatively, even in otherwise tranquil contexts, such as Ps 23:5. Outside of confessional and evangelical contexts, such passages (perhaps

A half-restored ancient ziggurat or step pyramid.

alongside "holy war" concepts in Joshua and the prophet's "Gentile oracles") serve as parade examples of the inferior morality of the Old Testament, which has not yet discovered the full implication of universal love. Even in relatively conservative contexts, the liturgical rubric is often unfortunately observed which eliminates these psalms from consideration for public worship (and "selected psalms" virtually never includes them).

Problems within the canon of Scripture, however, are never solved by creating a canon within the canon. And only the whole of Scripture, as usual, can provide the definitive solution. A minute part of the explanation can rest on cultural differences. It seems true that the ancient (like the modern) Near East indulged in coarse, hyperbolic language of this sort more readily than we (cf even Luther in more modern times). Parallels to this can be found in the literature of Israel's neighbors. Much more to the point is the realization, which one stresses repeatedly throughout the Old Testament, that Israel was "church" and state combined. This meant that Israel's political (and very concrete) enemies were normally also God's enemies. Individual curses dare not be read as effusions of personal vengeance, but must be read in solidarity with the entire covenant people and its destiny under God. The real subject of these psalms is not individuals or nations whom one should love or pray for as an absolute alternative. The enemies are archetypes of the demonic, of that primal evil that always and everywhere opposes God, His work, and His people. Ultimately, of course, the Antichrist or Satan indwells the wicked instead of Christ (and since we remain *simul peccator*, influences also us). The deeper realization is that no human power will ultimately exorcise it. A major biblical application of this struggle against the Antichrist occurs in the citations of Ps 109 as fulfilled in the person and activities of Judas Iscariot (cf similarly "Edom" and "Babylon," who stand for evil).

Vengeance is God's alone (Rm 12:19) but wickedness that refuses to be forgiven can only be destroyed. Christ took all of God's vengeance upon Himself. He dwells in us, and we not only can but must join Him in both prayer and labor for the final "judgment," which will at once spell the uprooting of all evil and final triumph of God's original, paradisiacal order.

We return to consideration of the form-critical structure of the laments and thanksgivings. The structural elements considered thus far suffice for the laments, but, as already noted, the two forms tend to merge into one.

The suddenness with which a psalm of thanksgiving often follows the lament without transition has often seemed very puzzling. One proposal suggests that after the lament and before the thanksgiving, a priestly "oracle of salvation" (Grm *Heilsorakel*—or "formula of absolution") intervened. This would assure the worshiper that God has favorably heard and answered his prayer. Psalm 22:21b may even preserve evidence of such a ritual in its otherwise incomprehensible "you have rescued me" at the point of transition from lament to thanksgiving.

In other respects, from data within the psalmic thanksgivings themselves, as well as by historical reports elsewhere in the Old Testament, the worship setting of this form is often as obvious and undeniable as anywhere. For example, in Ps 22:25–31 the worshiper often publicly acknowledges his deliverance before the congregation, and also announces the payment of his vow, which, in part, includes a sacrifice. It is no accident that Old Testament vocabulary uses the same word (Hbr *todah*) to denote both thank offering and thanksgiving psalm (the word is also etymologically related to the "praise" words). We see again the usual Old Testament pattern of sacrifice and prayer as normally inseparable complements (cf Ps 141:2, the familiar Vespers versicle). The usual practice appears to have been to recite the thanksgiving prayer either before or during the presentation of their offering.

Minor Types. Before we proceed with the fifth major category, the royal psalms, let us consider other minor types that have not yet been discussed. "Pilgrimage Songs" are plainly among these. As already noted, the relation of this type to the "Psalms of Ascent" (120–134) is uncertain (only Ps 122 gives clear internal indications of describing pilgrimage). Psalm 84 with its longing for Zion plainly belongs in this category, and there are allusions elsewhere to such pilgrimages (Pss 87; 121; 126; cf Is 2:3 with Mi 4:2).

Closely related are the processional hymns, or "entrance liturgies," as they are often called. In these psalms, pilgrims or other worshipers ritually ask about the conditions for admission into the sanctuary and receive symbolic catechetical instruction. We have two clear examples, Pss 15 and 24:3–

6, though Pss 48; 68; and 132 are also possibilities. Modern theory has often suggested that the ark, representing Yahweh, was the "King of glory" at the head of the procession. Although speculative, this is not beyond the realm of probability (cf 2Sm 6; 1Ch 15). At any rate, allusions in other psalms (42:4; 55:14; 118:19–20) make it plain that processions played a prominent role in Old Testament worship.

Gunkel himself preferred to speak of "Torah liturgies," that is, occasions when the priest gave instruction (Hbr *torah*), especially on worship procedures. At least outside of the Psalter, he thought he could discern other types of liturgies, e.g., "oracular" ones (priestly guidance in times of crisis, as when a king leaves for battle), and "prophetic" ones, concerned with typical prophetic themes (e.g., Is 12; 33). This reflects the great and generally wholesome accent that form criticism succeeded in putting on Israel's public worship as not only the major setting for most of the psalms, but also with great influence on the rest of Israel's life and literature.

Last but not least among the minor categories, we must include the wisdom psalms. Although not great in number, they require more than passing attention, because Ps 1 plainly bids us approach the entire Psalter as a Wisdom Book. Initially, that tends to be less help than hindrance for us, because of our grave difficulties in understanding wisdom. Psalm 1 certainly illustrates many of these difficulties (the apparent moralism, if not works-righteousness, the facile division of mankind into "two ways," etc.).

Suffice it to say here that "wisdom" deals with ultimates, with the entire created order, accessible in part after the fall to reason and experience in "general revelation," but ultimately available and testable only within "special revelation" (Bible and Gospel). Wisdom literature tends to *assume* that theological background, and to express itself in more universal language. At least two wisdom psalms (127 and 133) demonstrate this, and humanly speaking, could just as well have appeared in the Book of Proverbs. Other wisdom products, however, show greater signs of explicit theological reflection, and exhibit greater use of mainline biblical vocabulary. The bulk of the wisdom psalms are of that character (1; 37; 49; 73; 112; 119; 128; and perhaps 139). Echoes of wisdom language or procedures are apparent also in other psalms (e.g., 78:1–2; 34:12; 62:12). Above all, as Ps 1 probably intends to remind us, it is possible to consider the entire Psalter a wisdom book because it deals with the same ultimate issues of life and death, of suffering and retribution, etc. Wisdom, for all its uniqueness of expression, was in no sense an alien element in ancient Israel.

A depiction of the triumphal entry, from the Codex de Predis.

Royal (Messianic) Psalms. We have saved the "best wine," the royal psalms, till last. They form a natural capstone to the Psalter in the eyes of both tradition and of much modern scholarship. ("Royal" and "messianic," of course, are substantially synonymous). As noted above, Gunkel did not initially consider this a major form—no clear structure is discernible. At the same time, however, the importance of the royal psalms almost justifies a separate category, because, as we have noted, the king (alongside the righteous sufferer; cf below) is undeniably one of the two major characters in the Psalter.

Gunkel pursued the matter little further than attempting to determine the various settings of the psalms of this type: a king's enthronement (2; 101; 110), anniversary of the enthronement (21; 72), anniversary of the Davidic dynasty and its sanctuary on Zion (132), a royal wedding (45), the king's departure for war (20; 144:1–11), celebration of the king's victorious return (cf Ps 18 with 2Sm 22), etc. There has been no lack of critical debate about specifics of those associations, but in broad thrust there is no doubt about general agreement. Neither has there been much critical concern about the relatively "secular" nature of the contexts, as the above captions indicate.

Inevitably, however, the question of the compatibility of such interpretation with traditional and New Testament messianic interpretation presses to the fore. It is to be noted that Gunkel viewed these psalms as expressed by or about one of Israel's monarchs on some specific historical occasion not as idealizations (let alone predictions) of some future regent. On both sides there are those who would deny the possibility of any compatibility of the two views (historical and messianic), but we defend their ultimate unity (both are aspects of the "one, literal sense").

The royal psalms are to be read in the light of especially 2Sm 7, Nathan's pivotal messianic prophecy of perpetuity to the Davidic dynasty. His household received the same covenant that was the foundation of Israel's entire existence. We do not dismiss the grandiose language of these psalms as merely the traditional, fulsome bombast of ancient Near Eastern court style.

Their primary subject is not any particular Old Testament king, but the *office* of kingship under the promise. The terms of the promise were partly "fulfilled" again and again in Israel's kings (potentially even by those who were externally unfaithful to it). Since these kings could never completely live up to the promise, this always reminded Israel that another king would fully and finally come to establish an eternal kingdom. Nor is this something "read in"; the Old Testament context alone suffices to show that the ultimate, messianic import was part of the speaker's original vista and intent.

The nations indeed conspired against the Lord and His anointed (Ps 2:1–2) throughout Israel's history, but that very real history was of a piece with the ultimate battle of the kingdoms of this world against God's kingdom (a central biblical motif). In reply, God repeated Nathan's decree (2:7) and made their enemies a footstool (110:1), but not apart from Christ's definitive victory. Precisely because the Israelite kingdom was a microcosm of the eternal kingdom, the Israelite king could lay claim to the "ends of the earth" (2:8), but the reality was available to them essentially only as it still is to us—in Word and Sacrament. (Even after Christ's advent, but before the consummation, we continue to pray the psalms like ancient Israel did.) Israel's kings apparently exercised authority over the regular, Aaronic priesthood (cf 1Ch), thus possessing a special priesthood "after the order of Melchizedek" (110:4). But the full potential of that ultimately eternal order could not emerge until great David's greater Son occupied His throne (the Book of Hebrews). Israel's king was indeed God's "son," "begotten" (adopted) in the unique covenant relation.

Messianic and Christological interpretation of the royal psalms (cf especially the "dynastic oracles" of the prophets) does not require us to divorce ourselves from the realities of Israel's history any more than it does from our own. But it does require us to define the word *history* in the Bible's own sacramental and eternal sense. It is not less than history, but more than mere history because it addresses eternal issues. In Christ, the history of Israel's monarchy is also part of the history of our salvation. We will not read into the ancient texts a consciousness of all the details of the fulfillment, but we will read out of them their full prophetic and typological, Christological, and prophetic significance. The relevance of much of the entire Old Testament as Scripture and Gospel is at stake.

Characters

The **righteous sufferer**, whom we recognize to be ultimately none other than our Lord, is one of the two major figures of the Psalter. The other is **the**

OUTLINE

The Psalms are divided into ancient collections or "books," each ending with a doxology (41:13; 72:18–20; 89:52; 106:48; 150 or 145–50). Early Jewish commentaries suggested that the five books of the Psalms are comparable to the five Books of Moses (Gn through Dt). These divisions for the Psalms may have taken place as early as the third century BC.

Book	Principal Authors	Possible Historical Context
I. Pss 1–41	Intensely personal psalms of David	Life of David; 11th century BC; time of the tabernacle
II. Pss 42–72	Psalms of David and the kingdom; nationalistic	Reigns of David and Solomon; 11th and 10th centuries BC; time of the first temple
III. Pss 73–89	Psalms of Asaph and the Sons of Korah; nationalistic	Reign of Solomon; 10th century BC; some difficult to date
IV. Pss 90–106	Anonymous psalms and laments	Historical context less clear; some of the psalms refer to earlier writers such as Moses (Ps 90) and David (e.g., Ps 122), but others refer to the time of exile in Babylon (Ps 137), 6th century BC
V. Pss 107–50	Songs of ascents and praise; psalms of David	

Many believe Pss 90–106 were brought together after both Israel and Judah had fallen. The Babylonian captivity crushed the hopes of a great nation established by King David. In answer to that defeat, these psalms direct the people's attention to God as the everlasting King. Alongside the books of the Psalms appear some other obvious collections, such as the following:

> Yahweh Psalms (1–41)
>
> Elohim Psalms (42–89)
>
> Hallel Psalms (111–118)
>
> Songs of Ascents (120–134)
>
> Hallelujah Psalms (146–150)

For more on these collections and the broader structures of the books of Psalms, see "Historical and Cultural Setting" above.

king of the royal psalms, who, of course, is ultimately a messianic figure too (cf below). One interpretation would identify these two figures. Allegedly, it was originally the king who prayed the laments in his capacity as corporate personality or Israel reduced to one. Only later were they supposedly democratized and made available to all the faithful. Such a construction is, in a sense, attractive from the standpoint of messianic inter-

Christ as the Man of Sorrows with Mary and St. John, by Lucas Cranach the Elder.

pretation, but, on other grounds, it is too speculative and too beholden to other very questionable reconstructions for one to embrace it. The New Testament still gives us ample warrant to make the same ultimate typological and predictive application to Christ in both cases.

The sufferer in the Psalms does not always plead innocent, however. Partly on the basis of Egyptian analogies, scholarship has grown accustomed to speaking of two types of confessions: (a) the "negative confession" in which the worshiper denies his guilt and asks God's justice on His enemies (the type of which we have just been speaking), and (b) the "positive confession," where the speaker concedes his culpability and implores God's forgiveness. The latter are especially known as "confessional" or "penitential" psalms (cf above). One will not simplistically identify the latter type with Christ in the same way as the former, but it remains profoundly true that the latter cannot be validly prayed outside of the covenant either, that is, apart from an imputed righteousness and in unity with its Giver (*Christus et pro nobis et in nobis;* "Christ both in us and for us").

Narrative Development or Plot

Many of the psalms explicitly provide or imply stories, especially stories of rescue or divine favor. The superscriptions at times provide explicit stories that one can find in the Historical Books of Scripture. For more thoughts on plot in the psalms, consult the sections on Authors and Genre above.

Text and Translations

A glance at the footnotes in the Hebrew Bible will demonstrate that the textual condition of individual psalms varies widely, all the way from vir-

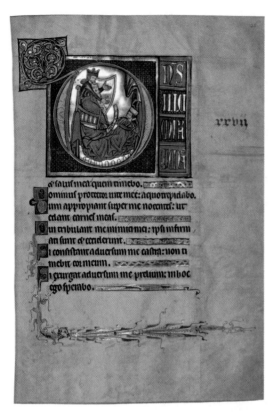

David playing his harp for Saul. (Psalm 26 in De Brailes Psalter c 1250.)

tually perfect to very troubled. Nor are the reasons for the variations any clearer than in the case of similar variations elsewhere in the Old Testament. Sometimes apparent textual corruptions can be attributed to a linguistically more archaic original, which later copyists would more readily misunderstand. But other unknown variables were obviously involved as well.

There is some evidence of early editing in the second and third books of psalms, called the Elohistic Psalter. Scribes apparently changed the divine name "Yahweh" to "Elohim" to provide consistency. For more on this, see pp 542–43.

A further point worth mentioning in the textual history of the Psalter is the three separate Latin translations made by St. Jerome (attesting, of course, to the importance and popularity of the psalms). At the bidding of one of the popes, Jerome first attempted only a revision of an older Latin translation—the so-called "Roman Psalter" because it has been used in modern times at St. Peter's in Rome. Later Jerome undertook a more thorough revision, based on the Hexapla; this is the so-called "Gallican Psalter" because it was first adopted by Gregory of Tours. It has major importance because it is the translation preserved in most editions of the Vulgate, and hence the basis of most Roman Catholic usage until Vatican II. These first two efforts of Jerome were based primarily on the Greek—hence, important as witnesses to the history of the Greek text, but twice removed from the Hebrew original. Jerome's third and most thoroughgoing revision was based on Hebrew and completed during his sojourn at Bethlehem, with the assistance of rabbinical scholars. To text-critical scholars this is, of course, the most important of Jerome's three versions, but the very familiarity of the masses with older versions of the Psalter prevented the third translation from receiving the same acceptance eventually accorded to his translations from the Hebrew of other biblical books.

Numbering Systems

The Psalter has varying numbering systems, both for some of the psalms themselves as well as for verses within them. *LBC* employs the system common in English, Protestant Bibles. Variations occur between the Hebrew edition, the LXX, the Vulgate, and even translations into modern languages.

Differences in versification arise from different attitudes toward the superscriptions: in Hebrew, German, and other Bibles they are usually (unless very short) counted as v 1 (if long, occasionally even as two verses), whereas in English they are not counted at all. Different numbers for the psalms themselves arise from different combinations, going back to the Septuagint, but via the Vulgate still often current in Roman Catholic Bibles and derivative literature. Since Pss 9 and 10 are combined, while 147 is divided into two, the result is that throughout most of the Psalter the Catholic number is one lower than that familiar to most Protestants (e.g., our Ps 23 is Ps 22). The LXX also combines our Pss 114 and 115, but then promptly divides 116 into two, so that displacement in numbering is only temporary.

Numbering systems usually total 150, which for unknown reasons (humanly speaking) apparently became fixed very early as the canonical maximum. The LXX, however, preserves a "Ps 151," superscribed, "A genuine, though supernumerary, Psalm of David, composed when he engaged Goliath in single combat." Two more psalms are appended in many Nestorian Syriac manuscripts, and Hebrew originals of all three, plus three additional psalms (six in all) are attested at Qumran (not to be confused with the community's own compositions, the *Hodayot*). Whether we have here psalms that were really Deuterocanonical in some circles, or simply the attraction of other liturgical favorites to a closed canonical collection, is a matter of considerable debate. Qumran also attests to a different sequence of psalms in some cases. Especially since the synagogue lectionary had 153 Torah readings, strenuous attempts have been made to discern some cycle of liturgical accompaniments by the 150 psalms, but with no sure results.

DOCTRINAL CONTENT

Summary Commentary

Book I, Pss 1–41; Called the "Yahweh Psalter"

Ps 1 The first psalm shows us the destiny of both the righteous and the wicked. The wicked will, at the final judgment, find themselves alienated from God and, ultimately, inheritors of eternal damnation. No one is exempt from this most frightening fate. Yet God has provided the way of righteousness.

Ps 2 Those who plot against God's elect incite God's wrath. The Lord, not human beings, anointed Israel's king and elected this nation for His plan of salvation.

Ps 3 This psalm recounts a dark period in David's life. His enemies, including his own son, have overwhelmed and opposed him. Despite his foes' claim that David's sins preclude him from salvation, David remains confident that God will protect and deliver him.

Ps 4 David complains that his enemies are speaking ill of him as king in an attempt to shame him. He reminds them that God sets apart the godly from those who behave in such a manner.

Ps 5 Boasting and deceit inevitably lead to destruction. David's petition reveals that God leads us out of such sins and covers us with His favor.

Ps 6 The first penitential psalm. David pleads with the Lord for deliverance from anxiety, physical discomfort, and sickness caused by a growing awareness of his sinful condition.

Ps 7 David, confident of his righteousness, petitions the Lord to judge him and his enemies justly. He repeatedly asserts that the righteousness of God's justice must destroy unrepentant sinners, and he compares God's wrath to that of a soldier preparing to meet his foe.

Ps 8 David thanks the Lord, our Ruler, for His great and inestimable blessing, for establishing such a kingdom and calling and gathering His people.

Ps 9 "The wicked are snared in the work of their own hands," David observes in this psalm. Because the Lord reigns, the righteous can "be glad and exult" (v 2) in His name.

Ps 10 The psalmist confidently prays that God will root out those who are wicked and take advantage of the weak and poor throughout Israel so that they "may strike terror no more" (v 18).

Ps 11 David confesses his confidence in the Lord's unmovable favor. The Lord "tests the righteous" (v 5). God's faithfulness and mercy toward us, however, never wanes or fails.

Ps 12 A cry for help in the face of treachery and deceit.

Ps 13 In moments of fear and frustration, our prayers can easily slip into blaming God for our problems. Asking "How long, O Lord?" (v 1) is okay. The psalm ends with confidence in the Lord.

Ps 14 This psalm clarifies the depth of human sinfulness, while it also illumines the greatness of redemption.

Ps 15 Sincerity and the righteous treatment of others, as taught in the Ten Commandments, are emphasized as the foundation to genuine worship.

Ps 16 The psalm praises the Lord for numerous earthly blessings but moves toward a climactic expression of hope for life in God's presence beyond the grave.

Ps 17 David begs for protection from a bloodthirsty enemy and trusts confidently in the Lord.

Ps 18 David exults, "The LORD . . . is worthy to be praised" (v 3) and recounts a time when the very cords of death were dragging him down into the abyss. The Lord hears his appeal and comes to his rescue.

Ps 19 The heavens continually declare God's praise, and the forces of nature daily show forth His glory as they faithfully carry out the duties He has assigned them.

Ps 20 The people desire God's blessing for their king as he prepares to lead them into battle.

Ps 21 This psalm not only offers thanks to God for Israel's king (vv 1–7) but also encourages him with promises of the Lord's blessing (vv 8–12).

Ps 22 Facing great opposition, the psalmist initially feels that God has forsaken him and is ignoring his prayers. After remembering God's faithfulness and deliverance, he believes that God will deliver him and commits himself to telling that message to others.

Ps 23 The Good Shepherd Psalm. In faith, David declares that since Yahweh is his shepherd, he "shall not want" (v 1).

Ps 24 A call for God's people to worship, noting His creation and glory. Possibly written for the return of the ark of the covenant to the tabernacle (2Sm 6:12–15).

Ps 25 This acrostic psalm includes prayers for victory, teaching, forgiveness, and deliverance.

Ps 26 Pleas of one falsely accused of wrongdoing.

Ps 27 David's confession of confidence in God, followed by a prayer for help, forgiveness, and guidance.

Ps 28 Facing personal crisis, David realizes he is unable to protect and save himself. He needs God to be his strength and shield.

Ps 29 God's power is a terrifying thing. The sound of His voice brings forth creation, shakes the mountains and trees, and unleashes the great flood that destroyed the earth.

Ps 30 David summarizes his feelings and God's response in v 5. Trusting in God's deliverance, David knows that the sorrow he feels will be replaced with joy as God comforts him.

Ps 31 David says that he hates those who trust in worthless idols; he trusts in the Lord (v 6).

Ps 32 The second penitential psalm. Luther wrote, "The beginning of this psalm teaches two things: first, that all are in sins [no one is righteous] and no one is blessed; second, that no one is capable of meriting the forgiveness of sin, but it is the Lord alone who forgives freely by not imputing [guilt]" (AE 10:147). Psalm 32 also shows the physical, mental, and spiritual implications of being silent in sin.

Ps 33 God's people are always to put their trust in Him alone and not in arms, generals, national defenses, and so on.

Ps 34 The Lord turns His countenance of favor toward His children, saves them, and blesses them. The Lord turns His countenance away from the wicked and condemns them to eternal death, though His will is to save all people.

Ps 35 David appeals to God Almighty as divine warrior and righteous judge. He prays that God will come to his defense and rescue him from those who were once close friends but who now accuse, slander, and condemn him with malice.

Ps 36 The wicked continuously plot against the Lord's servants, but His steadfast love is a refuge to those who know Him.

Ps 37 This psalm stresses two things: the righteous are blessed of God in due season, and divine punishment will overtake the wicked.

Ps 38 The third penitential psalm. The Lord chastises His children in order to turn them from temptation and sin and to keep them safe and faithful to Him.

Ps 39 Veiled in uncertainty is a flickering faith that puts its hope in God and in His strength and promise to rescue all who call on His name.

Ps 40 One who has fallen away from God now cries out for His fatherly kindness and mercy.

Ps 41 Two experiences afflict David: he is sick, and he suffers at the hands of enemies (traitors) who want his throne and his life.

Book II, Pss 42–72; Called "Elohim Psalter," Pt. 1

Ps 42 The psalmist experiences despair at the seeming victory of the godless and his separation from God's merciful presence at the temple.

Ps 43 The psalmist desires vindication for the cause of his sufferings. He asks God for the light and truth that come from His dwelling so that he might return to His sanctuary in joyful worship.

Ps 44 The psalmist recounts God's past faithfulness but complains that God is now against His people, letting them suffer defeat despite their faithfulness to Him. They petition Him to help them once more.

Ps 45 The psalmist uses a royal wedding to portray our King, who is God, and the fulfillment of His kingdom in His Son.

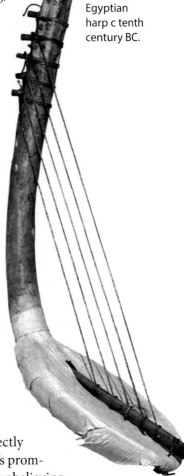

Egyptian harp c tenth century BC.

Ps 46 The almighty and Most High God controls nature, safeguards His chosen city against attacking foes, and stands over all nations at war. He is our sure fortress. In mercy, He makes Himself accessible and is, therefore, "God with us."

Ps 47 All nations are called to praise God for what He has done for and in Israel. Israel is called to praise Him as their great King, demonstrating His universal rule and salvation.

Ps 48 The Lord of heaven and earth makes His abode with humankind, where He is a strong fortress that shatters every enemy. He is, therefore, worthy of all praise, and we rightly "tell the next generation" (v 13) what He has done.

Ps 49 Wealth and earthly goods cannot buy off death. Those who foolishly rely on them find a very different end than those whose fortune and trust is in the Lord.

Ps 50 God comes as a judge to reprimand His people for the unbelief that hides behind careless ritualism and hypocritical religiosity.

Ps 51 The fourth penitential psalm. This anguished cry of confession from the depths of guilt finds God's absolution and renewal on the certain footing of grace alone (*sola gratia*).

Ps 52 A deeply personal lament of David as he speaks directly to a vicious enemy (vv 1–7). Confident prayer remembers God's promises, and it trusts and waits on God's justice and love. In an unbelieving world, the wicked attack what is good, boast, and even thrive in their evil.

Ps 53 When evil fools encamp against God's people, He saves and restores them.

Ps 54 The psalmist prays for deliverance amidst persecution by family and even strangers! He is confident that God will help as He always has.

Ps 55 The author finds himself in a town full of wickedness and violence, betrayed by a trusted friend and colleague, with no one to help except God. He turns to the Lord in prayer, entrusting his life to God's hand with confidence.

Ps 56 The psalmist finds himself in great peril from enemies and turns to God with confidence. Even in the midst of danger, David rejoices in God's love and His certain deliverance from death.

Ps 57 David turns to God for help. Chased by Saul, his king and father-in-law, David flees for his life and hides in a cave to avoid discovery. He confidently asks God for deliverance and praises God for rescuing him even before it happens (cf 2Sm 22).

Ps 58 David challenges the leaders of the people by condemning the unjust and dishonest.

Ps 59 Includes a prayer for help in times of need (vv 1–7) and assurance of deliverance (vv 8–17). When surrounded by enemies, we turn to God in confidence and trust.

Ps 60 God disciplines those He loves, and He tests His people to build their faith and strengthen the relationship of grace.

Ps 61 David turns once more to God for help in time of need, asking God to restore him to his throne in Jerusalem and bless him in the years and generations ahead.

Ps 62 Hymn of peace and confidence in God, who alone provides security and hope. Wealth deceives people by promising happiness. In the end, wealth, power, and fame turn out to be lies because they do not deliver what they seem to promise.

Ps 63 On the run, cut off from God's tabernacle and the capital city, Jerusalem, David turns to God in prayer and praise for His love and salvation.

Ps 64 The psalmist's enemies conspire against him and seek his destruction, but he turns to the Lord in prayer and receives deliverance.

Ps 65 David praises God for the forgiveness of sins, peace in the world, and prosperity in the land—a straightforward song of praise to God for His awesome grace.

Ps 66 A psalm that can be offered by any believer in any time of hardship. The Lord's deeds of salvation, culminating in the ministry of Christ, assure His people that He will make all things, even hardships, work out for their ultimate good (Rm 8:28–29).

Ps 67 A psalm of benediction (cf Nu 6:24–26). There is only one way of salvation, which Israel's God provided in the work of His Son, Jesus.

Ps 68 This psalm seems to be an order of service for a procession at the Jerusalem temple (or the tabernacle). In His sanctuary, God provides His salvation. Without this sanctuary, there is only judgment.

Ps 69 David offers this prayer for help in the midst of attacks and sufferings imposed on his enemies.

Ps 70 An urgent plea for God to remember His people and receive His deliverance from evil.

Ps 71 A psalm for an older believer struggling with assaults on his faith, including temptations to think that his faith was in vain.

Ps 72 Possibly a coronation psalm for Solomon, pleading for God's help. The psalmist realizes that even the best of the Davidic kings fell short of the ideal.

Book III, Pss 73–89; Called "Elohim Psalter," Pt. 2

Ps 73 The psalmist expresses doubts and struggles, yet passes through them to a faith renewed by God's faithfulness and promises.

Ps 74 Likely written after the destruction of Jerusalem and the temple in 587 BC. The psalmist feels rejected by God yet confesses that He is king and reminds Him of the covenant.

Ps 75 God judges the wicked and delivers the believer according to His timetable. If He seems delayed, we should not lose heart.

Ps 76 God is majestic in both judgment and salvation.

Ps 77 The author expresses certain struggles of faith and doubt which plague many believers. Even strong believers and spiritual leaders among God's people may find themselves troubled by times of weakness in their faith. But God's powerful Word strengthens us.

Ps 78 Second-longest psalm in the Psalter. Refers to the divisions between the Northern and Southern Kingdoms of Israel. God's dealings with Israel of old point to His acts toward us today. The psalm culminates in God's deeds to and through David, highlighting the importance of the covenant with David.

Ps 79 The psalm laments Jerusalem's destruction, perhaps in 587 BC, and calls for God to remember His people with compassion.

Ps 80 This psalm begs God to restore His people after their fall before foreign armies. The psalmist recognizes that God's acts of salvation in the past speak assurances for His salvation in the future. Israel repeatedly turned away from the Lord, thus incurring His judgment as a call to repentance.

Ps 81 Even while worshiping the one true God, His people were not listening to His Word. Here God laments the plugging of their ears (v 11), longing for the day they will turn again in repentance. God loves to speak to His people!

Ps 82 Alerts faithful Israelites and all believers that God concerns Himself with the care of individuals. He rebukes the powerful.

Ps 83 The psalmist feels overwhelmed by his enemies, who plot against him. His only recourse is to run to God Most High, whose great deeds he remembers in prayer.

Ps 84 The author has been separated from the sanctuary, where God is rightly worshiped. He now longs to return.

Ps 85 The psalmist feels distress and fear at his exposure to his enemies.

Ps 86 Ascribed to King David, this psalm points to God's steadfast love (vv 5, 13, 15) as the reason why prayers are answered. He asks for protection against enemies and expresses confidence that God shall indeed act.

A singer and two tambourine players from Israel's kingdom era (ninth–eighth century BC).

Ps 87 God includes people of all nations among His believers, all of whom may claim to be born in Zion (v 5).

Ps 88 This psalm evokes feelings of sadness and abandonment. The psalmist is so overcome by troubles that he wonders if God will hear him. God inclines His ear (v 2) toward His people, always ready to hear and answer us according to His mercy.

Ps 89 Speaks primarily of David, who enjoyed God's faithfulness (vv 2, 24) and promises. Even when David sinned and felt the weight of God's Law (vv 38–47), he still relied completely upon God. "How long, O LORD?" (v 46) easily comes to the lips of all who, because of their sins, have suffered under the weight of God's Law.

Book IV, Pss 90–106

Ps 90 A lament, when the frailty of life stands in stark contrast to God's eternal strength.

Ps 91 A strong confession of faith and example of life entrusted to God's protective safety, urging all readers to seek the Lord's refuge when fearful times arise.

Ps 92 The only psalm tied specifically to the Sabbath. While the Sabbath could be described by what could not be done on that day, this psalm shows what should be done: praise and celebration of God's great works.

Ps 93 The psalmist affirms that the Lord has always reigned and will do so forever. This confident confession celebrates God's almighty and eternal reign over even the most chaotic powers in creation.

Ps 94 The psalmist pleads for God to take vengeance on His enemies, repaying the oppressors so that justice returns.

Ps 95 In the midst of national crisis, this psalm assures people that God is king over all. The opening verses have been sung in the Church for centuries as the *Venite* (Latin for "O come").

Ps 96 A psalm for joyous occasions (cf 1Ch 16:23–34). Proclaim the marvelous deeds of God's salvation to all nations!

Ps 97 Joyfully proclaims the power and majesty of God's rule over creation. When people stand before God to be judged, only two responses are possible: terrified humiliation or joyful thanksgiving.

Ps 98 The psalm's sole purpose is to praise the victorious God and His marvelous works.

Ps 99 The psalmist proclaims that the Lord is King over all creation, highlighting His holiness, which evokes awe, reverence, and even fear. The psalm recalls Israel's leaders Moses, Aaron, and Samuel.

Ps 100 A thankful doxology, expressing joy that the Lord established Israel in His steadfast love.

Ps 101 The king, as God's servant, makes pledges and demands as he leads the people.

Ps 102 The fifth penitential psalm. This lament confesses a deep faith in the Lord's care and the security that comes from God's creative and eternal strength.

Ps 103 A call to praise the Lord, introducing psalms that do likewise (Pss 103–6). The weaknesses of mankind are contrasted with God's mighty rule.

Ps 104 The psalmist summons himself to praise God as Creator and Preserver of creation. God is indeed Creator of all. He continues to care for His world.

Ps 105 Pss 105–6 stand together as they recall God's promises to Abraham, focusing on God's grace. God frees His people from slavery.

Ps 106 The psalm begins with praise but then moves to confession. One of the most important words in this psalm is "nevertheless" (v 44). Despite Israel's persistent disobedience, God consistently upheld His promises and saved them.

Book V, Pss 107–150

Ps 107 Focuses on the time of restoration from the exile. History unfolds the prevailing deeds of God's steadfast love. Because of sin, this world is chaotic and inhospitable.

Ps 108 A response to stress which emphasizes God's help. Drawn from 57:7–11 and 60:5–12, with a few variations.

Ps 109 David calls for judgment and punishment on those who falsely accuse him. He believes his enemies have removed themselves beyond the reach of God's grace.

Ps 110 A royal psalm in which the Lord addresses the king. The world looks for the visible manifestation of God. David sees that manifestation prophetically in one of his future descendants: Jesus.

Hallel Psalms, Pss 111–118

Ps 111 An acrostic psalm praising God's works. Luther suggested that the words of v 4, "the Lord is gracious and merciful," should be painted in golden letters around a portrait of the Lord's Supper (AE 13:375).

Ps 112 An acrostic psalm focused on the person who fears the Lord by keeping in mind His words and works. The fear of the Lord leads us in the wisdom of generosity and contentment.

Ps 113 The first psalm of the Egyptian "Hallel" (113–118). A general call to praise. The Lord is not overwhelmed. He is exalted on high, and He reaches down low with His salvation.

Ps 114 The only Hallel psalm pointing back to the exodus by which God rescued the needy.

Ps 115 The psalmist encourages Israel not to look to the outward manifestations of strength as did the idol worshipers, but to remember God's steadfast love. Through the promises of His blessings, God calls His people beyond imagination to the truth of His existence.

Ps 116 Describes the Lord as a deliverer and expresses love for Him.

Ps 117 This shortest psalm celebrates God's grace with unlimited range of vision.

Ps 118 The last song of the Hallel (113–118), which offers thanks for national deliverance while anticipating the life of Christ.

Ps 119 The Great Psalm of the Word. The psalmist's words of devotion become as timeless as the Law (Hbr *torah*; "instruction") and God's promises, which he loves. He prays for right understanding of God's teaching. The psalm celebrates God's universal actions and nature, which are offered to all people in His life-giving Word.

Songs of Ascents, Pss 120–134

Ps 120 The tongue is a powerful tool of peace or war. God warns of His approaching judgment on lying lips that are eager for war. However, He also invites people to call on Him for peace and salvation.

Ps 121 Written for a pilgrim viewing Jerusalem's hills. He finds that God, who created all things, is his helper.

Ps 122 Focuses on the entry to Jerusalem as the place of God's judgment and the peaceful gathering of His people.

Ps 123 Our eyes are to be upon God, both to receive His blessings and to do His bidding. However, when our time of service is filled with contempt from others, we grow tired of waiting for God's justice.

Ps 124 Strength and safety come only by God's hand. We are in danger from flood and snare, the overwhelming and the enticing. But God is faithful for His name's sake. He rescues us so that we will continue to bless and call on His name.

Ps 125 God's blessing transforms us into mountains surrounding His dwelling place. We are built on His Word as an unchanging rock, and we become pillars by His grace.

Ps 126 God gives the expectation that times of sudden refreshing will come from Him.

Ps 127 Credited to Solomon, this psalm describes the value of the home and children and may also refer to the building of the temple.

Ps 128 Likely a pilgrim song, recited by travelers in the company of their families as the mountains of Jerusalem came into view.

Ps 129 God has already begun to judge, but the psalmist describes a more complete judgment still to come.

Ps 130 The sixth penitential psalm. The psalmist is in a state of emotional desolation, overwhelmed with misery and guilt. Yet, as he realizes God hears his pleas and grants him full forgiveness, his darkness slowly gives way to light and the hope of "plentiful redemption" (v 7).

Ps 131 Before God and the mysteries of existence, we are like little children. And like little children, we can find solace in God's love for us.

Ps 132 One of David's sons, the Anointed One, will be enthroned forever. He will clothe His people with righteousness and salvation. This psalm curses the enemies of God's Anointed, and He will "clothe [them] with shame" (v 18).

Ps 133 Living in unity is as soothing as being anointed with oil, as refreshing as dew from the mountains on a parched desert. Descriptions of the goodness and pleasure of unity and brotherhood remind us that we often experience discord, strife, and disunity instead.

Ps 134 The priests on duty at the temple during the night are urged to bless the Lord, and yet the Lord blesses us.

Ps 135 God's almighty power is evident in His creation and in His acts of redemption. The true God is contrasted with the man-made deities of false religions.

Ps 136 This great psalm of thanksgiving praises God for His acts of creation and redemption, both in history and in the lives of His people. Every detail, at every stage, is a sign of God's steadfast love, which, throughout human history, endures forever.

Ps 137 By abandoning God for false religions and the evil ways of the surrounding cultures, the people lost everything. Now, in their exile, they appreciate what they threw away.

Ps 138 God's name and Word are above everything, including all of the claims of the false gods. He cares for His children, the work of His hands, and His hands will protect them and bring His plans for them to completion. God's hand is against His enemies.

Ps 139 A meditation on God's attributes: His omniscience, His omnipresence, His omnipotence, and His holiness. The psalmist's wonder segues into anger at those who hate God and destroy His gift of life. That God knows our every thought, word, and deed can be terrifying to a sinner. This psalm, above all, proclaims God's love, which He expresses in His personal care and involvement in all of His creation.

Ps 140 God's judgment is harsh against those who use their words to harm others—through lies, gossip, slander, or other "poisonous" speech—as well as those who harm others through violence or subtle traps. God is on the side of the poor, the weak, and the oppressed.

Ps 141 Sinners will fall into the traps they have made for themselves and will ultimately be cast down.

Ps 142 David prays to the Lord, pouring out his complaints and troubles. God restores him to the fellowship of faith.

Ps 143 The seventh penitential psalm. The psalmist pleads for God's mercy, admitting that neither he nor anyone else can stand before God's judgment. He trusts in God's righteousness and in His name, not his own. This penitential psalm is a profound description of a repentant heart, which receives God's grace. The psalmist, giving up on himself, trusts in God's "steadfast love" (v 8).

Ps 144 The Warrior Psalm. Joyful song of victory by King David, after defeating enemies in battle.

Ps 145 The Mission Psalm. God is our King, and all generations and all the earth must hear about Him. He abounds in mercy, which extends to all His works. The Lord will draw near to those who fear Him (who have been broken by the Law).

Hallelujah Psalms, Pss 146–150

Ps 146 Do not put your faith in human beings—in politicians, social elite, or individuals, none of whom can save and all of whom will die. Rather, put your trust in God.

Ps 147 God has built Jerusalem and brought the exiles home. His Word that governs nature has been given to the children of Israel in Scripture. The Lord has forgiven those whom He had punished, gathered them from exile, and restored the Holy City.

Ps 148 Moving from the heavens to the earth, the psalm catalogs the whole range of the created order. The praise of creation culminates with praise for God's redeemed people.

Ps 149 Describes a festival procession to the Temple Mount. Joyous praise of God is interrupted with invocations for God's "vengeance" and "punishments" (v 7). And yet, despite God's judgment, He "adorns the humble with salvation" (v 4).

Ps 150 A tenfold "hallelujah!" in the heavens and in the place of worship, with every musical instrument; everything that breathes should praise the Lord because of His mighty deeds and His "excellent greatness"!

Specific Law Themes

The Psalms include a multitude of themes and each psalm has its unique emphases. As a result, the following comments are most general.

The psalms forewarn us that persecutors will assail God's people, who must contend for what is good and right in a world devastated by sin and unbelief. Furthermore, God's people will likewise suffer because of their personal failures. At times the Lord may allow them to endure under suffering until He determines their deliverance according to His good purposes (e.g., the exile in Babylon and domination by foreign powers). The psalmists at times express frustration with these truths in vivid complaint.

Specific Gospel Themes

The psalms also amply illustrate the Lord's saving righteousness and steadfast love for His people. He provides for their needs and protects them even in the midst of trials. Life is His gift to them, for which the psalmists frequently offer thanks and praise. A chief blessing prophesied in the psalms is the coming of the Messiah, which was fulfilled in the atoning death of Jesus, as many New Testament passages confirm.

Specific Doctrines

If one hears the Psalms as God's very Word, then, of course, one finds in them a magnificent summary of biblical theology (Luther called the Psalter a "Bible in miniature"). They express God's truth in such incomparable terms that it really is overwhelming to attempt any "theology of the Psalter." That being so, the Psalter is obviously not intended to make the rest of the Old Testament superfluous. The day of the medieval breviary with its schedule of reading the entire Psalter through each month or even each week has passed. Probably any comparable discipline within Protestantism has also faltered, and what happened with the Psalter is undoubtedly only a repetition on a smaller scale of what has happened with reading the entire Bible.

The Psalter's continued use in Christendom provides a convenient point of departure for rethinking the entire issue of the unity of Scripture, specifically of recovering the entire "older testament." The diligent reader will soon discover that, like the whole Bible, the Psalter's real subject is not man, his devotion, inspiration, or experience, but God as He still creates, elects, redeems, sanctifies, reigns, reveals, judges. And perhaps even in contrast to one-sided conservative accent on theology and doctrine, the Psalter's insistent poetry and doxology is a salutary reminder that its horizons must extend far, far beyond what the saints below can ever grasp, even now merging "mystically" with the angelic liturgy and pressing on eternally to sing forever—"together with angels and archangels and all the company of heaven."

Nonetheless, a few specific passages should be mentioned. The Church has long called upon Pss 2, 110, and other messianic psalms not only for teaching the doctrine of Christ but also for the doctrine of the Trinity (2:7; 110:4; see also 33:6) since the Lord creates, redeems, and sanctifies His people (Ps 104).

Psalm 19:12 and the penitential psalms were key to the Reformation, which emphasized both the need for confession and the treasure that is absolution, since no one can discern the depths of his sins. Psalm 51:5 has long been a key passage for the doctrine of original sin, along with Pss 130:3; 143:2. The Psalms likewise teach that justification, or forgiveness, is God's chief blessing (32:1–2; 130:3–4). They are naturally the source of the doctrine and practice of prayer, providing lively examples for both public and private use at God's invitation (50:14–15). They commend prayer for rulers (consider 127:1; 144:10) through whom the Lord extends blessings to His people.

Image of the Trinity in the Packham-Clifford book of hours (c 1314–13).

For doctrinal insights on specific types of psalms, see pp 557–69. See also Luther and Gerhard below.

Application

Book I, Pss 1–41; Called the "Yahweh Psalter"

Ps 1 The Lord sets us on the way of righteousness and keeps us on it through His Word. The Word forever reminds us—even when we have succumbed to the various temptations of life—that, through the death and resurrection of

Jesus Christ, our destination is certain. We will stand holy before God in the final judgment as members of the congregation of the righteous.

Ps 2 Ultimately, the Messiah—the Anointed One—was born from the nation of Israel. God preserved Israel so that through the offspring of one of David's descendants, Mary, the Savior of humankind was born. Those who "take refuge in Him"—i.e., trust in Him for their salvation—are truly blessed.

Ps 3 Despite our miserable condition (and certain end), God shields us from our foes, lifts us, and directs our eyes to His great mercy displayed in the cross of Christ. He assures us that salvation belongs to Him and is given to those who trust in Him.

Ps 4 How often do we find ourselves speaking ill of people in positions of authority? of colleagues and peers? God's Word condemns unjust complaints. Through David, God encourages us to turn from our sinful ways and "trust in the Lord" (v 5). Such trust brings peace of mind and eternal peace.

Ps 5 God leads us out of sins and covers us with His favor. He declares us righteous and thus covers us through faith in Christ's atoning sacrifice for all of our sins.

Ps 6 The first penitential psalm. Scripture clearly reveals that the result of sin is death (Rm 6:23), but how seriously do we take this threat? Consider this: nearly 2,000 years ago, our sinful condition was so desperate that God sent His own Son to deliver us. God be praised! Through faith in Christ's redemption, our sins have been forgiven.

Ps 7 The righteousness of God's justice must destroy unrepentant sinners. What a startling truth for those who refuse to repent of their sins! Yet the Lord also offers salvation through Christ Jesus who is our only refuge.

Ps 8 Luther wrote, "Let us follow the example of this singer of praises as he prophesies to us. The Lord is our Ruler, too, and His kingdom is established and founded from the mouths of babes and sucklings. We entered it by Baptism, and we are called to it daily through Word and Gospel. With David we also hope to come to where we shall see the heavens. . . . He won the kingdom with great trouble and anguish. Now He is crowned with honor and adornment and has everything under His feet" (AE 12:135–36).

Ps 9 Our sin carries the most frightening of consequences—death and damnation. However, as David reminds us, if we acknowledge our sin and God's wonderful deeds on our behalf, especially through Christ, we can be confident of His mercy toward us so we, too, can "be glad and exult" (v 2) in His name.

Ps 10 When the weak suffer, it may seem that God has abandoned us. Whether we have taken advantage of the weak or have been the victim of oppression, there is hope. The Lord has compassion on those oppressed by sin.

Ps 11 Despite our lack of faith and even our wicked deeds, the Lord extends His grace as a refuge from our sinful nature and the sinful works of others. He does so audibly and visibly through Word and Sacrament, as a testament of His great and unending love for us.

Ps 12 Unchecked wickedness sometimes leads us to doubt that God is watching out for us. Such despair is a great evil and can ruin our souls, but it can also help us to appreciate our complete dependence on God and His unfailing promises to save and defend us.

Ps 13 When our prayers question God and His ways, we do well to remember that Jesus not only commanded us to pray but also graciously promised to hear our prayers and intercede for us before the Father. No matter how weak our prayers or deep our frustration, Jesus' grace makes up for their shortcomings.

Ps 14 Though atheism and irreligion are increasingly accepted, indeed even fashionable in modern societies, they are destructive beliefs that finally lead to moral abandon and eternal death. Because this psalm clarifies the depth of human sinfulness, it also illumines the greatness in Jesus' redemption. He atoned for all the sins of all people and graciously calls all, even the most perverse, to forgiveness and eternal life.

Ps 15 There are times that we come to worship God in an unworthy manner. For example, we may remain unreconciled with others or persist in behaviors we know to be wrong. As God's true temple and the mercy seat where full forgiveness is freely given, our Lord Jesus Christ still calls us unto Himself.

Ps 16 Far too often our prayers are simply laundry lists of earthly desires. This psalm reminds us of our greater need to thank and praise God and make spiritual blessings a priority. Those who have the Lord have the source of all good things, even everlasting life.

David penitent before the prophet Nathan. The painter illustrates David's depth of sorrow by placing him in a hole in the ground (c 1442).

Ps 17 A tragic consequence of the world's fall into sin is that we often suffer through no particular fault of our own. God's ability to turn injustice into good is best illustrated by Jesus' innocent death on the cross. That horrible miscarriage of justice worked life and salvation for all people.

Ps 18 The deliverance God provided to David reminds us of our own victory over the grave, achieved for us by the risen Lord Jesus. Honor Him who is worthy of all praise.

Ps 19 We so often fail in the fulfillment of God's perfect Word. Marvelous as the heavens are, and eloquent as nature's testimony to the greatness of the Creator, God's forgiveness and grace as revealed in His Word are even more glorious.

Ps 20 Today, we are easily tempted to place our confidence in certain leaders and technological wonders rather than in God. This is little more than old-fashioned idolatry. Pray humbly for the authorities God has placed over you. He unfailingly answers and acts on our behalf in accord with His good and gracious will.

Ps 21 Part of our Christian responsibility, as this psalm reminds us, is to offer thanksgiving and petitions on behalf of our ruling authorities. The Scriptures testify throughout that God establishes various governments of the world not only to serve His people's earthly needs, but even to further the spread of the Gospel.

Ps 22 We may feel alone and forsaken by God. But, as this psalm foretells, God Himself came to be our Redeemer. While many human beings have shared these feelings, this psalm finds its greatest fulfillment in Jesus Christ, who spoke it from the cross (Mt 27:46).

Ps 23 The Good Shepherd Psalm. Our Good Shepherd lovingly provides everything that we need in this life. How wonderful that our Shepherd does not withhold His blessings from us, but still cares for these needs and more: He gives us His own Son!

Ps 24 The Lord is ruler and judge over all. He is powerful to purify His people. This is why worship begins with Confession of sins and Absolution: we seek the King of glory.

Ps 25 God promises to answer prayer, but we may be impatient or tempted to question His answers. Even when our faithfulness fails, God is faithful. He hears our prayers and truly acts for our good. In faith, we patiently wait for Him.

Ps 26 In worship, we sometimes focus on ourselves instead of on God. God calls us to repentance so that He may bless us and forgive us. Strengthened in faith, we respond by telling others of the great things He has done.

Ps 27 Human beings are prone to fearful responses. We worry about problems in this life, acting as if we face them alone. Yet God is our light and our salvation. Since He has redeemed us, we have nothing to fear. "If God is for us, who can be against us?" (Rm 8:31).

Ps 28 As sinners, we cannot save ourselves. We recognize our helplessness and need for God's grace. Our Savior comes, giving us His strength and protecting us from our enemies by paying the penalty of our sins.

Ps 29 We sinners might be destroyed by the power of His holy, powerful voice. Yet "the Word became flesh and dwelt among us" (Jn 1:14). God came to us in Jesus to speak His love and grace. In Baptism, flood and voice combine to cleanse us (this psalm was traditionally used at Baptisms).

Ps 30 Though you weep in the darkness of sorrow, cry out to the Lord. Take confidence in God's promise to comfort you and dry your tears (Rv 7:17).

Ps 31 Too often, we devote our lives to worthless things and despise the things of God. Yet as God delivered David from his sin and enemies, He delivers us as well. Christ paid for our idolatry and indifference. His Spirit gives us the gift of faith so that we trust in the only true God. Now we join David in rejoicing in God's great salvation.

Ps 32 The second penitential psalm. God calls us to confess our sins quickly with contrite hearts in order to receive absolution. Only He can relieve the troubled heart. "If we confess our sins, He is faithful and just to forgive us our sins and to cleanse us from all unrighteousness" (1Jn 1:9).

Ps 33 The Lord is our hope. Through His Word and Spirit, almighty God grants us faith in His Christ and His steadfast love. Thus, He gives us hope in our hearts and minds and certainty of His salvation in His Son, Jesus Christ. All praise, laud, and worship belong to our God, Father, Son, and Holy Spirit.

Ps 34 The Lord answers us according to His mercy and timing. Bless Him for your deliverance and redemption in Christ.

Ps 35 The Lord forbids that we accuse an innocent person, that he or she might be wrongly punished in body, property, or reputation (cf Pr 22:1). He bids us to err on the side of the Gospel in the case of our neighbor, unless guilt is clear (cf Mt 18:15–18). As we endeavor to treat our neighbors fairly and with mercy, our merciful Lord justifies us according to His righteousness.

Ps 36 The Lord teaches us to rely on His grace and protection in the midst of sin and wicked works of those who test our faith. We pray that He would answer, for His steadfast love is precious.

Ps 37 Our Lord does not abandon us, His children, to the schemes of the wicked, but on the Last Day He will fulfill our salvation and eternally deliver us from our enemies of sin, death, and the devil.

Ps 38 The third penitential psalm. Sin that is not confessed becomes a burden on our bodies and souls and causes great despair. Here we see that God's divine will is ultimately for our good as believers. "O Lord, my salvation!" (v 22) is the beautiful confession that through the healing balm of the Lord's mercy, there is deliverance and absolution.

Ps 39 In the midst of this life of vapors, phantoms, and threats, we often push God away. Despite this, He hears and answers our prayers. For we are His children through His Word and Holy Baptism, and He is our safe harbor and anchor of salvation and protection.

Ps 40 As saints and sinners, we are unable to keep God's Law perfectly, though He requires that we do so. By the power of His Word and Spirit and by faith, He instills in us new desires. Our Lord Christ kept the Law perfectly and died on our behalf that we might live with Him in His kingdom.

Ps 41 The Lord allows suffering in our lives, that our sins might be punished in the temporal sense, though we often cannot tell why we are suffering. Repent of your sins and pray for the Lord's mercy according to His Word. Though His discipline may never seem to end, we know His love and mercy still abound for us.

Book II, Pss 42–72; Called "Elohim Psalter," Pt. 1

Ps 42 We should desire God's presence, hear His Word in public worship, and receive the salvation that He gives in the Word. In the midst of our suffering and troubles, and against all appearances to the contrary, our Lord Jesus is our Savior and dwells among us in preaching and Communion to save us.

Ps 43 Take confidence in the Lord and His gifts. In an ungodly world, you are assailed by sin, death, and the devil. Yet God will comfort you by His life-sustaining Word.

Ps 44 As we undergo affliction, we are tempted to believe that God has deserted us or is unfairly punishing us. God is always "for you" despite everything you see, feel, or think to the contrary. God is not sleeping but helps, redeems, and loves (Rm 8:32).

Ps 45 The grand picture of this King and this marriage—illustrating Christ and His Bride, the Church—stands in contrast to the hard realities of suffering and death that we continue to see in the Church and endure in life.

Ps 46 We as individuals, and as the Church, experience many troubles in this life on account of the devil, the world, and our own sinful nature. Yet amid every crisis of body or soul, God is with us in His Son so that we may face every upheaval.

Ps 47 God's promised salvation is for all nations and has been carried out in time and history by His Son, who became man precisely to be "lifted up" on the cross and so "draw all people" to Himself (Jn 12:32).

Ps 48 What Mount Zion and temple worship were for ancient Israel, Christ's Church at worship is for us—the place where God mercifully dwells to save by His Word. We rightly "tell the next generation" (v 13) what He has done.

Ps 49 In a culture saturated with great personal and national prosperity, our own relative wealth and advantage easily become false "gods" to which we look for all good things. Christ alone can pay the ransom price for sin and overcome death for us by His death and resurrection.

Ps 50 We mask our sin by merely "going through the motions" of Christian worship (confessing, hearing, communing). Sin is not magically waved away; true repentance turns away from sin as the horror and poison that it is, and clings to the perfect, once for all sacrifice of God's Son.

Ps 51 The fourth penitential psalm. Sin is an inheritance, born in us, ever damaging us. None of our works can ever set us free from terror, despair, or death. However, God has blotted out even the worst of our sins—like David's adultery and murder—by Jesus' sacrifice.

The temple of Solomon from the Dura Europos Synagogue, second century AD.

Ps 52 Does God care? Yes! God has overruled the way of the wicked by sending His own Son to suffer and even die at the hand of evil people so that, by His death and resurrection, He might comfort us by His enduring love.

Ps 53 We are all foolishly corrupt, doing iniquity and not good. We all fall away from Him. The salvation that comes for us out of Zion is Jesus, who took our foolishness—our iniquity and corruption—and saved us by the seeming foolishness of His cross (1Co 1:18–25).

Ps 54 In times of sudden testing, we easily become disillusioned and wonder if God has abandoned us. However, in every trouble, God is our sure helper. The deliverance He provides in Christ, who Himself knew persecution unto death, makes us triumphant despite every appearance to the contrary.

Ps 55 When troubles press hard, we may find it easy to give in to our feelings and give up on God. The psalmist's steadfastness challenges us to trust in God's mercy. Our Lord Jesus Christ, the Righteous One, faced a city full of violence and plots against His life. Betrayed by Judas, He endured the cross, where He turned to the Father with confidence and gave His life as the ransom price for ours.

Ps 56 When we face trials, we may be tempted to worry about our own welfare or feel like giving up in hopelessness. Instead, we can remember that our problems are nothing new. Through these experiences, God strengthens our faith and draws us closer to Jesus Christ, our Savior.

Ps 57 We often pray with uncertainty and hesitation, doubting God's love and interest in our lives. Trusting in Jesus, we have confidence that God listens to us as a loving father listens to his beloved children.

Ps 58 When you find yourself in a position of power over someone, treat that person as one precious to God, purchased by the blood of Christ. Ultimate justice was served on the cross (condemnation of sin) and at the empty tomb (public vindication of Jesus as our Savior).

Ps 59 Whatever He wills for us is best, even if we don't understand it at the time. The world and all that is in it is passing away. Empires come and go. Only God and His promise of salvation in Jesus Christ stand firm, stand fast, and stand forever.

Ps 60 God disciplines those He loves, and He tests His people to build their faith and strengthen the relationship of grace. Whether you experience victory or defeat, persist in prayer and service to your Lord. In His care, you "shall do valiantly" (v 12).

Ps 61 God often uses difficult times to strengthen our faith and redefine our priorities. If we have drifted away from the Lord, He can use a reversal of fortune in our earthly circumstance to make us aware of our precarious spiritual situation and bring us back to Him. David's prayer that the King would reign forever (v 7) is ultimately fulfilled in Christ Jesus, who embodies God's steadfast love.

Ps 62 Even when our lives fall apart, our center and foundation hold firm: Nothing can separate us from the love of God in Christ Jesus our Lord (Rm 8:38–39).

Ps 63 When we are in the "wilderness" and God seems distant, we may find ourselves tempted to focus on our troubles rather than turning to God in faith and confidence. David shows us the way to handle disaster and doubt: meditate on the Lord (cf Php 4:4–7). Faith looks beyond the circumstances to the cross of Christ and sees God's love, holding fast to His promises to His children.

Ps 64 When false rumors fly and your reputation suffers, seek divine justice. Turn to the Lord and put the situation in His hands. Do not try to "get even," but leave the outcome to God. Jesus also endured all kinds of plots and slander (Mk 15, esp vv 29–32). He knows how to justify you.

Ps 65 We have nothing except what God gives us, and the appropriate response to such amazing generosity, both spiritual and physical, is praise. David begins the list of gifts with the most important, the forgiveness of sins and the gift of faith.

Ps 66 Hardships may tempt us to abandon the faith, yet knowing that the Lord uses hardship to test our faith will strengthen us to hold on to our faith. The Lord's deeds of salvation assure His people that He will make all things, even hardships, work out for their ultimate good (Rm 8:28–29).

Ps 67 There is only one way of blessing, which Israel's God provided in the work of His Son, Jesus Christ. Thus, we believe in God's salvation through Christ and proclaim it to all the world.

Ps 68 The Lord is powerful to rebuke our enemies and He abounds in grace. We therefore turn to the Lord and His Word in faith, and we give Him praise.

Ps 69 Though afflicted, we still confess our sins before God. We also turn to Him in faith for deliverance from those who persecute us, asking for His strength and deliverance, lest we fail to remain faithful to Him.

Ps 70 With the psalmist, we acknowledge our spiritual poverty before God. Part of that acknowledgment is being watchful, lest through pride or faithlessness we ourselves turn away from Him. He will provide deliverance—if not in this life, then certainly in the life to come.

Ps 71 Truths of the faith learned in childhood are of no advantage if they are forsaken later in life. The Lord is faithful in His righteous, saving deeds. They are always the source of our eternal life. Cling to these in faith and faithfully give witness and praise.

Ps 72 Pray for your leaders. Like the Davidic kings, we often fail to live as we should. Yet our hope is in David's Son and Lord, Jesus Christ, who has brought us eternal salvation.

Book III, Pss 73–89; Called "Elohim Psalter," Pt. 2

Ps 73 Being troubled by doubt and envy does not mean that we have lost our faith. We are called to struggle against them. We find strength to do so in the certainty of the final outcome of God's promises.

Ps 74 When calamity strikes, we ought to see God calling us to repentance in it (Lk 13:1–5). In repentance, we flee to God for mercy, not because of anything in us but by what He Himself has done for our redemption.

Ps 75 God judges the wicked and delivers the believer according to His timetable, not ours. His seeming delay in this should not cause us to lose heart but to continue in repentance and faith. As He has fulfilled all His promises in the past, so He will act in both judgment and salvation.

Trumpets on Israelite coins produced during the Bar Kokhba Revolt.

Ps 76 We must tremble in fear before God's judgment over our sins. Yet we also trust in and rejoice in His mighty deeds for our salvation, by which He has delivered us from those who would seek our eternal, spiritual harm (Col 2:15).

Ps 77 Self-confidence and personal efforts may blind us to our ultimate source of strength. As we focus on the Gospel, the message of God's mighty deeds for our redemption, He will strengthen our faith.

Ps 78 God's dealings with Israel point to His acts toward us today. Israel's history teaches us to repent of our own lack of faith. Also, God's saving deeds in Israel's history, especially in His acts toward and through David, point us to what Christ has done so that we may have God's ongoing salvation.

Ps 79 Originally written as a lament over Babylon's destruction of Israel, this psalm remains applicable to all Christians who suffer hardship and struggle at the hands of unbelievers. Christians throughout the world become the taunt of the unbelievers around them as they are either explicitly derided or condescendingly treated because of their faith and trust in God. This psalm is well-prayed by such sufferers, as it assures us that God is reliable and His deliverance is trustworthy.

Ps 80 In what ways have we suffered as a result of our turning away? God's pattern of salvation through history provides reliable assurances: God has saved us before; He shall yet save again!

Ps 81 God loves to speak to His people! He especially loves to tell you repeatedly of His great love for you, shown to you in the death and resurrection of His Son. With His Word God feeds His people (v 16), nourishing them with eternal life.

Ps 82 Justice in this world is hard to come by. Your heavenly Father has already judged you impartially by laying all of your sins upon Jesus. This provides you with salvation and endurance, even in the face of worldly injustice.

Ps 83 God's children do not stop praying, even when He appears to keep silent. God is faithful. He answers your prayers in His time and according to His good pleasure, yet always acting for your benefit and eternal life (Rm 8:28).

Ps 84 Many homebound Christians long for worship in God's house. Meanwhile, many other Christians, especially those in the height of their strength, neglect the worship of the Lord to their own detriment. God gives strength to His people (vv 5–7) through the hearing of His Word.

Ps 85 Christians may suffer from deep fears and insecurities. Rightly heeded, these fears chase us to Jesus. When God forgave your iniquity and covered your sin (v 2) through the death and resurrection of Jesus Christ, He destroyed your enemies of sin, death, and hell.

Ps 86 Rather than feeling overwhelmed by the obstacles that confront us (v 14), keep the eyes of your faith focused upon the Lord, for He alone is God (v 10). Because of the Lord's steadfast love, He cannot overlook or neglect His children.

Ps 87 Your true identity before God is not rooted in your nationality, your language, your family ties, your wealth, or any other earthly thing. God claims you to be His own in Baptism, through which you become His own child (vv 5–6), no matter who you are or from where you came (v 4).

Ps 88 Surely the loneliness spoken of here has been felt by many suffering Christians! Yet even in sorrow and suffering, we may confess the Lord to be the "God of [our] salvation" (v 1).

Ps 89 God's steadfast love of old (v 49) and His faithfulness (vv 2, 24) are shown most clearly in Christ, whose death and resurrection provide the remedy for all troubles (v 48).

Book IV, Pss 90–106

Ps 90 How quickly life flies by: grass withering, leaves falling and blowing away. Even more heartbreaking is to stand by a casket and stare at a lifeless body or to look in a mirror and see age steal youth and energy. Yet in spring the flowers bloom and the grass turns green. The grave is empty on Easter morning. Jesus has risen!

Ps 91 How encouraging it is to know of God's protection. Our security comes from His promises kept. Jesus trampled Satan once and for all when He gloriously rose from the dead. We walk in victory even during dangerous times because He is with us and will not let us be separated from His love.

Ps 92 In worship, you receive the strength of God's steadfast love and faithfulness. No doubt there are days you wonder if going to worship is worth the effort. But focus on what God has done for you in Jesus, who is faithful to His promises.

Ps 93 A storm may still crash into a church. The members may come back to see destruction, not beauty. Does the Lord reign? Indeed, He does. By His resurrection, He rules over our lives now and forever.

Ps 94 We pray that all will see the glory of God's justice in Jesus on the cross, turn from their wicked ways, and join with us in the life of righteousness, which includes caring for and protecting widows, orphans, and others who are helpless and oppressed.

Ps 95 Some days we struggle to come into God's presence with exuberance and humility. He is our Creator, who has formed and protected us by His strong hands. And wonderfully more—He is our Good Shepherd, who has made us the sheep of His loving hand.

Ps 96 Too many people see faith in God as a relic of the past with little to say about life today. People turn away from the true God in idolatrous pursuits. Do we give up? No. First, sing to the Lord! Join with others in worshiping the splendor and majesty of the Creator. Then, speak of His salvation in Jesus day after day.

Ps 97 The cross is where God's justice is served and His anger appeased on our behalf. The empty tomb is the assurance that we are preserved for life everlasting. We rejoice because His judgment is that we are His saints, the upright in heart, through faith.

Ps 98 The defeats of life are discouraging. Thanks be to God that He is victorious for us! Sin and death are conquered. Satan's head is crushed. Eternally, we are God's children. All creation is waiting for that final day of redemption, for the Lord's victory is an empty tomb on Easter morning.

Ps 99 Despite the psalmist's confidence that God in all His holiness reigns, we see an ordinary world ruled by people who are too often distant from God's ways and words. Yet the holy Savior is present just as He was in the Most Holy Place when we, His people, gather together to praise His holy name.

Ps 100 How unfortunate when we fail to make a joyful noise to the Lord. Yet even so, we know that He is good. He gave His Good Shepherd, Jesus, to make Good Friday and every day a time to offer Him our thanks.

Ps 101 The Church has not always been led by people of integrity. But Jesus was blameless, a man of perfect integrity. He comes to us with His royal and loyal love, shown perfectly on the cross. He brings us into the one "nation" made blameless in Christ's blood—the Church.

Ps 102 The fifth penitential psalm. When you lament, turn your attention to God's answer to these prayers: Jesus Christ. He stepped into our world and took on our groans and death, restoring confident hope at the appointed time on Easter morning. In Him we find the face of God, our Savior.

Ps 103 How many times do we need God's forgiveness? It's impossible to count. Day after day, our transgressions should bring His anger. But over and over again, He removes our iniquities. Where are they sent? To the cross, where Jesus takes the anger. Therefore, we bless the Lord.

Ps 104 More and more, we hear about nature with no mention of the Creator. Yet God is indeed Creator of all. He continues to care for His world. Even death cannot compare to God's power, as a stone obeyed His command and rolled away from the tomb on Easter morning.

Ps 105 All God's promises find their fulfillment in Jesus, who hung on the cross and then ushered in a new era by rising from the grave. Gathered together by Jesus as Abraham's true descendants, we now belong to the Church, which knows no geographical boundaries.

Ps 106 As we struggle with temptation (Gal 5:17), we can be sure that God is good. He will remain faithful (2Tm 2:13), granting us true repentance and new life in Christ.

Book V, Pss 107–150

Ps 107 You are the redeemed of the Lord. In Jesus God has restored the peace we long for. Our sins are forgiven, and where there is forgiveness of sins, there is life and every blessing. Speak up and tell others it is so.

Ps 108 From time to time, old defeats come back to haunt us. Perhaps a future challenge reminds us of a past failure. At times like this, we remember that God, who delivered us in the past, is with us in the present and the future.

Ps 109 The wicked will not always prevail. As we look to God for salvation, we know His justice will prevail upon our enemies who remain in sin. He declares us justified and His dear children through Jesus.

Ps 110 Chiefs and kings may exalt themselves. But in the Lord Jesus, the divine and the human become one in order to destroy the enemies of God and of His creation. As He raised His head at the resurrection, so He raises us to confident hope.

Hallel Psalms, Pss 111–118

Ps 111 As the psalmist records the Lord's deeds in his life, make a list of such blessings in your own life as a way to celebrate the Lord's works of creation, redemption, and sanctification.

Ps 112 The psalm describes the blessings for the righteous. Ask the Lord for a firm heart to trust in Him, subduing your selfish nature and reveling in His goodness.

Ps 113 As Hannah and Mary offered their praises to the Lord, so lift up your voice in praise. Celebrate the truth that He is the only God and none can compare with Him.

Ps 114 Tremble before the Lord as you recall your sin and confess it. Yet stand firm in his blessings of redemption, as described in the exodus and the conquest of Canaan.

Ps 115 Surrender every idolatrous thought as you would cast aside the false gods of the nations. Bless the Lord, who remembers you now and forevermore.

Ps 116 Bend the knees of your heart in sincere prayer, for the humble will not stumble and fall as do the liars. Confess Him with a true heart even as He confesses your name before the angels in heaven.

Ps 117 If God's love had to be merited, there would be no reason to praise Him. His love would also be severely limited. But because His love is His alone to give, it is great, and it reaches to people of all nations.

Ps 118 Luther's favorite psalm. We may sometimes wonder, "Where is the steadfast love of God?" Where is that "good action" of God for His people? He revealed His steadfast love in humble Israel, in the Child of the Virgin Mary. He veiled His greatest gift in what is least among people so that His gift might be received by all.

Ps 119 The Great Psalm of the Word. God's Word is our beloved guide to life. It reveals God's trustworthy promises and eternal mercy. The psalm's length presents

Assyrian playing a flute (645 BC).

God's Word like a diamond with 22 facets, each displaying a distinct light. By exhausting every letter of the alphabet, the psalmist demonstrates the breadth of the Word and his own boundless dedication to it. The Gospel radiates through the psalm as the psalmist describes God's promises, which save His people (cf vv 41, 58). God's Word is loved because of its message of steadfast love (cf vv 76, 88, 159). God is merciful, and this mercy brings life (cf v 156).

Songs of Ascents, Pss 120–134

Ps 120 Prayer is a refuge for those who are distressed. Rather than mourn as one dwells with the wicked, pray for them and for the Lord's deliverance.

Ps 121 We are pilgrims on a journey to our heavenly home (Php 3:20–21). This psalm reminds us to focus on the Lord, who oversees our journey. Allow nothing in creation to frighten you. Our God is eternally alert and goes above and before us.

Ps 122 Like David, we are welcomed to the Lord's house and can rejoice at the invitation. We are drawn to a heavenly Jerusalem (Heb 12:22). At the throne of Christ, the eternal Son of David, we find a place of peace (Rm 5:1; 8:1).

Ps 123 The Lord's mercy and justice will reach you in His time. Continue to look to Him and reach out to Him for strength.

Ps 124 We need this psalm's reminder that our strength and safety come only by God's hand. We are in danger from flood and snare, from the overwhelming and the enticing. Yet our help is in His name.

Ps 125 Ask the Lord to make you upright in heart and to surround you with His care and peace.

Ps 126 May God give us the expectation that times of sudden refreshing will come from Him. Perhaps now you are in a time of sowing with bitter tears; do not despair of His grace. Trust in His power to do the unimaginable through overflowing kindness.

Ps 127 Our houses and the families within them are God's gifts. However, our walls are fragile and our rooms are empty without His blessing. The Lord leads us to value His gifts and to commit them to His watchful care. He will preserve us unto life everlasting.

Ps 128 May God grant us the blessings of a life lived under the fear and respect of God. May we see our families as the kindness of God. In our relationships with our children and our grandchildren, God shows His power and mercy.

Ps 129 We may feel some part of the afflictions of this psalm. Yet, the afflictions shall not prevail! The blessings of the Lord are with us through Christ.

Ps 130 The sixth penitential psalm. In honesty, we must admit the depths of our sinfulness. When we are overwhelmed, God hears our pleas for mercy. He does not remember our sins, but rather grants us free forgiveness through the work of Christ, who gives us hope. Christ plunges into our depths to raise us in salvation.

Ps 131 Pray today for a childlike faith that simply trusts God's promises, hope, and peace.

Ps 132 Our sins would make us God's enemies. And yet, God dwells with us and clothes us with His righteousness and salvation. In David's Son, Jesus Christ, the incarnate God tabernacles with His people. God swore an oath to work this salvation, and, like David, we can trust His promises.

Ps 133 Our families, our communities, and our churches often experience discord, strife, and disunity. Yet Christ's prayer is that we may be one (Jn 17:11). He bestows that unity through the Holy Spirit in the refreshing waters of Baptism.

Ps 134 The night is an emblem of darkness and sorrow. Yet Christ is present in the darkness. He gives His blessing from the sacrificial mountain in Jerusalem by the continual ministry of the Church through Word and Sacrament.

Ps 135 When we know God only through His creation—the lightning and the storm—He can be terrifying. He punishes sin, as He did with Pharaoh, the Canaanite kings, and worshipers of false gods. Yet God has compassion on His people, those whom He has chosen and claims as His own.

Ps 136 The psalm is all about God's action, not ours. It invites us to join our praises to those of all creation as the redeemed praise Him for His mighty deeds.

Ps 137 We are exiles in the new Babylon—the world system with its abominations and its beast (Rv 18)—and must endure its temptations and tribulations. Yet we can also look for our deliverance, clinging to God's promises of redemption delivered by one wholly innocent: Jesus, God's own Child.

Ps 138 David's victories prefigure the victories of David's Son, Jesus Christ, and the victories of those who have been baptized into Him. Salvation is not only for David or for the Israelites but for all nations who will come to faith through God's Word.

Ps 139 This psalm gives a clear answer to today's controversy about the value of human life and when life begins, clearly condemning abortion and other assaults on developing children. And yet, this psalm, above all, proclaims God's love, which He expresses in His personal care and involvement in all of His creation.

Ps 140 Those who are persecuted for righteousness' sake are bearing the cross. Jesus too—the Son of David prefigured in this psalm—endured the vicious words and violent actions of "evil men" (v 1; Mt 26:57–68; 27:32–44). In Christ, we receive our vindication, our forgiveness, and assurance.

Ps 141 God, through the Office of the Ministry and other authorities, rebukes us for our sins. These are all to bring us to repentance. The "evening sacrifice" (v 2) of Christ's final atonement for sin makes our prayers acceptable before God. In Him, we will "pass by" (v 10) the snares of the wicked.

Ps 142 Our sins isolate us from others. We are shut out of the community of the righteous. These words of David are even more true of David's Son, Jesus Christ. He was persecuted, deserted, imprisoned, and tormented.

At His burial, He was imprisoned in a cave. But His Father raised Him to live in the company of those made righteous through His blood.

Ps 143 The seventh penitential psalm. Confess to the Lord that you are sinful and unclean. Ask Him to remove every shred of your pride and replace it with the robe of Christ's righteousness.

Judean warriors defending a tower at Lachish.

Ps 144 The Warrior Psalm. In our sins—such as our propensity for lying and swearing falsely—we are God's enemies. And yet, God shows us His favor, despite our insignificance, particularly through the Son of Man, the Son of David, Jesus Christ. The Church has historically seen this psalm as foreshadowing Christ, our true King.

Ps 145 The Mission Psalm. The Lord draws near to us in Christ, our King. His Word resounds from generation to generation, bringing the kingdom of God to all the world and to us. Boldly proclaim the Gospel!

Hallelujah Psalms, Pss 146–150

Ps 146 Your Lord is Christ, the Son of Man in whom there is salvation, who on earth fed the hungry, healed the blind, and ministered to everyone in need. You were buried with Him in Baptism so you can share His new life and claim all of these promises.

Ps 147 We need not depend on our strength, but we can "hope in His steadfast love" (v 11). The same Word that called the universe into existence and still governs its every detail is manifest in the Holy Scriptures and proclaimed in the Church for our salvation.

Ps 148 Our insensibility to God's goodness and glory is a sign of how far we have fallen. In all of His manifold creation, God has "raised up a horn for His people" (v 14). Through Christ, God has gathered together His own people into the Church, declaring them to be His saints and dwelling near them.

Ps 149 Salvation is a gift, a kind of clothing, and the pleasure the Lord takes in His people is not on account of their works. Rejoice in your King, who was bound and suffered the punishment due to the nations. We have fellowship with Him in the Church.

Ps 150 Of the many reasons to praise God, for us the most joyous are "His mighty deeds" (v 2) by which He has redeemed us in Christ and brought us to faith.

CANONICITY

From a human perspective, the principles of selection that led to the Psalter are never specified. We probably do well to think of the book as we do our best hymnbooks today. Among the factors would be: applicability to "all sorts and conditions of men," suitability for public worship, beauty and poetic distinction, theological faithfulness, and so on. Like the canonical process in general, the selections were a product of the Spirit's guidance over a considerable period (this to be distinguished, of course, from the inspiration of the songs to begin with).

The examples of doublets in the Psalter and repetition of passages in the Books of History show how the psalms built upon one another. They stemmed from practices at the tabernacle, temple, and events in the life of Israel. The third major division of the Hebrew Bible, the Writings (Megilloth), began with the Psalms. In fact, Psalms often stood as a title for the Writings (e.g., Lk 24:44). The New Testament confirms their authority among Jews and Christians, who received the Psalter without question.

Hula valley flowers, north of the Sea of Galilee. The psalms often describe creation praising its Maker.

LUTHERAN THEOLOGIANS ON PSALMS

Luther

"Many of the holy fathers prized and praised the Psalter above all the other books of the Scripture. To be sure, the work itself gives praise enough to its author; nevertheless we must give evidence of our own praise and thanks.

"Over the years a great many legends of the saints, . . . books of examples, and histories have been circulated . . . [and] the Psalter has been neglected. It has lain in such obscurity that not one psalm was rightly understood. Still it gave off such a fine and precious fragrance that all pious hearts felt the devotion and power in the unknown words and for this reason loved the book.

"I hold, however, that no finer book of examples or of the legends of the saints has ever come, or can come, to earth than the Psalter. If one were to wish that from all the examples, legends, and histories, the best should be collected and brought together and put in the best form, the result would have to be the present Psalter. For here we find not only what one or two saints have done, but what he has done who is the very head of all saints. We also find what all the saints still do, such as the attitude they take toward God, toward friends and enemies, and the way they conduct themselves amid all dangers and sufferings. Beyond that there are contained here all sorts of divine and wholesome teachings and commandments.

"The Psalter ought to be a precious and beloved book, if for no other reason than this: it promises Christ's death and resurrection so clearly—and pictures his kingdom and the condition and nature of all Christendom—that it might well be called a little Bible. In it is comprehended most beautifully and briefly everything that is in the entire Bible. It is really a fine enchiridion or handbook. In fact, I have a notion that the Holy Spirit wanted to take the trouble himself to compile a short Bible and book of examples of all Christendom or all saints, so that anyone who could not read the whole Bible would here have anyway almost an entire summary of it, comprised in one little book.

"[The Words of the Saints.] Beyond all that, the Psalter has this noble virtue and quality. Other books make much ado about the works of the saints, but say very little about their words. The Psalter is a gem in this respect. It gives forth so sweet a fragrance when one reads it because it relates not only the works of the saints, but also their words, how they spoke with God and prayed, and still speak and pray. Compared to the Psalter, the other legends and examples present to us nothing but mere silent saints; the Psalter, however, pictures for us real, living, active saints.

"Compared to a speaking man, a silent one is simply to be regarded as a half-dead man; and there is no mightier or nobler work of man than speech. For it is by speech, more than by his shape or by any other work, that man is most distinguished from other animals. By the carver's art even a block of wood can have the shape of a man; and an animal can see, hear, smell, sing, walk, stand, eat, drink, fast, thirst—and suffer from hunger, frost, and a hard bed—as well as a man.

"[The Hearts of the Saints.] Moreover the Psalter does more than this. It presents to us not the simple, ordinary speech of the saints, but the best of their language, that which they used when they talked with God himself in great earnestness and on the most important matters. Thus the Psalter lays before us not only their words instead of their deeds, but their very hearts and the inmost treasure of their souls, so we can look down to the foundation and source of their words and deeds. We can look into their hearts and see what kind of thoughts they had, how their hearts were disposed, and how they acted in all kinds of situations, in danger and in need. The legends and examples, which speak only of the deeds and miracles of the saints, do not and cannot do this, for I cannot know how a man's heart is, even though I see or hear of many great deeds that he does. And just as I would rather hear what a saint says than see the deeds he does, so I would far rather see his heart, and the treasure in his soul, than hear his words. And this the Psalter gives us most abundantly concerning the saints, so that we can be certain of how their hearts were toward God and of the words they spoke to God and every man. . . .

"What is the greatest thing in the Psalter but this earnest speaking amid these storm winds of every kind? Where does one find finer words of joy than in the psalms of praise and thanksgiving? There you look into the hearts of all the saints, as into fair and pleasant gardens, yes, as into heaven itself. There you see what fine and pleasant flowers of the heart spring up from all sorts of fair and happy thoughts toward God, because of his blessings. On the other hand, where do you find deeper, more sorrowful, more pitiful words of sadness than in the psalms of lamentation? There again you look into the hearts of all the saints, as into death, yes, as into hell itself. How gloomy and dark it is there, with all kinds of troubled forebodings about the wrath of God! So, too, when they speak of fear and hope, they use such words that no painter could so depict for you fear or hope, and no Cicero or other orator so portray them.

"And that they speak these words to God and with God, this, I repeat, is the best thing of all. This gives the words double earnestness and life. For when men speak with men about these matters, what they say does not come so powerfully from the heart; it does not burn and live, is not so urgent. Hence it is that the Psalter is the book of all saints; and everyone, in whatever situation he may be, finds in that situation psalms and words that fit his ease, that suit him as if they were put there just for his sake, so that he could not put it better himself, or find or wish for anything better.

"[The Communion of Saints.] This also serves well another purpose. When these words please a man and fit his case, he becomes sure that he is in the communion of saints, and that it has gone with all the saints as it goes with him, since they all sing with him one little song. It is especially so if he can speak these words to God, as they have done; this can only be done in faith, for the words [of the saints] have no flavor to a godless man.

"Finally there is in the Psalter security and a well-tried guide, so that in it one can follow all the saints without peril. The other examples and legends of the silent saints present works that one is unable to imitate; they present even more works which it is dangerous to imitate, works which usually start sects and divisions, and lead and tear men away from the communion of saints. But the Psalter holds you to the communion of saints and away from the sects. For it teaches you in joy, fear, hope, and sorrow to think and speak as all the saints have thought and spoken.

"In a word, if you would see the holy Christian Church painted in living color and shape, comprehended in one little picture, then take up the Psalter. There you have a fine, bright, pure mirror that will show you what Christendom is. Indeed you will find in it also yourself and the true ['Know yourself'], as well as God himself and all creatures. . . .

"To this may God the Father of all grace and mercy help us, through Jesus Christ our Lord, to whom be praise and thanks, honor and glory, for this German Psalter and for all his innumerable and unspeakable blessings to all eternity. Amen, Amen." (AE 35:253–57)

"[Types of Psalms.] The entire Psalter may be treated in a fivefold fashion, that is, we may divide it into five groups. First, some psalms *prophesy*. They speak, for example, of Christ and the church or what will happen to the saints. This class includes all the psalms that contain promises and warnings—promises for the godly and warnings for the ungodly. Second, there are psalms of *instruction*, which teach us what we should do and what we should avoid, in accordance with the law of God. This class includes all the psalms that condemn human doctrines and praise the Word of God. Third, there are psalms of *comfort*, which strengthen and comfort the saints in their troubles and sorrows but rebuke and terrify the tyrants. This class includes all the psalms that comfort, exhort, stimulate endurance, or rebuke the tyrants. Fourth are the psalms of *prayer*, in which we call on God, praying in all kinds of distress. To this class belong all the psalms that lament or mourn or cry out against our foes. Fifth, are the psalms of *thanks*, in which God is praised and glorified for all his blessings and help. This class includes all the psalms that praise God for his works. These are the psalms of the first rank, and for their sake the Psalter was created; therefore it is called in Hebrew *Sefer Tehillim*, that is, a praise book or book of thanksgiving.

"Now, we should understand that the Psalms, with all their verses, cannot always be classified so precisely and exactly into these groups. At times one psalm might contain two, three, or even all five classifications, so that one psalm may belong in all five divisions, with prophecy, instruction, comfort, prayer, and thanksgiving lying next to one another. However, this is the intention, that the reader may understand that the Psalter deals with these five topics. The classifications are a help, so that we might more easily understand the Psalter, become adapted to it, and also be able to learn and keep it." (Bruce A. Cameron, trans. *Psalms with Introduction by Martin Luther* [St. Louis: Concordia, 1993], pp 6–7)

For more of Luther's insights on this book, see *Lectures on the Psalms I, II* and *Selected Psalms I, II,* and *III* (AE 10–14) and *Exhortation of Psalm 127* (AE 45:311–37).

Gerhard

"The teachers of the early Church with unanimous agreement accepted this book as canonical and honored it with great praises. Athanasius (Epistle *ad Marcellin.*) calls it 'the epitome of all Scripture.' Basil (on Psalm 1) calls it 'a compendium of all theology, the common medical office of souls, the common repository of good teachings, useful to everyone according to his will.' Augustine calls it 'the teacher of little children, the adornment of youth, the comfort of old age, the register and summary of every page of theology.' Luther calls it 'the little Bible and the epitome of the Old Testament.' Elsewhere, he wrote this brief poem on the dignity and usefulness of the Psalter:

> What the sun is in the heaven, I think
>
> In all the sacred writings are the Psalms of David, king.
>
> The sun is leader of the planets, repeller of the dark.
>
> It nurtures everything with heavenly light and heat.
>
> Thus the strings of David drive darkness from the mind
>
> And with their living message bring love to souls . . . .[5]

"The Psalter, then, is a golden necklace, woven and composed of three things: (1) of the gold of doctrine and instruction, (2) of the pearls of comfort, (3) and of the jewels of prayer.

"The Psalter is: (I) *The epitome and compendium of all Holy Scripture,* which is clear: (1) from the scope and goal of Scripture, which is Christ, and (2) from the distribution of Scripture into Law and Gospel—both are treated in the Psalter.

---

5   *Quod sol in coelo est, inter tot biblica scripta / Davidis psalmos regis id esse reor. / Sol planetarum ductor caligine pulsa / Omnia coelesti luce, calore fovet. / Sic mentis tenebras pellunt Davidica plectra / Atque animas vivis alloquiis amant etc.*

"(II) *The catalog and summary of theological commonplaces.* In this respect we compare it with a piece of jewelry in which are: (1) the gold of comfort in the truth of doctrine; (2) the silver of proof against the errors of heretics; (3) the gems of admonition to virtues—the love of God, thanksgiving, and a love for one's neighbor; (4) the pearls of consolation. Babylas, from Ps. 116[:7]: 'Return, O my soul, to your rest.'

"(III) *A repository of illustrations.* In this respect it is compared with a highly polished mirror. Set forth in it are: (1) An example of the Church Militant, which is subject to the cross. (2) The example of true repentance. Origen, from Ps. 50[:16]: 'To the wicked, God said . . . .' Mauritius, from Ps. 119[:137]: 'Righteous are You, O Lord.' Bernard, from Ps. 51[:17]: 'I have lived recklessly. I have nothing to return to the Lord except that He does not despise a contrite heart.' (3) A mirror of faith and constancy.

"(IV) It is *a manual and handbook.*

"The Psalter is: (1) A theater of the works of God, for the things for which we must watch are exhibited within it. (2) A rich meadow filled with roses, where we gaze at the many lovely flowers. (3) A paradise that has not merely the bare fragrance of the flowers but also the fruits. (4) A broad sea in which lie precious pearls that only those can find who endure its tempestuous storms. (5) The school of heaven in which we speak with God, our teacher. (6) The compendium of the entire Scripture. (7) A mirror of divine grace that reflects the pleasant face of our kind Father. (8) A most careful anatomy of our soul that indicates all the states and affections of the soul and the remedies for those affections." (ThC E1 § 144)

Late Bronze Age gold rosette from the Canaanite level of Tel Akko, northern Israel.

QUESTIONS PEOPLE ASK ABOUT PSALMS

Psalm Superscriptions

The Middle Ages and even the Reformation attached mystical significance to the psalm superscriptions, e.g., "The Sheminith" (literally, "the eighth") of Ps 6, and "The Doe of the Dawn" of Ps 22. At the other extreme, much modern scholarship has tended to discount their antiquity or value (or both) almost entirely. A consistent—if extreme—example was offered by the New English Bible, which did not even deign to include them in its translation. Most versions continue simply to transliterate many of the superscriptions because translations and interpretations of them in modern times continue to vary. Extreme skepticism about their antiquity is unwarranted, however, not only because we find comparable elements in Sumerian, Akkadian, and Ugaritic compositions, but also because of the weight that the New Testament places on some of them (e.g., references to David in Mk 12:35–37; Ac 2:29–36).

The Hebrew texts are ancient but were not necessarily written with the psalms they describe. The ancient versions (especially Septuagint and Peshitta) frequently vary significantly from the Hebrew textual tradition. The Masoretic Hebrew text contains some 34 "orphan" psalms (as those lacking superscriptions are sometimes known), while the LXX has only two orphans and the Peshitta differs from both. The variations are not enough that one has cause to be suspicious of the antiquity and reliability of all the superscriptions, but there are enough differences so that it is apparent that the tradition varied widely.

Types of Superscriptions

There are many types of superscriptions. Some simply describe the type of composition, such as a song (*shir*), psalm (*mizmor*, originally implying stringed accompaniment), praise (*tehillah*), and prayer (*tephillah*). Perhaps of the same type, but more technical (and certainly more obscure) are *maskil* (presumably related to the wisdom root meaning "teach; be prudent/successful"); *miktam* (Pss 16; 56–60) and *shiggaion* (Ps 7; Hab 3; cf Akkadian *shegu*—"lamentation").

Other terms appear to be the names of melodies or modes according to which the psalms were to be chanted. The *Sheminith* ("eighth") of Ps 6 would appear to belong here, as also *Lilies* (sometimes in various combinations; Pss 45, 69, 80); "The Dove on Far-off Terebinths" (Ps 56); and especially "The Doe of the Dawn" of Ps 22. If these explanations are at all correct, they are comparable to the names of tunes appearing in most modern hymnals, which may be just as enigmatic (e.g., titles "Toplady" and "Redhead #77," which are common settings for "Rock of Ages").

Some of the superscriptions are almost certainly musical directions, roughly comparable to our "allegro," "forte," etc. This would seem to be the import of *neginoth* in Pss 4; 6; 54; 55; 61; 67; 76, apparently specifying accompaniment with stringed instruments. Two of the most common of the superscriptions are possible music directions. Fifty-five times (mostly in the first three books) we meet Hbr *lammenatseach*. The Chronicler applies the term to various overseers or superintendents of temple construction, but also to the musical director or "choirmaster," and hence its nearly universal rendition in English. Rather curiously, the

Doves and other creatures somehow inspired the music of psalmists, according to some superscriptions. This is a turtledove.

Septuagint and Targum relate the word to one of the biblical expressions for "duration, eternity" (translated in Gk, *eis to telos*). Whether they understood that in some end-of-the-world sense, or simply took it to mean something like "full rendering" is not clear. Some Akkadian and Egyptian hymns end with a notation, "to the end," but whether that influenced later tradition, and, if so, whether it provides any clue to the original meaning of the Hebrew phrase is also unknown.

"Selah" is surely the most (in)famous of the superscription notes in the Psalter. It occurs 71 times in 39 psalms, mostly in Books I–III, plus three occurrences in Hab 3. While its total omission (as in the New English Bible) is scarcely justifiable, it is probably advisable to pass over it in public recitation of the psalms, as suggested in some editions. In grammatical form, the best explanation appears to be an imperative of the verb "to lift up, exalt." Thus the word is commonly taken to signal something like an increase in the volume of either the choir or of the musical accompaniment. Presumably, the Septuagint's *diapsalma* is related to this understanding; it implies an interlude or refrain of some sort, and since Selah seems generally to occur at the close of a strophe, modern scholars often agree.

In addition to the number of superscriptions apparently having musical reference, a number of others plainly specify the liturgical occasion for their use in temple worship. Most of these superscriptions have reference to the psalms accompanying the daily morning and evening sacrifices in the temple (the *tamid*)—in some cases conceivably even rooting in tabernacle services before the time of David. Psalm 92 is prescribed for the Sabbath; similar rubrics for other days of the week are found only in the versions, but that does not prove their lateness (Ps 24 for Sunday, 93 for Wednesday, and 81 for Thursday). Psalm 30 is characterized as "a song at the dedication of the temple," but, tantalizingly, we are not told which temple (Solomon's of the tenth century or Zerubbabel's of the sixth).

Do Good Works Save Us?

Psalm 7:8 urges: "The LORD judges the peoples; judge me, O LORD, according to my righteousness and according to the integrity that is in me."

Psalm 143:2 states: "Enter not into judgment with Your servant, for no one living is righteous before You."

Ephesians 2:8–9 asserts: "For by grace you have been saved through faith. And this is not your own doing; it is the gift of God, not a result of works, so that no one may boast."

It has been held that the sentiments expressed by David in Ps 7:8 are the direct opposite of those voiced in the other two passages listed. Since Ps 7:8 is not the only passage of such a tenor, we can dispose of difficulties connected with a whole class of Scripture texts if we show it to be in agreement with declarations like Ps 143:2 and Eph 2:8–9. The reader may compare especially Ps 18:20–24 and Is 38:3.

Psalm 7:8 and similar declarations are thought to exalt self-righteousness—trust in one's own goodness and merits. Numerous other texts assert that people are saved by grace and not by anything they have achieved or earned. The discrepancy between these two sets of texts is only superficial. Study Ps 7:8 closely. David does not say that he is without any sin whatever, that his own merits will open for him the gates of paradise, that he is relying on his virtuous conduct and charitable deeds for eternal salvation. He is asserting his innocence with respect to certain foul deeds. Why should he not? He had not committed the wrongs attributed to him by his enemies who are mentioned in the preceding verses. His prayer is that God may "judge" him. That term here evidently has the meaning to vindicate someone or to protect someone against unjust treatment. This meaning is found frequently in the Scriptures, especially in the Psalms. David is saying, as it were: "Lord, You know that I am not guilty of the evil deeds with which my enemies charge me. Bring to light my righteousness and my integrity." There is, then, in these passages nothing that denies the cardinal truths that all are sinful and that our salvation is entirely due to God's grace and the redemption of Christ.

The Efficacy of Prayer

Psalm 18:41 declares: "They cried for help, but there was none to save; they cried to the LORD, but He did not answer them."

Matthew 7:8 promises: "For everyone who asks receives, and the one who seeks finds, and to the one who knocks it will be opened."

Upon first reading, these two statements seem to be in disagreement. Both speak of prayer. The Matthew passage declares that no prayer is in vain; the psalm passage apparently states that a prayer was offered by certain people and was not heard. The words of Jesus (Mt 7:8) predicate a universality that the words of David (Ps 18:41) seemingly deny. The difficulty is easily explained. That God hears every prayer is a blessed truth that is proclaimed in a number of passages in Holy Scripture (cf Mt 21:21; Lk 11:5–13; 1Jn 5:14). At the same time, however, it is true that there are many cries that the Lord does not answer. These vain, fruitless utterances come from the lips of God's enemies, the very kind of people described in Ps 18:41. The Scriptures assure us in solemn words that the prayers of the ungodly are not acceptable. See Ps 66:18: "If I had cherished iniquity in my heart, the Lord would not have listened"; 1Sm 28:6: "And when Saul inquired of the LORD, the LORD did not answer him, either by dreams, or by Urim, or by prophets." The so-called prayers of these people simply are not prayers at all. Such persons ridicule the idea of prayer; but when trouble arises, they wish to employ prayer as a means of extricating themselves out of their difficulties. God will not permit Himself to be manipulated in this manner. The seeming discrepancy involved in the above passages is removed, then, if the reader bears in mind that when the Bible says every prayer will be heard, it has reference to real prayers, the petitions sent up to God by His children.

The Lot of the Christian on Earth

Psalm 112:1–3 exhorts: "Praise the LORD! Blessed is the man who fears the LORD, who greatly delights in His commandments! His offspring will be mighty in the land; the generation of the upright will be blessed. Wealth and riches are in his house, and his righteousness endures forever."

John 16:33 affirms: "I have said these things to you, that in Me you may have peace. In the world you will have tribulation. But take heart; I have overcome the world."

The difficulty posed by these two texts has been observed by many Bible readers, but others have not been perplexed by it to any considerable degree. One may note, as elsewhere, that biblical wisdom speaks generally and is not intended to be pressed into every aspect or moment of a person's life. The following considerations show that there is no problem here: (1) God delights in blessing His children. If He does good to the evil and to the unjust, He certainly will not overlook or ignore those who trust in Him. We may say that the text from Psalm 112 states what gifts God's children may expect from Him if conditions will permit. (2) The welfare of the Church may require that Christians be not provided with riches and other earthly advantages. Suppose the first Christians had all been people of wealth and political influence, enjoying the favors of the mighty, having slaves to do their bidding and beautiful homes to shelter them. Would the Church in that case have been established far and wide, growing as a mustard seed? Toils and persecutions were required to erect this structure. The blood of the martyrs became the seed of the Church. If that blood had not been shed, the Christian Church in all probability would have been small and insignificant, doomed to speedy extinction. There are cases, then, where the spreading of God's kingdom demands that His children pass through tribulation. In those instances God departs from the principle laid down in Ps 112:1–3 and elsewhere, making an exception. (3) Frequently the welfare of individual Christians requires that riches be kept from them. They may become puffed up if they meet with earthly success and quickly forget their dependence on the goodness of God. To save them from spiritual disaster, the Lord may keep them in very humble circumstances, not following the rule announced in Ps 112.

On the basis of such considerations Christians easily harmonize the above texts. They argue thus: We know that God gladly furnishes us the good things of this earth. If He does not do it, it is for some great and good purpose; we shall not question His love or wisdom.

FURTHER STUDY

Lay/Bible Class Resources

Alden, Robert L. *Psalms: Songs of Discipleship.* 3 vols. Everyman's Bible Commentary. Chicago: Moody, 1976. ♪ Brief, popular treatment by a well-informed scholar.

Andrus, Debb. *Psalms: Conversations with God.* GWFT. St. Louis: Concordia, 1994. ♪ Lutheran author. Twelve-session Bible study, including leader's notes and discussion questions.

Brug, John F. *Psalms, Parts 1 & 2.* PBC. St. Louis: Concordia, 2003, 2004. ♪ Lutheran author. Excellent for Bible classes. Based on the NIV translation.

Etter, Mark, Diane Grebing, and Paul Grime. *Selected Psalms.* Leaders Guide and Enrichment Magazine/ Study Guide. LL. St. Louis: Concordia, 2010. ♪ An in-depth, nine-session Bible study covering different types of psalms with individual, small group, and lecture portions.

Kidner, Derek. *Psalms.* TOTC. 2 vols. Downers Grove, IL: InterVarsity Press, 1973–75. ♪ Written in a simple expository style. This commentary's strong point is the theological insight Kidner gives to each psalm. He manages to treat the Psalms in-depth from a conservative perspective without a lot of technical jargon. His introduction also contains helpful material on structure and content.

Life by His Word. St. Louis: Concordia, 2009. ♪ More than 1,500 reproducible one-page Bible studies covering each chapter of the canonical Scriptures. Page references to *The Lutheran Study Bible.* CD-Rom and downloadable.

Mueller, Steven. *An Introductory Course: Psalms.* Journeys through God's Word. St. Louis: Concordia, 1998. ♪ Lutheran author and theologian. Twelve-session Bible study, including discussion questions. Leader's guide sold separately.

Saleska, Tim. *Psalms.* God's Abiding Word. St. Louis: Concordia, 2002. ♪ Lutheran author and theologian who specializes in the Psalms. Ten-session downloadable Bible study for advanced students of the Bible, including leader's notes and discussion questions.

Church Worker Resources

Anderson, Bernhard W. *Out of the Depths: The Psalms Speak for Us Today.* 3rd ed. Louisville: Westminster John Knox, 2000. ♪ An introduction, which includes appendices with very helpful summaries of how the psalms might be individually categorized. Appendix C lists all the New Testament references to the Psalms in a very convenient way.

Bonhoeffer, Dietrich. *Psalms: The Prayer Book of the Bible.* Minneapolis: Augsburg, 1970. ♪ A devotional resource in which a well-known Lutheran theologian gives direction on how the Psalms are to be read Christologically.

Bullock, C. Hassell. *Encountering the Book of Psalms: A Literary and Theological Introduction.* Encountering Biblical Studies. Grand Rapids: Baker, 2001. ♪ Best introduction to the Psalms. It covers all major topics in a very readable and thorough way and is full of charts and pictures which will prove helpful for anyone writing notes on the Psalms.

Davidson, Robert. *The Vitality of Worship: A Commentary on the Book of Psalms.* Grand Rapids: Eerdmans, 1998. ♪ A theological commentary from a critical perspective, which reflects on personal and public devotional use of the Psalter.

Leupold, Herbert C. *Exposition of the Psalms.* Grand Rapids: Baker, 1959. ♪ Reprint of a rich resource by a careful Lutheran scholar. Often includes homiletical suggestions.

Mays, James. *Psalms.* Interpretation: A Bible Commentary for Teaching and Preaching. Louisville: Westminster John Knox, 2011. ♪ Themes and insightful comment on particular psalms from a more conservative expert. As the subtitle indicates, the book is designed to guide teachers and preachers by example.

FURTHER STUDY

Academic Resources

Alexander, Joseph A. *The Psalms Translated and Explained*. Grand Rapids: Baker, 1979. ઠ An old classic expository study of the Psalms. Studies some of the difficult passages with discerning maturity.

Bratcher, Robert G., and William D. Reyburn. *A Handbook on Psalms*. New York: UBS, 1991. ઠ Designed for those translating the Psalms into different languages. Treats translational issues and gives good, concise commentary on the Psalms. A very helpful resource for ascertaining basic meaning and argument.

Craigie, Peter C., Marvin E. Tate, and Leslie C. Allen. *Psalms 1–50, 51–100, 101–150*. 3 vols. WBC. Dallas: Word Books, 1983, 1990, 2002. ઠ Written by evangelical scholars working from a critical perspective. Volume one by Craigie is especially good for the notes on the text and its explanation. Throughout are good bibliographies for individual Psalms. A good resource on the individual psalms.

Dahood, Mitchell. *Psalms*. Vols. 16, 17, and 17A of AB. New York: Doubleday, 1966–70. ઠ For the advanced and the well-informed student with special reference to the place of Ugaritic in ancient literature (as Dahood saw it). Dahood applies his various possibilities whenever theoretically possible, employing very little self-criticism, and thus leaving others to sift and choose. Dahood's procedures are virtually impossible to discuss without a good knowledge of the Hebrew language.

Firth, David, and Philip S. Johnston, eds. *Interpreting the Psalms: Issues and Approaches*. Downers Grove, IL: InterVarsity Press, 2006. ઠ An academic introduction to the Psalms, which prepares readers for working with specialized studies.

Goldingay, John. *Psalms*. 3 vols. Baker Commentary on the Old Testament Wisdom and Psalms. Grand Rapids: Baker, 2006. ઠ A detailed academic commentary, interacting with insights from historical figures.

K&D. *Biblical Commentaries on the Old Testament: The Book of Psalms*. 2 vols. Grand Rapids: Eerdmans reprint (n.d.). ઠ This century-and-a-half old work from Lutheran scholars should not be overlooked. Despite its age, it remains a most useful commentary on the Hebrew text.

Keel, Othmar. *The Symbolism of the Biblical World: Ancient Near Eastern Iconography and the Book of Psalms*. Translated by Timothy J. Hallett. Winona Lake: Eisenbrauns: 1997. ઠ An important resource for looking at the "thought world" of the Book of Psalms by comparing it with ancient Near Eastern iconography. This work is filled with information, pictures, drawings, etc. The index makes it easy to look up the pages where particular psalms are discussed.

Kraus, Hans-Joachim. *Psalms 1–59, 60–150*. 2 vols. Translated by Hilton C. Oswald. A Continental Commentary. Minneapolis: Fortress Press, 1993. ઠ An important standard, more technical commentary that incorporates some historical critical and form critical presuppositions. Good commentary on individual verses as well as the structure of each of the psalms, with some good theological exposition.

———. *Theology of the Psalms*. Translated by Keith Crim. A Continental Commentary. Minneapolis: Fortress Press, 1986. ઠ This volume treats the Psalms thematically and theologically.

Limburg, James. *Psalms*. Westminster Bible Companion. Louisville: Westminster John Knox, 2000. ẟ A non-technical treatment of the Psalms by a Lutheran theologian working from a critical perspective. Insight into the major themes of each psalm, oriented to Christian theological comment.

Luther, Martin. *First Lectures on the Psalms*. Vols. 10 and 11 of AE. St. Louis: Concordia, 1974, 1976. ẟ Luther's earliest lectures on the Bible, covering most psalms from 1–126, illustrating his transition from medieval interpretation and theology to Reformation views focused on Christ. The translation is of Luther's scholia, with some glosses included in footnotes.

———. *Selected Psalms*. Vols. 12–14 of AE. St. Louis: Concordia, 1955–58. ẟ Luther's more mature teaching on the Psalms, ranging from 1519 to the 1530s. Special emphasis on the significance of the psalms from the vantage point of Good Friday and Easter.

Moll, Carl Bernhard, and Thomas J. Conant. *Book of Psalms*. LCHS. New York: Charles Scribner's Sons, 1884. ẟ A helpful older example of German biblical scholarship, based on the Hebrew text, which provides references to significant commentaries from the Reformation era forward.

Neale, John Mason, and Richard Frederick Littledale. *A Commentary on the Psalms: From Primitive and Mediaeval Writers*. 3 vols. London: Joseph Masters and Co., 1874. ẟ Excerpts from Church Fathers on how they interpreted the psalms and how they were used in the church. Illustrates the pre-Reformation allegorical method.

Perowne, J. J. Stewart. *The Book of Psalms*. 2 vols. Grand Rapids: Zondervan, 1976. ẟ A reprint of a nineteenth-century conservative classic.

Petersen, David L., and Kent Harold Richards. *Interpreting Hebrew Poetry*. Minneapolis: Fortress Press, 1989. ẟ An overview of commonly held interpretative perspectives.

Reardon, Patrick Henry. *Christ in the Psalms*. Ben Lomond, CA: Conciliar Press, 2000. ẟ A reflective, devotional, and historical-liturgical approach to the Psalms, written by a former Episcopal priest who converted to Eastern Orthodoxy.

Watson, Wilfred G. E. *Classical Hebrew Poetry: A Guide to its Techniques*. Sheffield, England: JSOT Press, 1984. ẟ A comprehensive description of the many different figures of speech used in Hebrew poetry with many examples from the Psalms. A good resource when investigating poetic techniques more closely.

Weiser, Artur. *The Psalms*. Translated by Herbert Hartwell. OTL. Philadelphia: Westminster, 1962. ẟ Throughout points to the unifying covenant theme. Suffers at times from Weiser's hypothesis of a covenant festival.

PROVERBS

The fear of the Lord is the beginning of knowledge

Solomon transformed Jerusalem from a highlands city into a hub of international commerce. His father, David, captured Jerusalem as a Jebusite (Canaanite) stronghold and turned it into the capital of his growing kingdom. Solomon's marriage to a daughter of Pharaoh demonstrated his international standing, wedding the culture that previously enslaved Israel. Herds of horses followed from Egypt and from Kue in Asia Minor. Solomon traded the herds and other goods to Hittites and Syrians to the north and east. He ruled over his nearer neighbors: Philistines, Moabites, Ammonites, Edomites, and Sidonians. Tyrian workmen crafted the cedar beams for the temple Solomon built in the Lord's name. Sheban caravans brought spices from the distant Saudi and African coasts. Solomon's leadership made Jerusalem an international landmark.

Along with goods from distant lands came people with different ideas. Biblical wisdom notes the common themes observed from the different cultures that explored God's orderly creation, while warning against the corruptions of foreign influence. Proverbs conveys these tensions of fascination and revulsion, seeking to distinguish the foolish from the wise. The beginning of biblical wisdom is "fear of the Lord," which means trust in God whose Word made Israel great.

Double-walled gate at Megiddo, built during Solomon's reign. The view looks to the Jezreel Valley. Note the wooden beams used between stones. It is believed that the use of such beams made the construction more stable during the frequent earthquakes that occur in Israel.

OVERVIEW

Authors
Solomon; Agur; Lemuel; Lemuel's mother; unnamed wise men

Date
Tenth century BC for most of the book; late eighth or early seventh for some parts

Places
Jerusalem; Israel

People
King Solomon; Solomon's son (Rehoboam) or a student; King Hezekiah; court officials; Agur; Lemuel and his mother; a woman who fears the Lord

Purpose
To bestow God's wisdom

Law Themes
Because foolishness is rebellion against God, fools condemn themselves to destruction; instruction curbs the misdeeds of fools and guides the deeds of the wise

Gospel Theme
Christ, God's wisdom, delivers us from self-destruction and brings forth righteousness

Memory Verses
Fear of the Lord (1:2–7); Wisdom and creation (8:22–31); the woman who fears the Lord (31:30–31)

TIMELINE

1009–970 BC	Reign of David
970–931 BC	Reign of Solomon
972 BC	Rehoboam born
931 BC	Israel divided under Rehoboam
715–686 BC	Reign of Hezekiah (Judah)

Historical and Cultural Setting

First Kings describes Solomon's reign and the historical environment in which Proverbs, Ecclesiastes, and the Song of Solomon developed. See pp 321–22.

COMPOSITION

Authors

The Book of Proverbs is a collection of collections, though it is not possible to say with certainty how many collections went into the book. The more important issue is their relation to Solomon. Higher criticism is generally no longer quite so skeptical of the Israelite origins of official, professional wisdom in connection with Solomon as it once was. However, it still entertains grave doubts about any but the most distant Solomonic connection with the Book of Proverbs—though these doubts have also moderated somewhat.

The precise wisdom topics that 1Ki 4:29–34 credits to Solomon (trees, beasts, birds, reptiles, fish) cannot easily be collated with the contents of Proverbs, but the two are probably not meant to be equated. Our most direct evidence for Solomonic involvement in the Book of Proverbs is found in the book's various superscriptions, but even these indicate that we cannot be simplistic about the matter. Both at Pr 1:1 and 10:1 we have "the proverbs of Solomon." This most likely means that technically the superscription of 1:1 applies only to chs 1–9, not the entire book.[1] A third superscription appears at 25:1: "These also are proverbs of Solomon which the men of Hezekiah king of Judah copied." The relatively rare Hebrew verb for copying may leave room for some editing by Hezekiah's men, but would suggest indeed quite faithful copying. In addition, there are the superscriptions to chs 30 and 31, each associated with "Massa" in some way (cf "oracle" in ESV), but *not* clearly attributed to Solomon.

Frankincense and myrrh were celebrated trade goods in Solomon's day.

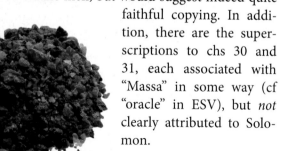

---

1 The possibility cannot be precluded that the superscription was placed at the head of a collection during its editorial history and intended to apply to that larger collection, such as proverbs before the references to further collections in chs 22–31. Cf the retention of a postscript at Ps 72:20 despite the fact that its collection was later added to a much larger collection.

If "Massa" in Pr 30:1 and 31:1 is correctly rendered as a proper noun, the reference would appear to be to a north Arabian tribe mentioned elsewhere, and indicating a non-Israelite source for these chapters. That interpretation might parallel other biblical references to Edomite wisdom, especially if one could argue, as some have, from the similarity of Jb 38:3–38 (whose roots are often sought in the same area) to Pr 30:4 (both in form and vocabulary). On the other hand, *massa* is also a standard Hebrew word for "oracle" (common in the prophets), and that rendition is possible in both cases.

We have no lead on either Agur or Lemuel from any other source, either biblical or extrabiblical. The latter was often traditionally taken as a pen name for Solomon, describing him as "toward/dedicated to God" or the like. The Vulgate also treats Agur at Pr 30:1 as a pen name. The Septuagint apparently recognizes no proper names in any of the four cases, indicating at least one ancient tradition of translation.

Are there other preliminary collections in the book besides those with the five headings? Beginning at Pr 22:17, there is a discernible change of style. In the Septuagint we meet the heading "Words of the Wise." Because the text has parallels with the Egyptian "Teaching of Amenemope," nearly all scholars agree that a new subcollection begins here (the superscription apparently having fallen out of the Hebrew textual tradition at some point). This would give us at least six previous collections, but it may be that some of them should be further divided. If the phrase "These also are sayings of the wise" of 24:23 is not a superscription, it suggests a transition or an incorporation of material from another source, possibly a seventh. Also the final two chapters may be a composite of four different chapters (see below on the Septuagint). Other scholars, of course, divide the book still further, but it seems safe to say that we have at least six or seven earlier "books of proverbs" behind the canonical Proverbs. Each collection has some of its own characteristic vocabulary, and there is some evidence of influence or dependence of some of them on others.

Septuagint Evidence

The Septuagint probably also preserves evidence, at least toward the end of the book, of an earlier period when some sequences in the book were still a bit fluid. Various additions and omissions appear throughout, but the order remains the same until 24:22, when the Septuagint inserts part of the "words of Agur" (30:1–10), followed by 24:23–24. Next comes the rest of ch 30 (vv 11–33), followed by the first part of ch 31 (1–9). Following this are chs 25–29 (Hezekiah collection), and the book concludes with the praise for a good wife, like the Hebrew. As usual it is hard to say whether the

Septuagint's variation represents a deliberate departure from the Masoretic Hebrew tradition, but more likely it reproduces an alternate Hebrew textual tradition preceding translation. As noted, there are a number of other variations between the Greek and Hebrew texts of Proverbs, including some material not found in the Hebrew at all. Thus the textual situation is similar to a number of other books. Qumran probably teaches us that we must take both the Greek and the Hebrew versions seriously.

Date of Composition

Early criticism tried to create an evolutionary sequence for Proverbs. Just as in the study of prophecy, it was assumed that simple, brief utterances must be early, with developed, complex ones a sure sign of lateness (and probably also of degeneracy). By that criterion, Pr 10:1–22:16 was confidently declared the earliest part of the book, and 1–9 the latest (also because of its theology), with the rest of the material fitted somewhere in between. Archaeological evidence from all over the ancient Near East would cast aside these assumptions, but their influence still lingers. We should now expect long as well as short wisdom compositions in *any* period!

The critics tended to date most of the composition as well as collection of the work in the fifth to third centuries BC. In contrast, scholarship today would even acknowledge *pre*-Solomonic roots of much of the material. Even the final form of the book may be dated to the time of the copyists of Hezekiah, who reigned from 715 to 686 BC.

Purpose/Recipients

The stated purpose of the Book of Proverbs is to provide its readers with godly wisdom (1:2–7) so that they avoid the self-destruction that is sin or foolishness. The introduction to the collection of proverbs by King Hezekiah's men provides a more specific context in which the words were used: the preparation of young men for the royal court. However, much of Proverbs describes life and choices at street level, making the collection attractive to a general audience and not just to the elite.

Literary Features

Genre and Collections

From a purely formal standpoint, it is relatively easy to distinguish three types of collections in Proverbs: (1) simple chains of sayings; (2) arrangement of a number of maxims according to some principle; and (3) longer teaching poems. In assessing the literary character of Proverbs, it is convenient to proceed from the simpler style of proverbs and the briefer collections to the more complex and longer composition of chs 1–9. This approach is not intended to suggest an evolutionary development, but is a convenient way to explore the contents and organize comments about them.

Sentential Wisdom. Proverbs 10:1–22:16 is entitled "The Proverbs of Solomon" (a note missing in the Septuagint). It includes some 375 examples of simple "sentential wisdom," unrelated and unreflective sayings strung together according to no overarching scheme. In chs 10–15 especially the proverbs tend to present contrast (antithetical in form). Only occasionally may one discern use of a content or catchword principle of arrangement, for example, a few concerned with the "king" in 16:12–15. The existence of the monarchy is also presupposed in 21:1 and 22:11, and there is no reason why Solomon should not be considered the immediate example. Both the everyday practicality of their contents and the classical poetic parallelism usually exhibited (essentially typical of popular sayings of any time or place) suggest roots in "folk wisdom." Nevertheless, some one-seventh of them have at least indirect reference to "Yahweh," making plain that they are theological and cannot be divorced from the total canonical context of covenant and salvation history in Israel (*Heilsgeschichte*).

Court Wisdom. Not much more can be said of the Hezekiah collection in Pr 25–29. If the superscription at 25:1 means that its contents were first reduced to writing in the time of Hezekiah, it certainly is testimony to the faithfulness and accuracy of the preceding oral tradition. Frequent mention of the king attests to the Solomonic roots of this material. Studies have even suggested Egyptian roots for some of it, possibly going back to the Twelfth Dynasty (early second millennium). Editorial activity by the "men of Hezekiah" over the collectors of 10:1–22:16 may be evident in the grouping of sayings (e.g., fools in 26:3–12; sluggards in 26:13–16; troublemakers in 26:17–28), a greater use of multiple-line sayings, and less antithetical parallelism (except in ch 28). Since chs 28–29 are more like 10:1–22:16, some

Judean prisoners with hands raised in surrender or perhaps prayer.

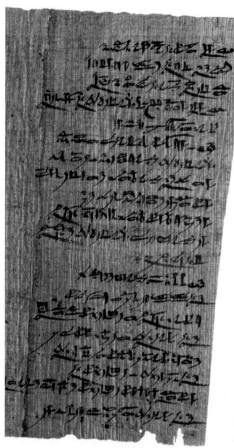

The "Teaching of Amenemope" in hieratic script. Each saying appears on its own line.

have thought of two subcollections involved here as well. Some have found significance in the fact that there are 137 proverbs in this collection, while the numerical value of the letters in the Hebrew for "Hezekiah" is 136. Such an association is by no means impossible, because we now know that this "play" with numbers (and sometimes the attachment of all kinds of mystical symbolisms to them) was by no means a late, but a very early interest of Near Eastern people.

Exhortations. The collection beginning with Pr 22:17, however, raises more questions. Not only is the literary structure somewhat more complex (mostly two- or three-verse exhortations with the second or third verse giving the reasons for, or consequences of, good or bad action) but there is the matter of the phenomenal parallelism of much of the section with the "Teaching of Amenemope" (an Egyptian sage who lived sometime in the latter half of the second millennium BC, well before Solomon). Some conservative scholars have been loathe to concede any kind of dependence (forgetting about the radical theological transference in any event), and some critics have thought simplistically of Israelite dependence, often editing the Hebrew severely according to the Egyptian and forgetting the relative freedom with which such material is often transmitted under any circumstances. Despite efforts to the contrary, there appears to be no reasonable doubt that the Egyptian material came first, but the ultimate relation of the Egyptian and biblical contexts is much more complicated. Sometimes the contacts are between the texts almost verbatim, while at other points the variation is considerable. A common source might stand behind both. Especially after 24:22 the divergence may be greater still and, as noted above, this may be a subsidiary collection altogether. (Some possible Amenemope parallels have been noted in other parts of the Book of Proverbs.)

The clearest indication of some internal relation of the two may appear at Pr 22:20. The Hebrew is at best difficult, but, as elsewhere, seems to be clarified when read alongside its Egyptian counterpart. Most likely, ESV's "thirty sayings" is correct, corresponding to the 30 "houses" or chapters of Amenemope. Without too much difficulty, it appears possible to count 30 such discrete sayings in the Hebrew, concluding at 24:22.

Numerical Sayings. Proverbs 30:7–9 is the first of the numerical sayings in the chapter introduced in Agur's name, followed by five more in vv 15–33. This type of numerical parallelism (in 6:16–19 and often also found in prophetic poetry) was once considered a late development, but we now know from Ras Shamra that it was an ancient and favorite device of poets. Many other lexicographical affinities with Ugaritic literature are especially evident in this section. The prominence of zoological subjects would suggest possible Solomonic connections also in this chapter (cf 1Ki 4:33).

Appendix about Women. The final two chapters comprise a sort of double appendix. Perhaps it was originally four appendixes; we noted above the different distribution of the material in the Septuagint. And this is only the beginning of conundrums on the proper translation and interpretation of at least aspects of these chapters.

Proverbs 31:1–9 is the only example in the book of a type that is very common in extrabiblical literature: vocational wisdom or career instruction for a young prince or potential king. Aramaisms in this section may point to extra-Israelite provenance. However, in no other known case is it the *mother* who gives the instruction, as here. The contents of the instruction, however, are relatively commonplace as wisdom goes: warnings against loose women and excessive drink, a reminder to attend to social justice, and so on.

Head of woman or female goddess (ninth–eighth century BC).

The final portion of Proverbs (31:10–31) is really an independent poem, the famous acrostic on "an excellent wife," following upon the previous example of a mother's ideal activity (though it also concludes in the Septuagint, where the sequences are different). Its completely practical and unromantic perspective views the wife primarily as a prudent manager of her household. Nevertheless, it is a testimonial to the dignity and status of women in Israelite homes and hence also the importance of the family, as also in their Jewish and Christian successors. Its final accent is on the fear of the Lord over surface appearances (v 30). This makes a fitting end to a book that has had so much to say about contentious and immoral women.

Wisdom Personified. Women also play a prominent role in the structure of the first collection of the book, chs 1–9. These chapters orient the reader and set the tone for the less explicitly theological material later in the book. Both because of its stylistic and theological development, this collection was once unanimously regarded as the latest section of the entire book. The first feature is perhaps most evident in ch 2, which is virtually all one long sentence, and the latter climaxes, of course, in the personification (hypostatization) of wisdom in ch 8.

Carved depictions of a lively, fruitful tree or plant were common in ancient Near Eastern art. They are thought to be examples of the tree of life, sometimes mentioned in ancient literature.

The preface or prologue (1:2–7 may be read as a single, unbroken sentence in the Hebrew) has many formal parallels, and much of the favorite vocabulary of wisdom is clustered here. Between the prologue and the first of the discourses stands the well-known theme of Yahwistic wisdom (1:7). Since it also appears in essence near the end of the collection at 9:10, we may have an example of literary "inclusion" (cf 15:33; Jb 28:28; Ps 111:10). The "fear of the Lord," which means "trust in the Lord," implies a starting point and also controlling principle for all wisdom. Luther well summarizes its opposite to make the point: "Educate a devil, and all you have is an educated devil." Trust in the Lord must be sincere in order for the desired results to follow, which the Lord bountifully promises.

In Pr 1:20–33 we meet the first of many passages where wisdom is personified. This literary feature climaxes in ch 8, where wisdom has ceased to be a mere personification and becomes a full-fledged "incarnation" as God's workman. Also noteworthy is the plural form of the Hebrew for "wisdom" in 1:20 and a few other passages; either it is an archaic, Phoenician form, or it is a construction (also ancient) analogous to the "plural of majesty" in "Elohim." Wisdom is here presented as stationing herself in the market, inviting busy men to follow. If the picture is not simply literary, it may reflect the actual behavior of some wisdom teachers, though it sounds more like what we know of some prophets.

Proverbs 2:16–19 provides the first of the many warnings against the "forbidden woman," in apparent contrast to "Lady Wisdom." So also Pr 5; 6:20–35; 7; and 9:13–18. These passages are so prominent that the contrast almost structures all of chs 1–9. Two parallel terms are used in the Hebrew, literally the "strange (woman)" and the "foreign/unfamiliar (one)." Both expressions are ambiguous and have occasioned much debate. The explanation that the passages are about foreign religion, not promiscuity or adultery as such, seems at best incomplete. The competing Canaanite religions were usually fertility cults that included promiscuity. Also, warnings against affairs with especially foreign women are also present in ancient Egyptian wisdom literature. It may well be that paganism, its fertility rites, and adultery are simultaneously condemned, especially when we note that the outcome of all such liaisons is often described as "death" (e.g., 2:18–19), a way outside of Yahweh's order of life that can ultimately lead only to utter ruin.

Two short poems (Pr 3:13–18 and 19–20) briefly interrupt the series of didactic addresses. The first one begins and ends with the common wisdom concern (cf also Ps 1) with "blessedness." Also significant is the comparison in Pr 3:18 of wisdom with "a tree of life" (also in 11:30; 13:12; 15:4). The figure has all kinds of parallels in ancient Near Eastern mythology and glyptic art. In biblical context, however, there is no reason to doubt that it was ultimately nourished by the narrative of Gn 2–3. The second poem (vv 19–20) is virtually a little hymn to God the Creator and is especially significant in anticipating the fuller account of wisdom's role in creation in 8:22–31; hence, we may well consider it in the personal sense already here.

Proverbs 1–9 begin to move to their climax in ch 7. Chapters 7 and 8 offer the two major expressions of increasingly explicit theology. Although in form ch 7 continues the theme of the rivalry between Lady Wisdom and the forbidden woman, the former (general revelation) is here plainly identified with Torah (special revelation). The very word *torah* is used in the Hebrew text of 7:2, and v 3 appears to be a reference to the use of phylacteries (cf Dt 6:8).

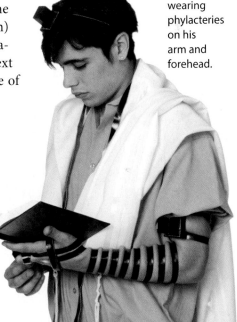

Young man wearing phylacteries on his arm and forehead.

Characters

The speaker and the hearer in chs 1–9 are called "father" and "son," though these titles may also describe the teacher-student relationship. Addresses to the son are key components to the book's structure. These characters give us a sense of how instruction took place in ancient Israel.

In Proverbs, wisdom is an attribute of God and of His people, though it is often personified as a dear mother or beloved bride. (This is likely because Hbr *chokmah* is grammatically feminine.) The common feminine imagery does not prevent Solomon from describing wisdom as God's "master workman" in Pr 8:22–31, a Christological passage (cf Jn 1:1–8; 1Co 1:24; Col 2:2–3). Chapters 1–9 contrast the appeals of Wisdom and Folly, who call out to people in the marketplace.

Proverbs mentions many different kinds of fools (see *TLSB*, p 1016). Although "wisdom" and "righteous" stand together in only one proverb (10:31), the book equates wise people with the righteous (cf 9:9–10).

Narrative Development or Plot

The first nine chapters of Proverbs present quests and accounts of creation. The address of a father to a son implies a storied setting for the book where the two sit together as the father seeks to teach his son and the son grows in wisdom. The characters of Wisdom and Folly depict women on a quest in the marketplace, seeking converts to their way of life (cf 1:20–33). Just as Wisdom and Folly seek hearers, the hearer is sent on a quest for wisdom (3:13–18). His goal is hampered by the adulteress, who would deceive him (cf ch 5). Chapter 8, the high point of the narrated section and of the whole book, describes God's work as Creator, working through wisdom.

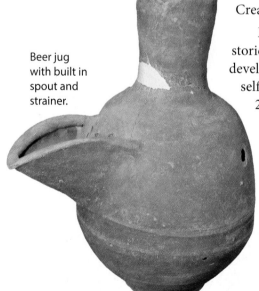

Beer jug with built in spout and strainer.

Many brief proverbs later in the book also imply stories, filling the mind with vivid images of setting and development. For example, the sluggard exhausts himself while making excuses to avoid work (e.g., 22:13; 26:13–15). A warning against alcohol abuse tells a story of a hangover in the form of a riddle (23:29–24:2).

Chapter 31 mirrors the father to son addresses found at the beginning of the book with a mother to son address (31:1–9). The book closes with an account of an excellent wife who proves her worthy wisdom through industriousness (31:10–27) so that her family praises her (vv 28–29).

Resources

On Proverbs as a collection of collections, see pp 622–21.

Text and Translations

As noted above, there are two literary editions of Proverbs (LXX and MT). The Hebrew text is in good order, though with some difficult passages. The LXX has some issues of corruption but also includes unique material that may be based on a Hebrew text that is not currently available to us. It also rearranges some of the content.

DOCTRINAL CONTENT

Summary Commentary

1:1–7 Solomon's introduction reminds us of the difference between true wisdom and the wisdom of the world.

1:8–19 Solomon warns against joining sinners in their adventurous plots, cautioning that the greedy and violent finally receive their punishment.

1:20–33 God's will is freely proclaimed and may be universally received.

Ch 2 Two roads exist for every person—the way of righteousness and the way of evil.

3:1–12 God punishes those who stubbornly resist His mercy and refuse to follow His commands. But He promises abundant blessings to all who, in faith, receive His gracious love and salvation through the merits of Jesus Christ.

3:13–35 Solomon, parent and teacher, emphasizes the blessings God gives through the wisdom He imparts. These blessings include the treasures of peace, security, and confidence, apportioned to those who trust in the Lord for forgiveness, new life, and eternal salvation. The blessings of those possessing true wisdom contrast with the condemnation accorded those who resist and scorn God's favor.

Ch 4 Little or no formal education existed in Old Testament times. Instead, the head of the household taught his family, including small children, in the ways of the Lord. Through this instruction, Israelites came to understand their identity as God's chosen people, to know God's saving love and promises, and to anticipate the coming of the Savior. Godly parents warn their children of the temporal and eternal consequences of wickedness.

Continued on p 634.

OUTLINE

I. Introduction (1:1–7)

  A. Superscription (1:1)

  B. Solomon's Preface (1:2–7)

II. Extended Discourses on Wisdom (1:8–9:18)

  A. First Address to a Son: Avoid the Company of Sinners (1:8–19)

  B. First Poem about Wisdom: Wisdom's Call and the Fate of Those Who Refuse to Listen to Her (1:20–33)

  C. Second Address to a Son (ch 2)

    1. Wisdom comes from God to protect you (2:1–15)

    2. An example of wisdom's protection: protection from the adulterous woman (2:16–19)

    3. Admonition to live righteously (2:20–22)

  D. Third Address to a Son: Wisdom Leads to a Proper Relationship with Yahweh (3:1–20)

  E. Fourth Address to a Son: Wisdom Leads to a Proper Relationship with One's Neighbor (3:21–35)

  F. An Address to Sons: Solomon's Parents Taught Him to Value Wisdom (4:1–9)

  G. Fifth Address to a Son: Wisdom Teaches the Difference between Wicked and Righteous People (4:10–19)

  H. Sixth Address to a Son: Advice for Living a Righteous Life (4:20–27)

  I. Seventh Address to a Son: Wisdom Teaches How to Avoid Adultery (ch 5)

  J. Eighth Address to a Son (6:1–19)

    1. Wisdom allows you to avoid entanglements with your neighbor (6:1–5)

    2. Wisdom is not compatible with laziness (6:6–11)

IV. The Words of Wise People (22:17–24:22)

    A. Introduction (22:17–21)

    B. Advice for Living with Your Neighbor (22:22–23:14)

    C. Advice from Your Father (23:15–24:22)

V. More Words of Wise People (24:23–34)

VI. Solomon's Proverbs Copied by Hezekiah's Men (chs 25–29)

    A. Superscription (25:1)

    B. Advice for Kings (25:2–27)

    C. All about Fools (25:28–27:4)

    D. Dealing with Family, Friends, and Other People (27:5–22)

    E. Guidance for Kings (27:23–29:27)

        1. Pay attention to your flock (27:23–27)

        2. Justice for poor people (28:1–11)

        3. Beware of wicked people (28:12–28)

        4. Wicked people endanger a kingdom (29:1–15)

        5. Final advice for a king (29:16–27)

VII. Agur's Proverbs (ch 30)

    A. Superscription (30:1)

    B. Agur's Prayers and Advice (30:2–10)

    C. Numerical Sayings (30:11–33)

VIII. King Lemuel's Proverbs (31:1–9)

    A. Superscription (31:1)

    B. Three Pieces of Advice for Kings (31:2–9)

IX. An Acrostic Poem about an Ideal Wife (31:10–31)

Ch 5 God shows us what sin looks like, why we sin, and where sin takes us. That is what Solomon does with his son. He gives him a vivid look at the road to and from adultery. What's more, he shows the sheer joy of deep, lasting intimacy within marriage.

6:1–19 God's Law shows us not only our sins but also their motivations and consequences.

6:20–35 The Sixth Commandment, "You shall not commit adultery," holds high God's institution of marriage and protects us from the deadly consequences of sexual immorality. Proverbs teaches us to weigh the heavy consequences of sexual immorality before we act.

Ch 7 Whether male or female, husband or wife, the one who commits adultery chooses immediate gratification over faithfully keeping one's commitments to God and spouse. More significant, this willful sin walks away from God and God's order in His creation, in which He reserves sexual intimacy for the marriage of one man and one woman.

Ch 8 The Lord is our Wisdom. His words and atoning works call from the heights and the crossroads of life for all humanity to hear. As such, He hates the sins of pride, arrogance, evil, and perverted speech (v 13).

9:1–12 The gracious invitation of Wisdom extends to all who live apart from the life she longs to bring.

9:13–18 God's Law warns against the deadly foolishness all around us.

10:1–5 The material blessings enjoyed by families should be pursued by prudent and diligent work done honestly. God blesses such labor and uses it to provide for the needs of His people.

10:6–23 The words we speak can be either a source of life and comfort, edifying those around us, or a source of strife and wickedness, stirring up hatred and division.

10:24–32 Both the righteous and the wicked face challenges. Yet the righteous, who travel the way of the Lord and who live in the fear of the Lord, are blessed with stability, joy, and the promise of everlasting life.

11:1–11 The distinction between the righteous and the wicked is not confined to the private or spiritual realms of life but also manifests itself in public words and actions.

11:12–12:11 Proverbs teaches the wisdom of living by righteousness as taught by the Lord.

12:12–16:9 In these proverbs, the characteristics of foolish and wise people are contrasted. The foolish are gullible and believe everything. They are reckless, careless, and quick-tempered. But because wise people thoughtfully evaluate everything on the basis of God's Word, their words and actions are always prudent and cautious.

16:10–33 These proverbs are especially directed to kings and other public servants. God uses them for the welfare of those who act righteously and as agents of wrath for those who do evil.

17:1–6 The Fourth Commandment not only teaches children to honor their parents but also teaches parents to cherish and take seriously God's gift of raising their children.

17:7–24 God's people are not to use the Gospel as grounds for partiality in judging (24:23–24), for calling good evil or evil good (Is 5:20), or for failing to protect the innocent.

17:25–19:12 The Eighth Commandment warns against false testimony against our neighbor. We should put a stop to gossip before it begins, not only by defending the reputation of the one spoken about but also by calling the gossiper to repentance and safeguarding ourselves from what may do irreparable damage.

19:13–20:30 Children are born fools, since they are born sinful. No one should be surprised by their excesses and ill manners. Yet no one should abandon them to their sinfulness but nurture and admonish them through God's Word.

21:1–22:16 Folly is more than mere stupidity. It is an act of rebellion against God. It not only brings bad consequences in this life but also damns us for eternity. True wisdom does not come from studying hard in school or even from having much life experience. True wisdom flows out of trust in the Lord ("the fear of the LORD").

22:17–24:22 Solomon knows that true piety is more than simply avoiding evil but is based on trust in God. Thus, he urges us not to envy sinners but to fear the Lord, for the Lord has graciously promised us a glorious future (23:17–18; 24:1–4, 13–14).

24:23–34 These verses comprise two sets of three topics: conduct in court (vv 23–25, 28), speaking (vv 26, 29), and work (vv 27, 30–34). We are told to be just in judging and honest in our testimony. We are to speak the truth to our neighbor in all circumstances. We are to work hard on the most important priorities and not shirk work like the sluggard.

Ch 25 Righteous people who compromise their principles disappoint us. Hope remains not in the possibility of renewing their righteousness by trying harder next time but rather in God's righteousness, which is credited to all who trust in the Lord's mercy.

Chs 26–29 Israel was not holy, or set apart, because of their own greatness but because of God's extraordinary kindness in calling them to be His people, the people from whom the future Messiah would be born. For the righteousness of rulers and their subjects is borne out of the divine righteousness reckoned to human beings through faith in God's promises. The righteousness that saves is a righteousness that *only* comes through faith in God's promise; Christ's righteousness was substituted for our wickedness.

Ch 30 Agur demonstrates the futility of life without wisdom, and also the blessings obtained from God's Word.

31:1–9 King Lemuel was taught God's Word by his mother in order to equip him to serve his subjects.

31:10–31 Celebration of an excellent wife. The most basic human relationship, according to God's design, is the joining of a man and woman in holy matrimony.

Specific Law Themes

Proverbs does not treat foolishness as mere stupidity or lack of knowledge. Foolishness has a moral dimension. Because foolishness is rebellion against God, fools condemn themselves to destruction. God provides instruction to curb the misdeeds of fools and to guide the deeds of the wise. This instruction is evident in the order that God created but is also shared by those whom God makes wise, especially parents.

Specific Gospel Themes

The Lord watches out for us and wants us to discover the wisdom of His ways. He created the world through wisdom, and wisdom is His precious gift to us. He is on the side of those who seek wisdom and righteousness. Ultimately, God's wisdom is Christ, who delivers us from self-destruction and brings forth righteousness in our lives.

Specific Doctrines

Historically, the Book of Proverbs has helpfully illustrated and amplified the meaning and application of the Ten Commandments. For example, Pr 22:6 reminds parents and children about the value of steady discipline and instruction in the faith. Additionally, when people make mistakes, love seeks to cover their offenses (Pr 10:12). This does not mean justifying someone in his wickedness (17:15; 20:9) but appealing to the righteousness and mercy of God. Proverbs teaches that God's people are obligated to intervene for others and

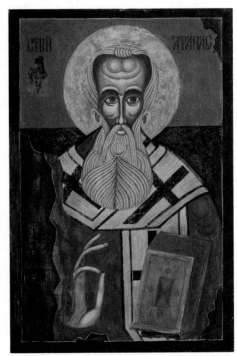

Bulgarian icon of Saint Athanasius the Great, doctor of the Church, who used Rm 8:22–26 to champion Christian orthodoxy against Arianism.

rescue them (24:11), answering Cain's question of whether one is to be his brother's keeper (cf Gn 4:9).

Proverbs 8, especially vv 22–31, is the high point of the book. The chapter has a clear internal structural unity of three strophes (vv 1–11, 12–21, 22–36) of 22 lines apiece (the number of letters in the Hebrew alphabet). The entire chapter provides the sharpest possible contrast to the frank portrait of the brazen seductress in ch 7. Especially in the second and third strophes, the first person personal and possessive pronouns become so prominent that we have a sort of self-proclamation by wisdom (cf some of Jesus' discourses in especially John). What wisdom really has to offer is herself—all that really and internally bestows life upon mankind. The third and climactic strophe (vv 22–36) gives a theological explanation for wisdom's superiority. It traces the horizons of wisdom and morality in a primordial and cosmic order: the order of creation.

Exegetical debate about vv 22–36 has long focused on two words, the Hbr roots *qanah* in v 22 and *'amon* in v 30. But the debate is also about interpretation. We have almost forgotten that v 22 was a major focus of the Christological debates of the Early Church. The Fathers were following the lead of the New Testament, which makes great use of the language and conceptuality of this passage on the primacy of wisdom to describe the primacy (pre-existence, divinity) of Christ (Jn 1; 1Co 1:24, 30; Col 1:15–17; 2:3; Heb 1:3; Rv 4:11; 22:13). However, Arian adoptionism appealed to the Septuagint's translation of *qanah* as "created" as a major argument against the Athanasian *homoousios* doctrine of Christ's eternal deity, which they supported by the translation "constituted." For conservatives who still refuse to divorce Old and New Testament, the matter dare not be decided only on a philological basis, as liberals attempt (as usual without definitive results). As here, hermeneutics will often not dictate one precise translation, but the philological option chosen must be demonstrably compatible with canonical teaching.

Usually *qanah* in the Old Testament means "get, acquire" and hence often "possess" (a favored translation already in antiquity). However, in a few passages, especially archaic ones (such as Pr 8 may well be), it denotes "create." Superficially, we now know it well in that sense in Ugaritic literature, especially of Asherah, the Canaanite "creatress of the gods"—except that "creation" in the strict sense is impossible in a mythological context (cf Gn 1), so that "procreate" would be more apropos! Apparently the word meant to "get" or "possess" in ways that varied with the context. "Beget" might be a good translation, both compatible with Christology and not reading into the context more specificity than is certainly there.

Other words in the context assume enlarged significance in the light of Christological fulfillment. The very next word in Pr 8:22 may mean either first in sequence ("beginning") or first in importance (cf 1:7). The two often coexist, but the parallel with "first" here and the "before" of v 25 tip the scales toward the priority of the former. Verses 23–25 continue the birth metaphor, while the "set up" of 23a may imply a royal installation (the same word in Ps 2:6), thus facilitating the messianic application.

The second major *crux* is the 'amon of Pr 8:30. The two main alternatives are (1) "master workman/foreman," etc., and (2) "little child/ward/nursling," etc. The former has the support of most of the ancient versions and is the most congenial to Christology, but the latter is not without ancient attestation and fits both the birth metaphors of vv 24–25 and the following context of vv 30b–31.

Despite questions about details, Pr 8 remains the major messianic text of canonical Wisdom Literature. In greatest possible contrast with the Early Church (and the New Testament), even conservative Christendom today sometimes appears to have lost the thread of its thought and, therewith, theological understanding of virtually the entire wisdom corpus.

After Pr 8, ch 9 easily appears anticlimactic. It revisits much of the contents of this entire collection (chs 1–9) and thence of the entire book. The "seven pillars" of wisdom's house (v 1) has engendered all types of debate and speculation. In some sense it probably implies completeness, that is, the cosmic extent of her invitation. In full scriptural context, it is ultimately not only proper, but necessary, to interpret especially vv 1–6 as an invitation

Remains of a typical Israelite house with a central courtyard surrounded by rooms. The walls around the courtyard were often built with large stone pillars.

to the "messianic banquet" or Eucharist (cf Is 55), a fitting climax to *all* of Proverbs indeed. It stands in explicit contrast to the rival "feast of fools," an initiation banquet to hell itself, with which the chapter ends.

Application

1:1–7 True wisdom is from the Lord, a message that is foolishness to those who reject it but God's very power to us who are being saved (1Co 1:18).

1:8–19 Through the Word and Sacrament (Means of Grace), God in Christ strengthens and preserves His people, just as He forgives all our sins for Jesus' sake.

1:20–33 His Law and His grace are for all people, for He desires all to be saved (1Tm 2:4). Those who turn their backs on God and His will face condemnation. But those who believe in Jesus as their Savior can rest secure, now and forever, in His love and care.

Ch 2 The way of evil is populated with those who reject God and His good and gracious will. The way of evil leads to certain and eternal death. The way of righteousness is traveled by God's forgiven children through faith in Christ Jesus, kept on the narrow path (Mt 7:13–14) by the working of the Holy Spirit through the Means of Grace. The path of righteousness leads to certain and eternal life.

3:1–12 Repent of your stubbornness and by faith pursue the Lord's abundant blessings. Christ will lead you in repentance and surround you with His grace.

3:13–35 Pray that the Lord would cultivate in you an enduring hunger for godly wisdom and life, a blessed foundation.

Ch 4 Godly parents warn their children of the temporal and eternal consequences of wickedness. The heavenly Father assures us of the grace and blessings God offers to those who love and trust in their Savior and who, relying on His Spirit's power, seek to walk in His light.

Ch 5 So much of God's teaching of the Law is exposé. God shows us what sin looks like, why we sin, and where sin takes us. Sin is never just a moral lapse or isolated infraction of one of God's Commandments; its consequences lead ultimately to death (Rm 6:23). How many of us might have been spared the horrific aftermath of sin if only we had looked beyond the sin to its consequences! The Gospel of Jesus Christ motivates us to take the higher road. We honor faithfulness in marriage and in all our relationships because of Him who was faithful to us in all things.

6:1–19 Consider a thought, an action, or a word by asking, Why am I doing this? Where could it take me? Can I do this in the name of the Lord? God hates sin so deeply that He sent His Son to take away sin's power—its curses and its eternal consequences. In Christ, we are forgiven and empowered to overcome sin. Good-for-nothings are made into God's precious and valuable sons and daughters.

6:20–35 Personal health, reputation, family, and career are at stake—and our relationship with God. Wisdom weighs the consequences and counts the costs. Wisdom, who is Jesus Christ, brings us the power and motivation to live worthy of our holy calling, especially where sexual purity is concerned.

Ch 7 The breaking of the Sixth Commandment has repeatedly brought death to marriage, family, friendships, and career. No talk of love, youthful naiveté, or even shared religious values can camouflage the destructive force of the sin of sexual intimacy outside marriage. The One who is faithful in all things offers forgiveness for all who have taken this deadly turn. The apostle Paul likens God's relationship with us to a marriage characterized by service and sacrifice (Eph 5:22–27). God's Word and wisdom light the way to sexual purity and marital faithfulness.

Christ blesses the Last Supper for His disciples. He is the Wisdom of God in the flesh who nurtures our faith.

Ch 8 Like Wisdom in ch 8, Christ calls us from worldly foolishness, judgment, and death to obedience, God's favor, and abundant life. Christ's eternal nature, His relationship with the Father, and His work in creation all mark Him as the very wisdom of God. He reaches out in love to all who love Him and diligently seek Him. In Christ, our Wisdom, we are rich beyond any human measure!

9:1–12 Jesus Christ calls the world to His banquet (Jn 6:32–59). Those who respond in faith will live forever in the company of Christ and His banqueting guests. Those who foolishly reject Him are dead in their sins.

9:13–18 Life in the Gospel saves us from a naive gullibility that sets us up for moral and spiritual disaster. The Law is the light that shows us the dirt in the house of our lives. The Gospel is the broom that sweeps it clean. The Gospel moves us from lazy moral laxity to wise discipline. The folly of sin gets a just punishment—death. The wisdom of our God-given faith brings eternal life.

10:1–5 We should be careful not to forget that it is God who provides us with all that we need to support our body and life. Likewise, we must never resort to wickedness or dishonesty in an attempt to secure a better profit for ourselves. The righteousness that comes through faith in Jesus not only delivers from death, but it also ensures that our heavenly Father will provide us with everything we need.

10:6–23 Always choose your words prudently, being careful never to speak gossip, lies, or slander about another person. Defend those whose reputation is under assault and forgive those who sin against you. Jesus was a victim of false accusations; the blood He shed on the cross covers all of our offenses.

10:24–32 The Lord is your hope, health, stronghold, and way. By His grace, seek a life of peace. Yet be ever ready to speak for what is true and good, in testimony to your Savior.

11:1–11 As you seek to live with integrity that reflects the righteousness we have received, express your righteousness in public ways—among your neighbors, in matters of commerce, and in your community. Although we may sometimes feel reluctant or unqualified to do this, by grace Jesus calls us the "salt of the earth" and the "light of the world" (Mt 5:13–16).

11:12–12:11 Worldly logic tells us that we become wealthy by hoarding what we have. But God's Word tells us that true riches come to those who give generously. We should always return a portion of our income to the service of God (who gives us all things) and support our neighbors according to their need. After all, this is God's wonderful way of dealing with His children. He has generously given us all that we need, including the life of His one and only Son for our salvation.

12:12–16:9 Throughout the day, like Proverbs, draw contrasts between the foolish and the wise. Befriend the foolish with cautious compassion, and the wise in gratefulness to the Lord who made them.

16:10–33 The authority of public servants has been instituted by God (Rm 13:1), and for that reason we owe them honor and obedience. Yet do not blindly follow authority but consider all things in view of God's Word.

17:1–6 Parents, are you taking seriously your responsibility to instruct your children in the Scriptures and the catechism (Dt 6:6–8)? Children, are you respecting your parents, holding them in the highest esteem, recognizing what good gifts God has provided you through them (Ex 20:12)? Our heavenly Father has given us His highest good in His Son, Jesus, and because Jesus delighted to do His Father's will, God now delights in you and me. In Jesus, we will receive the true crown of righteousness (2Tm 4:8), and by Him we call God our Father.

17:7–24 Ask the Lord to season your words with mercy and kindness so that His name is honored and your reputation guarded. The Father is our goodness and glory, whom we honor by faith.

17:25–19:12 What a difference between us and God! Our Lord has blessedly promised to put our sins as far from us as the east is from the west (Ps 103:12) and to remember our sins no more (Jer 31:34; Heb 8:12; 10:17). He will entertain no charge against us, now that there is no condemnation for those who are in Christ Jesus (Rm 8:1). What joy it would be if we let our Lord's forgiveness teach us to be as silent about the sins and shortcomings of our neighbor as God is pleased to be toward ours for Jesus' sake!

19:13–20:30 God's dear Son became a fool for our sakes, pierced and lashed to rescue us from foolishness and to deliver us into the arms of our dear Father. Share His nurture and admonition with the children in your life.

21:1–22:16 Ask the Lord to help you each day in the struggle against the sinful nature. By putting our trust in God and in His Son—Jesus Christ, Wisdom in human flesh—we are delivered from the consequences of our folly and we grow in the righteous behavior marked by wisdom.

22:17–24:22 Do not envy those who prosper through evil or who flout piety. Instead, entrust your life and your ways to the Lord of all wisdom and grace.

24:23–34 These verses admonish us to engage in the sort of decent conduct that enables societies to flourish. While all societies recognize the value of these behaviors, we Christians seek to live in such ways because the Gospel frees us to serve our neighbors in a God-pleasing way.

Ch 25 Our righteousness is passive (i.e., it is credited us apart from anything done on our part, solely through Christ's work on the cross). This passive righteousness frees, strengthens, and moves us to pursue what can be called "active" righteousness by keeping the Law to thank the Lord for His mercy.

Chs 26–29 By crushing the work of Satan, this Messiah would deliver the final blow to the catastrophic effects and consequences of sin upon humanity (Gn 3:15). This establishes the necessary context for reading these proverbs and instructions on human righteousness.

Ch 30 We cannot obtain enough insight, correct every injustice, or curb some of the most common sins. It is only through knowledge of the Holy One—God's only Son, Jesus Christ, who was crucified, died, and resurrected—that we are rescued from pressure of inadequacy, failure, and, ultimately, eternal damnation. Knowledge and soundness of mind gained from the Lord enable us to approach life in this world with confidence.

31:1–9 Although we may never find ourselves in kingly authority, let us learn from Lemuel's mother. Rather than focusing her teaching on how he could achieve financial and material success or how to increase his power, she taught God's Word to her son. God's Word from cover to cover bears witness first and foremost to another son: God's Son, who, at the appropriate time, took on human flesh and was born to a virgin mother. He did so to fulfill God's promise to bless all nations (Gn 12:2–3). Indeed, His death for the sins of the entire world (1Jn 2:2) opened up the gates to heaven.

31:10–31 Due to our active rebellion, the marriage relationship has been undermined. In His mercy, God still blesses our marriages. Since our relationship with the Creator is restored in Christ, this likewise serves to restore our marriages and all other human relationships. Call on Him to strengthen your marriage.

CANONICITY

Solomon's gift for writing proverbs was celebrated in Israel (1Ki 4:31–32; Ecclus 47:15). The Book of Proverbs was welcomed by Jews and early Christians without dispute. The New Testament refers to it in Rm 3:15 (Pr 1:16); Rm 12:20 (Pr 25:21–22); 1Pt 4:8 (Pr 10:12); 1Pt 4:18 (Pr 11:31); 2Pt 2:22 (Pr 26:11).

Extrabiblical "Wisdom"

Many remarkable parallels to biblical wisdom appear in other ancient Near Eastern cultures, probably more so than in any other area of biblical studies. However, the different forms of wise saying and their theological differences should be recognized.

For example, the Mesopotamian equivalents signify skill in especially magic and incantation, an interest that is obviously absent from the biblical collections. Both Mesopotamian and Egyptian discussions often take place in an atmosphere of fatalism or resignation to unalterable destiny. The extrabiblical examples are equally concerned with practical matters (admonitions to marital fidelity

Egyptian wisdom often appeared in magic texts. In this example, the god of wisdom, Thoth, appears as a baboon.

and warnings against indiscretions with women are prominent themes in both cultures), but especially Egyptian collections often exhibit an amoral "how to get ahead at all costs" or "it doesn't matter what you know but who you know" sort of cynicism.

Both Egypt and Israel were interested in the order that undergirded both cosmos and society (ethics) translated with terms such as *order*, *truth*, *rightness*, *righteousness*, etc. But profound differences also emerge in that Egyptian ideas of order (*ma'at*) were usually understood as another god rather than one aspect of a personal Creator's revelation.

The striking parallels between Pr 22:17–23:11 and the Egyptian "Teaching of Amenemope" cannot be easily dismissed. Certain similarities of Ps 104 with the "Hymn to the Sun" of Egypt's heretic-monotheist Pharaoh Akhenaton have often been noted. From all periods (and not only late ones) we find expressions of disillusionment or skepticism about facile dogmas, superficially comparable to Job and Ecclesiastes: the Egyptian "Song of the Harper" and "Dialogue of a Man with His Soul"; and from Mesopotamia the "Babylonian theodicy" and "Let me praise the lord of wisdom" ("*Ludlul bel nemeqi*").

Image of Akhenaton, who adapted Egyptian religion to
worship of one god—the sun.

Worthy of special attention are the novelistic "Sayings of Ahikar," perhaps originating in Assyria in the eighth century but circulated in various versions throughout the ancient Near East. Originally perhaps a maligned chancellor under Sennacherib, Ahikar is presented as the "counselor" and "father" of all Assyria. An Aramaic version was found among the ruins of the Jewish mercenaries of Elephantine (fifth century BC), and in the apocryphal Book of Tobit Ahikar appears as Tobit's nephew. In the late Old Testament period the book sometimes achieved quasi-canonical status (R. H. Charles includes it among the pseudepigrapha), and echoes of it are found in the Church Fathers, Talmud, and Koran.

Strangely enough, we do not so far have any real wisdom literature from Israel's immediate neighbors, although the Bible itself makes frequent mention of it. The mysterious East, and perhaps especially Edom and/or north Arabia, seems to have had a special reputation for wisdom (possibly the

"Massa" or oracle of Pr 30 and 31), but we lack details, and some scholars have developed hypotheses of influence on Israel from those quarters far beyond the evidence. Thus 1Ki 4:30 describes Solomon's wisdom as surpassing "the wisdom of all the people of the east and all the wisdom of Egypt." The next verse describes him as "wiser than Ethan the Ezrahite, and Heman, Calcol, and Darda, the sons of Mahol," all names that we can associate with the indigenous Canaanite culture of the area. The "Daniel" whose proverbial wisdom is said in Ezk 28:3 to have been exceeded by the king of Tyre may well be the same as the king who figures prominently in one of the three great Ugaritic epics. Otherwise, the large number of lexical, syntactical, and stylistic "Ugaritisms" that are evident in the Book of Proverbs establish a cultural continuity of Canaanite and Israelite wisdom expression.

Besides Ahikar (above) some intertestamental examples of wisdom must be noted. Some of them may be quoted or at least alluded to in the New Testament (cf also James as a New Testament wisdom book, often posing theological problems very similar to those of its Old Testament counterparts). Ecclesiasticus (c 200 BC) is quite comparable to Proverbs, while the pseudepigraphic Wisdom of Solomon (c 100 BC) contains longer compositions and sometimes shows marked Hellenistic influence. Wisdom influence is also very apparent in portions of Tobit, Baruch, and *1 Esdras* (e.g., the tale of the contest between the court pages won by Zerubbabel).

Timna, Israel, in the region of ancient Edom, remembered for its wise sayings.

LUTHERAN THEOLOGIANS ON PROVERBS

Luther

"[Proverbs] may properly be called a book of good works, for in it [Solomon] teaches how to lead a good life before God and the world.

"He pays special attention to the young people. In fatherly fashion he instructs them in God's commandments, with reassuring promises of how well things shall be with the righteous, and threats as to how the wicked will have to be punished. For young people are of themselves inclined to all evil. Because of their inexperience, they do not understand the wiles and wickedness of the world and the devil. They are far too weak to withstand bad examples and the causes of offense, neither are they able to govern themselves. If they are not instructed, they are ruined and lost even before they get their bearings.

"Therefore young people need and must have teachers and rulers who will exhort, warn, rebuke, and chastise them, who will hold them constantly to the fear of God and to his commandments in order to ward off the devil, the world, and the flesh. This, then, is what Solomon does abundantly and with all diligence in this book. He puts his teaching into proverbs, so that it can be grasped the more easily and kept the more readily. Anyone who intends to become righteous might well take this as a handbook or prayer-book for his daily use, read it often, and ponder his own life in it.

"For a man must go one of two ways: either he must let his father chastise him or he must let the executioner punish him. As they say, 'You may escape me, but you will not escape the hangman.' And it would be good to impress this constantly on the young people, so that they might know without any doubt that they must suffer either the father's rod or the executioner's sword, just as, in this book, Solomon is constantly threatening the disobedient with death. There is no other way out, for God leaves nothing unpunished. We see in our own experience that disobedient knaves perish in strange ways; they finally come into the executioner's hands just when they least expect it and feel most secure. Public testimony and signs of all this are the gallows, wheels, and places of execution at the gates of all the cities. Through his temporal government God has put them there to terrify all those who will not obey their elders and let themselves be instructed in God's word.

"Therefore in this book Solomon calls all those who despise God's word 'fools,' and all those who deport themselves according to God's commandments 'wise.' This does not apply solely to young people—though it is primarily they whom he has undertaken to teach—but to people of all stations from the highest to the very lowest. For just as youth has its own particular offenses against God's commandments, so every other group has its vices as well; and these are worse than the vices of youth. As they say, 'The older they are, the worse they get'; and again, 'Age is no cure for folly.'

"Even if there were nothing evil in the other and higher stations, no greed, pride, hatred, envy, etc., nevertheless this one vice would be bad enough, namely, that they try to be shrewd and smart when they ought not to be; everybody is inclined to do something else than what is committed to him, and to leave undone that which is committed to him. For example, whoever is in the spiritual office tries to be wise and active in the worldly office, and there is no end to his wisdom in this regard; in turn, whoever is in the worldly office has a head too small to hold all his superfluous knowledge about the conduct of the spiritual office.

"Of such fools all lands, all cities, all homes are full, and in this book they are diligently rebuked. Everyone is exhorted to take care of his own affairs and to do faithfully and diligently that which is committed to him; there is indeed no virtue beyond that of obedience, attending to that which is given him to do. Such people are called wise men; the disobedient are called fools, even though they do not want to be, or be called, disobedient men or fools." (AE 35:258–60)

Gerhard

"*The Proverbs of Solomon* are called by the Hebrews *mishle shelomoh*, the 'Parables or Proverbs of Solomon.'

"Solomon, also called Jedediah and Koheleth, wrote three books in accord with the number of his names. Nevertheless the latter part of this book (from c. 25 to the end) was copied from other books by Sebna and other scribes of King Hezekiah of Judah.

"The Greeks call them *Paroimiai*, 'Proverbs,' because they contain adages, parables, comparisons, and outstanding statements encouraging everyone to the virtues described in the Decalogue. It contains thirty-one chapters. It can be divided with regard to its efficient cause into the proverbs of Solomon and of other wise men, or with regard to its object and subject matter into: (1) general and specific statements—political, economic, ethical, and mixed; (2) into rules about faith and behavior.

"Solomon is commonly claimed to be the author of this book, yet some think that this book was collected by some other person from the statements of Solomon. We could justifiably call it 'The Book of Duties' or 'Holy Ethics' because it contains useful rules of life about the duties of the devout toward God and men. In addition, because this Book of Proverbs mentions the Son (30:4), Franciscus Davidis (*Disp. Albana tt. ij*, letter A), the ministers of Transylvania (bk. 2, c. 10), and Johannes Sommerus (*Refut. Carol.*, p. 41) reject it 'among the apocryphal books' in which we cannot safely place our confidence. Against these heretics, however, we set forth the unanimous consensus of the Israelite and Christian Church that never doubted the canonicity of this book. It contains 915 verses." (ThC E1 § 145)

FURTHER STUDY

Lay/Bible Class Resources

Dumit, Julene. *Proverbs: God's Gift of Wisdom*. GWFT. St. Louis: Concordia, 1995. ♫ Lutheran author. Ten-session Bible study, including leader's notes and discussion questions.

Ehlke, Roland C. *Proverbs*. PBC. St. Louis: Concordia, 2005. ♫ Lutheran author. Excellent for Bible classes. Based on the NIV translation.

Kidner, Derek. *Proverbs: An Introduction and Commentary*. TOTC. Downers Grove, IL: InterVarsity Press, 1975. ♫ A master of the Wisdom Literature, Kidner packs much information in his comments. However, he often misses the Gospel in Proverbs and does not relate to the text from a Christocentric perspective.

Life by His Word. St. Louis: Concordia, 2009. ♫ More than 1,500 reproducible one-page Bible studies covering each chapter of the canonical Scriptures. Page references to *The Lutheran Study Bible*. CD-Rom and downloadable.

Schurb, Ken, and Edward Engelbrecht. *Proverbs*. Leaders Guide and Enrichment Magazine/Study Guide. LL. St. Louis: Concordia, 2004. ♫ An in-depth, nine-session Bible Study covering the Books of Proverbs with individual, small group, and lecture portions.

Church Worker Resources

Bridges, Charles. *An Exposition of the Book of Proverbs*. London: Banner of Truth, 1968. ♫ A reprint of a classic resource. Bridges shows how Proverbs with its practical truths relates to the rest of Scripture.

Kidner, Derek. *The Wisdom of Proverbs, Job and Ecclesiastes: An Introduction to Wisdom Literature*. Downers Grove, IL: InterVarsity Press, 2008. ♫ Surveys the themes of biblical wisdom as reflected in these books. He interacts with contemporary thought on Wisdom Literature and compares Old Testament with apocryphal wisdom literature and other parallels in ancient Near Eastern thought.

Steinmann, Andrew. *Proverbs*. CC. St. Louis: Concordia, 2010. ♫ The best commentary available for Lutheran interpreters who seek careful historical consideration of the text, including philology and poetics, as well as Christological interpretation and application.

Academic Resources

K&D. *Biblical Commentaries on the Old Testament: The Proverbs of Solomon*. 2 vols. Grand Rapids: Eerdmans, 1950 reprint. ♫ This century-and-a-half old work from Lutheran scholars should not be overlooked. Despite its age, it remains a most useful commentary on the Hebrew text. Delitzsch carefully underlines the significance of the Hebrew text.

Scott, R. B. Y. *Proverbs/Ecclesiastes*. AB. New York: Doubleday, 1965. ♫ Draws parallels between Proverbs and pagan literature as he sees them. Exposition stresses the ethical content. Sometimes rather anemic.

Zöckler, Otto, and Charles Augustus Aiken. *The Proverbs of Solomon: Theologically and Homiletically Expounded*. LCHS. New York: Charles Scribner's Sons, 1870. ♫ A helpful older example of German biblical scholarship, based on the Hebrew text, which provides references to significant commentaries from the Reformation era forward.

ECCLESIASTES

Fear God and keep His commandments

Tradition attributed Ecclesiastes to Solomon's cynical older years, a suggestion that well matches the mood of the book and its poetic allusions to aging in 12:1–8. (See pp 661–62.) For an overview of Solomon's accomplishments and their historical context, see pp 321–22.

Historical and Cultural Setting

In keeping with the tradition of Solomonic authorship during his old age, we include the following observations based on 1 Kings and broader Near Eastern history.

Solomon's success as a ruler was diminished as he spent himself on selfish pursuits, especially foreign women and their idolatrous ways of worship. First Kings 11 states that the Lord grew angry with Solomon and raised up adversaries against him. Hadad the Edomite had fled David's reign to dwell in Egypt, where he was welcomed and prospered. Upon hearing of David's death, Hadad returned to Edom and fostered resistance to Solomon's reign. Similarly, a Syrian (Aramean) named Rezon escaped David but became king of Damascus. He, too, resisted Solomon. Finally, Jeroboam was a gifted servant of Solomon, entrusted with overseeing forced labor in north central Israel (tribes of Joseph—Ephraim and Manasseh). Like Hadad, Jeroboam fled to Egypt when Solomon suspected him of disloyalty.

While these three examples of local resistance would have troubled Solomon's reign, greater challenges were developing further afield in Egypt and Mesopotamia. The expansion of Israel under Saul, David, and Solomon corresponds to the beginning of the "Third Intermediate Period" of Egyptian history. The Egyptians became divided after the death of Rameses XI and were also resisted by the Libyans to the west and the Kishites to the south. In Solomon's latter years, he would have noted the increasing strength of Pharaoh Shoshenq I, who would eventually invade Judah in 927 BC, after Solomon's death.

Mask of Shoshenq I (biblical Shishak), who came to power in Solomon's later years and invaded Judah after Solomon's death.

A similar situation was developing to the north and east. A united Israel under Saul and David had successfully resisted invasions from the Arameans, who instead chose to fight their eastern neighbor, the Assyrians. Tiglath-pileser II defeated the Arameans in c 1100 BC. But after his death in 1076, there was a decline in Assyrian power. Toward the end of Solomon's reign arose Ashur-dan II, who inaugurated the Neo-Assyrian Empire that would ultimately conquer the northern tribes of Israel.

As a keen internationalist, Solomon would have noted these changes of power in Egypt and Assyria while he was trying to maintain peace within his own kingdom. He would realize that his heir required all his wisdom to maintain the kingdom of Israel. First Kings 12 tragically records the sins of Solomon's son, Rehoboam, whose decisions divided Israel precisely when their rivals were gaining strength. These historical circumstances could explain Solomon's anxiety expressed in Ecclesiastes (cf e.g., 2:18–23).

COMPOSITION

Author

The Hebrew title, "Qoheleth," is obviously based on the superscription (1:1), "The words of the Preacher [Qoheleth], the son of David, king in Jerusalem." The form *qoheleth* appears nowhere else in the Bible besides its seven occurrences in this book. It is a feminine form, which is usually understood as an abstraction—in this case an office, function, or a title (there are parallels to that usage). However, with one exception (7:27) a masculine verb form (predicate) follows in the text, presumably because the office was always filled by a man. It appears that the author of the book himself used the title as a pen name. Thus, it is an appropriate title for both the author and the work. The Greek translation is "Ecclesiastes," and its English equivalent would mean "Preacher."

MISUNDERSTANDING LUTHER

In 1566 Johann Aurifaber published a German edition of Luther's *Table Talk*,[1] which included the following saying attributed to Luther: "Solomon himself did not write the Book of Ecclesiastes, but it was produced by Sirach at the time of the Maccabees.—It is a sort of Talmud, compiled from many books, probably from the library of King Ptolemy Euergetes of Egypt."[2] In contrast, Conrad Cordatus recorded the statement as referring to the apocryphal book of Ecclesiasticus, which was written at the time of the Maccabees.[3]

Most scholars who consulted the *Table Talk* did not notice that Aurifaber's German edition likely contained a mistake. So they assumed that Luther suggested radical opinions about Ecclesiastes. In 1848 Förstemann and Bindseil published a new edition of the Aurifaber collection just as modern critical views were gaining acceptance. At that time, Franz Delitzsch noted the possible misunderstanding in the introduction to his commentary on Ecclesiastes, but this did not prevent critical scholars from citing Luther to support their radical view that Ecclesiastes was written after the Babylonian exile. Not surprisingly, modern critical judgment rejects Solomonic authorship virtually unanimously, but also many conservative scholars (Hengstenberg, Delitzsch, Young, Leupold, Harrison, Pfeiffer, etc.) agreed with the prevailing opinion introduced by someone misunderstanding Luther.

---

1   *Tischreden oder colloquia doct. Mart. Luthers* (Urban Gaubisch: Eisleben, 1566).
2   Page 533; WA TR 2:2776B attributes the saying to late 1532.
3   See WA TR 2:2776B.

The name Solomon is never explicitly used, but is clearly implied in the superscription "son of David, king in Jerusalem" (1:1) and similarly in 1:12 and 2:9. Various other allusions in the book plainly point in the same direction: the author's "great wisdom" (1:16), massive wealth, many servants (2:4–8), etc. Until modern times, there was only a minimal question about it.

Luther asserted that "this book was certainly not written or set down by King Solomon with his own hand. Instead, scholars put together what others had heard from Solomon's lips," and he cites 12:11 as evidence.

Date of Composition

The book asserts a tenth century BC origin with Solomon. Early critics attempted to place its composition late in the second century. The discovery of fragments of the book at Qumran and its familiarity to Jesus son of Sirach (second century BC) contradict such late dating. Possibly a majority of critics still cling to a third century date, but the trend among critics appears to be toward a somewhat earlier period.

Linguistic Arguments

The major argument for a postexilic date is linguistic. The situation is similar to that in Song of Solomon. No one who knows both classical and Mishnaic Hebrew will dispute the judgment that Qoheleth seems more like the latter, often in syntax as well as in vocabulary. Delitzsch is often quoted to the effect that if Ecclesiastes was really written by Solomon, the Hebrew language had no history, and he amasses some 96 words, etc., found elsewhere only in undeniably postexilic literature when Aramaic and Greek prevailed.[4]

The linguistic argument, however, is a very uncertain one. Archaeological discoveries in the past century have seriously weakened it. The supposed late and "Aramaic" cast of the language no longer carries much weight. Evidence at Ugarit shows that the elements thought to be Aramaic were ancient western Semitic elements. Albright, Dahood, and others have launched weighty arguments in favor of heavy Phoenician-Canaanite influence on the book's diction; while they themselves think of early postexilic provenance of the work, the arguments could also apply to Solomonic and/or to northern Israelite origins, possibly because that was the dialect in which discourses of that sort were ordinarily couched at the time. We simply lack sufficient Hebrew literature to construct with confidence any certain chart of the development of the language in different times and areas beyond the broadest generalities. As in the case of Song of Solomon, Persian or Sanskrit might explain what is often understood as Greek influence (due to Solomon's extensive trade contacts with the East; see pp 677–78). Elsewhere we have shown that Hellenistic traders were active in Israel from an earlier date than previously imagined (see p 868). Furthermore, an essentially Solomonic text might have been updated linguistically (a revision of Chaucer or even Shakespeare into modern English is a frequent and apt comparison).

---

4   Among the words regarded as late are *she-* instead of *'asher* as the relative pronoun, *pardes* (park or paradise), *zeman* (time), *kasher* (correct or kosher), etc. Syntactically, one notes the frequent use of the personal pronoun as a copula, the rare use of the waw-consecutive, etc.

Comparative Approaches

Instead of arguing for Greek influence, a more common comparative argument for lateness today seeks parallel developments in wisdom circles elsewhere in the ancient Near East. Ecclesiastes is widely understood as part of a late revolt against "wisdom orthodoxy," especially its allegedly rigid doctrine of reward and retribution for good or evil. There is no doubt that wisdom all over the ancient Near East entered into a crisis in late Old Testament times. On the other hand, we have evidences of periods of disillusionment (and even the entertaining of suicide) in both Egypt and Mesopotamia from much earlier periods (the "Song of the Harper," the "Dispute over Suicide," the "Pessimistic Dialogue between Master and Servant," even themes underlying the ancient and famous Gilgamesh Epic). One is surely justified in arguing that such moods are so recurrent, both individually and culturally, that a chronological case based on such parallels is extremely weak.

Remains of the original Jebusite walls of Jebus (Jerusalem).

Arguments about Internal Evidence

Another argument claims internal evidences militate against Solomon as the author. For example, the claim in 1:16 to have acquired more wisdom than "all who were over Jerusalem before me" has always aroused suspicion because only David ruled Jerusalem before Solomon (it had been a Jebusite city previously). But the statement does not specify kings, and Jerusalem was certainly an ancient city in Solomon's time. Similarly, 1:12 might easily be translated "I have *become* king" instead of ESV's "have been." Various times in the book (e.g., 4:13; 10:17) an objective or even critical viewpoint is adopted toward kingship, but if Solomon (or anyone else) wished to speak in traditional wisdom vein, that is exactly what one would expect (cf many parallels in Proverbs). Finally, it is often argued that the book refers to very difficult economic and social circumstances (cf 1:2–11; 3:1–15; 4:1–3; 7:1), such as would fit much of the postexilic period, but do not fit with Solomonic prosperity. However, wisdom speaks to circumstances that recur constantly in human experience, and there is nothing in Ecclesiastes that cannot easily be viewed in that way.

We have noted that all the arguments against the traditional position can be parried, if not refuted. Especially if one is ready to concede the possibility of later linguistic updating, little remains that hinders the conclusion that Solomon wrote the book.

Purpose/Recipients

As noted above, Ecclesiastes is written as a public address to the wise in which the speaker demolishes common opinion as "vanity of vanities" in order to prepare his hearers for a higher and truer wisdom.

One of the puzzling characteristics of the work is its frequent alternation of viewpoint, from what at least appears to be rank agnosticism to very traditional, orthodox-sounding assertions—and back again. Already the rabbis were concerned about what appeared to be contradictions. Some commentators have attempted the explanation that we have reflected here the vacillation in the author's own mind, his dialogue with himself as he struggled (barely successfully) to staunch the rising tide of skepticism about traditional values.

At one time, it was popular in critical circles to seek a literary solution to the problem. This took various forms, but they frequently proposed a double revision of Ecclesiastes: (1) by a wisdom editor, who sought to neutralize the book's strictures on the wisdom movement by stressing the merits of wisdom as a way of life; and (2) by an orthodox pietist who tried to render harmless various heresies in the work by adding passages stressing divine judgment and urging reverence toward God on the part of the reader. Among the passages commonly suspected are: 2:25; 3:15b, 17; 5:6b, 19; 7:18b, 29; 8:5; 9:7b; 11:9b; 12:1a, 13–14. However, the fact that the critics themselves could not agree on the alleged history of the book's formation, plus the absence of any kind of linguistic evidence that the suspect passages were added, has made this approach today a less-favored one. Even many critics are prepared to defend the book's essential unity.

Literary Features

Genre

Qoheleth is probably related to the Hbr noun *qahal*, which means "assembly" or "convocation" of almost any sort, including "congregation" or "church." However, the author describes himself as a speaker in a public wisdom assembly. He may address the general public whose "wisdom" is still largely that of this world. This audience he meets on its own terms—terms that he largely demolishes ("vanity of vanities") in order to prepare them for a higher and truer wisdom.

Characters

The main character is the speaker, whom the book and tradition maintained was Solomon. His references to old age suggest that the book was written in that season of life. Other figures who receive his counsel are mentioned in passing (cf the young, 11:9).

Narrative Development or Plot

The book's opening is almost anti-plot: everything repeats and nothing new develops. The author's personal experiences and experiments in life are presented in 1:12–2:26. He was on a quest to learn the best way to live, but his quest was frustrated. He shares both his frustrations and his insights. Subsequent sections convey further personal insights, culminating in ch 12 where he provides summary advice on the whole duty of man.

The challenges of aging are among the themes Solomon contemplated in Ecclesiates.

Resources

As noted above, there are similar themes in other Near Eastern compositions but Ecclesiastes does not acknowledge any of them as sources. Luther commented on the oral and public character of the book's presentation. One may envision Solomon as king addressing his court or another gathering while scribes record his thoughts. The poem about time in ch 3, and other poetic compositions in the book, may have been composed separately and incorporated into the work (e.g., the poem contrasting wisdom and folly in ch 7 shares similarities with many passages in Proverbs; Ec 12:9 acknowledges the author's editorial activity).

OUTLINE

Text and Translations

The Hebrew text of Ecclesiastes is in good order. The LXX follows it carefully, which leads to some stilted passages in the Greek.

DOCTRINAL CONTENT

Summary Commentary

1:1–11 Our lives, no matter how well lived, will not win favor in God's sight on the Last Day. Life is fleeting and has no meaning apart from God's love.

1:12–6:12 Our minds cannot fathom God's wisdom. The pursuit of pleasure can draw us away from the Lord and toward other altars, as Solomon turned to other gods and idols before returning to God. Toil and labor "under the sun" can drive one to the brink of grievous despair. Since God's will is unsearchable, we are hard pressed to answer eternal questions. Nevertheless, hold sacred the gifts of marriage, children, family, and the authorities put in place among us. Do not regard the accolades and accoutrements of the world as more important than the Lord and His gracious gifts. Wicked and foolish people sin against God in acts of religious complacency, empty devotion, and unfulfilled vows.

7:1–12:8 Avoiding God's wisdom is wickedness and folly, but finding such wisdom—as God gives it—preserves our life and gives us hope in the face of all frustrations. Other sources of wisdom offer little or no hope, certainly none in the face of God's final judgment. No matter in which nation we dwell, we are in the service of the King of heaven and earth and do well only by heeding His Word and by being ready and willing to serve. In this life, the wicked may fare better than those who do right. Although we see others getting away with doing wrong, we should not follow them. Rather than trying to make sense of everything that happens in life, recognize that God's purpose and plan prevail.

From a human, mortal perspective, it appears unfair that all people must die, as death deals equally with evil people as well as those who follow God. Yet God looks with favor

An ancient Jewish cemetery on the Mount of Olives, near Jerusalem.

upon the one who lives by faith. The twists and turns of life often tempt one to be foolish, because wisdom does not always quickly gain respect or results. We understand, as we conduct our lives, that God has the final say. The aches of old age make it difficult to envision anything hopeful and positive. Such bodily changes may overwhelm any joy we still have in life.

12:9–14 Solomon closes by emphasizing that the one searching for meaning in life should have come to the conclusions he offers. In particular, to avoid a meaningless life, one needs a right relationship with God.

Specific Law Themes

For natural man, life and success have no real significance. If one is foolish, that hastens destruction. If one has worldly wisdom, life remains dissatisfying. It inevitably ends with death and God's judgment. In view of these realities, the book repeatedly emphasizes the emptiness of life in a sin-filled world.

Specific Gospel Themes

The Creator graciously provides for us in every season and time. Life gains meaning and pleasure through fear, love, and trust in Him. True wisdom is also His gift, which leads to contentment ultimately provided in Christ Jesus.

Specific Doctrines

Read in full context, Ecclesiastes teaches that one does not have any warrant to evade the responsibilities of the time in which God has placed him. Like wisdom in general, one must remember the present, *before* it is too late. The refrain about God's judgment is focused primarily on the decisions of this life. However, at the very least, it is open to eternal matters. The writer of Ecclesiastes is aware that, once death comes, the judgment is irreversible. This entails the doctrine of man's creation as well as his fall into sin (Ec 12:7; Gn 3:19). There is certainly nothing here that contradicts other Scripture, but the interpreter must invoke "Scripture interprets Scripture" to expound its full impact.

The book's main point, however, remains to fight against any claim that human wisdom can discern God's ultimate purposes. The writer is not disillusioned, but *un*illusioned; not a cynic, but a realist. Even less is he any sort of closet atheist; God is obviously fundamental to his whole outlook. His worldview is still the traditional one (that is, a personal God, not "process"). God in His omnipotent and omniscient wisdom does have the answers, but He does not reveal them all (cf Job). He is the hidden God (*Deus absconditus*—not the inscrutable *moira* [Fate] of Greek cynicism). To the unbeliever He forever remains only hidden (despite "general revelation"), and even to the believer life's mystery is revealed only to the eyes of faith. God has given mankind his "portion," but He retains eternal matters in His own hand.

In wisdom one may catch a glimpse of God's own absolute freedom, but the more someone begins to grasp for it (rather than receiving it in grace), the more it eludes him. We should learn that neither science nor reason leads either to absolute certainty or to absolute freedom; rather absolute freedom, like absolute power, corrupts absolutely. (The greatest intellectual may turn out to be the silliest monster.) And even if all else fails, finally death unfailingly convinces a man of his utter finitude (Ec 12). Thus, the bulk of Qoheleth is one of the Bible's major proclamations of the Law (the second use, *usus elenchthicus*). It presents a clear, cold picture of a person's life without the covenant relationship with God.

Ecclesiastes 1:2–11 states the circularity of nature, which is indisputably true; the ultimate question is how one understands or interprets this, whether as the totality of reality or as evidence of God's covenant with nature (Gn 8:22). Similarly, with later statements on the unprovability of life after death, the question is whether or not more can be said at all. He who never questions, never doubts, is either a liar or unacquainted with revelation. There is truth to Bonhoeffer's treatment of Qoheleth as a manual on how to overcome doubt.

There are positive and corrective statements in the book. They are rather brief, for-

Solomon describes the fruitfulness of his vineyards and gardens (2:4–5), which grow, bear fruit, and decay into vanity through the seasons of life. Yet working, eating, and drinking remain among the basic joys of life (2:24).

mulaic, and undeveloped, but we have consistently noted this is characteristic of the entire wisdom genre. There is no more reason for reading them as superficial and half-hearted in the case of Ecclesiastes than of Proverbs and Job. And if read in full canonical context, the book has far more to say. Wisdom overcomes vanity and gains the fullness of life (its own limits as well as its divinely ordained fulfillment) only when it dares believe that the Creator is also the God who gave Himself to Israel, who encountered it in wrath and judgment, but also redeemed it—in Jesus Christ.

Application

1:1–11 Since life is both fleeting and routine, we need the Lord's wise Word to inspire and direct us. Faith worked in us by the power of the Gospel brings meaning to life and the certainty of forgiveness, eternal life, and salvation.

1:12–6:12 Life is confusing and can seem pointless. We know God's mercy only through the wisdom revealed to us in Holy Scripture, which is hidden in Christ (cf Jas 3:13–18; 1Co 1:30). When we return thanks to God for His gracious and simple gifts—house and home, flocks and herds, spouse and children—we focus on His fatherly mercy and kindness. Take pleasure in the Creator to gain proper appreciation of His gifts. For all that is done in the absence of faith will become chaff thrown into the devouring fire. Christ bids us to come to Him and be yoked to His light burden. Seek first His kingdom and His gifts, and all other things shall be given. God will judge the living and the dead on the Last Day. Temporal things cannot satisfy God's people. Eternity and the consummation of salvation are in Christ alone (cf Rm 8:18).

7:1–12:8 The only way to acquire wisdom is in the revelation that God has given us of Himself. Do not let the frustrations of life drive you to foolishness. Focus on the Lord and His wisdom. In our King, we find the hope of things to come and can face the end of life with confidence. Look for reasons to give thanks to Him each day, especially in the mercy He extends to you in Christ. When God blesses you with wealth, enjoy that blessing and be a blessing to others. Make proper use of the time God gives in life. Know that denying yourself simple pleasures does not gain God's favor. Simple and godly pleasures are only the beginning of the gifts of His love and forgiveness that He grants in Christ. The same God who consigned us to the grave because of sin has also promised us that we will be rescued from the grave and His eternal judgment. Through hearing the Word in our youth, He will prepare us. His promises will stay with us.

12:9–14 Justification based on God's favor toward us on account of Christ is received through faith. God has given His Word, and through it we have the ability to know His Commandments and promises. More important, we can know Him and how to avoid a meaningless life now and in eternity.

CANONICITY

The sequence of books in the Septuagint witnesses to the use of Ecclesiastes in early Judaism. Following the Davidic psalter come the books ascribed to Solomon—Proverbs, Ecclesiastes, and Song of Solomon—as son follows father.

The Mishnah records that the school of Hillel won out over the more conservative school of Shammai that questioned the sacred character of Ecclesiastes. Ecclesiastes was early assigned as a proper reading for a major Jewish liturgical festival: Succoth (Booths or "Tabernacles"). The book's somber message probably served as a damper on the excesses often associated with that autumn wine festival.

Family decorating their sukkah for the Festival of Booths (or Tabernacles).

The Tosefta clearly questions the book's canonicity, while assuming Solomonic authorship. The Talmud preserves considerable evidence of Jewish misgivings about the work (both authorship and canonicity), even in post-Mishnaic times. St. Jerome reported about Jews in his day who wished the book had not survived.

Among Christians, the New Testament does not speak to the issue of Solomonic authorship (in fact, the Scripture never clearly quotes or alludes to Ecclesiastes). Before the rise of higher criticism, the Church had little hesitation about the book; the Church Fathers and Reformers produced many (still useful) commentaries and preached countless sermons on it, though Luther complained about the great difficulty posed by the book. Nevertheless, he wrote an excellent commentary on it.

LUTHERAN THEOLOGIANS ON ECCLESIASTES

Luther

"This book is called in Hebrew *Qoheleth*, that is, 'One who speaks publicly in a congregation.' For *Qahal* means a congregation assembled together, that which in Greek is called *ekklesia*. . . . Now this book ought really to have a title [to indicate] that it was written against the free will. For the entire book tends to show that the counsels, plans, and undertakings of men are all in vain and fruitless, and that they always have a different outcome from that which we will and purpose. Thus Solomon would teach us to wait in confident trust and to let God alone do everything, above and against and without our knowledge and counsel. Therefore you must not understand this book to be reviling God's creatures when it says, 'All is vanity and a striving after wind.' For God's creatures are all good, Genesis 1[:31] and II Timothy 4 [I Tim. 4:4]; and this book itself says that a man shall be happy with his wife and enjoy life, etc. [Eccles. 9:9]. It teaches, rather, that the plans and undertakings of men in their dealings with the creatures all go wrong and are in vain, if one is not satisfied with what is presently at hand but wants to be their master and ruler for the future. That's how it always goes—backward—so that a man has had nothing but wasted toil and anxiety; things turn out anyway as God wills and purposes, not as we will and purpose.

"To put it briefly, Christ says in Matthew 6[:34], 'Do not be anxious about tomorrow, for tomorrow will have its own anxiety; it is enough that every day has its own evil.' This saying is really the interpretation and content of this book. Anxiety about us is God's affair; our anxiety goes wrong anyhow, and produces nothing but wasted toil." (AE 35:263–64)

For more of Luther's insights on this book, see *Notes on Ecclesiastes* (AE 15:1–187).

Gerhard

"*Ecclesiastes* is called by the Hebrews *qoheleth*, the feminine participle from the root *qhl*, 'he gathered.' Rabbi D. Kimchi believes that Solomon is so called because his soul had gathered an abundance of arts and wisdom for him. The feminine form has to do either with 'wisdom,' through which Solomon called together the people to himself and addressed them regarding necessary and useful matters, or with 'the soul,' which is the nobler part of man. In Eccles. 1:2 it is construed with the masculine. The Greeks call it *Ekklesiastes*, 'The Preacher,' because it speaks to the multitude generally, not to any one person in particular, as does Proverbs, according to Jerome's observation.

"The author of this book, by consensus of all, is Solomon, who undoubtedly set forth these teachings to his court either at table or in friendly conversation, as we gather from 1 Kings 10:8. Many of the Hebrews say that Solomon wrote this book in repentance after having lived a profligate life. Others say that with a prophetic spirit he foresaw the division of his kingdom under his son Rehoboam and was drawn into a contempt for fickle vanity. (See Ludovicus Vives, *Augustini de civ. Dei*, bk. 20, c. 3.)

"Ecclesiastes has twelve chapters. Its author explains the sum and goal of the entire book in the last chapter, v. 8, namely: 'Everything in the world is vanity.' Thus there is nothing more useful and necessary than to 'fear God and keep His commandments' (v. 13). There are, then, two chief parts: the first, concerning the vanity of human affairs and pursuits in the world; second, regarding the stability and usefulness of piety and the fear of God.

"Philaster (*Catal. haeres.*, c. 132) mentions that some heretics threw Ecclesiastes and the other books of Solomon out of the canon. In *De verbo Dei*, bk. 1, c. 5, Bellarmine accuses Luther of undermining the canonical authority of this book because [Luther] says in *Conv. serm.*, title *De lib. V. et N. T.*: 'The author of the book that is called Ecclesiastes seems to me to lack boots and spurs and rides only in slippers, as I myself used to do when I was still in the monastery.'[5]

---

5   StL 22:1411 (Table Talk).

"We respond. (1) We stated earlier what one must decide about the *Table Talk*. (2) Luther's words are being cut off as they are quoted. (3) Bellarmine, that copyist, has taken what Luther said about the Book of Ecclesiasticus or Sirach and applied this foolishly to the Book of Ecclesiastes. You see, Luther states clearly that he is speaking about that book that speaks out against tyrants, which Sirach made at the time of the Maccabees, which includes teachings about household responsibilities, which was collected from the library of Ptolemy Euergetes (all of which fits Sirach rather than Ecclesiastes). (4) Luther elucidated Ecclesiastes with a learned and useful commentary. Far be it from him to undermine its authority. (5) In his German Bible, Luther clearly counts this among the canonical books and separates it from the apocryphal books.

"Bellarmine will never be able to prove, therefore, that Luther undermined the canonical authority of Ecclesiastes. Rather, let him see how he can excuse the fact that a certain English Papist doctor in 1566 published a book entitled *Comitia Parlamentaria*, in which he tells a story about someone who had read the Book of Ecclesiastes and said that it was harmful. The doctor bears witness that he had heard this with his own ears. Heskinsius does not contradict him at all but says, 'This was a man to be respected, serious, prudent, devout, not unlearned,' and he adds: 'Hence it becomes quite clear how perilous a matter it is for laymen to read Scripture.' Heskinsius himself makes this judgment about Ecclesiastes: 'What frightens a person away from wisdom more strongly than the Book of Ecclesiastes? How shamefully the author seems to abuse wisdom, an outstanding gift of God, in this book!' " (ThC E1 §§ 146–47)

QUESTIONS PEOPLE ASK ABOUT ECCLESIASTES

Immortality of the Soul

Ecclesiastes 3:19–20 declares: "For what happens to the children of man and what happens to the beasts is the same; as one dies, so dies the other. They all have the same breath, and man has no advantage over the beasts, for all is vanity. All go to one place. All are from the dust, and to dust all return."

John 5:28–29 predicts: "Do not marvel at this, for an hour is coming when all who are in the tombs will hear his voice and come out, those who have done good to the resurrection of life, and those who have done evil to the resurrection of judgment."

The second text, as so many others, proclaims that there will be a general resurrection of the dead. The first has often been held to teach that death means annihilation and that hence the hope of the resurrection from the dead is vain. If the Ecclesiastes passage really teaches the utter destruction of the human person at death, then we must admit the existence of a discrepancy in the Scriptures. But does it contain such teaching? The text mentioned above merely asserts that as animals die, so must people die. The time comes when an animal breathes its last, and so it is with people. All go to one place. All are of the dust, and all turn to dust again. It is plain that the first text is speaking of the dissolution of the body that results from death. But what of the soul? Does the writer of Ecclesiastes know that a person has an immortal soul, or does he deny the existence of an imperishable element in the human being? That he firmly believes in the immortality of the soul is plain from 12:7, where he says: "The dust returns to the earth as it was, and the spirit returns to God who gave it." This, then, is clearly established: (1) The writer of Ecclesiastes states that death comes upon people and animals and that there is great similarity between the death of both. (2) He teaches just as clearly that the human spirit goes to God when a person dies and hence does not cease to exist.

The Justice and Mercy of God

Ecclesiastes 12:14 asserts: "For God will bring every deed into judgment, with every secret thing, whether good or evil."

Jeremiah 31:34 affirms: "No longer shall each one teach his neighbor and each his brother, saying, 'Know the Lord,' for they shall all know me, from the least of them to the greatest, declares the Lord. For I will forgive their iniquity, and I will remember their sin no more."

The one text speaks of God's righteous judgment, the other of His gracious forgiveness of sins. How shall we harmonize them? Hundreds of Bible passages could be adduced as parallels for the first text listed and just as many confirming the teaching of the second text. In fact, the whole Bible may be said to be divided into two great parts: one proclaims God's wrath and judgment; the other God's forgiveness. In dealing with the above texts, we are simply looking into the relationship between the Law and the Gospel. We are here therefore concerned not merely with two isolated statements, but with two great doctrines of the Bible, or with two grand divisions of the Scriptures.

Christ suffered for our justification.

God shall judge every work, even every secret deed, as to its moral value, whether it be good or evil, says the Ecclesiastes passage. The meaning evidently is that God is a righteous, impartial judge, and whatever is wrong will be treated by Him as wrong, and whatever is right will likewise receive its proper judgment. The sentiment expressed is similar to that found, for instance, in Ps 5:4–6. We need not multiply passages to show that the Scriptures proclaim the perfect justice and impartiality of our great God. It is universally agreed that they describe God as just, that is, as the almighty Ruler of the universe, who will punish the evildoing He has forbidden and give due recognition to the innocence of the righteous.

The text from Jeremiah is no less plain in asserting that God, when the days of the new covenant have come, will pardon the wrongdoing of His people and not remember their transgressions of His holy will. We are here reminded of the wonderful words proclaimed by the Lord Himself when He passed by before Moses: "The LORD, the LORD, a God merciful and gracious, slow to anger, and abounding in steadfast love and faithfulness, keeping steadfast love for thousands, forgiving iniquity and transgression and sin" (Ex 34:6–7). In the New Testament, for example, we hear Jesus say: "Be merciful, even as your Father is merciful. For He is kind to the ungrateful and the evil" (Lk 6:36, 35). It might seem that these texts describe the direct antithesis of justice. How can God be just and at the same time forgive evildoing? This question takes us into the very heart of the Scriptures, to the message of redemption through the substitutionary work of our Savior. Paul discusses this very matter, the relationship between God's justice and His forgiveness, and explains it authoritatively in Rm 3:21–26. God, who is merciful, wished to save the sinful race that His justice had to condemn. It seemed that either the mercy or the justice of God would have to be infringed or impaired. But the love of the heavenly Father had from eternity provided a way of escape, a method by which sin would be punished and still forgiveness of sins not be obstructed. Jesus, the Son of God, became humanity's Substitute. The punishment that the righteousness of God had to mete out to sinners was borne by Him. Hence no one can say that God is not just and does not punish sin. And now, since the penalty of all sins has been paid, the mercy of God freely pardons the guilty human race and provides for it eternal salvation. The message is sounded forth: in Christ we have the redemption through His blood, namely, the forgiveness of sins. The work of Christ, then, makes it possible for God to be just and to judge every evil deed without withholding from sinful beings the forgiveness of their sins. What at first sight seems to us very conflicting is all wondrously harmonized if we look at Christ. It is the glory of the Christian religion that it preserves inviolate the teachings both of God's justice and of God's mercy and grace.

FURTHER STUDY

Lay/Bible Resources

Brink, Kurt W. *Ecclesiastes: Enjoying God's Gifts*. GWFT. St. Louis: Concordia, 1996. ♫ Lutheran author. Six-session Bible study, including leader's notes and discussion questions.

Eaton, Michael A. *Ecclesiastes: An Introduction and Commentary*. TOTC. Downers Grove, IL: InterVarsity Press, 1983. ♫ Helpful, in a popular format. Compact commentary consulting the Hebrew and various translations. Written by a South African evangelical pastor and scholar.

Ehlke, Roland C. *Ecclesiastes/Song of Songs*. PBC. St. Louis: Concordia, 2004. ♫ Lutheran author. Excellent for Bible classes. Based on the NIV translation.

Kidner, Derek. *The Message of Ecclesiastes*. The Bible Speaks Today. Downers Grove, IL: InterVarsity Press, 1976. ♫ A brief, popular treatment from an expert on biblical wisdom, though he questions whether Solomon actually wrote the book.

Kidner, Derek. *The Wisdom of Proverbs, Job and Ecclesiastes: An Introduction to Wisdom Literature*. Downers Grove, IL: InterVarsity Press, 2008. ♫ The subtitle explains the focus of Kidner's book, which emphasizes the literary structure and theology of biblical wisdom.

Life by His Word. St. Louis: Concordia, 2009. ♫ More than 1,500 reproducible one-page Bible studies covering each chapter of the canonical Scriptures. Page references to *The Lutheran Study Bible*. CD-Rom and downloadable.

Teske, Steven, and James Bollhagen. *Ecclesiastes/Song of Solomon*. Leaders Guide and Enrichment Magazine/Study Guide. LL. St. Louis: Concordia, 2010. ♫ An in-depth, nine-session Bible study with individual, small group, and lecture portions.

Church Worker Resources

Bollhagen, James. *Ecclesiastes*. CC. St. Louis: Concordia, 2011. ♫ The most up-to-date commentary by a Lutheran pastor and theologian, who provides a Christological approach to interpreting and applying the book's message.

Garrett, Duane A. *Proverbs, Ecclesiastes, and Song of Songs*. NAC. Vol. 14. Nashville: Broadman, 1993. ♫ Accessible for laypeople as well as pastors. His verse-by-verse exposition usually conveys the message of the text well and succinctly. He argues for Solomonic authorship and has some references to the New Testament as well as to relevant Old Testament passages. He does refer to Christ on p. 305, but otherwise there is not much explicitly Christian theology in it.

Luther, Martin. *Ecclesiastes, Song of Solomon, and the Last Words of David (2 Samuel 23:1–7)*. Vol. 15 of AE. St. Louis: Concordia, 1972. ♫ There are few commentaries on Ecclesiastes that are explicitly Christian. Luther holds to Solomonic authorship and has great, broad comments as well as many fine exegetical details. A blessing to read.

Academic Resources

Ginsburg, Christian D., ed. *The Song of Songs and Coheleth*. New York: KTAV, 1970 reprint. ॐ A major resource by a Jewish scholar who converted to Christianity. It is especially known for its histories of the interpretation of the books.

Gordis, Robert. *Koheleth: The Man and His World—A Study of Ecclesiastes*. New York: Schocken, 1968 reprint. ॐ Pays close attention to the biblical idiom; includes rabbinical parallels. Sets Ecclesiastes in the traditions of the Persian and Hellenistic periods, rather than in that of Solomon.

K&D. *Biblical Commentaries on the Old Testament: The Song of Songs and Ecclesiastes*. K&D. Grand Rapids: Eerdmans, 1949 reprint. ॐ Both a philologically and theologically significant resource. This century-and-a-half old work from Lutheran scholars should not be overlooked. Despite its age, it remains a most useful commentary on the Hebrew text.

Leupold, H. C. *Exposition of Ecclesiastes*. Grand Rapids: Baker, 1966. ॐ A careful, discerning exposition of a difficult book. He has some good references to Christ and the Christian faith. His verse-by-verse commentary often does a good job of explaining the point of the text. However, Leupold denies Solomonic authorship and dates the book very late.

Longman, Tremper, III. *The Book of Ecclesiastes*. NICOT. Grand Rapids: Eerdmans, 1998. ॐ Argues that the original writer poses as Solomon and that a second writer added the introductory and concluding portions.

Scott, R. B. Y. *Proverbs/Ecclesiastes*. AB. New York: Doubleday, 1965. ॐ Stresses recent literary and historical research; interpretation itself is brief and critical in approach.

Zöckler, Otto and Taylor Lewis, eds. *Ecclesiastes, or Koheleth*. Translated by William Wells. LCHS. New York: Charles Scribner's Sons, 1898. ॐ A helpful older example of German biblical scholarship, based on the Hebrew text, which provides references to significant commentaries from the Reformation era forward.

SONG OF SOLOMON

Love is the very flame of the Lord

The Song of Solomon celebrates love, a common theme for all people of all times. What distinguishes the Song, however, is the way it connects human love to God's greater love in a poetry that mingles the earthly with the heavenly, the royal with the rural, and the ordinary with the eternal. These elements of the Song invite the reader to see something more than boy-meets-girl, and even something more than ruler-meets-servant. If love is "strong as death" and human passion shares in "the very flame of the LORD" (8:6), the meaning of the Song ascends beyond domestic life in ancient Israel.

The title of the Song itself invites one to discover something extraordinary. In Masoretic Hebrew Bibles, the title (or superscription) of the book is simply "Song of Songs." This is a Hebrew superlative expression that might be translated, "The best/highest/greatest song," "The Song *par excellence*," etc. (cf "vanity of vanities" in Ecclesiastes). Traditionally, it was often also understood as specifically the "best" of Solomon's songs in comparison with the total of 1,005 that 1Ki 4:32 reports he composed.

Both the Septuagint and the Vulgate translated the Hebrew title literally. From the Latin *Canticum Canticorum* is derived the English "Canticles," especially common still in Roman Catholic circles.

Lightning over the Negeb Desert. Solomon compares love to a lightning flash, the "flame of the LORD" (8:6).

OVERVIEW

Author
King Solomon

Date
c 970 BC (beginning of Solomon's reign)

Places
Jerusalem; sites throughout Israel (esp the north); Shunem

People
Solomon ("my beloved"); the Shulammite ("my sister, my bride") and her brothers; daughters of Jerusalem/Zion; the watchmen; David; Bathsheba

Purpose
God's love in Christ for you is "the very flame of the Lord," which alone conquers death and enables you to be faithful to Him and to the person with whom you are united in marital love

Law Theme
Religious promiscuity and unfaithfulness (idolatry), like sexual promiscuity and unfaithfulness, are destructive

Gospel Theme
In faithful love, God sent Christ to save the world; He grants to believers the priceless blessings of love for Him and marital love for spouses

Memory Verses
Love that pleases (2:3–7); captivated by the bride (4:9–10); the flame of the Lord (8:6–7)

TIMELINE

1048–1009 BC	Reign of Saul
1009–970 BC	Reign of David
970–931 BC	Reign of Solomon
972 BC	Rehoboam born
931–914 BC	Reign of Rehoboam (Judah)

The third title of the book, and the one most common in English-speaking Protestantism, is derived from v 1 of the book, which repeats the title, "Song of Songs," and then adds, "which is Solomon's." At least, that is the ordinary translation, implying the traditional understanding that Solomon wrote the song.

Historical and Cultural Setting

As noted earlier, rabbinic tradition held that Song of Solomon was written in Solomon's youth, before the practical issues of ruling dominated his thought (cf Proverbs) or the frustrations of personal error and politics led him to cynicism in old age (Ecclesiastes). These characterizations well fit how other Old Testament books describe Solomon's experience. For more on the poem's historical and cultural setting in the Solomonic era, see the introductions to Proverbs and Ecclesiastes.

Gazelles are among the favorite descriptive images used in the Song of Solomon.

COMPOSITION

Author

As in many of the psalmic superscriptions, the Hebrew prefix *lamedh* may imply authorship, and it may not (see p 551). Linguistically, it may also be a formula of dedication, imply genre of material ("Solomonic"), or other things. This is the first of many issues in interpretation of the book.

The six explicit references to "Solomon" in the book (1:1, 5; 3:7, 11; 8:11, 12) do not necessarily imply authorship and may be understood as historical references to a prototypal figure. Three additional references to an unnamed king (1:4, 12; 7:5) are ambivalent. No other scriptural passages speak to the issue. (The Song of Solomon is not quoted at all, or evidently not even alluded to in the New Testament—a fact to which, however, no further significance should be attached, as though its canonicity were in question.)

Liberal criticism almost unanimously rejects anything literally Solomonic about the work. The ascription to Solomon is supposed to have arisen partly because of his renown as a composer of songs (1Ki 4:32), partly because of his large harem (700 wives and 300 concubines, according to 1Ki

Continued on p 679.

ISSUES RAISED BY CRITICS

Critics have challenged the Solomonic authorship of the Song in the same way they have challenged Solomonic authority for Ecclesiastes. In both books the classical relative pronoun *'asher* is replaced by *she-*. There is no doubt that this may signal late (proto-Mishnaic) Hebrew, but, on the other hand, the appearance of this pronoun at many other points in the Hebrew Bible (even in the archaic Jgs 5) makes it unwise to conclude against Solomonic authorship. Some of the other postclassical syntactical features found in Ecclesiastes do not appear in the Song, possibly, however, because it is poetry instead of prose.

The allegation of Aramaisms in the book nowhere carries the weight it once did, since Ugarit has demonstrated their presence in the language of the area even in Mosaic times. At least two words (including *pardes* in 4:13, that is, "paradise," [translated as "orchard" in ESV] originally signifying an enclosed park or nobleman's private preserve; the word also appears in Ec 2:5 and Ne 2:8) are commonly argued to betray Greek influence. However, the same roots also appear broadly in Indo-European languages (e.g., Persian and Sanskrit). The use of "paradise" in the Hebrew text of the Book of Nehemiah, written in the fifth century BC, assures us that such terms entered Hebrew at least that early. Widespread Solomonic trade contacts could make plausible the assimilation of such terms into classical Hebrew. The many exotic plants and products mentioned in the book probably witness to the same mercantile associations, though skeptics see their mention as additional evidence of a much later provenance for the work.

Assuming the work is Solomonic, there is no reason why we should exclude the possibility of later linguistic restatement, but neither is there clear reason why we need to resort to any such hypothesis. A much more attractive explanation of the book's linguistic eccentricity suggests a northern or Galilean dialect. Our knowledge of the subject is scanty, but various evidences make the variations intelligible in that light. Solomon himself was a thorough product of the Jerusalem court, the home of classical Hebrew, but if the girl being wooed hailed from the North, use of a court poet skilled in that dialect would not be unusual. At any rate, one interpretation of "Shulammite" (twice in 6:13) understands it as a reference to Shunem (in the Esdraelon plain near Galilee; the LXX transliteration *Sounamitis* would support that view).

Tirzah, an early, important city in northern Israel.

Certain other geographical references in the book could support the hypothesis of a northern setting for the work (Lebanon, Hermon, Carmel, Tirzah), but others are southern (Engedi, Heshbon, Jerusalem), plus not a few of uncertain location. In 6:4 the beloved's beauty is compared to both Jerusalem and Tirzah, and much is often made of the latter reference. Conceivably, it is no more than a play on the name's possible meaning ("pleasing, charming"), but if the reference is topographical, as seems likely, it represents a major stroke in favor of very early, if not Solomonic, origin. Since Tirzah was an early capital of the Northern Kingdom, its favorable mention (like other northern references) seems unlikely at a time after the division of Israel into Northern and Southern Kingdoms (931 BC). It may be noteworthy that Samaria, Tirzah's successor as capital, is nowhere mentioned in the poem. The indiscriminate references to all parts of the land, and the absence of even a hint of knowledge of later divisions of territory would strongly suggest origin in the period of the United Monarchy. Also in favor of Solomonic authorship would be the book's great interest in the fauna and flora of the land, consonant with the notice in 1Ki 4:33 about Solomon's intent. Not only the several references to royalty, but the general aura of regal opulence and luxury, while certainly not decisive, are strongly suggestive of the Solomonic court.

11:3, which assuredly would both make him a great lover and require the greatest of "wisdom"), partly in an attempt to justify the work's popularity and ultimately to "baptize" and canonize it. The favored critical dating of the book is probably fifth to third century BC, that is, among the latest in the canon. Others, however, think of a late preexilic date, perhaps around 600 BC.

Nevertheless, the conservative will not lightly disregard the unanimous Christian tradition of Solomonic authorship until modern times. (The Talmud, as it does in other connections, speaks of Hezekiah, but it is unclear what that should mean—if it deserves credence to begin with.) A cogent philological case can still be made for the traditional opinion that the Song dates to the era of Solomon (tenth century BC).

Ivory flower carving found in Samaria.

Date of Composition

One ancient tradition associated the Song with Solomon's youth, when passion would have been strong; Proverbs with his more pensive middle age; and Ecclesiastes with his crabbed and cynical old age. While we cannot be absolutely sure, not even of Solomonic authorship (cf above), we have seen, nevertheless, that there is ample reason why we need not allow the "assured opinion" of higher criticism to stampede us into hasty abandonment of reasonable tradition.

Purpose/Recipients

The Song celebrates God's gift of faithful passion, blessed in the context of marriage. The poem, apparently delivered before the "daughters of Jerusalem" (1:4–5) and perhaps others, displays the joys of wedded love and the value of waiting to consummate the marriage. Read in its national and canonical significance, the song celebrates God's love in Christ for His Church.

Literary Features

Genre

Most agree that the poem is ultimately popular or folk poetry, not a learned composition, although that implies no artistic inferiority. The concreteness, even earthiness of the imagery, suggests the farmer's or peasant's close feeling for the countryside, and an urban suitor might readily adopt the idiom.

Both the rural context and the Near Eastern culture may help account for some of the sexual and physiological candor of the poem (sometimes concealed by euphemisms in translation). Israelite sensitivities were properly shocked and outraged by the nudity of Greek art and the Hellenistic gymnasium, but their verbal descriptions tended to be earthier and franker than are generally considered good taste in the West. Cultural feelings about taste and issues of basic morality should not be confused, however. Some similes are simply alien to our experience, e.g., the maiden's comparison to "a mare among Pharaoh's chariots" (1:9), or her hair to "a flock of goats leaping down the slopes of Gilead" (4:1). All of this magnifies the interpreter's task, but it is also a salutary reminder that the Holy Scriptures are no timeless revelation but very much bound to particularities of time and space, and any interpretative attempt to evade them is ultimately fraudulent.

Egyptian horses and chariot.

It is debatable whether or not the book is really to be classified as Wisdom Literature. Since it is not explicitly a teaching document, it is often held that it can be included as wisdom only for want of any better classification, or that the association with "wisdom" arose only because of its traditional ascription to Solomon.

On the surface, it is obvious that themes of love, sex, and marriage play a very prominent role in Proverbs too. This is true both on the level of repeated moral instruction in those areas, as well as in the metaphysical metaphors of "Lady Wisdom" versus the "forbidden woman" which structures especially Pr 1–9. Sometimes the similarity extends to the very vocabulary employed to discuss the subject (e.g., the "cistern" and "flowing water" of Pr 5:15–19 with the "fountain sealed" of Sg 4:12). One also notes the absence of the divine name Yahweh in most of the Song, as in many proverbs. An explicitly proverbial quality does occur in the Song, most obviously in the wise sayings of 8:6–8.

Furthermore, the themes of the Song fit squarely in the center of those that occupied wisdom in general. If one's major topic is "nature," or better, "creation," as wisdom's was, sexuality is bound to occupy a prominent place. If one's sweep is universal, considering what in one sense applies to all people everywhere, the mystery of human love and of sexual attraction will not be overlooked. No one knew better than wisdom that sex is one of the great levelers of mankind, that no matter what else may divide them, "male and female He created them." Little is done in life without some reference to sexuality, and most of life's ultimate questions cannot be posed without consideration of its origin and transcendental significance. (One may also note the wisdomlike introduction to Ps 45, which is quite parallel to the Song of Solomon.)

Characters

The book speaks in three main voices. The **"beloved"** is Solomon, identified in the passages with singular masculine pronouns (marked "He" in the ESV). Solomon, the son of David and Bathsheba, became Israel's king, renowned for wisdom. The **"Shulammite"** (6:13) is identified in the passages with singular feminine pronouns (marked "She" in the ESV). She was poor in comparison to Solomon and accustomed to outdoor work (cf 1:5–7). She may have been a resident of the northern city Shunam. The courtship of Solomon of Judah with a northern woman could represent the national union of Judah with the northern tribes of Israel, which would add a layer of historical, symbolic, and theological richness to the poem. The third voice in the song belongs to **a chorus**, which may be the daughters of Jerusalem (cf 1:4 with v 5) though these speakers are never directly titled ("Others" in ESV).

Shunem was located beside the good farmland in the Jezreel Valley.

Narrative Development or Plot

The story underlying the complex and cyclical nature of Song of Solomon is one of courtship, wedding consummation, and married love. These elements emerge and disappear throughout the poem, which celebrates each element without trying to present them in a chronological way. As is common in poetry, the Song places greater importance on the experience of the moment than on sequences.

Alongside the story underlying the Song, one may note the thematic structure presented in the outline below.

Resources

There appear to be ancient Near Eastern parallels, as with other Wisdom Literature. This seems especially true of certain Egyptian love lyrics (which would also suit a Solomonic milieu). The parallels are not exact (and may be coincidental), but a general similarity of atmosphere, situations, and favored metaphors seems evident. Three specifics are noteworthy: (1) the many allusions to nature, a parallelism of the awakening of love and sexual urges in humanity to the awakening of nature in spring; (2) the address of the lovers as "brother" and "sister" (though this is still common in the East today); and (3) the theme of lovesickness in the absence of the object of one's affections. More controversial are alleged parallels between the Song and mythological fertility rites (cf below).

Text and Translations

A few other observations about the book's text and style are in order before we proceed. Text-critically, there is little to comment on, because the Greek and Latin versions are almost slavishly close. Partially this answers to the high theological regard in which the work was apparently early held, but one also surmises that translators and copyists had little difficulty staying awake when dealing with such subject matter! At the same time, translational difficulties abound to the present day, partly because there are so many unique terms (many probably representing archaic survivals from an early period, some 50 of them appearing only once [*hapax legomena*]), partly also because of hermeneutical uncertainty about the precise social setting.

DOCTRINAL CONTENT

Summary Commentary

1:1 In the Song, Solomon elevates our sensibilities to their highest level. Nothing is so worthy of praise as that which extols God's love and devotion toward His beloved, His Bride, His people.

1:2–17 The first poetic cycle of the song. The Shulammite is of lowly birth. Her skin is weathered, and she is easily despised, but she is the love of her husband-king.

Ch 2 The second cycle. In a world of immediate gratification, it is tempting to satisfy our desires as quickly as they awaken. Such unbridled arousal

Continued on p 691.

OUTLINE

The overall structure appears to consist of four themes arranged in sections in the following order. The letters a, b, c, and d below refer to the four themes, or stages, in the relationship:

    a. The longing anticipation of courtship

    b. The excitement and splendor of the wedding ceremony

    c. The bliss of the couple's marriage consummation

    d. The infatuation and delight of married love

Within d appear three other themes, expanding the topic of marriage:

    a'. Married search and courtship: Solomon and the Shulammite are apart and yearn for reunion

    b'. Married appreciation of beauty: these are descriptions in praise of the beauty of the spouse, not unlike the premarriage descriptions of the beloved adorned in wedding attire for the marriage ceremony

    c'. Married consummation anew: the married couple reunites in joyful bliss

Divisions of the Book	Poetic Order of Themes
I. The Union: Four Cycles (1:2–5:1)	
A. First Cycle (1:2–17)	
1. Consummation (1:1–4)	c
2. Courtship (1:5–8)	a
3. Wedding (1:9–11)	b
4. Consummation (1:12–17)	c
B. Second Cycle (ch 2)	
1. Wedding-Consummation (2:1–7)	b-c
2. Courtship (2:8–15)	a
3. Wedding (2:16)	b
4. Consummation (2:17)	c

C. Third Cycle (3:1–4:7)

   1. Courtship (3:1–5)   a

   2. Wedding (3:6–11)   b

   3. Wedding-Consummation   b-c
      (4:1–7)

D. Fourth Cycle (4:8–5:1)

   1. Courtship (4:8–11)   a

   2. Wedding (4:12–15)   b

   3. Consummation (4:16–5:1)   c

II. The Reunion: Married Love (5:2–8:14)

A. Fifth Cycle (5:2–6:10)

   1. Search (5:2–8)   a′

   2. Praise (5:9–16)   b′

   3. Garden dialogue (6:1–3)   a′

   4. Garden dialogue (6:4–10)   b′-c′

B. Sixth Cycle (6:11–8:4)

   1. Search (6:11–13)   a′

   2. Praise (7:1–9)   b′

   3. Invitation (7:10–13)   a′

   4. Longing (8:1–4)   c′

C. Conclusion (8:5–14)

   1. Love: theological highlight   b′-c′
      (8:5–7)

   2. Love: application (8:8–12)   b′-c′

   3. Final appeal (8:13–14)   c′

HISTORY OF INTERPRETATION

The history of the book's interpretation is tortuous. This article will recount the history and evaluate the alternatives. Rabbis had misgivings about the book's surface secularity, if not eroticism, and it was even reported that some of its lyrics were being sung in local taverns! The superorthodox Rabbi Akiba took the lead in defense of the book, asserting that those who understood it in a secular vein would be excluded from the resurrection. His defense of it was characterized by superlative statements such as: "The world itself is not worth the day on which this book was given to Israel, for all the Writings are holy, but the Song of Songs is the Holy of Holies." And Akiba obviously carried the day, because, as we have seen, that superlative evaluation of the book is reflected in its association with the major Jewish festival of Passover, an association that we know from the Mishnah predates the destruction of the temple. A few grumbles about the book also surface a little later in the Mishnah, but for all practical purposes the matter was settled in Judaism (also for Christianity) until the rise of modern criticism.

The situation is not substantially different in the history of Christian interpretation. The Song is included without apparent question in the earliest canonical lists. The only major exception appears to be Theodore of Mopsuestia (d 428) of the more literal and historical minded school of Antioch. The details of his interpretation are lacking, but apparently he interpreted the book at least in part as referring to Solomon's love for Pharaoh's daughter. Whether he rejected all spiritual meaning or possibly even its inspiration seems unlikely, but we do not know for sure. In Constantinople (AD 553) the fifth ecumenical council emphatically rejected Theodore's opinion as "offensive to Christian ears." (In Reformation times Calvin denounced Castellio, and the Inquisition condemned Luis de Leon for similar positions.)

The Allegorical Approach

There is no doubt that, on all sides, even after the Reformation, the allegorical approach (or something very similar to it) held virtually unchallenged sway. In the Early Church, Origen is perhaps the most dexterous of the allegorists, and not even the historically minded Jerome veered in other directions. In the Middle Ages Bernard of Clairvaux stands out, like many other medieval mystics, applying the book especially to the individual soul. The allegory perhaps tended to be a bit more restrained after the Reformation and the hermeneutical theory accented the literal more, but important commentaries such as those of Spurgeon, Hengstenberg, and Keil did not differ significantly in ultimate result. Cocceius was even able to interpret the book as a history of the church, fulfilled in the Reformation. The headings of the Authorized Version clinched the triumph of allegorical interpretation of the book in the English-speaking world.

Solomon's broader life may help one interpret his song. As the king built the temple, so his love for the Shulammite built his kingdom, uniting north and south. This bond, in turn, foreshadowed Christ's love for His bride, the Church (Eph 5:25).

Some sort of spiritual-allegorical approach is likely the oldest approach to the book: describing God's love for His people in terms of human love. The general approach is common enough within the canon. For example, the negative imagery of adultery or "whoring after other gods" is apparent already in the Books of Moses, especially Deuteronomy, and is prominent in the prophets, especially Hosea, Jeremiah, and Ezekiel. Psalm 45, depicting on the surface a royal marriage, is a very parallel passage. (Many of these texts appear to have northern roots or associations, which might be related to the Song's possible own northern context.) In the New Testament the parallel "bride of Christ" metaphor is developed especially in Eph 5. Such parallels suggest a climate in which an understanding of the Song could develop and/or flourish.

Although the allegorical interpretation is preferable to many modern alternatives, it nevertheless has weaknesses. For example, details are made to represent something else, and it is no little trick to work out all such correspondences in a coherent way. In principle, the "spiritual" meaning has no intrinsic connection either with the text or with the history of which it speaks. In practice, this means sheer arbitrariness and subjectivity in interpretation.

For example, the Targum took the book as a historical allegory of Yahweh's dealings with Israel from the exodus to the return from the exile, and it was followed in this not only by various Jewish interpreters, but also by the great medieval Christian interpreter, Nicholas of Lyra, and even by a few modern interpreters. Traditional Roman Catholic interpretations focus on Mary (reflected in various references in the traditional liturgies of Marian festivals). She represents Israel, and with her occurs the mystical union between God and man. An amusing illustration of the problem with allegory occurs in Protestant circles. Spurgeon was uncertain whether Sg 6:13 ("Return, O Shulammite") represented Christ's call to the backsliding church or the siren call of lapsed Christians to the faithful, inviting them to apostasy—a dilemma Spurgeon resolved by preaching two sermons on the text!

The Dramatic Approach

Since about 1800, modern opinion has moved massively and almost unanimously away from allegory. However, it was easier to reject the traditional stance than it was to agree on a replacement. Nineteenth-century thought inclined strongly toward a dramatic instead of an allegorical interpretation, but there was no agreement on whether there were two or three main characters (and in either case a chorus of "daughters of Jerusalem" or the like was often added, following Greek examples). The two-character version received classical exposition at the hands of the generally conservative Lutheran exegete, Franz Delitzsch. Solomon, pictured as a shepherd, meets the Shulammite maiden during a royal tour of the North and, being physically attracted, brings her to Jerusalem to marry her. But he comes to love her truly before he wins her for his wife. Many details in the work, however, resist this construction: Solomon as a shepherd, the final scene in the girl's home village, etc.

More popular generally was the three-character dramatic hypothesis, often referred to as the "shepherd hypothesis." Ewald in the nineteenth century was its first major champion, but many have followed him, at least in general principle. In this reading, the book becomes a sort of prototype of the "eternal triangle." Solomon is no longer the shepherd (thus avoiding a major difficulty of the preceding version), but the villain of the piece. Solomon either abducts the girl to his harem or makes advances in the guise of a shepherd. However, the girl refuses to be swayed by promises of a luxurious life and remains faithful to her fiancé, a shepherd in her hometown of Shunem. Eventually, Solomon is impressed by the purity of the love of the rustic pair and allows the two to marry. (Especially this version easily lent itself to further allegory: Solomon stands for the world, while the girl represents the "Bride of Christ," who refuses to be seduced from her spouse; there would even be a certain historical aptness, in that Israel as a nation newly encountered the allurements of the world in the reign of Solomon.) However, the dramatic interpretation in any version suffers from almost as many detriments as the allegorical, and it finds very few defenders any longer.

More recent interpretations have followed quasi-dramatic lines, but they are even more speculative. There certainly is no more internal indication in the text of drama than of allegory. The closest we come is a possible dialogue, but mere dialogue does not constitute drama. (Gender differences, of course, are clearly indicated in the Hebrew, and already the ancient codex Sinaiticus sought to identify the speakers in marginal notations, as do some modern versions, e.g., B = bride, G = groom, and D = daughters of Jerusalem.) Instead of the conflict necessary for real drama, the expressions of love appear to remain on essentially the same level throughout; we have more the expression of a mood than dramatic action. The "stage instructions" that would have to be added for a drama embroil interpreters in further subjectivities. Above all, in the light of archaeological evidence, it appears that the dramatic form never really caught on at all in the East.

The Love Poetry Approach

Subsequent historical-critical attempts probably agree on little more than rejection of all the above interpretations. Increasingly any unity of the entire book was abandoned in favor of the view that it only contained a collection of love poems—but there is no agreement at all on how many. Most guesses probably range between five and thirty. In addition, literal exposition of the Song has increasingly come to be virtually synonymous with "erotic" interpretation, and many even speak of an "erotic hypothesis."

Comparative studies have led many to view the work as specifically a collection of popular, earthy wedding songs. One of the first hypotheses along these lines grew out of observations of wedding customs in modern Syria in 1873 by the Prussian consul in Damascus, J. G. Wetzstein. He observed a "King's Week" during which the bride and groom reigned as "king" and "queen," often sitting at a special table while songs were sung in honor of the bride especially. These songs (of the so-called *wasf* type) were stylized descriptions of the charms, physical and otherwise, of the beloved, enumerated often from head to foot or in reverse order. Possibly Solomon and the Shunammite, Abishag, became prototypes of the marriage rites in later communities, accounting for those names in the book. Wetzstein even thought he could discern echoes in the Song of a "sword dance" performed by the bride (cf 6:13–7:6), of a procession in which a threshing sledge served as a palanquin for the bride (cf 3:6–11), etc. Both the language and the festivities of the Syrians were often rather uninhibited.

Wetzstein's thesis is still influential, but not nearly as much as formerly. The "parallels" are often moot (e.g., the girl is never styled a "queen") and apply, at best, to only a small number of passages. In addition, Syria and Canaan were not identical cultures in antiquity, and the relevance of modern customs to biblical times is even more questionable. Hence, the modern critical disposition is probably to view the poems more as general love songs than as specifically wedding songs. The conservative might concede the possibility of some of the precanonical meaning or the Solomonic point of departure being exposed by such an hypothesis, but scarcely anything very significant for the exegesis of the book in its canonical context.

The Mythological Approach

Many comparative studies have favored a mythological or liturgical interpretation, according to which the poem(s) did not originally refer to human love at all, but to that of the gods. Usually the "sacred marriage" of Ishtar and Tammuz is thought of, represented by a "king" and a sacral prostitute in the earthly ritual. Only later and secondarily was the rite allegedly adjusted and applied to ordinary weddings. To make it acceptable in Yahwistic circles, it was perhaps "historified" by reference to Solomon and then eventually allegorized into the "marriage" of Yahweh and Israel.

This approach probably continues to grow among liberals, though most scholars are still cautious. The parallels are easily exaggerated and are certainly not self-evident in the text. The poem itself speaks only of the quite ordinary love of man and woman, not of the "cosmic fertilization" of pagan cult. If the pagan parallels and associations were nearly as close as many of these researchers allege, however, it is virtually impossible to see how the songs could ever have been regarded even as fit candidates for Holy Scripture.

It is highly debatable whether the imagery in the Song is really all that erotic; often it would seem that such interpretations tell us much more about the interpreters than about the text! Yet, at least on the first level of meaning, it does contain an element of truth that cannot simply be dismissed. Already 1:2–4 strikes the note of desire for union that runs throughout. In ch 3 the girl dreams that her beloved is in bed with her, but in her "mother's house" (v 4)—scarcely the place for affairs. Again in ch 5, she dreams that her lover is rattling the latch of her door, but finds no one when she rises, and when she again ventures into the street to look for him, the watchmen take her for a loiterer and administer a beating! In ch 8 she wishes that her lover were really her brother, who might enter her chambers without arousing suspicion and gossip.

But is not all this part of the verisimilitude of the poem? To long for and dream of the consummation, even to broach the ongoing question, "Why wait?" is part of the *reality* of the world of romance and courtship. Desire is not the same as illicit love.

Conservative Interpretation

Conservative thought, too, has moved in the direction of a more literal interpretation in the last century. A few conservatives such as Young even wish to limit its meaning to the "literal" one of expressing the beauty of monogamous love over against various degeneracies or perversions, ancient as well as modern. The ideal marriage might remind the reader of God's love for lost humanity, though that was not expressly part of the textual meaning. Such an interpretation of the book is not far removed from various nonerotic readings by critics, who find it to be only a lyrical expression of the essential rightness of the man-woman relationship.

Most conservatives, however, are not satisfied to leave it at that. Unless "canon" is understood only in a historical (non-normative) sense, some further spiritual meaning seems imperative; certainly to deny it would fly in the face of religious practice throughout the centuries. As usual, especially in wisdom precincts, a purely philological exegesis seems only to scrape the surface. If the message of the book were no more than that, it is hard to see (humanly speaking) how the book would ever have been received into the canon, all the more so since the theme is expressed so much more clearly many other times in Scripture. If the Song of Solomon, like its subject (marriage and sex), has more than merely a literal meaning, how shall we express the relationship? The unity of the various levels of meaning must be accented. It will not be a matter of a multiple or even a double sense, but of various aspects of the one literal sense (*unus sensus literalis*).

For all of the surface similarity with medieval interpretation, the Reformers' Christological interpretation was fundamentally different. Modern historicists and literalists often lump Christological interpretation with medieval interpretation as "allegory," but that represents an alien critique from a hostile audience. The Reformation principle might be styled theologically literal: the spiritual or theological meaning *was* the literal meaning, not some hidden, second sense under or behind it. It may sometimes appear to us that our ancestors did not always stress the historical component of that same literal sense as much as seems desired in our culture. But we will want to take care not to make a break in principle with their theological approach.

of passion leads to many sorrows, complications, and sins. Carelessness can ruin any earthly relationship. Mutual conversation and attention to each other is essential.

3:1–4:7 The third cycle. The Shulammite earnestly seeks her bridegroom. Like Solomon, our Lord spares no expense preparing for the marriage feast of the Lamb in His kingdom. He admires us the way a groom admires his bride on the wedding day.

4:8–5:1 The fourth cycle. Like Solomon calling the Shulammite, our Lord calls us to come out of our worldliness and to reside in communion with Him. The cedars of Lebanon were used to build the temple so that Israel and the Lord might dwell together.

5:2–6:10 The fifth cycle. When our Lord comes to us, we may be slow to hear and to believe. We may look for Him and not find Him where or as we want. Pray for your spouse (even if you have not yet met your spouse). Delight in the love that God gives you.

6:11–8:4 The sixth cycle. Out of all the queens, concubines, and virgins that Solomon had available to him, the Shulammite was his "only one." Within the blessing of holy wedlock, the intimacy of husband and wife is to be cherished and not neglected. But later, Solomon turned his heart away from her and from the Lord toward other interests (1Ki 11:3–4), though she longed for him (Sg 8:1–4).

8:5–14 The conclusion. The Lord loves us with a passion and He wants to preserve His dear ones till the end.

Specific Law Themes

An act of promiscuity and unfaithfulness, whether it be idolatry, broken personal loyalty, or adultery, is self-destructive and also leads others astray.

Specific Gospel Themes

In faithfulness, God loves His people and sent Wisdom (Christ) to save the world. He grants to believers the priceless blessings of love for Him and marital love for spouses.

Specific Doctrines

Marriage should be blessed as God designed it, "A man shall leave his father and his mother and hold fast to his wife, and they shall become one flesh" (Gn 2:24). God does not bless other sexual relations (cf Lv 18).

Every time and age must counter a host of aberrations in the area of sex and marriage. Natural revelation teaches a good deal about this (even when it is flouted); the special revelation of the Scriptures confirms, establishes, and enables believers to live in an ultimately different way. Treatment of women as sex-objects, sometimes accompanied by an overt misogyny, was as widespread at times in the biblical world as it is in ours. In contrast, wisdom and the Word teach that we should "let marriage be held in honor among all, and let the marriage bed be undefiled" (Heb 13:4), that the human body is indeed God's creation and not something to be ashamed of, as such, that sex is not intrinsically dirty nor is it a subject too secular to be of concern to the religious. While the world stands, the Church will always have to make such points. If such were not the case, human love would certainly be an unfit

symbol of divine love. Stress on a spiritual meaning alongside human love does not lessen, but enhances the message of the rightness of human love in proper context.

We cannot leave the urging of such themes to humanists over against an unbiblical puritanism and prudery. Having stressed that, however, we do well to remember that we live in a hedonistic age that does not care to hear of original sin or its destructive consequences. The truly biblical churchman needs to take care that he does not play into the enemy's hands by contributing to the secularization of the Church and its message.

Like Wisdom Literature in general, the conclusion to the Song stresses that its action takes place before God (8:6). Theologically, the Holy Spirit, the ultimate Author of all the biblical books, must have included that perspective. A proper interpretation of the book will stress both the indispensability of the elements (a literal, historical aspect), as well as the fact that a certain *double entendre* is built into whatever is sacred. To the believer, human love is both an echo of divine love and a transparency of another order of perfect love. Finally, all of nature longs for the new creation. It, too, shares in the redemption, now sacramentally, then eternally. The Song's use at the Jewish Passover even suggests its use at the Christian Easter (whose themes encompass nature). As Eph 5 and Rv 22 teach us, in Christ we see all this most clearly, all the while awaiting the consummation.

Application

1:1 Throughout history, the songs of God's people have been of the highest caliber, inspired by the Holy Spirit Himself, with names such as the Sanctus, the Kyrie, and the Gloria in Excelsis. The highest praise is always sounding from the mouths of the baptized as well as ringing in their ears.

1:2–17 The first poetic cycle of the song. The Church is the beloved of our Bridegroom, Christ Jesus. Her sins may be obvious, even to other sinners, but her Husband-King calls her holy and forgiven, beautiful and radiant in the glory of His grace.

Ch 2 The second cycle. God, in His passion to save us, sent forth His Son, born of a virgin, to redeem all who are under the Law's judgment and curse. Our Lord wants to hear our confession and our prayers, and even more so, He wants to give us His consolation and forgiveness. In Christ, your sins have been forgiven, and now, as He told the woman caught in adultery, "Neither do I condemn you; go, and from now on sin no more" (Jn 8:11).

3:1–4:7 The third cycle. What occupies our dreams and aspirations, our hopes and desires? The Lord commends to us the excellent and praiseworthy. His Word sets our hearts upon our Savior. With His holy, precious blood and with His innocent suffering and death, He has readied the marriage feast of heaven!

4:8–5:1 The fourth cycle. The Lord calls us holy, beautiful, stainless, pure. He calls us forgiven in His Gospel. Though we indulge daily and heartily in the things of this world, how much greater is it to partake of the things of God!

5:2–6:10 The fifth cycle. Life is often confusing. In such times of confusion, call on the Lord in prayer and seek Him in His Word. He promises to hear and to comfort you. If you are or were married, consider celebrating God's gift of a spouse by describing your spouse's best qualities. Whether you are married or single, rejoice in the love of your Lord.

6:11–8:4 The sixth cycle. In marriage vows, we promise to forsake all others. Thanks be to God that He does not forsake us when our hearts or thoughts stray. The Lord calls husband and wife to give each other their love and bear its fruit (Gn 1:28; Ps 127:3–5; cf Sg 7:12).

8:5–14 The conclusion. We are not to conform ourselves to the pattern of this world, but remain holy, set apart as a wall (v 10) unto the Lord.

CANONICITY

In the Hebrew canon, this work heads the subgrouping of the five Megilloth (scrolls for liturgical readings) because of its traditional liturgical association with the feast of Passover, the most preeminent occasion on the Jewish calendar when the Song of Solomon is interpreted as describing the marriage of the Lord and Israel during the exodus. The rest of the Megilloth follow in the chronological order of the festivals with which they are associated.

The Septuagint's placement of the book after Ecclesiastes (followed by all western versions) loses sight of the Passover association. For more on questions of canonicity, see p 696.

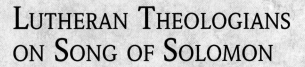

LUTHERAN THEOLOGIANS ON SONG OF SOLOMON

Luther

"The third book [the Song of Solomon] is a song of praise, in which Solomon praises God for obedience, as for a gift of God. For where God is not himself the householder and ruler, there is neither obedience nor peace in any station of life. But where there is obedience and good governing, there God dwells, he kisses and embraces his dear bride with his word, which is the kiss of his lips. Therefore when things go in a land or a home as nearly as possible according to the first two of these books [Proverbs and Ecclesiastes], then one may well sing this third book and thank God. For God has not only taught us this, but has himself also done it. Amen." (AE 35:260–61)

For more of Luther's insights on this book, see *Lectures on the Song of Solomon* (AE 15:189–264).

Gerhard

"*The Song of Songs* is called by the Hebrews *shir hashirim*, which in the Hebrew language means 'an outstanding or exceptional song.' The Greeks call it *Asma asmaton*, 'Song of Songs,' and also connect a mention of the author—that it was written by Solomon. First Kings 4:32 relates that Solomon composed many songs, but none of these is extant today except this one, which was more excellent than the rest.

"The interpreters differ regarding the aim [*scopus*] of this book, yet it is certain that it does not discuss marital love, much less excessive marital love. The Hebrews say: 'Heaven forbid! Heaven forbid that this be a song about obscene things! Rather, it is a metaphor. . . .' Otherwise, 'if it were not of great dignity, it would not be written in the catalog of the Holy Scriptures.' (I) Many of the ancients relate it to the spiritual marriage between Christ and the Church, as well as that of Christ and any faithful soul. Augustine, *De civ. Dei*, bk. 17, c. 20: 'The Song of Songs is a spiritual pleasure of holy minds in the marriage of the King and the queen-city, that is, of Christ and the Church. This pleasure, however, is wrapped in allegorical veils so that the Bridegroom might be desired more ardently and be seen with greater joy.' (II) Some think that in this book there is described the ardent affection of the king for the state of Israel and vice versa. (III) Luther relates it to the affection of the people of Israel toward God.

"It has eight chapters and consists of constant dialogue.

"Some of the ancient heretics used to say that the Song of Songs 'was written not by the Spirit of God but by the heavy breath of lust,' according to Philaster (*De haeres.*, c. 133). Beza attributes the same opinion to Castalion. This book was taken into the canon, however, by the common approval of both the Israelite and the Christian Church. In fact, among the ancient Hebrews, so great was their reverence for this book that they forbade anyone to read it—along with the beginning of Genesis and the beginning and end of Ezekiel—before his thirtieth year. The Christian interpreters seem to stand in the footsteps of those who think that the explanation of this song is not to be attained in youth but must be reserved for the solace of Christian old age and the provision [*viaticum*] of a devout departure. As examples, we have Bernard, Thomas Aquinas, and Jean Gerson, who spent the last days of their lives meditating upon and explaining this book.

"The common judgment of theologians attributes those three books we just listed—Proverbs, Ecclesiastes, Song of Songs—to Solomon (as we said earlier). Yet there are some who claim that the prophet Isaiah gathered the statements of these three books from the proverbs and songs that Solomon had composed and that had been preserved in the Israelite church until Isaiah's time.

"Proverbs was written especially for the *young* man, Ecclesiastes for the man in *full bloom*, and Song of Songs for the *old* man. Origen (prolog to *Homil. in cant.*, vol. 1, f. 71), Jerome (on Ecclesiastes 1), Theodoret (preface to his commentary on Song of Songs), and others of the ancients compare summaries of these books with the three parts of philosophy. Because according to the Stoics and Platonists all philosophy is divided into three parts—namely, physics, ethics, and dialectics (by which the Platonists understand metaphysics)—therefore they say that in Proverbs there is set forth the ethical part of philosophy, that is, useful discipline concerning behavior. In Ecclesiastes there is set forth the physical part of philosophy, indicating the nature of those things perceived by the senses and teaching the vanity of this present life and all things that are seen here, so that as we recognize their fluctuating and fragile character we may spurn them as fleeting, passing things and acknowledge that what is to come is firm and will endure forever. In the Song of Songs there is set forth theology and the metaphysical part of philosophy, which denotes the mystic union of bride and Bridegroom." (ThC E1 §§ 148–50)

Near Eastern women commonly veiled themselves as a sign of modesty, which also accented the beauty of their eyes and other facial features (Sg 4:13; 6:7).

697

Stained glass window in Notre Dame. This Tree of Jesse figure is Solomon,
holding a model of the church/temple.

FURTHER STUDY

Lay/Bible Class Resources

Dunker, Gary. *Song of Solomon: Love Is Strong as Death.* GWFT. St. Louis: Concordia, 2006. ♫ Lutheran author. Eleven-session Bible study, including leader's notes and discussion questions.

Ehlke, Roland C. *Ecclesiastes/Song of Songs.* PBC. St. Louis: Concordia, 2004. ♫ Lutheran author. Excellent for Bible classes. Based on the NIV translation.

Life by His Word. St. Louis: Concordia, 2009. ♫ More than 1,500 reproducible one-page Bible studies covering each chapter of the canonical Scriptures. Page references to *The Lutheran Study Bible.* CD-Rom and downloadable.

Marriage by God's Design: What the Bible Teaches about Marriage. St. Louis: Concordia, 2010. ♫ A four-session DVD-based study for large or small groups, explaining why God created His human creatures male and female, and why He instituted marriage for them.

Teske, Steven, and James Bollhagen. *Ecclesiastes/Song of Solomon.* Leaders Guide and Enrichment Magazine/Study Guide. LL. St. Louis: Concordia, 2010. ♫ An in-depth, nine-session Bible study with individual, small group, and lecture portions.

Church Worker Resources

Davis, Ellen F. *Proverbs, Ecclesiastes, and the Song of Songs.* Westminster Bible Companion. Louisville, KY: Westminster John Knox Press, 2000. ♫ Written by a scholar in a more popular style, arguing for layers of meaning in the Song, which speaks of human, natural, and divine relations.

Luther, Martin. *Ecclesiastes, Song of Solomon, and the Last Words of David (2 Samuel 23:1–7).* Vol. 15 of AE. St. Louis: Concordia, 1972. ♫ There are few commentaries on Ecclesiastes that are explicitly Christian. Luther holds to Solomonic authorship and has great, broad comments as well as many fine exegetical details. A blessing to read.

Academic Resources

Carr, G. Lloyd. *The Song of Solomon: An Introduction and Commentary.* TOTC. Downers Grove, IL: InterVarsity Press, 1984. ♫ Helpful in popular format, though more technical than other volumes in the series.

Gordis, Robert. *The Song of Songs and Lamentations: A Study, Modern Translation and Commentary.* New York: KTAV, 1974. ♫ A Jewish scholar seeks to explore the importance of what he considers secular love songs being included in the Old Testament canon. Many rabbinical references.

K&D. *Biblical Commentaries on the Old Testament: The Song of Songs and Ecclesiastes.* K&D. Grand Rapids: Eerdmans, 1949 reprint. ♫ Both a philologically and theologically significant resource. This century-and-a-half old work from Lutheran scholars should not be overlooked. Despite its age, it remains a most useful commentary on the Hebrew text.

Longman, Tremper, III. *Song of Songs.* NICOT. Grand Rapids: Eerdmans, 2001. ♫ Written by a well-known evangelical scholar, who takes a typological approach to interpreting the book. Holds that the Song is a compilation of several poems but treats the canonical form of the book as a unified composition.

Mitchell, Christopher W. *The Song of Songs.* CC. St. Louis: Concordia, 2001. ♫ The most thorough commentary on the Song, by a Lutheran scholar and philologist. The best resource available.

Pope, Marvin H. *Song of Songs.* Vol. 7C of AB. New York: Doubleday, 1977. ♫ Detailed philological study that takes a literal approach, regarding the book as a celebration of erotic love rooted in fertility rites.

Zöckler, Otto. *A Commentary on the Holy Scriptures: Song of Solomon.* LCHS. New York: Charles Scribner's Sons, 1898. ♫ A helpful, older example of German biblical scholarship, based on the Hebrew text, which provides references to significant commentaries from the Reformation era forward.

THE BOOKS OF THE PROPHETS

The Latter Prophets

In our English Bibles, the Books of the Prophets are divided into Major Prophets (five books) and Minor Prophets (twelve books).

MAJOR PROPHETS	MINOR PROPHETS	
Isaiah	Hosea	Nahum
Jeremiah	Joel	Habakkuk
Lamentations	Amos	Zephaniah
Ezekiel	Obadiah	Haggai
Daniel	Jonah	Zechariah
	Micah	Malachi

Scribes for the Hebrew Bible saw the matter differently. They described the Books of Isaiah, Jeremiah, and Ezekiel as the Latter Prophets (or simply "the Prophets") and placed Lamentations and Daniel among their third category of Old Testament books, the Writings. (On division and organization of the Hebrew canon, see p 1011.) They collected the Minor Prophets into the Book of the Twelve, which

During the era of the Latter Prophets (eighth century through fifth century), Assyrian and Babylonian armies crossed the great Euphrates River to raid Israel and Judah, bringing up captives.

was similar in length to the longer Prophetic Books. As a result, the Hebrew canon counted four scrolls of the Latter Prophets, matching the number of scrolls for four Former Prophets (many of our historical books; see pp 190–92). Thus, with the exception of Daniel, the Hebrew Latter Prophets correspond to what are usually simply referred to as the "Prophets" or prophetical books in English Bibles.

Introduction to the Prophets

No one disputes the importance of the Prophetic Books. Precisely how and why they are important, however, widely differs. Perhaps it is true to say that Christianity rates them higher than Judaism, and that this is one of the historic differences between the two religions, but one must be cautious.

In one sense, Judaism does accord the Books of Moses (the Torah) a certain priority, and regards the Prophets as commentary on them (as Christians readily agree). But even within Christianity, the significance of the Prophets varies drastically. Much of the traditional Christian importance attached to the Prophets arose because the prophets predicted and heralded the coming of Christ. However, even in this respect (as a look at the New Testament citations of the Old would demonstrate), prophecies about Christ are found with equal ease from virtually the entire Old Testament.

Abraham fresco from the synagogue at Dura Europos.

DEFINITION OF "PROPHET"

What is "prophecy"? The Bible answers this question from a fundamentally different standpoint than most modern scholarship. The modern answer is primarily sociological, while the Bible's answer is theological. Of course, the two are not fully separated from each other, but it is important that the approaches be carefully distinguished.

The Bible's own understanding of a prophet is someone who is a "spokesman, interpreter, mediator of God's will." In this sense, Abraham was a prophet (Gn 20:7) because he interceded with God for the welfare of Abimelech (though it is doubtful if Abraham had much else in common with the great prophets of the eighth century). Similarly, Aaron was a prophet to Moses (Ex 7:1–2) as his spokesman.

Moses is the preeminent prophet because of his unique role as representative and mediator of God's great revelation at Mount Sinai. Moses' functions or behavior may well have looked like those of the classical prophets, but the association is more theological: the great prophets were reformers, calling Israel back to its Mosaic roots. One of the few biblical passages that even approaches a theoretical discussion on prophecy is Dt 18:15–19, which emphasizes faithfulness to Moses as the standard of true prophecy. Christians, of course, would also invoke the name of Christ as the greatest—the incarnation and the fulfillment of all true prophecy.

Israelite Prophets and Other Prophets

There are some external parallels between Israelite prophets and the prophets of surrounding cultures. Some biblical prophets were originally called "seers" (1Sm 9:9). The ordinary Hebrew root for "see" is used (presumably for spiritual insight), but later another root (*chozeh*) is regularly used, apparently in a more specialized way, for the prophetic "vision" (presumably implying "inspiration"). The biblical vocabulary takes pains to underscore the *theological* chasm between Israelite prophecy and pagan clairvoyance. Hebrew has two common words for pagan prophets, usually translated "diviner" and "sorcerer," or the like, and always used negatively (one possible exception in Pr 16:10). Some interpreters compare the experience and behavior of Saul among the Israelite prophets (1Sm 10:5–6, 9–13) with the ecstasies, trances, and behaviors of pagan prophets (e.g., 1Ki 18:28–29, where a reflexive form of the Hebrew verb for prophesying is used: "they *made themselves* prophesy"). However, such comparisons do not describe equivalent activities, nor should they be used to argue that external signs of ecstasy were necessary or regular signs of genuine prophecy among the Israelites.

The idea of "prophecy" was not at all unique in Israel. In fact, the biblical descriptions of the false prophets and the difficulty in distinguishing them from the true prophets would indicate as much. The issue is complicated, however, with questions about terms (both in the Bible and outside of it), with the validity of "parallels," and with the course of prophecy within Israel.

At one time, parallel forms of prophecy were sought quite far afield, namely in Egypt and the major Mesopotamian cultures, but these appear to be of minimal help, at best. Discoveries closer to home—not surprisingly—have been more fruitful. For example, the major Hebrew word for "prophet" (*nabi'*) also figured prominently at Ebla in northern Syria.

Mari, to the east, on the middle Euphrates, was one of the major Amorite cultures, and illuminates the history of the patriarchs and of early Israel in many ways. The prominence of prophetic activity there suggests that it may well have been familiar to the patriarchs already. One common term at Mari is the *apilu*, an "answerer," apparently related to specific deities. Here we also meet the *muhhu*, a sort of "ecstatic," but also associated with idol worship. (The latter also appear elsewhere in Mesopotamia, alongside the *baru*, a "diviner" or "seer.") The Mesopotamian terms are often used of both men and women.

More significant is a certain similarity in the setting and content of the Mari oracles with the biblical ones. Oracles came from and were delivered in temples and had more secular uses as well. The Mari prophets, like their biblical counterparts, were very much involved in political and military affairs. There are both rebukes of the throne as well as oracles of assurance. Often a "messenger formula" ("Thus says [name]") is used, just as in the Bible. However, we find little comparable to the profound ethical and end time concerns of the biblical prophets.

When did prophecy surface among the Hebrews? The Bible is not concerned to answer those kinds of questions. However, the virtual ubiquity of some kind of prophecy makes it very likely that it was present from the outset.

Miriam, Moses' sister, is called a prophetess in Ex 15:20. The context of singing suggests, however, that we may have here a usage, similar to that found especially in 1Ch 25:1, where the word often implies to sing or play an instrument (perhaps because the Spirit was thought to inspire both activities). Elisha's call for a musician to stimulate prophecy (2Ki 3:15) may also illustrate the intimate connection of music and prophecy in ancient thought.

Prophecy appears to be well established by the time of the Judges, though the evidence is elusive. Deborah, who is also a judge, is labeled a "prophetess" (Jgs 4:4), and an unnamed "prophet" anticipates the call of Gideon (6:8). One wonders, however, if the prominence of the Spirit throughout the Book of Judges does not describe essentially the same activity as prophecy, albeit in different vocabulary. It may well be, as some have suggested, that in the kingdom period of Israel's history (1048–587 BC), the office of "judge" was divided among the "prophet" and the "king." In any event, by the time of Samuel, prophecy is obviously well established at the same time that kingship is fast taking root. As noted, 1Sm 9:9 records a change in the usual vocabulary from "seer" to "prophet," but we lack context to assess its significance. It is also unclear whether the expression "man of God" (v 10) or the various words translated as "oracle" and "seer" are merely alternate vocabulary. We continue to hear of "sons" and "schools" of the prophets in the ninth century in the time of Elijah and Elisha. Thereafter, these groups are not clearly described as active, but we are not sure whether the biblical silence implies absence.

As we noted earlier, Israelite prophecy, at least in its full theological dimensions, arose and operated largely as a counterweight to kingship and its paganizing tendencies. After the exile, when the monarchy failed to reestablish itself, prophets quickly faded from the scene too. The revival of prophecy, as well as of kingship, is plainly not expected until the messianic era—and, of course, the New Testament prominently proclaims the fulfillment of both of those hopes and promises.

True Versus False Prophecy

How were true and false prophecy distinguished? The truth question arises almost everywhere in Scripture where the topic of prophecy appears. If we remember, however, that the Bible's own definition of prophecy is a theological one, we will not be surprised to discover that the criterion of truth is also primarily a matter of revelation and faith.

Clay model of a sheep's liver used for divination by priests in Babylon. They examined the livers of sacrificed animals and predicted the future based on what they found (c 1900–1600 BC).

There may have been some external touchstones. Sometimes we hear that the false prophets sought bribes (cf Mi 3:5), but there is no indication that such was a characteristic of all. Many indications, however, that the false prophets tended to prophesy what their audiences wanted to hear is probably closer to the mark. The Micaiah story (1Ki 22) is a good example, as is Jeremiah's repeated complaint about his opposition, who proclaimed "peace, peace, when there is no peace" (6:14). Conversely, Jeremiah describes "war, famine, and pestilence" (28:8; cf 34:17) as characteristic of the tradition of true prophecy, and the scroll that Ezekiel is to eat has written on it "words of lamentation and mourning and woe" (2:10). In part such passages induced classical critics to set up preaching of judgment as a nearly infallible sign of genuine prophecy and cut out most other passages as additions from later times. That there was *some* truth in the observation that judgment was essential to the prophets' message is beyond denying, but it would be lovely, indeed, if matters were that simple! The great number of judgment oracles in the preexilic prophets corresponds to the great needs of the hour.

However, in their very preaching of judgment, the preexilic prophets looked forward also to God's coming work of redemption. And when the circumstances change after the judgment (cf Is 40–55), the prophets themselves are quick to change the dominant note of their preaching to hope and promise. The same explanation is undoubtedly to be given for the many positive and promissory oracles that are interspersed throughout the books of the preexilic prophets.

The two most important criteria for distinguishing true and false prophecy are found in two important passages in Deuteronomy. Not surprisingly, the criteria are theological. The first of these passages, Dt 13:1–5, describes what may unhesitatingly be called a *doctrinal* or *confessional* criterion. The test is in what the prophet teaches and preaches, whether or not it harmonizes with the rest of revelation. The rest of Deuteronomy, of course, is one of our major sources for spelling out the major articles of that doctrinal or confessional standard. Jeremiah's running battles with the false prophets of his day are good collateral reading, perhaps especially ch 23.

The second passage, Dt 18:21–22, sets forth as a standard the fulfillment or nonfulfillment of prophecy. Here "prophecy" is used in a sense largely for "prediction" or "*fore*telling." This passage of Deuteronomy is not alone in its stress on fulfillment of prediction as a major touchstone. The idea of predictive prophecy so suffuses biblical literature that it almost seems redundant to cite further examples. Perhaps we need note only the prominence of the apologetic argument from fulfillment of prophecy in Is 40–66, or quote the familiar refrain of Ezekiel: "When this comes . . . then they will know that a prophet has been among them" (33:33). In fact, the prophets were honored (and their writings received into the canon) after the exile—as they emphatically often had not been before—precisely because their predictions of destruction and captivity had proved utterly true.

Very often prophecies are explicitly introduced by an "if" clause (cf Is 1:19–20). In accordance with the ancient covenant formula (cf Dt 27), whether blessing or cursing would come depended on the response (not, of course, in the sense of meriting God's favor, but in the sense of being able to thwart it by unfaithfulness). If the people repented, God might relent and a prophecy of doom be suspended or revoked. If they rebelled, a prophecy of salvation might be set aside until God had, as it were, raised up children to Abraham from the stones (Mt 3:9). God illustrates this principle to Jeremiah through a potter's shaping of a vessel (ch 18), and it was one of the lessons God had to teach the pouting Jonah.

Typically with long-range prediction, the *entire* future stands before the prophet's eye, and the various periods or stages of fulfillment are not distinguished (cf even in the New Testament the telescoping of prophecies of the destruction of Jerusalem and of the end of the world, so that the separate events are described side by side).

In a very real sense, the problem of discerning true prophecy in Bible times must have been very similar to the one confronting believers today.

UNDERSTANDING CLASSIC CRITICAL VIEWS

Many documentaries and books about the Bible today begin with an attitude of doubt, questioning the reliability of the Scriptures. For much of the history of God's people, this was not the case. People trusted the testimony of the prophets about the Bible's history, authorship, and purpose. The following article will help you understand why attitudes changed and how these changes have affected people's beliefs. The article includes some challenging vocabulary, for which help may be found in the Bible dictionary at the end of volume 2. For more on these issues, see pp 10–11.

With the rise of Liberalism and higher criticism during the eighteenth century came a radical change in how the Prophetic Books were viewed. They continued to be regarded every bit as highly—possibly even more highly—than other books of Scripture. Yet the Prophetic Books (or remnants of them, after criticism) virtually became a canon within the canon, the essence of biblical religion that critical scholars preferred over other biblical teaching.

The first dimension of the critical view is historical; they regard the prophets as the *originators* or inventors of biblical religion. This view maintains that Amos in the eighth century had allegedly started the breakthrough into ethical belief in one God (monotheism), rising above more primitive notions of religion (ritualistic, legalistic). The true prophets were believed to be nearly all opposed to ritual, and preachers of judgment on those who failed to live righteously according to the newly evolved standards of morality. As a result, "prophets" was in practice reduced to only *two* prophets: Amos and Jeremiah. Some of the insights of the early prophets were thought to have been refined and advanced as time went on, but critics also decided that all too often there were fatal relapses and compromises with priestly, legalistic, and institutional forces that returned to mere ritual religion.

The other major dimension of the liberal view is somewhat theological. Much of the prophecy of the Bible was regarded as prophecy after the event, artificially placed in the mouths of earlier figures to express the theological conviction that whatever had happened must have been according to God's will. At most, they believed the prophets were "inspired" to see what *had* to happen sooner or later. What the prophets originally expressed in terms of probabilities or very long-range necessities was misunderstood or changed by later generations to imply detailed prediction.

The basic frame of reference for describing prophecy was no longer so much theological as it was sociological, psychological, and political. At the heart of classical historical-critical research, an incredible amount of effort was devoted to the attempt to pinpoint the precise historical occasion on which virtually every syllable of the prophets was spoken or written. It was this ideal that motivated the dividing and subdividing and distributing of verses and chapters among who knows how many prophets, disciples, editors, or redactors. By thus eliminating the "ungenuine" additions, the idea was to re-create as closely as possible exactly what the original stimulus to the prophetic word was, so that the modern "prophet" or preacher could do his best to mimic and apply the best examples and teachings from the prophets for the sake of modern hearers.

The critics taught a prophetic ministry that would use the great biblical figures as models of their own efforts toward a better life for all. The Social Gospel and its political and social relevance and activism followed as a matter of course. The early liberals were not as optimistic about human progress or the need for revolution as some of their later heirs were, but they started and worked with similar views and values.

Hardly anyone today would credit Amos and the other prophets with pioneering "ethical monotheism" in the crass and simplistic way the dogma was once propounded. As we have stressed, the origins of much of Israel's religion is often now pushed back several centuries prior to the prophets. But critics will still usually proclaim the prophets' importance for giving classical expression to it.

Orthodox Response

How did faithful Christians respond to the unbiblical beliefs presented above? There was no denying that classical criticism made contributions in the area of study of the prophets in two areas of critical strength: historical occasion and social consciousness. No doubt, tradition did at times accent the supernatural aspect of prophecy above other considerations. The futuristic or predictive aspect of prophecy was so highlighted that its date and circumstances did not receive appropriate attention. The concerns of private, individual piety and the promise of eternal life received such accent that it all but crowded off stage the prophet's obvious concern for public, social justice in this life. To the extent that those problems still exist, conservatism still stands to profit from the critics' emphasis on justice.

Traditional believers could laud the critical emphasis on the prophets' concern with ethics much more heartily if the critics also maintained an interest in eternal life (often not so much denied as quietly ignored). Sometimes the conservatives, with their accent on "messianic prophecy" seemed unwilling or unable to read or use much of the Old Testament except for a few traditional prophecies (and then only in Advent), so isolated from their historical context had they become; but, then, Liberalism was highly selective too!

The prophets may well remind traditional Lutherans that the alternatives to political and social action (as usually conceived) are not Pietism and quietism. The "two kingdoms" distinction of church and state is not only Lutheran social theory, but an essential part of Lutheran hermeneutics, especially of the prophets. The Lutheran Church sets in order and articulates its life of sanctification also according to its reading of the prophets—and vice versa.

Form Criticism

Form criticism and tradition criticism are more often used by scholars today than the literary dissections of earlier criticism (though the latter still flourishes in some circles). As elsewhere, the dominant concern was to penetrate behind the literary products to the preceding oral tradition. The prophets were viewed as speakers rather than writers. Short, futuristic—even messianic—sayings were regarded as genuine and primary.

Sigmund Mowinckel's influential form-critical classification of types of prophetic literature was first worked out on the basis of Jeremiah. They are often applied to other books as well. Mowinckel and others used the first four letters of the alphabet as follows: (A) oracles, couched in poetic form, and often in the first person, that is, God speaking directly through the prophet; (B) historical narratives especially concerned with recording the occasions of prophetic speeches or actions; (C) prose discourses or sermons; and (D) prophecies of hope. These became standard types of Israelite prophecy in commentaries. The descriptions of the Books of the Prophets in this resource may occasionally refer to these types, recognizing that some general classification is helpful if not applied rigidly.

Prophecy and Temple Services

Critics sometimes almost virulently promoted anti-priestly and anti-institutional views. However, the normative Israelite form of worship was from Moses, and if prophecy was reformatory, the prophets could scarcely have been totally opposed to the priests. The prophets themselves reprove false prophets in far harsher terms than they do faithless priests. Subsequent research has confirmed that the prophets certainly spoke at the temple in worship contexts even if they held no office there, and often the very vocabulary the prophets employed was derived from the worship with which most of their audience was perfectly familiar.

One cannot ignore, of course, the prophets' statements against mere ritualism. The prophets were forever condemning the Israelite tendencies to relapse into magical understandings of worship that characterized paganism. But there is no evidence that they ever rejected externals in favor of some spiritualistic "religion of the heart." If one read the prophets literalistically at this point, we would even have Isaiah condemning prayer (1:15) as much as other acts of worship!

Sometimes the prophets do express themselves very strongly (here as elsewhere) on the point of hypocritical worship. The classic example is Hosea

Egyptian scribes, tools in hand, prepare to work.

6:6 (and reiterated by our Lord, Mt 9:13; 12:7; etc.): "I desire steadfast love [*chesedh*] and *not* sacrifice"—but note the explanatory parallel, "the knowledge of God *rather than* burnt offerings." Hosea was not condemning the sacrifices but reminding his hearers that the sacrifices served the purposes of knowledge of God and mercy as one practiced His teachings and sought His mercy through the sacrifices. The rituals and their purposes could not be driven apart.

Conservative Evaluation

Perhaps the theological underpinnings of nearly all this sort of scholarship should be emphasized: the critical view was one of "community inspiration" as the Spirit guided the Church to reflect on the history of the prophets and to expand, contract, or adapt the experience and message according to ever-changing circumstances. As a result of these interests, the critics envisioned many writers and disciples contributing to the original prophet's work. They taught that the modern church in its use of Scripture must "go and do likewise!"

The conservative should not overreact. Luther observed that few of the Prophetic Books are put together in the type of logical order we might expect. Tradition and conservatism have usually assumed that the prophet himself was responsible for the final form of his book. We would scarcely care to deny that, but there is no theological reason why the role of disciples should not also be considered (cf e.g., Jeremiah and Baruch, his scribe, who may have contributed to the writing of the Book of Jeremiah and certainly contributed to its preservation).

No matter who put our Prophetic Books together, the result of the process is not one that the interpreter or preacher can safely ignore. There is an "alternation of weal and woe," that is, the juxtaposition of oracles of judgment with those of salvation. Surely more is involved than mere psychological relief. The oracles of promise at the conclusion of many prophetic books are more than well-wishing "liturgical appendices" as critics sometimes assumed. This is surely more than a purely formal matter of choral antiphonies.

The antiphonies of blessing and cursing in Dt 27 (cf Jsh 8) might well suggest the precedent for this common pattern in the prophetic literature. The import of the pattern appears to be essentially what the reformers called Law and Gospel—God confronts the believer in both judgment and salvation.

The most all-encompassing application of this principle is found in what appears to have been a sort of classical or traditional outline for Prophetic Books. One can illustrate it in almost pure form in the Book of Zephaniah, in the Septuagint sequence in Jeremiah, and, less clearly, in many other places. It takes a simple tripartite form: (1) oracles against Judah (and/or Israel), (2) oracles against Gentiles or foreign nations, and (3) promise of salvation to all, both Israelite and Gentile, who repent. Here we obviously have our "Law and Gospel" or "judgment and salvation" principle again, only with the first part divided into two.

A cuneiform receipt for Sarsekim (Jer 39:3) who sent a gold offering to Esangila, temple of Marduk (c 587 BC). Enlarged to show detail.

ISAIAH

Let us go up to the mountain of the Lord

Isaiah is such a remarkable figure that one hardly knows where to begin. Both in variety and forcefulness he excels, whether one measures from literary or from theological standpoints. Only a few of the early critics ever seriously disputed that evaluation, either because Isaiah allegedly was not "original" enough for their developmental scheme or because his social action accent was less prominent than in some other prophets. For tradition and conservatism, of course, Isaiah towers especially because of his prominent messianic pronouncements.

Historical and Cultural Setting

Isaiah lived through, witnessed, and commented on one of the major turning points in Israel's history—from the halcyon days of empire and independence under Uzziah through the fall of Samaria and the semi-escape of Judah only by accepting colonial status under the relentless pressure of the Assyrian colossus. Thanks to copious biblical as well as extra-biblical evidence, we have historical details about this period. Some of Isaiah's oracles are precisely dated in connection with specific historical events, and, within limits, even conservatives will legitimately theorize about the exact historical timing of many of the others.

Light breaks forth over the ruins of Judah's southernmost fortress at Kadesh Barnea, likely constructed under King Uzziah (792–790 BC). Isaiah prophesied both ruin and hope for the people of Judah.

OVERVIEW

Author
Isaiah the prophet

Date
c 740–681 BC

Places
Israel (Ephraim); Judah; Zion; Syria; Assyria

People
Isaiah; the prophetess; Shear-jashub; Maher-shalal-hash-baz; Uzziah; Jotham; Ahaz; Hezekiah; Rezin

Purpose
To comfort God's people with the good news of Zion's redemption

Law Themes
Judgment on false worship; Judgment Day; selfishness; woes against Israel and the nations; defeat by Assyria and Babylon; idolatry condemned

Gospel Themes
The remnant preserved; Immanuel; the Messiah's just reign; salvation promised to Ethiopia, Assyria, and the nations; the feast; mercy for Hezekiah; God's comfort for Zion; the Lord's Servant; Zion's deliverance; new heavens and a new earth

Memory Verses
Let us reason together (1:18–19); song of the vineyard (5:1–7); temple vision (6:1–13); Immanuel and His reign (7:14; 9:2–7); the Branch and the Spirit (11:1–9); the feast (ch 25); comfort (40:1–5); the Suffering Servant (52:13–53:12); the Lord's ways (55:6–11); new heavens and a new earth (65:17–25)

TIMELINE

792–740 BC	Reign of Azariah/Uzziah (Judah)
740 BC	The call of Isaiah
722 BC	Samaria (Israel) falls to Assyria
701 BC	Sennacherib besieges Jerusalem
696–642 BC	Reign of Manasseh (Judah)

Partly on the basis of the dated oracles, it is common to see two main phases of Isaiah's ministry, each concluded by a retirement or period of silence after rejection. The first phase peaks under the reign of Ahaz, ending in a withdrawal to a nucleus of faithful disciples, according to a common understanding of Is 8:16–18. Upon Hezekiah's accession, Isaiah takes heart and becomes vocal once more, only to retire again to an inner circle in the latter years of Hezekiah (cf 30:8–17). The picture is somewhat hypothetical, but not incompatible with the biblical data. In fact, much of the undated material in the Book of Isaiah, especially that focused on future time or almost on time itself (cf chs 40–66), may congenially be thought of as having been delivered to the faithful during those periods out of the public eye.

If such oracles were delivered in private to disciples (or only written down), we can understand that they were not precisely dated because their scope was God's time, whenever and however in the future their ultimate Author would see fit to fulfill them. To the faithful who believed that the prophet's thundering oracles of doom would come true first, and that the route of salvation for the remnant was only through suffering (for Christians, typical of the cross), Isaiah's oracles of restoration would be deeply meaningful.

King Uzziah's burial inscription records the reburial of the king's remains (c AD 50): "Hither were brought the bones of Uzziah king of Judah. Do not open."

COMPOSITION

Author

There is not the slightest debate about the historical circumstances of Isaiah of Jerusalem, and if we take the book as unified, these circumstances ultimately apply to all the oracles in it, even when further precision is impossible. The superscription specifies the reigns of Uzziah, Jotham, Ahaz, and Hezekiah (1:1), and in this case, not even critics challenge its applicability to Isaiah. Chapter 6, if presumed to record Isaiah's call, as is usually done, would pinpoint the beginning of his prophetic activity "in the year that King Uzziah died," about 740 BC.

Whether or not he outlived Hezekiah (d. 686 BC) is not entirely certain, but the reference in 2Ch 32:32 to a sort of biography of Hezekiah written by Isaiah, as he had earlier written one of Uzziah (2Ch 26:22), would suggest as much. Isaiah ceased to be active soon afterward. There is no way to test the reliability of the ancient tradition of his martyrdom under Manasseh by being sawn asunder within a hollow log. Yet the story is thoroughly credible. If the reference in Heb 11:37 is to Isaiah, its historicity is established, but the precise allusion there is uncertain.

The name Isaiah means "Yahweh is salvation" (essentially synonymous with the names Hosea, Joshua, and Jesus). The name is not only appropriate to the contents of the book, but Isaiah makes the name, and his life that embodied it, a "sign" or a "type" of his entire message, and thus also of the fulfillment, who in both name and life brought that message to fruition.

We know very little about further precise details of Isaiah's life, though we probably know more than for any other prophet except Jeremiah. Of his father Amoz (not to be confused with Amos), we know only the name (the biblical counterpart of the modern family name). If Isaiah was not a native of royal Jerusalem, he certainly was thoroughly at home there, and apparently spent his entire ministry there. That context helps account for the literary elegance, exalted ideas, and courtly bearing of the book. It also explains Isaiah's intimate involvement in the local and international politics of the period, as well as his theological concentration on Zion and its Davidic throne.

Whatever secular calling the prophet also pursued, if any, eludes us. The suggestion that Isaiah was a member of the ruling aristocracy, a court official, official advisor, and confidant of kings, conceivably of royal blood himself, is plausible, but not required by the evidence. Accent on the topic of biblical wisdom has popularized an understanding of Isaiah as a wisdom teacher not only because of the cast of some of his oracles but also because of his court associations, which we know were often characteristic of the "wise," as the ancient world heard that term. Many have explained Isaiah as a priest or at least a temple official because of his apparent presence inside the temple, where only priests had access, at the time of his call (ch 6). However, it is risky to extract certain information of that sort from a vision, and there could be other explanations for a layman's presence in the Holy Place. Most problematic is the tradition that makes Isaiah a physician by original profession because of his "medical" advice to Hezekiah (38:21).

Continued on p 724.

OUTLINE

Criticism has long been accustomed to distinguishing "I Isaiah" or "Isaiah of Jerusalem" (chs 1–39) from some unknown anonymous "II Isaiah" or "Deutero-Isaiah" (chs 40–66), (beginning with C. A. Doederlein in 1775).

Critical Opinions

It must be stressed that far more is at stake than merely whether or not there are two Isaiahs. As a matter of fact, virtually no one of critical mind thinks any longer of only two Isaiahs. Both parts of the book are further dissected by critics. "I Isaiah" and "II Isaiah" are only tags of convenience. Much material within chs 1–39 is dated later than the eighth-century figure, some of it even later than the bulk of chs 40–66. Similarly, chs 56–66 are usually considered separately as a "III Isaiah" or "Trito-Isaiah." However, the critics widely questioned the unity of those chapters, too, as is also true to a lesser extent of chs 40–55. The same principles that the critics use for the dismemberment of Isaiah are also employed for other Prophetic Books.

One must be aware of the extent to which the integrity of *all* of Scripture is implicated at this point, because the pattern of restoration through and after judgment, that is of Law and Gospel, forms a substructure to the entire Bible. It is given overt expression not only in the judgment-salvation polarity of the two halves of Isaiah, but in virtually every other Prophetic Book.

Critics propose a sixth-century date for Is 40–66 based on the correspondence of the material to a presumed stage in the history of Israel's religious development. It once was commonly asserted that monotheism, having first surfaced in the eighth-century prophets, received its classical expression by "Deutero-Isaiah." Few today would make the assertion in so unguarded a form, but the pattern remains (e.g., what was previously a mere "faith" in one God is now becoming a "certainty" or the like for "Deutero-Isaiah", they assume a *theoretical* polemic against idolatry, etc.). Given that assumption, parallel assertions in Scripture must be dated to about the time of the exile too. Allegedly, it was the shock of the exile, when Yahweh plainly could no longer be thought of as a mere national god bound to a people and their land, which first produced the historical situation needed for a full and virtually explicit worship of one God. This development was supposed to appear with biblical universalism. The God of Israel's history had now graduated into the status of sole universal Creator-Judge of heaven and earth, as the people's historical experience of creating a new nation became an eternal theme. This type of argumentation is so bound up with evolutionism that the conservative is constrained to reject it almost entirely.

The Unity of Isaiah

Nowhere in Scripture do we have so extensive and so sustained a prophecy of the future as we find in Is 40–66. However, shorter passages of the same sort appear also in chs 1–39 and in other Prophetic Books.

The New Testament in general, and also our Lord specifically and repeatedly, refers to prophecies from the earlier chapters as well as the later chapters as equally belonging to Isaiah. Many of these references are not just to the book, but to the person of Isaiah. For example, in Jn 12:38–41 quotations from both parts of the book are attributed to the man Isaiah in one breath. The cumulative evidence and the nature of the argumentation on the basis of the citations is such that it will not be dismissed as mere casual, popular reference by anyone who takes Christ's and the New Testament's testimony seriously.

I. Judgment on Judah and Jerusalem (chs 1–12)

  A. Title and Overview of the Book (ch 1)

  B. Second Title and the Pilgrimage of the Nations to Zion—the Theme of the Book (2:1–5)

  C. The Day of the LORD (2:6–22)

  D. Social and Moral Chaos (3:1–15)

  E. The Destiny of Zion's Daughters (3:16–4:1)

  F. Peace after Judgment (4:2–6)

  G. The Song of the Vineyard (5:1–7)

In Is 40–66 we have not only a single prediction or two, but a sustained projection of the prophet's vision into the future. He speaks as though he were contemporary with the exile—with Babylon, not with Assyria, as the enemy. The message can be extremely precise, as he brings comfort and promise to the exiles whose ordeal is about over. The major example is the specification twice by name of Cyrus (44:28; 45:1), though the figure of Cyrus is plainly implied elsewhere in the context. (The only real parallel in the Old Testament is the specification of Josiah in 1Ki 13 some three centuries before his historical appearance.) Since there is no evidence whatsoever of textual tampering at these points, the entire issue of the unity of Isaiah pivots to no little extent on these Cyrus passages. For liberals, they clinch the case for a contemporary, sixth-century date of these chapters, while for most conservatives these chapters represent the pinnacle of the predictive material in the entire context. (O. T. Allis, in particular, has demonstrated that the poetic parallelism and climactic structure of 44:26–28 would be destroyed if *Koresh* [Cyrus] were removed.)

We know that Isaiah was married (Is 8:3, where his wife is not named, but called only "the prophetess," probably not meant in a professional sense, but because she was married to a prophet). Two sons were given symbolic names, thus becoming walking prophecies or types (Isaiah explicitly includes them with himself as "signs and portents" in 8:18). The first was named Shear-jashub (7:3), "a remnant shall return," embodying one of Isaiah's chief themes. It is debated whether the name was primarily promise ("A remnant shall *certainly* return") or doom ("*Only* a remnant shall return"). Probably it was both at once. The name of the second son, however, is pure doom: Maher-shalal-hash-baz (8:1), "the spoil speeds, the prey hastes." Many scholars, including some conservative ones, believe that Immanuel ("God with us") was a third child of Isaiah's, but the position is fraught with considerable difficulty (cf below).

Great Isaiah scroll from Qumran.

Date of Composition

As noted above, God called Isaiah as a prophet in c 740 BC (the year King Uzziah died) and he served through the years of Hezekiah, down to 681 BC. It has traditionally been assumed that Isaiah had the visions of chs 40–66 in his later years, but we simply have no way of knowing. The fact that they appear last in Isaiah's book does not imply that they occurred last, precisely because much similar material is scattered throughout the first part of the book. The hypothesis of later composition is thought to account for the "mellowed" viewpoint and for the shift in vocabulary (cf below), but both the different subject matter and Isaiah's unrivaled literary abilities render the assumption moot. If he delivered such oracles publicly, it may have been among a closed circle of the faithful.

Purpose/Recipients

Isaiah wrote to warn the people of Judah to repent so that they might escape God's judgment, poured out through the Assyrians. However, the range of his prophecies of judgment spread in all directions to include virtually all nations known to ancient Israel and, indeed, all people throughout the world (chs 13–24). The universal scope of judgment in Isaiah's prophecies is complemented with the good news of Zion's redemption, which also becomes the means of salvation for all people (chs 2, 25).

Literary Features

Genre

Isaiah's style is exceptional. Rarely have "inspiration" in the poetic and the theological senses been wed so beautifully. Different genres are adopted in different parts of the book, but the same peerless ability is evident throughout. Some features of the style come through even in translation; many others are untranslatable. It is a matter that the conscientious reader cannot ignore, and in the original context it must have contributed inestimably to the impact of Isaiah's preaching. Play on words and startling similes are dominant throughout. Isaiah has an almost uncanny ability to find an apt figure or illustration to make his point (cf the lodge in a cucumber field, Is 1:8; or a child in a forest of few trees, 10:19). More technically, he is a master of all the formal devices of Hebrew poetry. And, as the novice in Hebrew often discovers to his dismay, we find in the Book of Isaiah a richness of vocabulary and synonyms unparalleled elsewhere in the Bible (someone has counted a total of 2,186 different words used).

There are many variations within the first chapters of Isaiah, but especially in chs 40–55, where the style is often called lyric or hymnic, because there are close connections with the style of the so-called enthronement psalms or hymns. (Scholars have debated in which direction the dependence lay, but it seems more likely that Isaiah adapted a familiar liturgical pattern both in applying its theme to current events and in projecting it upon the screen of ultimate fulfillment.) The eloquence in the latter chapters is more cumulative, and natural imagery tends to give way to human figures, especially personification. Triads, imperatives, and rhetorical questions are also much in evidence.

The more hymnic style of the latter half of Isaiah, so evident even in translation, also appears frequently in the earlier chapters. The shifts in style as well as vocabulary are easily credible in the case of a past master of the Hebrew language such as Isaiah. Change of vocabulary inevitably also attends change in style and subject matter. We shall not cite statistics here, but actual counts indicate a substantial continuity in vocabulary as well as variations. One of the most obvious of these is the frequent use of Isaiah's favorite name for God in all parts of the book: "the Holy One of Israel." Others would include references to the "highway," the "banner" (Hbr *nes*), etc.

Characters

Isaiah presents himself as Yahweh's willing spokesman, specifically called to speak His word to the people of Judah (ch 6). The prophet has special access to the kings of Judah (chs 7, 36–39) and is bold to rebuke them in the Lord's name while also relating God's comforting promises.

King Ahaz of Judah (735–715 BC) is a significant character in chs 6–12. Isaiah presents him as lacking trust in the Lord and unwilling to seek the Lord's counsel or even a sign. (See the first narrative described under "Narrative Development or Plot" below.)

King Hezekiah of Judah (715–686 BC) is the main character in chs 36–39. The prophet describes examples of his great faith, prayer, and turning to the Lord for help, yet ends his account of Hezekiah by pointing out his self-interest, which will lead to the downfall of Judah in the future. (See the second narrative described under "Narrative Development or Plot" below.)

Seventh-century BC Hebrew inscription from tomb of a royal steward (Kidron Valley). The inscription is attributed to Shebnah, a senior minister in King Hezekiah's court. See Is 22:15–16.

Cyrus II (559–530 BC), the king of Persia called "the Great," is mentioned by Isaiah in the prophecies of chs 44–45. Isaiah describes him as the Lord's "shepherd," who will restore Jerusalem and subdue nations. Cyrus conquered Babylon in 539 BC, and his policies were instrumental in returning the exiles to Jerusalem.

The Suffering Servant is the subject of four songs in Isaiah (42:1–9; 49:1–13; 50:4–11; 52:13–53:12). The servant is a humble ruler whom God has appointed to suffer on behalf of His people. The prophecies about the servant are fulfilled in the person and work of Jesus of Nazareth. (See *TLSB*, p 1178.)

Narrative Development or Plot

Since the Book of Isaiah is, in general, a collection of prophecies, it does not have an overarching storyline or plot. However, like other Prophetic Books, the oracles move from warnings of God's judgment to promises of redemption. Two sections of Isaiah are written with clear historical progressions.

The first narrative-based section, chs 6–12, opens with the Lord calling Isaiah to prophesy against the dullness and coming desolation of the kingdom of Judah. The prophet confronts King Ahaz with his lack of faith that the Lord can help the people overcome the threat of the Assyrians. The Lord promises the sign of Immanuel (ch 7) and the blessings of His future reign (ch 9, 11) while anticipating the judgment of Assyria and other nations. This section closes with praise for God's deliverance of the remnant of Israel, who will return from exile rejoicing.

The second narrative section, chs 36–39, describes the Assyrian army's advance against Jerusalem under the leadership of Sennacherib. Judah's king Hezekiah seeks the Lord's help by going to the temple and requests counsel from Isaiah. Isaiah sends word that the Lord will lead the Assyrian out of Judah and return him to his own land. Hezekiah prays for deliverance, and the Lord answers by sending His angel, who strikes down 185,000 Assyrians. The remaining Assyrians withdraw. The story then turns to Hezekiah's prayer for healing, which the Lord answers mercifully. The last chapter describes how Hezekiah shows off his storehouses to the Babylonian envoys. Isaiah warns him that the Babylonians will conquer Hezekiah's kingdom, though not during Hezekiah's lifetime. The narrative of chs 36–39 closely resembles 2Ki 18–20 and 2Ch 32.

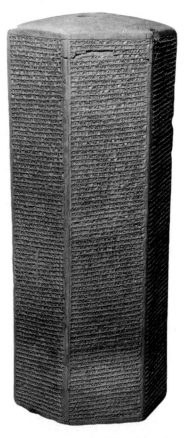

The Prism of Sennacherib records his principal campaigns, including the conquest of Judah.

Resources

The oracles of Isaiah provide examples of clear influence or interdependence among Israel's writers. However, in each case noted below, one cannot tell which author wrote his material first and influenced the other writer(s).

One of Isaiah's opening oracles (2:4) is worded like passages in Jl 3:10 and Mi 4:3. Since the Book of Joel is so difficult to date, it is unclear whether Isaiah influenced him or vice versa. Micah and Isaiah were contemporaries, and one likely influenced the style and wording of the other. Many other inner connections between Micah and Isaiah are traceable (cf Mi 4:1–4 and Is 2:2–5; Mi 2:1–5 and Is 5:8; Mi 5:9–14 and Is 2:6). Isaiah 36–39 is strikingly similar to 2Ki 18–20, and it is possible that Isaiah may have drawn his material from the account of Judah's kings or that he even served as their chronicle writer or editor. Another example of possible influence occurs with the prophet Obadiah, and others who prophesied against Edom. Isaiah condemned that nation in similar language. (See also the comment on the enthronement psalms, p 725.)

Text and Translations

The Masoretic text of Isaiah is in good shape, occasioning only a few, relatively routine, problems. The Septuagint, however, is so free—sometimes almost a paraphrase like a Targum—that its value as a witness to the original text is sharply reduced. Interest has focused on the phenomenal finds of Qumran, which yielded two manuscripts of Isaiah. One (usually referred to as IQIs[b]) was preserved only fragmentarily, but was virtually identical with the Masoretic text, thus establishing the antiquity of that textual tradition. The other Qumran copy (IQIs[a]) was complete, but differed somewhat at points, though still not significantly.

DOCTRINAL CONTENT

Summary Commentary

Chs 1–2 The Lord accuses Israel of ignorance and rebellion, yet plans for their repentance and forgiveness. A chief sin is corruption and indifference in their worship services. The Lord also describes Jerusalem's injustice and His wrath against idolatry. However, the Lord will gather the nations to His Church (the latter-day "Zion") through the Word.

Chs 3–5 The Lord prophesies that Judah will suffer due to a lack of sound leadership, despite its current prosperity. After judgment, Israel will receive rest and shelter. Isaiah describes God's gracious heart in the coming rule of the Messiah. Because Israel will not repent of unfaithfulness and unfruitfulness, the Lord will send Assyria to punish them with conquest and exile.

6:1–9:7 The Lord appears to Isaiah and calls him as a prophet. Isaiah is sent out with a message of condemnation, which must precede the hope that will arise through the Messiah. The Lord sends Isaiah to confront King Ahaz and to call him to trust the Lord firmly. Isaiah urges his hearers to repent, learn, and cling to the Word of God rather than to false spirituality. Ahaz does not heed the Lord's signs, so a different sign is given through the birth and name of Isaiah's second son. Judah will be all but swept away by Assyria.

Yet the Lord will still abide with and protect His people. The Lord promises deliverance from Assyria, but has the greatest deliverance in view—the blessing of a true, eternal King (cf 9:6–7). The Lord promises a future, everlasting Kingdom, fulfilling His promises to David and to Isaiah (7:14). The typically joyous birth announcement takes on even greater significance. Even the expectation of a prince's birth is surpassed here, for this child will deliver the oppressed and govern "with justice and with righteousness" as the Lord declares us just and sets us right through forgiveness and new life.

9:8–10:34 The Lord passes judgment on Assyria for her arrogance and oppression. He rebukes the wealthy and the greedy for destroying themselves and the helpless. The Lord plans to use, humble, and punish the proud Assyrians. The Lord calls all nations and individuals to genuine humility, which can only come about by seeing ourselves clearly in relation to the Lord and the standards He has commanded. The Lord notes that a remnant of Judah will turn away from the nations from which they have sought support.

Chs 11–12 The Lord describes the coming rule of the Messiah. The Assyrians were cut down like a tree (10:33–34). Now, Isaiah sees what is to happen several decades later. The axes of divine judgment will cut down the kingdom of David, the son of Jesse. The use of "Jesse" rather than "David" in 11:1, 10 indicates that this new king is not only of the lineage of David, but indeed a new David (Jer 30:9; Ezk 34:23–24; Hos 3:5). This promise of a Messiah is fulfilled in Jesus (Mt 1:6, 17; Lk 2:4; Ac 13:22–23). The Lord's people break out in song because of their salvation, proclaiming God's deeds to all people.

Ch 13 The Lord of hosts pronounces judgment on Babylon. He will consecrate an army for its destruction. The punishment depicted in ch 13 will find its most severe expression on Judgment Day, when sinners will face agonizing punishment and swift destruction.

Ch 14 Moved by compassion, the Lord will reverse the fortunes of Israel. As the chosen of the Lord, Israel will rule her enemies and settle in the land the Lord gives. The demise of Babylon's king demonstrates the final outcome for all who rely on oppression and wickedness to achieve their aims. His fall is a warning to never put ourselves in the place of God.

Assyria will destroy Philistia with fearsome efficiency. But in Zion, the Lord has founded a place of refuge for His afflicted people.

Chs 15–16 The complicated history of friendship and enmity between Israel and Moab will come to an end with Moab's bloody destruction. Yet even Moab's refugees will find shelter in the tent of the coming Davidic king.

Ch 17 Even great urban centers such as Damascus can offer no security against disaster. Yet, as with Israel, the Lord will preserve a remnant.

Ch 18 The Lord's plans are clearly signaled and sounded. All who dwell on earth should look and listen. The Lord makes known His message of salvation with unmistakable clarity—of Law and Gospel, of judgment and grace. Those who refuse to look and listen will be cut off from the Lord at an unexpected time.

Ch 19 As the Lord stirs up civil war in Egypt, the Egyptians will seek after wisdom, but will find only foolish counsel. The Lord destroys Egypt with a purpose: the Egyptians will come to know the Lord and worship Him alone. The Lord will accomplish Egypt's deliverance through both discipline and restoration.

Chs 20–21 The Lord commands Isaiah to walk naked and barefoot for three years as a sign to Cush and Egypt of their impending Assyrian exile. Through this unusual act, Isaiah proclaims the futility of earthly alliances that oppose the Lord's will. The Lord also appoints Isaiah to serve as a watchman and announce God's mighty acts, in particular the fall of Babylon.

Chs 22–23 Just as the Lord has spoken concerning the destruction of the nations, He speaks here of the destruction of Jerusalem, Tyre, and Sidon. God's own people will experience His wrath, for they have lived in ways indistinguishable from the nations.

Chs 24–27 The Lord now addresses the whole earth instead of individual nations. He proclaims that no one, not even the earth itself, will be spared the coming devastation. However, on Mount Zion, the Lord of hosts will prepare a feast and will swallow up death forever. Following judgment, the Lord will keep and protect His people as a pleasant vineyard. The Lord will keep in perfect peace those who trust in Him. Those made righteous through faith will experience the resurrection of their bodies and life everlasting.

Ch 28 When Ephraim stumbled in its own glory, it ignored the knowledge of the Lord and the beauty of His precepts. Jerusalem faces destruction because her inhabitants sought shelter in lies and falsehood instead of in the Word of the Lord. Yet the Lord will preserve a remnant founded on a precious cornerstone.

Ch 29 The visitation of the Lord will bring death and destruction to Jerusalem. Yet the Lord promises to do wonderful things with His people.

Chs 30–31 The Lord rescued Israel from slavery in Egypt; He forbids them from returning there for refuge. The people of Jerusalem will find no help by going down to Egypt. Only the Lord of hosts will protect and deliver Jerusalem. The Judeans despise the Word of the Lord, preferring illusions rather than truth. After a time of destruction, the Lord will be gracious to His people, binding them up and healing them in mercy.

Ch 32 Isaiah declares that a coming king will reign in righteousness, opening the eyes and ears of God's people. This promise is ultimately fulfilled by the Messiah. Those who are complacent will be laid low. But the pouring out of God's Spirit will make the lives of His people fruitful.

A granite statue of Amun protecting Cushite Pharaoh Taharqa (690–664 BC). The Cushites captured Egypt in 728 BC but were soon challenged by the Assyrians, who would bypass Judah to sack Thebes in 663 BC.

Chs 33–35 The Lord's judgments on the nations will certainly be fulfilled, but He will be gracious to His people. This includes His judgments about you and your family. Thanks be to God, our judge declares us "not guilty" on account of Christ. His sure Word of the Gospel saves us and makes us a new creation.

Chs 36–39 This section of Isaiah is a historical excursus explaining how the Lord defeated Assyria but prophesied Judah's exile in Babylon. The Rabshakeh entices and threatens Jerusalem to surrender or suffer. The people resist, remaining loyal to faithful King Hezekiah. In prayer at the temple, Hezekiah contrasts the idols of the nations with the one true God. Isaiah announces the Lord will rescue Jerusalem, and news comes that the king of Cush is approaching the Assyrians' southern flank. Isaiah prophesies that the Lord will rescue Judah amid hardship. The Lord answers Hezekiah's prayer for healing and forgiveness, but rebukes Hezekiah for expressing hope in Babylon as his ally against Assyria.

Chs 40–41 The Lord promises comfort and restoration for the Babylonian exiles. The Lord's messenger contrasts the Lord's faithfulness with the unfaithfulness of all people. The Lord lowers the nations but prepares for Israel's restoration. Israel has an incomparable God who watches over her.

Chs 42–44 The Servant establishes a new covenant to save the nations. Through the work of the Lord's Servant, the song of salvation reaches all people. Israel fails to believe and live as God's servant, and is punished with exile. The Lord bears witness in a courtroom setting that He is the only source of salvation. The Lord calls the idolaters back to court and swears that He alone is God. Through the work of God's Spirit, the chosen people grow in number.

Chs 45–48 The Babylonians regard themselves as uniquely wise and blessed through their astrological devotion, but they will be enslaved and humiliated. The Lord will humble mighty Babylon when He raises up Cyrus the Persian. The power and future of all nations are in God's hands. All people will confess Him and will submit in faith or in fear.

Jesus of Nazareth is the Suffering Servant of Isaiah's prophecies.

The Lord chastens Israel for stubbornness, indifference, and idolatry, noting that they were corrupt from the beginning. The Lord distinguishes His people from the nations and promises enduring peace through His Servant and His Spirit. This promise was fulfilled for your sake by Jesus of Nazareth (Mt 11:27–30).

49:1–52:12 Further description of the Servant-Savior is provided by the Lord. The Servant will administer not only the "sword" of God's Law but also the salvation delivered for you through the Gospel. The Lord contrasts His Servant's humility and obedience with Israel's rebelliousness. The Lord pleads for the people to believe in His salvation and describes the misery of living under His wrath.

52:13–53:12 In this final Servant Song, the Lord sacrifices the innocent Servant for the sake of ignorant, rebellious transgressors, making atonement for them. Few places in Scripture describe God's surpassing mercy for you in so touching a manner.

54:1–56:8 Although the Lord cast off Israel because of their sin, they will henceforth enjoy His vindication and everlasting love. The Lord's salvation will come not only for the chosen people of Israel but also for foreigners and outcasts. He invites all to seek Him in His Word and to receive His good and satisfying gifts.

56:9–59:21 Israel's leaders have forsaken their sacred duty. As Israel practices idolatry through a number of degenerate acts, they are openly mocking the Lord. By their sins, the people of Israel have separated themselves from God and from His salvation. The Lord heals and comforts all who are of a contrite and lowly spirit. But God's comfort and peace are withheld from the wicked, including those intent on backsliding in the ways of their own hearts. The Lord condemns all who draw near to Him only with words, those who seek their own pleasure above all else. But for those who share with their neighbors in need, the Lord promises healing. The Lord Himself, by His own arm, will act with zeal to accomplish both justice and salvation among His people.

Chs 60–62 The Redeemer of Israel will bring His penitent people out of the darkness of their sin into His everlasting light. The Servant/Messiah will come, bringing good news and everlasting joy to the redeemed of Israel. The mouth of the Lord announces the coming salvation that will be established in Jerusalem and proclaimed to the ends of the earth.

Chs 63–66 The Lord's steadfast love for His people is beautifully epitomized in the exodus from Egypt. Confessing their sins, the Lord's penitent people pray to Him as their Father, asking Him to reclaim them.

The Lord will repay the iniquities of those who reject Him, but His chosen servants—who seek Him in faith—will lie down in safety. The Lord threatens to punish all who follow their own devices and do not listen to Him. The retribution we deserve for our iniquities has been laid on Jesus. With His own blood, He made payment for all of our sinful deeds.

The Lord will bring about a new birth of joy and delight. In the Lord's new creation, we will completely forget the weeping and futility so characteristic of life in a fallen world. In their place shall be joy and gladness, fulfillment and satisfaction.

With hot rebuke, Isaiah closes his prophecy. Though he has emphasized God's grace and restoration in the preceding chapters, he ends with the fires of punishment because his hearers will not repent.

Specific Law Themes

Isaiah, like other prophets, derides the false worship of the Judeans who abuse the temple sacrifices by treating them as mere duty or as guarantees of God's favor despite their sins. Selfishness and idolatry are of special concern for him. Isaiah proclaims God's judgment against a wide variety of nations; his oracle of Judgment Day for all the earth builds on this theme of God's wrath. Many of his oracles concern the defeat of two empires: Assyria and Babylon, whom God uses to punish the kingdoms of Israel and Judah.

Specific Gospel Themes

Although Isaiah's denouncements of the nations are written with great skill, his oracles of promise and blessing make him one of the most popular prophets for readers. The Lord promises to preserve a remnant of His people despite their disobedience. The messianic prophecies regarding Immanuel are known to all through the many famous musical settings and hymns that broadcast them. In Isaiah, the Messiah will reign justly but He will also suffer on behalf of God's people, themes rehearsed in the New Testament story of Jesus of Nazareth. Isaiah prophesies salvation for Ethiopia, Assyria, and the nations, which is fulfilled as the Gospel spreads through Christian missionaries. Isaiah depicts the future paradise as a feast, which again is celebrated in the New Testament and Christian liturgy. Zion, as the people of God, is a constant theme for the prophet. Zion's rulers, such as Hezekiah, receive God's mercy. The book ends by prophesying a new heavens and a new earth.

Specific Doctrines

Isaiah's overwhelming importance requires some introductory, systematic comments about his major theological emphases. It is scarcely excessive to label him "*the* theologian of the Old Testament." This is stated without prejudice to other biblical literature, and minus the abstract scholastic form of "theology" focused on definitions of terms and logic.

Isaiah's call (ch 6) reflects the usual vertical vantage point of the prophets, standing at God's throne, from which height they can readily "see" horizontally far into the future. From that standpoint the temporal distinctions of ordinary humanity fade behind the eternal "now," and all of time becomes, as it were, one day as much as for God Himself (cf 2Pt 3:8).

The theme of creation, with its implication of a universal Creator of heaven and earth engaged in judging and redeeming in a "new creation," is extremely prominent in the latter half of Isaiah. Also the semitechnical word *bara'* ("create") is prominent, as in Gn 1. It would seem to be precisely the accent required also in oracles dealing with the source and scope of all history. In principle, it differs little from the theme of God's holiness or ineffable transcendence prominent in the first half of Isaiah.

As befits the times, the specific *expression* of the promises varies also: the "remnant" motif from the beginning of Isaiah mutates into "Suffering Servant" language, and the specifically *royal* messianism of the earlier chapters is almost totally submerged under the broader version of the restoration of Zion. Only a critical mind, which almost on principle seeks to *de*unify and *de*harmonize Scripture, will have difficulty recognizing the ultimate unity of only slightly different expressions. In fact, the accent on Zion is one theme that emphatically unites the two parts of the book, as well as the accents on holiness and faith.

Perhaps above all towers the theme of God's holiness, His being and status as wholly other, "God and not man." It receives classical expression in the Trisagion of the call (Is 6:3) and in the favorite title for God, "Holy One of Israel," but also appears in hundreds of other formulations. We plainly have here a major instance of the prophetic "reformation," underscoring ancient Mosaic teaching. Just as in the "holiness code" (Lv 17–26), the gift of the covenant means for Isaiah that Israel must be holy as her God is holy. That must be evident in political stance as well as in social demeanor. Sin in Isaiah's thought is preeminently "rebellion" (*pesha'*), unwillingness to recognize God's sovereignty over all aspects of life, whether in the public or private sector (let us not forget that Israel, unlike modern states, was church and state at once).

The other side of God's holiness, His glory (His holiness revealed), is obviously present by implication too. It receives explicit expression more in the latter half of Isaiah (and Ezekiel). These themes are so prominent also in Israel's worship, that one might well think of massive temple influence in this connection (and also Is 6 might point in that direction). God supplies the means for His people to assume His character, if they will receive it. If not, that same holiness requires damnation.

Traditional Lutheranism is disposed to put more stress on another Isaianic refrain, that of "faith." In this respect Isaiah shares with Habakkuk the title, "the St. Paul of the Old Testament." The only faithful response to God's holiness and the "cornerstone" (Is 28:16) of Israel's survival is "returning and rest . . . quietness and trust" (30:15). The meaning of "faith" in Isaiah should not simply be equated with Paul's, but neither should it be disjoined from it. On the surface it has much more the popular sense of "trust" (*fides qua*)

DID JESUS BRING PEACE?

Isaiah 9:6 declares: "For to us a child is born, to us a son is given; and the government shall be upon His shoulder, and His name shall be called Wonderful Counselor, Mighty God, Everlasting Father, Prince of Peace."

Matthew 10:34 warns: "Do not think that I have come to bring peace to the earth. I have not come to bring peace, but a sword."

Readers of the Bible have wondered why Jesus, who is called the Prince of Peace in the magnificent prophecy of Isaiah, declares that He did not come to bring peace on earth but a sword. The context of Matthew 10:34 shows in what sense the words of Jesus must be taken. He is not speaking of a war that the Christians will have to wage, but one they will have to endure. His meaning is that acceptance of the Gospel will not bring outward tranquility and peace upon His followers, but enmity, hatred, opposition, and persecution. Hence these passages are not contradictory. The one speaks of the character of Jesus and that of His kingdom, the other of the experiences of His followers here on earth.

or "firmness" (*'emunah*; 7:9b). But it plainly implies also the corresponding object of the trust and its content (*fides quae*), that is, ultimately the same divine work of judgment and salvation that Paul highlights so emphatically.

The motif of the "day of the LORD" is very prominent in Isaiah, perhaps climactically in Is 2. We need not enter here into the fruitless academic debate about the ultimate origins of the concept, holy war or temple worship (probably both). Neither can it be true that Amos, on whom Isaiah should be dependent, first deployed it as a theme of judgment instead of certain redemption.

The concept of the "remnant" runs throughout the book. Much of Isaiah's judgment and salvation or Law and Gospel message centers on this point. There is no other way for the people of God, the "holy seed" (6:13), to be formed than in the crucible of exile and restoration, death and resurrection. The theme is present in the bleak terms of Isaiah's call (6:11–13), and in the main word that appears in the name of his first son, Shear-jashub (7:3). It is debatable, but highly possible, that a remnant was already present in a circle of faithful disciples clustered about Isaiah.

Byzantine "Zion"

Temple Mount called "Zion"

Original "Zion"

Zion originally described the southeast hill on which stood Jebus, a Canaanite strong-hold (2 Sm 5:7). It came to include the Temple Mount north of it (e.g., Is 8:18) and, in Christian times, the larger hill to the west.

Finally, the twin motifs of Zion and the Messiah are nowhere so prominently displayed as in Isaiah. "Zion" themes are prominent enough throughout the book, but at the end of Isaiah *royal* messianism is almost completely submerged by stress on the universal kingship of God, and by the Servant themes. Use of the exodus and general covenant motifs appears more prominently nearer the end of Isaiah. Such variety is at least as attributable to one unusually resourceful poet, varying his figures with the topic.

It is important that "Zion" (the end times city of God) be distinguished (though not divorced) from the earthly Jerusalem, or Isaiah and other prophets will soon be embroiled in the crassest contradictions. The theme of the "inviolability of Zion" is necessary to Isaiah's message, but, of course, the earthly Jerusalem is doomed to destruction. The "gates of hell" cannot prevail against Zion (the Church), and after the earthly holocaust it will rise as the center of the messianic kingdom, the joy and desire of all the earth (cf 2:1–4). Isaiah celebrates the beginning of the realization of those promises, and the New Testament proclaims their fulfillment in Christ's kingdom (yet with a consummation in the kingdom of glory still awaited).

Climactically, Isaiah presents the theme of the Messiah, of the son of David enthroned in the city of David, the personal embodiment and type of the fulfillment of all election. Involved are not only some of the best-known prophecies in the Old Testament (Is 7; 9; 11), but others that are not so well-known (e.g., chs 32 and 33).

Before we conclude our brief survey of Isaianic theology, the phenomenal similarity of many of these motifs with three "Isaianic psalms" (Is 46–48) must be noted, most famously in the refrains of Immanuel, of faith, of God's transcendence, and of the "inviolability of Zion," in Ps 46, the Reformation psalm. Close connections between Isaiah and the Psalter also surface in the "hymns of Zion" in general, as in the enthronement and royal psalms.

Application

The opening chapters of Isaiah describe God's judgment against Judah and Jerusalem as well as the prophet's calling to admonish them. Among his warnings, Isaiah also prophecies the Lord's plans to save His people. These major themes have much to say about our lives.

Chs 1–12 In our sinfulness, we stand as God's enemies. However, rather than utterly destroy us, He longs to purify us by His righteousness. The Lords call us to purity in prayer and worship as taught by His Word. When we confess our sins, He promises faithfully to forgive us on account of Jesus' pure sacrifice.

Like Judah, our world today is filled with idols (wealth, power, beauty, and fascination with new religions). These cannot compare to the true God, who is powerful to judge and to save as He will when Christ returns. He calls you to fulfill His Word through Isaiah by sharing the Word with your family, friends, and neighbors. The Lord works through that illustrious Word to change your heart and those around you.

Although He chastens you, He will restore you through Jesus, the holy Seed that Isaiah prophesied. Christ reigns now in patience, calling those who doubt to repentance. Our King shall soon appear to exile the stubborn and to dwell with those He has chosen by grace through faith. The Lord abides with us still, even amid judgment and devastation. He is our Immanuel, and nothing can sweep Him away. The Spirit equips us to spread word of this blessed reign to all nations, to testify what the Lord accomplishes in Jesus Christ.

Chs 13–23 Through the prophet Isaiah, the Lord confronts both the people of Judah and also the surrounding nations. Isaiah sees not only the Lord's judgment upon these nations but also a hope-filled promise of future salvation (cf ch 19). We should fear God's wrath and repent of all evil, iniquity, and pride.

Whenever our relationship with the Lord stands in need of restoration because of our disobedience, our own actions and prayers alone cannot make things right. It is always God's compassion in Jesus Christ that restores us again and again. While the glorious king of Babylon remained in the grave (14:11), our King, the Lord Jesus Christ, rose from the grave. Through faith in Him, our guilt is taken away and our resurrection is assured.

Pride was the downfall of Moab (chs 15–16), and it is our downfall too. Those who trust in the works of their own hands are guilty of idolatry. When we fear, love, and trust in created things more than in the Maker of all things, we have forgotten the God of our salvation, who sent His Son, Jesus, to bear our sins of idolatry and to bless us with the refuge of His forgiveness. The Lord desires not our destruction, but that we turn to Him in repentant faith.

Although we are not called to imitate Isaiah's unusual witness to the world (ch 20), our actions and words should show that escape from God's wrath comes only through saving faith. Our trade and commerce can be carried out fairly and with honor. Christ clothes all who are ashamed and exposed because of sin. He covers our sin with His forgiveness. Our heavenly Father will deal generously with us by His surpassing grace.

Every Christian is called to serve as a watchman, announcing God's mighty acts as Isaiah did. However, God specially calls pastors to serve publicly as His watchmen, proclaiming both God's threats and promises. We can confidently rejoice in the salvation Jesus has won for us and in the promises of forgiveness and everlasting life announced by His watchmen.

Chs 24–27 The songs of thanksgiving and the visions of future mercy are among the most somber and joyous in the prophet's writings. When we do not heed the call of the watchmen, when we do not live lives of repentance, we are indistinguishable from unbelievers. Along with all of earth's other inhabitants, we stand before God as poor, miserable sinners. In thought, word, and deed, we have transgressed, violated, and broken His covenant. Although we deserve to suffer for our guilt, we can sing for joy that the Righteous One, Jesus Christ, has suffered in our place. "He was wounded for our transgressions; He was crushed for our iniquities" (53:5).

We are blessed to live and work under the leadership of many rulers and lords, but only the Lord is deserving of our faith and remembrance. We should always recognize that earthly authorities are only mortals through whom the Lord works on behalf of His people. Through His death and resurrection, Jesus has accomplished the salvation of sinners. His work guarantees that our bodies will also rise.

Chs 28–32 In this section of Isaiah we read how the Lord judges both Israel and Judah through the Assyrians and how it is foolish to expect that deliverance would come through the Egyptians.

Like the stubborn children of Israel, when we believe that human governments can help and profit us more than the Lord, we are guilty of idolatry. Though the help of people and nations may prove worthless, the help Jesus offers takes away our sin and shame, providing eternal protection. We must be careful not to become drunk with love of self, but always to seek the Lord in the beauty of His Word. Like the people of Jerusalem, we are often tempted to take refuge in pleasant-sounding lies. Instead, we should gladly learn the wonderful counsel of God's Word.

We should never despise preaching and God's Word in favor of smooth-sounding illusions that lead to perverseness. God's people should view adversity as the Lord's teaching tool. In adversity, we learn to walk in the way of the Lord and hear His Word. He has been merciful to all by sending His Son. Jesus is our King who reigns in righteousness and shares that righteousness with all who believe in Him, providing them with shelter from the storms of sin and death. In the waters of Holy Baptism, God pours out His Spirit upon us. By that Spirit, we are given Jesus' righteousness, resulting in lives of peace and trust forever.

Chs 33–39 The heart of the Book of Isaiah repeats many of the earlier themes and anticipates the great themes in the latter half of the book. These chapters hold the whole of the book together, turning from focus on Assyria to what the Lord would do in the days of Babylon and Persia. The Lord answers our prayers and guides the roles of leaders, all for the good of His people. Though troubles surround you, know that the Lord has them flanked and surrounded. When godly leaders are challenged, curb your complaints but cry out to the Lord on their behalf. The Lord is faithful to His Word and will deliver His people. He will not always grant you immediate relief from difficulty. He might use hardship to chasten and to teach. Take comfort in the wisdom of His ways. He demonstrated His zeal for you in the sufferings of Jesus for your redemption. The Lord will hear your prayer as surely as He heard Hezekiah's. No matter what difficulty or diagnosis you face, do not hesitate to make your request known to the Lord. He hears, forgives, and delivers His people according to His mercy, and He works through our hands for others' good. Prayer is our ever-ready strength, and the Lord is our ever-present ally. His Son will rule for your benefit and deliver you peace.

Chs 40–48 Although the themes of God's judgment do not disappear, the next chapters resound with messages of His mercy. The Lord's promises of comfort and restoration, fulfilled through John the Baptist's ministry, have personal consequences for you and for all people. Just as the Lord doubled the comfort and forgiveness for the exiles, He has doubled comfort and forgiveness for you in the person of His Son. Rather than defend your weaknesses, confess them before the Lord, who gives life through His Word.

Jesus Christ fulfilled the prophecies of the Lord's Servant (42:1–9) on your behalf. He frees you from your sins by His righteousness alone. Because you have received the Gospel, open your mouth to confess and to sing about Jesus' works—both His Law and His Gospel. He will lead you and never forsake you.

When you share God's Word with others, bear in mind that conversion and salvation are the Holy Spirit's work through the truth you share. Take comfort and confidence that He will fulfill His promises. The Lord of hosts is with you when you share the Word. Today, despite the difficulties that beset you, the Lord holds your future securely. In fact, He planned for your future through His beloved Son. As you reflect on your persistent weaknesses, recall also the Lord's patience (48:9–11) and the mercy announced for you in Christ.

Chs 49–55 Isaiah renews his prophecies of the Suffering Servant who would redeem Israel—a promise fulfilled in Jesus of Nazareth. Today, regard your sins with appropriate shame, but likewise see that the Lord, your Savior, has redeemed you. He will not forget you (49:15). He longs to restore you and your family. The Servant's obedience and suffering atoned for your sins and the sins of all the world. Walk in the light of His Word. In Him there is no disgrace.

Unrepentance lulls us into spiritual sloth, so that we do not discern the Lord's purposes in view of His Word. Wake up and listen! The Redeemer calls daily, and His mercies are new each morning. When the Lord calls and equips you for service, loose your bonds of fear and doubt. God's gifts and calling will suffice for you, and He will protect you.

Chs 56–66 In the last chapters of Isaiah, the prophet confronts us with our character and celebrates the characteristics of God. We often pursue personal pleasure and gain at the expense of our God-given responsibilities.

Like the people of Israel, we have our own collection of idols. When we fail to confess our sins and do not repent, we separate ourselves from God. In the darkness of our iniquity, our sins testify against us. Jesus came into the world to bridge the separation between God and sinners. All of our transgressions and iniquities were laid on Him at the cross, that we might know the bright light of His forgiveness.

Isaiah rightly depicts our sin as the equivalent of marital unfaithfulness (ch 62). Like an unfaithful wife, we deserve to be forsaken by our Bridegroom, Jesus Christ. But He has redeemed us with His own blood. He does not treat us as we deserve, but delights to make us His own holy people, made beautiful by His forgiveness.

On the Last Day, the Lord's overwhelming power will trample all His enemies, including all who reject the salvation purchased with Jesus' life-blood. His crimson garments bear witness to His decisive defeat of sin and death through His crucifixion and resurrection. He is indeed mighty to save, giving resurrection life to all who believe.

Spring gardens in Jerusalem teach us to long for the new heavens and new earth described by Isaiah (ch 65).

The Lord delights in those who are humble and contrite in spirit. But those who pursue self-chosen ways will be put to shame. Even the offerings they outwardly present to the Lord are regarded by Him as abominations. Although the glory of the Lord spans both heaven and earth, God Himself dwelt among us in the person of Jesus Christ. He became the sacrificial Lamb of God, whose death atoned for all our sins.

CANONICITY

As noted above, Isaiah was frequently cited by early Jews and Christians (cf Ecclus 48:17–25; Ac 8:26–40). The great Isaiah scroll at Qumran demonstrates the care with which his words were preserved.

Lutheran Theologians on Isaiah

Luther

"If anyone would read the holy prophet Isaiah with profit and understand him better, let him not ignore this advice and instruction of mine, unless he has better advice or is himself better informed. In the first place let him not skip the title, or beginning, of this book [Isa. 1:1], but learn to understand it as thoroughly as possible, in order that he may not imagine he understands Isaiah very well, and then have someone charge him with never having even understood the title and first line, let alone the whole prophet. For this title is to be regarded really as a gloss and a light upon the whole book. Isaiah himself, as though with his finger, points his readers to this title as stating the occasion and reason for his book. I say to him who ignores or does not understand the title that he should let the prophet Isaiah alone, or at least that he will not understand him thoroughly. For it is impossible to mark or perceive the prophet's words and meaning properly and clearly without this thorough understanding of the title.

"When I speak of the title [1:1], I do not mean only that you should read or understand the words 'Uzziah, Jotham, Ahaz, Hezekiah, kings of Judah,' etc., but that you should take in hand the last book of Kings and the last book of Chronicles and grasp them well, especially the events, the speeches, and the incidents that occurred under the kings named in the title [of Isaiah], clear to the end of those books. For if one would understand the prophecies, it is necessary that one know how things were in the land, how matters lay, what was in the mind of the people—what plans they had with respect to their neighbors, friends, and enemies—and especially what attitude they took in their country toward God and toward the prophet, whether they held to his word and worship or to idolatry.

Lands Surrounding Israel and Judah

"In addition it would be well also to know how these lands were situated with reference to one another, so that the strange and unfamiliar words and names might not make reading unpleasant and impede or obscure understanding. To do my simple Germans a service, I shall briefly describe the country surrounding Jerusalem or Judah, where Isaiah lived and preached, so that they may better see whither the prophet turned when he prophesied to the south or the north, etc. [geography follows; see map, p 345] . . .

"These are really the lands and the names about which Isaiah prophesies, the neighbors—enemies and friends—surrounding the land of Judah like wolves around a sheepfold. With some of them Judah made alliances and counter-alliances, but it did not help her at all.

What the Prophet Isaiah Treats

"After this, you must divide the prophet Isaiah into three parts. In the first part, like the other prophets, he handles two things. First he preaches a good deal to his people and rebukes their many sins, especially the manifold idolatry which has got the upper hand among the people. As godly preachers now and always do and must do with their people, so Isaiah too keeps the people in check with threats of punishment and promises of good.

"Second he prepares and disposes them to expect the coming kingdom of Christ, of which he prophesies more clearly and in more ways than any other prophet. In chapter 7 he even describes the mother of Christ, the Virgin Mary, how she is to conceive and bear him with her virginity intact. In chapter 53 Isaiah even describes Christ's passion together with his resurrection from the dead, proclaiming his kingdom as powerfully and plainly as if it had just happened, already at that time. This must have been a splendid and highly enlightened prophet. For all the prophets do the same: they teach and rebuke the people of their time, and they proclaim the coming and the kingdom of Christ, directing and pointing the people to him as the common Savior of both those who have gone before and those who are yet to come. Only, one of the prophets does more of this than another, one does it more extensively than another. Isaiah, however, does it most of all, and more extensively than any of the others.

"In the second part Isaiah has to do especially with the empire of Assyria and the Emperor Sennacherib. He also prophesies more and at greater length about this than does any other prophet, namely, about how the emperor would subdue all neighboring lands, including the kingdom of Israel, and inflict much misfortune on the kingdom of Judah. But there he stands like a rock, with his promise that Jerusalem shall be defended and freed by him from Sennacherib. And this is one of the greatest miracles to be found in the Scripture, not only because of the event, that so mighty an emperor should be defeated before Jerusalem, but also because of the faith with which men believed it. It is a miracle, I say, that anyone at Jerusalem could have believed him in such an impossible thing. Isaiah must, without doubt, have heard many bad words from unbelievers. Yet he did it; he defeated the emperor and defended the city. He must have stood well with God and been a precious man in his sight!

"In the third part Isaiah has to do with the empire at Babylon. Here he prophesies of the Babylonian captivity, whereby the people were to be punished and Jerusalem destroyed by the emperor at Babylon. It is here that he does his greatest work, comforting and upholding a people yet to be, in this destruction and captivity yet to come, in order that they might not despair, as if they were vanquished and Christ's kingdom would not be coming and all prophecy were false and vain. How rich and full his preaching: Babylon shall in turn be destroyed, and the Jews will be released and will return to Jerusalem. With proud defiance of Babylon, Isaiah even gives the names of the kings who shall destroy it, namely the Medes and Elamites, or Persians. He mentions particularly the king who shall release the Jews and help them back to Jerusalem, namely Cyrus, whom Isaiah calls 'God's anointed' [Isa. 45:1]. He does all this long before there is a kingdom in Persia. For he is concerned altogether with the Christ, that his future coming and the promised kingdom of grace and salvation shall not be despised or be lost and in vain because of unbelief and great misfortune and impatience amongst his people. This, indeed, would be the case, unless the people expected it and believed confidently that it would come. These, then, are the three things with which Isaiah deals." (AE 35:273–77)

For more of Luther's insights on this book, see *Lectures on Isaiah, Chapters 1–39; 40–66* (AE 16, 17).

Gerhard

"The prophetic books, so called because the prophets wrote them at God's command, follow the Mosaic or legal books, the historical books, and the doctrinal or poetic books in the canon of the Old Testament. Four major and twelve minor prophets are counted.

"Among the major prophets, *Isaiah* is set in the first position, and he is nineteenth in the order of the canonical books. He is set in the first rank, however, not because he is older than the rest, because chronology shows that Jonah, Hosea, and Amos were earlier in terms of time. Rather, he occupies the first place because of the dignity of his prophetic declarations and because his prophecy is longer than all the rest. Some add this reason: because he was related to the Messiah not only by faith but also by a kinship of blood. He is called *yesha'yahu*, as if to say, 'the Salvation of the Lord,' whose message Isaiah indeed included in his addresses. Isaiah is called 'the son of Amoz' (Isa. 1:1), and the rabbinic scholars claim in this regard that he was the brother of Amaziah, king of Judah, and father-in-law of Manasseh. He began to prophesy in the 3,160th year of the world, seven hundred years before the birth of Christ, while King Uzziah of Judah was still ruling, and he lived to the last days of Hezekiah (Isa. 1:1; 39:3). Therefore he was nearly a contemporary of Hosea, Amos, and Micah and spent the course of his life under four kings of Judah: Uzziah, Jotham, Ahaz, and Hezekiah (as is evident from the aforementioned passages).

"Of all the prophets, Christ selected this one to expound publicly in the synagogue of His own country because Isaiah sets forth his prophecies about the Messiah so clearly that he seems to act as an evangelist rather than a prophet.

"Augustine writes about him (*De civ. Dei*, bk. 18, c. 29): 'Isaiah, along with his rebukes of iniquities, his commands of righteousness, and his predictions of an evil future for a sinful people, also prophesied much more than the rest about Christ and the Church, that is, about the King and the city that He founded, so that there are some people who have called him an evangelist rather than a prophet.' Augustine means Jerome, who writes this about him (Epistle *ad Paulin.*): 'To me, Isaiah does not seem to compose a prophecy but the Gospel.' In the introduction to his commentary on Isaiah, Jerome writes: 'I shall explain Isaiah in such a way that I shall reveal him not only as a prophet but also as an evangelist and an apostle.' Also: 'This present writing contains all the mysteries of the Lord.' Also: 'Whatever there is of Holy Scripture, whatever human language can speak, whatever mortal senses can accept, these are contained in this book.' Jerome again writes (Epistle *ad Paulum et Eustochium*): 'Isaiah was a noble man, clear in expression, of urbane eloquence, who admitted no uncouth speech.'

"Jerome also says that Isaiah included in this book whatever human language and the mortal senses are capable of accepting about physics, ethics, logic, and the mysteries of Holy Scripture and that he did this with greater charm and eloquence and urbane elegance of diction than did the rest of the prophets.

"Amphilochius calls him 'an outspoken person' (*Opera*, p. 94). In *Seder Olam* the Hebrews say that Isaiah was born of royal blood and that his own kinsman, the idolatrous King Manasseh, sawed him in two with a wood saw after he had taught in his office for sixty years. Of the Christian theologians, Epiphanius (*De vitis Patriarch.*, c. *De Esaia*) and Jerome (*Ad Paulum et Eustochium*) make the same claim. They try to confirm this from Heb. 11:37.

"Isaiah's prophecy covers sixty-six chapters and can be divided into *introduction, narrative,* and *conclusion.* The narrative contains things both legal and evangelical. The legal material can be recounted according to the series of the four kings under whom he taught. Athanasius says about Isaiah: 'The majority of his prophecy is Gospel tidings with respect to the coming of the Word in the flesh and the sufferings that He took upon Himself for our sakes.' He concludes his prophecy with an address about the final judgment and the eternal punishments of the wicked, because of which Augustine writes: 'This prophet ends his book at that point when time [*seculum*] will end' (*De civ. Dei*, bk. 20, c. 21)." (ThC E1 § 151)

FURTHER STUDY

Lay/Bible Class Resources

Bartelt, Andrew H. *Isaiah: Here Am I! Send Me*. GWFT. St. Louis: Concordia, 1996. ♫ Lutheran author and theologian. Thirteen-session Bible study, including leader's notes and discussion questions.

Bartelt, Andrew H., Jane L. Fryar, and Edward A. Engelbrecht. *Isaiah: Parts 1 and 2*. Leaders Guide and Enrichment Magazine/Study Guide. LL. St. Louis: Concordia, 2006. ♫ In-depth, nine-session Bible studies with individual, small group, and lecture portions.

Borchert, Mark, and Edward A. Engelbrecht. *God's Abiding Word: Isaiah*. St. Louis: Concordia, 2003. ♫ An eleven-session, advanced study of Isaiah from Lutheran theologians. Explores the Law and the Gospel dynamic in the prophet's writings. Downloadable and reproducible.

Braun, John A. *Isaiah Parts 1 and 2*. PBC. St. Louis: Concordia, 2005. ♫ Lutheran author. Excellent for Bible classes. Based on the NIV translation.

Life by His Word. St. Louis: Concordia, 2009. ♫ More than 1,500 reproducible one-page Bible studies covering each chapter of the canonical Scriptures. Page references to *The Lutheran Study Bible*. CD-Rom and downloadable.

Motyer, J. A. *Isaiah*. TOTC. Downers Grove, IL: InterVarsity Press, 1999. ♫ Reads Isaiah conservatively and as a literary unity. Helpfully points out a major shift in the second half of Isaiah (from 48:20–21, Cyrus and Babylon are not mentioned again). His strength is in his broader theological explanation of the text.

Church Worker Resources

Leupold, Herbert C. *An Exposition of Isaiah*. Grand Rapids: Baker, 1977. ♫ A careful exposition of Isaiah and its messianic prophecies. Written by a Lutheran commentator who taught at Capital Seminary in Columbus, Ohio.

Luther, Martin. *Lectures on Isaiah*. Vols. 16 and 17 of AE. St. Louis: Concordia, 1968, 1972. ♫ The great reformer's lectures from 1527–30, which reflect his mature approach to biblical interpretation. Luther consulted the Hebrew text and reflected on the application of the prophecies and their New Testament fulfillment.

Oswalt, John N. *The Book of Isaiah*. 2 vols. NICOT. Grand Rapids: Eerdmans, 1986. ♫ Stresses the theological and doctrinal unity as well as a literary unity. Explains the details of the text by examining individual words or phrases that do not seem intelligible upon first reading.

Pieper, August. *Isaiah II: An Exposition of Isaiah 40–66*. Milwaukee: Northwestern, 1979. ♫ Lutheran theologian. One of the best expositions of Isaiah 40–66.

Quinn-Miscall, Peter. *Reading Isaiah: Poetry and Vision*. Louisville: Westminster John Knox Press, 2001. ♫ An introduction to the poetic and visionary form of the book, treating it as a unified whole.

Academic Resources

Alexander, Joseph A. *Commentary on the Prophecies of Isaiah*. Grand Rapids: Zondervan, 1978 reprint. ♪ A helpful old standard resource from a noted linguist.

Allis, Oswald T. *The Unity of Isaiah*. Nutley, NJ: Presbyterian and Reformed, 1950. ♪ Demonstrates the unity of the Book of Isaiah in a careful, discerning manner.

Childs, Brevard. *Isaiah: A Commentary*. Louisville: Westminster John Knox Press, 2000. ♪ Although Childs divides Isaiah along typical, critical lines, he also argues for interpreting it as a unified document with canonical standing. Special attention to the book's theology.

K&D. *Biblical Commentary on the Old Testament: The Prophesies of Isaiah*. 2 vols. Grand Rapids: Eerdmans, 1971 reprint. ♪ This century-and-a-half old work from Lutheran scholars should not be overlooked. Despite its age, it remains a most useful commentary on the Hebrew text.

Lessing, R. Reed. *Isaiah 40–55*. CC. St. Louis: Concordia, 2011. ♪ A thorough theological commentary from a Lutheran theologian, interacting extensively with the Hebrew text. Highly recommended for preachers.

Nägelsbach, Carl Wilhelm Eduard. *The Prophet Isaiah*. LCHS. New York: Charles Scribner's Sons, 1878. ♪ A helpful older example of German biblical scholarship, based on the Hebrew text, which provides references to significant commentaries from the Reformation era forward.

Westermann, Claus. *Isaiah 40–66*. OTL. Philadelphia: Westminster, 1969. ♪ A moderately critical study that includes insightful comments from a respected critical scholar.

Young, Edward J. *The Book of Isaiah*. 3 vols. NICOT. Grand Rapids: Eerdmans, 1965–72. ♪ The *magnum opus* of a great conservative scholar. Carefully interprets the many prophecies of Isaiah in their context; also stresses their messianic import.

———. *Studies in Isaiah*. Grand Rapids: Eerdmans, 1954. ♪ Especially important for a careful study of Isaiah 7.

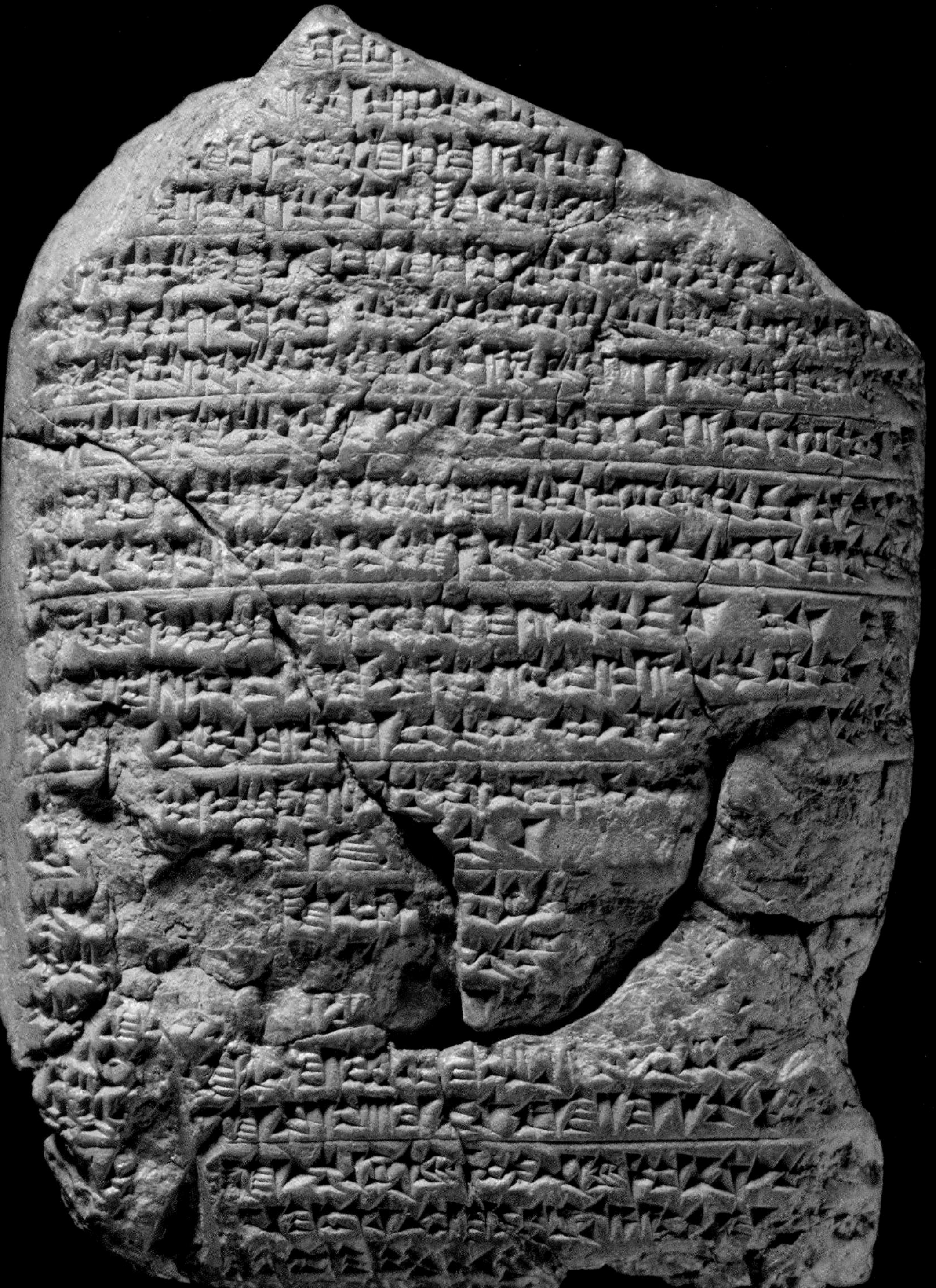

JEREMIAH

The Lord will make a new covenant

Along Israel's central ridge, about 3 miles northeast of Jerusalem, Jeremiah's priestly ancestors settled in the region of the tribe of Benjamin where they looked out over the Jordan Valley and upward to Jerusalem. In c 970 BC, Jeremiah's hometown of Anathoth became a city of exile for Abiathar, the chief priest who did not support Solomon's accession as king after David (1Ki 2:26). Jeremiah may have descended from this exiled priest but was at least associated with his descendants. The prophet was, therefore, born to controversy, which played a great role in his ministry at Jerusalem during the last days before the Babylonians overran the city, plundered Solomon's temple, and destroyed it.

Among the significant events of which Jeremiah was a contemporary, we may mention: the death of the great Assyrian king Ashurbanipal; the subsequent swift decline and fall of Nineveh (612 BC) and of the entire Assyrian Empire; the battle of Megiddo (609 BC) in which Judah's king Josiah lost his life; Nebuchadnezzar's subsequent defeat of Egypt at the battle of Carchemish (605 BC); and the rapid change of imperialist occupiers of Judah, from Assyria to Egypt to Babylonia and two or three deportations from Jerusalem, the last one accompanying its destruction. Jeremiah is, indeed, the prophet who witnessed the decline and fall of the Davidic kings.

Several other faithful prophets were active during Jeremiah's lifetime, but, as with all the prophets, Jeremiah does not mention them. Among these were Ezekiel, Daniel, Nahum, Habakkuk, and possibly Obadiah and Zephaniah. Of contemporaries, the false prophet Hananiah is featured prominently (Jer 28) because of his clashes with Jeremiah, as is the faithful prophet, Uriah, who had been extradited from Egypt and executed by Jehoiakim (26:20–23). In the same connection, we do, however, have mention of Micah (26:18), active a century earlier—the *only* time a prophetic book mentions another "writing prophet" by name!

We are better informed about the details of Jeremiah's life than of any other prophet, thanks mostly to copious information found within his book

The Babylonian Chronicle records the defeat of the Assyrians, Nebuchadnezzar's rise to power, and his victory over Jehoiachin of Judah in 597 BC. The Chronicle includes the principal events of each year, from 747 to 280 BC, with some gaps in the record.

itself. There is no prophet where detailed knowledge of the tortuous history of the period is as important for understanding as in the case of Jeremiah. Although very precise historical data are sometimes given, the problem is complicated by the often completely unchronological order in which Jeremiah's oracles occur—another reminder that presentation of history in biblical thought is not identical with the modern chronological and documentary ideals.

Historical and Cultural Setting

The question of Jeremiah's attitude toward Josiah's reformation and Jeremiah's relationship to the Book of Deuteronomy is an important one. Surprisingly, Jeremiah makes no clear reference to Josiah's reform, though he apparently was a staunch supporter of Josiah. Higher criticism, of course, attaches supreme importance to the issue, because of the pivotal role that Deuteronomy and the "Deuteronomic reformation" plays in its entire reconstruction of the history of Israel's religion (see pp 10-11).

Critical views have given contradictory answers about Jeremiah's attitude toward Josiah's reform, partly depending on their presuppositions. (E.g., the classically liberal viewpoint that Jeremiah could not possibly have supported Deuteronomy's sanction of sacrifice, public rituals, biblicism, etc.) A favorite proof text for those who think Jeremiah opposed the reform has always been Jer 8:8, condemning the "lying pen of the scribes" and those who trust in the "word of the LORD." But there is no clear indication that Jeremiah targeted the reform, only the usual prophetic concerns about insincerity, bribery, and so on. A few extreme scholars even argued for the dependence of Deuteronomy on Jeremiah, even though traditional chronology would separate the writing of the two books by nearly 1,000 years!

Many critics argue for Jeremiah's dependence on a Deuteronomistic editor, pointing especially to the discussion in 11:1–17, where Jeremiah stoutly exhorts his audience to "hear the words of this covenant" (but again the text lacks particulars). This camp argues that Jeremiah not only approved of this editor's theology, particularly its alleged program of centralization of worship, but also adopted its characteristic style in many of his sermons. The latter point builds on the undeniably "Deuteronomic" character of Jeremiah's sermons in their present form, but other explanations are possible, of course, and we return to the issue below.

A very popular middle—and sort of compromising—position argues that Jeremiah at first welcomed the reform, but later became disillusioned at some of its unfortunate developments and came to the realization that real regeneration would have to come from within rather than by law or statute. A few have tried to explain Jeremiah's famous "new covenant" discourse (31:31–34) as Jeremiah's later alternative to the Deuteronomistic quasi-legalism.

A Conservative Approach

The truth is that we have no direct information on Jeremiah's attitude toward Josiah's reform. Given conservative premises that Josiah's reformation was based on a Mosaic Book of Deuteronomy (or its equivalent), every likelihood would indicate that Jeremiah was in thorough sympathy with the movement. The few oracles certainly datable to the time of Josiah can just as easily imply approval of the reform as disapproval. Again the lack of specific mention may be for the same puzzling reason as the failure to mention other contemporary canonical prophets—perhaps a desire to avoid duplication.

What is often overlooked in this entire issue is its political dimension, perhaps because we so easily forget that ancient Israel was state as well as "church." The account of Jeremiah's near arrest and execution or lynching in Jer 26 concludes with the significant statement: "But the hand of Ahikam the son of Shaphan was with Jeremiah so that he was not given over to the people to be put to death." Careful reading of various references makes plain that Jeremiah had the closest association with some three generations of this influential family, which was also one of the mainstays of Josiah's throne. The father, Shaphan, had been something like state-secretary to Josiah in charge of temple renovation. When the Book of the Law was found, it was to him that Hilkah first reported it. Shaphan, in turn, read from the book to Josiah, and on the king's instructions, it is he and his son, Ahikam, who seek validation of its message from Huldah the prophetess. (Why not Jeremiah? Was it because

OVERVIEW

Author
Jeremiah the prophet with his scribe, Baruch

Date
628–c 580 BC

Places
Anathoth; Judah; Jerusalem; Egypt; Tahpanhes; Assyria; the Lord's house (temple); Topheth (Valley of the Son of Hinnom); Ammon; Edom; Moab; Babylon; the court of the guard

People
Jeremiah; Baruch; people of Israel and Judah; Zedekiah; Jehoiakim; false prophets; men of Anathoth; Nebuchadnezzar; Coniah (Jeconiah); the righteous Branch; Gedaliah; Nebuzaradan; Ishmael; Johanan

Purpose
To call Judah to repentance, announce the Babylonian exile, and prophesy the new covenant

Law Themes
The nations plucked up, broken down, destroyed, and overthrown; punishment of Judah by sword, famine, and pestilence; faithless shepherds; turn in repentance; forsaking the Lord and His covenant; idolatry; Judah cursed like Sodom

Gospel Themes
The nations built and planted; healing; the Lord will relent; the remnant will return; a righteous Branch to sit on David's throne; new covenant, new hearts; God's steadfast love and mercy; judgment of nations

Memory Verses
Broken cisterns (2:11–13); amend your ways (7:3); a proper boast (9:23–24); delight in the Word (15:15–21); the Lord tests the heart (17:5–10); the potter and the clay (18:6–11); the new covenant (31:31–34)

TIMELINE

722 BC   Samaria (Israel) falls to Assyria

628 BC   Jeremiah called to be a prophet

589 BC   Final siege of Jerusalem begins

587 BC   Babylonians take Jerusalem; temple destroyed

538 BC   Cyrus decrees that exiles may return to Judah

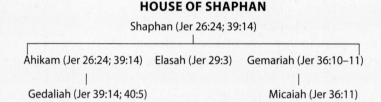

THE HOUSE OF SHAPHAN

The descendants of Shaphan, who likely served as royal secretary during King Josiah's reform (2Ki 22:3–20), were on friendly terms with Jeremiah. The following diagram identifies members of Shaphan's family who are mentioned in the Book of Jeremiah, encompassing three generations of Judean officials from the time of Josiah's restoration of the temple (c 633 BC) to the governorship of Gedaliah (587 BC) after the Babylonian conquest.

HOUSE OF SHAPHAN

Shaphan (Jer 26:24; 39:14)

Ahikam (Jer 26:24; 39:14)   Elasah (Jer 29:3)   Gemariah (Jer 36:10–11)

Gedaliah (Jer 39:14; 40:5)   Micaiah (Jer 36:11)

Seal (Bulla) belonging to "Gemaryahu Son of Shaphan." He is the Gemariah known to Jeremiah.

Jeremiah was of northern priestly descent, and thus somewhat an outsider?) The incident does at least suggest that Jeremiah's later cordiality with the family of Shaphan was due to shared religious convictions. Of course, this Hilkiah may even have been Jeremiah's father (1:1)!

After Josiah's death at Megiddo came the collapse of his policies (including, no doubt, his religious reform). The family of Shaphan, like Jeremiah, apparently continued in firm support of Josiah's reform and in opposition to the policies of Josiah's various relatives who succeeded him. Two of Ahikam's brothers also appear beside Jeremiah: Elasah, one of the two couriers who bore Jeremiah's letters to the exiles in Babylonia (Jer 29:3), and Gemariah, from whose house Baruch read Jeremiah's scroll in Jehoiakim's reign, and who vainly tried to prevent the king from burning it (ch 36). To the Babylonians, the Shaphan family and Jeremiah both appeared "pro-Babylonian." After the fall of Jerusalem, Jeremiah declined to journey to Babylon. We are not surprised that the Babylonians commended him to the care of Ahikam's son, Gedaliah, whom they had appointed governor of the captured province (39:14).

COMPOSITION

Authors

The book's superscription identifies Jeremiah as "the son of Hilkiah, one of the priests who were in Anathoth in the land of Benjamin." Of the father, we know nothing (unless, as seems very unlikely, he was the same priest who discovered the Book of the Law in the temple), but Anathoth (still bearing essentially the same Arabic name, 'Anata) lies on the second ridge of hills, a few miles northeast of Jerusalem. Mention of priestly descent makes it possible that Jeremiah was descended from David's priest, Abiathar, whom Solomon had banished to his home city, Anathoth, in favor of Zadok (1Ki 2:35). That would also mean Jeremiah had roots in Shiloh (Abiathar was descended from Eli) and thus in the heartland of the northern tribes, whose traditions might well have survived a century after the fall of Samaria. Such an association would explain Jeremiah's affinity with Hosea, another northern prophet (e.g., the covenant as marriage to Yahweh).

The superscription goes on (Jer 1:2) to date Jeremiah's call in the thirteenth year of the reign of Josiah (cf 25:3), that is, about 628 BC. How old he was at the time, we do not know. In Jeremiah's autobiographical account of his call, he describes himself as a *naʿar*, that is (usually) a "youth" of marrying age, probably not older than 20. His last recorded words (ch 44) were spoken in Egypt, where he had been kidnapped by Johanan after Ishmael's assassination of Gedaliah, sometime after 587. Thus, Jeremiah exercised a ministry of at least 40 years, perhaps somewhat more (628–c 580). Presumably, that length of activity is also reflected in the length of the book, second in length only to Isaiah among the prophets.

Jeremiah lived out his entire life in that chaotic and fateful period a century after the fall of Samaria (and the activities of the great eighth-century prophets) when we have almost a rerun of the earlier history of Israel's decline, only this time with Judah as the victim. In the three-cornered contest for world supremacy between Assyria, Babylon, and Egypt, Judah's foreign policy was largely based on expediency instead of principle, and Jeremiah is usually obliged to oppose it just as uncompromisingly as Isaiah had a century earlier. After Babylonian supremacy has largely been established, pro-Egyptian and anti-Egyptian factions wrack the court at Jerusalem as they had Samaria's in its final days (cf Hosea).

How did all the material in the Book of Jeremiah get put together in its present form? That Baruch played a prominent role, and that his scroll formed the core of the ultimate product appears likely, but one can only guess. The historical narratives in Jeremiah are often referred to as the "Baruch Biography," on the assumption that they stemmed from the prophet's constant companion and confidant. The supposition is by no means impossible or even unlikely, but it must be stressed that the Bible itself never makes such an assertion. All we are told is that "Baruch wrote on a scroll at the dictation of Jeremiah all the words of the Lord that He had spoken to him" (Jer 36:4), and after Jehoiakim had destroyed the first copy, "many similar words were added" (36:32) to the replacement.

Date of Composition

The major phases of Jeremiah's ministry may roughly correspond to the overall order of his book. Chapters 1–6 may stem largely from the beginning of Jeremiah's career, from his call to Josiah's reform (c 628–623). The second period of his ministry would be concurrent with the latter part of Josiah's reign, from the beginning of the reform until the king's death at Megiddo in 609. It is certainly striking that relatively few passages in the book can clearly be ascribed to this so-called silent period. Some question the dating of the early oracles to Josiah's time and believe that Jeremiah was not very active at all (or perhaps not even called) until around 609 BC. Chapters 7–39 (after a so-called "silent period"?) do seem to report primarily on events in a "third phase," between Megiddo in 609 BC and the sack of Jerusalem in 587 BC. Likewise, chs 40–45 describe events involving Jeremiah after the catastrophe.

Purpose/Recipients

The Lord appointed Jeremiah "a prophet to the nations" (1:5) to declare their overthrow (1:10). Like his contemporary, Ezekiel, Jeremiah warned those still in Jerusalem that there was no future for them as an independent kingdom. But unlike Ezekiel, Jeremiah suffered significant persecution since the people of Jerusalem rejected his message and King Jehoiakim even burned a scroll of his prophecies. Jeremiah preached God's judgment to deaf ears, and his oracles express to the Lord his frustrations.

Literary Features

Genre

In the Book of Jeremiah, oracles can readily be spotted by their poetic format in most versions. They appear especially in chs 1–25. Chapters 30–31 are prophecies of hope. Gentile oracles appear in chs 46–51. The middle twenty chapters are historical discourses or sermons. These two types are most characteristic of Jeremiah. The prose sermons, usually in the first person ("I"), are scattered throughout the book. This type is not only more extensive in Jeremiah than in any other prophetic book, but Jeremiah's prose is remarkably like that found in the Book of Deuteronomy.

Perhaps even more than Isaiah and Ezekiel, Jeremiah loves to repeat certain pet phrases, such as "Peace, peace, when there is no peace" (8:11); "accept discipline" (2:30; rendition of the Hebrew phrase varies); "early and late" or "persistently" (7:25); "terror on every side" (6:25); "the voice of mirth and the voice of gladness" (7:34); "not to make a full end" (4:27); and "sword, famine, and pestilence" (14:12). Three relatively unique patterns of introducing divine oracles in Jeremiah may also be noted: (1) "Thus says Yahweh [often with 'of hosts'], the God of Israel" (common in Kings, but not in the other prophets); (2) "Behold, I am about to bring . . ."; and (3) "The word which came to Jeremiah from Yahweh as follows" (or variations; its Hebrew uniqueness often obscured further by varying translations).

Consideration of Jeremiah's style also overlaps with the question of whether Moses wrote the Book of Deuteronomy. Critics assume that Deuteronomy was composed during the same period as Jeremiah. Conservatives argue that its very antiquity as a traditional sermon style, plus its historic association with Moses and the Torah, would make it more likely that Jeremiah would, on occasion, adopt the style of Deuternonomy for his messages. There is far more prose in Jeremiah than in any other prophet, and it generally has a Deuteronomic flavor.

Although Jeremiah's prose is relatively easy to render into English, that is not always the case with poetry. From a purely literary standpoint, Jeremiah's poetry is not quite the exquisite piece of art we behold in Isaiah, but it is of the first order nonetheless. The ancient, classical canons of Canaanite poetry are obviously still alive with Jeremiah, but perhaps employed more flexibly and spontaneously than in earlier writers. Whether that is a reflection of Jeremiah's apparently more emotional temperament, or whether it signals the beginning of the end for the ancient cultural patterns, is hard to say. In Jeremiah's contemporary, Ezekiel, and increasingly thereafter, the poetic standards appear to fall by the wayside or to be repeated without real mastery or comprehension.

Characters

As one of the largest books of the Old Testament, Jeremiah mentions numerous persons. The following are key figures in the book. For a more complete treatment of the characters, it is necessary to consult commentaries.

Baruch the scribe, son of Neriah, is described in chs 32, 36, and 43 as assisting Jeremiah with his message, sometimes at considerable risk. Baruch may have contributed to the book's wording, collection, and arrangement. See pp 755–56.

Kings of Judah are mentioned throughout the book. **King Jehoiakim** (609–598), who allowed his father Josiah's reform to unravel, was confronted by Jeremiah's preaching (cf chs 22, 26). This king burned Jeremiah's scroll (ch 36).

King Jehoiachin (598–597) reigned only three months after his father, Jehoiakim, until taken captive to Babylon (ch 22). Isaiah ends (ch 52) with the hopeful news that Jehoiachin has been released from prison in Babylon, anticipating the future restoration of the Davidic kings.

The contents of this krater were dedicated at a sanctuary, as the Hebrew word *holy* indicates. Ritual was the common means for expressing one's faith.

King Zedekiah (597–587) is the most frequently mentioned ruler in the Book and the last ruling king of Judah. He was a son of King Josiah, brother to Jehoiakim, and uncle to Jehoiachin. Zedekiah sough Jeremiah's counsel but did not follow it, likely due to political pressures. He died in exile at Babylon. See chs 32, 34, 37–39, and 52.

Governor Gedaliah (587 BC) was appointed to rule Judea for the Babylonians. He was the grandson of Shaphan, who served as secretary to King Josiah during his famous reform. Gedaliah supported Jeremiah but the governor was assassinated by Ishmael for cooperating with the Babylonians (chs 38–41). For more on this important family, see p 754.

Other significant characters include the Babylonian captain Nebuzaradan (chs 39, 52), the Judean captain Johanan (see chs 40–43), and the murderer Ishmael (see chs 40–41).

Narrative Development or Plot

As a collection of oracles and narratives with uncertain chronological order, the Book of Jeremiah does not have an overarching storyline or plot.

The first chapter relates Jeremiah's call as a reluctant prophet. Chapters 36–45 recount persecutions that Jeremiah suffered as he shared the Word of the Lord with various rulers, including descriptions of how the Lord rescued him from the persecutions. Chapter 52 recounts the fulfillment of Jeremiah's prophecy that Judah would fall, and also provides the hopeful message about Jehoiachin, the last surviving king of Judah whom the Babylonians released from prison.

Resources

For questions of Jeremiah's dependence upon the Book of Deuteronomy, see the "History and Cultural Setting" above.

Jeremiah 26:18, which cites Mi 3:12, is the only example in the prophets where one writer explicitly cites another prophet (however, cf Jer 25:11–12; Ezr 1:1; Dn 9:2). In this unique case, Jeremiah anticipates the literary practices of later Judaism and early Christianity, pointing to the growing canonical status of prophetic writings. Jeremiah's oracle against Edom (49:7–22) has a close relationship to Ob 1–9. The verbal parallelism is particularly striking between Jer 49:14–16 and Ob 1–4, and between Jer 49:9 and Ob 5. Jeremiah may also have used the Book of Joel. There are basically two possibilities: one prophet was dependent on the other or both used a common source. The Book of Jeremiah ends with what may be described as an appendix (52:1–27) borrowed from 2Ki 24:18–25:21.

Text and Translations

The Septuagint text of Jeremiah presents one of the most grievous text-critical problems in the entire Old Testament. The problem is twofold, concerning both the length and the arrangement of the material. The LXX text is roughly one-eighth (some 2,700 words) shorter than the Hebrew text. Most of the missing text consists of single verses or parts of verses, but sometimes longer portions are missing too. Some of the variations are readily explainable on normal text-critical principles; others are not. Some of the poetic regularity of the Hebrew text seems to be missing in the LXX, but that is a frequent casualty of translation. Usually the variations are ultimately no more serious than alternate, abbreviated, ways of saying the same thing. The Qumran discoveries have given us some shorter Hebrew manuscripts, demonstrating that the textual divergence predated the translation of the

OUTLINE

I. The Call of the Prophet (ch 1)

II. Warnings and Exhortations to Judah (chs 2–35)

   A. Earliest Prophecies (chs 2–6)

   B. The Temple Message (chs 7–10)

   C. Covenant and Conspiracy (chs 11–13)

   D. The Drought (chs 14–15)

   E. Disaster and Comfort (16:1–17:18)

   F. The Sabbath and Israel's Identity (17:19–27)

   G. The Potter and Israel (chs 18–20)

   H. Condemnation of Kings, Prophets, and People (chs 21–24)

   I. Foretelling the Babylonian Exile (chs 25–29)

   J. Promises of Restoration and the New Covenant (chs 30–33)

   K. Historical Appendix (chs 34–35)

III. Suffering and Persecution of the Prophet (chs 36–38)

   A. Burning of Jeremiah's Scroll (ch 36)

   B. Imprisoning of Jeremiah (chs 37–38)

IV. The Fall of Jerusalem and Related Events (chs 39–45)

   A. The Fall of Jerusalem (ch 39)

   B. Gedaliah and Jeremiah (chs 40–41)

   C. Jeremiah, Baruch, and Egypt (chs 42–45)

V. Judgment against the Nations (chs 46–51)

VI. Historical Appendix (ch 52)

LXX. The chart on p 763 illustrates how the texts are different from one another. For the sake of comparison, all the references in the chart are from the Hebrew (same as English) chapters and verses.

Early critics tended to favor the Septuagint text. The priority and superiority of the longer Hebrew text may well be established in due time, but it will have to be tested and weighed by the normal text-critical canons. The wide LXX variations at very least seem to suggest that the process of editing the Book of Jeremiah resulted in different editions. Perhaps the LXX provides us with one example where we have preserved the "first edition" of a biblical book, before it achieved final, canonical form. It is also possible that the shorter Hebrew texts and the LXX represent an editor's effort to shorten a very long and complex collection of the prophet's words that included quite a bit of repetition. The traditional Masoretic Hebrew text remains the standard for English translators.

Doctrinal Content

Summary Commentary

Ch 1 Jeremiah introduces himself and the historical context of his prophetic ministry, including the details of his call, two visions, and God's promises to be with him. God sent prophets like Jeremiah to convict His people of their sin so that they might repent and return to Him. In mercy, God patiently waited, providing ample time for repentance.

Chs 2–6 Through Jeremiah, God files charges against His people for breaking covenant with Him. He uses the powerful image of marital unfaithfulness—a capital crime under Mosaic Law—to drive home the seriousness of the charge. Judah's temporary repentance is only superficial—their hearts still stray far from the Lord. In this section, Jeremiah offers a glimmer of hope for the northern tribes, revealing God's plan to rescue a remnant of their people in the future.

In pronouncing judgment against His people, God warns them of an irresistible enemy advancing quickly from the north. Like a hurricane-force wind, Babylon's armies will sweep Judah away, leaving only a few survivors. Jeremiah grieves for Judah and its people, lamenting their imminent destruction. The same God who created the world by His powerful Word has pronounced judgment upon His sinful and rebellious people. From the lowliest individual in the streets to the highest official in the temple or king's palace, God's people have turned away from Him to other gods. Their rebellion appears clearly in their immoral behavior as they reject every prophet who calls them back to faith and to the obedience that comes from faith. Even in the midst of his grief, Jeremiah voices a note of hope—all is not lost.

Chs 7–10 God warns His people that mere possession of the temple and ritual observance of its worship laws will not save them. He condemns them for worshiping false gods, even in the temple compound, and for offering their children as burnt offerings to idols. Possession of God's Word cannot save them because their teachers have misrepresented it.

The Lord grieves over the sin of His people, which will cause their destruction. Although it breaks His heart, God must punish unrepentant sinners because He is just and righteous. Yet the Lord yearns to forgive them. Jeremiah contrasts the one true God with idols. Like scarecrows, idols are inanimate objects crafted by human hands; they have no power to harm or to help. God is all-powerful, so no one can escape His justice and judgment.

Chs 11–13 The people break God's covenant, incurring the curses pronounced when their ancestors entered the Promised Land. Persistent apostasy can have only one outcome: God's judgment. Jeremiah struggles to understand how a righteous God can tolerate the wicked and even allow them to prosper. God delays punishment of His people, allowing them plenty of time and opportunity to repent and return to Him in faith. Failing that, He will give them over to their enemies, and justice will be served—the land will be laid waste and its inhabitants exiled.

Jeremiah uses a loincloth to illustrate God's judgment against His people. The new loincloth, ruined by the elements, now resembles the spiritual condition of God's people. As a result, God will treat them like a person treats rags. The Lord uses the image of a full jar of wine to illustrate the fullness of His judgment against His people. No one, rich or poor, will be spared from the coming wrath. The time for repentance eventually runs out, and unrepentant sinners must then face the fullness of God's justice. The Lord has determined to send His people into exile because of their arrogance and idolatry. Their rebellion against Him is so ingrained that it has become part of their nature, like spots on a leopard.

Chs 14–15 Jeremiah describes a drought and its effect on the land and its inhabitants. As a result of their sins, the people do not deserve God's help, but in his prayer for aid, Jeremiah appeals to God's faithfulness (v 13). He expresses his frustration over false prophets who tell the people that peace lies ahead, though Jeremiah has warned them that destruction is coming.

THE ORDER OF JEREMIAH'S PROPHECIES

Not only is the LXX considerably shorter than the Hebrew text, but the material is arranged in a different sequence. The two outlines appear side by side below.

Masoretic Order	Septuagint Order
1. The prophet's call (ch 1)	1. The prophet's call (ch 1)
2. Various oracles, mostly of doom with some supplementation with prose sermons, and, toward the end, also of biographical narratives (chs 2–25)	2. Oracles of doom in Jerusalem and Judah (chs 2:1–25:13)
3. Mostly biographical material, containing various oracles and prophecies of hope, but not prose sermons (chs 26–45)	3. Gentile oracles (chs 25:15–38; 46–51)
4. Gentile oracles (chs 46–51)	4. Oracles of deliverance (chs 26–35)
5. An appendix relating Jerusalem's fall and immediately subsequent history (ch 52; essentially parallel to 2Ki 24:18–25:30)	5. Jeremiah's sufferings (chs 36–45)

As shown above, the Septuagint has essentially the same blocks of material, but in different sequence (in the chart, we give the rough Hebrew chapter and verse equivalences for the sake of convenience).

Students of prophecy will note at once that the LXX sequence is that of the classical prophetic outline of universal judgment followed by universal (offer of) salvation—in this case followed by the "Book of Suffering" which did not fit that outline. That order could, of course, represent a later rearrangement of the material, but such a thing appears unprecedented in prophetic manuscripts. Furthermore, it must be conceded that 25:15–38 has no immediate connection with its Hebrew context, while it makes a superb conclusion to the Gentile oracles.

God responds to Jeremiah's prayer for the people. They have refused to repent and return to Him; therefore, He will destroy them.

Jeremiah complains that everyone stands against him because of his negative message. He comes close to accusing God of deceiving him into thinking that his job as prophet was going to be easier than it has been. God calls Jeremiah to repentance for his doubt and promises to strengthen him for the work ahead.

Chs 16–17 Jeremiah's actions will reinforce his words of judgment and condemnation. Persistent sin can only result in condemnation by God and loss of all joy. God's grace will be known by all people—both the Judean exiles returning from a foreign land and by heathen nations who turn to the true God. However, the Lord will first deal with their sin of idolatry by destroying the people of Judah and desolating the land.

Only the person who trusts God and follows His Word will survive in eternity. Jeremiah prays for vindication from God and for justice against his accusers. He bristles against the injustice of being punished for doing God's will.

The Sabbath was a day of rest and worship under Mosaic Law (cf Ex 20:8–11; Dt 5:12–15). God set it aside as a blessing for His people. By continuing commerce on the Sabbath just as on any other day, God's people broke the covenant and turned their backs on Him.

A potter's wheel (cf Jer 18). The upper stone fit into the lower stone and was lubricated to spin.

Chs 18–20 Committed to their idolatry and self-centered lifestyles, the Judeans refuse to respond to the Lord's gracious invitation to repent of their sin. Their rejection of God is plainly seen in their mistreatment of His prophet Jeremiah.

Jeremiah proclaims God's judgment by breaking a piece of pottery near the valley where children had been sacrificed to pagan gods. As Jeremiah breaks the clay vessel, so God will break Jerusalem and reduce the population to destruction. The prophet complains bitterly about the opposition he has experienced in response to the dire warnings he preached to the people. His predictions of destruction stand unfulfilled, giving his enemies grounds to beat him, imprison him, and plot against his life. Jeremiah calls on the Lord for help and praises His name, but he cannot help expressing the anger and despair he genuinely feels.

Chs 21–24 God reveals His judgment on Jerusalem to the political and religious leaders of Judah: only those who surrender to the Chaldeans will live. God disciplines them for their lack of repentance and for ignoring His warnings. Even during this judgment, mercy and compassion shine through, providing a way of survival.

God challenges His people in Jerusalem to keep His covenant by helping other people, protecting the weak and vulnerable, and keeping Him first in their worship and their lives. In contrast, Jeremiah condemns Israel's leaders for their obsession with wealth and power and, at the same time, neglect and abuse of the needy. God tells these powerful people that they will not enjoy their dishonest gains.

God promises to give His people a new and righteous King who will save and protect them as long as He reigns over them. The Lord tells Jeremiah that He will safeguard the Judean people sent into Babylonian exile in 587 BC, but that His wrath remains on those still in Jerusalem. The good—the faithful—will return.

Chs 25–29 In a prophecy dating to 605 BC, God warns His people that He will soon destroy Jerusalem because of their idolatry and immorality. Ultimately, His judgment will fall on all nations, including Babylon.

If the people will confess their sin, God will forgive them and spare them. For Jeremiah's faithful proclamation, he is arrested and tried for treason (a capital crime).

Jeremiah narrowly escapes the death penalty under wicked King Jehoiakim when a high court official, Ahikam, and others intercede for him. Jeremiah predicts that God will let all who submit to the Babylonians live in their own land safely. To accomplish His purposes, the Lord uses people and nations and empires.

In 594 BC, Hananiah falsely predicts the return of the temple furnishings taken to Babylon in 597 BC and the Judean captives. Jeremiah warns the populace of Jerusalem that the worst is yet to come. God does not deal with sin merely with a "slap on the wrist" (as Hananiah thought). The future of God's people lies with the exiles, taken from Jerusalem to Babylon in 587 BC. God's judgment must fall upon His rebellious people. Yet God's favor rests upon the exiles, and they are encouraged to settle down for a long stay, after which God will return them to Jerusalem.

Chs 30–33 God tells Jeremiah to write down the prophecy of a future restoration. God will anoint a King to rule over His people, and the community will live in peace after the exile in Babylon. The exile is temporary, for God Himself will save the remnant and return them to their home. God could destroy them for their sin, but out of deep love and compassion He merely disciplines them with exile and promises them a new relationship, not based on the Law of Moses but on grace and faith.

Jeremiah's forebearers would have grazed their sheep in fields where Solomon exiled their patriarch, Abiathar, the last high priest of Eli's line (1Ki 2:26–27). On the allotment of lands to the Levites, see Jsh 21, esp v 18.

God tells Jeremiah to buy a parcel of land near Anathoth as a visible promise that life would return to normal after the exile (which would last a long time). Surrounded by the enemy army, it may have seemed foolish to buy land for the future, but obeying God is always the right thing to do. The Lord further charges His people with idolatry, a sin violating the First Commandment (cf Ex 20:4–6). Because they turned their backs on God, He will turn them over to the Babylonians for the city's destruction and the people's exile. Eventually, the Lord will restore the fortunes of His people, and the empty streets will once again ring with joy and laughter. God's discipline must work itself out at this point before He will show mercy to His rebellious people. God plans a wonderful future for His people, ultimately fulfilled in Christ Jesus, the Davidic King who will rule over His people as High Priest, who shall intercede for them.

Chs 34–35 When the Babylonians temporarily withdraw and it seems the danger is past, the rich once more enslave the servants they have freed. This reveals the unbelief and rebellion at the heart of God's people. Still, God does not reject them forever; He plans for their discipline and restoration. He uses the faithful Rechabite family to show His people what obedience looks like.

Ch 36 Jehoiakim of Judah destroys the written prophecies of Jeremiah, rejecting God's mercy and the chance to repent of his sins. In doing so, he seals his fate and the fate of the nation. Even at this late stage in Judah's history, God wants to spare the people and forgive their sins—if only they would repent and turn back to Him.

Chs 37–38 Jeremiah assures King Zedekiah and the city residents that the withdrawal of the Babylonians is only temporary. The Babylonians will certainly return and destroy the city, as God had ordained because of people's sin. Jeremiah's enemies secure permission from King Zedekiah to kill him for treason since he advised the city's soldiers to desert and predicted their defeat at the hand of the Chaldeans. Rather than risk outright murder, they confine Jeremiah to a dry cistern with the expectation that he will die of thirst or starvation. Ebed-melech, an official in King Zedekiah's administration, rescues Jeremiah with the king's permission. King Zedekiah arranges a private meeting with Jeremiah and learns that he can avoid capture and save the city by surrendering to the Babylonian army, yet Zedekiah fears his own advisers more.

Ch 39 After a siege of one and a half years, Zedekiah and his people experience the consequences of their idolatry and unbelief. Yet, as promised, God rescues a remnant of the people and will later return them to Judah. Nebuchadnezzar has Jeremiah released from custody and returned to his hometown. Before Jeremiah goes, he brings good news to Ebed-melech, who had rescued him from the dry cistern (38:7–13), that he will survive the fall of Jerusalem because he trusts in the Lord.

JEREMIAH AND THE LACHISH OSTRACA

Another topic relating to Jeremiah's lifetime is his possible mention in some of the 18 letters found by archaeologists in 1935 in the guardroom of Lachish, southwest of Jerusalem, which fell just before Jerusalem (cf Jer 34:7, where it is mentioned as still standing). Two mentions of prophets once led to intense speculation that Jeremiah (or even Uriah) was meant, and while that is unlikely, the texts do shed important extrabiblical light on the Hebrew language and prophetic activity in that period. Ostracon XVI is broken and refers only to "...iah the prophet" (unfortunately thousands of names besides Jeremiah concluded with that abbreviation for the divine name). Letter III mentions some unnamed prophet who had sent a warning of some sort, perhaps of possible sedition. Letter VI is also interesting in its complaint that some princes were "weakening the hands" of the people (discouraging, demoralizing)—precisely the same accusation made by the princes of Jerusalem against Jeremiah (38:4).

A Lachish ostraca (sixth century BC) refers to a "prophet," perhaps a contemporary or even Jeremiah himself.

Chs 40–41 Gedaliah, appointed governor by the occupying Babylonians, naively ignores warnings of an assassination plot against him. Ishmael murders a number of pilgrims and Gedaliah. Johanan, one of Gedaliah's soldiers, and his men overtake Ishmael. Johanan's faithfulness and mercy here contrast sharply with the treachery of Ishmael, who seeks advantage over others who are suffering. The Lord rescues Jeremiah and preserves a faithful remnant of the people in the land.

Chs 42–45 Jeremiah promises God's blessings to Johanan and his band of refugees if they will stay in Judah, but warns that God does not want His people to place their confidence in Pharaoh or his army. Johanan and the last of the royal family break their vow (42:5–6) and move to Egypt against God's will, taking Jeremiah with them. The Judean refugees who fled to Egypt are convinced that worshiping false gods brings them peace and prosperity. God reveals His heart while encouraging Baruch, Jeremiah's secretary. When God disciplines, even faithful servants like Baruch will feel the heat of His wrath. Yet God will protect Baruch throughout the turmoil ahead.

Chs 46–51 God declares that He will use Egypt's defeat by Babylon as a pattern for further military losses. Egypt, however, will survive. Jeremiah proclaims a series of oracles against the Philistines, Moab (fulfilled in 582 BC), the Ammonites (a prophecy fulfilled in 582 BC), the Edomites, Damascus (capital of Aram that came under Babylonian domination shortly after Jerusalem fell), the people of Kedar and Hazor (Babylonians overran them at the beginning of the sixth century BC), Elam, and finally, Babylon, whom God holds responsible for the destruction of Jerusalem and the captivity of its citizens. During the process of Babylon's destruction, the Israelites will come together to seek the Lord to make an everlasting covenant (50:4–5).

Ch 52 Jeremiah concludes on a hopeful note. Despite Judah's rebellion, God never forgot His promises.

Specific Law Themes

In the opening oracle, the Lord tells Jeremiah that the nations will be plucked up, broken down, destroyed, and overthrown. Jeremiah commonly warns about the punishment of Judah by sword, famine, and pestilence. He derides the faithless shepherds whom God and the community had entrusted with leadership in both the civil and religious spheres. A favorite expression of Jeremiah is the word *turn* used to describe repentance. Since the Judeans forsake the Lord and His covenant and pursue idolatry, they will be cursed like Sodom.

Specific Gospel Themes

Compared with a prophet like Isaiah, Jeremiah offers less consolation. However, the arrangement of his book is such that the overwhelming darkness of his oracles amplifies the brilliance of God's grace. Jeremiah records that nations will be built and planted as the Lord relents from His wrath and promises healing. The remnant will return. A righteous Branch will sit on David's throne. Jeremiah's most important Gospel theme is the new covenant and the promise of new hearts, which occur in what commentators call the "Book of Comfort" (chs 30–33). God is steadfast in love and mercy. As He judges the nations, He will deliver His people.

Specific Doctrines

Although Jeremiah repeats many earlier themes of biblical theology, such as those in Deuteronomy, theologians have turned to him especially for the doctrines of sin, the Lord's correction, repentance, and trust in Him.

For example, Jeremiah records how the Lord curses mankind's trust in self (17:5–6) because the human heart is desperately wicked (17:9–10). The Lord instructs sinners through discipline and correction (10:23–24; 30:11; 31:19) with the goal of restoring them through repentance and trust in the Lord alone (17:7). Jeremiah notes that Israel's basis of fellowship with God was not the sacrifices of the Mosaic covenant of themselves, but the Word of God that the people should hear and believe (7:21–23). Since Israel cannot fulfill the old covenant, the Lord promises to provide a new covenant focused on His Word and faith (ch 31). This becomes the most important prophecy of the book, the basis of New Testament revelation in Christ (Heb 8:8–13; 10:16–17), and the title of the New Testament feast of the Lord's Supper, which is called the "new covenant" (Lk 22:20; 1Co 11:25; cf Mt 26:28; Mk 14:24).

The Lord insists that Jeremiah speak His Word with boldness (Jer 15:19) and says that He will teach the people to invoke His covenant name, Yahweh, with genuine trust (23:5–6; 33:16). In fact, they can call on Him even to bless their enemies and conquerors, the Babylonians (29:4–7). In all these ways, the Book of Jeremiah shows its importance to Christian theology.

Application

Ch 1 Jeremiah records the historical context of his ministry. God provided ample time for Judah's repentance. He is likewise patient toward you, whom He calls to repentance and true faith in Christ. Idolatry and immorality eventually bring disaster upon sinners. God wants His people to repent and turn back to Him, averting disaster and receiving His mercy.

Chs 2–6 Through Jeremiah, God files charges of marital unfaithfulness against His people for breaking covenant with Him. God grants time for sinners to repent, but those who refuse to do so will face His justice. He also shows His grace by rescuing a remnant in order to replant them in the Promised Land and bring a Savior from their descendants. God had sent prophet after prophet to warn His people and call them to repentance because He loved them and wanted them back. Today, He calls you so that you may receive His gracious salvation. Repent of all pride, and pray for sincere faith and wisdom with kindness. Beware of spiritual leaders who prove faithless. Consider all things in view of God's Word, and respect those who teach God's Law and Gospel. He gives us new hearts and faithful leaders. In spite of our faithless acts, God continues to be faithful through His Son, Jesus, our Savior.

Chs 7–10 Mere possession of God's Word cannot save Judah because their teachers have misrepresented it. Without genuine, living faith, it is impossible to please God (Heb 11:6). Sin may start small, but it often grows until it takes over a person's life, leading even to such obvious evils as child sacrifice (consider today the abuse and neglect of children, who may be sacrificed to selfish interests). Because of the people's apostasy, God will bring His power to bear against them and their leaders. Yet God is so great, He can also do the impossible: save sinners without violating His own righteousness (cf Rm 3:21–26).

Chs 11–13 The people break God's covenant. Jeremiah struggles to understand how a righteous God can tolerate the wicked. Often we are

A red slipped Iron Age II goblet, found in the city of David, with two pouring vessels.

unable to understand God's justice or reconcile God's providence with the evil we experience. Yet God cannot be mocked. Sinners who resist His grace will face judgment and eternal condemnation. The Law, like an illustration, shows us our sins. In spite of our ruined state, God loves us. Do not test the Lord's kindness, but call on Him today with a repentant heart. The cup He longs to pour out for you is that of the new testament in His blood for the forgiveness of sins. The Lord has provided for our cleansing through Holy Baptism. He restores us by His faithful Word and makes us a new creation in Christ.

Chs 14–15 Jeremiah describes a drought and its effect on the land and its inhabitants. Take heart that the Lord does not delight in destroying sinners. God is righteous—He keeps His Word—and He will bring down the curses He threatened (Dt 28:15–68). "But God shows His love for us in that while we were still sinners, Christ died for us" (Rm 5:8). As witnesses, God's grace is sufficient for our weakness, and His Holy Spirit empowers us to share His Word faithfully.

Chs 16–17 God alone will provide strength for Jeremiah in his difficult ministry, just as He provides all we need in Jesus Christ. He is the blessed Bridegroom for His beloved Bride, the Church. The Lord explains to Jeremiah and His people the severity and magnitude of their sin. Those who turn away from the Lord must perish. God's Word often creates opposition in this world, as it did for Jeremiah and even for Jesus (Jn 7:7). Yet God does not abandon His faithful servants, though sometimes they must suffer and even die for their faith. Rest and worship are essential for the spiritual health and welfare of God's people. The Gospel of Jesus Christ draws us together in public worship so that we might rejoice in our salvation and return to our callings with renewed confidence.

Chs 18–20 Those who proclaim God's Word faithfully will likely face persecution as Jeremiah did. Yet believers stand in grace, confident of God's love. He makes us a new creation just as a potter reworks a lump of clay. As heinous as people's sin is, God stands ready to forgive and save, if only they will repent and turn to Him. Like Jeremiah, we are often weak and fearful in times of crisis because we doubt the Lord and trust in ourselves. When we are weakest, God's strength shines through more clearly (cf 2Co 12:10). He is ever our refuge and strength, who hears our confession and forgives all our sins.

Chs 21–24 God reveals His judgment to the political and religious leaders of Judah: only those who surrender to the Chaldeans will live. Keeping the Law means not only avoiding the wrong thing but also includes doing the right thing, such as having mercy. Today, as then, people sacrifice their integrity and compassion for temporary riches. God condemns the spiritual leaders of Judah for misleading His people. The Law is to be preached to unrepentant sinners, no matter how painful it may be, so that people are not deceived. The Gospel is to be preached to spirits crushed by the Law, bringing light and life through faith in Jesus Christ, our Savior. Today, the Lord calls us to repent of our sin and serve Him by faith. He graciously gives us His own heart and faithfulness in His Son born of David's line.

Chs 25–29 God, righteous and holy, must punish sin. Even if God's justice seems to delay, it always accomplishes its purpose. Like individual people, nations have gone their way without regard for God. For Jeremiah's faithful proclamation, he is arrested and tried for treason. Hard hearts resist every overture of mercy from God. Faithful proclamation of God's Word often brings serious, even fatal, opposition by the worldly powers. Pray daily for faithful leaders. Take heart, knowing that God's Word prevails, stronger than any opposing force, and it accomplishes its purpose: your salvation.

Chs 30–33 God's greater purpose of salvation will be accomplished in spite of the people's sin. He will rescue His people and reign over them through David's descendant, the Messiah. In Christ, the discipline of God works for our benefit. In Christ Jesus, God provides the sacrifice necessary to silence the accusations of the Law. By faith, Christians have a new and right relationship with God (cf Rm 3:21–26). When trouble surrounds you, cling to the Lord's commands and promises. Only He can create and sustain saving faith and faithful living in His people. In Jesus, the Lord sent a faithful King to rule over all His people and a High Priest to intercede. Entrust your cares to Him through prayer. His all-availing sacrifice and His compassionate rule will bless and keep you.

Chs 34–35 People seem willing to slavishly follow their own traditions and ignore the Law of God (cf Mt 15:1–6). (Consider, e.g., how holiday traditions spread easily though their spiritual meaning is often lost.) God patiently calls sinners to repentance, sending messengers and granting them ample time to turn back to Him in faith.

Ch 36 Jehoiakim of Judah destroys the written prophecies of Jeremiah. Persistent unbelief rejects forgiveness and grace, guaranteeing eternal condemnation for sin. God's desire for every person in every age is that they might turn and repent and believe in the Savior.

Chs 37–38 Jeremiah notes that the withdrawal of the Babylonians is only temporary. Sin brings terrible consequences. They are sometimes delayed, but they are inevitable. The world hates God and His Word and opposes those who proclaim its truth. Yet God rescues His people, even when they die, and gives them eternal life (cf Rm 8:31–39). Like Jeremiah, God's people today should never give up hope but rather trust in the Lord, especially when things are at their worst.

Ch 39 The people suffer under siege but not without promise. You cannot avoid what you fear by disobeying God and trusting your own wisdom. Instead, trust that the Lord never forgets His people.

Chs 40–41 Gedaliah trusts in his own wisdom and strength, setting the stage for his death and disastrous results for the survivors of Jerusalem. Yet, God is at work for the salvation of souls. Like Johanan, have mercy on those who suffer and are confused by life's troubles. Repent of evil ambitions, and make service to the Lord and His people your highest goal. In mercy, the Lord made your salvation His highest priority, suffering death on the cross to bring you new life.

Chs 42–45 God does not want His people to place their confidence in Pharaoh or his army. Human reason often wins out over trust in God and obedience to Him. God cannot tolerate such rebellion. Because God is wholly righteous, He must punish sin (Heb 12:6), although it causes Him great pain. God keeps His promises, even when His people break theirs, and He finally sends the Savior for all sinners.

Chs 46–51 Added to the prophecies is a note of comfort for the Judean exiles in Babylon: God will discipline, but not completely destroy them. He has mercy for others too. He promised to preserve some of the population and Moab's identity as a people, at least for a time. Though Moab disappeared from history before the New Testament era, some of its descendants received the blessings of the new covenant (Ru 4:14–17; Mt 1:5–6). Wise or foolish by the world's standards, salvation belongs to everyone who trusts in Jesus Christ, for He alone is "the way, and the truth, and the life" (Jn 14:6). Through destruction, God teaches other nations of His dominion over them so they may come to faith. At the same time, He spares those He has called by His name.

Ch 52 See 2Ki 25:1–21. Despite Judah's rebellion, God never forgot His promises. Years later, God sent Jesus Christ as the atoning sacrifice for the world's sin. All of God's promises find their Yes in Christ (2Co 1:20).

CANONICITY

The different texts for the Book of Jeremiah show that the Judeans did not immediately settle on a canonical form. However, they valued it greatly, as well as its author. For example, Jesus son of Sirach remembered Jeremiah's woes and the fulfillment of his words (Ecclus 49:6–7). During Jesus of Nazareth's earthly ministry, the crowds who heard Jesus spoke of Him as though He were a new Jeremiah (Mt 16:14), demonstrating the respect with which the prophet was honored.

LUTHERAN THEOLOGIANS ON JEREMIAH

Luther

"Few comments are needed for an understanding of the prophet Jeremiah, if one will only pay attention to the events that took place under the kings in whose time he preached. For his preaching had reference to the condition of the land at that time.

"In the first place the land was full of vices and idolatry. The people slew the prophets and would have their own vices and idolatry go unrebuked. Therefore the first part, down to the twentieth chapter, is almost entirely rebuke and complaint of the wickedness of the Jews.

"In the second place Jeremiah also foretold the punishment that was at hand, namely, the destruction of Jerusalem and of the whole land, and the Babylonian captivity, indeed the punishment of all nations as well. Yet, along with this, he gives comfort and promises that at a definite time, after the punishment is over, they shall be released and shall return to their land and to Jerusalem, etc. And this is the most important thing in Jeremiah. It was for this very thing that Jeremiah was raised up, as is indicated in the first chapter [1:11, 18], by the vision of the rod and the boiling pots coming from the north.

"And this was highly necessary; for since this cruel hardship was to come upon the people, and they were to be uprooted and carried away out of their land, many pious souls—such as Daniel [Dan. 9:2] and others—would have been driven to despair of God and his promises. For they would not have been able to think otherwise than that it was all over with them, that they were utterly cast off by God, and that no Christ would ever come, but that God, in great anger, had taken back his promises because of the people's sin.

"Therefore Jeremiah had to be there and proclaim the punishment and the wrath, telling the people that it would not last forever, but for a fixed time, such as seventy years [25:11–12; 29:10], and that afterward they would come into grace once again. With this promise he had also to comfort and sustain himself, or he would have had little consolation and happiness. For he was a sad and troubled prophet and lived in miserably evil days. Besides he had a peculiarly difficult ministry. For over forty years, down to the captivity, he had to say hard things to obstinately wicked people. Still it did little good. He had to look on while the people went from bad to worse, always wanting to kill him, and putting him to much hardship.

"On top of that he had to experience and see with his own eyes how the land was destroyed and the people carried away captive, amid great misery and bloodshed. Nor does this include what he had afterward to preach and suffer in Egypt, for it is believed that he was stoned to death by the Jews in Egypt.

"In the third place like the other prophets, Jeremiah too prophesies of Christ and his kingdom, especially in the twenty-third and thirty-first chapters [23:5–6; 31:31–34]. There he clearly prophesies of the person of Christ, of his kingdom, of the new testament, and of the end of the old testament.

"Now these three things do not follow one another in sequence; they are not separated from one another in the book in the way that they actually came along. Frequently in the first part there is something in a later chapter which really took place before that which is spoken of in an earlier chapter. So it seems as though Jeremiah did not compose these books himself, but that the parts were taken piecemeal from his utterances and written into a book. For this reason one must not worry about the order or be hindered by the lack of it.

"We learn from Jeremiah among others that, as usual, the nearer the punishment, the worse the people become; and that the more one preaches to them, the more they despise his preaching. Thus we understand that when it is God's will to inflict punishment, he makes the people to become hardened so they may be destroyed without any mercy and not appease God's wrath with any repentance. So the men of Sodom long ago had to not only despise the righteous Lot, but even afflict him because he taught them— even though their own affliction was at the door [Gen. 19:1–13]. Likewise Pharaoh, when about to be drowned in the Red Sea, had to oppress the children of Israel twice as much as before [Exod. 5:6–21]. And Jerusalem had to crucify God's Son when its own final destruction was on the way.

"So it goes everywhere even now. Now that the end of the world is approaching, the people rage and rave most horribly against God. They blaspheme and damn God's word, though they well know that it is God's word and the truth. Besides so many fearful signs and wonders are appearing, both in the heavens and among all creatures, which threaten them terribly. It is indeed a wicked and miserable time, even worse than that of Jeremiah.

"But so it will be, and must be. The people begin to feel secure and sing, 'Peace; all is well.' They simply persecute everything that accords with the will of God and disregard all the threatening signs, until (as St. Paul says [I Thess. 5:8]) destruction suddenly surprises them and destroys them before they know it.

"But Christ will be able to sustain his own, for whose sake he causes his word to shine forth in this shameful time of ours, just as at Babylon he sustained Daniel and those like him, for whose sake Jeremiah's prophecy had to shine forth. To the same dear Lord be praise and thanks, with the Father and the Holy Spirit, one God over all and to eternity. Amen." (AE 35:279–82)

Gerhard

"*Jeremiah* is called *Yiremyahu*, 'the elevated and exalted of the Lord.' He prophesied under Josiah, Jehoiakim, and Zedekiah.

"He was deported into Egypt along with the rest of the people of Judah by Johanan, son of Kareah. He died in Tahpanhes, stoned by his own people, and was buried there.

"Alexander Polyhistor writes this about him:

At the time of Jehoiakim, Jeremiah prophesied, whom God had sent. When he found the Jews sacrificing to a golden image whose name was Baal, he foretold that a disaster would overcome them because of this. As a result, Jehoiakim commanded him to be burned alive. [Jeremiah] also said that those whom the Assyrian king had captured would make pits of the same wood near the Tigris and Euphrates. King Nebuchadnezzar heard this, took along King Stibar of the Medes to help, and overthrew first the cities of the

Samaritans—Galilaea, Scythopolis, and Galatis—with 180[,000] foot soldiers, 120,000 cavalry, and 10,000 chariots. Next, he captured Jerusalem and took the king of the Jews alive and deported to Babylon the gold, silver, bronze, and everything else that had been in the temple with the exception of the ark and the tablets of the Law.

"Ludovicus Vives (commentary on Augustine's *De civ. Dei*, bk. 18, c. 25) quotes this from Alexander.

"Augustine himself writes this about the times when Jeremiah prophesied (*De civ. Dei*, bk. 18, c. 33): 'Jeremiah prophesied while Josiah was ruling in Jerusalem, Ancus Martius was ruler among the Romans, and the captivity of the Jews was approaching. His time of prophesying reached to the fifth month of the captivity, just as we find in his writing.' Augustine writes regarding Jeremiah that 'Plato heard him teach in Egypt' (*De doctr. Christ.*, bk. 2, c. 28). Later, however, he realized that this was false and retracted it (*Retractat.*, bk. 2, c. 4), and in *De civit. Dei*, bk. 8, c. 11, he writes: 'Plato was born a hundred years after Jeremiah.' A true reckoning of the chronology shows that there were about two hundred years between the births of Jeremiah and Plato. In *De civit. Dei*, bk. 18, c. 37, Augustine again teaches, correctly, that Plato was born not long after Ezra because Ezra died in the thirty-second year of Artaxerxes (as Nauclerus witnesses, vol. 1, *generat.* 54). Ezra died in the eighty-sixth Olympiad, and Plato was born in the eighty-eighth Olympiad, according to Apollodorus (*Chronica*). Whatever the situation may be, it is certain that Plato read the Books of Moses and of the prophets and transferred many things from them into his own books, as Eusebius proves (*Praeparat. evangel.*, bk. 11).

"Jeremiah's prophecy covers fifty-two chapters, which can be divided into *introduction*, which explains Jeremiah's calling to the prophetic ministry [*munus*]; *narrative*, which contains the prophecy itself, directed partly to the Jews and partly to the foreign enemies of the Jews, namely, the Gentiles; and *conclusion*, which includes a summary of the history of the city captured and the kingdom overthrown by the Chaldeans." (ThC E1 § 152)

James Sant's painting of "The Infant Timothy Unfolding the Scriptures" illustrates the importance of the prophetic Scriptures to the saints of the Old Testament and the New.

FURTHER STUDY

Lay/Bible Class Resources

Gosdeck, David M. *Jeremiah, Lamentations*. PBC. St. Louis: Concordia, 2004. ♪ Lutheran author. Excellent for Bible classes. Based on the NIV translation.

Harrison, Roland K. *Jeremiah and Lamentations: An Introduction and Commentary*. TOTC. Downers Grove, IL: InterVarsity Press, 1973. ♪ Canadian evangelical scholar. Emphasis on the historical data and its implications for Jeremiah's message. Somewhat popular. Compact commentary based on a variety of translations (the author worked on both the NKJV and NIV editions).

Life by His Word. St. Louis: Concordia, 2009. ♪ More than 1,500 reproducible one-page Bible studies covering each chapter of the canonical Scriptures. Page references to *The Lutheran Study Bible*. CD-Rom and downloadable.

Poellot, Daniel E. *Jeremiah and Lamentations: Perseverance in Hope*. GWFT. St. Louis: Concordia, 2004. ♪ Lutheran author and theologian. Eleven-session Bible study, including leader's notes and discussion questions.

Church Worker Resources

Laetsch, Theodore. *A Bible Commentary: Jeremiah*. St. Louis: Concordia, 1952. ♪ Professor at Concordia Seminary, St. Louis, for many years. Faithful Lutheran interpreter.

Thompson, John A. *The Book of Jeremiah*. NICOT. Grand Rapids: Eerdmans, 1979. ♪ Helpful, traditional interpretation, but linguistically and theologically rather weak.

Academic Resources

Bright, John. *Jeremiah*. AB. New York: Doubleday, 1965. ♪ An important, mildly critical resource from a respected biblical scholar. Attempts to comment on the prophecies in their chronological order rather than the traditional order found in the Hebrew and in English translations.

K&D. *Biblical Commentary on the Old Testament: The Prophesies of Jeremiah*. 2 vols. Grand Rapids: Eerdmans, 1971 reprint. ♪ This century-and-a-half old work from Lutheran scholars should not be overlooked. Despite its age, it remains a most useful commentary on the Hebrew text.

Nägelsbach, Carl Wilhelm Eduard. *Jeremiah and Lamentations*. LCHS. New York: Charles Scribner's Sons, 1891. ♪ A helpful, older example of German biblical scholarship, based on the Hebrew text, which provides references to significant commentaries from the Reformation era forward.

Orelli, Conrad von. *The Prophecies of Jeremiah*. Minneapolis: Klock & Klock, 1977. ♪ A reprint of a pithy resource; mildly reflects critical views of the late-nineteenth century.

LAMENTATIONS

Though He cause grief,
He will have compassion

There are numerous and striking similarities between some of the laments in the Book of Jeremiah and those in Lamentations (e.g., the phrase "daughter of" occurs about 20 times in each book; and "eyes flowing with tears" in Lm 1:16; 2:11 and Jer 9:1, 18). The calamities lamented are attributed to the same causes in both books (national sin, faithless priests and prophets, the perfidy of allies in whom vain hope had been placed, etc.). Furthermore, despite formal differences among the five poems (cf below), there is no doubt that the same mood pervades all of them. As a result, tradition uniformly attributed the book to Jeremiah. (See "Author.")

On the other hand, there are also numerous divergences from Jeremiah's undisputed laments (or "confessions"), some of which can be better paralleled with other books, especially some of the laments in the Psalter. The style of Lamentations is generally more elaborate than Jeremiah's; chs 2 and 4 are more like Ezekiel. Not all of the so-called divergences stand up, however. For example, one must dismiss as ultimately simplistic the frequent critical assertion that Lm 3:59–66, with its petition for God's judgment upon the wickedness of the Babylonians, conflicts with Jeremiah's consistent insistence that Babylon was God's own chosen instrument to effect His wrath upon Israel. Jeremiah's own oracles against Babylon, as e.g., in 25:12 and chs 50–51, would suffice to refute the charge, let alone more general knowledge of prophetic theology in its totality. Similarly, Lm 4:17 does not contradict Jeremiah's opposition to placing any hope in deliverance from Egypt, but simply records the fact that most of the populace did, in fact, entertain such vain hopes.

Historical and Cultural Setting

For an account of the book's setting, see the introduction to Jeremiah.

Clay figure of a mourning woman, found in the extensive tombs of Azor, Israel, south of Tel Aviv.

COMPOSITION

Author

Equally ancient and widespread (though not univocal) is the tradition that Jeremiah wrote this book. The Talmud can be cited on this point, and most of the ancient versions witness to it—if not in their titles, then in a brief prologue. Only the Syriac Peshitta of the ancient versions includes the name of Jeremiah in the title, as do also most of the English versions we are familiar with. The Vulgate, however, prefixes to the first chapter: "These are the lamentations of the prophet Jeremiah" and the Septuagint (at least some recensions) even more expansively: "And it came to pass after Israel had gone into captivity, and Jerusalem was laid waste, that Jeremiah sat weeping and composed this lament over Jerusalem and said . . . " (a prologue that stylistically suggests a Hebrew original). The traditional association of Jeremiah with Lamentations undoubtedly accounts for much of that prophet's unfortunate characterization as the "weeping prophet," a title that really does not apply to him.

It was this traditional ascription to Jeremiah that caused the Septuagint to sandwich Lamentations between Jeremiah and Ezekiel, a sequence that is still followed almost universally in the West. More attention has often been devoted to the question of authorship than it deserves (especially in comparison with the book's message and importance). We have seen that a strong *traditional* case for Jeremiah as the author can be made, but technically it is not possible to go further. Since nearly everyone agrees that the work was produced in the *time* of Jeremiah and almost certainly by an eyewitness or participant in the tragedy, the difference between the various traditions is, quite literally, only nominal.

Date of Composition

Jeremiah remained in Judah long enough before Johanan kidnapped him to Egypt (c 587 BC) that Lamentations might plausibly stem from that interval. If, however, we are to think of some other author, the book is of even more interest as possibly our only direct evidence of the mood and mentality of those whom Nebuzaradan had spared from deportation.

Quite a number of critics are convinced that the five poems in the book do not stem from a single hand, and considerable energy has been expended in attempts to establish the order and various circumstances in which they were originally written. Some commentators have sought to associate some of the poems (especially ch 1) with the 597 instead of the 587 deportation, and suggestions as late as Maccabean times have been made. A common suggestion is that chs 2 and 4 are the work of an eyewitness, to which were later added the laments of chs 1 and 3 and the prayer of ch 5 (the last three perhaps from about 540, in the depths of the exile). However, the great variety of these conjectures and their lack of common acceptance remain their best refutation.

Purpose/Recipients

The Book of Lamentations mourns the destruction of Jerusalem and its people while expressing hope and prayers that the Lord will restore Zion. The poems may have assisted the survivors in worship, directed toward repentance and the future.

Literary Features

Genre

The usual Hebrew name for this book, following the ancient pattern evidenced also in other biblical books, is simply its opening word, the exclamation *'ekah* ("How"). It was apparently a standard opening word for a dirge over a fallen city (cf Is 1:21, also addressed to Jerusalem prophetically). In the Hebrew text, its special character is also highlighted—not only in 1:1 but also at the beginning of chs 2 and 4. The word stands at the beginning of the poem, outside the metrical pattern and above the other lines of poetry (a style called anacrusis).

Exactly when the work began to be called Lamentations is not clear. The Babylonian Talmud and other early Jewish writings refer to it in this way (Hebrew, *qinoth*). It is likely that the Septuagint was dependent on such an early Hebrew tradition in labeling the book *threnoi,* and thence the *Liber Threnorum* of the Vulgate and most subsequent translations (cf our general term "threnody," which means "a song of lamentation for the dead").

Attention must also be given to the question of possible Mesopotamian influence on the style of the biblical Lamentations. In ancient Sumer, lamentation was a genre used for worship, and a lament over the destruction of Ur is especially noteworthy for its sometimes striking parallels with Lamentations. The Neo-Babylonian period was also noted for its threnodies over fallen cities, and influence from this quarter is even more plausible. Destruction of cities was certainly a common enough occurrence in the ancient Near East, and the ruin was normally attributed to the wrath of the god(s). Hence, it is possible that ancient literary conventions were at hand for commemorating such catastrophes and that our author availed himself of some of them. Nevertheless, the even greater differences in theology and other details, as well as the fact that some of the parallels are found also in entirely different genres, seem to indicate that whatever connection there is (if any), is more a matter of broad cultural continuum than of any direct influence.

A more substantial form-critical issue arises from the more individual expression of the poems at points. Chapter 3 is often regarded as an "individual lament" in contrast to the more communal or national reference of the other songs, and hence is often considered a later, independent composition, originally having nothing to do with the destruction of Jerusalem. The "I" is also much in evidence in the clearly communal lament of ch 1, indicating how easily the singular and plural forms of expression were interchangeable. Hence, it appears much more likely that the difference is purely formal, a matter of variation purely for the sake of variety. Perhaps by using the device of "corporate personality," the city is simply personified more directly at points, or the author more directly identifies himself with, and speaks in the name of, his beloved city at some points than at others.

All five of the poems are "alphabetic" in some sense (itself a major argument for unity of composition). The first four poems are also quite strictly acrostic, beginning with successive letters of the Hebrew alphabet. However, the acrostic principle is applied in different ways (something that is quite evident in the Hebrew text). Chapters 1 and 2 exhibit the simplest type of acrostic: each verse (with the curious exceptions of 1:7 and 2:19) consists of three lines, but only the first line begins with the requisite letter of the Hebrew alphabet. The general pattern is the same in ch 4, except that there are only two lines per verse. The acrostic pattern in ch 3 is more complicated: each verse again is composed of three lines, but each of those three lines begins with the same letter of the alphabet. As noted, ch 5 is the only poem not structured acrostically, but it does contain 22 verses, almost certainly one for each letter of the Hebrew alphabet. (Cf similarly Ps 33; 38;

OUTLINE

Each chapter of Lamentations is a separate lament poem (cf 2Sm 1:19–27; 3:33–34; Ps 79; 83; 89:38–51). Chapters 1–4 are written as acrostic poems, so that the first word of a poetic verse begins with a letter of the Hebrew alphabet (see pp 784–85). Because Hebrew has 22 letters, chs 1, 2, and 4 each have 22 verses. Ch 3 is different, devoting 3 verses for each Hebrew letter, yielding a total of 66 verses. Ch 5 has 22 verses, but does not strictly follow the alphabetic pattern.

A quite unique problem (that is, with the possible exceptions of Pr 31 and Ps 34) arises in the acrostics of chs 2–4, in that in these three chapters the Hebrew letter *pe* precedes *ayin,* the reverse of the normal alphabetic order (which is followed in ch 1). There is no convincing explanation for this oddity.

    I. The Desolation and Misery of Jerusalem (ch 1)

    II. The Lord's Anger against the Daughter of Zion (ch 2)

    III. The Lord Will Discipline and Have Mercy (ch 3)

    IV. Zion's Punishment Is Accomplished (ch 4)

    V. Plea That the Lord Would Not Forget Zion (ch 5)

and 103; Lm 5 also displays other structural differences from the rest of the poems; cf below.)

Acrostics, of course, are certainly used in the Bible outside of Lamentations (cf esp Ps 119). They are also known in both ancient Egypt and Mesopotamia, thus demolishing an earlier critical supposition that they evidenced late and degenerate formalism. Certainly in the case of Lamentations the use of what initially appears to be so cumbersome and constricting a device has not affected the writer's style, because on the literary power and beauty of the book there is no dispute.

Characters

The key character of the book is the city of Jerusalem, which, like a mother, mourns over her children, the people of the city who are frequently mentioned. Alongside her are the "daughters of Zion," which may refer to the young women of the city or to the surrounding towns.

As noted above, in ch 3 the writer frequently refers to himself and his experiences.

Narrative Development or Plot

As a collection of lament poems, Lamentations does not have a storyline or plot. However, the hope expressed in ch 3 is pivotal to the book, which allows mourners to set their past with its regrets behind them and to pray for renewal.

Resources

On the relationship between Lamentations and Jeremiah, see the introduction above.

Text and Translations

The traditional Hebrew text of Lamentations is in good order, and the ancient translations clearly follow the Hebrew text. The Dead Sea Scrolls preserve fragments of some copies (4QLam^a; 3QLam; 5QLam^a; 5QLam^b), which indicate some variations from the traditional text.

DOCTRINAL CONTENT

Summary Commentary

Ch 1 Jeremiah describes the terrible conditions in Jerusalem after it fell to the Babylonians and its leading citizens were taken captive. Contrasted with the wealth and beauty of its former days, the ruins lie as a testimony to God's just response against persistent sin and rebellion.

Ch 2 By the Lord's hand, Babylon has destroyed Jerusalem and razed its temple. The consequences of sin have left people slaughtered and the remaining citizens exiled to Babylon. God has turned His back on His people for turning their back on Him. Their worship of false gods violated the covenant dating back to the exodus from Egypt. Their sin has now born hideous fruit.

Ch 3 Jeremiah personally describes the great suffering of God's people at the hand of the invading Babylonians. He makes no excuse for their sin, but he encourages them (and us today) with God's great compassion and unfailing love. The people have been crushed but not utterly destroyed—their hope must be in the Lord and His great love for them.

Ch 4 Jeremiah contrasts the wealth of Jerusalem's past with the poverty of its residents after the Babylonian conquest. The sins of the religious leaders come into focus as the cause for the destruction of the city. A note of hope appears at the end with a veiled reference to the eventual return of the exiles from Babylon (v 22).

Ch 5 Jeremiah points out that the sins of all the people lie at the very root of their current suffering (cf v 16). Because of their unfaithfulness, they struggle just to get enough to eat; they find themselves subjected to abuse and humiliation. Lamenting in anguish, God's people appeal to the Lord for forgiveness and restoration.

This cuneiform tablet (front and back) confirms that members of the Judean royal house were prisoners at Babylon (sixth century BC).

Specific Law Themes

Lamentations describes how the Lord pours out His anger against the kingdom of Judah, which is depicted as a woman. As a result, Judah finds no comfort. She cries, mourns, weeps, and laments the siege and exile.

Specific Gospel Themes

The heart of the book, like the Book of Comfort at the heart of Jeremiah, declares that the steadfast love of the Lord never ceases; great is His faithfulness. The writer encourages the mourners to wait quietly for the salvation of the Lord, who will redeem them in His time.

Specific Doctrines

The theological significance of Lamentations is considerable, both on the immediately historical level, and also in the light of the New Testament. The reader must thoroughly appreciate the significance of the land as Israel's "inheritance" in order to empathize with the writer and his contemporaries. How could the God of the covenant allow to fall into the hands of infidels the "sacrament" and seal of His eternal covenant and promise, the seat of the son of David whom 4:20 calls "the breath of our nostrils, the Lord's anointed"? Was God powerless? Had His promises failed? Did He no longer care? Was there any prospect of future deliverance? Of return of the exiles? Would justice ever be meted out to their tormentors? What was the point of such suffering? With these questions of suffering, Lamentations can certainly be compared with Job and Habakkuk. In fact, Habakkuk, like Lamentations, also considers the subject in primarily national instead of individual terms.

The pain in Lamentations is still so great that the writer's immediate need was to articulate it rather than to theorize about its meaning. However, it is far more than just psychological venting; it is obviously also confession of sin. For all of the bitterness of the moment, Lamentations never questions either God's justice or His love. There is no attempt to evade or excuse their own responsibility. But if God is faithful, there must also be a future under Him and His Word, and (esp in ch 3) the writer's stubborn confidence in the God of the covenant swells to fervent exclamation of hope in His unfailing goodness.

Thus, Lamentations presents the consistent biblical and especially prophetic teaching of the meaning of judgment, of God's wrath, and of the "remnant." The deeper meaning of the disaster demonstrates God's method of leading His people to repentance, of the need for both judgment and salvation, of Law and Gospel. In total biblical context, Lamentations presents a major expression of the "death and resurrection" of Jerusalem as a type of Good Friday and Easter. The Church, not any modern nation or political entity, should be moved by the book to "national repentance." The believer, though crushed by God's judgments, remains confident of restoration and resurrection.

In Christ, the Church sees herself as the heir of the Old Testament people of God, returning to and fulfilling the rhythms of Israel's experience before God in the time of the consummation, and into that history all have been baptized. The Church's appropriation of the book and of the history it describes thus differs only superficially from that of Judaism on the "Ninth of Ab" (see "Canonicity" below): it not only confesses the destruction of Jerusalem as part of its history, but it sees the fullness of that history in God's judgment upon all people in Christ, though a final judgment is still to come. One would think especially in this connection of Jesus' own repeated comparison (and typology) of His death with the destruction of the temple. The typological significance of Lamentations is thus very close to that of the Book of Jonah.

Much of the vocabulary of Lamentations has entered into the Christian meditation on the cross, and it is not to be dismissed as mere literary accommodation. It is doubtful if Lamentations is ever directly cited in the New Testament. However, liturgical and homiletic usage of the book was profoundly faithful to the spirit and intent of the New Testament. Major examples would include: "Is it nothing to you, all you who pass by?" (1:12); "they hiss and wag their heads" (2:15; cf Ps 22:7); and the "wormwood and the gall" of 3:19.

One part of the book is relatively familiar to Christians today—the beautiful words of hope in 3:19–33. But their near exclusive use, or at least use apart from the context, suggests as strongly as anything how dire the danger is that our Gospel is becoming sentimentalized and universalized into "another Gospel." Lamentations can play a major role in holding before us the magnitude of God's righteous wrath, apart from which there is little need for "Gospel."

Application

Ch 1 Jeremiah describes the terrible conditions in Jerusalem after it fell to the Babylonians. The foundation of sin and rebellion is unbelief, a refusal to trust God and follow Him. Even in the face of His people's faithlessness, God proves Himself faithful to His promise of a Savior by preserving a remnant that will return to Jerusalem.

Ch 2 God has turned His back on His people for turning their back on Him. Despite the apostasy of God's people, He still loves them and will bring them back from their captivity to rebuild Jerusalem and the temple. From these people, God shall raise up a Savior for all nations.

Ch 3 The people have been crushed but not utterly destroyed—their hope must be in the Lord and His great love for them. We are often our own worst enemies, responsible for our suffering through our own choices. No matter how bad things get, our hope is always in the Lord because He loves us in Jesus Christ and never abandons us.

Ch 4 The sins of the religious leaders come into focus. Spiritual leaders carry a great responsibility for the welfare of God's people (cf Jas 3:1). God sustained His people, and through their descendants raised up a Savior for all, Christ the Lord.

Ch 5 Because of their unfaithfulness, the people of Jerusalem struggle just to get enough to eat; they find themselves subjected to abuse and humiliation. In our own lives, we easily forget God and our calling as His people at times when it seems that everything is going our way. God stands ready to forgive penitent sinners by restoring His blessing to us through the blood of Jesus Christ.

Jewish men praying together at the Western Wall, Jerusalem, during the Tish'ah b'Ab fast.

CANONICITY

In the Hebrew canon, Lamentations appears among the Writings, specifically among scrolls proper for liturgical reading on Jewish festivals (the Megilloth; the placement is not because of lateness of composition). In this case the liturgical association is most obvious and apropos—with the ninth day of the fifth month, Ab, on the Hebrew calendar (*Tish'ah b'Ab*), falling in late July or early August on the Gregorian calendar. This commemorates not only the fall of Jerusalem to Nebuchadnezzar on that date (cf 2Ki 25:8–9, though Jer 52:12 says the "tenth," apparently referring to a different phase of it), but also the capitulation to Titus in AD 70 and the fall of Betar (Bar Kokhba's revolt) in AD 135, all traditionally on the same date.

Christian liturgical use of the book also began very early in the Christian era, but associated with the last three days of Holy Week (especially in the Reproaches of the Tenebrae service).

LUTHERAN THEOLOGIANS ON LAMENTATIONS

Luther

"Sobs and complaints of this kind are usually uttered by those who struggle with unbelief and despair and cannot buoy up their heart or lay hold of any hope of salvation." (AE 8:72)

"Oh, we handle these poor young people who are committed to us for training and instruction in the wrong way! We shall have to render a solemn account of our neglect to set the word of God before them. Their lot is as described by Jeremiah in Lamentations 2.[:11–12]. . . . We do not see this pitiful evil, how today the young people of Christendom languish and perish miserably in our midst for want of the gospel, in which we ought to be giving them constant instruction and training." (AE 44:206)

"[God] stands hidden among the sufferings which would separate us from him like a wall, indeed, like a wall of a fortress. And yet he looks upon me and does not forsake me. He stands there and is ready to help in grace, and through the window of dim faith he permits himself to be seen. And Jeremiah says in Lamentations 3[:32–33], 'He casts men aside, but that is not the intention of his heart.' These people know nothing at all of this kind of a faith, and they give themselves over to thinking that God has forsaken them and is their enemy. They even lay the blame on other men or on the devil, and have simply no confidence at all in God. For this reason, too, their suffering is always an offense to them and harmful. And yet they go on doing their good works, as they think, quite unaware of their serious unbelief. But they who in such suffering trust God and hold on to a good, firm confidence in him, who believe that he is well-pleased with them, see in their sufferings and afflictions nothing but pure and precious merits, the costliest treasures which no man can assess. For faith and confidence make precious before God all that which others think most shameful." (AE 44:28)

Gerhard

"The Hebrews call *Lamentations* '*ekah* from its first word. The rabbinic scholars in their commentaries call it *qinoth*, 'complaints,' and the Greeks, *Threnoi*, 'Lamentations,' because of its subject matter. Rabbi Salomon thinks that this is the book that the king of Judah read from the beginning, then threw into the fire (Jer. 36:23). This, however, we can refute from c. 45 [of Jeremiah]. It contains the pathetic, mournful complaints about the wretched condition of the state of Israel into which it fell after the death of King Josiah. In the place of the introduction, the Septuagint translators present a summary of this book in these words: 'After Israel had been led into captivity and Jerusalem was deserted, it happened that the prophet Jeremiah sat down, wept, and mourned over Jerusalem with this lamentation. He sighed bitterly, cried out, and said,' etc.

"In the Hebrew text, Lamentations was written in this order: the first verse begins with ', the second with *b*, and so on to the end, keeping intact the order of letters of the Hebrew alphabet. In the third chapter, the first three verses begin with ', the second three with *b*, and so on, with each succeeding three verses keeping the pattern to the end of the alphabet. In the introduction to his commentary, Jerome believes that a mystery is not lacking here. The book consists of five chapters, which we can divide into lamentation and prayer." (ThC E1 § 153)

FURTHER STUDY

Lay/Bible Class Resources

Gosdeck, David M. *Jeremiah, Lamentations*. PBC. St. Louis: Concordia, 2004. ♪ Lutheran author. Excellent for Bible classes. Based on the NIV translation.

Harrison, Roland K. *Jeremiah and Lamentations: An Introduction and Commentary*. TOTC. Downers Grove, IL: InterVarsity Press, 1973. ♪ Canadian evangelical scholar. Emphasis on the historical data and its implications for Jeremiah's message. Somewhat popular. Compact commentary based on a variety of translations (the author worked on both the NKJV and NIV editions).

Life by His Word. St. Louis: Concordia, 2009. ♪ More than 1,500 reproducible one-page Bible studies covering each chapter of the canonical Scriptures. Page references to *The Lutheran Study Bible*. CD-Rom and downloadable.

Poellot, Daniel E. *Jeremiah and Lamentations: Perseverance in Hope*. GWFT. St. Louis: Concordia, 2004. ♪ Lutheran author and theologian. Eleven-session Bible study, including leader's notes and discussion questions.

Church Worker Resources

Gordis, Robert. *The Song of Songs and Lamentations: A Study, Modern Translation and Commentary*. New York: KTAV, 1974. ♪ A helpful translation and commentary from an eminent rabbi and biblical scholar.

Academic Resources

Hillers, Delbert R. *Lamentations*. Vol. 7A of AB. New York: Doubleday, 1972. ♪ Some critical overtones, but helpful.

K&D. *Biblical Commentary on the Old Testament: The Prophecies of Jeremiah*. 2 vols. Grand Rapids: Eerdmans, 1971 reprint. ♪ This century-and-a-half old work from Lutheran scholars should not be overlooked. Despite its age, it remains a most useful commentary on the Hebrew text.

Nägelsbach, Carl Wilhelm Eduard. *Jeremiah and Lamentations*. LCHS. New York: Charles Scribner's Sons, 1891 ♪ A helpful older example of German biblical scholarship, based on the Hebrew text, which provides references to significant commentaries from the Reformation era forward.

EZEKIEL

Son of man, I have made you a watchman

Groves of fruit trees cast shadows over dark-green, mid-summer fields that line the low-lying waterways between Erech and Babylon. On July 31, 593 BC, the exiled priest Ezekiel became a prophet as the Lord revealed to him a startling vision of His glory and inspired His servant to write.

In exile, the prophet lived "in the land of the Chaldeans by the Chebar canal" (1:3). Southern Mesopotamia was the homeland along one of the major irrigation canals whence the Neo-Babylonian dynasty of the conquerors hailed. From cuneiform inscriptions we know the canal was used to bring water to the ancient city of Nippur, a short distance southeast of Babylon itself. In 3:15 the prophet further indicates that the name of the "camp" was "Tel-abib" (the "mound of the flood," also, ultimately, the inspiration for the name of the modern Israeli metropolis, Tel Aviv).

Historical and Cultural Setting

The fact that the prophet had his own house (8:1) would indicate fair living conditions for not only the prophet but also for most of the rest of the exiles. We should avoid thinking of their living circumstances in the extremes of poverty or

Fishermen pass the irrigated fields along the Euphrates River. The Chebar, a canal of the Euphrates, is lost to us, but its region would have appeared like the modern river bottoms of Mesopotamia.

OVERVIEW

Author
Ezekiel the prophet

Date
593–570 BC

Places
Babylon; Chebar Canal; Jerusalem; Israel; Judah; mountains of Israel; temple of Jerusalem; Ammon; Moab; Mount Seir; Edom; Philistia; Tyre; Sidon; Egypt

People
Ezekiel; exiles; cherubim and other angels; elders of Judah and Israel; Nebuchadnezzar; servant David; prince of Tyre; Pharaoh; Gog

Purpose
To explain why God's glory departed from Israel and how His glory would return

Law Themes
Death and God's wrath comes to Israel by the sword; Israel has not walked in God's statutes; in anger, God withdraws His glory and blessings; idolatry as spiritual adultery; defilement; exile; famine and pestilence

Gospel Themes
God keeps His covenant; new hearts; gift of the Spirit; the Good Shepherd; cleansing; restore the fortunes; God's glory returns; the new temple

Memory Verses
The watchman's calling (3:17–19); a new heart (11:19–20); the Lord desires to save us (18:21–23, 32); the Good Shepherd (34:20–24); a prophecy of Baptism (36:25–27); the Lord's glory returns (43:2–5)

TIMELINE

722 BC	Samaria (Israel) falls to Assyria
593 BC	Ezekiel's first vision
587 BC	Babylonians take Jerusalem; temple destroyed
573 BC	Ezekiel's vision of a new Jerusalem
538 BC	Cyrus decrees that exiles may return to Judah

795

wealth. The Babylonians in general were much more benign in their policy of deportation than the Assyrians had been. But the lot of deportees or refugees is never a happy one, and it probably was a long time before many were able to pick up the pieces of their shattered lives. However, that many had gotten back on their feet a half-century or more later is evidenced by the poor response, especially by the younger generation, when they had the opportunity to return to Judea after Cyrus's edict; a little later we even know from Babylonian records of a fairly well-to-do Jewish business establishment, "Murashu & Sons." It will not do, however, to see Ezekiel's days as ones of semi-assimilated prosperity and equanimity.

The massive Babylonian Talmud includes 63 tractates. It contains Rabbinic wisdom collected at Babylon by descendants of the exiles, compiled fifth century AD.

Perhaps above all, whatever their physical circumstances, subjectively and psychologically the exiles were often simply devastated, as not only the Book of Ezekiel witnesses but also the contemporary Lamentations and Ps 137. No doubt, humanly speaking, if Ezekiel had not given the theological interpretation of deserved divine judgment to the catastrophe, the exiles would have soon joined the countless numbers of others in similar circumstances all through the corridors of history who simply dropped from sight.

In contrast to Ezekiel's predecessors, and especially to his contemporary Jeremiah, Ezekiel is apparently held in some esteem by fellow Judeans. He is

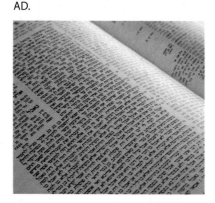

seemingly the first to benefit from the "authentication" that the fulfillment of prophecies of exile lent to prophecy. Despite the vocabulary of his call, there is not the slightest hint of anything like persecution. The elders of the exile consulted him (14:1; 20:1), and sometimes large crowds even listened to him, apparently more in uncomprehending amusement at his antics (20:49; 33:30–32) than in assent to his message (at least until after the fall of Jerusalem). But their amusement was a far cry from the violent reception often accorded the earlier prophets.

COMPOSITION

Author

Ezekiel's father, Buzi (1:3), was a priest, and the priestly coloration of the book (especially the final nine chapters) make it plain that Ezekiel, too, lived and moved and had his being in that world of thought, whether or not he ever officially functioned in priestly capacity. Although his priestly background can be exaggerated, he still differs markedly from Jeremiah, who, though a priest, evinces remarkably little interest in such matters (though not for the reasons or quite to the degree to which many spiritualistic critics would have it). Perhaps the different interests of these prophets marks the beginning of a new era, when the purged and purified rites and institutions could serve their divinely intended purpose (especially chs 40–48). It should also be noted that, whereas Jeremiah's descent was probably from the "disenfranchised" line of Abiathar, Ezekiel was linked to the main priestly line of Zadok, whom Solomon had chosen to replace disloyal Abiathar (1Ki 2). Thus one is not surprised when Ezekiel himself strongly underscores the divine legitimacy and prerogatives of the Zadokites (40:46; 43:19).

Ezekiel is a late contemporary of Jeremiah, though, as usual, they make no mention of each other. Many aspects of their prophecies run parallel to one another. However, in contrast to Jeremiah, who was active in Judah in its last days and even spurned the conquerors' offer to grant him safe conduct out of the country, Ezekiel's entire ministry was spent among the exiles in Babylonia. Both because of the extrabiblical literature and the record of his own book, we are nearly as well-informed about the external circumstances of his life as of Jeremiah's. Ezekiel, however, reveals far less of his inner, personal life than Jeremiah.

Ancient thrones typically included figures of winged guardians, like the cherubim in Ezekiel's vision. This Egyptian example was found at Megiddo, Israel.

Much attention was once drawn to Ezekiel's allegedly bizarre personality. Epilepsy, catalepsy, autohypnosis, schizophrenia, aphasia, levitation, paranoia—all were suggested as descriptions for Ezekiel. Some conservatives overreacted in fear that study of the subject was almost intrinsically irreverent or a denial of inspiration. Fortunately, that furor has abated. Even if it were possible to psychoanalyze Ezekiel, the most that we would learn would be a little about the form of his original delivery, but nothing of its contents. One may note that God and special inspiration are not bound to "balanced personalities," but He may employ the entire range of human personality in communicating His message.

Perhaps the same circumstance explains Ezekiel's apparent austerity. The terms of his call say as much: "Like emery harder than flint have I made your forehead . . ." (3:9). Sometimes it is asserted that one of the few revelations of Ezekiel's humanity is seen when he calls his wife the "delight of his eyes" (24:16), but this is canceled out by the fact that when his wife dies on the day that the final siege of Jerusalem begins, it does not deter him from preaching to the people. It must be countered, however, that the latter was at God's explicit command—and Ezekiel, in contrast to Jeremiah, *was* married, and apparently happily. Beyond this, however, many oracles in the book suggest that Ezekiel was ultimately quite an ordinary mortal: themes of divine compassion and tenderness (cf "shepherd" in ch 34), and almost lurid descriptions of sexuality (chs 16 and 23), etc.

Date of Composition

In his own superscription to the book, Ezekiel relates the date of his call to the "fifth year of the exile of King Jehoiachin" (593 BC). This is nearly always taken to imply that Ezekiel himself was among the aristocracy that Nebuchadnezzar deported to Babylon in 598 after Jehoiakim's foolhardy revolt. The preceding reference to the "thirtieth year" is not immediately clear in its meaning. Most likely, it refers to the prophet's age when God called him to be a priest or prophet (the age at which Levites were allowed to commence official functions), but there are other explanations.

The last dated prophecy in Ezekiel (29:17) is in the "twenty-seventh year" (571 BC, after Jehoiachin's exile). Thus, Ezekiel has a total recorded ministry of slightly over 20 years.

Purpose/Recipients

Like Jeremiah, Ezekiel's major task was to warn those still in Jerusalem that there was no future for them as an independent kingdom. This was also the direction of the bulk of his oracles. (The great community of themes and accents among Jeremiah and Ezekiel are based on this common warning.)

Literary Features

In the modern era, Ezekiel received light attention. Critics dismissed him as the first fanatic in the Bible. Suddenly, around 1920, Ezekiel became a storm center of criticism. Three issues came under intense debate: (1) the unity and composition of the book; (2) the place or places where Ezekiel exercised his ministry; and (3) the date of the prophet's ministry. Despite the impressive external unity of the book, scholars began to divide it into smaller units and attributed them to multiple authors, as earlier scholars had done with other Prophetic Books. In contrast to the clear statement of the book that

Ezekiel exercised his entire ministry in the exile in Babylon, many began to argue that he really spent part (or even all) of it in Judea. As a famous assertion has it, it was not a heavenly hand that brought Ezekiel to Jerusalem (8:1), but a literary device that transferred him to Babylon!

One may concede it is remarkable that only four chapters in the entire book focus on the people of Babylon among whom Ezekiel lived (33–34, 36–37). Not only does he address his denunciations in chs 3–24 to the people of Jerusalem, but his action prophecies, requiring witnesses, portray people a thousand miles away. All in all, Ezekiel is phenomenally well-informed about events back in Jerusalem.

These bare facts scarcely add up to the radical critical construction put on them. At best, the new hypotheses raised more questions than they answered. If the Babylonian setting was really an editorial artifice, one would expect it to be more conspicuous than it is in the book. On the other hand, both language and imagery offer considerable indirect evidence of original Babylonian provenance. It has been characteristic of exiles in all ages to keep themselves well-informed of circumstances and developments in their homeland, and as Jeremiah's letter indicates, correspondence between the groups would have been regular. Finally, we may note that the Prophetic Books afford many other examples of both spoken and acted prophecies to distant audiences, most obviously and regularly in the Gentile oracles.

Most of the radical attempts to redate Ezekiel need not detain us; they never did have much of a following.

Genre

From the standpoint of classical Hebrew stylistic canons, Ezekiel rates as noticeably inferior to Jeremiah and, even more so, to Isaiah and Amos. That, of course, has nothing to do with the validity of his inspiration in the theological sense, nor does it imply that Ezekiel's oracles do not have a remarkable impact and power of another sort. It may be a matter of individual ability, but it may also signal the massive cultural breakup throughout the ancient Near East as a result of the political convulsions of the time.

Ezekiel makes little use of the shorter and more classical forms of prophetic oracles, instead composing long literary dissertations. His prose is often wordy and repetitive. Even when he writes poetry, the old glory seems to have departed. In form as well as vocabulary, one may begin to speak of "post-classical Hebrew." Nevertheless, let it be clear that these are technical, literary judgments. No one who takes the trouble to read Ezekiel will dismiss him in any broader sense as less forceful or less important.

The ancient prophetic tradition of action prophecies or "symbolic actions" receives climatic expression in Ezekiel. Resort to such behavior was not only encouraged, but virtually mandated by the dumbness that God laid on Ezekiel almost from the moment of his call until the fall of Jerusalem. Thus, like Isaiah and Jeremiah, his entire life became an action prophecy, a "type" or embodiment of his message. His own explanation for his behavior, of course, was simply that the "hand/spirit of Yahweh" had induced it.

Possibly even more so than Jeremiah, Ezekiel is characterized by many favorite phrases. They should not so much be labeled "stereotyped" as viewed as the repeated blows of a hammer. Among them are: (1) "Son of man," that is "(mere) creature/human being," as God consistently (93 times) addresses the prophet; (2) Israel as a "rebellious house"; (3) the command to "set his face against [name]"; (4) God's action "for His name's sake"; and (5) "They shall know that I am God/a prophet has been among them."

Characters

Ezekiel is the main human character of the book, since the Lord repeatedly addresses him as "son of man," an Aramaic expression that characterizes his weakness and humble state. Ezekiel is supremely concerned to be the pastor, the watchman of God's flock. In this way, we begin to get the measure of the man and his message. For more on Ezekiel, see "Author" above.

Cherubim are described as supporting God's throne in chs 1, 3, and 9–11. These angelic beings are carefully depicted but play a largely passive role in the story, more like objects or elements of the throne than interactive beings. Ezekiel presents the most detailed description of such beings in Scripture.

Exiles are the recipients of the prophet's messages in the first part of the book, though the people still in Judea are usually addressed.

Like other prophets, Ezekiel often directs his prophecies against rulers and decries their unfaithfulness (cf "shepherds" in ch 34). He makes special mention of the king of Tyre and the Egyptian Pharaoh, whom God will punish due to their self-indulgent wealth.

Narrative Development or Plot

Since the Book of Ezekiel is primarily a collection of visions and oracles, it does not present a typical, overarching storyline or plot. Yet the oracles of the book are presented constantly with first person ("I") accounts of the prophet's experiences as God calls him and commissions him to share his

OUTLINE

The book virtually divides itself into three major sections: (1) call and oracles of judgment on Israel (chs 1–24); (2) oracles of judgment on foreign nations, or Gentile oracles (chs 25–32); and (3) oracles and visions of restoration (chs 33–48). (Sometimes chs 40–48 are considered a separate, fourth section.)

I. Ezekiel's Call and Oracles of Judgment on Israel (chs 1–24)

  A. Ezekiel's Inaugural Vision and Commissioning (chs 1–3)

    1. Ezekiel's inaugural vision (ch 1)

    2. The prophetic commissioning of Ezekiel: part 1 (ch 2)

    3. The prophetic commissioning of Ezekiel: part 2 (ch 3)

  B. Prophecies of Judgment against Israel (chs 4–24)

    1. The first action prophecies of Jerusalem's siege and exile (ch 4)

    2. More action prophecies and the first judgment oracle (ch 5)

    3. Judgment for idolatry on the mountains (ch 6)

    4. "The end has come" (ch 7)

    5. The glory of God versus four abominations in the temple (ch 8)

    6. Those without the mark are slain (ch 9)

    7. The glory mounts the throne over the cherubim and wheels (ch 10)

    8. After promising "one heart" and "a new spirit," the glory departs the temple (ch 11)

9. An action prophecy of the prince's exile and two false proverbs about true prophecy (ch 12)

10. False prophets and prophetesses (ch 13)

11. Cases of casuistry (ch 14)

12. Jerusalem is a useless vine (ch 15)

13. Jerusalem the whore (ch 16)

14. The allegory of the cedar sprig and the Messiah planted by Yahweh (ch 17)

15. The wicked will die, and the righteous will live (ch 18)

16. A lament for Israel's princes (ch 19)

17. Review of the old covenant and promise of the new (20:1–44)

18. Yahweh's punishing sword is drawn (20:45–21:32)

19. Judgment on the bloody city for her abominations (ch 22)

20. Two lewd sisters whore against Yahweh (ch 23)

21. The cooking pot; the death of Ezekiel's wife (ch 24)

II. Oracles against Other Nations (chs 25–32)

A. Oracles against the Ammonites, Moab, Edom, and the Philistines (ch 25)

B. An Oracle against Tyre (ch 26)

C. A Lament over Tyre (ch 27)

D. Tyre's King Is Expelled from Eden (ch 28)

E. Judgment for Egypt, Recompense for Babylon, and a Horn for Israel (ch 29)

F. Egypt Will Fall, and Pharaoh's Arm Will Be Broken (ch 30)

G. Like Assyria the Cedar, Pharaoh Will Descend to Sheol (chs 31–32)

III. Oracles and Visions of Israel's Restoration (chs 33–48)

A. Oracles of Israel's Eschatological Restoration (ch 33–39)

1. The watchman; the fall of Jerusalem (ch 33)

2. Yahweh will save His sheep through His messianic Shepherd (ch 34)

3. An oracle against Mount Seir (ch 35)

4. Yahweh will sprinkle His people with clean water to give them a new heart and spirit (ch 36)

5. Resurrection of dry bones to become a people united under the new David (ch 37)

6. In the latter days, Gog will attack and be defeated by God (ch 38)

7. Yahweh will defeat Gog and pour out His Spirit on His people (ch 39)

visions and action prophecies. The story linking the oracles is that of a man compelled to share surprising revelations from God, and who dutifully carries out God's will as His "watchman," warning the exiled Judeans and those still in Jerusalem about God's wrath.

As Ezekiel proclaims God's Word, he sees a vision in which the Lord withdraws from His temple in Jerusalem due to the people's unfaithfulness. When the prophet's wife dies, the Lord forbids him from mourning for her as a sign that the exiles cannot mourn over Jerusalem. At this point, the book presents a series of oracles against the nations (chs 25–32) until the Lord directs Ezekiel back to prophecies about Israel and its future. He receives promises that Israel will be restored and finally overcome her enemies. God shows him the new temple, which symbolizes the future of Israel (chs 40–48). The Spirit of the Lord returns to hallow the new sanctuary and Israel.

Resources

As noted above, Ezekiel wrote in what may be described as both a stylistically inferior yet unique composition with compelling content. His writing does not bear the marks of extensive influence from the earlier, grander prophets, though he is well acquainted with biblical content, such as the history of Israel.

Text and Translations

The general sense of the Hebrew text remains clear, but obscurities abound in details. Text-critically, the Masoretic text of Ezekiel must be rated as the worst of the Major Prophets, with only Hosea, Samuel, and some psalms exceeding it in textual difficulties among compositions of the Old Testament. The Septuagint often differs markedly from the Masoretic Hebrew text. The general consensus is that the LXX often goes back to a superior prototype, but so far we have little Qumran illumination on the subject, and each instance must continue to be judged on its own merits.

DOCTRINAL CONTENT

Summary Commentary

Chs 1–3 The presence of the exiles "in the land of the Chaldeans" far from home is a manifestation of God's judgment upon an unfaithful people. But a remnant has remained faithful, among them Ezekiel the priest, whom God chooses as His instrument to explain why that judgment had come. Ezekiel describes the revelation of God's glory and voice. God calls Ezekiel to witness.

Chs 4–5 Ezekiel's action prophecies illustrate the dreadful judgment that God would visit upon the Israelites for their infidelity. The Lord condemns Israel for its brazen, sometimes worse-than-heathen misbehavior. Because God loves deeply, He responds vigorously to those who violate His covenant.

Chs 6–7 The Lord condemns the people, but, for the first time, salvation is clearly declared for the contrite remnant. Because God Himself was brokenhearted at their previous faithlessness, He will remember them now and so fulfill for them His promises, including the promise of the Savior.

Chs 8–11 At the beginning of Ezekiel's visionary visit to Jerusalem, he is led to witness four "abominations" that entail rank syncretism or even outright rejection of the true faith. The vision in ch 9 vividly describes God's final judgment on His disobedient people. But a remnant, bearing a mark of salvation on their foreheads, will escape. The vision of the throne-chariot on which the glory sat, first described in ch 1, is repeated and expanded in ch

10. Using the metaphor of Jerusalem as a cooking pot with meat inside, God contradicts the inhabitants' arrogant self-assurance that the city walls will protect them. Ezekiel's outcry at Pelatiah's sudden death provides an occasion for the comforting Gospel sermon that follows. God certainly will not make a full end of the remnant of Israel, but will provide salvation.

Chs 12–19 Action prophecies forecast the forthcoming deportation after Jerusalem's fall and its attendant horrors, followed by refutations of two complaints the people are using to discount God's warnings. God does not answer the prayers of those who do not pray in His name, not even when false prophets claim to speak for Him. Ezekiel emphasizes that righteousness (faith and life) is not transferable from one person to the next. Jerusalem is a vine that is good for nothing but burning, a vivid illustration of the city's fall in 587 BC. In a long allegorical satire, Ezekiel equates idolatry with adultery. The underlying theme is one of base ingratitude. The livid chapter on Israel's whoredom is followed by a beautiful affirmation of God's unwavering faithfulness to His everlasting covenant. Ezekiel then builds a glorious picture of God establishing His eternal kingdom in a descendant of David (and Jehoiachin): the Messiah. Life or death depends upon whether or not one believes and, as a result, lives out that faith. Ezekiel laments because God withdrew His blessings from Judah, whose leaders rebelled against Him.

Chs 20–24 God recounts how generations of Israelites compounded their sins. God desired to pour His wrath against them but, by His grace, stilled His own hand. While the elders come seeking counsel, God speaks only to Ezekiel and reveals how the withdrawal of His blessings will ultimately lead to Israel's repentance. God's hand draws His sword of judgment: Nebuchadnezzar. Like a prosecuting attorney, Ezekiel presents God's charges against Judah, who has forgotten her Lord (22:12). Both the Northern and Southern Kingdoms of Israel prostituted themselves by worshiping foreign gods and forming alliances with foreign governments. By God's own hand, the Babylonians besiege Jerusalem (24:2). Finally, Ezekiel must hold in his sorrow over the death of his wife as a sign to the exiles that they have no right to mourn over the destruction of the temple and Jerusalem.

Ch 25 Ezekiel pronounces seven prophecies against nations surrounding Israel. He begins by accusing Moab of believing that Judah is like the other nations (25:8), when in truth they are called and blessed by God. Similarly, the Edomites joined forces with the Babylonians besieging Jerusalem. God reaches out to the Philistines, that they may know He is God.

Chs 26–28 The Lord speaks against Phoenicia and its principal city, Tyre. People who pride themselves on criticizing and persecuting God's

An artist's depiction of Alexander the Great's troops assaulting Tyre (332 BC). This conquest partially fulfilled Ezekiel's prophecies against the city, which became a possession of the Greeks.

people will suffer His wrath here or in the grave. Yet, there is hope and beauty for the repentant. God requests that nations sing a funeral lament over the destruction of Tyre. Her ruins remain as Tyre's legacy of disgrace to surrounding nations. The sin of self-pride brought unrighteousness (28:15). God also speaks against Sidon. He will make His glory known in judgment (28:22–23) but finally in mercy. He directs Israel back to His covenant with their namesake Jacob—"Israel" (Gn 28:13–15; 32:28).

Chs 29–32 At God's command, Egypt never again rises to its former greatness. God sends Babylon, the most ruthless of nations (30:11), as the executioner of His divine plan of justice. He compares Egypt to Assyria, a nation that grew in power under God's guidance and whose capital once repented (cf Jnh 3). But proud Assyria turned away from God. All nations over time have collapsed under the weight of their own pride. After the fall of Jerusalem, God commands Ezekiel to record laments for Pharaoh. God lists nations like Egypt who turned away and are no more (32:22–30).

Chs 33–39 God changes Ezekiel's focus. No longer does Ezekiel speak against the nations. Instead, God calls Ezekiel to serve once again as Israel's watchman "to warn the wicked to turn from his way" (33:8). It would do little good for God to replace Israel's bad shepherds with other earthly rulers. Human society cannot lift itself out of the quicksand of pervasive corruption. In place of unfaithful shepherds, God will provide one Shepherd, Jesus Christ ("My servant David"; 34:24). He describes the tranquility of the new creation. Although God has spoken against Edom (25:12–14), He does so again. Nothing can hinder God's plan of salvation. He will push out those who interfere with His salvation, so all may know that He is God (35:4, 9, 11–12, 15). Ezekiel prophesies the return of God's people to the land promised. He characterizes Israel's sin by referring to the holiness code of Lv 11:1–15:33. Their return will "vindicate the holiness of [God's] great name"

(36:23). God carries Ezekiel to a valley filled with dry bones and calls him to prophesy over them. Ezekiel prophesies that God will unite Israel again.

Chs 40–48 Symbolism forms the basis for the rest of Ezekiel. Already God has promised to deliver His people from captivity. He now describes an even greater deliverance through His promised Messiah. Ezekiel begins a temple tour and sees the exacting standards by which God measures mankind. People from every direction, tribe, and nation will flow into God's presence. Ezekiel notes how holy the place is by mentioning that only the sons of Zadok can approach and minister there. Having completed their tour of the temple complex, the man of bronze leads Ezekiel out the east entrance, heading back to the location where their tour had begun. Ezekiel watches the glory of the God of Israel (43:2) enter the restored temple from the east, whence it had departed (11:22–24). God reiterates Levitical standards for His priests with some new regulations and gives the Israelites a prince, not a king; the heavenly Father is Israel's King, who embodies Israel's role in worship, enacting roles of both a priest and a king. Ezekiel's guide takes him to the inner court, where a stream of water begins flowing, transforming the Salt Sea (cf Rv 22:1–2). Each tribe is welcomed back. The idealized promised land is the prophetic symbol of a place in time in which the type of worship described previously will be possible.

Specific Law Themes

Death and God's wrath come to Israel by the sword of the Babylonians because Israel has not walked in God's statutes. Their idolatry appears as spiritual adultery to God. They are defiled by their sins. In anger, God withdraws His glory and blessings from the temple and from the kingdom of Judah. The Judeans must go into exile to spare the land. Famine and pestilence hound them.

Specific Gospel Themes

Despite the failures of Israel and Judah, God keeps His covenant. He creates new hearts for them and grants them His pure Spirit. He will replace their unfaithful leaders with Himself as the Good Shepherd. By cleansing the people and the land, He will restore their fortunes. His glory will return to fill the new temple and create a new and holy nation.

Specific Doctrines

Ezekiel's prophecies determined the shape of the future more than any other prophet. It is no exaggeration to think of him as the first postexilic prophet, perhaps in specific contrast to Jeremiah as the last preexilic prophet. Ezekiel's overriding concern is with God's holiness and/or His glory. If Isaiah can be said to champion God's transcendence, Ezekiel places the greater accent on His incarnational presence on earth. Jeremiah, by contrast, stresses God's immanence. All three know of His paradoxical indwelling in the temple. The net effect can only be judgment on the faithless, but promise and the presence of God for the faithful. This retributional pattern was as old as revelation itself, not a new mechanistic and corporate doctrine that Jeremiah and Ezekiel struggled to adjust to individual, personal circumstances. Ezekiel also prominently includes what critics alleged is a Deuteronomic phrase of acting "for My name's sake." He uses it with essentially the same import as Jeremiah.

In developing the main theme of God's transcendence as well as its applications, Ezekiel is the major refutation for the way critics have pitted prophet against priest. For Lutheran sacramental doctrine, Ezekiel will remain a major source and inspiration. The immediacy and subjectivism of "prophetic religion" and of "justification by faith" are inseparably linked with the mediacy and physical presence of the Sacraments, of an inscripturated Word. Atonement and incarnation, salvation and new creation, form the foundation of the biblical fabric. Virtually everything else that may be asserted about Ezekiel follows from those two points: transcendence in its verbal and sacramental dimensions.

The doctrine of sin is a good first example of the thoroughness of Ezekiel's theology. If anything, Ezekiel sees "total depravity" in all its heinousness over against divine perfection in even sharper contours than Jeremiah. Sin is ritual and sacral indeed, but social and moral at the same time—that is, applying to the "whole man," body and soul. Individual accountability also is stressed at least as much as in Jeremiah, yet even more clearly within a corporate, congregational context. Both ruin and revival, when and if they come, will affect the "heart" and "spirit" as much as the "bones" and ultimately also the earthly valley or stage. God's holiness necessarily implies the strict exclusion of the unregenerate, but it also means that His honor, His "name" (reputation) is at stake so that there is also a dynamic toward restoration, in the hope that all may know "that I am the LORD" (more than 30 times in the book).

Ezekiel's emphasis on repentance (cf 18:23; 33:11) has received special attention from theologians due to the Lord's clear statements of human responsibility for sin, our active role in repentance, and the Lord's desire to save people rather than condemn them. Similarly, the Lord's testimony that

He alone can change a person's heart and give new life through the Spirit highlights God's active role in our repentance and salvation through the Son of David, Jesus, which sinful human beings could not accomplish through their own abilities (11:19–20; 34:16–27; 36:26–27). Justification and sanctification are God's Work. Ezekiel's prophecy regarding Baptism and its effects is likewise important for understanding the divinely bestowed blessings of the Sacrament and that the water may be applied by sprinkling or pouring (36:25–27).

Angelology (of the cherubim, the heavenly guide) is also important to Ezekiel. The baroque character of Ezekiel's visions and actions ushers in the age of the apocalyptic literature with all its supernaturalist, end-of-the-world accents that are also structural for Daniel and the New Testament. Ezekiel is often called, albeit with slight exaggeration, the "father of apocalyptic literature."

A mural from the Dura Europos synagogue depicts Israel's dry bones rising to life (third century AD).

Application

Chs 1–3 Ezekiel will call the exiles to repentance and describe God's mercy promised to them. Today, God does not send us visions with new revelations, but works through the Word. Through repentance and absolution, He desires to raise us with Christ in newness of life. God calls Ezekiel to witness to all sorts of conditions of men, even though prospects are bleak and the audience is hostile. As the Lord strengthened Ezekiel, He will also strengthen us to proclaim the Gospel. Our life may be one of lamentation, mourning, and woe, but that may be the only way to break through pride and lead us to see how hopeless our natural condition is. If, however, God's accusing message is ingested, His word of forgiveness in Christ's atonement will be "as sweet as honey."

Chs 4–5 Ezekiel's action prophecies illustrate God's wrath. The outpouring of His wrath on obstinate unbelievers reminds us that He operates by the same principle in salvation; His Son bore the wrath our sins deserved. His love is costly—a price we could never pay: complete holiness.

Chs 6–7 The Lord condemns the people. The Law is necessary to the message of salvation. A weak preaching of the Law inevitably sets one up for a deficient or weak understanding of the Gospel. Thanks be to God there is a day of mercy, too, which Ezekiel will proclaim and we may celebrate with joy in Christ, our Savior.

Chs 8–11 Ezekiel witnesses four "abominations." Only when people realize the ever-present and insidious depth of their bondage to sin will they feel any need for a Savior. The road to perdition is broad, but God does not fail to place His mark of salvation on all who repent (9:4). The vision of the throne-chariot shows that the glory of our incarnate Lord will not depart forever. Those who remain in Jerusalem must face judgment (cf Gal 4:26). Thanks be to God; He gives us His Word and Spirit, new hearts, and new lives in His promises of mercy.

Chs 12–19 Action prophecies show that God's overarching purpose in judgment is to bring forth repentance and create trust in His salvation. All religions do not lead to the same place. We should not think that salvation can come from any other human source, but only from the righteousness of God. By catastrophe, the Lord prepares the way for restoration and salvation. In Christ, the true vine, we can bear much fruit (Jn 15:1–11). If the Lord can restore someone who has fallen as far as Jerusalem, He can restore anyone. His grace is broad enough to cover even your greatest sin. Ezekiel describes how God makes a new creation for you, established through Christ's birth, life, death, and resurrection.

Chs 20–24 Verse by verse, God recounts how generations of Israelites compounded their sins. God desired to pour His wrath against them (20:8, 13, 21) but, by His grace, stilled His own hand (20:9, 14, 22). God would have us make repentance a way of life. When difficulties or even disasters enter your life, let them remind you of the need for daily repentance and the refreshing blessings of the Gospel extended to you through Christ. Both the Northern and Southern Kingdoms of Israel prostituted themselves. Modern lewdness in films, songs, and on the Internet similarly mislead people today by alienating them from God. Repent of lusts and from spiritual adulteries that mix true devotion with falsehood. Our sins profaned His most glorious temple—the body and life of His Son. Yet the Father quietly gave Him over to death so that we might have life. Thankfully, Jesus cleanses our pain-filled hearts and will wipe away all our tears.

Ch 25 Ezekiel pronounces prophecies against nations surrounding Israel. God will not allow nations or individuals to mock Him. He will call straying people to repentance. Bear His name with repentant joy and sincere faith so that others may know the Lord. When you see someone struggling, pray for him and actively seek his good. Leave vengeance to God, who continues to reach out to people who do not know Him. He desires the salvation of all (1 Tm 2:3–4), as He emphasizes to Ezekiel (Ezk 18:23, 32).

Chs 26–28 The Lord speaks against Phoenicia and its principal city, Tyre. Mocking the Lord brings His retribution. Though Tyre will sink down, those who trust the Lord will rise up in blessing. His arm is stretching out to oppose His enemies and to reach His people, to save them from themselves. Pride may replace wisdom in our lives. In response to our self-delusion, Jesus humbled Himself by taking up the cross to bear our sin and raise us up from the depths of corruption. Notice God's gracious promise of Israel's return from their Babylonian captivity (28:24). He promises to hallow and glorify His people through Christ Jesus (cf Rm 8:18; 1Co 1:30).

Chs 29–32 Egypt's influence over the Mediterranean area comes to an end. Mercenary faith lusts after material possessions and lacks sincere devotion. Repent of self-interested religion and call upon the Lord with sincere devotion. Our ultimate reward is in His mercy and the homeland He has promised in Christ. The grave awaits us all. But the One who "spread terror in the land of the living" also holds the keys of death and hell (Rv 1:18). Our champion, the resurrected Lord, will deliver us.

Chs 33–39 As a watchman for the Lord, Ezekiel carries God's Word to His people. God's Word remains effective: God's Law causes despair in sinful hearts, leading them to repent. Then, God's Word reaches out with the life-giving power of the Gospel to absolve the sinner and create a new life. Christians, serve the Lord with confidence, knowing that the Good Shepherd is ever vigilant to deliver from evil. Jesus is the Good Shepherd who faithfully provides God's Word to all generations. God had made a promise of a land inheritance to Abraham (Gn 12:2–3). Included in that promise were these words: "and in you all the families of the earth shall be blessed" (Gn 12:3), a messianic promise God fulfills in Christ and through Holy Baptism in His name. The dead receive life. The people receive hope of restoration. God's Word is effective and still has power to give new life and hope. Gog represents the evil forces arrayed against Christ's Church. God's Word seals the doom of this unholy alliance. His powerful Word, through Ezekiel and through Christ, provides comfort to Christians today. "The gates of hell shall not prevail" (Mt 16:18). Judgment on His enemies is mercy for His people.

Chs 40–48 Temple symbolism forms the basis for the rest of Ezkiel. Ezekiel begins his temple tour and sees the exacting standards by which God measures man. Because God holds us to His standards, we find ourselves woefully inadequate. Yet God graciously covers our inadequacies with Christ's blood and makes us partakers of His holiness. Traditionally, Gentiles could pass no farther than the outer court, while Israelites could pass farther. By the blood of Jesus Christ, our great High Priest, all may enter God's presence (Heb 9:11–14). The sacrifices proclaimed the atonement fulfilled when Jesus Christ "offered for all time a single sacrifice for sins" (Heb 10:12). In the symbolism of this vision, we see a glimpse of the Lord's heavenly dwelling place, which He prepares for us in Christ. What Ezekiel describes anticipates the coming of the greatest Son of David, your Lord Jesus Christ, who hallows your worship and presents your prayers to the heavenly Father. God's grace transforms what was dead to bring forth new life. How great is His power! How gentle His kindness toward you.

CANONICITY

In the second century BC, Jesus son of Sirach celebrated God's revelations to Ezekiel (Ecclus 49:8–9). Scribes of the Qumran community were copying his work.

However, the rabbis had their questions about Ezekiel. Objections, especially from the more conservative school of Shammai, are supposed to have been of three sorts: (1) alleged contradictions with the Books of Moses, especially in the laws of chs 40–48 and the "creation" context of ch 28; (2) the alleged immorality of chs 16 and 23; and (3) fears of gnostic, theosophic, or other sectarian misuses of the call account and the apocalyptic portions. Some of the fears were eventually met by a proscription of reading the book until the age of 30 (the age at which Ezekiel and other priests could be called to service), but, above all, the difficulties are reported to have been solved by the lavish use of "midnight oil" (300 jars of it) in one Rabbi Hananiah's study, who resolved all problems to the satisfaction of the other rabbis (Menah 45a; Hag 13a)! In addition, there is a Talmudic statement about Ezekiel, as of other books, that the "Great Synagogue" wrote Ezekiel (see Bava Batra 14b). At most, this may preserve some authentic memory of compilers' activities.

Ezekiel's visions of the future temple are echoed in Revelation's visions of the heavenly Jerusalem. Christians welcomed the book into their canon without issue.

LUTHERAN THEOLOGIANS ON EZEKIEL

Luther

"This vision in the first part of Ezekiel [1:4–28], however, is nothing else than a revelation of the kingdom of Christ in faith here upon earth, in all four corners of the whole world as said in Psalm 19[:4]: *In omnem terram*. This is how I understand it (let someone else improve on it). For no one can be a prophet, as St. Peter testifies, unless he have the Spirit of Christ [II Pet. 1:21]. . . . To put it briefly: this vision is the spiritual chariot of Christ in which he rides here in the world, meaning thereby his entire holy church. . . .

"This vision, moreover (as Ezekiel himself shows in chapters 8–9), signified the end . . . of the priesthood, the worship, and the church organization instituted and given them by Moses. For all of these were instituted only until Christ should come, as St. Paul says in Romans 8[:2–3] and II Corinthians 3[:6], as Christ himself says in Matthew 11[:13], and as the Epistle to the Hebrews says repeatedly. . . .

"For this prophecy contains two things. The first is that Israel and Judah shall return to their land after their captivity. This came to pass through King Cyrus and the Persians, before the birth of Christ, at the time when the Jews returned to their land and to Jerusalem from all countries. They also came to Jerusalem every year to the feasts, even from foreign countries where they maintained their residence, drawing many Gentiles with them and to them.

"But the hope of the Jews that there shall yet be another physical return, when all of them together shall come back into the land and set up again the old Mosaic order of things, this is something they have dreamed up themselves. There is not a letter in the prophets or in Scripture which says or signifies anything of the kind. It is written, indeed, that they shall return out of all lands whither they have been driven; not all of them, however, but only some of them out of all lands. . . .

"The second thing, and the best thing in this prophecy . . . is that God promises to create something new in the land, to make a new covenant unlike the old covenant of Moses that they dream about. This is plain from Jeremiah 31[:31–32] and from many more passages. No longer are there to be two kingdoms but one kingdom, under their King David who is to come; and his shall be an everlasting kingdom, even in that same physical land.

"This, too, has been fulfilled. For when Christ came and found the people of both Israel and Judah gathered again out of all lands so that the country was full, he started something new: he established the promised new covenant. He did this not at a spiritual place, or at some other physical place, but exactly in that same physical land of Canaan, and at that same physical Jerusalem—as had been promised—to which they had been brought back out of all lands. . . .

"These two things Ezekiel teaches us when he comforts the people concerning the return from Babylon, but even more when he prophesies the new Israel and the kingdom of Christ. That is his vision of the chariot, and also really his temple, in the last part of his book [40:2–48:35]. . . .

"Ezekiel says neither that this city shall be called Jerusalem, nor that it shall stand at the place where Jerusalem was situated. . . . He says, 'It shall be called *Dominus ibi*,' 'There God,' or 'God there,' that is, 'Where God himself is.' The temple shall not be in the city. . . . There shall also be a great flow of water out of the temple into the Dead Sea [Ezek. 47:1–12] . . . but this in no way squares with the topography of Israel.

"Besides the tribes and the land of Israel are very differently divided and arranged, so that the city and the temple shall not lie in the land of any tribe of Israel, though Jerusalem was previously located in the land of the tribe of Benjamin [Josh. 18:28]. All this and much more is plainly given in the text. . . .

"Therefore this building of Ezekiel is not to be understood to mean a physical building, but like the chariot at the beginning [1:4–28] so this building at the end [40–48] is nothing else than the kingdom of Christ, the holy church or Christendom here on earth until the last day." (AE 35:284–290)

Gerhard

"*Ezekiel, yechezqe'l*, means 'strength of God.' Theodoret (commentary on Ezek. 1:3) notes that he could boast of two gifts: both 'priesthood and prophecy.' He prophesied at the same time as Jeremiah, but he lived in the city of Babylon, while Jeremiah lived in Jerusalem. The author of the preface to Marsilius Patavinus's *Defens.* writes the following about him:

> By revelation of the Holy Spirit he foresaw the four Gospels about six hundred years before Christ's incarnation. He uttered a perfect prophecy of the four Gospels with a similitude of four animals, the first of which was a man; the second, a lion; the third, a calf; and the fourth, an eagle. In each of these, each mystery regarding Christ is figured: in the face of a man, His birth in the flesh; in that of the lion, the roaring of the preaching of the Gospel or the mystery of His resurrection; in that of the calf, the eternal priesthood; in that of the eagle, the mystery of spreading His divinity, which had to be published to the Church throughout the world.

"Gregory's statement is in harmony with this: 'Our Redeemer: a man by His birth, a calf by His death, a lion by His resurrection, an eagle by His ascension.' Nevertheless others explain that prophetic vision in other ways. (See Justin, *Quaest. et resp. ad orthod.*, q. 44, p. 325.)

"Ezekiel died in Chaldea at the hands of a leading man of his own people whom he had reproached because of his idolatry. After his slaying, he was buried in the land of the Spyrii [*Spyriorum*] in the district of Maur in the tomb of Shem and Arphaxad, the ancestor of Abraham.

"According to Jerome (Epistle *ad Paulin.* and the introduction to bk. 1 of his commentary on Ezekiel), among the Jews, no one is allowed to read the beginning of Genesis or the Song of Songs or the beginning and end of Ezekiel until he has reached the age of the priestly ministry, that is, his thirtieth year.

"It has forty-eight chapters in which we have, with the exception of a prologue, a prophecy partly rebuking, partly comforting." (ThC E1 § 154)

FURTHER STUDY

Lay/Bible Class Commentaries

Kuschel, Keith. *Ezekiel*. PBC. St. Louis: Concordia, 1994. ჰ Lutheran author. Excellent for Bible classes. Based on the NIV translation.

Life by His Word. St. Louis: Concordia, 2009. ჰ More than 1,500 reproducible one-page Bible studies covering each chapter of the canonical Scriptures. Page references to *The Lutheran Study Bible*. CD-Rom and downloadable.

Roehrs, Walter R. *Ezekiel: I Am the LORD*. GWFT. St. Louis: Concordia, 1995. ჰ Lutheran author and theologian. Eleven-session Bible study, including leader's notes and discussion questions.

Taylor, John B. *Ezekiel*. TOTC. Downers Grove, IL: InterVarsity Press, 1969. ჰ Compact commentary from an evangelical author. Helpful but somewhat critical. References the English Revised Version, RSV, and KJV.

Church Worker Resources

Allen, Leslie C. *Ezekiel*. 2 vols. WBC. Waco: Word, 1994, 1990. ჰ An evangelical scholar showing special interest in the redaction of the text. Helpful for textual criticism.

Block, Daniel I. *The Book of Ezekiel*. NICOT. Grand Rapids: Eerdmans, 1997, 1998. ჰ A thorough, recent work from an evangelical scholar, which is generally conservative and very helpful.

Eichrodt, Walter. *Ezekiel*. OTL. Philadelphia: Westminster, 1970. ჰ Perhaps the best of the "biblical theology" movement. Only mildly critical.

Academic Resources

Greenberg, Moshe. *Ezekiel*. Vols. 22 and 22A of AB. New York: Doubleday, 1983. ჰ Philologically strong. Detailed commentary by a Jewish scholar. Very conservative and insightful. But, obviously, must be supplemented from a Christian viewpoint.

Hummel, Horace. *Ezekiel*. 2 vols. CC. St. Louis: Concordia, 2005, 2007. ჰ The best available commentary, strong philologically and rich in theology. Written by a skilled Lutheran theologian who assesses critical views.

K&D. *Biblical Commentaries on the Old Testament: Ezekiel*. 2 vols. Grand Rapids: Eerdmans, 1950 reprint. ჰ This century-and-a-half old work from Lutheran scholars should not be overlooked. Despite its age, it remains a most useful commentary on the Hebrew text.

Levenson, Jon D. *Theology of the Restoration of Ezekiel 40–48*. Decatur, AL: Scholars Press, 1976. ჰ A stimulating resource; sometimes critical.

Schröder, Fr. Wilhelm Julius. *A Commentary on the Holy Scriptures: Ezekiel*. LCHS. New York: Charles Scribner's Sons, 1890. ჰ A helpful older example of German biblical scholarship, based on the Hebrew text, which provides references to significant commentaries from the Reformation era forward.

Zimmerli, Walther. *Ezekiel*. 2 vols. Hermeneia: A Critical and Historical Commentary on the Bible. Philadelphia: Fortress, 1979, 1983. ჰ Exhaustive detail. Argues that the book is the product of the prophet's disciples. Relatively critical, but helpful.

APOCALYPTIC LITERATURE

Klaus Koch's study of the history of critical investigation of apocalyptic literature has a revealing title that may be translated freely, "Thoroughly Puzzled
by Apocalyptic" (*Ratlos vor der Apokalyptik*). But this insightful title is insipidly
rendered in the official English translation, *The Rediscovery of Apocalyptic*. The
ultimate issue is theological, of course, and it provides a parade example of
interpretive issues. The characteristic liberal distaste for the subject, it is safe
to say, is rooted in the fact that apocalyptic literature in the Bible highlights
just about everything that Liberalism prefers not to highlight: supernatu-
ralism, original sin, salvation by grace alone instead of human cooperation,
predictive prophecy, verbal inspiration, particularism, final judgment, bodily
resurrection, etc. That same list of qualities explains, at least in part, why apocalyptic plays so central a role in orthodoxy. Käsemann's oft-quoted dictum,
"apocalyptic . . . was the mother of all Christian theology," is a gross exaggeration, of course, but contains some insight.

Classic Liberal Views

As in so many other areas of biblical study, Wellhausen forms the major water-
shed, and he continues to cast a long shadow over contemporary thought on
the subject. Wellhausen's point of departure in this respect was the assumption of a fundamental break between the "prophetic spirit" of preexilic Israelite
religion and the "Judaism" of the postexilic period, the legalism, supernatural-
ism, and particularism of which allegedly stifled prophetism. The apocalyptists were put down as inferior imitators of the great prophets, who partly in
response to the trauma of the exile and its aftermath, and partly in dependence on Iranian and Zoroastrian "dualism," developed prophetic ideas in an
unfortunate and regressive manner. Although the prophets allegedly had

anticipated "salvation *in* history" (that is, in continuity with the present and with mankind's full cooperation), the disillusioned, pessimistic apocalyptists preached a utopian "salvation *from* history" (that is, sudden divine intervention and transformation from on high).

Such a view had profound implications for the understanding of the nature of the unity of the testaments and for the interpretation of the New Testament. The standard Wellhausenian view of such matters is often referred to as the "prophetic connection theory." That is, Jesus and the preexilic prophets should be directly connected; for all practical purposes, one should skip over the half a millennium between the exile and Christ in order to connect such greats as Amos, Isaiah, and Jeremiah with the teaching of Jesus. The exilic, postexilic, and intertestamental prophets and writers were a barrier rather than a blessing in this view. (So pervasive was this prejudice in Germany that scholarly research in the area all but ceased throughout much of the first half of the twentieth century.) In this understanding, the "historical Jesus" was a great ethical teacher, the last and greatest of the prophets, and the "Christ of faith" (the apocalyptic Son of Man, incarnate, and resurrected) was largely a construct of the primitive church.

Confessional Response

How shall the confessional theologian react to all this discussion, proceeding from his axioms of special inspiration, unity of Scripture, and the like? Perhaps above all, he will want to stress a prophetic-apocalyptic-Jesus continuity. Continuity does not imply identity (there are developments and adaptations along the way), but continuity nonetheless, and of a positive sort. Apocalyptic literature certainly highlights certain themes found already in classical prophecy (and, inchoately, even earlier), especially conflict motifs, the hopelessness of the human predicament unless God intervenes, etc. Furthermore, in making such points, the conservative will want to stress how the critical dissections of the prophetic literature nourish the critical dogma of prophetic-apocalyptic disjunction. Passages in the Prophetic Books that stress themes or use language considered "apocalyptic" are regularly declared "not genuine" and later additions by the critics. After they eliminated such materials from consideration, their critical notion of what is genuinely "prophetic" is also easily upheld. A better—and more fateful—example of critical argumentation in a circle can hardly be found!

Date of Apocalyptic Literature

If the more apocalyptic passages in the prophetic writings cannot blithely be declared ungenuine, it is not so easy for critics to claim that apocalyptic passages are later in composition than the texts that surround them. This, of course, has a very direct bearing on the question of the date of Daniel. If some of the proto-apocalyptic sections of prophecy (perhaps especially Jl 3–4; Is 24–27; Ezk 38–39; and Zec 9–14) stem from some time well into the postexilic period, the critical assumption of a still later date for more developed apocalyptic literature like Daniel is very difficult to counter. We, of course, possess a fair number of extracanonical apocalyptic works (*Enoch*, *4 Ezra*, or 2 Esdras, etc.), which formally have much in common with Daniel, and which are usually dated in a period around the turn of the testaments, commencing with Daniel itself. However, many examples could surely be found in world literature of styles of writing that were ahead of their time literarily, and whose lead was not widely followed until a much later era.

Partly because of the critics' circular argumentation, critical literature commonly attributes to the apocalyptic genre a number of unique characteristics. A conservative can only assent to these lists with reservations. For example, it is commonly asserted that, whereas the classical prophet was primarily a man of the spoken word, the apocalyptist was not only primarily a writer, but perhaps his "visions" were no longer even actually seen. His almost exclusive use of prose instead of the poetry in which prophetic oracles were often couched was supposed to confirm

Israelites held back the darkness with olive oil lamps. This footed example comes from Lachish (Iron Age II).

the point. It seems very doubtful, however, that we know enough of the phenomenology of either prophetic or apocalyptic inspiration or of the transmission and writing down of their messages to make such claims.

Similarly, it is stated that the classical prophet spoke publicly, but apocalyptic was nearly "anonymous" or even "pseudonymous." At the least, this assertion exceeds the evidence, failing to describe a book such as Ezekiel. The following are characteristics commonly associated with apocalyptic literature.

Supposed Dualism

Critics describe apocalyptic literature's view of time and history as "dualistic." No doubt, apocalyptic literature has a sharply honed sense of the distinction between the present age and the future or coming age, the two set apart, by history's climactic act of divine intervention, the final judgment. As noted above, criticism usually intends by this language to contrast the alleged escapism and utopianism of apocalyptic literature with the "sober, realistic" confidence in human potential of their heroes, the prophets.

The term "dualism" is not totally objectionable, but careful distinctions are imperative. Earlier critics were convinced that apocalyptic literature was beholden to the genuine Zoroastrian dualism of light and darkness (Ormazd and Ahriman). However, biblical "dualism" is perhaps best illustrated by the contrast between light and darkness in especially Isaiah (cf John in the New Testament). In a way, it is no real dualism at all. Evil enters the picture only with the rebellions of Satan and mankind, and it maintains power only because the Almighty allows it. It is one of apocalyptic literature's central proclamations that the evil one and all his works have in principle already been judged, and that the time is but short before his final elimination—but, of course, the idea was anything but alien to earlier biblical writers!

Sense of Time

Often the apocalyptic interest in God's definitive management of time and history expresses itself in terms of well-defined dispensations or kingdoms (especially the four of Daniel). Here too, however, we recognize no more than a sharpening of the general biblical sense of time. God's battle with evil leading up to the end goes on nonstop, but, at least to creatures of space and time, there will be an inevitable periodicity about it, certain occasions when the struggle is especially evident. Since God's victory is not only future but present, the Lutheran dogmatic language of the "two kingdoms" and/or of "Law/Gospel" is faithful for describing all human history. The Church lives in an already/not-yet situation.

The Will of God and of Mankind

Critics often refer further to the apocalyptic outlook as "deterministic." This is scarcely acceptable at all. Indeed, apocalyptic literature expresses in no uncertain terms the basic biblical hope that the one transcendent God is firmly in control and calls all the final shots. But there is no indication that human beings have no will. God holds people responsible.

Transcendence

In connection with all of this, critical literature also regularly makes a great point of apocalyptic literature's heightened stress on God's transcendence. It argues that apocalyptic literature fills the gap between God and mankind by the development of elaborate angelic hierarchies and a corresponding development in demonology. These motifs are certainly more prominent in apocalyptic literature, and proper names begin to appear (Satan, Michael, Gabriel, etc.). However, the angelology of Daniel differs little, if any, from that of Ezekiel and Zechariah, and, in fact, the similarity is a major argument against dating Daniel so much later, as critics do.

Resurrection

Belief in a final, bodily resurrection in connection with the final judgment is regularly hailed by critics as one of apocalyptic literature's major developments. It was, allegedly, only another aspect of its despair in historical possibilities and tendency to sit back and wait for God to make everything right again. Again we have a partial truth here. Critics are often loathe to concede any type of Old Testament belief in life after death except for perhaps the most shadowy type of existence in Sheol. They misread passages that, at very least, are capable of more positive interpretations. (Cf also the debate between the Sadducees and the Pharisees on the subject.) But, no doubt, the theme of resurrection is more central in apocalyptic literature than earlier literature. Properly understood, we undeniably have here a major factor in "cumulative revelation," as well as a major example of God preparing the seedbed for receptivity to the Gospel of our Lord's resurrection (to radical critics, of course, Jesus' resurrection is only an expression of the preaching and expectation of the historical Jesus).

Carey, Greg. *Ultimate Things: Introduction to Jewish and Christian Apocalyptic Literature.* Atlanta: Chalice Press, 2006. ᛜ An overview by a New Testament scholar.

Collins, John J., et al. *The Encyclopedia of Apocalypticism.* 3 vols. New York: Continuum, 2000. ᛜ Extensive treatment by a well respected Roman Catholic scholar of the Old Testament.

Morris, Leon. *Apocalyptic.* Grand Rapids: Eerdmans, 1972. ᛜ A very careful, well-informed introduction and treatment of apocalyptic literature and its proper interpretation.

Murphy, Frederick J. *Apocalypticism in the Bible and Its World: A Comprehensive Introduction.* Grand Rapids: Baker Academic, 2012. ᛜ A recent introduction by a scholar of intertestamental and New Testament studies.

Russell, D. S. *The Method and Message of Jewish Apocalyptic: 200 B.C.–A.D. 100.* Philadelphia: Westminster, 1964. ᛜ A neoorthodox treatment of apocalyptic literature.

DANIEL

A kingdom that shall stand forever

Virtually all challenges for biblical study arise in connection with the Book of Daniel. We encounter not only nearly all the standard issues here—and those often in heightened form—but quite a few relatively unique ones as well. Perhaps nowhere has the impact of higher criticism been so great or so startling as here, and it is no accident that Daniel regularly takes its place as a litmus test for either orthodoxy or "critical orthodoxy" (alongside Jonah, the unity of Isaiah, and whether Moses wrote the Books of Moses).

In addition, conservative interpreters are sometimes sharply divided on the proper interpretation of many key portions of the book between millennial (mostly premillennial and dispensationalist) and amillennial outlooks. (The same cleavage appears at other points in the Old Testament, especially in the latter portions of Ezekiel and Zechariah, but scarcely to the same degree or with the same trouble as with Daniel.) Hence, the Book of Daniel becomes a proving ground for one's methods of biblical interpretation.

The introductory problems of the Book of Daniel almost reduce themselves to one: whether the book was written by a historical Daniel in the Babylonian exile, or whether it is written in Daniel's name to lift the hopes of victims of Seleucid persecution somewhere between the beginning

Lion from the procession street of Nebuchadnezzar II, ruler of Babylon.

OVERVIEW

Author
Daniel

Date
c 605–536 BC

Places
Judah; Babylon; Shinar; Media; Persia; Susa in Elam; Greece; Tigris River; Egypt

People
Daniel, Hananiah, Mishael, and Azariah (the Judeans); Nebuchadnezzar; chief of the eunuchs; wise men and Chaldeans; Darius the Mede; Cyrus the Persian; Belshazzar; various rulers; Gabriel and Michael

Purpose
To comfort the people of God by demonstrating that the Most High God rules over the kingdom of men

Law Themes
Babylon holds Judah captive; Judah has failed to obey God's voice and has violated God's covenant; open shame; apocryphal events, including the profaning of the temple and the abomination that makes desolate; God's final judgment; everlasting contempt

Gospel Themes
The Most High God rules the kingdom of men; He keeps His covenant; mercy for the oppressed; His Anointed One will rule a kingdom that shall never be destroyed; an everlasting dominion; everlasting life

Memory Verses
The everlasting Kingdom (2:44–45); the King of heaven (4:37); the Son of Man receives dominion (7:13–14); the saints receive dominion (7:27); God's great mercy (9:18); the resurrection (12:2–3)

TIMELINE

722 BC	Samaria (Israel) falls to Assyria
605 BC	First Judeans, including Daniel, exiled to Babylon
538 BC	Cyrus decrees that exiles may return to Judah
536 BC	Daniel's final vision
516 BC	Second temple completed

of Seleucid persecution in 167 BC and Judas Maccabeus's rededication of the temple in 164. Taking the book itself literally, it is quite easy for the conservative to answer that basic question by asserting the historical value of the book. In addition, of course, we have the clinching testimony of our Lord, who in Mt 24:15 refers to "the abomination of desolation, spoken by Daniel the prophet." The preposition *by* makes it plain that Christ is thinking of a person by that name (and of the "abomination" as foreshadowing events beginning to be fulfilled in connection with His own life and work).

Historical and Cultural Setting

The rapid collapse (627–605 BC) of the Assyrian Empire made way for the conquests of the Neo-Babylonians. The Assyrians attempted to form a military alliance against the Babylonians by uniting forces with the Egyptians. However, as the Egyptians moved through Israel, King Josiah of Judah interfered and died at the Battle of Megiddo (609 BC), opening the way for conquest of his own kingdom. The Assyrian-Egyptian alliance could not withstand the Babylonians, who defeated the alliance decisively at the Battle of Carchemish. That same year, in 605 BC, the Babylonians took Jerusalem and carried away young Daniel and other Judeans, with the full destruction of Jerusalem taking place later in 587 BC.

Yet the Babylonians themselves were susceptible to overthrow. In 538 BC, Cyrus II the Great led the Persians to take Babylon. In the interest of pleasing his subjects, whom the Babylonians had exiled, Cyrus granted the Judeans and others the right to return to their homeland and restore their temples. Although the Babylonians rebelled against the Persians during the reign of Xerxes I (486–465 BC), the Persians governed the Near East until the invasion of Alexander the Great of Macedon in 332 BC.

Clay brick imprinted with "Cyrus king of the world, king of Anshan. . . . The great gods delivered all lands into my hands and I made this land dwell in peace."

COMPOSITION

Author

The Book of Daniel contains no heading or other explicit statement about its source. Yet literal Danielic authorship is plainly the implication of the text (cf the situation with Moses' authorship of the Pentateuch, written largely in the third person). At times Daniel speaks in the first person and asserts that visions were given to him (cf chs 7–9), and presuming that the book is a unit, it is easy to assume that he also wrote the rest of the book, including the narratives about himself in the first part. Both the narratives and the visions are independently arranged in chronological order, but the fact that the visions commence before the narratives end also attests to unity of composition. It is true that we apparently know nothing else about Daniel besides the information contained in the book, but that is certainly the case with other biblical authors and ancient writers.

Conservatives are generally inclined to argue that the Daniel mentioned in Ezekiel (14:14, 20; 28:3) is identical with the author of the biblical book, that is, that Ezekiel is referring to his renowned contemporary. However, the parallelism with the much more ancient personages of Noah and Job makes that position questionable. Ezekiel's reference could be to some equally ancient figure of which we know nothing else except perhaps the garbled Ugaritic legends about Dan'el. Liberals usually assume that it is precisely that ancient legendary figure to which the unknown author of Daniel attributed his "visions." Even on liberal premises that seems rather unusual, because writings in someone else's name (pseudepigrapha_ usually appeal to figures occupying a much more central and well-known position in biblical history than an ancient Daniel would.

Critics also question unity of authorship. They search for sources and try to reconstruct stages of transmission. The use of both Aramaic and Hebrew in the book raises inevitable questions. In addition, many critics argue for a much earlier origin (third century or possibly even earlier) of the "legends" in the first part of the book than of the visions in the latter. The former are often supposed to have originally circulated independently in the eastern Jewish diaspora, and to evince, on the whole, a much more moderate and tolerant attitude toward Gentiles than the nakedly hostile visions composed in Maccabean times to counter Seleucid tyranny. Some think of only an oral form of the earlier "legends" while others think in terms of written sources, but it is obvious that the conservative cannot agree to such premises.

The original independence of the various "legends" is supposed to be demonstrated by the fact that in each one Nebuchadnezzar converts to and legitimizes Judaism, while in each succeeding story he reappears as an intolerant and vainglorious heathen. To this we can only answer that superficial and repeated "conversions" are no novelty in our day either!

Date of Composition

Critics question virtually every early chronological reference in the book. Allegedly, the author's historical memory is so imprecise and garbled that he must have written long after the events of the Babylonian and Persian periods (see "Daniel and History," pp 844–49). As they read the book, the author becomes reasonably precise and accurate only when he approaches his "predictions" of the second-century Maccabean events of which he was a contemporary (7:1; 8:14; 11:21–39). Almost precisely the same construction was placed on the Book of Daniel by Porphyry, a Neoplatonist philosopher and anti-Christian polemicist of the third century AD. Jerome, in his famous and still useful commentary on Daniel, answered the charges.

The book, however, gives us considerable data about its date. It opens with a reference to "the third year of the reign of Jehoiakim" (1:1), that is, probably 605 BC, when it is reported that Daniel was deported to Babylon after Nebuchadnezzar took Jerusalem. The latest internal reference is apparently to the "third year of Cyrus" (10:1; cf "Darius the Mede" on pp 845–46), that is, perhaps 536 or thereabouts, depending on the point of reference in Cyrus's career. How long afterward the book itself was composed we cannot tell, but probably not too much later.

Purpose/Recipients

The book has the dual intent of comforting those in the "fiery furnace" of the Babylonian exile, as well as assuring them that present tribulations and deliverances are the vestibule to and prophecies of events at the end of historical time. The exile will not be permanent, but eventually all earthly kingdoms (specifically those in closer prospect) will pass away, and God's eternal kingdom will be established. Times may well get even worse. This portends not God's failure but the imminence of His final triumph.

Literary Features

Genre

Daniel is nearly always classified as apocalyptic literature, and the greatest example of that literature in the Old Testament. (See also "Apocalyptic Literature" on pp 817–21.) However, much of Daniel 1–6 is written as historical narrative, through which the apocalyptic visions are introduced and described.

Characters

The Book of Daniel presents some of the most memorable characters in the Old Testament, the first being the author, who repeatedly demonstrates courage and divine wisdom in tense circumstances. Similarly, the other Judeans are presented with the same traits (chs 1, 3). Alongside these faithful Judeans are presented a variety of pagan rulers whose religious and cultural views keep them from understanding the Lord and His ways. However, as the Lord acts miraculously and providentially on behalf of His people, the truth about Him is revealed. The Babylonian rulers Nebuchadnezzar and Darius the Mede respond in humble faith. In contrast, the callous Belshazzar does not repent and suffers defeat. Officials of the king are similarly callous and also hatch conspiracies against the righteous.

Alongside the human figures, Daniel describes two angels who bring visions to him and help him understand them: Michael and Gabriel.

Narrative Development or Plot

The book describes the struggle of the Judeans to maintain their faith and way of life while living, working, and prospering in a pagan environment. Their religious beliefs and practices continually distinguish them from their neighbors in Babylon, which leads to threatening situations. In each case, the Lord intervenes to rescue the Judeans or to humble the rulers who threaten them. The first six chapters of the book unfold as historical narrative, whereas the later chapters are largely occupied with the visions during Daniel's mature years.

Resources

As noted above, the Book of Daniel is a unified composition. The prophet may have compiled it from documents prepared at different points in his life, as indicated by the different languages used. The apocryphal additions to Daniel appear to have been composed and perhaps circulated independently before being inserted into the book by later editors (e.g., Susanna is added at different points).

Text and Translations

As noted above, conservatives regard the book as a composition of the Babylonian and Persian eras; critics regard the book as dating from the Greek era. The nature of the text speaks to this question of the book's history.

OUTLINE

Daniel is particularly easy to outline. Each chapter is a separate section. The only exception is the last section, which covers chs 10–12. In chs 1–6, Daniel describes what happens to him in third person ("he"). In chs 7–12, Daniel describes what happens to him in first person ("I").

I. Judeans Steadfast in Practicing Their Faith (ch 1)

II. Nebuchadnezzar's Dream: Four Kingdoms and the Establishment of the Kingdom of God (ch 2)

III. God's Faithful Servants Are Rescued from Death (ch 3)

IV. Nebuchadnezzar Judged for His Arrogance against God (ch 4)

V. Belshazzar Judged for His Arrogance against God (ch 5)

VI. God's Faithful Servant Is Rescued from Death (ch 6)

VII. Daniel's Vision: Four Kingdoms and the Establishment of the Kingdom of God (ch 7)

VIII. Daniel's Vision concerning the Post-Babylonian Kingdoms (ch 8)

IX. Daniel's Prayer and Vision concerning Jerusalem during the Post-Babylonian Kingdoms (ch 9)

X. Daniel's Vision concerning the Post-Babylonian Kingdoms (chs 10–12)

These sections are organized in two interlocking structures (chiasms). This thoughtful literary development attests to the book's unity.

Section	Reference	Literary Type	Language
Prologue	Ch 1	Story	Hbr
First Structure			
A. Nebuchadnezzar dreams of four kingdoms and God's kingdom	Ch 2	Dream Story	Aram
B. Nebuchadnezzar sees God's servants rescued	Ch 3	Story	Aram
C. Judgment on Nebuchadnezzar	Ch 4	Dream Story	Aram
C´. Judgment on Belshazzar	Ch 5	Vision Story	Aram
B´. Darius sees Daniel rescued	Ch 6	Story	Aram
A´. Daniel has a vision of four kingdoms and God's kingdom	Ch 7	Vision	Aram
Second Structure			
D. Details on the post-Babylonian kingdoms	Ch 8	Vision	Hbr
E. Jerusalem restored	Ch 9	Vision	Hbr
D´. More details on the post-Babylonian kingdoms	Chs 10–12	Vision	Hbr

Original Languages

Daniel is written in both Hebrew and Aramaic (the latter in the older literature often referred to as "Chaldee," because it begins at 2:4 with a speech of the "Chaldeans"). In addition, a number of Persian loanwords appear throughout, and in the Aramaic section there are three words of Greek origin (a number of others once thought to be Greek have turned out not to be). The three Greek words in 3:5 are all names of musical instruments, which were easily diffused beyond the country of origin, especially in the days of Greek and Persian confrontations in which our book is set. We cannot presently document those Greek musical terms elsewhere earlier than the time of Plato in the fourth century BC, but that scarcely proves the Greeks or Persians were not using them earlier. At most we might consider that scribes made minimal updates of Oriental names for these instruments so that their readers could identify them, especially since the instruments themselves appear to be of Mesopotamian origin. In any event, the presence of only *three* Greek words in the book is strong evidence against late Maccabean origin. The Persian terms really pose no historical problem either, because Daniel himself served at least a number of years under Persian rule, and the book probably took final shape in that period.

The major linguistic debates have always raged around the Aramaic of Daniel. Older critics argued that the book could scarcely have been written in Babylon because it exhibited a western instead of an eastern dialect of Aramaic. But that argument has been quietly abandoned. The language is now regarded as "Imperial Aramaic" (*Reichsaramäisch*), for a long time the common language of nearly the entire Near East. Its existence can be documented almost throughout the biblical period, but it became especially prominent in the Persian empire during the reign of Darius I (522–486 BC).

The Aramaic of Daniel closely resembles that of Ezra and of the Elephantine Papyri found in Egypt, both from the latter part of the fifth century. These slightly later parallels certainly do not veto the possibility of the actual composition of the Aramaic of Daniel in the sixth century; at most we might have to reckon with a subsequent modernization of Daniel's original Aramaic dialect (as in the case of the other biblical books, and no theological problem, if properly understood). This conclusion is, if anything, confirmed by the discovery of the Aramaic literature at Qumran, especially the *Genesis Apocryphon* (perhaps composed as early as the third century), which exhibits many and striking traits different and indisputably later than the language of Daniel.

Essentially the same situation obtains in the Hebrew portions of Daniel. The language is similar to that found in other biblical literature of the exilic and early postexilic periods (Ezekiel, Haggai, Ezra, Chronicles), but differs markedly from that of Ecclesiasticus, written only shortly before the second century date proposed for Daniel by critics. As noted above, the Hebrew of Daniel contains a number of Persian administrative terms, where we would expect to see Greek influence if the book were written nearly two centuries after Alexander's conquests.

It has been argued that the very existence of a sizable chunk of Aramaic in Daniel should testify to late composition, when the Hebrew language had waned. The Aramaic sections of Ezra, as well as the Aramaizing Hebrew of Nehemiah, both much earlier than the critical date for Daniel, should suffice to refute that thesis. Not only did Aramaic often supplant Hebrew very early on, in educated circles even well before the exile (2Ki 18:26; Is 36:11), and, no doubt, especially in the East, but the evidence now is that the nationalistic and religious movement spearheaded by the Hasidim and Maccabees was accompanied by a revival of the Hebrew tongue.

Why Daniel is written partly in Hebrew, partly in Aramaic, and what the relation is between the two portions are questions that have never been answered to everyone's satisfaction. The question is, of course, related to that of the original unity of the book (see above). The situation is somewhat similar to that in Ezra. Ezra 4:28 begins use of Aramaic. In Daniel, it begins in the middle of a verse (2:4) with a speech of the "Chaldeans" to the king, but continues on long beyond that speech until the end of ch 7. Even more puzzling is the fact that the Aramaic thus straddles the two obvious divisions of the book according to contents: the narratives in chs 1–6 and the visions in 7–12. The Qumran manuscripts attest to the transition from Hebrew to Aramaic and from Aramaic back to Hebrew. They likewise confirm that the Song of the Three Holy Children (apocrypha) was a later addition.

The Septuagint

For whatever reason, the Septuagint differs radically from the Masoretic text, more so than in the case of any other Old Testament book. The deviations are not so prominent in Dn 1–3 and 7–12, which agree reasonably well with the Masoretic text except for the apocryphal additions (see below). In chs 4–6, however, the difference is at times almost drastic, characterized by expansive paraphrase and many additions. The relationship to the traditional Hebrew text is complicated. The Septuagint is plainly based on another line of textual tradition, and one which we now sometimes (only sometimes) find supported by the Hebrew manuscripts of Daniel at Qumran. Some critics think that the "Prayer of Nabonidus" (cf p 848), discovered at Qumran is related to the LXX variations, at least in ch 4, but there appears to be no firm evidence of that. Others also profess to find the LXX text an "actualization" of the Masoretic text, that is, interpreting Daniel's visions more clearly in the light of Maccabean controversies, but one suspects that the desire to harmonize the texts influences this conclusion.

These deviations were so many and serious that the Early Church apparently repudiated the LXX text for Daniel and substituted the more literal translation of Theodotion. As a result, the original LXX translation was all but forgotten until modern times. For a long time it was known only through Paul of Tella's sixth-century Syriac translation of Origen's Hexapla, and later though the discovery of a tenth-century rendering of the Hexaplaric version, the "Codex Chisianus." The Chester Beatty papyri gave us about one-third of a much better text, and now, with the help of Qumran discoveries, a good share of it can be reconstructed.

The Theodotion Version

Theodotion's text, the one used by most of the Church Fathers (apparently as early as Clement of Rome in the first century) is by no means identical with the Masoretic text either (it, too, includes the apocryphal additions) but is far closer to it than LXX. Sometimes Qumran readings support Theodotion, too, indicating that he had access to a Hebrew text type much closer to the Masoretic text than that underlying LXX. However, since we encounter "Theodotionic" readings in authors who lived earlier than Theodotion, it may be that he did not translate directly from the Hebrew but merely revised some earlier version. Obviously, text critics still have much to learn about the book's early textual history, but one important thing is clear nonetheless: the obvious primacy and authority accorded the Hebrew/Aramaic edition, as St. Jerome would later style it.

Jerome's remarks, in the preface to his commentary to Daniel, are in the context both of praising the church for having preferred Theodotion over the unreliable LXX, and of dismissing some of Porphyry's arguments against Daniel because they were based on the apocryphal additions. Nevertheless, Jerome included the apocryphal additions in his commentary, as he had in the Vulgate translation.

Apocryphal Additions

Three apocryphal additions to Daniel are usually counted, but five different compositions are really involved. They are briefly described here but given full treatment in the section on the Apocrypha, as noted in the cross-references below. There is considerable variation in the ancient versions as to the place of their insertion in the canonical text, but that of the Vulgate is the most familiar. Unlike the apocryphal additions to Esther, these additions do not appear to be deliberate expansions of the original text, but in all likelihood had circulated independently before becoming attached to Daniel.

After Dn 3:24 of the canonical text we meet the first of the three additions, really two originally independent ones combined editorially: The Prayer of Azariah (vv 26–45) and The Song of the Three Holy Children (vv 52–90). See *LBC* 2:134–41.

Easily the most popular of the apocryphal additions to Daniel is the story of Susanna, appended to the book as ch 13 in the Vulgate, but appearing at the beginning of the book in Theodotion. These two ancient translations also have somewhat different versions of the story. See *LBC* 2:116–25.

Finally, at Vulgate ch 14, we have Bel and the Dragon, really two separate tales, as the title suggests. See *LBC* 2:126–30.

DOCTRINAL CONTENT

Summary Commentary

Ch 1 God punishes unrepentant King Jehoiakim of Judah and allows many Judeans to become exiles in Babylon. Yet Daniel and his friends will learn that the Lord is still in control, even though they are in the hand of Nebuchadnezzar (chs 2–6). They determine not to violate God's laws, even though they live in a heathen environment. God, the source of all wisdom, blesses and preserves them in faithfulness.

Ch 2 The many Babylonian wise men are unable to recount or interpret Nebuchadnezzar's dream, and their gods are mute idols. But Daniel is confident that his God will help him recount the dream and interpret it. God reveals through Nebuchadnezzar's dream the final dissolution of all earthly kingdoms. Nebuchadnezzar is impressed with the wisdom Daniel has received from the God of heaven. This gives Daniel an opportunity to reveal more about the true God and His promise of a Savior.

Ancient Christian depiction of the Three Holy Children, wearing loose-fitting Mesopotamian garments.

Ch 3 Nebuchadnezzar builds a golden statue and at its dedication commands all people to worship it. Such worship is forbidden in the First Commandment (Ex 20:3–6). The three youths who did not obey the idolatrous king's command are delivered because God's angel protected them.

Ch 4 Nebuchadnezzar wants others to know how the eternal King has changed his life and so drafts a decree. He has learned that God rules all earthly kingdoms. Daniel interpreted the dream for the king and urged him to humble repentance. Since Nebuchadnezzar went on living as before, God caused him to live like a beast for a period of time. Afterward Nebuchadnezzar praises the King of heaven, who is able to humble those who walk in pride.

Ch 5 Belshazzar hosts a great feast at which he and his guests drink toasts to their idols from the sacred vessels of the Jerusalem temple. God, whom Belshazzar mocks, suddenly shows His presence. Daniel reminds Belshazzar of how God chastened Nebuchadnezzar for his pride. Belshazzar does not learn from this lesson; he is humbled and his kingdom given to another.

Ch 6 Daniel is cast into the lions' den for continuing to pray to the true God. When Daniel is saved from death, Darius issues a new decree ordering all people in his kingdom to fear the God of Daniel.

Ch 7 Daniel has a vision of four beasts coming out of the great sea. He also sees the Ancient of Days preside over a court of judgment and condemn the fourth beast to be burned. Daniel sees "one like a son of man" (v 13) coming with the clouds of heaven, who is given eternal rule over the whole earth. Daniel's visions are interpreted to mean that the Ancient of Days will destroy all earthly kingdoms, and that the saints of the Most High will possess an everlasting kingdom.

Ch 8 In a vision of a ram and a male goat, God assures His people that His sanctuary will be restored. The angel Gabriel explains that wars between Persia and Greece will lead finally to the emergence of Antiochus IV, who will defy God and His people. But Daniel is assured that God has appointed this evil ruler's end.

Ch 9 Daniel fervently longs for the restoration of Jerusalem and the temple. His search of the Scriptures leads him to Jeremiah's prophecy that the captivity would end after 70 years. Daniel is aware that Israel's sins brought God's curse on them. His long prayer is a heartfelt confession of sins and an earnest plea for the Lord's mercy. God demonstrates His love for Daniel by immediately responding to his prayer. The angel Gabriel directs Daniel to expand his vision of the future. Daniel is to think not of seventy years but of seventy times seven and future fulfillment.

Chs 10–12 Daniel continues to grieve over the fate of his people and Jerusalem. Once again, the Lord sends a divine messenger to strengthen Daniel and prepare him spiritually for the word of truth he will hear. The Lord's messenger reveals to Daniel the coming conflicts between Persia and Greece, Egypt and Syria, culminating in the wicked reign of that "contemptible person," King Antiochus IV Epiphanes (175–164 BC). The vision concludes with encouragement for Daniel: Michael is in charge of Israel; the people will be delivered; and those whose names are written in God's book will rise to everlasting life in the end.

Specific Law Themes

Babylon holds Judah captive. Since Judah failed to obey God's voice and has violated God's covenant, the Babylonians defeat them and impose exile, leading to open shame. God reveals to Daniel numerous ominous events that include the profaning of the temple and the abomination that makes desolate. Daniel likewise sees God's final judgment, at which point the wicked will experience everlasting contempt.

Specific Gospel Themes

Throughout the book, the experiences of the Judeans confirm that the Most High God rules the kingdom of men. The Lord keeps His covenant and mercifully delivers His oppressed people. He gives Daniel a vision of His Anointed One, who will rule a kingdom that shall never be destroyed, which is fulfilled in Jesus Christ. Daniel also sees the resurrection of the dead and the promised life everlasting.

Specific Doctrines

Daniel introduced a major figure of prophecy: the "son of man," whom we meet for the first time in Dn 7. Old Testament scholars have discussed the question of whether the son of man is an individual or a collective figure (representing Israel, "the saint of the most high"). Despite the critical favor for the collective interpretation, the individual interpretation is surely the primary intent of Dn 7. The common critical appeal to Dn 7:18, 27 does not contradict this; the Kingdom is, indeed, given to both the son of man and to the saints. There are aspects of truth to the collective understanding. The "son of man," following basic Hebrew idiom, is also *a man* (cf its use in this sense in the contemporaneous Ezekiel), the only true man (not only Israel collectively reduced to one), the last and end times Adam (cf Rm 5), come to redeem mankind from the beast and to restore him to his original, created glory. But first and foremost, the figure is obviously also divine, a transcendent and preexistent heavenly being who is thus in a position to effect such a change in mankind's status. Daniel's prayer of confession summarizes biblical teaching from the prophets generally on the topics of sin and righteousness (ch 9).

The figure is ultimately "messianic" as the New Testament makes plain (the identification further supported by the pseudepigraphical *Book of Enoch*). As even radical criticism recognizes in its perverse way, there is little doubt that "son of man" was designed by the Holy Spirit as a major magnet around which New Testament Christology (and that of our Lord Himself) crystallized, and to which the other component parts of Old Testament prophecy were attracted (the future prophet, priest, and king, as well as the Suffering Servant).

Daniel is also important for his teaching on the role of angels as God's servants and messengers, naming the ranking angels Michael and Gabriel while describing their activities in distinction from other angels (7:10; 8:16; 9:21; 10:13).

Application

As you read Daniel, take to heart the example of this great leader of God's people who devoted himself to God's Word amid the disappointments and temptations of exile. Beware of overinterpreting the symbolism of Daniel's prophecies, a mistake that has led many people into error. Instead, cling to this general message: your God reigns, and He works to deliver you from evil, especially in the gift of His Son, Jesus, the Anointed One (9:24–26).

Ch 1 Daniel and his friends bear witness to the Lord by keeping His Word. The Lord likewise uses the testimony of Christians today to proclaim His saving name and work, even in the most challenging circumstances. When you are tempted by worldly pressures to sin against the Lord, call to mind the example of these God-fearing youths. Your Lord, the Savior, is with you even now, and He will not forsake you.

Ch 2 Daniel is confident that his God will help him. Today, when life's mysteries or challenges threaten you, turn for guidance and comfort to the Lord and His Word. He knows all things and will hear your prayer. We are not able to know the mysteries of God, except what the Father has revealed to us in Christ (Rm 16:25–27). His Kingdom awaits its full revelation at the end of history. Today, pray for opportunities to proclaim the Gospel to others. The true God of heaven blesses and watches over you and will keep you to the end.

Ch 3 Nebuchadnezzar's golden statue was an obvious example of idolatry. Today, the gods we are tempted to worship may take subtler forms: material things, power, self. Only one "image" brings life and salvation—the incarnate Son of God (Col 1:15–20). You have God's promise that "He will command His angels concerning you to guard you in all your ways" (Ps 91:11). You can be sure that His angels are watching over you at all times.

Ch 4 Like Nebuchadnezzar, we need constantly to be reminded that, though earthly kingdoms have great power and authority, the Most High rules. Thankfully, He rules mercifully (cf vv 34–37). He may allow trouble and illness in our lives to discipline us for our good (Heb 12:3–11). When this happens, we may trust His loving purpose and call on Him for strength and healing.

Ch 5 Belshazzar's example is a warning for us all. "Do not be deceived: God is not mocked" (Gal 6:7). God calls for repentance and faith. The fall of Babylon made a deep impression on the biblical writers (Is 21:9; Rv 18:2) and came to symbolize the end of the world. All human history will end. Only the kingdom of God is forever, and He rules for the sake of our justification.

Nabonidus Cylinder records king Nabonidus rebuilding the temple of the moon and the sun gods. Includes a petition for the protection of his son, Belshazzar.

Ch 6 Daniel suffers for continuing to pray to the true God. These events are a preview of God's ultimate triumph over all the forces of evil. Then every knee shall bow (Is 45:23; Php 2:10), and every nation will come and worship the Lord (Rv 15:4). The devil, that roaring lion (1Pt 5:8), means deadly woe, but we tremble not (*LSB* 656)! For Christ is our protector.

Ch 7 Daniel has a vision of four beasts, followed by a vision of the Ancient of Days, who presides over a court of judgment. This judgment scene, repeated in v 26, is a prelude to the final judgment, when all people will appear before the throne of God. The "son of man" is Jesus, fully divine and fully human, Son of Mary and Son of the Most High, whose kingdom will never end (Lk 1:32–33). Daniel was perplexed over what he saw; this may be comforting to us, since we do not fully comprehend God's ways and purposes either. An element of mystery surrounds His promises and their future fulfillment, but we know that God has given us the Kingdom in His dear Son (Lk 12:32).

Ch 8 The vision of a ram and a male goat represents coming war. When trouble comes into our lives, no matter what its source, we also may ask, "How long?" Whether our time of suffering is long or short, we know that God hears our prayers and will help us according to His timetable. Take comfort in Christ's victory.

Ch 9 The pattern of Daniel's prayer of repentance is one that we continue to follow in worship and private devotions. We are confident of being heard because Jesus is seated at the right hand of the Father. God's vision of the future surpasses all our thinking and calculating. We walk by faith and not by sight (2Co 5:7), trusting that the One who kept His promise to send the Messiah, the Anointed One, will keep all His promises to us in His own time and way.

Ch 10–12 That Daniel is strengthened by an angel reminds us of Jesus' experience in Gethsemane (Lk 22:43) and His promise that angels watch over us (Mt 18:10). At times, evil rulers have persecuted the people of God, bringing great affliction on them. But such suffering will be only for the time appointed by the Lord. Believers have always been curious about when the end of the world is coming. Some have tried to precisely determine that date based on the various numbers found in Dn and other biblical books. Jesus made clear that no one knows that day and hour (Mk 13:32; trying to guess the year has led to numerous false prophecies). The angel's advice to Daniel, to "go your way," is good for us all. Know that you are in God's hands, and take comfort that He has allotted a place in heaven for you.

CANONICITY

Critics would diminish the reliability and the authority of the Book of Daniel. However, it seems very unlikely that a writer would have been as deficient in recent historical knowledge as critics assume him to have been. His work would not have achieved any lasting popularity or authority (let alone canonicity), if it were so deficient.

Daniel is not included in the middle or prophetic section of the Hebrew canon (where it was first placed by the Septuagint), but rather appears among the Writings (*Kethubim*). A good case can be made for the antiquity of many of these (e.g., Ruth, Job, Psalms, or Proverbs). It is abundantly clear that canonical position is not directly related to date of composition. Josephus's assertion that the third part of the canon contained only four books (evidently Psalms and the Wisdom Books), all hymnic and preceptive, may even suggest that Daniel was transferred to the Writings at a late stage. If so, the reason may be related to the traditional explanation for Daniel's failure to be included among the prophets, namely, that he possessed the prophetic gift but not the prophetic office. Not only was his office primarily a political or administrative one, but a large portion of his book has a narrative and visionary (apocalyptic) character rather than a prophetic one in the ordinary sense.

A related argument pointed to the omission of Daniel in Ecclesiasticus's catalogue of famous Israelites (ch 44). Some have concluded that since Jesus son of Sirach wrote around 180 BC, that should prove that Daniel had not yet been composed at that time. However, the list in Ecclesiasticus is not exhaustive; another most notable omission is Ezra. Evidence from Qumran has further neutralized such critical suggestions. There are two Hebrew manuscripts from Cave XI, plus fragments from others, including one commentary that refers to "Daniel the prophet" like Mt 24:15. These attest not only to the Book of Daniel's popularity but to its canonical status only a very short time after critics would date the work. Thus we have indirect, but strong evidence of regard for Daniel at least as far back as the third century (with the likelihood then of still earlier roots). If the pseudepigraphic *1 Enoch* 14:18–22 (probably written no later than 150 BC) quotes Dn 7:9–10, as seems likely, we have further evidence of Daniel's early use as Scripture—too early if it had first been written scarcely a decade previously. Other marginally canonical works of the same period also allude to Daniel and his book (1Macc 2:60; Baruch 1:15–3:3; Sibylline Oracles III, 397). New Testament writers and other early Christians welcomed use of the book.

LUTHERAN THEOLOGIANS ON DANIEL

Luther

"Daniel came to Babylon some years before the destruction of Jerusalem, during the reign of King Jehoiakim. King Nebuchadnezzar had had Jehoiakim captured and bound, and would have brought him to Babylon too, had he not changed his mind and let him remain. As it was, Nebuchadnezzar brought some of the best people back with him (including Daniel) as well as vessels from the temple in Jerusalem. We can read all about this in II Kings 24, and in II Chronicles 36. . . .

"From this book [of Daniel] we see what a splendid, great man Daniel was in the sight of both God and the world. First in the sight of God, he above all other prophets had this special prophecy to give. That is, he not only prophesies of Christ, like the others, but also reckons, determines, and fixes with certainty the times and years. Moreover he arranges the kingdoms with their doings so precisely and well, in the right succession down to the fixed time of Christ, that one cannot miss the coming of Christ unless one does it wilfully. . . .

"In the sight of the world, too, Daniel was a splendid and great man. For we see here that he rules the first two kingdoms as their chief prefect. It is as though God were to say, 'I must provide leaders [*Leute*] for these kingdoms, even if I have to let my Jerusalem and my people be destroyed in order to do so.' Though Daniel was never a king, and never had great wealth or honor out of it, nevertheless, he did possess and perform the functions, duties, and offices of a king. That is the way the world operates: those who work most about the place have the least, and those who do nothing get the most; in the words of the gospel saying, 'One sows and another reaps' (John 4[:37]). Indeed, what is worse, he had to take hatred, envy, perils, and persecution as his reward for it all, for that is the reward with which the world is accustomed to repay all services and benefits.

"However this does not hurt Daniel. He is the dearer to God because of it, and God rewards him all the more bountifully, looking upon Daniel as king in Babylon and Persia. For God reckons and judges according to the deed and fruit, not according to the person and name. Daniel is therefore, in deed the true king of Babylon and Persia, even though he lacks the royal person and name, and gets out of it no wealth but only unhappiness and all kinds of peril. Behold how God is able to console and to honor his captive Jews [Judeans], by taking the son of a townsman from destroyed Jerusalem and making him a twofold emperor, in Babylon and Persia. In short, among all the children of Abraham, none was so highly exalted in the world as Daniel. Joseph was indeed great in Egypt with King Pharaoh. David and Solomon were great in Israel. But they were all little kings and lords compared with the kings of Babylon and Persia; and it was among these that Daniel was the chief ruler. He miraculously converted them to God, and doubtless produced great fruit among the people in both empires; through him they came to a knowledge of God and were saved. This is well indicated by the documents and decrees of these emperors that the God of Daniel was to be honored in every land (Daniel 2 and 6).

"This Daniel we commend to the reading of all good Christians, to whom he is comforting and useful in these wretched, last times. But to the wicked he is of no use, as he himself says at the end [12:10], 'The wicked shall remain wicked and shall not understand.' For the prophecies of Daniel, and others like them, are not written simply that men may know history and the tribulations that are to come, and thus satisfy their curiosity, as with a news report, but in order that the righteous shall be encouraged and made joyful, and strengthened in faith and hope and patience. For here the righteous see and hear that their misery shall have an end, that they are to be freed from sins, death, the devil, and all evil—a freedom for which they yearn—and be brought into heaven, to Christ, into his blessed, everlasting kingdom. This is how Christ too, in Luke 21[:28], comforts his own by means of the terrible news, saying, 'When you shall see these things, look up and raise your heads, because your redemption is near,' etc. For this reason we see that here too Daniel always ends all his visions and dreams, however terrible, with joy, namely, with Christ's kingdom and advent. It is on account of this advent, the last and most important thing, that these visions and dreams were given, interpreted, and written.

"Whoever would read them with profit must not depend entirely on the histories or stick exclusively to history, but rather refresh and comfort his heart with the promised and certain advent of our Savior Jesus Christ, who is the blessed and joyful redemption from this vale of misery and wretchedness. To this may he help us, our dear Lord and Savior, to whom with the Father and the Holy Spirit be praise for ever and ever. Amen." (AE 35:294, 313–16)

For more of Luther's insights on this book, see "Preface to the Prophet Daniel" (AE 35:294–316).

Gerhard

"*Daniel, Dani'el,* 'the judgment of God' or 'judged by God.' If what the rabbinic scholars say here and there about Daniel's prophecy is true, it was taken into the canon after the Babylonian captivity but not without some hesitation. After it could not be excluded, however, it was thrown back into the last class of writings of the Old Testament. The Hebrews put Daniel among the *Kethubim,* or holy writings, and they argue at great length whether one ought to include his prophecy among the immediate works of the Holy Spirit or ascribe it to the common and ordinary gift of prophecy. Regarding this matter, one can look at Rabbi Samuel Valerius (introduction to his commentary on Daniel) and Rabbi Joseph Albo (*Fundam.,* bk. 3, c. 10). On the other hand, Galatinus (*De arcan.,* bk. 4, c. 14) correctly advises that we must consider him a prophet. In Dan. 9:23 and 10:11 he is called *'ish chamudoth,* 'a man of desirable things,' so to him may be attributed a name in proportion to the subject matter that was revealed in him. He is also called 'a man most desired,' to show that he is especially dear to God. Jerome (Epistle *ad Paulin.*) calls him 'the polyhistor ['very learned man'] of the whole world.' Epiphanius mentions that his father was called Sabaea (*Haeres.* 55).

"The first part of the book—that is, from the beginning to those words of c. 2: 'The Chaldeans said to the king of Syria,' etc.—is told in Hebrew. The second part, which runs from there to the vision of Belshazzar's third year (that is, to the end of c. 7), is written in Hebrew letters but is written in Syriac, that is, in Chaldaic. The third part, to the end of c. 12, is again written in Hebrew.

"It consists of twelve chapters, the first six of which contain historical material; the latter six, prophetic." (ThC E1 § 155)

FURTHER STUDY ━━━━━━━━━━━━━━━━━━━━━

Lay/Bible Class Resources

Baldwin, Joyce. *Daniel: An Introduction and Commentary.* TOTC. Downers Grove, IL: InterVarsity Press, 1978. ₰ Modern commentary that avoids higher critical and millennialist approaches. Very helpful resource. Laconic in spots; should be used with caution in the visionary chapters.

Bollhagen, James F., Erwin J. Kolb, Ken R. Schurb, and Andrew E. Steinmann. *Daniel.* Leaders Guide and Enrichment Magazine/Study Guide. LL. St. Louis: Concordia, 2009. ₰ In-depth, nine-session Bible studies with individual, small group, and lecture portions.

Deterding, Paul, *Daniel: Encouragement for Faith.* GWFT. St. Louis: Concordia, 1996. ₰ Lutheran author and theologian. Thirteen-session Bible study, including leader's notes and discussion questions.

Jeske, John C. *Daniel.* PBC. St. Louis: Concordia, 2006. ₰ Lutheran author. Excellent for Bible classes. Based on the NIV translation.

Life by His Word. St. Louis: Concordia, 2009. ₰ More than 1,500 reproducible one-page Bible studies covering each chapter of the canonical Scriptures. Page references to *The Lutheran Study Bible.* CD-Rom and downloadable.

Young, Edward J. *The Prophecy of Daniel: A Commentary.* Grand Rapids: Eerdmans, 1949. ₰ Another careful exposition; amillennial. Good, but somewhat dated. Avoids higher critical and millennialist approaches.

Church Worker Resources

Collins, John J. *Daniel. With an Introduction to Apocalyptic Literature.* Grand Rapids: Eerdmans, 1984. ₰ Critical, but helpful on apocalyptic literature.

Jerome, Saint. *Jerome's Commentary on Daniel.* Translated by Gleason L. Archer. Eugene, OR: Wipf & Stock Publishers, 2009. ₰ An important ancient commentary from the translation of the Latin Vulgate.

Leupold, Herbert C. *An Exposition of Daniel.* Grand Rapids: Baker, 1969. ₰ A careful exposition of Daniel, emphasizing the biblical basis for amillennialism.

Porteous, Norman W. *Daniel.* OTL. Philadelphia: Westminster, 1965. ₰ A critical treatment with an attempt to deal with the theological significance of the Book of Daniel.

Academic Resources

K&D. *Biblical Commentaries on the Old Testament: Daniel.* Grand Rapids: Eerdmans, 1955 reprint. ₰ This century-and-a-half old work from Lutheran scholars should not be overlooked. Despite its age, it remains a most useful commentary on the Hebrew text.

LaRondelle, Hans. *The Israel of God in Prophecy: Principles of Prophetic Interpretation.* Berrien Springs, MI: Andrews University Press, 1983. ₰ A discerning study and refutation of dispensationalism.

Steinmann, Andrew. *Daniel.* CC. St. Louis: Concordia, 2008. ₰ Excellent commentary from a Lutheran interpreter. References all recent works as well as important ones from the Church Fathers and the Reformation (Hippolytus, Jerome, Luther, Calvin).

Whitcomb, John C. *Darius the Mede.* Philippsburg, NJ: Presbyterian and Reformed, 1959. ₰ A standard resource from the conservative viewpoint.

Zöckler, Otto. *A Commentary on the Holy Scriptures: Daniel.* LCHS. New York: Charles Scribner's Sons, 1890. ₰ A helpful older example of German biblical scholarship, based on the Hebrew text, which provides references to significant commentaries from the Reformation era forward.

DANIEL AND HISTORY

Critics have long raised questions about the historical reliability of some points in the Book of Daniel. These objections begin with the opening verse, specifically its reference to a Babylonian deportation in Jehoiakim's third year. This article explores these historical issues by describing the critics' concerns and plausible explanations for what Daniel recorded.

The Deportation

Not only was the historicity of the event itself once nearly universally denied by the critics, but they noted a discrepancy in the assertion of Jer 46:2 that Nebuchadnezzar's first year (when such a deportation would have to have occurred) was Jehoiakim's *fourth*, not his third year. The discrepancy is probably easily explained by the different methods of reckoning a king's first year in Judah and Babylon. The event itself, a Babylonian invasion under Nebuchadnezzar (apparently the first of four) in connection with his consolidation of power after the defeat of Egypt at Carchemish in 605 BC, is plainly chronicled also in 2Ki 24 and 2Ch 36. Typically, however, critics were not convinced until archaeologists discovered the Babylonian Chronicles in the 1950s, which confirmed at least the basic outline of the biblical history (though critical doubts remain about details).

The Identity of Belshazzar

Daniel 5:11 refers to Belshazzar as a "son" of Nebuchadnezzar. In 7:1 (cf 5:30) Belshazzar is called a "king" of Babylon. Only in a very technical sense do the objections hold. It is widely accepted today, even in critical circles, that we have nothing more serious here than use of popular idioms (which seem to be characteristic of Daniel in general). "Son" in the generic sense of "descendant" or "successor" is widely attested in the ancient Near East, and "king" is readily understandable in the popular sense of regent or the acting ruler. We now know that technically Belshazzar was a son of Nabonidus, one of Nebuchadnezzar's successors as the result of a plot. Belshazzar served as regent in Babylon during his father's long and frequent absences at the oasis of Teman in northern Arabia. This neglect of his duties contributed to the people of Babylon hailing Cyrus as a deliverer when he conquered the city.

The Identity of Darius the Mede

Much more intractable, however, are the problems occasioned by the repeated references in the Book of Daniel to a "Darius the Mede." For critics this is probably the parade example of what they regard as the writer's gross historical confusion. In Dn 5:31 Darius appears as the successor to Belshazzar, after the fall of Babylon, where we would expect Cyrus. In 6:28 Cyrus appears to succeed Darius, but in 9:1 Darius is described as the son of Ahasuerus, a name otherwise associated with Xerxes (see pp 425–26, 460). The well-known sequence of Persian rulers is: Cyrus, Cambyses, Darius (Hystapes), Xerxes. Along with this, critics pointed out, Darius Hystapes was no Mede, but a Persian. He was a successor to Cyrus who had annexed Media to create the "Medo-Persian" empire.

No absolutely definitive solution is at hand for the way Daniel presents the history. Yet, as usual, more positive readings of the passages are at least possible. Some conservatives have followed the solution proposed by Whitcomb and tentatively seconded by Albright. Considerable evidence is marshaled to identify Darius the Mede with a Gobryas or Gubaru, who was one of Cyrus's main lieutenants in the capture of Babylon and its subsequent administration (the Hebrew indicates Darius "was *made* king" [9:1], a strange idiom for Cyrus himself, and evidently using "king" again in a popular sense). Darius here may be understood as a royal title of honor, comparable to Caesar or Augustus, and

Gold model of a chariot with figures in Median garb
(Achaemenid Persian, fifth through fourth centuries BC).

Gobryas may well have assumed it especially in Cyrus's absence. In this way, 6:28 equates the rules of Darius and Cyrus, rather than asserting a succession. Gobryas may actually have been a Mede, for we know that Medes figured prominently in the capture of Babylon. Possibly the term "Mede" was another honorific title, perhaps singling out that part of the dual name of the empire (Medo-Persian) because of fond memories of the ancient alliance of Babylonia and Media against Assyria. Who this sixth-century "Ahasuerus" may have been (Darius's father in 9:1) we have no clue, only that he cannot have been the fifth-century Persian ruler Xerxes, who lived much later. Perhaps again the Oriental love for a plethora of royal titles is involved.

Other conservatives (especially Wiseman and Steinmann), however, prefer to deploy some of this data toward an identification of Darius the Mede with none other than Cyrus the Great himself. "Darius" may still be regarded as honorific, but we know that Cyrus was actually related to the Medes through his mother, and did bear the title "king of the Medes." "Made king" of 9:1 then would imply God as the agent, and in 9:28 "Darius" and "Cyrus" would simply be equated. In addition, we know that Cyrus was about 62 years old when he conquered Babylon (5:31). "Ahasuerus" as Cyrus's father is no more readily explainable than for Gobryas.

Still others have sought to identify "Darius the Mede" with Cambyses, Cyrus's son, who for a time served as coregent with his father. Obviously, we still await further discoveries in order to arrive at a definitive identification of Darius the Mede.

The Four Kingdoms

For most critics, Daniel's presumed error about Darius's being a Mede is only a symptom of its confusion about the Medes in general. Here a basic interpretative issue throughout the book is broached, namely the identification of the four kingdoms in both ch 2 and chs 7–12. In order to defend the work as applying primarily to the presumed author's own Greek (Seleucid and Maccabean) period, critics are forced to argue that the four empires are Babylonia, Media, Persia, and Greece. But then, of course, they are able to object that there was no independent Median empire between the fall of Babylon and Cyrus's rule (Media as an independent entity flourished as a sort of early contemporary of the Neo-Babylonian empire, preceding Cyrus's meteoric rise). To the conservative this view looks like a classical case of circular argumentation, with the critics only making further trouble for themselves by their misidentification of the four kingdoms. If Scripture interprets Scripture, the fourth empire must be the Roman one at the time of Christ, and the three preceding kingdoms accordingly will be Babylonia, Medo-Persia, and Greece. A *combined* Medo-Persian empire following Cyrus's capture of Babylon fits the historical facts perfectly.

Internal evidence outside of the visions indicates that the writer thought of a combined Medo-Persian entity, namely the giving of Belshazzar's kingdom to the "Medes *and* Persians" (5:28) and Darius's concern with the "law of the Medes *and* the Persians" (6:8, 12).

The Chaldeans

Still another famous and related charge of error to the author of Daniel is his use of "Chaldean." The term is used in a double sense in the book. Its use in an ethnic sense occasions no problems. The "Neo-Babylonian" dynasty to which Nebuchadnezzar belonged was really a "Chaldean" one, originally of a tribe or province of southern Babylonia (just north of the Persian Gulf), but because of its dominance at this time the tribal name was often used for "Babylonian" (e.g., Dn 1:4; 3:8; 5:30; 9:1; cf Is 13:19; 3:14; 48:14, 20; Ezk 23:22).

However, Daniel also uses "Chaldean" in a more restricted sense of "wise men," "intelligentsia," "astrologers," or at least some subdivision of these circles. Since this usage is not confirmed by inscriptional evidence and is found nowhere else in the Old Testament, critics are quick to conclude that its use in that sense here is out of place, that idiom allegedly not having arisen until much later when the genuine ethnic sense of "Chaldean" had been forgotten. In reply, conservatives cite support from Herodotus; writing c 450 BC (closer to the traditional dating of Daniel than to the critical dating of the book) the Greek historian uses "Chaldean" in the same dual sense as the Bible. Not surprisingly, the ruling Chaldean dynasty had apparently quickly put its own men into all positions of authority and influence in Babylon. This would, of course, include much of the priesthood (cf Dn 3:8), wisdom circles, and astrologers (2:2; 4:7; 5:7). Critics have further objected that Daniel would never have been initiated into such an elite caste (let alone made its head), but assuming that this did not involve becoming a pagan priest (something the text nowhere intimates; 2:48), there are no grounds for such an assertion. It should also be noted that Herodotus also supports the account of Dn 5 that Babylon was conquered during a feast, without the inhabitants of the city even knowing that it was taking place.

Food Laws

The critics offer yet another circular argument for late composition of the book regarding the concern of Daniel and his companions in 1:8 for "kosher" food laws and the attendant "separatism" which it evinces. The critics reason that if the priestly portions of the Books of Moses (specifically here Lv 3:17; 6:26; 17:10–14; and 19:26) had not even been composed by Babylonian times, then the Judeans could not be concerned about such food laws. Even if one would agree to their opinions about the dating of the Books of Moses, it would be

847

strange if the Hebrews, almost alone among ancient peoples, had no such ritual concerns at all in connection with food! There is evidence also outside the Books of Moses that such "separatism" predated the exile (Hos 9:3; Am 7:17). Furthermore, food choice is scarcely the only concern at this point. Apparently Daniel and his friends also decline to "defile themselves" because, as was common, the food had been consecrated to idols. Eating it involved participation in a pagan sacrificial rite (cf Ex 34:15; 1Co 8).

Nebuchadnezzar's Madness

A final major complaint against Daniel's historical credibility has to do with the story of Nebuchadnezzar's madness in ch 4. This was apparently a condition known as "boanthropy" in which the afflicted person imagines himself to be a cow or a bull. The argument states that there is a lack of extrabiblical evidence corroborating the story. On three counts, however, the critical argument appears to be inaccurate. Independently from the Bible, we have three ancient notices that appear to point in the same direction: (1) Josephus's preservation of a report by the Babylonian priest, Berossus, that Nebuchadnezzar was "ill" prior to his death; (2) Eusebius's report of another early tradition about strange behavior by the king toward the end of his life; and (3) an inscription from Nebuchadnezzar himself confessing a strange interlude of four years when he did not engage in his usual activities.

Critics had long suspected that the story had originally been told about Nabonidus, the "nature boy" with his extended absences at the oasis in Tema. Unlike Nebuchadnezzar, Nabonidus was despised by his subjects, a situation that could lead to a derogatory legend. Supposedly, the tale was transferred to the well-known Nebuchadnezzar centuries later when virtually all memory of Nabonidus had faded. When in 1955 from Qumran Cave IV a "Prayer of Nabonidus" came to light, it was widely hailed in liberal circles as confirmation of the long-standing critical assumptions. In it Nabonidus, "king of Assyria and Babylonia" (sic), reports that he suffered from a "serious inflammation" for seven years, but when he prayed and confessed his sins, a Jewish priest of the exile came and explained matters to him. Especially in the light of other evidence possibly linking the Qumran community with groups that had returned relatively recently from Babylonia to Palestine, the critics now argued that the Prayer of Nabonidus was evidence for the original Babylonian basis for Dn 4. They asserted that memories of Nabonidus would survive in Israel even less easily than in his native Babylonia, and when they disappeared, the fascinating story was attached to the famous name of Nebuchadnezzar instead.

However, entirely apart from the preference that conservatives would accord the canonical version on dogmatic grounds, it seems fair to subject the

Qumran tale to the same critical treatment given Dn 4. We certainly have no other evidence of Nabonidus's madness, and his description as king of both Assyria and Babylonia scarcely encourages confidence in the document's reliability. It is just as easy to suppose that Nebuchadnezzar's experience was popularly transferred to the despised Nabonidus instead of the experience of Nabonidus being transferred to Nebuchadnezzar. In the light of the other apocryphal legends that were attracted to Daniel, it is quite plausible that Nabonidus's prayer is another apocryphal example. In fact, the differences in the two stories are great enough that one may wonder whether they have any relationship to one another at all! Since the Qumran version is undocumented anywhere else, it is even possible that it was first composed later, in Maccabean times.

Conclusion

As these examples show, there is still much to learn about the Book of Daniel, which describes historical persons and events during a major time of upheaval for large numbers of people. Over the span of Daniel's life, Judah fell to the Babylonians and the Babylonians fell to the Persians. Readers should not rush to judgment and conclude that they know more about events than ancient authors, such as Daniel. Students of the Holy Scriptures should read Daniel on its own terms rather than on the speculative complaints of the critics.

THE BOOK OF THE TWELVE

The Minor Prophets

The Greek title "Book of the Twelve" (*dodekapropheton*) describes a fourth of the Latter Prophets in the Hebrew canon. Jesus son of Sirach perhaps referred to this title when he provided the earliest known description of the collection: "May the bones of the twelve prophets revive from where they lie, for they comforted the people of Jacob and delivered them with confident hope" (Ecclus 49:10; early second century BC). The title "Book of the Twelve" is also better than our familiar translation of the Latin title, "Minor Prophets." In some cases, it does seem that these prophets were "one-theme" prophets or nearly so, in contrast to the many themes covered by the longer Prophetic Books. However, the Latin title makes it sound as though these prophets were less important, which is not the case.

Critical scholars have sometimes pointed to this collection of various Prophetic Books to justify their theories about the works of many writers being compiled to make longer Prophetic Books, such as Isaiah, Jeremiah, Ezekiel, and Daniel. However, the manuscripts demonstrate that the shorter Prophetic Books retained the names of their authors. They did not become incorporated into larger or other books. These facts speak against the theories of the critics and commend to us the traditional view that the larger books of Isaiah, Jeremiah, Ezekiel, and Daniel are the works of those prophets and not compiled from many prophets. (Cf also the theory that the Book of the Twelve was created to correspond to the twelve tribes of Israel.)

We still have no good explanation for the sequence of books in the collection of the "Twelve." Since the books from Nahum to Malachi are nearly in chronological order (Zephaniah is out of place), chronological considerations were likely a factor. However, the Septuagint has a different order that is even less chronological. Whatever the explanation for the sequence, these books were likely brought together because they filled a scroll of roughly the same size as the three preceding Latter Prophets. This would have happened after Malachi wrote his book (c 430 BC), but no more precise date for the collection is known.

A medieval depiction of Christ among the 12 minor prophets, from St. Jerome's *Explanatio in Prophetas et Ecclesiasten*.

HOSEA

You will call Me "My Husband"

Hosea likely lived in the Northern Kingdom of Israel. One of the highest peaks in Gilead is still known today in Arabic as *Jebel Osha* (Mount Hosea) and Gilead is mentioned as part of Israel before Tiglath-pileser II annexed it in 732 BC (Hos 6:8; 12:11). There is a predominance of rural imagery in the Book of Hosea, but that does not confirm that Hosea came from Gilead. In 7:5 there is a reference to "our king" (Jeroboam?), apparently in connection with governmental intrigues in the Northern Kingdom.

Further evidence for Hosea's northern origins is indirect, but scholars do not contest it. For example, Hosea includes themes for the Northern Kingdom: covenant, law, God's love, coolness toward kingship, etc. In contrast, themes for the Southern Kingdom are in short supply (Zion, temple and its sacrifices, Messiah, etc.). Hosea repeatedly refers to Ephraim, which was a common title for the Northern Kingdom drawn from its leading tribe.

Historical and Cultural Setting

During Hosea's lifetime, the Assyrians were close to losing their kingdom to the kingdom of Urartu, located between the Tigris River and the Caucasus Mountains. However, when Tiglath-pileser III came to power (744 BC), he drove back the Urartu armies, and expanded and consolidated Assyrian power. This is the beginning of the Sargonic Age, the last great years of the Assyrian rule, which contributed to the decline and fall of Israel in 722 BC.

This eighth-century Samarian ivory carving uses the common artistic theme of a woman looking out from a balcony. Note the elaborate hair decoration.

OVERVIEW

Author
Hosea the prophet

Date
c 740–715 BC

Places
Israel (Ephraim; capital, Samaria), including Jezreel Valley; Bethel (Beth-aven); Gilead; Judah; nations of Assyria, Egypt, Lebanon

People
Hosea and Gomer; "No Mercy," "Not My People"; Kings Uzziah, Jotham, Ahaz, Hezekiah, Jeroboam, Joash, Jehu

Purpose
Hosea reminds Israel of the Lord's loving faithfulness and calls them away from unfaithfulness to a new life

Law Themes
Israel's unfaithfulness; unfaithful priests and princes; adultery and drunkenness; unfruitfulness; idolatry; conquest of Samaria; stumbling

Gospel Themes
The Lord's faithfulness; children of God; redemption; healing in repentance; God's fatherly love; the Lord answers and looks after His people

Memory Verses
My husband (2:16–17); lack of knowledge (4:4–6); God will revive us (6:1–3); break the fallow ground (10:11–12); bands of love (11:1–4); dew to Israel (14:4–9)

TIMELINE

793–753 BC	Reign of Jeroboam II (Israel)
752–732 BC	Reign of Pekah (Israel)
c 740–715 BC	Hosea written
724–722 BC	Assyria besieges Samaria
605 BC	Nebuchadnezzar besieges Jerusalem

The prophet Hosea has been associated with the region of Gilead.

Hosea wrote about unfaithfulness while the kingdom of Israel strayed after other gods during the long and stable reign of Jeroboam II (793–753 BC) and later rulers. One may cautiously align three subdivisions of Israel's history with three sections of Hosea's book (cf outline below), concluding that Hosea did most of his writing during the last years of Israel. However, one must acknowledge that the book's references to politics are indirect. Hosea 1–3 may reflect the calm days of Jeroboam's stable reign (some would push its extent up to 5:7). Hosea 4–9 may reflect the Syro-Ephraimitic alliance against Ahaz (cf Is 7) or the chaotic conditions of much of that period in general. Hosea 10–14 can be read as originating in the last days of Israel under Hoshea. (The king's name matches the prophet's in meaning: "Yahweh saves.") There are no clear references to the cataclysmic events of the Assyrian conquest in 722 BC, though the reference in 11:11 to return from Egypt and Assyria has been associated with the exile.

Hosea is one of the great eighth-century prophets, including Amos, Micah, and Isaiah. Hosea was the only Old Testament prophet, so far as we know, who was both a native of and active in the Northern Kingdom of Israel, also known as "Ephraim" after its leading tribe. (Amos was active in the Northern Kingdom but came originally from Judah.) Hosea's ministry in the kingdom that fell first might be the reason that he was listed first among the "Twelve." (He is not chronologically the earliest, since the traditional dates for both Jonah and Amos precede him.)

Since Hosea is regarded as a northern prophet, one might wonder why the superscription to his book (1:1) lists four kings of Judah before mentioning only one king of Israel. One may note that after Jeroboam II, Israel's kings did not last long in office (see pp 372–73). Such short reigns and lack of dynasties would make it difficult for northern kings to serve as historical points of reference. From a more conservative viewpoint, it may also be legitimately argued that a northern prophet listed the southern kings first and in great detail, because they alone were the bearers of the messianic promise (cf also 3:5).

COMPOSITION

Author

Hosea means "Yahweh saves." He was the son of Beeri (1:1) and was apparently married to the prostitute Gomer, daughter of Diblaim. Gomer bore him three children: two sons, Jezreel and Lo-Ammi ("Not My People"), and a daughter, Lo-Ruhamah ("No Mercy"). Hosea's unusual family circumstances were central to his message as a prophet. In ch 3, God commanded him to love an immoral woman (presumably Gomer). Hosea bought her (redeemed her from slavery?) and kept her secluded from her former associates. Scholars debate whether the passage about marrying a prostitute was historical reality or an example of symbolism. Because the topic is sexual, some scholars have even attempted to psychoanalyze Hosea, though removed from him historically by thousands of years! Such approaches are best avoided. The simplest explanation for the family drama that Hosea describes would be that it reflects real experiences. This interpretation yields a superb basis for the theological application to Israel's history—the nation deserved exile but the Lord eventually restored a remnant (Hos 1–3).

Date of Composition

The superscription would give Hosea a fairly long ministry of at least 27 years (c 740–715) during which he would have written his book. As the book does not refer to the monumental fall of Samaria (722 BC), he may have completed it before that event. However, one needs to bear in mind that his book does not give direct evidence of historical events.

Purpose/Recipients

Hosea reminds Israel of the Lord's loving faithfulness and calls them away from unfaithfulness to a new life. He focuses his prophecies on the people of the Northern Kingdom, Israel, whom he compares with an unfaithful bride.

Literary Features

Genre

The Book of Hosea may be divided into two major genres. The first relates the story of Hosea (chs 1–3) in prose and poetry. The second is a collection of poetic oracles (chs 4–14). Hosea's style is somewhat unique among the prophets and contrasts greatly with the elegant, classical Hebrew of Amos or Isaiah. It is not flowing and regular, but staccato and jagged. Jerome, the

Early Church Father who translated the Vulgate, described Hosea's writing as broken up by commas and clauses (*commaticus*). Hosea's northern dialect, which differed from the Hebrew used in Jerusalem, would have been less familiar to later copyists. These differences in style and dialect may explain the text-critical problems of the book (see below).

These comments are not meant to condemn Hosea's writing style. He often wrote with striking and effective pictures that appear suddenly and are not developed beyond a bare simile or metaphor. He also included many plays on words.

Characters

The Lord and Israel are major characters in the Book of Hosea, but the drama of their relationship is acted out in the persons of **Hosea** and his unfaithful wife, **Gomer**. She bore him three children: two sons and a daughter. Hosea gave the children symbolic names that illustrated God's attitude toward Israel's present and future: Jezreel ("God sows" punishment), Lo-Ruhamah ("No Mercy"), and Lo-Ammi ("Not My People").

The character of Gomer causes the major debate surrounding the Book of Hosea. Interpreters wonder whether the account of the prophet's marriage to an adulteress is literal, or symbolic (allegorical, parabolic, or visionary) of the country's faithlessness to its "lord" or husband (cf Is 54; Ezk 16, 23). Another aspect of the issue is whether or not Hosea knew of his wife's character before he married her.

The old rule of interpretation that a text has "one *literal* sense" would tip the scales in favor of taking the story literally—and it, no doubt, does so for the majority of both liberal and conservative interpreters. (Usually a text gives indications if the author wants it to be understood in some non-literal fashion.) Among the defenders of a literal intent are Irenaeus, Theodore of Mopsuestia, Augustine, Luther, Laetsch, and probably a majority of modern interpreters. Defenders of an allegorical intent (many of whom one is surprised to find here) include the Targum, Jerome, most medieval commentators, Calvin, Gunkel, Gressmann, von Rad, Young, and many evangelicals. A sort of middle position (really more a subdivision of the allegorical understanding) defends the view that the prophet saw this "marriage" as a vision (Origen, Ibn Ezra, Kimchi, Hengstenberg, Keil, etc.). These examples show us that theology is not the deciding factor in people's opinions.

The major argument for an allegorical, parabolic, or other "spiritual" understanding is that a righteous God would never command a prophet to marry such an unfaithful woman, especially in the light of Old Testament laws (Lv 19:29; Dt 23:17) that exclude prostitutes from the congregation of holy Israel and prescribe stoning for an adulteress. Similarly, then, the argument goes, how could such a prophet have an effective ministry, any more than a modern pastor would under such circumstances? And what kind of an example would that set for God's people?

However, many of the prophets' lives served as action prophecies (e.g., Ezekiel, see p 800), and Hosea fits readily into the pattern. Such behavior would highlight in the extreme a major theological point the Lord wanted to make through Hosea, namely, that God elected and continued to love a people who had not merited His love in the slightest (cf Dt 7:7; Ezk 16). Also, one of the major weaknesses of any allegorical approach is that there are no convincing symbolic meanings for the names of Gomer and Diblaim.

Israelite marriages were typically held beneath a canopy. This painting depicts the wedding of Mary and Joseph.

There is a certain undeniable attractiveness for the centrist view that Hosea was not aware of Gomer's character at the time of their marriage. "Wife of whoredom" in Hos 1:2a is then understood as Hosea's own sad statement about what he learned later about his wife (2:2 is then often understood as containing an actual divorce formula after Gomer strayed from Hosea). But just as God planned to restore Israel after the "divorce" of the exile (cf Is 50, 54), so Hosea later reclaimed his wife. Chastened and repentant, she no longer lusted after her former ways but was content to be faithful to her husband ("lord").[1]

Narrative Development or Plot

The structure of the Book of Hosea may be viewed in different ways. However, the first part of the book (chs 1–3) certainly relates the story of Hosea's family as an illustration of God's relationship to Israel. Gomer marries Hosea and bears his children. He anticipates trouble for the children (1:2–9) as well as a hopeful future (1:10–2:1). At some point, Gomer leaves Hosea. Commentary follows with themes of trouble and hope (2:2–23) as in the first chapter. Hosea redeems a woman and marries again. Apparently, the woman is Gomer. The second marriage is presented as trouble (3:1–4), then

---

1 The double use of the Hebrew *ba'al* for both religious and marital "lords" makes this interpretation easier to hold, and it undeniably is part of the text's *theological* meaning, regardless of Gomer's real character.

OUTLINE

The organization of Hosea presents complex problems. Commentators agree that the first three chapters revolve around Hosea's personal issues. Beyond ch 3, various oracles are added. The following outline provides an overview:

I. Superscription (1:1)

II. Hosea's Personal Issues as Prophecies (1:2–3:5)

    A. Names of Hosea and Gomer's Children Presage Israel's Judgment (1:2–9)

    B. Great Reversal of the Curse (1:10–2:1)

    C. Divorce Proceedings with New Betrothal and Marriage (2:2–15)

    D. Images of Great Reversal (2:16–23)

    E. A Second (?) Marriage to Gomer (ch 3)

III. Various Oracles (chs 4–14)

    A. Yahweh's Lawsuit against Israel (ch 4)

    B. Court Called to Order (5:1–7)

    C. Warfare and False Repentance (5:8–6:6)

    D. Israel's Guilt Congenital, but Not Incurable (6:7–11)

    E. Israel Becomes like All Nations in Apostasy and Judgment (ch 7)

    F. Sow the Wind, Reap the Whirlwind (ch 8)

    G. Days of Festival and Punishment (ch 9)

    H. Israel's Utter Destruction (ch 10)

    I. Possibility of "Second Exodus" (11:1–11)

    J. Israel as Deceiver (11:12–13:1)

    K. Israel's Final Judgment (13:2–16)

    L. Promise of Restoration (ch 14)

Possible explanations for the arrangement are further described under "Narrative Development or Plot" above.

as a promise (3:5). These weal and woe themes then manifest themselves in God's dealings with Israel throughout the oracles in the rest of the book (4:1–5, 15a and 5:15b–6:3; 6:4–11:7 and 11:8–11; 13:12–13, 16 and 14:1–9).

As described above, the book possibly also includes chronological divisions of material: Jeroboam II has relatively peaceful and prosperous last years (chs 1–3); political and economic problems in the Northern Kingdom, as Assyrian pressure grows (chs 4–9); and Israel's last days before the fall of Samaria in 722 BC (chs 10–14). However, the oracles at the end of the book do not correspond precisely to these historical considerations, as the prophet worked his composition to present his theological arguments. For example, consider the division of the following theological accents: accent on Israel's guilt (chs 4–8); accent on Israel's punishment (chs 9–11); and accent on both (chs 12–14), but ending with promise or hope in ch 14.

Resources

A persistent historical and theological theme in Hosea is the exodus from Egypt (2:15; 7:16; 8:13; 9:3, 6; 11:1; 12:9, 13; 13:4). He describes Israel going back to Egypt as a pronouncement of exile and judgment. Remembering that the Lord delivered His people from Egypt is evidence of His mercy, expressed most beautifully in 11:1, which Matthew saw fulfilled typologically in the calling forth of the boy Jesus from Egypt to become the Redeemer of Israel (Mt 2:13–15).

Text and Translations

The state of the Hebrew text is easily the most problematic in the entire Old Testament (followed by Ezekiel and Samuel). We do not have a clear understanding of why this is the case, though some scholars wonder whether it is a consequence of Hosea's northern dialect. Chapters 1–3 are in somewhat better shape than the rest of the book, but that is a relative matter. Of course, many of the problems are trivial and critics have at times exaggerated and aggravated the problems. One should note that only the precise details are ordinarily affected; rarely is the main thrust and message of Hosea at stake. Nevertheless, there is no denying that in many instances the traditional Hebrew text drives translators toward conjecture, causing English versions to differ from one another.

The Septuagint frequently goes its own way. Since there were already issues in the Hebrew text, the Septuagint translators also resorted to conjectures about the meaning of the text.

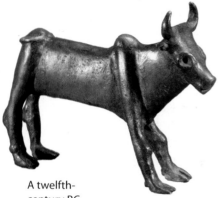

A twelfth-century BC bronze calf found at Samaria.

DOCTRINAL CONTENT

Summary Commentary

Hosea most often presents prophecy that is specifically religious or theological rather than focusing on social ills, as a prophet such as Amos does. Both conservative and liberal interpreters have tended to spiritualize the material, while critics have pursued historical matters to the neglect of Hosea's theology.

Chs 1–3 Hosea dramatically depicts the wretched condition of God's people at that time through the prophet's tragic marriage and the suffering it inflicts on his children (1:2–11). God warns Israel that He will punish her for the idolatrous insistence that Baal will provide for her needs. At the same time, the Lord more earnestly urges Israel to repent and avoid judgment. Despite Israel's complete disregard for the covenant, the Lord promises to renew His marriage with Israel. To this end, He will even marshal creation as His witness and servant (2:14–23). In obedience to the Lord's request, Hosea redeems Gomer and renews his commitment to her, despite her unfaithfulness. This prophesies God's desire to restore Israel as a pure people after the exile.

Chs 4–8 God's judgment against Israel focuses on the priests and their failure of leadership, because they have permitted and even encouraged the people to engage in gross idolatry. God warns Israel and Judah that putting their hope in foreign kings is useless. As long as they continue in idolatry, they may seek God, but they will not find Him; only in repentance can they be healed (ch 5). Although Hosea earnestly encourages Ephraim and Judah to return to the Lord, his pleas continue to fall on deaf ears. Rather than trusting the Lord, Israel's leaders persist in seeking help from foreign nations such as Assyria and Egypt (chs 6–7). Topping the list of Israel's misdeeds is idolatry—their rejection of the Creator and their devotion to calves made of gold.

Chs 9–14 Hosea alternately speaks about Israel's past and future. He reminds the people of how faithfully the Lord has treated His children. At the same time, however, Hosea warns Israel of impending judgment as a result of the nation's apostasy. Even as the Lord continues to speak of His unrequited love and longing for Israel, His firstborn, He anguishes over the people's endless iniquity and willful disobedience (11:1–12:1). Rather than follow the example of their forefather Jacob, who in faith strove with God and so received a blessing, the Israelites of Hosea's day set themselves in a fight against the Lord and so inevitably fall under a crushing defeat. Israel's never-ending idolatry and disobedience provokes the Lord's most violent description of judgment (e.g., 13:16). The overwhelming evidence of Israel's apostasy shows that Hosea's indictment was true. The book ends with a plea for Israel to return to the Lord (ch 14).

Specific Law Themes

Hosea provides one of the most profound presentations of Law and Gospel in all of Scripture. He relates how Israel is plagued with unfaithfulness since they "whore" after idols (4:7–19). Especially devastating is the unfaithfulness of the priests and princes. The prophet describes their activities with imagery of adultery and drunkenness (7:4–5); they will stumble in their sins (4:4–5). The Lord will remember their iniquity (9:9) because they do not remember their Lord. Samaria will be conquered and devastated for its devotion to the golden calves (8:5–6; 10:5; 13:2). As a consequence of the people's sin, they will experience unfruitfulness (4:10). Even if they bear children and prosper, the children will not grow up (9:16).

Specific Gospel Themes

In contrast with the unfaithfulness of Israel's leaders and the people generally, Hosea emphasizes the Lord's faithfulness (2:16–20) and His love, the latter related in the terms "steadfast love" and "knowledge of God" (6:6). The Lord describes the people as His children (1:10–11; 11:10). Although He disciplines them, He will also restore them. Even while the people persist in their sin, the Lord reflects on His willingness to redeem them (7:13). The prophet describes the repentance and restoration of the people as their healing (6:1–2; 7:1a; 14:4). In contrast to the silent idols, the Lord answers and looks after His people (2:21–23; 14:8).

Specific Doctrines

The New Testament cites Hosea more often than any other minor prophet. As a consequence, he is perhaps the greatest among those books. Alongside the themes of Law and Gospel, Hosea's writings illustrate other doctrines. God's people—the Church—are not finally defended by human institutions but by God Himself (1:7). Nor is the existence of God's people dependent on maintaining a certain governance or rites (3:4–5). What God desires from man is deeper, demonstrated in love for God and for one's neighbors (6:6), though this love does not come naturally to people, who are hardened in their wills and must be loosed by God's Word (6:5). A theologian's common description of man's resistant will, comparing it to a hard block of wood, comes from this passage as well as others in the Old Testament (FC SD II 19–23). As God wishes to save us, not destroy us, He softens the wrath we deserve (11:8–9). Our great sin against Him is to trust in someone or something other than Him, our only Savior (13:4, 9). In 13:14, the Lord raises questions that He would address in Christ Jesus, who died and rose to remove the plagues and the sting of the grave for us.

Application

Chs 1–3 Although it pains us to admit, our wealth often begins to lead us into the same failings as those of Israel in Hosea's day, putting our trust in things rather than in the Lord. It tends to dominate our interests at the expense of family, friends, and neighbors. Fortunately for us, however, the God of Israel never wavers in His commitments. God's Law continues to show us our sins and to make us want to be rid of them. Through Christ, all our waywardness and idolatry is forgiven, and a new and all-inclusive covenant has been enacted. Through Hosea's ministry, God shows mercy and pledges to gather, restore, and lead His people into a better future.

Chs 4–14 Today we also see failures in leadership, not only among the clergy and secular leaders, but also in parents. We need to hear Hosea's prophetic exhortations, not only to prevent us from slipping into thanklessness, but also to check our inclinations toward willful sins and outright rebellion. Hear the Father's roar (Hos 11:10)! Tremble and return by faith in Christ, who bore God's judgment for you and for your peace. Offer yourself, your family, and your congregation to the Lord in repentant prayer. Acknowledge lack of control and beg God's forgiveness, restoration, and health. By grace, God's Holy Spirit will enable you to see things aright. He will ransom and redeem His people through His Son's compassionate love.

CANONICITY

As noted above, Jesus son of Sirach remarked on the usefulness of the Book of the Twelve. Jews at Qumran copied Hosea's text as well as a commentary on the book. Matthew cited and applied the Book of Hosea to the life of Jesus (Hos 11:1; Mt 2:15). Its place in the biblical canon has never been questioned.

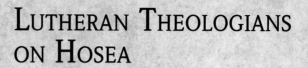

Lutheran Theologians on Hosea

Luther

"Hosea lived and preached, as he himself indicates in the title [1:1], at the time of the second and last Jeroboam, king of Israel. This was the same time in which Isaiah and also Amos and Micah were living in Judah; but Hosea was the oldest of them.

"Jeroboam too was a fine and prosperous king who did much for the kingdom of Israel, as II Kings 14[:23–27] testifies. Nevertheless he persisted in the old idolatry of his ancestors, the kings of Israel. Thus although there were truly many fine men in the nation at that time, they still could not make the people righteous. For the devil had to inflict this misery on the people, that they always killed the prophets and sacrificed their children to the idols, and so filled the land with bloodguiltiness, because of which he here in chapter 1[:5] threatens Jezreel.

"It appears, however, as though this prophecy of Hosea was not fully and entirely written, but that pieces and sayings were taken out of his preaching and brought together into a book. Nevertheless we can trace and discover in it this much at least, that he performed the two offices fully and boldly. First he preached vigorously against the idolatry of his time and bravely rebuked the people, together with the king and his princes and priests. It was surely for this reason that he, like the others, tasted death. He had to die as a heretic against the priests and as a rebel against the king, for that is a prophetic and apostolic death, and in this way Christ himself had to die. Second he also prophesied powerfully and most comfortingly about Christ and his kingdom, as is shown particularly in chapters 2, 13, and 14.

"But no one should think because he uses the words 'harlot' and 'harlotry' many times, and in chapter 1[:2–3] takes a 'wife of harlotry,' that he was unchaste in words and deeds. For Hosea is speaking allegorically; this 'wife of harlotry' is his lawfully wedded wife, and with her he begot legitimate children. The wife and children, however, had to bear those shameful names as a sign and rebuke to the idolatrous nation. For it was full of spiritual harlotry, that is, idolatry, as Hosea himself says in the text, 'The land commits great harlotry by forsaking the Lord' [1:2]. In the same way Jeremiah wore the wooden yoke and carried the cup [Jer. 27:2; 25:17]. Indeed it was common for all the prophets to be doing some strange thing as a sign to the people. So here Hosea's wife and children had to have names of harlotry as a sign against the whoring, idolatrous nation. For it is incredible that God should order a prophet to practice harlotry, as some interpret this passage in Hosea to mean." (AE 35:317–18)

For more of Luther's insights on this book, see *Lectures on Hosea* (AE 18:1–76).

Gerhard

"The first among the minor prophets is *Hosea*. Although his prophecy has more chapters than that of Daniel, yet he yields to Daniel in length. *Hoshea* means 'savior,' and he is so called because he announced salvation to the house of Judah and was supposed to be a type of Christ, the Savior. In *Synops.*, Dorotheus notes that he was born in the town of Belemoth of the tribe of Issachar; Drusius (on Hosea, part 3) reads 'Bethshemesh,' which he lists among the cities of that tribe (see Josh. 19:22). Jerome approves this and writes: 'Hosea was born of the tribe of Issachar in Bethshemesh.' These words are quoted in the *Glossa ordinaria* on Josh. 1:1. His father is called Beeri (Hosea 1:1), but his estate and situation are unknown. The rabbinic scholars have the rule: 'When the name of his father is expressed in the beginning of any prophet, we take it to mean that the father was a prophet.' This rule, however, has not been proved with sufficient strength.

"Hosea prophesied before the Babylonian captivity at the time of King Jeroboam under four kings of Judah: Uzziah, Jotham, Ahaz, and Hezekiah. He was a contemporary of Jonah (2 Kings 14:[25]), of Isaiah (Isa. 1:1), of Amos (Amos 1:1), and of Micah (Mic. 1:1)—all of whom foretold destruction for the kingdom of Israel. Jerome speaks as follows regarding this prophet's style (*Prolog. super duod. prophetas*): 'Hosea is chopped up and speaks as if in [individual] statements.' Augustine, *De civit. Dei*, bk. 18, c. 28: 'The more deeply the prophet Hosea speaks, the more difficult it is to penetrate him.'

"The book has fourteen chapters, and we can divide it into the title and the prophecy itself, which uses both invective and comforting discourse." (ThC E1 § 156)

FURTHER STUDY

Lay/Bible Class Resources

Collver III, Albert B. *Hosea, Joel, and Amos: Faithfulness amid Unfaithfulness.* GWFT. St. Louis: Concordia, 2010. ♪ Lutheran author and theologian. Eleven-session Bible study, including leader's notes and discussion questions.

Eickmann, Paul. *Hosea/Joel/Amos.* PBC. St. Louis: Concordia, 2005. ♪ Lutheran author. Excellent for Bible classes. Based on the NIV translation.

Hubbard, David Allen. *Hosea.* TOTC. Downers Grove, IL: InterVarsity Press, 1989. ♪ RSV, with other translations consulted. Written by an American evangelical scholar.

Life by His Word. St. Louis: Concordia, 2009. ♪ More than 1,500 reproducible one-page Bible studies covering each chapter of the canonical Scriptures. Page references to *The Lutheran Study Bible.* CD-Rom and downloadable.

Norden, Rudolph F. *Hosea: Critic and Comforter for Today.* GWFT. St. Louis: Concordia, 1996. ♪ Lutheran author and devotional writer. Ten-session Bible study, including leader's notes and discussion questions.

Church Worker Resources

Luther, Martin. *Lectures on the Minor Prophets.* Vol. 18 of AE. St. Louis: Concordia, 1975. ♪ The great reformer's lectures from the 1520s, which reflect his mature approach to biblical interpretation. Luther consulted the Hebrew text and reflected on the application of the prophecies and their New Testament fulfillment.

Mays, James L. *Hosea.* OTL. Philadelphia: Westminster, 1969. ♪ Moderately critical. Examines the theory of several strands of authorship; his thrust is on Hosea's message.

Stuart, Douglas. *Hosea-Jonah.* Vol. 31 of WBC. Waco, TX: Word Books, 1987. ♪ Thoroughly conservative, even taking New Testament fulfillment into account. Possibly the best modern commentary presently available for Hosea.

Ward, James M. *Hosea: A Theological Commentary.* New York: Harper & Row, 1966. ♪ Stress on the text and its meaning. An independent (non-series) work, semi-technical, and "moderate" in theological outlook.

Academic Resources

Andersen, Francis I., and David Noel Freedman. *Hosea.* Vol. 24 of AB. New York: Doubleday, 1980. ♪ A very detailed resource, generally conservative, with some departures from common scholarly opinion.

Dearman, J. Andrew. *The Book of Hosea.* NICOT. Grand Rapids: Eerdmans, 2010. ♪ A historical and theological treatment by an evangelical scholar who examies the canonical form of the text.

Ferreiro, Alberto, and Thomas C. Oden, eds. *The Twelve Prophets.* Vol. 14 of ACCS. Downers Grove, IL: InterVarsity Press, 2003. ♪ Citations from Early Church Fathers and other significant Christian teachers.

K&D. *Biblical Commentary on the Old Testament: The Twelve Minor Prophets.* 2 vols. Grand Rapids: Eerdmans, 1971 reprint. ♪ This century-and-a-half old work from Lutheran scholars should not be overlooked. Despite its age, it remains a most useful commentary on the Hebrew text.

Schmoller, Otto. *Hosea.* LCHS. New York: Charles Scribner's Sons, 1898. ♪ A helpful, older example of German biblical scholarship, based on the Hebrew text, which provides references to significant commentaries from the Reformation era forward.

Wolff, Hans W. *Hosea.* Hermeneia: A Critical and Historical Commentary on the Bible. Philadelphia: Fortress, 1974. ♪ An exhaustive, critical work, translated from the German. If adapted with theological discretion, it includes useful observations, especially on linguistics.

JOEL

Rend your hearts and not your garments

Joel's prophecy opens with a depiction of Judgment Day as a relentless locust plague, a terror to a farm-based economy.

Apart from references to the temple in Jerusalem, the prophet Joel gives us very little information about the setting of his work. He describes a great locust plague; however, in Judah and throughout the ancient Near East, locust plagues were recurring events, which makes it difficult to locate the events of Joel in history. As a result, less is known about Joel's historical situation and personal circumstance than for any other prophet. Where facts are lacking, theories and opinions rush to fill in the gap. Guesses as to Joel's date range over more than half a millennium, through the entire history of the Latter Prophets, describing him as one of the earliest prophets to one of the latest.

As shown below, the best solution for dating the Book of Joel is to identify the earliest date after which the text was likely written and let that suffice. However, further analysis is also provided for those who wish to explore the range of scholarly opinion.

Historical and Cultural Setting

Some of the arguments in favor of placing Joel earlier in history, at the time of King Joash (835–796 BC), are the following: Joel wrote after the victory of Jehoshaphat over the Moabites and Ammonites (cf Jl 3:2; 2Ch 20:1–26); Joel mentioned the Phoenicians, Philistines, Egyptians, and Edomites as enemies of Judah (Jl 3:4, 19) but he did not mention later enemies, such as Assyrians, Babylonians, and Persians; appropriate temple practices prevail, as in the earlier period of history (Jl 1:9, 13–14, 16; 2:1, 14–17; 2Ch 23:16–17; 24:14).

Composition

Author

With assurance we can say that Joel was the son of Pethuel (1:1), and that his oracles center on a locust plague affecting Jerusalem and the temple. The strongly liturgical cast of the book might suggest that he was a priest or temple prophet, but that is a guess. Some regard even his name ("Yahweh is God") as merely descriptive and a mark of anonymity, but that is surely speculative.

Date of Composition

A traditional viewpoint, still defended by conservatives, makes Joel one of the earliest of the prophets, perhaps second only to Obadiah, whom they date some 20 years earlier. Because no specific king is mentioned, many dated Joel's ministry in the ninth century under the regency of the priest Jehoiada during Joash's minority after Athaliah's deposition (835 BC; see "Historical and Cultural Setting" above). Among the major arguments was appeal to Joel's

OVERVIEW

Author
Joel the prophet

Date
After the reign of Jehoshaphat (873–848 BC) or later

Places
Judah; Jerusalem; Valley of Jehoshaphat

People
Joel, son of Pethuel; elders; priests

Purpose
To call for fasting and repentance before the day of the Lord, depicted by a plague of locusts and a coming battle

Law Themes
Punishment brought by locusts; the day of darkness; fasting and mourning; judgment of the nations

Gospel Themes
Grace and mercy for the repentant; consecration; the gift of the Spirit; a harvest of blessings; refuge from enemies

Memory Verses
The day of the Lord (2:1–2); return to the Lord (2:12–13); the outpouring of the Spirit (2:28–29))

TIMELINE

931 BC	Israel divided under Rehoboam
873–848 BC	Reign of Jehoshaphat (Judah)
c 848–800 BC	Joel written
792–740 BC	Reign of Azariah/Uzziah (Judah)
722 BC	Samaria (Israel) falls to Assyria

relatively classical style, considerably different from that of many known postexilic figures. That historical argument was buttressed by Joel's location in the Hebrew canon. However, the early appearance of the book among the Minor Prophets does not guarantee that it is earlier in date, especially since we know about other sequences for the books in antiquity (see p 851).

With the rise of historical criticism in the nineteenth century, a late postexilic date became more popular, and still prevails among critics today. Just how late varies, but many are prepared to situate Joel as late as the fourth century, not long before the arrival of Alexander the Great (a few even in Maccabean times). The arguments for a later date are even less conclusive than those for an early one. The major argument for Joel's alleged lateness is the general, universal character of the references; specific sins are not mentioned. There is no denying the observations, but they tell us little about date.

Related to this is an argument that Joel wrote in an early apocalyptic style. However, "apocalyptic" is an exceedingly difficult style to date (see pp 817–21). Another consideration is Joel's preoccupation with matters at the temple, allegedly pointing to postexilic circumstances when little else was left to Judah besides its temple. But the Bible presents such worship as intrinsic to the lives of Judeans during all periods after Solomon built the temple.

Joel's alleged frequent quotation of early prophecy (as these supposedly were beginning to assume canonical status) is supposed to be characteristic of late prophecy. The argument is undercut by indications that prophets in all ages often drew on a common pool of traditional phrases and imagery.

Finally, we may note that it once was fashionable for critics to cite linguistic evidence when arguing that a prophetic book was written after the exile. The discovery of Ugaritic texts and the words they used have now all but demolished that approach because these texts demonstrate that often West Semitic terms were much older than the critics assumed. Somewhat related was

Greek traders brought pottery and other goods to Canaanites and Israelites already in the second millennium BC. This Mycenaean krater (mixing bowl) was found in a tomb at Dan.

the former argument that mention of trade with "Greeks" in Jl 3:6 forced a date near the Hellenistic period, but archaeology has shown that trade with the Aegean region even predated Israel.

Purpose/Recipients

To call the people of Judah for fasting and repentance before the day of the Lord, which is depicted by a plague of locusts and a coming battle. A key verse states, " 'Rend your hearts and not your garments.' Return to the LORD your God" (2:13).

Literary Features

Genre

Joel is written as a series of poetic oracles with prose included at 2:30–3:8. In critical circles, it was widely held (and still often is) that Joel himself was responsible for only the first half of the book (1:2–2:27; the locust plague itself). The latter half (2:28–3:21) was supposed to have been contributed by some later writer ("Deutero-Joel"), who linked his work to the first half by adding a reference to the day of the Lord at four points (1:15; 2:1b, 2a, 11b). Such opinions are mere speculation. The real issue here is the relationship between present and future or between historical events mentioned in the book and those anticipated by its prophecies.

Characters

Two main characters speak in the Book of Joel: (1) **the prophet**, who is the main speaker at the beginning of the book, and (2) **the Lord**, who is the main speaker at the close of the book. Both the Lord and His prophet call the people of Judah to repentance. The object of their message is, first of all, the elders and priests of Judah, along with the people of the land who gather at the temple to fast and pray.

Narrative Development or Plot

Although Joel is not written as a story, one can detect a storyline in the pronouncements from the prophet and the Lord, for whom the prophet speaks. The people are losing their crops with which they worship the Lord at His temple. Although no specific sins are described, the prophet calls for their repentance and prayers so that the Lord might preserve their sustenance with which they worship Him. As total disaster seems inevitable, the people respond to the prophet's message and gather in prayer. The Lord has pity on them and restores the bounty of the land. As the people know and confess

OUTLINE

Superscription (1:1)

I. Catastrophes Current and Coming (1:2–2:17)

  A. The Current Catastrophe: The Locust Plague (1:2–20)

    1. Description of the locust plague (1:2–12)

    2. Call to fast at the temple (1:13–14)

    3. A lament and prayer (1:15–20)

  B. The Coming Catastrophe: The Day of the Lord (2:1–17)

    1. Blow a trumpet in Zion (2:1–2)

    2. The Lord's army as locusts (2:3–11)

    3. Call to return to the Lord (2:12–14)

    4. Call to fast and pray at the temple (2:15–17)

II. The Lord's Response (2:18–3:21)

  A. To the Locust Plague: Healing and Restoration (2:18–27)

  B. To the Coming Day of the Lord (2:28–3:21)

    1. Salvation for the survivors who escape (2:28–32)

      a. All will be prophets (2:28–29)

      b. Ones calling on the name of the Lord will be saved (2:30–32)

    2. Judgment of the Nations (ch 3)

      a. Summons and accusations (3:1–12)

      b. The nations are sentenced, while Judah is blessed (3:13–21)

Him as their God, He also promises a future restoration when He will pour out His Spirit and deliver His people while the world is beset with turmoil and war.

Resources

Joel has some 22 parallels with 12 other Prophetic Books. Because of Joel's many parallel passages, it is regarded as either the original prophetic source or the latest conglomerate of quotations from the other prophets. One cannot tell whether Joel was written before the other books or if Joel was written after them.

A related consideration is Amos's alleged dependence on Joel: there certainly are a number of parallels, and some argue that it was these parallels that led scribes to place Joel in the canon next to Amos. There are also some close parallels with Obadiah, and possibly Jl 2:32 ("as the LORD has said") is quoting Ob 17.

Text and Translations

The text of Joel is well preserved in the manuscript tradition. The ancient translations include some variants but nothing too significant.

DOCTRINAL CONTENT

Summary Commentary

1:1–2:17 Joel summons the people of Judah to assemble and hear the Lord's judgment for their sin: successive waves of locust swarms will come and devastate their land. Then wildfires and drought will dispose of what remains. Desperation and starvation will result from the people's refusal to repent. The locust hordes that God threatens to unleash on Judah will be as devastating as the invasion of a human army. In light of the impending locust plague, Joel urges the people to repent of their sin and return to the Lord, offering the hope that He might yet relent and hold off the disaster.

2:18–3:21 Along with dire predictions about a locust plague and famine, Joel assures the people that the Lord will not abandon them or allow them to be mocked by their pagan neighbors. After the devastation, the Lord promises to pour out His life-giving Spirit. His purpose in so doing is to deliver the gifts of salvation. Prophesying about Judgment Day, Joel announces that the Lord will punish His enemies, while vindicating and finally delivering His people. Given the inevitability of judgment, dreadful punishments await those who reject God and His purposes.

Specific Law Themes

Joel warns the people that God's punishment is coming on them through a plague of locusts that will devour their crops (chs 1–2). He also frequently refers to fire that will complete the devastation (cf 2:3). For sinners, the "day of the LORD" is a day of darkness that should drive them to fasting and mourning. The unrepentant nations will suffer the Lord's wrath on the ulti-mate day of the Lord when He gathers them to a great battle that they will lose (3:1–16).

Specific Gospel Themes

Joel's theme of repentance is one of hope because the Lord promises grace and mercy to those who turn from their ways. Along with the theme of repentance appears consecration, by which the priests set apart the people as holy (1:13–18). The Lord becomes a refuge for them. He promises the gift of the Spirit, that He will dwell in them and work among them from the greatest to the least (2:28–29). The people will reap a harvest of blessings by which to honor their Savior.

Joel prophesied the outpouring of the Spirit at Pentecost.

Specific Doctrines

Theological explanation of history is at the heart of the significance of the Book of Joel. As a matter of interpretation, we are compelled to take the prophecies about the locusts literally, but not for their own sake. These locusts are also symbols for the final judgment—which will be a lit-eral event! Every day is judgment day, but there is also a final Judgment Day to which current disasters point us. Joel thus clari-fies as briefly and classically as any prophet the way we are to view history and the end times. Joel shows that though the Lord may punish His people for specific sins—even sending calamities—that is not His ulti-mate will for them. He likewise may soften or even suspend His punishments for spe-cific sins because of His great forgiveness and love (2:12–13).

The prophecy of Joel is likewise sig-nificant for its promise about the work of the Holy Spirit in the last days, which was fulfilled in the outpouring of the Holy Spirit on the Day of Pentecost (2:28–29).

Through Christ, God gives His Spirit to "all flesh" and not just to the specially anointed leaders of Israel as a chosen people. God and His Word dwell in and work through us.

Application

1:1–2:17 The scorched earth Joel describes continues to have relevance today, with natural disasters and warfare looming ever larger. In our own lives, unchecked sins bring about disastrous consequences. In such times of sorrow and despair, however, never forget that God often uses bad things to bring us to repentance and to accomplish His good and gracious will. The ultimate example of this is Christ's mournful death, which atoned for the sin of the world. Through His Son's death and resurrection, God promises to raise us from the dead and give us eternal life in a new heaven and new earth. When our own sins likewise kindle God's wrath and threaten to bring us under His judgment, consider the question posed by Joel: "Who can endure the awesome day of the Lord?" Thanks be to God, we have a Savior, our risen Lord Jesus Christ, who has already endured God's wrath and judgment for us.

2:18–3:21 To be sure, the Lord will not tolerate rebellion, and He fully expects us to sincerely repent of our sins. When we return to the Lord, He is faithful and just and forgives us of all our unrighteousness. Knowing that the Lord's judgment may come any time, we should remain ever watchful and strive to be ready for that day. By His grace, the Lord enables us to do this very thing, as we call on Jesus' name and trust that He will save us. Repent daily and strive continually to enter by the narrow gate. Receive limitless grace from the One who is the way, the truth, and the life. Through Him, you shall indeed come home to the Father.

CANONICITY

If Joel was written early and therefore frequently referenced by other prophets, that would show substantial regard for this book. The canonicity of the book is affirmed by Ac 2:16–21 (Jl 2:28–32) and by Rm 10:13 (Jl 2:32). See also the comments of Jesus son of Sirach from the early second century BC (p 851).

LUTHERAN THEOLOGIANS ON JOEL

Luther

"Joel was a kindly and gentle man. He does not denounce and rebuke as do the other prophets, but pleads and laments; he tried with kind and friendly words to make the people righteous and to protect them from harm and misfortune. But it happened to him as to the other prophets: the people did not believe his words and held him to be a fool.

"Nevertheless Joel is highly praised in the New Testament, for in Acts 2 St. Peter quotes him. Thus Joel had to provide the first sermon ever preached in the Christian Church, the one on Pentecost at Jerusalem when the Holy Spirit was given [Acts 2:1–16]. St. Paul too makes glorious use of the saying, 'Everyone who calls upon the name of the Lord will be saved' [Rom. 10:13], which is also in Joel 2[:32].

"In the first chapter he prophesies the punishment which is to come upon the people of Israel. They are to be destroyed and carried away by the Assyrians; and he calls the Assyrians cutting, swarming, hopping, and destroying locusts [1:4]. For the Assyrians devoured the kingdom of Israel bit by bit until they had completely destroyed it. In the end, however, King Sennacherib had to suffer defeat before Jerusalem; Joel touches on that in chapter 2[:20] when he says, 'I will remove the northerner far from you.'

"In the second place, at the end of the second chapter and from that point on [2:28–3:21] he prophesies of the kingdom of Christ, and of the Holy Spirit, and speaks of the everlasting Jerusalem.

"He speaks of the valley of Jehoshaphat [3:12] and says that the Lord will summon all the nations thither for judgment. The ancient fathers understand that to refer to the Last Judgment. I do not condemn this interpretation, but hold, nevertheless, that this is really Joel's meaning: even as he calls the Christian Church the everlasting Jerusalem, so he calls it also the valley of Jehoshaphat. He does so because through the word all the world is summoned to the Christian Church and is there judged, and by the preaching is reproved as being all together sinners in the sight of God, as Christ says, 'The Spirit of truth will reprove the world of sin' [John 16:8]. For valley of Jehoshaphat means valley of judgment. Thus also does Hosea call the Christian Church the valley of Achor." (AE 35:318–19)

For more of Luther's insights on this book, see *Lectures on Joel* (AE 18:77–123).

Gerhard

"*Joel*. Some translate *Yoel* as 'beginning,' others as 'the descent of the Lord.' He was born and buried in Canaanite land, in the district of Beth-horon, the son of Pethuel (*Pathuel*), which they translate as 'the breadth' or 'entry of the Lord' or 'God who opens.' He was of the tribe of Reuben. Because he makes no mention at all of Israel and the ten tribes, it is assumed from this that whatever the prophet says is related to the kingdom of Judah and Jerusalem. Jerome claims that he prophesied at the same time and under the same kings as did Hosea. There are some who believe that he followed Isaiah and Hosea, who foretold the devastation of the kingdom of Judah at the hands of the Babylonians, and that he began to prophesy, after the devastation of the kingdom of Israel that Hosea predicted, concerning the kingdom of Judah that would soon be destroyed by the Babylonians. All the circumstances of time show that he prophesied at the time of King Hezekiah.

"The book has three chapters, which contain partly an exhortation to repentance and partly the comfort offered to those who repent." (ThC E1 § 157)

FURTHER STUDY

Lay/Bible Class Resources

Collver III, Albert B. *Hosea, Joel, and Amos: Faithfulness amid Unfaithfulness*. GWFT. St. Louis: Concordia, 2010. ♪ Lutheran author and theologian. Eleven-session Bible study, including leader's notes and discussion questions.

Eickmann, Paul. *Hosea/Joel/Amos*. PBC. St. Louis: Concordia, 2005. ♪ Lutheran author. Excellent for Bible classes. Based on the NIV translation.

Hubbard, David Allen. *Joel and Amos*. TOTC. Downers Grove, IL: InterVarsity Press, 1989. ♪ Compact commentary based on the NIV, with other translations consulted. Written by an American evangelical scholar.

Life by His Word. St. Louis: Concordia, 2009. ♪ More than 1,500 reproducible one-page Bible studies covering each chapter of the canonical Scriptures. Page references to *The Lutheran Study Bible*. CD-Rom and downloadable.

Church Worker Resources

Luther, Martin. *Lectures on the Minor Prophets*. Vol. 18 of AE. St. Louis: Concordia, 1975. ♪ The great reformer's lectures from the 1520s, which reflect his mature approach to biblical interpretation. Luther consulted the Hebrew text and reflected on the application of the prophecies and their New Testament fulfillment.

Academic Resources

Allen, Leslie C. *Joel, Obadiah, Jonah, and Micah*. 2nd ed. NICOT. Grand Rapids: Eerdmans, 1994. ♪ An evangelical scholar writing from a critical perspective. The commentary is generally conservative.

Craigie, Peter C. *Hosea, Joel, Amos, Obadiah, and Jonah*. Vol. 1 of *The Twelve Prophets*. Philadelphia: Westminster, 1984. ♪ An evangelical scholar writing from a critical perspective.

Crenshaw, James L. *Joel*. Vol. 24C of AB. New York: Doubleday, 1995. ♪ Dates the work of the prophet Joel to after the exile. Gives special attention to Hebrew terms and sentence structures.

Ferreiro, Alberto, and Thomas C. Oden, eds. *The Twelve Prophets*. Vol. 14 of ACCS. Downers Grove, IL: InterVarsity Press, 2003. ♪ Citations from Early Church Fathers and other significant Christian teachers.

K&D. *Biblical Commentary on the Old Testament: The Twelve Minor Prophets*. 2 vols. Grand Rapids: Eerdmans, 1971 reprint. ♪ This century-and-a-half old work from Lutheran scholars should not be overlooked. Despite its age, it remains a most useful commentary on the Hebrew text.

Schmoller, Otto. *Joel*. LCHS. New York: Charles Scribner's Sons, 1898. ♪ A helpful, older example of German biblical scholarship, based on the Hebrew text, which provides references to significant commentaries from the Reformation era forward.

Sweeney, Marvin A. *The Twelve Prophets*. Vol. 1 of *Berit Olam*. Collegeville, MN: Liturgical Press, 2000. ♪ Treats the literary structure of the Book of the Twelve as a whole, using critical approaches, then provides specific commentary on each book. Based on the NRSV.

Wolff, Hans Walter. *Joel and Amos*. Hermeneia: A Critical and Historical Commentary on the Bible. Philadelphia: Fortress, 1977. ♪ Analysis of Joel's structure and the setting of his work written from a moderately critical view. Thorough, translated from the German.

An orthodox Jew announces the beginning of a festival with a blast on a ram's horn trumpet (Hbr *shophar*), the most common musical instrument in the Bible, which is mentioned in Jl 2:1, 15.

AMOS

Let justice roll down like waters

Near Tekoa, Amos's home, rounded hilltops suddenly give way to steep valleys, creating an undulating landscape. The ancient town is situated some 12 miles south of Jerusalem on the edge of the wilderness of Judea where today stands acres of Byzantine rubble. Although Amos was a native of Judah, he directed nearly all of his preaching against the Northern Kingdom of Israel and perhaps also delivered a good share of his prophecies there. Why Amos's activity was so one-sidedly northern is not clear. However, his prophecies show that the idea of "all Israel" was never abandoned. Theologically, as well as politically, the Southern Kingdom of Judah continued its claim on the northern tribes.

There are no serious problems in dating Amos. The superscription is not doubted (even if critical scholars believe it to be a later editorial addition). The two kings that Amos mentioned in the superscript reigned at essentially the same time: Azariah/Uzziah of Judah (792–40 BC) and Jeroboam II of Israel (793–53 BC).

Historical and Cultural Setting

The period during which Amos wrote is well-known, both from biblical and Assyrian records. Its background is sketched in 2Ki 14:1–15:7 and in 2Ch 25–26. Archaeologically, it is also the period of the famous Samaria Ostraca, which catalog deliveries of fine wine and oil to the northern capital. Amos's preaching is linked with the politics of the period, especially the policies of Jeroboam II. At this time the Assyrians defeated Israel's old competitors, the Arameans. But the Assyrians were too weak to follow through against Israel. As a result, Jeroboam regained most of the territory Israel had previously lost (as Jonah had predicted in 2Ki 14:25; alluded to also in Am 6:13). He conquered Damascus, the capital of Syria, and even Hamath, a city of the Hittites, about 200 miles north of Damascus. In the Southern Kingdom, Uzziah subdued the Philistines, made vassals of the Amorites, built strong outposts in the Judean wilderness, fortified Jerusalem with towers, and maintained a large standing army. Jeroboam and Uzziah maintained peace with one another and independently regained much of the former Davidic empire for their separate kingdoms.

Economically, Israel prospered because it did not yet have to face the Assyrians. These days of peace and prosperity were similar to the golden era of the united kingdom under David and Solomon. Citizens concluded that this prosperity must be a sure sign of God's favor and blessing and that a greater "day of the Lord" (cf Am 5:18–20) must be just around the corner. But underneath the prosperity Amos saw only rot. This was not primarily social and economic, as the secular-minded scholars read it, but religious and covenantal. When everything was prospering

OVERVIEW

Author
Amos the prophet

Date
c 792–740 BC

Places
Judah; Jerusalem; Zion; Israel; Samaria; Bethel; Gilgal; Dan; Syria

People
Uzziah; Jeroboam; Joash; Ben-hadad; Amaziah

Purpose
To warn Israel and Judah that God would punish them for injustice and for idolatry, though a remnant would be saved

Law Themes
The nations condemned; the Lord as a lion; only a remnant; unfaithful worship; the day of the Lord

Gospel Themes
The remnant; seek the Lord and live; the booth of David; restoration of Israel; the Lord relents

Memory Verses
Let justice roll down (5:21–24); the fortunes of Israel restored (9:13–15)

TIMELINE

793–753 BC	Reign of Jeroboam II (Israel)
c 792–740 BC	Amos written
752–732 BC	Reign of Pekah (Israel)
724–722 BC	Assyria besieges Samaria
605 BC	Nebuchadnezzar besieges Jerusalem

The Ugaritic alphabet written with cuneiform symbols. Developed c fifteenth century BC.

externally, the Lord called Amos to preach that Israel's current heresy—adding to the long series of precedents—was finally filling the cup of God's wrath to overflowing. No prophet portrays the impending doom with greater darkness. Critics usually minimize the little bit of promise the book does contain, but, no doubt, it was not a time for a message of hope.

COMPOSITION

Author

The name Amos, used in the Bible only for this prophet, comes from a root meaning "to bear" or "to place a load upon." The name may describe his experience as a prophet, given the bleak and unwelcome message God called him to share.

"Shepherds" in Am 1:1 translates a rare Hebrew word, used elsewhere in the Bible only in 2Ki 3:4 of King Mesha of Moab. Since the root is found in Ugaritic describing those who had charge of a shrine's flocks, some researchers have suggested that Amos was also a sanctuary worker. However, Amos described himself in 7:14b as a "herdsman and dresser of sycamore figs," which would indicate that "shepherd" should be taken in its ordinary sense as a farm worker. At most, the use of the rare word for shepherds would indicate that Amos worked on estates or plantations owned by the temple.

Amos's Ministry

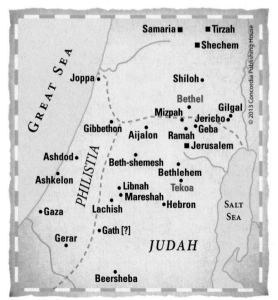

© 2013 Concordia Publishing House

God called Amos especially to "prophesy" (7:15). His comment (7:14a) that he was "no prophet, nor a prophet's son" (which has also spawned much debate) would seem to mean that he was no *professional* prophet. He did not come from a hereditary guild or company of prophets (cf 1Sm 10:5; 19:20). We have no account of Amos's call, though the visions in Am 7–9 are widely suspected to preserve some of that information (cf also the "lion's roar" in 3:8). Besides a possible reference to people opposing him (5:10), we have the account of Amos's clash with

Amaziah, priest of Bethel, in 7:10–17 and his apparent expulsion from the North (7:13).

We cannot tell whether the oracles in the book are in chronological order, so we do not know when Amos was expelled from the North. As a result, we also do not know how much or what part of his ministry was actually carried out on northern soil. Neither can we guess how long he served as a prophet, though most interpreters suppose that it was relatively short. There is no other personal information, and no clue to his manner of death.

Compared to other prophets, critics have been quite gentle with Amos. They found him congenial to their own views, as they understood him. They attributed the entire book to Amos except for the following portions: (1) two or three of the initial Gentile oracles, especially the one against Judah (Am 2:4–5); (2) the three creation doxologies in the book (4:13; 5:8–9; 9:5–6); and (3) the concluding promise about the Messiah (9:11–15). At one time rejection of the messianic oracle was virtually a test for whether one was a proper critic, but recent times have seen an increasing number of defections from that view.

Date of Composition

Amos probably wrote in the decade 760–750, just before the middle of the eighth century. That places him just after the activity of Jonah (2Ki 14:25) and just before the ministry of Hosea. With further information, we may someday be able to date the prophecies more precisely since Amos mentioned that he recorded them during the "two years before the earthquake" (1:1). This earthquake must have been unusually severe, because it apparently is the same one alluded to much later in Zec 14:5, and we also now know it archaeologically from the excavations at Hazor.

Some scholars have tried to link Am 8:9 with a solar eclipse known from Assyrian records to have occurred on June 15, 763 BC. But Amos's wording in the passage does not allow us to establish that he was referring to the same event.

The eighth-century remains of Hazor (stratum VI) have earthquake damage.

Purpose/Recipients

Amos wrote stringent rebukes of ritualism and temple abuses in Israel and Judah. He likewise sharply attacked the social abuses that prevailed in an era of prosperity in order to warn the people and call them to repentance. His prophecies are almost totally about judgment with the exception of his sparkling conclusion, which caps the prophecies with hope in God's Messiah.

Literary Features

Genre

Amos's rural background does not mean that he was uneducated. Rural imagery is prominent enough in the book, but its language is pure and superb classical Hebrew (possibly second only to Isaiah's). The book is a series of pronouncements and visions from the Lord, mostly poetry with brief prose. The poetic style exhibits classical simplicity, the oracles are carefully balanced, and there is a discernible unity of design throughout.

The literary style of Amos is stimulating because he crafted his message with expressive references to nature and rural life:

Overloading a wagon describes sinners straining God's mercy (2:13).

The roaring of a lion describes the pressure the Lord placed on His prophet (3:8).

A shepherd finding parts of a devoured sheep describes how the Lord will recover a remnant of Israel (3:12).

Pulling a stick from a fire illustrates Israel's narrow escape from total destruction (4:11).

The constellations demonstrate God's majesty (5:8).

Ripe summer fruit illustrates how soon the nations would decay (8:1).

Characters

Significant characters in Amos are the various nations against which he pronounced judgment. He singled out one outstanding sin for each nation while using a formulaic statement to indicate that there were further offenses ("For three transgressions . . . and for four"; 1:3, etc.). For example, Amos denounced Syria for cruelty (1:3–5), Philistia for slave trade (1:6–8), Phoenicia for truce-breaking (1:9–10), Edom for refusing to make peace (1:11–12), Ammon for aggression (1:13–14), and Moab for vengeance (2:1–3). Finally, he reached the chief objects of his prophecies. He denounced Judah for idolatry (2:4–5) and Israel for pride (2:6–16) and focused on these two nations for the remainder of the book.

The prophet famously denounced the arrogant Israelite women as "cows of Bashan" (4:1). He described his confrontation with Amaziah, the priest at the idolatrous shrine of Bethel, who reported him to King Jeroboam (7:10–17). This incident likely caused Amos to be expelled from the North.

The chief speaker and character in the prophecies is the Lord, who roars His judgment (3:8), grieves over His people's sin (5:1–25), and appeals for their repentance (5:4, 6, 14). He reminds them of the other nations He has destroyed as well as His special relationship to the nation that He rescued from Egypt (3:2).

Narrative Development or Plot

Because the Book of Amos is a collection of pronouncements and visions, it does not have a storyline or plot. However, the opening series of prophecies against the nations moves in a circle, addressing those nations around Israel/ Judah before pouncing on them as the main subjects. There is a brief story of Amaziah, the priest of Bethel, confronting Amos for his prophecy about King Jeroboam (7:10–17), which concludes with the Lord's pronouncement of judgment against Amaziah and Israel.

The book does end with a twist. In the middle of ch 9, it turns sharply away from the themes of judgment to declare the restoration of Israel in the messianic age.

Resources

Amos championed the teachings of Moses. Many of Amos's points were also anticipated by Samuel, Elijah, and other prophets reported in the former Prophetic Books. Regardless of questions about Amos's precise relations with other prophets, he remains a classical example of some of the major themes of prophecy before Israel went into exile, and one of the first prophets for whom we have detailed records. Amos is commonly referred to as the "prophet of justice" (Hbr *mishpat*), and that accent is often compared with those of other eighth century prophets, such as Isaiah's stress on holiness and Hosea's on love.

Text and Translations

Amos's clear, pleasing style perhaps relieved copyists from having problems with the book; text-critical questions are few. Mischief easily begins, however, with translating an important term in the book: "justice." This happens simply because there is no adequate English equivalent for Hbr *mishpat*. The older translation "judgment" is not much better. (Here is an example of the

OUTLINE

Superscription (1:1–2)

I. Judgments against the Nations (1:3–2:16)
  A. Syria (1:3–5)
  B. Philistia (1:6–8)
  C. Tyre (1:9–10)
  D. Edom (1:11–12)
  E. Ammon (1:13–15)
  F. Moab (2:1–3)
  G. Judah (2:4–5)
  H. Israel (2:6–16)

II. Declarations concerning Israel (chs 3–6)
  A. Accusations Lodged against Israel (chs 3–4)
    1. Yahweh's exclusive relationship with Israel (3:1–2)
    2. Prophecy verified (3:3–8)
    3. Proclamation concerning Israel's guilt and punishment (3:9–15)
    4. Condemnation of the rich women of Israel (4:1–3)
    5. Indictment of sacrificial sins (4:4–5)
    6. Failure to respond to Yahweh's rebuke (4:6–13)
  B. Lamentation for Israel (5:1–3)
  C. Exhortation to Seek Yahweh (5:4–17)
  D. Judgment on the Day of Yahweh (5:18–6:14)
    1. The day of Yahweh (5:18–20)
    2. Detestable ritual practices (5:21–27)
    3. Warning to the secure and complacent (6:1–7)
    4. Certain destruction for the prideful house of Israel (6:8–14)

III. Visions (chs 7–9)

 A. Visions That Do Not Come to Pass (7:1–6)

  1. Vision of the locusts (7:1–3)

  2. Vision of the fire (7:4–6)

 B. Visions That Do Come to Pass (7:7–9:10)

  1. Vision of the plumb line (7:7–9)

  2. Historical interlude (7:10–17)

  3. Vision of the summer fruit (8:1–14)

  4. Vision of the Lord beside the altar (9:1–10)

 C. Restoration of David's Booth (9:11–15)

frequent impossibility of fully translating a term and of the need for knowledge of the original languages.) The major problem is that Amos's "justice" is inevitably heard in the modern secular sense as a universal ideal toward which all good men will strive. To hear biblical vocabulary in that sense is simply to distort it, and transform it into a totally different creature.

One can scarcely stress too much that the biblical term "justice" (Hbr *mishpat*) and its synonym "righteousness" are not only ethical and "religious" but include one's standing before the eternal God. Defining justice and meeting its requirements in a fully God-pleasing manner are gifts of His covenantal grace, no matter how the biblical ideals compare with morals in other cultures. "Justice" is *solely* a result of God's "judgments" pronounced from His heavenly court, and one's response to them reveals whether the ultimate judgment is saving or damning. God's justice calls for salvation plus response, or justification as well as sanctification.

Bowls were used for drinking parties (Am 6:6), similar to the Greek symposia. This glass bowl, possibly eighth century BC Phoenician, was found in a hoard of goods at Nimrud.

Doctrinal Content

Summary Commentary

Chs 1–2 Amos denounces the nations surrounding Judah and Israel and threatens them with fiery judgment and political defeat. Like its unbelieving neighbors, Judah is guilty of listening to false prophets and worshiping in ways unbecoming the one true God. Likewise, Amos accuses Israel of breaking virtually every part of the covenant. The people worship other gods, withhold justice from the innocent, and shamefully exploit the poor and vulnerable.

Chs 3–6 Because Israel has completely abandoned the covenant—through worshiping idols, perpetrating injustice, and showing indifference to the poor—the Lord threatens to allow an invading enemy to wreak havoc on the land. The prophecy intersperses vivid descriptions of divine judgment with the divine lament "yet you did not return to Me." The Lord sings a funeral dirge over impenitent Israel, for He is soon to come in judgment against the nation for abandoning the covenant. The people of Israel are living under the delusion that their prosperity is a sign of God's approval and that their perfunctory offering of sacrifices is keeping the Lord satisfied, even though they act unjustly and honor other gods. God's first expectation has ever been and will always be "You shall have no other gods before Me" (Ex 20:3).

Samarian ostracon found in the treasury of King Ahab of Israel. Potsherds were used for book-keeping.

Chs 7–9 By means of symbolic visions involving locusts, fire, and a plumb line, the Lord warns His people that He will punish their apostasy. However, these threatening visions, Amos's repeated intercessions on behalf of the people, and God's forbearance did not drive them to repentance. Amaziah the priest rebukes Amos and orders him out of Israel. The prophet responds by uttering some of his most chilling words of judgment. Amos does so with good reason for, on top of all their other sins, the people of Israel have now dared to openly despise the prophetic word even as it is being spoken to them. His next vision, the basket of summer fruit, points again to the Lord's judgment that will soon cut down the people of Israel for their idolatrous worship, their greed, and their callous mistreatment of their brethren. In his fifth and final vision report, Amos makes two main points: (1) Because Israel has abandoned the covenant, it has forfeited its claim to a privileged status before God. Thus the nation will be destroyed, leaving only a tiny remnant. (2) Yet the Lord provides a means of escape. Amos's prophecy unexpectedly ends with a word of hope. A day of rich blessing is coming, for the Lord will fulfill His covenant promises, bring about restoration, and establish the eternal kingdom of His Messiah.

Specific Law Themes

Amos pronounces God's judgment upon the pagan nations around the Near East before condemning Judah and Israel with them (chs 1–2). The Lord presents Himself as an angry lion that would devour the people and recounts how He destroyed other nations that rebelled against Him in the past (chs 3–4). The people take fatal confidence in their offerings and other elements of their worship, which only condemn them further (chs 5–6). They expect that the "day of the LORD" will be "light" for them, whereas Amos announces that it will be only darkness (5:18).

Specific Gospel Themes

The Book of Amos leaves very little room for Gospel themes. However, one can see them in the account of the remnant since at least a portion of the people will survive. The Lord continues to call them to repentance, emphasizing His gracious nature. Amos 9:11–15 is the brightest moment, when the Lord promises to restore "the booth of David" (9:11; a messianic image for the house of David, which is fulfilled in Jesus of Nazareth). He promises to relent from finally destroying the people (9:15).

Specific Doctrines

Amos's theme of "justice" brings to focus the Lutheran concern that the two aspects of God's reign be properly distinguished as Law and Gospel. Amos is a major reminder that those principles are derived from Scripture. The interpreter must use Law and Gospel to grasp and expound properly what Scripture says about itself. Specifically, the "church" and "state" components that were combined in the Old Testament theocracy must be carefully distinguished in the New Testament "kingdom of grace." The justice that the Church proclaims is that *sacrificial* "justice" we have in the covenant with Christ. In the Gospel alone we escape condemnation, no matter how fine a moral code we pursue.

The persistent grace of God is not an obvious theme in Amos. However, in canonical context, it is hidden everywhere and informing everything, and becomes clear especially in the prophet's accent on election (cf Am 3:2).

Amos does, of course, heavily accent the importance of Israel and Judah as "state," the kingdom of God's power where His love can manifest itself only through the rule of law. Amos emphatically reminds us that we, too, still live in God's kingdom of power and have responsibilities before God here.

Application

Chs 1–5 Through the prophet Amos, the Lord roars for justice among the nations. Seeing those around us condemned might tempt us to be smug, though it ought to show us that unless we repent and do what is right, the same fate can befall us. Vices destroy our communities today, despite the great blessings we have enjoyed from God's hand. God calls His Church today to repentance precisely because He wishes to avert the shame and sorrow that will inevitably result when we take the way of selfishness and greed. He daily calls us to receive anew the forgiveness Christ won for us. Amos teaches us that grace and faith are the true basis for worship and a right relationship to the Lord. His invitation ever stands: "Come to Me, all who labor and are heavy laden, and I will give you rest" (Mt 11:28).

Chs 6–9 As happened in Judah and Israel, people today interpret material prosperity as a sign that they need not humble themselves and turn away from complacency. They are just as slow to heed God's Word and are equally intractable in their bad behavior. This scenario reminds us just how dangerous it is to ignore God's Word and to defy those sent to call us to repentance. Though guilty ourselves of similar failings, we take comfort in Christ's loyalty and unbounded forgiveness. His death has paid the debt of our rebellion, and His resurrection assures us that even as He lives, so also shall we. Treasure the Word! As the conclusion to Amos shows, our God is gracious and continually stands ready to receive the repentant heart and lift it up with His Word of forgiveness and peace in Jesus, great David's greater Son.

CANONICITY

The canonicity of Amos has never been questioned and is affirmed by the following New Testament references: Ac 7:42 (Am 5:25) and Ac 15:15–17 (Am 9, 11–12). See also the quotation from Jesus son of Sirach about the Book of the Twelve (p 851).

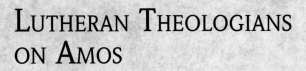

LUTHERAN THEOLOGIANS ON AMOS

Luther

"Amos [1:1] does specify his time: he lived and preached in the days of Hosea and Isaiah. He attacks the same vices and idolatry, or false sanctity, as does Hosea, and he also forewarns of the Assyrian captivity.

"He is violent too, and denounces the people of Israel throughout almost the entire book until the end of the last chapter, where he prophesies of Christ and his kingdom and closes his book with that. No prophet, I think, has so little in the way of promises and so much in the way of denunciations and threats. He can well be called Amos, that is, 'a burden,' one who is hard to get along with and irritating, particularly because he is a shepherd and not one of the order of prophets (as he himself says in chapter 7[:14]). Besides he comes out of the land of the tribe of Judah, from Tekoa, into the kingdom of Israel, and preaches there as a foreigner. It is for this reason that they say the priest Amaziah, whom he rebukes in chapter 7[:10–17], beat him to death with a club.

"In the first chapter Amos is difficult and obscure, where he speaks of three and four sins. Many have knocked themselves out over it, struggling with it at great length. But the text, I believe, shows clearly that these three and four sins are but one sin. For he always names and cites only one sin. Against Damascus, for example, he names only the sin that 'they have threshed Gilead with iron chariots,' etc. [1:3].

"But Amos calls this sin 'three and four' because the people do not repent of the sin or acknowledge it; rather they boast of it and rely upon it as though it were a good deed, as false saints always do. For a sin cannot become more grave, great, or weighty than when it tries to be a holy and godly work, making the devil God and God the devil. So, too, three and four make seven, which is the completeness of numbers in the Scriptures, where one turns back and begins to count again, both the days and the weeks.

"Amos is quoted twice in the New Testament. The first time is in Acts 7[:42–43], where Stephen cites Amos 5[:25–27] against the Jews and shows by it that the Jews have never kept God's law from the time they first came out of Egypt. The second time is in Acts 15[:16–17], where St. James in the first council of the apostles quotes from the last chapter of Amos [9:11–12] as a proof of

Christian liberty, that the Gentiles under the New Testament are not bound to keep the laws of Moses which the Jews themselves have never kept and could not keep, as St. Peter preaches in Acts 15[:10]. These are the two most important bits in Amos, and they are two very good bits." (AE 35:320–21)

For more of Luther's insights on this book, see *Lectures on Amos* (AE 18:125–90).

Gerhard

"Amos (*'Amos*) means 'burden.' He is called this because he is a vehement prophet who foretold to the people a harsh burden, that is, serious punishment, because of their wickedness. In his German preface, Luther renders it 'burdened with rebukes' (cf. AE 35:320; WA DB 11/2:227). Because of this, he immediately says in the inscription *debre 'Amos*, as if he were saying 'heavy words,' 'which the land does not endure,' as Amaziah would say in false accusation (Amos 7:10). Jerome translates it as *bastazon* ['bearing']. The Latin prologue on this prophet says that he is called 'burdened' because he 'is filled with spiritual grace.' Yet it is inappropriate to call grace a burden. Rabbi Phinees gives as an explanation for his name that 'he had a burdened or hindered tongue.' This comes, however, from an uncertain tradition.

"Amos was born in the town of Tekoa in the tribe of Judah, which was six miles south of Bethlehem. Although he was a shepherd, he became a prophet (Amos 1:1; 7:14). He prophesied at the time when Uzziah, otherwise called Azariah, was ruling the kingdom of Judah and when Jeroboam, son of Joash, was controlling the government of the kingdom of Israel. Therefore he was a contemporary of Isaiah and Hosea but was later than Jonah with regard to time.

"Jeroboam, whom [Amos] had rebuked because of the two golden calves, killed him by piercing his temples with a spike.

"The principal theme of the prophecy is that it foretells the overthrow of the kingdom of Israel, for he specifically prophesied to the kingdom of Israel or the ten tribes, as is apparent from Amos 1:1; 3:1; 4:1; 5:1. He expresses few words regarding the kingdom of Judah, and these in passing (Amos 2:4; 6:1).

"It consists of nine chapters altogether, which can be divided into two parts. The first is the general inscription (Amos 1:1). The second is the prophecy itself, which contains the threats of the Law directed partly against the foes of God's people (Amos 1:[2]–2:[3]), partly against the people of Judah (Amos 2:4–5), partly against the Israelites (Amos 2:6–9:[10]), and, finally, consolations of the Gospel (Amos 9:11–15)." (ThC E1 § 158)

Is God the Author of Evil?

Amos 3:6 asks: "Is a trumpet blown in a city, and the people are not afraid? Does disaster come to a city, unless the LORD had done it?"

Deuteronomy 32:4 asserts: "The Rock, His work is perfect, for all His ways are justice. A God of faithfulness and without iniquity, just and upright is He."

Is God the highest, purest, and best Being imaginable? Scripture answers yes in a number of places. How shall we harmonize these passages that apparently describe God as the author of evil with this biblical teaching? Texts of this nature, besides Am 3:6, are Is 45:7, Jer 18:11, 2Th 2:11–12, and others. Several important truths must be pointed out. We must bear in mind, in the first place, that the Amos passage alludes not to *moral* wrong, but to *physical* calamities, earthquakes, storms, and the like. These afflictions could not befall a city if God, the Ruler of the universe, did not allow them. And let no one imagine that it militates against His holiness and goodness when He permits these catastrophes to overwhelm a city or country. Sometimes God uses them to punish evildoers and chasten His children for their own good. These visitations serve His own great purposes, the glory of His name and the welfare of people, inasmuch as they urge people to repent of their sins. In regard to these matters we are in the position of children to whom some of the things their father does seem cruel and indefensible until they gradually grasp the meaning of sin and its consequences (cf Heb 12:5–11). Some people say, "If God were kind and good, He would never send famines, plagues, storms, and wars." They do not consider that this is a sinful world, in which there must be punishment and correction. Here, then, there is no difficulty.

A more baffling question is, "What is the relationship of God to moral evil? If our Lord did not give the robber air to breathe and food and drink to strengthen his body, his robberies could not be committed." This no one can deny. But does this fact show that God approves of the evil deeds of this man? Surely not. "He makes His sun rise on the evil and on the good, and sends rain on the just and on the unjust" (Mt 5:45), even though the unjust employ the means of sustenance for carrying out their sinful designs. God permits wrongs to be done, but He does not sanction them. God treats people as responsible beings and does not by means of His almighty power hinder the execution of their wicked plans until the time He has allotted them is ended. But He pleads with them to repent. In all these situations there is nothing that could be urged against the holiness of God.

Perhaps the weightiest question remains. Does not the Bible say that God now and then does more than merely permit moral evil? Does it not say that on certain occasions He even causes it? A text that is especially quoted in this connection is 2Th 2:11–12: "Therefore God sends them a strong delusion, so that they may believe what is false, in order that all may be condemned who did not believe the truth but had pleasure in unrighteousness." "God sends them a strong delusion" simply means that He will withdraw His restraining hand and permit Satan to make his vicious attacks. God will at times let people fall into sins and errors; but in every such case this action of God is a punishment inflicted for willful departure from, and rejection of, the truth. Among the clearly revealed ways of God is this one, that He punishes wrongdoing by permitting people to lapse into deeper and more reprehensible sin. An important text to note is Rm 1:24–32, where Paul ascribes the moral corruption of the unbelieving world to God's just judgment for the suppression of the truth given them and for the idolatry which they indulged in. There is no conflict here between the various attributes of God. The Lord is both good and just. The judge in a criminal court may in the course of a year condemn several criminals to be executed and still be a very kindhearted person. Goodness and justice are parallel virtues; one does not exclude the other. We should remember that whenever sinful deeds are said to have been caused by God, His retributive or punitive justice is referred to, which made Him cease restraining the sinner. Hence we no longer regard the texts listed above as disagreeing with each other.

FURTHER STUDY

Lay/Bible Class Resources

Collver III, Albert B. *Hosea, Joel, and Amos: Faithfulness amid Unfaithfulness.* GWFT. St. Louis: Concordia, 2010. ♪ Lutheran author and theologian. Eleven-session Bible study, including leader's notes and discussion questions.

Eickmann, Paul. *Hosea/Joel/Amos.* PBC. St. Louis: Concordia, 2005. ♪ Lutheran author. Excellent for Bible classes. Based on the NIV translation.

Hubbard, David Allen. *Joel and Amos.* TOTC. Downers Grove, IL: InterVarsity Press, 1989. ♪ Compact commentary based on the NIV, with other translations consulted. Written by an American evangelical scholar.

Kettner, Edward G., Elaine Richter, and Kevin S. Golden. *Minor Prophets: Amos, Jonah, Habakkuk.* Leaders Guide and Enrichment Magazine/Study Guide. LL. St. Louis: Concordia, 2009. ♪ In-depth, nine-session Bible study with individual, small group, and lecture portions.

Life by His Word. St. Louis: Concordia, 2009. ♪ More than 1,500 reproducible one-page Bible studies covering each chapter of the canonical Scriptures. Page references to *The Lutheran Study Bible.* CD-Rom and downloadable.

Motyer, J. A. *The Day of the Lion: The Message of Amos.* Downers Grove, IL: InterVarsity Press, 1974. ♪ Written in a popular style from an English evangelical scholar.

Church Worker Resources

Cripps, Richard S. *A Commentary on the Book of Amos.* Rev. ed. Minneapolis: Klock & Klock, 1981. ♪ An old standard; critical.

Lessing, R. Reed. *Amos.* CC. St. Louis: Concordia, 2009. ♪ The best available pastoral commentary, written by a conservative Lutheran scholar. Thorough treatment of the Hebrew text.

Luther, Martin. *Lectures on the Minor Prophets.* Vol. 18 of AE. St. Louis: Concordia, 1975. ♪ The great reformer's lectures from the 1520s, which reflect his mature approach to biblical interpretation. Luther consulted the Hebrew text and reflected on the application of the prophecies and their New Testament fulfillment.

Mays, James L. *Amos.* OTL. Philadelphia: Westminster, 1969. ♪ Somewhat helpful; mildly critical. Written from a moderately critical viewpoint.

Stuart, Douglas. *Hosea–Jonah.* Vol. 31 of WBC. Waco, TX: Word Books, 1987. ♪ Thoroughly conservative, taking New Testament fulfillment into account.

Sweeney, Marvin A. *The Twelve Prophets.* Vol. 1. *Berit Olam.* Collegeville, MN: Liturgical Press, 2000. ♪ Treats the literary structure of the Book of the Twelve as a whole, using critical approaches, then provides specific commentary on each book. Based on the NRSV.

Academic Resources

Andersen, Francis I., and David Noel Freedman. *Amos.* Vol. 24A of AB. New York: Doubleday, 1989. ♪ Thorough treatment of the Hebrew text; highly detailed.

Carroll R., M. Daniel. *Amos—The Prophet and His Oracles.* Louisville: Westminster John Knox, 2002. ♪ A review of academic research on the Book of Amos from Wellhausen through the end of the twentieth century.

K&D. *Biblical Commentary on the Old Testament: The Twelve Minor Prophets.* 2 vols. Grand Rapids: Eerdmans, 1971 reprint. ♪ This century-and-a-half old work from Lutheran scholars should not be overlooked. Despite its age, it remains a most useful commentary on the Hebrew text.

Paul, Shalom. *Amos.* Hermeneia: A Critical and Historical Commentary on the Bible. Minneapolis: Fortress, 1991. ♪ Thorough commentary from a Jewish scholar who focuses on history of interpretation and critical issues.

Schmoller, Otto. *Amos.* LCHS. New York: Charles Scribner's Sons, 1898. ♪ A helpful, older example of German biblical scholarship, based on the Hebrew text, which provides references to significant commentaries from the Reformation era forward.

OBADIAH

The day of the Lord is near

Edom embraced a tract of very mountainous country about 110 miles long and 30 miles wide. It was bounded on the north by the land of Moab and the southern shore of the Dead Sea; on the east by the Midianites; and on the south by the Gulf of Aqaba, an arm of the Red Sea on the east side of the Sinai Peninsula. From the southern shore of the Dead Sea (c 1,275 feet below sea level), the Arabah depression slowly rises to sea level at the Gulf of Aqaba. The descendants of Esau who inhabited this rugged country were often at odds with Israel and the later kingdom of Judah. Obadiah's prophecy refers to one such occasion, when the sons of Edom attacked refugees from Jerusalem and Judah.

Historical and Cultural Setting

Obadiah is the shortest book in the Old Testament canon (only 21 verses long) but, as St. Jerome noted, both theologically and historically it often poses problems far out of proportion to its size. (In many ways its contents and problems are similar to those of Nahum.) Obadiah's very brevity makes it easy to overlook.

The date and occasion of Obadiah's message are difficult to pin down. The prophet obviously speaks of some devastation of Jerusalem in which the Edomites were implicated. But which one? Friction, often bitter, was a constant in Israel's history, and Edom is repeatedly scored also by other prophets. (Cf Nu 20:14–21; Jgs 11:16–18; 1Sm 14:47–48; 2Sm 8:14; 1Ki 11:14–25; 2Ch 20:10–30; Am 1:6, 9, 11.) There are three main possibilities, and all three have their champions (see "Date of Composition" below). Theological viewpoint apparently plays only a minimal role in deciding.

The descendants of Esau found refuge in the red sandstone mountains southeast of Canaan. The small tree at center left provides a sense of scale.

COMPOSITION

Author

The name Obadiah ("serving Yahweh") was fairly common in ancient Israel (cf 1Ki 18:3–16; 2Ch 17:7–9; Ne 10:5; 12:25). Yet we know very little about this particular prophet. He was likely an eyewitness of Edom's cruelty to his fellow Judeans.

Date of Composition

Older conservative scholars favored a quite early date for the Book of Obadiah, relating it to the Philistine and Arab attack in the reign of Jehoram of Judah, c 850 BC (cf 2Ki 8:20; 2Ch 21:16–17). That would, of course, make Obadiah the earliest of the "writing prophets," preceding even the early dating of Joel by some 20 years. That dating is almost entirely out of favor today. However, there is no good reason why the possibility should not be seriously entertained, particularly if critical developmental theories are discarded.

Recent scholars, in contrast, have often favored a relatively late date, perhaps around 450 BC, when various Arab tribes from the desert (the later Nabateans) began to press into historic Edomite territory east of the Arabah, and the Edomites, in turn, increasingly moved west into southern Judah (the beginning of the "Idumea" of New Testament times, from which the Herodians came).

The majority of scholars, however, probably prefer to think of the destruction of Jerusalem by Nebuchadnezzar in 587 BC as the most likely occasion for Obadiah's activity. That was Luther's preference already in the sixteenth century. There is various evidence of Edomite complicity in that catastrophe (Ezk 35:10; Lm 4:21–22; Ps 137:7), though details are lacking. This position must concede, however, that Obadiah does not refer explicitly to either Jerusalem's razing or to the Babylonian captivity (the "exiles" of v 20 might have appeared in many periods).

Purpose/Recipients

Obadiah decries the abuses of Edom against fugitives from Judah, warning them before the ultimate judgment of "the day of the Lord" against all nations. He announces to the Judeans that God will restore His people and have victory over Edom.

Literary Features

Genre

Obadiah describes his work as the result of a vision (v 1). In contents the book is little more than a single Gentile oracle against Edom (vv 1–14), broadening in the final verses (15–21) to proclaim a great reversal, when final judgment will overtake *all* nations and Zion will be restored. Yet Obadiah is seen as not only a lovely miniature and epitome of many major prophetic themes but as a meaningful promise also for the Christian Church.

Critics have separated Obadiah at various points, but most commonly a seam is said to be detectable between vv 14 and 15. Since at this point the subject shifts from condemnation of Edom to "the day of the Lord—upon *all* nations," it is often argued that the latter part of the book is no longer the particularized prophecy of Obadiah, but a more universalized, apocalyptic addition of a later period. However, the progression from particular to general is readily explainable. No doubt, as time goes on, "Edom" (like "Babylon") increasingly takes on universal significance as a symbol of "all the kingdoms of the world," but that symbolism was present to some degree in all periods. Otherwise, too, Obadiah shows many signs of theological and literary unity.

Characters

The Edomites and the fugitives from Judah are the two main sets of human characters. Jacob and Esau, the forebearers of the nations, likewise came into view. They represented their descendants who continued to struggle with one another.

Narrative Development or Plot

Like other Prophetic Books, Obadiah is a series of oracles and does not have a storyline or plot. Nonetheless, the deep story of Jacob's struggle with his brother Esau (Gn 27–28, 32–33) is essential to understanding the prophecies and the final triumph of the Lord's kingdom over pagan Edom.

OUTLINE

Superscription (v 1a)

I. The First Proclamation against Edom: Humiliation (vv 1b–4)

II. The Second Proclamation against Edom: Displacement (vv 5–7)

III. The Third Proclamation against Edom (vv 8–18)

   A. Doom and Accusation (vv 8–15)

   B. Restoration for Jacob (Judah) and Destruction for Esau (Edom) (vv 16–18)

IV. Israel's Restoration and the Kingship of Yahweh (vv 19–21)

Resources

Many prophets (Isaiah, Ezekiel, Amos) condemn Edom in language very similar to Obadiah's. There are especially close affinities between Joel and Obadiah scattered throughout both of those two books. For example, compare Jl 2:32b with Ob 17a. When Joel adds "as the LORD has said," he may be referring to what the Lord told Obadiah: "in Mount Zion there shall be those who escape." Especially significant is the close relation between Jeremiah's oracle against Edom (49:7–22) and Ob 1–9. The verbal parallelism is particularly striking between Jer 49:14–16 and Ob 1–4, and between Jer 49:9 and Ob 5.

In the case of both Joel and Jeremiah there are basically two possibilities: one prophet was dependent on the other or both used a common source. Again, these positions are defended, often, it would seem, depending as much as anything on prior decisions about the date of Obadiah's activity.

Text and Translations

Like other prophets, Obadiah appears often to use the "prophetic perfect" (i.e., the future described as already past, because the prophet is so sure of the fulfillment of his oracles due to his vantage point in Yahweh's throne room). The Hebrew "imperfect" also causes difficulties. The KJV, RSV, and NRSV translate, in effect, "you should not have" in vv 12–14, but a much more likely translation would seem to be, "you should/must not," depicting the prophet speaking to contemporaries (cf ESV and NIV).

DOCTRINAL CONTENT

Summary Commentary

1–9 Esau and his descendants have been arrogant and worldly since Esau sold his birthright to Jacob for a bowl of stew. The nation has a long record of hostility toward God's people Israel and, by extension, toward God. Obadiah announces God's judgment on Edom's behavior. Yet it is easy to forget that God, in His mercy, has given Edom a long time to repent and come to Him. The centuries that have passed demonstrate God's patience with Edom.

Artist's depiction of Esau embracing his estranged brother, Jacob. Cf Gn 33.

10–14 After years of indifference punctuated by hostility, Edom faces a choice when God sends Babylon to punish Israel. Edom could show the compassion Jesus later described in Mt 25:34–40. Instead, Edom chooses destructive, self-serving action. The underlying spiritual hostility that led to such a choice seals Edom's fate.

15–18 God will judge nations and individuals according to their deeds, and all will come up short (Rm 3:9–20).

19–21 Throughout history, God has used nations such as Edom and Israel as object lessons. Edom paid the price for spiritual arrogance and indifference; Israel was punished for unfaithfulness. However, God remained faithful to His people. He kept His promises and preserved a faithful remnant.

Specific Law Themes

The Edomites offend the Lord in part because of the pride they take in their security, as though the ruggedness of their homeland will shield them indefinitely from judgment. As a consequence, the Lord will see to it that foreigners pillage their dwellings even as the Edomites have pillaged Judah. Just as the Lord has set aside a Day of Judgment for the nations, He will also set one for Edom.

Specific Gospel Themes

The entire Book of Obadiah is promissory to Israel. The one major prophetic theme that is missing is judgment on Israel. The day of the Lord calls down divine judgment upon His nation's foes and assures His people that the God who is surely on their side will eventually set all things straight. Those who escape the current trials shall dwell in a renewed kingdom even as those who suffer now, awaiting Christ's reappearing, will rejoice in the kingdom of heaven.

Specific Doctrines

Obadiah describes the offense the Lord takes at idolatry and idolatrous self-confidence (v 3) as well as the universal judgment (v 15) and the kingdom of God (v 21).

Application

1–21 Like sinful Judah, we fall prey to the consequences of our sins, including the taunts and gloating of sinners today. Like Edom, God gives us opportunities (Eph 2:10) to either participate in His good work of compassion or to turn our backs on those in need. He has already extended His compassion toward us in the sacrifice and blessing of Jesus. There are times when we are spiritually arrogant and deserve punishment. But God keeps calling us to repentance and to believe His promise of salvation. To all who listen to His Word, He has given the privilege of serving as witnesses to point others to His grace in the one Savior, Jesus Christ. God continues patiently to offer our world His grace and postpones judgment so that more people may repent (2Pt 3:9). "Now is the favorable time; behold, now is the day of salvation" (2Co 6:2).

CANONICITY

One might wonder why so short and specific a book would appear in the Bible. But that would overlook the important general themes Obadiah announces. As noted above under "Resources," it is possible that other prophets valued and cited Obadiah at a very early date. He was, of course, included among the 12 prophets mentioned by Jesus son of Sirach in early second century BC (see p 851).

LUTHERAN THEOLOGIANS ON OBADIAH

Luther

"Obadiah does not specify the time when he lived. However his prophecy applies to the time of the Babylonian captivity, for he comforts the people of Judah that they shall return to Zion.

"His prophecy is directed especially against Edom, or Esau, which bore a special and everlasting hatred against the people of Israel and Judah, as usually happens when friends turn against each other; especially when brothers fall into hatred and hostility against each other, such hostility knows no measure.

"So here the Edomites hated the Jewish people beyond all measure, and had no greater joy than to see the captivity of the Jews, boasting and mocking them in their misery and wretchedness. Almost all the prophets denounced the Edomites because of their hateful wickedness. Even Psalm 137[:7] complains of them and says, 'Remember, O Lord, against the Edomites the day of Jerusalem, how they said, "Rase it, rase it! Down to its foundations!" '

"This hurts beyond measure when men mock and laugh at those who are wretched and troubled, defying them and boasting against them. It constitutes a great and strong assault [*Anfechtung*] upon their faith in God and a powerful incentive to despair and unbelief. Therefore God here appoints a special prophet against such vexatious mockers and tempters, and comforts those who are troubled, strengthening their faith with threats and denunciations against such hostile Edomites—those who mock the wretched—and with promises and assurances of future help and rescue. In such distress this is truly a needed comfort, and [the one who brings it] a veritable Obadiah.

"At the end he prophesies of Christ's kingdom, that it shall not be at Jerusalem only, but everywhere. For he mixes all the nations together, Ephraim, Benjamin, Gilead, the Philistines, the Canaanites, Zarephath. This cannot be understood to refer to the temporal kingdom of Israel, for according to the law of Moses these tribes and people had to remain separate and distinct in the land." (AE 35:321–22)

For more of Luther's insights on this book, see *Lectures on Obadiah* (AE 18:191–204).

Gerhard

"Obadiah ('*Obadyah*) means 'servant of God' or 'God's handiwork,' from the root '*bd* and *yh*, which is contracted from *yhwh* ['Jehovah']. It is not clearly evident as to his tribe and when he prophesied. Some make the probable claim that he lived around the beginning of the Babylonian captivity and addressed the people of Judah who had not yet been taken to Babylon. He is not the Obadiah mentioned in 1 Kings 18:3 because, with regard to time, he came later and was almost a contemporary of Jeremiah.

"Before he had begun to prophesy, he had reached the rank of semi-centurion or 'captain of fifty' under King Ahaz of Israel. After two semi-centurions had been consumed by fire from heaven, King Ahaz had sent him to arrest the prophet Elijah, but he deserted the king, took up with the prophet, and became his disciple. Some of the rabbinic scholars claim that he was a proselyte from Edom because the little book of his prophecy was written especially against the Edomites, that is, the Chaldeans and heathen who afflicted Israel.

"It contains a single chapter that has two parts. The first is of the Law, in which he predicts the final destruction of the Edomites, who were rejoicing over the disaster that had befallen the people of Judah, and convicts them for their sins as the cause for their destruction. The latter part is of the Gospel, and in it he prophesies the spiritual liberation of the true Israelites, which Christ would accomplish. Some entire statements against the Edomites are common also to Jeremiah 49 and Ezekiel 25." (ThC E1 § 159)

FURTHER STUDY

Lay/Bible Class Resources

Baker, David W., T. Desmond Alexander, and Bruce Waltke. *Obadiah, Jonah and Micah*. TOTC. Downers Grove, IL: InterVarsity Press, 1988. ṩ Compact commentary based on the NIV, with other translations consulted. United Kingdom and American evangelical scholars.

Kettner, Edward G., Elaine Richter, and Kevin S. Golden. *Minor Prophets: Amos, Jonah, Habakkuk*. Leader's Guide and Enrichment Magazine/Study Guide. LL. St. Louis: Concordia, 2009. ṩ In-depth, nine-session Bible study with individual, small group, and lecture portions.

Life by His Word. St. Louis: Concordia, 2009. ṩ More than 1,500 reproducible one-page Bible studies covering each chapter of the canonical Scriptures. Page references to *The Lutheran Study Bible*. CD-Rom and downloadable.

Spaude, Cyril. *Obadiah/Jonah/Micah*. PBC. St. Louis: Concordia, 2004. ṩ Lutheran author. Excellent for Bible classes. Based on the NIV translation.

Weidenschilling, J. M. *Obadiah, Jonah, and Micah: Mercy in the Middle*. GWFT. St. Louis: Concordia, 2004. ṩ Lutheran author. Twelve-session Bible study, including leader's notes and discussion questions.

Church Worker Resources

Allen, Leslie C. *Joel, Obadiah, Jonah, and Micah*. 2nd ed. NICOT. Grand Rapids: Eerdmans, 1994. ṩ An evangelical scholar writing from a critical perspective. The commentary is generally conservative.

Jenson, Philip Peter. *Obadiah, Jonah, Micah: A Theological Commentary*. New York: T&T Clark, 2008. ṩ Brief commentary on literary and theological elements. Written by an Anglican; based on NRSV with reference to the Hebrew.

Luther, Martin. *Lectures on the Minor Prophets*. Vol. 18 of AE. St. Louis: Concordia, 1975. ṩ The great reformer's lectures from the 1520s, which reflect his mature approach to biblical interpretation. Luther consulted the Hebrew text and reflected on the application of the prophecies and their New Testament fulfillment.

Stuart, Douglas. *Hosea–Jonah*. Vol. 31 of WBC. Waco, TX: Word Books, 1987. ṩ Thoroughly conservative, taking New Testament fulfillment into account.

Academic Resources

K&D. *Biblical Commentary on the Old Testament: The Twelve Minor Prophets*. 2 vols. Grand Rapids: Eerdmans, 1971 reprint. ṩ This century-and-a-half old work from Lutheran scholars should not be overlooked. Despite its age, it remains a most useful commentary on the Hebrew text.

Kleinert, Paul. *Obadiah*. LCHS. New York: Charles Scribner's Sons, 1898. ṩ A helpful, older example of German biblical scholarship, based on the Hebrew text, which provides references to significant commentaries from the Reformation era forward.

Raabe, Paul R. *Obadiah*. Vol. 24D of AB. New York: Doubleday, 1996. ṩ Currently the most thorough and best commentary, written by a conservative Lutheran scholar.

JONAH

Should I not pity Nineveh?

The Galilean hills encircle the town of Gath-hepher, located in the traditional territory of Zebulun in northern Israel, about 4 miles north of Nazareth. Second Kings 14:25 describes this town as the home of the prophet Jonah, and locals today can point to a tomb in the region that is thought to belong to him. What is more, modern Muslim popular piety has shrines dedicated to the prophet Jonah not only in Galilee but also in the regions of Joppa and Nineveh.

Jonah had predicted the victories of Jeroboam II in restoring "the border of Israel from Lebo-hamath as far as the Sea of the Arabah" (2Ki 14:25). Since Jeroboam II reigned from c 786 to 746, that means Jonah was active in the first half of the eighth century, making him an early contemporary of Amos. That the reports in Kings and the Book of Jonah have no contact beyond the prophet's name is scarcely surprising in and of itself; not even the names of many "writing prophets" with far larger books are so much as mentioned in the books focused on Israel's kings.

Historical and Cultural Setting

From the end of the ninth century BC to the mid-eighth century, the Assyrians competed with the kingdom of Urartu, which weakened the Assyrians' hold of or their influence on kingdoms such as Aram and Israel. Two periods of Assyrian history offer credible points of contact with the story of Jonah. During the reign of Adad-nirari III (c 810–782), son of the famous Semiramis, there were great religious stirrings in the empire, including even one

OVERVIEW

Author
Jonah the prophet

Date
c 790 BC

Places
Israel; Nineveh (Assyria); Tarshish; Joppa

People
Jonah; Amittai; mariners; ship's captain; king of Nineveh

Purpose
To describe God's mercy toward the people of Nineveh and toward all who repent

Law Themes
Evil; flight from God; indifference; Sheol; fasting and sackcloth; God's appointed testing

Gospel Themes
God's appointed mercy; steadfast love; God turns/relents; pity

Memory Verses
God's powerful Word (3:6–10); God's character (4:2)

- -

TIMELINE

931 BC	Israel divided under Rehoboam
793–753 BC	Reign of Jeroboam II (Israel)
c 790 BC	Jonah written
722 BC	Samaria (Israel) falls to Assyria
715–686 BC	Reign of Hezekiah (Judah)

Reconstructed Nergal Gate, the northwest entry into Nineveh.

This Late Bronze-Age drinking vessel of Aegean origin was found at Ugarit, Syria, and is painted with an octopus decoration. It illustrates the movement of people and cultural exchange in the region.

that encouraged putting "your trust in Nabu and no other god" (akin to the belief in one God taught by Israelite prophets). Another possibility a little later is Ashur-dan III (773–754), during whose reign two severe plagues and an earthquake (cf Am 1:1) are known to have wracked the populace, which could have made them open to a message of repentance.

COMPOSITION

Author

Neither the Book of Jonah itself nor other Scripture ever asserts that Jonah himself wrote it, as tradition has tended to assume, and hence authorship by Jonah is not guaranteed. However, the tradition is well grounded by the prayer in ch 2, which should be viewed as coming from Jonah, given its personal character. Indeed, Jonah may have been closely associated with the book's composition.

Date of Composition

The usual critical dating in the fifth to fourth century BC is based on several assumptions. For example, some have argued that the word *was* in 3:3 meant that Nineveh was no longer standing when the book was written, though such wording hardly demands that the city had passed away. Critics also once commonly attempted to buttress a late dating by arguing that the Aramaic language influenced some features of the writing (alleged "Aramaisms") or that other late expressions appeared in the text. However, evidence from the c 1400 BC texts discovered at Ugarit shows that many such "Aramaisms" are even older than Israel! This has made even critics very cautious about such arguments. Furthermore, there is evidence that such "Aramaic" idioms were more common in northern rather than in southern Canaan—and Jonah hailed from northern Galilee, where one would most likely find such influences. Finally, ideas about the evolution of religion from local interests in Israel to the religious life of other nations, such as the Assyrians, led some critics to conclude that Jonah had a more developed—and therefore later—theology. This is an assumption that largely ignores the evidence of the Bible itself.

There appear to be no compelling reasons why one should question an eighth-century date for the Book of Jonah.

Purpose/Recipients

Jonah critiques Israel's view of itself as God's specially chosen people while affirming the surpassing mercy of God for other nations—even nations hostile to His chosen people. The book applies the theme of repentance both to the prophet and to the people of Nineveh. The events related in the book explore the boundaries of God's mercy and patience as well as the role of mankind in God's mission. It is a story of both personal and national repentance.

Literary Features

The Book of Jonah has long been one of the most visible outposts along the liberal-conservative battle line. Strict conservatives do not hesitate to draw the line at this point, and liberals have reserved much of their ridicule about "fundamentalist literalism" for the traditional way of reading Jonah. Whether one reads Jonah as factual or fictional is determined largely by prior ideas about interpretation and also confessional commitments.

Genre

Jonah is an unusual member of "the Twelve" (see p 851). Unlike most prophetic literature, which consists primarily of oracles ("A"-type prophecy), this book is almost exclusively narrative ("B"-type prophecy) about Jonah, except for ch 2. Commentators have had a hard time deciding exactly what genre Jonah is.

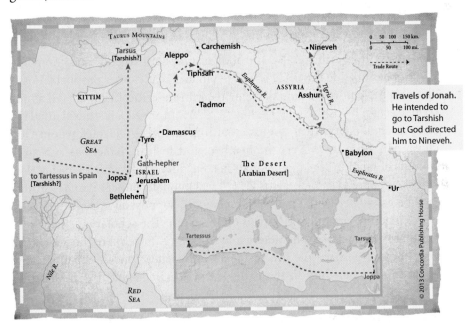

Travels of Jonah. He intended to go to Tarshish but God directed him to Nineveh.

© 2013 Concordia Publishing House

OUTLINE

Jonah, as good literature, presents the true story and events of the prophet's life as the scenes of a play, as shown by this outline.

Scene I Account of Jonah's Call and His Reaction (1:1–3)

Scene II Onboard Ship in the Midst of a Storm at Sea (1:4–17)

Scene III Inside the Great Fish (ch 2)

Scene IV Yahweh Gives Jonah His Assignment a Second Time (3:1–3)

Scene V Jonah Delivers the Message; Nineveh's Response (3:4–10)

Scene VI Jonah's Prayer in Nineveh (4:1–3)

Scene VII Jonah Sits outside the City of Nineveh; Yahweh Teaches a Lesson on Mercy (4:4–11)

At one time, critics called the book a "prophetic legend" and compared it with tales outside the Bible about Jonah and many other prophets. Possibly "prophetic novel" would describe the current critical view as well as any term. Certain British scholars (Cheyne, G. A. Smith, etc.) have explained the story as an allegory. They propose that Jonah represents Israel, whom God chose (Gn 12:3) to convert the heathen. But instead, Israel has run away from its obligation. The name Jonah means "dove," with which Israel is elsewhere compared (Ps 74:19; Hos 7:11; 11:11). Jonah's father's name, Amittai, may be associated with "truth" (Hbr 'emeth), supposedly to signify Israel's commission to uphold and spread divine truth. The scholars further point out that the cuneiform characters for *Ni-nu-a* (Nineveh) are those of a fish and a house (perhaps the fish inside a tomb). They conclude that, because Israel shirked her duty in the exile, she was "swallowed" by the monster

Babylon (the metaphor is used in Jer 51:34–44) and disgorged (allowed to return) only upon repentance. Israel still remains dissatisfied that the Gentiles have not been punished and has only reluctantly resigned herself to the task. Most such allegorical approaches collapse when it comes to trying to work out all details. As a result, critics have also tended to favor the idea that Jonah is a parable, which is hardly different from allegory except that a parable may require fewer details for its interpretation.

The more traditional approach, which is preferable, reads the story of Jonah at face value as an artfully crafted historical narrative that describes real events from the prophet's life. For more on the Book of Jonah as history, see below the section on "Specific Doctrines" and the side article "The Prophet Jonah and the Great Fish."

Characters

As the namesake of the book, **Jonah** is the main character. The events of the book recount his travels and his reactions to the Lord, who is unrelenting in pursuit of His mission for Jonah. The **sailors** in ch 1 are important to the story, not just for their role in tossing Jonah overboard, but especially in illustrating the effect of the prophet's message on the human heart. They turn from fearing the storm and divining God's purposes by lot to fearing/trusting the Lord and making vows to Him. The **Ninevites** add further surprise to the story because they respond so fully to the Lord's message through the half-hearted prophet. The book ends with the sailors and Ninevites trusting in the Lord, but with the prophet in despair because the Lord does not share his disdain for the enemies of Israel.

Narrative Development or Plot

The events in the Book of Jonah present a dynamic travel story that moves on both a physical and a spiritual level. The story tracks the movement of Jonah from Jerusalem to Nineveh where the Lord has asked him to fulfill a mission. Spiritually the story tracks the changes in Jonah from unrepentance and resistance against God's mission to his repentant fulfilling of God's mission. It ends with the prophet falling into despair and leaves the reader wondering whether the prophet will welcome the Lord's insights about His mission to Nineveh and move from despair to mercy for the Ninevites.

Resources

There are clear parallels with Joel (3:9 with Jl 2:14 and 4:2 with Jl 2:13), but one cannot tell which book influenced the other.

Text and Translations

The prose in Jonah is good, classical Hebrew for the most part, and the psalm (ch 2) is even antique in flavor. The straightforward character of the book probably explains why there are few text-critical problems (cf Joel and Amos). Some minor linguistic updating may have taken place after the eighth-century composition.

DOCTRINAL CONTENT

Summary Commentary

Ch 1 Jonah turns his back on God, but God stops Jonah from his folly. God could punish Jonah or send someone else to Nineveh. However, God loves Jonah so much that He sends a storm to interrupt his flight and to eventually bring him back into a healthy relationship with his Savior. God uses Jonah's disobedience as a learning opportunity for him and for the ship's crew. Jonah has an opportunity to compare his indifference and hostility toward Nineveh with the sailors' concern for his life. And the sailors are able to learn of the true God through Jonah's confession of faith and God's control of the sea. Jonah thinks he will die by drowning in the sea, and that should be the outcome of his refusal to obey God. But God has other plans for Jonah. The great fish saves him from drowning and gives him pause to consider his situation and his role in carrying out God's will.

Ch 2 Jonah deserves death, not deliverance. Yet the Lord graciously rescues him by miraculous intervention. Jonah recognizes the greatness of the Lord's compassion and expresses his thanks in prayer.

Ch 3 God is concerned for all people, even those we might write off. Jonah has a precious opportunity to preach God's Word to Nineveh, but his heart is not in it. He does not seem to understand the extent of God's concern for people who are enemies of Israel, and he hopes that misfortune will come to them. The people of Nineveh hardly seem like "good prospects" for conversion. However, the message they hear is from God, and God makes sure that it bears the fruit of repentance.

Ch 4 The book has a suspended ending, leaving us to wonder whether Jonah abandoned his callous attitude toward Nineveh and welcomed the Lord's desire to save them.

Specific Law Themes

The book opens with a common Old Testament theme: a nation's evil, which has grown so steep it draws the Lord's special attention (1:2). Jonah's flight from God and his indifference to the Lord's mission are likewise described as evil and provoke God's wrath (1:8). Jonah comes to repentance only after being thrust down to "Sheol" (2:2). When Jonah finally reaches Nineveh, the message of God's wrath drives the Assyrian leaders to fast and to wear sackcloth as expressions of their repentance. When Jonah finally has a chance to rest, God is not through with him. He appoints a test by which He will break the prophet out of his self-pity. God is everywhere, energetically changing people's lives with the threats of the Law.

Specific Gospel Themes

The Book of Jonah beautifully reveals how God's wrath serves His greater purpose of having mercy on Jonah, the sailors, and the Ninevites. In fact, God appoints mercy for Jonah through the blessings of creation. He abounds in steadfast love (4:2) and even turns/relents from "disaster" (literally, "evil"; 3:10). In the end, God's pity and patience surprise the reader and would turn Jonah's heart toward faith and trust (4:11).

Specific Doctrines

Miracles, providence, and history are key elements in the story of Jonah, as well as God's missionary zeal for saving the nations, which manifests itself boldly in the account. The conservative support for reading the Book of Jonah as history finally rests (as in the case of the unity of Isaiah and Mosaic authorship of the Pentateuch) chiefly in the testimony of the New Testament and of our Lord. The two relevant texts are Mt 12:39–41 and Lk 11:29–32.

Critics commonly point out the fact that the "sign of Jonah" is presented a bit differently in Matthew and Luke. In Luke it is the preaching of judgment by the Son of Man, who fulfills the prophetic role of Jonah for the present unbelieving generation. In Matthew the sign is the Son of Man's "three days and three nights in the heart of the earth," corresponding to the period Jonah spent "in the belly of the great fish." However, the distinction makes little difference: it is precisely Christ's death and resurrection that seals His condemnation upon those who refuse to believe. In both cases we clearly have Christ's own explicit interpretation, presenting Jonah's "death and resurrection" as an anticipation and forecast of His own. It is interesting that Jonah is the *only* prophet Jesus ever directly compares Himself to—possibly because Jonah's home was close to Nazareth. Such a comparison implies that Jesus viewed the story of Jonah as history. There is an inner unity between the anticipation (prophecy) and the climax (fulfillment; cf Jnh 1).

For those who argue that Jesus was only presenting a literary comparison (for which any parable or other tale might also serve as historical fact), the clinching refutation would appear to be Jesus' reference to the "men of Nineveh." He obviously regards them not only as historical figures but as still available to "rise up at the judgment with this generation and condemn it" (found in both Luke and Matthew!).

There can be little doubt that the major stumbling block to understanding the book as history is not only a bias against miracles or God's providence in general, but the rampant, repeated, and self-evident record of God's intervention in the book. (On the distinction between providence and miracles, see *TLSB*, p 1674.) How does one argue against the idea that there are too many or too grand a set of miracles, especially since Jesus compares the events to one of the greatest miracles in biblical teaching: the doctrine of the resurrection of the body?

Documented instances in modern times of men who were swallowed and regurgitated alive by whales may help some people accept the story more easily, but ultimately the matter is miraculous. The fast-growing (castor bean?) plant (4:6) cannot be matched by even the fastest growing varieties in tropical climates. (Consider also the way the storm subsides after Jonah has been thrown overboard.)

The major "improbability" is, of course, the core of the book: that an Israelite prophet would journey to Nineveh to begin with, let alone successfully convert the entire city. However, Elijah and Elisha not too long previously illustrate prophetic activity in the neighboring areas of Tyre and Damascus. (Also other aspects of their ministries have many parallels—the miracles, the antipagan preaching, the despondency they sometimes felt, etc.) The "Gentile oracles" in most of the prophets clearly indicate Yahweh's *claim* on all nations (cf esp Jer 13) even if they were not ordinarily delivered abroad. Jonah's own reasons for reluctance to obey are not explicitly stated.

Application

Chs 1–2 When we break God's Law and receive punishment, He often turns the situation into a learning experience and an opportunity for us to confess and praise Him. The apostle Paul, like Jonah, once felt that he had "received the sentence of death," but the God "who raises the dead" delivered him (2Co 1:8–10). All sinners deserve the sentence of everlasting death. But the God to whom salvation belongs has, in Christ, rescued us and given us new life.

3:1–5 Do you assume some people are unable or unwilling to respond to the Gospel? We have the immense privilege of sharing God's Law and Gospel with the world around us. We have opportunities to be part of His plans. May we never be found guilty of neglecting our mission to make disciples of all nations. Faithfully fulfill your role as His witness. Leave conversion in God's hands; He has promised that His Word will bear fruit, and He is concerned that all people have the opportunity to be saved. Thank God, His Word bore the fruit of repentance in Nineveh and also in your life.

3:6–4:11 Jesus declared that "the men of Nineveh will rise up at the judgment . . . and condemn" His own generation of hearers who failed to repent (Mt 12:41). God continues to call us to repentance for our sins of thought, word, and deed. The men of Nineveh furnish us with an example to follow. May they not condemn us on the Day of Judgment! May the Holy Spirit rather lead us daily to repent of our sins and trust Christ for pardon and peace.

CANONICITY

The apocryphal books of Tobit and Ecclesiasticus cite the Book of Jonah, offering eloquent testimony that Israelites regarded the book as canonical at an early date. See also p 851.

The story of Jonah was a popular artistic theme in early Christian catacombs.

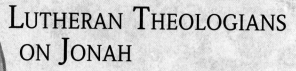

LUTHERAN THEOLOGIANS ON JONAH

Luther

"As Jerome indicates, there are some who contend that this prophet was the son of the widow at Zarephath near Sidon, who fed Elijah in the famine, as described in I Kings 17[:8–24] and Luke 4[:26]. The reason they give is that Jonah [1:1] here calls himself a son of Amittai, that is, a son of the True One, because his mother said to Elijah when he had raised him from the dead, 'Now I know that the word of your mouth is true' [I Kings 17:24].

"Let anyone believe this who will; I do not believe it. Jonah's father's name was Amittai, in Latin *Verax*, in German *Wahrhaftig*; he was from Gath-hepher, a town in the land of the tribe of Zebulun, Joshua 19[:13]. For it is written in II Kings 14[:25], 'King Jeroboam restored again the border of Israel from Hamath as far as the Sea of the Arabah, according to the word of the Lord, the God of Israel, which he spoke by his servant Jonah, the son of Amittai, the prophet of Gath-hepher.' Moreover the widow at Zarephath was a Gentile, as Christ indicates in Luke 4[:25–26]. But Jonah here in chapter 1[:9] confesses that he is a Hebrew.

"So we gather then that this Jonah lived at the time of King Jeroboam [II], the great grandson of King Jehu, at the time when King Uzziah reigned in Judah. This was also the time at which the prophets Hosea, Amos, and Joel were living in the same kingdom of Israel in other places and towns. From this we can readily gather what a splendid and valuable man this Jonah was in the kingdom of Israel. God did great things through him, for it was through his preaching that King Jeroboam was so successful and won back all that Hazael, king of Syria, had taken from the kingdom of Israel [II Kings 10:32–33; 13:3, 7; 14:25].

"But greater than all he did in his own nation were his attacks upon the great and mighty kingdom of Assyria and his fruitful preaching among the Gentiles; among them he accomplished more than could have been accomplished among his own people with many sermons. It was as though God willed to demonstrate by him the word of Isaiah, 'He who has not heard, shall hear it,' as an illustration of the fact that they who have the word richly despise it thoroughly, and they who cannot have it accept it gladly. Christ himself says, in Matthew 21[:43], 'The kingdom of God will be taken away from you and given to the nations producing the fruits of it.' " (AE 35:323–24)

For more of Luther's insights on this book, see *Lectures on Jonah* (AE 19:1–104).

Gerhard

"*Jonah* (*Yonah*) means 'dove,' and the reason for this name is not clear. He belonged to the nation of Judah and was born at Gath Hepher, a city in the tribe of Zebulun (Josh. 19:13).

"Epiphanius says he was born in Gath or in Havathamaum in the tribe of Dan, not far from Azotus, a city of Palestine, near the sea. [Epiphanius] also says he was the widow of Zarephath's son, whom the prophet Elijah raised from the dead in Zarephath of Sidon and whose mother later said to him: 'Now I know that you are a man of God and that [the Lord's word] in your mouth is the truth' [1 Kings 17:24]. For this reason, he says, the boy was called 'the son of Amittai,' that is, 'the son of truth,' because the truth was again brought out into this light when the prophet Elijah was speaking.

"Jonah's father was Amittai [Jon. 1:1]. Jonah prophesied at the time when Jeroboam, son of Joash, was king of Israel and Phul Belochus ruled in Assyria and Babylon, as we gather from 2 Kings 14:25, where Jonah's prophecy is mentioned. God sent him to Nineveh, the chief city of the Assyrian monarchy (Gen. 10:11). Because at first he refused this call, he was enveloped in peril. After being divinely freed from this, he faithfully fulfilled the duties of the calling entrusted to him, and with his preaching of repentance, he brought the people of Nineveh unharmed out of the imminent destruction he had prophesied for them.

"The book consists of four chapters and has two parts: (I) The account of Jonah turning his back and refusing his divine call, for which God punished him (Jonah 1) but later freed him miraculously (Jonah 2). (II) The account of Jonah accepting the repeated call and, by his prediction of imminent destruction, bringing the Ninevites to repentance (Jonah 3). This bothered him, but the divine oracle restrained him (Jonah 4).

"Jerome is greatly surprised that the Septuagint translators translated 'forty days' (Jon. 3:4, etc.) as 'three days' because in the Hebrew they have no commonality of syllables, accents, or words. Augustine struggles mightily to explain these difficulties and is unable to extricate himself sufficiently (*De civ. Dei*, bk. 18, c. 44). We give the simple response, however, that the Greek text here is corrupt because some copies do have 'forty.' " (ThC E1 § 160)

THE PROPHET JONAH
AND THE GREAT FISH

Perhaps no story in the Bible is more frequently challenged than that of Jonah being swallowed by a large fish and remaining in its belly three days. The theology of those who in all simplicity adhere to the Scriptures is often termed a "Jonah-and-the-whale" theology. Some people call this story an allegory or a parable, which means that in their view we are here dealing with a fictitious story, which was invented for teaching purposes.

Is it possible to regard this story as a parable invented by a prophet or instructor to illustrate some great truth? The Bible indeed contains many parables. The story of the 10 servants (Lk 19:11–27), which on the face of it reads like the account of a historical event, is called a parable, the term implying that the incidents are merely imagined. The story of Jonah, however, is not a parable. Two considerations exclude such a view. In the first place, the story itself does not indicate that it is the product of someone's imagination. Nor is

The image of Jonah swallowed up and expelled by the great fish was associated by early Christians with Jesus' death and resurrection.

there any hint that the book was intended to be a parable. From beginning to end the Book of Jonah purports to hand down historical truth. We cannot but conclude that it was the intention of the writer to have the readers look upon what he relates as reality. In the second place, our Lord in the New Testament treats the story of Jonah's extraordinary experience as historical truth. Matthew quotes Jesus (12:40): "For just as Jonah was three days and three nights in the belly of the great fish, so will the Son of Man be three days and three nights in the heart of the earth." These words of Jesus confirm the historicity of the story of Jonah, and in the light of His clear utterance any attempt to give the Old Testament account the character of a parable or an allegory should be abandoned. But now we have to face the great host of critics who exclaim that the story of Jonah, if taken literally, relates a ridiculous impossibility. The argument they present is that a whale has so small a gullet that it could not possibly swallow a man. We are told that it feeds on small animals, such as crustaceans and mollusks, its throat being so narrow that nothing larger than a man's fist can pass it. Such an argument, however, does not worry the Christian in the least. If God could provide a fish to be at hand when Jonah was thrown into the sea, He could also make its throat large enough to let the body of a man be passed into the monster's stomach. But what is very remarkable is that the objection of the critics rests on an assumption that is altogether false. It is true, the "right whale," also called the whalebone whale, has the throat described, but the sperm whale, or cachalot, has a gullet that, to quote the manager of a whaling station, "can take lumps of food eight feet in diameter." It is likewise possible that a large shark can swallow a man and spit him out again, according to some modern accounts. (See CC Jnh, p 187.)

In a carefully written article, supplied with all required references and published in the *Princeton Theological Review* (October 1927), Ambrose John Wilson of Oxford, England, has gathered the helpful information for reaching correct conclusions in this matter. The words of the whaling station manager just quoted are taken from his article. We are here told that it is just the cachalot, a sperm whale, which is found in tropical and subtropical waters, though it has been found as far north as Iceland. As to its swallowing abilities, Mr. Wilson quotes the same man as saying that the largest thing they had found in a whale was "the skeleton of a shark sixteen feet long." The article submits two accounts of persons having been swallowed by the sperm whale. It informs us that this whale "for the most part subsists on the octopus, the bodies of which, far larger than the body of a man, have been found whole in its stomach." The sperm whale, so it says, "swims about with its lower jaw

917

hanging down and its huge gullet gaping like some submarine cavern. Only too easy to be swallowed by it!" It seems, then, that here there is ample reason to reject the claim that a whale has not a big enough gullet to take a person into its stomach. Other writers, we may add, tell us that sharks have been caught of sufficient size to swallow an individual. The sacred account with its parallel passage does not say that the animal receiving Jonah was a whale. The Greek word (Mt 12:40) merely signifies a great sea creature.

But there remains the objection that it is unlikely that a person could live in such a house of flesh for three days and three nights. If our great God wishes to preserve someone in such a situation, He can well do it, we reply. In addition we can quote Mr. Wilson's article again, which devotes a special section to the question, "Could a man live in a whale?" We read: "The answer seems to be that he certainly could, though in circumstances of very great discomfort. There would be air to breathe—of a sort. This is necessary to enable the fish to float. The heat would be oppressive. 104 to 106 degrees Fahrenheit is the opinion of one expert; a provision maintained by his 'blanket' of blubber, 'often many feet in thickness,' which is needed 'to enable him to resist the cold of ocean' and 'keep himself comfortable in all waters, in all seas, times, and tides' . . . but this temperature, though high fever heat to a human being, is not fatal to human life. Again, the gastric juice would be extremely unpleasant, but not deadly. It cannot digest living matter; otherwise it would digest the walls of its own stomach."

The writer then proceeds to tell of two instances where a man was swallowed by a sperm whale and came out alive from his gruesome prison, one being that of Marshall Jenkins, who is said to have had this extraordinary experience in 1771. And in 1891, while taking part in a whaling expedition, James Bartley was gulped down by a furious whale who had been harpooned. On the second day after his imprisonment and the killing of the monster he was found in its stomach in an unconscious condition, but was revived, and after three weeks had regained his health. Mr. Wilson states in the second article, published in the *Princeton Theological Review* (October 1928), that the reliability of the story of James Bartley has been attacked; but he shows that what has been argued against it does not amount to disproof. Whatever view one may take of the stories alluded to, it must be clearly understood that we Christians do not need them in order to accept the account of the Book of Jonah as true. Its credibility for us rests on far higher grounds than such occurrences. But they may serve to silence some critics who take delight in referring to the story of Jonah as a "good fish story."

FURTHER STUDY

Lay/Bible Class Resources

Baker, David W., T. Desmond Alexander, and Bruce Waltke. *Obadiah, Jonah and Micah*. TOTC. Downers Grove, IL: InterVarsity Press, 1988. ᕝ Compact commentary based on the NIV, with other translations consulted. United Kingdom and American evangelical scholars.

Kettner, Edward G., Elaine Richter, and Kevin S. Golden. *Minor Prophets: Amos, Jonah, Habakkuk*. Leader's Guide and Enrichment Magazine/Study Guide. LL. St. Louis: Concordia, 2009. ᕝ In-depth, nine-session Bible study with individual, small group, and lecture portions.

Life by His Word. St. Louis: Concordia, 2009. ᕝ More than 1,500 reproducible one-page Bible studies covering each chapter of the canonical Scriptures. Page references to *The Lutheran Study Bible*. CD-Rom and downloadable.

Spaude, Cyril. *Obadiah/Jonah/Micah*. PBC. St. Louis: Concordia, 2004. ᕝ Lutheran author. Excellent for Bible classes. Based on the NIV translation.

Weidenschilling, J. M. *Obadiah, Jonah, and Micah: Mercy in the Middle*. GWFT. St. Louis: Concordia, 2004. ᕝ Lutheran author. Twelve-session Bible study, including leader's notes and discussion questions.

Church Worker Resources

Allen, Leslie C. *Joel, Obadiah, Jonah, and Micah*. 2nd ed. NICOT. Grand Rapids: Eerdmans, 1994. ᕝ An evangelical scholar writing from a critical perspective. The commentary is generally conservative. However, in this case, the author interprets the Book of Jonah as a parable.

Jenson, Philip Peter. *Obadiah, Jonah, Micah: A Theological Commentary*. New York: T&T Clark, 2008. ᕝ Brief commentary on literary and theological elements. Written by an Anglican; based on NRSV with reference to the Hebrew.

Laetsch, Theodore. *Commentary on the Minor Prophets*. St. Louis: Concordia, 1956. ᕝ Professor at Concordia Seminary, St. Louis, for many years. Faithful Lutheran interpreter.

Lessing, R. Reed. *Jonah*. CC. St. Louis: Concordia, 2007. ᕝ The most extensive and best available pastoral commentary, written by a conservative Lutheran scholar. Thorough treatment of the Hebrew text.

Luther, Martin. *Lectures on the Minor Prophets II*. Vol. 19 of AE. St. Louis: Concordia, 1974. ᕝ The great reformer's lectures from the 1520s, which reflect his mature approach to biblical interpretation. Luther consulted the Hebrew text and reflected on the application of the prophecies and their New Testament fulfillment.

Stuart, Douglas. *Hosea-Jonah*. Vol. 31 of WBC. Waco, TX: Word Books, 1987 ᕝ Thoroughly conservative, taking New Testament fulfillment into account.

Academic Resources

Cary, Philip. *Jonah*. Brazos Theological Commentary on the Bible. Grand Rapids: Brazos, 2008. ᕝ A theological commentary by a professor of philosophy and Augustine, focused on typology.

K&D. *Biblical Commentary on the Old Testament: The Twelve Minor Prophets*. 2 vols. Grand Rapids: Eerdmans, 1971 reprint. ᕝ This century-and-a-half old work from Lutheran scholars should not be overlooked. Despite its age, it remains a most useful commentary on the Hebrew text.

Kleinert, Paul. *Jonah*. LCHS. New York: Charles Scribner's Sons, 1898. ᕝ A helpful, older example of German biblical scholarship, based on the Hebrew text, which provides references to significant commentaries from the Reformation era forward.

Sasson, Jack M. *Jonah*. Vol. 24B of AB. New York: Doubleday, 1990. ᕝ A thorough, scholarly commentary on the Hebrew text.

MICAH

Walk humbly with your God

From the rounded Shephelah hills of Judah, villagers looked eastward over the valleys leading to the plains of Philistia. The eighth-century prophet Micah hailed from the village of Moresheth (Mi 1:1), located not far from the Philistine city of Gath (v 14). This was frontier territory for Israel in the days of their first kings when young David slew Goliath of Gath. The site of Moresheth is likely the largely unexcavated Tell-ej-Judeideh, a few miles north of Lachish.

In the eighth century, about 250 years after David, the kingdoms of Israel and Judah were mature monarchies. The visions the Lord gave Micah looked northeast to Jerusalem and Samaria where dynasties ruled. (In the region of Moresheth, archaeologists have found numerous jar handles stamped as belonging to the king of Judah, showing that the area was specially tied to the ruler at Jerusalem.) The Lord showed Micah how abusive leaders exploited their privileges over God's people. He likewise showed Micah the distant empire of Assyria preparing for invasion.

Historical and Cultural Setting

Micah wrote about leadership—spiritual and political leadership—at a time when Israel and Judah prospered in the shadow of a great empire: the Assyrians. After the Assyrians declined during the early eighth century, they gained new strength under the Sargonic rulers, descendants of Sargon II. Conditions in Israel steadily grew worse after the death of King Jeroboam (910 BC). They had no ability to resist the offense of Tiglath-pileser or his successors. Shalmaneser defeated the Northern Kingdom and led its citizens captive into exile (722 BC) before returning to attack Judah.

When Assyrian troops marched through Israel on their way to Jerusalem, the Judeans had neither the strength to offer significant resistance nor a sufficient ally in the Egyptians. This was because the Libyan pharaohs ruled a divided and disorganized Egypt. The Kushite pharaohs who succeeded them (c 747 BC) likewise struggled to govern and could not compete with the expanding powers of the Assyrians.

King Sennacherib receives officials while awaiting the defeat of the Judeans defending Lachish (701 BC). Micah lived in the region and may have witnessed the conflict.

Rulers of Judah had their jars stamped "[Belonging] to the King" or with a royal seal.

Micah opens with a clear superscription about the reigns of "Jotham, Ahaz, and Hezekiah" as the period of his ministry (the same as in Is 1:1). Likewise, the preserved oracles support the information that Micah's visions were "concerning Samaria and Jerusalem," that is, partly occurring before the fall of the Northern Kingdom, Israel.

COMPOSITION

Author

The name Micah means "Who is like Yahweh?" and it has often been supposed that the opening question in the book's doxology (7:18) is a play on the name. Some 13 other biblical figures also bear the name, but the major namesake of the eighth-century prophet is another great prophet a little over a century earlier, Micaiah son of Imlah (1Ki 22). "Micaiah," is simply a longer form of "Micah."[1]

As noted above, about the only personal information we have on Micah is his home in Moresheth (1:1, 14). Not even the name of the prophet's father is mentioned. Commentators often seek to explain various features in Micah's preaching as reflecting his small-town background; there may be partial truth in the explanation, but one should be cautious. Those origins might help explain the feeling with which Micah condemns exploitation and oppression of the poor (cf Amos). However, note that a number of small villages, including Micah's home, are also so singled out for judgment in 1:10–16. Micah, unlike his great contemporary Isaiah, reveals no interest in the political machinations of the times, and provincial origins could account for that. Isaiah was a court preacher; Micah may be viewed as a country preacher.

The sarcasm of Mi 2:11 and the contrast he draws between himself and other prophets in 3:5–8 show that Micah was not a professional prophet, or he at least distanced himself from most "prophetic" figures. Micah 2:6–7 may hint at the popular opposition aroused by his preaching.

---

1   In the Hebrew Bible, a marginal note (*Kethib*) at Jer 26:18 even refers to our prophet by the longer form, but apparently the shorter version was generally preferred to minimize confusion.

Date of Composition

The superscription to Micah connects his prophetic ministry with the reigns of Jotham (750–735), Ahaz (735–715), and Hezekiah (715–686). Jeremiah 26:18 specifies that Micah predicted Jerusalem's destruction about a century before the event took place. It cites Mi 3:12 as written during Hezekiah's reign. This provides important information for dating the composition of the book. The passage in Jeremiah is also interesting because it is the only example among the Major and Minor Prophets where one prophet quoted another by name (however, cf Jer 25:11–12; Ezr 1:1; Dn 9:2).

Purpose/Recipients

Micah's preaching against Samaria seems clearest in the opening oracle, predicting its fall (Mi 1:2–7), and in 6:9–16, where "the statutes of Omri, and all the works of the house of Ahab" are denounced.

Micah called out against the leaders of Judah and Israel (1:2), who indulged themselves. They did not see the problems that threatened their subjects, including the threat of exile for the daughters of Zion (1:16; 4:10; 5:7). Yet Micah also prophesied the coming of a faithful Shepherd, who would stand guard over His people and spring to their defense with the strength of a young lion. This Ruler would come from a shepherd's town (Bethlehem), ascend to the "tower of the flock" (4:8; David's palace/throne), and renew the kingdom. Micah's Shepherd is Jesus (5:2, 4; Mt 2:6).

Literary Features

Genre

The Book of Micah is a collection of the visions he recorded throughout his ministry. Visions may be introduced with the word *Hear* (1:2; 3:1; 6:1), which occurs at key points in the book. Nineteenth-century literary critics were quite severe with Micah, offering numerous doubts about the authenticity of the visions. They nearly always

---

OVERVIEW

Author
Micah the prophet

Date
c 750–686 BC

Places
Judah; Jerusalem; Zion; Moresheth; Bethlehem; Lachish; Israel; Samaria; Gilgal; Bashan; Gilead; Gath; Assyria; Babylon; Egypt; Euphrates River

People
Kings Jotham, Ahaz, and Hezekiah; remnant of Israel; leaders of Judah and Israel

Purposes
To indict the shepherds of Israel and Judah for exploiting and misleading the people and to prophesy the Lord's work as a shepherd for the remnant

Law Themes
Nakedness and shame; remnant; exile; false prophets

Gospel Themes
Remnant; Zion; shepherd; cut off; God's patience

Memory Verses
Remnant gathered (2:12–13); the Ruler from Bethlehem (5:2–5a); what is good (6:8); compassion again (7:18–20)

TIMELINE

931 BC	Israel divided under Rehoboam
750–735 BC	Reign of Jotham (Judah)
750–686 BC	Micah written
722 BC	Samaria (Israel) falls to Assyria
715–686 BC	Reign of Hezekiah (Judah)

regarded Mi 1–3 (with the likely exception of 2:12–13) as genuinely written by Micah. However, critics applied the following dogma to the rest of the book: preexilic, true prophets always heralded doom; therefore, Micah could not have written the comforting prophecies attributed to him. This odd reasoning led to extensive surgery on the book, resulting in assumed authors titled "Deutero-Micah" and "Trito-Micah." The content does not require multiple authors, and such critical notions are unsound.

The Lord showed Micah that the Messiah would come from the shepherds' hills of Bethlehem Ephrathah (5:2).

Micah 4 commonly refers to "Zion," which may have been a principle in the composition of this oracle. Critics regarded Mi 4–5 as a later addition because 4:10 correctly predicted that Babylon would be both the locale of Judah's captivity and the origin of the return. We must remind ourselves that the general theme of restoration after judgment was at least as old as Deuteronomy and commonly found in the lives of Israel's earlier leaders (e.g., David).

Micah 6–7 is similar to 1–3, only somewhat milder in tone. Much of ch 7 has the quality of a hymn or psalm.

Characters

The chief character of Micah's visions is the Lord, who confronts the people of Samaria/Israel and Judah with their sins. In particular, the Lord distinguishes the oppressive rulers, priests, and prophets from the poor and weak, who are exploited. The prophet laments after seeing the visions of judgment (1:8–9). The Babylonians and Assyrians arrive as instruments of the Lord's wrath.

The Lord also promises a "remnant" assembled from the lame and afflicted, whom He shall restore. To that end, He promises a ruler in Israel who comes from Bethlehem, whom later Jews and Christians identified as the Messiah, Jesus (Mt 2:5–6; Jn 7:42; cf *ALEN*, p xcix).

Narrative Development or Plot

Since the Book of Micah is a collection of visions or oracles, it does not have a storyline or plot. However, the book does present the threat of doom (chs 1–3) followed by the promise of restoration (chs 4–5), and repeats this theme in its final chapters. (See the outline below.)

Some commentators see the book presenting a lawsuit in which the Lord is the plaintiff, Israel and Judah are the defendants, and the mountains are witnesses. The oracles present God's indictment, His people's weak defense, and God's judgment; Judah receives the sentence with repentance and trust.

Resources

Micah is the fourth of the great eighth-century BC prophets, including Amos, Hosea, and Isaiah. Yet he is often overshadowed by the others, especially his fellow Judean, Isaiah. As a result, he is sometimes called "the neglected prophet" or "little Isaiah." Many inner connections between Micah and Isaiah are traceable (e.g., Mi 4:1–4 and Is 2:2–5; Mi 2:1–5 and Is 5:8; Mi 5:9–14 and Is 2:6). If Amos is the prophet of justice, Hosea of love, and Isaiah of holiness, Micah champions and synthesizes all three of these themes (cf especially 6:8) from the eighth century.

Text and Translation

The Hebrew text of Micah alternates between full clarity and points of difficulty (e.g., Mi 1:10–16). In at least three instances, translators face special challenges (2:7–10; 6:9–12; 7:11–12). For these texts, readers may wish to consult various English translations.

DOCTRINAL CONTENT

Summary Commentary

Chs 1–3 The Lord acts as the witness for the prosecution in the case against His sinful people represented by their capital cities, Samaria and Jerusalem. He marks His appearing with dramatic signs in the creation, pointing forward to what will happen on Judgment Day—all the earth needs to take note of what happened to Israel and Judah. Micah condemns the wickedness of the rich and powerful oppressors and proclaims the Lord's judgment against their covetous behavior. Yet in mercy, the Lord promises to gather a remnant out of Israel and shepherd them. The very people whom God charged to administer justice, to give sound teaching, and to preach His Word are abusing their authority for personal gain. Micah proclaims that the Lord will refuse to hear their cry for deliverance when judgment comes.

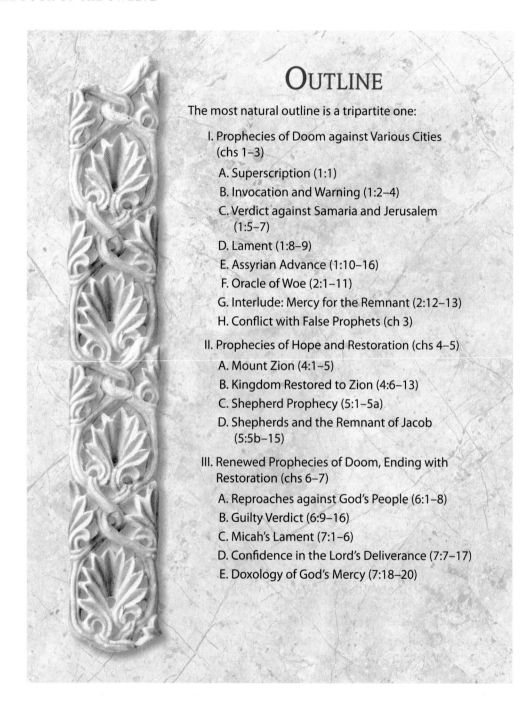

OUTLINE

The most natural outline is a tripartite one:

I. Prophecies of Doom against Various Cities (chs 1–3)

    A. Superscription (1:1)

    B. Invocation and Warning (1:2–4)

    C. Verdict against Samaria and Jerusalem (1:5–7)

    D. Lament (1:8–9)

    E. Assyrian Advance (1:10–16)

    F. Oracle of Woe (2:1–11)

    G. Interlude: Mercy for the Remnant (2:12–13)

    H. Conflict with False Prophets (ch 3)

II. Prophecies of Hope and Restoration (chs 4–5)

    A. Mount Zion (4:1–5)

    B. Kingdom Restored to Zion (4:6–13)

    C. Shepherd Prophecy (5:1–5a)

    D. Shepherds and the Remnant of Jacob (5:5b–15)

III. Renewed Prophecies of Doom, Ending with Restoration (chs 6–7)

    A. Reproaches against God's People (6:1–8)

    B. Guilty Verdict (6:9–16)

    C. Micah's Lament (7:1–6)

    D. Confidence in the Lord's Deliverance (7:7–17)

    E. Doxology of God's Mercy (7:18–20)

Chs 4–5 Micah prophesies of a time when the Lord will bring about His reign of peace and justice by bringing people from all nations to worship at His heavenly temple. Micah also proclaims the time when the Lord will gather His faithful people and reign over them as King. Though the nations assemble against Jerusalem, the Lord promises that in the end all the nations will be threshed out like grain. The Lord does not guarantee that the city of Jerusalem will escape capture, but He does promise a ruler from the house of David who would bring lasting peace and security. (This is a famous prophecy of the birth of Jesus Christ.) The Lord is with His holy remnant, even when they live in the midst of their enemies.

Chs 6–7 The Lord's indictment of Israel is based on the evidence of His saving acts. Yet by their sins, the people act as though serving the Lord wearied them. The Lord clearly reveals in His Word what He requires of His people. Their problem is not a failure to know but a failure to do. The Lord plans to punish the wickedness of powerful city people. He will curse them, not bless them. They will be derided and condemned. Whoever breaks God's laws, especially by using positions of power to exploit the weak, will ultimately face God's judgment. At the time of Micah's ministry, there was corruption and dissolution in the public and private spheres of life. Yet the prophet's conclusion speaks of a coming time when God would gather His dispersed people and vindicate them before the nations. In the closing doxology, Micah describes the Lord's loving and forgiving nature, confidently asserting faith in Him.

Specific Law Themes

Hearing the destruction the Lord threatens, Micah laments and states that he will "go stripped and naked" as an extreme expression of his mourning (1:8). Indeed, he anticipates the shameful nakedness the people will suffer as the conquering foreigners march them away from their homeland, stripped of their identity (1:11; their clothing would have distinguished them from other tribes of people). The devastation will be so thorough, only a remnant of Israel will survive and go into exile. The prophets and others who should have led the people faithfully instead mislead them and oppress them (ch 3). These are some of the major themes of the Law's condemnation in the oracles.

Specific Gospel Themes

The Lord takes the remnant theme, common in the Old Testament prophets, and turns it from a word of condemnation into a word of hope and of

His mercy (2:12; 4:7; 5:7–8; 7:18). He will gather and restore the remnant of Israel. Zion, where atoning sacrifices were offered, will be their rallying place as the Word of God is restored to them and given also to the nations (ch 4), a prophecy of New Testament mission activity. Whereas previously the people suffered under oppressive leaders, the Lord promises to raise up a shepherd from Bethlehem (5:2–5a), fulfilled in Jesus Christ. With the expression "cut off" (5:9–13), the Lord describes the remnant's victory over those who oppressed them and the removal of temptations that misled them. The people who tried God's patience will themselves wait patiently as He fulfills His promise to deliver them (7:7–10, 18–20).

Specific Doctrines

The doctrine of sin is an important element of the book; 2:1–2 illustrates how sin begins as covetousness in the human heart. God's "latter day" mission prophesies about the mission of the New Testament Church and the role of God's Word in it (4:1–4). Christ as king and God's rule are prophesied in 5:2. These are important background for the New Testament teaching of the kingdom of God. Micah 6:3–5 reproaches the Lord's people for unfaithfulness, illustrating the call to repentance. This passage is also the basis of the Reproaches used in the Chief Service for Good Friday (*LSB Altar Book*, pp 518–22), which congregations do well to use. God is most properly worshiped through justice, kindness, and humility (6:8) toward others. Micah 7:19 describes how God will not hold the sins of His people against them on Judgment Day but will purify His people from them.

Application

Chs 1–3 If we abuse our authority as parents, employers, pastors, or teachers, we kindle God's wrath and displeasure. When we serve our own interests at the expense of others, especially those who are powerless and needy, the Lord would drive us to confess our sin, ask forgiveness, and amend our ways. As we have received God's mercy in Christ, He calls us to show mercy by looking after the interests of others (Php 2:1–7). Micah's prophecies against Israel and Judah are especially appropriate in evaluating our works and compelling us to repentance.

Chs 4–7 In this world, hostility, distrust, and conflict will persist among various nations and cultures. Our Father remedies such disunity by leading people to faith in Christ Jesus. As we are baptized into Christ, we are made into God's temple, and cultural and national hostilities are abolished

(Gal 3:26–29). In heaven, we will experience this reality in its fullness. Until then, the Lord has not promised us victory over all our earthly enemies, but He has given us victory over sin, death, and the power of the devil through Jesus, the Son of David, born at Bethlehem in "the fullness of time" (Gal 4:4). Through Word and Sacrament, God continues to gather people into His kingdom, people who confess their sins and look to Him for salvation. As Micah says in closing, "Who is a God like you, pardoning iniquity?" (7:18).

CANONICITY

In the early sixth century, the elders of Judah cited Micah's prophecy, illustrating the authoritative character of the book not long after it was composed (Jer 26:16–19). Jewish scribes bound it into the Book of the Twelve (Minor Prophets; see p 851). The evangelist Matthew described the fulfillment of Micah's prophecy about Bethlehem (Mt 2:5), and Christians received the book into their canon without question.

A shepherd in Bethlehem walks his sheep to pasture. Micah 5:4–5a describes the coming Davidic Messiah as a shepherd.

LUTHERAN THEOLOGIANS ON MICAH

Luther

"The prophet Micah lived at the time of Isaiah. Micah [4:1–3] even uses the words of Isaiah 2[:2–4], and thus one notes that these prophets who lived at the same time preached almost the very same word concerning Christ, as though they had consulted one another on the matter.

"Micah is one of the fine prophets who rebukes the people severely for their idolatry and constantly refers to the coming Christ and to his kingdom. In one respect he is unique among the prophets, in that he points with certainty to Bethlehem, naming it as the town where Christ was to be born [5:2]. For this reason he was famous under the Old Covenant, as Matthew certainly shows in chapter 2[:3–6].

"In short he denounces, he prophesies, he preaches, etc. Ultimately, however, his meaning is that even though Israel and Judah have to go to pieces, Christ will yet come and make all things good. So, too, we now have to rebuke, denounce, comfort, and preach, etc., and then say, 'Even though all be lost, Christ will yet come at the Last Day and help us out of all misfortune.'

"In the first chapter Micah is difficult, a fact to which the original Hebrew contributes. He makes numerous plays on words, such as *Zaanan* for *shaanan*, and *Achzib* and *Mareshah*, etc., twisting the words to give them an ominous meaning. It is as if I were to say, 'Rome, you shall become a room full of emptiness'; or, 'Wittenberg, you shall become a *weiter Berg*,' etc. The grammarians will surely notice this and also observe the pains we have taken." (AE 35:324–25)

For more of Luther's insights on this book, see *Lectures on Micah* (AE 18:205–77).

Gerhard

"*Micah* (*Mikah*) means 'humiliated.' He came from the city of Mareshah in the tribe of Judah (Josh. 15:44). He prophesied at the time of Jotham, Ahaz, and Hezekiah, the kings of Judah, as is evident from the inscription (Mic. 1:1), and was a near contemporary of Isaiah, with whom he agrees in many matters. Therefore he was different from that Micah who foretold the death of wicked King Ahab (1 Kings 22:8; 2 Chron. 18:7), for he came a long time after him.

"The book has seven chapters that contain both addresses of the Law, in which he predicts the overthrow of the kingdoms of both Judah and Israel because of their wickedness and idolatry, and the comforts of the Gospel regarding the coming of the Messiah and the spiritual liberation He would provide, a type of which was the corporeal liberation from the Babylonian captivity. Before all the prophets, [Micah] has the singular distinction of naming the place of the Lord's birth (Mic. 5:2)." (ThC E1 § 161)

Sunrise over the Dead Sea. Cf Mi 7:19.

The birth of Jesus was prophesied in Mi 5:2. Note how the artist includes
a lamb, the animal of sacrifice, at the base of the manger.

FURTHER STUDY ————————————

Lay/Bible Class Resources

Baker, David W., T. Desmond Alexander, and Bruce Waltke. *Obadiah, Jonah and Micah*. TOTC. Downers Grove, IL: InterVarsity Press, 1988. ♫ Compact commentary based on the NIV, with other translations consulted. United Kingdom and American evangelical scholars.

Life by His Word. St. Louis: Concordia, 2009. ♫ More than 1,500 reproducible one-page Bible studies covering each chapter of the canonical Scriptures. Page references to *The Lutheran Study Bible*. CD-Rom and downloadable.

Spaude, Cyril. *Obadiah/Jonah/Micah*. PBC. St. Louis: Concordia, 2004. ♫ Lutheran author. Excellent for Bible classes. Based on the NIV translation.

Weidenschilling, J. M. *Obadiah, Jonah, and Micah: Mercy in the Middle*. GWFT. St. Louis: Concordia, 2004. ♫ Lutheran author. Twelve-session Bible study, including leader's notes and discussion questions.

Church Worker Resources

Allen, Leslie C. *Joel, Obadiah, Jonah, and Micah*. 2nd ed. NICOT. Grand Rapids: Eerdmans, 1994. ♫ An evangelical scholar writing from a critical perspective. The commentary is generally conservative.

Laetsch, Theodore. *Commentary on the Minor Prophets*. St. Louis: Concordia, 1956. ♫ Professor at Concordia Seminary, St. Louis, for many years. Faithful Lutheran interpreter.

Luther, Martin. *Lectures on the Minor Prophets II*. Vol. 18 of AE. St. Louis: Concordia, 1975. ♫ The great reformer's lectures from the 1520s, which reflect his mature approach to biblical interpretation. Luther consulted the Hebrew text and reflected on the application of the prophecies and their New Testament fulfillment.

Mays, James L. *Micah*. OTL. Philadelphia: Westminster, 1976. ♫ Moderately critical, interpreting the text according to theories of its transmission. Sometimes helpful.

Academic Resources

Anderson, Francis I., and David Noel Freedman. *Micah*. Vol. 24E of AB. New York: Doubleday, 2000. ♫ A magisterial work, much concerned with a unified text. More philological than theological, and rather technical.

Ferreiro, Alberto, and Thomas C. Oden, eds. *The Twelve Prophets*. Vol. 14 of ACCS. Downers Grove, IL: InterVarsity Press, 2003. ♫ Citations from Early Church Fathers and other significant Christian teachers.

Hillers, Delbert R. *Micah*. Hermeneia: A Critical and Historical Commentary on the Bible. Philadelphia: Fortress, 1984. ♫ Moderately critical resource. A solid study, defending the unity of the book. However, the overall hermeneutical framework is not theological but sociological (Micah dreams of a better age).

K&D. *Biblical Commentary on the Old Testament: The Twelve Minor Prophets*. 2 vols. Grand Rapids: Eerdmans, 1971 reprint. ♫ This century-and-a-half old work from Lutheran scholars should not be overlooked. Despite its age, it remains a most useful commentary on the Hebrew text.

Kleinert, Paul. *Micah*. LCHS. New York: Charles Scribner's Sons, 1898. ♫ A helpful older example of German biblical scholarship, based on the Hebrew text, which provides references to significant commentaries from the Reformation era forward.

Smith, John Merlin Powis, et. al. *A Critical and Exegetical Commentary on Micah, Zephaniah, Nahum, Habakkuk, Obadiah, and Joel*. ICC. Edinburgh: T&T Clark, 1911. ♫ Liberal and critical, but excellent help on text-critical issues.

Wolff, Hans W. *Micah: A Commentary*. Minneapolis: Augsburg, 1990. ♫ A classical "redaction critical" work, which tries to reconstruct the history of the present text through many centuries. Less useful, though good insights or details are found along the way. Extensive bibliography.

NAHUM

A stronghold in the day of trouble

In many ways, the Book of Nahum is similar to Obadiah (see pp 895–903), which also lacks personal information. The superscription tells us that this seventh-century prophet Nahum was from Elkosh, but that helps little because of its uncertain location. Among the suggested locations of Elkosh are: (1) northern Galilee; (2) southwestern Judah (cf 1:15), near Micah's home; (3) Capernaum (which means, "village of Nahum"); and (4) near Nineveh (where some claim to have discovered Nahum's tomb), perhaps because the vivid description of Nineveh's fall was thought to require an eyewitness. The most likely location is Judah, since the prophet addresses the people of that region.

Historical and Cultural Setting

Nineveh, the capital city of the Assyrian Empire, was a powerful and great city. It was established by Sennacherib (704–681 BC) on the east bank of the Tigris River. Its location on an important trade highway between the Mediterranean Sea and the Persian Gulf made it known as the greatest of all ancient cities (cf Jnh 3:3).

As Nahum wrote, the Assyrian Empire reached the height of its power, bypassing tiny Judah for the greater glory of conquering and occupying Egypt. However, the Assyrians' dominance would not last long. In c 664 Psamtik expelled the Assyrian troops from Egypt. By c 612–609 the Neo-Babylonian Empire had overrun Assyria in keeping with Nahum's prophecy of Nineveh's destruction.

Bodyguards at the palace of Sennacherib. Nahum prophesied Nineveh's destruction.

OVERVIEW

Author
Nahum the prophet

Date
c 663–612 BC

Places
Elkosh; Nineveh; Assyria; Judah; Israel; Thebes

People
Nahum; people of Judah; the king, nobles, and troops of Assyria

Purpose
The Lord fights for those who take refuge in Him

Law Themes
The Lord is jealous and avenging; Nineveh is destroyed

Gospel Themes
The Lord frees oppressed Judah; His Word and feasts are for His people

Memory Verses
The Lord's promise (1:7–8); good news for Judah (1:15); the Lord opposes Assyria (2:13)

TIMELINE

793–753 BC	Reign of Jeroboam II (Israel)
715 BC	Hezekiah repairs temple
c 663–612 BC	Nahum written
640–609 BC	Reign of Josiah (Judah)
629 BC	Josiah purges high places
605 BC	Nebuchadnezzar besieges Jerusalem

COMPOSITION

Author

Little is known about the prophet, but the name Nahum means "comfort" or "the comfort of Yahweh." This suggests that his prophecy, a word of judgment against Nineveh, brought comfort to the people of Judah. Some critics have classified him as a chauvinistic, nationalistic prophet, comparable to the "false prophets" that so exercised contemporaries, such as Jeremiah (cf Hananiah in Jer 28). Such a judgment is itself narrow and fails to appreciate how Nahum's sharp focus connected with the broader themes of biblical theology (see "Specific Doctrines" below).

Date of Composition

The date of Nahum's composition is relatively certain. The contents of the book virtually force a date within a half-century span. The comparison of Nineveh's impending fate to that of Thebes, the upper Egyptian capital, in c 663 BC sets the earliest possible date. At the other end, Nineveh's fall in 612 sets an obvious latest possible date (and even those who do not regard Nahum as prophecy are reluctant to date it very long after that significant event).

Can we be more precise? Conservatives tend to date the Book of Nahum as close to 663 BC as possible, partly in order to highlight its predictive aspect. Others, who diminish prophecy, tend to move closer to a 612 date. How much closer varies, but two favorite suggestions are: (1) 625 BC, shortly after the death of the empire's last great ruler, Ashurbanipal, when Nineveh was first beset by the Medes; or (2) near 612 BC, not long before the city fell to a Medo-Babylonian coalition.

Purpose/Recipients

This short book communicates a message of comfort to God's people in Judah: that the dreaded Assyrian Empire is about to come to an end. For the people of Nineveh, the capital city of Assyria, Nahum's warning of impending destruction should have brought them to repentance. But they did not repent, and Nineveh was destroyed.

Literary Features

Stylistically, Nahum easily heads the list of the Minor Prophets. Many of his deft, vivid, word-pictures are fully worthy of Isaiah, who is regarded as the best of all "writing prophets." Some of Nahum's forcefulness is evident even in translation, but much is inevitably also lost. Nahum has been called the last of the great classical Hebrew poets, and it has been observed that his rhythm "rumbles and rolls, leaps and flashes, like the horsemen and chariots that he describes." Similar praises could easily be multiplied. Readers who wish to capture the literary strength of the book may wish to read it aloud from start to finish.

Genre

Nahum, like Obadiah, is largely a single Gentile-oracle (not against "Edom," but Nineveh/Assyria). Chapter 1 is not only more varied than the later chapters, but it shows signs of adaptation or condensation. Remnants of an acrostic (alphabetic) poem appear in the first part of the chapter. Efforts to recover the original form of the acrostic poem have proved entirely futile, and some commentators deny the existence of such an underlying pattern altogether. However, it does appear that the letters of the Hebrew alphabet can be followed fairly accurately down to *lamedh*, the twelfth letter.

It may well be that Nahum adapted or supplemented earlier compositions in order to make his theological direction unmistakably clear at the outset of the book. Critics might deny the chapter to Nahum altogether, or blame its alleged deterioration on later scribes. However, the superscription's styling of the book as both an "oracle" (*massa'*) and a "vision" (*chazon*) may be the prophet's way of acknowledging that he combined portions of earlier writings. Some critics have attempted to relate the two terms to "genuine" and "ungenuine" portions of the book. Both terms are used so broadly of prophetic messages, however, that such conclusions can scarcely be made.

The Babylonian Chronicle describes how the Babylonians conquered Nineveh.

Scandinavian scholars have regarded the book as a liturgy and Nahum as a prophet writing for worship services, such as a New Year's festival. (Together with Obadiah, Joel, and Habakkuk, Nahum has been a favorite subject of such efforts.) In this theory, the book is read for broad themes, with Assyria only as a current illustration and Nahum as a symbol of comfort rather than as a person. This hypothesis is unthinkable to a conservative interpreter. However, there is no denying that much of Nahum's language reads like psalms that were used at the temple, and a passage like 1:15 at least makes specific reference to liturgical acts.

Characters

The chief character is the **Lord**, described as an avenging warrior. The object of His wrath is **Nineveh and its people**, the capital city of the Assyrians and the bane of Judah, whom the Lord defends. Nahum especially noted the role of charioteers in the coming defeat of Nineveh.

An Assyrian chariot.

OUTLINE

Title (1:1)

I. The Divine Warrior (1:2–15)

  A. A Partial Acrostic Poem of the Lord's Wrath and Care (1:2–8)

  B. Doom for Nineveh and Deliverance for Judah Are Announced (1:9–15)

II. The Future Destruction of Nineveh (chs 2–3)

  A. Nineveh Besieged and Pillaged (2:1–10)

  B. The Lion Taunt (2:11–13)

  C. Woe to the City of Bloodshed (3:1–3)

  D. The Sorceress-Prostitute Taunt (3:4–7)

  E. The Comparison-with-Thebes Taunt (3:8–11)

  F. Final Taunts (3:12–19)

Narrative Development or Plot

The Book of Nahum is an oracle, a divinely inspired message uttered by a prophet sent by God. As such, the book does not have a storyline or plot. However, the book follows a clear outline: God's judgment regarding Nineveh (ch 1), God's verdict (ch 2), and God's execution of His plans (ch 3). As a result, the book relates Nineveh's downfall while the Lord preserves little Judah upon the mountains.

Resources

As noted above, ch 1 likely contains an adaptation of an earlier alphabetical poem. Nahum's description of the day of the Lord and other expressions show similarities to the writings of other Israelite prophets, which is not surprising.

Text and Translations

The Hebrew text is well preserved, despite the conclusions of some critics that the alphabetical poem in ch 1 was corrupted.

DOCTRINAL CONTENT

Summary Commentary

Ch 1 Nahum foretells God's swift and final destruction of Nineveh and the Assyrian Empire. With mighty power, God executes His avenging wrath against His adversaries, who plot evil against Him and His people. The Lord, who is "a jealous and avenging God" (v 2), demands exclusive devotion (Ex 34:14; Dt 4:24).

Ch 2 Nahum mockingly describes the sudden, devastating siege and capture of Nineveh, the city once known for its ruthlessness and cruelty.

Ch 3 For Nineveh, God's patience came to an end. The evil nation of Assyria that had tyrannized surrounding peoples, acquiring wealth and power at their expense, was overthrown, and it disappeared from the annals of history. God's wrath is revealed against all unrighteousness (Rm 1:18).

Specific Law Themes

"The LORD is a jealous and avenging God" (Na 1:2). This proclamation of Nahum does not indicate God is consumed with envy, as a jealous person might be. Instead, this indicates that the Lord will not tolerate people serving other gods (Ex 20:5). And within the great city of Nineveh were wicked and cruel people who practiced witchcraft and worshiped many false gods.

That the Lord is "avenging" is best understood in light of Is 10:10–11 and Zep 2:13–15, which show us that the Lord will not allow the pride and arrogance of a wicked city to stand.

Although Jonah preached a message that the people of Nineveh responded to and were saved (3:10), Nahum preached at a time when the people of Nineveh would not repent. Nahum's warning of ruin was fulfilled in 612 BC when the city was destroyed.

Specific Gospel Themes

Throughout Nahum, the Lord is portrayed as a warrior who fights for those who trust in Him (cf Ex 15:3). This was a message of hope for those in Judah who had been under constant threat from the Assyrian Empire for generations. The promise of the destruction of Judah's enemy was a message of hope and a sign that the Lord had compassion for His people. This image of the divine warrior who protects His people is a powerful reminder that God does not abandon His people, whether Israel in the Old Testament or His Church today.

Specific Doctrines

Nahum emphasizes the justice and universality of God's action in world history. He concentrates on the application of that justice to a major scourge of God's people (as most other prophets do). Assyria did God's will by punishing Israel for its sins, but the Assyrians deserved God's judgment themselves. Biblical theology reminds us that the judgment on Nineveh becomes part of our history. God also judges our imperiousness. The dominant teaching in Nahum has to do with God's wrath, tempered with promises of comfort and protection for God's people (1:6–7). In this way, the book defines the "good news" (1:15), the Old Testament expression translated as "Gospel" in the New Testament.

Application

Chs 1–2 God will not leave unpunished those whose way of life is violence and force (cf Mt 26:52). God has revealed a different way, one of mercy and peace through His Son, the Prince of Peace. As God mercifully delivered ancient Judah from Assyrian oppression, so He rescued us from sin, death, and the devil through the victory of our Lord Jesus Christ.

Ch 3 Because of our sins, we also deserve His wrath and displeasure. Yet "God has not destined us for wrath, but to obtain salvation through our Lord Jesus Christ" (1 Th 5:9). God's wrath was poured out on Christ, and by faith in Him we have pardon and peace.

CANONICITY

As noted above, Jesus son of Sirach remarked on the usefulness of the Book of the Twelve (p 851). Scribes at Qumran copied a commentary on the book (4QpNah) and copies of Nahum itself show up in other collections (e.g., Mur 88; 8 Hev XII gr). The apostle Paul cited Nahum as Scripture (Rm 10:15)

LUTHERAN THEOLOGIANS ON NAHUM

Luther

"The prophet Nahum prophesies about the destruction that the Assyrians were to inflict upon the people of Israel and Judah, as it was then actually accomplished by Shalmaneser and Sennacherib. This destruction took place because of the people's great sins. It was limited, however, in that the righteous remnant were to be preserved, as Hezekiah and those like him then experienced. Therefore it seems that Nahum came before Isaiah, or was at least his contemporary.

"Next Nahum announces the destruction of the kingdom of Assyria, especially of Nineveh. While this city was very righteous in the time of Jonah, it afterward became full of wickedness again, and greatly afflicted the captives of Israel. Therefore even Tobit announces the final ruin of Nineveh's wickedness, and says, 'Its iniquity will bring it to destruction.' True to his name (for Nahum means *consolator*, or comforter), he comforts God's people, telling them that their enemies, the Assyrians, shall in turn be destroyed.

"At the end of chapter 1[:15], he talks like Isaiah 52[:7] of the good preachers who proclaim peace and salvation on the mountains, and bids Judah joyfully to celebrate. Though that can be understood to refer to the time of Hezekiah, after Sennacherib, when Judah was rescued and survived against King Sennacherib, nevertheless, this is a general prophecy referring also to Christ. It declares that the good news and the joyous worship of God, taught and confirmed by God's word, shall remain in Judah. Thus he is, and is properly called, a real *Nahum*." (AE 35:326)

For more of Luther's insights on this book, see *Lectures on Nahum* (AE 18:279–315).

Gerhard

"*Nahum* (*Nachum*) means 'preacher or teacher of repentance' or 'comforter.' It is not evident as to when he lived and prophesied. From the circumstances, we can draw the probable conclusion that he lived before the Babylonian captivity, around the end of the kingdom of Hezekiah, and that he was a contemporary of Micah, ninety years after Jonah. His native city was Elkosh, an unknown city (Nah. 1:1). Some think that Elkosh was a district in the tribe of Simeon. He preached destruction to the Assyrians, who were going to afflict the Lord's people, but especially to the city of Nineveh, the metropolis of the Assyrian kingdom. Although the Ninevites had repented at the time of Jonah, through which they had escaped the punishment divinely foretold them, later they nevertheless returned to their old wickedness, zealously practiced every kind of evil, insulted God, and grievously afflicted His people. Consequently, they finally fell into their long-deserved punishment.

"The book has three chapters that contain both the prophecy of the destruction of the Assyrians (Nahum 1) and his explanation of the reasons for it (Nahum 2–3)." (ThC E1 § 162)

FURTHER STUDY

Lay/Bible Class Resources

Baker, David W. *Nahum, Habakkuk, Zephaniah*. TOTC. Downers Grove, IL: InterVarsity Press, 1988. ♫ Compact commentary based on the NIV, with other translations consulted. American evangelical scholar.

Collver III, Albert B. *Nahum, Habakkuk, Zephaniah: The Lord Delivers His Faithful*. GWFT. St. Louis: Concordia, 2010. ♫ Lutheran theologian. Nine-session Bible study, including leader's notes and discussion questions.

Life by His Word. St. Louis: Concordia, 2009. ♫ More than 1,500 reproducible one-page Bible studies covering each chapter of the canonical Scriptures. Page references to *The Lutheran Study Bible*. CD-Rom and downloadable.

Westendorf, James J. *Nahum/Habakkuk/Zephaniah*. PBC. St. Louis: Concordia, 2005. ♫ Lutheran author. Excellent for Bible classes. Based on the NIV translation.

Church Worker Resources

García-Treto, Francisco. "The Book of Nahum, Introduction, Commentary and Reflections" in vol. 7 of *The New Interpreter's Bible*. Nashville: Abingdon, 1996. ♫ Written by an evangelical scholar, based on the NIV and NRSV.

Luther, Martin. *Lectures on the Minor Prophets*. Vol. 18 of AE. St. Louis: Concordia, 1975. ♫ The great reformer's lectures from the 1520s, which reflect his mature approach to biblical interpretation. Luther consulted the Hebrew text and reflected on the application of the prophecies and their New Testament fulfillment.

Maier, Walter A. *Nahum*. St. Louis: Concordia, 1987 reprint. ♫ A detailed, thorough study by a Lutheran interpreter.

Robertson, O. Palmer. *The Books of Nahum, Habakkuk, and Zephaniah*. NICOT. Grand Rapids: Eerdmans, 1990. ♫ Written by a conservative, American Evangelical scholar, with special emphasis on the context and structure of the book.

Sweeney, Marvin A. *The Twelve Prophets*. Vol. 2 of *Berit Olam*. Collegeville, MN: Liturgical Press, 2000. ♫ Treats the literary structure of the Book of the Twelve as a whole, using critical approaches, then provides specific commentary on each book. Based on the NRSV.

Academic Resources

Christensen, Duane L. *Nahum: A New Translation with Introduction and Commentary*. Anchor Yale Bible. New Haven, CT: Yale University Press, 2009. ♫ A unique commentary that applies the author's logoprosodic analysis to Nahum's poetry as well as thorough philology.

K&D. *Biblical Commentary on the Old Testament: The Twelve Minor Prophets*. 2 vols. Grand Rapids: Eerdmans, 1971 reprint. ♫ This century-and-a-half old work from Lutheran scholars should not be overlooked. Despite its age, it remains a most useful commentary on the Hebrew text.

Kleinert, Paul. *Nahum*. LCHS. New York: Charles Scribner's Sons, 1898. ♫ A helpful, older example of German biblical scholarship, based on the Hebrew text, which provides references to significant commentaries from the Reformation era forward.

Fresco-Mosaic of Jesus Christ as the the Good Shepherd. In the Bible, leaders are described as shepherds who should care diligently for the people (cf Na 3:18). The Gospels describe Jesus as a faithful leader of God's people.

HABAKKUK

The righteous shall live by his faith

In 612 BC, the Chaldeans besieged Nineveh, which fell after only three months. After absorbing the Assyrian Empire, Babylonian troops headed southward toward Judea. Jerusalem's outer walls, built by Manasseh at the beginning of the seventh century (2Ch 33:14), could not withhold the approaching Babylonians when Judean rulers rebelled against them at the end of the seventh century.

Habakkuk probably served as a prophet during the last days of King Josiah's reign and the first days of King Jehoiakim's reign in Judah sometime around 605 BC. When he delivered his prophetic message, the predicted Chaldean invasion of Judah was close at hand, so close that the people of Habakkuk's time would live to see it. He was a contemporary of other prophets active in Judea and Jerusalem, such as Zephaniah and Jeremiah.

Historical and Cultural Setting

The rise of the Neo-Babylonian Empire was a surprise. The Assyrians attacked and burned Babylonia in 689 and again in 648 BC. However, in 626 BC, the Babylonian ruler Nabopolassar advanced against the Assyrians. Although the Assyrians pushed his troops back temporarily, Nabopolassar soon led them forth again, keeping the Assyrians in retreat or under siege. His son and successor, Nebuchadnezzar II, defeated the Egyptians at Carchemish in 605 BC, which cleared the way for their advance against Egypt and—what to them was a minor state—Judah.

The Babylonians destroyed the temple complex built by Solomon. The Western Wall in Jerusalem is a retaining wall built by Herod for the second temple. Jews still gather at the wall today for prayers.

OVERVIEW

Author
Habakkuk the prophet

Date
c 605 BC

Places
The Lord's temple (Jerusalem); Chaldea; Lebanon; Teman

People
Habakkuk; the Chaldeans; all people

Purpose
The Lord shows that He works even through evil nations such as Babylon to accomplish His good purposes

Law Themes
Evil, which God permits to afflict His people; the need for patience; woes against drunkenness and idolatry; God's wrath

Gospel Themes
The Lord supplies patience; the righteous shall live by faith; God remembers mercy; faith and joy in the midst of trouble

Memory Verses
Habakkuk's complaint (1:2–4); a message for the arrogant and the righteous (2:2–4); a mercy prayer (3:2); rejoice always in the Lord (3:17–19)

· ·

TIMELINE

640–609 BC	Reign of Josiah (Judah)
605 BC	Nebuchadnezzar besieges Jerusalem
c 605 BC	Habakkuk written
599 BC	Nebuchadnezzar takes captives
587 BC	Jerusalem temple destroyed

While these military and political changes took place, Habakkuk was troubled by the fact that God appeared to be ignoring the sin and violence that abounded in the land of Judah (cf e.g., Ezk 8). When Habakkuk cried out to God, the Lord answered that He soon would raise up the Chaldeans, that bitter and hasty nation, terrible and dreadful, to punish Judah for its sinfulness. Habakkuk was then perplexed that God had chosen a nation worse than His own people to punish them.

COMPOSITION

Author

The Book of Habakkuk has many broad similarities with Nahum, beginning with its superscription that characterizes the work again as, in effect, both an oracle and a vision. The superscription tells us little else, and in truth, everything stated about the prophet is deducted from its contents, from speculation, or from tradition.

The first conundrum is the prophet's name. Beginning in the middle ages, interpreters sought to explain the name in association with the Hebrew term meaning to grasp or embrace. However, the name is similar to the Akkadian name for a kitchen herb, presumably current in Judah because of the massive Mesopotamian influences. (Cf other names from plants, "Susanna" means lily; "Hadassah" [Esther] means myrtle, etc.)

Habakkuk's name may derive from the Akkadian name for the Asian herb, basil.

Habakkuk himself appears to give us some information about his inspiration. If Hab 2:1 is to be taken literally, it reports that the prophet took his stand "on the tower" to watch until a vision came in answer to his complaint (cf Is 21:8). When the vision did come, he was commanded to "make it plain on tablets" (2:2; possibly a display of placards). Habakkuk 3:16 may describe physical sensations in the prophet as his prayer was answered.

Some have tried to interpret ch 3 to mean Habakkuk was a "liturgical" or temple prophet. Others take "prophet" (3:1) to mean "singer," as in Chronicles, and cite especially 3:19b as evidence.

Later legend and tradition mentioned Habakkuk often, perhaps because the book itself says so little. The most important tale appears in one of the apocryphal additions to Daniel (14:33–39), entitled "Bel and the Dragon" (see *LBC* vol. 2, pp 127–33). Here Habakkuk appears as a Judean who miraculously carries pottage to, and finally rescues, Daniel after he had been cast to the lions a second time. The Old Greek version of the LXX described Habakkuk as "the son of Jesus from the tribe of Levi" (v 1; "Jesus" was a common Israelite name).

Date of Composition

Early critics tended to date most of the book as late as possible. For example, Bernhard L. Duhm's influential suggestion emended *kasdim* (Chaldeans) in 1:6 to *kittim* (Greeks; a change of only one consonant in Hebrew), and similarly *yain* (wine) in 2:5 to *yawan* (Greece). This allowed him to date the entire book around the time of Alexander the Great, toward the end of the fourth century. In time, Duhm's approach fell out of favor, and the Qumran scrolls have destroyed the argument. (It is interesting, however, that although the Dead Sea manuscript plainly reads *kasdim* [Chaldeans], the accompanying midrashic commentary applies it to the *kittim,* by whom the Qumran community meant the Hellenistic party and/or the Seleucids [cf Dn 11:30].)

Purpose/Recipients

The prophet opened the book with a complaint against God. But the ultimate target of Habakkuk's message was the people of Judah and Jerusalem who would face the Babylonian threat (cf "Chaldeans" in 1:6). Habakkuk is unique among the Prophetic Books of the Old Testament in that he never directly addressed God's people, who would read his message. Yet, by making his message plain (2:2), he enabled people to understand who the Lord is and what He will be doing for them (v 20).

Literary Features

Genre

Like the works of other Israelite prophets, the Book of Habakkuk is an oracle. However, it presents a debate between the prophet and God (chs 1 and 2), ending with a psalm of submission (ch 3).

Commentators often thought that a compiler borrowed ch 3 from a liturgical collection, where perhaps this psalm already possessed its present superscription linking it with Habakkuk. Initially the absence of the psalm from the Qumran Habakkuk scroll caused some to believe that it had been

OUTLINE

Title (1:1)

I. The Debate between Habakkuk and God (1:2–2:5)

  A. The Argument about Divine Justice (1:2–11)

    1. Habakkuk's first complaint: lack of justice in Judah (1:2–4)

    2. The Lord's response: His plan for avenging evil (1:5–11)

      a. Preparations for retribution (1:5)

      b. Means identified as the Chaldeans (1:6)

      c. Chaldeans described (1:7–11)

  B. The Second Argument (1:12–2:5)

    1. Habakkuk's second complaint: how can God look on as "the wicked swallows up the man more righteous than he?" (1:12–2:1)

    2. The Lord's response: His rule is sure, and He will judge the wicked in His own time (2:2–5)

II. The Lord's Justice Is Certain: Woes to the Arrogant Oppressors (2:6–20)

  A. The Plunderer Plundered (2:6–8)

  B. The Fortified Dismantled (2:9–11)

  C. The Citizens Crushed (2:12–14)

  D. The Shameless Put to Shame (2:15–17)

  E. The Idolater Silenced (2:18–20)

III. Habakkuk's Psalm of Submission (ch 3)

borrowed. However, that appeal is today widely regarded as an argument from silence, and most commentators would probably agree that the psalm provides an integral crown and climax of the book.

The book's unique structure has provoked various opinions about its genre. The first two chapters of Habakkuk initially exhibit a neat balance of two laments (1:2–4 and 1:12–17) and two replies (1:5–11 and 2:1–5). Habakkuk 2:6–19 continues with a prophetic speech of doom, structured around five "Woes," and concludes (v 20) with a liturgical piece. This structure led some early critics to compare the book with classical Greek dramas and even to suggest that it had been intended for dramatic performance. Other critical scholars seized upon the apparent Akkadian background of the prophet's name as possible evidence of cultic (fertility) associations for the book. Also, the French scholar Humbert worked out a detailed theory according to which the book originated among the temple prophets associated with the Jerusalem temple in the last quarter of the seventh century. He suggested that the present order of the oracles stems from a liturgical festival c 602, awaiting Nebuchadnezzar's imminent invasion to deliver them from Jehoiakim's evil rule. The major evidence for Humbert's theory is the psalm (ch 3), replete with typical psalmic superscription, "Selah" (its only occurrence outside the psalter), and even a "colophon" to the choirmaster. But much of ch 1 is also a quite typical individual lament, chs 1 and 2 have an almost antiphonal structure, and ch 2 concludes with what can easily be understood as a rubric or versicle.

The critics are certainly right to pay attention to the oracle's structure, but its meaning cannot be determined through comparisons with Greek or Akkadian culture, nor can the specific circumstances for its writing be isolated as thoroughly as Humbert proposed.

Characters

Who is the subject of the laments, and/or against whom are the woes of Hab 2 directed? Conversely, who are the righteous in 1:2–4, 13? Are the same people in view in all instances, or different ones? Are the evils spoken of internal (Judah's) or external (some foreign oppressor)? Habakkuk gives no specific historical references, and in the light of other prophets, the moral concerns could apply to Gentile nations as well as to Israel (or to both). Just about every empire in the history of the Near East from Assyria on has been suggested as playing a role.

Certainly in the broader canonical context, and perhaps quite specifically, the prophet's aim is all ungodliness, whenever it manifested itself.

Narrative Development or Plot

Habakkuk is divided into three major parts: the terrible judgment to come through the Chaldeans (ch 1); the five woes with which God threatens Chaldea (ch 2); and the majestic appearing of God and Habakkuk's response (ch 3). Although the book does not have a storyline or plot, it shares the common movement from condemnation to mercy and restoration found throughout the prophets.

Habakkuk contains a series of questions and responses relating to life's constant problems: "Lord, why are You not doing anything about the evil that surrounds us?" (1:1–14). God does act, but not as we expect, so we then ask "Why?" (1:5–17). God answers the "why" as far as the wicked are concerned (2:6–20). God emphasizes His answer by His person and by His action (3:1–15). The response of God's people to God's answers and actions is a psalm of praise and trust (3:16–19).

This is not merely a dramatic construction, the artistically executed plan of a skillful writer, but the natural result of the manner in which God dealt with His prophet. The book was intended as an urgent call to repentance for the wicked, as a message of consolation for the little flock of believers, and as an admonition for the latter to continue steadfast in their trust and confidence in the promised salvation and Savior.

Resources

As noted above, Hab 3 can be regarded as a psalm, which could have existed as a separate composition before it was incorporated into the present work.

Text and Translations

The Hebrew text of Habakkuk presents some challenging readings. The Qumran commentary (1QpHab), the Scroll of the Minor Prophets (Mur 88), the Greek Scroll at Nahal Hever (8 Hev XII gr), and LXX manuscripts have variant readings, though most are spelling changes that do not affect meaning. Although the Qumran commentary did not include text for ch 3 of the book, the other early witnesses did.

DOCTRINAL CONTENT

Summary Commentary

Ch 1 Habakkuk experiences firsthand the oppressive policies of Jehoiakim, king of Judah (609–598 BC; 2Ki 23:36–37), and he feels surrounded by unchecked evil because of failure to enforce God's Law. Habakkuk grumbles against God. God's response to Habakkuk's complaint describes the powerful and arrogant nation that He will raise up to punish Judah for the sins in that nation's midst.

Babylonian warriors.

Like others of great faith, Habakkuk argues and wrestles with God, waiting for answers to explain God's incomprehensible ways (cf Gn 18:23–32; Jer 20:7–18; 2Co 12:7–9). Yet Habakkuk does not lose patience but waits to hear what God will say.

Ch 2 God responds to Habakkuk's complaint by urging patient trust, for in due time the instrument of Judah's chastisement (Chaldea) will itself suffer judgment for its cruel misdeeds.

In a series of five "woes," the prophet derisively pronounces God's judgment against the sins of Babylon: greed, pride, violence, shameful abuse of neighbors, and idolatry. Habakkuk's words remain a sober reminder of God's displeasure with human sin in all of its manifestations.

Ch 3 As Habakkuk reflects on a terrifying manifestation of God's glory and power, he prays for mercy, quietly confident of God's ultimate deliverance even in the midst of great distress. The book that begins with a complaint now ends with an expression of joyful confidence in the God of salvation.

Specific Law Themes

The major issue in Habakkuk centers around the problem of evil. In many respects, this prophet echoes the Book of Job or certain psalms when he asks the age-old question: Why do You permit evildoers to flourish, allowing them to oppress the righteous? (1:13). This is a question to which there are only partial answers. The Lord seems silent in response to the injustices and sufferings of His people, who can only wait.

Excessive love of wine (or wealth) besets the arrogant; this reckless bravado led to their downfall (2:5). The wealth the Chaldeans had accumulated from the nations they oppressed would be plundered by the survivors of those very nations (2:7–8). Habakkuk ridicules idols as a product of human imagination. Silent and dead, the idols are able to teach no one (2:19). Those intoxicated with pride most often deal treacherously with others and are themselves in danger of destruction (Pr 16:18).

Specific Gospel Themes

Habakkuk is told to wait and attend his own life (2:3). He is to live by faith that God will eliminate evil in His own proper time. Waiting for the Lord is an act of faith and hope (Ps 33:20–22). In contrast to the arrogant person, the one who lives by faith is righteous, trusting in God's promises while waiting for the Lord to act (Hab 2:4).

The message of the Book of Habakkuk can well be summarized in God's statement of promise: "the righteous shall live by his faith" (2:4), and the prophet's statement of faith, "I will rejoice in the LORD; I will take joy in the God of my salvation" (3:18). The book is a source of continuing encouragement for all who live by faith and wait for the Lord's final return and the end of all evil.

Specific Doctrines

The problem of the book is the problem of evil—in world history, in the Church, in the human heart—the realization that every human "solution" contains the seed of its own dissolution and often only exacerbates the problems.

God's answer is primarily to trust, to have faith that God will work all things for good (cf Rm 8:28). The posture of the faithful supplicant, then, will always be one of waiting. There finally is no other answer to the problem of evil but the answer of faith.

The Lord's answer to Habakkuk in 2:4, "the righteous shall live by his faith," had monumental impact upon the Church's teaching twice in history. First, it shaped the teaching of early Christians in contrast to legalism, as shown by the number of times Hab 2:4 is referenced in the New Testament. Second, this passage played a similar role during the Protestant Reformation, which directed the Church's teaching back to the New Testament emphasis of justification by God's grace through faith. As a result, Habakkuk's little book still profoundly affects the Church's doctrine and focus. Luther wrote, "Here we see that the prophets preached and stressed faith in the Christ as much as we do in the New Testament; here we see that Habakkuk is so bold as to condemn all other works and attribute life exclusively to faith. For he states plainly enough that the unbeliever will succeed in nothing. Let him pray and wear himself and work himself to death. His works already stand condemned as counting for nothing at all; nor will they help him. And the believer shall live by faith without works" (AE 19:197).

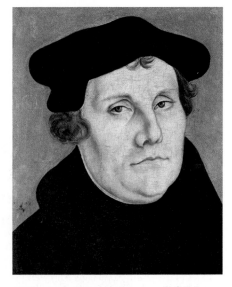

Hab 2:4 influenced New Testament authors and reformers such as Martin Luther.

Application

Chs 1–2 Human beings dare never sit in judgment of God's ways, which are beyond human discernment (Rm 9:20; 11:33). We, however, can place our trust in Him, confident that in the end He will carry out His beneficial will in our lives. We need to remember that God hears our prayers and that, though we struggle when facing life's perplexing questions, nothing can separate us from His love (Rm 8:38–39). The Lord promises to answer those who call on Him, though in His own time and manner. God's Word is the light for our path (Ps 119:105).

3:1–16 Much in our lives brings anguish, fear, and even feelings of helplessness to our hearts (Ps 25:16–18; Ac 14:22). God does humble us under His mighty hand, but He does so in order to exalt us (1Pt 5:6). We also need to hear God's "woe" and humbly repent of our sin. As the Lord was present in His holy temple, so He is present with us in His Holy Word and Sacraments to pardon and cleanse.

3:17–19 When we look to ourselves and our own strength, we have reason only to despair. But when we are cast down and experience inner turmoil, we say, "Yet I will rejoice in the LORD; I will take joy in the God of my salvation" (Hab 3:18).

For thoughts about Habakkuk's series of questions and responses, see "Narrative Development or Plot" above.

CANONICITY

The "pesher" or spiritual "commentary" on Hab 1–2 is among our prize finds from Qumran. Like other Dead Sea Scrolls, it tells us much about the principles of interpretation prevalent among the Jews there (often comparable to, or at least illuminating those of the New Testament). They treasured Habakkuk's message. Early Christian references to Habakkuk demonstrate a similar regard: Ac 13:40–41 (Hab 1:5); Mt 24:28 (Hab 1:8); and the quotations of Hab 2:4 in Rm 1:17; Gal 3:11; and Heb 10:38.

The Nubian Ibex and other Near Eastern antelope
are known for sure-footedness (cf Hab 3:19).

Lutheran Theologians on Habakkuk

Luther

"This Habakkuk is a prophet of comfort, who is to strengthen and support the people, to prevent them from despairing of the coming of Christ, however strangely things may go. This is why he uses every device and stratagem that can serve to keep strong in their hearts the faith in the promised Christ. His message is as follows.

"It is indeed true that because of the people's sins the lands shall have to be destroyed by the king of Babylon. But Christ and his kingdom shall not fail to come on that account. On the contrary, the destroyer, the king of Babylon, shall have little good out of his conquest, for he too shall perish. For it is God's nature and work to help when there is need and to come in the midst of the proper season. As Habakkuk's song says, 'In wrath he remembers mercy' [3:2]; or as the proverb puts it, 'When the rope holds tightest, it breaks.'

"In the same way we must support Christians with the word of God in anticipation of the Last Day, even though it appears that Christ is delaying long and will not come. For Christ himself says that he will come when men least expect it—when they are building and planting, buying and selling, eating and drinking, marrying and giving in marriage [Luke 17:27–28]—in order that at least some, though not all, can be preserved in faith. For in this matter preaching and believing are essential, as we see every day. . . .

"Habakkuk certainly has a name appropriate to his office, for Habakkuk means an embracer, one who embraces another and takes him in his arms. This is what he does in his prophecy: he embraces his people and takes them in his arms. That is, he comforts them and supports them, as one embraces a weeping child or person to quiet and compose him with the assurance that things will go better, if God so will." (AE 35:327–28)

For more of Luther's insights on this book, see *Lectures on Habakkuk* (AE 19:105–237).

Gerhard

"*Habakkuk* (*Chabaquq*) means 'embracer,' 'comforter,' or 'wrestler.' Where and when he lived are not expressed. From the circumstances, we draw the probable conclusion that he lived around the time of Jeremiah or a little earlier, because he prophesies concerning the Babylonians, who were going to destroy the kingdom of Judah. In the apocryphal additions to Daniel, [Habakkuk] is mentioned as having brought food to Daniel in the lions' den.

"The book has three chapters that contain: (1) the complaint about the serious sins of the people of Judah; (2) the prophecy of the punishments that would come at the hands of the Chaldeans; (3) comfort regarding their coming liberation; and (4) an exhortation to patience and prayers, whose form he prescribes." (ThC E1 § 163)

FURTHER STUDY

Lay/Bible Class Resources

Baker, David W. *Nahum, Habakkuk, Zephaniah*. TOTC. Downers Grove, IL: InterVarsity Press, 1988. ๑ Compact commentary based on the NIV, with other translations consulted. American evangelical scholar.

Collver III, Albert B. *Nahum, Habakkuk, Zephaniah: The Lord Delivers His Faithful*. GWFT. St. Louis: Concordia, 2010. ๑ Lutheran theologian. Nine-session Bible study, including leader's notes and discussion questions.

Kettner, Edward G., Elaine Richter, and Kevin S. Golden. *Minor Prophets: Amos, Jonah, Habakkuk*. Leaders Guide and Enrichment Magazine/Study Guide. LL. St. Louis: Concordia, 2009. ๑ In-depth, nine-session Bible study with individual, small group, and lecture portions.

Life by His Word. St. Louis: Concordia, 2009. ๑ More than 1,500 reproducible one-page Bible studies covering each chapter of the canonical Scriptures. Page references to *The Lutheran Study Bible*. CD-Rom and downloadable.

Westendorf, James J. *Nahum/Habakkuk/Zephaniah*. PBC. St. Louis: Concordia, 2005. ๑ Lutheran author. Excellent for Bible classes. Based on the NIV translation.

Church Worker Resources

Luther, Martin. *Lectures on the Minor Prophets II*. Vol. 19 of AE. St. Louis: Concordia, 1974. ๑ The great reformer's lectures from the 1520s, which reflect his mature approach to biblical interpretation. Luther consulted the Hebrew text and reflected on the application of the prophecies and their New Testament fulfillment.

Robertson, O. Palmer. *The Books of Nahum, Habakkuk, and Zephaniah*. NICOT. Grand Rapids: Eerdmans, 1990. ๑ Written by a conservative, American Evangelical scholar, with special emphasis on the context and structure of the book.

Smith, Ralph L. *Micah–Malachi*. Vol. 32 of WBC. Waco, Texas: Word Books, 1984. ๑ Written by an American evangelical from a conservative perspective.

Sweeney, Marvin A. *The Twelve Prophets*. Vol. 2 of *Berit Olam*. Collegeville, MN: Liturgical Press, 2000. ๑ Treats the literary structure of the Book of the Twelve as a whole, using critical approaches, then provides specific commentary on each book. Based on the NRSV.

Academic Resources

Andersen, Francis I. *Habakkuk*. Vol. 25 of AB. New York: Doubleday, 2001. ๑ The most detailed of the modern commentary on the Hebrew text, focused on interpreting the final form of the text in its cultural context.

K&D. *Biblical Commentary on the Old Testament: The Twelve Minor Prophets*. 2 vols. Grand Rapids: Eerdmans, 1971 reprint. ๑ This century-and-a-half old work from Lutheran scholars should not be overlooked. Despite its age, it remains a most useful commentary on the Hebrew text.

Kleinert, Paul. *Habakkuk*. LCHS. New York: Charles Scribner's Sons, 1898. ๑ A helpful, older example of German biblical scholarship, based on the Hebrew text, which provides references to significant commentaries from the Reformation era forward.

ZEPHANIAH

Seek refuge in the name of the Lord

Modern Samaritans burn away the offcasts of Passover sacrifices (cf the practices in Lv 3–4). King Josiah restored the feast of Passover in an effort to reform Judean religion.

Zephaniah's superscription says only "in the days of Josiah." Since Josiah reigned over 30 years (640–609 BC), the dating is not precise. Majority opinion, probably correctly, favors the period before Josiah's reformation (c 625) when the dire religious situation described in the book seems most likely to have existed. Usually, however, the date is not put much before 625, because of possible problems with the prophet's youth. (See "Author" below.) He was a contemporary of Habakkuk and Jeremiah, who also prophesied in Jerusalem and Judah.

Historical and Cultural Setting

Josiah came to the throne of Judah in 640 BC following the religiously disastrous reigns of Manasseh and Amon. The Assyrian Empire was in decline during the last quarter of the seventh century, and Babylon was rising in importance (see "Historical and Cultural Setting," p 947). Zephaniah prophesied at a time when the Judean people were rebellious against God. They had come to believe that the Lord would neither help nor harm them. They were worshiping idols and not seeking the Lord. They valued only wealth, real estate, and business (1:12–13).

COMPOSITION

Author

Zephaniah, whose name may be translated "The LORD protects," is the neglected prophet among those of the seventh century, especially when measured against the breadth, depth, and variety of his oracles. One cannot help but wonder whether he gets less attention because his book is an epitome of the prophetic messages during this era.

We have no more personal information about the prophet than that given in the superscription. The genealogy is unusually long, going back four generations to Hezekiah. Inevitably, that has raised more questions than answers. On the one hand, one wonders what its purpose might have been if Zephaniah's great-great-grandfather was not the well-known king. (The name Hezekiah does not seem to have been too common.) On the other hand, if that was the intent, why was not "the king" added to the name, which would remove all ambiguity? It is difficult, but not impossible, to squeeze the required number of generations into the time available, but the brief time span does suggest that Zephaniah, like Jeremiah, may have been relatively young, at least at the time of his call. For that reason, he is occasionally referred to as the "young prophet." If he was of royal blood, his inclusion of "the king's sons" in the denunciations of Zep 1:8 would carry extra weight.

OVERVIEW

Author
Zephaniah the prophet

Date
640–609 BC

Places
Judah; Jerusalem; Israel; Philistia; Moab; Ammon; Assyria

People
Zephaniah and his forebears; King Josiah, son of Amon; the Israelites; the Philistines; Moabites; Ammonites; Cushites; Assyrians

Purpose
Zephaniah announces God's wrath against the nations as a warning for Judah, whom he calls to repent

Law Themes
God's wrath against the nations, including His chosen people; the day of the Lord

Gospel Themes
The day of the Lord; the remnant preserved; the nations seek the Lord; the Lord is in our midst

Memory Verses
The Lord's awesomeness (2:11); the nations changed (3:9–13); quieting Zion (3:16–17)

. . . .

TIMELINE

793–753 BC	Reign of Jeroboam II (Israel)
696–642 BC	Reign of Manasseh (Judah)
640–609 BC	Zephaniah written; reign of Josiah (Judah)
628 BC	Jeremiah called to be a prophet
605 BC	Nebuchadnezzar besieges Jerusalem

The name of Zephaniah's father has also aroused speculation. Cushi would ordinarily translate as "Ethiopian," or more properly, "Nubian" (cf Moses' wife, Nu 12:1). The name may imply partially foreign ancestry, but one can say no more.

Inevitably, there have also been those who wanted to make Zephaniah a priest. Temple language and allusions do appear in the book (e.g., Zep 1:7, 9; 2:1), but not enough to prove the case. Some have also used the prophet's name as support for this thesis. One could translate it as "Yahweh is Zaphon." Zaphon was an important Canaanite god, somewhat like the spirit of the "mountain of the gods" in Canaanite mythology, which also bore this name. If this applies, the name may have polemical or apologetic significance: Yahweh really is what Zaphon only claims to be. It is argued that a priest might be more likely to bear such a name. That, however, is not only uncertain, but the historical significance of the name may long since have fallen into disuse. Hence, later generations usually explained the name with reference to another root: "Yahweh has hidden" (or "treasured," "cherished," etc.).

Date of Composition

The book's opening words make plain that it was written in the latter half of the seventh century BC.

At one time, the hypothesis was popular that Zephaniah's ominous predictions of invasion referred to a Scythian threat. Because Herodotus's reference to such an invasion of Israel is not substantiated by the wealth of information on the period that we now possess, the whole idea is largely abandoned today. At any rate, the assumption has no more merit here than in the case of Jeremiah's early oracles (chs 1–6).

Purpose/Recipients

Zephaniah proclaimed God's wrath against Judah and the Gentile nations because of their shamelessness. He described the coming day of the Lord, which would affect all people. Finally, he celebrated how the Lord would restore the remnant of Israel.

Literary Features

Genre

Zephaniah, like other prophets, wrote a series of oracles and "woes," which he introduced as "the word of the LORD" (1:1). Zephaniah is an almost perfect example of the classical threefold prophetic outline. Each of the three chapters corresponds to a type of prophetic oracle: judgment on Judah, judgment on Gentile nations, and promise of restoration (cf outline below). Zephaniah frequently used the "prophetic perfect" in his pronouncements of God's promises (see p 898).

Characters

The **Lord**, who threatens wrath but also promises restoration, is a chief character in the prophecies of Zephaniah. He speaks against a variety of nations and their leaders: Judah, Philistia, Moab, Ammon, Cush, and Assyria. But in the last chapter the message is extended to all people.

Narrative Development or Plot

As a collection of oracles, the Book of Zephaniah does not have a storyline or plot. Like other prophetic books, it moves from themes of judgment to redemption. The joy-filled celebration of God's mercy toward Israel in 3:9–20 contrasts sharply with the bitter day of the Lord in ch 1.

Resources

Zephaniah's themes are reminiscent of the eighth-century prophets Isaiah and Micah, from whom he may have drawn inspiration for his writing style. He often used expressions previously used by other prophets: Zep 1:7 (Jl 1:15; 2:31); Zep 3:14–20 (cf passages in Isaiah; see Bible center-column references); Zep 1:14–15 (Jl 2:1–2).

The weathered likeness of Pharaoh Neco (610–595 BC), who defeated Josiah in the Battle of Megiddo.

Text and Translations

The Hebrew texts of Zephaniah have few textual variants. The LXX follows the Hebrew in most cases.

DOCTRINAL CONTENT

Summary Commentary

Ch 1 The Lord declares that final judgment will come worldwide, then pronounces specific judgments against faithless Judah. God's day of wrath

OUTLINE

Title (1:1)

I. The Day of the Lord Is a Day of Wrath (1:2–3:8)

    A. The Lord's Just Wrath against Judah (1:2–2:3)

        1. The Lord's universal judgment (1:2–3)

        2. Condemnation of Judah (1:4–6)

        3. The day of the Lord is near (1:7–14)

        4. Description of the day of wrath (1:15–18)

        5. Judah's last chance to repent (2:1–3)

    B. The Lord's Just Wrath against the Nations Surrounding Judah (2:4–15)

        1. West—Philistia (2:4–7)

        2. East—Moab and Ammon (2:8–11)

        3. South—Cush (2:12)

        4. North—Assyria (2:13–15)

    C. The Lord's Just Wrath and Concern for Jerusalem (3:1–8)

        1. The evil of "the oppressing city" (3:1–5)

        2. The Lord's concern for Jerusalem (3:6–8)

II. The Day of the Lord Is a Day of Restoration (3:9–20)

    A. The Conversion of the Nations (3:9–10)

    B. The Remnant of Judah Is Saved and Purified (3:11–13)

    C. Judah Sings a Song of Victory Because of Its Restoration (3:14–20) would come swiftly on the people of Judah because of their materialism, worldliness, and general disobedience.

Ch 2 Zephaniah urges the people of Judah to seek the Lord, then describes the devastation that will fall on neighboring nations because of their sins.

Ch 3 The city of Jerusalem, including its leaders, refuses to return to the Lord. Such impenitence brings upon them God's day of wrath. But the Lord will preserve a remnant of faithful people. Along with the remnant in Israel, nations from around the world will call on the name of the Lord and serve Him. Once proud and haughty, these people will now praise God because the Lord has paid the price for their rebellious deeds. Therefore, Zephaniah urges God's people to fear no evil but instead to rejoice over their coming salvation.

Specific Law Themes

The day of the Lord will be one in which evil is punished and His remnant is purified. No one will be able to buy salvation, no matter how much wealth has been accumulated (1:18). Zephaniah emphasizes the universal character of God's judgment since the day of the Lord will be a worldwide event.

Specific Gospel Themes

Zephaniah brings a message of salvation for all people (3:9). Divine grace exists with divine fury. The Lord promises to save a remnant of all the people. Ultimately, this remnant is all those who have put their trust in Him, both the believing people of Judah and the baptized in the Church today. Thus, the day of the Lord is a day of grace and favor for all those who believe. Just as that day would reach all nations with God's wrath, Zephaniah prophesied the worldwide promise of God's grace and mercy.

Judean warriors defend Lachish against Assyrian attack. Note the Judeans' distinct headdress and circular shields.

Specific Doctrines

Zephaniah famously proclaimed God's great wrath, which inspired the medieval Latin poem/hymn *Dies Irae*. This dramatic message has been shared and sung in the church perpetually since the thirteenth century. As recently as the mid-twentieth century, *The Lutheran Hymnal* (St. Louis: Concordia, 1941) included two hymns based on the poem (*TLH* 607, 612).

Application

1:2–6 Like the rebellious people of Judah, we also deserve God's anger when we replace God and His Word with what we find exciting, entertaining, or perhaps financially beneficial. We, too, are guilty of arrogance, pride, and boasting. But God's Law shows us our sin and drives us to repentance. He forgives our sins because Christ, our Savior, suffered judgment in our place.

1:7–18 Zephaniah's prophecy is meant as a warning for us (cf 1Co 10:6), as Jesus preached, "Repent and believe in the gospel" (Mk 1:15). The final Day of Judgment will come unexpectedly, as a thief in the night (1Th 5:2). We have all missed the mark of God's perfection and deserve only His punishment, now and eternally. However, God so loved the world that He sent His only Son to endure the punishment for our sins. All who believe in Jesus have no need to fear the Day of Judgment.

Chs 2–3 Fear may hinder us from witnessing of God's love and mercy; how wrong and foolish that would be! God has redeemed us in Christ. He will always be with us, and someday He will take us to the heavenly Jerusalem.

CANONICITY

Two commentaries on Zephaniah were found at Qumran (1QpZeph; 4QpZeph). Portions were likewise preserved in the manuscripts of Murabba'at (Mur 88) and the Greek text at Nahal Hever (8 Hev XII gr). These examples demonstrate the value Jewish scribes placed upon the book. Christians received it into their canon without question.

LUTHERAN THEOLOGIANS ON ZEPHANIAH

Luther

"Zephaniah lived in the time of the prophet Jeremiah, for as the title [1:1] shows, he prophesied under King Josiah, as did Jeremiah. For that reason he prophesies the very same things as Jeremiah, namely, that Jerusalem and Judah shall be destroyed and the people carried away because of their wicked life, devoid of repentance.

"Unlike Jeremiah, however, he does not name the king of Babylon as the one who is to inflict this destruction and captivity. He says simply that God will bring misfortune and affliction upon the people so that they may be moved to repentance. For none of the prophets was ever able even once to persuade this people that God was angry with them. They relied continually on the claim that they were, and were called, God's people; and whoever preached that God was angry with them had to be a false prophet and had to die, for they would not believe that God would leave his people. It was then as it is today: all who teach that the church errs and sins, and that God will punish her, are denounced as heretics and killed.

"Now Zephaniah prophesies this disaster not only for Judah, but also for all the surrounding and neighboring lands, such as the Philistines, Moab, the Ethiopians, and Assyria. The king of Babylon is to be God's rod upon all lands. In the third chapter Zephaniah prophesies gloriously and clearly of the happy and blessed kingdom of Christ, which shall be spread abroad in all the world. Although he is a minor prophet, he speaks more about Christ than many other major prophets, almost more than Jeremiah even. He does so in order to give the people abundant comfort, so that they would not despair of God because of their disastrous captivity in Babylon, as if God had cast them off forever, but rather be sure that after this punishment they would receive grace again and get the promised Savior, Christ, with his glorious kingdom." (AE 35:328–29)

For more of Luther's insights on this book, see *Lectures on Zephaniah* (AE 18:317–64).

Gerhard

"*Zephaniah* (*Tsephanyah*) means 'the Lord's secretary' or 'the examiner for the Lord.' He was the son of Cushi, the great-great-grandson of Hezekiah. He prophesied at the time of Josiah, king of Judah, and was a contemporary of Jeremiah, according to Augustine (*De civit. Dei*, bk. 18, c. 33). Ludovicus Vives, commentary on this passage [of Augustine], says regarding Zephaniah: 'The Hebrews say that he was a prophet and the son, grandson, and great-great-grandson of prophets, for his father was Cushi, his grandfather was Gedaliah, his great-grandfather was Amariah, his great-great-grandfather was Hezekiah, all prophets. For they say that all the forefathers whom someone names in the title were also prophets.' This rule of the rabbinic scholars, however, is uncertain.

"Zephaniah prophesied chiefly about the overthrow of the kingdom of Judah. The book consists of three chapters, the first of which is a threat containing the prophecy of visitation by the Chaldeans; the second, an exhortation to repentance; and the third, a mixture of warning and consolation that contains a prophecy about the calling of the Gentiles and the extension of the Church that was to be awaited at the time of the Messiah." (ThC E1 § 164)

FURTHER STUDY

Lay/Bible Class Resources

Baker, David W. *Nahum, Habakkuk, Zephaniah.* TOTC. Downers Grove, IL: InterVarsity Press, 1988. ♪ Compact commentary based on the NIV, with other translations consulted. American evangelical scholar.

Collver III, Albert B. *Nahum, Habakkuk, Zephaniah: The Lord Delivers His Faithful.* GWFT. St. Louis: Concordia, 2010. ♪ Lutheran theologian. Nine-session Bible study, including leader's notes and discussion questions.

Life by His Word. St. Louis: Concordia, 2009. ♪ More than 1,500 reproducible one-page Bible studies covering each chapter of the canonical Scriptures. Page references to *The Lutheran Study Bible.* CD-Rom and downloadable.

Westendorf, James J. *Nahum/Habakkuk/Zephaniah.* PBC. St. Louis: Concordia, 2005. ♪ Lutheran author. Excellent for Bible classes. Based on the NIV translation.

Church Worker Resources

Luther, Martin. *Lectures on the Minor Prophets.* Vol. 18 of AE. St. Louis: Concordia, 1975. ♪ The great reformer's lectures from the 1520s, which reflect his mature approach to biblical interpretation. Luther consulted the Hebrew text and reflected on the application of the prophecies and their New Testament fulfillment.

Robertson, O. Palmer. *The Books of Nahum, Habakkuk, and Zephaniah.* NICOT. Grand Rapids: Eerdmans, 1990. ♪ Written by a conservative, American Evangelical scholar, with special emphasis on the context and structure of the book.

Smith, Ralph L. *Micah-Malachi.* Vol. 32 of WBC. Waco, Texas: Word Books, 1984. ♪ Written by an American evangelical from a conservative perspective.

Academic Resources

Berlin, Adele. *Zephaniah.* Vol. 25A of AB. New York: Doubleday, 1994. ♪ A literary commentary by a Jewish writer, working from a critical perspective. Attention to the Hebrew text and the history of its interpretation in Judaism.

K&D. *Biblical Commentary on the Old Testament: The Twelve Minor Prophets.* 2 vols. Grand Rapids: Eerdmans, 1971 reprint. ♪ This century-and-a-half old work from Lutheran scholars should not be overlooked. Despite its age, it remains a most useful commentary on the Hebrew text.

Kleinert, Paul. *Zephaniah.* LCHS. New York: Charles Scribner's Sons, 1898. ♪ A helpful, older example of German biblical scholarship, based on the Hebrew text, which provides references to significant commentaries from the Reformation era forward.

Sweeney, Marvin A. *The Twelve Prophets.* Vol. 2 of *Berit Olam.* Collegeville, MN: Liturgical Press, 2000. ♪ Treats the literary structure of the Book of the Twelve as a whole, using critical approaches, then provides specific commentary on each book. Based on the NRSV.

HAGGAI

I will fill this house with glory

When the Babylonians conquered Jerusalem in 587 BC, they left the temple of the Lord in utter ruin. About 50 years later, when the first Judeans returned from exile in Babylon, they dreamt of restoring the temple. Haggai, along with Zechariah and Malachi, was a "postexilic" prophet who urged the restoration of the temple and faithful sacrifices. These three prophets proclaimed God's message after the people of Judah began to return to their homeland from exile. In many respects, we enter a different world with the three postexilic prophets.

Historical and Cultural Setting

In the middle of the sixth century BC, the Persians suddenly appeared from the region of modern Iran to conquer not only the Babylonian Empire but also eventually Egypt (525 BC). Among the first acts of Emperor Cyrus II was a reversal of some key Babylonian policies. Cyrus allowed exiles to return to their homelands and supported the rebuilding of local temples. In 538 BC, the first wave of Judean exiles started out for Jerusalem, and by 536 BC, they had laid the foundation for rebuilding the temple. Shortly after, though, they gave up, discouraged by the opposition posed by their neighbors. (See Ezr 4.)

The Samaritans or their predecessors and their neighbors had opposed the Judeans from the outset. The Persian emperor Cambyses II (528–23) had always been less enthusiastic than his father, Cyrus, about encouraging a measure of local self-governance. Only after Cambyses died and Darius emerged as victor did Haggai urge the people to rebuild the temple (1:2). God sent Haggai and Zechariah to encourage the people to finish what they had started (520 BC). Four years later, the temple was finished and dedicated (Ezr 6:15–18).

The walls of Darius the Great's palace depict men bringing tribute to the Persian king.

COMPOSITION

Author

As is the case with most of the prophets, we have an almost total lack of information about the biography or personal circumstances of the postexilic prophets. They are content to be heralds, servants of the Lord.

The historical activity of Haggai (and Zechariah) is confirmed by independent mention twice in the Aramaic portion of Ezra (5:1; 6:14). Since neither prophet is mentioned until about 520 BC, it is sometimes thought that they had only recently arrived in Judah together with a fresh group of exiles. There are patristic traditions that they had previously preached in the exile itself. This may be, but it is equally possible that they had come as children with their parents nearly two decades earlier (c 538) and witnessed the gradual drift of the community into demoralization and despair. Certainly, if many of them took the earlier prophecies of restoration literally, especially perhaps those of Isaiah, the disparity with the facts at hand would have been almost too much to bear. If Hg 2:3 indicates that he had himself seen the first temple, his old age at this time could explain why his prophetic activity was of such short duration.

Ecclesiastical tradition tended to regard Haggai as a priest, partly because of his name ("festive one," derived from the common word for "pilgrimage festival"), but that is not a necessary conclusion. Both Haggai's overriding concern to get the temple rebuilt and his third oracle (2:10–19) would indicate great interest in temple matters and close contacts with the priests. If anything, however, the text would suggest that he was not himself one of the priests.

Date of Composition

One striking contrast between Haggai and the preexilic prophets is the precise dating of Haggai's oracles. Perhaps this practice of dating is partially anticipated in

Ezekiel, but its only real parallel is in the nearly contemporaneous oracles of the first half of Zechariah. Modern scholars would be thrilled to have such precise information about earlier prophecies, but as we have noted many times, the Bible's ultimate interest is not with time, but with God's Time, "in, with, and under" our time.

The Cyrus Cylinder describes the king of Persia defeating Babylon in 538 BC.

As the text of Haggai stands, we have four precisely dated oracles, all in the second year of Darius (520 BC), and covering a period of not quite four months: (1) on the first day of the sixth month (1:1); (2) on the twenty-first day of the seventh month (2:1); and (3 & 4) two oracles on the twenty-fourth day of the ninth month (2:10, 20).

Purpose/Recipients

Haggai's book is very short, containing only 38 verses. The objective of Haggai's messages was primarily practical: to urge the Judeans to resume and complete the rebuilding of the temple in Jerusalem that had been interrupted earlier (c 530 BC) by the opposition of the people who were occupying the land when the Judeans returned from exile.

Literary Features

Genre

Haggai wrote prose oracles, which distinguished his writing in the Book of the Twelve. He made it unmistakably clear that he had a message directly from God through expressions such as the following: "The word of the LORD came by the hand of Haggai the prophet" (1:1; 2:1; cf 2:10, 20); "thus says the LORD of hosts" (1:2, 5, 7, 9; 2:4, 6, 8, 11, 23). Practically no question has been raised about the authenticity and integrity of the book.

Not only is all of Haggai in prose, but the style is very pedestrian (though helpfully direct and very much to the point). Critics are only too happy to use these facts to describe Haggai's work as drastically inferior to the work of earlier prophets, a complaint that they extend to most of the rest of the postexilic period. From a purely literary standpoint it is undeniable that Haggai's style is not as strong. But theologically, style is entirely beside the point. No doubt, it reflects the radical cultural changes and trauma that the community had experienced.

OUTLINE

I. The Command to Rebuild the Temple (1:1–11)

II. The People Obey (1:12–15)

III. The Glory of This Temple Will Surpass Solomon's (2:1–9)

IV. The People's Faithful Response to the Lord Will Remove Their Defilement (2:10–19)

V. Zerubbabel Is the Lord's Chosen Leader (2:20–23)

Characters

Haggai wrote his oracles to the **Judeans** who had resettled Jerusalem and Judea. The intimidated settlers, who feared retaliation from the neighbors and from Persian authorities, abandoned their plans to restore the temple. Haggai is recorded as addressing the people directly or primarily only once (1:13), when he assured them that Yahweh was with them in their resolve to proceed with the construction. His references to the "remnant" (1:14; 2:2) betrayed the nagging question in the background about whether or not they really were the true Israel, the heirs of the promise. The first two oracles were addressed to the two leaders who figure prominently also in the Book of Zechariah: the **governor Zerubabbel** and the **high priest Joshua,** who were aroused to action and successfully led the people to complete the temple in 516 BC.

An example of an Egyptian signet ring.

The fourth and final oracle (2:20–23), delivered on the same day as the preceding one, is addressed to Zerubbabel alone. Picking up the theme of shaking the kingdoms of this world again, Haggai heaped up messianic language and applied it to Zerubbabel, grandson of King Jehoiachin. He called Zerubbabel "servant," "chosen" or elect one, and "signet ring" (used to represent the owner in sealing letters and documents). This promise about God's chosen is very similar to some in Zec 3, 6. It is the major point of the Book of Haggai and the postexilic period.

Narrative Development or Plot

As the Book of Haggai is a collection of oracles, it does not have a storyline or plot, even though the oracles are written in prose. They read almost like a series of letters, tracking the historic events from God's command to build, to the people's faithful response, and to the continuing challenges they face in a hostile and ever-changing world.

Resources

A unique feature of Haggai's and Zechariah's accounts is the way they drew upon the Persian dating formulas. This shows how subject and dependent Judah was to the Persian Empire.

Text and Translations

The text of Haggai generally poses no great problems, but many critics see a problem at the end of ch 1. The date given for the beginning of building activity (twenty-fourth day of the sixth month, about a month after Haggai's initial sermon) seems to introduce something rather than conclude it. Critics propose ways to amend the text. However, the most likely explanation would seem to be stylistic in consistency. There is no text-critical support for changing the text.

The LXX is helpful for the few cases where the Hebrew text is less clear, though the LXX also apparently included some additions to the text at 2:9, 14. No one knows what to make of the LXX superscriptions to Pss 137, 144–148, linking them with Haggai and Zechariah.

The traditional messianic title "desire of all nations" (cf 2:7 in KJV) may be based on a mistranslation. Both context and the plural Hebrew verb indicate that the Hebrew noun also should be pointed as a plural, meaning "desirable/costly things" or "treasures." In a broader sense, the picture is plainly messianic in case. The aid from the Persians that supported reconstruction (Ezr 6:8–9) would be only a preliminary fulfillment. When temple and treasure were redefined in Christ, the full import of Haggai's promise appeared, and Heb 12:26 reminds us that some of their promise aspects still remain in the time of the Church.

DOCTRINAL CONTENT

Summary Commentary

Ch 1 The Lord chastises His people for being concerned about their own houses while His sacred house lies in ruins. The people of Judah obey the Word of the Lord and begin the task of rebuilding the temple. They demonstrate repentance for their previous selfishness. The Lord in turn promises to be with them, and He stirs up the spirit of the people and their leaders to work hard.

Ch 2 The Lord encourages His people to continue their work of rebuilding the temple with the assurance that He will be with them and that in the future, the glory of this house will be greater than the first temple. But the people have not received the blessings they expected from the Lord. And the offerings they bring to the Lord are unclean (v 14) because of their earlier failure to rebuild the temple. But the Lord promises to bless them. The people of Judah need to realize that without this blessing, both the temple building project and their crops will suffer.

Haggai concludes by looking to the future. The time was coming when the Lord would overthrow the kingdoms of the world and make His chosen servant Zerubbabel the one through whom the promise of the Savior would be realized.

Specific Law Themes

Haggai rebuked the Judeans for their timid and self-serving response to the challenge of rebuilding the temple—they did nothing. He explained that the reason they failed to prosper and receive God's blessings was that they were living with the results of their sinful behavior (1:9–11). When the congregation did step forward and build the temple, the size and simplicity of the building reminded them again of all that they had lost (2:3). Haggai concluded his prophecies with a message for all nations, that the Lord would shake the empires and exercise judgment over them.

Specific Gospel Themes

Haggai provides an unstated promise of God's blessing along with his encouragement to rebuild the temple (1:6–11). He highlights the trust ("the people feared the LORD;" 1:12) that follows as the people returned to their work. The promises of blessing become explicit in ch 2. The Lord will not only bless the people but they will have His Spirit continuously (2:5). They shall live as God's chosen people, and their governor, descendant of King David, is the object of special promises that are finally fulfilled in his descendant, Jesus of Nazareth.

Specific Doctrines

Haggai prophesied about the importance of the temple and pure worship for the sake of the covenant relationship between God and His people in the Old Testament. The prophet's interest in Zerubbabel illustrated the cooperative service of prophecy and kingship in Israel. The first "prophet" in the classical sense was Samuel, who served alongside King Saul. After Haggai and Zechariah's interest in Zerubbabel, prophecy diminished as a companion office to the role of the king/governor. Haggai preserved the emphases on the calling of prophet, priest, and king while anticipating that God had something greater in view.

Front and back of a Persian gold daric (Darius) coin.

Haggai prophesied that the kingdoms of this world would not last. In contrast, God's Spirit abides with His people, and He will fulfill His purpose for them (2:5b–9; Heb 12:26–29). The ultimate "treasure" of the nations would come in fulfillment to the promise that God made to Zerubbabel, from whose line would come the Messiah, who would cleanse the temple and restore the kingdom (cf Mt 1:12, 16).

Application

Ch 1 The Lord's work suffers today when we take care of our own material wants and needs but fail to support the work of proclaiming the Gospel. Jesus had a different priority. He came to serve, giving His life as a ransom for us. Though He was rich, for our sakes He became poor so that we might become rich (2Co 8:9). The riches we have received in Him move us to become rich in our love for Him and others. Through Word and Sacrament, God is present with us today. His Spirit stirs us to repentance and gives us a burning desire to serve Him.

Ch 2 Do we at times become discouraged thinking that God's Church and the preaching of His Word count for nothing in this world? The Lord assures us that this is where we find our greatest treasure: forgiveness of sins and peace in Christ our Savior. We need the Lord to bless us, for without Him, we can do nothing. By His bodily presence in Christ, He has demonstrated His gracious kindness to us. We can depend on Him to provide for all our needs, both spiritual and physical.

When we see the world in turmoil, with wars and rumors of wars across the globe and evil increasing all around, how often do we find ourselves foolishly wondering whether the Lord is in control? We need to remember that just as He did in the past, so today the Lord continues to govern all things in the interest of His kingdom. Through Jesus, the promised descendant of David and Zerubbabel, we receive forgiveness for our sins of doubt and worry.

CANONICITY

Hebrews 12:26–28 quoted from and alluded to Hg 2:6, demonstrating the book's usefulness in the Early Church. The book was copied in other collections as well (e.g., Mur 88; 8 Hev XII gr, the latter based on reconstructions).

Haggai 2:6 prophesies the stormy skies that will accompany Judgment Day. Above, migrating birds brave a stormy sky. Each year millions of birds migrate through Israel.

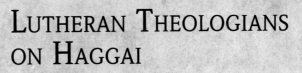

LUTHERAN THEOLOGIANS ON HAGGAI

Luther

"Haggai is the first prophet given to the people after the Babylonian captivity, and by his prophecy the temple and the worship of God were set up again. In addition Zechariah was later given to him as a companion for a period of two months, so that by the mouth of two witnesses the word of God might the more surely be believed. For the people had fallen into great doubt whether the temple would ever be rebuilt.

"It is our opinion that Daniel is speaking of this prophet, where he says in chapter 9, 'From the going forth of the commandment to restore and rebuild Jerusalem to the coming of Christ, the prince, there shall be seven weeks, and three score and two weeks,' etc. For although a decree had gone out earlier from King Cyrus that the temple should be rebuilt at Jerusalem at his (the king's) expense, yet it was hindered until the time of Haggai and Zechariah. When God's commandment went out through their prophesying, then the work went ahead [Ezra 1:1–4; 4:4–6:15].

"Haggai denounces the people, however, because they had given no thought to setting up the temple and the worship of God, but had feverishly grubbed and scraped only for their own property and houses. For this reason they were afflicted with famine and with loss of produce, wine, grain, and all sorts of crops. This was an example to all the godless, who pay no heed to God's word and worship and are always filling their own bags. It is to them alone that this text applies, when he says, 'Their bag shall be full of holes' [1:6].

"So we find in all the histories that when men will not support God's servants or help to maintain his word, he just lets them go and grub for themselves, and scrape incessantly. However in the end he punctures the bag full of holes; he blows into it so that it disintegrates and vanishes, and no one knows what has become of it. God intends to share their food or they'll not have any.

"He prophesies also of Christ in chapter 2[:6–7], that he shall soon come as a 'comfort of all nations,' by which he indicates in a mystery that the kingdom and the laws of the Jews shall have an end, and the kingdoms of all the world shall be destroyed and become subject to Christ. This has already taken place, and continues to take place until the Last Day when it will all be fulfilled." (AE 35:329–30)

For more of Luther's insights on this book, see *Lectures on Haggai* (AE 18:365–87).

Gerhard

"*Haggai* (*Chagay*) means 'festal' or 'celebrating a feast' or 'diligent.' He began to prophesy after the Babylonian captivity, in the second year of King Darius of the Persians, as is evident from Ezra 5:1 and Hag. 1:1. The greatest historians say that this Darius was the son of Hystaspes. The predecessor of this Darius, King Cambyses (whom Ezra calls Ahasuerus and Artaxerxes [*Arthasasta*]), had hindered the restoration of the temple. This Darius, however, finally gave the Jews the power to rebuild the temple. Because the Jews were remiss and lazy in this work and were more concerned about rebuilding their own private dwellings than the temple, God summoned up this prophet, Haggai, and two months later his colleague, Zechariah, both of whom rebuked this yawning of the people and prophesied about the excellence of the second temple that would be gained for it through the coming of the Messiah.

"This book has two chapters, the first of which is an exhortation to go through with the building of the temple, and the second of which is a consolation regarding the preservation of this temple until the coming of the Messiah." (ThC E1 § 165)

FURTHER STUDY

Lay/Bible Class Resources

Baldwin, Joyce. *Haggai, Zechariah, Malachi*. TOTC. Downers Grove, IL: InterVarsity Press, 1972. ♦ Compact commentary that interacts with a variety of English translations and with the Hebrew text. British evangelical scholar.

Deterding, Paul. *Haggai, Zechariah, Malachi: Return to the Lord*. GWFT. St. Louis: Concordia, 2005. ♦ Lutheran author. Eleven-session Bible study, including leader's notes and discussion questions.

Hartzell, Eric. *Haggai/Zechariah/Malachi*. PBC. St. Louis: Concordia, 2005. ♦ Lutheran author. Excellent for Bible classes. Based on the NIV translation.

Life by His Word. St. Louis: Concordia, 2009. ♦ More than 1,500 reproducible one-page Bible studies covering each chapter of the canonical Scriptures. Page references to *The Lutheran Study Bible*. CD-Rom and downloadable.

Church Worker Resources

Luther, Martin. *Lectures on the Minor Prophets*. Vol. 18 of AE. St. Louis: Concordia, 1975 ♦ The great reformer's lectures from the 1520s, which reflect his mature approach to biblical interpretation. Luther consulted the Hebrew text and reflected on the application of the prophecies and their New Testament fulfillment.

Smith, Ralph L. *Micah–Malachi*. Vol. 32 of WBC. Waco, Texas: Word Books, 1984. ♦ Written by an American evangelical from a conservative perspective.

Sweeney, Marvin A. *The Twelve Prophets*. Vol. 2 of *Berit Olam*. Collegeville, MN: Liturgical Press, 2000. ♦ Treats the literary structure of the Book of the Twelve as a whole, using critical approaches, then provides specific commentary on each book. Based on the NRSV.

Taylor, Richard. *Haggai, Malachi*. Vol. 21a of NAC. Nashville: Broadman & Holman, 2004. ♦ Evangelical, with emphasis on theology of the books. Based on the NIV.

Verhoef, Pieter A. *The Books of Haggai and Malachi*. NICOT. Grand Rapids: Eerdmans, 1987. ♦ A careful exposition of the text written by a conservative evangelical from South Africa; sees Haggai and Malachi as preparing unique and unified compositions.

Academic Resources

K&D. *Biblical Commentary on the Old Testament: The Twelve Minor Prophets*. 2 vols. Grand Rapids: Eerdmans, 1971 reprint. ♦ This century-and-a-half old work from Lutheran scholars should not be overlooked. Despite its age, it remains a most useful commentary on the Hebrew text.

McCurdy, James Frederick. *Haggai*. LCHS. Charles Scribner's Sons, 1898. ♦ A helpful, older example of German biblical scholarship, based on the Hebrew text, which provides references to significant commentaries from the Reformation era forward.

Meyers, Carol L., and Eric M. Meyers. *Haggai, Zechariah 1–8*. Vol. 25B of AB. New York: Doubleday, 1987. ♦ Most detailed commentary on the Hebrew text; written from a critical viewpoint by archaeologists. Based on themes, argues that the prophecies of Haggai were edited with Zechariah 1–8 to form a composite text.

ZECHARIAH

Not by might, nor by power, but by My Spirit

The rubble of Jerusalem's former glory surrounded Zechariah as the Word of the Lord came to him. The Lord called Zechariah as prophet about two months after the prophet Haggai in 520 BC. But unlike his fellow prophet who recorded only a handful of oracles, Zechariah continued to write, sharing unique insights from the Lord about the hope of Israel and the coming kingdom of God. The result is the longest book of the Minor Prophets.

Historical and Cultural Setting

Because the prophecies of Haggai and Zechariah occurred at nearly the same time and under similar circumstances, see the introduction to Haggai to learn more about the setting (p 971).

COMPOSITION

Author

The name Zechariah means "Yahweh remembers." There are several other Old Testament persons that carried the same name (cf 2Ch 24:20; 26:5; Is 8:2). The prophet is further identified as the son of Berechiah and the grandson of Iddo. It seems that Berechiah died before Iddo, his father, which would account for the fact that Ezra and Nehemiah mention only Iddo and omit Berechiah's name (cf Ezr 5:1; Ne 12:4). Alongside Haggai, Zechariah played a major role in rebuilding the temple. In addition, Ne 12:16 lists him as a son of the priest Iddo, who had returned from the exile (12:4) together with Zerubbabel. No definite information

The base of a Jerusalem tower that collapsed during the Babylonian conquest in 587 BC.

OVERVIEW

Author
Zechariah the prophet

Date
520–518 BC

Places
Jerusalem and Zion; Judah; Bethel; Israel; Bashan; Megiddo; Babylon; Shinar; Damascus; Tyre, Sidon, and Lebanon; Philistia; Greece

People
Zechariah; Joshua the high priest; Zerubbabel, governor of Judah; the Israelites; Heldai, Tobijah, Jedaiah, and Hen; Sharezer and Regemmelech; King Darius

Purpose
Zechariah supports the rebuilding of the Jerusalem temple and prophesies about the fulfillment, in Christ, of the old covenant

Law Themes
A call to return to the Lord in repentance; dishonesty condemned; the whirlwind among the nations; the doomed flock

Gospel Themes
The Lord chooses His people; the Branch prophecy of forgiveness; the temple restored; nations seek the Lord; the coming King; the day of the Lord

Memory Verses
The vision of Joshua (ch 3); by the Lord's Spirit (4:6); the humble King (9:9); the doomed flock (11:4–6); they are My people (13:7–9)

• •

TIMELINE

605 BC	Nebuchadnezzar besieges Jerusalem
538 BC	Cyrus decrees that exiles may return to Judah
520 BC	Zechariah begins to receive God's Word
516 BC	Second temple completed

is available regarding the extent of Zechariah's ministry both as a priest and as a prophet. The last dated prophecy in his book was spoken in the fourth year of Darius, 518 BC (Zec 7:1). Some have assumed, on the basis of Ne 12:16, 26, that he was still active in the days of Nehemiah, but that text refers to the Levites named in Ne 12:22–25, not the priests.

Criticism quite unanimously regards only the first eight chapters of Zechariah as "genuine," that is, written by Zechariah. Critics often refer to the remainder (Zec 9–14) as "Deutero-Zechariah." Sometimes they divide further and consider chs 12–14 a "Trito-Zechariah." As in other cases, these arguments from the critics are speculative and not rooted in either clear history or long respected traditions about the Book of Zechariah.

Nehemiah's reference to Zechariah as the head of a priestly house is very instructive. We suspect that many prophets (among them the contemporary Haggai) may have been priests as well as prophets because of the convergence of priestly and prophetic interests in their books, but in the case of Zechariah, there is no doubt (cf also Ezekiel).

Date of Composition

Jewish and Christian scholars alike regarded Zechariah as the author of this book until 1644 when Hugo Grotius expressed doubt about Zechariah as the writer of chs 9–14. Grotius contended there was strong evidence that these six chapters were written several hundred years later by one or several other authors. As a result, many different theories have been advanced.

Both because of the contents of the book, and because of three precise dates after the manner of Haggai, there is no serious question about the date or circumstances of Zechariah's work. The first date (Zec 1:1), the eighth month of the second year of Darius (that is, Oct/Nov 520; the day is not specified on this occasion) is roughly a month before the last recorded utterances of Haggai (2:10). The two prophets make no mention of each other, which is commonly the case. A second date at the beginning of the visions (Zec 1:7) is some three months later, "the twenty-fourth day of the eleventh month" (of the same year), that is, Feb/March 519. The third and final date in the book occurs in 7:1; the fourth day of the ninth month of the *fourth* year of Darius, that is, Dec/Jan 519/8, nearly two years later than the visions. Thus, in contrast to Haggai, Zechariah's recorded ministry lasts a bit longer, extending somewhat over two years. How much longer he ministered, and whether or not he lived to witness the dedication of the temple in the sixth year of Darius, cannot be stated with certainty. Ezra 6:14 is often interpreted that way but remains a bit ambiguous.

In some respects, Zechariah's message appears to correspond to a slightly later situation in the struggling Judean community than Haggai's, as the slightly later dating of his oracles would lead one to expect. The intense hopes aroused by Darius's accession appear to have abated, and the prophet has the task of assuring the people that though God has not restored the Kingdom to Israel as expected, God's promises continue undiminished.

Purpose/Recipients

In the face of the disillusioning realities of continuing foreign rule, economic uncertainty, and internal apathy, Zechariah sustained the faith of the congregation in the divine promises. By his concentration on the temple—and the theology of purification or sanctification accompanying it—Zechariah played a major role, under God, in the preservation of Israel until the new kingdom dawned with Christ.

Literary Features

Genre

The bulk of the Book of Zechariah consists of visions, presented in an "apocalyptic" style similar to the styles of Ezekiel and Daniel. The visions may be classified as first person oracles, all reported in the same general pattern. They are preceded and followed by explanations. Presumably the explanations were added because the visions by themselves were difficult to interpret—this is a standard feature of the apocalyptic genre. Zechariah's influence on later apocalyptic writings (also of the New Testament) is immense.

In addition to the explanations of the visions, other oracles appear to have been inserted (e.g., Zec 2:6–13; 4:6b–10). They were probably added as sermons to explain or expand upon the surrounding visions.

As noted above, critics commonly deny the unity of the last six chapters of the book. As chs 9 and 12 both begin with a sort of superscription ("An oracle"; translated as "burden" in ESV), two originally independent collections are supposed. Since, in addition, the same "superscription" may appear at the beginning of Malachi, it is commonly held that originally the compilers of the prophetic canon had before them merely three collections of anonymous oracles. In order to obtain a total of *twelve* Minor Prophets (one for each tribe in Israel?), two of these compilations were attached to the end of Zechariah. The third was outfitted with the artificial name Malachi on the basis of one of its major formulations (Mal 3:1). Such critical speculations

OUTLINE

I. Introductory Oracle (1:1–6)

II. Eight "Night Visions" (1:7–6:8)

    A. A Horseman (1:7–17)

    B. Four Horns (1:18–21)

    C. A Man with a Measuring Line (ch 2)

    D. Joshua the High Priest (ch 3)

    E. A Golden Lampstand (ch 4)

    F. A Flying Scroll (5:1–4)

    G. A Woman in a Basket (5:5–11)

    H. Four Chariots (6:1–8)

III. Crowning of Joshua (6:9–15)

IV. Fasting Sermons (chs 7–8)

V. Victory of Messianic King over Rivals (ch 9)

VI. Denunciation of False Shepherds (10:1–5)

VII. The Return of Israel (10:6–12)

VIII. Allegory of the Good Shepherd (ch 11)

IX. Final Eschatological Battle of the Nations against Jerusalem (12:1–9)

X. Israel Laments Its Rejection of the Good Shepherd (12:10–14)

XI. Repudiation of False Prophecy (13:1–6)

XII. The Salvation of God's People (13:7–9)

XIII. Varied Pictures of the Last Day (ch 14)

    A. Mount of Olives Split in Half to Protect the Righteous (14:1–5)

    B. Unique Day (14:6–7)

    C. Living Waters (14:8)

    D. The Lord is One (14:9)

    E. New Jerusalem (14:10–15)

    F. The Feast of Booths (14:16–19)

    G. The Restoration of All Creation to Its Original Holiness (14:20–21)

lack objective support. An increasing number of scholars argue for the traditional division of the books and the unity of composition and authorship.

Characters

Joshua, the high priest, is on trial and is clad in "filthy garments" as a visible sign of his sin (Zec 3:3; cf Job 9:31). The prosecuting attorney is "**the Satan**," as in Job 1–2 ("Satan" is not used as a proper noun, as we meet it a century later for the first time in 1Ch 21:1). But plainly it is not so much the high priest who is being personally charged. The high priest served as mediator and representative of the whole congregation ("Israel reduced to one," as is sometimes also said of prophets and kings). By God's favor, Joshua will be clad in "pure vestments" (Zec 3:4; that is, Jerusalem's future purity and glory, her "righteousness" in the Messiah's kingdom, in contrast to her present humiliation and sin).

The enigmatic figure of Zerubbabel plays a somewhat less central role in Zechariah than in Haggai.

Narrative Development or Plot

As a collection of oracles, the Book of Zechariah does not have a storyline or plot. However, there is a general progression from the desolate state of Israel upon its return from exile to the renewal it will experience in the time of the coming Messiah.

Resources

The imagery of Zechariah's visions likely stem from the works of other prophets. For example, in the third vision (2:1–5) two angels impress upon a man with a measuring line the futility of his attempts to measure Jerusalem's area, because its future population will exceed all humanly measurable bounds (cf Is 54; Ezk 40–48). The lack of visible walls need not disturb the people, because Yahweh will be incarnate in His "glory" (Zec 2:5) to protect it (cf Ezk 43). Here we plainly have the continuation of Isaiah's theme about the "security of Zion." An oracle before the fourth vision (Zec 2:6–13) climaxes with rhapsodies (vv 10–12) as in Is 40–55, and concludes with the same liturgical refrain we met in Hab 2:20 and Zep 1:7; man's part is faithful silence in view of the final judgment. Since Jer 23:5 and 33:15, the title "Branch" had described the Messiah (cf also Is 4:2; 11:1). "My servant the Branch" (Zec 3:8) recalls "My servant David" in the messianic prophecies of Ezk 34 and 37. The same metaphor appears in Is 53:2. In this way, Zechariah shows increased awareness that the true Israel, the remnant, is more church than state. The two symbolic staffs, "Favor" and "Union" (Zec 11:7) are similar to Ezekiel's two sticks in 37:16. Apparently, they represent two aspects of the blessings or salvation that the populace stood to receive under the rule of the Good Shepherd: God's gracious, covenantal care for His elected flock and the healing of the schisms that rend Israel (church). Apparently echoing Ezk 38–39, Zec 12:1–9 describes the final, last-ditch attack of heathendom upon Judah and Jerusalem.

Text and Translations

Scribes have introduced a variety of readings to the Hebrew text over the centuries, which may include some glosses to explain the text. They do not significantly affect the readability of Zechariah. In some places the LXX likely preserves more reliable readings.

DOCTRINAL CONTENT

Summary Commentary

1:1–6 When God's Word produces changes of heart and life, it bears beautiful fruit. The people of Judah have to learn that lesson from their tragic past lest their return from exile end in sorrow. When God's Word meets resistance and rejection, then there will be a repeat of the same shuddering outcome seen in war-damaged Jerusalem.

1:7–6:8 The prophet next records a series of eight visions. At a moment when God seems remote and uncaring, Zechariah sees that He is guiding events for good. The Angel of the Lord is among His people, interceding for them and preparing for the rebuilding of the temple and city. However, Zechariah's soul wilts before the forces arrayed against the holy people from his own day to the end of time. Almighty God stiffens the prophet's backbone and restores his courage by the sight of even mightier powers fighting on the side of God's people. He sees that a measuring line will not do when seeking to determine the extent of God's kingdom (2:1–13). God's promise to dwell in Jerusalem's earthly temple pales in splendor to what is to come. God used earthly leaders like Joshua and Zerubbabel to accomplish His work in this world (4:1–14). Rebuilding the temple was a most important project for the Jerusalem community of believers, many of whom had returned from exile in Babylon. Nevertheless, the ever-present temptation to idolatry came to the people of Jerusalem who had worked so hard at rebuilding the temple (5:5–11). God made it clear that idolatry had no place among them; that wicked woman had to be carted off to Babylon. In the last of the eight visions (6:1–8), the Lord reveals to the people of Jerusalem, who have suffered devastation, that He is indeed powerful and active. His authority is likened to strong horses pulling four chariots, patrolling the earth in all directions.

6:9–15 In the midst of the book, a crown made from gifts of gold and silver becomes an object lesson to teach about the coming Branch, who will fill the offices of King and Priest. Not everyone in Zechariah's day whole-heartedly believes God's promises that accompany this lesson.

Chs 7–8 In the last dated section of Zechariah's prophecies, priest and people alike need to learn the lessons from Judah's history lest the errors that caused such distress be repeated. In a series of seven oracles (8:1–17), the Lord of hosts contrasts His future blessings with the judgment His people had suffered in former days. God then tells the people of Bethel that their fasts will become joyful worship. He promises a great movement of people from the Gentile world who will seek the Lord and entreat His favor.

Chs 9–14 The final section of the book describes the Messiah and His kingdom. The Lord's saving work on behalf of His people is foretold using illustrations based on Old Testament history. God's enemies suffer defeat for breaking His Holy Law. Chapter 11 begins with a lament over the Lord's coming judgment, followed by a description of how He abandoned His flock and no longer had pity on them. This chastisement is God's "strange" work. His "proper" work is to comfort. The day is coming, declares the Lord, when His people, represented here by Jerusalem and Judah, will be delivered from their enemies (12:1–9). Zechariah concludes by prophesying intense mourning for all people until the messianic kingdom is fulfilled.

Specific Law Themes

Zechariah opens with a call to repentance and emphasis on faithfulness to the covenant. The visions reveal the problems of corruption, dishonesty, and self-absorption that occur at all levels, from the people generally to the priests especially. In particular, the Lord threatens to again scatter the people who only recently returned from exile (7:14)! He expresses this with the image of a whirlwind. The latter portion of the book focuses especially on the failure of the leaders of Judah ("shepherds," chs 9–11) to care for the people ("the flock"). In this way, the message of Zechariah is especially relevant for leaders in the Church today or in society generally.

Holy Land shepherd with flock. A shepherd's role was a common illustration for political and spiritual leadership.

Specific Gospel Themes

Zechariah comforts and encourages the people of Judah by emphasizing their election by grace: God has chosen them to be His people, and their current sins and difficulties have not overturned God's good and gracious will toward them. Borrowing the prophetic imagery of "the Branch" that springs up anew from the stump of Judah, Zechariah prophesies that the Lord will work forgiveness for the people through the high priest Joshua, which anticipates the ministry of the greater "Joshua," Jesus. Israel's priesthood and temple ministry remain valid and valuable to the Lord's people, His continuing instrument for forgiveness and restoration. Zechariah foresees the day when the Lord will put away the kings of the world and will reign over the people humbly and directly (9:9; ch 14). This will be the great day of God's salvation.

Specific Doctrines

Zechariah has been called "one of the most comforting of the prophets" (AE 35:330). He provides some broad, general messianic prophecies (Zec 3:9; 6:12; 8:22; 13:1; 14:9). However, he also provides specific prophecies that have New Testament fulfillment recorded: the Palm Sunday entry of Jesus into Jerusalem (9:9; Mt 21:5); payment for Judas's betrayal (11:12–13; Mt 26:15; 27:9–10); piercing of Jesus' side (12:10; Jn 19:37); smiting of the Shepherd (13:7; Mt 26:31).

The "Zion" and "David" themes in Zechariah are like two sides of one coin. In them one readily sees the importance of the Book of Zechariah from the standpoint of Christian theology. Zechariah's accent on the priestly role of the Messiah adds still another major dimension to its Christology. The second part of the book is even more immediately applicable to Christ, and His death and resurrection. Chapters 9–14 became one of the primary sources of early Christian teaching about the Messiah. Zechariah is often known as the "Prophet of Holy Week," an accolade that is ultimately valid for the entire book but is especially evident in four prominent New Testament quotations from the last six chapters (9:9 in Mt 21:5 and Jn 12:12–15; 11:12 in Mt 27:3–10; 12:10 in Jn 19:37; and 13:7 in Mt 26:31 and Mk 14:27).

Zechariah's clear message of repentance (1:3) continues to play an important role in the life of the Church. In conjunction with this, theologians have drawn on his emphasis on the Holy Spirit, whom God gives to those who repent, so that they might be comforted and strengthened for their calling (4:6; 12:10).

Another observation from Zechariah is that the angels may intercede for God's people on earth (1:12).

Application

1:1–2:13 God keeps returning with open arms, beckoning us to repent. He pities the guilty with a Father's heart. If you experience dismal moments, do not succumb to the despairing thought that God has forsaken His people. Zechariah saw a glorious future for the people of Judah, but he did not understand how great would be the fulfillment of God's promises in Jesus Christ and the heavenly Jerusalem. Likewise, the eyes of our faith today see only dimly the glory that will be revealed to us.

2:14–3:10 The Joshua of Zechariah's day would have sunk under Satan's accusations if a greater Joshua (Jesus) had not stepped forward to reverse a grim situation. The first Joshua was no private person but represented his whole people in the filth of their sin. However, the promised Branch was on the way, who on Good Friday removed the iniquity of Joshua and his people. The greater Joshua has robed us in righteousness. We enjoy the peace and safety of His kingdom.

Chs 4–13 People of all nations will become one in the Holy Christian Church. There is a vast difference between the Old Testament kingdom of Israel and the kingdom restored by the Messiah. Luther described the former as weak because it was based on Israel's obedience. Of the latter he said: "This kingdom is founded on God's mercy without our own goodness or merit, and therefore it will stand fast to all eternity" (AE 20:304). Like Israel, we all fall short of God's glory. Because of His compassion, He called Israel back to Him and likewise keeps calling us. Zechariah warns about false worship and false prophets. Throughout history, false religion has been a serious problem. People today may not call on Baal or Rimmon for help, but idols and false prophets are still evident. Luther wrote: "Many a person thinks that he has God and everything in abundance when he has money and possessions" (LC I 5). Idols may be gone from our eyes but not from our hearts. Only when Christ comes again in glory will there be an end to all false religion.

Ch 14 Zechariah's description of Jerusalem's future anticipates John's vision: "I saw the holy city, new Jerusalem, coming down out of heaven from God, prepared as a bride adorned for her husband" (Rv 21:2). Both foresee a day when the Lord will use His mighty power to crush all His enemies and make all things new and holy.

CANONICITY

As with the other Minor Prophets, Jewish teachers and scribes, such as Jesus son of Sirach (Ecclus 49:10) and the Dead Sea community, valued Zechariah's book. The New Testament references establish the canonicity of the book and support the traditional Jewish and Christian Church position in reference to its unity.

LUTHERAN THEOLOGIANS ON ZECHARIAH

Luther

"This prophet lived after the Babylonian captivity. With his colleague, Haggai, he helped to rebuild Jerusalem and the temple and to bring the scattered people together again, so that government and order might be set up in the land again. He is truly one of the most comforting of the prophets. He presents many lovely and reassuring visions, and gives many sweet and kindly words, in order to encourage and strengthen the troubled and scattered people to proceed with the building and the government despite the great and varied resistance which they had till then encountered. He does this down to the fifth chapter.

"In the fifth chapter, under the vision of the scroll and the bushel, he prophesies of the false teachers who are later to come among the Jewish people, and who will deny Christ; and this still applies to the Jews at the present day.

"In the sixth chapter he prophesies of the gospel of Christ and the spiritual temple to be built in all the world, because the Jews denied him and would not have him.

"In the seventh and eighth chapters a question arises which the prophet answers, encouraging and exhorting them once more to build the temple and organize the government. And with this he concludes the prophecy about the rebuilding in his time.

"In the ninth chapter he proceeds to the coming times, and prophesies first in chapter ten [9:1–6] of how Alexander the Great shall conquer Tyre, Sidon, and the Philistines, so that the whole world shall be opened to the coming gospel of Christ; and Zechariah [9:9] has the King Christ coming into Jerusalem on an ass.

"In the eleventh chapter, however, he prophesies that Christ shall be sold by the Jews for thirty pieces of silver [11:12–13], for which cause Christ will leave them, so that Jerusalem will be destroyed and the Jews will be hardened in their error and dispersed. Thus the gospel and the kingdom of Christ will come to the Gentiles, after the sufferings of Christ, in which he, as the Shepherd, shall first be beaten, and the apostles, as the sheep, be scattered. For Christ had to suffer first and thus enter into his glory [Luke 24:26].

"In the last chapter [14], when he has destroyed Jerusalem, he abolishes also the Levitical priesthood along with its organization and utensils and festivals, saying that all spiritual offices shall be held in common, for the worship and service of God, and shall not belong to the tribe of Levi only. That is, there shall be other priests, other festivals, other sacrifices, other worship, which other tribes could observe, indeed, even the Egyptians and all the Gentiles. Surely that is the outright abolition and removal of the Old Covenant." (AE 35:330–31)

For more of Luther's insights on this book, see *Lectures on Zechariah* (AE 20).

Gerhard

"*Zechariah* (*Zekaryah*) means 'the memory of the Lord' or 'mindful of the Lord.'

"His visions are not much different from those of Daniel.

"He was the son of Berechiah, grandson of Iddo. Because the names fit, some think that he was the man of whom Christ says that the Jews killed him between the temple and the altar (Matt. 23:[35]). The more correct claim, however, is that Christ is speaking about Zechariah, the son of Jehoiada, whom Scripture says the Jews stoned in the court of the temple, that is, between the temple and the altar of the burnt offerings (2 Chron. 24:21). This Jehoiada was also called Berechiah.

"This Zechariah of ours prophesied also after the Babylonian captivity and was given to Haggai as a colleague after Haggai had already been preaching for two months. The book consists of fourteen chapters in which are contained: (1) an exhortation to the people from the Babylonian captivity that they should repent genuinely (Zech. 1:1–7); (2) the mention of visions through which they are advised about the blessings they already have received and that are yet to come (through c. 7); (3) instruction about true fasting and the true worship of God (through c. 8); (4) a prophecy about the complete destruction of the enemies of the people of Israel, about the coming of Christ, and about His blessings to the Church (to the end of the book)." (ThC E1 § 166)

FURTHER STUDY

Lay/Bible Class Resources

Baldwin, Joyce. *Haggai, Zechariah, Malachi*. TOTC. Downers Grove, IL: InterVarsity Press, 1972. ♪ Compact commentary that interacts with a variety of English translations and with the Hebrew text. British evangelical scholar.

Deterding, Paul. *Haggai, Zechariah, Malachi: Return to the Lord*. GWFT. St. Louis: Concordia, 2005. ♪ Lutheran author. Eleven-session Bible study, including leader's notes and discussion questions.

Hartzell, Eric. *Haggai/Zechariah/Malachi*. PBC. St. Louis: Concordia, 2005. ♪ Lutheran author. Excellent for Bible classes. Based on the NIV translation.

Life by His Word. St. Louis: Concordia, 2009. ♪ More than 1,500 reproducible one-page Bible studies covering each chapter of the canonical Scriptures. Page references to *The Lutheran Study Bible*. CD-Rom and downloadable.

Church Worker Resources

Leupold, Herbert C. *An Exposition of Zechariah*. Grand Rapids: Baker, 1965. ♪ A very helpful resource, careful in its interpretation of apocalyptic writings. Written by a Lutheran commentator who taught at Capital Seminary in Columbus, Ohio.

Luther, Martin. *Lectures on the Minor Prophets*. Vol. 18 of AE. St. Louis: Concordia, 1975. ♪ The great reformer's lectures from the 1520s, which reflect his mature approach to biblical interpretation. Luther consulted the Hebrew text and reflected on the application of the prophecies and their New Testament fulfillment.

McComiskey, Thomas F., ed. *The Minor Prophets: An Exegetical and Expository Commentary*. Grand Rapids: Baker, 2009. ♪ Originally published as three volumes. Written by American conservative evangelicals.

Petersen, David L. *Zechariah 9–14 and Malachi*. OTL. Louisville: Westminster John Knox, 1995. ♪ Mainstream work that looks for different divisions or collections of material within Zechariah. Critical, but not extreme.

Academic Resources

Chambers, Talbot W. *Zechariah*. LCHS. New York: Charles Scribner's Sons, 1898. ♪ A helpful, older example of German biblical scholarship, based on the Hebrew text, which provides references to significant commentaries from the Reformation era forward.

K&D. *Biblical Commentary on the Old Testament: The Twelve Minor Prophets*. 2 vols. Grand Rapids: Eerdmans, 1971 reprint. ♪ This century-and-a-half old work from Lutheran scholars should not be overlooked. Despite its age, it remains a most useful commentary on the Hebrew text.

Meyers, Carol L., and Eric M. Meyers. *Haggai, Zechariah 1–8*. Vol. 25B of AB. New York: Doubleday, 1987; and *Zechariah 9–14*. Vol. 25C of AB. New York: Doubleday, 1993. ♪ Most detailed commentary on the Hebrew text; written from a critical viewpoint by archaeologists. Based on themes, argues that the prophecies of Haggai were edited with Zechariah 1–8 to form a composite text.

MALACHI

Behold, I send My messenger

Traditionally, Malachi has been regarded as the last of the Old Testament prophets, corresponding to his book's position in the English Bible and similar versions. It must be stressed, however, that even by conservative reckoning, Malachi is not the latest book in the Old Testament. The latest book is Chronicles, which appears last in the Hebrew order of books (see p 1011). Chronicles is probably to be dated around 400 BC, perhaps a generation after Malachi.

Historical and Cultural Setting

During the fifth century BC, the Judeans were subject to the mighty Persian Empire, which controlled Egypt and sought to expand into Greece. However, the empire's efforts to expand were frustrated by a variety of factors, such as revolts in Egypt and Babylon, not to mention the tenacious Greeks that we read about in the accounts of the ancient historian Herodotus.

Yet the Persian Empire remained strong, advancing its building projects, economy, and cultural interests despite the uprisings and lack of military success in foreign lands. Little Judah sought its own improvements at this time, completing the reconstruction of the walls of Jerusalem in 445 BC. The Persian rulers would regard them as of little interest, a matter for local officials. Malachi probably wrote his book around 430 BC during the long and stable reign of Artaxerxes I (464–24 BC).

The massive Tomb of Artaxerxes illustrates the wealth of the Persian Empire. Workmen may have carved it at the same time the prophet Malachi was writing his little book.

COMPOSITION

Author

Surprisingly, the first question about the Book of Malachi is whether we even know its author's name. Virtually without exception, critics believe that the superscription (assumed to be an editorial addition) mistakenly coined the name on the basis of Mal 3:1, where God promises to send "My messenger" ("Malachi" in Hebrew; the word might also be translated, "My angel"). Presumably, the book's editor identified this figure with the prophet himself, either taking "My messenger" to be his personal name, or understanding it as applying to his ministry.

The arguments against "Malachi" as a proper noun are both text-critical and based on the name's meaning. For one thing, the name Malachi (or its full form Malachiah) is not found elsewhere in the Old Testament and other early Hebrew writings. It is often argued that use of so singular a name would be especially unlikely in the postexilic period when the Hebrew mal'ak was increasingly used for "angel," and at a time when the interest in angels was becoming increasingly prominent.

The text-critical evidence, at best, points to ancient uncertainty about the name. The Septuagint took malachi to mean "by the hand of His messenger" (though it does entitle the book Malakias or Malachi). The Aramaic Targum added further opinion and identified the author with Ezra: "by the hand of my messenger, whose name is called Ezra the scribe." Jerome, probably due to his training under rabbis, accepted the tradition that Ezra was the author. Other rabbinic traditions, however, described Malachi as his own person with a Levitical genealogy.

Despite all this, the Book of Malachi undeniably bears the stamp of one individual personality. The balance of probability would seem to favor "Malachi" as a proper noun, but grounds are lacking to dismiss the other possibility out of hand. In any event, following universal convention on both sides, we shall speak of "Malachi" as the personal name of the author of the last book in the Minor Prophets.

Date of Composition

The book does not plainly state when the prophet lived. There are, however, some hints: the temple has been rebuilt (Mal 3:10); a governor is ruling (1:8); many of the same religious and moral defects of Nehemiah's time (laxity in tithes and offerings, improper marriages) are prevalent. Accordingly, it seems that Malachi was a contemporary of Nehemiah and may even have helped to prepare the way for some of the reforms that Nehemiah effected.

The fact that the temple has obviously been restored and the worship reinstituted means the book was written after the temple dedication in 516 BC. It appears that some time has elapsed, due to the fact that the priests are already weary of the rituals and sloppy in their execution. Reference to a raid on Edom (Mal 1:4) helps little, because that was a recurrent event (e.g., Obadiah). Likewise, poor harvests and locust plagues (3:6–12; cf Joel, Haggai) were also recurring events. Tiny Jerusalem appeared to be forgotten not only by the world but also by God, so the people wondered why they should weary themselves in His service (2:17). In general, the ritual and ethical problems confronted by Malachi are similar to those Ezra and Nehemiah combated in the middle of the fifth century, but it is difficult to be more precise.

Sometimes it is argued from the use of the usual term for a Persian satrap or "governor" (*pechah*; 1:8) that Malachi could not have been active while Nehemiah was on the scene, but the term apparently could also be used much more flexibly.

Purpose/Recipients

Malachi's predominant concern was with the purity and correct execution of the temple worship. The three main abuses that concern Malachi are: (1) the degeneracy and lassitude of the priesthood; (2) intermarriage with pagan women and often heartless divorce of their first partners; and (3) the congregation's failure to pay the sacred dues, to the detriment of especially the Levites. The first three oracles (chs 1–2) concentrate more exclusively on current problems in the community, while the remainder of the book looks forward to future events and the end times.

Literary Features

Genre

Malachi's form is different from most of the other prophetic books. Rather than recording a series of oracles or discourses, it presents and answers rhetorical questions. It is arranged in six speeches or oracles, each introduced by this standard pattern: (1) Yahweh or the prophet first advances an argument; (2) a challenge or question is uttered by the people or the priest; (3) a defense by Yahweh, sometimes in words of reproach and doom.

This style has caused some interpreters to argue that Malachi committed his ideas to writing from the outset. Some assert that the spirit of the legalist, catechist, and scribe is supposedly beginning to quench the spirit of prophecy. Even more negatively, some, who note (correctly) that Malachi's method anticipates a method common among the rabbis and in the Talmud, characterize him as a scholastic rabbi. These opinions fail to appreciate the prophet's style. Although his writing lacks the poetry of earlier prophets, it does not lack in powerful teaching.

Characters

Malachi taught that a herald or forerunner would introduce the heavenly Messiah (cf Is 40:3, 9). The New Testament cites the prophecies and applies them to John the Baptist. Obviously, by New Testament times, it was a major aspect of messianic hope. (Cf Mal 4:5 and the identification of the "messenger" with Elijah, the great embodiment of prophecy.) The Christian community, of course, no longer awaits the arrival of "Elijah" (cf the orthodox Jewish tradition of leaving an empty place for him at the Passover table).

Narrative Development or Plot

As noted above, Malachi is written in the form of questions and answers and so does not have a storyline or plot. However, the book shows a clear progression from present struggles to the future judgment and the glory of the messianic age.

Resources

As noted above, Malachi is not known for his creativity, though he does express his concerns in a unique way compared to the other prophets. Malachi repeats and reinforces specific teachings of the Law of Moses.

Text and Translations

Malachi 4:1–6 in Christian versions (following the Septuagint) is 3:19–24 in the Hebrew Bible. No textual problems of note are exhibited in Malachi.

DOCTRINAL CONTENT

Summary Commentary

1:1–5 God impresses the truth of His love for Israel (Jacob) by contrasting what happened to them with what happened to Edom (Esau).

OUTLINE

Title (1:1)

I. God's Love (1:2–5)

   A. The Lord Reminds Israel of His Love (1:2)

   B. The Lord Defeats Judah's Enemies (1:3–5)

II. Condemnation of the Priests (1:6–2:9)

   A. The Lord Is Father and Master of All (1:6)

   B. How the Priests Have Despised the Lord's Name (1:7–2:9)

     1. Offering polluted sacrifices (1:7–14)

     2. Failing to teach rightly (2:1–9)

III. The People Must Be Faithful through Proper Marriage Practice (2:10–16)

   A. The Lord Iws Father and Creator of All (2:10)

   B. The People Are Faithless to Their Spouses and God's Laws (2:11–16)

IV. The Lord Will Establish Justice through His Messenger (2:17–3:5)

   A. The Lord Accuses the People (2:17–18)

   B. God Will Send His Messenger to Establish Justice (3:1–5)

V. A Call to Return to the Lord in Repentance (3:6–15)

   A. The People Accused of Robbing God (3:6–9)

   B. The Lord Offers Blessings in Return for Full Tithes (3:10–12)

   C. The People Accused of Harsh Words against God (3:13–15)

VI. The Ones Who Fear the Lord Are Remembered by Him (3:16–4:3)

VII. Final Words (4:4–6)

   A. A Call to Observe the Law of Moses (4:4)

   B. The Promise of a Greater Prophet (4:5–6)

1:6–2:9 The Lord calls to account His Old Testament priests for the way they despised Him, as evidenced by their worship practices. He condemns the priests for failing to live up to the expectations He presented in His Word. Our fallen human nature makes us quick to serve our own interests by giving leftovers rather than firstfruits.

2:10–16 The people of Israel were guilty of breaking one of the covenant laws by marrying foreign, idolatrous wives. The Creator's first command to Adam and Eve was to "be fruitful and multiply" (Gn 1:28). After creating Eve, the Lord brought her to Adam and instituted marriage. He spoke the Sixth Commandment to guard this union (Ex 20:14). Yet throughout history, humans have violated God's rules for marriage.

2:17–3:5 The people in Malachi's day ask, "Where is the God of justice?" (cf 2Pt 3:4). The Lord makes it very clear that the Day of Judgment is coming. He wants all people to be prepared for that day.

3:6–4:6 Jeremiah's complaint, "Why does the way of the wicked prosper?" (Jer 12:1), resounds in Malachi's day. Many of Jacob's children think nothing of robbing God by withholding their full tithes because it seems to them that evildoers prosper. The Lord assures those who fear Him that their service has not been in vain and that they will be spared on the Day of Judgment. Malachi concludes with the Lord's announcement that Judgment Day is coming.

Specific Law Themes

The book opens with a harsh statement, "Esau I have hated" (1:3), intended to illustrate the depth of God's love and choice for Israel. No matter how one translates or interprets the statement, it remains one of the harshest in the entire Bible. From this point, Malachi turns back to Israel's priests, who serve closest to God's nearer presence at the temple. He takes the Lord's chosen ones to task for their unfaithfulness on the heels of His rejection of Esau/Edom. He adds to their offenses a series of practical issues: divorce, unfaithfulness in offerings, etc., and closes by announcing the day of the Lord's return in judgment.

Specific Gospel Themes

Just as Malachi opens harshly against Esau/Edom, he opens with words of love and faithfulness for Israel. While calling Israel to repentance, he reminds them that the Lord will be feared (i.e., trusted) not only in Israel but also among the nations (1:14). God is a Father to His people, not a distant

creator or heartless judge (2:10). To restore the people He prepares a messenger—fulfilled in the person of John the Baptist. What is more, He who cannot forget His people (3:16) will send the "sun of righteousness" (4:2).

Specific Doctrines

Malachi opens his book with very sharp teaching about election, which Paul quoted in Rm 9:13, making Malachi's teaching key to all future discussions of the doctrine and the issues that surrounded it. Malachi likewise powerfully addresses the problems of unfaithful worship, which is a symptom of unbelief.

Malachi, like other prophets, unites worship and ethics, matters external and internal. Malachi is thus a major example of the principle that "He who does not pray at specified times and places probably does not pray at all."

Malachi briefly, but clearly, condemns mixed marriages (2:10–16). These often included the men divorcing their first, Jewish wives to wed foreign women (cf Ezra and Nehemiah). Such marriages were probably often contracted for economic or other security reasons, but Malachi sees clearly the inevitable religious dimension: indifference toward the only true religion and profanation of the temple (v 11), not to speak of breach of covenant with their first wives (v 14).

Malachi associates the congregation's current social and economic distress with their "robbing God" by failure to bring "the full tithes" (3:6–12). The ultimate inseparability of spiritual and material blessing is a standard part of the Bible's perspective.

Malachi stands on the threshold of four hundred years of prophetic silence between the Old and New Testament revelations. God's people will have His Word spoken and written by Moses and the prophets in the

The Egyptian winged sun disk spread widely as a symbol for divinity, as this Persian example shows. Some scholars suggest that Mal 4:2 refers to such imagery, which was also found in Judah.

previous century, but no new message will be given them by God until, as Malachi prophesies, the great forerunner of the Messiah will appear—John the Baptist, who will prepare the way for Him. The Messiah is the capstone of the Old Testament and the cornerstone of the New, the Alpha and the Omega, the beginning and the end, the first and the last, even Jesus Christ, Son of God and Son of Man, Savior of the world, King of kings and Lord of lords forever.

Application

Ch 1 To justify rebellion against God, human beings sometimes question God's love as though God has dealt with them unfairly. Despite all rebellion, God maintains His steadfast love for sinners. In the New Testament, He demonstrated this love conclusively when Christ died for all on the cross (2Co 5:15). As a result, believers know for certain that nothing can separate us from His love (Rm 8:38–39).

2:1–9 God expected His Old Testament priests to act faithfully, and He has similar requirements for His pastors and teachers today (cf Ti 1:9). How blessed are those who have such servants of the Lord! And how important it is for us to pray that they remain faithful in their calling. For we all need what a devoted Christian leader proclaims: repentance and the forgiveness of sins in Christ, our Lord.

2:10–3:5 Like the Judeans in Malachi's day, Christians also violate God's will concerning the marriage relationship in various ways. We need His admonition about marriage and family as well as His forgiveness. With the command and blessing of marriage, the Lord provides a rich portion of His Spirit, who is faithful and keeps us in good faith. That's why He sent the Messenger of the new covenant, Jesus Christ, to suffer and die for the sins of the world. Christ will come again, "not to deal with sin but to save those who are eagerly waiting for Him" (Heb 9:28).

3:6–15 It is true that the wicked often prosper in this life. Though God does promise that His people may enjoy worldly blessings, He also warns that they can expect suffering too. Because of Christ's death and resurrection, we can be certain of His eternal blessings (Eph 1:3, 11–14).

3:16–4:6 For those who refuse to repent and believe the Gospel, it means utter destruction. But for those who fear His name, the Last Day will be a day of rejoicing. John the Baptist called the people of his day to repentance and faith in the coming Savior. How great a message for us to hear!

CANONICITY

Both the genuineness and the canonicity of the Book of Malachi are unquestioned. These New Testament quotations establish and corroborate the same: Mt 11:10; Mk 1:2 (Mal 3:1); Mt 11:14; 17:12; Mk 9:11 (Mal 4:5); Lk 1:17 (Mal 4:5–6); Rm 9:13 (Mal 1:2–3).

The Messiah promises, "I am . . . the life" (Jn 14:6). Mosaic in Punta Arenas Cathedral.

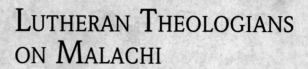

LUTHERAN THEOLOGIANS ON MALACHI

Luther

"The Hebrews believe that this Malachi was Ezra. We let that pass, because we can know nothing certain about him except that, so far as we can gather from his prophecy, he lived not long before Christ's birth and was certainly the last prophet. For he says in chapter 2 [3:1] that Christ the Lord shall come soon.

"He is a fine prophet, and his book contains beautiful sayings about Christ and the gospel. He calls it 'a pure offering in all the world,' for by the gospel the grace of God is praised, and that is the true pure thank-offering. Again he prophesies of the coming of John the Baptist, as Christ himself in Matthew 11[:10, 14] interprets that of which Malachi [3:1; 4:5] writes, calling John his messenger and Elijah.

"Beyond that he also denounces his people severely because they do not give the priests their tithes and other services [3:8–10]. Even when they gave them, they did it faithlessly; sick and blemished sheep, for example, whatever they did not want themselves, had to be good enough for the poor priests and preachers [1:8–14]. This is the way it usually goes. Those who are true preachers of the word of God must suffer hunger and privation, while false teachers must always have their fill. To be sure, the priests too are denounced along with the offerings, because they accepted those offerings and sacrificed them. Such was the work of dear Sir Avarice.

"But God here declares that he is greatly displeased with this. He calls such faithlessness and wickedness an offense against himself. On account of it God threatens to leave them and to take the Gentiles as his people.

"Afterward he denounces the priests particularly because they falsified the word of God and taught it faithlessly and thereby deceived many [2:6–10] and because they abused their priestly office by not rebuking those who offered blemished things or were otherwise unrighteous, and by praising them instead and calling them righteous, just to gain contributions and profit from them. In this way avarice and concern for the belly have always injured the word and worship of God; they always turn preachers into hypocrites.

"He denounces them also because they grieved [betrübten] their wives and despised them, and thereby defiled their own sacrifices and worship [2:13–16]. For the law of Moses forbade the offering of impure [betrübte] sacrifices to God; and those who were impure dared not sacrifice or eat of the sacrifice. This is what they brought about who grieved their wives and made them weep, and tried to justify their actions by the example of Abraham, who had to cast out and grieve his Hagar [Gen. 21:9–14]. However Abraham had not done this because of ill will, just as he had not taken Hagar to wife because of a whim [Gen. 16:1–4]." (AE 35:332–33)

For more of Luther's insights on this book, see *Lectures on Minor Prophets I* (AE 18:389–419).

Gerhard

"*Malachi* (*Mal'aki*) means 'messenger' or 'angel.' The rabbinic scholars think that this Malachi is Ezra, whose canonical book is extant, which they conclude from the fact that he reproves the same sins that Ezra rebuked. Augustine, *De civit. Dei*, bk. 20, c. 25: 'There are some who believe that the prophet Malachiel or Malachi, who is also called "the angel," is also Ezra the priest whose other works have been taken into the canon. Jerome says that this is the opinion of the Hebrews concerning him.' This argument, however, is not strong. Some think that the name Malachi is not a proper name but the common title for all the prophets and that we can take this name to mean Haggai, who is also called 'the angel of the Lord' (Hag. 1:13). This, however, is just as uncertain as the notion that this was Ezra.

"There are some who think that this was the angel who came down from heaven and took on human form to prophesy to Israel what God had commanded. Jerome attributes this idea to Origen. Epiphanius, on the other hand, writes that he was born in the town of Sopha in the tribe of Zebulun and that he was given the name 'Angel' because he was endowed with an excellent form and blameless behavior.

"This Malachi was the last prophet of the Old Testament, whom, in the order of the New Testament, John the Baptist followed as the forerunner of the Messiah. This Malachi of ours prophesied about John in 3:1 and 4:5. Augustine, *De civit. Dei*, bk. 17, c. 24: 'During that entire time from when the Jews returned from Babylon and after Malachi, Haggai, and Zechariah, who prophesied at that time, and Ezra, they did not have prophets until the coming of the Savior.'

"The book has four chapters that we can divide into two parts. The first of these is the rebuke in which the priests and the people are charged both because of their negligence and deceits in divine worship and their greed in the sacrifices and because of their violation of the marriage laws and because of their blasphemies (Malachi 1–2). The second part is consolatory, in which the coming of the Messiah, as well as of His forerunner, John the Baptist, is foretold (Malachi 3–4)." (ThC E1 § 167)

Fresco-Mosaic of John the Baptist, forerunner of the Messiah.

FURTHER STUDY ———————————

Lay/Bible Class Resources

Baldwin, Joyce. *Haggai, Zechariah, Malachi.* TOTC. Downers Grove, IL: InterVarsity Press, 1972. ♪ Compact commentary that interacts with a variety of English translations and with the Hebrew text. British evangelical scholar.

Deterding, Paul. *Haggai, Zechariah, Malachi: Return to the Lord.* GWFT. St. Louis: Concordia, 2005. ♪ Lutheran author. Eleven-session Bible study, including leader's notes and discussion questions.

Hartzell, Eric. *Haggai/Zechariah/Malachi.* PBC. St. Louis: Concordia, 2005. ♪ Lutheran author. Excellent for Bible classes. Based on the NIV translation.

Life by His Word. St. Louis: Concordia, 2009. ♪ More than 1,500 reproducible one-page Bible studies covering each chapter of the canonical Scriptures. Page references to *The Lutheran Study Bible*. CD-Rom and downloadable.

Church Worker Resources

Kaiser, Walter C., Jr. *Malachi: God's Unchanging Love.* Grand Rapids: Baker, 1984. ♪ A very helpful resource by an evangelical scholar, following a careful method of interpretation.

Luther, Martin. *Lectures on the Minor Prophets.* Vol. 18 of AE. St. Louis: Concordia, 1975. ♪ The great reformer's lectures from the 1520s, which reflect his mature approach to biblical interpretation. Luther consulted the Hebrew text and reflected on the application of the prophecies and their New Testament fulfillment.

Taylor, Richard. *Haggai, Malachi.* Vol. 21a of NAC. Nashville: Broadman & Holman, 2004. ♪ Evangelical, with emphasis on theology of the books. Based on the NIV.

Verhoef, Pieter A. *The Books of Haggai and Malachi.* NICOT. Grand Rapids: Eerdmans, 1987. ♪ A careful exposition of the text written by a conservative evangelical from South Africa; sees Haggai and Malachi as preparing unique and unified compositions.

Academic Resources

Hill, Andrew E. *Malachi.* Vol. 25D of AB. New York: Doubleday, 1998. ♪ Exhaustive study of the Hebrew text prepared by a conservative evangelical scholar.

K&D. *Biblical Commentary on the Old Testament: The Twelve Minor Prophets.* 2 vols. Grand Rapids: Eerdmans, 1971 reprint. ♪ This century-and-a-half old work from Lutheran scholars should not be overlooked. Despite its age, it remains a most useful commentary on the Hebrew text.

Packard, Joseph. *Malachi.* LCHS. New York: Charles Scribner's Sons, 1898. ♪ A helpful, older example of German biblical scholarship, based on the Hebrew text, which provides references to significant commentaries from the Reformation era forward.

Petersen, David L. *Zechariah 9–14 and Malachi.* OTL. Louisville: Westminster John Knox, 1995. ♪ Mainstream work that looks for different divisions or collections of material within Zechariah. Critical, but not extreme.

Smith, Ralph L. *Micah–Malachi.* Vol. 32 of *WBC.* Waco, Texas: Word Books, 1984. ♪ Written by an American evangelical from a conservative perspective.

Sweeney, Marvin A. *The Twelve Prophets.* Vol. 2 of *Berit Olam.* Collegeville, MN: Liturgical Press, 2000. ♪ Treats the literary structure of the Book of the Twelve as a whole, using critical approaches, then provides specific commentary on each book. Based on the NRSV.

ORDER OF BOOKS IN HEBREW BIBLE

The Law
(*Torah*)

Genesis
Exodus
Leviticus
Numbers
Deuteronomy

Prophets
(*Nevi'im*)

Former Prophets

Joshua
Judges
Samuel
Kings

Latter Prophets

Isaiah
Jeremiah
Ezekiel
Book of
   the Twelve
   Hosea
   Joel
   Amos
   Obadiah
   Jonah
   Micah
   Nahum
   Habakkuk
   Zephaniah
   Haggai
   Zechariah
   Malachi

The Writings
(*Kethuvim*)

Psalms
Proverbs
Job
Song of Solomon
   (Canticles)
Ruth
Lamentations
Ecclesiastes
   (Qoheleth)
Esther
Daniel
Ezra and
   Nehemiah
Chronicles

The Christian Bible orders its books differently from the Hebrew tradition. Whereas the Hebrew Bible ends with Chronicles, the last book added to the Hebrew canon, the Christian order for the Old Testament ends with the prophet Malachi, who prophesied the coming of John the Baptist and Jesus.

Art Credits